THE WESTERN EXPERIENCE

THE WESTERN EXPERIENCE

EIGHTH EDITION

MORTIMER CHAMBERS

University of California, Los Angeles

BARBARA HANAWALT

The Ohio State University

THEODORE K. RABB

Princeton University

ISSER WOLOCH

Columbia University

RAYMOND GREW

University of Michigan

Boston   Burr Ridge, IL   Dubuque, IA   Madison, WI   New York   San Francisco   St. Louis
Bangkok   Bogotá   Caracas   Kuala Lumpur   Lisbon   London   Madrid   Mexico City
Milan   Montreal   New Delhi   Santiago   Seoul   Singapore   Sydney   Taipei   Toronto

McGraw-Hill Higher Education

A Division of The **McGraw-Hill** *Companies*

THE WESTERN EXPERIENCE

Published by McGraw-Hill, a business unit of The McGraw-Hill Companies, Inc., 1221 Avenue of the Americas, New York, NY, 10020. Copyright © 2003, 1999, 1995, 1991, 1987, 1983, 1979, 1974 by The McGraw-Hill Companies, Inc. All rights reserved. No part of this publication may be reproduced or distributed in any form or by any means, or stored in a database or retrieval system, without the prior written consent of The McGraw-Hill Companies, Inc., including, but not limited to, in any network or other electronic storage or transmission, or broadcast for distance learning.

Some ancillaries, including electronic and print components, may not be available to customers outside the United States.

This book is printed on acid-free paper.

2 3 4 5 6 7 8 9 0 DOW/DOW 0 9 8 7 6 5 4 3

ISBN 0-07-242437-0

Vice president and editor-in-chief: *Thalia Dorwick*
Executive editor: *Lyn Uhl*
Sponsoring editor: *Monica Eckman*
Editorial coordinator: *Angela Kao*
Marketing manager: *Janise Fry*
Media technology producer: *Ginger Warner*
Senior project manager: *Jean Hamilton*
Senior production supervisor: *Lori Koetters*
Freelance design coordinator: *Gino Cieslik*
Senior supplement producer: *Rose M. Range*
Photo research coordinator: *Ira C. Roberts*
Photo researcher: *PhotoSearch, Inc.*
Cover Design: *Gino Cieslik*
Typeface: *10/12 Palatino*
Compositor: *GAC Indianapolis*
Printer: *R. R. Donnelley*

The credits for this section begin on page C-1 and is considered an extension of the copyright page.

Library of Congress Control Number: 2002107630

www.mhhe.com

About the Authors

Mortimer Chambers is Professor of History at the University of California at Los Angeles. He was a Rhodes scholar from 1949 to 1952 and received an M.A. from Wadham College, Oxford, in 1955 after obtaining his doctorate from Harvard University in 1954. He has taught at Harvard University (1954–1955) and the University of Chicago (1955–1958). He was Visiting Professor at the University of British Columbia in 1958, the State University of New York at Buffalo in 1971, the University of Freiburg (Germany) in 1974, and Vassar College in 1988. A specialist in Greek and Roman history, he is coauthor of *Aristotle's History of Athenian Democracy* (1962), editor of a series of essays entitled *The Fall of Rome* (1963), and author of *Georg Busolt: His Career in His Letters* (1990) and of *Staat der Athener*, a German translation and commentary to Aristotle's *Constitution of the Athenians* (1990). He has edited Greek texts of the latter work (1986) and of the *Hellenica Oxyrhynchia* (1993). He has contributed articles to the *American Historical Review and Classical Philology* as well as to other journals, both in America and in Europe. He is also an editor of *Historia*, the international journal of ancient history.

Barbara Hanawalt is the King George III Chair of British History at The Ohio State University and the author of numerous books and articles on the social and cultural history of the Middle Ages. Her publications include *The Middle Ages: An Illustrated History* (1999), *'Of Good and Ill Repute': Gender and Social Control in Medieval England* (1998), *Growing Up in Medieval London: The Experience of Childhood in History* (1993), *The Ties That Bound: Peasant Life in Medieval England* (1986), and *Crime and Conflict in English Communities, 1300–1348* (1979). She received her M.A. in 1964 and her Ph.D. in 1970, both from the University of Michigan. She has served as president of the Social Science History Association and has been on the Council of the American Historical Association and the Medieval Academy of America. She is currently second vice president of the Medieval Academy of America. She was an NEH fellow (1997–1998), a fellow of the Guggenheim Foundation (1998–1999), an ALCS Fellow in 1975–1976, a fellow at the National Humanities Center (1997–1998), a fellow at the Wissenschaftskolleg in Berlin (1990–1991), a member of the School of Historical Research at the Institute for Advanced Study, and a senior research fellow at the Newberry Library in 1979–1980.

Theodore K. Rabb is Professor of History at Princeton University. He received his Ph.D. from Princeton, and subsequently taught at Stanford, Northwestern, Harvard, and Johns Hopkins universities. He is the author of numerous articles and reviews in journals such as *The New York Times*, and the *Times Literary Supplement*, and he has been editor of *The Journal of Interdisciplinary*

History since its foundation. Among his books are *The Struggle for Stability in Early Modern Europe* (1975), *Renaissance Lives* (1993), and *Jacobean Gentleman* (1999). He has won awards from the Guggenheim Foundation, the National Endowment for the Humanities, the American Historical Association and The National Council for Historical Education. He was the principal historian for the PBS series, *Renaissance,* which was nominated for an Emmy.

Isser Woloch is Moore Collegiate Professor of History at Columbia University. He received his Ph.D. (1965) from Princeton University in the field of eighteenth- and nineteenth-century European history. He has taught at Indiana University and at the University of California at Los Angeles where, in 1967, he received a Distinguished Teaching Citation. He has been a fellow of the ACLS, the National Endowment for the Humanities, the Guggenheim Foundation, and the Institute for Advanced Study at Princeton. His publications include *Jacobin Legacy: The Democratic Movement under the Directory* (1970), *The Peasantry in the Old Regime: Conditions and Protests* (1970), *The French Veteran from the Revolution to the Restoration* (1979), *Eighteenth-Century Europe: Tradition and Progress, 1715–1789* (1982), *The New Regime: Transformations of the French Civic Order, 1789–1820s* (1994), *Revolution and the Meanings of Freedom in the Nineteenth Century* (1996), and *Napoleon and His Collaborators: The Making of a Dictatorship* (2001).

Raymond Grew is Professor of History Emeritus at the University of Michigan. He has also taught at Brandeis University, Princeton University, and at the Écoles des Hautes Études en Sciences Sociales in Paris. He earned both his M.A. and Ph.D. from Harvard University in the field of modern European history. He has been a Fulbright Fellow to Italy and a Fulbright Travelling Fellow to Italy and to France, a Guggenheim Fellow, and a Fellow of the National Endowment for the Humanities. In 1962 he received the Chester Higby Prize from the American Historical Association, and in 1963 the Italian government awarded him the Unitá d'Italia Prize; in 1992 he received the David Pinkney Prize of the Society for French Historical Studies and in 2000 a citation for career achievement from the Society for Italian Historical Studies. He has twice served as national chair of the Council for European Studies, was for many years the editor of the international quarterly, *Comparative Studies in Society and History,* and is one of the directors of the Global History Group. His recent publications include essays on historical comparison, global history, Catholicism in the nineteenth-century, fundamentalism, and Italian culture and politics. His books include *A Sterner Plan for Italian Unity* (1963), *Crises of Development in Europe and the United States* (1978), *School, State, and Society: The Growth of Elementary Schooling in Nineteenth-Century France* (1991), with Patrick J. Harrigan, and two edited volumes: *Food in Global History* (1999) and *The Construction of Minorities* (2001).

This book is dedicated
to the memory of David Herlihy
whose erudition and judgment
were central to its creation
and whose friendship and example
continue to inspire
his coauthors.

Brief Contents

Contents

Chapter 1

THE FIRST CIVILIZATIONS 3

Chapter 2

THE FORMING OF GREEK CIVILIZATION 37

Chapter 3

CLASSICAL AND HELLENISTIC GREECE 73

Chapter 4

THE ROMAN REPUBLIC 103

Chapter 5

THE EMPIRE AND CHRISTIANITY 137

Chapter 6

THE MAKING OF WESTERN EUROPE 177

Chapter 7

THE EMPIRES OF THE EARLY MIDDLE AGES (800–1000): CREATION AND EROSION 209

Chapter 8

RESTORATION OF AN ORDERED SOCIETY 247

Chapter 9

THE FLOWERING OF MEDIEVAL CIVILIZATION 289

Chapter 10

THE URBAN ECONOMY AND THE CONSOLIDATION OF STATES 329

Chapter 11

BREAKDOWN AND RENEWAL IN AN AGE OF PLAGUE 341

Chapter 12

TRADITION AND CHANGE IN EUROPEAN CULTURE, 1300—1500 401

Chapter 13

REFORMATIONS IN RELIGION 435

Chapter 14

ECONOMIC EXPANSION AND A NEW POLITICS 473

Chapter 15

WAR AND CRISIS 513

Chapter 16

CULTURE AND SOCIETY IN THE AGE OF THE SCIENTIFIC REVOLUTION 551

Chapter 17

THE EMERGENCE OF THE EUROPEAN STATE SYSTEM 589

Chapter 18

THE WEALTH OF NATIONS 633

Chapter 19

THE AGE OF ENLIGHTENMENT 667

Chapter 20

THE FRENCH REVOLUTION 699

Chapter 21

THE AGE OF NAPOLEON 737

Chapter 22

FOUNDATIONS OF THE NINETEENTH CENTURY:
POLITICS AND SOCIAL CHANGE 769

Chapter 23

LEARNING TO LIVE WITH CHANGE 805

Chapter 24

NATIONAL STATES AND NATIONAL CULTURES 845

Chapter 25

EUROPEAN POWER: WEALTH, KNOWLEDGE, AND IMPERIALISM 885

Chapter 26

THE AGE OF PROGRESS 927

Chapter 27

WORLD WAR I AND THE WORLD IT CREATED 963

Chapter 28

THE GREAT TWENTIETH-CENTURY CRISIS 1005

Chapter 29

THE NIGHTMARE: WORLD WAR II 1061

Chapter 30

THE NEW EUROPE 1111

EPILOGUE: THE PRESENT IN HISTORICAL PERSPECTIVE 1165

Maps

Boxes

HISTORICAL ISSUES BOXES

CHRONOLOGICAL BOXES

Books of Related Interest

New edition coming soon
Sherman, *Western Civilizations: Sources, Images, and Interpretations,* Volume I: To 1700, 6th edition, ISBN 007-2565675

New edition coming soon
Sherman, *Western Civilizations: Sources, Images, and Interpretations,* Volume II: From 1600, 6th edition, ISBN 007-2565659

New edition coming soon
Sherman, *Western Civilizations: Sources, Images, and Interpretations,* From the Renaissance to the Present, 4th edition, ISBN 007-2819642

Annual Editions: Hughes, *Western Civilization,* Volume I, 10th edition, ISBN 0-697-39378X
Annual Editions: Hughes, *Western Civilization,* Volume II, 10th edition, ISBN 0-697-39377-1

New edition coming soon
Wolf, *Personalities and Problems: Interpretive Essays in World Civilizations,* Volume I, 3rd edition, ISBN 007-2565640

New edition coming soon
Wolf, *Personalities and Problems: Interpretive Essays in World Civilizations,* Volume II, 3rd edition, ISBN 007-2565667

New edition
Tierney and Scott, *Western Societies: A Documentary History,* Volume I, 2nd edition, ISBN 007-064844-1

New edition
Tierney and Scott, *Western Societies: A Documentary History,* Volume II, 2nd edition, ISBN 007-064845-X

Preface

When this book was originally conceived, the authors who came together shared several concerns. First, several of us were very active in what was then the newly growing field of social history, and we wanted a textbook that would introduce students to these exciting issues and ways of thinking about history. Secondly, we wanted the textbook not merely to set forth information but to serve as an example of historical writing. That means we cared a lot about the quality of the writing itself and also that we wanted the chapters to be examples of a historical essay that set up a historical problem and developed arguments about that problem using historical evidence. Thirdly, we recognized that for American students the *Western Civilization* textbook needed to provide an overview of that civilization, giving students an introduction to the major achievements in Western thought, art, and science as well as the historical context for understanding them. And lastly, we were determined that our book would treat all these various aspects of history—politics, culture, economics, etc.—in an integrated way. Too many books, we felt, dealt with these topics separately, even in separate chapters, and we sought to demonstrate and exemplify the connections. To that end, *The Western Experience* is designed to provide an analytical and reasonably comprehensive account of the contexts within which, and the processes by which, European society and civilization evolved. Now in the eighth edition, this book has evolved with the strength of prior revisions, including the seventh edition's entire rewriting and reordering of the six chapters that cover the Middle Ages.

To continue that evolution, the eighth edition includes substantially revised selected chapters to make difficult concepts more understandable and to remove material that interfered with the general flow of the text. We have worked conscientiously to make the text more readily comprehensible for the student readers, while preserving an analytical framework and the latest historiographical information.

Features of *The Western Experience*, Eighth Edition

Each generation of students brings different experiences, interests, and training into the classroom—changes that are important to the teaching-learning process. The students we teach have taught us what engages or confuses them, what impression of European history they bring to college, and what they can be expected to take from a survey course. Current political, social, and cultural events also shape what we teach and how we teach. Our experience as teachers and the helpful comments of scores of other teachers have led to a rewriting and reordering throughout the book as we have sought to make it clearer and more accessible without sacrificing our initial goal of writing a reasonably sophisticated, interpretive, and analytic history.

Among the changes that we have made in this edition to clarify the text is the use of a **color-coded thematic grid** in each chapter. This enables students and teachers to pick out which of the seven themes are developed in each chapter. A teacher can aid the students to follow through the themes, such as changes in gender roles, the economy, or warfare in various periods. Such a grid makes comparative questions easier to address and permits students to trace different responses to historical change over time. The grid also helps teachers to plan lectures and lessons and coordinate them with supplementary books or audio and visual materials in the course.

The **maps** in *The Western Experience* are already much admired by instructors and much copied in other textbooks. In the eighth edition students will be able to use a URL link to the same maps in an interactive format on the website for the text. The URL location of the website will be available in the book, so that students can have immediate access to the map they wish to work on.

To encourage students to move beyond rote learning of historical "facts" and to think broadly about history, the authors have added **"Questions for Further Thought"** at the end of each chapter. These are too broad to be exam questions; instead they are meant to be questions that stimulate the students to think about history and social, political, and economic forces. Some are comparative, some require students to draw on knowledge of a previous chapter, some ask about the role of great leaders in politics, and some ask about how the less famous people living at the time perceived the events surrounding them.

The Online Learning Center can be accessed through the McGraw-Hill Higher Education website. The Online Learning Center contains a Student Center, Instructor Center, and an Information Center. The features included in the Online Learning Center are PowerPoint presentations, quizzes, flash cards, audio pronunciation, a new "Who am I?" game, and map and chronology exercises. The

integration of the Online Learning Center as an instructional component makes teaching and learning with *The Western Experience* much more accessible and enjoyable.

◆ INCORPORATION OF RECENT HISTORIOGRAPHY

For us the greatest pleasure in a revision lies in the challenge of absorbing and then incorporating the latest developments in **historical understanding.** From its first edition, this book included more of the results of quantitative and social history than most general textbooks of European history, an obvious reflection of our own research. Each subsequent edition provided an occasion to incorporate current methods and new knowledge, a challenge that required reconsidering paragraphs, sections, and whole chapters in the light of new theories and new research, sometimes literally reconceptualizing part of the past. That evolution continues with this edition.

We have taken into account recent work in all aspects of history, including economic, intellectual, cultural, demographic, and diplomatic history as well as social and political history. Most striking of all are the new perspectives that arise from work in **gender studies and cultural studies,** which we have sought to incorporate in this text.

◆ A BALANCED, INTERPRETIVE, AND FLEXIBLE APPROACH

At the same time, we recognize that the professional scholar's preference for new perspectives over familiar ones makes a distinction that students may not share. For them, the latest **interpretations** need to be integrated with established **understandings and controversies,** with the history of people and events that are part of our cultural lore. We recognize that a textbook should provide a coherent presentation of the basic information from which students can begin to form their historical understanding. We believe this information must be part of an interpretive history but also that its readers—teachers, students, and general readers—should be free to use it in many different ways and in conjunction with their own areas of special knowledge and their own interests and curiosity.

◆ OVERARCHING THEMES

Throughout this book, from the treatment of the earliest civilizations to the discussion of the present, we pursue certain key themes. These seven themes constitute a set of categories by which societies and historical change can be analyzed.

(1) *Social structure* is one theme. In early chapters, social structure involves how the land was settled, divided among its inhabitants, and put to use. Later discussions of how property is held must include corporate, communal, and individual ownership, then investment banking and companies that sell shares. Similarly, in each era we treat the division of labor, noting whether workers are slave or free, male or female, and when there are recognized specialists in fighting or crafts or trade. The chapters covering the Ancient world, the Middle Ages, and the early modern period explore social hierarchies that include nobles, clergy, commoners, and slaves or serfs; the treatments of the French Revolution, the Industrial Revolution, and twentieth-century societies analyze modern social classes.

(2) Another theme we analyze throughout this book is what used to be called the *body politic*. Each era contains discussions of how political power is acquired and used and of the political structures that result. Students learn about the role of law from ancient codes to the present, as well as problems of order, and the formation of governments, including why government functions have increased and political participation of the population has changed.

(3) From cultivation in the plains of the Tigris and Euphrates to the global economy, we follow changes in the organization of production and in the impact of *technology*. We note how goods are distributed, and we observe patterns of trade as avenues of cultural exchange in addition to wealth. We look at the changing economic role of governments and the impact of economic theories.

(4) The *evolution of the family and changing gender roles* are topics fundamental to every historical period. Families give form to daily life and kinship structures. The history of demography, migration, and work is also a history of the family. The family has always been a central focus of social organization and religion, as well as the principal instrument by which societies assign specific practices, roles, and values to women and men. Gender roles have changed from era to era, differing according to social class and between rural and urban societies. Observing gender roles across time, the student discovers that social, political, economic, and cultural history are always interrelated; that the present is related to the past; and that social change brings gains and losses rather than evolution in a straight line—three lessons all history courses teach.

(5) No history of Europe could fail to pay attention to *war*, which, for most polities, has been their most demanding activity. Warfare has strained whatever resources were available from ancient times to the present, leading governments to invent new ways to extract wealth and mobilize support. War has built and undermined states, stimulated science and consumed technology, made heroes and restructured nobility, schooling, and social services. Glorified in European culture and often condemned, war in every era has affected the lives of all its peoples. This historical significance, more than specific battles, is one of the themes of *The Western Experience*.

(6) *Religion* has been basic to the human experience, and our textbook explores the different religious institutions and experiences that societies developed. Religion affects and is affected by all the themes we address, creating community and causing conflict, shaping intellectual and daily life, providing the experiences that bind individual lives and society within a common system of meaning.

(7) For authors of a general history, no decision is more difficult than the space devoted to *cultural expression*. In this respect, as elsewhere, we have striven for a balance between high and popular culture. We present as clearly and concisely as possible the most important formal ideas, philosophies, and ideologies of each era. We emphasize concepts of recognized importance in the general

history of ideas and those concepts that illuminate behavior and discourse in a given period. We pay particular attention to developments in science that we believe are related to important intellectual, economic, and social trends. Popular culture appears both in specific sections and throughout the book. We want to place popular culture within its social and historical context but not make the gulf too wide between popular and high or formal culture. Finally, we write about many of the great works of literature, art, architecture, and music. Because of the difficulties of selection we have tried to emphasize works that are cultural expressions of their time, but that also have been influential over the ages and around the globe.

Attention to these seven themes occasions problems of organization and selection. We could have structured this book around a series of topical essays, perhaps repeating the series of themes for each of the standard chronological divisions of European history. Instead, we chose to preserve a narrative flow that emphasizes interrelationships and historical context. We wanted each chapter to stand as an interpretive historical essay, with a beginning and conclusion. As a result, the themes emerge repeatedly within discussions of a significant event, an influential institution, an individual life, or a whole period of time. Or they may intersect in a single institution or historical trend. Nevertheless, readers can follow any one of these themes across time and use that theme as a measure of change and a way to assess the differences and similarities between societies.

◆ STRONG COVERAGE OF SOCIAL HISTORY

To discuss history thematically is to think comparatively and to employ categories of social history that in the last generation have greatly affected historical understanding. The impulse behind social history was not new. As early as the eighteenth century many historians called for a history that was more than chronology, more than an account of kings and battles. Closer to our own time, Virginia Woolf asked why there was not a history of ordinary people rather than kings and monarchs. Although in the nineteenth century historical studies gave primary place to politics,

diplomacy, and war (using evidence from official documents newly accessible in state archives), the substantial changes brought about by the Industrial Revolution and colonialism led historians to begin to look at economic and social history. Intense interest in social history came in the 1960s and 1970s when the academic world opened its doors to students from the working class and the availability of computers and large data sets made it possible to trace the life patterns and accomplishments of workers, minorities, and women. But even those working with qualitative sources documented the daily life in ancient Rome or Renaissance Florence or old New York as reflected in styles of dress, housing, diet, and so on. Historical museums and popular magazines featured this "pots and pans history," which was appealing in its concreteness but tended (like the collections of interesting objects that it resembled) to lack a theoretical basis. Historians writing the history of those who were often illiterate have found abundant sources to bring the lives of ordinary people into our understanding of a society beyond the tiny minority who were the powerful, rich, and educated (and who left behind the fullest and most accessible records of their activities). The ordinary people now have a place within a larger interpretive framework, borrowing from the social sciences, especially anthropology, sociology, economics, and political science. Still an arena of active and significant research, social history has also expanded, strengthened by new work on the history of women. With the development of a stronger theoretical sense, these interests have grown into gender studies that give a fresh new dimension to familiar historical issues. Social history has changed in another way, too, shifting away from explanations that gave priority to social structure and material factors and toward cultural studies.

◆ CHRONOLOGICAL/CONCEPTUAL ORGANIZATION AND PERIODIZATION

These developments in social history, which have greatly expanded the range of evidence and issues that historians must consider, have changed our ideas of periodization. The mainstay for organizing historical knowledge has been the rise and fall of dynasties, the formation of states, and the occurrence of wars and revolutions. But we all know that people did not wake up on the morning after the war between Sparta and Athens, or Waterloo, or even the Second World War to find their family structures and basic economic needs radically altered because a balance of political power or a change of dynasty had occurred. The periodization most appropriate for describing changes in culture and ideas, economic production, or science and technology is often quite different, and changes in everyday life and popular culture often occur on a still different scale. We have sought a compromise for *The Western Experience*. It maintains the traditional chronological sequence of the introductory European history course. At the same time, insofar as each chapter is an interpretive essay, the information it contains illustrates arguments to describe a period of European history. For all these reasons, chapters also have topical emphases, and sometimes a cluster of chapters is required to treat a given era.

Pedagogical Features of the Eighth Edition

◆

The eighth edition of *The Western Experience* continues the precedent of earlier editions with its high-quality book production, and the inclusion of full color, clearly focused maps, and a highly accessible format. This edition offers more than 100 maps and 400 illustrations, each with an explanatory caption that enhances the text coverage. It features a variety of pedagogical devices to help students tackle the content without sacrificing subtlety of interpretation or trying to escape the fact that history is complex.

◆ COLOR CODED GRID OF SEVEN THEMES

Positioned at the start of every chapter, this grid highlights the seven themes developed in each chapter.

CHAPTER 28. THE GREAT TWENTIETH-CENTURY CRISIS							
	Social Structure	Body Politic	Changes in the Organization of Production and in the Impact of Technology	Evolution of Family and Changing Gender Roles	War	Religion	Cultural Expression
I. TWO SUCCESSFUL REVOLUTIONS	▓	▓	▓	▓	▓	▓	
II. THE DISTINCTIVE CULTURE OF THE TWENTIETH CENTURY			▓	▓			▓
III. THE RETREAT FROM DEMOCRACY		▓	▓				▓
IV. NAZI GERMANY AND THE U.S.S.R.	▓	▓	▓				
V. THE DEMOCRACIES' WEAK RESPONSE	▓	▓				▓	▓

◆ PRIMARY SOURCE BOXES

These excerpts from primary sources are designed to illustrate or supplement points made in the text, to provide some flavor of the issues under discussion, and to allow beginning students some of that independence of judgment that comes from a careful reading of historical sources.

OEDIPUS' SELF-MUTILATION

◆

In Sophocles' tragedy King Oedipus, Jocasta, the mother of Oedipus, hangs herself after learning that she has married her own son. An attendant then narrates what follows. (Those he "should never have seen" are the daughters Oedipus fathered by his mother-wife.)

"We saw a knotted pendulum, a noose,
A strangled woman swinging before our eyes.
The King saw too, and with heart-rending groans
Untied the rope, and laid her on the ground.
But worse was yet to see. Her dress was pinned
With golden brooches, which the King snatched out
And thrust, from full arm's length, into his eyes—
Eyes that should see no longer his shame, his guilt,
No longer see those they should never have seen,
Nor see, unseeing, those he had longed to see,
Henceforth seeing nothing but night . . . To this wild tune

He pierced his eyeballs time and time again,
Till bloody tears ran down his beard—not drops
But in full spate a whole cascade descending
In drenching cataracts of scarlet rain.
Thus two have sinned; and on two heads, not one—
On man and wife—falls mingled punishment.
Their old long happiness of former times
Was happiness earned with justice; but to-day
Calamity, death, ruin, tears, and shame,
All ills that there are names for—all are here."

From E. F. Watling (tr.), Sophocles, *The Three Theban Plays*, Penguin Classics, 1971, pp. 60–61.

◆ **HISTORICAL ISSUES BOXES**

These boxes explain major controversies over historical interpretations so that students can see how historical understanding is constructed. They encourage students to participate in these debates and formulate their own positions.

TWO VIEWS OF COLUMBUS

◆

The following two passages suggest the enormous differences that have arisen in interpretations of the career of Christopher Columbus. The first, by Samuel Eliot Morison, a historian and a noted sailor, represents the traditional view of the explorer's achievements that held sway until recent years.

1. "Columbus had a Hellenic sense of wonder at the new and strange, combined with an artist's appreciation of natural beauty. Moreover, Columbus had a deep conviction of the sovereignty and the infinite wisdom of God, which enhanced all his triumphs. One only wishes that the Admiral might have been afforded the sense of fulfillment that would have come from foreseeing all that flowed from his discoveries. The whole history of the Americas stems from the Four Voyages of Columbus, and as the Greek city-states looked back to the deathless gods as their founders, so today a score of independent nations unite in homage to Christopher the stout-hearted son of Genoa, who carried Christian civilization across the Ocean Sea."

From S. E. Morison, *Admiral of the Ocean Sea: A Life of Christopher Columbus* (Boston: Little, Brown, 1942), pp. 670–671.

2. "For all his navigational skill, about which the salty types make such a fuss, and all his fortuitous headings, Admiral Colón [Christopher Columbus] could be a wretched mariner. The four voyages, properly seen, quite apart from bravery, are replete with lubberly mistakes, misconceived sailing plans, foolish disregard of elementary maintenance, and stubborn neglect of basic safety—all characterized by the assertion of human superiority over the natural realm. Almost every time Colón went wrong, it was because he had refused to bend to the inevitabilities of tide and wind and reef or, more arrogantly still, had not bothered to learn about them.

From Kirkpatrick Sale, *The Conquest of Paradise: Christopher Columbus and the Columbian Legacy* (New York: Knopf, 1990), pp. 209–210, 362.

◆ MORE HEADING LEVELS

We have given particular attention to adding more descriptive content guides, such as the consistent use of three levels of headings. We believe these will help students identify specific topics for purposes of study and review as well as give a clear outline of a chapter's argument.

◆ CHRONOLOGICAL CHARTS

Nearly every chapter employs charts and chronological tables that outline the unfolding of major events and social processes and serve as a convenient reference for students.

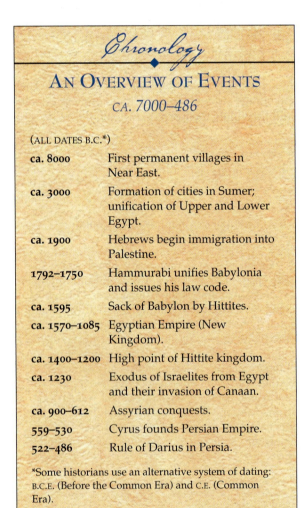

Chronology

AN OVERVIEW OF EVENTS
CA. 7000–486

(ALL DATES B.C.*)

ca. 8000	First permanent villages in Near East.
ca. 3000	Formation of cities in Sumer; unification of Upper and Lower Egypt.
ca. 1900	Hebrews begin immigration into Palestine.
1792–1750	Hammurabi unifies Babylonia and issues his law code.
ca. 1595	Sack of Babylon by Hittites.
ca. 1570–1085	Egyptian Empire (New Kingdom).
ca. 1400–1200	High point of Hittite kingdom.
ca. 1230	Exodus of Israelites from Egypt and their invasion of Canaan.
ca. 900–612	Assyrian conquests.
559–530	Cyrus founds Persian Empire.
522–486	Rule of Darius in Persia.

*Some historians use an alternative system of dating: B.C.E. (Before the Common Era) and C.E. (Common Era).

Available Formats

To provide an alternative to the full-length hardcover edition, *The Western Experience*, Eighth Edition, is available in two-volume and three-volume paperbound editions. Volume I includes chapters 1 through 17 and covers material through the eighteenth century. Volume II includes chapters 15 through 30 and the Epilogue, and covers material since the sixteenth century. Volume A includes chapters 1 through 12, Antiquity and the Middle Ages; Volume B includes chapters 11 through 21, The Early Modern Era; and Volume C includes chapters 19 through 30 and the Epilogue, The Modern Era. The page numbering and cross-references in these editions remain the same as in the hardcover text.

Ancillary Instructional Materials

McGraw-Hill offers instructors and students a wide variety of ancillary materials to accompany *The Western Experience*. These supplements listed here may accompany *The Western Experience*. Please contact your local McGraw-Hill representative for details concerning policies, prices, and availability, as some restrictions may apply.

◆ FOR THE STUDENT

Student Study Guide/Workbook with Map Exercises, Volumes I and II: Includes the following features for each chapter: chapter outlines, chronological diagrams, four kinds of exercises—map exercises, exercises in document analysis, exercises that reinforce the book's important overarching themes, exercises in matching important terms with significant individuals—and essay topics requiring analysis and speculation.

New Multimedia Supplements for the Student:

- *The Online Learning Center:* A fully interactive, book-specific website featuring links to chapter- and topic-appropriate sites on the World Wide Web, and a guide to using the Internet. Some outstanding tools included on the site:
  - Chapter outlines

- Interactive "drag and drop" exercises ask students to match up significant individuals and key terms with the correct identifications.
- An audio function helps students pronounce difficult terms.
- Self-tests offer students a chance to find out in what areas they need more study.
- Essay questions
- Map exercises are also included.
- Links with exercises
- New animated maps

◆ FOR THE INSTRUCTOR

An integrated instructional package is available in either print or electronic format.

Instructor's Manual/Test Bank: This fully revised and expanded manual includes chapter summaries, lecture and discussion topics, and lists of additional teaching resources such as recommended films, novels, and websites. In addition, the test bank for the seventh edition of *The Western Experience* includes more questions than ever before. Types of questions include multiple choice, identification, sentence completion, essay (both factual and interpretive), and critical thinking exercises (such as map analysis or source analysis questions).

Computerized Test Bank: A computerized test bank is available in Windows or Mac formats.

Overhead Transparency Acetates: This expanded full-color transparency package includes all the maps and chronological charts in the text.

The Instructor's Resource CD-ROM: Allows instructors to create their own classroom presentation using resources provided by McGraw-Hill. Instructors may also customize their presentations by adding slides or other electronic resources. In addition, this CD allows instructors access to all their instructional materials (including the test bank) in one integrated instructional package. The IRCD includes the following resources: a PowerPoint slide show, electronic overhead transparencies (maps and chronological charts from the text), the instructor's manual (with hyperlinks to appropriate maps and timelines to help the instructor build lecture presentations), and the test bank.

The Online Learning Center: Available to the instructor and includes the Instructor's Manual and PowerPoint slides in addition to students' resources.

Acknowledgments

Manuscript Reviewers and Consultants, eighth edition: Sig Sutterlin, Indian Hills Community College; John Tanner, Palomar College; Fred Murphy, Western Kentucky University; Guangquin Xu, Northwest Arkansas Community College; Tyler Blethen, West Carolina University; Gunar Freibergs, Los Angeles Valley College; Neil Heyman, San Diego State University; Laura Pintar, Loyola University; Vickie Cook, Pima Community College; Owen Bradley, University of Tennessee; Elizabeth McCrank, Boston University; Mary DeCredico, U.S. Naval Academy; Richard Cole, Luther College; Ron Goldberg, Thomas Nelson Community College; Thomas Rowland, University of Wisconsin-Oshkosh; Dan Brown, Moorpark College; Charles Steen, University of New Mexico; George Monahan, Suffolk Community College; Anne Quartararo, U.S. Naval Academy; Edrene Stephens McKay, Northwest Arkansas Community College; Valentina Tikoff, DePaul University.

Manuscript Reviewers and Consultants, seventh edition: Frank Baglione, Tallahassee Community College; Paul Goodwin, University of Connecticut; Robert Herzstein, University of South Carolina; Carla M. Joy, Red Rocks Community College; Kathleen Kamerick, University of Iowa; Carol Bresnahan Menning, University of Toledo; Eileen Moore, University of Alabama at Birmingham; Frederick Murphy, Western Kentucky University; Michael Myers, University of Notre Dame; Robert B. Patterson, University of South Carolina at Columbia; Peter Pierson, Santa Clara University; Alan Schaffer, Clemson University; Marc Schwarz, University of New Hampshire; Charles R. Sullivan, University of Dallas; Jack Thacker, Western Kentucky University; Bruce L. Venarde, University of Pittsburgh.

Manuscript Reviewers and Consultants, sixth edition: S. Scott Bartchy, University of California, Los Angeles; Thomas Blomquist, Northern Illinois

University; Nancy Ellenberger, United States Naval Academy; Steven Epstein, University of Colorado at Boulder; Laura Gellott, University of Wisconsin at Parkside; Barbara Hanawalt, University of Minnesota; Drew Harrington, Western Kentucky University; Lisa Lane, Mira Costa College; William Matthews, S.U.N.Y. at Potsdam; Carol Bresnahan Menning, University of Toledo; Sandra Norman, Florida Atlantic University; Peter Pierson, Santa Clara University; Linda Piper, University of Georgia; Philip Racine, Wofford College; Eileen Soldwedel, Edmonds Community College; John Sweets, University of Kansas; Richard Wagner, Des Moines Area Community College.

Focus Group Reviewers from Spring 1992: Michael DeMichele, University of Scranton; Nancy Ellenberger, United States Naval Academy; Drew Harrington, Western Kentucky University; William Matthews, S.U.N.Y. at Potsdam.

We would like to thank Lyn Uhl, Monica Eckman, and Angela Kao of McGraw-Hill for their considerable efforts in bringing this edition to fruition.

Introduction

Everyone uses history. We use it to define who we are and to connect our personal experience to the collective memory of the groups to which we belong, including a particular region, nation, and culture. We invoke the past to explain our hopes and ambitions and to justify our fears and conflicts. The Charter of the United Nations, like the American Declaration of Independence, is based on a view of history. When workers strike or armies march, they cite the lessons of their history. Because history is so important to us psychologically and intellectually, historical understanding is always shifting and often controversial.

Historical knowledge is cumulative. Historians may ask many of the same questions about different periods of history or raise new questions or issues; they integrate the answers and historical knowledge grows. The study of history cannot be a subjective exercise in which all opinions are equally valid. Regardless of the impetus for a particular historical question, the answer to it stands until overturned by better evidence. We now know more about the past than ever before, and we understand it as the people we study could not. Unlike them, we know the outcome of their history; we can apply methods they did not have, and often we have evidence they never saw.

Humans have always found pleasure in the reciting and reading of history. The poems about the fall of Troy or the histories of Herodotus and Thucydides entertained the ancient Greeks. The biographies of great men and women, dramatic accounts of important events, colorful tales of earlier times can be fascinating in themselves. Through these encounters with history we experience the common concerns of all people; and through the study of European history, we come to appreciate the ideals and conflicts, the failures and accidents, the social needs and human choices that formed the Western world in which we live. Knowing the historical context also enriches our appreciation for the achievements of European culture, enabling us to see its art, science, ideas, and politics in relationship to real people, specific interests, and burning issues.

We think of Europe's history as the history of Western civilization, but the very concept of a Western civilization is itself the result of history. The Greeks gave the names east and west to the points on the horizon at which the sun rises and sets. Because the Persian Empire and India lay to their east, the Greeks labeled their own continent, which they called Europe, the west. The distinction between Western civilization and others, while frequently ethnocentric, arbitrary, and exaggerated, was reinforced by the many encounters that Europeans had with other peoples and civilizations. The view that the Western civilization is all one can be easily challenged in every respect save its cultural tradition.

The Western Experience gives primary attention to a small part of the world and thus honors that cultural tradition. The concentration on Europe nevertheless includes important examples of city and of rural life; of empires and monarchies and republics; of life before and after industrialization; of societies in which labor was organized through markets, serfdom, and slavery; of cultures little concerned with science and of ones that used changing scientific knowledge; of non-Christian religions and of all the major forms of Christianity in action.

Throughout this book, from the treatment of the earliest civilizations to the discussion of the present, certain themes are pursued. These seven themes constitute a set of categories by which societies and historical change can be analyzed: social structure, the body politic, changes in the organization of production and in the impact of technology, the evolution of the family and changing gender roles, war, religion, and cultural expression. The themes are developed more fully in the Preface. These themes help readers integrate the narrative of events with a deeper understanding of how societies and individuals responded to changing circumstances. By following through the themes in the text, readers will have a basis of comparison of historical responses to politics, the economy, family and gender roles, war, religion, and culture. The themes are a constant of human history, but each period, sometimes each generation, had different responses to them. Readers of this book will find many ways to enrich their understanding of history. It introduces historical methods; it provides a framework for what they already know about Western society; and it challenges preconceptions about the past, about how societies are organized, and about how people behave. Historical study is an integrative enterprise that must take into account long-term trends and specific moments, social structure and individual actions.

A college course alone cannot create an educated citizen. Nor is history the only path to integrated knowledge. Western history is not the only history a person should know, nor is an introductory survey necessarily the best way to learn it. Yet, as readers consider and then challenge interpretations offered in this text, they will exercise critical and analytical skills. They can begin to overcome the parochialism that attributes importance only to the present. To learn to think critically about historical evidence and know how to formulate an argument on the bases of this evidence is to experience the study of history as one of the vital intellectual activities by which we come to know who and where we are.

Mortimer Chambers
Barbara Hanawalt
Theodore K. Rabb
Isser Woloch
Raymond Grew

▲ GREAT HALL OF BULLS, LASCAUX CAVES
An example of animals depicted in a prehistoric cave painting.
Musée des Antiquités St. Germain en Laye/Dagli Orti/The Art Archive

The First Civilizations

The subject of this book is the Western experience—that is, the history of European civilization, which is the civilization of modern Europe and America. Yet we do not begin with the mainland of present-day Europe, for our civilization traces its origins to earlier ones in Mesopotamia and around the Mediterranean Sea. Human beings began to abandon a nomadic existence and live in settled agricultural villages about 8000 B.C. This change in human lifestyle points to some of the themes that will run through this book—for example, the rise of technology to contain rivers and to survey and map areas for farming, or the art of cutting and assembling huge stones to build walls and pyramids.

By about 3000 B.C. humans had created settlements of some size along the banks of the Tigris, Euphrates, Nile, and Indus rivers. People's efforts to build a better life transformed the agricultural villages into something we can recognize as cities—having a scale and pattern crucial for the development of civilization. In these valleys, types of behavior and institutions first appeared that have persisted, in varying forms, throughout all periods of Western civilization.

Powerful kingdoms and great empires, centered on sizable cities, gradually arose in Mesopotamia and in Egypt. Their achievement of literacy and their many written records; their long-distance trade; their invention of increasingly ingenious tools, utensils, vehicles, and weapons; their development of monumental architecture and representative art; and their advances in medicine, astronomy, and mathematics marked the change from primitive life and constituted civilization.

	Social Structure	Body Politic	Changes in the Organization of Production and in the Impact of Technology	Evolution of Family and Changing Gender Roles	War	Religion	Cultural Expression
CHAPTER 1. THE FIRST CIVILIZATIONS							
I. THE EARLIEST HUMANS	■		■	■			■
II. THE FIRST CIVILIZATIONS IN MESOPOTAMIA	■					■	
III. EGYPT			■			■	■
IV. PALESTINE						■	
V. THE NEAR EASTERN STATES					■		

I. The Earliest Humans

Our first task as we try to grasp historical chronology is to gain a sense of the overwhelmingly long period that we call "prehistory." The astronomer Carl Sagan reckoned that, if the entire history of the universe were plotted out over the span of one year, everything that we usually think of as European history—the subject of this book—would have taken place in the last two or three minutes of the year.

All human beings are members of the species *Homo sapiens* ("thinking human being"), which evolved, according to present evidence, about 400,000 years ago. The immediate predecessor was *Homo erectus,* which may have emerged as long ago as 1.5 million years. Back in time beyond *Homo erectus* is an area of doubt and controversy. There is growing support for the theory that humanity originated, in the form of *Homo habilis,* roughly "skillful human being," in east Africa about 2 million years ago. As to mankind's emigration from Africa, recent excavations in the nation of Georgia (part of the former Soviet Union) have discovered two skulls that are considered the most ancient human remains outside Africa. They date to about 1.7 million years ago and suggest that people emigrated when they became carnivorous and had to expand their territory in search of meat; they also show that the emigration must have been under way by this time.

As historians seek to understand earliest mankind, they must remember that there is no *inevitable* pattern of development in social groups. Hunter-gatherers can remain such indefinitely, and small farming communities may never turn into anything else.[1] But there seem to be certain patterns through which many societies have developed and out of which civilization arose.

At least in the part of the world treated in this book, humanity did change from people who gathered and hunted food wherever they could into farmers in small villages. This change led in turn to an increase in population and the forming of larger, long-lived towns.

◆ HUMAN BEINGS AS FOOD GATHERERS

Human beings have always had to try to come to terms with their environment. For the greatest part of their time on earth, they have struggled simply to hunt and gather food. Only at a later stage did people live in stable settlements—first villages, then cities.

Labor in Early Communities In all observed societies, labor is divided on the basis of sex. In the earliest societies, both hunting and gathering food were the means of survival. Current research suggests that women may have done most of the gathering as well as caring for the young. If hunting animals required longer expeditions, we may guess that men usually performed this duty. Even

---

[1]A point convincingly made by Johnson and Earle, p. 6 (see recommended readings at end of chapter).

later, as agriculture became the basis of the economy, modern research suggests that women must have continued their domestic tasks, such as cooking and tending children.

We can surely guess that quarrels of some kind broke out between societies. One hunting band, for example, might have had to turn aside the claims of another band to certain territory. In such clashes, we may guess that men assumed leadership through their strength and thus created a division of roles based on sex that gave them dominance of their communities. One result of this social division has been a comparative lack of information about the role of women in history; the reconstruction of this role, the restoring of women to history, has been a leading theme of historical research in the present generation.

The Old Stone Age   The period during which people gathered food is often called the Old Stone Age, or Paleolithic Age, and ranges from the beginning of human history to about 11,000 B.C. Even in this early period, some human beings developed a remarkably sophisticated kind of painting, the earliest demonstration of the role of artistic creation as another theme in the history of civilization. The most striking creations known from food-gathering societies are a series of cave paintings that survive at their finest in Lascaux in France and Altamira in Spain (28,000–22,000 B.C.). Most of the paintings show wild animals, enemies of human beings and yet part of their essential support. The paintings may have a quasi-religious meaning as symbolic attempts to gain power over the quarry; scars on the walls suggest that people threw spears at the painted animals, as if to imitate killing them. If so, the cave paintings provide our earliest evidence for one of the main themes of history: the attempt to communicate with forces outside human control through symbolic action, art, and thought—that is, through religion and ritual acts.

◆ HUMAN BEINGS AS FOOD PRODUCERS

The Discovery of Agriculture   About 11,000 B.C., according to recent research, there occurred the most important event in all human history: People turned from hunting animals and gathering food to producing food from the earth. This event, the rise of agriculture, is called the Neolithic Revolution and introduced the Neolithic Age, or New Stone Age.[2] The word *revolution* usually implies dramatic action over a short time, which was in no way true of this one. Yet revolution it was, for it made possible the feeding of larger populations. The rise of agriculture gave continuity to human existence and demanded long-term planning and the practice of new skills and specialties. Those people not needed in agriculture could engage in hunting (for this skill was still needed), weaving, pottery, metalwork, and trade. Agriculture, once mastered, became another enduring theme throughout history and has always been the largest single factor in the economy of the world. Indeed, increasing the food supply was the imperative step to be taken on the path to cities and civilization.

Patterns in Population   But *why* did this revolution take place? What caused people to turn from the pattern of roaming the countryside that had lasted hundreds of thousands of years? The driving force was probably an inevitable increase in population. As mankind multiplied in the later, or "upper," Paleolithic Age, it became imperative to develop a continuous food supply and to have a secure reserve over the whole year. But traditional foraging might not guarantee such a supply. As people hunted animals, they inevitably made their prey scarcer. Even gathering fruit and grains required ever longer journeys. Therefore farming became a necessity. People grew grain in the summer and stored it in winter, but not all single families could be certain of enough food at all times. Storage of food became a task for the community, and this led to social cooperation, which in turn required social control—an approach to political organization and government.

Moreover, when people invested labor in their settlements and began to depend on land, protecting and even expanding their territory became of immense importance. Therefore one effect of the agricultural revolution was the impetus to gain control over territory—sometimes through negotiation, but sometimes through war. War is

---

[2]The Mesolithic (Middle Stone) Age, beginning around 8000 B.C., was limited to northwestern Europe.

another of the constantly recurring themes of Western civilization. The reasons for making war will vary considerably through the centuries, and the tools of war will become ever more sophisticated; but the willingness to seize a weapon, shed other people's blood, and risk one's own life to gain or to protect territory descends from the earliest permanent human settlements.

◆ EARLY NEAR EASTERN VILLAGES

The First Settlements   The Neolithic Revolution first occurred probably in the hills of what is now southern Turkey and northern Iraq, especially in the Zagros hills east of the Tigris River. But, again, why was *this* region the cradle of agriculture? Historians have concluded that only this location held a sufficient supply of animals for domestication along with the needed vegetables and cereals. The earliest known settlements, dating from about 9000 B.C., were unwalled and unfortified, and their people lived in simple huts. About 8000 B.C. the first somewhat larger villages appeared. The oldest seem to have been Jericho and Jarmo, but even these were still small settlements; by about 8000 B.C. Jericho may have had 2,000–3,000 people. The population of Jarmo, settled about 7000 B.C., is estimated at about 150, crowded into twenty to twenty-five houses of baked clay.

Invention, Travel, Trade   As villages became permanent, they also became more versatile in their inventions; our first evidence of pottery, for example, comes from what is now Syria and dates from about 8000 B.C. This invention allowed the storage of food and sustained the population in periods when hunting and gathering were more difficult. Another invention, the art of weaving, was practiced in Anatolia, now within modern Turkey, by about 7000 B.C. and provided both new occupations and new resources for a village.

About this time, too, people began to travel in crude rafts and in carts with wheels. Potters gradually learned to fashion their wares on the surface of a turning wheel, and thus could make in minutes what had previously taken hours; and the pot, the raft, and the wheel combined to provide the means to transport grain and other goods. Thus arose another institution of all later societies: the mutually profitable exchange of goods in

trade, pursued by people skilled enough to make a living at it. Some archaeologists have suggested that a number of towns were formed not for the sake of local agriculture but to serve as trading centers. Trade needs safe routes and a guarantee of safety for traders, which in turn require some kind of political protection, mutual understanding between communities, and control.

Agricultural Communities   The early farmers were naturally much concerned with fertility. When people feared that their own efforts might not solve life's problems, they turned to divine powers for help. These societies therefore sought to communicate with goddesses in the form of statuettes of unmistakable earth-mothers with large buttocks and breasts, whose fertile bodies, it

---

Chronology

AN OVERVIEW OF EVENTS
CA. 7000–486

(ALL DATES B.C.*)

ca. 8000	First permanent villages in Near East.
ca. 3000	Formation of cities in Sumer; unification of Upper and Lower Egypt.
ca. 1900	Hebrews begin immigration into Palestine.
1792–1750	Hammurabi unifies Babylonia and issues his law code.
ca. 1595	Sack of Babylon by Hittites.
ca. 1570–1085	Egyptian Empire (New Kingdom).
ca. 1400–1200	High point of Hittite kingdom.
ca. 1230	Exodus of Israelites from Egypt and their invasion of Canaan.
ca. 900–612	Assyrian conquests.
559–530	Cyrus founds Persian Empire.
522–486	Rule of Darius in Persia.

*Some historians use an alternative system of dating: B.C.E. (Before the Common Era) and C.E. (Common Era).

was hoped, would make the soil productive. Such figures also signify the importance of human mothers, for the villages flourished only if women produced and sustained each new generation.

So by stages there arose agrarian communities with communal gods, domesticated animals, simple technologies and economies, and some regulation of social behavior. Yet we must remember how painfully slow was the transition from nomadic hunters to food-producing villagers. And still another 4,000–5,000 years were to separate such agricultural villages from the first civilizations.

II. The First Civilizations in Mesopotamia

History has been called an argument without end. It is still not definitely clear where civilization began, but the region of Mesopotamia has at least some claim as the cradle of civilization. The historian can point to the forming of cities, as distinct from farming towns, in this region, and Mesopotamia was also home to one of the two earliest systems of writing. From these beginnings arose two of the earliest civilizations, those of Sumer and of Babylonia. Both have left behind them written documents that are priceless sources for the thoughts and practices of these societies.

◆ THE EMERGENCE OF CIVILIZATION

We may define civilization as a social organization with more complex rules than those that guided dwellers in caves or the earliest farmers. In a civilization, there are more sophisticated divisions of authority and labor, including duties, powers, and skills that pass down within certain families. A sensational excavation in A.D. 2000 at the site of Tell Hamoukar, in modern Syria, has revealed that people were living there by about 4000 B.C. and that they developed the earliest known civilization at this site about 3700 B.C. (the ancient name of the city has not yet been found). Among the signs of civilization found here are monumental architecture and seals used, perhaps by officials, to stamp valuable goods. Further knowledge of this site must await more excavation.

The Beginnings of Government The establishment of firm authority requires the acceptance by both governors and the governed of their status; we shall see this balance throughout history, but we shall also observe its collapse when conflict leads to the replacement of one governing group by another. Rulers, however named, often arise from among the heads of powerful families. But there may be other sources of political strength. Seeking social order, people give authority to a man or woman who seems to have some special quality of leadership or ability.

An equally essential part of the social cement, in all periods of civilization, has been law, formally accepted codes of behavior, as distinct from the simple customs of a village. Law may develop slowly, but eventually it is recorded in detailed law codes, which tell us how societies controlled their people. Such codes can also tell us about ethical values, divisions between citizens, and social structure.

There is tension, in any civilization, between control and freedom. Law codes not only control people but are also a way of restraining one citizen from interfering with another. Such restraint in turn guarantees some liberties, and law exists partly to make us more free. The constant discussion and refinement of law is another permanent theme of our history.

The Power of Cities Cities are larger and therefore stronger than villages; they have the power to dominate the hinterland and its inhabitants. In many early civilizations, one society even enslaved parts of another society. Slavery, though deplorable in modern eyes, allowed the enslavers more varied occupations by freeing them from the mundane requirements of existence. As people began to use their freedom, however obtained, to pursue special skills, some gained a reputation for religious knowledge and became the state's communicators with divine powers; and such is the strength of religious belief that these priests could form a class of advisers whom even kings could not ignore.

Other citizens used their new freedom to develop new arts and crafts. Along with improved techniques of pottery, weaving, and domestication of animals, a major step forward took place when workers discovered how to blend other

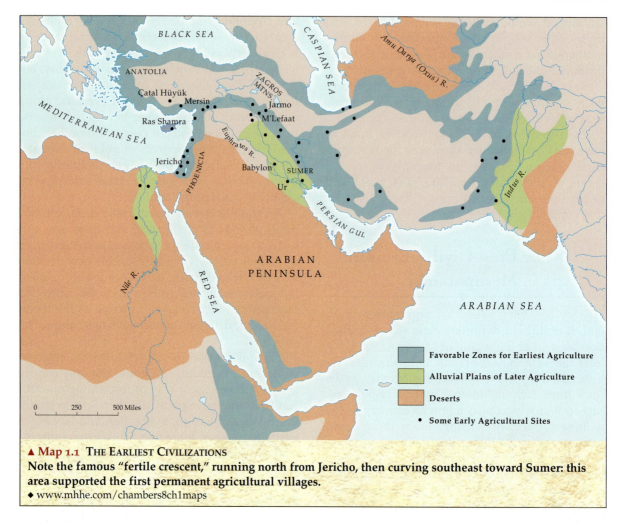

▲ **Map 1.1** **THE EARLIEST CIVILIZATIONS**
Note the famous "fertile crescent," running north from Jericho, then curving southeast toward Sumer: this area supported the first permanent agricultural villages.
◆ www.mhhe.com/chambers8ch1maps

metals with copper to fashion bronze, especially for weapons. As the first cities reached significant size, humanity thus entered the Bronze Age, which started about 3000 B.C. and ended between 1200 and 1000 B.C.

◆ SUMER

Cities of Sumer Mesopotamia (the "land between the rivers") is a rich alluvial plain created by deposits from the Tigris and Euphrates rivers. At the southern end of this plain, within modern Iraq, arose a civilization with a more advanced scale of development than that of the people of Tell Hamoukar. This took place in the area known as Sumer. Geography both nourished and threatened the Sumerians. The land was fertile, yet the rivers could roar over their banks, carrying away

homes and human lives. Also, the land was open to invasion. Thus survival itself was often uncertain, a fact reflected in a strain of pessimism in Sumerian thought.

The people of Sumer and their language appear to be unrelated to any other known people or language. By about 3000 B.C. Sumer contained a dozen or more city-states—in other words, cities that were each independent of the others, each ruled by its own king (known as the *lugal*) and worshiping its own patron deity, a god that was thought to offer protection to the city. Sumerian religion held that rule by the king was a divine gift to the people and that the king ruled in the service of the gods. Thus religion and government, two of the large themes of civilization, were combined to comfort the people and, at the same time, to organize and control society.

Sumerian cities were much larger than the early farming villages already mentioned. One of them, Uruk, had a population estimated at 50,000 by around 3000 B.C. and a walled circumference of ten miles. The citizens of each city were divided into three classes: nobles and priests, commoners, and slaves. These classifications are the first example of what we shall often meet in history: a recognized, legal division of people into social orders. The king was not considered divine, but rather a servant of the gods. In practical political terms, he held power only so long as he could command support from the powerful priests and nobles.

The City and Its God   At the center of a Sumerian city usually stood a ziggurat, a terraced tower built of baked brick and culminating in a temple, probably for the patron god of the city. A ziggurat might be a stupendous structure: The wall surrounding one was some thirty-six feet thick. The Old Testament contains many echoes from Sumer, and it seems likely that the story in the Bible of the Tower of Babel was ultimately based on the memory of a ziggurat.

In Sumerian culture, the patron god theoretically owned the whole city; but in fact, much of the land was private property, held mainly by powerful men and their families but also by private citizens. Most houses were of a single story and were jammed into narrow streets, but some richer houses had two stories and an open court. The people were monogamous, and women held property and took part in business but did not hold political office.

Trade and Mathematics   Geography also forced Sumerians to devise the art of trading. Trade was essential for the growth of Sumerian cities because, despite the region's astonishing fertility, it lacked good timber and stone. Sumerians

▲ **A ziggurat from Ur. The stairway leads up to a room in which a god could rest and take his pleasure. The ziggurat formed the core of a temple compound, while around it were storehouses.**
Georg Gerster/Comstock

pioneered the art of building in baked brick, but to obtain other materials they had to export such goods as metalwork, a craft at which they became outstanding.

Perhaps to bolster their expertise in the essential art of trading, the Sumerians developed a precise system of mathematical notation. Their system was the sexagesimal, in which the number 60 (*sexaginta* in Latin) is one of the main elements; this system has the advantage of including 3, 10, and 12 as factors. One of the longest-lasting legacies of Mesopotamia to our world is this system: Even today, the foot has 12 inches; the day, twice 12, or 24, hours; the minute and hour, 60 units each; and the circle, 360 degrees.

Sumerian Writing   Historians have long disputed whether the Sumerians or the Egyptians first developed the art of writing; recent research may show a slight lead in favor of Egypt. In any case, the Sumerians were writing by about 3000 B.C. The most important intellectual tool ever discovered, writing enables people to keep records, codify laws, and transmit knowledge. All the record keeping, libraries, and literature of later times are made possible by this invention. Their script was pictographic: Each sign was originally a stylized picture of the article that the scribe had in mind.

In time, scribes reduced the complexity of the system by simplifying pictures and by combining several pictures into one. In this process of abstraction, the meaning of a sign might change. For example, a crude picture of a star was simplified into four wedge-shaped marks and given the meaning of "god" or "heaven."[3] In another kind of refinement, the Sumerian script became at least partly alphabetic and phonetic rather than remaining purely a system of pictographic writing. Sumerian texts were written on clay tablets by pressing the end of a reed or bone stylus into the wet clay; the resulting wedge-shaped marks are called *cuneiform* (Latin *cuneus*, meaning "wedge"), a name used for all such scripts in whatever language they occur. *Scripts* are not *languages:* They are symbols that can be used to write several

[3]The Sumerian system of writing is excellently described by S. N. Kramer, *The Sumerians*, 1963, pp. 302 ff.

▲ A relief showing the Sumerian hero Gilgamesh holding a conquered lion, from the reign of Sargon II of Assyria, eighth century B.C. The relief shows the long continuation of the Sumerian legend.
Giraudon/Art Resource

languages, as the Latin script is used to write all the languages of western Europe.

The Epic of Gilgamesh   Sumerian literature has left us a priceless document, a moderately long and stirring narrative known as the Epic of Gilgamesh. There evidently was a king in Sumer with this name (about 2700 B.C.), but in the epic, Gilgamesh is a great hero and ruler, said to be part man and part god. The woodless geography of Sumer dictates part of the story, as Gilgamesh sets out to recover cedar from northern lands (probably what is now Syria). He travels with his companion Enkidu, who is killed by the storm god, Enlil. Gilgamesh, mourning the loss of his friend and confronted with the near certainty of death, plods on through the world in search of eternal life. He finds the plant that restores youth, but a serpent swallows it while Gilgamesh is bathing. In sorrow he returns home, and the epic ends with his death and funeral.

The epic is profoundly pessimistic and gives us a key to the Sumerian view of the universe. The gods, who created the world, established the standards by which people had to live. The storm god, Enlil, lived in heaven. Normally kind and fatherly, Enlil made the rich soil of Mesopotamia fertile and was credited with designing the plow. At times, however, when Enlil had to carry out the harsh decrees of other gods, he became terrifying.

The Fate of Humanity in Sumerian Thought   This fearful alternation between divine favor and divine punishment doubtless reflects the uncertainty bred in the Sumerians by the constant threat of floods. When the rivers overflowed and destroyed the crops, the Sumerians thought the gods had withdrawn their favor, and they rationalized such treatment by assuming that they had somehow offended the gods or failed to observe their requirements.

In Sumerian mythology, humanity was almost completely dependent on the gods. Indeed, Sumerian myth taught that the gods had created people merely to provide slaves for themselves. In another Sumerian epic, *The Creation of Mankind*, Marduk the creator says, "Let him be burdened with the toil of the gods, that they may freely breathe." Other Sumerian myths foreshadow the biblical accounts of eating from the tree of knowledge in paradise and of the flood that covered the earth.

Sargon of Akkad and the Revival of Ur   Wars among the cities of Sumer weakened them and prepared the way for the first great warlord of Western history: Sargon, of the area called Akkad, named for a city just north of Babylon. Sargon ruled from 2371 to 2316 B.C.[4] and conquered all Mesopotamia; his kingdom even reached the Mediterranean Sea. From the name Akkad, the language of Sargon is called Akkadian; it is of the Semitic linguistic family and includes both Babylonian and Assyrian. Thus, through Sargon, we meet one of the most important of all groups of peoples in Western civilization, the Semites. The difference between Semites and other peoples of the region—indeed, between most peoples—is linguistic, not "racial." The peoples of the region spoke a number of related languages including Akkadian, Hebrew, and Canaanite. Akkadian, also written in cuneiform, now replaced Sumerian as a spoken language, although Sumerian continued as a written language until about the beginning of the Christian era.

Sargon and his successors ruled from Akkad until about 2230 B.C., when invasion, and perhaps internal dissension, dissolved the Akkadian kingdom. The Sumerians then regained control of southern Mesopotamia and established the so-called Third Dynasty of Ur. The chief ruler of this period was Ur-Nammu (2113–2096 B.C.). He created another practice that we will see again and again in history when he issued the first law code and spelled out regulations and penalties for a broad range of offenses. He also established standard weights and measures, a recognition of the importance of trade to the people of his state. Ur-Nammu's law code is preserved in only fragmentary form, but it is clear that he laid down fines in money rather than calling for physical retribution: "If a man has cut off the foot of another man . . .

---

[4]Dates in early Near Eastern history are in constant revision. For dates in this chapter, we normally rely on the *Cambridge Ancient History,* 3rd ed., 1970–2000.

he shall pay ten shekels . . . If a man has severed with a weapon the bones of another man . . . he shall pay one mina of silver." (Some historians assign this code to his son Shulgi.)

◆ THE BABYLONIAN KINGDOM

Ur declined, toward the year 2000 B.C., and was destroyed by neighboring peoples in 2006. A Semitic people called Amorites soon established their own capital at Babylon, within the region known as Babylonia. Hammurabi, the sixth king of the dynasty in Babylon itself, finally succeeded in unifying Mesopotamia under his rule.

Hammurabi and His Law Code Hammurabi (1792–1750 B.C.) is a towering figure whose greatest legacy is the most significant of all the documents written down to this time: a stone column, now in the Louvre Museum in Paris, recording in cuneiform script a long series of legal judgments published under his name. This so-called Code of Hammurabi, like the earlier one of Ur-Nammu, is not a complete constitution or system of law; rather, it is a compilation of those laws and decisions that Hammurabi thought needed restating. Its form is important. The code begins with a preamble, in which the god Marduk declares that he is giving his laws to Hammurabi; this preamble thus validates the laws by assigning them a divine origin.

The code includes 280 sections, much more carefully organized than any earlier one that we know (see "Hammurabi's Law Code," p. 13). Hammurabi has always been considered the primary example of the lawgiver, the man who grasped the organizing power of royal declarations of law; his example was to be followed by many other potentates, whether or not they consciously looked back to the Babylonian model. The sections of the code, like those of Ur-Nammu's code, are all arranged in the form, "If *A* takes place, *B* shall follow," for example, "If a man strikes his father, they shall cut off his hand."

Hammurabi recognized three classes within his society: We follow the historian H. W. F. Saggs[5]

and call them gentleman (one of the landowning families), landless free citizen, and slave. The penalties for various offenses were not uniform; rather, they differed according to the status of the victim. Sometimes the code allowed monetary compensation rather than physical retaliation. For example, "If a man destroys another man's eye, they shall destroy his eye"; but "If a man destroys the eye of another man's slave, he shall pay one half the slave's price." The penalties were severe, to say the least, and the rule of strict retaliation between members of the same class has given us the saying "an eye for an eye, a tooth for a tooth"[6] as a motto for Hammurabi's principles.

Women and the Family in the Code But Hammurabi was not concerned merely with retaliation. Among the most forward-looking provisions in his code were those regarding the family. Hammurabi evidently recognized the vulnerable position of women and children in his society and took care to protect them. If a man's wife became ill, he could marry another woman but had to continue to support the first wife; and she, if she wished, could move out and keep her dowry, that is, the contribution made by her family when she was married. A widower could not spend his dead wife's dowry but had to save it for her sons; and a widow could keep her dowry.

Hammurabi regulated marriage with care, evidently wanting to secure a stable life for future generations. He dealt with breach of promise by decreeing that, if a man had paid a marriage price to his potential father-in-law and then decided not to marry the young woman, the woman's father could keep the marriage price. If a man wanted to divorce a wife who had not produced children, he could do so but had to return her dowry.

The Code and Society The code is not wholly a progressive document. Some decisions in the code reflect a double standard for the sexes. A wife could divorce her husband for adultery and reclaim her dowry, but only if she had been chaste; if not, she was thrown into the river (and, presumably,

---

[5]*Civilization before Greece and Rome*, 1989, p. 44.

[6]This formulation also reaches us through the Bible (Exod. 21:24).

Hammurabi's Law Code

Here are some excerpts from the "judgments" laid down by Hammurabi in his famous law code.

"When Marduk [the patron god of Babylon] sent me to rule the people and to bring help to the country, I established law and justice in the language of the land and promoted the welfare of the people. At that time I decreed:

"1. If a man accuses another man of murder but cannot prove it, the accuser shall be put to death.

"2. If a man bears false witness in a case, or cannot prove his testimony, if that case involves life or death, he shall be put to death.

"22. If a man commits robbery and is captured, he shall be put to death.

"23. If the robber is not captured, the man who has been robbed shall, in the presence of the god, make a list of what he has lost, and the city and the governor of the province where the robbery was committed shall compensate him for his loss.

"138. If a man wants to divorce his wife who has not borne him children, he shall give her money equal to her marriage price and shall repay to her the dowry she brought from her father; and then he may divorce her.

"142. If a woman hates her husband and says, 'You may not possess me,' the city council shall inquire into her case; and if she has been careful and without reproach and her husband has been going about and belittling her, she is not to blame. She may take her dowry and return to her father's house.

"195. If a son strikes his father, they shall cut off his hand.

"196. If a man destroys the eye of another man, they shall destroy his eye.

"197. If he breaks another man's bone, they shall break his bone.

"200. If a man knocks out a tooth of a man of his own rank, they shall knock out his tooth."

From Robert F. Harper (tr.), *The Code of Hammurabi*, Gordon Press, 1904, 1991 (language modified).

drowned) along with her lover. Nowhere does the code state that a husband will suffer the same punishment if he has been unfaithful.

At the end of his long document, Hammurabi added a proud epilogue, reading in part, "The great gods called me, and I am the guardian shepherd whose beneficent shadow is cast over my city. In my bosom I carried the people of the land of Sumer and Akkad; I governed them in peace; in my wisdom I sheltered them." He thus combined the power of both law and religious belief to create a civic order for his society.

◆ MESOPOTAMIAN CULTURE

Hammurabi's subjects used all manner of commercial records (bills, letters of credit, and the like), and their knowledge of mathematics was amazing. They built on foundations laid by the Sumerians, using the sexagesimal system, with the number 60 as the base. They had multiplication tables, exponents, tables for computing interest, and textbooks with problems for solution.

The Mesopotamians also developed complex systems of astrology (the art of predicting the future from the stars) and astronomy. It is not certain which science inspired the other, but we have both astrological predictions and astronomic observations from the second millennium. The Babylonian calendar had twelve lunar months and thus had only 354 days, but astronomers learned how to regularize the year by adding a month at certain intervals. When the Hebrews and Greeks wanted to order time through a calendar, they learned the method from the Babylonians. In fact, the calendars of both Jerusalem and Athens were also lunar, with 354 days and a month added from time to time.

III. Egypt

The early cities of Mesopotamia had turbulent histories, falling now to one warlord, now to another. The kingdom of Egypt, by contrast, achieved a nearly incredible permanence. The

Chronology

DATES IN EGYPTIAN HISTORY
3100–332

The basic source for Egyptian chronology is a list of the rulers compiled about 280 B.C. by Manetho, an Egyptian priest, who wrote in Greek. He grouped the kings into thirty dynasties (later chronicles added a thirty-first). Modern scholars accept Manetho's divisions and have established these approximate dates B.C.:

Archaic Period (Dynasties 1–2)	3100–2700
Old Kingdom (Dynasties 3–6)	2700–2200
First Intermediate Period (Dynasties 7–10)	2200–2050
Middle Kingdom (Dynasties 11–12)	2050–1800
Second Intermediate Period (Dynasties 13–17, invasion of Hyksos)	1800–1570
New Kingdom, or Empire (Dynasties 18–20)	1570–1085
Postempire (Dynasties 21–31)	1085–332
Conquest of Egypt by Persia	525
Conquest of Egypt by Alexander the Great	332

► Top: The ceremonial palette of King Narmer is a symbolic representation of the unification of Upper and Lower Egypt. This side of the palette shows the king, wearing the white crown of Upper Egypt, smashing the head of an enemy. The god Horus, in the form of a falcon, holds a rope attached to a captive of Lower Egypt, a region symbolized by six papyrus plants.

► Bottom: On this side of the palette King Narmer has completed his conquest of Lower Egypt and wears the red crown of that kingdom. He is reviewing the bodies of decapitated victims. The exotic beasts with necks intertwined may symbolize the unity of the two Egypts.
Hirmer Fotoarchiv

basic element in the long history of Egyptian civilization is the Nile River. The Nile overflows its banks each summer, reviving the land with fresh water and depositing a thick layer of alluvial soil for cultivation. Only this yearly flood protected the early Egyptians from starvation.

The geography of Egypt must also have played a part in the social organization of the state. In

▲ **An example of a hieroglyph. The man on the left says (reading from right to left), "Seize [it] well."**
The worker on the right replies (from top to bottom), "I will do as you wish." From the tomb of
Ptahhotep (Old Kingdom, Dynasty V. ca. 2565–2423 B.C.).

effect, Egyptians could live only along the Nile
and could not withdraw into any kind of interior.
Moreover, the need to live close to the river isolated
Egypt from other peoples and allowed a long,
generally unbroken development. The climate is
usually equable, and the river was a friend, not the
potential enemy that it was in Sumer.

These conditions allowed the kings to control
their subjects through governors and, if need be,
with troops up and down the river. The narrow
bed of the Nile as it flows down to the Mediterranean Sea is almost a metaphor for the highly
"vertical" structure of Egyptian society. Egyptians
must have thought that the regularity of their
agricultural life was a gift from the gods. The
kings and their servants saw to the maintenance
of religion, and the faith of Egypt was a large factor in the strength and longevity of their society.

◆ THE OLD AND MIDDLE KINGDOMS

Unification of Egypt and Its Kings Historians
treat Egyptian history in three periods: the Old,
Middle, and New Kingdoms. These periods in
turn are divided into some thirty-one groups of
kings, or dynasties. Early Egypt was divided into
two regions, Upper Egypt (the Nile Valley) and
Lower Egypt (the river delta, where the water
spreads into a shape like the Greek letter delta). A
king, Menes (also known as Narmer), who lived
about 3100 B.C., unified Upper and Lower Egypt
and established a capital at Memphis. By the beginning of the Old Kingdom (about 2700 B.C.), the
land had been consolidated under the strong central power of the king, who enjoyed a supremacy
that we can hardly imagine today. The king (he
was not called *pharaoh* until the New Kingdom,
which began about 1570 B.C.) was the owner of all

Egypt and was considered a god as well. The whole economy was a royal monopoly; serving the king was a hierarchy of officials, ranging from governors of provinces down through local mayors and tax collectors. Artisans, peasants, and servants, all working for the king, nourished the whole system.

The supreme monuments of the Old Kingdom are the three immense pyramids, tombs for kings, built at Giza (now within the city of Cairo) between 2600 and 2500 B.C. These staggering feats of engineering dwarf any other monuments from any age. The Egyptians were the unchallenged masters in cutting and manipulating stone. They fitted the tremendous blocks in the pyramids together with nearly perfect tightness. Building such a pyramid may well have been the chief activity of the king during his rule. The ability to move and arrange such huge weights was a sign of an omnipotent ruler.

Religion   The king was seen as a god—specifically, the incarnation of the god Horus, who is represented in art as a falcon. Here Egypt differs from the Mesopotamian kingdoms, in which the ruler was not considered divine. Thus Egypt offers another example of the political power of re-

▲ THE PYRAMIDS OF GIZA. Left to right, the pyramid of
Menkaure, Khefre, and Khufu (the "Great" pyramid).
Henning Bock/AKG London

ligion in organizing early societies. Other gods, who occupied lesser positions in Egyptian religion, appeared in a variety of forms, often as animals, and in origin were probably deities of the villages up and down the Nile. The Egyptians believed in a pleasant life after death, in which people would perform their usual tasks but with more success. The king, already a god, would become a greater god; soothsayers, priests, and administrators would hold even higher positions. For everyone who had lived a good life, there would be delights such as boating and duck hunting.

In Egyptian mythology, the god who ruled over the dead was Osiris, originally a god of fertility. Myths taught that he had given Egypt its laws and shown the people how to prosper. Legend also told that he was murdered by his treacherous brother and his body cut into fragments, which his loving wife and sister, Isis, reassembled, thus resurrecting him. Osiris' son, Horus, was identified with the king, who was, as we have said, considered the incarnation of Horus on earth and the center of the world.

In harmony with their expectation of survival beyond death, the Egyptians made careful preparations for the physical needs of the afterlife, especially by placing favored possessions, such as jewelry and wine cups, into a tomb and embalming and making mummies of the dead. Statues sat in the tombs of kings as receptacles for their spirits in case their bodies should be destroyed.

Maat   The Egyptians recognized an abstract ethical quality called *maat*, which Egyptologists translate roughly as "right order." *Maat* existed if everything was in the order that the gods had ordained. *Maat* was a kind of primeval and cosmic harmonizing force that arranged all created things in the right relationships. All ancient societies valued order—most of them had a monarchic system that naturally prized discipline—but the notion of *maat* seems to show a new way of advocating moral behavior. When a society can give a name to the abstract idea of right order, a subtler kind of thinking is taking place. Right order would, indeed, help to hold Egyptian society together. The king maintained *maat* and acted in accordance with it; he could not, therefore, be evil or act wrongly. Thus *maat* illustrates another

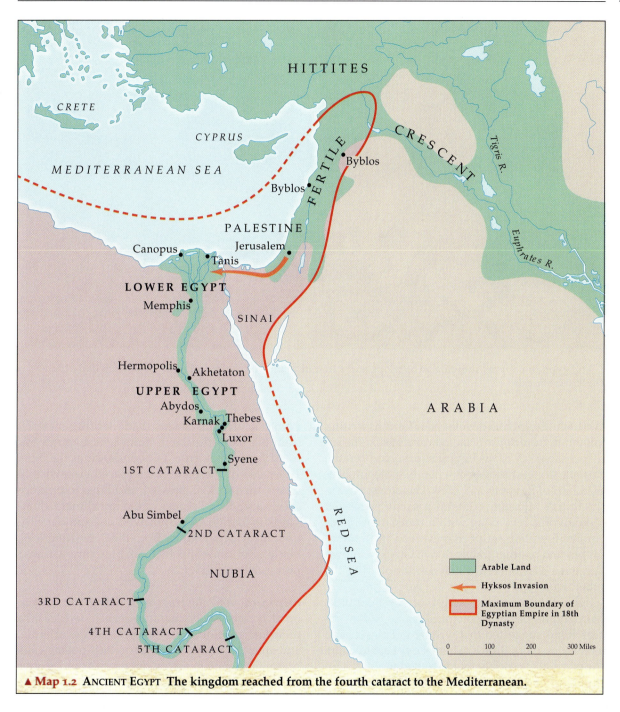

▲ **Map 1.2** ANCIENT EGYPT **The kingdom reached from the fourth cataract to the Mediterranean.**

frequent use of religion throughout history: as a carefully crafted tool to promote and maintain social order and political control. Egyptian religion also taught that Osiris, ruler of the next world, judged human beings and decided whether the dead truly deserved admission to the hereafter.

At a later period Osiris is shown in art accompanied by 42 judges, who weigh the merits of the deceased against the demands of *maat*. The Egyptian judgment of the dead may be the earliest example of the need and reward for ethical conduct in life.

▲ **An Egyptian papyrus showing an antelope and a lion in a game of chess; a playful scene from daily life.**
The British Museum.

Writing Egyptians developed a form of writing known as *hieroglyphs* ("sacred carvings"). The indispensable key to the Egyptian past has been the Rosetta stone, discovered when Napoleon occupied part of Egypt in A.D. 1798. This stone, now in the British Museum, contains a partly preserved hieroglyphic text along with a translation in the cursive Egyptian script that evolved from hieroglyphs and another translation in Greek, a known language that offered a way of deciphering the other two.

Like the cuneiform script of Mesopotamia, hieroglyphs began as pictorial signs. Recent research has suggested that writing in Egypt began as early as about 3200 B.C. If so, Egypt could claim the prize as the society that invented writing, a little ahead of Sumer. Hieroglyphs sometimes use merely a picture of the object represented; for example, a small oval represents "mouth." But at some point the scribes decided to use the pictures as phonetic signs; thus *ra* continued to mean "mouth" but was also used for the sound of the consonant *r*. Fully developed hieroglyphs, like Sumerian cuneiform, are therefore a combination of pictograms and phonetic signs.

Papyrus The Egyptians made writing material from the papyrus plants (from which comes our word *paper*) that grew in abundance in the Nile. The reeds of the plant were placed crosswise in layers, then soaked, pressed, and dried to produce sheets and rolls. Because of the dry climate, thousands of papyri have survived in legible condition; most papyri come from the New Kingdom, but in later times much Greek literature was also preserved on papyri.

Literature and Instructions Egyptians developed a rich, lively literature. Their works, like their art, are full of mythology and the afterlife, and their hymns to various deities, poems celebrating the king's victory over death, and stories about the gods all reflect the serene Egyptian confidence in the beneficence of divine powers. Various texts, collectively known as the *Book of the Dead*, provide charms and other methods of ensuring a successful transition to the other world.

Success in this world appears as the central concern of another literary genre, appropriately known as "instructions" or "instructions in wisdom." These books, in which a wise man gives advice about how to get ahead in the world, offer a key to Egyptian social attitudes, especially the supreme position of the king. The writers counsel discretion and loyalty:

> If you are a man of note sitting in the council of your lord, fix your heart upon what is good. Be silent—this is better than flowers. Speak only if you can unravel the difficulty . . . to speak is harder than any other work. . . . Bend your back to him that is over you, your superior in the king's administration. So will your house endure with its substance, and your pay be duly awarded. To resist him that is set in authority is evil.[7]

Love Poetry   We also have Egyptian love poetry: "I love to go to the pond to bathe in your presence, so I may let you see my beauty in my tunic of finest royal linen, when it is wet." And there are meditations, songs, ghost stories, and fables of all kinds. In fact, not until the Greeks did the ancient world have another literature with variety and beauty equal to that of Egypt.

Mathematics and Medicine   The Egyptians were pioneers in applied science. The need for careful planting in the silt deposits of the Nile forced them to master arithmetic, geometry, and the art of surveying; an unusually rich overflow might wipe out the boundaries between plots of land, and when this happened the land had to be remeasured.

Medicine in Egypt depended largely on driving out demons from the body. The Egyptians believed that a separate god ruled over each organ and limb, and treatment consisted largely in finding the right chant to appease the appropriate deity and then delivering it in the right tone of voice. Sometimes a sorcerer simply threatened a demon by promising to invoke the aid of the gods if it did not depart at once.

An Approach to Diseases   But medicine was not based entirely on magic. We have recipes for toothache, for depression, for constipation, and much more. The Edwin Smith Papyrus, a treatise on surgery, discusses some forty-eight medical problems, classified according to the various parts of the body. Whenever possible, the author gives a diagnosis and suggests a treatment through surgery. A verdict is often given in one of three forms—"An ailment that I will treat," "An ailment with which I will contend," or "An ailment not to be treated"—probably according to whether the prognosis was favorable, uncertain, or unfavorable. This text is a witness to the birth of a kind of inquiry that transcends haphazard

▲ **Queen Hatshepsut of Egypt (1503–1482 B.C.), history's first female ruler, pictured as a sphinx, which was a divine animal. Surrounding her face are a lion's mane and a ceremonial false beard.**
The Metropolitan Museum of Art, Rogers Fund, 1931 (31.3.166).

---

[7]Adolf Erman, *The Ancient Egyptians: A Sourcebook of Their Writings,* 1966, pp. 61–62 (language modified).

folk medicine. Such maturing and broadening of knowledge independent of magic characterize the civilizing process throughout history.

◆ THE NEW KINGDOM

The Invasion of the Hyksos   A major disaster struck Egypt about 1630 B.C., the invasion of the Hyksos (the name means roughly "rulers of foreign lands"). Historians are still not certain who these invaders were, but they were probably a group of western Asiatic peoples from Syria and Palestine. Part of their success was due to their use of the horse-drawn chariot in war. They seized and controlled mainly the region of the delta, but by about 1522 B.C. Egyptian warriors from Thebes had counterattacked and had driven the Hyksos from the delta and back into their homeland. The period following their expulsion is called the New Kingdom or the Egyptian Empire.

The Eighteenth Dynasty   During the Eighteenth Dynasty the rulers in Thebes, now called *pharaohs*, strengthened the power of the central government over the nobles and organized Egypt into a military state. They enlarged their domain by invading Asia (campaigning in what is roughly modern Syria), where they clashed above all with another kingdom known as Mitanni.

Hatshepsut (1503–1482 B.C.)   Within the Eighteenth Dynasty there reigned the most powerful female ruler of ancient times, Hatshepsut. This dynamic woman seized power and in 1503 B.C. had herself crowned king of Egypt, representing this act as the will of the god Amon. It was an act of breathtaking audacity in a social system in which men had always held the absolute power of monarch. Perhaps to emphasize her right to rule as king, she had herself portrayed as a sphinx with a beard.

▲ **Akhnaton and Nefertiti in a familial scene hold three of their children while the sun-disk blesses and cherishes them. The style of art (round bellies, slender bodies, elongated jaws) is typical of the Amarna period.** M. Büsing/Bildarchiv Preussischer Kulturbesitz.

Hatshepsut wanted to be remembered above all as a builder, the restorer of Egypt. "I have repaired," she proclaimed on inscribed walls, "what was destroyed by the Hyksos; I have raised up what was in pieces ever since the Asiatics had been in the Delta, overthrowing what had been made." Her great temple tomb in the Nile valley is among the most majestic of temples in Egypt.

Thutmose III (1504–1450 B.C.) Thutmose III, Hatshepsut's successor, became Egypt's greatest military leader. He made seventeen expeditions into Asia and expanded the empire as far as the Euphrates River. He proudly recorded his victory over Mitanni (about 1465 B.C.). His successors, exploiting these conquests, grew rich on the tribute paid by subject peoples. With this economic power the Egyptians expanded their trade, honored their gods with more temples, and continued working the rich copper mines in the Sinai peninsula.

Akhnaton's Religious Reform After the conquests of Thutmose III, a dramatic conflict of religions took place in the New Kingdom. This struggle arose from a contest between the pharaoh and certain priests and nobles, as each party strove to make its own god the supreme one. Thus the apparent religious battle—not for the last time in history—was, in reality, a political one. Although this battle was but one event during the centuries of the New Kingdom, the reforming aims of one side in this conflict have fascinated modern observers.

Early in his reign, King Amenhotep IV (1379–1362 B.C.) began to oppose the worship of Amen-Re, for centuries the traditional god of Thebes, and sponsored the worship of the *aton,* the physical disk, or circle, of the sun. Supported by his wife, Nefertiti, Amenhotep appears to have been trying to overcome the influence of priests and bureaucrats in Thebes. To advertise the new faith among his people, he changed his own name to Akhnaton, meaning "he who serves Aton." He moved his capital from Thebes to a completely new city called Akhetaton, "the horizon of Aton" (a village called El Amarna today), where he built a temple to Aton. He composed a soaring hymn in praise of Aton, hailing him as the creator of the world—an account of creation comparable to

those of the Sumerians and the Israelites.[8] Doubtless through his desire, art of the Amarna period became realistic; the king was shown with a pot belly and elongated head and jaw, and this style reached into portraits of common people as well.

There is evidence that Akhnaton fought the worship of other gods, and some historians have gone so far as to call him the first monotheist. But such a conception is anachronistic and overlooks how Aton was worshiped: The royal family alone worshiped the god, while the Egyptian people were expected to continue to worship the pharaoh himself. Artistic scenes show priests and nobles in attitudes of reverence, but they are addressing their prayers to the pharaoh, not directly to Aton.

The Reaction against Akhnaton The more conservative priests, and probably most Egyptians, continued to worship Amen-Re, and Akhnaton's religious reform ended with his death. The next pharaoh changed his name from Tutankhaton to Tutankhamen, thus indicating that Amen-Re, the older chief deity, was again in favor. The royal court moved back to Thebes, and the city named for Aton, Akhetaton, was abandoned and destroyed. Akhnaton's name was savagely hacked off monuments and king lists, and he was now known as "the criminal of Akhetaton." The young king Tutankhamen reigned for only nine years and was buried with dazzling splendor. His tomb, discovered in A.D. 1922 intact with all its treasures, is one of the most stunning finds in the history of Egyptology.

Ramses II (1294–1227 B.C.) In the Nineteenth Dynasty, the New Kingdom emerged from the period of religious conflict with renewed strength and was led by ambitious pharaohs, the most famous of whom was Ramses II. He fought a major, though inconclusive, battle with the Hittite kingdom of Asia Minor in 1290 B.C., at Kadesh in Palestine and carried on the war until 1274 B.C. At this time the two kingdoms signed a peace treaty;[9]

---

[8]Strong resemblances have been seen between this hymn and Psalm 104. See J. A. Wilson, *The Culture of Ancient Egypt*, 1951, p. 227.

[9]Both the Hittite and Egyptian texts of this document are translated in J. B. Pritchard (ed.), *Ancient Near Eastern Texts Relating to the Old Testament*, 1969, pp. 199–203.

▲ **Syrian subjects presenting tribute to the pharaoh of Egypt on a wall painting at Thebes in the period of the empire.**
C. M. Dixon/British Museum

this may have been the world's first nonagression pact and brings forth another of the themes that run through history, namely diplomacy and negotiation between states.

Ramses II devoted much of Egypt's wealth to amazing building projects. At Karnak, for example, he completed an enormous hall of columns sacred to Amen-Re, who had now fully regained his old position. Ramses' supreme achievement as a builder is the colossal temple that he had carved out of the rocky cliffs along the Nile at Abu Simbel. In front of the temple sit four 65-foot high statues of the king. The building of the Aswan Dam by the modern Egyptians would have drowned the temple and its statues beneath the water of an artificial lake; but an international group of engineers preserved Ramses' desire to be remembered for all time by cutting the outer monuments free and raising them above the level of the water.

◆ A VIEW OF EGYPTIAN SOCIETY

Administration and Slavery   In antiquity, communication by ship was greatly superior to overland transportation in animal-drawn carts

because of the greater speed and economy of sailing. The Nile therefore imposed a natural administrative unity on Egypt. The kings secured their power through the help of ministers and advisers, especially the class of priests, while a complex bureaucracy carried out the routine work of government and saw to the economy, which was a royal monopoly with the exception of marketing the simplest household products.

Slaves existed, but the economic difference between free citizens and slaves was not always vast. Both classes worked the fields, labored on the pyramids, and were indeed the ultimate economic basis for the regime, although their own lives changed little from one generation to another.

Education   For all its controls, the Egyptian hierarchy did allow youths to enter and rise through education. The kings and their gods needed all manner of scribes, treasurers, and functionaries, and Egyptian children might learn the art of writing in a school run by a temple or a palace or even from a private teacher in a village. They normally studied from age four to age sixteen and could then enter the army or the royal service. Scribes were also needed for the arts of medicine and architecture and for the priesthoods; most priests were men, but some were women.

Women and the Family Men and women viewed marriage as most desirable and often married as teenagers. The desire for children was universal as insurance against the future. One wise man of the Eighteenth Dynasty advised, "Take a wife when you are young, so that she might give you a son. Happy is the man with a large family, for he is respected on account of his children." On marriage, a woman obtained the title "mistress of the house," and the house and its management were her responsibilities. Agricultural work was by far the main occupation of Egyptians, and women participated in the task; they also went shopping, a fact noted with surprise by the Greek historian Herodotus on his visit to Egypt.

Most women were peasants with little education, but they had certain powers not granted, for example, to women of Israelite or Greco-Roman societies. Most remarkably, in view of the critical importance of ownership of land in Egypt, land passed down from mother to daughter; probably, it has been said, because it is always clear who one's mother is, while paternity can be uncertain. Likewise, men commonly identified themselves by citing the name of their mother, not of their father.

Women and Occupations This method of passing on property meant that women could own and manage both land and other property. Thus a woman did not have to turn her property over to her husband at the time of marriage. Women could also initiate legal action, buy and sell property, and execute wills. But women were legally equal to men only within their own class. Most women were peasants and shared the daily work of planting crops, picking fruit, and carrying baskets; above all, they had to produce children.

Men normally held the important positions in the state and the bureaucracy (again the amazing position of the queen Hatshepsut should be remembered). Below this level of political influence, women performed tasks like overseeing weavers, singers, and cooks; some were treasurers in private businesses. A respected occupation was that of midwife, and midwives delivered most Egyptian babies. A great many women were singers, dancers, and professional mourners at funerals. Among higher positions open to women were priesthoods, often including priestesses who chanted or played instruments in temples.

Women were buried along with their men, sharing in the elegance of the tomb according to the rank of their husbands. Privileged women could be given in death a profusion of jewels, necklaces, and other ornaments.

The Permanence of Egypt We must not overlook the turmoil within Egyptian history: the invasion of the Hyksos, wars in Asia, the collapse of the New Kingdom, and its conquest by Assyria and then by Persia (see "Dates in Egyptian History"). Yet there remains the awesome *permanence* of Egypt: No other state, in the history of the nations we call Western, ever survived so long. On the whole, over the span of some thirty centuries, life flowed predictably, like the Nile, making severe demands but bringing the material for a well-earned reward.

IV. Palestine

We have already discussed the Semitic societies of Babylonia and Assyria and turn now to Semites in the area of Palestine. They include the Phoenicians, who were famous as sailors and explorers; they also developed a simple alphabet that became the mother of all the scripts of Europe. Even more important to the Western experience was the society of Israel, which gave the Western world its greatest book—the Bible.

◆ CANAANITES AND PHOENICIANS

The region of Palestine was originally inhabited by a group of Semitic tribes known as the Canaanites, among whose cities were Jericho and Jerusalem. By about 1200 B.C. the Canaanites had settled mainly in Phoenicia, a narrow region along the Mediterranean Sea (roughly modern Lebanon). The Phoenicians drew part of their culture from the Mesopotamian and Egyptian states nearby, but they were also brilliant innovators.

The Phoenician Alphabet Their outstanding contribution was a simplified alphabet with twenty-two characters that was later adopted by

▲ **Several translations of "I am Darius," in Phoenician, Akkadian, hieroglyph, and Greek.**

the Greeks and became the ancestor of Western alphabets. The political and social importance of this invention is impossible to overstate. It ended the long period during which people had to learn thousands of pictorial symbols to be reasonably literate and writing was a mysterious art known to only a few. Especially in the hands of the Greeks, writing brought a knowledge of law codes and historical records within the intellectual reach of ordinary citizens and led to reevaluation of the past and a critical spirit about received tradition.

Phoenician Exploration The Phoenicians lacked the military power to create an empire, but they influenced other cultures, especially through trade on both land and sea. They established trading posts or colonies far from Palestine, the most famous of which was Carthage, a powerful city on the north coast of Africa that controlled parts of North Africa and Spain. The Greek historian Herodotus records that some Phoenicians for the first time sailed completely around Africa.

Among the Phoenician articles of trade was a reddish dye that the ancients called *purple;* cloth dyed in this color became a luxury and has remained a mark of royalty or eminence. The Phoenicians' wide explorations made them masters of the sea, and because of their sailing ability they provided the navy for the Persian Empire.

They and other Canaanite peoples had thus developed a high urban civilization by the time the Israelites began their invasion of the Palestinian coast.

◆ HEBREW SOCIETY AND THE BIBLE

South of Phoenicia is the region of Palestine that today is known as Israel, also settled in antiquity by speakers of the Semitic Hebrew language. The Hebrew Bible, or Old Testament, provides a continuous record of how this people viewed its past, but before historians can use the narratives and chronicles of the Jewish and Christian sacred books as a source, they must take a stand on the credibility of the documents. Scholars in the nineteenth century questioned whether the Old Testament contained unchallengeable, divinely revealed truth. Archaeology in recent years has often confirmed the Bible, at least in questions of geography and topography, but literal accuracy is not, after all, the central issue to the historian. Religious traditions of any society, whether or not they are strictly verifiable, can instruct us about a society, just as do law codes and lists of kings.

The Israelite chroniclers concentrated on a single god and on humanity's relationship to him. This great theme, varied in countless ways, fuses the Old Testament into a story about one god and the history of his chosen people. Unlike

Mesopotamian epics, the Bible deals with real people and real times; it combines ethics, poetry, and history into the most influential book in the Western tradition.

The Early Hebrews and Moses   Hebrew tradition tells that a nomadic tribe led by Abraham migrated into Palestine from the east. A probable date for this movement is about 1900 B.C. His grandson, Jacob, is said to have organized the settlers into twelve tribes under the leadership of his twelve sons. Jacob himself also took the name Israel (meaning "God strove" or "God ruled"), and this name is also used for the people.[10] Israel was therefore a tribal society, unlike the urban society of Sumer or the unified monarchy of Egypt.

Egypt and the Exodus   Some Israelite tribes settled in Canaan. Others migrated to Egypt, according to the Bible to escape a severe famine, although immigration into Egypt had long been allowed. They remained there, but evidently suffered such harsh conditions that they determined to return to their homeland. Their return took place probably about 1240–1230 B.C., in the "exodus" (see "The Salvation of Israel," p. 26). At their head was Moses, who led them across the Sinai peninsula during a period of general unrest in the Near East. Their return was the critical formative event in their history. Moses organized the tribes of Israel and some neighboring Canaanites into a confederation bound by a covenant to the god he named YHWH (by convention, we write this word Yahweh; in English it later became Jehovah) and placed all the people in Yahweh's service. Moses proclaimed the new covenant between God and his people on Mount Sinai, in the wastes of the desert. According to the Old Testament Book of Exodus, he received his instructions directly from Yahweh. These instructions, a document of the greatest historical interest, include the Ten Commandments, in which Yahweh issues the terse order, "Thou shalt have no other gods before me." That is, the Commandments do not deny the existence of other gods; rather, they insist that Yahweh

be worshiped as the supreme one (such a doctrine is known as henotheism). So far as we can tell, this was the first time that any people in Western civilization accepted one god above all others.

But *why* did Israel accept one god as the highest, in contrast to the rest of the ancient world, in which families of deities were the rule? Was Moses perhaps influenced by Akhnaton's worship of Aton as the supreme god? We do not know, but we may guess that Moses saw the need to unify his people so that they would be strong enough to regain their home in Palestine; and what could forge a stronger bond than having the whole people swear allegiance to one god above all?

Moses also laid down a code of laws, which, unlike earlier codes, is a series of laws prescribing ethically right conduct. Far more than other ancient codes, this one respects people over property, lays down protection for the oppressed, and insists on respect for parents. This code appears to be the first intervention of religion into the private behavior of human beings. The historical reality of Moses, the fact that his laws are connected with the experience of a people, and the power of the ethical concerns of that people have given the faith of Israel an immediacy to which Sumerian or Egyptian religion could hardly pretend.

Israel and Its Society   Early Israelite society was clearly father-dominated through the patriarchs and God, whom they considered their supreme father. This structure led to a patriarchal family and shaped the legal status of women. Marriage occurs through purchase throughout the Old Testament, and a daughter might be bestowed on a man as a kind of salary, as in the moving story of Jacob and Rachel. Jacob loved Rachel dearly, and this is the point of the story, but he worked seven years to gain her in lieu of the purchase price (Gen. 29). Sometimes women were awarded as prizes for military success.

Some women did indeed rise above such a level of dependence on the family, and their heroism is all the greater. For example, the book of Ruth tells the story of Naomi, a woman of Bethlehem who moved to Moab (east of the river Jordan and the Dead Sea). When she planned to return to Bethlehem, her loving Moabite daughter-in-law Ruth refused her orders to remain behind. Ruth toils faithfully in the field and meets Naomi's relative Boaz, whom she marries. Her grandson is Jesse

---

[10]The book of Genesis (32, 35) gives two versions of how Jacob changed his name. In the first, he wrestles with an angel, who then designates him as he who "strove with God and with humans"; in the second, God appears to him and tells him that his name shall be Israel.

THE SALVATION OF ISRAEL

◆

The Old Testament book of Exodus narrates the escape of the Israelites from Egypt and preserves the hymn of praise sung by Moses and his people after they reached the holy land. The poem celebrates the strength of God and his generosity in saving Israel. It also shows that Israel saw itself as having a special compact with God.

"I will sing to the Lord, for he has triumphed gloriously; the horse and his rider he has thrown into the sea. The Lord is my strength and my song, and he has become my salvation; this is my God, and I will praise him, my father's God, and I will exalt him. The Lord is a man of war; the Lord is his name. Pharaoh's chariots and his host he cast into the sea; and his picked officers are sunk in the Red Sea. The floods cover them; they went down into the depths like a stone. Thy right hand, O Lord, glorious in power, thy right hand, O Lord, shatters the enemy. . . . Thou hast led in thy steadfast love the people whom thou has redeemed, thou hast guided them by thy strength to thy holy abode . . . the sanctuary, O Lord, which thou hast made for thy abode, the sanctuary, O Lord, which thy hands have established. The Lord will reign for ever and ever."

From Exodus, 15, Revised Standard Version of the *Bible*, National Council of Churches of Christ, 1946, 1952, 1971.

and her great-grandson is David, who became King of Israel and whom Christians consider an ancestor of Jesus (Matthew 1). Again, there is the strong figure of Deborah. The book of Judges (5) preserves her hymn of praise to God, which many scholars consider the oldest passage in the Bible. She was also one of the judges, leaders of the villages of Israel before there was a united kingdom, and is said to have served forty years.

The Israelite Monarchy By a series of attacks on Canaanite cities and by covenants made with other tribes, the Israelites established themselves in Palestine. About 1230 B.C. they invaded Canaanite territory in a campaign aimed at expansion. Biblical stories say that Joshua, the successor of Moses, led the tribes of Israel across the Jordan River and followed God's instructions to take the Canaanite city of Jericho by siege. Many modern scholars would modify the biblical account and assume a more gradual process of occupation.

During the years of the conquest of Canaan, Israel still lacked a central government. The "judges" managed to reunite the people in periods of crisis, but the tribes then habitually drifted apart. They were also under pressure from the Philistines, a warlike people living along the coast of Palestine. According to the Bible, the people finally demanded a king, evidently wanting to imitate the practice of the Canaanites and also as protection against the Philistines: "We will have a king over us; then we shall be like other nations, with a king to govern us, to lead us out to war and fight our battles" (1 Sam. 8:20). The first king was Saul (1020?–1000?). His successor, David (1000?–961?), captured Jerusalem and made it Israel's capital. The entire nation now took the name Israel, and during his reign David extended the kingdom to its farthest boundaries. He conquered the neighboring kingdoms of Edom, Moab, Ammon, and Zobah; in modern terms, his domain included modern Israel, Lebanon, much of Jordan, and part of Syria even north of Damascus.

Solomon Solomon, David's son and successor (961?–922?), was famed for his wisdom. Like all great kings of the period, Solomon was a builder. He left behind him the physical memorial that symbolized the faith of Israel through the centuries—the Temple in Jerusalem. But the temple could not compare in size with his magnificent palace and citadel, whose stables, according to tradition, housed twelve thousand horses.

Solomon's autocratic rule and extravagance caused resentment among his people, who were heavily taxed to pay for his palace and army. After his death the kingdom split into two parts. The northern half, centered on the ancient town of Shechem, retained the name of Israel; the southern half, ruled from Jerusalem, was now called Judah. Weakened by internal quarrels, the northern kingdom of Israel was conquered in 722 B.C. by the

JEREMIAH REPROACHES ISRAEL

The people of Israel discovered henotheism, but to maintain it was not easy. The prophet Jeremiah warned his people that they were backsliding into worshiping false gods such as Baal, rather than retaining allegiance to the one true God.

"The Lord said to me, 'There is revolt among the men of Judah and the inhabitants of Jerusalem. They have turned back to the iniquities of their forefathers, who refused to hear my words; they have gone after other gods to serve them; the house of Israel and the house of Judah have broken my covenant which I made with their fathers. Therefore, thus says the Lord, Behold, I am bringing evil upon them which they cannot escape; though they cry to me, I will not listen to them. . . . The Lord once called you, "A green olive tree, fair with goodly fruit"; but with the roar of a great tempest he will set fire to it, and its branches will be consumed. The Lord of hosts, who planted you, has pronounced evil against you, because of the evil which the house of Israel and the house of Judah have done, provoking me to anger by burning incense to Baal.'"

From Jeremiah, 11, Revised Standard Version of the *Bible*, National Council of Churches of Christ, 1946, 1952, 1971.

Assyrians to the northeast, who deported much of the population into Babylonia.

The Dissolution of Israel Judah was now the only Israelite kingdom. The Greeks called this people *Ioudaioi*, from which comes the name Jews. Judah also fell in 586 B.C. to the Neo-Babylonian Kingdom ruled by Nebuchadnezzar. The captives were deported to Babylon, in the so-called Babylonian captivity, but later in the same century they were allowed by King Cyrus of Persia to trickle back into Palestine. In general the Jews became pawns of the various forces that ruled Palestine until A.D. 1948, when a revived Jewish state—the republic of Israel—took its place among sovereign nations.

The Faith and the Prophets Judaism was also shaped by a few resolute critics, known as the prophets: men of the people, tradesmen, and preachers, such as Amos, Micah, Hosea, Jeremiah, and Isaiah. These prophets were not kings and had no military power that could make the people listen to their message. The most authoritative prophet had been Moses, and all successors looked back to him for guidance. The later prophets spoke one general message: Israel was becoming corrupt and only a rigid moral reform could save it. Worship of Yahweh had sometimes been blended with that of the gods, or Baalim, of the Canaanites. Luxury, promiscuity, and extravagance were weakening the discipline of Israelite society (see "Jeremiah Reproaches Israel"). Perhaps most important, they warned that worship of Yahweh had become, for many, only a matter of form and ritual. They insisted that their people should put their faith in God and live in a just and righteous manner.

But even as they denounced the prevalent wickedness, the prophets promised that God would forgive Israel if the people repented and that he would further prove his love to Israel by sending a Messiah. The word *Messiah* (*mashiah* in Hebrew) means a person or even a thing possessing a divine power or purpose; referring to people, it came to mean one "anointed" by God to perform a special mission. From about 200 B.C. onward, Jewish thought held that a king would some day appear, a descendant of David, who would restore the power and glory of Israel on earth. The famous Dead Sea Scrolls (discussed in chapter 5), ranging in date from the second century B.C. through the first century A.D., often speak of the awaited Messiah. Christians, too, developed their theory of a Messiah, who would return to rule on earth over all humanity: To them, the "anointed one" (*ho christós* in Greek) is Jesus, but to Jews, the hero is still unborn or unknown.

The Preservation of the Faith Another event that strengthened Judaism was the organization of the sacred writings. Ezra, who wrote about 445 B.C., is the prototype of a new kind of spiritual leader—the scribe and scholar. He collected and published the first five books of the Old Testament (the Pentateuch); later scholars collected the

▲ **An extreme rarity, the only example of frescoes in a Jewish synagogue showing scenes from the Bible. From Dura Europus, ca. A.D. 239; now in a museum at Damascus.**
Princeton University Press/Art Resource.

books of the prophets. The Temple in Jerusalem, destroyed during the Neo-Babylonian invasion, had been rebuilt during the sixth century B.C. and, in the absence of a free Jewish state, assumed even greater importance as the nucleus of the faith. It fell once more, in A.D. 70, this time to the Romans, who destroyed it. But part of the western wall of the outer court survived, and at this site the Jews were permitted to gather and pray.

◆ THE JEWISH LEGACY

The Jews are the only society originating in the ancient Near East whose social and religious traditions have continued to influence modern European civilization. For reasons that no one can fully explain, adversity has never broken the Jewish spirit, and over many centuries the Jews have persisted as a society even without an independent state. Their faith provided the most persuasive answer to the problem that also troubled their neighbors—the nature of the relationship between humanity and God.

To Israel, there was only one supreme god; unlike the gods of the pagans, he was an exclusive and intolerant one. He judged severely, but he was also prepared to forgive those who sincerely regretted wrong behavior. He had created the world but stood outside the world; he had no association with the world of nature and never appeared as an animal or in any other form. Above all, he was a god for everyone, not just for nobles, priests, and kings. Christianity, the religion of medieval and modern Europe, and Islam, the chief religion of the Near East, are both children of Judaism and have drawn on the morality and ethics of the older faith.

V. The Near Eastern States

A series of general disruptions about 1250 to 1150 B.C. left no state dominant for the next few centuries until the Assyrians began their conquests. They became the first people to accomplish a political unification of large parts of the Near East (see map 1.3). The Persians, the next great imperialists of this region, built on foundations laid by the Assyrians and ruled with an administrative skill that only the Roman Empire would equal in ancient times. The Persians also developed a widely accepted religion, Zoroastrianism, some of whose doctrines persisted long after the Persian Empire had disappeared.

◆ THE ASSYRIAN STATE

The Assyrians The Assyrians were descended from Semitic nomads who had entered northern Mesopotamia about 2500 B.C. and founded the city of Ashur, named after their chief god. From this name comes the designation *Assyrian* for the people. Their language was a Semitic dialect closely resembling that of the Babylonians, and they wrote in the cuneiform script that had originated in Sumer and had remained in general use.

Assyrian Conquests About 900 B.C. the Assyrians began their most important period of conquest and expansion. They became masters of the upper reaches of Mesopotamia, and their territory included Babylonia to the south, the cities of Palestine to the west, and northern Egypt. By the middle of the seventh century B.C. their dominion embraced most of the Near East.

If any one concept could characterize Assyrian society, it would be militarism. The army was especially dominant and efficient. In administering their empire, the Assyrians faced a greater challenge than any earlier state in absorbing large kingdoms such as Egypt and Babylonia. They ruled with a degree of control unknown in any of the earlier conglomerates.

Assyrian Rule The Assyrian kings exacted heavy payments of tribute as the price of leaving the conquered territories in peace. Some peoples, such as the inhabitants of Judah, escaped further burdens, but other less independent peoples had to accept a vizier, or governor, serving the king. In some cases the imperial government deported subject peoples who might prove troublesome—for example, those inhabitants of Israel who were dispersed within the Assyrian domain. Assyrian armies stationed in the provinces were a further guarantee of stability. We must also record that

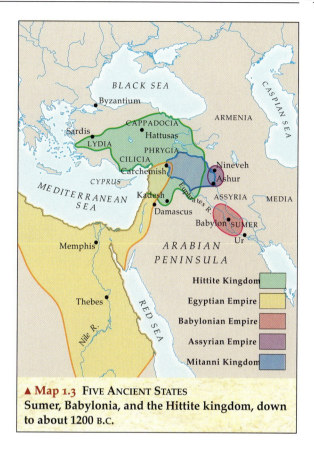

▲ **Map 1.3** **Five Ancient States**
Sumer, Babylonia, and the Hittite kingdom, down to about 1200 B.C.

Assyrian kings took pride in their brutal treatment of enemies and victims. Certainly, brutality has always existed in war, but the boast of one king is repellent:

> 3000 of their combat troops I felled with weapons.
> . . . Many of the captives taken from them I burned in a fire. Many I took alive; from some (of these) I cut off their hands to the wrist, from others I cut off their noses, ears, and fingers; I put out the eyes of many of the soldiers. . . . I burnt their young men and women to death.[11]

Language became another means of unifying the Assyrian domain; the Semitic language known as Aramaic (originally spoken by the Aramaeans, who controlled parts of Mesopotamia from about 1100 to about 900 B.C.) was ultimately spoken everywhere in lands dominated by Assyria. It later became the common tongue of the Near East and was the official language of the

---

[11]From H. W. F. Saggs, *The Might That Was Assyria*, 1984, p. 261.

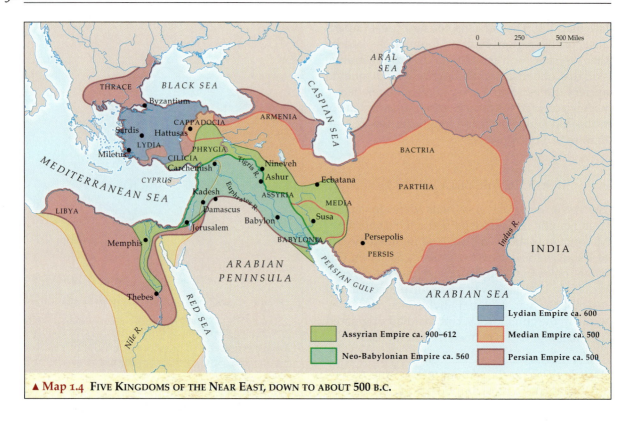

▲ **Map 1.4** FIVE KINGDOMS OF THE NEAR EAST, DOWN TO ABOUT **500** B.C.

Persian Empire. In Palestine, Aramaic was spoken by the Jews, including Jesus.

Assyrian Art and Writings   For all their harsh militarism and their brutal rule over their conquered subjects, the Assyrians created magnificent works of art. Much of the wealth extracted from the empire was spent on glorifications of the king and his conquests. Most notable are the reliefs cut on the palace walls at Nineveh, the capital, and elsewhere. The last powerful Assyrian king, Ashurbanipal (668–627 B.C.), also created a library of cuneiform texts. The largest single group of these texts covers omens, divination, or observations of the stars, because Assyrian kings relied heavily on omens and their interpretation by priests to guide royal policy.

It is hardly surprising that the subjects of the Assyrians watched for any chance to rebel. Finally, in 612 B.C., a combination of forces led by Babylonians captured Nineveh, and the Assyrian empire collapsed. Within a few years Assyria was reduced to a primitive state of nonurbanized living. Greek explorers 200 years later found it only sparsely populated.

◆ **THE CHALDEANS AND THE MEDES**

The Assyrian Empire gave way to two successor states: the Chaldean, or Neo-Babylonian, Kingdom and the Kingdom of the Medes. The Chaldeans, the dominant tribe within a new kingdom based on Babylon, were the most learned astronomers of antiquity. They kept minute records of eclipses, charted a plan of the heavens, and calculated the length of the year mathematically. Their discoveries were passed on to the Greeks and Romans and influenced all medieval and modern astronomy.

Babylon, the capital of the Neo-Babylonian Kingdom, was notorious as a center of luxury and wealth. Nebuchadnezzar (604–562 B.C.), the most famous king of the Chaldean dynasty, built lavish temples to the gods and is said to have constructed a terraced roof garden known as the Hanging Gardens, which was considered one of the Seven Wonders of the ancient world. It was he who captured Jerusalem in 586 B.C., destroyed the city and its holy temple, and scattered thousands of Jews within Babylonia, a tragedy recorded by the prophet Jeremiah.

The Iranians Down to this point we have met the Sumerians, the Egyptians, and some Semite peoples. We come now to a people who spoke an Indo-European language, the Iranians. No documents have been found in the original Indo-European language, but from this language almost all the modern languages of Europe descend. Germanic languages including English, Greek, Latin, Romance languages, Slavic languages including Russian, and the languages of India, Pakistan, and Iran all belong to this family. Perhaps about 6000–5000 B.C. the Indo-European peoples began a slow dispersion across Europe and parts of Asia. Some of them finally settled on the Indian subcontinent, while others moved westward into Greece, Italy, central Europe, and Asia Minor.

A new people, the Iranians, appeared, another branch of the family that spoke Indo-European languages. Two noteworthy Iranian societies were the Medes and the Persians. The Medes, living in the area of Media to the east of Mesopotamia, formed a coherent kingdom about 625 B.C., and they took part in the capture of Nineveh in 612 B.C. We know little of their society because no written documents from Media have yet been found.

Their neighbors, the Persians, lived in the same general area and eventually subdued the Medes. Yet the Medes had enough prestige to be named first in official documents in which both Medes and Persians are mentioned. The Greeks, too, used *Medes* (Medoi) as the term embracing both Medes and Persians, and they called their two wars with the Persian Empire the *Medic* wars.

◆ THE PERSIAN EMPIRE

Cyrus (559–530 B.C.) The Persians proceeded to form the largest, most efficient state down to their time. The founder of the Persian Empire was King Cyrus. His actions show him as a determined imperialist, and his first conquest was his victory over Media, to the north, in 550 B.C. A few years later Cyrus led his forces into western Asia Minor and conquered the kingdom of Lydia. This advance brought the Persian Empire westward as far as the Aegean Sea, which separates Asia Minor from Greece, and set the stage for a direct clash between the vast empire of the Near East and the new culture of the Greeks; but this clash was not to come for another two generations.

To secure the southern flank of his growing empire, Cyrus led his forces against the neo-Babylonian empire and captured Babylon. The inhabitants evidently welcomed him, for they offered little resistance. Their judgment was sound; Cyrus treated the city with moderation, not

◄ **An Assyrian relief showing Ashurbanipal's soldiers attacking a city. Some soldiers swim to the attack; others scale the walls with ladders while defenders fall from the ramparts.**
Hirmer Fotoarchiv.

▲ **Part of the Bisitun inscription in Iran, showing King Darius of Persia (522–486 B.C.) receiving the submission of rebels. Carved in three languages, this inscription provided the key to deciphering cuneiform writing.**
Photography by Dr. G. G. Cameron, The University of Pennsylvania (Neg ANEP Plate 462).

sacking it as an Assyrian conqueror might have done. In fact, his administration was marked by a notable toleration of the customs and religions of the people he brought under his control. We have seen that he allowed as many as 40,000 refugees from Judah to return to their homeland.

Cambyses and Egypt   Cyrus' successor, Cambyses (530–522 B.C.), made the third conquest that completed the Persian Empire: He conquered Egypt

in 525 B.C., and the rich valley of the Nile remained under Persian rule until Alexander the Great captured it in 332 B.C.

Darius (522–486 B.C.)   The most skillful administrator of the Persian Empire was Darius. He left behind a superb monument—a proud summary of his reign written in three languages (Old Persian, Akkadian, Elamite). Carved under a relief showing Darius and some of his captives, this text survives high on the face of a rock at Bisitun in Iran. In a series of paragraphs, each beginning "Saith Darius the king," he records his conquests, including that of Babylon, and the defeat and mutilation of his enemies. He also clarifies that he is the only source of law: "As was said by me, thus it was done." The tone and physical setting of this grandiose monument confirm the lofty position of the king in the Persian state. A later inscription on his tomb also proclaimed his devotion to justice: "I am a friend to right, not to wrong. Whoever does harm, I punish him according to the damage he has done." This statement reminds us of the insistence on restitution built into Hammurabi's code and shows how some Near Eastern kings, for all their unchallengeable power, tried to earn a reputation for fairness.

The Administration of the Empire   Darius divided his empire into some twenty satrapies, or provinces, each ruled by a satrap ("protector of the realm"). The king, naturally, was the supreme head of the state, but the satraps had a high degree of independence; they dispensed justice, designed foreign policy, and were in charge of finance. Each satrap, for example, was responsible for collecting an assigned amount of revenue from his province. This system of delegating authority became the model for the Roman Empire when it expanded Rome's domain outside Italy.

The Greek historian Herodotus, writing in the fifth century B.C., mentions with admiration the Persian system of roads begun by Cyrus and perfected by Darius. A great highway ran across the empire from the capital at Susa westward to Sardis in Lydia, a distance of more than one thousand miles. The first long highway built anywhere, this road served trade and commerce and also bound the far-flung empire together.

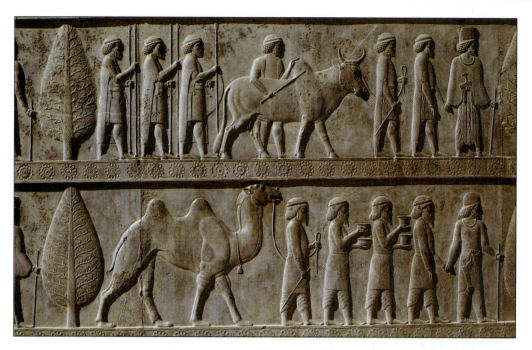

▲ **Two panels on a staircase of the great reception hall at the Persian capital, Persepolis. In each panel an official leads a messenger whose followers bear tribute for the king of Persia.**
George Holton/Photo Researchers

Some Features of Persian Rule The Persian kings ruled their immense empire from several capital cities, of which Susa and Persepolis were the most famous. The king was the absolute and supreme ruler. His word was law, and he was surrounded with pomp and ceremony; his isolation from his subjects contributed to his reputation for awesome power, which went far to establish the aura of magnificence that has colored monarchy in the Roman Empire and the subsequent kingdoms of Europe.

Royal Persian Women Mothers of the king of Persia had privileges uncommon in the Near Eastern kingdoms.[12] "Mother of the king" and "wife of the king" were technical terms, and the king's mother had direct access to the monarch. She had no formal political power but could intervene, even with the all-powerful king, for the sake of members of her family. The king's wife ranked below his mother and formed, with his mother, the center of the royal court. She could possess large

holdings of land and treasure, riches beyond the dreams of any influential Greek woman.

Zoroaster The Persian king was never considered divine, but he often served as a priest and claimed to have received his authority from the god of the Persians, Ahura Mazda. The prophet who formed the Persian faith was Zoroaster (also known as Zarathustra). We are not sure of the date of his life and work, but a number of historians think he lived about 600 B.C. or soon after.

Zoroaster was not considered divine; rather, he taught that the supreme god, Ahura Mazda, a god of light, had created the world and directed the heavens and seasons. The Persian conception of God as creator of the world, and of light and darkness, seems to have influenced Judaism to some degree. Within the book of the prophet Isaiah, God says, "I form light and create darkness. . . . I made the earth, and created humankind upon it; it was my hands that stretched out the heavens" (ch. 45).

The Dualist Religion of Persia Around Ahura Mazda gathered good deities such as "Truth," "Righteous Thought," "Devotion," and so on,

---

[12]For these facts, see M. Brosius, *Women in Ancient Persia,* 1996, pp. 21–31.

whose ideals humanity should follow. But the Persian faith taught that Ahura was opposed by Ahriman, a wholly evil spirit—a devil, in fact. Thus Zoroaster taught a dualist religion, that is, one with two divine forces, although only Ahura is the true god whose message we are to hear. A concern with the devil was to expand greatly in the New Testament. Another similarity to Christian thought is found in Zoroaster's proclamation that, after thousands of years, a day of judgment will see the final triumph of good, and those people who have followed Ahura in morally good lives will gain paradise, while the rest will suffer in the realm of endless night. Zoroaster also rejected such ancient practices as the sacrifice of animals. The faith he taught demanded recognition of the one good spirit and a life of devotion to Ahura's ideals. His noble thought far outlasted the Persian Empire and still has followers today in Iran and in India.

In this chapter we have observed several historical themes. The rise of agriculture, which enabled humanity to live in permanent villages, led to the expansion of such villages into cities. In the cities, civilization arose with more ingenious tools that led to monumental architecture. Trade and its companion, writing, emerged. Monarchy became and remained the form of government, and rulers issued law codes to control their societies.

SUMMARY

The mighty legacy of the ancient Near Eastern societies—including the art of writing, monumental architecture, the development of pottery and weaponry—also influenced the development of their neighbors, the Greeks. The Greeks further learned from the older societies the use of coinage, the measurement of time, and forms of diplomacy. They added to this heritage a radical individualism and a passion for logical argument; their policies and institutions have influenced our own, even more directly and profoundly than those of the Near East, as will be apparent when we turn to the Mediterranean and the peoples of Greece.

QUESTIONS FOR FURTHER THOUGHT

1. This chapter has looked at religious practices in several societies. How does the religion of Israel resemble some other religions? How does it differ from them?

2. In the forming of societies, which contributes more, intellectual skills or the dominance and administration of a strong government?

RECOMMENDED READING

Sources

Lichtheim, Miriam. *Ancient Egyptian Literature: A Book of Readings.* 3 vols. 1973–1980. Excellent gathering of original sources in modern translation.

Metzger, B. M., and M. D. Coogan (eds.). *The Oxford Companion to the Bible.* 1993. Best general introduction to the Bible.

The New Oxford Annotated Bible. 1991. The New Revised Standard Version, with helpful annotation throughout.

Pritchard, James B. (ed.). *Ancient Near Eastern Texts Relating to the Old Testament.* 1969. More than the title implies; a wide-ranging collection of cuneiform and hieroglyphic texts on many subjects, with brief commentaries by eminent scholars.

Sandars N. K. (tr.). *The Epic of Gilgamesh,* 1972. The great Sumerian epic, in a highly readable translation with informative introduction.

Studies

Albright, William Foxwell. *The Biblical Period from Abraham to Ezra.* 1963. A brief history of Israel from a giant in the field.

The Cambridge Ancient History. 3d ed. 12 vols. 1970–2000. The standard history of the ancient world; chapters by numerous scholars, with large bibliographies.

Childe, V. Gordon. *What Happened in History.* 1985. Compact but profound analysis of history by a great anthropologist.

Crawford, H. *Sumer and the Sumerians.* 1991. A new history of the earliest civilization.

Dandamaev, Muhammad A. *A Political History of the Achaemenid Empire.* 1990. The Persian empire and its organization.

Ehrenberg, Margaret. *Women in Prehistory.* 1989. On women's roles in the rise of agriculture and in the early cities.

Frankfort, Henri. *The Birth of Civilization in the Near East.* 1956. A comparison of early Mesopotamian and Egyptian history.

Frye, Richard N. *History of Ancient Iran.* 1984. All-inclusive history of Persia.

Gardiner, Sir Alan. *Egypt of the Pharaohs.* 1969. A detailed political narrative.

Gimbutas, Marija. *The Goddesses and Gods of Old Europe, 6500–3500 B.C.: Myths and Cult Images.* 1984. Challenging work that argues for a matriarchal structure in earliest Europe that gave way to male domination.

Grimal, Nicolas. *A History of Ancient Egypt.* 1992. A recent complete history in one volume.

Hallo, William W. *Origins: The Ancient Near Eastern Origins of Some Modern Western Institutions.* 1996. Excellent example of the comparative method in history.

Hallo, William W., and William K. Simpson. *The Ancient Near East: A History.* 2d ed. 1998. American textbook survey of Mesopotamian/Egyptian history.

Johnson, Allen W. and Timothy Earle. *The Evolution of Human Societies: From Foraging Group to Agrarian State.* 2d ed. 2000. Anthropological study that allows deductions about developments in earliest times.

Kemp, Barry J. *Ancient Egypt: Anatomy of a Civilization.* 1989. Social and intellectual history.

Kramer, Samuel Noah. *The Sumerians: Their History, Culture, and Character.* 1963. Full portrait of Sumerian society by a leading authority.

Lamberg-Karlovsky, C. C., and Jeremy A. Sabloff. *Ancient Civilizations: The Near East and Mesoamerica.* 1979. Good coverage of the agricultural revolution, tools, early cities.

Læssøe, Jørgen. *People of Ancient Assyria, Their Inscriptions and Correspondence.* 1963. Good collection of original Assyrian texts.

Lerner, Gerda. *The Creation of Patriarchy.* 1986. Studies, from a feminist perspective, the rise of the social system in which men assume roles of command and leadership.

Meyers, Carol L. *Rediscovering Eve: Ancient Israelite Women in Context.* 1988. Women in Israelite society and in the Bible, with attention to folk customs.

Oates, Joan. *Babylon.* 1979. A survey for the nonspecialist.

Redford, Donald B. *Akhenaten: The Heretic King.* 1984. Highly readable study of this king in historical setting.

Reeves, Nicholas, and Richard H. Wilkinson. *The Complete Valley of the Kings: Tombs and Treasures of Egypt's Greatest Pharaohs.* 1996. A stunning photographic record of Egyptian architecture.

Robins, G. *Women in Ancient Egypt.* 1993. Well-illustrated treatment.

Roux, Georges. *Ancient Iraq.* 3d ed. 1992. Detailed, readable survey of ancient Mesopotamia.

Saggs, H. W. F. *Civilization before Greece and Rome.* 1989. Chapters on law, trade, religion, and so on; not a continuous narrative.

———. *Everyday Life in Babylonia and Assyria.* Rev. ed. 1987.

———. *The Greatness That Was Babylon.* 1988. General history of Mesopotamia; good survey of everyday life.

———. *The Might That Was Assyria.* 1984. Sympathetic portrait of this militaristic society.

Shanks, Hershel (ed.). *Ancient Israel: From Abraham to the Roman Destruction of the Temple.* Rev. ed. 1999. Eight chapters by experts, forming a concise modern history.

Wilson, John A. *The Culture of Ancient Egypt.* 1951. A timeless classic, superb for the history of ideas.

▲ A magnificent mask of gold foil, found pressed on the face of a ruler of Mycenae, ca. 1500 B.C. This is one of the first Europeans on whose faces we can look.

THE FORMING OF GREEK CIVILIZATION

*G*reek civilization has been praised by our own more than any other for its creativity, its artistic genius, its intellectual daring. It created forms of thought and expression that have been imitated ever since: philosophy, drama, epic poetry, and history. It also assigned a leading role to reason, debate, and logical argument. This civilization honored personal heroism and independence, and its literature is the oldest one with many individually known writers.

In Greece, for the first time, we see another theme that runs through Western civilization: a body politic, a political system with laws fashioned by the people and with guaranteed participation for citizens. The Greeks developed a civic culture that broke with the Near Eastern traditions of monarchy. They lived in independent communities, or city-states. These cities were normally dominated by an upper class of some kind, but even this structure extended power beyond the all-powerful ruler of older civilizations.

Citizens of Greek city-states took pride in their temples, their civic traditions, the qualities of their own state, their participation in its life. In Athens the government was a democracy in which the male citizens themselves, not their representatives, made political decisions directly. This democracy allowed no role for women, foreigners, or slaves. Sparta, Athens' leading rival, chose by contrast a severe, authoritarian form of rule and was the only Greek state to retain monarchy after it had vanished in all others.

These two states led Greece into its most brilliant victories in war, the defeat of forces twice sent from the vast Persian Empire. They also became the nuclei of alliances that followed this triumph with tragedy, as their rivalry escalated into the long, destructive Peloponnesian War.

CHAPTER 2. THE FORMING OF GREEK CIVILIZATION							
	Social Structure	Body Politic	Changes in the Organization of Production and in the Impact of Technology	Evolution of Family and Changing Gender Roles	War	Religion	Cultural Expression
I. CRETE AND EARLY GREECE	▓			▓		▓	
II. THE GREEK RENAISSANCE	▓	▓				▓	▓
III. THE POLIS	▓	▓	▓	▓	▓		
IV. THE CHALLENGE OF PERSIA					▓		
V. THE WARS OF THE FIFTH CENTURY		▓			▓		

I. Crete and Early Greece (ca. 3000–1100 B.C.)

◆

The first important society in the Greek world developed on the island of Crete, just south of the Aegean Sea. The people of Crete were not Greek and probably came from western Asia Minor well before 3000 B.C. They traded with the nearby Greeks and left their influence in art, in religion, and in a system of writing. They were followed in history by a number of cities in Greece governed by monarchs. The most imposing such city was Mycenae, where tombs have disclosed stunning works of art. Greek legend also tells of a war against Troy in which Mycenae was the leading Greek power.

◆ CRETAN CIVILIZATION

We have no reliable historical narratives about early Cretan civilization. Therefore we must rely on archaeological evidence, found especially in a magnificent villa at Knossos. The historian must recognize that archaeological evidence often calls for much conjecture in its interpretation. The villa is known as the Palace of Minos; the civilization of Crete is thus often called Minoan.

King Minos and His Palace   Greek legend told of the Minotaur ("Minos-bull"), a monster that lived

in a labyrinth (surely a memory of the complex palace) and devoured girls and boys sent to it as tribute. The myth suggests that Greeks had at least a dim recollection of a ruler called Minos, and the historian Thucydides tells of Minos, the powerful king who "cleared the seas of piracy, captured islands, and placed his sons in control over them."

Other palaces on Crete exist, but none is so elegant as that at Knossos. For our knowledge of the palace, and much of Cretan culture generally, we must thank (Sir) Arthur Evans, a wealthy Englishman who began to excavate at Knossos in 1900 and spent some forty years at his task: he named the palace the Palace of Minos and restored much of it, including its colorful wall paintings.

The Palace of Minos was built over a period of about 700 years from ca. 2200 to ca. 1500 B.C. It was an extensive structure, with a vast eastern courtyard, an impressive grand staircase leading to upper rooms, and many wings and storage chambers. The palace even had a plumbing system with water running through fitted clay pipes.

The walls of the palace at Knossos were decorated with frescoes showing the Cretans' delight in nature. Gardens, birds, and animals are vividly portrayed, and one spectacular painting shows young men vaulting over the horns of a bull. The absence of walls around the palace suggests that Minoan civilization was essentially peaceful.

▲ MAP 2.1 EARLY GREECE DURING THE BRONZE AGE, ca. 2000–1100 B.C.
◆ www.mhhe.com/chambers8ch2maps

Cretan Society and the Roles of Women Knossos was clearly the wealthiest of the Cretan cities, and the king was served by an efficient bureaucracy. The rulers were probably men; one wall painting shows a man, often identified as a priest or king, leading an animal to some kind of ceremony. Women were respected in this society, and jeweled ladies in elegant gowns appear in Minoan wall paintings.

Some historians have argued that women on Crete had actual political power in a system of matriarchy, or rule by women. This theory de-

scends from a book published in 1861 by a Swiss scholar, Johann Bachofen, who theorized that early societies worshiped a goddess called the Great Mother, Mother Goddess, or Earth Goddess. Only over time, the theory holds, did men wrest political power away from women. Statuettes of women are known from Crete, holding snakes or grain in their hands and thus dominating nature. This much need not surprise us, since the earth is a noun of the feminine gender in many languages and is clearly the mother of all crops. But these facts fall short of proving the existence of a true

matriarchy on Crete; it is better simply to accept that these figurines probably represent goddesses of nature.

On the other hand, paintings found at Knossos show women in elegant coiffures, dressed in splendid robes and wearing dramatic makeup. Their faces show no hint of hard labor; these women, at least, enjoyed an upper-class lifestyle, whether or not they had political influence.

A Cretan Empire?   Much of the wealth of Crete came from trade, and Cretan pottery has been found far and wide throughout the Mediterranean world. About a dozen sites in the Greek world, probably trading posts, are called *Minoa*, obviously named after Minos. But we cannot speak of a true Cretan empire with political control of wide areas like the dominions of Assyria or

▼ **Roman wall painting, showing Theseus having killed the Minotaur; he is surrounded by grateful Athenian children, whom he has saved from possibly being devoured by the half-man, half-beast monster.**
Scala/Art Resource, NY

▲ **This marble statuette of a goddess is a product of the Cycladic culture (named for its home in the Cyclades Islands of Greece), which preceded the coming of the Greeks. Carved ca. 2800 to 2300 B.C., the statuette represents the early emphasis on female rather than male gods. Neolithic art preferred abstraction to Paleolithic realism and points the way toward later abstract thought. In the twentieth century, artists like Brancusi and Mondrian returned to this type of noble, elegant simplicity.**
© British Museum.

◄ **A wall painting from Knossos, showing athletes vaulting over the horns of a bull. The figure at the right will catch the leaper in the center. The location of this painting in the palace suggests that the sport was a kind of ceremony. The bull may represent raw nature being tamed in this agricultural society.**
Erich Lessing/Art Resource, NY

Persia, for Crete lacked the population to conquer and permanently subdue overseas possessions.

◆ CRETE AND THE GREEKS

Minoan civilization reached its height between 1550 and 1400 B.C. Greek art of this period shows Minoan influence, and at least two Greek goddesses, Athena and Artemis, were probably adopted from Crete.

Cretan Writing The Minoans also had interchange with the Greeks through writing. Clay tablets have been found at Knossos in two similar scripts, called Linear A and Linear B. Both scripts are syllabic: Each symbol represents a sound, such as *ko*, rather than a letter of an alphabet. The language written in Linear A, the older script (used ca. 1700–1500 B.C.), has not yet been deciphered; but Linear B, the younger of the two scripts (used ca. 1450–1400 B.C.), has been deciphered as an early form of Greek. The decipherment was the work of a brilliant English architect, Michael Ventris, not a professional classical scholar. He achieved this feat in 1952 and tragically died in a motoring accident in 1956. The tablets contain

inventories, rosters, and records of all kinds, listing footstools, helmets, vessels, seeds, and the like. They thus show that the rulers on Crete governed through fairly elaborate bureaucracies.

That these Linear B tablets were written in a form of Greek is a startling discovery, for it shows

▼ **Throne room at Palace of Knossos.**
Bridgeman Art Library

▲ A "marine style" vase by a Greek artist, about 1500 B.C., clearly imitating Cretan models. Sea creatures were often used in Minoan pottery in a free, naturalistic style.
C. M. Dixon

▲ A large vase from Crete in the Late Minoan II style, ca. 1450 to 1400 B.C., when Cretan art came under Greek influence and became more disciplined and geometric. Note the double ax motif; found in the palace at Knossos.
C. M. Dixon

that the Greeks, who at this time had not developed writing of their own, learned to write their language in a Cretan script. Their presence on Crete during this period suggests that Greeks had come to dominate Knossos, perhaps through outright military seizure. Probably the only Greek community that could have done this was that of Mycenae.

The Collapse of Cretan Civilization   About 1380 B.C., a catastrophe, whose causes are uncertain, engulfed Knossos and other Cretan cities; several of the stately palaces were burned or destroyed. A massive earthquake shook the island at this time, but the disaster may also have been connected with a quarrel or rebellion against Greek rule.

Some historians have tried to link the collapse of Knossos with a tremendous earthquake on the island of Thera (or Santorini) about seventy-five miles north of Crete. This earthquake is now dated to about 1625 B.C. It must have done damage on Crete, but the exact relationship, if any, between this natural disaster and the destruction of Knossos remains unclear.

◆ MYCENAEAN CIVILIZATION
(ca. 1600–1100 B.C.)

The Greeks, the people who spoke and imported the Greek language, began to settle in Greece about 2000 B.C., arriving from the Balkan areas to the north; they were members of the general family of Indo-Europeans who had started to migrate into Europe at an uncertain time, perhaps around 5000 B.C. (see chapter 1, p. 31). They called themselves Hellenes and their country Hellas; the Greeks still use these names, and only in West European languages are they called *Greeks*, a name given them by the Romans.

▲ A tablet in Greek, written in the Linear B script, from Pylos, about 1200 B.C. Note that each line contains a brief listing, probably items from an inventory, followed by a number. Such tablets reveal a complex bureaucracy within the monarchy at Pylos during the Mycenaean Age.
C. M. Dixon

The City of Mycenae

Geography divides Greece into many small valleys and forced the Greeks to develop independent communities with kings, but without the direction—or oppression—of a central ruler like a pharaoh. By about 1600 B.C., the Greeks had created wealthy, fortified cities, among which the most prominent was Mycenae, a huge citadel built on a hill in the Peloponnese. The years from 1600 to 1100 B.C. are therefore often called the Mycenaean Age.

The Work of Heinrich Schliemann

Another pioneer of archaeology, the German Heinrich Schliemann, is mainly responsible for the rediscovery of Mycenae. Arriving here in 1876, he discovered six graves, probably those of a ruling dynasty, containing gold masks and ornaments of stunning workmanship. The graves at Mycenae have given us a glimpse of the wealth and artistic accomplishments of this city. They contained such luxuries as masks of gold foil that were pressed on the

faces of the dead and a complete burial suit of gold foil wrapped around a child, as well as swords, knives, and hundreds of gold ornaments. Tablets written in Linear B, attesting a palace bureaucracy, have been found at Mycenae and other sites of the Mycenaean Age.

The Zenith of Mycenaean Power and the Trojan War

Between 1400 and 1200 B.C., Mycenae reached the height of its prosperity and created the most imposing monuments in Bronze Age Greece. A mighty decorated gateway with a relief of lions carved over it, known as the Lion Gate,

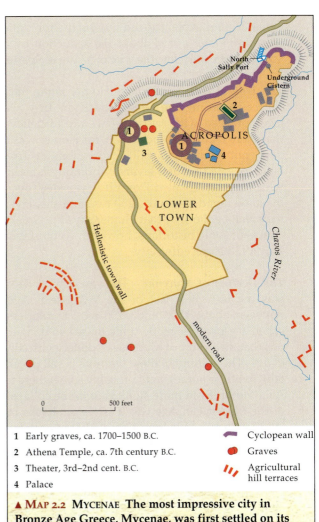

1 Early graves, ca. 1700–1500 B.C.	▬ Cyclopean wall
2 Athena Temple, ca. 7th century B.C.	● Graves
3 Theater, 3rd–2nd cent. B.C.	⫽⫽ Agricultural hill terraces
4 Palace	

▲ **MAP 2.2** **MYCENAE** The most impressive city in Bronze Age Greece, Mycenae, was first settled on its citadel. As the population expanded, a lower town developed, also surrounded by a wall. Outside the walls were terraced agricultural plots.

formed the entrance to the walled citadel. Some rulers were buried in immense vaulted beehive-shaped tombs, of which the grandest and best preserved is the so-called Treasury of Atreus, named by archaeologists for the legendary father of King Agamemnon; but we do not really know which ruler or rulers were buried here.

Each city of the Mycenaean Age was probably independent under its own king. The only time these cities appear to have united was during the war against Troy, a rich city of obscure ethnic origin in Asia Minor near the Dardanelles. The evident wealth of the city must have offered a tempting prey to pirates and looters. Such was probably the real cause of the war against Troy, but Greek legend explained the war by the romantic story in Homer's *Iliad* about the seduction by a Trojan prince of Helen, the wife of a king of Sparta.

The Troy of Homer   Because Homer is the only source recording the Greek attack on Troy, we must proceed with caution if we are to believe that there really was such a war, for Homer was a poet, not a historian. Still, excavations at Troy have revealed several layers of building, among which one layer, called Troy VII A, was destroyed by some invaders about 1250 B.C., and this layer may well be the Troy that Homer says the Greeks attacked; some historians, however, would favor Troy VI, the preceding city.

The Decline of Mycenae   The war against Troy was the last great feat of the Mycenaean Age. Between about 1300 and 1200 B.C., marauders, called sea-peoples, made trade by sea so dangerous that the export of Mycenaean pottery virtually ended. The identity of these warriors is still uncertain, but their homes were probably somewhere in Asia Minor. Even more significant to the collapse of the Mycenaean Age was a series of attacks by land, lasting roughly from 1200 to 1100 B.C.; around 1100 B.C., Mycenae itself was overrun, though not obliterated. This invasion by land was probably the work of a later wave of Greeks who spoke the Doric dialect of the Greek language. Between about 1200 and 1100 B.C., these Greeks made their way southward from central Greece and settled mainly in the Peloponnese, especially in Corinth and Sparta, which became the most important cities in which Doric Greek was spoken.

▲ **Picture of elegant little set of scales found in a Mycenean grave, used to weigh out gold in the next world, 16th c. B.C.**
National Archaeological Museum, Athens, Greece

The Dark Age   The period 1100–800 B.C. is called the Dark Age of Greece, because throughout the area there was sharp cultural decline: less elegant pottery, simple burials, no massive buildings. Even the art of writing in Linear B vanished, perhaps because the more learned class was killed off, or perhaps because the economy was so weakened that the keeping of records became pointless. Nor do we have written sources about the period. But the decline was not a total collapse. Farming, weaving, making pottery, the Greek language in spoken form, and other skills survived.

The invasions of the twelfth century B.C., in which the Dorian Greeks played at least a part, ended forever the domination of the palace-centered kings. The shattering of the monarchic pattern of the Mycenaean Age may even have been liberating. If these monarchies had survived, Greece might have developed as Egypt and Asia Minor did, with centralized rule and priests who interpreted religion in ways that justified kingship. Self-government in Greece might have been delayed for centuries, if it appeared at all.

II. The Greek Renaissance (ca. 800–600 B.C.)

◆

It is really the historian who is in the dark during the Greek Dark Age. At least near the end of this period, there must have been a revival of confidence and a nourishing of civic life.

▲ The "Lion Gate," the entrance to the citadel at Mycenae, built about 1350 B.C. Two lionesses stand guard over the city; note the depth of the entranceway and the width of the threshold. In early civilizations, power could be demonstrated by moving enormous stones.
Michael Holford Photographs

With the passing of time, Greek culture revived after the Dark Age and entered a period of extraordinary artistic and intellectual vitality. Poetry and art broke new frontiers; the economy expanded, partly through overseas colonization; and the *polis,* or independent city-state, emerged. Historians borrow a term from a later period and call this movement the Greek Renaissance.

◆ GREEK RELIGION

The Greeks brought with them, during their earliest immigration around 2000 B.C., the worship of some of their gods, above all Zeus, the sky god, whose name is Indo-European; his counterparts are Dyaus in early India, Jupiter in Rome, and Tiu in Norse myths. Other gods were adapted from other regions: Apollo, the sun god, from western Asia Minor; Aphrodite, goddess of love, from Cyprus; Athena, goddess of wisdom, and Artemis, the hunter goddess, from Crete. At a much later stage, Greeks adopted some Egyptian gods (Isis, for example), but there is no solid evidence for the belief, recently put forth, that they received all or even many of their gods from Egypt (see "The Debate over Black Athena," p. 48).[1]

The Relationship of Greeks to Their Gods   Greek gods are not the remote, transcendent deities of Mesopotamian peoples. They intervene in human affairs, they assist their favorites, and they are anthropomorphic: That is, they are humanlike superbeings, differing from people only in their physical perfection and immortality. Even Mount Olympus, their legendary home, is an actual mountain in northern Greece.

---

[1]Herodotus, the first historian, writing around 440 B.C., does say this, but he was perhaps so impressed with the antiquity of Egypt and with the resemblance of gods in the two cultures that he drew this false conclusion.

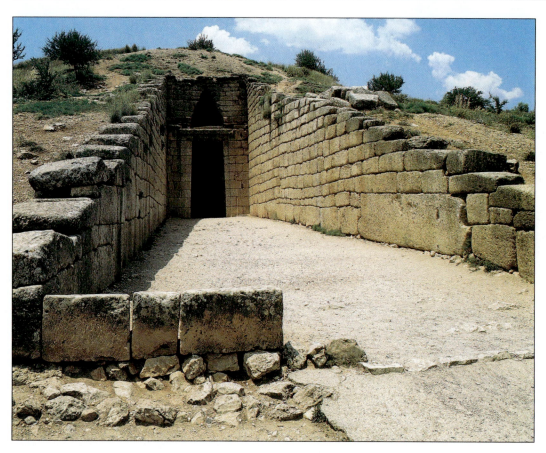

▲ The most spectacular tomb at Mycenae, the "Treasury of Atreus," built in beehive style about 1300 B.C. The long entrance alley and the tomb itself are almost perfectly preserved.
Michael Holford Photographs

The Greeks never developed a code of behavior prescribed by religion, as Israel did. Some acts, such as killing a parent or leaving a relative unburied, were obviously wrong, as were offenses against generally accepted conduct, such as betraying a friend. If people became too arrogant, Nemesis, an avenging force, would sweep down on them and destroy them. But on the whole, Greek religion had no spirit of evil and scarcely any demanding spirits of good.

The gods were viewed as generally benevolent, but they had to be appeased through offerings and suitable ceremonies. The most remarkable feature of Greek religion—especially in contrast to monarchies of Egypt and Mesopotamia—was that the Greeks had priests and priestesses for their temples and smaller shrines but no priestly class that intervened in politics. To put it simply, the Greeks had no church. The societies all around

▼ The "warrior vase" from Mycenae, showing armed warriors departing for battle; at the left, a woman waves her farewell.
C. M. Dixon

▲ **MAP 2.3** ARCHAIC AND CLASSICAL GREECE, ca. 800–400 B.C.
◆ www.mhhe.com/chambers8ch2maps

Greece seem to have needed priestly hierarchies to interpret religion and sacred lore. Only thus could they be sure that they were not offending divine powers.

Forms of Worship Why the Greeks felt they could worship without such a hierarchy we do not know, but the reason must be connected to the independence of the six to seven hundred individual Greek city-states. There was no king, pharaoh, or emperor who had the power to install such a system. Religion and civic life were inter-

twined, and the beautiful temples all over Greece were built by decision of the governing power, but not at the orders of priests or viziers.

Most gods were common to all Greeks, and their worship is a sign of a Panhellenic culture that arose during the Greek Renaissance. Each locality, while recognizing the several gods generally, could have its own patron. For example, various gods had temples in Athens, but Athena was accepted as the protecting goddess of the city. Zeus, though worshiped everywhere as the chief god, was the main local deity at Olympia. Apollo

The Debute over Black Athena

◆

Martin Bernal, in Black Athena, *has set forth the challenging thesis that Greek civilization and even much of the Greek language rest on cultural borrowings from Egypt and the Levant from about 2100 to about 1100 B.C. Bernal also holds that anti-Semitic nineteenth-century scholars deliberately concealed the contribution of Egypt and the Phoenicians. This excerpt, in Bernal's words, summarizes his thesis.*

"The scheme I propose is that while there seems to have been more or less continuous Near Eastern influence on the Aegean over this millennium, its intensity varied considerably at different periods. The first "peak" of which we have any trace was the 21st century. It was then that Egypt recovered from the breakdown of the First Intermediate Period, and the so-called Middle Kingdom was established by the new 11th Dynasty. This not only reunited Egypt but attacked the Levant and is known from archaeological evidence to have had wide-ranging contacts further afield, certainly including Crete and possibly the mainland. . . . It is generally agreed that the Greek language was formed during the 17th and 16th centuries B.C. Its Indo-European structure and basic lexicon are combined with a non-Indo-European vocabulary of sophistication. I am convinced that much of the latter can be plausibly derived from Egyptian and West Semitic. This would fit very well with a long period of domination by Egypto-Semitic conquerors. . . . [I] discuss some of the equations made between specific Greek and Egyptian divinities and rituals, and the general belief that the Egyptian were the earlier forms and that Egyptian religion was the original one."

From Martin Bernal, *Black Athena,* Vol. 1, Rutgers University Press, 1987, pp. 17–23, abridged.

Mary R. Lefkowitz and Guy MacLean Rogers, professors of classics at Wellesley College, have edited a 500-page volume, Black Athena Revisited, *in which 24 scholars give their reactions to Bernal's theories. The following is one excerpt from the discussion.*

"No expert in the field doubts that there was a Greek cultural debt to the ancient Near East. The real questions are: How large was the debt? Was it massive, as Bernal claims? Was it limited to the Egyptians and the Phoenicians? . . .

"All of the contributors agree that the early Greeks got their alphabet from the Phoenicians; but little else. Indeed, in terms of language, the evidence that Bernal has presented thus far for the influence of Egyptian or Phoenician on ancient Greek has failed to meet any of the standard tests which are required for the proof of extensive influence. . . .

"Similarly, in the area of religion, Egyptian and Canaanite deities were never worshiped on Greek soil in their indigenous forms. . . .

"Archaeologists, linguists, historians, and literary critics have the gravest reservations about the scholarly methods used in *Black Athena.* Archaeologists cite a constant misconstruing of facts and conclusions and misinterpretation of such archaeological evidence as there is. . . . Linguists see Bernal's methods as little more than a series of assertive guesses, often bordering on the fantastic."

From Guy MacLean Rogers, *Black Athena Revisited,* University of North Carolina Press, 1996, pp. 449–452, abridged.

---

was the chief god at Delphi and supposedly inspired the oracle, a woman who gave guidance to inquirers after payment of a fee. New research supports the ancient tradition that she inhaled vapors from a chasm.

This woman, or the priests who interpreted her answers, was careful to express these answers in ambiguous language, so that the oracle could be justified no matter what happened. The historian Herodotus reports that, when King Croesus of Lydia asked whether he should invade Persia, he was told that "if Croesus crosses the Halys River [the frontier of Persia], he will destroy a mighty kingdom." He took this to be encouraging, attacked Persia—and destroyed his own kingdom.

The Greek faith in this oracle is another sign of growing common identity among the Greeks. Though never more than a small village, Delphi was adorned with treasure houses built by the various cities to house the gifts they dedicated to Apollo when seeking his guidance.

◆ PUBLIC GAMES

Another sign of a growing community among Greeks is the founding of Panhellenic athletic games in 776 B.C. This date is commonly agreed to mark the beginning of the "historic" period of Greek civilization: broadly speaking, the period when writing began and we begin to have fairly solid dates for events.

The first games were held at Olympia, in the Peloponnese, and were dedicated to Zeus; thus, from the beginning the games were connected with religion and demonstrate that religion can have wide uses in a community. But they were also a way of celebrating human perfection and heroism, an aspiration typical of Greek civilization. Originally, the Olympics featured only foot races and wrestling, but gradually they came to include horse and chariot races, boxing, javelin throwing, and other events. Only the winner gained a prize, an olive wreath, but victory also brought rich awards from one's city and lifelong glory; the modern myth of the "amateur athlete" was unknown to the Greeks. In imitation of the Olympics, other cities founded games, and there was eventually one set of Panhellenic games (that is, open to all Greeks) each year, as well as games in many individual cities. The games also give us some of our dates in the archaic period, for the Greeks themselves used the Olympic games especially as chronological reference points.

◆ COLONIZATION (CA. 750–550 B.C.)

The growth in population during the Dark Age probably strained the natural resources in Greece, especially the limited farming land, and finally drove the Greeks into foreign colonization. In effect, the mainland Greeks, starting around 750 B.C., tried to relieve social tension by exporting their surplus population. They colonized vigorously from ca. 750 to ca. 550 B.C., and by the end of this period Greeks were spread throughout the Mediterranean. Wherever they went, they settled on the edge of the sea, never far inland. Colonies, when founded, were wholly independent cities, and among them are some of the great ports of modern Europe: Byzantium (today Istanbul in Turkey), Naples, Marseilles, and Syracuse.

This expansion overseas led to a revival of trade after the stagnation of the Dark Age. The Greeks now had access to a greater food supply, above all grain from southern Italy and the Black Sea. Trade brought prosperity to many Greek cities and, even more important, spread Greek civilization throughout the Mediterranean.

◆ THE ALPHABET

Origin of the Alphabet The Greeks apparently lapsed into illiteracy when the Linear B script vanished, soon after 1200 B.C.; but by about 750 B.C. their trade had brought them to Palestine and into contact with the Phoenicians, who used a Semitic script called the alphabet. This alphabet had only twenty-two characters, but their precision and versatility made this script far easier to master than pictorial cuneiform scripts (see p. 10). Fortunately for the future of European literacy, the

▼ A comparison of Greek and Phoenician alphabets.

▲ **Map 2.4** Greek Colonization, ca. 750–550 b.c.

Greeks adopted the alphabet and gave even greater precision to their script by changing some of the characters, which were all consonants, to vowels.

Two versions of the Greek alphabet developed. A Western version made its way to Cumae, a Greek town in Italy, and then to the Etruscans, the people in Italy who then controlled Rome. They passed it on to the Romans, who turned it into the alphabet used throughout the Western world. The Eastern version became the standard alphabet in Greece itself. Much later, many letters of the Greek alphabet were used in the Cyrillic script of Russian and other Slavic languages. Thus large parts of the world today use one or another derivative of the Phoenician alphabet in the form it was received from the Greeks.

The Alphabet and Greek Life The Greeks first used the alphabet in public for the proclamation of laws, which ordinary people could read and

grasp; information could circulate more rapidly, with dynamic consequences for political life. Later, from about 500 b.c., especially in Athens, people began to publish all kinds of public decisions and records on prominently displayed stone inscriptions; these were not simply boastful monuments to a king's victories but were documents enabling citizens to understand, criticize, and control the activities of the state.

◆ ARCHAIC LITERATURE

The Homeric Epics The greatest literary creations of the Greek Renaissance are the epic poems about the glorious heroes who had supposedly led the war against Troy. The supreme achievements of this poetic tradition are two epics ascribed to Homer, the *Iliad* and the *Odyssey*. The *Iliad* is a portrait—in rolling, majestic verse—of a warrior aristocracy in which greatness in combat is the highest virtue.

The chief hero is the proud warrior Achilles, who withdraws from the siege of Troy when his concubine is taken from him; he then allows his friend Patroclus to wear his armor in combat and, after Patroclus is killed by the Trojan hero Hector, avenges his friend's death by killing Hector in a scene of savage power. The gods take sides with their favorites, but the *Iliad* is essentially a poem about men and women.

The *Odyssey,* by contrast, celebrates cleverness rather than sheer military prowess. Its hero, Odysseus, makes his way home after the Trojan War through dozens of adventures that test his skill and tenacity and that enable Homer to explore human character and behavior in widely different situations. Eventually Odysseus reaches his home, the island of Ithaca, and drives off a band of suitors who are wooing his faithful wife Penelope.

▼ **An Etruscan vase (about 520 b.c.), with a scene from Greek literature. Odysseus and his men escape from the Cyclops, Polyphemus, by putting out his only eye (Homer's *Odyssey*, Book 9). This scene is found on several other vases from Greece.**
Michael Holford Photographs

The Homeric Question   These epics were probably first recited at feasts by traveling bards, but over the years they became known to all through presentation at festivals and finally through study in schools. We have no idea who wrote these great epics. This is the famous "Homeric question." Neither ancient Greeks nor modern scholars have been able to prove whether a person named Homer really lived, whether the epics are the work of one writer or several, and whether they were originally composed orally or in writing.

It is clear, however, that the texts we have date from long after the Trojan War of ca. 1250 b.c. Most scholars date the poems to around 750 b.c., and this disparity raises the question of how any knowledge of the war could have been preserved. The traditions were evidently passed down through the centuries. The poems themselves were probably composed orally, recited for generations, and written down later, after the Greeks had become fluent in the art of writing. In any case, Homer remained the chief inspiration for Greek literature in all periods.

Hesiod   Homer never speaks in the first person (except to invoke the Muses to inspire him), but his successors began to express their own thoughts and feelings and to create a literature of intensely frank self-expression. The first major post-Homeric poet was Hesiod of Boeotia (in central Greece), whose *Works and Days* dates from around 700 b.c. Hesiod was a farmer, and his poem is a farmer's almanac, celebrating agriculture and, in the "days" of the title, telling the reader when to plow and plant. The poem also contains a bitter attack on the injustice of aristocratic landlords ("gift-devouring rulers") toward their peasants.

In his other surviving poem, the *Theogony*, Hesiod recounts the genealogy of the various gods. He narrates frankly the bloody rise of Zeus to supreme divine power. The god Cronus had castrated his own father, Uranus, to gain rule over the world and had killed his own children except Zeus, who escaped. After a long struggle, Zeus won the final battle and became the supreme god. This conflict resembles similar sagas in Hittite literature, in which gods kill and mutilate one another. But the difference in the Greek conception is that the supremacy of Zeus is seen not just as

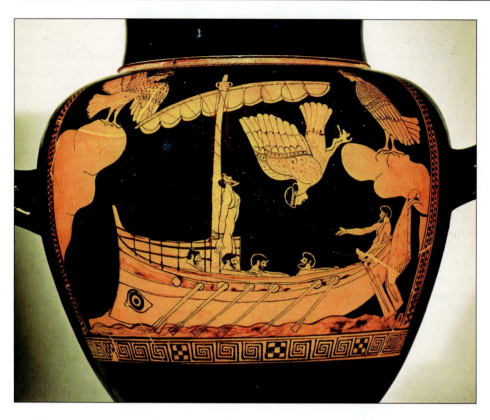

◀ A superb red-figure vase (the figures are left in the natural red of the clay), illustrating a scene from Homer's *Odyssey*, Book 12. Odysseus, bound to the mast of his ship, listens to the song of the Siren, who guides him into troubled waters; by the Siren Painter, about 490 to 480 B.C. Michael Holford / British Museum

another act of vengeance but as a fulfillment of the proper divine order.

Archilochus   About 650 B.C. Greek poets began to work with more personal themes. Archilochus of Paros has left us brief poems of brilliant vigor and audacity, written as bursts of self-revelation, a typically Greek kind of literature that has no predecessors in the ancient Eastern cultures. He was a traveler, a man of action, and a mercenary soldier who fell in battle. He criticizes traditional forms of chivalry and can be cynical about supposed aristocratic conduct. He boasts, for example, that he once threw away his shield to save his life and laughs off this unmilitary act: "Never mind, I'll buy another one just as good." His love poetry can be astonishingly frank. In one poem he tenderly yet passionately describes his seduction of a girl, including his own sexual fulfillment.

Sappho   The most intense and subtle poet of the age was Sappho of the island of Lesbos (about 600 B.C.). We have only one complete poem from her pen and many short quotations (see "Sappho's

Love Poetry," p. 53). In her poetry she writes about an association of young women, but it is not certain precisely what kind of group this was. They worshiped Aphrodite and the Muses, minor goddesses who inspired poetry and other arts.

The most tantalizing question, to which the surviving fragments of her work supply no exact answer, is what kind of experiences the group shared. Sappho was a widow and apparently taught the girls poetry, dance, music, and elegant dress as preparation for marriage. Sometimes she sings of the beauty of the girls, sometimes of her pain when one leaves the circle (probably to marry) or is unresponsive to her affection. At other times she speaks frankly of the pleasures of love, and there is little question that she shared physical love with some of the girls. But, unlike Archilochus, she does not boast of her sexuality or of her conquests; rather, she writes of shared experience and love felt mutually. In its exact evocation of emotion, its inventive images, its individuality, her poetry reveals a writer of the highest originality and power. One exquisite poem, in four short lines, expresses loneliness in heart-breaking simplicity:

SAPPHO'S LOVE POETRY

◆

The poetry of Sappho of Lesbos is amazingly sensitive and original. This short excerpt from a poem frankly acknowledges her need for love.

"You have come, and done,
And I was waiting for you

The following is addressed to a young woman.

"He seems to be a god, that man
Facing you, who leans to be close,
Smiles, and, alert and glad, listens
To your mellow voice.

"And quickens in love at your laughter
That stings my breasts, jolts my heart
If I dare the shock of a glance.
I cannot speak,

"My tongue sticks to my dry mouth,
Thin fire spreads beneath my skin,

To temper the red desire
That burned my heart."

My eyes cannot see and my aching ears
Roar in their labyrinths.

"Chill sweat slides down my body,
I shake, I turn greener than grass,
I am neither living nor dead and cry
From the narrow between.

"But endure, even this grief of love."

From Guy Davenport (tr.), *7 Greeks*, New Directions, 1995.

The moon has set,
so have the Pleiades; it is midnight.
The hour goes past,
but I lie alone.

III. The Polis

◆

"The human being," said the Greek philosopher Aristotle, "is a political creature." By this he probably meant that humans normally want to live within a community of people sharing cultural traditions and common citizenship. The Greek city, at its largest, had about 40,000 adult male citizens. Originally, monarchs ruled, as they did at Mycenae, but over the years most cities reached at least an approach to government by a body of citizens. In their cities, the Greeks created architecture, dramas, and philosophic writings that are still worshiped and imitated.

◆ ORGANIZATION AND GOVERNMENT

For the social and political history of Western civilization, the most important event in the Greek Renaissance was the emergence, soon after 800 B.C., of the independent city-state, the *polis* (plural,

poleis). Physically, the polis had a central inhabited area (the *astu*), often surrounding a citadel called the *acropolis* ("high city"). Over time, the acropolis came to be reserved for temples, shrines, treasuries, and other official buildings. Within the astu, the nucleus of the city, the people dwelt in closely packed houses, each normally built on more than one level, without internal staircases but with the rooms opening to a courtyard. A wall usually surrounded the astu; outside it, but still part of the polis, were suburbs and fields. Those who owned land might live in the urban center and walk or ride a donkey to their land. Or they might live in smaller villages, which were still legally part of the polis.

General Structure of the Polis Greek cities usually had a large open space, the *agora*, that served as a main public square and civic center. Although used as a public market, the agora was always a sacred place and, like the acropolis, it housed temples and official buildings. In Athens, the agora was also the site of trials, of buildings containing laws and other documents, and of many freestanding inscriptions on marble recording further public business.

In a Greek polis, only male citizens could vote, pass on their property through wills, and generally participate in civic life. Females did not vote but, like men, were protected against seizure and violence. Outside this group, and without civic rights, were slaves and resident aliens. No citizen of a polis had rights in any other polis; thus poleis were both cities and small states.

Population of the Poleis   When Greeks referred to the size of the citizen body, they reckoned only adult males, and by this measure the poleis ranged from a few hundred citizens to tens of thousands. Athens, the largest, had between thirty-five and forty-five thousand citizens; if to this we add the estimated number of women, children, resident foreigners, and slaves, the total population of Athens and the outlying villages, which were also part of the polis, was between two and three hundred thousand (the whole region is known as Attica). Sparta, by contrast, probably had an adult male population of no more than twelve thousand.

Origins of Self-Government   Despite considerable diversity within the six to seven hundred poleis, one development seems to have been common to all those poleis that we know anything about, namely, the growth of some kind of self-government by the male citizens. The major social problem that Greek poleis solved was how to harness the energies of all the citizens in support of a city rather than allow the rivalries inherent in such crowded quarters to erupt into civil war. In many poleis (Corinth, for example), oligarchy (a system in which a small number of citizens governed) held sway, while other cities, especially Athens, developed control of affairs by the masses.

Evolution toward self-government is rare in history, and the various forms of self-government that arose in Greece may, like the Greeks' lack of a priestly class, be the result of topography and the scale of their towns. In a small state, locked within a ring of hills, no monarch could long remain a remote, transcendent figure like the rulers of Eastern kingdoms. Homer attests that the Greeks of the Mycenaean era had kings, but by about 700 B.C. they had vanished—though we can seldom say precisely how—in nearly all poleis. Sparta, the

most authoritarian Greek state, was an exception and retained a system with two kings, each descended from a royal family, ruling together. The Spartans apparently felt safer in a system in which one king could act as a control over the other.

Hoplites and Society   The wealthier classes—using the term loosely, we may call them aristocrats, but there was no hereditary nobility—must have governed, if Homer is to be believed, through assemblies that originated as the armed forces of the poleis. But as populations increased and armies came to include citizens outside the circle of the elite, the upper classes could no longer ignore the wishes of others. In particular, Greek infantry soldiers, called hoplites (Greek *hopla,* arms), may have been an impetus toward self-government, because numbers of armed citizens could more effectively demand a say in political decisions. It is significant that the first Greek legal codes defining citizens' rights were published soon after the disappearance of kings, within the seventh century B.C.—evidence that the populace was no longer willing to accept direction from the wealthy.

Tyrants and Tyranny   Also in the seventh century we hear of the first popular leaders who united the masses and overturned the rule of the old aristocracy. These men installed themselves as "tyrants" (the Greek word *tyrannos* meant an autocrat who ruled without strict legal foundation, not necessarily a cruel oppressor). The tyrants, though certainly no sponsors of democracy, did help to undermine rule by the traditional aristocracy and in a way opened the path to self-government. They sometimes built grandiose temples and other public works to beautify their cities and ensure the support of the people. Some sponsored industry and trade of their city's products overseas. Most saw to the buildup of armies, doubtless for their own security. On the whole, tyrants forced progress within their cities and helped lead the cities away from the rule of the older aristocratic class.

Greek Armies   In the period of the Greek Renaissance we also see the formation of the armies that were to make the Greeks supreme in battle against their neighbors. Infantry soldiers, or hoplites, were grouped into the formation called the phalanx. This was a close-packed formation of men, usually eight deep. A soldier carried a shield on his left arm and protected his right side by standing close to his neighbor's shield. The weapons were either swords or, especially in the fourth century B.C., long spears. The phalanx became a formidable instrument in battle, especially when moving forward to attack.

As the ranks pushed forward, one adversary or the other would give way. Once the front ranks of either side were broken, the Greeks normally broke off the battle, for they lacked the manpower to sustain huge casualties. Infantry soldiers had to provide their own equipment. This meant that they were men of the middle class, and many historians have concluded that solidarity among the hoplites contributed to the growth of political consciousness and pointed the way to a greater degree of self-government.

◆ THE ECONOMY OF THE POLEIS (CA. 700–400 B.C.)

A Modest Lifestyle   The poleis were sufficiently similar to allow a general picture of their economy. The basic activity was agriculture, but in many areas of Greece the soil is thin and rocky, not suited to raising grain or pasturing animals. A shortage of food was therefore a constant threat to economic stability. Some states, as we have seen, drained away part of their excess population through colonization and imported grain from areas on the fringe of the Greek world.

All Greek dwellings were modest, and sanitation was primitive, although the Athenians had a main drain under their central market. Grain, and occasionally fish, were staples of the diet; meat was usually reserved for festival days. Breakfast, if taken at all, was a lump of bread dipped in olive oil, which also served as fuel for lamps and even as a kind of soap. Sugar was unknown; the only sweetening agent was honey. With few luxuries available, Greeks could subsist on small incomes. Fishing and farming were suspended in winter, so Greeks had considerable leisure time, which they spent mainly in public places, as is still true today.

Coinage and Public Expenses   The development of an economy based on coinage was slow. Coinage itself began in the kingdom of Lydia, in western Asia Minor, about 600 B.C. or a little later. Soon the Greeks began to use coins, but at first they played little part in daily trade: The smallest coin was usually a drachma, said to have been at that time the price of a sheep. In the fifth century the use of coinage expanded rapidly, as fractions of the drachma came into use. Taxation in poleis paid for the upkeep of walls, drains, roads, harbors, and the like, though Greeks had little grasp of the mechanics of public finance. There were no permanent military treasuries until the 300s B.C., a surprising fact since the cities were so often at war. Infantry soldiers had to arm themselves, but they were paid at the expense of the state. When large projects such as public buildings and maintenance of ships were planned, the expenses were assigned to citizens who were judged capable of bearing the cost.

Use of Slave Labor   A great social-economic historian, M. I. Finley, once asked the challenging question: Was Greek civilization based on slave labor? Undeniably, slave owners had freedom to pursue civic affairs. Many Greeks looked down on manual labor as beneath their dignity, and it was usually the task of poor citizens or slaves. The troubling institution of slavery was accepted by all ancient societies and was justified by philosophers like Aristotle, who asserted that nature had divided humanity into natural masters and natural slaves—the latter including all "barbarians," that is, non-Greeks. Nor did anyone in antiquity ever recommend abolishing slavery on the ground that it was morally wrong: The only criticism of it was the occasional warning to manage it efficiently.

Greeks commonly obtained slaves through conquest of other territory, though kidnapping and even the sale of children added to recruitment. An ordinary slave might cost about 150 drachmas, roughly four months' pay for a laborer, but a highly skilled one could cost much more.

Industry   Greece, unlike Rome, did not use gangs of slaves in agriculture, and industry was rarely more than household craft. The only industries in which slaves worked together in large numbers were mining and stone quarrying, where conditions were atrocious. These industries and domestic service were the only tasks always assigned to slaves. In a unique exception to this rule, Athens had a police force composed of three hundred slaves from Scythia. The Athenian writer Xenophon said, "A man buys a slave to have a companion at work." Potters, shoemakers, and stonecutters might have a slave or two, though a few larger workshops are known: One shield maker, for example, had 120 slaves.

The availability of slaves and the prejudice against manual labor may explain why some slaves worked, along with citizens, on the building of the Parthenon in Athens and were paid the same as free men—one drachma a day, about the same wage paid to soldiers and sailors—and it partly explains the lack of inventions among the Greeks that could have made industry more productive.

◆ SPARTA AND ATHENS (ca. 700–500 B.C.)

We know little about the internal workings of most poleis, and the two we know best, Sparta and Athens, were not typical; but their importance requires detailed discussion.

Early Sparta   Sparta, the most influential of all the Dorian states, chose to solve its problem of overpopulation by conquering Messenia, the territory to its west, in a war usually dated 736 to 716 B.C. Many, probably most, of the Messenians were then enslaved. Only males of demonstrably pure Spartan descent could be full citizens, and they were each given an allotment of land to be worked for them by the enslaved Messenians, who were known as *helots*. They were public slaves, with no rights whatever, but they differed from other slaves in Greece in that they could not be bought and sold. Spartan landowners spent their lives in constant military training in order to maintain control over the helots, who outnumbered them by about seven to one.

Around 650 B.C. the Messenians tried to rebel, but the uprising failed, and the Spartans responded by making their army more invincible and their state even more rigid. The new arrangements, attributed to a lawgiver named Lycurgus, date from about 600 B.C. The identity of Lycurgus was obscure even in antiquity, though such a man

apparently lived around 800 B.C., and many historians believe that Spartan reformers of around 600 B.C. ascribed their system to him in order to give it the appearance of ancient authority.

Sparta's Government   In the Spartan regime, oligarchy, or rule by a small number, was tempered with some measure of democracy. The public assembly included all males over the age of thirty, who elected a council of twenty-eight elders over age sixty to serve for life and to plan business for the assembly. The assembly also chose five *ephors* ("overseers") each year; they received foreign delegates, summoned the assembly to meet, and in general acted as a check on the power of the kings. When proposals came before the assembly, voting was limited to yes or no, without debate. As a further safeguard against too much popular control, the ephors and council could simply dismiss the assembly if, in their opinion, it made the wrong choice. Thus, the limited democracy of Sparta yielded to its ultimate faith in oligarchy. To Greek political philosophers, Sparta was a superb example of a "mixed" constitution, in which the kings represented the element of monarchy, the council, oligarchy, and the citizenry, a kind of democracy.

For a time Sparta tried to dominate some other Peloponnesian states by outright conquest. But by around 560 B.C. this policy had failed, and about 530 B.C. the Spartans sought strength through alliance rather than warfare by forming an alliance, known as the Peloponnesian League, with their neighbors. The league is one of the earliest examples of alliance in the Greek world and is a rare instance of the Greeks' transcending the normal exclusiveness of city-state politics. The Spartans led the league but did not wholly control it, and action required approval of the member states.

Men and Women in Spartan Society   The Spartan male dedicated most of his life, from age seven through age sixty, to soldiering. The warriors lived and trained together, and their discipline could be sadistic. As tests of their courage and resourcefulness, young men were taught to steal if necessary, to go without food and shelter, even at times to kill a helot.

Spartan women also had a lifestyle that other Greeks found extraordinary. Again the military commitments of the state played a role in shaping social practices, for the girls trained in games in order to become physically strong mothers. Spartan men, living with one another, seldom visited their wives, and if a marriage was childless, a woman could bear a child by a man other than her husband. These customs were meant to ensure enough manpower for the army and to focus loyalty on the state, not on the individual family.

Spartan Isolationism Spartans were cut off from the other Greeks by two mountain ranges, and they traded little with other people, even adopting an intrinsically worthless iron currency to maintain their isolation.

Their lifestyle was one of extreme austerity. They rarely traveled, did not welcome visits by foreigners, and deliberately shielded themselves from new ideas that might have inspired intellectual pursuits such as philosophy or historical writing. Their short, abrupt speech is usually called "laconic" from the name of the plain where they lived, Laconia.

Though they did make fine pottery, at least until about 525 B.C., when the art declined, their military regime left little time for or interest in the arts. Thus the isolation of Sparta from other Greeks was both geographic and psychological, but it reflected the deliberate choice of the people.

Early Athens The city of Athens also had expansionist beginnings, extending its domain by about 700 B.C. to include the whole plain of Attica. It was a large polis with widespread trading interests, and its political currents were strong and turbulent. As the people experimented again and again with their constitution, their political history became the most varied of all the city-states of Greece.

Athens, like other states, once had kings; but the monarchy ended in 683 B.C. (we do not know exactly how), and the city was managed by three (later nine) *archons,* or administrators, elected annually by an assembly in which all adult male citizens could vote. After their year in office, the nine archons moved permanently into a council called the Areopagus, which eventually numbered about

▲ **An Attic kouros, or young man, in the "severe" style, about 510 B.C. The figure is one of ideal physical perfection, typical of the humanity-centered aesthetics of Greece.**
Nimatallah/Art Resource, NY

three hundred men. Because it comprised senior men with permanent membership, the Areopagus was probably more influential than the board of archons in setting public policy.

Draco and Homicide Law

Our first information about a reform in Athens after the monarchy is dated around 621 B.C. when Draco, an otherwise unknown statesman, codified the law on homicide, apparently distinguishing between voluntary and involuntary homicide. This reform was a large step forward, for early societies often looked on any kind of homicide as defiling the community in the eyes of the gods. This reform was also another in the series of law codes that established a recognized basis for justice and did away with forcing citizens to rely on the dictates of tribal elders.

Crisis in the Athenian Economy

An economic crisis in the 500s B.C. forced Athens into far-reaching social changes, the likes of which no Greek state had ever seen. As often happens in history, economic conditions demanded a social response. Down to about 600 B.C. the Athenian economy was trying to do the impossible, namely, feed the growing population of Attica from its own limited area; this strategy caused a nearly desperate social and economic crisis. Some farmers had evidently borrowed food from others who were better off and had gone so deeply into debt in the form of grain that they had lost their own land and had even fallen into slavery by pledging their bodies as security for more food.

Their frustration might have exploded into violent revolution had the Athenians not found a rational solution by giving (probably in the 570s) powers of arbitration to Solon, who had been archon in 594 B.C.[2] He was a poet and statesman whose courageous, compassionate work has made him a towering figure in Greek history, indeed in the history of civilization.

---

[2]That Solon was archon in 594 B.C. is fairly certain, and most historians follow ancient sources in dating his reforms to this year as well. But the assumed linkage between his archonship and his reforms was probably only an inference drawn in antiquity, and there is good reason to think that the reforms took place in the 570s; see C. Hignett, *A History of the Athenian Constitution*, 1952, p. 316.

Solon and Economic Reform

Aware that the poor farmers could probably never repay their debts, Solon took the daring step of canceling all agricultural debts and forbade further borrowing against the body. At one stroke the enslaved men were free, but the land they had lost probably remained in the hands of its new owners, who were thus compensated for the cancellation of debt. This legislation left many families without land and made them seek work elsewhere, but the crucial fact was that Solon had prevented civil war. Such arbitration by a private citizen without an army to fight with is heretofore unknown in history.

Because an economic crisis had threatened the community and brought him to power, Solon determined to transform the economy of Athens. He decreed that no product from the soil could be exported except olive oil; by this means he forced the Athenians to cultivate olive trees, which they could grow more successfully than grain. He also changed the commercial weights used by the Athenians, making them the same as those more widely used in Greece, a reform that brought Athens into a wider circle of trade.

Solon's Political Reforms

Solon now seized the opportunity to reform the Athenian state with the aim of breaking the grip of the wealthy and those with eminent family backgrounds on public office. He therefore divided all Athenian citizens into four classes based on their income from farmland and allowed members of the two highest classes to hold office. The significance of this reform is that men could improve their status economically and thus achieve positions of leadership regardless of their ancestry.

Solon also created a court of appeal, the Heliaea, somehow drawn from the people, but our sources tell us little of how it worked. His chief contribution was to see the common people as a group with grievances and to take bold steps to help them. He thus pointed the state toward eventual democracy, but he did not want to go too far and by no means gave the masses supreme power; in his own poetry he declared, "I gave the people just enough privilege and no more." Nor did his legislation, humane though it was, wholly end the agricultural problem; freeing farmers

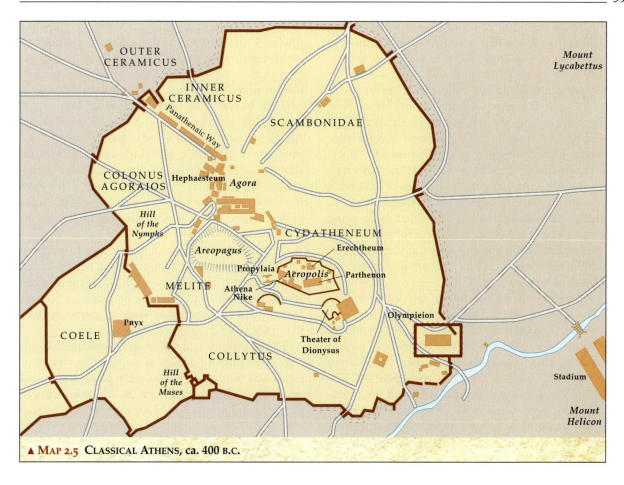

▲ MAP 2.5 CLASSICAL ATHENS, ca. 400 B.C.

from servitude was not the same as guaranteeing them enough to eat, and the agony of those peasants who had lost their land continued.

The Tyrant Pisistratus Pisistratus, a popular Athenian military leader supported by poorer farmers from the hill country in eastern Attica, saw his chance in this turmoil. In 561 B.C. he and his followers seized power; though twice driven out, he returned in 546 with a mercenary army to gain permanent control and ruled from that year until his death in 528.

Pisistratus fits well the pattern of the Greek tyrants sketched earlier. He rewarded his supporters with grants of land, surely taken from the estates of landowning aristocrats who had opposed him, thus completing the work of Solon, who lacked the power and probably the will to redistribute land. And like many another "big city

boss," he saw to a splendid program of public works. He built temples to Athena and Zeus and established a yearly festival to the god Dionysus. By encouraging dramatic contests at this festival, he opened the way for the development of Athenian tragedy in the next century.

He ruled by cloaking his despotic power in legal form. The assembly still chose archons, but from trusted men picked by the tyrant himself. The legal facade was actually one of his chief contributions, for the Athenians now became familiar with democratic procedures, which gave them experience with the working of real democracy when it came into existence at the end of the sixth century.

Cleisthenes and Demokratia Pisistratus' son, Hippias, ruled securely until 514 B.C., when a conspiracy frightened him into using terror as a means to maintain his control. He forced many Athenians into exile, including Cleisthenes, the leader of the Alcmaeonids, a powerful family. While in exile in Delphi, Cleisthenes and his supporters enlisted the help of the Spartans to overthrow Hippias. According to Herodotus, Cleisthenes and his family had spent lavishly to rebuild the temple at Delphi, and the Delphic priests had the oracle urge the Spartans to "liberate the Athenians." Moreover, Hippias had given his daughter in marriage to the son of a Persian vassal ruler, and this move may have looked to the Spartans like a dangerous act that could bring about Persian influence over Greece. In any case, a Spartan force led by the king Cleomenes drove out the Pisistratid family in 510 B.C. and ended the Athenian tyranny.

Cleisthenes returned to his native city and in 508—perhaps to secure his own political supremacy—carried the social revolution further by proposing a scheme whereby the masses would actually direct the state. The Greek word *demos* means "the people," but in Greek political language it also means "the masses," and the domination of the Athenian state by the whole mass of voters came to be called *demokratia*. Participation extended only to the adult male citizens of Athens, for women, aliens, and slaves did not vote; but this system was by far the closest to a democracy that had ever existed.

Cleisthenes anchored his system in popular support by a stroke of genius: He created a council of five hundred members (called the *boulé*) to prepare business for the assembly; all male citizens above age thirty were eligible to serve in it for a year. In later times (and perhaps from the beginning, though our sources do not say so) councillors were chosen by drawing lots, and no man could serve more than twice. There was a fair chance that every eligible Athenian would be chosen to serve during his lifetime, and this widespread participation in the council ensured that the people would want to maintain the new regime. Within about fifty years this new council came to surpass in political power the old Areopagus council, which continued to exist.

The End of Regional Factions in Athens Our sources tell us that the Athenians were loosely divided into three groups in Attica: those who lived in the central plain, or along the coast, or "beyond the hills" in eastern Attica. Cleisthenes set out to break up these regional factions through a complex system of building blocks. Every man was now enrolled as a citizen within the single village, or *deme,* in which he lived, and which kept registers of its citizens. These villages throughout Attica were then grouped into ten tribes, so composed that each tribe contained citizens from all parts of Attica. The council's five hundred men included fifty men from each tribe and were, like the tribes, automatically a cross section of Athenian citizens. Thus within the council, too, no local faction could dominate.

As a result, when the council met to prepare business for the assembly, no single region could dominate the discussion. Each of the ten tribes fought as a unit in the army, and here, too, men from all over Attica, not from a single region, stood together in each tribal regiment.

The sovereign body was, as before, the assembly, including all adult male citizens, whether landowners or not. The assembly passed laws and resolutions brought before it by the council, elected magistrates, voted for or against war, and

▲ **Athenians used sherds of pottery, called ostraka, to vote men out of town for ten years. The sherd at the lower left bears the name Hippokrates; the others are directed against Themistocles, son of Neocles.**
Scala/Art Resource, NY

accepted alliances with other states. Unfortunately, as a democratic assembly, it was vulnerable to being misled or corrupted by unscrupulous politicians. Sometimes it gave way to disastrous or vindictive decisions.

The Use of the Lot in Elections   After passing his reforms in 508 B.C., Cleisthenes vanishes from our sources, but the Athenians continued to refine his system, especially through the use of the lot. In 487 B.C. they began to choose their nine annual archons, the executive committee, by drawing lots from a slate of candidates. Later, in the fifth and fourth centuries, all manner of officials, such as public auditors and managers of public land and mines, were so chosen. The theory behind this practice held that many men were equally honest and capable of serving in a democracy and choosing officials by lot reduced corruption and angry competition in the process of selection.

Choosing civic officials by lot greatly diminished the prestige of such positions and caused the most ambitious men not to bother to seek them. As a result, political power shifted to the ten generals, who were elected annually and could be reelected. From this point onward, the great Athenian politicians competed for the position of general.

Ostracism   Also in 487 B.C., for the first time, a man was expelled from Athens for ten years by the process of ostracism. In this colorful procedure, the whole people could vote once a year to expel any man whom they considered potentially dangerous. They voted by scratching a name on *ostraka,* or potsherds. If the total number of votes was six thousand or more, the "winner" had to depart Attica for ten years; but neither his property nor his family suffered any penalty. Aristotle attributed the practice to Cleisthenes himself, but this statement remains controversial.

IV. The Challenge of Persia

By the beginning of the "classical" period of Greek history, lasting from about 500 to 323 B.C., the Greek states had reached the political form they would retain for more than two centuries. But almost at once they faced their supreme chal-

Chronology

CHRONOLOGY OF THE PERSIAN WARS

(ALL DATES B.C.)

499, autumn	Greek cities of Ionia in Asia Minor revolt from Persian Empire.
498	Athens and Eretria (on island of Euboea) take part in burning Sardis in Persian Empire.
496	Persians besiege Miletus, the leading city in the revolt.
494	Fall of Miletus.
493	End of Ionian revolt.
492, spring	Persian expedition to northern Greece suffers heavy losses in storms.
490, mid-August	Battle of Marathon near Athens; Persians defeated.
486, November	Death of King Darius of Persia; accession of Xerxes.
484, spring–**480,** spring	Xerxes prepares for new invasion of Greece.
480, spring	Persian army sets out from Sardis.
480, late August	Battles of Thermopylae and Artemisium.
480, late September	Battle of Salamis.
479, early August	Battle of Plataea.
479, mid-August	Battle of Mycale on coast of Asia Minor (according to Herodotus, fought on the same day as Plataea).

lenge, a clash with the great Persian Empire. In two brief but intensely dangerous wars, they turned the Persian armies back. Their morale was heightened because they were fighting for their own land, and the poet Aeschylus, in his play *The Persians,* records their battle cry: "Now the struggle is about everything." Daring and even trickery played their parts in the remarkable victory.

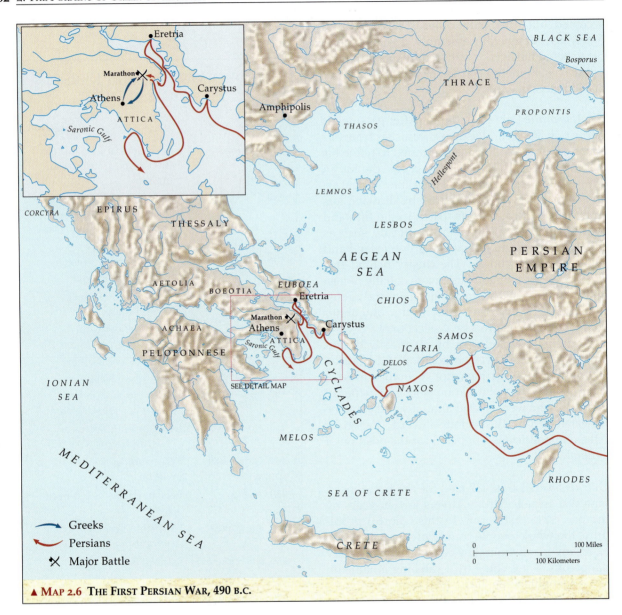

▲ **MAP 2.6 THE FIRST PERSIAN WAR, 490 B.C.**

◆ THE INVASION UNDER DARIUS AND MARATHON (490 B.C.)

King Darius of Persia (r. 522–486 B.C.) had expanded his empire throughout Asia Minor, including the Greek cities in the region called Ionia, on the west coast. Some of these Greeks sought their liberty from Persian control in 499 B.C. in the "Ionian revolt." The rebels obtained a promise of help from the Athenians, who sent them twenty warships. The historian Herodotus declares that "these ships turned out to be the beginning of trouble for both Greeks and non-Greeks," since they led directly to the two Persian wars. The revolt collapsed in 493 B.C., and Darius now proposed to invade Greece itself, largely for the sake of revenge against Athens, which had helped the rebels in the burning of Sardis, one of his cities.

After a brief campaign in 492, he sent a fleet across the Aegean in 490. The Persians first

Greeks

Persians

✗ Major Battle

▲ **MAP 2.7** THE SECOND PERSIAN WAR, 480–479 B.C.
Note the canal cut through Mt. Athos in 492 B.C.

attacked Eretria, on the island of Euboea, and then landed in Attica on the beach at Marathon, a village north of Athens. The Athenian infantry routed them in a brilliant victory and even marched back to Athens in time to ward off a Persian naval attack. A later legend told of an Athenian, Eucles, who ran back to Athens in his armor with the good news; he cried out, "Hail, we rejoice," and dropped dead (the origin of the marathon race). The Athenians never forgot this

immortal feat of arms; they lost only 192 men, whose burial mound still stands at Marathon, and the Persians lost about 6,400.

◆ THE SECOND PERSIAN WAR
(480–479 B.C.)

Preparations for War   To avenge this defeat, Darius' son, Xerxes (486–465 B.C.), readied a huge force and swore that this time there would be no mistake. Fortunately for Greece and Europe, the Athenians were guided by a shrewd strategist, Themistocles. In 483 B.C., seeing the Persian menace on the horizon, he had persuaded the Athenians to use some newly found veins of silver in their mines to increase greatly the size of their fleet.

With this money they raised the number of their ships to two hundred. These ships were the famous triremes, on which nearly two hundred men rowed, seated in three banks. So swift and strong were these ships that they became, in effect, missiles, capable of smashing and disabling the enemy's ships. By thus greatly multiplying the striking power of one man, the trireme became the naval equivalent of the phalanx, in which hundreds of men could strike together on land.

The Invasion of 480 and Thermopylae Early in 480 some thirty Greek states, also fearing annihilation, formed a military alliance and entrusted to the Spartans command on both land and sea. A few months later Xerxes began his march toward Greece with a force of perhaps sixty thousand men and six hundred ships, in a grandiose amphibious invasion of Europe. The first Greek force sent out in 480 against the Persians was defeated at the pass of Thermopylae in central Greece. The Spartan king in command, Leonidas, dismissed many of his allies, with the result that the Spartans defended the pass almost alone in a stand always remembered for its heroism. A poet, in two simple, grave lines on a stone, immortalized the heroism of the three hundred Spartans and their king who fell there: "Stranger, tell the Spartans that we lie here, faithful to their orders." At the same time, a sea battle at nearby Artemisium was inconclusive.

Themistocles and the Victory at Salamis As the Persian forces continued southward, the Athenians abandoned Athens and the Persians burned the city down. This burning was a reply to the actions of the Athenians and other Greeks, who had burned the Persian city of Sardis in the Ionian revolt in 498. In this nearly desperate situation, Themistocles devised a brilliant trick. He sent a slave to the Persian king with a false message: Themistocles wished him well and advised him that, if he attacked the Greek fleet with his own at

▲ Themistocles, the great Athenian strategist, was ostracized about 472 B.C. This ostrakon, cast against him, says, "Themistocles, son of Neocles, let him depart" *(ITO).*
American School of Classical Studies at Athens: Agora Excavations.

once, he would win the decisive battle practically without a blow.

The Persians were taken in by the ruse and sent their ships into the narrows between Athens and the island of Salamis, where the Greek fleet, lying in wait, utterly defeated them. His navy shattered, Xerxes, who had watched the battle from a height, abandoned Greece and marched back toward the Dardanelles (see "'They Have a Master Called Law,'" p. 65).

The Battle of Plataea (479 B.C.) Yet the Persians could still have won the war, for a large Persian army remained in central Greece. The reckoning with this force came in a battle in 479 B.C., at the village of Plataea. Once more a Greek army, under the Spartan general Pausanias, crushed the Persians; out of perhaps fifty thousand Persians, only a few thousand survived.

The Greeks won a further battle at Mycale on the shore of Asia Minor in 479. The Ionian Greeks now proclaimed their freedom and thus completed the work of throwing off Persian control that they had begun twenty years earlier. Thus

> ## "They Have a Master Called Law"
>
> *As King Xerxes leads his army into Greece in 480 b.c., he asks a former king of Sparta, who is accompanying him, whether the Greeks will really fight against the Persians.*
>
> "Now, Demaratus, I will ask you what I want to know. You are a Greek and one from no minor or weak city. So now tell me, will the Greeks stand and fight me?" Demaratus replied, "Your Majesty, shall I tell you the truth, or say what you want to hear?" The king ordered him to tell the truth, saying that he would respect him no less for doing so.
>
> "Your Majesty," he said, "I am not speaking about all of them, only about the Spartans. First, I say they will never accept conditions from you that would enslave Greece; second, that they will fight you in battle even if all the other Greeks join your side."
>
> Xerxes said, "Demaratus, let's look at it in all logic: why should a thousand, or ten thousand, or fifty thousand men, if they are all free and not ruled by a single master, stand up against such an army as mine? If they were ruled by one man, like my
>
> subjects, I suppose they might, out of fear, show more bravery than usual and, driven into battle by the lash, go up against a bigger force; but if allowed their freedom, they wouldn't do either one."
>
> Demaratus said, "Your Majesty, I knew from the beginning that if I spoke the truth you wouldn't like my message, but, since you ordered me to do so, I told you about the Spartans. They are free men, but not wholly free: They have a master called Law, whom they fear far more than your soldiers fear you. And his orders are always the same—they must not run away from any army no matter how big, but must stand in their formation and either conquer or die. But, your Majesty, may your wishes be fulfilled."
>
> From *Herodotus*, book VII, Chaps. 101–104, abridged, trans. M. H. Chambers.

the Greeks crowned the most brilliant victory in the history of their civilization.

V. The Wars of the Fifth Century (479–404 b.c.)

After a brief period of cooperation, the two leading Greek cities, Athens and Sparta, led their allies into the long, tragic war that fatally weakened the Greek poleis.

◆ THE ATHENIAN EMPIRE

The victorious Greeks continued the war against Persia in 479 and 478 b.c., liberating, for example, the Greek city of Byzantium on the Bosporus from Persian control. But in 478 Sparta returned to its perennial isolationism and withdrew from the alliance that had been formed to oppose Persia. In response, many of the newly liberated Greek states met on the island of Delos in 478 and formed an alliance, known as the Delian League, to continue the war and take further vengeance on

Persia. Athens was recognized as head of the league and determined which members should supply ships to the common navy and which members should contribute money.

The military campaigns, often fought under the command of the Athenian general Cimon, were successful until the warfare between Greeks and Persians ended about 450. Meanwhile, Athenian control of the league had become stricter through the years. Sometimes Athens forcibly prevented members from withdrawing from the league; sometimes it stationed garrisons or governors in the supposedly independent member states. Athenian domination became unmistakable in 454, when the league transferred its treasury from Delos to Athens. The cash contributions were now nothing but tribute to Athens, and the alliance of equals had become an Athenian empire.

◆ THE AGE OF PERICLES

The Golden Age of Athens   The leading statesman in the period of the Athenian empire was Pericles (490?–429 b.c.), an aristocrat from a wealthy family who had the support of the common people. Now that the archonship was no longer a position for an ambitious man, Pericles held only the post of general, to which he was reelected from 443 to 429. He was a powerful orator and a highly competent general and was renowned for his personal honesty; moreover, his policies generally favored the common people.

He won them over by establishing pay for Athenian jurors and for those who served in the council. These measures not only supported the people but worked to assure the fullest possible participation in government by all citizens. In 447 B.C. he proposed that the Athenians restore the damage done by the Persian invasion of 480 and rebuild the temples on the Acropolis.

Between 447 and 432 B.C. they built for their goddess Athena the most nearly perfect of all Greek temples, the Parthenon. Inside it was a statue of Athena bearing more than a ton of gold. It was the work of the sculptor Phidias, who probably directed the reliefs on the temple as well. They also built a magnificent gateway to the Acropolis. These public works both beautified the city and served the political aim of providing work for the people.

Moreover, Pericles' lifetime coincided with the zenith of Athenian literature, when Athenian drama, especially, reached its highest development in the plays of Sophocles (a friend of Pericles) and Euripides. (On drama see further chapter 3, p. 81.) So brilliant was this era, and so strongly marked by his leadership, that historians often call the era from 450 to 429 the Age of Pericles. His political dominance drew praise from the historian Thucydides because "he controlled the masses, rather than let them control him. . . . Though the state was a democracy in name, in fact it was ruled by the most prominent man."[3]

The Athenian Judicial System   The expansion of the empire must have been one of the causes of the development of the Athenian judicial system. Juries were chosen by lot and comprised two to five hundred or even more citizens drawn from all classes. There was no detailed body of civil or criminal law, and in trials there was no judge,

merely a magistrate to keep order. Juries had wide powers of interpretation without the possibility of appeal from their decision. Nor were there professional attorneys, although a man facing trial could pay a clever rhetorician to write a courtroom speech for him. Juries heard all manner of cases with the exception of homicides, which were tried by the Areopagus council (see p. 57). Critics of this system saw it as too democratic, but it expressed the spirit of the Greek state: that the average citizen could and should play a part in governing the city.

◆ THE PELOPONNESIAN WAR
(431–404 B.C.)

"Historical laws" are difficult to establish and dangerous to use, but the observation of the British historian Lord Acton is hard to resist: "Power tends to corrupt." The Athenian empire, which had emerged out of the heroic victory in the Persian Wars, became more and more dominating over its subject states—its former allies. This movement and the resentment that it caused brought about the long war that sealed the doom of the Greek city-states. By far the longest and most dramatic of all collisions in Greek history, the Peloponnesian War also received an immortal analysis from the greatest of ancient historians, Thucydides of Athens (ca. 455–ca. 395 B.C.).

The Outbreak of War   In the 430s aggressive action by Athens convinced the allies of Sparta that they must declare a preventive war on Athens. First, in 435 Corinth, an ally of Sparta, went to war with one of its colonies, Corcyra (today the main city on the island of Corfu). The quarrel threatened to become Panhellenic when Corcyra appealed for help to Athens in 433. Despite the warning of ambassadors from Corinth that any assistance would make war inevitable, the Athenians signed an alliance with Corcyra and actually fought with their new allies in a naval battle against Corinth.

Second, also in 433, the Athenians ordered the town of Potidaea, in northern Greece, to demolish its walls, send hostages to Athens, and banish its magistrates. Though Potidaea was a member of the Athenian empire, these demands infuriated the allies of Sparta, especially Corinth. The allies

[3]Thucydides 2.65.

▲ **A portion of the frieze within the Athenian Parthenon, showing officials carrying the robe that will be presented to Athena. On the right, gods sit in conversation, awaiting the procession; note that they are portrayed as larger than the human beings.**
Hirmer Fotoarchiv

demanded a meeting of the Peloponnesian League (see p. 56) and voted to declare war on the Athenians and their allies.

The Opposing States Thucydides gives his opinion that these events were only the immediate, incidental causes of the war: "The truest cause, though the least talked about openly, was that the growth of Athenian power frightened the Spartans and finally compelled them to go to war."[4] This judgment seems accurate, for neither the affair of Corcyra nor that of Potidaea threatened the Spartans directly; more menacing was the general disturbance of the balance of power caused by Athenian boldness.

This war, known as the Peloponnesian War, opposed two kinds of states. Sparta, though the head of the Peloponnesian League, controlled no empire and maintained itself through its own resources. Athens relied on its empire to provide grain for its people and tribute to pay for its navy. Sparta had the strongest army in Greece, and Athens was the chief naval power.

The Archidamian War (431–421 B.C.) The first ten years of the war are called the Archidamian War, so named for Archidamus, one of the kings of Sparta when the war began. Fighting opened in 431 B.C. but was inconclusive for several years. Sparta sought to break Athenian morale by invading Attica annually, ravaging farms, and then departing for the Peloponnesian harvest. But the Athenians withdrew behind their "long walls" that reached down to their harbor until the enemy left, and Pericles refused to allow the Athenian infantry to challenge Sparta on the field. Instead, the Athenians launched raids by sea against coastal towns in the Peloponnese, but these raids left Sparta untouched. Far more damaging to Athens than the Spartan invasions was a devastating plague (not yet identified with any known disease) that attacked the Athenians, packed inside their walls, in 430 and later years. The plague took thousands of lives within the crowded, unsanitary city; Thucydides survived it and has left us a horrifying description of its effects on the body.

Unfortunately for Athens' effectiveness in the war, Pericles died in 429 B.C. None of his successors could maintain his stable leadership, and

[4]Thucydides 1.23.

▲ **A Roman copy of an idealized portrait of Pericles, the leading Athenian statesman of his time. The helmet symbolizes his position as commander.**
Scala/Art Resource, NY

some were unscrupulous demagogues playing only for their own temporary power. In the 420s both sides achieved certain successes, but the casualties that all parties suffered in the next few years made them ready to end, or at least suspend, the war. A peace treaty, supposed to last for fifty years, and making Athens and Sparta allies, was signed in 421 B.C. It is called the Peace of Nicias for the Athenian general who led the negotiations.

The "Suspicious Truce" (421–415 B.C.) and the Affair of Melos At this point the Greeks could have turned their backs on war, for both Athens and Sparta had shown courage and neither had gained a decisive advantage. Thucydides called the next few years a time of suspicious truce, but

during this period one event demands attention, the brutal subjugation of the small island of Melos by the Athenians in 416.

The Athenians sailed up to this neutral island and commanded the Melians to join the Athenian empire. Thucydides describes the negotiations in a brilliant passage, called the Melian Dialogue, in which envoys on each side argue their cases. It is by no means clear how he could have known what was said by either side, and this dialogue is probably based on his own conjectures. In any case, the Melians protest that they are so few in number that they cannot in any way threaten the Athenians, to which the Athenians reply that it is precisely their weakness that makes them dangerous: If the Athenians allow so small a state to remain neutral, this will show weakness in the Athenians themselves and may tempt their subjects to rebel.

In the Dialogue the Athenians brush aside all arguments based on morality and justice and finally seize the island, kill most of the adult men (probably two to three thousand), and sell the women and children as slaves. Without explicitly stating any moral conclusion, Thucydides shows the Athenians giving way to the corrupting influence of war; as he says in another passage, "War teaches men to be violent."[5]

The Syracusan Expedition In 415 B.C. another occasion for war arose. The people of Segesta, a city in Sicily, appealed to Athens for help in a war they were fighting against Syracuse, the leading power on that island. In commenting on the death of Pericles, Thucydides noted that his successors were often lesser men of poor judgment. It was so now, as Alcibiades, a talented young political leader of enormous ambition and—as it later turned out—few scruples, persuaded the Athenian assembly, against the advice of the Athenian general Nicias, to raise a large fleet and attack Syracuse, with him as one of the generals. This campaign in effect reopened the Peloponnesian War despite the peace treaty of 421 B.C.

Thucydides makes it clear that a quick, resolute attack might well have succeeded, but the Athenians failed to strike when they had a clear advantage. One event that blunted the Athenian attack

[5]Thucydides 3.82.

▲ **Map 2.8** **Greece in 431 b.c. on the Outbreak of the Peloponnesian War**
Shows the members of the alliances headed by Athens and Sparta.

was the loss of Alcibiades. He was recalled to Athens to stand trial on two scandalous charges: that he had been part of a gang of rowdies that had mutilated small statues of the god Hermes and that he and his friends had mocked some religious ceremonies known as mysteries. Fearing that his political enemies would be able to secure his conviction, he defected to Sparta and advised them how to fight the Athenians. His defection left Nicias, who had opposed the campaign from the start, in command.

In Syracuse, the Athenians finally decided to break off the campaign, but they lost a critical battle in the harbor and could not sail away. Trying to retreat toward the interior of the island, they were cut off and decimated. Those who survived this calamity were imprisoned in terrible conditions in a quarry at Syracuse; as Thucydides grimly says, "Few out of many returned home."[6]

[6]Thucydides 7.87.

Athens Defeated The disaster in Sicily led to many defections among Athens' subjects, but Sparta still could not strike the final blow. The war dragged on for another eight years until, in 405 B.C., the Spartan admiral Lysander captured the Athenian fleet at a spot called Aegospotami, in the Dardanelles. Athens, now unable to bring grain through the straits, had to surrender in desperate hunger in 404. It abandoned its empire and, as a guarantee for the future and a symbol of humiliation, had to pull down the "long walls" that had protected the population during the war. Sparta proclaimed this event, in language often used by victors in war, as the "liberation of Greece" and imposed on the Athenians a cruel regime (known as the Thirty Tyrants). Pro-Spartan and anti-Spartan factions assailed one another during the rule of this hated clique, with atrocities and murders committed on both sides. After eight months the Spartan king, Pausanias, restored the democracy in 403 B.C.

Athens never regained its former power, although democracy survived for long years after the war. The quality of political leadership had declined after the death of Pericles, as Thucydides observed. Several times when the war could have ended, ambitious politicians raised support for rash ventures that ended in disaster, of which the Sicilian expedition was only the most notable.

Looking back at the fifth century B.C., we can see that, in interstate politics, the Greek poleis made little constructive use of their brilliant victory over the invaders from Persia. Freed of a foreign enemy, they divided themselves into two blocs that turned against one another and, like characters in a Greek tragedy, involved themselves in the catastrophe of the Peloponnesian War.

Summary

◆

The Athenians lost their empire, which had made them the richest polis in Greek history. Sparta, persuaded by its allies to go to war in 431, had shattered the Athenian empire, but this empire had been no threat whatever to Sparta's isolated life within the protecting mountains of the Peloponnese. The losses in manpower had been heavy on both sides, but Sparta could less easily sustain these losses because of its smaller population, and in the fourth century it could put fewer and fewer troops in the field.

Besides these losses, there now came a failure of will, a spirit of pessimism and disillusion among Athenian intellectuals. Such a collapse of civic morale all but destroyed the sense of community that was the very heart of the polis. Self-centered individualism replaced the willing cooperation between citizens. Many thought uncontrolled democracy had led to social decline and military disaster, and they contrasted the discipline of Sparta, the victor, with the frequent chaos of Athenian policy. Thucydides often speaks critically of "the masses" and "the rabble," and similar ideas run through the work of Plato and other philosophers, who asked what had gone wrong with democracy and what system should replace it.

Questions for Further Thought

◆

1. There was no single ruler of ancient Greece, as there was in Egypt. If there had been such a ruler, how might Greek history and society have been different?

2. In what ways would you have liked to live in ancient Greece? What features of Greek life would you have found undesirable?

RECOMMENDED READING

◆

Sources

Herodotus. *The Histories*. Robin Waterfield (tr.). 1998. A new translation with precise notes by Carolyn Dewald.

Homer. *The Iliad*. Robert Fagles (tr.). 1990. A stirring translation in verse.

———. *The Odyssey*. Robert Fagles (tr.). 1996. A worthy companion to Fagles' *Iliad*.

Thucydides. *The Peloponnesian War*. Rex Warner (tr.). 1972. The masterpiece of Greek historical writing.

———. *The Landmark Thucydides*. Robert B. Strassler (ed.). 1996. The Crawley translation, older but still a classic, with many helpful maps, notes, and appendixes.

Studies

Boardman, John. *Greek Art*. 1973. One of many books by this great authority.

Boardman, John, et al. (eds.). *The Oxford History of Greece and the Hellenistic World*. Sixteen chapters by leading authorities on topics like art, literature, religion, and history.

Burkert, Walter. *Greek Religion*. 1987. By the most original and profound expert of our times.

———. *The Orientalizing Revolution*. 1992. Brief but close-packed study of Eastern influence on Greek art, religion, and culture.

Burn, A. R. *Persia and the Greeks: The Defence of the West, c. 546–478 B.C.* 2d ed. 1984. Accurate narrative of the Persian Wars.

Chadwick, John. *The Decipherment of Linear B*. 2d ed. 1970. Study of the Cretan scripts, with notes on the method of decipherment.

Drews, Robert. *The Coming of the Greeks*. 1988. Important on the arrival of the Greeks and movement of Indo-European peoples.

———. *The End of the Bronze Age: Changes in Warfare and the Catastrophe, ca. 1200 B.C.* 1993. Suggests that Mediterranean cities fell as chariot warfare gave way to massed infantry attacks.

Ehrenberg, Victor. *From Solon to Socrates*. 1968. Standard textbook on the central period of Greek history, with good references to sources.

Fantham, Elaine, et al. *Women in the Classical World*. 1994. Chapters on women in both Greece and Rome. Many good illustrations.

Finley, M. I. *The World of Odysseus*. 2d ed. 1977. Brilliant discussion of the historical material in Homer, both Iliad and Odyssey.

Flacelière, Robert. *Daily Life in Greece at the Time of Pericles*. 1965. Social and economic history of Greek life.

Forrest, W. G. *A History of Sparta, 950–192 B.C.* 1980. Brief history of Sparta, taking the story down through the state's collapse.

Garlan, Yvon. *Slavery in Ancient Greece*. Rev. ed. 1988. Thorough treatment of this institution.

Green, Peter. *The Greco-Persian Wars*. 1996. Modern, accurate narrative of the two Persian Wars.

Guthrie, W. K. C. *A History of Greek Philosophy*. 6 vols. 1962–1981. Encyclopedic history, brilliant and sensitive.

Hansen, Mogens Herman. *The Athenian Democracy in the Age of Demosthenes: Structure, Principles, and Ideology*. 1991. History of the democracy with careful attention to how it functioned.

Kagan, Donald. *The Archidamian War*. 1974. Detailed history of the first part of the Peloponnesian War (followed by two other volumes).

Keuls, Eva C. *The Reign of the Phallus*. 2d ed. 1993. Brilliant but one-sided work arguing that females were severely restrained in classical Greece; many illustrations.

Lawrence, A. W. *Greek Architecture*. 1987. Introductory survey of temples and private buildings.

Lazenby, J. F. *The Spartan Army*. 1985. History and operation of the Spartan army.

Lenardon, Robert J. *The Saga of Themistocles*. 1978. Readable, sound study of the great strategist.

MacDowell, Douglas M. *The Law in Classical Athens*. 1978. Good discussion of all aspects.

Morrison, J. S., and J. F. Coates. *The Athenian Trireme: The History and Reconstruction of an Ancient Greek Warship*. 1986. Essential treatment, solving at last the problem of how the Greek trireme was built.

Page, Denys L. *History and the Homeric Iliad*. 2d ed. 1966. Especially good on Near Eastern connections with the epic.

Patterson, Cynthia B. *The Family in Greek History*. 1998. The most recent study.

Pomeroy, Sarah B. *Goddesses, Whores, Wives, and Slaves*. 1975. The pioneering work that opened the modern study of women in the ancient world; includes chapters on Rome.

Renault, Mary. *The King Must Die*. 1958. An evocative historical novel set in the mythical time of Theseus.

Sealey, Raphael. *Women and Law in Classical Greece*. 1990. Carries the discussion beyond Athens into other Greek societies.

Wycherley, R. E. *How the Greeks Built Cities*. 1976. Greek town planning with description of major urban public buildings.

▲ A superb statue of the god Apollo from the west pediment of the Temple of Zeus at Olympia. In a commanding gesture, the god controls a centaur and symbolically brings Hellenic rationality to bear over an undisciplined universe. The statue combines the power and dignity of a god with the ideal perfection of a human being.
Erich Lessing/Art Resource, NY

CLASSICAL AND HELLENISTIC GREECE

The Peloponnesian War left the two main Greek political alliances, those built around Athens and Sparta, weak and demoralized. The war thus prepared the way for the conquest of Greece in the next century by the Macedonian king Philip II. His son, Alexander the Great, went on to conquer Egypt, Persia, and vast stretches of Asia Minor.

Despite the tumultuous conditions of Greek politics—and perhaps because of the uncertainties and upheavals—the fifth and fourth centuries witnessed an extraordinary flowering of intellectual and artistic achievement. This burst of creative energy was concentrated in time and space to a degree that was unprecedented in history and, some would argue, has never been duplicated. The theme that runs through Greek civilization now became the inquiry into philosophy and analytical thought. In these years the Greeks wrote their greatest tragic dramas; they invented historical writing; and philosophers probed virtually every phase of human existence. Within society, the classical structure of the family and the several roles of women now become visible.

During the last decades of the fourth century, the Greeks, having lost the world of the independent polis, embraced the larger world of Alexander's empire, which brought them into contact with other peoples. There followed a series of intellectual experiments, especially in science and technology, art and literature, philosophy and religion. The Greek language took deeper roots in the Near East and ultimately became the language for the Christian New Testament.

CHAPTER 3. CLASSICAL AND HELLENISTIC GREECE							
	Social Structure	Body Politic	Changes in the Organization of Production and in the Impact of Technology	Evolution of Family and Changing Gender Roles	War	Religion	Cultural Expression
I. CLASSICAL GREEK CULTURE							
II. THE RISE OF MACEDONIA							
III. THE HELLENISTIC AGE							

I. Classical Greek Culture (ca. 500–323 B.C.)

◆

In less than two centuries, Greek society went through a profound intellectual transformation, apparent above all in literature, philosophy, drama, and historical writing. In all these spheres, reasoned argument became supreme. This cultural trait was hardly to be found among their older eastern neighbors. This era was one of Athenian preeminence, and the study of this "golden age" inevitably focuses on Athens.

◆ GREEK PHILOSOPHY

The Inspiration for Philosophic Thought The supreme intellectual invention of the Greeks is the special search for knowledge called philosophy—the attempt to use reason to discover why things are as they are. Philosophy is born when people are no longer satisfied with supernatural and mythical explanations of the world or of human behavior. It is hard to say just why Greeks gradually became skeptical about the accounts that they inherited in their own mythology, but around 600 B.C. they began to suspect that there was an order in the universe beyond manipulation by the gods—and that human beings could discover it.

Life in Greek poleis was conducive to argument and debate, and such conditions encouraged rational inquiry and even dispute. And philosophy, like drama and history, became a means to analyze and understand change and upheaval. Yet philosophy never turned its back on religion.

The earliest philosophers were seeking nothing less than a cosmic plan, a divine world order.

The Beginnings of Philosophy in Miletus The first Greek philosophers lived in the city of Miletus, a prominent trading center on the western shore of Asia Minor in the region of Ionia. Its citizens had direct contact with the ideas and achievements of the Near East, and these intellectual currents must have helped form the city as a center of thought. Soon after 600 B.C., certain Milesians were discovering a world of speculation in an apparently simple yet profoundly radical question: What exists? They sought their answer in some single primal element. One philosopher, Thales, for example, taught that everything in the whole universe was made of water, a notion that echoes Babylonian myths of a primeval flood. He may have reasoned that water is found in several states—as ice, as mist, and as water itself. Moreover, all the first civilizations—Sumer, Egypt, Babylonia—were nourished by great rivers.

The hypothesis of Thales inspired various replies. For example, one of his pupils, Anaximander of Miletus, held (probably about 560 B.C.) that the origin of everything was an infinite body of matter, which he called "the boundless." A whirling motion within the boundless divided its substance into the hot, which rose to form the heavens, and the cold, which sank and assumed form in the earth and the air surrounding it. A further separation into wet and dry created the oceans and the land. Human beings, he thought, had emerged from the sea; in this way he expressed a primitive theory of evolution. This

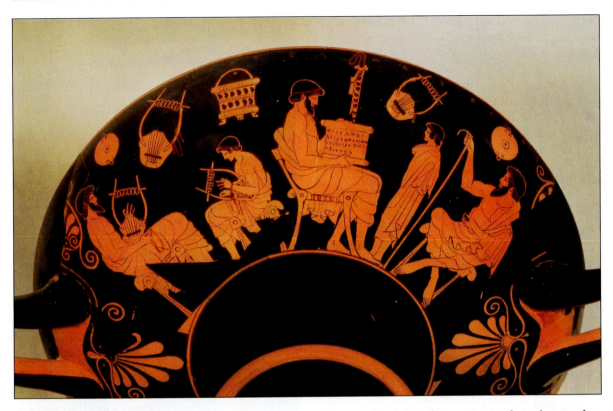

▲ **An Attic red-figure vase (about 470 b.c.), showing scenes from a school. At left, a master teaches a boy to play the lyre; at right, a boy learns to recite poetry from a scroll held by a master while another master supervises the class.**
Johannes Laurentius, 1992/Bildarchiv Preussischer Kulturbesitz

theory points toward a common later classification of all matter into four elements: earth, air, fire, and water. Moreover, he said, all things will pass away into that from which they came: Thus—a dark but clearly religious statement—will they "pay the penalty for their wrongdoing according to the ordinance of time."

Pythagoras and Numbers Among the theories proposed to explain the order or substance of all things were those of Pythagoras of Samos (around 530 b.c.), who developed a strikingly different theory to explain the structure of the world. He saw the key to all existence in mathematics and approached the universe through the study of numbers. He discovered the harmonic intervals within the musical scale and stated the Pythagorean theorem in geometry about the area based on the sides of a right triangle. Pythagoras went on to say that all objects are similar to numbers, by

which he probably meant that objects always contain a numerically balanced arrangement of parts. He lacked, of course, the experimental methods of modern physicists; yet his theory is remarkably similar to the modern discoveries of mathematical relationships within all things, including even the genetic code in our bodies.

The Atomic Theory Yet another way of looking at the universe came from Leucippus and his contemporary, Democritus of Abdera, about 450 b.c. They saw the world as made up of invisibly small particles, or atoms (*a-toma* in Greek, meaning "things that cannot be divided"), which come together and cohere at random. Death, according to this theory, leads simply to the redistribution of the atoms that make up our body and soul and thus need hold no terror for humanity. The validity of the atomic theory was eventually to be recognized in the modern era. It is another example of the ability of Greek theorists to hit part of the scientific truth, even though they could not prove it in laboratories.

The Sophists Around 450 B.C. philosophers turned away from speculations about the structure of the universe and toward the study of human beings and the ways they led their lives. The first Greeks to undertake this study were those commonly known as Sophists (*sophistés* in Greek means "expert" or "learned man"). They came to Athens from various places and challenged nearly all accepted beliefs. One of the early Sophists, Protagoras, declared that "man is the measure" of everything; that is, human beings and their perceptions are the only measure of whether a thing exists at all. The very existence of the gods, whom people cannot really perceive, is only an undemonstrable assumption. From such a statement it is only a short step to the belief that it is almost impossible to know anything; in the absence of objective knowledge, the only recourse is to make your way through the world by coolly exploiting to your own advantage any situation you encounter.

The Sophists also drew an important distinction between human customs on the one hand and the law of nature on the other. Thus they argued that what was made or designed by people was arbitrary and inferior; what existed naturally was immutable and proper. This argument called into question all accepted rules of good behavior. Freed of moral constraints, the Sophists suggested that intellectual activity was valuable only in helping one succeed in life. They accepted pupils and said they could train these pupils for success in any calling, since in every line of work there are problems to be solved through reasoning. They taught the art of rhetoric, persuasive speech making that could be used to sway an assembly or to defend oneself in court. Their pupils, they implied, could gain power by analyzing the mechanics of politics and by using the skills the Sophists taught them.

Socrates of Athens The main critic of the Sophists was Socrates (469–399 B.C.). He was active during the intellectually dynamic period before and during the Peloponnesian War. Socrates faulted the Sophists for taking pay for teaching,

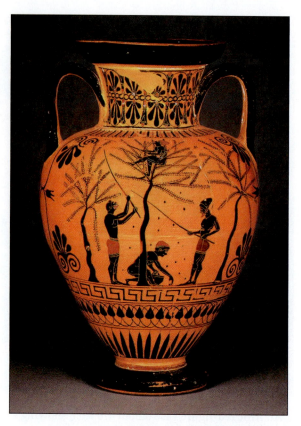

▲ The olive was one of the basic crops in Greek agriculture. In this black-figure vase (the figures are painted black while the background is the natural red of the clay), two men knock olives off a tree at harvest time, while another climbs the branches and a boy gathers the fruit.
British Museum (PS227411)

yet failing to recognize moral absolutes and teach ethically right behavior. In the course of his critique, Socrates transformed philosophy into an inquiry about the moral responsibility of people. His basic questions were not, What is the world made of and how does it operate? but rather, What is right action and how can I know it is right? His mission was to persuade the young men of Athens to examine their lives in the pursuit of moral truth, for "the unexamined life is not worth living."

His technique was to engage his pupils in a dialogue of questions and answers and to refute, correct, and guide them by this "Socratic" method to the right answers. He held that no man is wise who cannot give a logical account of his actions and that knowledge will point to the morally right choices; this belief led to his statement that "knowledge is virtue," one of several Socratic theses that seem paradoxical, for even ignorant men may be virtuous. Another such paradox is his statement that he was the wisest of men because he knew that he knew nothing. It was through ironic statements like these that he made people think critically and thus discover moral truths. The Roman orator and essayist Cicero said that Socrates had brought philosophy down from the heavens and placed it in the cities of the world.

Socrates' Trial and Death

Socrates had political critics, for he was the tutor of several Athenians who had opposed democracy during the last years of the Peloponnesian War. One, Critias, was a member of a pro-Spartan oligarchy known as the Thirty Tyrants, who ruled Athens after the war. Alcibiades, who joined the Spartan side during the war, was another of his followers. As a result, Socrates was suspected of sympathy with the enemies of Athenian democracy, and in 399 B.C. he was brought to trial on charges of "worshiping strange gods and corrupting the youth"—a way of implying that Socrates had connections with enemies of the democratic state.

One can understand why Athenian jurors, who had just regained their democratic constitution from a short-lived oligarchy that fell in 403, would have wanted to punish anyone who had collaborated with the oligarchs. But there is little reason to think that Socrates was disloyal to the state. Nevertheless, persuaded by Socrates' enemies and acting in misguided patriotism, the jury convicted him. He proposed as his penalty a fine of 100 drachmas, which was about two months' pay, thus not a trifling sum; but when he also ironically requested the honor of dining rights at the town hall, the jury reacted in anger by voting for the death penalty (see "Socrates Is Sentenced to Death," p. 78).

Socrates accepted his fate and declined to seek exile. Perhaps he thought that life outside his polis, at age seventy, offered little pleasure. He may also have wanted to show his young followers that the duty of a good man was to obey the laws of the state. He drank a cup of poison with simple courage.

Plato: What Is Reality?

Our knowledge of Socrates' thought comes mainly from the writings of his most famous pupil, Plato (428–347 B.C.), for Socrates wrote nothing. Plato continued Socrates' investigation of moral conduct by writing a series of complex and profound philosophical books, mainly in the form of dialogues in which Socrates is the main speaker. In these works, Plato went far beyond the ironic paradoxes proposed by Socrates and sought truth through a subtle process of reasoning and inquiry that modern readers still endlessly discuss and probe.

Plato made his greatest impact on the future of philosophy with his theory of knowledge. Socrates' answer to the question, How can I know what is right? was simply that one must listen to one's conscience. Such reliance on the inner voice within each human being did not satisfy Plato, who believed that we must go beyond the evidence of our senses to find ultimate reality and truth. Moreover, Socrates thought that everyone could recognize and practice right behavior; but Plato believed that moral goodness was restricted to the elite who could master it through philosophic study. He developed and taught his theories in his school in Athens called the Academy.

The Republic

According to Plato, we see objects as real, but in fact they are only poor reflections of ideal models, or "forms," which are eternal, perfect originals of any given object or notion.[1] In his *Republic*, Plato illustrates our lack of true perception with a famous metaphor. Imagine men sitting in a cave, facing a wall, with a fire behind them. As others carry objects through the cave, in front of the fire, the men see only vague shadows of the objects and therefore cannot make out the reality. Everything that we see is like these imprecise shadows; so what we see as justice, for example, is nothing but an approximation of the true "form" of justice. Only through long training in philosophy can we learn how to perceive and understand the true ideal forms, which exist outside our world.

Plato presents this thesis in several dialogues, of which the most widely read is *The Republic*.

---

[1]Plato used the Greek word *idéa*, which means an image that one can see. Thus "form" is a better translation than the English "idea," even though the latter is widely used.

SOCRATES IS SENTENCED TO DEATH

◆

Plato's version of Socrates' words to the jury that sentenced him to death:

"You too, gentlemen of the jury, must look forward to death with confidence, and fix your minds on this one belief, which is certain: that nothing can harm a good man either in life or after death, and his fortunes are not a matter of indifference to the gods. This present experience of mine has not come about mechanically; I am quite clear that the time had come when it was better for me to die and to be released from my distractions. . . . For my own part I bear no grudge at all against those who condemned me and accused me, although it was not with this kind intention that they did so, but because they thought they were hurting me. . . . However, I ask them to grant me one favor. When my sons grow up, gentlemen, if you think that

they are putting money or anything else before goodness, take your revenge by plaguing them as I plagued you; and if they fancy themselves for no reason, you must scold them just as I scolded you, for neglecting the important things and thinking that they are good for something when they are good for nothing. If you do this, I shall have had justice at your hands, both I myself and my children.

Now it is time that we were going, I to die and you to live; but which of us has the happier prospect is unknown to anyone but God."

From Hugh Tredennick (tr.), Plato, *The Last Days of Socrates*, Penguin Classics, 1954, 1972, 1980, p. 76.

Like other Athenian intellectuals, Plato opposed democracy as a political system dominated by emotion rather than logic. His repudiation of democracy intensified when a jury was persuaded to condemn Socrates to death, even though he had served the state as a soldier and had committed no crime. Socrates is the main speaker in the *Republic,* and in the work's long debate over the right form of state he expresses severe criticisms of democracy as a volatile, unpredictable, and ineffective system. Yet it is by no means certain that these opinions were really those of the historical Socrates. It is probable that Plato was the real antidemocrat and that he put these opinions into the mouth of Socrates for dramatic purposes. Whatever its source, Plato's denunciation of broad participation by the people in governing has remained a challenge to political theorists ever since.

Plato's Ideal State Looking back at the death of his teacher at the hands of a popular court, Plato sought to demonstrate that people without a philosophical education should never exercise political power. Their chief disqualification was that they had no grasp of reality, because they were unable to perceive the forms.

Government should therefore be in the hands of men who had received an education in philosophy. This ruling elite would see to it that "every-

one will do his proper task." In Plato's preferred system, a second class, warriors, would defend the state; a third class, workers, would produce the needed material goods. Plato sums up his conception of good government in an epigram: "The state will be ruled well when philosophers become kings and kings become philosophers."[2]

Like other visions of a perfect state, Plato's *Republic* has had little effect on actual constitutions, but it remains the most widely read philosophical book of all time. Its analyses probe nearly every problem of philosophy, from statesmanship to the nature of perception, the power of language, and psychology. Many threads run through the book, but one above all: the question, What is justice? As we have seen, the issue of justice was central to Greek thought and also to the debates in the history of Thucydides. Indeed, it recurs throughout the whole fifth century. That the pupil of Socrates, who had seen his teacher condemned in what he considered a brutal distortion of justice, should have been obsessed by this question emphasizes the degree to which Plato was a product of the Athenian society of his time.

Aristotle: Form and Matter Plato had a pupil of equal genius, Aristotle (384–322 B.C.), who was for a time the teacher of Alexander the Great of Mace-

---

[2]Plato, *Republic,* 473 c.

◄ An Attic relief, showing the goddess Athena leaning on her spear and gazing at a tablet, perhaps a list of men fallen in battle. If so, this would justify the name often given to this relief, the "Mourning Athena." Acropolis Museum, Athens

donia. Aristotle founded a school within a grove in Athens called the Lyceum. His investigations, in which he was assisted by his pupils in Athens between 336 and 322 B.C., embraced all fields of learning known to the ancients, including logic, metaphysics, astronomy, biology, physics, politics, and poetry.

Aristotle departed from Plato's theory of an ideal reality that cannot be perceived by the senses. Rather, he saw reality as consisting of both form and matter. In this way, he turned his pupils to empirical sciences, the study of what can be seen to exist. He also had an overall theory of the world of nature. For Aristotle each object has a purpose as part of a grand design of the universe. "Nature does nothing by accident," he said. The task of the philosopher is to study these individual objects to discover their purpose; then he may ultimately be able to determine a general pattern.

Aristotle and the State Like Plato, Aristotle wanted to design the best state. In one of his works, the *Politics,* he classified the types of political constitutions in the Greek world and distinguished three basic forms: monarchy, aristocracy, and moderate democracy. He warned that monarchy can turn into tyranny; aristocracy, into oligarchy; and moderate democracy, into radical democracy, or anarchy.

Of the three uncorrupted forms, Aristotle expressed a preference for moderate democracy— one in which the masses do not exercise too much power. The chief end of government, in his view, is a good life for both the individual and the community as a whole. This idea is an extension of the view expressed in his *Ethics,* that happiness is the greatest good of the individual. To achieve this end, people must seek moderation, often called the Golden Mean: a compromise between extremes of excessive pleasure and ascetic denial—a goal that reflected the Greek principle of harmony and balance in all things.

Aristotle's Physical Theories Aristotle's conception of the universe remained influential in scientific speculation for two thousand years. By 350

▼ **The so-called Temple of Concord from Agrigento, Sicily. Superb example of a fifth-century Doric temple. The stone was of inferior quality and was originally covered with stucco, still visible on some columns.** John Snyder/Corbis Stock Market

B.C. philosophers generally recognized four elements: earth, air, fire, and water. Aristotle gave the elements purpose and movement. Air and fire, he said, naturally move upward; and earth and water, downward. He explained movement by saying that elements seek their natural place. Thus, a stone falls because it seeks to return to the earth. It also seeks to be at rest; all motion is therefore involuntary and unnatural and must be accounted for by an outside force.

To the four elements Aristotle added a fifth, ether, the material of which the stars are made. He explained that the stars move in a natural circular motion, and outside the whole universe there exists an eternal "prime mover," which imparts movement to all the other parts. This prime mover, or God as Aristotle finally designates him, does not move or change; God is a kind of divine thought or mind that sets the whole universe in motion.

Aristotle and the World of Nature Among the most original and fascinating of all Aristotle's works are his writings on biology, which are based on extensive firsthand observation. In the *Generation of Animals*, he studies the birth and reproduction of animals, birds, fish, insects, and human beings. In the *Parts of Animals*, he discusses the functions of the various parts of the body.

Aristotle believed that nature, the creator of living things, designed every part with a specific function. Thus, for example, the lion and wolf were given no vertebrae in the neck because nature intended that they should have rigid necks for charging their prey. Such explanations are called *teleological* (from the Greek word *telos*, meaning "aim, goal"), and they remained influential for many centuries. Even more influential was Aristotle's effort to classify all that he observed in separate categories. His organizing principles remained the basis for the study of nature until the scientific revolution of the seventeenth century.

◆ GREEK TRAGEDY

One of the most lasting achievements of the fifth century B.C. was the creation and perfection of a new literary and theatrical form, tragedy. Greek dramas were written in the most sublime poetry since Homer, and they first appeared in Athens, at religious festivals honoring the god Dionysus. At these celebrations, also marked by dancing and revelry, dramatic performances addressed increasingly profound moral issues.

Themes in Greek Tragedy The writers of tragedies derived most of their plots from tales of gods and heroes in Greek mythology; therefore drama never lost its close connection with religion. Their central themes include questions fundamental to all religions: What is humanity's relationship to the gods? What is justice? And if the gods are just, why do they allow people to suffer? That tragic drama arose at this time and in this place may be the result of the new confidence of the Athenians following their victory over Persia and the founding of the Athenian empire. Their inspiration may also have derived from their awareness of how short-lived triumphs can be. Greek tragedy relentlessly pursued its main theme—that worldly success can lead to arrogance, and arrogance to folly. Destruction, often sent by the gods as punishment, can be the inevitable result.

The Production of Plays In the fifth century these dramas were performed before audiences of as many as fifteen thousand people of all classes, often during religious festivals. The plays not only moved and inspired but also provided an education in ethics for citizens, who were gripped by the complex debates over which persons were acting justly and which ones should suffer retribution for moral error and crime. Just as philosophy explored the subject of ethical responsibility and right conduct, so do the dramas—but with far greater emotional power. Greek tragedies are still performed and filmed, and they continue to inspire operas, plays, and ballets more than two thousand years after their creation.

Aeschylus: Fate and Revenge Playwrights presented dramas in sets of three, accompanied by a comic playlet known as a satyr play (probably meant to relieve the heavy emotion of the main drama). Only one such "trilogy" has survived: the *Oresteia*, the tragedy of Orestes, the son of Agamemnon, by Aeschylus, which was produced in 458 B.C. Its central theme is the nature of justice, which Aeschylus explores in a tale of multiple murders and vengeance. Agamemnon, the leader of the war against Troy, found his fleet becalmed and had to sacrifice his daughter to revive the winds so that he could fulfill his oath to make war on Troy. On his return, his wife, Clytemnestra, kills him and is in turn killed by her son, Orestes, who is finally tried and acquitted in an Athenian court presided over by the goddess Athena. The cycle of retribution runs its course as the themes of fate and revenge focus on the family, all developed through majestic poetry and intense emotion.

Sophocles: When Is Civil Disobedience Justified?
Sophocles wrote mainly during the Peloponnesian War of 431–404 B.C. He changed the form of drama by adding a third actor (Aeschylus never had more than two actors on the stage at any time) in order to concentrate more on the interplay of characters and the larger issues of society that they explore. He also shows a greater interest in personality than does Aeschylus.

His *Oedipus the King* is perhaps the most nearly perfect specimen of surviving Greek tragedy; its central concern is the relationship of the individual and the polis. The play is about Oedipus, the revered king of Thebes, who has unknowingly committed the terrible crimes of killing his father and marrying his mother. As the play opens, some unknown offense has brought a plague on his people. Oedipus orders a search to discover the person who has caused this pollution. As the search narrows with terrifying logic to Oedipus himself, he discovers that his crimes of patricide and incest, though unintentional, have disturbed the order of the universe and his polis in particular. The only remedy is for him to serve justice and atone for his offenses. When the truth emerges, Oedipus' wife-mother hangs herself and Oedipus, in a frenzy of remorse and humiliation, plunges the brooches from her robe into his eyes and begins a life of wandering as a blind outcast; the once powerful monarch is now a broken, homeless fugitive (see "Oedipus' Self-Mutilation," p. 83).

Sophocles' *Antigone* continues the saga of Oedipus' family as his daughter Antigone grapples with another dilemma about justice. One of her brothers has been killed while attacking his own city, Thebes. Antigone wants to give him a traditional burial despite his traitorous actions, but the ruler of Thebes forbids such honor for an outlaw. Antigone must therefore decide which laws to obey—those of the gods or those laid down by a man.

Antigone defies the ruler by burying her brother and thus willingly goes to prison, where she hangs herself in heroic loyalty to her beliefs. The play, like most Greek tragedies, raises moral questions that still resonate: When is civil disobedience justified, and is it our duty to resist laws that we consider wrong?

Euripides: Psychology and Human Destiny
The Athenian poet Euripides, a contemporary of Sophocles, emphasized above all the psychology of his characters. Reacting to the violence of his times, he throws his characters back on their own searing passions. They forge their own fates, alienated from their societies. As a result, we see in Euripides how the workings of the mind and emotions shape a person's destiny. His intense, even fanatical, characters determine the course of events by their own often savage deeds. Compared with Aeschylus and Sophocles, Euripides seems less confident in a divine moral order. In this uncertainty, he reflects the wavering spirit of his age.

In Euripides' *Medea,* for example, Jason, Medea's husband, has deserted her for a princess of Corinth. Driven by overwhelming emotion to take revenge, Medea kills the Corinthian girl and then turns on her own children. As love and hatred battle within her, she weeps over her children but, despite a momentary weakening of will, completes her vengeance and kills them. The powerful woman has found her own way of dealing with the terrors of the world. We should note that she is not punished for her horrible crime, as probably would have happened in a tragedy of Aeschylus or Sophocles.

◆ GREEK COMEDY: ARISTOPHANES

Comedy abandoned these serious themes and satirized contemporary situations and people in the real world. Almost the only comedies that have come down to us are those written by the Athenian Aristophanes, a younger contemporary of Sophocles and Euripides. Again and again he emphasized the ridiculous in individual lives as well as in society at large. Aristophanes used fantasy and burlesque to satirize the Peloponnesian

OEDIPUS' SELF-MUTILATION

◆

In Sophocles' tragedy King Oedipus, *Jocasta, the mother of Oedipus, hangs herself after learning that she has married her own son. An attendant then narrates what follows. (Those he "should never have seen" are the daughters Oedipus fathered by his mother-wife.)*

"We saw a knotted pendulum, a noose,
A strangled woman swinging before our eyes.
The King saw too, and with heart-rending groans
Untied the rope, and laid her on the ground.
But worse was yet to see. Her dress was pinned
With golden brooches, which the King snatched out
And thrust, from full arm's length, into his eyes—
Eyes that should see no longer his shame, his guilt,
No longer see those they should never have seen,
Nor see, unseeing, those he had longed to see,
Henceforth seeing nothing but night . . . To this wild
tune

He pierced his eyeballs time and time again,
Till bloody tears ran down his beard—not drops
But in full spate a whole cascade descending
In drenching cataracts of scarlet rain.
Thus two have sinned; and on two heads, not one—
On man and wife—falls mingled punishment.
Their old long happiness of former times
Was happiness earned with justice; but to-day
Calamity, death, ruin, tears, and shame,
All ills that there are names for—all are here."

From E. F. Watling (tr.), Sophocles, *The Three Theban Plays,*
Penguin Classics, 1971, pp. 60–61.

War, political leaders, intellectuals—including Socrates—and the failings of democracy. Whatever his political motives in writing his satires, they sometimes exposed the folly of human behavior more devastatingly than the tragedies did. And they were particularly cutting in their depiction of the absurdities of arrogant persons in Athenian society.

The earliest of Aristophanes' eleven surviving plays is *The Acharnians* (425 B.C.), an antiwar comedy from the early years of the Peloponnesian War (Acharnae was an Athenian village). Aristophanes continued his antiwar theme in other plays, notably *Lysistrata,* which he wrote after the disastrous Athenian expedition to Syracuse. In this comedy the women of Athens, despairing of any other means of ending the long war, go on a sex strike that humiliates their blustering menfolk, and they succeed in enlisting the other women of Greece in their cause.

Aristophanes reserved some of his sharpest attacks for the democratic leaders who succeeded Pericles. In *The Knights* (424 B.C.) a general tries to persuade an ignorant sausage-seller to unseat Cleon, one of those leaders:

Sausage-Seller: Tell me this, how can I, a sausage-seller, be a big man like that?

General: The easiest thing in the world. You've got all the qualifications: low birth, marketplace training, insolence.

Sausage-Seller: I don't think I deserve it.

General: Not deserve it? It looks to me as if you've got too good a conscience. Was your father a gentleman?

Sausage-Seller: By the gods, no! My folks were scoundrels.

General: Lucky man! What a good start you've got for public life!

Sausage-Seller: But I can hardly read.

General: The only trouble is that you know anything. To be a leader of the people isn't for learned men, or honest men, but for the ignorant and vile. Don't miss the golden opportunity.[3]

◆ HISTORICAL WRITING

Drama is one way of examining the human condition; writing history is another. The constant wars in the fifth century B.C. prompted some men to

---

[3]From L. S. Stavrianos, *Epic of Man to 1500,* 1970.

seek to explain why war was their perpetual companion. They looked to the past to understand what causes war and how people behave during conflict. In so doing, they invented a new literary form: history.

Herodotus: Father of History   Herodotus, a Greek from Asia Minor and a contemporary of Sophocles, is rightly called the "Father of History," for he was the first to write a sustained narrative of political events, in his case, the Greek victory over Persia. Yet his narrative was no mere chronicle, for he laid down forever the historian's main question: Why do events happen? Again, Herodotus understood that a major war could also be a clash between two differing cultures. He therefore began by trying to learn the history of the Persian Empire in order to explain its pressure on Europe.

The most impressive dimension of his work is his demonstration that all the cultures of the ancient world were interconnected. Using travelers' tales, interviews, and oral tradition, much as a modern anthropologist does, Herodotus described the character and outlook of the several peoples of the Near East. He also reduced centuries of Near Eastern history into order, chronicling the dynasties and successions from one monarch to another. He did this without the help of any earlier narrative, and the structure he gave to the history of the Persian Empire has not been shaken. He explained the growth of the Persian Empire as the work of powerful, ambitious monarchs, constantly striving for a larger realm. In the end, Herodotus shows his Greek heritage with his verdict that the Greek victory in the Persian Wars was the inevitable triumph of a free society over a despotic one. He also brings the supernatural into his work through dreams, omens, and oracles, and he declared that the Athenians—"next to the gods"—were mainly responsible for the Greek victory.

Thucydides: Analysis of War   Greek historians "published" their work by giving readings, perhaps also allowing copies to be made. Thucydides, a younger contemporary of Herodotus, is said to have heard Herodotus read, and this experience may have inspired him when, as a participant in the Peloponnesian War, he decided to write its history. He did not live to finish his work,

▲ Roman wall paintings often show scenes from Greek drama and mythology; this painting shows Medea, in Euripides' play, about to kill her children. "My friends, I am resolved to act, to slay my children quickly and depart from this land."
Naples, Archeological Museum. Photo, © Luciano Pedicini

which breaks off in 411, seven years before the end of the war. Thucydides has a narrower theme than Herodotus, for he concentrates on a limited period and area.

Yet he is the more profound inquirer into causation, he weighs evidence more carefully, and he analyzes more keenly the motives of statesmen and warriors. He offers far fewer anecdotes than Herodotus; wit and humor are totally absent. His entire first book, out of the eight that make up his history, explores the causes, both immediate and long-term, for the outbreak of the war. Thucydides brings to bear on events the kind of logical and unemotional analysis that philosophers developed in the late fifth century. Throughout his work he presents a series of speeches and debates about various issues and decisions in order to lay bare the motives of the participants. The speakers are usually contemptuous of moral principles, and arguments based on justice and mercy, if brought up at all, are ruthlessly swept aside by whichever person or force has the upper hand. It is by no means clear that Thucydides himself rejected compassion, but he presents the whole war as a cold pursuit of power. It was by such rigorous analysis that he brought order out of the cruelties and disruptions of his age.

In Thucydides' view, the Athenian state was in good order under Pericles because he could control the Athenian people. His political successors, by contrast, allowed the masses to influence decisions, with tragic consequences for Athens, including above all the expedition to Sicily in 415 b.c. Thucydides combines accuracy and concentration on detail with descriptive powers that rival those of the dramatists, particularly when he brings a scene of horror to life. No reader can avoid feeling a chill over the clinical description of the plague that attacked Athens in 430 b.c. or the shattering defeat of the proud armada that sailed against Syracuse. He is the undisputed master among ancient historians, and for gripping narrative power and philosophical breadth he remains unsurpassed (see "Thucydides: The Melian Dialogue," p. 86).

◆ THE FAMILY IN CLASSICAL GREECE

Recovering Greek Attitudes Greek society assigned certain roles to people according to their sex. Men were the rulers and leaders, and in no Greek state did women vote or hold offices, with the exception of certain priesthoods. They were, however, citizens and so could not be violated or sold into slavery.

Thus, roughly half the citizens of Greek poleis must have been women, but to reconstruct their place in Greek society is not easy, mainly because nearly all our sources were written by men. Probably there was no single view of women in Greek society, as we can see from our oldest source, the Homeric poems. In the *Iliad*, the story opens as Achilles and Agamemnon quarrel over a concubine who is nothing but a sexual slave, while the Trojan hero Hector honors and cherishes his wife, Andromache; equally, in Homer's *Odyssey* Penelope, the wife of the absent Odysseus, is an admired model of wisdom and fidelity.

As we look from the idealized figures of Homer to the women of the polis, we see a much less benign attitude toward women. Certainly

▼ **An Attic kouros, or young man, called the Kritios boy, leaning on one foot; shows a movement away from the severe toward a more natural style.**
Hirmer Fotoarchiv

THUCYDIDES: THE MELIAN DIALOGUE

◆

In 416 B.C., the Athenians mercilessly inform the people of the small island of Melos that they must join the Athenian empire. Thucydides presents the cold logic of their demand.

Athenians: We will use no fine phrases saying, for example, that we have a right to our empire because we defeated the Persians, or that we have come against you now because of the injuries you have done us. And we ask you not to imagine that you will influence us by saying that you have never done us any harm. You know as well as we do that the strong do what they have the power to do and the weak accept what they have to accept.

Melians: So you would not agree to our being neutral, friends instead of enemies, but allies of neither side?

Athenians: No, because it is not so much your hostility that injures us; rather, if we were on friendly terms with you, our subjects would regard that as a sign of weakness in us, whereas your hatred is evidence of our power.

Melians: We trust that the gods will give us fortune as good as yours, because we are standing for what is right against what is wrong.

Athenians: Our opinion of the gods and our knowledge of men lead us to conclude that it is a general and necessary law of nature to rule wherever one can. This is not a law that we made ourselves, nor were we the first to act upon it when it was made. We found it already in existence, and we shall leave it to exist forever. We are merely acting in accordance with it, and we know that you or anybody else with the same power as ours would be acting in precisely the same way.

From Rex Warner (tr.), Thucydides, *The Peloponnesian War*, Penguin Classics, 1954, 1980, pp. 403–404 abridged.

---

there was no equality between the sexes. A woman was always under the control of her *kyrios,* or master—at first her father, then her husband, then her father again if she became divorced or widowed. Her father gave her in marriage with a dowry, normally at about age fifteen, to a man perhaps ten to fifteen years her senior. Xenophon describes the education of a young wife in obedience and household skills, and the picture is like the training of a young animal (see "The Training of a Wife," p. 87).

Women and Property   A wife's main duty, apart from managing the household, was to provide a male heir in order to maintain the family's hold over its property. In Athens, if the family had no male heir, the property came to a daughter, but she held it only temporarily. In this respect Athenian women were far less privileged than, for example, Egyptian women. The heiress must then be married to the nearest available male relative, thus preventing the property from passing from the family. Yet the duty of women to provide heirs did not cause Greeks to think of a woman as a mere breeding machine. On the contrary, the power, possessed only by women, to bear children seems to have made them objects not only to be cherished but also to be feared.

Restrictions in Women's Lives   Widows and heiresses had to be given new husbands in order to maintain control of property within the family. Since women could thus be transferred from one husband to another, Greeks were not sure about their fidelity; adultery by women was a grave threat because it could bring outsiders into the family and threaten the preservation of property within the correct line. It is always clear who a child's mother is, but doubts can exist about the identity of a father. Such suspicions may partly account for some passages by Greek poets and philosophers in which women are viewed as undisciplined, emotionally unstable, and sexually inexhaustible. By contrast, infidelity in men was looked on as permissible.

To preserve a woman's fidelity, the door of the home was considered her proper frontier, but such restrictions were not possible for families without servants; yet even when women did go out, they were normally accompanied by a handmaiden, a slave, or a relative. The statesman Pericles, in a speech given him by Thucydides, says

The Training of a Wife

The Athenian writer-soldier Xenophon wrote a work in which one Ischomachus explains how he trained his wife in her duties. He instructs her as follows.

"Your duty will be to remain indoors and send out those servants whose work is outside, and superintend those who are to work indoors, and to receive the incomings, and distribute so much of them as must be spent, and watch over so much as is to be kept in store, and take care that the sum laid by for a year be not spent in a month. And when wool is brought to you, you must see that cloaks are made for those that want them. You must see too that the dry corn [i.e., grain] is in good condition for making food. You will have to see that any servant who is ill is cared for.

"There are other duties peculiar to you that are pleasant to perform. It is delightful to teach spin-ning to a maid who had no knowledge of it when you received her; to take in hand a girl who is ignorant of housekeeping and service; to have the power of rewarding the discreet and useful members of your household, and of punishing anyone who turns out to be a rogue. The better partner you prove to me and the better housewife to our children, the greater will be the honour paid to you in our home."

From E. C. Marchant, (tr.), *Xenophon*, Vol. 4, Harvard University Press, 1979, pp. 7. 35–42 abridged.

---

that the most honored woman is she who is least talked about in society.

Some Greek thinkers were able to rise above such a limiting view of a woman's place. Plato, in his *Republic*, recommended that women share in education with men, although he stopped short of what we would call a truly liberal attitude to sexual equality.

The Power of Women in Myth In several ways, then, men could feel uncertain about their control over women. If we have rightly understood some of this uncertainty, we may be near to understanding why women of Greek drama such as Clytemnestra, Antigone, and Medea are such powerful characters, far stronger and more dangerous than the men in Greek plays. Again, in mythology the "furies," who could drive people mad, were female; Greeks tried to appease them by calling them the "kindly ones." Female too were the powers called Nemesis and Ate, which brought punishing destruction on those who became too arrogant and self-confident; so were the three Fates who spun out the thread of life and cut it off at the end.

Men, Women, and Sex Men, unlike women, were allowed to find sex where they liked. Ele-gant single women were paid companions at men's social affairs; the most famous courtesan of all, Aspasia, had a long affair with the statesman Pericles and bore him a son. Only these women could participate in the refined intellectual life of the city. Poorer women worked, for example, as seamstresses, nurses, or sellers in the market. Prostitutes, who were normally slaves or foreigners, were not difficult to find; a man might have sex with a slave whom he owned. Homosexuality between men was tolerated and is often illustrated in ribald scenes on Greek pottery.

Yet we must not expect perfect consistency where such emotions are at play. By modern Western standards, and even some ancient ones, Greek women suffered severe restrictions. On the other hand, women whose households had slaves may have had to work less than many women in modern emancipated societies. Our museums contain copious statues of beautiful Greek maidens. And many of the most revered deities are women: Athena, who was respected for her warlike nature and never had lovers in myth, was also the protecting goddess to the Athenians, who held her in affection and built for her one of the world's architectural masterpieces, the Parthenon. Aphrodite, who could involve human beings in ruin through sexual passion, was treasured as the model of ideal beauty and was so portrayed in hundreds of statues.

It is impossible to estimate in scientific terms the emotional love between Greek men and women. The recommendation of Plutarch, that a man should sleep with his wife three times a month, suggests that love played only a modest part in marriage. On the other hand, gravestones from many poleis show the affection in which some women were held; typically, a woman is seated, members of her family stand nearby, and a

▼ **The "Getty Bronze," a fourth-century statue in a soft, relaxed style. Surviving bronze statues from Greece are rare.**
Collection of the J. Paul Getty Museum, Malibu, California (77.AB.30)

son or her husband takes her hand in a quiet farewell.

II. The Rise of Macedonia

The Peloponnesian War had caused terrible losses in manpower for the Greek city-states. Instead of the needed healing period, there followed decades of interstate warfare—the perennial tragedy of Greece—that further weakened the poleis. These battles opened the way for an old kingdom from the north of Greece, Macedonia, to become the leading power in the Greek world. Moreover, the Macedonian king Alexander the Great drove the Greek language and many features of Greek culture deeply into Asia Minor and Egypt.

◆ THE DECLINE OF THE INDEPENDENT POLEIS

Athens had lost the Peloponnesian War and Sparta had imposed on the Athenians a puppet regime, known as the Thirty Tyrants, in 404 B.C.; but within a few months popular opposition swept this group away. As the Athenians sought to regain power, they revived their naval league in 394 B.C., though with many fewer members than it had had in the fifth century. But their arrogance had not subsided. Despite their promises to respect the independence of the league's members, the Athenians began to demand tribute from them as they had done under the Delian League. Rebellions followed, and this second league collapsed about 355 B.C.

By now there were no longer only two dominant cities in Greece. The polis of Thebes was becoming an important power, siding now with Athens, now with Sparta, in a series of never-ending quarrels. There was no clear trend in these struggles except that the constant intrigue and war, spanning several decades, drained the energies of all the antagonists. In 371 B.C. the brilliant Theban general Epaminondas won a victory over Sparta and thus finally exploded the long-held belief in Greece that the Spartan infantry was invincible. The Thebans liberated Sparta's slaves, the

▲ **Map 3.1** **Macedonia under Philip II, 359–336 b.c.**

helts, and helped them to found their own city, called Messene, in the Peloponnese.

The Spartans thus lost much of their territory and many of the slaves who had worked their land. A shortage of manpower accelerated the decline in Sparta's strength. Aristotle informs us about 335 B.C. that Spartan armies in the field had fewer than one thousand men, rather than the four or five thousand who had gone into battle during the wars of the fifth century. Epaminondas himself died in another battle near Sparta in 362

B.C., and no comparable leader in any polis took his place. The era of independent city-states was all but over, doomed by the constant wars of the fourth century.

◆ PHILIP II OF MACEDONIA

The Rise of Philip Macedonia, a kingdom in northern Greece, emerged as a leading power under an ambitious, resourceful king, Philip II, who reigned between 359 and 336 B.C. With shrewd political skill Philip developed his kingdom, built up a powerful army, and planned a program of conquest.

Using both aggression and diplomacy, Philip added poleis and large territories to his kingdom and extended his influence into central Greece. The great Athenian orator Demosthenes (384–322 B.C.), in a series of fiery speeches called "Philippics," beginning in 351, called on his countrymen to recognize the danger from Macedonia and prepare to make war against it. But by the time the Athenians responded, it was too late to halt the Macedonian advance.

Philip's Victory and Death Philip won a decisive battle against Athens and several other poleis at Chaeronea in 338 B.C. All the city-states of southern Greece, except isolated Sparta, now lay at his mercy. He could have devastated many of them, including Athens, but his sense of tactics warned him not to do so. Instead, he gathered the more important poleis into an obedient alliance called the League of Corinth, which recognized Philip as its leader and agreed to follow him in his next project, an invasion of Persia.

But before Philip could open his Persian war, he was murdered in 336 B.C. by one of his officers who apparently had a personal quarrel with the king. Some historians have wondered whether Philip's wife or his son, Alexander, may have been involved in a plot to kill Philip and put Alexander on the throne; but tempting as such speculations may be, the sources do not give them clear support.

◆ ALEXANDER THE GREAT

The empire built by Philip now passed to his son, Alexander III (r. 336–323 B.C.), known as Alexander the Great, and never has a young warrior prince made more effective use of his opportunities. During his brief reign Alexander created the largest empire the ancient world had known and, more than any other man, became responsible for the eastward expansion of the Greek world.

Alexander's Invasion of Persia In the next year, 335, a rumor of Alexander's death caused a democratic revolution in the city of Thebes. Alexander marched on Thebes and sacked it with the utmost

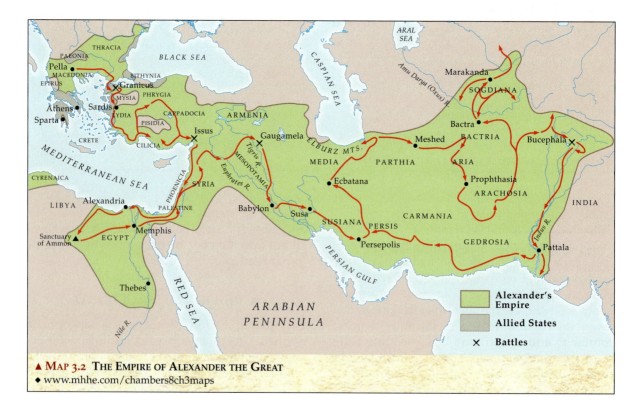

▲ MAP 3.2 THE EMPIRE OF ALEXANDER THE GREAT
◆ www.mhhe.com/chambers8ch3maps

▲ **The Venus of Cyrene in Rome (early third century B.C.), a most elegant, graceful depiction of ideal female beauty.**
Scala/Art Resource, NY

Persian Empire. The Persia that he attacked was a much weaker state than the one that had conquered Babylon or the one that Xerxes had led against the Greeks in 480 B.C. Intrigue and disloyalty had weakened the administration of the empire. Moreover, the king, Darius III, had to rely on Greek mercenary soldiers as the one disciplined element in his infantry, for native troops were mainly untrained. The weakness of Persia helps explain Alexander's success, but in no way does it diminish his reputation as one of the supreme generals in history. His campaigns were astonishing combinations of physical courage, strategic insight, and superb leadership.

Alexander in Egypt Alexander swept the Persians away from the coast of Asia Minor and in 332 B.C. drove them out of Egypt, a land they had held for two centuries. The Egyptians welcomed him as a liberator and recognized him as their pharaoh. He appointed two Egyptians to administer the country, along with a Greek to manage the finances; he was to follow this pattern of dividing power throughout his reign.

▼ **The head of Alexander the Great in heroic profile; the obverse of a silver coin issued by Lysimachus, one of Alexander's bodyguards, who after his master's death became king of Thrace.**
Gift of Mrs. George M. Brett. Courtesy, Museum of Fine Arts, Boston.

brutality, destroying every building except temples and the house of the poet Pindar. Having thus warned the Greek cities against any further rebellions, Alexander began the invasion of the

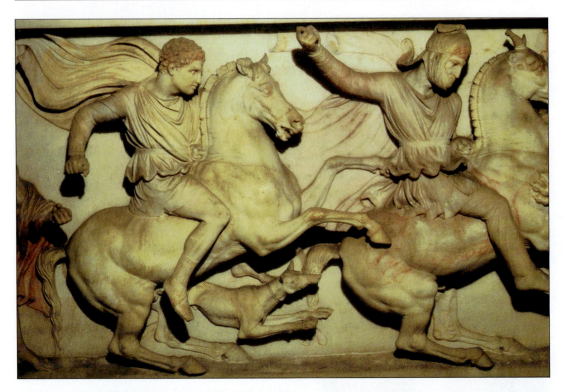

▲ A scene from the magnificent "Alexander Sarcophagus" found at Sidon, now in the Archaeological Museum, Istanbul; fourth century B.C. Alexander, left, is shown hunting, accompanied by a Persian. Although we have no reason to think Alexander was ever buried in this sarcophagus, the scene symbolizes Alexander's heroism and virility and calls attention to his conquest of the Persian Empire.
C. M. Dixon

While he was in Egypt (also in 332), Alexander founded the city of Alexandria. He intended this city to serve as a link between Macedonia and the valley of the Nile, and he had it laid out in the grid pattern typical of Greek city planning. Although he did not live to see it, Alexandria remained one of the conqueror's most enduring legacies: a great metropolis throughout history.

Victories and Death of Alexander In the next season, 331 B.C., Alexander fought Darius III at Gaugamela, winning a complete victory that guaranteed he would face little further opposition in Persia. Darius III was murdered by disloyal officers in 330 B.C., and Alexander assumed the title of king of Persia. Again he followed his policy of placing some areas in the control of natives: Babylonia, for example, was given to a Persian named Mazaeus.

The expedition had now achieved its professed aim; yet Alexander, for whom conquest was self-expression, continued to make war. During the next few years he campaigned as far east as India, where he crossed the Indus River (see map 3.2), and finally, in 326 B.C., he began his march back. But at Babylon in 323 B.C., he caught a fever after a bout of heavy drinking, and within a few days he died, not yet thirty-three.

The Reputation of Alexander Alexander is a figure of such stature and power that he defies easy interpretation, and even today radically different biographies are written about this most famous man in Greek history. Part of our difficulty is that our best narrative source for his life, the Greek historian Arrian, lived four centuries after Alexander's death, and Arrian, for all his merits, was not the kind of probing historian who might have given us a rounded psychological portrait of the king. Yet it is clear that along with Alexander's courage and drive, perhaps as their necessary accompaniment, came a personality sometimes barely containing a raging animal. He ordered the execution of a number of his friends for supposedly being aware of conspiracies against him; another friend he murdered himself in a sudden fury. On the other hand, Arrian tells the moving story of Alexander's pouring a cup of water, offered him by his parched troops, into the desert because he refused to drink if his men could not.

Nor do we know just what Alexander was trying to accomplish. There is little reason to believe the popular myth that he hoped to conquer the world. His goal may have been a stable empire that would maintain his vast conquests, but if so he failed, for he had designated no successor and the empire disintegrated on his death.

Alexander's Rule Alexander established democratic regimes in the Greek states in Asia Minor that he had freed from Persian rule. But he also established some policies that brought Persians and their ways into his regime. We have seen that he used Persians as administrators. He also had young Persians trained in Macedonian style and even enrolled them within Macedonian regiments. These measures were intended to strengthen his empire by enlisting support from natives. Some historians have gone further and have declared that Alexander had a vision of the unity of the human race and was trying to establish an empire in which different peoples would live in harmony as within one family, but this view is widely, and rightly, rejected as sentimental and too idealistic.

Other historians focus on his acts of cruelty and vindictiveness and see him as a paranoiac tyrant. In any case, no portrait of him should overlook his patronage of scholarship, which extended even to his bringing scientists and geographers with him as he invaded Persia. His foundation, Alexandria, became the intellectual center of the next age. However we interpret Alexander, he has remained the prototype of a world conqueror. Some of his successors sought to maintain his memory by putting his portrait on their own coins, and even Roman emperors issued

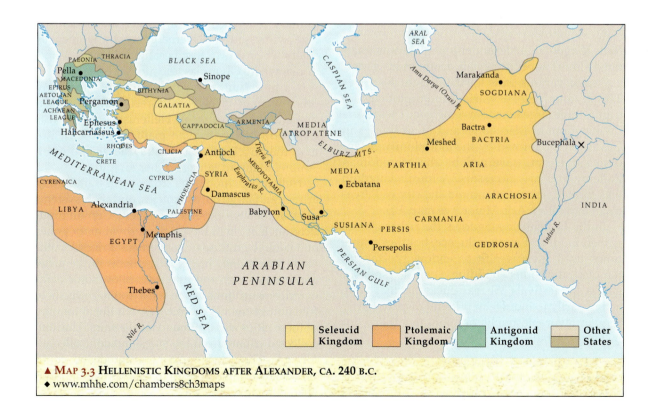

▲ **MAP 3.3** HELLENISTIC KINGDOMS AFTER ALEXANDER, CA. 240 B.C.
◆ www.mhhe.com/chambers8ch3maps

medallions portraying him, as if to borrow his glory and power for their often threatened reigns.

III. The Hellenistic Age (323–30 B.C.)

The Classical Age of Greek civilization began about 500 B.C. and ended in 323 B.C., with the death of Alexander the Great. The next period, the Hellenistic Age, began with that event and extended to the death of Cleopatra VII of Egypt in 30 B.C. During this period the Greeks carried their culture throughout the Near East in the movement known as Hellenization. Broadly speaking, Hellenization refers to the increasing use of the Greek language and customs among non-Greeks. This movement had begun well before the death of Alexander, but his invasion of the Persian Empire gave a decided stimulus to such a widespread acceptance of Greek culture. The Greeks in turn received legacies, especially in religion, from the peoples whom they met in this age.

◆ THE DISSOLUTION OF ALEXANDER'S EMPIRE

New Kingdoms   Alexander's empire was shattered almost at once after his death, as his generals seized various parts for themselves. By about 275 B.C., after years of warfare and diplomatic intrigue, three large kingdoms emerged. These were the kingdom of Macedonia and its territories in Greece; Syria, formed by the Macedonian Seleucus; and Egypt, governed by the Macedonian Ptolemy and his successors. A fourth kingdom was formed about 260 around the city of Pergamum in western Asia Minor (see map 3.3).

In the Hellenistic kingdoms the richer classes gained more and more influence, but they sometimes used their wealth to endow spectacular temples and other buildings and to sponsor games and festivals. We may guess that they were acting partly to indulge in prideful display, partly to gain favorable public opinion. In Athens, for instance, Attalus II of Pergamum (r.[4] 158–138)

---

[1]The letter *r*. before a date or series of dates stands for "reigned."

donated a magnificent stoa, or colonnaded building, that was rebuilt in A.D. 1956.

Kingdoms and Leagues   The subsequent history of these kingdoms is one of continual warfare until they were all eventually absorbed by the Roman Republic. The king of Macedonia controlled northern Greece. The poleis in the south retained their autonomy, and some of them formed defensive leagues to protect their independence from the monarchy. The most influential were the Aetolian League in western Greece and the Achaean League on the northern coast of the Peloponnese.

These leagues tried to strengthen themselves by awarding citizenship in the league to all citizens of their member cities; but this principle of confederation for mutual security arrived too late in Greek history to take firm root before Greece fell to the expanding Roman Republic. As to the Egyptians and inhabitants of the Near East, they had long seen their rulers as divine or semidivine beings, and the Hellenistic kings in these areas exploited this tendency and established themselves as absolute monarchs who owned the kingdom.

Hellenistic Rulers   Remarkably, considering the military roots of these kingdoms, the Hellenistic Age witnessed the reemergence of women as rulers. Their power first became evident in Macedonia, where Olympias, the mother of Alexander, was a more important political figure than any other woman in classical Greece. The most famous and skillful of all Hellenistic queens was Cleopatra of Egypt, who manipulated such Roman military leaders as Julius Caesar and Mark Antony to the advantage of her kingdom.

Hellenistic monarchs ruled through strong armies and large bureaucracies, and their systems of taxation were extremely efficient. Certain products, such as oil in Egypt, were royal monopolies and could be traded only at official prices. Greeks usually held the chief public offices in the army and bureaucracy, and rulers did allow some democratic institutions, such as a town council, to function in Near Eastern cities, but the autonomy of these cities was limited to local affairs. The king collected tribute from the cities and controlled all foreign policy, and he alone granted and could cancel such rights of self-government as the cities enjoyed.

◆ ECONOMIC LIFE

Agriculture and Industry   One of the sharpest contrasts between the classical and Hellenistic worlds was the scale of economic activity. In classical Greece, farmers worked small plots of land, and industry and commerce were ventures of small entrepreneurs. In the Hellenistic states of Egypt and the Seleucid kingdom, vast estates predominated. Industry and trade operated throughout the Near East on a larger scale than ever before in the ancient world, requiring the services of bankers and other financial agents.

The Hellenistic world prospered as ambitious Greeks, emigrating from their homeland to make their fortunes, brought new vigor to the economies of Egypt and the Near East. They introduced new crops and new techniques in agriculture to make production more efficient. For example, Greeks had long cultivated vines, and they now enhanced the wines of Egypt. At the same time, they improved and extended the irrigation system and could thus devote more acreage to pasturing animals, which provided leather and cloth for the people and horses for the cavalry.

Trade and Finance   The growth of long-distance trade was even more remarkable. The Hellenistic rulers encouraged these efforts by establishing a sound money system, building roads and canals, and clearing the seas of pirates. Traders ventured eastward to India and, in the west, beyond the Mediterranean to the Atlantic coasts of Africa and Europe.

Unfortunately, the resulting prosperity was not evenly distributed. Rulers and members of the upper classes (usually Greek) amassed great fortunes, but little of this wealth filtered down to the small farmers and laborers. This great disparity between rich and poor led to increasing social conflict.

Hellenistic Cities   Agriculture remained the major industry in the vast lands of the new kingdoms, but it was in the numerous Greek cities founded by Alexander and his successors that the civilization that we call Hellenistic took form. Most of these new cities were in western Asia, in the Seleucid kingdom. Alexander had founded the brilliant city of Alexandria, in Egypt, but the Ptolemies who ruled Egypt did not follow his example by founding many cities. They considered a docile, rustic civilization far easier to control than citizens of a politically active urban society.

Some Hellenistic cities were magnificently ornate and spectacular. Besides their political institutions the Greeks brought from their homeland many of the amenities of polis life—temples, theaters, gymnasiums, and other public buildings. Pergamum, an outstanding example of city planning, contained a stupendous altar to Zeus, a renowned library, and a theater high above the main city with a superb view. The city may have had as many as one hundred thousand inhabitants (under the Roman Empire its population was about two hundred thousand), while Alexandria, the largest of all, had at least a half million people.

Local families in the upper classes copied Greek ways and sent their children to Greek schools. Moreover, a version of Greek, *koiné* ("common") Greek, became an international tongue. Now, for the first time, people could travel to virtually any city in the Mediterranean world and make themselves understood.

◆ LITERATURE, ART, AND SCIENCE

Libraries and Scholars   The most significant literary achievements in the Hellenistic Age were in the field of scholarship. The kings of Egypt took pride in constructing a huge library in Alexandria that probably contained, by 200 B.C., a half million papyrus rolls. Along with the library, they built the Museum, a kind of research institute, where literary, historical, and scientific studies flourished, each employing its own experts. One of the main interests of literary scholars in Alexandria was the literature of the classical period, and among their achievements was the standardization of the Greek text of Homer. By comparing the many versions that had been handed down in manuscripts over the centuries, scholars were able to establish the text on which modern versions of Homer are based.

The specialization of scholars was characteristic of the growing professionalism of the age. Whereas the citizen of fifth-century Athens could be a farmer, a politician, and a soldier at the same

▲ Panels from the altar to Zeus at Pergamum, in the Pergamon-Museum, Berlin, showing gods in combat with giants. Greek art preferred abstraction to reality, and such scenes probably represent the triumph of Greek civilization over non-Greek peoples. The violence and dramatizing are in the "baroque" tradition of Hellenistic art of the second century B.C.
C. M. Dixon

time, now each of these roles was filled by a professional. The army consisted of professional soldiers, while professional bureaucrats ran the government.

A New Spirit in Art Hellenistic rulers also wanted to glorify their cities and provided generous subsidies for art and architecture. The architecture of the age sometimes emphasized size and grandeur, as compared with the simplicity and human scale of classical architecture. Thus, the Altar of Zeus from Pergamum, now in Berlin, included a great stairway, flanked by a frieze four hundred feet long. The figures on the frieze, typical of Hellenistic sculpture, are carved in high relief, with an almost extravagant drama and emotionalism that make them seem to burst out of the background. Hellenistic sculpture also differed from that of the classical period through its devotion to realism. Instead of creating figures of ideal perfection, artists now showed individuality in faces and bodies (see picture of bronze statue of boxer), even depicting physical imperfection or frank ugliness.

Hellenistic Science   Advances in the field of science drew strength from the cross-fertilization of cultures in the Hellenistic Age. The Greeks had long speculated about the nature of the universe, and the Near East had an even longer scientific tradition, particularly in the fields of astronomy and mathematics. After Alexander's conquests joined the two cultures, other conditions favored scientific advance: the increased professionalism of the age, the use of Greek as an international language, and the facilities of the Museum in Alexandria. The result was a golden age of science that was not surpassed until the seventeenth century.

Euclid's Geometric Theorems   Unlike their eastern neighbors, Greeks had a strong desire for theoretical understanding, even beyond the solving of immediate mathematical and engineering problems. Their work in the realm of theory descends from their skill in philosophic debate.

In mathematics, Euclid (about 300 B.C.) compiled a textbook that is still the basis for the study of plane geometry. Some of his theorems were already known, and others (for example, his demonstration that nonparallel lines must meet somewhere) may seem obvious. His accomplishment was to construct a succession of elegant proofs for these theorems, each based on earlier proofs, starting with the simple proposition that the shortest distance between two points is a straight line. The analytical method of his proofs is a characteristic of Greek thought, for Greek

▲ **Bronze statue of a boxer from Rome, second century B.C. Greek sculptors had abandoned statues of ideal beauty and were now experimenting with scenes of frank realism. Note the boxer's battered face and bandaged hands.**
Scala / Art Resource, NY

philosophers believed that knowing something entailed being able to prove it. The restatement of Euclid's theorems through the study of geometry in schools around the world has made him perhaps the most widely read Greek author.

Archimedes: Advanced Mathematics and Engineering   The greatest mathematician of antiquity—indeed, one of the greatest ever, in the class of Newton and Einstein—was Archimedes of

Syracuse, who also lived during the Hellenistic era (287?–212 B.C.). He calculated the value of *pi* (the ratio between the circumference and diameter of a circle); he developed a system for expressing immensely large numbers, by using 100 million as the base (as we use 10); and he discovered the ratio between the volumes of a cylinder and a sphere within it, namely, 3:2. In a testament to his love of theoretical knowledge, he wanted this proportion engraved on his tombstone.

Archimedes was also a pioneer in physics; he demonstrated that a floating body will sink in a liquid only to the point at which it displaces its own weight. He understood the principle of using the lever for lifting massive weights and is said to have proclaimed, "Give me a place where I can stand and I will lift the earth" (that is, standing outside the earth entirely and with a long enough lever). He also invented the water screw, still used for irrigation in Egypt. As the Romans besieged Syracuse in 212 B.C., he devised engines to fight them off; but, tragically, he was murdered by a Roman soldier as the city fell—while he sat drawing a mathematical figure in the sand.

Aristarchus and the Orbit of the Earth About 250 B.C., Aristarchus, an astronomer and mathematician, advanced a heliocentric theory of the movement of the planets. The view that the earth revolves around the sun was not new, but Aristarchus refined it by stating that the earth revolves on its own axis while it, together with the other planets, circles the sun. Not until the sixteenth century did astronomers prove the soundness of Aristarchus' system; meanwhile, the Greek astronomic tradition continued to follow an older geocentric theory, which held that the earth was the center of the solar system and that the sun revolved around it. The false geocentric theory was, however, the basis for the most important Hellenistic text on astronomy, the *Almagest* of Ptolemy of Alexandria (about A.D. 140). This book systematized the Greek study of astronomy and remained the accepted text on the subject for more than one thousand years.

Other Mathematical Discoveries Hellenistic scientists also made important advances in the realm of measurements. Hipparchus calculated the length of the average lunar month to within one second of today's accepted figure. Eratosthenes

about 225 B.C. computed the circumference of the earth to be about twenty-eight thousand miles, only three thousand miles more than the actual figure. Other scientists worked out the division of time into hours, minutes, and seconds and of circles into degrees, minutes, and seconds.

◆ PHILOSOPHY AND RELIGION

Philosophies of Comfort The change in lifestyle from the relative security of the polis to the increasing uncertainties of a larger world shifted the direction of Greek philosophy. Plato and Aristotle had been philosophers of the polis in the sense that they were concerned with the individual's role in the intimate world of the city-state; the ideal state in their theories would have only a few thousand citizens. But when the city-state came to be governed by a large kingdom headed by a remote ruler, individual men and women could hardly influence its policies even though they were caught up in its wars and its many changes of fortune.

Moreover, the large Hellenistic cities lacked the cohesiveness, the sense of belonging among citizens, that had made the classical poleis internally united. In such conditions, philosophers sought means of accommodation with the larger Hellenistic world that was shaping their lives. They tried to provide people with guidance in their personal lives and were less concerned about the nature of the political framework. Thus, the two most important schools of Hellenistic philosophy, Epicureanism and Stoicism, were philosophies designed to provide comfort and reassurance for the individual human being.

Epicurus and Atomism Epicurus, who taught in Athens during the generation after Alexander, believed that people should strive above all for tranquillity, which he sought to provide through the atomic theory of Democritus. Our bodies and souls, Epicurus taught, are made up of atoms that cohere only for our lifetimes. When we die, the atoms will be redistributed into the universe again, and nothing of us will remain behind to suffer any desire for the life we have lost. Because death therefore holds no terrors, we should concern ourselves only with leading pleasurable lives, above all avoiding physical and mental pain. Sensuality, gluttony, and passionate love, in

Epicurus' view, are equally unrewarding, since they may lead to disappointment and pain. Thus, the wise person withdraws from the world to study philosophy and enjoy the companionship of a few friends. Some later Epicureans came close to advocating an almost heedless pursuit of pleasure, but such was not the message of Epicurus, whose philosophy was intended as a powerful antidote to anxiety and suffering.

Zeno and the Universe of Stoicism   A different approach to life's problems was that of a contemporary of Epicurus—namely, Zeno of Cyprus—who founded a philosophical school known as Stoicism, so named because he taught his pupils in a building in Athens called the Stoa. Zeno was a man of Semitic ancestry, and the fact that he taught at Athens is a notable example of the mixing of cultures that took place in the Hellenistic age. A later Stoic, Chrysippus, stated Stoicism in its best-known form: One must act in accordance with nature, choosing one's actions with attention to reason. Such a program will lead one to virtue. A successful life includes pleasure; good health is desirable, provided one uses it in the pursuit of virtue. If one acts in accordance with nature, one cannot be other than happy.

To Stoics, the universe was wholly created and held together by a force sometimes called fire, sometimes *pneuma* or "breath." At certain intervals, the universe is destroyed by fire, but it is born again, and we are reborn with it. Because a single divine plan governs the universe, to find happiness one must act in harmony with this plan. One should be patient in adversity, for adversity is a necessary part of the divine plan and one can do nothing to change it. By cultivating a sense of duty and self-discipline, people can learn to accept their fate; they will then become immune to earthly anxieties and will achieve inner freedom and tranquillity.

Ethical Duties of the Stoics   The Stoics did not advocate withdrawal from the world, for they believed that all people, as rational beings, belong to one family. Moreover, to ensure justice for all, the rational person should discover his or her place in the world and consider it a duty to participate in public affairs.

The Stoics advanced ideas that were to have a profound influence on later Western history, espe-

cially as they were interpreted in the Roman and Christian visions of civilization: the concept that all humanity is part of a universal family; the virtues of tolerance; and the need for self-discipline, public service, and compassion for the less fortunate members of the human race. Stoicism is thus part of a great intellectual revolution that led some thinkers to consider similarities among humans more important than differences.

Again, while most earlier Greeks had accepted without question the institution of slavery, the Stoics believed that the practice of exploiting others corrupted the owner (the slave could endure bondage by achieving inner freedom). Stoicism became the most influential philosophy among the educated of the Hellenistic Age and achieved great influence among the Romans, who adopted with conviction the ideals of discipline and fulfillment of public and private duty.

New Religions   The search for meaning in life preoccupied all levels of Hellenistic society, but none so painfully as the great masses of the poor. The answers of philosophy were addressed to an intellectual elite: wealthy scholars, as it were, meditating in the study. But the poor—lacking the education, leisure, and detachment for such a pursuit—looked elsewhere for spiritual and emotional sustenance in their daily encounters with the problems of life. For many, religion answered their need for escape and consolation.

Among the new religious practices were the Near Eastern mystery cults that had some features in common as a result of the frequent intermingling of cultures in the cosmopolitan Near East. They are called mystery cults because they centered on the worship of a savior whose death and resurrection would redeem the sins of humanity; their rituals were secret, known only to the participants, and were elaborate, often wildly emotional; and they nourished hope by promising an afterlife that would compensate for the rigors of life on earth. One of the most popular mystery cults was the worship of the Egyptian deities Isis and Osiris. In Egyptian mythology, Osiris had been murdered and dismembered but was reassembled and saved by Isis, his devoted wife; he then became the god of the underworld. Thus, the myth suggested that its followers might also attain salvation and life after death.

SUMMARY

All these political, scientific, and intellectual explorations were parts of the legacy of Alexander, the Macedonian who brought Greek civilization and the Greek language into the world beyond the Mediterranean Sea. Greek was to be the language in which the New Testament was written, and therefore some historians have also seen his campaigns as preparing the way for Christianity and have even called Christianity his most important legacy. Be this as it may, the Greeks and Macedonians could not maintain permanent control over the remains of Alexander's empire. Not Greece but Rome became the uniting force that passed the legacy of classical civilization to medieval and then to modern Europe.

QUESTIONS FOR FURTHER THOUGHT

1. The Greeks invented historical writing. In looking at the past, what are the most important questions a historian should ask?

2. The Greek city-states and their system of alliances gave way to the rising power of Macedonia. How might the Greek states have preserved their strength and political power?

RECOMMENDED READING

Sources

Aristotle. *The Athenian Constitution.* P. J. Rhodes (tr.). 1984. The great philosopher's brief history and description of the Athenian state, with helpful commentary.

Arrian. *The Campaigns of Alexander the Great.* Aubrey de Sélincourt (tr.). 1958. Our main source for the life of the great conqueror.

Carey, Christopher (tr.). *Trials from Classical Athens.* 1997. Translations of selected courtroom speeches in Athenian cases.

Demosthenes. *Public Orations.* A. W. Pickard-Cambridge (tr.). 1963. Collects the statesman's orations on public policy, such as his opposition to Philip II.

Grene, David, and Richmond Lattimore (eds.). *The Complete Greek Tragedies.* 9 vols. 1953–1991. The best collection of modern translations.

Lefkowitz, Mary, and Maureen B. Fant. *Women's Life in Greece and Rome: A Source Book in Translation.* 1982. Translated documents and literary excerpts on all features of women's lives.

Plato. *The Republic.* Desmond Lee (tr.). 1974. The central work of Greek philosophy.

Plutarch. *Nine Greek Lives.* Robin Waterfield (tr.). 1998. Biographies of prominent statesmen and commanders, including Pericles and Alexander the Great.

Xenophon. *A History of My Times.* Rex Warner (tr.). 1979. A narrative, often less than profound, of Greek history down to 362 B.C.

Studies

Bosworth, A. B. *Conquest and Empire: The Reign of Alexander the Great.* 1988. Now the standard treatment of Alexander's life and reign.

Burford, Alison. *Land and Labor in the Greek World.* 1993. Modern treatment of land tenure and agriculture in Greece.

Cawkwell, George. *Philip of Macedon.* 1978. Macedonia before Philip II, father of Alexander, and the expansion of the kingdom.

Dodds, E. R. *The Greeks and the Irrational.* 1951. Brilliant investigation of the Greek mind, showing its irrational and psychological complexity.

Dover, K. J. *Greek Homosexuality.* 1989. Scientific, nonsensational study of this social phenomenon. By today's leading Hellenist.

———. *Greek Popular Morality in the Time of Plato and Aristotle.* 1994. Goes beyond the ethical doctrines of philosophers to discover the values of ordinary Greeks.

Errington, R. Malcolm. *A History of Macedonia.* Catherine Errington (tr.). 1990. Compact one-volume treatment, carrying the story down through Alexander's successors.

Garland, Robert. *The Greek Way of Life: From Conception to Old Age.* 1990. Reconstruction of normal life cycle of Greeks in classical and Hellenistic age.

Golden, Mark. *Children and Childhood in Classical Athens.* 1990. Groundbreaking study of how children interacted with adults.

Green, Peter. *Alexander to Actium: The Historical Evolution of the Hellenistic Age.* 1990. The most comprehensive historical and cultural survey; a colossal study.

Hammond, N. G. L. *The Macedonian State: The Origins, Institutions, and History.* 1989. By the leading expert on Macedonia of the last half century.

Just, Roger. *Women in Athenian Law and Life.* 1989. Brief, admirably up-to-date treatment of marriage, inheritance, freedom and seclusion, and more.

Kitto, H. D. F. *Greek Tragedy: A Literary Study.* 1969. Probably still the best general book on one of the supreme achievements of the Greeks, written without literary jargon.

Lacey, W. K. *The Family in Classical Greece.* 1984. Survey of the family in Greek world, especially in Athens and Sparta.

Lloyd, G. E. R. *Aristotle: The Growth and Structure of His Thought.* 1968. Good survey of all areas of Aristotle's philosophy.

Long, A. A. *Hellenistic Philosophy: Stoics, Epicureans, Sceptics.* 2d ed. 1986. Readable survey of the postclassical Greek philosophers.

Osborne, Robin. *Classical Landscape with Figures: The Ancient Greek City and Its Countryside.* 1987. How the countryside influenced the development of the Greek city.

Parker, Robert. *Miasma: Pollution and Purification in Early Greek Religion.* 1990. Important study of pollution concerning birth, death, crime, and disease, and its purification.

Pickard-Cambridge, A. W. *The Dramatic Festivals of Athens.* 2d ed. by John Gould and David M. Lewis. 1968. Detailed description of dramatic festivals, costumes, and much more.

Pomeroy, Sarah B. *Women in Hellenistic Egypt.* 1989. Especially good on the status of women in this society.

Rowe, C. J. *Plato.* 1984. Modern introduction with ample bibliography.

Sansone, David. *Greek Athletics and the Genesis of Sport.* 1988. On the place and history of games in Greek society.

Sinclair, R. K. *Democracy and Participation in Athens.* 1988. On the opportunities for average citizens to share in running the Athenian state.

Stockton, David L. *The Classical Athenian Democracy.* 1990. Comprehensive description of the working of the state, not excessively technical.

Tarn, W. W. *Alexander the Great.* 1979. Beautifully written biography by the leading Alexander scholar of his day, sometimes giving way to hero worship.

Travlos, John. *Pictorial Dictionary of Ancient Athens.* 1980. Precise locations of and essays on all major buildings and sites in Athens.

Vlastos, Gregory. *Socrates: Ironist and Moral Philosopher.* 1991. Most important recent study of style and significance of Socrates' thought.

Walbank, F. W. *The Hellenistic World.* 1982. The best brief survey of the period.

White, K. D. *Greek and Roman Technology.* 1984. Describes entire range of classical technology.

Wood, Ellen Meiksins. *Peasant-Citizen and Slave: The Foundations of Athenian Democracy.* Rev. ed. 1989. Argues that Athenian agriculture was managed more by free peasants than slaves.

▲ "Noble" Romans, those whose ancestors had been consuls, had the right to have masks representing them carried in funeral processions. This republican noble of about 30 B.C. shows the masks of two of his ancestors.
Scala/Art Resource, NY

THE ROMAN REPUBLIC

The Greeks flourished in small, intensely competitive communities, but the Romans formed a huge, long-lived empire. The Greek historian Polybius, who lived many years in Rome, has left us his analysis of Rome's successful policy. Drawing on theories of Aristotle, he praised Rome for its mixed constitution. He saw the element of monarchy in the two Roman consuls. The Roman Senate represented oligarchy, or the rule of a few. And the Roman common people supplied the element of democracy. The state, he thought, so long as it was balanced on these three supports, could not fail to prosper and expand.

The history of Rome brings to the fore another of the themes that run through the Western experience: the use of warfare as a deliberately chosen instrument of policy. Sometimes Rome got its way through diplomacy, but when this failed the military machine did not. An army is not a democracy but a body governed by a few experienced men—in fact, an oligarchy.

The Romans exploited the family as a force, a weapon, in society. Political power was based on the strength of a man's family and on the alliances he formed with other families. The state united first the Italian peninsula, then the whole Mediterranean basin. Finally, the Romans came to know a culture that they recognized as superior to their own: that of Greece. The poet Horace said that "Greece, once captured, conquered its captor," as Greek literature and art inspired those of Rome.

In the process of domination, a series of warlords became so powerful that, through their rivalry, they destroyed the republic and the political freedom that Rome had achieved. The response was the formation of an even more powerful autocracy, from which Europe was to descend: the Roman Empire.

CHAPTER 4. THE ROMAN REPUBLIC							
	Social Structure	Body Politic	Changes in the Organization of Production and in the Impact of Technology	Evolution of Family and Changing Gender Roles	War	Religion	Cultural Expression
I. THE UNIFICATION OF ITALY	■	■		■	■	■	
II. THE AGE OF MEDITERRANEAN CONQUEST	■	■			■		
III. THE ROMAN REVOLUTION		■	■	■	■		
IV. THE END OF THE ROMAN REPUBLIC		■			■		
V. THE FOUNDING OF THE ROMAN EMPIRE		■				■	

I. The Unification of Italy (to 264 B.C.)

The inhabitants of Italy greatly outnumbered those of Greece in antiquity. Unlike the Greeks, they became unified under the leadership of a single city, Rome. This movement required centuries, and during this period Rome itself was transformed from a monarchy into a republic with a solid constitution. Families were not only the binding force of the household but became the building blocks of political power. Guided by the Roman Senate, the city expanded its territory until the whole peninsula of Italy was under Roman control.

◆ THE GEOGRAPHY OF ITALY

Italy is not, like Greece, divided into many small valleys or islands. The main geographic feature is the Apennine range, which runs diagonally across Italy in the north and then turns southward to bisect the peninsula. North of the Apennines, the Po River flows through a large, fertile valley that was for centuries the home of Celtic peoples known as Gauls. The hills of Italy, unlike those of Greece, are gentle enough for pasturing. The landscape is of unsurpassed beauty; some of the best Roman poetry—by Virgil, Horace, and Catullus—hymns the delights of the land and the pleasure of farming. But the geography of Italy could also be a challenge. The mountains divide the land into sections and made the task of unifying Italy a long and arduous one.

◆ EARLY ROME

The legends about the founding of Rome by Aeneas, a Trojan hero who reached Italy after the Trojan war, or by Romulus and Remus (two mythical sons of the war god Mars) are myths, so we must depend on archaeology to recover early Roman history. Pottery finds suggest that the site of Rome, along the Tiber River in the plain of Latium, was inhabited as early as 1400 B.C. Ancient scholars relied on myths to date the "founding" of Rome in 753 B.C. We need not take this date seriously as the moment at which Rome came into existence, but there must have been considerable habitation in the area by that time, especially on the seven hills that surround the city. About 625 B.C. the settlers drained the marshes below the hills and built a central marketplace, the Forum. This area was to be forever the center of Roman history.

Etruscan Origins Besides the Romans themselves, two other peoples laid the basis for Roman

▲ **This sarcophagus is from a late sixth-century Etruscan tomb. The reclining couple on the lid reflects the influence of Greek art on the style of the Etruscans.**
Alinari/Art Source, NY

history. The first were the Etruscans, who actually dominated early Rome from about 625 to 509 B.C. The name *Roma* is Etruscan, and at least some of the kings of Rome, as their names show, were Etruscans. The origin of the Etruscans themselves is obscure and has provoked a famous controversy. Some ancient sources say that they were a native European people, but the Greek historian Herodotus asserts that they arrived from Asia Minor. In any case, the Etruscans appeared in Italy soon after 800 B.C., in the region north of the Tiber River known as Etruria (their name is preserved in modern Tuscany). Their language is still mostly undeciphered even though thousands of short Etruscan inscriptions exist.

The Etruscans had a technologically advanced culture and traded with Greeks and Phoenicians; Greek vases, especially, have been found in Etruscan tombs, and Etruscan art largely imitates that of the Greeks. They also bequeathed to the Romans the technique of building temples, and they introduced the worship of a triad of gods (Juno, Minerva, Jupiter) and the custom of examining the innards of animals to foretell the future.

Greek Influence　The second non-Roman people who helped shape Roman culture were the Greeks. Beginning about 750 B.C., they established some 50 poleis in southern Italy and on the island of Sicily. So numerous were the Greek cities in southern Italy that the Romans called this region *Magna Graecia* ("Great Greece") and thus gave us the name *Greeks* for the people who have always called themselves Hellenes.[1]

Greek culture from these colonies influenced the Etruscans and, in turn, the Romans. For example, from the village of Cumae, the oldest Greek colony in Italy, the Etruscans learned the Western version of the Greek alphabet and passed it on to Rome; it became the basis for the alphabet used throughout the Western world. And virtually all Roman literature is inspired by Greek models.

---

[1]The name *Graikoi* (*Graeci,* or Greeks) was sometimes used, according to Aristotle (*Meteorology* 352) and other sources, for the people generally called Hellenes. The name probably comes from one or more villages in central Greece called Graia; one such place is mentioned in Homer (*Iliad* 2.498).

▲ The art of Etruscan tombs often showed dancing and banqueting in the afterlife. This fifth-century painting, from the Tomb of the Lionesses at Tarquinia, shows two dancers with jugs of wine.
Scala/Art Resource, NY

The Founding of the Roman Republic   About 500 B.C. (the Romans reckoned the date as 509) Rome freed itself of its last Etruscan king and established a republican form of government. Roman tradition held that the brother of the last Etruscan king, Tarquinius Superbus, raped a noble matron named Lucretia, who killed herself in shame. This event led to an uprising against the arrogant ruler and to a republican government. The uprising was supposedly led by one Brutus, who became leader of the new state; centuries later, his descendant, Marcus Brutus, was one of the assassins of Julius Caesar and was also seen as a liberator. This legend, true or not, shows why the Romans hated the name *rex* (king) and why they insisted on divisions of power in every phase of their constitution. After the founding of the Republic, the Etruscans gradually declined as a power until they were finally absorbed by the Romans in the fourth century.

◆ THE EARLY CONSTITUTION

A large part of the history of the Roman Republic concerns the development of its constitution; this was never a written document but rather a set of carefully observed procedures and customs. The Roman system, like that of Sparta, had three major components, which tended to offset and balance one another. The executives were two officers called consuls, who were the supreme civil and military magistrates. On occasion the Romans appointed a man as "dictator," whose authority surpassed that of the consuls, but his office was limited to six months. There was also an advisory body of elder statesmen called the Senate.

Finally, there were assemblies that included all adult male citizens.

The Assemblies The consuls were elected annually by the Assembly of the Centuries (or Comitia Centuriata), which was made up of the entire army divided, in theory, into 193 groups of 100 men each; in this assembly the wealthier citizens voted first and could determine the result if most of them voted the same way. This arrangement illustrates the hierarchical and conservative instincts of the Roman mind; so does the law providing that, in cases in which the two consuls disagreed, one could block the action of the other, and the consul advocating no action prevailed. Consuls possessed a right known as *imperium*, which gave them the power to command troops and to execute any other assignments they might receive from the Senate.

There were two other assemblies, the more important being the Assembly of Tribes (Comitia Tributa), which was divided into thirty-five large voting blocs called tribes. Membership in a specific tribe was determined by a man's residence. This tribal assembly elected officers who did not command troops and therefore did not have imperium; and these magistrates, known as quaestors and aediles, looked after various financial matters and public works. The other body, actually the oldest of the three, was the Assembly of Curiae (Comitia Curiata), or wards of the city; this assembly met only to validate decisions taken elsewhere and

▼ **This temple in central Rome, from the second century B.C., perhaps dedicated to Portunus, the god of harbors, is a typical Roman temple with a closed room for an image of the god. An altar stood in front. The columns are in the Greek Ionic order, and the temple has a deep basement, common in Etruscan building. Thus the temple unites the three cultures that went into the making of Rome.**
Trëe.

▲ **Many inscriptions, written by professional painters in favor of this or that candidate in elections, have been found on the walls of Pompeii, the city buried in the eruption of A.D. 79.**
Alinari/Art Resource, NY

gradually lost importance. In time, the Assembly of Tribes became the most active of the three assemblies and passed most of Rome's major laws.

The Senate The Senate, which existed in the period of the kings, was the nerve center of the whole state. It did not, in the Republic, pass laws, but it did appoint commanders, assign funds, and generally set public policy. The letters SPQR (standing for "The Senate and the Roman People") were carried on the army's standards and showed the preeminent status of this body. The Roman Senate house, which still stands (rebuilt about A.D. 290) in the Forum, was thus the shrine of Roman power. The senators in the Republic (usually about 300) were men who had held elected offices, and membership was for life. Their solid conservatism acted to restrain hot-headed politicians, and more than once they provided the moral leadership that saw the state through a mil-

itary crisis. Indeed, the word *patres* (fathers) was often used to refer to the Senate.

The Power of the Family Rome had no political parties in the modern sense, but the Senate did have factions, often based on families, that were rivals in the struggle for power. Modern historians have learned how to tell the story of the Republic through the study of the family. Alliances, divorces, marriages, and adoptions could all add to the political power of the family. A larger unit, the *gens* (or clan), included a group of related families consisting of, for example, all Romans whose second name was Cornelius or Aemilius. The great clans and their subdivisions contrived to maintain such firm control over high office that by about 100 B.C. it was rare for any man to reach the consulship who had no previous consul in his family. Such an outsider (for example, the orator Cicero) was referred to as a "new man."

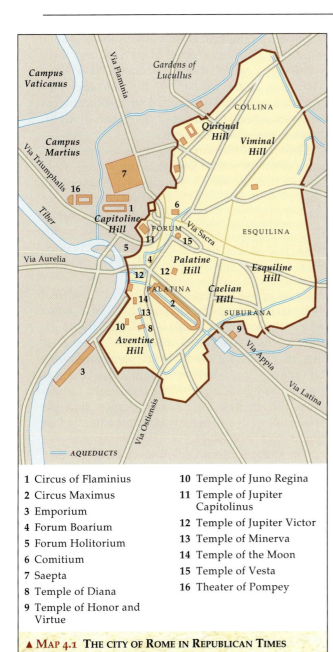

1 Circus of Flaminius
2 Circus Maximus
3 Emporium
4 Forum Boarium
5 Forum Holitorium
6 Comitium
7 Saepta
8 Temple of Diana
9 Temple of Honor and Virtue
10 Temple of Juno Regina
11 Temple of Jupiter Capitolinus
12 Temple of Jupiter Victor
13 Temple of Minerva
14 Temple of the Moon
15 Temple of Vesta
16 Theater of Pompey

▲ **Map 4.1** **The city of Rome in Republican Times**

Patron and Client Free men of lower standing often attached themselves to an influential citizen and became his clients, while he was their patron. Clients received financial and political support from the patron, whom they in turn followed in political and private life. The size of a man's clientele was an accurate gauge of his power in the state. The Claudian clan is said to have moved to Rome bringing with it a large band of dependents.

The patron-client relationship was recognized in Roman law, which prescribed penalties against a patron who defrauded or mistreated a client.

◆ THE STRUGGLE OF THE ORDERS (494–287 B.C.)

Patricians and Plebeians Within the citizen body, the Romans established a distinction that had no parallel in any Greek state. The patricians, a small number of clans (about five to seven percent of the whole people), were recognized as being socially and legally superior to the vast majority, who were called plebeians. Ancient sources do not explain how the distinction arose; it was probably based on wealth gained from owning land and on the less easily defined criterion of social eminence. Membership in the patrician class was based on birth (or, occasionally, adoption), and originally only patricians could belong to the Senate (the *patres*) and hold office.

The plebeians did win a number of privileges in a long process called the struggle of the orders (or classes). When the struggle ended, the plebeians could point to significant gains, but the great families were still secure in their domination. Indeed, one effect of the struggle of the orders was to make the state an even more efficient machine for conquest: The plebeians could now feel that they had a more favorable position within the system and were thus more willing to fight for their country.

Concessions to the Plebeians The plebeians' first victory in the struggle came in 494 B.C., when they evidently threatened to secede from the state.[2] They now obtained the right to elect annually two men, called tribunes, to represent them; the number eventually rose to ten. The powers of the tribunes reveal the Roman genius for political compromise in the interests of a united state. The patricians evidently recognized that spokesmen for the people were a necessary evil, and oaths were exchanged that made it a religious crime to violate or injure the body of a tribune. The

---

[2]The sources give contradictory dates for, and accounts of, many events in Roman history down to about 280 B.C.; the order adopted here cannot always be proved right in every detail.

Chronology

THE STRUGGLE OF THE ORDERS

The main stages by which the Roman plebeians attained a measure of equality with the patricians are as follows:

494 B.C. First "secession" of plebeians; appointment of two tribunes (later rising to ten).

450 The Laws of the Twelve Tables, Rome's first written law code, is published.

445 The Lex Canuleia permits marriage between patricians and plebeians.

367 Licinian-Sextian laws limiting amount of public land anyone could hold.

366 First plebeian consul.

287 Laws passed by plebeians are binding on the whole state; final victory of plebeians.

"sacrosanctity" of the tribunes allowed them to interfere in any action, since no one could lay hands on them. Out of this protected status arose the famous veto power of the tribunes (sometimes called *intercession*); they could forbid any magistrate from acting and could even arrest consuls. Such power might have threatened to cause anarchy, but in fact, because it reassured the plebeians, it proved to be a stabilizing influence.

Other concessions to the plebeians included the publication of a code of laws, in 450 B.C., on the so-called twelve wooden tablets, and the right, in 445, to intermarry with patricians. Intermarriage created a patrician-plebeian aristocracy that replaced the original one restricted to patricians alone.

The Licinian-Sextian Laws The plebeians won their greatest victory in 367 B.C. Two tribunes, Licinius and Sextius, carried a bill that reserved one consulship every year to a plebeian (there were occasional exceptions, but the principle remained). Their bill also created another office— that of praetor, a kind of assistant consul who also held imperium. His main duty, probably taken away from the consuls, was to be the chief officer

for cases at civil law. Eventually in the Republic eight praetors were elected every year, but there were never more than two consuls at a time. Therefore, as the road to the highest office narrowed, a praetor who wanted to become consul was well advised to observe the generally traditional ways of Roman politics.

The laws of Licinius and Sextius also restricted the amount of public land that any citizen could occupy (the precise acreage allowed is disputed). This measure was supposed to prevent the upper classes from occupying more than a fair share of public land for themselves; but over the years they did precisely this, and the lower orders were often denied their proper amount of farming territory.

The End of the Struggle of the Orders The final concession to the plebeians came in 287 B.C., when a law (the Lex Hortensia)[3] established that decisions of the Assembly of Tribes (or Comitia Tributa, in effect, an assembly of plebeians) were binding on the whole state. Thus the common people now had the absolute legal right to pass laws; but in practice most legislation had the sponsorship of the Senate before it came before the Assembly of Tribes.

The struggle of the orders was a bitter conflict, and only the need to remain united against outside enemies kept it from degenerating into civil war. It led to greater power for the plebeians; but the patrician-plebeian upper class managed to control the changes in the constitution before they could lead to actual direction of affairs by the masses.

◆ ROMAN SOCIETY IN THE REPUBLIC

The Structure of the Roman Family The forceful part played by the family in Roman politics was reflected in the organization of the family itself. The Romans accepted direction from the top in most areas of their society, and this kind of structure was built into the family of patricians and plebeians alike. The father of the family, the *paterfamilias,* was the absolute owner of the whole family, which included children, land, other

---

[3]All Roman laws were named for their proposers, in this case one Hortensius; since *lex* (law) is a feminine noun in Latin, the adjective naming it must end in *-a.*

property, animals, and slaves. So long as he lived, his sons, even if married with their own households, remained in his power. On the death of the father, each of his sons became a *paterfamilias* in his own family. Such a severe system differs from anything known in Greece but has parallels in Israelite society.

Women in the Early Republic   The nature of the Roman state, an organization aimed at military defense and expansion, required a constant supply of soldiers. Therefore society designed a role for women that would guarantee the fulfillment of motherhood. Roman legend told that Romulus, the city's mythical founder, led a raid against the Sabines, a neighboring tribe, in which the Romans seized thirty virtuous women to become their wives. This "rape of the Sabines," as it became called, supposedly gave the infant city of Rome a class of strong, loyal women.

▼ **Marble bust of Julius Caesar.**
Archaeological Museum Naples/Dagli Orti/The Archive

Other legends reaffirm the heroic role of women in the early Republic. For example, about 490 a Roman commander, Coriolanus, took sides with a neighboring people in attacking Rome itself. Only the pleas of his wife and his mother persuaded him to halt his troops and lead them away. The legend further says that the women asked the Senate only one reward for their service to the state, namely, to recognize Female Fortune (Fortuna Muliebris) as a goddess and dedicate a temple to her.

Customs in Marriage   Despite these tributes to the virtues of Roman women in legend, the early Republic generally kept women in the position of second-class citizens. A young woman normally married at about age fourteen, as in Greece, and was transferred to her new family and lost her right to her native family's property. Her husband was sometimes considerably older and might have been married before, perhaps having lost a wife in childbirth. Wives were legally within the power of their fathers or husbands (again as in ancient Israel), and their chief virtues were considered to be silence and obedience. The sources tell stories about women legally executed by their families for adultery or other offenses.

Women in the Later Republic   But this system could not last forever. As Rome became wealthier, the narrow framework of women's lives was loosened, and they began to own significant property. Marriage less often involved the placing of a woman under the absolute power of her husband. The reason for this change was not necessarily a wish to respect women's rights; rather, it was that wealthy families with well-off daughters did not wish to lose control over their property by transferring their wealth out of the family.

Marriages now became less stable, and we find women of prominent families, especially in Rome itself, moving in society and even from husband to husband, with a freedom impossible in Greece. In apparent alarm at the emancipation of women, Marcus Cato, a prominent conservative, spoke in favor of an existing law that forbade women to possess jewelry and wear colored dresses; but his opposition to this luxury tells us that women were doing so in the second century B.C. Despite Cato's dislike of such women's liberation, we do not find in Rome that undercurrent of fear of the mysterious powers of women that can be seen in Greek myth and literature.

Women and Family Politics   As in Greece, Roman women could not hold office or vote, but they greatly surpassed Greek women as influences behind the scenes. One especially eminent woman was Cornelia, the daughter of Scipio Africanus, the victorious general in the second Punic War. On the death of her husband she refused all offers of marriage, including one from a king of Egypt, and devoted herself to the education of her twelve children, among whom were the tribunes Tiberius and Gaius Gracchus. She was a woman of high education who maintained a salon and whose letters were praised for their elegant style; indeed, she had a position and prominence unparalleled by that of any woman in classical Greece.

Other women in the Republic also became important as links between powerful families in marriage alliances, which were arranged by fathers, often for the political advantages they could bring with them. One notable such marriage made Julius Caesar the father-in-law of Pompey and cemented the alliance of the two men during Caesar's rise to supreme power. Julia, the daughter of the first emperor, Augustus, was also married to men favored by this emperor in order to continue his family line. The influence of women in politics continued to grow enormously during the Roman Empire, when the long periods of an emperor's reign allowed wives and mothers of rulers to learn and control the levers of power in the imperial court. Yet we must not exaggerate the degree to which Roman women were liberated. In all periods, as in Greece, sarcophagi and tomb reliefs portray men with their wives in conventional poses, and one gravestone for a woman praises her for her domestic virtues: "She was chaste, she was thrifty, she remained at home, she spun wool."

Religion and Roman Values   Roman religion consisted largely of forms of worship that upheld Roman tradition. Within the household, the father acted as the priest and led the family in its worship of household gods—for example, Janus, the god protecting the doorway; Vesta, the spirit of the hearth; and household spirits known as Lares and Penates.

◀ **A late Republican gravestone showing one Lucius Vibius and his wife and child. Roman realism is evident in the portraiture. The face of the man suggests the determined conservatism that shaped the Roman character during the Republican period.**
Scala/Art Resource, NY

Public religion, on the other hand, was closely connected with the interest of the state. Priesthoods were mainly political offices, held only by men. Women were, however, responsible for one of the most important religious duties: It fell to six virgins to maintain the sacred fire of Vesta that guarded the hearth of the state. These Vestal Virgins were held in high honor and lived in a spacious, elegant villa in the Forum; by a remarkable exception, these women were freed of the power of their father.

Roman religion, unlike Greek, often served to maintain conservative old Roman values, such as *pietas* (proper devotion), *dignitas* (the respect that was owed to a good citizen), and *gravitas* (the wish to take things seriously). As to Roman rites, they seem to have been designed mainly to placate the gods, almost to keep them at arm's length, through sacrifices. The Romans believed that their gods would protect them if the gods were shown proper devotion, or *pietas*. The Romans also went to elaborate lengths before declaring war, seeking reasons to believe that the war was just and holy. Eventually some rites hardened into patterns whose original meaning had been forgotten; but so long as the priests did not deviate from routine, the Romans assumed that the gods were satisfied and would not frustrate their enterprises.

Roman Mythology Nearly all of Roman mythology was an adaptation of Greek legend, and Roman gods were often Greek deities with Roman names. The Greek father-god, Zeus, became Iuppiter, or Jupiter; his wife, Hera, became Juno; Athena became Minerva; Hermes became Mercury; and so on. Romans worshiped these gods officially in public and also in the home along with the household deities, these latter being minor gods with no connection to the Greek pantheon. Perhaps because Greek myths often show gods behaving spitefully or immorally, the Romans also created certain uplifting ideals—such as Virtus (manly conduct), Pax (peace), Fides (loyalty), and Pudor (modesty)—and transformed them into gods.

◆ EARLY ROMAN LITERATURE

It may seem surprising that it took the Romans centuries to develop a literature. Homeric epic is older than the Greek city-states themselves, but

Rome had been independent of the Etruscans for the better part of three centuries before a significant literature emerged. Evidently the Romans needed contact with Greek civilization, which came about during the age of conquest, to stimulate their own literary efforts. After the first Punic War, one Naevius wrote an epic poem about Rome's victory (thus imitating Homer), but it has not survived.

Comedy The earliest preserved Latin literature is the comedies, influenced by the Greeks, of Plautus (250?–184? B.C.) and Terence (190?–159? B.C.). These playwrights imitated Greek New Comedy, as it is called, in which the plays were entirely fiction. The Romans did not approve of Old Comedy, such as the plays of Aristophanes, which savagely lampooned active politicians.

Plautus filled his comedies with stock situations and characters, such as mistaken identities, lecherous old men, and frustrated romances. One of his plays about mistaken identities, the *Menaechmi*, gave Shakespeare the model for his *Comedy of Errors*. Terence wrote comedy in a more refined and delicate style than Plautus. His characters are less earthy, and the humor emerges from more subtle situations or such human foibles as greed.

Roman Historians: Polybius Historical writing, too, began rather late in Rome, around 200 B.C., and the writings of the earliest Roman historians are all lost, surviving only through quotations in other writers. The earliest preserved historical narrative on Rome is from the Greek writer Polybius (200?–118? B.C.). He was deported from Greece as a hostage to Rome in the 160s, where he met many Roman statesmen and became an expert in Roman history. He wrote a general history of the Greco-Roman world from the first Punic War down to his own times, largely to demonstrate the inevitable domination of the Mediterranean by the Romans.

Polybius believed that much of Rome's success in government was due to its well-designed constitution—a commendable mixed form of state that would long maintain Rome's power. He traveled widely and insisted on the need to visit sites in order to grasp the importance of geography to history. His work is analytic and methodical and attempts to revive the high standards of historical writing that Herodotus and Thucydides had established. He is both the most important historian of the Hellenistic Age and the most reliable guide to earlier Roman history.

◆ EARLY EXPANSION OF ROME

Rome's First Conquests   While the Romans were developing their form of government, they were also expanding their holdings on the Italian peninsula. Sometimes they could use peaceful diplomacy, for example, by making a treaty with neighboring peoples in the plain of Latium. More often they turned to outright military conquest in wars that were clearly long and strenuous. They gained one important victory over the last remaining Etruscan stronghold, the town of Veii, just across the Tiber River, which they took and destroyed in 396 B.C.

The Invasion by the Gauls   The period of conquest was not uniformly successful and in fact included one major disaster. In 390 B.C. a marauding tribe of Gauls left their stronghold in the Po valley and captured the city of Rome. The event led to an action that Roman tradition remembered as a heroic deed performed by wealthy Roman women. Rome negotiated a ransom with the Gauls to secure their withdrawal, but only a contribution from women brought the funds up to the full amount demanded. The state honored the women by proclaiming that laudatory orations could be spoken at their funerals. Rome then renewed its policy of expansion, showing the resilience that made it, in the words of the historian Edward Gibbon, "sometimes vanquished in battle, always victorious in war."[4] By the 290s Rome dominated the Italian peninsula as far south as the Greek city-states of Magna Graecia.

The Roman Army   No small element in Rome's military victories was the new formation of its army. The Greek phalanx gave way to the system of maniples, or groups of either 60 or 120 men, each commanded by a centurion (roughly a lieutenant in a modern army). The advantage of this system was that the army had both power and versatility, because the maniples could maneuver

---

[4]*Decline and Fall of the Roman Empire,* chap. 38.

independently and could hold together even if the main unit, the legion (6,000 men), lost its formation. About 100 B.C. the maniple was replaced by the cohort (*cohors*), usually a group of 600, but this change was not one of principle, and the cohorts maintained the flexibility of the maniples.

Pyrrhus Invades Italy   In the 280s some of the Greek cities of southern Italy, threatened by the growing imperialism of Rome, enlisted Pyrrhus, the king of Epirus (near modern Albania), to save their independence with a campaign against Rome. He brought a large force that included 20 war elephants, a weapon that the Romans had never before confronted. Pyrrhus fought two successful battles in 280 B.C., but at a heavy cost in casualties to his own men (hence the phrase "a Pyrrhic victory"). The Romans again rebounded from defeat, and Pyrrhus abandoned his allies in 275, leaving the Romans free to pursue their conquests. By 265 B.C. Rome controlled the entire Italian peninsula but had not yet mastered the Po valley.

The Roman Federation   Rome showed great administrative skill in organizing the conquered communities by establishing different degrees of privilege and responsibility among them. Residents of a few favored communities received the most highly prized status, full Roman citizenship. This status meant that they were on the same legal footing as the Romans; they had the protection of Roman law, they could make legal wills to pass on their property, and they could even hold office in Rome. Members of some other communities became citizens who could not vote but had the right of intermarriage with Romans. At a lower level of privilege were the allied states (*socii*). They enjoyed Rome's protection from other peoples and were also liable to provide troops.

This carefully designed system of confederation enabled the Romans to solve an administrative problem that had frustrated the Greek poleis: how to control a large territory without having to demolish or transform the conqueror's own institutions. Even more important, the creation of this chain of alliances greatly expanded the manpower available to Rome in its progressive domination of the Mediterranean. And as the various communities under Rome's control came more and more to resemble Rome in social structure, they could climb the rungs up to full Roman citizenship: a powerful stimulus to loyalty that served Rome well in all its conquests.

II. The Age of Mediterranean Conquest (264–133 B.C.)

Rome had now established its control over the whole Italian peninsula. There followed a period of imperialistic expansion that many historians consider partly involuntary, as Rome became embroiled with other Mediterranean powers. One result, important for the future history of Europe, was the inevitable forming of a system of administering Rome's new territories.

◆ THE PUNIC WARS

Rome—by which we now mean not only the ancient city but also the group of peoples in Italy allied with the city—at last had the strength in population to become a world power. The Romans achieved that goal in three wars with Carthage, a city that had been founded by Phoenicians about 700 B.C. and over the next century had established its own Mediterranean empire. By the time Rome had unified the Italian peninsula, Carthage controlled cities in northern Africa, parts of Spain, the islands of Corsica and Sardinia, and much of Sicily. It was beyond comparison the leading naval power in the western Mediterranean and could live off the tribute paid by its possessions. With good reason a German historian called Carthage "the London of antiquity."

The First Punic War The first war between Rome and Carthage began in 264 B.C. with a conflict over Messana (modern Messina) in Sicily. It provides a perfect example of how two states can stumble into war. This town was governed by a corps of Italian mercenary soldiers known as Mamertines ("sons of Mars," the Roman god of war). Under threat of conquest by the neighboring city of Syracuse, the Mamertines received troops from Carthage as protectors into their town. Then, when the Carthaginians showed no wish to leave,

Chronology

THE ROMAN PROVINCES

The dates when some of the major Roman provinces were legally established. (The actual conquests were sometimes earlier.)

241 B.C.	Most of Sicily (completed in 211).
227	Corsica and Sardinia, administered as one.
197	Nearer and Farther Spain.
146	Macedonia; Africa (former territory of Carthage).
129	Asia (former territory of Pergamum).
ca. 120	Transalpine Gaul.
ca. 81	Cisalpine Gaul.
62	Syria.
16–13	Three Gauls (northern France, formerly conquered by Julius Caesar).

the Mamertines appealed to Rome to drive them out.

After a hesitant debate, the Romans sent a small force to assist Messana. But, when Carthage replied with more troops of its own, the quarrel escalated into a contest for control of the whole island of Sicily. This was the first of the three Punic Wars, so named from the Latin word *Poeni* for the Phoenicians who had founded Carthage. Roman tenacity finally won this war in 241. In this combat the Romans showed the virtues of which they were most proud—above all determination (*constantia*) and the refusal to be defeated no matter how heavy the casualties. Carthage abandoned Sicily entirely, large parts of the island passed to Rome, and it became the first Roman province (a territory outside Italy controlled by Rome).

In 238 B.C. the Carthaginian garrison on the island of Sardinia rebelled, and the Romans took the opportunity to seize the island. The Carthaginians were also forced to hand over the neighboring island of Corsica, and the two islands, administered together, formed the second Roman province. Carthage was furious over this humiliation, which made a second war with Rome all but inevitable.

The Second Punic War and Hannibal The second of the three wars (219–202 B.C.) was the most critical of all. Carthage, still angry over Rome's seizure of Sardinia and Corsica, sought to build up an empire in southern Spain as some compensation for its losses. In 219 B.C. a quarrel arose over Saguntum, a town in Spain to which Rome had promised protection. The great figure on the Carthaginian side was Hannibal, whose father had made him swear undying hatred of Rome. In 219 he seized Saguntum, thus in effect opening war with Rome. A brilliant and daring strategist, second to almost none in history, he determined to carry the war to the enemy. In autumn 218 he led his army from Spain through the snow across the Alps and down into Italy. He brought with him 37 elephants, the irresistible weapon in ancient war (all but one of them soon died).

Once in Italy Hannibal hoped to arouse the tribes of Gauls in the Po valley and end the alliances of the various peoples with Rome, following which he would conquer Rome itself. Despite his energy, his twofold strategy failed. In 216 B.C. he won a stupendous victory over the Romans at Cannae, in southeastern Italy, which has remained a classic study for strategists ever since; but not even then could he bring about a revolt of the allies. Their loyalty is a testimony to Rome's enlightened statesmanship. At least half of them remained faithful to Rome, and without their help Hannibal's manpower was no match for that of Rome.

▲ **Map 4.2** **Italy in 265 B.C., on the Eve of the Punic Wars**

Publius Cornelius Scipio While Hannibal was in Italy, the Roman commander Publius Cornelius Scipio, only 26 years old, carried the war into Spain. Scipio was the first man given such a command without having held higher office. He apparently had absolute faith in the favor of the gods and could inspire his men with this conviction. In 209 B.C. he captured the important city of New Carthage and by 206 he controlled most of Spain. In 204 he landed in Africa, near Carthage itself, where his victories brought about the recall of Hannibal from Italy and set the stage for a final clash between these two great generals and their forces. Scipio won the decisive battle in 202, at Zama in North Africa. In honor of the victory, Scipio received the name *Africanus* and proudly added it to his traditional Roman name. Besides

paying Rome a huge indemnity, Carthage had to give up all its territory except its immediate surroundings in Africa and was forbidden to raise an army without Roman permission.

Thus the second war ended in a hard-earned victory for Roman perseverance and skill; but a large bill would later have to be paid. Hannibal had laid waste large tracts of farming land in southern Italy and had driven many farmers off their soil. In casualties, too, the cost to Rome had been severe: It is estimated that Roman military manpower fell from about 285,000 in 218 to about 235,000 in 203.

The Third Punic War After the second war, Rome made an alliance with Masinissa, the king of Numidia, just west of Carthage. Over the years

Masinissa began to plunder Carthaginian territory and drove Carthage to the point of armed resistance against him. In Rome a bitterly anti-Carthaginian group was led by Marcus Cato, whose name has become symbolic of narrow intolerance. He and his group argued that Carthage was still dangerous; he constantly urged that it be destroyed. Finally he succeeded in persuading Rome to declare war against Carthage and in making it a campaign of punishment (149–146 B.C.).

Another Scipio, known as Scipio Aemilianus, captured Carthage in 146. The Romans utterly destroyed the city and formally cursed the site (the tale that they poured salt into the soil is only a modern fiction), and the territory became the Roman province called simply Africa. The conquest of the territory formerly held by Carthage in Europe was complete when Rome conquered almost all of Spain by 133 B.C.

◆ EXPANSION IN THE EASTERN
MEDITERRANEAN

Wars with Macedonia and Syria   In the following decades the Romans continued their conquests until they had mastered the whole Mediterranean basin. Historians have long debated whether this policy represented deliberate imperialism or was at least partly accidental. Certainly the first stage was forced on Rome by the king of Macedonia, Philip V (r. 221–179 B.C.). He drew Rome into war by forming an alliance with Hannibal in 215 B.C. and thus opened the gate through which, over centuries, Roman troops and administrators poured as far east as Armenia and changed the course of European history.

During this era Rome also became involved in war with Antiochus III, the Macedonian ruler of Syria, the kingdom founded by Seleucus after the death of Alexander. Roman forces defeated his army at Magnesia in Asia Minor in 190 B.C.—another significant moment in Rome's expansion, as Roman legions left Europe and fought in Asia Minor for the first time.

Annexation of Greece   For a time, the Romans tried to stay out of Greek affairs and proclaimed that they were allowing the Greeks freedom. To the Greeks, freedom meant the liberty to do as they liked, but for the Romans it meant behaving as obedient Roman clients. After further quarrels and battles, the Roman Senate realized that outright annexation of the Greek mainland was the only way to secure Rome's interests.

Therefore, in 146 B.C., Macedonia and Greece were combined into a province. This decision brought the Romans into permanent contact with Greek culture, which they passed on over the centuries to Europe. They had already destroyed Carthage, and as they took over Greece their dominance in the Mediterranean could not be denied or reversed. But this domination came at a price. Without the need for unity against outside enemies, Roman society began to lose its cohesiveness; this in turn led to the decline of the Republic.

The Province of Asia   Some experienced rulers in the region were shrewd enough to perceive what had happened and began a process of accommodation to Rome. For example, in 133 B.C., the last king of Pergamum died without leaving a successor and the Romans found that he had willed his kingdom to Rome—surely because he had seen that the kingdom of Pergamum could not long survive without Roman protection. Four years later Rome created the province of Asia, based on the territory of Pergamum (see map 4.3). This province possessed great wealth and offered tempting opportunities for a governor of Asia to enrich himself through corruption; the post became highly desirable for ambitious politicians and also brought with it a posting to the pleasant climate of the beautifully built Greek cities.

◆ THE NATURE OF ROMAN EXPANSION

Organization and Force   Rome's success in its domination of the Mediterranean rested on certain unique historical conditions. Early in its history, events had forced the city to seek defensive alliances. After the expulsion of the Etruscan monarchs, for example, Rome had to unite militarily with its neighbors in the plain of Latium against a possible Etruscan counterattack. Constant wars in the fourth and third centuries, such as the invasion by the Gauls in 390 B.C., further emphasized the need for common security.

The result was a commitment to, and mastery of, military force that proved to be unsurpassed,

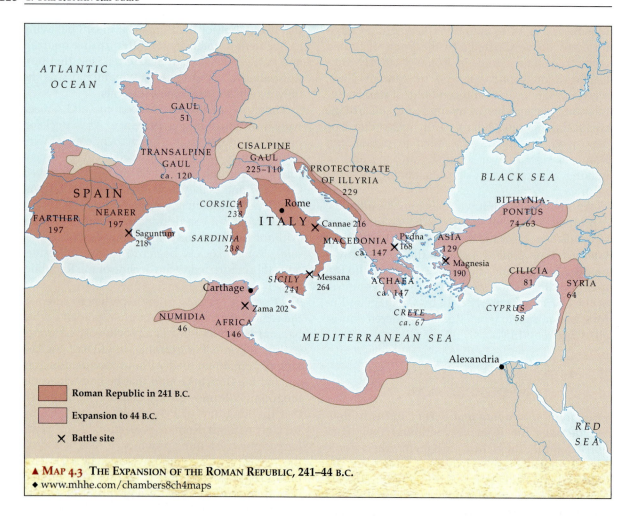

ATLANTIC
OCEAN

GAUL
51

TRANSALPINE
GAUL
ca. 120

CISALPINE
GAUL
225–110

PROTECTORATE
OF ILLYRIA
229

BLACK SEA

SPAIN

CORSICA
238

Rome

ITALY

BITHYNIA-
PONTUS
74–63

FARTHER
197

NEARER
197

✕ Saguntum
218

SARDINIA
238

Cannae 216 ✕

MACEDONIA
ca. 147

Pydna ✕
168

ASIA
129

✕ Magnesia
190

CILICIA
81

SYRIA
64

SICILY
241

✕ Messana
264

ACHAEA
ca. 147

Carthage ●

✕ Zama 202

CRETE
ca. 67

CYPRUS
58

NUMIDIA
46

AFRICA
146

MEDITERRANEAN SEA

Alexandria ●

■ Roman Republic in 241 B.C.

■ Expansion to 44 B.C.

✕ Battle site

RED
SEA

▲ **MAP 4.3** **THE EXPANSION OF THE ROMAN REPUBLIC, 241–44 B.C.**
◆ www.mhhe.com/chambers8ch4maps

and this military force soon developed into a highly effective and (when necessary) utterly ruthless policy of conquest. Scipio Aemilianus, for example, forced the people of Numantia, in Spain, to surrender in 133 B.C., by reducing them to cannibalism and even cut off the hands of four hundred young men in a neighboring city who had advocated aiding their Spanish brethren. The Senate at home considered Aemilianus' achievements worthy of a triumphal parade, the highest military honor that Romans could bestow on a successful commander.

Provincial Administration The Latin word *provincia* means "a duty assigned to a magistrate," and the Romans extended the meaning to denote the various regions that they acquired through conquest. The Senate chose the governors for the various provinces, often giving them the title *pro-*

consul ("in place of a consul"). These governors ruled their provinces with absolute power, though they could not violate Roman law or act illegally against Roman citizens. Some provincial governors ruled fairly, but others were notorious for their corruption. From the Roman view, the advantage of the system was its efficiency: Rebellions were not common, and troops stationed in the provinces could maintain control without resorting to massacres.

***Tax Collectors, or* Publicani** The provinces furnished financial support for the Roman Republic. Some had to pay tribute in various forms, usually food, while others were assigned a fixed sum of money. In order to obtain these taxes, the state devised a convenient but corruptible system of tax collection. Companies of tax collectors, known as *publicani,* bid for the contracts to collect the taxes of certain provinces, especially Asia. The collectors paid the state a fixed sum in advance and then made their profit by collecting taxes in excess of what they had paid. The governor of the province was supposed to see that the *publicani* did not collect more than a specified sum. Unfortunately, however, the collectors could use their funds as bribes to persuade the governor to overlook their rapacity.[5]

The Equestrians   The tax collectors came from a class known as equestrians. The *equites* originally formed the cavalry in Rome's military forces, but over the years the equestrians stopped fighting on horseback and became a social class, roughly the businessmen of Rome. Equestrians did not serve in the Senate. They had to be of high financial standing, and some of them could far outstrip senators in wealth. They held no political offices but formed companies to build roads and aqueducts and to conduct businesses of all kinds.

III. The Roman Revolution (133–27 B.C.)

The year 133 B.C. saw the final conquest of most of Spain, in the west, and the acquisition of the province of Asia, in the east. This was also the beginning of the Roman revolution, a long political transformation that ended the Roman Republic. Imperialism demanded powerful military commanders, and the selfish rivalry among them burst the bounds of the constitution.

◆ SOCIAL CHANGE AND THE GRACCHI

The Changing World of Italy   The breakdown of the Roman Republic has been called Hannibal's legacy, for the ravages of years of fighting up and down Italy had brought many farmers to the point of ruin. On the other hand, wealthy citizens had enriched themselves with booty and the spoils of war. The less fortunate had often lost their land or were willing to sell it to these newly wealthy men. There had also been a great increase

---

[5]Cicero, a firm supporter of the *publicani,* called them "the flower of the Roman equestrians, the ornament of the state, and the foundation of the Republic."

Chronology

THE ROMAN REVOLUTION

The main landmarks in the Roman revolution were as follows:

133 B.C.	Tiberius Gracchus elected tribune; is killed in riot.
123–122	Gaius Gracchus tribune; equestrians gain control of extortion court; Gaius killed.
107	First consulship of Marius.
91–88	War with Italian allies.
81–79	Sulla's dictatorship.
70	First consulship of Pompey and Crassus.
66	Pompey given command against Mithridates in Asia.
59	Julius Caesar consul, receives command in Gaul.
58–50	Caesar's conquest of Gaul.
49	Caesar invades Italy, opening of civil war.
44	Caesar murdered.
31	Battle of Actium, defeat of Mark Antony.
27	Supremacy of Octavian, later called Augustus; beginning of Roman Empire.

in the slave population on Italian soil from prisoners of war, and these slaves depressed the wages paid to private workers.

Often the displaced farmers had little choice but to join the ranks of the permanently unemployed. Their poverty threatened to impede the recruitment of soldiers into the Roman army, for Rome had nothing like a modern war treasury, and only men who had enough money to buy their own armor could be drafted into the legions. Without sufficient recruits, the gains from the conquests might be lost. Moreover, those who could no longer find work lost the spirit of cohesion and loyalty to their society. They became prey to demagogues and many became supporters of this or that warlord. The Senate, which might have provided moral leadership to the state, also showed itself unable to stand firm as the long revolution rolled on.

Tiberius Gracchus   Two ambitious young Roman statesmen, Tiberius and Gaius Gracchus, moved to solve the problems of those who had lost their land. Their mother, Cornelia, was a well-known daughter of a great family; her father was Publius Cornelius Scipio Africanus, who had won the war against Hannibal. She had married a prominent plebeian politician, Tiberius Gracchus. Because patrician or plebeian status came down through the male line, her sons were plebeian, though descended from the loftiest aristocracy.

Tiberius, the older brother (162–133 B.C.), became tribune in 133 and proposed a bill to the Assembly of Tribes that would assign parcels of publicly owned land to dispossessed farmers. The state would obtain and redistribute such land by enforcing a long-ignored law that limited the amount of public land that anyone could occupy. To serve in the Roman army, a man had to have at least a modest amount of wealth, and Tiberius' aim, a moderate one, was to create prosperous farmers and thus increase the supply of potential recruits for the army. He made the mistake of not submitting his bill for the approval of the Senate before proposing it. Angered at this slight, some senators found another tribune willing to oppose the bill with his veto. Tiberius then persuaded the people to remove that tribune from office. This action was both illegal and dangerous. Once such a step had been taken, what tribune would be safe in the future from an identical threat? But the people followed Tiberius and passed the bill.

Tiberius Murdered   The distribution of land was in progress when Tiberius decided to run for re-election. This move was a breach of custom, for tribunes held office for only one year. Some of his opponents feared that he might seize permanent leadership of the propertyless and lead them into social revolution. A group of senators, late in 133, took the law into their own hands and provoked a riot in which Tiberius was clubbed to death—an event that gave grim warning of a new intensity in Rome's political struggles. Above all, this action violated the taboo against assassination of a tribune, and this first step, once taken, became easier to repeat. Despite Tiberius' death, the distribution of land continued, and his enemies even took credit for the success of the project.

Gaius Gracchus   Tiberius' younger brother, Gaius, became tribune ten years later, in 123 B.C. He was the harsher and less compromising of the two plebeians. He remembered that some senators had inspired the murder of his brother, and he wanted to reply with several measures that sought to limit the powers of senators. He proposed, and the people accepted, that the Senate's freedom in assigning governors to provinces should be restricted. One of the most important powers of the Senate was membership in the extortion court, which investigated cases of alleged extortion by provincial governors and tax collectors. The jurors, all senators, were usually not severe in judging governors, who were fellow members of the Senate. Gaius had a bill passed that assigned the seats on this jury to members of the equestrian class.

All tax collectors were equestrians, and it was now they who had the potential to favor members of their group who might be accused and brought to trial for extortion. Gaius' arrangements were later revised, but he was the first to make the extortion court the subject of a bitter political quarrel.

The Fall and Death of Gaius Gracchus   Gaius had also followed his brother Tiberius in authoring a bill that continued the distribution of public land. It included provisions for the founding of colonies where more citizens could be settled. But he committed a major blunder in proposing to found a colony of Roman citizens on the site of Carthage, the hated enemy in the three Punic wars. This ill-judged action aroused widespread criticism.

Like his brother, Gaius Gracchus came to a violent end. He failed to be elected to a third year as tribune, and his enemies asserted that he and his followers were planning a revolution. The Senate then ordered one of the consuls for the year 121 B.C. to "see to it that the state suffered no harm," thus inviting the consul to use force to suppress the younger Gracchus. This resolution, which was later passed against others whom the Senate wanted to eliminate, was known in Roman politics as the "last decree" (*Senatus consultum ultimum*). When the consul raised up a mob to hunt Gaius down, he had one of his own slaves kill him.

The Gracchi and History   The Gracchi had unleashed a whirlwind when they invited the Assembly of Tribes to take a more activist role. It is true that the people had long possessed the right to legislate in this assembly, but they had not always had the will; nor had ambitious tribunes always dared to use such a weapon. But now demagogues began to turn more and more to this assembly to pass bills in favor of their military patrons. From this moment began the slow but sure Roman revolution.

◆ THE YEARS OF THE WARLORDS

The Gracchi could not protect themselves from the violence of the Senate because they had no army. But as Roman conquests brought the state into further wars, powerful generals appeared who did have the support of their armies and used it to seize power. Their struggles against one another undermined the republican constitution and the state finally collapsed into dictatorship.

Marius and a Changed Roman Army   The first general to play this game was Gaius Marius (157?–86 B.C.), from the countryside near Rome. In Roman terminology, he was a "new man" or *novus homo*, that is, a man none of whose ancestors had been consul. He was a roughneck, of little education, but stalwart and fearless. He is a crucial figure because he changed, radically and forever, the membership of the Roman army and the direction of its loyalty. He gained high prestige by winning a war (111–106 B.C.) against Jugurtha, the king of Numidia in North Africa. Marius had obtained this command after the generals who had been sent out by the Senate had proved incompetent; and Marius showed his hatred for the feeble aristocrats who had thoroughly bungled the campaign.

Marius' reputation grew even more after he drove back an attempted invasion (105–101 B.C.) by some Germanic tribes moving toward northern Italy. Such was his stature in this period that he was consul for five consecutive years and dominated politics from 107 to 100 B.C.

In order to raise large numbers of men for his army, Marius abolished the old requirement that a soldier had to own at least a modest amount of property, and he also accepted volunteers instead of just drafting men for service (the men so enrolled were known as *capite censi*, "enrolled by head count"). As a result, the army came to be composed largely of poor men who served their commander, received booty from him, relied on him as their main patron, and expected him to obtain for them a grant of land that they could farm after they were discharged. Thus Marius converted the army into an instrument for ambitious commanders during the remaining years of the Republic and even throughout the Roman Empire.

The War with the Italians   The Italian peoples who were Rome's allies had never been granted Roman citizenship, and in 91 B.C. another reform-minded tribune, Marcus Livius Drusus, tried to carry a bill that would have made them citizens. The Senate declared his law null and void, and Drusus, like the Gracchi, was murdered. At this outrage some of the allies proclaimed themselves independent and opened a war that continued until 88. In the end the Romans negotiated with the Italians and allowed them to acquire citizenship. But the fact that it required a war to obtain this concession shows that both the Roman upper classes—the senators and equestrians—and the Roman masses were still protective of their privileges.

Sulla the Dictator   The Italian War made the reputation of another powerful general, Lucius Cornelius Sulla (138?–78 B.C.). He was a man without any scruples, a glutton and sensualist who helped himself to whatever women he liked. In the 80s civil war broke out in Rome over who should obtain the command in a war against Mithridates, the king of Pontus in Asia Minor (r. 120–63 B.C.). One group rallied behind Sulla and his legions, seeing in him the best vehicle for their own ambitions. In 88 he invaded the city of Rome with his supporters—the first but not the last time that Romans themselves marched on and seized the ancient city.

Mithridates had extended his kingdom until it included the Roman province of Asia and even large parts of the Greek mainland. In 88 B.C. he gave orders for the massacre of at least 80,000 Romans and Italians residing in Asia Minor—a testimony to the unpopularity of Roman rule in this province. This massacre could not go unanswered, and Sulla received the command against Mithridates.

Sulla departed for his campaign in 87 B.C., and during his absence Marius and his supporters seized Rome in turn. They conducted a reign of terror, publishing lists ("proscriptions") of those to be killed either with or without "trials" and exhibiting their maimed bodies and even their heads in the streets. But as soon as Sulla was free of his Eastern war, he returned to Italy and once more occupied Rome (November 82). Our sources tell us that he had thousands of his opponents executed and had himself named dictator without limit of time, thus breaking the customary six-month limit for holding that office.

Sulla's Reforms   For all Sulla's brutality and self-indulgence, he did have a political program: to reshape the state on strictly authoritarian and conservative lines. Two forces, he thought, had menaced the rigid control over Rome that the Senate should enjoy: the tribunes of the people, who had made the Assembly of Tribes more conscious of its power, and the generals who had used the loyalty of their armies to gain political leverage. To deal with the first of these threats, Sulla forced through a law that blocked tribunes from holding any other office; they also had to wait ten years to be reelected. These measures were meant to discourage any ambitious politicians from seeking this office.

Sulla handled the army commanders through a law that forbade them to leave their provinces or make war outside their borders without instructions from the Senate; thus, no ambitious commander could blunder into a war or make himself into a conqueror. Sulla further established minimum ages at which a man might hold the various offices in a political career (a consul, for example, had to be 42 or older). He also canceled the work of Gaius Gracchus on the jury system; as one might expect from this strict traditionalist, he gave all the seats on the juries back to senators.

Sulla resigned the dictatorship in 79 B.C., a rare act in any supreme ruler, but he evidently thought

▲ This idealized statue of the first century B.C. shows the ruthless tyrant Cornelius Sulla in the dignified pose of a classical orator.
Giraudon/Art Resource, NY

he had put the Senate so firmly in control that he was no longer needed; he died in 78. To his enemies he was pitiless, and his executions of Roman citizens were horrifying, but he was also a political strategist. He had done his part for the conservative cause by putting the Senate in charge, but this body proved unable to manage the next generation of warlords.

The Rise of Pompey Sulla had used the tool forged by Marius—an army loyal to a commander—and another warlord soon followed his example, namely Gnaeus Pompeius (106–48 B.C.), usually called Pompey. He first gained a reputation in 77 B.C., when he was sent to Spain to end a revolt there. After completing this task, and while his army was still intact, he helped suppress a rebellion of slaves in Italy led by a Thracian slave named Spartacus. This campaign was already under the command of another ambitious Roman, Marcus Licinius Crassus, the richest man of his time. Pompey and Crassus were rivals, but they worked together in suppressing the revolt. No sooner did the slave revolt collapse in 71 B.C. than the joint commanders, Pompey and Crassus, marched their armies to the gates of Rome and demanded both consulships for the year 70. Pompey was legally unqualified for this office, for he was only 36 and had held no previous magistracy. If Crassus, Pompey's rival, had refused to join in this bargain, he might have preserved the Sullan system. But, like him, the Senate also lacked the will to enforce the constitution and resist the two men, and they won election as consuls. This was little short of a coup d'état.

During their consulship Pompey and Crassus canceled several of Sulla's arrangements. They restored to the tribunes their right to propose legislation, and they mixed senators and equestrians in the always controversial juries. At the end of their year in office, both consuls retired without demanding any further appointment—an action that, though at first surprising, was really consistent with Pompey's ambitions. He wanted to be the first man in the state, but he disliked committing himself to open revolution. A modern historian has compared him to Shakespeare's Macbeth: He would not play false and yet would wrongly win.

Pompey's Military Commands In 67 B.C. Pompey obtained an extraordinary command to deal with pirates operating in the Mediterranean who were interfering with the grain supply for Rome—a critical matter since the city had to live on grain shipped to its harbor. Pompey fulfilled his orders and cleared the seas in a swift campaign. He also recognized the economic roots of piracy and settled many of the captured pirates on land that they could cultivate in Asia Minor and Greece. Then in 66 B.C. he received through the Tribal Assembly an even more important command in Asia Minor, where Rome was involved in war with Mithridates, Sulla's old enemy, who was still on his throne.

Another Roman general, Lucullus, had practically wiped out Mithridates' forces, so Pompey's campaign was essentially a mopping-up operation. But Pompey took action that had permanent results; he set up a system of client kings, rulers of smaller states whose loyalty to Rome was ensured by the device of "friendship" (*amicitia*). This arrangement was an informal bargain through which Rome would protect local rulers, who paid no taxes to Rome but were expected to assist with manpower and resources when needed. He also captured Syria in 64 B.C.; it became a Roman province in 62 B.C.

Cicero: Nonmilitary Statesman During Pompey's absence overseas, Marcus Tullius Cicero (106–43 B.C.) became the chief nonmilitary statesman in Rome. Like Marius, he was a "new man" from the countryside, but unlike Marius, Cicero chose a career in law and administration rather than in the military. His administrative skill won for him each successive political office at the earliest possible legal age. He was genuinely dedicated to compromise and political negotiation and thought that such procedures would establish the combined rule of the two upper classes, the senatorial and equestrian.

Cicero was elected consul for 63 B.C. One of his defeated rivals for the office, Catiline (Lucius Sergius Catilina), formed a conspiracy to take over the city by force. Cicero learned details of this plan and denounced Catiline in four famous speeches (the "Catilinarian" orations). He obtained the Senate's support to execute some of the captured conspirators without trial (a wholly illegal act); Catiline himself died in battle against an army of the state.

Cicero was the most versatile Latin writer of his time, and his polished prose style became the model in Latin for clarity and elegance. He also wrote philosophical treatises. Cicero's treatises do not follow the doctrines of any particular school; he was equally interested in Stoicism, the thought of Plato, and several other schools, and he chose whatever seemed persuasive from Greek writings for his own theories. In *On the Republic*, for example, Cicero accepted the Platonic view that wise leaders ought to govern the state, but he disregarded the more technical aspects of Plato's philosophy.

Cicero and Other Factions Cicero's political speeches are a continuous record of his career and his frustrated ambitions. He enjoyed his political success as a "new man" and sought a place for himself among the upper classes, believing that they should guide the state along established constitutional lines. Unfortunately, most politicians in the later Republic felt little allegiance to the constitution and selfishly followed their own personal advantage. Cicero never became a magnetic leader around whom others gathered. His letters are a frank and often painful record of the compromises forced on him in the treacherous world of Roman politics.

Pompey Returns to Rome When Pompey returned to Rome in 62 B.C. from his Eastern victories, he had two political aims. He wanted the Senate to ratify the arrangements he had made in Asia Minor; and he requested a grant of land for his men. This latter request, as we have seen, was nothing unusual. It reflected the relationship between a general and his troops, which was that of patron and client—one of the oldest traditions in Rome. But some senators, either jealous or fearful of his prestige, combined to frustrate his wishes. This short-term victory practically doomed the Senate and the Republic, for it drove Pompey into a political alliance with Julius Caesar, who proved to have the revolutionary will that Pompey lacked.

◆ THE FIRST TRIUMVIRATE

The Partners and Their Desires Gaius Julius Caesar (100–44 B.C.), a descendant of an old patrician family, returned to Rome in 60 B.C. from his post as governor of Spain. Intellectually, he was a brilliant man who wrote elegant, lean Latin. Politically, he is an example of the aristocrat who bases his power on the common people. In this respect he resembles Pericles in Athenian history. Caesar had enemies within the Senate, where many looked on him as a brash upstart or a potential tyrant. They refused his request to be allowed to run for the consulship of 59 in absence and then lead a triumphal parade through the city. Faced with this direct affront to his dignity, Caesar made a political bargain with Pompey. Crassus joined them because he was at odds with some powerful senators over a financial matter. The three formed a coalition known to historians as the First Triumvirate ("body of three men"; it had no official mandate or status). Their united influence at the polls over their clients elected Caesar as one of the consuls for 59. To confirm the bargain in a manner

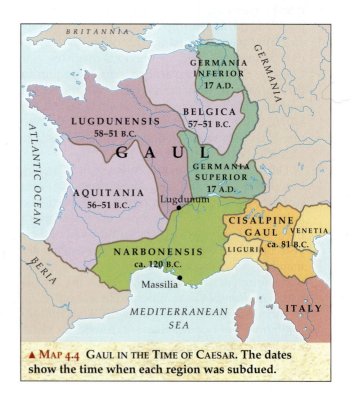

▲ MAP 4.4 GAUL IN THE TIME OF CAESAR. The dates show the time when each region was subdued.

customary in Roman politics, Pompey married Caesar's daughter, Julia.

Caesar's Consulship and the Gallic War Caesar's influence secured allotments of land for Pompey's army and the approval of his arrangements in the East. Crassus' financial quarrel was also settled to his satisfaction. Caesar then secured for himself the command over Cisalpine Gaul (the Po valley) and the coast of Illyria for a guaranteed period of five years beginning on March 1, 59 B.C.

About this time the governor of Transalpine Gaul (Provence, in the south of France) died, and the Senate added this province as well to Caesar's command.

Caesar intervened in the politics of the Gallic tribes and opened a series of campaigns that finally brought the whole area of modern France and Belgium under Roman rule. The Romans implanted in Gaul the Latin language (the origin of modern French), Roman technology, and Roman ways in general. Caesar narrated and defended

▼ **Perhaps the most spectacular classical monument in Europe, the Pont du Gard was built in the first century** A.D. **to carry water to Nîmes (ancient Nemausus) in France. The water ran through a trough above the top layer of arches. The aqueduct is an example of the Romans' mastery of hydraulic technology and construction in arches.**
Michael Holford Photographs

his actions in his *Commentaries on the Gallic War,* which to this day remains a superb textbook in political-military decision making.

The Gallic War lasted from 58 to 50 B.C. Caesar's two partners in the triumvirate, Pompey and Crassus, were always suspicious of each other, but they maintained fairly good relations and even held a second consulship together in 55. They also had Caesar's command in Gaul renewed for another five years, so that it would not expire until March 1, 49, and they obtained commands for themselves. Crassus went out to Syria, from which he launched a disastrous campaign against the kingdom of Parthia, across the Euphrates River. Here he lost his life in 53 B.C. Pompey was given command over the two provinces of Spain, which he governed through assistants, preferring to remain at the center of power near Rome.

◆ THE SUPREMACY OF JULIUS CAESAR

The Break between Caesar and the Senate   Caesar's conquest of Gaul greatly enriched the state, but to his enemies it was a cause of dismay. They feared that he might use his victories and his popularity among the people to become another, and perhaps a permanent, Sulla. As protection against Caesar, his enemies in the Senate began to draw Pompey into their camp. Some of them had quarreled with him in the past, but they were willing to gamble that they could eliminate him when they no longer needed him.

As 49 B.C. opened, the Senate met in a state near hysteria. A small band of implacable senators forced through a motion ordering Caesar to lay down his command, even though he was then taking no action beyond remaining in his province of Cisalpine Gaul. The Senate passed a decree establishing martial law (that is, the "last decree," which had been invented for use against Gaius Gracchus) and ordered Pompey to command the armies of Rome against Caesar. The ill-advised Pompey accepted the command; but in doing so he signed his own death warrant and condemned the Republic to extinction in yet another civil war.

The Attack on the Tribunes of the People   Finally, the Senate defied the oldest of Roman traditions by threatening the lives of any tribunes who opposed these extreme measures. They thus handed Caesar a superb theme for his own propaganda: He could proclaim that he was defending the rights of the tribunes, of the common people of Rome who had elected them, and of the men in his army who had loyally served in the Gallic wars.

Caesar's Invasion of Italy   Caesar saw that his enemies were in effect challenging him to war and decided that he had no course but to fight for his dignity and, as he could now assert, for the people and their sacred tribunes. On about January 11, 49 B.C., he spoke the words, "The die is cast," and crossed the boundary of his province, the small Rubicon River north of Ravenna, thus invading his own country at the head of Roman legions. Yet perhaps his conscience was not wholly clear: The biographer Plutarch records the tale that, on the night before the crossing, he dreamt that he was having sexual relations with his own mother.

Caesar advanced swiftly, and Pompey and his followers had to retreat to Greece; Caesar pursued them and won a decisive battle in 48 B.C. at the town of Pharsalus, in Thessaly. Pompey sought refuge in Egypt, but advisers to the pharaoh realized that Caesar had won the victory and that it was not safe for them to give Pompey protection. As Pompey approached the shore, he was stabbed to death by a former Roman officer of his. His head was cut off and his body thrown into the sea. Caesar followed to Egypt in October 48 B.C. and found that Pompey was dead. He now intervened in a civil war between the young king, Ptolemy XIII, and his sister, the famous Macedonian ruler Cleopatra VII. Caesar arranged that Ptolemy and Cleopatra should share the rule and proceeded to have a long affair with the queen. A boy, called Caesarion (the Little Caesar), was born.[6] Politics played as much a role as love, because Cleopatra's affection guaranteed Roman control over the rich resources of Egypt; Caesar did not follow the usual practice of making Egypt a province but left it as a kingdom to be ruled by Cleopatra and Ptolemy. After other victories Caesar returned to Rome in 46.

---

[6]Scholars have always been uncertain whether Caesar was really the father of this boy.

▲ **An arena in El-Djem, Tunisia, imitating the Colosseum in Rome. Built in the second/third century A.D., this arena could seat 50,000 spectators. Wild animals were housed in the long rectangular pit in the center. Roman buildings were widely copied throughout the Empire as other cities sought to identify themselves with the great capital.**
Photo Researchers, Inc.

Caesar's Rule to 44 B.C. Caesar now decided to make his rule impregnable and assumed the positions of both dictator and consul. On the model of Sulla, he extended his dictatorship beyond the legal six-month limit; then, in 44, he had himself named dictator for life. He swept aside all restraints on his power that Roman tradition might have imposed and took complete authority to pass laws, declare war, and appoint men to office.

As dictator, Caesar saw to a series of rapid reforms in many areas of Roman life. He raised the membership of the Senate to about nine hundred, packing it with many of his veteran officers. From this time onward the Senate lost its former authority as the bulwark of the state. He scaled down his large army by settling many of his soldiers in newly founded colonies and extended Roman citizenship into some of the provinces. His most lasting reform was one by which we still regulate our lives—the establishment of a calendar based on the old Egyptian reckoning of 365 days, with one day added every fourth year. This "Julian" calendar lasted until 1582, when it was revised by Pope Gregory XIII to our present Gregorian calendar.

THE MURDER OF JULIUS CAESAR

The biographer Plutarch, who wrote about A.D. 120, looked back to describe the scene when Caesar was killed, 44 B.C.

"The place chosen for this murder, where the Senate met on that day, contained a statue of Pompey, one of the adornments for the theater he had built; this made it clear to all that some divine power had guided the deed and summoned it to just that spot. As Caesar entered, the Senate rose as a sign of respect, while those in Brutus' faction came down and stood around his chair. Tillius Cimber seized Caesar's toga with both hands and pulled it down from his neck, which was the signal for the assassination. Casca was the first to strike him in the neck with his sword, but the wound was neither deep nor fatal, and Caesar turned around, grasping and holding the weapon. Those who knew nothing of the plot were terrified and did not dare run away or help Caesar or even utter a sound. But those who came prepared for the murder whipped out their daggers, and Caesar was encircled, so that wherever he turned he met with blows and was surrounded by daggers leveled at his face and eyes and he was grappling with all their hands at once. Everyone was supposed to strike him and have a taste of the murder; even Brutus stabbed him once in the groin. Some say that, as he fought off all the rest, turning his body this way and that and shouting for help, he saw Brutus draw his dagger and pulled his toga down over his head and let himself fall at the base of Pompey's statue, whether by chance or because he was pushed by the assassins. There was blood all around the statue, so that it seemed that Pompey was presiding over the vengeance taken against his enemy, who now lay at his feet and breathed out his life through his wounds. They say he was struck 23 times, and many of the assassins were wounded by one another as they all directed their blows at his body."

Plutarch, *The Life of Caesar*, chap. 66, trans. M. H. Chambers.

The Death of Caesar   The full effect of Caesar's plans was not to be realized, for on March 15, 44 (the date known as the Ides of March), after four years of supremacy, he fell to the daggers of conspirators led by two of his lieutenants, Marcus Brutus and Gaius Cassius. His autocracy had been a grave affront to the upper class; because he had undermined their dignity as members of the governing class, they united against Caesar and carried out the most famous political murder in all history. It is said that Caesar was warned that morning of an imminent conspiracy and that he brushed the warning aside. As the Senate met near a theater built by Pompey, the killers plunged on him; when he recognized his protégé, Marcus Brutus in the group, he said in Greek, "You, too, my boy?" and covered his head with his toga as he fell. His body was carried to the Forum and burned on a rock that still stands in a small temple built to his memory after his death (see "The Murder of Julius Caesar," above).

Caesar's character is baffling and controversial, even as it was to his contemporaries. He was pitiless toward Gauls and Germans, and he enriched himself by selling prisoners of war as slaves; but indifference toward captured foreigners was common in the ancient world. In Rome he showed too little respect for the Senate and republican forms once he became dictator, and for this mistake he paid with his life. On the other hand, in the civil war he was generous enough to dismiss opposing generals whom he had captured, and they lived to fight him another day. Such actions may have rested on cool calculation of their value as propaganda, but they may also show genuine gallantry. No one can question Caesar's fiery leadership. He was wiry and tough, he ignored heat and rain, he swam unfordable rivers, and his troops followed him into Italy with enthusiasm and fought with amazing discipline.

Caesar clearly thought that the old institutions of the Senate and the assemblies were obsolete. "The Republic," he is said to have remarked, "is only a name without body or face, and Sulla did not know the ABCs of politics in resigning his dictatorship."[7] The political weakness of the late Republic largely confirms this harsh evaluation. But in the end Caesar's arrogance was too much for the experienced politicians whom he needed for his administration. His career thus blends triumph and tragedy. He rose to the absolute summit of Roman politics, but in doing so he destroyed both the Roman Republic and himself.

IV. The End of the Roman Republic
◆

Julius Caesar's dictatorship had all but killed the Roman Republic, but after his death the question still remained whether the republican constitution could be revived. Some politicians tried to restore the republic, and the issue hung in the balance for thirteen years, until Caesar's adopted son, Octavian, eliminated his rival, Mark Antony, and gained supreme control.

◆ THE SECOND TRIUMVIRATE

Antony and Octavian Brutus, Cassius, and the other assassins imagined that republican government could be restored with Caesar out of the way. Yet partisans of Caesar commanded armies throughout the Roman world, and they were not men who would meekly surrender their powers to the Senate. One survivor was Marcus Antonius, or Mark Antony, a follower of Caesar and consul for the year 44 B.C. Antony tried to seize for himself the provincial command in Cisalpine Gaul, even though the Senate had already assigned it to another governor for the year 43. The Senate turned on him, with Cicero, now a senior statesman, leading the attack. The state sent an army out to bring Antony to justice, and it must have seemed to many that the old institutions of the Republic had indeed come back to life.

Among the commanders whom the Senate put in action against Antony was a young man of 19—Caesar's grandnephew, whom Caesar adopted in his will. His name, originally Gaius Octavius, became Gaius Julius Caesar Octavianus upon his adoption; modern historians call him Octavian, but he called himself Caesar. He used his name skillfully to win a following among Caesar's former soldiers, but he also played the part of a discreet young supporter of the Senate in its battle against Antony. Cicero, the chief supporter of the old constitution, naively wrote of Octavian after their first meeting, "The young man is completely devoted to me."[8]

Formation of the Second Triumvirate Octavian had been assigned the duty of capturing Antony, but they both recognized that the Senate was really seeking the destruction of the Caesarian faction from which they both derived their political support. If either man were overthrown, the Senate would soon discard the other. Octavian thus calculated his own advantage and turned his back on the duty of attacking Antony. The two Caesarians formed an alliance near Bologna in 43 B.C. They brought into their partnership a lesser commander, Marcus Lepidus; then, following the example of Sulla and others, they invaded Rome and made themselves the military rulers of the ancient capital.

Faced with their armies, the Senate had to acknowledge their leadership, and a tribune proposed a law that turned the state over to their control for a period of five years; their official title was Triumviri (body of three men) "to provide order for the state"—a charge broad enough to supply a legal basis for nearly any action they might wish to take. Thus was formed the Second Triumvirate. In due course they had their collective power renewed for another five years.

Brutus and Cassius, seeing that they did not have popular support, left for the East and in 43 B.C. were given control over all the eastern provinces. But in 42 B.C. the triumvirs eliminated these enemies at the Battle of Philippi in northern Greece. To reward their troops with land, the rulers had already marked out the territory of no fewer than eighteen prosperous towns in Italy. The rule of the Second Triumvirate (43–33 B.C.)

---

[7]Suetonius, *Life of Caesar,* chap. 77.

[8]*Letters to Atticus,* 14.11 (April 25, 44 B.C.).

was thus made secure by the seizure and redistribution of property. A series of "trials" mounted against those who had had the bad luck to be on the losing side provided further security. As in the time of Marius and Sulla, the autocrats brushed aside the traditional guarantees of Roman law as they coldly purged their enemies. The number of the slain was said to be the largest ever. Cicero had placed himself in special danger through a series of orations denouncing Antony (the "Philippics," a term recalling Demosthenes' attacks on Philip II of Macedon; see p. 90). He paid the price and was murdered on Antony's orders in 43 B.C.

◆ OCTAVIAN TRIUMPHANT

Antony and Cleopatra   Suspicion now began to grow between the two major partners, Antony and Octavian (Lepidus had been forced into retirement when he tried to take control of Sicily away from Octavian). They now both lusted for supreme power, and Antony did his own cause grave harm by remaining in the East for long periods. On the one hand, he fought a disastrous war against the Parthian kingdom, which had taken certain Roman territories after the death of Crassus in 53. On the other, he carried on a long affair with Cleopatra VII of Egypt. Octavian stayed in Rome and skillfully exploited the rumors that surrounded this romance with Cleopatra. In particular, Octavian falsely asserted that Antony was planning to place this Eastern queen in command of the state.

Octavian's Victory over Antony   The final break between the two men came in 32 B.C. Octavian raised a large force from Italy and the western provinces; led by his skillful general Marcus Agrippa, this force defeated Antony in 31 B.C. at Actium, a promontory on the western coast of Greece. Antony shamefully abandoned his men and sailed back to Egypt with Cleopatra, and his army surrendered to Octavian.

The next year Octavian unhurriedly advanced on Alexandria for the reckoning with Antony and Cleopatra. Antony took his own life, and Cleopatra soon did the same—according to the version immortalized in Shakespeare, by letting a poisonous snake bite her. With Cleopatra's death ended the last Macedonian kingdom and,

therefore, the Hellenistic Age, which had begun with the death of Alexander the Great in 323 B.C.

V. The Founding of the Roman Empire

Those Romans, like Cicero, who had hoped for the restoration of the Republic lost their hopes or their lives. Only one warlord from the Republic, Octavian, had survived the confused years after Julius Caesar. By a supreme political charade, he combined his own autocracy with the restoration of the forms of the Republic. This skillful compromise in effect created the Roman Empire, which he ruled until his death in A.D. 14.

◆ AUGUSTUS AND THE PRINCIPATE

When Octavian returned to Rome in 29 B.C. from his conquest of Egypt, he performed the ceremony of closing the gates of the temple of Janus, the double-headed god who looked both ways; this act symbolized the arrival of a state of peace. His supremacy was beyond challenge. The issue now was whether he would solve the problem that had defeated Caesar: how to rule without seeming to be an autocrat. He achieved this by restoring the appearance—but no more—of republican government. His designated candidates ran for office, and a willing Senate executed only the policies that he favored. Republican structures remained intact, but they were managed by his loyal men. At no time did he announce that he was converting the Republic into an empire. As a result, there is no official beginning for the Roman Empire; the best date is probably 27 B.C., for in that year Octavian laid the foundations of his system.

Octavian Becomes Augustus   On January 1, 27 B.C., Octavian appeared in the Roman Senate and announced that the state had returned to peace and that he needed no more extraordinary authority. He resigned his commands and took credit for restoring the Republic. But he arranged that the Senate, full of his loyal creatures, should "voluntarily" give him an enormous provincial command, consisting of Spain, Gaul, and Syria. Most of the legions were concentrated in these provinces; thus Octavian was the legal commander of most of the Roman army. Egypt was handled in a special manner. It was treated as a private possession of Octavian's and managed by his own appointee; therefore it was strictly not one of the Roman provinces.

The older, more pacified provinces (Asia, Africa, Greece, and others) were ruled by governors appointed by the Senate; thus historians speak of "imperial" (governed by the emperor) and "senatorial" provinces. Through this arrangement, Octavian showed respect to the Senate, which Caesar had largely ignored. This is another element in the statesmanship that Octavian was careful to display.

A few days later the Senate met again and conferred on Octavian the name Augustus, meaning "most honored" or "revered." This title brought with it no powers, but its semidivine overtones were useful to Augustus (as we shall now call him) in establishing his supremacy. In 23 B.C. he resigned the consulship but received two additional powers from the Senate. His imperium was extended to cover not only his provinces but the whole Roman world. He also obtained the authority of a tribune (*tribunicia potestas*). As a patrician (by his adoption into Caesar's family), Augustus could not actually be a tribune. Yet his having the "power" of a tribune suggested that he was the patron and defender of the common people of Rome. This power also gave him the legal right to veto any actions and to offer legislation. He was usually called the *princeps,* an old republican word meaning roughly "first citizen," but not an official title. This was another of his skillful pretensions to have restored the Republic. Modern writers often refer to the system that Augustus established as the Principate.

◆ AUGUSTUS, THE FIRST ROMAN EMPEROR

The Administration   The long reign of Augustus from 27 B.C. to A.D. 14 laid down many abiding features of the Roman Empire. He provided a cash payment from the public treasury to soldiers

▼ The Ara Pacis (Altar of Peace) was built in Rome in 13 B.C. to celebrate the establishment of peace by Augustus. Relatives of the imperial family are portrayed in idealizations of their stations in life rather than in strict Roman realism.
C. M. Dixon

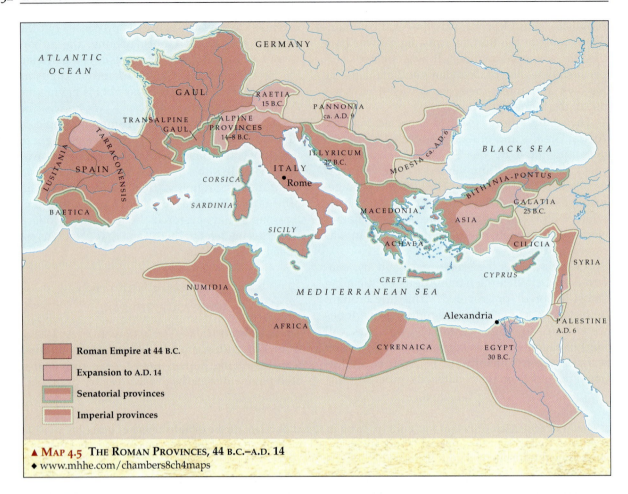

▲ **MAP 4.5** THE ROMAN PROVINCES, 44 B.C.–A.D. 14
◆ www.mhhe.com/chambers8ch4maps

Legend:
- Roman Empire at 44 B.C.
- Expansion to A.D. 14
- Senatorial provinces
- Imperial provinces

who had served for twenty years, thus securing the loyalty of the legions to the state, not to their generals. To collect the money, he had to establish a reliable civil service and reform the taxation system, enrolling in effect the whole Roman world. He made the Empire more secure by extending and solidifying the northern frontier (see map 4.5) to reach the Rhine and Danube rivers. His control was all but absolute, but most people were relieved at the ending of the long period of civil war.

He created a permanent fire department and a postal service. He formed a body of soldiers in Rome, the Praetorian Guard. This force of some nine thousand men served as the city's police force and as Augustus' personal bodyguard, but after a few decades it came to play a decisive and violent role in the designation of new emperors.

The Manipulation of Religion   Augustus also assumed the office of Pontifex Maximus, or high priest, and made attempts to revive the old Roman religion, probably as a device to promote political stability. He also grasped the possibilities of a ruler-cult. First, he assigned Julius Caesar a place among the Roman gods and built a Temple to the Deified Julius. He also called himself *Divi Filius*, or son of the divine Julius, though he was only the adopted son of Caesar. This verbal trick invited people to imagine that Augustus might some day become divine like Caesar. The poets Virgil and Horace, who wrote at his court, discreetly referred to Augustus as a future deity; and, in fact, Augustus was deified on his death, a political action that was imitated on the deaths of several later emperors who were thought to have ruled well. He also sponsored the building of temples to "Rome and Augustus"—a further suggestion, though not an offensive demand, that the emperor should be worshiped. It also became customary to make an offering to the Genius (protecting spirit) of the emperor.

Part of the religious revival was the rebuilding of scores of temples, but temples were by no means the only Augustan buildings; a famous saying was that "he found Rome made of brick and left it made of marble." The prosperity of the later years of Augustus' rule reflects the general peace that he brought to the Roman world. Freed of the expense of wars, Rome enjoyed a confidence that expressed itself in artistic and literary creativity.

Legislation, Women, and the Family Part of Augustus' program was the revival and maintenance of traditional Roman values. In this effort religion naturally played its part, but he also intervened in the areas of marriage and the family. His proclaimed intention was to restore the old Roman values of chastity and stability within the family, and the historian has little reason to doubt his sincerity. But a more realistic purpose was surely to rebuild the population of Italy after the losses in the civil wars. He therefore awarded special privileges to fathers of three or more children. The Augustan laws even penalized both men and women who did not marry or have children: for example, unmarried persons could not inherit a trust, and childless persons forfeited half their inheritances.

The legal rights of women also advanced under his legislation. Augustus issued strong laws against adultery, and women could now accuse a husband of adultery through a witness. Moreover, freedwomen (that is, former slaves) could now marry any man in Rome with exception of senators, and their children held the rank of citizens. A beautiful monument from the Augustan period, the Altar of Peace (Ara Pacis), prominently displayed women of Augustus' family—the first time that women were shown alongside men in public monumental art. Augustus was probably not working for what we would see as women's liberation, nor did he have the fixed purpose of bringing women's rights up to the level of those enjoyed by men; but these actions were at least a partial result of his work toward the repopulation of Italy.

SUMMARY
◆

The Roman Republic never gave so much power to the people as the Athenian democracy did. The dominant forces were the great political families, allied through strategic marriages. As success in war created powerful commanders, their rivalry shattered the republican constitution. Augustus was Caesar's adopted son and also his final successor, the last warlord of the Republic. He rose to power in shameless disloyalty and bloodshed. Through his careful control of the army and magistrates, he then gave Rome three decades of healing after the civil wars, and the success of his work is shown by the fact that the state did not relapse into civil war after his death. His personality seems to lack the panache of Caesar, who was invincible in the field and a talented man of letters, but his greatness before history is that he formed the structure from which modern Europe has descended—the Roman Empire.

QUESTIONS FOR FURTHER THOUGHT
◆

1. What features and conditions of life in Rome were especially conducive to the constant expansion of Rome's territorial holdings?

2. The Roman Republic had a constitution that resembled that of a Greek city-state in many ways, but it collapsed and gave way to one-man rule. How might Roman statesmen and the Senate have preserved the republican constitution?

RECOMMENDED READING

◆

Sources

Caesar, Julius. *War Commentaries*. Rex Warner (tr.). 1960 and reprints. An unsurpassed textbook in political-military decision making.

Cicero. *Selected Political Speeches*. Michael Grant (tr.). 1977.

———. *Selected Works*. Michael Grant (tr.). 1960.

Gardner, Jane F., and Thomas Wiedemann (eds.). *The Roman Household: A Sourcebook*. 1991. Translated sources of all kinds on marriage, inheritance, and relations within the family.

Livy. All surviving portions of his history of Rome are in four volumes published by Penguin (various translators). 1965–1982.

Mellor, Ronald (ed.). *The Historians of Ancient Rome: An Anthology of the Major Writings*. 1998. Collection in one volume of long excerpts from the Roman historians.

Plutarch. *Fall of the Roman Republic*. Rex Warner (tr.). 1972. Biographies of Caesar, Pompey, Cicero, and other leading politicians of the Republic.

Polybius. *The Rise of the Roman Empire*. Ian Scott-Kilvert (tr.). 1979. A generous selection from the surviving portions of the historian of Roman imperialism.

Sallust. *Jugurthine War and War with Catiline*. S. A. Handford (tr.). 1963.

Shelton, Jo-Ann (ed.). *As the Romans Did: A Sourcebook in Roman Social History*. 2d ed. 1998. Compilation of many interesting sources, arranged by categories (families, housing, education, and so on).

Studies

Bradley, Keith R. *Discovering the Roman Family*. 1991. Chapters on child labor, the role of the nurse, divorce, and so on.

Cornell, T. J. *The Beginnings of Rome*. 1995. Extensive narrative of all aspects of the early Republic. Now the best source.

Cornell, T. J., and J. Matthews. *Atlas of the Roman World*. 1982. Historical narrative, well illustrated by excellent maps.

Dixon, Suzanne. *The Roman Family*. 1992. On the development and practices of the family, following her *The Roman Mother*, 1988.

Dupont, Florence. *Daily Life in Ancient Rome*. 1992. On housing, amusements, the economy, the family.

Earl, Douglas. *The Age of Augustus*. 1980. The best survey of political and social life in the Augustan age.

Gardner, Jane F. *Women in Roman Law and Society*. 1986. On the legal position of women and its changes in Roman life.

Habicht, Christian. *Cicero the Politician*. 1990. Admirably concise treatment, placing Cicero within the circle of Roman politicians.

Keaveney, Arthur. *Sulla: The Last Republican*. 1983. Study of Sulla, stressing his program of reform.

Keppie, Lawrence. *The Making of the Roman Army: From Republic to Empire*. 1984. Good history and analysis of the working of the army.

Kleiner, Diana E. E. *Roman Sculpture*. 1992. Complete history and survey of sculpture down to A.D. 330, superbly illustrated.

Meier, Christian. *Caesar*. 1995. The most modern, comprehensive biography of Rome's greatest warrior.

Nicolet, Claude. *The World of the Citizen in Republican Rome*. 1980. On the relation between citizen and state: taxation, military service, membership in assemblies, and so on.

Pallottino, Massimo. *A History of Earliest Italy*. 1991. Culture, economics, and history of the peoples of Italy by a great Etruscologist.

Rawson, Beryl (ed.). *The Family in Ancient Rome*. 1986. Essays on various topics.

Richardson, Lawrence, Jr. *A New Topographical Dictionary of Ancient Rome*. 1992. Lists all known buildings and topographic features; first work to consult on any such question.

Richlin, Amy. *The Garden of Priapus: Sexuality and Aggression in Roman Humor*. 1983. On the often ribald content of Latin literature.

Scullard, H. H. *From the Gracchi to Nero*. 5th ed. 1982. The best textbook narrative of the central period of the Republic and the early Empire.

Seager, Robin. *Pompey: A Political Biography*. 1979. Brief, readable study of the man involved in many central political crises.

Stockton, David. *The Gracchi.* 1979. The best modern study of the two politicians who discovered and used popular support.

Syme, Ronald. *The Roman Revolution.* Originally 1939. The greatest study of the classical world in the last century; brilliant analysis of the collapse of the Republic. For advanced students.

Zanker, Paul. *The Power of Images in the Age of Augustus.* 1988. Architecture, coinage, and other types of art as part of the Augustan program of propaganda.

▲ Gaius Octavius, given the title "Augustus" by the Roman Senate, is portrayed as ruler and military commander in this idealized statue.

Chapter 5

THE EMPIRE AND CHRISTIANITY

The history of the Roman Empire is one of amazing continuity. The system of government devised by Augustus and maintained by his successors gave the Empire two centuries of solid prosperity. Historians call this the period of the *Pax Romana,* "the Roman Peace," and the Empire as a system of government remained an ideal in Europe for centuries. In the history of the Empire, one of the main themes is the working of a cohesive political organization. The carefully crafted administration managed the greatest of all ancient Empires, and its remains—stadiums, public baths, marketplaces, temples, official buildings—have inspired imitations down into our own times.

At the beginning of the third century, the Empire entered a period of crisis. Control of the army became the key to power, and emperors and would-be emperors followed one another in confusing succession. When order finally returned during the fourth century, the old Roman Empire was no more. In the East, the Byzantine Empire was formed; in the West, the Empire steadily declined, finally ceasing to be governed by Roman emperors in A.D. 476.

But even as antiquity was passing, ancient peoples were laying the basis for a new form of civilization. A change of religion became the second large historical theme in the Empire, as a new set of beliefs emerged: Christianity, which was destined to transform the life and culture of the Western heirs of the Roman Empire.

CHAPTER 5. THE EMPIRE AND CHRISTIANITY							
	Social Structure	Body Politic	Changes in the Organization of Production and in the Impact of Technology	Evolution of Family and Changing Gender Roles	War	Religion	Cultural Expression
I. THE EMPIRE AT ITS HEIGHT							
II. THE PERIOD OF CRISIS							
III. THE LATE ROMAN EMPIRE							
IV. CHRISTIANITY AND ITS EARLY RIVALS							

I. The Empire at Its Height

Three unifying elements preserved the Roman Empire that Augustus founded. First was the figure of the emperor, whom all subjects identified as the head of the regime. With some exceptions, the emperors were competent, stable rulers until about A.D. 200. Second were the civil servants and city councils, who collected taxes and maintained urban life. Third was the army, both the ultimate security of the emperor himself and the protector of the frontiers. The three elements supported one another, and the failure of any one of them threatened the other two and thus the fabric of the state (see "Tacitus on the Powers of Augustus," p. 139).

◆ THE SUCCESSORS OF AUGUSTUS

The Julio-Claudian Dynasty The first emperor, Augustus, had no male heir. His last wife, Livia, was from the old patrician clan of the Claudians and evidently persuaded him to adopt her son, Tiberius, and to designate Tiberius as his successor. She thus played a leading role in the shaping of the imperial dynasty.

After the death of Augustus in A.D. 14, the Senate recognized Tiberius as ruler and thus confirmed the principle of dynastic succession, establishing the fact that an empire, not a republic, now existed. The dynasty founded by Augustus is known as the Julio-Claudian, because of a complex series of marriages between the Julian and Claudian clans. This dynasty reigned until

A.D. 68. Much can be said against the rule of the Julio-Claudians. Tiberius was morbid, suspicious, and vengeful. His successor, Gaius (nicknamed Caligula), suffered from insanity and was murdered by the emperor's bodyguard, known as the Praetorian Guard. Claudius was gullible and was manipulated by his assistants and wives, the last of whom probably poisoned him to secure the throne for her son Nero. Nero ruled with some efficiency for his first five years but then became one of the worst emperors, whose tyranny led to a rebellion in Gaul. When the revolt spread to Rome, he saw that he was doomed and killed himself.

Yet these emperors did maintain, and even expand, the heritage left by Augustus. Claudius, for example, saw to the conquest of southern Britain, which became a Roman province in 47. He established new provinces and founded the city of Cologne in what is now Germany. Moreover, the Empire remained at peace internally, and the provincial administration that Augustus had established continued to function effectively.

Imperial Administration The process of centralization of power in the person of the emperor and away from the Senate continued. Tiberius transferred election of magistrates from the people to the Senate; in effect, those whom he "recommended" were automatically elected. Claudius turned many affairs of state over to his trusted assistants, usually Greeks who had been freed from slavery (thus called *freedmen*), who helped to found the bureaucracy that more and more ran the Empire.

TACITUS ON THE POWERS OF AUGUSTUS

◆

The first emperor of Rome, Augustus, maintained that he had restored the Republic after years of civil war. The historian Tacitus, writing about A.D. 120, gave a different evaluation of his work.

"After Brutus and Cassius were killed, the state had no military force.... Even the party of Julius Caesar had no leader left but Augustus, who laid aside the title of Triumvir and called himself a consul. For controlling the people, he contented himself with the rights of a tribune. When he had seduced the army with gifts, the people with distributions of food, and everyone with the pleasure of general calm, he began little by little to increase his authority and to gather to himself the powers of the Senate, the magistrates, and the laws. No one opposed him, since the strongest men had fallen either in battle or through legalized executions, and the rest of the no-bles, according to who was more ready to accept servitude, were awarded gifts and public offices; since they profited from the new arrangements, they preferred their present security to the previous uncertainties. The provinces, too, accepted this state of affairs, since the former government by the Senate and people was suspect, owing to the struggles among the powerful and the greed of local governors; the protection of the laws had been worthless, because the laws were constantly overturned by violence, intrigue, and finally outright bribery."

From Tacitus, *Annals*, Book 1, ch. 2, trans. M. H. Chambers.

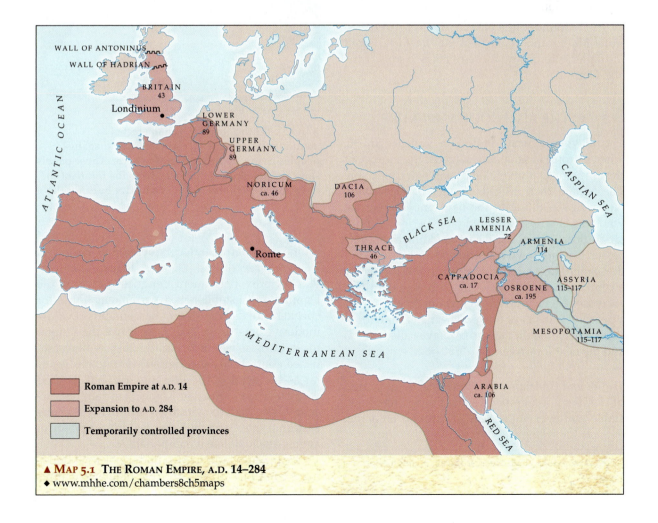

Roman Empire at A.D. 14

Expansion to A.D. 284

Temporarily controlled provinces

▲ MAP 5.1 THE ROMAN EMPIRE, A.D. 14–284
◆ www.mhhe.com/chambers8ch5maps

Interventions by the Army   Another factor that weakened senatorial power was the frequent interference in affairs of state by the Praetorian Guard. The Guard first intervened in politics in 41, when it forced the Senate to recognize Claudius as emperor. It did the same for Nero in 54. This repeated invasion of civil authority by the Praetorian Guard was a step on the road toward militarization; within little more than a century, the emperors were to become totally dependent for power on their ability to buy the good will of the soldiery. The army, which had kept the emperors secure, sometimes became a force beyond control.

The military played a significant role in the struggle over the succession after Nero's death in 68, as troops in various quarters of the Empire backed their own candidates for emperor. The year 69 is often called "the year of the four emperors" because in the course of the year four men claimed to be emperor. Vespasian finally stabilized the situation and emerged as sole ruler late in 69. He founded the Flavian dynasty (so called from his second name, Flavius), which lasted through his reign and those of his two sons, Titus and Domitian.

◆ THE FIVE GOOD EMPERORS

The Flavian dynasty ended in violence in 96, when a group of senators instigated the murder of the emperor Domitian, Vespasian's despotic son. The Senate then picked a quiet older senator, Nerva (r. 96–98),[1] to be the new emperor. Nerva, who was childless, adopted an experienced military officer, Trajan, and designated him as his successor. The next two emperors, also childless, did the same. This system remained in use for nearly a century: An emperor would choose a qualified successor and adopt him as his son, thus ensuring a peaceful transfer of power. The men thus chosen were so capable that historians have called Nerva and the next four rulers the "five good emperors."

Trajan and Hadrian   On the whole, in the period of the five good emperors, the Empire remained stable and even expanded. Trajan was an active

---

[1]The letter *r.* before a date or series of dates stands for "reigned."

▲ In A.D. 113 the emperor Trajan erected a monumental column to celebrate his war against peoples living across the Danube River. These panels show preparations for the war. Note the figure of the river god at the bottom, under a bridge built for the army.
Trëe.

military emperor and conquered the region of Dacia, north of the Danube River. This was Rome's only permanent conquest north of the Danube and established a permanent home for speakers of Latin; their descendants occupy modern Romania. In 116 Trajan drove the Empire to its farthest extension to the east as he established control over the Tigris-Euphrates valley as far as the head of the Persian Gulf; but he died while trying to return to Rome. Hadrian, his successor, decided to withdraw from this extreme eastern position; he thus changed from a policy of aggressive to defensive imperialism.

Trajan and Hadrian also undertook vast building programs. Trajan erected many structures throughout the Empire. Especially, he built a huge new forum (the Forum of Trajan) in central Rome and placed there an impressive column, which preserves a series of scenes recording episodes in his wars north of the Danube. This new Forum had a large group of buildings—shops, offices, a library—to the east of his column. Hadrian's most famous building project is Hadrian's wall (much of it still stands), built across Britain to protect the frontier between the Roman province of Britain and the areas controlled by Celtic tribes to the north. In Italy, among other projects, he had built an immense luxurious "villa," actually a small town, south of Rome near Tivoli.

Hadrian continued the development of a frank autocracy. Laws now came down straight from the emperor and were known as "decisions" (*constitutiones*). Often the Senate was not even formally invited to approve such laws. He sought advice from an informal council known as the "friends" (*amici*) of the emperor, which included the leading experts in Roman law. One of these, Salvius Julianus, collected the edicts that Roman praetors had issued over the centuries, in an attempt to standardize the procedures of civil law; this action pointed the way toward the great codification of law in the sixth century under the emperor Justinian (see chapter 6). Hadrian's laws, though issued without any pretense of democratic process, were generally fair and humane. They tried to improve the condition of soldiers and slaves and gave women the same rights in court as men.

Antoninus Pius, Marcus Aurelius Hadrian arranged the succession of the next two emperors, Antoninus Pius (r. 138–161) and Marcus Aurelius (r. 161–180), who are the last of the "five good emperors." The rule of Antoninus was peaceful, and under the reign of Marcus Aurelius the Empire

▼ **The emperor Hadrian had this famous wall built across Britain to mark off the Roman Empire and keep foreign peoples out.**
C. M. Dixon

enjoyed its last years of prosperity. Meanwhile, hostile new peoples were massing to the north and east of the imperial frontiers. In the final years of Marcus' reign, the gathering storm broke in all its fury, and he had to spend years fighting invasions by peoples on the Danube River and in the East.

One campaign was especially disastrous, because the army returning from Asia Minor in the 160s brought with it a devastating plague that spread through much of Europe. This plague must have been one cause of the later weakening of Rome, but the nearly total lack of records prevents our knowing how many died.

Unfortunately, Marcus abandoned the principle of adoption and passed the throne to his worthless son, Commodus (r. 180–192), whose extravagance and cruelty were reminiscent of Nero and Domitian. His murder on the last day of 192 opened a period of terrible instability, to which we shall return (pp. 149–151).

◆ ROMAN IMPERIAL CIVILIZATION

The Economy of the Cities   The first two centuries of the Empire are often called the "higher" Empire. In this period Italy and the provinces reached a level of prosperity and of flourishing population that Europe would not see again for a thousand years. The results of Roman censuses, which have partially survived, indicate that Italy at the death of Augustus contained about 7.5 million inhabitants. (In about 1500, the earliest date at which we can make a comparable estimate, the same area contained about 10 million people.)

Cities in the Empire   In the Western provinces, cities were, for the most part, small; to judge from the area enclosed by Roman walls, most towns contained only a few thousand residents. Yet they usually imitated Rome with temples, markets, arenas, courthouses, and other public buildings and thus displayed an authentic urban character. In the East, cities were often much larger. Alexandria in Egypt is estimated to have had about 400,000 inhabitants; Ephesus in Asia Minor, 200,000; Antioch in Syria, 150,000. The size of the cities in the East is surely one reason why the economy in the Eastern part of the Empire was stronger than that in the Western part.

Largest of all the imperial cities, and a true wonder of the ancient world, was Rome. Estimates of its size generally suggest about 1 million inhabitants. Not until the eighteenth century would European cities again contain such a concentration of people; in the 1780s, for example, Paris held about 600,000 people. Roman civil engineering maintained, even under crowded conditions, acceptable standards of public hygiene and supplied enormous quantities of pure water and food.

Agriculture   Agriculture still remained the basic support of the economy, supplying, according to rough estimates, more than 75 percent of the total product of the Empire. One important change in Italian agriculture in the last century of the Republic had been shrinkage in the number of small peasant farms. They gave way to great slave-run estates, called *latifundia*, which generally produced cash crops. The owners of the big *latifundia* were wealthy senators and equestrians, even entrepreneurs from outside the traditional governing classes. Trimalchio, a freed slave who appears as a character in Petronius' novel, the *Satyricon*, boasted that he could ride from Rome to the area near Naples without leaving his own land.

The managers of these vast plantations favored varied forms of agriculture—cultivating vines, olives, and fruit and raising large numbers of cattle, sheep, and goats. Only enough grain was cultivated to feed the resident staff of workers, most of them slaves. The great estates also supplied the cities with building stone, lumber, and firewood; huge quantities of wood were required, for example, to keep the Roman baths at comfortable temperatures. In the view of many historians, extensive deforestation and overgrazing led inevitably to erosion of the land and the loss of fertile topsoil—principal reasons for the economic decline of Roman Italy. Even ancient peoples had the power to injure their environments.

Economies in the Provinces   In the provinces, the "Roman peace" favored the development of what had once been backward areas to the point that they threatened Italy's economic leadership. The wine market, for example, passed into the hands of Spanish cultivators in the second century, for Spanish wine rivaled Italian in quality and was

▲ An arch built by the emperor Trajan at Beneventum. Some panels show sacrifices to the gods, and the whole was intended to commemorate Trajan's generosity to his people. Triumphal and commemorative arches were among the proudest monuments in Rome and have been imitated in many modern cities.
Nimatallah/Art Resource, NY

cheaper to produce, thanks to lower labor costs. In some areas of industry, too, the provinces began to outrun Italian production.

One of the main Italian industries was pottery, but by about A.D. 50 pottery made in Gaul had replaced Italian pottery even in Italy and had also taken over the market in the provinces and military camps. Thus Rome's success in establishing a commercial network created markets for products from the provinces and eventually contributed to Italy's own economic decline.

City Life in Italy   The upper class in Rome lived on a far higher scale, and was more widely separated from the common people, than the rich of Greece. The wealthy had running water tapped into their homes, slaves to tend them hand and foot, and elegant country villas for recreation.

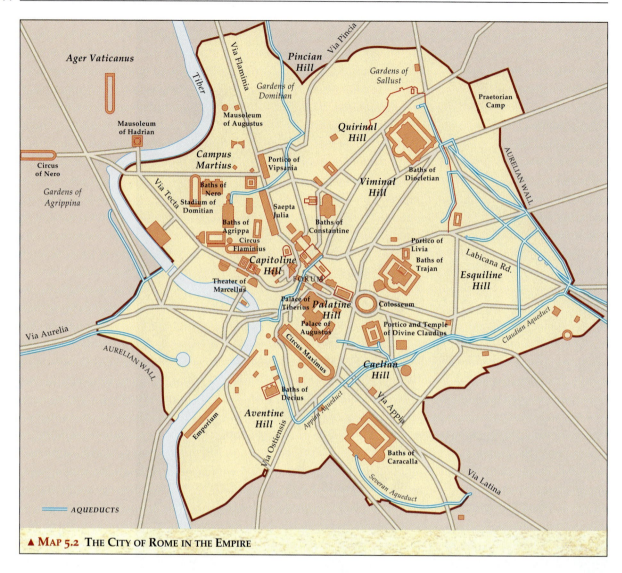

▲ MAP 5.2 THE CITY OF ROME IN THE EMPIRE

Hadrian's villa, or country retreat, near Rome was the size of a small city. These villas approached economic self-sufficiency, because slaves manufactured articles of light industry (clothing, leather goods, domestic utensils) on the farms.

A modern feature of Roman cities was the existence of suburbs and resorts. Pompeii was a commercial town, but its neighbor Herculaneum was a residential suburb. Both towns, buried and thus preserved by the volcanic eruption of Mt. Vesuvius in 79, contain examples of the airy Roman house, built around a central open court, or atrium, and decorated with graceful wall paintings.

The Working Classes The workers of Rome had no such elegant housing, living rather in flimsy and inflammable apartments in high-rise buildings. They often had to plod up a hundred steps or more to their crowded rooms. A bed was the only place for sitting or eating, and the window opened to a noisy street. Rooms lacked running water, but a complex system of aqueducts gave easy access to water outside the home, and Rome always took pride in its enormous, cheap public baths.

There were associations in Rome for every kind of worker: fishermen, engineers, cobblers, silk workers, and so on. Despite their small, crowded apartments, city laborers had working conditions that were beyond the dreams of a Near Eastern peasant. They worked only about six or seven hours a day, and the Roman year contained about

160 holidays, to which the state added from time to time special days of celebration. The modern American actually works longer hours than the ancient Roman, despite our labor-saving devices.

Social Conditions The major amusements for the people during days of leisure were public games, especially chariot races, which brought honor and wealth to the skilled charioteers, in arenas such as the huge Circus Maximus. Besides races, the Romans gave themselves over to brutal contests, which sometimes went on to death, between professional gladiators or between men and animals. The main arena for these spectacles was the grandiose Colosseum, begun by the emperor Vespasian in the 70s. It held about 50,000 spectators, and much of it still stands in central Rome, probably the one monument that most vividly recalls the classical city.

Rome was wealthy enough to support roughly half its population at public expense through free allotments of food, especially grain, which was the most common item in the diet. In the less prosperous years after 200 the cost of these subsidies placed a heavy strain on the Empire's economy.

The Mixture in Society Social mobility became easier under the Empire. For example, some Greeks who had been freed from slavery enjoyed enviable careers as secretaries to emperors or as businessmen. The need for more troops opened new opportunities for provincials, who entered the Roman legions, especially during the second century and later; and even the Senate began to include men born in the provinces. In time the Empire became less "Roman," for in both manpower and economic strength the primacy of Italy was of the past.

▼ **A well-preserved apartment house (second to third century A.D.) in the city of Ostia, which served Rome as a port. The dwelling space is located over shops on the ground floor. The tradition of snack bars everywhere in Rome and Italy is an old one.**
C. M. Dixon

Women and the Family The gains in the status of women continued in the Empire, above all within the families of the ruling elite, who lived in remarkable luxury. But more than this, women in the court of the emperor could even achieve political power comparable to that of such queens in the Hellenistic age as Cleopatra. Livia, the last wife of Augustus, is said to have met with ambassadors of foreign states in the absence of Augustus and to have seen to the advancement of her political favorites. As we have seen, Augustus adopted her son, Tiberius, who became the second emperor of Rome; when Augustus died and was officially proclaimed a god, Livia became the priestess of his cult and received the title Augusta, a parallel to his own name Augustus.

Later in the history of the Julio-Claudian dynasty, Agrippina the Younger, a descendant of Augustus, showed equal political skill in getting her son chosen as the emperor Nero. She married the emperor Claudius, who already had a son from another marriage, and then persuaded Claudius to adopt her son; she probably poisoned Claudius and then obtained the support of the Praetorian Guard for Nero, whom the Senate recognized as emperor. Her influence over Nero in his early years made her almost a co-emperor, and her face appeared on official coins along with his.

The faces of other mothers and wives of emperors were struck on coins, and there were statues to women of the imperial court at many places in the Empire. Of course, not many women could attain such eminence, and the traditional values remained for most women: chastity and deference to the husband, loving care toward the children. In a famous epitaph, a Roman butcher said of his wife,

> She preceded me in death, my one and only, chaste in body,
> loving in spirit, faithful to her faithful husband, always
> cheerful, never neglecting her duty through greed.

Roman Law A complex system of law and procedure was one of the chief cultural contributions of Roman civilization. Roman law had already developed under the Republic, but its further development under the Empire made it even more all-embracing. The Stoic philosophy influenced Roman legal thought, through the idea that the universe is inherently rational and that life should be guided by reason. Moreover, Roman legal thought recognized a kind of natural law, valid for all people, which could be discovered through rational inquiry. At times, especially in periods of crisis, weaker members of society could not always obtain justice; but the overriding social purpose of Roman law was to provide justice rather than simply maintain the stability of the state. As an example, "natural law" denied the legality of slavery.

The Growth of the Roman Legal System The assemblies of the Republic, both that of the Centuries and that of the Tribes (see chapter 4), issued laws mainly on large public issues, such as distributions of land or assignments of military commands overseas. Another influence on the law came from magistrates, especially praetors, who issued edicts that explained the principles by which they would interpret the law during their year in office; these edicts acquired the authority of tradition and ultimately passed into permanent law.

Normally, cases came before a judge, who was a private citizen relying on the advice of other private citizens who were reputed to understand the law but did not actually practice law. These advisers were called jurists (*iurisprudentes* or *iurisconsulti*), and their opinions constantly influenced the growth of the law, especially in the first two centuries of the Empire. They could also rise to high political office. Among the most important jurists were Ulpian, Paulus, and Gaius. They delivered written responses, with authority delegated to them by the emperors, to questions raised by presiding judges and relied mainly on "natural law" for their opinions. Their responses thus shaped Roman laws, even when the laws themselves were issued by emperors as *constitutiones*. They also wrote voluminous commentaries on the law, and their opinions are widely preserved in the final great codification of the law by Justinian in the sixth century.

Citizens and Noncitizens in Roman Law The Romans distinguished their own citizens from the other peoples under their control. Roman citizens were subject to the "civil law" (*ius civile*), or law

◀ **The Sacred Way leads into the Roman Forum through the Arch of Titus, which was erected to celebrate the end of the great Jewish rebellion in A.D. 70. A triumphal procession would enter the Forum through this elegantly placed arch and parade up to the Temple of Jupiter on the Capitoline Hill.**
Trëe

applying to citizens. The number of people subject to this law grew constantly as citizenship was extended to more and more inhabitants. Finally, the emperor Caracalla decreed that all free men and women in the Empire should be citizens, thus subject to the *ius civile.*

Down to the time of this mass grant of Roman citizenship, inhabitants of the Empire who were not citizens had the right to maintain many of their own customs, which came to form the *ius gentium,* or law applying to other nations. These two kinds of law fell, logically enough, to two magistrates for administration, the "urban praetor" (*praetor urbanus*) and the "traveling praetor" (*praetor peregrinus*). But when all free men and women became citizens, the *ius gentium* in this sense was no longer needed.[2]

The Romans' respect for their law is consistent with the remarkable cohesiveness that one sees throughout their society. In war they were often brutal, but then so were many others in all periods of history. Rome's achievement in designing and preserving a system of laws governing the behavior of citizens toward one another has served as a model for much of the law of Western Europe. Codes of law, as we have also observed, are a feature of several other ancient societies, but in richness and complexity the codifications of the late Roman Empire easily surpass all the rest.

Engineering and Architecture The Romans showed brilliance in the fields of engineering and construction. The most enduring monument to Roman civilization is the impressive network of roads found everywhere from Britain to Africa. Originally designed as highways for the rapid movement of legions, these roads became trade routes in more peaceful times and eliminated all barriers to travel.

---

[2]In Roman legal theory, *ius gentium* came to mean a kind of universal law observed by all nations, in effect, a system of law that could be discovered by reason.

From the earliest times the Romans also built aqueducts that converged toward the cities, sloping down and carrying fresh water from the mountains; Rome's imposing system of sewers was constantly flushed by water from the aqueducts. The Romans placed more emphasis on personal cleanliness than did any other civilization until modern times. Several emperors commissioned the building of immense public baths, of which the grandest of all were the Baths of Caracalla at Rome, built in the third century. The English city of Bath is named for the facilities that the Romans built there.

Roman temples, imitating those of the Greeks, were supported by columns, usually in the Corinthian style, crowned with a bell-like acanthus flower. Their temples had large interiors and were often completely walled at the rear, because Romans performed their ceremonies indoors. They were the first to grasp the possibilities of using arches and vaults on a large scale, thus giving their buildings a vastness that the Greeks could not achieve.

Large Buildings in Concrete   The Romans also invented concrete, which is inexpensive and can be laid by relatively unskilled labor. It can be shaped into forms impossible in marble, and it is lighter in weight and can easily be supported in vaulted buildings. One of its most successful applications is the spacious Pantheon—built in the time of Augustus and then rebuilt under Hadrian—covered by a dome with a striking opening in the center. Sculpture and architecture coincided in triumphal arches, which often bear reliefs depicting the historical event that the arch commemorates.

Literature in the Empire: Virgil   In Rome, literature was generally the entertainment of the upper classes. In Greece, by contrast, dramas were presented before as many as fifteen thousand spectators, many of them people of the lowest social rank. Augustus, the first emperor, favored several of the most famous Latin poets at his court. Perhaps the leading Latin poet was Virgil (70–19 B.C.). He borrowed from Greek models, as Roman poets often did. His early poems, the *Bucolics* (also called *Eclogues*) and *Georgics,* are polished hymns of praise to the Italian landscape that reflect the style of Theocritus and Hesiod; but the gentle, human spirit of Virgil himself is always present. The best qualities of Virgil appear when he treats civilized emotions—mercy, compassion, and sadness; then his work echoes with a graceful melancholy.

These qualities appear in his patriotic epic, the *Aeneid,* which adopts and transforms materials from Homer. In this work Virgil narrates the wanderings of Aeneas, the Trojan whose descendants were the legendary founders of Rome. Leaving his native city after the fall of Troy, Aeneas reached Carthage and had a romance with its queen, Dido; but his sense of duty compelled him to abandon her in order to reach Italy and fulfill his destiny. Virgil's aim was to sing the glory of Rome and its salvation by Augustus after the civil wars of the late Republic. Virgil knew Augustus, was a favorite at Augustus' court, and at times wrote what could be considered official propaganda.

Satire: Horace, Juvenal   A contemporary of Virgil's was Horace, whose *Odes, Epodes,* and *Satires* examine love, amusement, annoyance, contentment—in short, the feelings of everyday life. He too was well connected with the court of Augustus. Now and then Horace makes an attempt at serious patriotic verse, but these poems are self-conscious and moralizing and do not speak with the real Horatian voice of gentle, amusing irony.

Juvenal, a more pungent satirist than Horace, wrote shortly after A.D. 100. He took as his motto "Indignation inspires my poetry" (*facit indignatio versum*). His poems denounce the excess of pride and elegance in Roman society. His language is colorful, often bitter and obscene. One of his richest and wisest satires concerns the vanity of human wishes. After reviewing the foolishness of human beings, Juvenal gives his advice in a famous epigram: One should pray for "a sound mind in a sound body" (*mens sana in corpore sano*).

Poetry of Love   There was also a rich literature of sexuality. The poet Ovid (43 B.C.–A.D. 17) wrote a handbook for seduction, *The Art of Love,* and a treatise on love affairs. Perhaps because of his frankly sexual subject matter, Augustus exiled him to a distant town in the Black Sea region: a reminder that the peace and order under the Empire did not always guarantee personal freedom. The poet Propertius (47 B.C.?–2 B.C.?) and others also wrote of their mistresses; and the Greek satirist Lucian (A.D. 120?–185?) has left a racy *Dialogue of the Courtesans*.

Historians: Livy   The histories of Rome written during the Republic were usually the work of men directly involved in politics. Under the Empire this situation changed because political contest had almost vanished. It therefore seemed appropriate to look back on the Republic and write a final history of its politics and imperialism. Titus Livius, or Livy, undertook this task during the reign of Augustus, when the decisive political transformation occurred. Livy narrated Roman history from its legendary beginnings until 9 B.C. Because he usually drew on the work of earlier historians, he was sometimes unable to escape the influence of the myths that had clouded the history of the early Republic; thus he is at his best when he uses a good source such as the Greek historian Polybius.

Livy's *Roman History* is a kind of prose epic, filled with patriotism and admiration for the great men who had led Rome when the Republic was conquering the Mediterranean. He also suggests that Rome had declined in moral standards. Livy was the last writer in Latin to attempt a full history of Rome. His work inspired many later writers who looked back at the Republic as the Golden Age of Rome; it was accepted as authoritative until soon after 1800, when historians began to be more skeptical about Roman tradition.

Tacitus   The leading Roman historian in intellectual stature was Cornelius Tacitus (55?–120?). His first major work is the *Histories*, in which he treats Roman history from 69, the year of the four emperors, through the death of Domitian in 96, emphasizing the analysis of character. Deeply influenced by satire, the dominant literary form of his age, Tacitus loved to fashion stinging epigrams aimed at members of the governing class, and he treated nearly all his main characters as selfish or corrupt. His disillusioned attitude was partly the result of his being an outsider, probably from southern Gaul; he saw Roman society through the cool eyes of a man from a province who became a senator and even rose to the office of consul.

His most important work is the *Annals*, which covers the reign of the Julio-Claudian emperors from Tiberius through Nero. Tacitus looked back at the early Empire from the vantage point of a later period. Though he said he wrote "without anger or partisanship" (*sine ira et studio*),[3] he found little good to say about the first emperors, and few modern critics would call him impartial. At his best, Tacitus sets a high standard of accuracy, but his wish for accuracy was sometimes at war with his desire to send a moral message about the failings of this or that regime.

II. The Period of Crisis (192–284)

◆

The Roman Empire, at its height, was in modern language the superpower of the Western world. There was no other state or system that could be called an empire, and certainly none that could challenge or threaten it. But in the third century of our era the Empire faltered and stumbled. The three unifying elements all appeared to be at the end of their strength. Emperors proved to be either weak or corrupt; the civil service was demoralized; and the army was broken up into factions that supported now one emperor, now another. The collapse of these three bulwarks of the state brought the economy crashing to ruin.

◆ THE CRISIS OF LEADERSHIP

The centuries of the "Roman peace" ended with the death of the emperor Commodus in 192, and in the following years the political balance shifted to the military. The next generation faced an all but fatal military and political crisis. Wars broke out on the European frontiers, and most emperors could survive only a few years. During the third century, dozens of emperors claimed the throne, but many of these men were really no more than political gamblers or warlords who for a short time purchased the loyalty of their soldiers. Thus two of the stabilizing elements of the Empire—the strong, effective emperor and the disciplined army—began to fall apart.

---

[3] *Annals*, 1.1.

◀ The ancient Greek city Ephesus, on the coast of Turkey, remained prosperous in the Empire. Tiberius Julius Celsus, consul in A.D. 92, endowed this magnificent library, which his son completed about 135.
Comstock

The Roman Senate, which had once been the inspiration and bulwark of the state, now had neither interest nor ability to intervene in affairs of state, while the emperors assumed more and more dictatorial powers and governed through court favorites. The economy of the Empire, too, nearly collapsed during this period, largely because defense costs had risen as raiders plundered the wealth of the Empire on several frontiers. Moreover, the emperors had been supplying the inhabitants of Rome with free food and public games, or "bread and circuses," in the phrase of Juvenal the satirist—a fairly effective means of political domination, but a heavy drain on the economy. Adding to these financial problems was a shortage of silver, on which the imperial currency was based. The emperors resorted to debasing the currency, but this action forced people to hoard what silver they had and actually drove more of the metal out of circulation.

A further problem was the increasing reluctance of people of independent means to hold civic offices, which paid no salary. Moreover, office holders were forced to pay from their own pockets any deficiency in the collection of taxes. Finally, the government had to compel people to take office, a step that pointed to the practice of binding people to their occupations. This in turn led to the collapse of the third crucial element of stability in the state, the efficient administrators and civil servants. Many of the emperors during the century of crisis were men of little leadership; but some of them must have been among the ablest rulers in the history of Rome, for otherwise the Empire would have totally disintegrated.

◆ WEAKNESSES IN THE INSTITUTION OF SLAVERY

Like most other ancient states, Rome used slaves widely. The historian's task is not simply to denounce this repugnant system, but to understand its place in Roman society. No earlier society had organized the institution of slavery to such a degree or used slaves in such large numbers. Ancient slavery, unlike slavery in the United States, never comprised members of only one ethnic group. Anyone might have the bad luck to be rounded up and forced into slavery. During the late Republic, the number of available slaves increased dramatically, as Rome overran Greece, Asia Minor, Spain, and Gaul. Julius Caesar reports in his *Gallic War* that he once sold 53,000 Gauls into slavery in a single day. One owner of a large estate mentioned in his will that he owned no fewer than 4,116 slaves. Of the 7.5 million inhabitants of Italy at the death of Augustus, an estimated 3 million were slaves.

The mounting flood of cheap slaves allowed the expansion of the great plantations during the last century of the Roman Republic. In most places slaves were more or less adequately fed. On the other hand, in Sicily they were often turned loose without shelter to feed off the land.

Slaves had a better life in the cities, where they served as artisans, hairdressers, secretaries, and personal servants. Slaves from the East, Greeks in particular, commonly tutored the children of the free classes. Slaves supplied much of the entertainment in ancient society. Girls and boys who could sing, dance, or recite were highly valued; there was also active traffic in beautiful young slaves of both sexes, often for sexual purposes. Gladiators were slaves and reputedly fought harder because of it. If they prevailed over an opponent, they might win their freedom; if they lost, they forfeited nothing more than a miserable existence.

Judged solely as an economic system, ancient slavery offered the Empire certain advantages. It permitted a calculated use of labor in relation to land and capital. But in the long run, the slave system of antiquity also had serious weaknesses, which we must include in the causes for the decline of the Empire in the West. Rome declined in part because its economy could no longer support the army needed to defend the frontiers against invaders. Why was the economy not equal to the task? One principal reason was that the slave system could not resolve two problems that every economy must face: the creation of incentives, to ensure that workers will labor hard and well; and the recruitment of replacements for the aging and the dead. The possibility of being freed provided some incentive to workers, but on the whole the plight of the slave was scarcely to be envied.

Especially in the countryside, the principal incentive that bent slaves to their tasks was the dread of punishment. For this reason, they were best employed in work that required little skill, diligence, or effort. The association of slavery with physical labor drained work of its dignity and dampened interest in technological innovation. And, in the view of most historians, demoralized slaves were poor producers of children, even when they were allowed to marry. Why pass misery down the generations? And conquests ceased from the time of Hadrian, a fact that threatened the continued supply of slaves.

◆ THE PLIGHT OF THE POOR

Within the free population, the spread of the great estates in the last century of the Republic had driven many small cultivators off the land. Many displaced workers drifted to the Roman metropolis, where free bread and circuses purchased their docility. In many provinces, too, rural depopulation and the abandonment of cultivated fields had become a major problem in the centuries after Augustus.

Faced with shrinking numbers of cultivators and taxpayers, the Roman government sought desperately to reclaim and resettle the abandoned fields. For example, Marcus Aurelius initiated a policy of settling foreigners on deserted lands within the Empire. The state also sought to attract free Roman cultivators back to the countryside. The free cultivator who settled on another's land was called a *colonus*, and the institution was called the *colonate*.

The Poor and the Land   Roman policy toward the *coloni* and other free cultivators was ambivalent and shifting. In many cases the *colonus* did well, with a light and fixed rent that he paid to the landlord, or *dominus*. He could sell the land he improved or pass it on to his heirs, and he could depart from it at will. But by the fourth century the picture was much worse: The *colonus* was bound to the soil, as were his children after him, and he was subject to the personal jurisdiction of his lord. The long-term interests of society dictated that resettlement within family-owned farms should be encouraged. On the other hand, the hard-pressed government could not overlook any source of revenue, and it often resorted to outrageous fiscal practices. It ruthlessly requisitioned food; it forced settlers to pay the taxes of their absent neighbors; and it subjugated settlers to the authority of their landlords, who could be held responsible for collecting from them services and taxes. By the fourth and fifth centuries, under conditions of devastating fiscal oppression, some peasants preferred to flee the Empire rather than face ruin at home.

III. The Late Roman Empire

The crisis of the third century came close to a disaster that might have carried the Empire straight to its death. But some of the many emperors, both desperate and determined, managed to hold off invasions on the frontiers. The system designed by Augustus and maintained by his successors proved to have enough resources to weather the storm. As the Empire regained stability, it could not return to the old system in which the Senate provided a measure of guidance and contributed efficient governors. The only promise for the future lay in a strict vertical system. Meanwhile, in the world of faith the old Roman deities commanded less and less devotion, and a change of gods could not be halted or reversed.

◆ RESTORATION UNDER DIOCLETIAN

The Rule of Diocletian (r. 284–305) The political crisis of the third century finally ended in 284 when Diocletian, a high army officer, seized the imperial throne. He was from the peasantry of Illyria and was a strong, ruthless man who ruled through an authoritarian bureaucracy. Recognizing that the Empire was too large and too unstable to be directed by one man, Diocletian enlisted three associates to assist him in ruling. The two senior men (Diocletian and Maximian) bore the title Augustus; the two younger (Galerius and Constantius) were known as Caesar. Modern historians call this arrangement the Tetrarchy (rule of four). Each of the four rulers was placed wherever he was needed.

In order to solve the financial crisis, Diocletian had every plot of land taxed at a certain amount, to be paid to the emperor's agents. Trades and professions were also taxed so that the burden would not fall solely on landowners. The cities in the Empire had long had a local council or *curia*; the officials, called *curiales*, were personally responsible for the required tax and had to pay it themselves if they could not collect it from others. Diocletian tried to hold back inflation with a famous Edict on Prices, which fixed maximum prices for nearly all goods and also fixed maximum wages. But natural economic forces led to

▲ The Tetrarchs (Diocletian and his corulers), shown supporting each other, on a corner of St. Mark's cathedral in Venice: Diocletian and Maximian are on the right; Galerius and Constantius on the left. The heads on the swords are Germanic.
Michael Holford Photographs

further inflation, and he had to let the edict lapse after a few years.

Diocletian's severe rule stabilized the Empire, though it is hard to find in it much to praise. Many of his practices continued throughout the fourth century, especially his establishment of a despotism that resembled the ancient kingdoms of the Near East in its absolute monarchic rule. All laws came directly from the emperor, and the jurists, who had shaped the growth of law in the first two centuries of the Empire, played no further role. Thus Rome had moved from a "principate," the system of Augustus, to a "dominate" (*dominus*, "master").

The Accession of Constantine   Diocletian retired in 305, and soon afterward his system of shared rule broke down. Years of complex intrigue and civil war followed, as several leaders fought for the throne. One of the ruling circle was Constantius, the father of Constantine. When Constantius died in 306, Constantine began to fight for supreme power; in 324 he defeated his last rival and became sole emperor of Rome. Thus forty years after the accession of Diocletian, the Empire once again had a single ruler. In 330 Constantine renamed the old Greek city of Byzantium as New Rome and established it as his capital; popular usage gave it the name Constantinople.

◆ CONSTANTINE AND THE BUREAUCRACY

By the end of his reign in 337 Constantine had set the pattern that remained throughout the fourth and later centuries. The whole state was now one rigid structure, almost one massive corporation that brutally discouraged individual initiative.

The economy was in virtual stagnation. Members of all trades and professions were grouped into *corpora,* or corporations, and to change professions was difficult. To make certain that the various day-to-day services would be performed, the state made professions hereditary. A small class of farmers managed to remain independent, but the general trend was toward converting agricultural workers into near slaves. A totally impassable gulf existed between the monarch's court and the common people. Even within the court the emperor stood apart from the rest, surrounded by ceremony. Fourth-century rulers wore expensive cloaks dyed in purple, and courtiers had to kiss a corner of the emperor's robe when approaching the throne. Diadems, the custom of kneeling before the emperor, and other marks of royalty became traditional and have remained so in European monarchies.

◆ THE DECLINE OF THE WESTERN EMPIRE

After Constantine's death in 337, the chief administrative question for more than a century was whether one man could be strong enough to rule as

▲ The emperor Constantine tried to increase his glory by commissioning colossal portraits of himself, such as the one in Rome shown here. The original full-length statue was some forty feet tall.
Hirmer Fotoarchiv

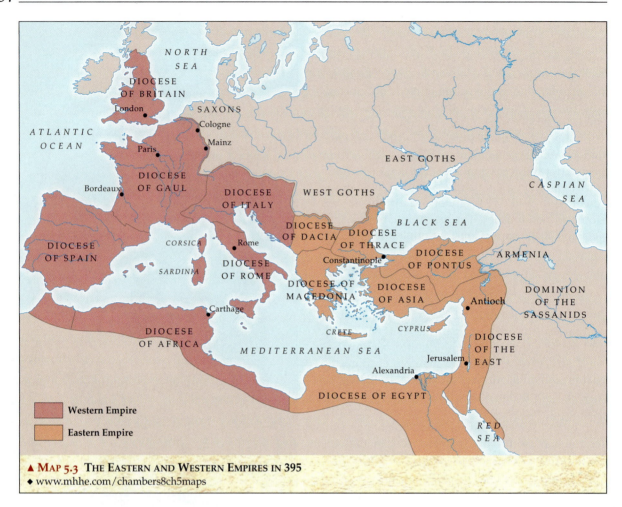

▲ **MAP 5.3** THE EASTERN AND WESTERN EMPIRES IN 395
◆ www.mhhe.com/chambers8ch5maps

sole monarch. For most of the time, this solution proved impossible, and some kind of shared rule became common. On the death of Theodosius in 395, the Empire split into an Eastern half and a Western half, with the dividing line just east of Italy.

In the last centuries of the Empire, society became more and more rigid; it did not, and perhaps could not, allow people to move freely from one class to another. As the central government weakened, local estates, usually called *villas,* became self-sufficient units with hunting lands and workshops that supplied the goods that the local population needed; they therefore became the main economic and political units of the Western Empire. At the same time, trade was declining because of a shortage of new markets and the constant threat of invasions along the frontiers. Moreover, a shortage of labor caused fertile lands to lie fallow and mines to remain unexploited.

The "Fall" of Rome? Such was the background for the dramatic turning point in history that is the end of the Western Empire. The formal end of the Western Empire is traditionally dated to 476, when a Germanic warlord, Odovacar (sometimes Odoacer), deposed the youth whom we call the last Western emperor, Romulus Augustulus, and the Senate resolved not to try to name any further Western emperors. To symbolize the end of the Western emperors, an embassy was sent to Constantinople to surrender the imperial insignia. Modern readers inevitably think of this event in the terminology imposed by the historical masterpiece of Edward Gibbon—that is, as the "decline and fall" of the Empire. But no political structure as large as the Roman Empire really falls like a tree in a forest without further influence or legacy. Moreover, some emperors in Constantinople, notably Justinian in the sixth century, saw

Chronology
The "Fall" of Rome

476 is known to all readers of history as the year of the fall of Rome, but the true chronology is more complex.

393 Theodosius I, ruling in Constantinople, installs his son Honorius as emperor in the West.

395 Death of Theodosius; the division of the Empire into Eastern and Western parts is maintained.

423 Death of Honorius in West; other Western emperors continue to be appointed.

474, June 24 Leo I, emperor in East, appoints Julius Nepos as emperor in West.

475 Nepos appoints Orestes, a former lieutenant of Attila the Hun, as Master of the Soldiers. Orestes insists that his young son, Romulus Augustus (or Augustulus), be recognized as Western emperor. Nepos flees to Salona in Dalmatia. Romulus is proclaimed emperor in Ravenna on October 31, but the act is without legal force, and Nepos continues to be recognized as official Western emperor.

476 The German warlord Odovacar (sometimes Odoacer) leads a rebellion against Orestes and kills him, August 28. He deposes Romulus in Ravenna (September 4) and exiles him with a pension to Campania. The Roman Senate sends an embassy to Zeno, the Eastern emperor (r. 474–491), proclaiming no further need for a Western emperor; but Zeno continues to recognize Nepos until his death.

480, April or May Nepos is murdered in his villa at Salona.

ca. 520 Marcellinus, in his Latin *Chronicle* written in Constantinople, states that the Western Empire (*Hesperium imperium*) "perished" with the deposition of Romulus Augustulus in 476, thus establishing this date for the "fall" of Rome.

themselves as the head of the whole traditional Empire, West and East, and tried to reunite the two geographic parts.

The Survival of the Eastern Empire Even though historians take care to speak of the transformation of the Empire rather than of its disappearance, there is no doubt that the Empire in the West did pass away, while the Eastern part, based on Constantinople and called by historians the Byzantine Empire, survived for nearly another thousand years. The problem is to explain why the Western regions could not maintain themselves under a continuous government while no similar dissolution threatened the Eastern portion of the Empire.

Theories about the Fall Some historians have been enticed into trying to state the one great cause for the fall of Rome—and this quest may be

impossible. Gibbon, for example, blamed the destructive work of barbarism and religion. But to say that Rome declined because of invasions by Germans, Franks, and Goths only pushes the inquiry back one step: Why were these peoples able to defeat an Empire that had ruled the civilized world for centuries? And why did the Eastern part of the Empire not decline along with the Western?

Some historians suggest that the emperors unintentionally paved the way for the fall of Rome by exterminating possible political rivals in the upper class, thus weakening the group that could have supplied leadership for the state. Others have advanced an economic argument, saying that the Empire was bound to decline because it never really emerged from a domestic economy. But this second theory is hardly convincing, for some societies—admittedly much less complex than the Empire—have existed for many centuries with no more than a domestic economy. If there had been no convulsions and strains in the Empire, the production of goods and food could have continued more or less unchanged. Other historians have proposed exhaustion of the soil and fluctuating cycles of rainfall and drought in order to explain Rome's economic depression, but there is little exact knowledge about the cycles of crops and weather conditions that would indubitably account for the fall of the Empire.

A Crisis in Manpower   Still other historians have suggested that the weakness of the Western Empire was due to a shortage of manpower. This explanation does have some merit, because the Eastern cities appear to have been more populous than the Western ones, and thus they had more strength and resilience. The numerical inferiority of the West became even more serious when the villas became self-sufficient units and there was no longer a centralized military system. It was much easier for outsiders to invade the Empire when they met haphazard resistance from local forces. As early as the third century, many Germanic captives and volunteers entered the army, which was scarcely "Roman" in any true sense. The Germanic troops felt little loyalty to Roman tradition and were unwilling to submit to severe discipline. Thus the army—the power base of the Augustan age—sank and pulled the Empire down with it. Also, the relocation of the capital to Constantinople moved the administrative center even farther from the Western provinces and probably accelerated the dissolution of the regions of Italy and Gaul.

The Routes of Invasion   But the shortage of manpower was not the only factor in the weakening of the Western Empire. Possibly an even stronger threat was simply the physical geography of Europe. The Western Empire seems to have been far more vulnerable to invasion than the Eastern Empire. Warlike peoples streamed along the Danube valley and through the terrain of Central Europe into the Western provinces, which offered a less hazardous route than the journey south through the difficult mountains of the Balkans, Greece, and Asia Minor into the Eastern Empire.

Social Conditions and Decline   Other conditions, too, made the Western Empire less able to resist invasion. In the late second and third centuries the emperors had deliberately increased the prestige of the army and depressed the Senate and the civil service. The creature that they fashioned soon began to rule them, for the armies and their leaders made and unmade emperors at will. The only way to preserve civilian control over the military machine would have been to entrust more responsibility to the Senate and to maintain strong civil servants. But the emperors simply continued along the path of absolute coercion, stifling initiative and making the lower classes apathetic and resentful. These conditions gave citizens only slight motivation to defend their oppressive government; domination by invaders may have seemed not much worse than being in the grip of the Roman state.

We must also consider the large number of holidays and many forms of amusement within the city of Rome: To what degree did such luxuries contribute to the transformation of the Western Empire? There is evidence here and there that the masses in the city gradually lost their feelings of responsibility. For example, in 69, as Tacitus reports, the crowd cheered with pleasure as rival troops fought in the streets for the throne.[4] When the masses no longer had to exert more than minimal effort to survive, they abandoned the discipline and civic cooperation that had created the Empire. The people shunned public office, non-Italians supplied the troops, and appeals for traditional Roman firmness in danger found little response.

The Role of Christianity   Finally, historians must take into account the great upheaval in ideas and faith. We cannot express this view in the language of science or statistics, but the new religion, Christianity, may also have weakened the defenses of the Empire. This thesis was first supported by Edward Gibbon, who had rejected the Catholic faith in his own life and scorned Christianity. But even as we recognize Gibbon's prejudices, we must

---

[4]*Histories*, 3.83.

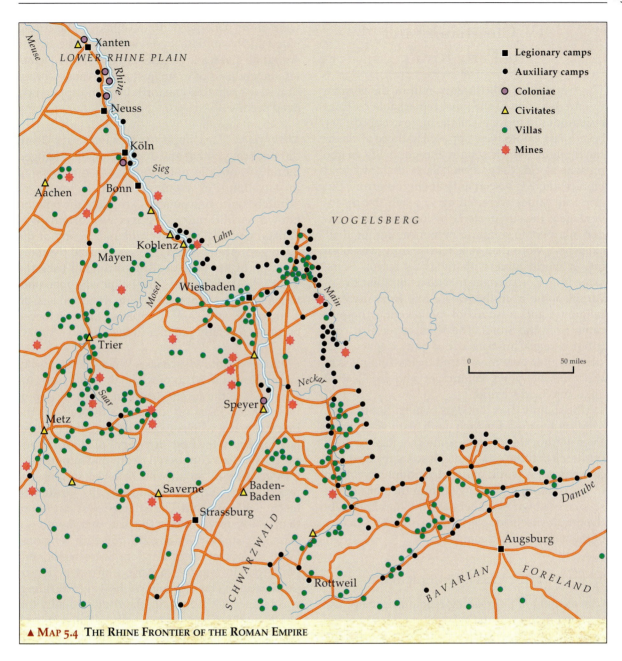

Legend:
- ■ Legionary camps
- ● Auxiliary camps
- ◉ Coloniae
- △ Civitates
- ● Villas
- ✳ Mines

▲ **MAP 5.4** THE RHINE FRONTIER OF THE ROMAN EMPIRE

allow that he may have hit a part of the truth. In the Roman scheme the emperors, governors, and administrators stood far above the people, and Roman religion provided little spiritual compensation for a low rank in the world. The Christian faith offered something better: the message that all persons are potentially equal in the eyes of

God and may hope for a better afterlife through salvation. As the Western Empire came under constant attack, the increasing number of Christians may have been less than eager to fight to preserve the old system. This spiritual rejection, as we might call it, worked along with the mighty pressures of invasion to cause the "fall" of Rome.

IV. Christianity and Its Early Rivals

◆

The triumph of Christianity within the Roman Empire was one of the most remarkable cultural revolutions in history—all the more extraordinary because its values were opposed to those of classical thought, which sought the good life in the present world. *Carpe diem,* "Seize the day," said Horace; there is no certainty about tomorrow. But classical values were failing to reach the disadvantaged, the subjugated, the losers. Small wonder that people sought a new meaning for their existence. More than this, Christianity was born into a world alive with religious fervor. Some came from Zoroastrianism with its promise of salvation, some from the Jews, some from mystery religions; and a strain of philosophic thought came from the Stoics. The Jews, especially, contributed zeal. Christians added to this legacy their striving after pure morals and their willingness to welcome everyone, commoner and intellectual alike, into God's world.

Christianity then found its own battles to fight. Martyrs testified for their faith with their lives. Even within the church, some theologians took positions that the established leaders rejected and denounced. A world of debate and interpretation of Christian thought flowed from the pens of the scholars known as Fathers of the Church. Finally the Empire itself adopted Christianity. The victory of the new faith was complete.

◆ THE MYSTERY RELIGIONS

One element of a spreading religious ferment under the Empire was the growing popularity of the so-called mysteries, which promised a blessed life after death to those who were initiated into secret (therefore "mysterious") rites. Through these rites, the believer attained a mystical identification with the renewing cycles of nature. The mysteries are generally described in various sources as thrilling, bringing one into another world, carrying one to a summit of emotion and perception.

The Mysteries of Eleusis The oldest and most famous rites were held each fall at Eleusis, a day's

walk from Athens. A drama-filled night culminated in the initiate's conviction that he or she would be given a lovely life after death by Demeter, the goddess of grain, just as she caused beautiful new grain to come forth from the apparently dead seed.

Mithraism This hope for survival after death did not bring with it any expectation of a changed moral life, nor did initiation lead to membership in any kind of community of believers or "church," with one notable exception: the religion known as Mithraism. Mithras was originally a Persian god of light and truth and an ally of the good god, Ahura Mazda; he symbolized the daily triumph of life over death by bringing back the sun to the dark heavens. Initiation was open only to men, and Mithraism—with its emphasis on courage, loyalty, self-discipline, and victory—became especially popular in the Roman army.

Christianity and Mysteries When Christians began, around A.D. 30, to proclaim the good news (or "gospel") of the recent death and resurrection of their leader, Jesus of Nazareth,[5] throughout the Empire, many who responded thought they were hearing about the best "mystery" of all: A historical person had conquered death and promised a blessed afterlife to all who believed in him. Yet much early Christian literature was written to teach believers that Christianity was far more than a "mystery." In fact, the historian should not class Christianity among the mystery religions. First, rites in mystery religions were secret, and participation required a period of instruction or purification. The experience, however thrilling, was temporary. Above all, the rituals usually did not lead to forming a community of believers or a church. Christianity, by contrast, demanded that every believer practice love and justice in new communities made up of Jew and Greek, slave and free, male and female, rich and poor, educated and ignorant.

---

[5]"Jesus" was his name. After his death he was called *ho Christós,* "the anointed one," or the Messiah, by his followers. Thus the names "Christ" and "Jesus Christ," though universally used, are not historically accurate, and "Jesus, called the Christ" is cumbersome.

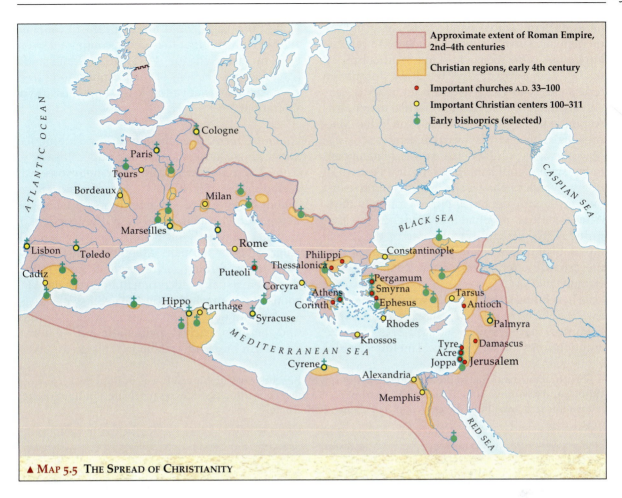

▲ MAP 5.5 THE SPREAD OF CHRISTIANITY

Characteristics of Christianity This new religion hardly looked "religious." Christians had no temples or other holy places, no priests, no ordinary sacrifices, no oracles, no visible gods, no initiations; they made no pilgrimages, did not practice divination, would not venerate the emperor, and challenged the final authority of the father (or oldest male) in family life. No wonder some pagans accused Christians of being atheists who undermined traditional society. The roots of these radical beliefs and practices go back to the long Judaic tradition and its sacred writings. Christians maintained that prophecies in the Hebrew Bible, which in the light of new revelation they began to call the *Old* Testament, had foretold the coming of Jesus as the Messiah, the deliverer of the Jewish people, and the future lord of the world.

Like the Jews, Christians emphasized their god's wish to create a community of men and women who practiced justice and mercy. All the first Christians had been Jews, but they parted company with Jewish tradition by insisting that Jesus' life, his sacrificial death, and his resurrection all meant that God's community had become open to everyone, on absolutely equal terms, from every background.

◆ THE JEWS IN THE ROMAN EMPIRE

The Jews and Other Powers The Jews had been favored subjects of the Persian Empire until Alexander's invasion of the East (334–323 B.C.) swept away Persian rule. In the Hellenistic Age they were governed during the third century B.C. by the Ptolemies of Egypt and then by the Seleucid kings of Syria, who began to force Greek culture on them and finally outlawed the Jewish religion altogether. One Seleucid king, Antiochus IV (r. 175–164 B.C.), defiled the holy Temple in Jerusalem by erecting within it an altar to Zeus and an image of himself. Pious Jewish nationalists responded under the leadership of Judas Maccabaeus with guerrilla warfare. This successful Maccabean Revolt (167–164 B.C.) is remembered today with Hanukkah, the eight-day Festival of Lights, which celebrates the reported miracle of a one-day supply of oil that burned for eight days. After a century of virtual independence, the Jews in Judea (the province created out of the Jewish kingdom of Judah) fell under Rome's control after the arrival in Jerusalem of the Roman general Pompey in 63 B.C.

When Julius Caesar was at war with Pompey in 47 B.C., he had the help of a Jewish force, and he rewarded the Jews with reduced taxes and exemption from military service. The Romans also agreed that Jews could not be called to court on the Sabbath and that they could continue to worship in their synagogues, even in Rome itself. Thus, despite the loss of their century-long freedom, the Jews enjoyed at least some measure of toleration.

Roman Control over the Jews   Rome permitted client kings, local rulers who pledged loyalty to Rome, to rule Judea. The most notorious was Herod the Great (r. 40–4 B.C.), hated by most Jews, whom he sought to win over by remodeling the Temple in Jerusalem into one of the wonders of the ancient world. But Herod's son was a weak ruler, and the Romans assumed direct control over Judea through civil servants from Rome; they were usually called procurators, the most famous of whom was Pontius Pilate.

Constant quarrels between the Roman officers and the Jews reached a climax in A.D. 66, when Jerusalem burst into rebellion. This great Jewish

▼ A Mithraeum, or shrine to the savior god Mithras, with benches for worshipers. It was built in the second or third century within a large first-century apartment. On the altar, Mithras is shown sacrificing a bull to Apollo. Above this level was built the church of San Clemente in Rome.
C. M. Dixon

IV: CHRISTIANITY AND ITS EARLY RIVALS **161**

War, as the Romans called it, lasted until 70, when the Romans under the emperor Titus demolished the Temple, except a remnant of the Western Wall, at which Jews were allowed to pray once a year. This portion of wall still stands and is a holy shrine to Jews today. Hoping to retain the favor of the Jews by respecting their god, the Romans did not at first try to eliminate the Jewish faith itself; but they finally did attempt its suppression after another Jewish rebellion (131–135). Nonetheless, Judaism retained its coherence and strength, assuring its people that God would one day send them their redeemer.

Jewish Factions   The attractiveness of Hellenistic culture, combined with the insult of Roman occupation, led to a continuing crisis of identity among the Jews. After the Maccabean Revolt, three principal factions arose, each stressing the part of Jewish tradition that it considered most essential for the survival of the Jews as God's people.

First, the landed aristocracy and high priests formed the Sadducees, religious conservatives who rejected belief in an afterlife and in angels because they did not find such teaching in the five Books of Moses (the Pentateuch, called the *Torah* by Jews).

A second faction, the Pharisees, were pious middle-class laypersons who taught the resurrection of the dead, believed in angels, and accepted gentile converts.[6] During the century following the Roman expulsion of the Jews from Jerusalem in 135, the spiritual heirs of the Pharisees, the great rabbis, organized their oral legal traditions, which updated the practice of the Torah, into a book called the Mishnah. This compendium became fundamental for all subsequent Jewish thought and was augmented in the East by an authoritative commentary (the Gemara) to form the Babylonian Talmud, or general body of Jewish tradition. A similar process in the West created the less elaborate Persian Talmud.

The Essenes   The third faction was the Essenes, who have drawn the most attention in recent years because of the astonishing discovery of the

---

[6]The Latin word *gentiles* (akin to *gens;* see p. 108) means "foreigners," those born to non-Jewish mothers.

Dead Sea Scrolls, documents found from 1947 onward in eleven caves near the Dead Sea. Although scholarly debate continues, the consensus is that the writers were ascetic priests who settled at Qumran, fifteen miles into the desert east of Jerusalem, after the Maccabean Revolt; they were evidently protesting against the leadership of the Temple by high priests whom they considered corrupt and unworthy.

These rolls and many fragments of leather have given historians an extraordinary view of the apocalyptic beliefs and strict practices of this protesting faction, which was active from ca. 150 B.C. to A.D. 70. The Essenes were convinced that evil in the world had become so powerful—even prevailing in the Temple—that only a cataclysmic intervention by God, which would soon arrive, could cleanse the world and open the way for righteousness to prevail.

Doctrines of the Essenes   A certain "Teacher of Righteousness," the priestly champion of the forces of light, is thought to be the anonymous author of many of the scrolls; his opponent in Jerusalem, who he says serves the powers of darkness, is called the Wicked Priest. The scrolls foresee at least two God-anointed leaders: the Messiah of David (a military commander) and the Messiah of Aaron (a high priest). The writers also predict the return of the "Teacher."

The relations of the Essenes at Qumran to Jesus and the first Christians remain much debated. The Essenes never appear in the Christian Bible, or New Testament. To be sure, in the spectrum of Jewish factions, these two groups could hardly have differed more widely. The Essenes were exclusive, hierarchic, priestly, and withdrawn from society. Jesus and his followers welcomed everyone; they were egalitarian, uninterested in sacrifices in the Temple, and wholly "in the world."

◆ ORIGINS OF CHRISTIANITY

The Person of Jesus   The modern historical investigation of Jesus of Nazareth has challenged scholars for two centuries. He seems to have been a charismatic Jewish teacher, yet he wrote nothing that we know of. His existence and his execution by the Romans are confirmed by such first- and second-century historians as Josephus, Tacitus, and Suetonius.

For details we must sift the writings of early converts, such as Saul of Tarsus (who did not know Jesus) or the authors of the Gospels (the first four books of the New Testament), which focus on Jesus' power over evil forces, his message of hope and moral demands, his healing miracles, and his radical inclusiveness (even lepers were welcomed into the faith). But ancient writers had little interest in presenting his biography in chronological order or in probing his inner life. We know almost nothing about his career as a youth and young adult apart from his being raised a Jew in Galilee;

◄ **The church of Santa Costanza in Rome, built in the early fourth century as a mausoleum for Constantia and Helena, daughters of the emperor Constantine, contains some of the oldest Christian mosaics. This scene from daily life shows workers bringing in the grape harvest.** Erich Lessing/Art Resource, NY

thus, despite the efforts of many, it is impossible to write a biography of Jesus.

Jesus as Teacher   As his followers recalled his career, Jesus was born of a virgin named Mary, who was betrothed but not yet married to a man named Joseph, in the last years of Herod the Great, at a date that modern scholarship sets about 4 B.C. At around age thirty, Jesus went to John the Baptist, an outspoken prophet, to be baptized—that is, to become purified through a ritual washing—and join his apocalyptic movement, which foresaw the coming end of the world. Soon afterward John was imprisoned, and Jesus began a program of itinerant teaching and healing, apparently rejecting John's apocalyptic message by proclaiming instead the "good news" that God's rule had already begun *before* the final judgment. Jesus affirmed the Pharisees' belief in resurrection, yet he urged his disciples to pray that God's will be done here on earth as it is in heaven, that God's kingdom should come to people here. Jesus was, therefore, a man in the tradition of the Hebrew prophets, who brought their message to the people directly.

In the Sermon on the Mount, the summary of Jesus' basic principles recorded in the Gospel of Matthew, Jesus declared that when God rules, the poor, the meek, the pure in heart, the peacemakers, and the justice seekers will be honored. He said too that prayer and piety were matters of personal commitment, not public gestures to win society's acclaim.

Doctrines of Jesus   With all other Jews, Jesus believed that God was a gracious, welcoming God. The related questions were: To *whom* is God gracious? and, therefore, Whom must I treat as my neighbor? As Jesus demonstrated by his fellowship at open meals, every person was potentially such a neighbor, especially a person in need.

Jesus' fellowship at meals reached its climax at his last supper at the time of Passover, a Jewish religious holiday. At this meal he urged his disciples to continue a ritual practice in memory of him, using bread and wine to symbolize the gift of his body and the sacrifice of his blood. The early Christians regularly did so, calling this meal the eucharist, or thanksgiving. Jesus' doctrines included the assurance that belief in his message

would bring redemption from sin and salvation with eternal life in the presence of God; above all, he called himself the Son of Man—but also the Son of God, who would sit at God's right hand.

Jesus' Death   For the passing of Jesus, only Christian sources give us a narrative, which we cannot compare with others. Christian writers state that the high priests in Jerusalem accused Jesus of blasphemy (he had challenged their authority in the Temple), of pretending to be God's Messiah and a king, and of opposing paying taxes to the Roman emperor. The Roman governor, Pontius Pilate, apparently feared that a riot, led by Jesus' enemies, was about to break out at the Passover. He washed his hands to make himself innocent of Jesus' blood and handed him over to the crowd, which then brought about his crucifixion, a horribly painful form of execution (about A.D. 30).

Jesus' followers became convinced that God raised him from the dead after three days and that this resurrection confirmed the truth of his deeds and words despite his rejection and persecution. The Christians further believed that he ascended bodily into heaven but would return to save his followers and establish his kingdom. Armed with this conviction, they followed the example of Stephen, the first Christian martyr, and began to convert other Jews to their faith.

Paul and His Mission   A Pharisee, Saul of Tarsus (in today's southern Turkey), known to us as Paul, became a leader in persecuting Jews who had become Christians. Then, about A.D. 33, on his way to Damascus to organize further persecutions, he saw on the road an apparition of the risen Jesus, who asked him to explain his hatred. Paul realized he had been given a special mission to the gentiles and became Christianity's tireless advocate, traversing the Roman world, organizing Christian communities of both Jews and gentiles, and advising their members through his letters. He was executed in Rome about A.D. 62 while planning a mission to Spain (see map 5.6).

Paul became the best known of all the early Christian teachers. His letters, or epistles, written to give specific guidance to the congregations he founded, were widely circulated and then collected as part of the Christians' authoritative Scriptures. Luke devotes nearly half of the Acts of

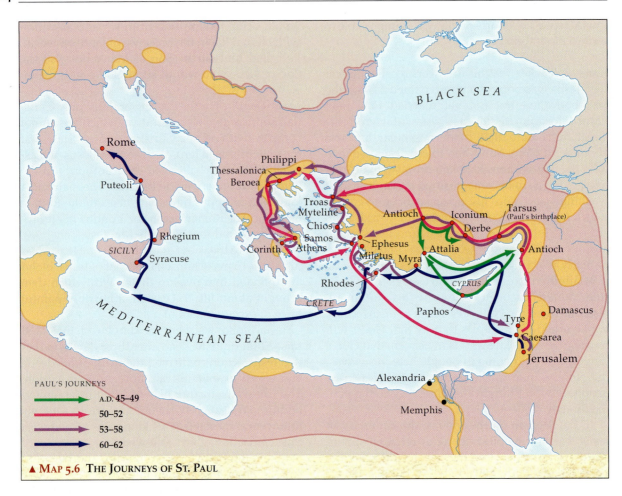

PAUL'S JOURNEYS

→ A.D. 45–49
→ 50–52
→ 53–58
→ 60–62

▲ **MAP 5.6** THE JOURNEYS OF ST. PAUL

the Apostles to Paul's career as a courageous witness who fought with burning missionary fervor for his new lord.

Paul and the Conversion of the Gentiles Above all, Paul rejected the policy of some early Jewish Christians who wanted to restrict membership in the new faith to Jews or to gentiles who had become Jews through circumcision. In one of his tautly argued letters in the Bible's Book of Romans he asked: "Is God the God of the Jews only? Is he not also the God of the Gentiles? Yes, of the Gentiles also." By rejecting circumcision as a condition of membership, Paul helped firmly establish the Christian church on the basis of personal faith, not limited by ethnic identity, bloodlines, or observation of the Mosaic law.

He and later Christian teachers saw themselves as the direct heirs of the Jewish tradition, from which they drew their concept of one God and

their notions of creation and the early history of humanity. The first human beings, Adam and Eve, had disobeyed God, thus introducing sin and death into the world. By nature Adam was the founder of the human race; by grace—in Christian theory, that gift from God that redeems sinners and gives them life after death—Jesus was its second founder, restorer, and redeemer.

Paul and Christian Communities Paul taught Christians to regard themselves as citizens of heaven and to begin living with one another in humility and love, in joyous expectation of their final destiny. Christians were sure that God would soon consign their world's system of honor and shame based on violence, pride, and class discrimination to the trash heap of history. Paul also redefined the notion of the Messiah. For Jews, this leader would someday arrive and create another kingdom on earth. For Paul, the messianic age had begun with Jesus, interrupting the age of violence and death as the sign and promise of what the future would bring.

Paul's vision of human freedom and a renewed human community characterized by mutual service is one of the most compelling social images in Western culture. Taking this message throughout the lands of the eastern Mediterranean, Paul and his successors brought converts by the thousands into the new church.

Persecutions The Roman government adopted a general policy of toleration toward the many religious sects of the Empire, seeking the blessings of all divine powers on the Empire. The Romans even paid for sacrifices to be performed on behalf of the Empire in the temple in Jerusalem. They asked only that veneration be shown on official occasions to the traditional gods and to the deceased and deified emperors—little more than public patriotism. But the Christians, like the Jews

▼ **The fourth-century sarcophagus of Junius Bassus, in classicizing style, showing Adam and Eve in Eden with the threatening serpent.**
Scala/Art Resource, NY

before them, refused even this apparently small compromise with polytheism.

Rome's attitude toward Christians wavered between lack of interest and cruel persecution. The first serious persecution took place under Nero in A.D. 64. A vast fire had ravaged the crowded areas in central Rome, and Nero had many Christians brutally killed as scapegoats. The historian Tacitus, in reporting the affair, declares that Christians were thought guilty of a wicked style of life, but he makes it clear that the persecution was based on a false charge (*Annals*, 15.44). From time to time other anti-Christian actions took place, but it is unlikely that the mild doctrines of Christians were the reason. Their main offense was, rather, their stubbornness or *contumacia*, which caused many in the Roman world to see them as enemies of society. The emperor Trajan, giving instructions to his civil servant Pliny, agreed that laws against Christians should be followed, but he warned against anonymous accusations, which he would not tolerate.

Occasional persecutions and long periods of peace marked the history of the Church—that is, the Christian community—into the fourth century. Then, in the period 303–313, came the Great Persecution under Diocletian and his successors, when the rulers sought to eliminate what they saw as a potential menace to the state. Their unsuccessful efforts testify to the widespread strength of Christianity. Moreover, the persecutions created a list of venerated Christian martyrs, which led to the cult of saints, thereafter an integral part of Christian piety.

Female Martyrs In Christian thought, women could receive God's favor just as men could. Therefore Roman officials persecuted women as well as men. Our sources (called Acts of the several martyrs) record many stories of horrific punishments inflicted on women. According to Christian sources, virgins were thrown into brothels and women were fastened naked to trees by one foot and left to perish as they hung downward. One woman of Alexandria boldly refused to abandon her faith and is said to have been tortured to death by having boiling pitch poured over her body.

A famous martyr was St. Perpetua, who was put to death in Carthage in 203. A narrative in

Latin records her fate. The emperor Septimius Severus had forbidden any subjects to become Christians, but Perpetua and five others fearlessly confessed their Christianity. Her mother was a Christian, but her father was a pagan. In vain he begged her to renounce her faith in order to spare his family the disgrace of having a Christian daughter. She was tried before a procurator, who also urged her to recant, but she refused the customary sacrifice for the emperor. Perpetua and her slave, who became St. Felicitas, welcomed their martyrdom; they and their fellow Christians were mauled by wild animals before being killed by the sword.

St. Agnes and St. Cecilia   The narratives of the martyrs are meant to show the steadfast courage of early Christians and the solace they found in their faith. Christian sources preserve, for example, the story of St. Agnes, in the time of Diocletian. She was exposed in the stadium of Domitian in Rome (now the Piazza Navona, where a church stands bearing her name), but her nakedness was covered by the miraculous growth of her hair. She was then tied to a stake to be burned, but the flames would not touch her and the emperor had her beheaded.

Again, St. Cecilia, the purported inventor of the organ and the patron saint of music, was according to tradition imprisoned in her own bath to be scalded. She emerged unscathed and was then beheaded (the date of her death is uncertain). A church to her memory stands on the spot of her house in Rome, where she lived with her husband, whom she converted.

An Emperor Becomes the Church's Patron   One of the most amazing changes of face in Roman history is the radical shift in the policy of the government toward the Christians initiated in 313 by the emperor Constantine. In the traditional story, first appearing around the period 318–320, Constantine had a dream on the evening before he was to fight a rival for supremacy over Italy in 312, at the Milvian Bridge near Rome. In the dream he was told to decorate the shields of his soldiers with the Greek letters *chi* and *ro*, the monogram of Christ: "In this sign you shall conquer." Constantine won the battle

▲ **The fourth-century emperor Valentinian I shown as Christian ruler in a colossal statue from Barletta in southeast Italy. In one hand, he holds an orb (restored) to signify his imperial power; in the other, the cross to show his devotion to the Church. The portrait thus unites the two forces that sustained the later Empire.**
Scala/Art Resource, NY

and thereafter recognized divine power in the name of Christ.

At what point Constantine himself converted to Christianity is debated. In any case, in 313, at a conference held at Milan, he ended the age of persecutions by extending complete freedom of worship to the Christians and ordering the return of their confiscated goods. As to Constantine himself, his conversion had certain political reasons, for there were now so many Christians that he naturally wanted to include them within the state. But his own letters and actions show a serious personal commitment to Christianity.

The Victory of Christianity   Just before his death in 337, Constantine received baptism from the bishop Eusebius of Nicomedia, but Christianity was not yet the official religion of the Empire. The emperor Julian, known as the Apostate, turned his back on the church and tried in the period 361–363 to restore the position of the traditional gods, but by then the wave of Christianity could not be stopped. In 391 and 392 Theodosius the Great forbade the practice of all religions except the form of Christianity recognized by the government, thus transforming in one move the character of both the Empire and Christianity. He reversed Rome's long-standing policy of religious toleration and changed the Church from a brave alternative society sharply critical of "this world" into a friend of worldly power; it thus began attracting some "converts" who sought personal gain rather than spiritual renewal.

Christianity and Roman Law   The law had been moving for many years toward more humane regulations, partly under the influence of philosophic conceptions of "natural" law that could apply to all mankind. For example, the old supreme power of the father had long since fallen away. Christianity moved this spirit forward. Constantine and his successors gave more and more privileges to the church. Christians became exempt from the much-resented burdens of civil service in local curiae. Churches could own property and enjoyed exemptions from certain taxes, and bishops were allowed to judge the legal disputes of the members of their congregations. The clergy had the power to preside over the freeing of slaves by their owners, and freed slaves became citizens at once. Thus the Church acquired a privileged juridical status that it would retain, in many Western lands, until the eighteenth and nineteenth centuries.

Constantine repealed the old laws of Augustus that regulated marriage and punished celibacy—a lifestyle now tolerated more easily because celibacy in priests was seen as a virtue. Emperors tried, though without great success, to discourage the ease with which people could be divorced (St. Jerome writes of a man living with his twenty-first wife, a woman who had already had twenty-two husbands), and cases in divorce could be heard by priests. Women were given greater protection with regard to dowries; husbands had less power over a dowry during marriage, and it became easier for a wife to recover it after divorce (Hammurabi of Babylon had long ago seen to similar rights for women).

◆ BATTLES WITHIN CHRISTIANITY

Usually the Christian community did not bother to define matters of dogma or discipline until disputes threatened its internal unity. The losers in these disputes, if they did not amend their beliefs, were regarded as heretics (from the Greek word *hairesis*, meaning "choice"—that is, a wrong choice). This word was used from the earliest days of Christianity.

The Heresies of Marcion and Montanus   A heresy that threatened the character of the Christian revelation was that of Marcion of Sinope in Asia Minor (ca. 150). He sought to reform Christianity by restricting it to the message of St. Paul alone. He therefore edited his version of the New Testament, which included and recognized as divine only the Gospel of Luke and the Epistles of Paul.

Another heresy was that of a bishop from Asia Minor, Montanus (ca. 170–200), who maintained that certain living believers were prophets who were continuously receiving direct inspiration from the Holy Spirit. Women were prominent among these prophets, and Montanus' ideas eventually won the allegiance of the great North African writer Tertullian. The movement forced Christians to ask: Who should rule the Christian congregations—teachers, who could only interpret texts from the past, or living prophets, who might expect continuing new revelations?

Christian Responses to Heresy   Christians who accepted the standard doctrines of the Church branded the ideas of Marcion and Montanus as heresy. Because such heresies have vanished over the centuries, one might well ask: What is their historical importance? The answer is that they stimulated the early Church to redefine its positions. Out of the turmoil and disagreement, the Church emerged stronger, even though the price was sometimes the blunt suppression of sincerely held opinions.

Orthodox theologians of the second century answered Marcion by defining the canon of sacred writings to include, in effect, the modern Bible—the entire Old and New Testaments. And the Church answered Montanus by declaring that the age of divine inspiration had come to an end. All the truths needed for salvation, the Church now said, were complete with the work of St. John, the last inspired author (ca. 100), and no new revelations were needed. In the fourth century, too, the Church refused to accept as inspired certain other writings, calling them the Apocrypha (obscure or unclear writings).

The Government of the Church   Evidence from the first century indicates that James, a relative (perhaps a brother) of Jesus, was the recognized head of the Christians in Jerusalem. During this period, too, we meet the terms deacon (*diakonos*), bishop (*episkopos,* or "overseer"), and elder (*presbuteros*), which at first were nearly synonymous. Then, in the second century, the bishop became the elected leader of a group of elders (later called priests) and of deacons (both men and women), who became responsible for collecting donations, distributing charities, and managing the Church's material affairs.

Bishops gained the right to appoint priests, define doctrine, maintain discipline, and oversee morals. This political structure gave Christianity a stable administration and a hierarchy that no ancient mystery religion enjoyed. In the West, the number of bishops remained small; they thus obtained power over fairly large areas. Bishops in cities with the largest Christian communities—Rome, Alexandria, Antioch—became the most influential. Finally, the bishop of Rome became the head of the Church in the West. The general name for a bishop was *papa,* or father, but eventually the bishop of Rome was the only one who could so call himself (in English, *pope*).

Women in the Church   The role of women in early Christianity presents some contradictions to the historian. The figure of Mary, mother of Jesus, was of course universally revered, and Gospel accounts associate other women with Jesus: Mary Magdalene and another Mary are said to have been the first to see Jesus risen from his tomb. Paul names one Junia in the Book of Romans as "outstanding among the apostles." Other gifted women served as teachers and coworkers with Paul.

On the other hand, the Christian writer Tertullian says of women, "You give birth to suffering and anguish. You are Eve. The Devil is in you. You were the first to abandon God's law. You were the one who deceived man." Such a stern condemnation of women reminds us of the much milder words of Paul commanding women to be silent in church: "Let the woman learn in silence with all subjection. But I suffer not a woman to teach, nor to usurp authority over the man, but to be in silence" (1 Tim. 2).

Widows and Virgins in the Church   But as the church developed it made more and more use of the devotion and abilities of women. Widows, for example, had always inspired compassion as people in need of help, and special honor was paid to widows who had led a chaste life and could show that they had done good works. Their duty was to pray at home but also to visit the sick and pray at their bedsides. But, in accordance with Paul's words, they were not to teach the Gospel.

Later, in the third and fourth centuries, widows and virgins could become deaconesses and thus rise higher in status within the church. Though they were members of the clergy, they still could not teach or interpret the scriptures. Their main duty was to maintain order and assist the male clergy in performing duties such as baptism, especially for women. They continued to visit the sick and to pray at their bedsides; in doing so they confirmed the church's role as the loving protector of humankind.

Powerful Christian Women   If women could not perform the duties reserved for priests, they could still be powerful behind the scenes. St. John Chrysostom (345?–407), a priest at Antioch

▲ Mosaic of the Three Magi, kings or wise men, Balthasar, Melchior and Gaspar in Saint Apollinare Nuovo, 6th century A.D. Ravenna.
San Apollinaire Nuovo Ravenna/Dagli Orti (A)/The Art Archive

and later archbishop at Constantinople, complained that influential women could get their favorites chosen as priests. Among the women whom he accused of greed and immorality was the empress Eudoxia, wife of the emperor Arcadius (r. 383–408). In the end she got Chrysostom exiled to a remote place in Armenia.

Women, especially those in the court, could also contribute stupendous fortunes to the founding of churches. St. Helena, the mother of the emperor Constantine, founded churches in Palestine, and others are known to have endowed hospitals and monasteries. Above all, historians have pointed to the ability of women in the field of conversion as their most important contribution to the early church. Paul refers to the power of women to maintain and pass on the faith in a letter to his lieutenant Timothy: "Recalling your tears, I long to see you so that I may be filled with joy. I am reminded of your sincere faith, a faith that lived first in your grandmother Lois and your mother Eunice" (2 Tim. 1). Again, St. Helena was a Christian before her son Constantine became one and probably influenced his conversion. St. Monica, the mother of St. Augustine, was a Christian and lovingly worked for the conversion of her husband and for the salvation of her son.

Donatists In 303, Diocletian issued an edict ordering that churches and sacred books should be destroyed throughout the Empire. Some Christians sought to escape punishment by surrendering their copies of the Scriptures. Those who did so were called *traditores* ("those who handed over" the Scriptures—thus our word *traitor*), and the more steadfast Christians hated them. When the persecutions ended in 313, a party of North African Christians led by a bishop named Donatus declared that the "traitors," even if repentant, had forever lost membership in the Church; all the sacraments they had ever administered—all baptisms, marriages, ordinations, and the like— were declared worthless. Because the traitors were many, acceptance of the Donatist program would have brought chaos to the North African church.

The result was violent schism, which mounted on occasion to civil war. Refusing to accept the rule of traitors, the Donatists established their own bishops and hierarchy. In response, the more forgiving orthodox Church declared that the sacraments conferred grace on the recipients *ex opere operato,* simply "from the work having been performed," and that the spiritual state of the priests at the time did not matter. This attitude remained the official Christian doctrine until challenged during the Protestant Reformation of the Middle Ages.

Arius and Arianism The heresy of Donatus, which insisted on proper order in the church, partakes of the Roman heritage of law and discipline within the Western church. Another heresy reflects the Greek interest in theosophical and philosophical issues. This was the movement beginning about 311 when Arius, an Alexandrian priest, began to teach that Jesus was not coequal with God the Father but had been created by him at a moment in time. Arius stated, "There was a time when he [Jesus] was not." The teachings of Arius raised a furor in Egypt and soon throughout the Empire. To restore peace, Constantine summoned the first "ecumenical" council (that is, one representing the entire inhabited world) of the Church, which met at Nicaea in Asia Minor in May 325. The council condemned Arius in the "Nicene Creed," which declared that Jesus was coeternal with the Father and of one substance with God.

Arius was exiled but was later allowed to return to Alexandria. Arianism persisted in many places, and even Constantine gradually moved to a more tolerant policy toward it. A later council, meeting at Constantinople in 381 under the emperor Theodosius, restated the Nicene Creed. These declarations had behind them the full power of the state and could be enforced as a matter of law, although belief might waver with political currents. Finally, at the Council of Chalcedon of 451, Jesus was clearly defined as one person with two natures. As a human being, he was the son of Mary; as God, he was coequal with the Father and had reigned and would reign with him eternally. This definition has since remained the belief of Christians in general.

The Church and Classical Culture Christian writers, although they proclaimed themselves enemies of pagan culture, had no choice but to accept classical traditions. The basic grammars and texts, the authoritative models of argument and style, were all pagan. To defend the faith, Christian apologists had to master the art of rhetoric and use the arsenal of pagan learning. This Christian accommodation with pagan learning had decisive repercussions. Nearly all the texts of the great classical authors have reached us in copies made by Christians, who believed they were useful in education. Paradoxically, these outspoken enemies of pagan values actually preserved a rich cultural heritage that they sought to undermine.

◆ THE FATHERS OF THE CHURCH

Christianity became the chief religion of Europe partly because it reached the people through the languages and thought of Greco-Roman civilization. Even before the birth of Jesus, Greek-speaking Jews in Alexandria had translated the Old Testament into Greek; this version, said to have been made by seventy-two scholars, is called the *Septuagint* (from the Latin *septuaginta,* meaning "70"), and the authors of the New Testament referred to it and wrote their own works in the common Greek of the day. On the basis of these sacred texts, there grew an ocean of commentary and persuasion by the so-called Fathers of the Church, the leading theologians of the second to fifth centuries.

Origen and Eusebius The most learned Church father writing in Greek was Origen (185?–253?), a priest in Alexandria. Both the volume and the profound scholarship of his writings were a wonder of late antiquity. He worked especially on the text of the scriptures by comparing the original Hebrew and the Septuagint; he also wrote extensive commentaries on books of the Bible and a tract, *Against Celsus,* in which he answers the arguments of an elitist critic of the Christians. Another highly influential Greek father was Eusebius of Caesarea (260?–340?). His most original work was a history of the Church, which became the model for later such histories. The most learned man of his time, he also wrote a *Chronicle* of universal history, which is one of our most important sources for ancient history in general.

The Latin Fathers: Ambrose and Jerome Among the fathers who wrote in Latin was Ambrose, bishop of Milan from 374 to 397. His most important doctrine was that the Church must be independent of the emperor and that bishops should have the right to chastise rulers. In 390 Ambrose excommunicated the emperor Theodosius after he had massacred the rebellious citizens of Thessalonica, forbidding him to receive the eucharist and thus placing him outside the body of the Church. Theodosius admitted his guilt and repented, and the popes of later centuries who struggled with secular officials owed much of their power to the resolute example of Ambrose.

Jerome (340?–420) succeeded Eusebius as the most learned Church father of his time. His translation of both the Old and the New Testaments into Latin, usually called the Vulgate version of the Bible, is probably the most influential book ever written in the Latin language. It became the medium through which the Judeo-Christian writings permeated the Latin-speaking nations of Europe and was the biblical text most often used during the Middle Ages. It also assured that Latin would survive deeply into the Middle Ages as the medium of debate and would thus provide a necessary link to the classical past.

▲ An early mosaic (ca. 400) showing Christ holding a book and surrounded by apostles in Roman dress. Two women, perhaps saints, crown St. Peter and St. Paul, with the holy city of Jerusalem in the background. The commanding figure of Jesus resembles that of Jupiter in Roman art. From the church of Santa Pudenziana, Rome.

Scala/Art Resource, NY

Augustine Augustine (354–430), the best known of the fathers, was born in North Africa of a pagan father and a Christian mother and accepted Christianity under the influence of Ambrose in 387 (see "Augustine Is Brought to His Faith," p. 172). He became bishop of Hippo in North Africa in 395 and spent the remaining years of his long life writing, preaching, and administering his see.

In his voluminous writings Augustine had something to say about almost every question of Christian theology. He profoundly influenced, for example, Christian teachings on sexual morality and marriage. Like some of his pagan contemporaries, he believed that the world was already filled with people. "The coming of Christ," he wrote, "is not served by the begetting of chil-

dren." He therefore urged all Christians to a life of celibacy, even though this would cause their number to decline: "Marriage is not expedient, except for those who do not have self-control." He banned all sexual activity for the unmarried. Within marriage, husband and wife should unite sexually only for procreation, and even the pleasure they took in this act, representing a triumph of libido over reason, was a small, though pardonable, sin.

The Working of Grace Augustine was passionately interested in the operations of grace (see p. 172). He sought the work of grace in his own life, and the result was his *Confessions,* an intensely personal autobiography; it is both a record of his

Augustine Is Brought to His Faith

◆

St. Augustine describes how, after many struggles to overcome his lustful nature, he was inspired at age thirty-one to pick up and read in the New Testament; this was the critical moment in his conversion.

"And, not indeed in these words, but to this effect I spoke often to you: 'But you, O Lord, how long? Will you be angry forever? Do not remember against us the guilt of past generations.' I sent up these sorrowful cries—'How long, how long? Tomorrow, and tomorrow? Why not now? Why is there now no end to my uncleanness?'

"I was saying these things and weeping in the most bitter contrition of my heart, when I heard the voice of a boy or girl, I do not know which, coming from a neighboring house, chanting, and often repeating, 'Take up and read; take up and read.' Immediately my face changed, and I began to consider whether it was usual for children in any kind of game to sing such words; nor could I remember ever hearing anything like this. So, restraining the torrent of my tears, I rose up, interpreting it as nothing but a command from heaven to open the Bible, and to read the first chapter I saw. So I returned to where I had put down the apostles. I grasped it, opened it, and in silence read the first paragraph I saw—'Not in rioting and drunkenness, not in debauchery and lust, not in strife and envy; but let Jesus Christ be your armor, and give no more thought to satisfying bodily appetites' [Romans 13–14]. I read no further, I did not need to; for instantly, as the sentence ended—by a light of security that poured into my heart—all the gloom of doubt vanished."

From *Confessions*, 8.12, J. G. Pilkington (tr.), in Whitney Oates (ed.), *The Basic Writings of Saint Augustine*, vol. 1 (Random House, 1948), p. 126, language modified.

early life, when he gave way to material and sexual temptations, and a celebration of the providence that had guided him in his struggle toward God. This masterpiece of introspective analysis is a type of literature virtually unknown in the classical tradition.

In theological matters, Augustine distinguished between God the creator (the author of nature) and God the redeemer (the source of grace), and insisted that these two figures not be confused. God as creator had given humanity certain powers, such as intelligence superior to that of beasts, but those powers, injured by the original fall of Adam and Eve, are insufficient to earn salvation. Only through grace, which Jesus' sacrifice had earned, could humanity hope to be saved. Moreover, God had already decided on whom he would bestow grace; hence, even before we are born, we are all predestined either to heaven or to hell.

Augustine on Salvation   Augustine deeply pondered the problem of sin—the breaking of God's law—and quarreled with Pelagius, a British monk who argued that sin was only the result of a wrong choice and that people could achieve per-

fection, do good works, and thus attain salvation. For Augustine, sin descended from Adam into every human being, and doing good works, no matter how many, could not guarantee salvation, which was the gift of God alone through his grace. Humanity's salvation must await a glorious transformation at the end of time.

Augustine further believed that the power of grace might redeem the whole course of human history. In his greatest work, *The City of God*, he set out to show that there was order in history: Behind the manifold events of the past the hand of God was evident, directing people through his grace to their destiny. Into this immense panorama, Augustine brought the sacred history of the Jewish Testament, the history of his own times, and the Christian expectation of resurrection. He held that the grace of God united the chosen in a form of community or city that stood against the community of those joined by the love of earthly things. The city of God, in which live those chosen for salvation, was as yet invisible, and the elect who were its members should recognize that this present earth was not their true home. Augustine saw history as moving in a straight line toward humankind's salvation, as

▲ The cathedral in Syracuse, Sicily. The interior, in powerful historical symbolism, shows a Doric temple to Athena (fifth century B.C.) with its original columns, now supporting the walls and roof of a Christian church built in the seventh century A.D.
Art Resource, NY

compared with cyclical views among some Greeks. Therefore, to Christians of his own troubled age and to those of later ages, Augustine held out the beckoning vision of a heavenly city, a celestial Jerusalem, where at last they would be at home with God.

SUMMARY

In the history of the Roman Empire, several great themes are seen. The body politic soon lost direct elections by the people, and the structure of society became constantly more monarchic. As success in war led to an established empire, a long period of peace nourished the economy and saw the development of urban centers throughout Europe. The Empire managed to avoid a near-collapse, and within its survival the Christian religion won the victory of faith. Christians felt able to ignore or transcend the "fall" of Rome—an event that the modern world sees as a possible model of its own fate. The transformation of the Empire, as it is better called, is a challenge and a warning to all who read history; it is also the recognized end of the ancient world and the beginning of a long period in which new nations would use the legacy of antiquity in their own development.

QUESTION FOR FURTHER THOUGHT

1. It may well surprise the historian that the Roman Empire, which controlled almost all of Europe in its time, suffered a catastrophic decline. By what means, if any, might this decline have been mitigated or even prevented?

RECOMMENDED READING

Sources

Early Christian Writings: The Apostolic Fathers. M. Staniforth (tr.). 1968.

Suetonius. *Lives of the Caesars.* Robert Graves (tr.). 1972.

Tacitus. *Annals of Imperial Rome.* Michael Grant (tr.). 1978.

———. *The Histories.* Kenneth Wellesley (tr.). 1976. The two works give the history of the Empire in the first century A.D. by the leading Roman historian.

Studies

Barnes, Timothy D. *The New Empire of Diocletian and Constantine.* 1982. Detailed study of the reigns of the two emperors who restored the power of Rome.

Birley, Anthony. *Marcus Aurelius: A Biography.* 1987. Study of the only philosopher-king in Roman history.

Bradley, Keith R. *Slaves and Masters in the Roman Empire: A Study in Social Control.* 1987. Modern treatment of slave families, freeing of slaves, rewards and punishments.

Brown, Peter. *Augustine of Hippo: A Biography.* 1986. Masterly treatment of the greatest of the church fathers.

———. *The World of Late Antiquity, AD 150–750.* 1971. One of many illuminating books by this great scholar. Brief, well illustrated.

Cameron, Averil. *The Mediterranean World in Late Antiquity, AD 395–600.* 1993. A brief, accessible modern survey.

Cross, Frank M. *The Ancient Library of Qumrân and Modern Biblical Studies.* 1976. Good introduction to the study of the Dead Sea Scrolls.

Frend, W. H. C. *The Rise of Christianity.* 1984. Most extensive one-volume history of the early church down to about A.D. 600.

Galinsky, Karl. *Augustan Culture.* 1996. Art, architecture, literature, and culture of the age.

Lieu, Judith, et al. (eds.). *The Jews among Pagans and Christians in the Roman Empire.* 1992. Essays on various aspects of Jewish life and society in the Empire.

MacMullen, Ramsay. *Christianizing the Roman Empire.* 1986. The spread of Christianity, with attention to conversion of Constantine and results.

———. *Constantine.* 1988. Biography of the emperor who pointed the Empire toward Christianity.

———. *Paganism in the Roman Empire.* 1981. Study of pagan beliefs, worshipers, and cults in the Empire.

Musurillo, Herbert (ed.). *The Acts of the Christian Martyrs.* 1979. Translations of accounts of torture and martyrdom in early Christianity.

Nicholas, Barry. *An Introduction to Roman Law.* 1988. Study of principles of the law, with attention to its influence in medieval and modern times.

Stambaugh, John E. *The Ancient Roman City.* 1988. Study of development of the city; comparisons with other ancient cities.

Wells, Colin. *The Roman Empire.* 2d ed. 1995. The best one-volume modern narrative.

Whittaker, C. R. *The Frontiers of the Roman Empire: A Social and Economic Study.* 1994. On the Germans and other neighbors of the Empire.

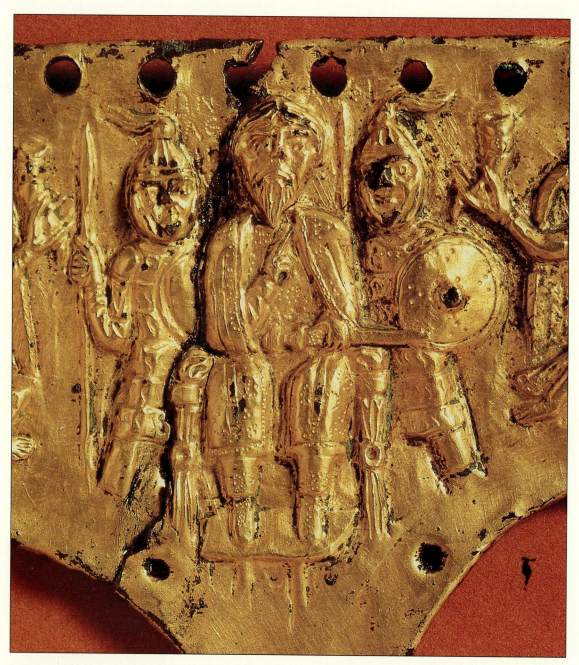

▲ The gilded copper relief of the Lombard king Agilulf, shown flanked by his warriors, shows Germanic adaptation of kingship in imitation of the Roman emperors. The Lombards conquered much of the Italian peninsula in 568. Agilulf became king shortly afterward.
Scala/Art Resource, NY

THE MAKING OF WESTERN EUROPE

The "Dark Ages" is the popular conception of the period after the decline of the Roman Empire in Western Europe, but the period was one that saw continuities as well as radical changes. In the period of roughly the fifth through the eighth centuries A.D., the composition and customs of Western Europe's population changed with the invasion of various Germanic and Hunnish peoples. The former Celtic and Roman populations gradually intermarried with the invaders; classical Latin ceased to be the ordinary language of people and instead evolved into Spanish, Portuguese, French, and Italian. Roman law blended with the law of the invaders. Settlement patterns also changed. Those Romans wealthy enough to have country villas moved from the cities to the country. The invaders, who had lived in forests and practiced agriculture in villages, also preferred to live in the countryside. Roman cities fell into a decline, and aqueducts, roads, walls, baths, and the general infrastructure that made the cities comfortable were no longer maintained. But with all these changes, some semblance of the earlier glory of Rome remained, particularly among educated churchmen.

Christianity continued to gain widespread acceptance among the Roman population and among the invading tribes. Although most of the tribes initially converted from paganism to the heresy espoused by Arius (see chapter 5), eventually the population of Western Europe became Roman or Catholic Christians. Paganism lingered, and Jews continued to live in the West. Monasteries, religious communities for men and women, provided a refuge for those who wished to lead a life of prayer and scholarly pursuits. Heroic missionaries went among the tribes and brought them Christianity along with Roman civilization and writing. It was a period of major spiritual expansion.

For the ordinary people, both Roman and tribal, these centuries were ones of violence, danger, and movement. Waves of invasions made agriculture and even survival unpredictable, but eventually the movement stopped and kingdoms were established so that agriculture and trade resumed. Even during these political disruptions innovations were improving agriculture, including a better plow, a new system of crop rotation, the horse collar, and the stirrup.

CHAPTER 6. THE MAKING OF WESTERN EUROPE							
	Social Structure	Body Politic	Changes in the Organization of Production and in the Impact of Technology	Evolution of Family and Changing Gender Roles	War	Religion	Cultural Expression
I. THE NEW COMMUNITY OF PEOPLE							
II. THE NEW POLITICAL STRUCTURES							
III. THE NEW ECONOMY							
IV. THE EXPANSION OF THE CHURCH							

I. The New Community of Peoples

The civilization that took root in the west and north of Europe after the decline of the Roman Empire was the direct ancestor of the modern Western world. Historians call the millennium between the fall of the Roman Empire and approximately 1500 the Middle Ages, or the medieval period of European history. The Early Middle Ages witnessed the emergence of new types of social and cultural organization from the shambles of the Roman Empire; this new civilization embraced both the former subjects of the Empire and peoples from beyond its borders. The Greeks and Romans called all these peoples *barbarians* because of their unintelligible languages and strange customs.[1] There was no single barbarian nation: These peoples were many and differed considerably in language and culture.

◆ THE GREAT MIGRATIONS

Among the barbarian peoples were the Celtic tribes in northern Scotland and in Ireland. (The common name for the Celtic Irish was, confusingly, Scots.) These Celts escaped the Roman domination that had befallen their cousins, the Britons and Gauls. The underlying culture of

France and Spain remained Celtic. Although Roman occupation imposed its government and civilization on the Celts, it did not destroy their own culture.

More numerous and more formidable than the Celts were the Germans, who were settled in a great arc that stretched from Scandinavia to the Black Sea. Historians have given these peoples the generic names of Germans or Goths, based loosely on their membership in the Germanic linguistic group to which their various dialects belonged. The term does not imply unity of culture, a self-designation by the people, or a relationship to modern Germans. Many of the Germanic tribes had long been exposed to Mediterranean influences and had some understanding of the Roman economy, warfare, and culture. From about 350, Christianity spread among the Germans north of the Danube, but in its Arian form. Beyond this Germanic cordon lived the still pagan Slavic tribes, also identifiable by their linguistic group, and the most numerous of the barbarians. When the tribes migrated, they traveled as family groups with their possessions, abandoning the land on which they had previously lived.

Huns and Germanic Peoples Germanic tribes had for centuries challenged the Roman frontiers because their primitive, unproductive economies forced them to search constantly for new lands to plunder or settle. The wealth and splendor of the Roman world attracted the Germans. The Romans

---

[1] The Greeks invented the word *barbaros* to imitate the strange sounds of unintelligible languages.

Chronology

THE GERMANIC INVASIONS

ca. 310	Goths and other Germans on the Danube.
ca. 350	Huns invade Europe, destroy Ostrogoths, and drive Visigoths to seek settlement south of the Danube in Byzantine territory.
378	Battle of Adrianople: Visigothic defeat of Byzantine army.
ca. 400	Franks, Alamans, Burgundians, Vandals, and others cross the Rhine into Gaul.
410–412	Visigoths sack Rome and move on into Gaul.
429	Visigoths in Spain and South Gaul.
ca. 430–500	Anglo-Saxons in England, Vandals in Africa, Franks in Gaul, Alamans in Alsace and upper Danube, Burgundians in Rhone Valley.
(d. 461)	St. Patrick: Conversion of Ireland.
(r. 485–511)	Clovis: Conversion of Franks to Roman Christianity.
(r. 493–526)	Theodoric and the Ostrogothic kingdom of Italy: Boethius and Cassiodorus.
(r. 527–565)	Justinian: Conquest of Vandal kingdom of North Africa and part of Spain and Italy.
(r. 590–604)	Pope Gregory the Great: Mission of Augustine (597) to England.
(664)	Council of Whitby: United English Christians under the papacy.
(r. 714–741)	Charles Martel: Defeats the Arabs at Tours (Poitiers) in 732.
751	Pepin III: Becomes King of Franks with papal support, anointed by pope in 754.

brought them into the Empire initially as slaves or prisoners of war, then as free peasants to settle on deserted lands, and finally as mercenary soldiers and officers. By the fourth century, however, the barbarian penetration of the Empire became more violent because the barbarians themselves were being invaded and forced southwestward by nomadic hordes from central Asia.

The nomads who sowed tumult in the barbarian world were the Huns, a people probably of Mongolian or Tatar origin. Perhaps in reaction to climatic changes that desiccated their pastures, the Huns swept out of their Asiatic homeland and terrorized Western Europe. Unlike the Germanic tribes, they had no previous contact with Rome or Christianity. Their great chief Attila (r. 433?–453), the "scourge of God" according to Christian writers, established his horde on the plain of the middle Danube and from there led the Huns on raids into both Gaul and Italy. With Attila's death in 453, the Hunnic empire disintegrated, but the Huns had already given impetus to the great movement of peoples that marks the beginning of the Middle Ages.

Visigoths   The Visigoths (or West Goths) were the first of the Germanic tribes that the Huns dislodged. Fleeing before the Huns, the Visigoths asked the Byzantine emperor to settle them in a depopulated area south of the Danube. In 376 the

▼ VISIGOTHIC FIBULAE
Fibulae were decorative pins used to fasten clothes. These sixth-century Spanish examples are typical of the sophisticated metalwork practiced by medieval artisans. Gems set in gold and bronze reveal the outline of an eagle form, as well as a delight in pattern that was characteristic of the age.
Walters Art Gallery, Baltimore

emperor Valens admitted them into the Empire. Although the Visigoths were willing to settle peacefully, the Byzantine officials treated them miserably, raping their women and forcing them to sell children into slavery in return for food. The starving Goths rebelled and Valens led an expedition against them. The triumph of the Visigothic cavalry over the Byzantine army at the battle of Adrianople in 378 showed the superiority of the Gothic mounted warrior (the prototype of the medieval knight) over the Roman foot soldier.

Continuing their westward movement, the Visigoths sacked Rome in 410, the first time in 800 years that a foreign army had occupied Rome. The Visigoths took gold and silver treasure, slaves, and movable property. The devastated Romans asked the Visigoth leader what he would leave for them, and he is reputed to have replied, "Your lives." Crossing the Alps into Gaul, the Visigoths established in 418 the first autonomous kingdom on Roman soil. At its height in the mid-fifth century, the kingdom of the Visigoths extended from Gibraltar to the Loire River. Another Germanic people, the Franks, conquered the Visigothic kingdom in Gaul in the sixth century and confined the Visigoths to Spain.

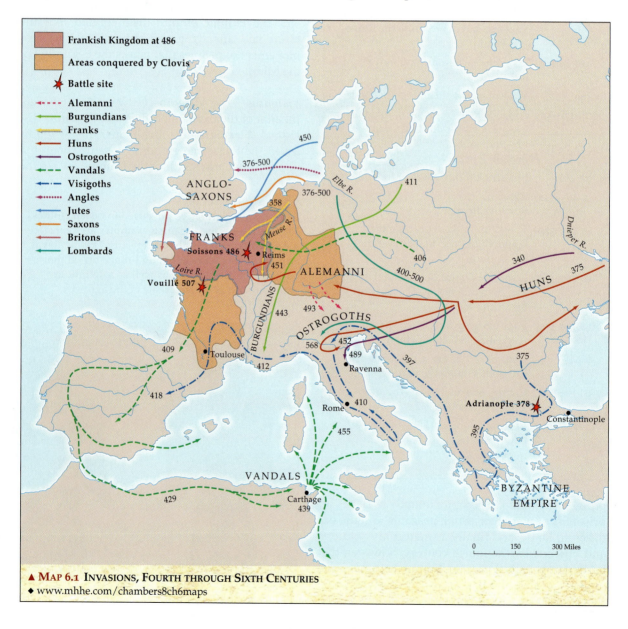

▲ **Map 6.1** Invasions, Fourth through Sixth Centuries
◆ www.mhhe.com/chambers8ch6maps

Vandals and Burgundians   The Vandals were another Germanic people that the Huns forced out of their territory. Coming from eastern Germany, the Vandals crossed the Rhine River into Gaul in 406. Perhaps eighty thousand in number, they continued south through the Iberian Peninsula (Spain) and crossed to North Africa, where they established a permanent kingdom in 429. Like the Visigoths, the Vandals were Arians, and they persecuted orthodox Christians. They became so powerful on the Mediterranean Sea that in 455 they were able to plunder Rome. This act, the cruelty involved in their religious persecutions, and their piracy in the Mediterranean earned the Vandals a reputation for senseless violence, which the modern word *vandal* still reflects. The Vandal kingdom survived until the Byzantine emperor Justinian destroyed it in the sixth century.

The Burgundians, another Germanic tribe from eastern Europe, followed the Vandals into Gaul, probably in 411. These Germans established an independent kingdom in the valleys of the upper Rhône and Saône rivers in 443, which gave the region its permanent name, Burgundy (see map 6.1).

Ostrogoths   The ease with which all these Germanic peoples invaded the Roman frontiers shows that the Empire had lost virtually all authority in the West by the middle of the fifth century. The emperor Valentinian III was the last Roman to exercise any real power in the West. A series of feeble emperors were raised to the throne and then deposed or murdered by German officials, who were the effective rulers. One of these rulers, Odovacar, deposed the last emperor in 476. Although no more than a palace mutiny, this coup marks the final passage of power from Roman to German hands in the West.

The Ostrogoths (eastern Goths) moved into the territory vacated by the Visigoths at the invitation of the Byzantine emperor. Young Theodoric, son of one of their kings, was sent as a hostage to Constantinople. There he learned at least something of Greek and Roman culture, although he continued to adhere to Arian Christianity. The emperor so favored him that he was even made a Roman citizen. When Theodoric united all of the Ostrogoths under his command, they became too dangerous to keep in the East and the emperor dispatched Theodoric and the Ostrogoths to deal with

▲ SUTTON HOO DRAGON OF ANGLO-SAXON ENGLAND
There were many metallic buckles and pins found at Sutton Hoo, the ship burial site of the East Anglian king Anna, who died in 654. Shown here is a dragon, made of gilt bronze and garnet. The body, extending from the head—with its jaws, teeth, and garnet eye—to the tail, is embellished in a style common at the time, with intricate beasts intertwined in long ribbonlike patterns.
© British Museum (PS199015)

Odovacar. Theodoric led his troops into Italy in 489 and conquered it, overthrowing Odovacar in 493.

Germanic Tribes in Gaul   In the third and fourth centuries the Germanic tribes living just beyond the Roman frontier in the Rhine valley coalesced into two large federations, the Alemanni in the upper valley and the Franks in the lower valley. The Alemanni pushed beyond the Rhine into the middle of Gaul and founded a kingdom in 420. They give to both modern French and Spanish their names for Germany (*Allemagne, Alemania*). The Franks slowly penetrated into northern Gaul, moving across the valley of the Seine up to the Loire River. By the fifth century they had separated into two peoples: the Salian, or "salty," Franks, who occupied the lands from the shores of the British Channel to the Loire valley (excluding only Brittany); and the Ripuarian, or "riverbank," Franks, whose history is wrapped in obscurity but who seem to have settled between the Rhine and Meuse rivers. The first-mentioned king of the Salians, a figure who stands on the dark margin between legend and history, was called Merovech, and he gave his name to the first dynasty of Frankish kings, the Merovingians.

Anglo-Saxons in Britain The Romans had withdrawn their legions from Britain in 407 to defend Rome against the Visigoths, leaving the island open to invasion. The Germanic settlement of Britain differed from the conquests on the continent. Rather than traveling as family groups, the Angles, Saxons, Jutes, and even some Franks came in small bands under the authority of chiefs. These Germanic peoples did not settle and assimilate with the native peoples (the Britons) as they did in most other Roman provinces; they either exterminated the Britons or pushed them westward into Cornwall and Wales.

For a few decades in the early sixth century the Britons in Britain unsuccessfully rallied against the Germanic invaders under a king whom later sources call Arthur, but after 550 the invaders triumphed and imposed their language on the region. So sharp was the linguistic change thus enforced that modern English, apart from place names, shows little trace of the speech of the original Britons.

The Early Slavs The Slavic tribes living to the east of the Germans embarked on their own extensive migrations. In the fifth and sixth centuries some Slavic tribes pushed their settlements as far west as the Elbe River and as far north as the Baltic Sea; they are the ancestors of the modern West Slavs—the Poles, Czechs, and Slovaks. During the same years, other Slavic tribes penetrated into the Balkan peninsula and Greece; their descendants are the modern South Slavs—the Serbs, Croats, Bulgarians, and Macedonians. Still other tribes moved east beyond the Dnieper River and north into the forest regions of Russia; they are the ancestors of the modern East Slavs—the Russians, Ukrainians, and Belarussians (or White Russians).

◆ GERMANIC SOCIETY

Much of what we know about Germanic society comes from a Roman historian and writer, Cornelius Tacitus (ca. A.D. 56–120). While he lived before the period of the invasions, he knew of Germanic customs from talking to Germanic soldiers and slaves. In recent years archaeology has

done much to supplement his account of the these peoples.

Social Structure Germanic society was composed of chiefs who distinguished themselves by success in battle, free warriors and their families, and some slaves. The Germanic free warrior owned land, and individual ownership existed as far back in their history as our knowledge goes. Individual ownership allowed some families to become richer than others. Germanic society was not egalitarian. Families with a common ancestry were linked together into kindreds (groups of near relatives). The kindred fought, migrated, settled, and held certain forms of property (forests and wastelands) in common.

The kindred also adjudicated disputes among its members and avenged injuries done to them. Compensation was defined in money for loss of a person's life. The amount of compensation, called a *Wergeld* (literally, "man money"), depended on the social rank of the individual. Offenders could also pay the family compensation for the loss of an arm, eye, teeth, or nose. The wergeld helped to prevent feuds.

Kindreds grouped together to form a tribe, a people, or a nation; members of a tribe always looked upon themselves, rightly or wrongly, as descendants from a common ancestor. Before the Germanic invasions of the Roman Empire, the tribes or peoples did not usually have kings; only the invasions, which required a continuing military command, made the king (who also served as chief priest) usual within Germanic society.

The Valued Role of Women A sensitive indicator of social values in any society is the status of women. Tacitus praises the Germans for their chastity and fidelity. German women, Tacitus also tells us, were mature at first marriage, and their husbands were their equals in age. Women were so valued in marriage that the family of the groom paid a dower (or marriage gift) to the bride, which was hers to keep and pass on to her heirs. When Germanic laws were recorded in the sixth century, the value placed on killing a woman of marriageable age was among the highest wergelds a murderer could pay.

Women made essential contributions to the Germanic household at every social level. A free

German male who aspired to be a warrior needed a wife who would tend his fields and watch over his flocks and herds during his absences on campaigns. The chief or king similarly looked for a wife who could collect his dues, pay his retainers, and manage his lands. The social importance of Germanic women was not, however, an unmixed benefit. According to Tacitus, they worked harder than the men did. In addition to doing much of the agriculture, women brewed, spun cloth, and made clothing for their families. They were often the prized booty for raiding expeditions and constant targets of abduction. Their life expectancy seems to have been shorter than that of males, and their resulting smaller number added to their social value.

Comitatus or Warrior Bands Warfare was a way of life and an integral part of the economy for the Germanic peoples. While herding, agriculture, and hunting provided much of their daily needs, the Germans also raided other peoples and eventually the Roman territory to get metals, slaves, and precious objects. The warriors were organized into bands under the leadership of a chief. Tacitus called this warrior band a *comitatus* ("following"), in which young warriors would join the retinue of an established chief, follow him to battle, and fight under his leadership in return for his protection and a share of his booty. Historians have traced the origins of feudalism to the comitatus (see Chapter 8).

Law and Procedures Germanic laws were not written down until the sixth century, and reliance on oral tradition explains several peculiarities of Germanic institutions. To recall the ancient laws, the Germans consulted old, respected men of the community, who could remember past customs. One of the most distinctive features of tribal government was its reliance on large councils or assemblies. The chief or king had only limited power and never made decisions alone; he always acted in an assembly or council of free warriors who aided him in making his judgments.

To confirm the making of contracts within the community, Germans (and the medieval world after them) relied heavily on symbolic gestures publicly performed. In conveying property, for example, the former owner would hand over a twig or a clod of earth to the new owner in the presence of witnesses. But since the memory of witnesses was often unreliable as a record of such agreements, the Germans also determined truth or falsehood, guilt or innocence, in disputes by investigating the character of the litigants or by appealing to magic. In a practice known as *compurgation,* twelve good men would swear to the honest reputation and presumed innocence of the accused. Or the accused would undergo an *ordeal* (the word originally meant "judgment"), such as stepping barefoot over hot irons or immersing a hand in boiling water; if the feet or hand showed no severe burns, the accused was declared innocent. Sometimes two litigants would simply fight before the court (trial by combat) on the assumption that an innocent man could not be vanquished.

All these practices influenced the development of medieval law and government. The use of juries in trials, a common practice of Europe in the Middle Ages, was based on the assumption that the entire community, represented by sworn men, should determine when a law was violated. The medieval king, like his early Germanic predecessor, was also expected to make his major decisions with the advice of senior men, assembled in councils (see "Tacitus on the Early Germans," p. 184).

The Literary Legacy of Germanic Poetry Since the Germans made little use of writing, their literature was preserved by oral transmission. They favored poetry, more easily memorized than prose, for literary expression. The earliest surviving examples of Germanic poetry were not written down until the ninth century, but they still provide an authentic reflection of Germanic culture, testifying to a violent age.

In the Anglo-Saxon epic *Beowulf,* the king of the Danes, Hrothgar, is powerless against the terrible monster Grendel; his plight illustrates the weakness of tribal kingship. Hrothgar must appeal for help to the hero Beowulf, a great warrior who comes from a tribe in southern Sweden. Beowulf succeeds in defeating Grendel by tearing off his arm. Grendel flees and dies. When Grendel's mother, a sea-witch, comes seeking revenge, Beowulf chases her to her underwater cave, where he finds a giant's ancient sword and slays Grendel's mother. Beowulf becomes king and dies

TACITUS ON THE EARLY GERMANS

The short book by Cornelius Tacitus, Germania, *published in 98, is virtually the only surviving portrait of early Germanic society. In this passage Tacitus describes the customs of the Germans in government.*

"On matters of minor importance only the chiefs deliberate, on major affairs the whole community; but, even where the people have the power to decide, the case is carefully considered in advance by the chiefs. Except in case of accident or emergency they assemble on fixed days. . . . When the mass so decide, they take their seats fully armed. Silence is then demanded by the priests, who on that occasion have also power to enforce obedience. . . . If a proposal displeases them, the people roar out their dissent; if they approve, they clash their spears.

"One can launch an accusation before the Council or bring a capital charge. The punishment varies to suit the crime. The traitor and deserter are hanged on trees, the coward, the shirker and the unnaturally vicious are drowned in miry swamps under a cover of wattled hurdles. The distinction in the punishment implies that deeds of violence should be paid for in the full glare of publicity, but that deeds of shame should be suppressed. Even for lighter offences the punishment varies. The man who is found guilty is fined so and so many horses or cattle. Part of the fine is paid to the King or State, part to the injured man or his relatives."

From H. Mattingly (tr.), *The Germania* (Penguin Classics, 1970), pp. 11–12.

---

years later in his last major fight against a dragon. The poem is rich in descriptions of drinking halls, court intrigues, kingship, and personal loyalties of a follower to his leader. Other than Grendel's mother, women do not play a role in the poem. Christian elements appear in the earliest written version, indicating that the poem underwent transformation over the years it was recited.

Religion and Superstition   Germanic religion displayed an abiding sense of pessimism. The Germans saw nature as a hostile force controlled by two sets of gods. Minor deities, both good and bad, dwelt in groves, streams, fields, and seas and directly affected human beings. Through incantations, spells, or charms, people tried to influence the actions of these spirits. Such practices strongly influenced popular religion and mixed with it a large element of superstition, which lasted through the Middle Ages and long beyond.

The higher gods lived in the sky and took a remote interest in human affairs. Chief among them was Woden, or Odin, god of magic and victory. Woden; his wife, Friia or Frig; Thor, the thunderer; Ti or Tyr, the god of war—all give their names to days of the week in all Germanic languages, including English.

The Art of Metal Working   Because they changed their homes so frequently, the Germans developed no monumental art—no temples, palaces, or large statues—before settling within the Empire. Their finest art was jewelry made from precious metals, often embodying forms of animals (see photos on pages 179 and 181). This animal style, probably originating in the steppe region of eastern Europe and Asia, strongly influenced early medieval art; even the lettering and illuminations in the manuscripts of that epoch reflect some of its motifs.

◆ GERMANS AND ROMANS

Historians have estimated, although on flimsy evidence, that the Germans who settled within the Roman Empire constituted no more than 5 percent of the total population. The Germans did not exterminate the Romans; rather, through gradual settlement and intermarriage with Romans, the Germans adopted lives that made them almost indistinguishable from their Roman counterparts. Some historians have argued that both Romans and Germans came to resemble the indigenous Celts.

Historians no longer speak confidently, as they once did, of the Germans being responsible for the

SIDONIUS APOLLINARIS ON LIVING WITH GERMANS

A Roman of patrician birth and training living in Gaul, Sidonius (ca. 431–ca. 480) wrote a series of letters to friends commenting on the loss of the Latin language, the wreck of the Roman Empire, and the crudity of the Germanic tribes.

"Though you descend in the male line from an ancestor who was not only consul—that is immaterial—but also (and here is the real point) a poet . . . yet here we find you picking up a knowledge of the German tongue with the greatest ease; the feat fills me with indescribable amazement. . . . You can hardly conceive how amused we all are to hear that, when you are by, not a barbarian but fears to perpetrate a barbarism in his own language. Old Germans bowed with age are said to stand astounded when they see you interpreting their German letters; they actually choose you for arbiter and mediator in their disputes. You are a new Solon in the elucidation of Burgundian law. . . . You are popular on all sides; you are sought after; your society gives universal pleasure. You are chosen as adviser and judge; as

soon as you utter a decision it is received with respect. In body and mind alike these people are as stiff as stocks and very hard to form; yet they delight to find in you, and equally delight to learn a Burgundian eloquence and a Roman spirit.

"Let me end with a single caution to the cleverest of men. Do not allow these talents of yours to prevent you from devoting whatever time you can spare to reading. Let your critical taste determine you to preserve a balance between the two languages [Latin and German], holding fast to the one to prevent us making fun of you, and practicing the other that you may have the laugh of us."

From O. M. Dalton, *The Letters of Sidonius,* 2 volumes, V. v. To his friend Syagriius (Clarendon Press, 1915).

---

destruction of the Western Roman Empire. Even before entering the Empire, many Germans, particularly those settled near the frontiers, had achieved a cultural level that resembled that of Romans living in those areas. In the northern part of Gaul, Celtic influences had already reemerged, and Roman influence proved to be a rather thin veneer on the region and its peoples. Assimilation, however, was slow and had a definite impact on Roman society. In the course of time, the Germanic chiefs and armies obtained perhaps a third of the territory of the former Western Empire. Some of them paid Romans for the confiscation. One Roman in Gaul wrote to a friend that he had lost all his lands, but eventually the Visigoth who took them sent him a payment much lower than the value of the land. Even this amount was enough that he could hold up his head in Roman society again. The letters of Sidonius Apollinaris (431–480) are eloquent about the experiences of the Roman patricians (see "Sidonius Apollinaris on Living with Germans," above).

Changes Following Settlement   The settling tribes changed the landscape and language of the

areas they invaded. Before the invasions the tribes had lived in nucleated villages (houses in a central area and fields surrounding the housing area). When they moved into the Roman Empire, the Germanic tribes showed a preference for continuing this settlement pattern rather than living in cities. Since those Romans who had villas also preferred to live in the countryside, urban populations shrank and the infrastructure of the cities, such as aqueducts, disappeared. With education abandoned except in the Church and among some Romans, the Latin language was no longer commonly written or spoken, and vernacular languages (the romance languages, or languages derived from the Roman one) began to develop.

As the invaders settled and established states modeled as much as possible on their understanding of Roman government, they needed written law rather than oral tradition. The Germanic law codes, modeled on Roman law codes but codifying Germanic law, included the schedule of wergelds and the power of kings. The codes allowed Romans to continue under their own laws.

Intermarriage in the population was inevitable. The Roman middle class married with the invaders. Most of the humble Germanic free warriors settled as cultivators on the land. If there were anxieties among Roman or Germanic parents about intermarriage or among free warriors becoming peasants, these anxieties are not expressed in written accounts.

Christianity and the Tribes By the time many of the tribes entered Europe, they had already converted to Christianity. The conversion began with Ulfila (ca. 310–ca. 381), the son of Christian parents who lived in the land of the Goths. His parents had been captured by the Goths so that he grew up a Gothic-speaking Christian. He received a Christian education and was consecrated in 341 by the bishop of Constantinople, who was the leader of the Arian party. Ulfila brought the Arian version of Christianity to the Goths and translated the Bible into their language. From these early missionary activities Arian Christianity spread to the Visigoths, Vandals, and Ostrogoths.

The difference between the Arian Goths and the Roman Christians was one of the most serious barriers to peaceful settlement of the tribes. Most of the Arian kings persecuted the native Christian population. Only the Franks, under Clovis, converted to Roman Christianity. Because of this early conversion, the Frankish rulers developed a close relation with the Roman Church.

II. The New Political Structures

By the beginning of the sixth century, the initial wave of tribal migrations into the West had eased and the tribes began to settle, forming monarchies and recording their law in imitation of the Romans. While the Western Empire was undergoing a major reconfiguration of its political landscape that only partially resembled its Roman past, the Eastern Empire continued to flourish.

◆ THE EARLY BYZANTINE EMPIRE

The name Byzantine is, strictly speaking, a historical misnomer. The inhabitants of the Eastern Empire recognized no break between their civilization and that of classical Rome. Throughout their history they called themselves *Romans*, even after Rome had slipped from their power and

they had adopted Greek as their official language. Indeed, modern Western historians sometimes forget that the Roman Empire did not fall in the East until 1453.

Capital at Constantinople Byzantine history began when the emperor Constantine transferred the capital of the Roman Empire from the West to the East in 330. The emperor probably had many motives for moving the capital further east, including the larger Christian population in the east. It was also the wealthiest and most populous part of the Empire, and Constantine found, as had his predecessor, Diocletian, that it was easier to

▼ **This Byzantine gold cup, dating from the sixth or seventh century, was found at Durazzo in modern Albania. Four female figures in gold repoussé symbolize the cities of Rome, Cyprus, Alexandria, and Constantinople. The detail shows the figure of Constantinople. The representation of cities in allegorical form indicates the prominence of urban centers in Byzantine thought and society.**
Metropolitan Museum of Art, Gift of J. Pierpont Morgan, 1917 (17.190.1710) Photograph © 2001 The Metropolitan Museum of Art, New York.

▲ Emperor Justinian, Ravenna
The mosaics—patterns made from small chips of tinted glass backed with gold leaf—that cover the wall of the church of San Vitale in Ravenna are one of the greatest achievements of the Byzantine era. Here, the emperor Justinian is surrounded by both priests and warriors, emphasizing his power over the religious as well as the secular domain.
Scala/Art Resource, NY

raise both money and troops to defend the Empire. The most threatening of the external enemies were also on the eastern frontier, including the Persian Empire and various Germanic tribes.

Constantine chose as his new capital the site of the ancient Greek colony of Byzantium, located on a narrow peninsula that appears as a hand trying to connect Europe and Asia. The official name of the rebuilt city was New Rome; however, it soon came to be called the City of Constantine, or Constantinople, after its founder.

The location of this capital influenced the character of Byzantium and the course of its history. The city stood at the intersection of two heavily traveled trade routes: the overland highway from the Balkans to Asia Minor and the maritime route between the Black and Mediterranean seas. Moreover, the city at once acquired the aura of a Christian city, the capital of the Christian empire. Because of his close association with the emperor, the bishop of Constantinople enjoyed the high status of patriarch, and in the entire Church only the bishop of Rome ranked above him.

Abandonment of the West The successors of Constantine had no intention of abandoning the powers of the old Roman Empire in either the West or the East. However, the Eastern emperors lacked the resources to come to the aid of the Western emperors. They could only try to preserve the boundaries in the East by a combination of warfare against the barbarians and paying tribute to them to remain in peace within the borders. When the Visigoths and Ostrogoths became rebellious, the emperors paid them to go west. The idea of restoring the Empire to its former size, power, and glory was never lost. The emperor whose actions best illustrate this aim was Justinian.

◆ JUSTINIAN THE GREAT (R. 527–565) OF BYZANTIUM

Justinian pursued three principal goals in his reign: the restoration of the Western provinces to the empire, the reformation of laws and institutions, and an ambitious program of splendid public works.

Justinian and Theodora   Historians have much information, or at least many allegations, about Justinian from his court historian, Procopius. While the emperor lived, Procopius praised him in two official histories: *On the Wars* recounts Justinian's victorious campaigns, and *On Buildings* describes his architectural achievements. But after Justinian's death, Procopius also wrote one of the most vicious character assassinations in history. *The Secret History* paints Justinian, empress Theodora, and several high officials of the court as monsters of public and private vice. Historians still have not satisfactorily reconciled the contradictory portraits that the two-tongued Procopius has left to us.

Justinian's name is linked to that of his empress, Theodora, with whom he shared power. Born in about 500, Theodora became a famous actress and a celebrated courtesan before she was twenty. She traveled through the cities of the Empire, earning her way, according to Procopius, by skilled prostitution. In her early twenties she returned to Constantinople, where she mended her morals, but lost none of her charm, and married Justinian. She was, in sum, an outsider, with no roots in the social establishment of the capital and no inclinations to respect its conventions.

Theodora's influence on her husband was decisive from the start. In 532 the popular factions of Constantinople rose in a rebellion known as the Nike Revolt. The two parties at the chariot races at the hippodrome in Constantinople were known as the Blues and the Greens. In addition to supporting their own horses and drivers, they had taken different sides on religious and political divisions in the Empire. Uniting against Justinian and Theodora, they rebelled. Justinian panicked

and planned to flee. But in a moving speech, as recorded by Procopius, Theodora urged her husband to choose death rather than exile. Justinian remained and crushed the uprising.

Reconquest of the West   To restore imperial rule over the lost Western provinces, Justinian attacked the kingdoms of the Vandals, Ostrogoths, and Visigoths and sought a precarious peace with the Persians beyond his eastern frontier. By 554 his troops had destroyed the Vandal kingdom in North Africa and established Byzantine rule there; had forced the Visigoths in Spain to cede the southern tip of the Iberian peninsula; and had triumphed, at least for a while, over the Ostrogothic kingdom in Italy (see map 6.2). Although Justinian finally controlled only Sicily and southern Italy, Ravenna became the glorious center of Byzantine conquest in Italy. The Greek presence remained strong in these places throughout the Middle Ages. Ravenna preserves churches with mosaics of Justinian and Theodora.

Justinian sought to reconcile the Eastern and Western branches of the Church, which were bitterly divided over a theological question concerning the nature of Christ.[2] He had the pope abducted from Rome and taken to Constantinople, where he bullied him into accepting an unwelcome compromise. Justinian's coercive tactics did not bring union and peace to the Church, and all the conflicting parties bitterly resented them.

Codex Justinianus   In 528 Justinian appointed a commission to prepare a systematic codification of Roman law. The result was the *Corpus Iuris Civilis* ("Body of Civil Law"), often called Justinian's Code. It consisted of four compilations: the *Codex*, an easily consulted arrangement of all imperial edicts according to topics; the *Digest*, or *Pandects*, a summary of legal opinions; the *Institutes*, a textbook to introduce students to the reformed legal system; and the *Novellae*, a collection of new imperial edicts issued after 534. These

---

[2]The Monophysite theory holds that Jesus has one nature, partly divine and partly human; he was not, in other words, simply true man. Condemned as heretical at the Council of Chalcedon (451), the belief remained strong in the East. The orthodox view is that Jesus has two natures, one human and one divine, and is both true God and true man.

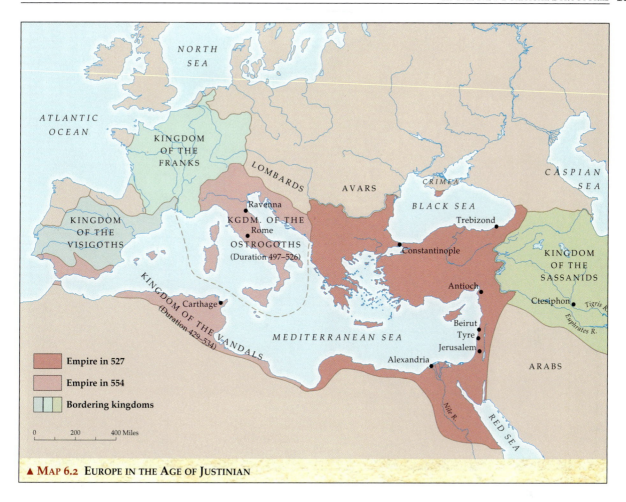

▲ **MAP 6.2** EUROPE IN THE AGE OF JUSTINIAN

works are the last major ones written in Latin in the East; the language of the Empire was now Greek.

It would be hard to exaggerate the importance of the *Corpus Iuris Civilis.* It has remained for all subsequent generations the largest and richest source of information concerning the legal institutions and thought of Roman antiquity. In the Middle Ages international and commercial law were based on it, as was much of Church law. The modern legal systems of most Western countries incorporate the principles of Roman law as preserved in the Corpus.[3]

---

[3]The British Commonwealth and the United States (except Louisiana) follow common law, based on cases decided in medieval England; but common law too was strongly influenced by Roman legal concepts.

Hagia Sophia The destruction that the Nike revolt caused in Constantinople gave Justinian an opportunity to start a rebuilding program. The most spectacular of his many new churches, palaces, and public works was the great church of Hagia Sophia, or Holy Wisdom. Begun in 532 and completed in 537, it became the model for churches all over the Empire. As Procopius described it, its great dome seemed to float in the air, as if suspended by a chain from heaven. Hagia Sophia is one of the acknowledged architectural masterpieces of the world. Like other Byzantine churches, it was decorated with brilliant mosaics, but most of these were destroyed by the iconoclasts (people who regarded the use of icons for worship as a form of idolatry) in the eighth and ninth centuries. Because of the iconoclastic movement, the richest examples of the early mosaics

▲ INTERIOR OF HAGIA SOPHIA
Hagia Sophia, the monumental project of the emperor Justinian, is a lasting reminder of the power of the Byzantine Empire. The saucerlike dome, which rises 180 feet, is carried on four pendentives (the wedge-shaped supports that allow a circular dome to rest on a square structure) and is a notable achievement of Byzantine engineering. The original mosaics were destroyed during the iconoclastic controversy, redone afterwards, and whitewashed by the Turks after the conquest of Constantinople in 1453.
© 1993 Tibor Bognár/Corbis Stock Market

are not to be found in Constantinople and Asia Minor but rather in areas that were no longer under Byzantine rule in those centuries. San Vitale and San Apollinare in Ravenna, Italy, are particularly noted for early Byzantine mosaics.

Historical Assessment of the Reign Justinian was remarkably successful in all his ambitious policies until the last years of his reign. Beginning in 542, terrible plagues (the same type of plague as the Black Death in the fourteenth century) repeatedly struck the imperial lands. Justinian was waging a two-front war against the Persians to the

east and the resurgent Ostrogoths on the western frontier. The strains on human resources left the entire Empire on the defensive at his death.

Historians have viewed Justinian's policies as unrealistic, excessively ambitious, and ultimately disastrous. Memories of ancient Roman greatness blinded him to the inadequacy of his own resources. Yet Hagia Sophia and the *Corpus Iuris Civilis* ensure him a permanent reputation in both the East and the West.

In the years following Justinian's death, new invaders overwhelmed the frontiers and wrested from his successors most of the territorial acquisitions of his reign. These emperors could not recover the Western provinces of the old Roman Empire, and the Byzantine Empire, unable to remain a universal state, had to find its way as an Eastern, and exclusively Hellenic, Empire.

▼ Baptism of Clovis I

Although this depiction of Clovis comes from a fourteenth-century manuscript, it suggests the continuing power of his image and particularly the importance of his conversion and baptism, which is here commemorated some 800 years after the event. Even as the bishop performs the baptism, he is helped by an angel from above. Apart from its content, this miniature is a splendid example of the way the initial letters of chapters were decorated by medieval monks.
The Huntington Library, San Marino, CA

◆ THE FRANKISH KINGDOM

Unification under Clovis The founder of the kingdom of the Franks was Clovis (r. 485–511),[4] putative grandson of Merovech, king of the Salians. Clovis' great accomplishment was the political unification of nearly the whole of Gaul, corresponding roughly to most of modern France. Already king of the Salians, he had himself elected king of the Ripuarians and thus ruled a united Frankish people. According to the bishop and historian Gregory of Tours (538–594), one of the reasons Clovis succeeded in becoming the sole ruler was that he killed all his relatives who might challenge him. His sons added both Burgundy and Provence to the kingdom, nearly completing the conquest of Gaul.

No less important than military force for unification was Clovis' conversion, probably about 496, to Roman, rather than Arian, Christianity. Gregory of Tours tells us that Clovis' wife, Clotilda, urged him to convert and that he had promised to be baptized if he won a battle that he was losing. Winning it, he and all his troops were baptized. This step facilitated his conquests and made possible the peaceful assimilation of the diverse peoples he ruled. As the first barbarians to accept Roman Christianity, the Franks became the "eldest daughter" of the Western Church and soon its acknowledged sword and champion.

The Later Merovingians Clovis had established a strong Frankish kingdom in Gaul, but his Merovingian successors, known traditionally as the "do-nothing kings," showed the weaknesses of tribal monarchy. Unable to conceive of the kingdom as anything but a private estate, they divided and redivided their lands among their heirs. Frankish custom dictated partible inheritance, that is, all surviving sons inherited the property equally. To resolve territorial disputes, the Merovingians relied primarily on violence to define their powers. The history of their reigns is largely a dismal story of intrigue and destructive feuds. Nevertheless, they enlarged their territory by subjugating the Burgundians and Alamans.

---

[4]His name is really a cognate of Louis; thus, by this historical oddity, all the long line of French kings named Louis are misnumbered.

Amid wars and rivalries among the Merovingians, the character of Frankish society was changing; the decisive shift was in the technique of making war. The introduction of the stirrup, probably in the early eighth century, gave a final advantage to the mounted warrior over the foot soldier: He could now strike a hard blow without falling from his horse. This improvement confirmed the superiority, which had been evident for several centuries, of cavalry over infantry. Since horses were expensive, war became a preeminently aristocratic occupation; therefore, a new functional and social division appeared in Frankish society. In the past most freemen had been both peasants and warriors. Now freemen who could not afford horses and arms—a majority of the population—became full-time peasants; those freemen who could afford the new implements of battle became full-time fighters and formed the new military aristocracy.

Because of the Merovingian kings' negligence, their chief household official, known as the mayor of the palace, gradually took over the real powers of government. The mayor's functions were to manage the palaces and supervise the royal lands; he was also able to distribute the lands largely as he saw fit. Using this privilege, some of the mayors began to supply the aristocracy with the estates they needed to maintain expensive animals and arms. The mayors thus built a following among the new military aristocracy. One mayor, Pepin of Heristal (d. 714), who already administered the eastern lands of the kingdom, gained control over the western lands in 687, thus unifying nearly the whole kingdom of Gaul under his administration.

Charles Martel   Pepin's son and successor, Charles Martel, or "The Hammer" (r. 714–741), succeeded in defeating the Arab advance into Europe at the battle of Tours in 732 (see p. 223). This great victory saved the Frankish lands from invasion and stopped the advance of the Arabs in Europe. He cultivated the support of the warrior aristocracy by granting them land for their service. He encouraged Christian missionaries to convert newly conquered people. With the aid of these two groups, Charles began to extend Christianity and Frankish domination over the Germanic tribes settled beyond the Rhine River.

Pepin the Short   Charles' son, Pepin the Short (r. 741–768) continued the policies of his father. The continuing support of the military aristocracy and the new sympathy of the ecclesiastical hierarchy enabled the mayor Pepin to effect a major constitutional change. In 751 an assembly of Frankish notables declared that the last Merovingian king, the feeble Childeric III, was not truly a king and recognized Pepin as their legitimate sovereign. Pepin had sent a delegation to the pope asking about the legitimacy of the change and had been assured that it was better that the person with the power of the king be actual king.

Threatened with attack on Rome by the Lombards, a Germanic people who had been harassing Italy, Pope Stephen visited King Pepin's court in 754 and anointed him king. The act left the implication that the Frankish king had a special tie to the papacy and to the Roman past. Twice Pepin came to Italy with troops and defeated the Lombards, confirming papal possession of the Patrimony of St. Peter (Rome and its environs). Later popes would repeatedly point to this Donation of Pepin as establishing the Papal States. By building strong Christian and Roman influences within his kingship, Pepin strengthened and transformed his reign. He bequeathed to his successors a monarchy founded on the support of great warriors and priests and dignified by association with the Christian and Roman past.

◆ KINGSHIP IN ITALY AND SPAIN

Theodoric and the Ostrogothic Kingdom in Italy
After the Visigoths had left Italy for southern Gaul and Spain, the Ostrogoths, led by King Theodoric (r. 493–526), settled in Italy (see p. 181). A shrewd ruler, Theodoric founded a kingdom in Italy that provided more than thirty years of peace. The Roman Christian bishops had helped the Ostrogoths conquer Italy even though they were Arian heretics. Theodoric, like Clovis, understood the importance of the Church and practiced a policy of toleration, even hiring Roman Christians for his government.

Theodoric made no attempt to combine the Gothic state with the remnants of the Roman one. He allowed the Goths to continue with their laws and customs while the native population continued under Roman law. But in his own government, he imitated Roman rulers. Knowing Byzantine traditions well from his youth in Constantinople, he issued law codes and kept a court in Ravenna similar to that of Byzantium. All officials were Romans rather than Goths.

Theodoric was liberal to the Roman population, returning two-thirds of the taxes to them and taxing the Goths as well as the Romans to keep the treasury full. He even undertook to rebuild cities. Toward the end of his reign, perhaps in response to the Church's attempt to put down Arianism, he became more suspicious of the Romans in his administration (see p. 204). After Theodoric's death, Justinian's wars set off bloody fighting in Italy.

Lombards A weakened Italy could not withstand the incursion of another Germanic tribe, the Lombards. Entering Italy in 568, they knew little about the Roman civilization or Christianity. Pope Gregory the Great bribed them not to attack Rome itself. After Pepin defeated them in the mid-eighth century, the Lombards settled in northern Italy (now called Lombardy).

Visigothic Kingdom The Visigoths could not control the vast territory that they had initially taken in Gaul and Iberia; Clovis defeated them in 507 and drove them into Spain. United under King Leovigild (r. 569–586), they gained control over most of the Iberian peninsula. Like Theodoric in Italy, Leovigild realized that he could rule only with the cooperation of the Roman landlords and bishops. As in Ostrogothic Italy, the period of Visigothic rule allowed Roman/Christian culture to flourish.

The Visigoths remained Arian until the reign of Leovigild's son, Reccared (r. 586–601). When he converted to Roman Christianity, most of his bishops also became adherents of that Church. The close relationship between the bishops and kings in Spain became important for the course of Spanish politics. The bishop of Toledo anointed the Visigothic kings in a ceremony similar to the ordination of a priest. Attacks on the kings were equated with attacks on Christ. The Visigothic kingdom fell in 711 to Muslim invaders, who had only to kill the king to subdue the country.

◆ ANGLO-SAXON ENGLAND

The invasions in the fourth through sixth centuries divided England into more than twenty petty dynasties and kingdoms. Unlike invaders into other lands, the invaders of England did not find Roman populations or Christian bishops, and the invaders themselves were not yet Christian converts. The story of Christianity in the British Isles is told later in this chapter. The invaders retained the Germanic government of kings and chieftains and warrior bands. In addition to Beowulf, a number of other poems date from this period, including *The Wanderer* and *The Seafarer*, which describe the adventurous lives of warriors and the loss of a powerful chief and protector.

The numerous petty dynasties coalesced into seven fairly stable kingdoms, traditionally known as the heptarchy: Northumbria, Mercia, East Anglia, Essex, Sussex, Kent, and Wessex (see map 6.3). The first kings to exert a stable hegemony over England were the rulers of Northumbria in the seventh and eighth centuries. This was the golden age of Northumbrian culture; the monastery at Wearmouth-Jarrow then counted among its members Bede the Venerable (see p. 206), the greatest scholar of his day. But Northumbrian rule was short-lived, and by the late ninth

▲ **MAP 6.3 ANGLO-SAXON ENGLAND**

century leadership passed to Egbert of Wessex and his successors.

III. The New Economy, 500–900

The great achievement of the Early Middle Ages was the emergence of the single-family peasant farm as the basic unit of agricultural production. There were three reasons for this development. First, many owners of villas found that they could not purchase new slaves and found it more economical to settle their slaves on family farms for which they paid rent to the estate owner. Second, changes in warfare, specifically the new supremacy of the mounted warrior, made fighting an expensive profession and converted many free warriors into full-time cultivators. Finally, a series of technological innovations in agriculture aided the peasant farmer in supporting himself, his family, and the new relationship between landlord and peasant farmer. As in the ancient world, most of the wealth came from agrarian pursuits, including the production of grains, wines, olive oil, and linen and woolen cloth.

◆ AGRICULTURAL INNOVATIONS

The Heavy-Wheeled Plow   The most fertile agricultural region of Europe is the great alluvial plain that stretches from southeast England and France to the Urals. The peoples of the ancient world had not been able to farm it efficiently. The light plow of antiquity only scratched the heavy soils of the north. The light plow was suitable enough for the thin soil and dry climate in the Mediterranean, where the best strategy was only to pulverize the surface in order to retain moisture. On the northern plain, however, the earth had to be cut deeply and turned to form the furrows needed to carry away excess water from the abundant rains. Thus, a heavier, more powerful plow was needed. Archaeological evidence has shown that such a plow emerged simultaneously among the Germans and the Slavs in the sixth century.

Other changes in farming techniques accompanied the development of the heavy plow. The Mediterranean plow required only two oxen to pull it, while the northern plow needed as many as eight. Thus, peasants in the north often kept oxen collectively and therefore needed to live in communities rather than in isolated individual settlements. Since the Germanic peoples had been accustomed to living in villages before they settled in former Roman territory, their agricultural arrangements suited their living preferences.

Efficient Use of Horses   At the same time, new techniques allowed peasants to use horses in addition to oxen as draft animals. The Romans had harnessed the horse with almost incredible inefficiency. Pliant straps around the horse's throat and belly could strangle a heavily loaded horse. Horses could pull only light chariots with this harness. In the ninth century northern Europeans developed a collar and harness that rested the load on the horse's shoulders, making the horse efficient for pulling wagons and plows. At about the same time, the tandem harness appeared, which permitted teams of horses to be hitched one behind the other. The horseshoe, introduced at this time, gave the animal better traction and protected its sensitive hooves.

Horses were faster than oxen for plowing and carting, but they were also a more expensive investment. They cost more to buy and, unlike oxen, they could not live on grass alone but had to be fed grain as well. As a consequence, horses were not universally used in agriculture in the Middle Ages.

The Three-Field System   Northern Europeans also developed a new method of crop rotation: the three-field system. An estate's arable land was divided into three large fields of several hundred acres each, with two-thirds of the land cultivated each year on a rotating basis. The system was first documented in 763. A field was planted in winter wheat, then in a spring crop—oats, barley, peas, or beans—then permitted to lie fallow for a year. (See map 8.1 for an illustration of the three-field system.) The older two-field system, based on the yearly alternation of winter wheat and fallow, continued to be used in Mediterranean lands, where spring crops were difficult to raise because rain was scarce in the spring and summer. The north, however, had abundant year-round rainfall.

The three-field system kept a larger portion (two-thirds) of the soil in crops each year. The

▲ Bad and Good Regiment, ca. 1125

This manuscript illustration shows a typical medieval plow team of oxen. The heavy plow used on the plains of Northern Europe included three indispensable parts: a colter, or knife, to cut the soil; a share, or wedge, to widen the breech and break up the clods; and a moldboard to lift the earth and turn the furrow.
Photo, D. Pineider, Biblioteca Medicea Laurenziana, Florence

fallow became pasture for village animals, and their manure returned the soil to fertility. With only one-third rather than one-half of the land lying fallow, the other two-thirds produced grain and other crops. Yields from the new crop rotation show the increased productivity: In the Mediterranean system, one bushel of planted grain yielded only two or three bushels at harvest, while in the new system the yields might be as high as seven bushels harvested.

A spring crop of legumes restored fertility to the soil, provided a more varied diet for the people, and lessened the risk of total failure, because two crops were planted in one year. A spring crop of oats was used for fodder and thus helped support a larger number of animals, which in turn provided manure for more abundant crops. Barley was turned into beer.

The agricultural innovations spread through Europe at a glacial pace, but their eventual adoption profoundly affected the new Western civilization. They allowed northern Europe to support a denser population and established a tradition of technical innovation that has remained alive and unbroken to the present.

Peasant Life A glimpse of the life of peasants comes from the estate books of the great abbey of Saint-Germain-des-Prés near Paris. The list of peasants shows that remnants of the old Roman *latifundia* system were still present, since some of the inhabitants were called slaves and others were free. Both the status listings and the names show that there had been considerable intermarriage among the original population of the estate and the newly settled Franks. Thus, Maurisius (a Roman name), a half-free man, was married to Ermegardis (a Germanic name). The peasants paid rent for their farms and had to provide labor for their lords, such as carting, plowing, harvesting, and hay making on the estate. True manorialism did not develop until the eleventh century (see chapter 8).

The settlement of the Germanic peoples as peasants brought its own revolution in the roles of men and women. Women, children, and slaves

▲ FRENCH ILLUMINATIONS OF PEASANTS
The division of labor by sex was a prominent part of the peasant economy. Men did the heavy field work including beating the grain of the stalk with a flail. Women did spinning and weaving. The symbol for the peasant man was the flail and for the woman the spindle.
The Giraudon/Art Resource, NY

had done all the agriculture during the period before migration, but once settled, men became the farmers as had been true in the ancient world. Handling the heavy plow and the large oxen teams was considered men's work. Women, in addition to caring for children, tended to domestic animals, produced cheese, brewed beer and mead (a fermented honey drink), and took up the Mediterranean women's tasks of spinning and weaving. As in ancient Greece, a special house was set aside for young women to spend a few years spinning and making cloth for the estate. The medieval artistic symbols for men and women reflected this agricultural shift: Peasant women were depicted with a spindle, and peasant men were shown at the plow or with a flail for beating grain from sheaves.

◆ TRADE AND MANUFACTURE

One of the central issues that economic historians of the early Middle Ages have debated is the decline of trade and towns as the political power of the Roman Empire waned in the West. Henri Pirenne laid out his thesis in *Mohammed and Charlemagne* (1935), arguing that the Germanic invaders did not destroy the Roman political and cultural life but tried to preserve it where they

could. It was only the Arab conquest of land surrounding the Mediterranean in the eighth century that brought Roman trade patterns to an end. Modern archaeology indicates that Northern Europe was developing trade routes and commercial goods before the Arabs dominated the Mediterranean.

Trade and Commerce The Mediterranean had been a great commercial artery for the exchange of Western goods, for the spices and fine cloths of the Levant, and for papyrus and grain from Egypt. Trade in Eastern luxury items never disappeared, because the Church and wealthy individuals demanded such items as silk, dyes, perfumes, olive oil, wine, and papyrus. Jews and Syrians carried on the trade with the East. Slaves (the word *slave* derives from *Slav,* which were the people most often sold) were traded to the East to pay for the luxury goods. Evidence of trade in gold from sub-Saharan Africa (Sudan) existed from the sixth century and became important by the tenth century through the Iberian Peninsula. Salt, tin, and copper were exported to Africa. Archaeological evidence, however, indicates that this trade was of minimal importance to the Western economy and that the trade that had characterized the western Mediterranean in Roman times had all but disappeared with the Visigothic and Vandal invasions in the fifth century. The eastern Mediterranean continued to provide vital trade until well into the seventh century.

A northern trade was gaining in importance. The Frisians were the most active traders, relying on the Rhine River to export cloth and luxury items into the hinterland of Europe. Through ports on the North Sea, the Frisians also traded with England, the coast of France, Denmark, and other Baltic countries. The cloth they traded, which was valued for its thick, waterproof quality, probably was the surplus production of estates and monasteries in northern Europe.

Towns and Production   Some historians have argued on the basis of written evidence that Roman towns continued to flourish and to manufacture goods for the surrounding countryside. Again, archaeology shows that the inhabited area of those Roman towns that continued to exist had shrunk to little more than ecclesiastical buildings, inns, and some residences. The thriving Roman pottery centers were gone, and towns ceased to serve as administrative centers except for Church business. Craft production was done at the village and estate level. Little trade moved any of this production around the hinterland. Luxury objects were circulated only among elites, both in the Church and in lay society.

IV. The Expansion of the Church

The Church in the early Middle Ages was both a dynamic leader, guiding the West in the period of the collapse of Roman authority, and the preserver of the classical educational traditions of literacy, rhetoric, and logic. The development of monasticism provided a new opportunity for pious men and women to live a life of prayer and service in a world in which much was changing. Within the walls of monasteries and nunneries as well as in bishops' residences, classical learning was preserved, copied, and taught. Missionaries went to frontier areas and converted to Christianity people who had never been exposed to the Roman civilization. The missionaries brought both Christian and Roman traditions to these peoples and incorporated into Christianity some of the traditions they found among these peoples as well. By the

beginning of the seventh century, all of Christian Western Europe had abandoned Arianism and adopted Roman Christianity. Concurrent with the monastic movements and missionary activities, the papacy developed as the religious and often the political leader in the West. Powerful popes filled the void left by the Roman state, carrying on diplomacy and legitimizing kings.

◆ ORIGINS OF THE PAPACY

The papacy—*pope* derives from *pappas,* a Greek word for *father*—had its origins in the bishopric of Rome. The pope's authority gradually grew in importance and power so that he became the head of the Roman Catholic Church.

Doctrine of Petrine Succession   According to the traditional Catholic (and medieval) view, Jesus himself endowed the apostle Peter with supreme responsibility for his church: "And I say unto thee, thou art Peter and upon this rock I will build my church, and the gates of hell shall not prevail against it" (Matt. 16:18). In the Aramaic language that Jesus spoke, as well as in Greek and Latin, *Peter* and *rock* are the same words, implying that the Church was to be founded upon Peter. This play on words has been called the most momentous pun in history. Medieval tradition further held that Peter became the first bishop of Rome and was martyred there about the year 60. Historical evidence does not conclusively establish Peter's presence in Rome.

Growth of Papal Primacy   Several factors led to the predominance of the Bishop of Rome and the subsequent growth of papal power. Rome was the city of the Caesars, the capital of the world, and the center of Latin culture; people were accustomed to seeking guidance from Rome. As the authority of the emperors waned and disappeared in the West, people still looked to Rome for leadership, and increasingly its bishop provided it. The emperors, eager to use the Church as an adjunct to their own imperial administration, favored the concentration of religious authority in the West in the Bishop of Rome's hands. During the invasions, the papacy represented the orthodox Christian practice as opposed to the Arian heresy of the Germanic invaders and so became the focal point of orthodox Christians in the West.

The idea of the primacy of the pope gained support in the fourth and fifth centuries, largely through the activities of powerful popes such as Pope Leo I (r. 440–461). It was he who sent a delegation to Attila the Hun to persuade him not to attack Rome. Leo I also addressed the issue of papal primacy in numerous letters and sermons, identifying the living pope as the successor of Peter and enjoying the same powers that Peter had as the chosen disciple. Although the popes were not exercising an autocracy over the Church, their prestige in the Western world was unrivaled. Some church leaders expressed doubts about the primacy of the pope, maintaining that all bishops were equal in authority. The patriarch of Constantinople, primate of the Eastern Christians, did not recognize the superior authority of the papacy.

Gregory the Great The popes increasingly assumed responsibility for the security of Italy and the defense of the Church. They negotiated with a sequence of invaders—Huns, Vandals, Ostrogoths, and Lombards—and repeatedly sought help from the distant and distracted Eastern emperors. The pope who best exemplifies the problems and accomplishments of the early medieval papacy is Gregory I (r. 590–604).

When Gregory became pope, the Lombards were plundering the Roman countryside and threatening Rome with destruction and starvation. Under these difficult conditions, Gregory maintained the productive capacity of the Church's estates, kept food coming to Rome, ransomed captives, aided widows and orphans, and organized the defense of the city. Gregory finally negotiated a truce with the Lombards in 598, although they continued to pose a threat to the security of Rome for more than a century.

Gregory was no less solicitous for the welfare of the entire Church. During his pontificate Gregory gave new momentum to missionary efforts and achieved some remarkable successes. The Spanish Visigoths were converted from Arian to Roman Christianity during Gregory's reign. By establishing a tradition of active involvement in the affairs of the world, to which most of his medieval successors would faithfully adhere, Gregory widened enormously the influence of the Roman see.

Like many of the early church leaders, Gregory came from a Roman patrician background and

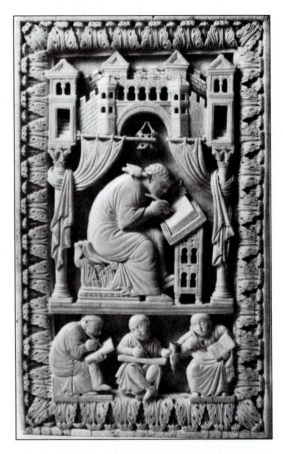

▲ **Pope Gregory the Great was one of the key figures in the transition from the ancient world to the Middle Ages. He is regarded—along with Jerome, Ambrose, and Augustine—as one (and the last) of the four fathers of the Latin Church. His efforts to defend Rome against the Lombards and to advance missionary work gave added prestige to the papal see.**
Art Resource, NY

had been educated to be an imperial administrator. Using the experience of his career in the civil administration of the declining Roman state, he organized the estates belonging to the papacy around Rome to provide a more solid financial base for the papacy. This action by Gregory is an example of the survival of Roman governmental genius in the service of the Church.

◆ MONASTICISM

Even more effective than the papacy in shaping medieval civilization were the monks. The ascetic ideal of fleeing the world in order to devote oneself to worship is common to many religions. Beginning in the third century, highly devout Christians who sought refuge in permanent prayer and isolation began to live apart from the daily world. The most renowned of these was St. Anthony, who lived a life of rigid asceticism in the desert of Egypt for more than twenty years (started ca. 285). Some of the early Syrian hermits, such as Simon Stylites, lived on a pillar for years, eating only millet seeds. The Church Father Jerome criticized hermitic excesses, commenting that if beards made a man holy, all goats were holy.

It became more common for people who wished to follow an ascetic life to live and work together in cenobitic ("living in common") monasticism. Even Anthony found that the numbers of people who flocked to his isolated retreat had to be organized and given rules for guidance. Egypt was the home of the first true monasteries and nunneries, with the days divided by work and prayer. St. Basil, the father of Greek monasticism, spent a year in Egypt before establishing a monastery (ca. 360) in Greece. The Basilian order, which is still in existence today, established the tradition of shared meals, sleeping quarters, and common prayers. It became the predominant order in the Eastern Empire. Double houses, monasteries and nunneries with communities of the opposite sex attached to them, were common in early monasticism in the East and in Gaul and Anglo-Saxon England.

Benedict and the Benedictine Rule

The man who designed the most common Western form of monasticism—St. Benedict, a Roman patrician—founded a community at Monte Cassino in ca. 520 and drew up a rule, or manual of conduct, for its members. The Benedictine rule dealt with all the main problems of monastic life, including food (the rule provided for an allotment of wine each day) and clothing, discipline, prayer, the work of monks, and sleeping arrangements. The rule was a flexible one, applicable to many individual communities. The abbot was to be elected for life, with full authority over the community, but he was to consult the elder and even the younger monks. One of the most famous regulations required some manual labor, lending to it a dignity that both the Greeks and Romans had denied. "Idleness," said the regulation, "is the enemy of the soul." The core vows for joining the Benedictine

order were poverty, chastity, and obedience (see "The Rule of St. Benedict on the Clothing of Monks," p. 200).

Early Nunneries

From the earliest days of monasticism, women joined communities of nuns. St. Jerome designed a rule for the women in his family and their friends. St. Basil's mother and sister were already living in a nunnery when he founded his monastic order. St. Scholastica, Benedict's sister, lived in a nunnery near Monte Cassino. In Anglo-Saxon England abbesses, such as Hilda of Whitby (657–680), headed double monasteries and had such prestige that princes and kings consulted them. Abbess Hilda encouraged learning at Whitby; five of its monks went on to become bishops.

Relationship of Monasteries to Lay Society

The monks exerted an extraordinary influence on every level of medieval civilization. They were the most successful agriculturists of the age, first as farmers in their own right and then, gradually, as

▼ **St. Benedict Presenting His Rule**
This fourteenth-century image depicts Saint Benedict presenting his rule to a group of nuns. His connection with female spirituality went back to his own lifetime, because his sister, Scholastica, was also devout and lived at a convent near Benedict's at Monte Cassino.
Bibliotheca Seminario Vescovile/Photo, © P. Tosi/Index, Florence

THE RULE OF ST. BENEDICT ON THE CLOTHING OF MONKS

◆

The rule of St. Benedict (ca. 480–ca. 550) tried to anticipate all the needs of monks and all the problems that might arise in monastic communities in terms of regulation of work, prayers, relations among the monks, visitors to the monastery, travel, and monastic vows. This humane rule became the basis of monastic rules in Western Europe.

"The clothing distributed to the brothers should vary according to local conditions and climate, because more is needed in the cold regions and less in warmer. This is left to the abbot's discretion. We believe that for each monk a cowl and tunic will suffice in temperate regions; in winter a woolen cowl is necessary, in summer a thinner or worn one; also a scapular for work, and footwear—both sandals and shoes.

"Monks must not complain about the color or coarseness of all these articles, but use what is available in the vicinity at a reasonable cost. However, the abbot ought to be concerned about the measurements of these garments that they not be too short but fitted to the wearers.

"Whenever new clothing is received, the old should be returned at once and stored in a wardrobe for the poor. To provide for laundering and night wear, every monk will need two cowls and two tunics, but anything more must be taken away as superfluous. When new articles are received, the worn ones—sandals or anything old— must be returned.

"Brothers going on a journey should get underclothing from the wardrobe. On their return they are to wash it and give it back. Their cowls and tunics, too, ought to be somewhat better than those they ordinarily wear. Let them get these from the wardrobe before departing, and on returning put them back.

"For bedding the monks will need a mat, a woolen blanket and a light covering as well as a pillow.

"The beds are to be inspected frequently by the abbot, lest private possessions are found there. A monk discovered with anything not given him by the abbot must be subjected to very severe punishment. In order that this vice of private ownership may be completely uprooted, the abbot is to provide all things necessary: that is, cowl, tunic, sandals, shoes, belt, knife, stylus, needle, handkerchief and writing tablets. In this way every excuse of lacking some necessity will be taken away."

From Timothy Fry (ed.), *The Rule of St. Benedict in Latin and English with Notes* (Liturgical Press, 1980), pp. 261–265.

---

managers of ever larger estates; thus, they set an example of good farming practices and estate management from which laypeople could benefit.

Monasteries and nunneries came to play a major role in early medieval society and government. Powerful families often established religious communities on their lands. The abbots and abbesses were often closely related to these prominent laypersons, and they administered the monastery's lands and resources in the interest of their lay relatives. Monasteries, in other words, became integrated into the structures of local power.

Kings, too, relied heavily on monastic farms to supply food for their administrations and armies and often appropriated part of the monks' income to finance their own needs. Able abbots served as advisors and administrators for the kings.

Education and Preservation of Learning Culturally, monks and nuns were almost the only people who were literate and learned. The Benedictine rule assumed that the monk could read; and the monasteries, although not expressly obliged to do so, maintained both libraries and schools for the training of young monks and nuns and, sometimes, lay children.

Monasteries organized *scriptoria*, or writing rooms, in which manuscripts that were needed for liturgy or education were copied. The great bulk of the surviving Latin literary works of both pagan and Christian antiquity were preserved in libraries, the monks were virtually the only intellectuals in society. Monastic scribes wrote nearly all the administrative records, lay and ecclesiastical, that have survived from the early Middle Ages.

The Appeal of the Ascetic Life Part of the monks' importance to society came from their communal organization, which enabled them to cope effectively with the problems of a turbulent

▼ **This Spanish manuscript illumination of daily life in the monastery shows that the writing of manuscripts was one of the monks' principal occupations. In addition, one of the monks is ringing the bells that marked the different services of the day and that also served to remind the surrounding countryside of the activities of the monastery.**
The Pierpont Morgan Library / Art Resource, NY

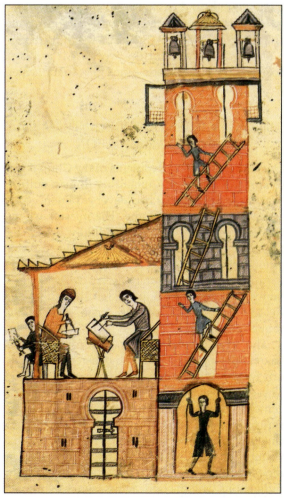

▲ Centula Abbey, after Eleventh-Century Manuscript
Centula Abbey, in northwestern France, was founded in 790 by Angilbert, a poet-scholar in Charlemagne's circle. This seventeenth-century engraving after a lost eleventh-century manuscript depicts the heart of a vast complex that included three churches (all known) and seven villages and that housed more than three hundred monks.
Bibliothèque Nationale de France, Paris

copies made in monasteries and nunneries. Sometimes monks decorated, or illuminated, the manuscript pages; manuscript illuminations are among the loveliest art forms that have come from the age. Because they maintained the schools and

age. Monasteries and nunneries provided a haven for people like Gregory the Great, St. Benedict, and St. Scholastica, to compensate for the disappearance of Roman intellectual life. At the same time, they extended charity to the poor and to pilgrims who stopped at their doors. Brothers and sisters with more practical skills were useful in monastic work and administration. In a turbulent age, the community provided a valued sense of continuity over generations.

Asceticism seems peculiarly suited to an age of transition. The ascetic, by his or her life, calls into question the accepted attitudes of the age. The monks rejected both the classical and barbarian systems of values and thus helped uproot or weaken attitudes such as the classical aversion to physical labor and the barbarian love of violence.

Finally, the monks and nuns were thought to ensure God's blessings for the world. Establishments of men and women who spent their life in prayer and charitable works were a hope and inspiration for those who did not have the opportunity to withdraw from the world. All ranks of society valued and made pious gifts to monasteries and nunneries.

◆ MISSIONARIES AND POPULAR RELIGION

One of the major achievements of the Church was to spread Christianity, including Roman culture, to parts of Europe that had never experienced extensive contacts with Rome. The missionary initiative was often made individually before the time of Gregory the Great. St. Patrick was a Briton who was captured and became a slave in Ireland. Escaping from his captors, he went to Gaul, where he was ordained a bishop. He returned to Ireland in 430 and converted the Irish, establishing monasteries there.

The Irish monks converted northern Anglo-Saxon England, establishing monasteries in northern England, including Lindisfarne and Whitby. These monasteries and nunneries became great centers of learning and religious crafts. They preserved many texts that were destroyed on the continent during the invasions. The illuminated manuscripts of these Celtic/Anglo-Saxon monasteries combined elements of Christianity with the indigenous designs of dragons, snakes, animals,

and plants, as can be seen in the *Book of Kells* and the *Lindisfarne Gospel*.

Benedictines as Missionaries Gregory the Great understood the potential of the Benedictines as missionaries. According to legend, he saw some fair-haired Anglo-Saxon children in the slave market and asked about their origins. Being told that they were Angles, he commented that they looked like angels. Further questions revealed that the Angles still worshiped trees and stones. Gregory sent a bishop, Augustine, to England with other priests in 597. Augustine found that the Kentish king's wife, Bertha, the great-granddaughter of Clovis and Clotilde, had been prevailing on the king to convert, and he eventually did convert to Roman Christianity.

The conversion of the Frisians and other groups to the east of the Rhine was more challenging. Anglo-Saxon Benedictines moved into this rough land with the blessings of the pope. Willibrord (later called Clement, 658–739) went to Frisia, and Winfrith (later Boniface, 675–754) went into Bavaria. They established churches where the pagans had formerly worshiped trees, sometimes even cutting down the sacred trees to build the church.

Elements of the former religion remained a part of Christianity, so that many of the days that had been pagan holidays were coordinated with saints' feasts. Conversion was gradual, and the new converts only partially understood the religion. Christianity brought the converts into contact with the wider world of the old Roman culture, including the Latin language and writings, and into potential trade and political contacts with other Christian peoples.

Council of Whitby As the Roman variety of Christianity, brought by Augustine of Canterbury, spread in England, it came into conflict with the Irish and Anglo-Saxon versions. The two versions had differences in the date for the celebration of Easter and in some points about monasticism.[5] Finally, at the Council of Whitby in 664, the king of

---

[5]Irish Christians set the date of Easter later than the Romans (reflecting later springs in the north), applied the tonsure (the haircut symbolizing clerical status) in their own way, and conceived differently the role and powers of the bishop.

Northumbria questioned both sides about their belief in St. Peter. When both agreed on Peter's primacy, he concluded that his people should observe Roman practices.

The Role of Miracles One of the convincing tools of conversion was miracles and stories of miracles. Stories of how saints cured sick people who worshiped at their tombs or how saints punished the ungodly when they stole sacred objects from churches conveyed a persuasive message about the power of the Christian God and his faithful followers. The miracle stories are historians' best source of popular culture during the early Middle Ages, because they record instances in daily life that were changed because of divine intervention.

◆ THE CHURCH AND CLASSICAL LEARNING

Christian writers had an ambiguous attitude toward classical texts: Many prominent Christian writers condemned classical literature as foolishness and an incitement to sin, and yet the classical authors provided both the language for study and philosophical texts that demanded reconciliation with Christian teachings. Christianity itself was a religion founded on a book, the Bible, and Christian theologians had to have the skill to read and interpret the sacred texts. Because the Church had not yet established its own schools, its scholars studied in secular schools, learning the techniques of philosophical argument and rhetorical expression that were traditional among pagan scholars.

Preservation of Classical Texts Christian scholars preserved a tradition of literacy in the fifth and sixth centuries, but their output accurately reflects the difficult conditions of their times and the biases of their own mental outlook. An important part of their literary effort was devoted to the preparation of textbooks that would preserve a modicum of ancient learning and the ability to read the ancient authors. One of the most influential of these textbooks was *Introductions to Divine and Human Readings* by Cassiodorus, a sixth-century monk and official in

◀ PHILOSOPHY CONSOLING BOETHIUS, EARLY ELEVENTH CENTURY
In his *Consolation of Philosophy*, Boethius described the embodiment of philosophy as a mature woman who had grown as tall as the heavens and carried a scepter and books. This image, from an eleventh-century manuscript, depicts philosophy as equal in height to the building whose solid facade and row of small windows may be the prison in which Boethius wrote his famous work.
Bibliothèque Nationale de France, Paris

Theodoric's government. In it he listed the religious and secular books that he thought a monk should copy and read. This book is about as appealing to modern readers as a library catalog, but at the time it was carefully studied and used to determine the holdings of medieval libraries.

Another sixth-century Christian scholar in Theodoric's service, Boethius, translated portions of Aristotle's treatises on logic from Greek into Latin; these translations were the main source of early medieval writers' limited but significant familiarity with Aristotelian logic until the thirteenth century. Boethius wrote on many other subjects as well and is most famed now for his *Consolation of Philosophy*, a meditation on death that does not mention the Christian religion. Boethius wrote the *Consolation* while imprisoned by Theodoric at the end of his reign. The book helped preserve the dignity of learning by showing the role that reason and philosophy play in solving human problems. In Spain classical learning was preserved by Isidore, bishop of Seville, in his *Etymologies,* which were a vast encyclopedia of ancient learning, covering in twenty books subjects from theology to furniture and providing a rich source of classical lore and learning for medieval writers.

Christian Writings Scholars also helped through original works to shape the character and interest of the age, especially by writing *exegeses,* or comments and interpretation, on the Bible. In this field the most important writer after St. Augustine was Pope Gregory. His commentary on the Book of Job made extravagant use of allegory in explaining the biblical text and set the style for biblical exegesis in the medieval world. Pope Gregory also taught readers, notably through his *Dialogues,* about the lives of the saints and the miracles that God wrought through them. Gregory had an ability to simplify works of theology and wrote the *Pastoral Care* as instruction for bishops.

Since Christians viewed history as a vast panorama illustrating and proclaiming God's miraculous providence, the study of history also evoked great interest among scholars. One of the most influential accounts was the *History of the Franks* by Gregory, bishop of Tours. Like many of

▲ CHI-RHO, *BOOK OF KELLS*
The Greek letters *chi* **and** *rho,* **the first two letters of Christ's name, were frequently used as symbols of Christianity by early believers. This page, from the late eighth-century Irish manuscript** *The Book of Kells,* **is an example of the complex interlacing that was characteristic of Anglo-Saxon manuscript illumination in this period.**
The Board of Trinity College Dublin

the early medieval historians, Gregory began with creation; he then recounted the history of the human race up to 591.

Learning and Scholarship Scholarship on the continent sank to its lowest level in the seventh and early eighth centuries, but it flourished in Ireland in the seventh and in England in the early eighth century. Scholars there enjoyed the relative shelter of an insular home. They had the zeal of new converts and a strong monastic system that supported the schools. Since they did not speak a language derived from Latin, they could learn a correct Latin in schools without being confused by related vernacular forms. Thus, their Latin was closer to classical Latin than that used on the continent.

The finest English scholar was undoubtedly Bede the Venerable (673?–735), whose *Ecclesiastical History of the English People,* an account of the conversion of the English and the growth of their Church, established his fame even until today. His high sense of scholarship is evident in his excellent Latin and in the careful way he cites his sources: oral interviews with knowledgeable eyewitnesses, documents from local archives, and accounts written at his request. His book is the product of a medieval writer, not a modern one; Bede recounted miracles, and the principal theme of his history is the story of salvation. But his belief that history was the unfolding of God's plan did not lead him to distort the material in his sources. He is a man who in any age would be recognized as a scholar.

SUMMARY
◆

By the close of the seventh century, Europe was much changed from the days of the Roman Empire. The new Visigothic kingdom controlled the territory that would become modern Spain, the Merovingians ruled over the former Roman province of Gaul, which had roughly the borders of modern France. Anglo-Saxon England under the Northumbrian hegemony included all of modern England. In Italy the pope had proved a powerful force not only in religion but also in politics. The people who moved into the old Roman Empire came as settlers. While their customs of governing were different from those of the Roman population, they soon blended their own practices with those of the Romans. Christianity proved one of the most powerful tools of assimilation because it taught both the Christian and Roman culture. Missionaries, drawn from the Benedictine monastic order, went beyond the borders of the old empire and converted those who had no exposure to the Roman world. The monastic orders provided a refuge for those who wanted to live a life of prayer and those who wanted to read classical philosophy and Christian theological texts. The preservation of texts was largely the work of monasteries. The medieval economy was based on agriculture, and the period of the sixth and seventh centuries saw the development of new technologies: stirrups for the better use of horses for fighting, the horse collar that allowed horses to replace oxen, the heavy-wheeled plow for cultivating the fields of northern Europe, and a crop rotation system that permitted two-thirds of the land to be cultivated each year. With increased agricultural production, Europe was on the verge of greater wealth, which would be concentrated in the north rather than on the Mediterranean. In Europe and the eastern Mediterranean major political changes were again on the horizon as the Franks continued to consolidate their power, the Byzantine Empire faced renewed invasions, and Islam inspired the Arabs to conquer the old Persian Empire and much of the Byzantine Empire.

QUESTIONS FOR FURTHER THOUGHT

◆

1. What were the problems that the Germanic folk encountered in trying to assimilate with the Romans? What problems did the Romans have in living side by side with the tribesmen?

2. Historians have long argued that three elements went into the making of what we call "medieval civilization"—Roman government and culture, Germanic government and social customs, and Christianity. What elements did each of these contribute to the emerging medieval culture in the West?

3. What was the influence of the technological developments in the sixth and seventh centuries on warfare and on agriculture?

RECOMMENDED READING

◆

Sources

Colgrave, B. (ed.). *The Life of Bishop Wilfrid . . . , Two Lives of Saint Cuthbert . . . , Felix's Life of Saint Guthlac, and The Earliest Life of Gregory the Great.* 1985. The hagiographies of the missionary saints.

Gregory of Tours, *History of the Franks,* trans. Ernest Brehaut, 1916.

*Herlihy, David (ed.). *Medieval Culture and Society.* 1968. A collection of primary sources that illustrate social and cultural aspects of the Middle Ages.

*Mattingly, H. (tr.). *Tacitus on Britain and Germany: A Translation of the "Agricola" and the "Germania."* 1967. A description of the life and culture of Germanic tribes including his experience living in Roman Britain.

*Peters, Edward. *Monks, Bishops, and Pagans: Christian Culture in Gaul and Italy, 500–700.* 1975. A collection of primary sources related to the early western church.

*Procopius. *Secret History.* Richard Atwater (tr.). 1964. A scandal-filled history of Justinian's reign.

Studies

*Brown, Peter. *The Cult of the Saints: Its Rise and Function in Latin Christianity.* 1980. Locates the cult of the saints not in popular religion but in the power structures of late ancient society.

*Burns, Thomas S. *A History of the Ostrogoths.* 1984. Based on archaeological as well as literary evidence.

Carver, Marvin. *Sutton Hoo: Burial Grounds of Kings.* 1998.

*Duby, Georges. *The Early Growth of the European Economy: Warriors and Peasants from the Seventh to the Twelfth Century.* Howard B. Clark (tr.). 1974. The early medieval economy viewed in terms of "gift and pillage."

*Dunbabin, Jean. *France in the Making: 843–1180.* 1985. On the formation of the political structure of France and the growth of a strong monarchy.

*Fleckenstein, Josef. *Early Medieval Germany.* Bernard F. Smith (tr.). 1978. Germanic institutions from the migrations to the eleventh century.

Fossier, Robert (ed.). *The Cambridge Illustrated History of the Middle Ages. Vol. 1: 350–950.* Janet Sondheimer (tr.). 1989. Essays by French scholars, including four on Eastern Europe. Full bibliographies; lavishly illustrated.

*Geary, Patrick. *Before France and Germany: The Creation and Transformation of the Merovingian World.* 1988. A comprehensive summary of recent research, stressing the importance of the Roman heritage for the growth of Frankish institutions.

*Herrin, Judith. *The Formation of Christendom.* 1987. A survey of the development of the Christian world from Constantine to the mid-ninth century, with particular emphasis on the Western debt to Byzantium.

*Herwig, Wolfram. *History of the Goths.* Thomas J. Dunlap (tr.). 1988. Stresses the instability of Gothic tribal formations.

Hodges, Richard, and David Whitehouse. *Mohammad and Charlemagne: The Origins of Europe.* 1983. A reevaluation of the Pirenne thesis using archaeological evidence. The authors explore the shift of trade from the Mediterranean to northern Europe.

James, Edward. *The Franks*. 1988.

*Lawrence, C. H. *Medieval Monasticism: Forms of Religious Life in Western Europe in the Middle Ages*. 2d ed. 1989. On the Rule of Benedict, the rise of Cluny, and other topics.

*Lynch, Joseph. *The Medieval Church: A Brief History*. 1992. A very readable introduction to the history of the church.

*Moorhead, John. *Justinian*. 1994. A lively discussion of the reign of Justinian in the context of his times.

Pirenne, Henri. *Mohammed and Charlemagne*. 1935. A classic discussion of the effects of Islamic conquests on the rise of the Franks and the interruption of Mediterranian trade.

Stenton, Frank. *Anglo-Saxon England*. 1971. Basic introductory text.

*Straw, Carole. *Gregory the Great: Perfection in Imperfection*. 1988.

*Wallace-Hadrill, J. M. *The Barbarian West*. 1962. Brief and readable essays.

Wemple, Suzanne Fonay. *Women in Frankish Society: Marriage and the Cloister, 500 to 800*. 1981. An important study of a neglected topic.

Wickham, Chris. *Early Medieval Italy: Central Power and Local Society, 400–1100*. 1981. Mainly social history of the decline of unity within Italy after the fall of the Roman Empire.

*Available in paperback.

▲ This twelfth-century silver reliquary from Aachen represents Charlemagne as emperor, saint, and protector of the Church. After his death, through all the subsequent medieval centuries, Charlemagne was remembered and viewed as the ideal Christian emperor.
Scala/Art Resource, NY

THE EMPIRES OF THE EARLY MIDDLE AGES (800–1000): CREATION AND EROSION

Europe's fate was inextricably bound with that of the old Roman world in the period of the seventh through the eleventh century. New conquests, the spread of Christianity to previously non-Christian peoples, and the rise of a new religion, Islam, had major impacts on the West. Combining conquest with missionary activity, the Frankish kings, like the Byzantine emperors, spread their power and Christianity to the Slavs of eastern Europe and previously unconverted Germanic tribes in the north of Europe. Islam influenced the course of history for both Western Europe and the Byzantine Empire. Muhammad, the founding prophet of Islam, enjoined his followers, the Muslims or, believers in Islam, to do battle for their faith. The leaders who followed Muhammad rapidly conquered Byzantine provinces but were turned back at Constantinople. They conquered the Persian Empire and moved west, conquering the Iberian Peninsula. The Byzantine Empire recovered from the Arab and other attacks to play an active role in the politics of Eastern Europe and the Arab world. In the West Pepin's son, Charlemagne, unified the Frankish lands under his control and conquered large portions of northern and eastern Europe to form the Carolingian Empire.

The old Roman world was now divided into three vast Empires: Charlemagne's empire was largely located in northwest Europe and the northern Mediterranean. The Byzantine Empire included parts of Turkey and the areas to the north and west of Constantinople. The Arabic Caliphate extended from Persia all along the southern Mediterranean and included the Iberian Peninsula. In addition there were the smaller political units of Anglo-Saxon England and the Kievan state.

The formation of large political units and the conversion of populations to new religions had widespread effects. The position of women changed with new religious laws. Intellectual revival occurred with the peace and patronage fostered by the regimes. And new military and political arrangements arose. But all these political units had inherent internal weaknesses that made them unable to withstand new invasions of Turkish peoples and war parties from Scandinavia. The empires broke up into smaller political units more capable of dealing with immediate problems of defense.

CHAPTER 7. THE EMPIRES OF THE EARLY MIDDLE AGES							
	Social Structure	Body Politic	Changes in the Organization of Production and in the Impact of Technology	Evolution of Family and Changing Gender Roles	War	Religion	Cultural Expression
I. The Byzantine Empire							
II. Islam							
III. Carolingian or Frankish Empire							
IV. The Vikings, Kiev, and England							

I. The Byzantine Empire (632–1071)

The Byzantine Empire developed a decisively Eastern orientation. The characteristic was already observable in Justinian's reign. Although Justinian's great codification of Roman law was in Latin, he issued his own edicts in Greek, now the common language of the Empire. Court ceremonials resembled those of an Eastern ruler, in which the subjects were distanced from the ruler by space, dress, and submissive behavior. Social organization was also undergoing changes that made large estates look more like those in the West (see chapter 6) and forced a reorganization of the army that eventually created a rural elite and a subservient peasant class. Although Byzantium remained wealthy, aggressive in defending its borders, and expansive in its missionary activity, it was under constant attack and its physical territory shrank to an area in Europe and Asia surrounding Constantinople.

◆ STRAINS ON THE EMPIRE

Heraclius and the Persian Wars   Heraclius (r. 610–641) came to power amid repeated military disasters. The Avars, a nomadic tribe from Central Asia, and Slavs invaded the Balkans right up to the walls of Constantinople. While the Avars withdrew again to above the Danube River, the Slavs remained in the Balkans. The aggressive

Persians took Antioch, Jerusalem, and Alexandria. The Persians even removed from the Church of the Holy Sepulcher in Jerusalem the cross on which Jesus was crucified. Raising money through treasures donated by the churches, Heraclius strengthened the army and then boldly opened a successful war against the Persians in 622. The Persians agreed to a humiliating peace and returned the Holy Cross.

The Persian wars left Byzantium financially depleted and its army exhausted. The Empire was not in a position to defend itself immediately against a new menace on its borders. After the death of Muhammad in 632, his Muslim followers from the Arabic world embarked on a tidal wave of conquests, overrunning much of the Empire in scarcely more than ten years.

Effects of Territorial Losses   A century elapsed before the Byzantines were able to take the offensive against the Muslims. The Empire had lost Egypt and Syria, but the loss had positive as well as negative effects. Those regions had never become entirely Greco-Roman and had resisted Byzantine administration, taxation, and religion. These regions embraced the Arian (see chapter 5) and monophysite (see chapter 6) heresies. Their religious beliefs were closer to Islam, thus making the Arab conquest easier. Furthermore, the economic importance of Constantinople as the major trading city for the West increased after the Arab conquest of Egypt. Asia Minor, Antioch, and Jerusalem, however, had been of major importance to Byzantium, and the Empire tried to reconquer them (see maps 6.2 and 7.1).

Military Revival The emperor Leo III (r. 717–741) beat back a Muslim attack on Constantinople in 717 and 718 and then began to reconquer Asia Minor. The military revival reached its height under the great warrior emperors of the ninth through eleventh centuries. Byzantine armies pushed the Muslims back into Syria and waged successful wars in southern Italy, the Balkan Peninsula, and the Caucasus. Their principal military accomplishment was in the Balkan Peninsula, where they defeated the nomadic people known as the Bulgars. The modern Bulgarians are entirely Slavic in language and culture and retain only the name of the original nomads. During

the late ninth and tenth centuries, Byzantium experienced once again a period of stability, wealth, and artistic glory.

Leo III and Iconoclasm   While Leo III's military campaigns marked the turn of the tide against the Arab expansion, his religious policies plunged the Empire into turmoil. Leo had grown up in Asia Minor, where he had contact with both Islam and heretical Christians, and he absorbed some of their suspicions that the use of holy images, or icons (from the Greek *eikon*, "image"), in worship was akin to idolatry. He introduced *iconoclasm* ("image-breaking") in the Empire in 726. Not only did he forbid the veneration of images within churches, he pursued a policy of actively destroying them. Iconoclasm was a drastic policy,

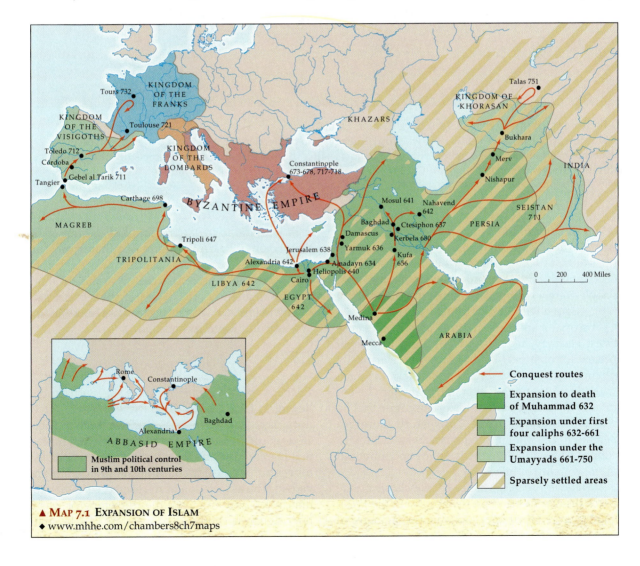

▲ **MAP 7.1** **EXPANSION OF ISLAM**
◆ www.mhhe.com/chambers8ch7maps

▲ ICONOCLAST WHITEWASHING AN IMAGE OF CHRIST, CA. 900
Byzantine iconoclasts, protesting the worship of images and the leadership of a Latin pope, destroyed the decorations of numerous churches. This page from a Psalter illuminated around 900 depicts the obliteration through whitewashing of an icon of Christ.
Moscow, Historical Museum; photo, Ecole des Hautes Etudes, Paris.

because many of the worshipers had come to regard particular icons, images of Jesus, Mary, and the saints, as being efficacious as intercessors for divine help. Leo and the iconoclasts argued that people were worshiping pieces of wood and stone rather than God, Jesus, or Mary.

Historians still do not agree about Leo's motives. He may have used iconoclasm as a legal pretext for obtaining land to support the army. By seizing the holdings of the monasteries, which strongly advocated the worship of images, he enriched the treasury. Other historians argue that he was attempting to make Christianity more appealing to the Muslims, whom he was seeking to conquer, by emulating the Islamic condemnation of the worship of images.

Whatever the reasons, Leo's iconoclastic policy had a disastrous effect on relations with the West; it antagonized the popes and was a major factor in their decision to seek out a Frankish champion in the person of Pepin the Short (see chapter 6). The veneration of images was restored temporarily in the Byzantine Empire between 784 and 813 and then permanently after 843. But the iconoclastic policy helped to widen the cleavage between the Western and Eastern churches.

◆ BYZANTINE GOVERNMENT

Position of the Emperor The Byzantines believed that if the Empire performed the sacred duty of aiding the salvation of the human race, God would never permit its destruction, an idea that inspired Byzantines with the courage to resist for centuries a nearly continuous onslaught of invaders. The association of the sacred with the secular in the Empire meant that the emperor was a holy figure as the head of the state. A Christian emperor could not claim divinity (as pagan Roman emperors had), but the emperor lived surrounded by ceremony that imparted an aura of sanctity to his person; and the term *sacred,* used much as we use the word *public,* was liberally applied to his person, palace, and office.

Although the Byzantine emperor was head of both Church and state, recent historians have pointed out that his powers over the Church were restricted. He could not repeal the Nicene Creed or personally flout laws of Christian morality. Since he was not a priest, he could not say Mass or administer the sacraments. Yet the emperor exercised a wide authority over ecclesiastical matters. He supervised the discipline of the Church, set the qualifications for ordinations, created bishoprics and changed their boundaries, investigated the monasteries and reformed them when necessary, and appointed patriarchs and at times forced their resignation. Even dogma and practice were not beyond his influence, as Leo III demonstrated in his initiation of iconoclasm. The emperor summoned councils, supervised their proceedings, and enforced their decisions. Because of the emperor's extensive powers, the clergy was largely limited to performing the sacred liturgy and administering the sacraments.

Elaborate Bureaucracy The emperor, like his predecessors in the old Roman Empire, enjoyed absolute authority and governed with the aid of an elaborate civil service. In Byzantium all justice flowed from the emperor, and he or his chief official could hear appeals from any local court in the Empire. The Byzantine government supported such refinements as an effective fiscal system, a state postal service, and even a secret police, ominously called the *agentes in rebus* ("those doing things"). Western governments had none of these innovations.

At a time when Western governments operated almost without a budget, the Byzantine government collected large revenues from the 10 percent tariff on trade and from the profit from the state monopolies. The government also employed skilled diplomats, whom contemporary observers celebrated for their ability to keep enemies divided and for their liberal use of bribes, tributes, and subsidies. In contrast to this elaborate bureaucracy, Western kingdoms functioned with a rudimentary administration and without a professional civil service.

Literate and trained laymen largely staffed the bureaucracy. Eunuchs (castrated men) were preferred for important positions in the government because it was believed that they would not be tempted by sexual intrigue and would have no wife or children to compete with the emperor for their loyalties. Eunuchs performed managerial functions that in the West were assumed by queens and women of the court.

◆ THE TWO CHURCHES

The contrasting experiences in the early Middle Ages deeply affected the character and spirit of the two major branches of Christianity. The differences between the two Churches clarify other contrasts in the history of the Eastern and Western peoples. The Eastern Church developed and functioned under the supervision of the emperor. In the West, on the other hand, the collapse of central authority in the Roman Empire gave the clergy a position of leadership in secular affairs.

Theological Differences Both the Eastern Church and the Western Church considered themselves catholic (that is, universal) and orthodox (that is, holding true beliefs); the terms *Roman Catholic* and *Greek Orthodox* used to identify the Churches today are exclusively modern usages. The two Churches maintained nearly identical beliefs. Perhaps the principal, or at least the most famous, disagreement was and still is the *filioque* dispute (meaning "and from the son"), which concerns the relationship between members of the Trinity: the Father, Son, and Holy Spirit. The Eastern Church held, and still holds, that the Holy Spirit proceeds only from the Father, while the Western Church maintained that the Holy Spirit proceeds from the Father "and from the Son."

The Eastern Church permitted, as the Western Church did not, divorce for reasons of adultery and the ordination of married men to the priesthood, although bishops had to be celibate.

Languages in Liturgy The most significant liturgical difference between the two Churches was that the Eastern Church allowed the use of vernacular languages—Greek, Coptic, Ethiopian,

Syriac, Armenian, Georgian, Slavonic, and others—in the liturgy. Liturgical usage added great dignity to these Eastern languages and stimulated their development. The East Slavs, for example, possessed a rich literature in Slavonic within a century after their conversion to Christianity. Western vernacular literature was much slower in developing. On the other hand, the toleration of many vernacular languages weakened the unity of the Eastern Church. An Eastern cleric using his own vernacular language could not easily communicate with clerics from other regions, whereas a Western cleric who used Latin could make himself understood anywhere in the West. Because of linguistic differences from their neighbors, Eastern churches tended to develop in isolation from one another. Moreover, the toleration of many vernacular languages made difficult the revival of classical learning. In learning Latin, a Western cleric also acquired the ability to read the great Latin classics, while an Eastern cleric who did not know Greek was blocked from the Greek classics. Eastern cultures were thus deprived of access to scholarship of the ancient world.

The Eastern Church remained thoroughly decentralized because of its diverse languages. It developed into a loose confederation of independent national churches that relied on secular authority (on the model of the emperor's control over the Greek church) to defend their temporal interests. In contrast, with the unity of Latin as its liturgical and literary language, the Western Church began to develop a centralized control over Christianity in the West under the papacy. The popes' power was often strong enough to defy secular rulers (see chapter 8).

Missionary Activities   The two Churches came into direct conflict in the Balkans over the conversion of the Slavs. Two Christian brothers of Slavic descent, Cyril and Methodius, set out in about 862 as missionaries from the Byzantine Empire to preach to the Slavs. Cyril developed a Slavonic script based on Greek letters called the Cyrillic alphabet. The brothers used the Yugo-Slav or South Slav dialect, translating the Bible and the liturgy into Slavonic. With modifications, the Cyrillic alphabet remains in use in parts of Eastern Europe and Russia today.

Cyril and Methodius had their first success with the conversion of the Serbs. Then the Bulgarians, now settled in a kingdom in the Balkans, requested missionaries. In their peace settlement with the Byzantine Empire, the Bulgarians had been allowed to settle in the Balkans in exchange for converting to Christianity. They too adopted the Cyrillic alphabet and adhered to the Eastern Church.

In the West the sword opened the way for missionaries. The papacy relied on the Frankish rulers to expand the boundaries of the Western Church through conquest. The struggles between Rome and Constantinople for conversion of the Slavic peoples brought about the area's religious configuration that still exists today. Croatia, Albania, and Moravia (the Czechs and Slovacs) came under the Roman Church, but the Serbs and the rest of the Balkan area adhered to the Greek Church. Russia was converted to the Eastern Church in the tenth century.

◆ BYZANTINE ECONOMY AND SOCIETY

Urban and Rural Population   The outstanding feature of Byzantine civilization, compared with that of Western Europe, was the continuing vitality of its cities. At one time the Byzantine Empire included such great urban centers as Alexandria, Antioch, Beirut, Constantinople, Trebizond, and Tyre. At its peak under Justinian, Constantinople probably contained more than three hundred thousand inhabitants. The city had paved and illuminated streets and splendid churches and palaces. Urban society was, however, marked by a wide division between rich and poor. The rich lived among magnificent surroundings in huge palaces; the poor, in sprawling slums. Crimes committed in broad daylight were commonplace.

Rural society was organized on a theme system. The themes were administered by generals, who became the elite of the Empire. Soldiers and sailors were paid by granting them their own farms. They fought in their own theme army or navy to defend their land. These soldier/farmers made decisions concerning the use of uncultivated or common lands, assumed (or were required to assume) collective responsibility for the payment of taxes, and elected judges and other officials to supervise the village government. The village organization was similar to the one that developed in the West.

Trade and Manufacture   The Byzantine Empire was wealthy compared with other states of the age. One great source of wealth came from the commerce that passed through the ports and gates of Constantinople. The Slavs from the north carried amber, fur, honey, slaves, wax, and wheat; Armenians and Syrians from the east brought clothing, fruit, glass, steel, and spices; merchants from the west contributed arms, iron, slaves, and wood. The vigorous commerce attracted large colonies of foreign merchants. The commercial importance of Byzantium is revealed in the prestige of its gold coin, the *bezant*. Its weight and purity were kept constant from the reign of Constantine to the late eleventh century; no other major system of coinage can match its record of stability.

Constantinople was also the producer of luxury items. When the Persian Empire blocked the trade in silk from China and India across the land routes (the Great Silk Road), Justinian tried to find other ways to import silk from China. He experimented with sending missionaries to Ethiopia and the Arabian peninsula to create a route through the Red Sea. Finally, two monks who had

▲ SILK TEXTILE
A splendid example of the quality of silk manufacture in Constantinople around the year 1000, this textile shows the eagle, an ancient symbol of power and victory, holding in its beak a ring while resting its claws on a row of pearls. This particular work of craftsmanship is said to have been used to transport the remains of St. Germain, who died in Ravenna in 448, back to Auxerre in France.
Giraudon/Art Resource, NY

▼ AGRICULTURE
Cultivating their own plots was the principal work of Byzantine peasants. This manuscript illustration shows the various labors of digging, harvesting, and watering taking place in a fanciful landscape.
Bibliothèque Nationale de France, Paris

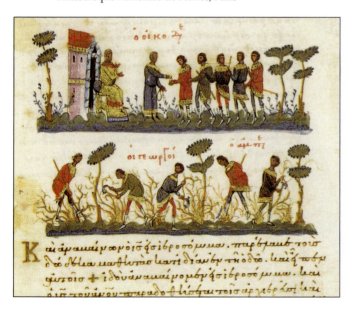

returned from northern India revealed to him the secret of silkworm cultivation and weaving, which the Chinese had known for at least two millennia. Justinian established silk production as a state monopoly; it enriched the state and meant that the emperor controlled the distribution of prestigious quality silk fabrics and dyes among aspiring tribal kings who wished to imitate the emperor. The best silk, rich purple-dyed cloth, was reserved for the imperial family. So significant was the symbolic value of purple silk that it became a particular distinction of legitimacy to "be born in the purple," indicating that the emperor's mother gave birth in a chamber hung with purple cloth. One emperor, Constantine Prophyrogenitus ("born in the purple," r. 913–957), took it as a name.

Byzantine artisans producing luxury goods such as silk were organized into *guilds* (organizations of craftsmen who trained skilled workers and organized artisans to ensure quality products). The *Book of the Prefect,* written in about 950 and describing the duties of a city's chief administrative officer, mentions twenty-one craft guilds; most of these made luxury products. The artisans were famed for gold work, glass objects, ivories, jewelry, icons, and reliquaries, all of which were shipped everywhere in the known world. The government closely regulated prices and movement of goods and maintained state monopolies.

Limited Role of Women Women in the Byzantine Empire continued as they had in the ancient world. Their lives centered around the home, and their contact with men outside the family was strictly limited. They wore veils over their heads, but not their faces. Whereas in Western monasticism nuns performed charity work and ran schools, Byzantine nuns were strictly cloistered and performed none of these functions, which were reserved for monks. Only at the imperial and aristocratic level could women play an active role, including acting as regent and even becoming sole ruler, as did Empress Irene (r. 797–802) and Theodora (r. 1042, 1055–1056). It was another Theodora, a regent, who initiated the return to icon veneration in 843. Aristocratic women played a role in administering family lands.

The streets and fields were not devoid of women. Poor women had no recourse but to aid in family agriculture, to become street vendors of food and drink, or even enter into the theater and prostitution.

The law placed women and children under the protection of male relatives, so they could not act legally on their own. Nonetheless, the law afforded women the protection of their dowries—

▼ Women Weaving and Spinning
Textile production was an important industry in Byzantine culture. This manuscript illustration depicts one woman weaving on a simple rectangular frame and another woman spinning.
Bibliothèque Nationale de France, Paris

the goods, money, and land that the wife brought to the marriage. The dowry was an important economic asset to the family, and the husband could administer but not sell it during the marriage. On his death the wife regained it for her widowhood. Widowhood did not leave women legally free, as it did in the West, because the Eastern Church intervened and discouraged women from remarrying.

◆ BYZANTINE CULTURE

Education   Byzantine wealth supported a tradition of learning that benefited not only the clergy but also many laymen. There were three types of institutions of higher learning: a palace school, primarily for laymen, trained civil servants in language, law, and rhetoric; a patriarchal school instructed priests in rhetoric and theology; and monastic schools taught young monks the mystical writings of the past. With the demise of public grammar schools in the sixth and seventh centuries, the poor depended on their guild for what education they received. A general shift in education reflected the shifts connected with the medieval period of Byzantine history. In the past, boys, particularly sons of the elite, had been trained in the Greek and Latin classical authors. That became obsolete, and instead, they learned Greek from a Psalter (containing the biblical Psalms) and other devotional literature.

Scholarship   Scholars used the Greek rather than the Latin language almost exclusively after the sixth century. They composed school manuals, histories, saints' lives, biblical commentaries, and encyclopedias of ancient science and lore. With the revival of the Empire under the Macedonian dynasty (ca. 870–1025), interest in learning gained prestige once again. Constantine VII Porphyrogenitos wrote books on history and supported scholarship. On the whole, Byzantine scholars did not show the fascination with Aristotle and science that the Arabs and the Western scholars did, but concentrated instead on Plato and religious writers. Their greatest accomplishment was the preservation of classical Greek literature. With the exception of some few works preserved on papyri, virtually all that the Western world possesses of classical Greek authors has come down through Byzantine copies, most of which date from the tenth to the twelfth centuries.

Art and Architecture   With the final rejection of iconoclasm in the middle of the ninth century, art and architecture flourished once again. Byzantine artisans designed and decorated many churches throughout the Empire. Their work is found in such places as Messina and Palermo in Sicily and Venice in Italy. Artists were summoned to such distant places as Kiev to aid in the design, construction, and decoration of churches.

The mosaics make vividly concrete the Byzantine concepts of empire, emperor, and church. The emperor is always presented as the august figure that Byzantine ideology made of him. Christ is never shown as suffering; he is, in other words, always God and never man. The reason for this seems to have been the close association that the figure of Christ bore to the living emperor. To show Christ as suffering would suggest that the emperor too might be a weak and vulnerable man. The mosaics have no sense of movement, admission of human frailty, or recognition of the reality of change. Operating within this picture of the world, the artists nevertheless portrayed their solemn figures with a rich variety of forms, garments, and colors. Byzantine mosaics may be static, but they are neither drab nor monotonous.

Popular Culture   Byzantine popular culture had both secular and spiritual sides. The population entered vigorously into the theological debates over the nature of Christ (divine or human or both in the same person) and the use of icons. One Byzantine theologian observed that, when he went to the marketplace and asked the price of bread, he received an argument on the nature of Christ. Theological debate was not confined to arguments in councils of churchmen. Instead, the laity's involvement could lead to riots.

The Hippodrome in Constantinople and similar sports centers in other cities continued some of the entertainments of the Roman coliseums. Chariot racing was the most popular sport, but animal shows, theater, and other spectacles also enjoyed considerable vogue. The spectators divided into rival fan groups called the "Blues" and the "Greens," whose members adopted strange haircuts and clothing, carried weapons, and generally acted as rowdy sports fans. These "clubs" could form more serious factions if they involved themselves in religious or political issues and were responsible for some of the more serious riots.

◆ DECLINE OF THE BYZANTINE EMPIRE

Social Transformations   The theme system that Heraclius had created to recruit an army and navy of free peasant-warriors began to collapse. From the early tenth century these free peasant-warriors, apparently to escape mounting fiscal and military burdens, began to abandon their farms to more powerful neighbors. In the eleventh century many of them became serfs; they gave up their freedom of movement and paid landlords a rent for their property. The disintegration of the theme system reduced the military manpower and led to a rural aristocracy of landlords, which in turn weakened the strength of the central government.

The emperors tried to limit the size and number of great estates, but by the late eleventh century, their weaker successors preferred to purchase the loyalty of the rural aristocracy by distributing imperial estates to them. The aristocracy was also gaining control over ecclesiastical lands, as the Church granted them entire monasteries to administer in the name of the Church. But, in fact, these concessions represented virtual gifts of monastic properties to lay lords. Byzantium was being transformed from a disciplined society of peasant-warriors under a strong central government to a society with a dependent peasantry, strong local landlords, and a weak central government.

Defense of the Empire   Without a pool of free peasants to recruit for the army and navy, the emperors had to seek outside help. To maintain control of the sea, essential to the security of Constantinople, they sought the support of the growing naval power of Venice. Emperors in 998 and 1082 gave generous trading concessions to the Venetians, which were major steps in the growth of Italian (and Western) naval strength in the waters of the eastern Mediterranean. The problem of land defense was even more pressing. A new people, the Seljuk Turks, had recently emerged from the steppes to threaten the Eastern frontiers.

The Seljuk Turks   The Byzantines gave the name *Turk* to a number of nomadic tribes that lived in the region east and north of the Caspian Sea (modern Turkestan). In the eleventh century, members of one tribe, the Seljuks, penetrated beyond the eastern borders of the Empire into Asia Minor. They shattered the largely mercenary army of the Byzantines and took the emperor captive at Manzikert in 1071.

As the Byzantine defenses broke down, Asia Minor lay open to the Seljuk forces. One Turkish chieftain, Suleiman, established himself and his warriors at Nicaea, only a few miles from Constantinople. The virtual loss of Asia Minor forced the Byzantine emperor to appeal to the West for help, a request that led to the First Crusade. This appeal signaled the end of the Byzantine Empire as a great power in the East.

East-West Schism   The second disaster of the eleventh century was the formal schism between the Eastern and Western branches of the Church in 1054. Major dogmatic differences were less important in the schism than were rivalry, disputes, and snobbery. Competition over the conversion of the Slavs and control over the churches in southern Italy contributed to the rancor. Furthermore, the Byzantines resented the papal claim to primacy within the Church. Rome by this time appeared to them as a provincial town without an empire or a subject territory; the Byzantines considered Constantinople, the seat of wealth and power, the more appropriate capital for the Church.[1]

Perhaps even more fundamental, the rupture of relations reflected the breakdown in communications between the East and the West. After Justinian's reign, the two halves of the Roman Empire and the two halves of the Church ceased to speak or understand a common language, making misunderstandings more difficult to resolve.

The schism of 1054 destroyed the hope for a united Christian Church. Even today, more than nine hundred years after the event, adherents of

---

[1]In the tenth century the Byzantines told Liutprand, bishop of Cremona, that they, and not the residents of Rome, were the true Romans and that Rome was a town inhabited exclusively by "vile slaves, fishermen, confectioners, poulterers, bastards, plebeians, underlings."

the Western and Eastern traditions are still trying to overcome the rift. Only in 1965 did the pope and the Greek patriarch formally remove the excommunications of 1054.

II. Islam

Sometime about 610 in the Arabian town of Mecca, a merchant's son named Muhammad began to preach to the people, summoning them to repentance and reform. Gradually, he brought his teachings together to form a new system of religious belief that he called Islam. The explosive impact of his preaching must be reckoned as one of the most extraordinary events of world history. Within a century after Muhammad's death his followers had conquered and partially converted territories larger than the old Roman Empire. Today Islam remains the faith of perhaps 800 million people, more than an eighth of the world's population.

◆ THE ARABS

The Arabian peninsula, the homeland of the Arabs, profoundly influenced their culture and history. Its vast interior and northern regions have steppes, wastelands, and some of the hottest and driest deserts of the world. The Arabs, however, adapted to this harsh environment. They supported themselves by raising sheep and camels that provided nearly all their necessities: meat, milk, wool, skins for clothes and tents, and fuel from dried camel dung. The Arabs were extremely proud of their family, race, language, skill, and way of life. The harsh environment and their fierce pride made them spirited, tenacious, and formidable warriors.

The Arabian peninsula was in a state of intense political and social ferment on the eve of Muhammad's appearance. The stronger political powers—the Persians, Byzantines, and Abyssinians across the Red Sea—tried repeatedly to subdue the Arabs but could not dominate them in their desert home. Religious ferment was no less explosive. Several prophets, preaching new religious beliefs, had gained followers in Arabia before Muhammad. Their success indicated a growing dissatisfaction among the Arabs with their traditional paganism, which gave no promise of an afterlife and offered no image of human destiny and the role of the Arabs in it. Both Christianity and Judaism had won numerous converts, but neither one was able to gain the adherence of most Arabs. The religious leader who by the force of his vision fused all these contending pagan, Christian, and Jewish ideas into a single, commanding, and authentically Arabian religion was Muhammad.

◆ MUHAMMAD

Historians have little certain information about the founder of Islam. Muhammad was born at Mecca about 570 or 571. His father died before his birth, and his mother died when he was 6. Raised by his uncle, Muhammad worked as a camel driver in caravans. He may have been illiterate and may have had no direct knowledge of the Jewish and Christian scriptures; but he did acquire a wide, if sometimes inaccurate, knowledge of the history and teaching of those two religions. At about the age of twenty-five Muhammad married the widow of a rich merchant. Freed from economic concerns, he gave himself to religious meditations in the desert outside Mecca.

Preaching In 610 Muhammad heard the voice of the angel Gabriel speaking to him, and he continued to receive such revelations in increasing frequency and length for the remainder of his life. After his first revelation from Gabriel, Muhammad began to preach publicly about personal moral reform, but only his wife and a small group of relatives initially accepted his teachings. The people of Mecca feared him because his strictures against paganism seemed to threaten the position of Mecca as a center of pilgrimages. Rejected in his native city, Muhammad accepted an invitation to expound his ideas in Medina, about 270 miles to the north.

Hijra Muhammad's emigration from Mecca to Medina is called the *hijra* and occurred in 622, which later became the year 1 of the Islamic calendar. The *hijra* was a turning point in Muhammad's career for two reasons: He became the political leader and governor of an important town, which gave him a base for the military expansion of the

Islamic community; and his responsibilities as head of an independent town affected the character of his religious message. More and more, his message was concerned with public law, administration, and the practical problems of government.

Muhammad was more successful in making converts at Medina than he was at Mecca. He told his followers that God ordered them to convert or conquer their neighbors. With the support of his followers, Muhammad marched against the Meccans, defeating them in battle in 624 and taking Mecca in 630. He destroyed all the pagan shrines, keeping only the Kaaba (Arabic for "square building"), which Muslim tradition says that Abraham built. By his death in 632, Muhammad had given his religion a firm foundation on Arabian soil.

◆ THE RELIGION OF ISLAM

Instructed by the angel Gabriel, Muhammad passed on to his followers the words or prophecies of Allah (from *al ilah,* meaning "the God").

The collection of prophecies is known as the *Koran;* and Allah, in Islamic theology, is its true author. The Koran was written down in its present version in 651 and 652. It imparts to the sympathetic reader a powerful mood, one of uncompromising monotheism, of repeated and impassioned emphasis upon the unity, power, and presence of Allah. The mood is sustained by constant reiterations of set formulas praising Allah, his power, knowledge, mercy, justice, and concern for his people.

The chief obligation that Muhammad imposed on his followers was submission (the literal meaning of *Islam*) to the will of Allah. Those who submit are Muslims. (*Muhammadan*, which suggests that Muhammad claimed divinity, is an inappropriate usage.) Muhammad was little concerned with the subtleties of theology; he was interested in defining for Muslims the ethical and legal requirements for an upright life. Unlike Christianity, Islam retained this practical emphasis; jurisprudence, even more than speculative theology, re-

▼ KORAN, NINTH THROUGH TENTH CENTURY

The Koran, the sacred book of Islam, in a ninth- or tenth-century printing. From the ninth century the design of sacred books followed specific forms that remained standard in Islamic art. Color and gilding are added not only as ornament but also to separate verses; the leafy projection to the left signals the beginning of a new chapter. Courtesy of the Freer Gallery of Art, Smithsonian Institution, Washington, D.C.

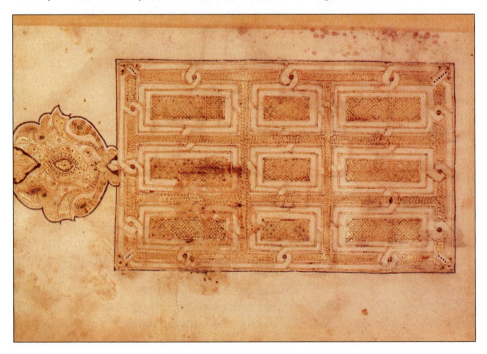

▲ PILGRIMAGE GUIDE
**This sixteenth-century illustration of a pilgrimage
guide written around 900 shows the Kaaba at Mecca.
The Kaaba, said to have been built by the Prophet
Abraham, is the black rectangular building
surrounded by domed arcades.**
Courtesy of The Arthur M. Sackler Museum, Harvard
University Art Museums, The Edwin Binney, 3rd Collection
of Turkish Art at the Harvard University Art Museums,
© President and Fellows of Harvard College, Harvard
University

mained the great intellectual interest of Muslim
scholarship. Also in contrast to Christianity, Islam
did not recognize a separate clergy and church,
for there was no need for specialized intermediaries between Allah and his people. Allah was the
direct ruler of the faithful on earth; he legislated
for them in the Koran, which was administered

through Muhammad, the Prophet, and his successors, the caliphs. Church and state were not separate entities, at least in theory. There was only the
single, sacred community of Allah.

Relationship to Other Religions The message of
Islam exerted a powerful appeal to the Arabs.
Compared with Christianity and Judaism, Islam
was a starkly simple belief, easily explained and
easily grasped. It was an effective fusion of religious ideas from Arabic paganism, Christianity,
Judaism, and perhaps Zoroastrianism. Judaism influenced the legal code regulating diet and behavior. Judaism and Christianity provided the notion
of prophecy, for Muhammad considered himself
the last of a line of prophets that began with Abraham and included Jesus. More than that, the Bible
tells that Abraham fathered Ishmael by Hagar, an
Egyptian slave girl (Gen. 16–17), and Muslims believe that Ishmael was their ancestor and lies
buried with Hagar in the Kaaba at Mecca. Christianity contributed the concepts of Last Judgment,
personal salvation, heaven and hell, charity to the
poor and weak, and a universal religion. Christianity, or perhaps Zoroastrianism, suggested the
figures of Satan and evil demons. Paganism contributed the veneration of the Kaaba and the requirement of pilgrimage to the sacred city.

Islam was based on religious ideas already familiar to the Arabs. Perhaps more important, Islam appealed strongly to the intense racial and
cultural pride of the Arabs. The Koran was written in their native language, Arabic, and only in
Arabic could Allah be addressed. Islam was seen
as the final revelation, completing the message
that God had partially conveyed through the Hebrew prophets and Jesus. The Arabs, a people
who had hitherto played a negligible role in history, were given an important mission in life: to
carry to the world the ultimate saving message.
The Arabs saw themselves as replacing the Jews
as God's chosen people, with a sacred right to his
holy places, including Jerusalem (see "The Koran
on Christians and Jews," p. 222).

◆ EXPANSION OF ISLAM

Conquests Several factors aided the extraordinary expansion of Islam in the first century of its
existence. Islam fused the once contending Arab
clans and tribes into a unified and dedicated force.

The Koran on Christians and Jews

◆

In the Koran, Muhammad proclaims that the faith of Islam also welcomes "the people of the Book"—that is, Christians and Jews who have the Bible as their sacred book—and that Islam is the fulfillment of these earlier faiths.

"Believers, Jews, Christians, and Sabaeans [of the kingdom of Saba in southwest Arabia]—whoever believes in Allah and the Last Day and does what is right—shall be rewarded by their Lord; they have nothing to fear or regret. To Moses We [that is, Allah] gave the Scriptures and after him We sent other apostles. We gave Jesus the son of Mary veritable signs and strengthened him with the Holy Spirit. And now that a Book [the Koran] confirming their Scriptures has been revealed to them by Allah, they deny it, although they know it to be the truth and have long prayed for help against the unbelievers.

"May Allah's curse be upon the infidels! Evil is that for which they have bartered away their souls. To deny Allah's own revelation, grudging that He should reveal His bounty to whom He chooses from His servants! They have incurred Allah's most inexorable wrath. An ignominious punishment awaits

the unbelievers. The unbelievers among the People of the Book, and the pagans, resent that any blessings should have been sent down to you from your Lord. But Allah chooses whom He will for His mercy. His grace is infinite.

"Abraham enjoined the faith on his children, and so did Jacob, saying: 'My children, Allah has chosen for you the true faith. Do not depart this life except as men who have submitted to Him.' Say: 'We believe in Allah and that which is revealed to us; we believe in what was revealed to Abraham, Ishmael, Isaac, Jacob, and the tribes; to Moses and Jesus and the other prophets. We make no distinction between any of them, and to Allah we have surrendered ourselves. Your God is one God. There is no God but Him.' "

From *The Koran,* N. J. Dawood (tr.) (Penguin Books, 1968), condensed.

The Arabs, long familiar with camels, were masters of desert warfare. Their enemies, relying on horses, could not challenge them on desert terrain. Using the desert much as English imperialists later used the sea, the Arabs moved armies and supplies with facility across vast arid stretches, struck the enemy at places and times of their own choosing, and retreated to the safety of the desert when the odds turned against them. Moreover, the Arabs' immediate neighbors, the Byzantines and Persians, were mutually exhausted by their recurrent wars. Both the Byzantine and Persian empires included large Semitic populations that were linguistically and culturally related to the Arabs and could, therefore, comprehend the message of Islam.

The Arabs were able to make and hold their conquests through a unique combination of fanaticism and toleration. Warriors were inspired by the Prophet's promise of vast rewards to those who died in the Holy War against the nonbelievers and by the very real prospect of considerable booty if victorious. The Prophet, however, also enjoined a policy of partial toleration toward Chris-

tians and Jews, who were both known as the "people of the Book" (the Bible). Thus, Christians and Jews continued to live under their own laws, but they paid a special tax for the privilege. Many Persian, Greek, and Semitic people converted voluntarily because they found the religion close to their own beliefs. Finally, because the Arabs did not have the numbers and the skills to govern all the territories they conquered, they opened the ranks of government to men from the newly conquered peoples. This move added stability to Arabic rule.

Islam expanded most rapidly in the period following Muhammad's death in 632 and coinciding with the rule of the first four caliphs, as Muhammad's successors were called. Arabian forces seized the Byzantine provinces of Palestine and Syria, overran Persia, and conquered Egypt by the 640s. By 661 the Arabian Empire was firmly established as a world power.

Umayyads   Islamic conquests continued under the caliphs of the Umayyad family, who were the first line of hereditary rulers of the Arab Empire.

The Umayyads moved the capital from Mecca to Damascus. Under their rule the Muslims conquered North Africa and overran the kingdom of the Visigoths in Spain. After crossing the Pyrenees into the kingdom of the Franks, Muslim raiders were finally defeated by Charles Martel at Tours in 732. This battle, 100 years after Muhammad's death, marked the extent of the Arabs' western advance and stabilized the frontier of Islam for the next several centuries (see map 7.1).

Sunni-Shiite Schism   As the territory under Islamic control grew to enormous size, internal dissensions shattered Islamic unity. Relations among the various peoples who had accepted Islam became fractious, and religious divisions appeared. Islam had been an open and fluid religion at the death of Muhammad, but scholars and teachers gradually elaborated a theology that a majority of the believers accepted as orthodox. The scholars based the new orthodoxy not only on the Koran but also on the *Sunnas,* or traditions, which were writings that purported to describe how the first companions of Muhammad or how Muhammad himself dealt with various problems. Some Muslims, however, rejected the new orthodoxy of the *Sunnites,* as they came to be called. Those who opposed the Sunnites were called the *Shiites* ("party" or "faction" of Ali).

This earliest schism was more a political than a religious one. The Shiites maintained that only the descendants of Muhammad's son-in-law, Ali (r. 655–661), who was the fourth caliph, could lawfully rule the Islamic community; they rejected the Umayyads (and later the Abbasids) as usurpers. Shiism soon became a cloak for all sorts of antagonisms, protests, and revolts. It struck deep roots among the mixed populations, reflecting the dissatisfactions of non-Arabs with the Arab preponderance and channeling the antagonism between the poorer classes and their masters.

The growing social and religious dissensions finally destroyed the Umayyad caliphate. A descendant of Abbas, the uncle of Muhammad, revolted against the Umayyads, captured Damascus, and ruthlessly massacred the caliph's family in 750. This victor founded the Abbasid dynasty. Only one member of the Umayyads, Abdurrahman, escaped. He fled to Spain, where he set up an independent caliphate at Córdoba in 755. Other independent regimes soon arose: Morocco in 788,

Tunisia in 800, eastern Persia in 820, and Egypt in 868. All became virtually independent under their local dynasties. The new Abbasid caliph moved the capital from Damascus to a new city, Baghdad. The Abbasid dynasty, which endured until 1258, marked a high point in Islamic culture, but the political community of Islam was never again to be united.

◆ ISLAMIC ECONOMY AND SOCIETY

Despite disunity, medieval Islamic civilization reached its peak of prosperity, refinement, and learning in the ninth and tenth centuries. Arabic, the language of the Koran, served to unify literature, learning, and commerce across the Islamic lands.

Diverse Economic Systems   As Islam expanded, it embraced numerous economic systems. The Bedouins in the Arabian peninsula, the Berbers in North Africa, and the Turkish people of Eurasia continued to have a pastoral economy. The majority of those living in Egypt, Persia, Sicily, and Spain lived from settled agriculture. The inhabitants of cities, especially those along the caravan routes that tied the Middle East to India and central Asia, relied on commerce.

The universal language, Arabic, made commercial communications easy. Muhammad had been a merchant, and Islamic law favored commerce. Maritime commerce in the Mediterranean provided, until the sixteenth century, the chief commercial link among India, Egypt, and the West. A large collection of letters from Jewish merchants living in Cairo in the eleventh and twelfth centuries has survived and marvelously illuminates trade and many other aspects of social life in the medieval East.[2]

Trade and Manufacture   Commercial exchange stimulated agriculture within the Arabic world.

---

[2]These letters are called the *Geniza documents. The geniza* was a storeroom attached to a synagogue; records mentioning God's name (including merchants' letters) could not be destroyed and were stored in the geniza. The geniza of the Cairo synagogue was sealed up and not rediscovered until the nineteenth century. Its contents were then sold to collectors of Jewish documents and to libraries and thus dispersed throughout the world. For examples of these extraordinary records, see S. D. Goitein, *Letters of Medieval Jewish Traders,* 1973.

Cultivators in Sicily and Spain adopted new plants from Asia, such as rice, and new techniques of cultivation, such as irrigation. Muslims from Persia to Spain practiced an agriculture remarkably advanced for the age. Trade also stimulated urban artisans to improve the quality of their products. The steel of Damascus and Toledo, the leather of Córdoba, and the fine cotton, linen, and silk of many Eastern towns (damask, for instance, was named for the weaving of Damascus) were desired and imitated in the West. Merchants shipped these products to India and Indonesia, where they were traded for spices and other products.

Cosmopolitan Cities A vigorous urban life, concentrated in the cities of Damascus, Baghdad, Cairo, and Córdoba, distinguished medieval Islamic society. According to travelers' reports, Damascus had 113,000 homes and 70 libraries. Baghdad surpassed all other cities in the number of palaces, libraries, and public baths. Products from almost all parts of the known world could be purchased at the markets, or bazaars, in all the major cities. The streets teemed with slaves, servants, artisans, merchants, administrators, and beggars. The aura of the Islamic cities was preeminently cosmopolitan.

Advances in Technology The Arabs, often borrowing from China, India, and Byzantium, improved on what they found. Byzantium had used Greek fire, a compound based on naphtha, which could burn on water or be put in clay pots with a fuse and hurled across a wall, causing fires where it landed. Said to be a Syrian invention, the Byzantines kept it as a military secret, but the Arabs eventually got the formula. The Arabs also improved on siege weapons and fortress building that they learned from the Byzantines. Serving as a conduit to the West of inventions from China, they introduced the windmill and the spinning wheel as well as paper making, block printing, and specialized textile weaving.

Law and Government Because Islam recognized no distinction between church and state, the caliph was the supreme religious and civil head of the Muslim world. He was not free, however, to change the laws at will, since Allah had already provided all the laws his people needed. The caliph's role was primarily a military chief and a judge. Administration at the local level was done by a judge whose task was to see that the faithful lived according to the law of the Koran.

Mixed Role for Women In the early days of Islam, women played a major role in conversion. Muhammad's wife, Khadija, was his first convert. His second wife, daughter of a wealthy Meccan, was an early convert who shared the exile in Medina before Muhammad married her. The wives of two of the first caliphs were also early converts.

The Koran placed a high value on preserving and enhancing the family. It encouraged people to marry and enjoined men to support their wives. It allowed male Muslims to have as many as four legal wives, but only if they could support them and treat them all fairly. Divorce was difficult because the husband had to allow his divorced wife to keep gifts he had given her and support her and her children. Women could inherit from their male kin, but their portion was less than a male heir would receive: "A male child shall have the equivalent of two female children."

The position of women depended on their social class and on the period in which they lived. Islamic society became more restrictive of women in later centuries. Muhammad had urged his wives to live in seclusion, but eventually the harem (rooms reserved for women) was recommended for all women after puberty. But the strict seclusion of the harem was something that only the very wealthy could afford for their wives, daughters, and concubines. Peasant and artisan women would have to be in public. Women who left the seclusion of home did so with a veil covering the head and face.

◆ ISLAMIC CULTURE

The Islamic conquests brought the Arabs into contact with older and more accomplished civilizations than their own, particularly with the intellectual achievements of the Greeks, which they were eager to preserve. During the eighth and ninth centuries, scholars translated into Arabic many Greek authors: Aristotle, Euclid, Archimedes, Hippocrates, and Galen. Islamic scholars were especially interested in astronomy,

WRITING MEDIEVAL WOMEN'S HISTORY

One of the most important new directions for historical writing has been the history of women. Books and articles on women from all time periods and all countries are now abundant, and courses on women's history are readily available. Writing the history of women in the Middle Ages, however, presents major interpretive problems.

Very few writings by women survive from the Middle Ages. Not very many women in the West were literate, and those who were knew vernacular languages rather than Latin, the language of learning. Still, learned nuns left devotional literature, plays, and histories. Arabic was the language of both literature and speech, and some women's poems in Arabic survive. Greek women wrote histories. Another source of women's own thoughts were accounts of their visions or of their lives that their priests recorded.

Most information about women, therefore, is filtered through sources written by men. Men wrote about women from a number of motives, and these biases must be taken into consideration when interpreting the sources. Religious sources, for instance, seek to organize society and instruct believers. To understand and interpret these sources, a historian needs to know a great deal about the context in which they were written. The strictures from the Koran, for example, could be read as being very repressive of women. When seen in the context of Muhammad's desire to preserve and strengthen the family, however, they take on a different meaning. Add the pre-Islamic context, and the Koran can be viewed as improving the position of women by protecting them against abuses they had previously experienced.

Other sources, such as laws, provide sparse information about the women they seek to regulate and protect. The researcher does not know whether the laws were actually applied. A variety of other sources help to elucidate this information. Court cases, of course, provide ready information when they are available. But historians have creatively used archaeological evidence and even place names. For example, the Anglo-Saxons had the custom that the husband presented the wife with a gift, the *morgangifu*, the day after the marriage. Present-day names such as Mayfield or Morgay Farm indicate that these were bridal gifts to women. The historian's craft is partly one of solving mysteries; the study of women's history provides rich opportunities for the historically minded sleuth. Both the subject itself and the problems of researching it contribute to the dynamics of the field.

astrology, mathematics, medicine, and optics, and in these areas their writings exerted a great influence on the Western world.

Medical Education Al-Razi (known as Rhazes in the West) of Baghdad was director of the state hospital in Baghdad, and he had practical experience with medicine and medical education. He wrote some 140 medical treatises, including a description of smallpox. Among the accomplishments of the Abbasid caliphate were courses in pharmacy and licensing of all people practicing medicine.

Mathematics and Astronomy Arabic mathematicians adopted their impressive numbering system from the Hindus, but made the critical addition of the zero, which is itself an Arabic word. The use of the zero allows figures to be arranged in columns and allows the use of a decimal system. Italian merchants became familiar with the Arabic numbers shortly before the year 1200 and carried them back to the West. Arabic mathematicians also developed algebra. Astronomers and astrologers invented an improved astrolabe (which measures the angular declination of heavenly bodies above the horizon) and were able to improve the astronomical tables of antiquity.

Philosophy and Theology Scholars also wrote philosophical and theological treatises. The most important Islamic philosopher was the Spaniard ibn-Rushd, or Averroës (1126?–1198), who wrote commentaries on Aristotle and exerted a profound influence on Christian as well as Islamic philosophy in the Middle Ages. Islamic philosophical speculations nourished intellectual life in the West in two ways: Western philosophers

◄ **Abu-Zayd Visiting a Muslim Village**
This thirteenth-century illustration is a leaf from the *al-Hariri Magamat* (Assemblies of Entertaining Dialogues), a collection of tales set in various parts of the Muslim world. Here, the main character, Abu-Zayd, visits a lively village whose inhabitants carry on their daily tasks of spinning, agriculture, and worship.
Bibliothèque Nationale de France, Paris

gained a much broader familiarity with the scientific and philosophical heritage of classical Greece through translations made from Arabic, chiefly in Spain; and Islamic philosophers explored issues central to religious philosophy much earlier than did Christian thinkers. What is the relation between faith and reason, between an all-powerful God and the freedom, dignity, and individuality of the human person? In posing these problems and in suggesting answers, the Muslims stimulated and enriched thought in the West.

Centers of Culture Baghdad under the Abbasid dynasty was a great cultural center. Caliph Harun al-Rashid's reign (r. 786–809) was the high point of Islamic culture. The *Arabian Nights* was first written in this period and put into its present form in the fourteenth century. The stories convey a glamorous and idealized, but not a false, picture of the luxurious life at Baghdad. Harun's son Al-Mamun (r. 813–833) reigned even more splendidly than his father did. He was also a patron of learning. Al-Mamun founded an observatory for the study of the heavens and established a "House of Wisdom" (sometimes referred to as the first Islamic institution of higher education), where translations were made and a library collected for the use of scholars.

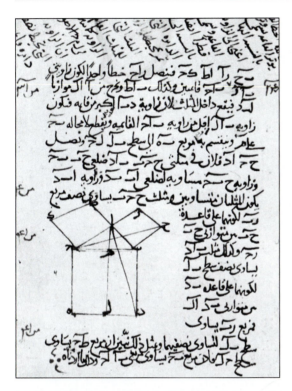

▲ This thirteenth-century Arab commentary on the *Geometry* of Euclid illustrates the proof of the Pythagorean theorem. Mathematics was one science in which the Arabs surpassed the classical achievements.
© British Museum

embarked on the reconquest of the Iberian Peninsula, and Christian fleets broke the Islamic domination of the western Mediterranean islands. The Byzantine offensive gave rise to the First Crusade, which wrested Jerusalem from Islamic control in 1099. In the East, Turkish nomads infiltrated the Abbasid caliphate in considerable numbers, and the Seljuks (converts to Islam) seized Baghdad in 1055. Turkish rulers gained supremacy in all the eastern Islamic states over the next few centuries.

The Arabic economic base was changing. By the thirteenth century, maritime and commercial supremacy on the Mediterranean Sea passed

▼ FORMS OF THE FIXED STARS, CA. 1009–1010
One of the earliest examples of Islamic book illustration, this manuscript, written around 1009–1010, contains seventy-five drawings noting the forms of the fixed stars. Sagittarius, shown as an armed rider, is traced from the pattern of the constellation and indicates the sophistication of Muslim astronomy.
The Bodleian Library, University of Oxford. MS. Marsh 144, page 273

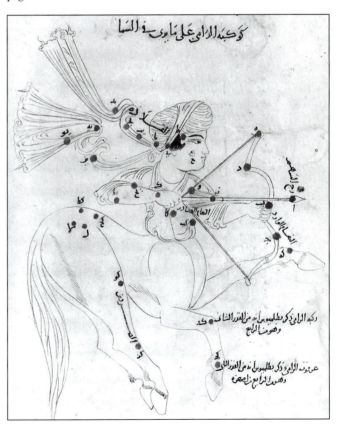

Spain was a notable center of medieval Islamic civilization. The brilliance of Islamic-Spanish civilization is best reflected in three great architectural monuments: the mosque (now a cathedral) at Córdoba, the Alhambra Palace in Granada, and the Alcazar at Seville. Jewish communities in Spain, the most creative of Jewish communities in the West, contributed to the high quality of intellectual life. It was also in Spain that Western Christians came into intimate contact with Islamic learning and drew from it the greatest benefits.

◆ DECLINE OF MEDIEVAL ISLAMIC CIVILIZATION

The earliest indication of decline was the growing military weakness of the various Islamic states in the face of new invasions in the middle of the eleventh century. In the West, Christian armies

▲ MOSQUE AT CÓRDOBA, 784 – 990
Begun around 784, the Mosque at Córdoba was enlarged throughout the ninth and tenth centuries. The flexible plan of parallel aisles creates a complex visual forest of double-tiered arches that originally supported a wooden roof. This immense structure, with 850 columns and 19 aisles, was one of the largest buildings in the Islamic world.
Fridmar Damm/Leo de Wys

to Italians and other Westerners. Arabian coins largely disappeared from circulation in the West, documenting a headlong retreat from commerce. Simultaneously, the Islamic states no longer supported their warriors with salaries but with grants of land, which weakened central authority. The growing importance of an aristocracy of rural warriors seems to have brought a new militarism and rigidity into society.

To be sure, Islamic civilization continued to support some great cultural centers and to inspire some great artists and thinkers; but after the eleventh century it began to lose the qualities of openness, flexibility, and intellectual daring that

had so distinguished it in the ninth and tenth centuries.

III. The Carolingian, or Frankish, Empire

The Frankish Empire was already strong when Charles the Great (r. 768–814) became its king. Charles Martel, Charlemagne's grandfather, had defeated the Arabs in a battle at Tours in 732, thus sparing Frankish lands the same fate that befell the Visigothic kingdom in Spain. Charles Martel's

▲ The remarkable series of rooms and courtyards that make up the Alhambra Palace in Granada are one of the supreme achievements of Islamic art. The delicate tracery, the elegant details, and the constant presence of running water create a mood of luxury and refinement that can still be experienced by the visitor today.
J. Messerschmidt/Leo de Wys

EINHARD ON CHARLEMAGNE

◆

The most important Western ruler of the Early Middle Ages was Charles the Great, or Charlemagne. A member of his court, Einhard, wrote of his life and describes him as follows.

"Charles was large and strong, and of lofty stature; his height was seven times the length of his foot. In accordance with the national custom, he took frequent exercise on horseback and in hunting. He often practiced swimming, in which he was so skilled that none could surpass him. He was temperate in eating, and particularly so in drinking, for he hated drunkenness in anybody, much more in himself and in members of his household. While dining, he listened to reading or music. The subjects of the readings were the stories and deeds of older times; he was fond, too, of St. Augustine's books, and especially of 'The City of God.'

"Charles had the gift of ready and fluent speech, and could express himself with the utmost clearness.

He was not satisfied with a command of only his native language, but studied foreign ones, and was such a master of Latin that he could speak it as well as his native tongue; but he could understand Greek better than he could speak it. He zealously cultivated the liberal arts, held those who taught them in great esteem, and conferred high honors on them. He also tried to write, and used to keep tablets under his pillow, so that in leisure hours he might train his hand to form the letters; but as he began his efforts late in life, he had poor success."

From Einhard, *Life of Charlemagne*, S. E. Turner (tr.) (University of Michigan Press, 1960).

son, Pepin the Short, had elevated the family role in government from that of mayor of the palace to that of king of the Franks. Forming an alliance with the Frankish aristocracy and the pope, he had deposed the last of the Merovingians and was crowned king (see p. 192). Through careful alliances with the aristocracy, continued warfare with neighbors, and good management, the Frankish kings established a large empire in the former Roman province of Gaul and extended their control beyond the Rhine River. Charles the Great was a worthy successor to his able ancestors.

◆ CHARLEMAGNE

Pepin's son Charles the Great, or Charlemagne, pursued the policies of his predecessors with unprecedented energy. His biographer, the court scholar Einhard, says that he was a large man, "seven times the length of his own foot," and that he delighted in physical exercise, particularly hunting, riding, bathing, and swimming. His taste for food and women seems to have been no less exuberant. Perhaps more remarkable in this man were his intellectual curiosity and alertness. He was probably illiterate; Einhard says that he kept tablets by his bed to practice forming letters at

night, though with "poor success." But Einhard also says that he spoke and understood Latin, comprehended Greek, and enjoyed the company of learned men (see "Einhard on Charlemagne," above). The vast empire that Charlemagne built (called the "Carolingian" Empire from "Carolus," his Latin name) was in large measure a personal accomplishment, a tribute to his abounding physical energy and intelligence.

Victorious Wars   Charlemagne's success as king depended on his success in waging long wars on every frontier. He perceived that spreading Christianity along with conquest led to submission to Frankish authority among pagan peoples. Where permanent conquest and conversion were not possible, the expeditions would still weaken neighboring enemies and prevent them from striking into the Frankish domains. At the pope's request Charlemagne campaigned four times in Italy against the Lombards and against factions in Rome opposed to the pope. He suppressed the independent Bavarians and overcame the Saxons after thirty-three years of fighting, thus bringing them fully and finally into the community of Western peoples. His conversions could be brutal. When the Saxons resisted Christianity, he threatened to kill them if they did not convert. These victorious wars added new territories to his empire (see map 7.2).

Imperial Title   On Charlemagne's fourth visit to Italy in 800, when he was praying before St. Peter's altar on Christmas night, Pope Leo III crowned him emperor of the Romans. The coronation added nothing to his possessions but still was of great symbolic importance. It confirmed the alliance of the papacy and the Frankish monarchy. The coronation proclaimed the complete political and cultural autonomy of the Western community of peoples from Byzantine (Roman) control.

◆ CAROLINGIAN GOVERNMENT

Imperial Ideology   The coronation added much to Charlemagne's dignity, and a grandiose imperial ideology developed around his person. But the elevation at the hands of the pope also led to later conflicts between future emperors and popes over who had the right to grant imperial power. A cult developed around the emperor that played a vital role in preserving the unity of the Empire. In imperial propaganda Charlemagne became the new David (the ideal king of the Old Testament), the new Augustus (the greatest of the pagan emperors), and the new Constantine (the champion of the Church). By presenting the emperor as a figure of such sanctity and brilliance, the government hoped to make rebellion against him unthinkable. Idealization of the emperor might thus accomplish what armies could not do alone.

Administering the Empire   The emperor was the head of the government. He ruled with the aid of a small group of officials. The chaplain, head of the palace clergy, advised the emperor and the entire court in matters of conscience. The chaplain also supervised the chancery, or secretariat, where the official documents were written. The chief lay official, the count of the palace, supervised the administration, judged cases that the emperor did not personally handle, and acted as regent during the emperor's frequent absences. Other officials included the chamberlain, who looked after the

royal bedroom and treasury; the seneschal, who kept the palace in food and servants; and the constable, who cared for the horses.

At the local level the fundamental administrative unit was the county, which resembled in its extent the Roman provinces. The count was the administrator, judge, and military leader of the county.

Charlemagne's chief administrative problem was to maintain an effective supervision and control over the local officials. He used three devices to resolve this problem. First, Charlemagne himself traveled widely to ascertain how the land was being administered and to hear appeals from the decisions of the counts. Second, he appointed special traveling inspectors, called *missi dominici* (or "emperor's emissaries"), to inspect a particular county every year. These men scrutinized the behavior of both the lay and the ecclesiastical officials, heard complaints, published imperial directives, and reported their findings to the emperor. Third, Charlemagne required that the important men of his realm, both laymen and ecclesiastics, attend a general assembly almost every year. There they reported on conditions in their local areas, advised the emperor on important matters, and heard his directives. Many of the imperial directives have survived. Divided into chapters (*capitula*), these informative records are known as *capitularies*.

Currency   To promote unity, Charlemagne also standardized weights, measures, and money throughout his Empire. The monetary system came to be based on a single minted coin, the silver *denarius,* or penny. Twelve of these made a *solidus*, or shilling (although such a coin was not actually minted), and twenty shillings made a pound.

◆ THE CAROLINGIAN RENAISSANCE

The Frankish rulers—Pepin, Charlemagne, and their successors—promoted learning within their domains in what is now called the Carolingian Renaissance. These rulers were interested in education for several reasons. In the sixth and seventh centuries, when the continent was divided among many small kingdoms, different styles of writing, known as *national hands* (Visigothic, Merovingian,

▲ MAP 7.2 CAROLINGIAN EMPIRE UNDER CHARLEMAGNE
The dates indicate the years in which the regions were added to the Empire. Marches were the frontier provinces (except Brittany, which was a maritime province) specially organized for the military defense of the Empire. Magdeburg was the episcopal see that took the leadership in converting the Danes and Slavs to Christianity. Aix-la-Chapelle, also called Aachen, was the capital of the Empire. The tributary peoples were those beyond the frontiers of the Empire over whom the emperor exercised a loose authority. They owed allegiance to him but were never integrated administratively into the Empire.

Lombard, and so on), had developed; and numerous variant readings had slipped into such basic texts as the Bible and the Benedictine rule. The Latin grammar used by scholars had also absorbed many regional peculiarities.

Literate persons in one part of Europe had great difficulty recognizing or reading a text written in another. The widespread decline in education had left few persons who could read at all. Poorly educated priests could not properly perform the liturgy, on which God's blessings on the community were thought to depend; and varia-

▼ **This ninth-century manuscript illumination from the first Bible of Charles the Bald displays the Carolingian minuscule, which is the model for the lowercase letters used today in what printers call Roman type.**
Bibliothèque Nationale de France, Paris

tions in religious rituals were also growing. Both situations weakened the unity of the Church as well as the state.

Carolingian Minuscule   Pepin and Charlemagne sought to remedy the lack of literacy. One great achievement of this educational revival was a reform in handwriting. About the year 800, monks at the monasteries of Corbie and Tours devised a new type of formal literary writing, a "book-hand," using lowercase letters and known as the Carolingian minuscule. Previously, the book-hands had been based on various styles of capital letters only and were difficult to read rapidly. The Carolingian minuscule used capital letters for the beginning of sentences and smaller (or lowercase) letters for the text. Our modern printing is based on this Carolingian innovation. It was easier to read a page written in this way; also, more letters could be written on a page, and thus more books were produced at less expense. Use of this graceful new script eventually spread across Europe.

Latin Language   Another achievement of this educational revival was the development of a common scholarly language. Carolingian scholars perfected a distinctive language now known as medieval Latin, which largely retained the grammatical rules of classical Latin but was more flexible and open in its vocabulary, freely coining new words to express the new realities of the age. Medieval Latin was also clearly different from the vulgar, or Romance, Latin spoken by the people. The establishment of medieval Latin as a distinct language of learning thus freed the Romance vernaculars to develop on their own. One of these vernacular languages is Old French, whose oldest surviving text dates from 842.[3]

The Latin created by the Carolingian scholars enabled travelers, administrators, and scholars to make themselves understood in all parts of Europe; and it continued to serve this function until the modern era. Even when it disappeared as an international language, it helped promote

---

[3]At Strasbourg in 842, Charles the Bald and Louis the German, two of the sons of Louis the Pious, took an oath that was recorded in Latin, Old French, and German. The oath at Strasbourg not only preserves the oldest surviving text in Old French but also marks the first use of German in a formal legal document.

European unity. All the modern vernacular tongues of Europe developed under the strong influence of these scholars' Latin. One of the reasons why it is possible to translate quickly from one European language to another is that their learned vocabularies are in large measure based on common Latin models.

Standardization of Texts A further achievement of the educational revival was the standardization of important texts. Pepin sought to standardize the liturgy on the basis of Roman practice and Charlemagne continued his policy. Charlemagne had Alcuin of York, an Anglo-Saxon scholar who served as a sort of minister of cultural affairs from about 783 until 794, prepare a new edition of Jerome's Vulgate translation of the Bible. This edition became the common biblical text for the entire Western Church. Charlemagne procured from Monte Cassino a copy of the Benedictine rule and

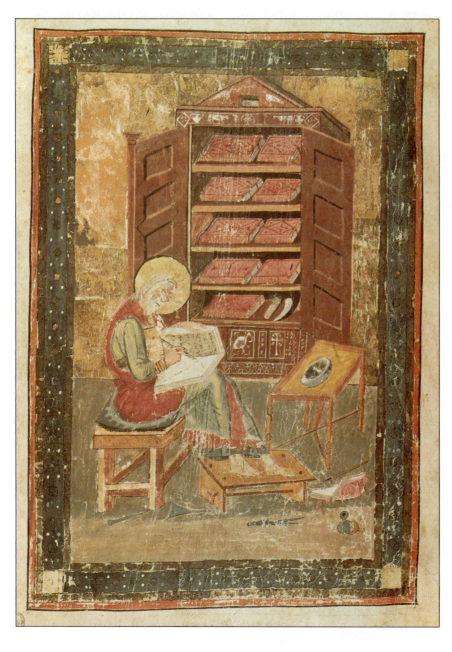

◄ Ezra Restoring the Bible
The image of Ezra restoring the Bible, in this eighth-century English manuscript, gives the work of the medieval monk an exalted self-justification. Here we see a biblical figure doing exactly what monks did—namely, writing and copying. In this case, Ezra was purifying the text of the Bible, and the implication was that monks were engaged in the same task. The vivid depiction of the bookshelves, with their open doors, and the table and stool is clearly an attempt to bring to life a scene from a monastery of the time.
Scala/Art Resource, NY

had it copied and distributed, so that monks everywhere would follow a standard code.

Schools and Curriculum   Expanding educational opportunities were essential for the success of Charlemagne's program. To increase the supply of locally trained scholars, he ordered all bishops and monasteries to establish schools to educate boys. Charlemagne himself set the example by founding a palace school for the sons of his own courtiers. Alcuin helped devise the standards for the school curriculum, based on the seven liberal arts. He divided the curriculum into the *trivium,* or verbal arts (grammar, rhetoric, and logic), and the *quadrivium,* or mathematical arts (arithmetic, astronomy, geometry, and music). In the twelfth century this curriculum would become the standard program of study for a bachelor of arts at universities.

Court Scholars   Charlemagne brought scholars from all around Europe to his court, including Anglo-Saxons and Italians. They formed an academy to discuss major intellectual issues in imitation of the classical world and used names drawn from the Bible or classics when they met together. Charlemagne was known as David and Alcuin as Horace.

Most of the scholars were grammarians and educators, engaged in producing teachers' manuals, textbooks, and school exercises; they went back to the Latin classics for models of correct grammar, usage, and vocabulary rather than for aesthetic satisfaction or philosophical insights. Their work was neither original nor possessed of rhetorical grace, but it was of the greatest importance for the intellectual growth of Europe. The revived mastery of correct Latin equipped scholars of later generations to return to the classical heritage and to recover from it philosophic and aesthetic values.

◆ CAROLINGIAN SOCIETY AND CULTURE

Aristocratic Culture   While Charlemagne was trying to raise the educational level of his people and the clergy, popular culture remained chiefly oral. The upper classes, including Charlemagne himself, enjoyed heroic poems of warfare, but

only a fragment of this poetry remains. Fighting and hunting were the chief occupations of the aristocrats, and with the many wars and the large forests, they had much to occupy themselves. The aristocrats surrounded themselves with as much luxury as they could make on their estates or could purchase from traveling merchants. They bought goods whose origins were in Byzantium, and they had gold and silver objects made for them by local craftsmen.

Economy and Society   As described in chapter 6, the agricultural economy was gradually improving as new tools and farming techniques permitted cultivation of the fertile river-valley soils. Large landed estates, farmed by serfs, provided most of the food. Ordinary woolen and linen cloth was made on these estates, which also produced wine, cheeses, and other food. Aside from Venice and some Mediterranean port cities, the towns were small. Many of the artisans worked directly on estates rather than in towns, and long-distance trade was conducted by traveling merchants.

Art and Architecture   The increased prosperity is visible today in the number of fine churches and monasteries that date from this period. As Charlemagne conquered new territories, monks, nuns, and clergy moved into them and established new religious foundations. The period was one of major building. Byzantine architecture became the model for most of the churches, including the magnificent one that Charlemagne built at Aix-la-Chapelle (modern Aachen) and that still stands today.

Mosaics in imitation of Byzantine models graced many church walls, and if mosaics were too expensive, wall painting took their place. The clergy commissioned artisans to make ecclesiastical objects, especially reliquaries for the bones of saints, out of precious metals and precious gems and stones.

◆ DECLINE OF THE CAROLINGIAN EMPIRE

Division of the Empire   Charlemagne at his death left a united and apparently strong empire to his single surviving son, Louis the Pious. Louis, a weak and indecisive man, soon lost control over

▲ This small (8 5/8 inches) ivory depiction of the
Virgin was probably executed at Aachen, one of the
capitals of Charlemagne, in the ninth century. Note
that the Virgin holds spindles in her left hand;
spinning was typically woman's work. But
surprisingly, she also wears armor — gauntlets on
her wrists and what look to be shoulder pieces.
Though a woman doing woman's work, she is a
militant, imperious figure, strikingly different from
the motherly madonnas of later medieval art.
Metropolitan Museum of Art, Gift of J. Pierpont Morgan, 1917
(17.190.49) Photograph © 2001 The Metropolitan Museum of
Art, New York.

his own family, and his sons rebelled against him.
After Louis' death, the three surviving sons partitioned the Empire at the Treaty of Verdun in 843
and established their own kingdoms (see map 7.3;
see also footnote on p. 233).

As the family of Carolingian rulers divided
amid civil wars and partitions of territory, the loyalty of the military aristocracy also waned. The
new rulers conquered no new lands; so they had
no new offices or properties with which to buy the
loyalties of the aristocracy. The office of count, appointive under Charlemagne, became hereditary
under his successors. The Carolingian rulers no
longer summoned the great men of the realm to
the yearly assemblies and no longer dispatched

▲ MAP 7.3 PARTITION OF THE FRANKISH EMPIRE

the *missi dominici* on their circuits. The institutional and moral bonds tying their central governments to the peripheral territories were thus
broken or abandoned.

▲ MAP 7.4 INVASIONS OF SOUTHERN EUROPE, NINTH
THROUGH TENTH CENTURIES

New Invasions   Under Charlemagne's weak successors, invasions of the Frankish Empire resumed, and centrifugal forces tore at the empire as well. To the south, Muslims from North Africa invaded Sicily and southern Italy in 827, attacked the valley of the Rhône in 842, and raided Rome in 846. Concurrently, from the east a new nomadic people, the Magyars, established themselves by about 895 in the valley of the Danube; from this base for the next fifty years, they struck repeatedly into the areas that are now France, Germany, and Italy (see map 7.4). Eventually they settled in modern-day Hungary. But none of these raids were as devastating to the Carolingian lands as those of the Scandinavians.

IV. The Vikings, Kiev, and England

For both Western and Eastern Europe, the migration and raids of the Vikings (Danes, Norwegians, and Swedes) altered the political map during a long period from the mid-eighth to the early tenth century. The Scandinavian migrations had a profound effect throughout the northern part of Europe, including the founding of the Kievan Rus principality and the invasion of Anglo-Saxon England and Carolingian France.

◆ THE VIKINGS

Scandinavia's sparse farmland could not support the populations that developed there. Parts of the population had migrated out in the fourth century and joined the Germanic invasions of Europe. The ninth and tenth centuries saw a resurgence of out-migration. Contemporary sources called them Northmen or Vikings (a name applied to all Scandinavians in the eighth century); the East Slavs called them Verangians.

Viking Ships and Exploration   One major factor in the migration of Northmen was their ships. These were shallow draft craft equally capable of traveling up rivers and on the high seas. A large square sail propelled the ship in winds and oarsmen propelled it in the calm. The ships were large enough to carry horses and provisions as well as men.

▲ **PICTURE-STONE**
This carving shows a Viking horseman at the top with his round shield and helmet. In the center section is a Viking boat. The prow was raised and cut into the shape of a dragon's head or some other ferocious beast. A rudder was used to guide the boat. The two occupants are shown wearing chain mail, the typical armor of the time.
Werner Forman / Art Resource, NY

The ships permitted both exploration and trade. As skilled and versatile seamen, the Vikings' explorations took them as far as a western territory they called Vinland, undoubtedly part of the North American continent. Iceland, settled as a result of these explorations, became a major center of medieval Scandinavian culture. The Vikings were constantly at war with one another because there was no stable kingdom; a defeated chief, rather than becoming a vassal under his conqueror, often preferred to seek out new land overseas.

Eastern Expansion   To the east the Vikings engaged in both trade and raiding. In about 830, Vikings from Scandinavia, known as the Rus,

▲ MAP 7.5 INVASIONS OF NORTHERN EUROPE, EIGHTH THROUGH NINTH CENTURIES
◆ www.mhhe.com/chambers8ch7maps

were invited to intervene in wars among the East Slavs. They staked out their own claims in Novgorod and Kiev, eventually establishing a principality composed largely of East Slavs (see more later in this chapter). The internal river systems of central Europe provided a conduit to Constantinople and the Black Sea. Some Vikings came to trade with Byzantium and Persia, but others made their wealth by hiring themselves out as mercenaries to the Byzantine emperor (see map 7.5).

Western Expansion   In England and on the continent, the Vikings appeared first as merchants and

pirates, then as conquerors and colonists. Vikings, chiefly Danes, began raiding England in 787. One story tells of the attack on London: Unable to move up the Thames River because of London Bridge, the Vikings attached ropes to the pilings holding up the bridge and rowed downstream as the tide was going out; the pilings easily pulled out and the Vikings raided upstream. By 866 a Danish army landed in eastern England and established a permanent settlement. In Ireland and Scotland, Norwegians were the invaders and settlers. Dublin was a Norwegian settlement.

On the continent Danes began their attack along the western coast of France as early as 800, eventually penetrating far inland. Viking raiding parties even ventured around the Iberian Peninsula into the Mediterranean Sea and up the Rhône valley. In 911 the Viking Rollo secured from Charles the Simple, the king of France, the territory near the mouth of the Seine River, which became known as Normandy (from the name *Northmen*).

Conversion to Christianity   Christianity only gradually made inroads in Scandinavia. Some Vikings converted in order to carry on trade in Western Europe. In the middle of the ninth century Anskar, a Dane trained in a Saxon monastery, made conversions in Denmark and southern Sweden, establishing churches and winning adherents among the nobility. The conversions, however, were often incomplete. Gravestones in the shape of a cross display carvings of the old gods as well. Burials continued to have grave goods (objects from daily life for use of the dead in afterlife), often with some Christian objects as well. Christianity did not have a strong enough hold to dissuade the Vikings from attacking and looting monasteries in England and France.

Treatment of Women   The violent nature of Scandinavian society suggests that women were treated roughly. Polygamy was normal and concubines common. Other evidence, however, indicates that women were esteemed and played the role of advisers in politics. Archaeology has also indicated the value placed on women. For instance, one ship burial at Oseberg in Sweden is that of a noblewoman who was fifty years old. Her grave contained another woman, perhaps a servant (thirty years old), several beds with quilts and cushions, a chair, two lamps, tapestries, and spinning and weaving implements.

Poetry and Sagas   The Edda are the legends of the Norse gods, telling their exploits and fights. They were recorded in the thirteenth century in both poetry and prose. According to the "Lay of Volund," warriors who died in battle joined the following of Odin in a great banquet hall, Valhalla. But the entire company of gods and heroes would be doomed to destruction by fire during a cosmic twilight when the ravaged earth would sink entirely into the sea. The myth

▲ JEWELRY OF VIKING HANDICRAFT AND PLUNDERED COINS

The Viking artisans were skilled at stone and wood carving as well as making fine jewelry. They used their own designs, which included serpents, animals, and plants intertwined. They also incorporated plundered objects such as coins directly into their designs.

© Universitetets Oldsaksamling, Oslo. Photo: Ove Holst/University Museum of National Antiquities Oslo, Norway

became the basis for Richard Wagner's opera *Götterdammerung*.

The sagas, although written down in Iceland during the thirteenth century, are prose stories that actually cover the Viking period to about 1000, when Iceland converted to Christianity. The sagas are adventure stories recounting a fierce sense of bravery and violence on the part of both men and women. In the Eddic poems Gudrun does not slay her brothers after they kill her husband, Sigurd, whereas in the *Gisla Saga* the widow has her brother killed after he kills her husband. *King Harald's Saga* recounts Harald's adventures traveling down the Eastern rivers to Constantinople and his exploits as a Verangian Guard (mercenary) in Constantinople. The saga describes his invasion of England in 1066 and his defeat.

◆ THE KIEVAN RUS PRINCIPALITY

The East Slavs invited the Vikings to aid them in their internal wars in the first half of the ninth century. The Vikings then became instrumental in establishing the first East Slavic state centered around Kiev on the Dnieper River and Novgorod on Lake Ilmen.

Origins   The *Primary Chronicle,* the most detailed and important source for the origin of the Rus state, recounts that the Rus (Vikings or Verangians) ruled Novgorod. Prince Oleg (r. 873?–913) united the two cities of Novgorod and Kiev under his rule. In 907 he led a fleet, allegedly containing two thousand ships, on a raid against Constantinople. The Byzantine emperor granted both tribute and trading concessions in order to purchase peace with the Rus. Oleg's successors completed the unification of the East Slavic tribes, bringing together an area that stretched from the Baltic to the Black Sea and from the Danube to the Volga rivers.

In 988 the Kievan ruler, Vladimir, converted to the Eastern form of Christianity and imposed baptism on his subjects. As was so often the case, the influence of a woman was important in the conversion. In exchange for military help in the defense of Byzantine territory, Vladimir demanded a Byzantine princess in marriage. The woman in question, Anna, sister of the emperor, would not marry Vladimir unless he converted to Christianity. He agreed, and she arrived with a group of missionaries. The missionaries translated the Bible and the liturgy by adapting the Cyrillic alphabet to East Slavic—the forerunner of modern Russian.

Reign of Yaroslav the Wise   The Principality of Kiev (see map 7.6) reached its height of power under Vladimir's son Yaroslav (r. 1015–1054). Yaroslav won self-government for the Rus Church from the patriarch of Constantinople in 1037. The head of the independent Church was called the *metropolitan* and lived in Kiev, which became the ecclesiastical as well as the political capital of the East Slavs.

During his reign Yaroslav had prepared the first written codification of East Slavic law, the *Russkaia Pravda.* He patronized church building, bringing in skilled Byzantine artisans to decorate them. The cathedral at Kiev was the masterpiece. Yaroslav, a writer himself, promoted learning in his principality and assembled many scribes to translate religious books from Greek into Slavic. Although located in the power axis of Byzantium, Kiev kept close ties to Western Europe. The family of Yaroslav had marriage connections with the ruling dynasties of Byzantium, England, France, Germany, Norway, Poland, and Hungary. Yaroslav's own daughter Anna married King Henry I of France. Charters with her signature survive, carefully inscribed with Cyrillic letters; she seems to have been the only layperson in the French court who could write.

Agriculture and Trade   Kiev was a leader in the agricultural revival of early medieval Europe; its fertile steppes produced abundant crops. The Rus peasants were plowing with horses at a time when oxen were still common in the West. Most of the population were free peasants, but there were some serfs and slaves.

The Rus traded with the Scandinavians, the steppe peoples, the Muslims at Baghdad, and especially the Byzantines. Every year a great fleet of boats, led by the princes themselves, assembled at Kiev and floated down the Dnieper River to the Black Sea and across to Constantinople. Amber, fur, honey, slaves, and wheat were exchanged for silks, spices, and other luxuries of the East. In recent years Russian archaeologists excavating at Novgorod have uncovered numerous commercial documents written on birch bark that documented this lively trade.

Kievan Cities   Trade supported the development of urban centers. Within the many towns, a wealthy aristocracy of princes, warriors, and great merchants rubbed shoulders with artisans, workers, and large numbers of destitute persons. Kiev in the eleventh century was one of the great cities of the age. A German chronicler, Thietmar of Merseburg, said it had 400 churches, 8 marketplaces, and unnumbered inhabitants. Kiev must have included 20,000 to 30,000 people—more people than any contemporary Western city.

▲ **MAP 7.6** PRINCIPALITY OF KIEV

Kievan Government The head of the Kievan government was the prince, who selected nobles, called *boyars,* to aid him in governing. The towns had large citizen assemblies, called *veches,* that the prince also consulted for advice. The government was thus based on a balance of monarchic, aristocratic, and popular elements. The prince, unlike the Byzantine emperor, was not the fountain of justice. Most cases were settled in popular courts from which there was no organized system of appeal, features that brought Kievan justice closer to the Germanic system.

Learning and Literature The clergy established a formal educational system primarily to train the clergy; but their schools were open to the sons of ruling families. A number of women, too, were educated in convents. Birch bark letters discovered by archaeologists show that women could read and perhaps write. Their letters are about business and love.

The *Primary Chronicle,* the literary masterpiece of the age, recounts the conversion of the Rus to Christianity and their battles against the pagan peoples who surrounded them. The poetry of

▲ **Yaroslav Presenting Model of Church**
Although now destroyed, a group of eleventh-century frescoes in St. Sophia Cathedral in Kiev once depicted the family of Prince Yaroslav. This re-creation of the frescoes in a drawing by the seventeenth-century Dutch artist A. V. Westvelt shows Yaroslav presenting a model of a church to Prince Vladimir.
Courtesy, General Research Division, New York Public Library. Astor, Lenox, Tilden Foundations.

medieval Rus is represented by a short heroic epic titled *Song of Igor's Campaign*, which records an unsuccessful campaign that the Rus princes conducted in 1185 against the pagan Polovtsi, a people from the steppes.

Art and Architecture   Christianity had an immense influence on architectural and artistic development. The East Slavs built many churches based on Byzantine models. The familiar "onion" domes of Russian churches, for example, were a late effort to imitate in wood the domes on ecclesiastical structures at Constantinople. The Kievan principality appreciated magnificence and splendor in its churches and liturgical services. It hired Byzantines to train its artisans and to decorate its churches with icons.

Decline of the Principality of Kiev   As was true of the Byzantines, Arabs, and Carolingians, both internal and external troubles destroyed the peace of the land after Yaroslav's death. Like the Carolingians, Yaroslav divided his territory among all male heirs. The result was frequent bickering and civil wars. These internal struggles left the people unable to resist the renewed menace of the steppe nomads. In 1061 the Cumans, a nomadic Turkish people, began harassing the frontier, and they eventually cut off Kiev from contact with the Black Sea. This sundering of the trade route to

Constantinople was a disaster for commerce and culture because it deprived Kiev of contact with the Byzantine Empire and the Western world.

◆ ANGLO-SAXON ENGLAND

The Viking attacks on England had begun in the late eighth century, and by 793 the famous centers of Anglo-Saxon learning, Lindisfarne and Jarrow, were looted and destroyed. The Vikings successfully established themselves in the north of England and were pushing south when they encountered King Alfred of Wessex (r. 871–899).

Alfred the Great   King Alfred, after experiencing military defeats by the Danes in the early years of his reign, reorganized the defense of the kingdom. He reformed the militia to keep a larger and more mobile army in the field and built fortresses to defend the land and ships to defend the coast. His reforms proved successful. Before 880 several Danish chiefs received baptism as part of a treaty with Alfred, and in 886 the Danes agreed to confine themselves to a region in the north and east of England. This region, which the Danes continued to dominate for several generations, was later known as the *Danelaw,* in recognition of the fact that the Danish laws in force there differed from the English laws of other parts of the country.

Chronology

CHRONOLOGICAL CHART

Byzantium	Islam	Frankish Empire	Vikings/England/Rus
Heraclius (r. 610–641)	Muhammad (d. 632)	Merovingians	
Defeat of Persia (622–629)	Hijra (622)		
Loss of Egypt, Syria to Arabs	First four caliphs (632–666)		Council of Whitby (664)
	Expansion into N. Africa		
Leo III (r. 717–741)	Conquest of Visigoths	Charles Martel (714–741)	Bede (d. 735)
Iconoclasm	Defeat at Tours (732)		
Siege of Constantinople (718)			
Bulgarian wars	Umayyads in Córdoba	Pepin becomes king (741)	
			Viking invasions
	Harun al-Rashid (r. 786–809)	Charlemagne (r. 768–814)	
		Imperial coronation (800)	
		Louis the Pious (r. 814–840)	
	Disintegration of Arab Empire	Division of Empire (843)	
Cyrillic alphabet			Alfred of Wessex (r. 871–899)

Intellectual Life Anglo-Saxon England was perhaps the most literate country of Europe at the time. Schools and tutors educated upper-class boys and girls in Old English. There was an audience for poetry and prose.

Alfred renewed intellectual life in England. He gathered a group of scholars and began a program of translating into Anglo-Saxon the works of such writers as Bede, Gregory the Great, and Boethius. During his reign, an unknown author compiled a history of England known as the *Anglo-Saxon Chronicle.* Continued thereafter by various authors and now extant in several versions, the *Chronicle* is an indispensable source for the later Anglo-Saxon period in English history.

SUMMARY

The period from the seventh to the beginning of the eleventh century included the rise of a new religion, Islam, and an Arab conquest of the southern Mediterranean; a revival of the Byzantine Empire; the rise of Kiev; prosperity in Anglo-Saxon England; and the Carolingian Empire. But all these empires and kingdoms had internal weaknesses that left them too disorganized to resist fresh invasions. The Arabs, Byzantines, and Kievans lost territory to Turkish tribes. In the West Vikings, Magyars, and Muslim pirates disrupted peace. The Vikings plundered and eventually settled in large parts of Ireland, England, and France. The Carolingian Empire split into French-speaking and German-speaking halves.

Western Europe owed a debt to the Islamic civilization that came to influence almost every aspect of medieval Western life over the next few centuries. Western farmers imitated Muslim techniques of irrigation and learned to grow new plants, such as rice, citrus fruits, and peaches. Merchants adopted the Arabic numbers and probably some Islamic forms of business partnerships. Muslim mathematicians made enormous contributions to the development of algebra. These works provided the foundations for Islamic learning and preserved the thought of these writers through a period when Greek texts were not being widely copied in the West. Recovering from the latest invasions, Europe was on the threshold of a period of immense creativity in which Islamic contributions would play a large role.

QUESTIONS FOR FURTHER THOUGHT

◆

1. In both chapter 6 and chapter 7, one of the dominating themes was the migration of various peoples from Northern and Eastern Europe (Germanic tribes, Vikings, and Slavs), from Central Asia (Huns, Avars, Bulgarians), and from the Arabian Penninsula. Why were these people on the move? Speculate on both the conditions that might stimulate movement and those that attracted them to the West.

2. We have seen in chapter 6 that, aside from some outstanding figures such as Boethius and Bede, intellectual life suffered in the West during the invasions. What brought about the flourishing of Arabic, Carolingian, Anglo-Saxon, and Russian learning during the subsequent centuries? What political conditions give rise to intellectual advances?

3. The decline and fall of empires continues to challenge historians to look for causes. In this chapter we have seen the Byzantine, Arabic, Carolingian, and Kievan Empires go into decline after a period of expansion, consolidation, and brilliance. What influence does the personality of the emperor or ruler have, and what influence do internal and external events have on the fate of empires? Compare these empires to the Roman one.

RECOMMENDED READING

◆

Sources

Cross, Samuel Hazard (ed.). *Russian Primary Chronicle: Laurentian Text*. O. P. Sherbowitz-Wetzor (tr.). 1968. The major primary source for early Russian history.

*Dmytryshyn, Basil. *Medieval Russia: A Source Book, 850–1700*. 3d ed. 1991. Primary sources for the period covered.

*Einhard, *The Life of Charlemagne*. 1962. Personal account by someone who lived in Charlemagne's court.

*Ibn, Khaldun. *The Mugaddimah: An Introduction to World History*. Franz Rosenthal (tr.). 1969. Reflections on societies and empires by a North African Muslim; written in the fourteenth century.

The Meaning of the Glorious Koran. M. Marmaduke Pickthall (tr.). 1948. Interpretation of Koran.

*Vernadsky, George (ed.). *Medieval Russian Laws*. 1964. Review of early Russian laws.

Zenkovsky, Serge A. (ed.). *Medieval Russia's Epics, Chronicles, and Tales*. 1974. Includes sermons and saints' lives.

Studies

Bulliet, Richard W. *The Camel and the Wheel*. 1990. On Arabic society and economy.

Fine, John V. A. *The Early Medieval Balkans: A Critical Survey from the Sixth to the Late Twelfth Century*. 1983. The only work of its kind in English.

*Geanakoplos, Deno J. *Byzantine East and Latin West: Two Worlds of Christendom in the Middle Ages and Renaissance*. 1966. The Western debt to Byzantium.

Hussey, J. M. *The Orthodox Church in the Byzantine Empire*. 1986. History of Orthodox Church in Byzantium.

Keddie, Nikki, and Beth Baron (eds.). *Women in Middle Eastern History: Shifting Boundaries in Sex and Gender*. 1991. Essays explaining the position of women in Islam.

Laiou, Angeliki E. *Gender, Society, and Economic Life in Byzantium*. 1992. A study of the lives of women, peasants, and more ordinary people in thirteenth- and fourteenth-century Byzantium.

Levin, Eve. *Sex and Society in the World of the Orthodox Slavs, 900–1700*. 1989. A study of the birch bark letters.

*Lewis, Bernard (ed.). *Islam from the Prophet Muhammad to the Capture of Constantinople*. Vol. 1: *Politics and War*. Vol. 2: *Religion and Society*. 1987. Collected essays.

Mango, Cyril. *Byzantium: The Empire of New Rome*. 1980. An introduction to the civilization of the Eastern Empire, with effective use of archaeological data.

*Martin, Janet. *Medieval Russia, 980–1584*. 1995. Short history of medieval Russia that also covers recent interpretations.

Meyendorff, John. *Imperial Unity and Christian Divisions: The Church 450–680*. 1989. An attempt to portray the divisions from the Eastern rather than the Western perspective.

*Ostrogorski, George. *History of the Byzantine State*. Joan Hussey (tr.). 1969. The basic reference for all matters of political history.

*Riché, Pierre. *Daily Life in the World of Charlemagne*. Jo Ann McNamara (tr.). 1975. A very good read on social and cultural history of the period.

Sawyer, P. H. *Kings and Vikings: Scandinavia and Europe A.D. 700–1100*. 1984. Excellent summary of recent research on the Vikings.

Stenton, Frank. *Anglo-Saxon England*. 1971. Basic introductory text.

Walther, Wiebke. *Women in Islam*. 1993.

---

*Available in paperback.

▲ URBAN GROWTH IN THE TWELFTH CENTURY

The economic prosperity and population growth of the twelfth century permitted the development of urban centers for trade and commerce. Urban centers continued to prosper throughout the Middle Ages. They all had walls and defensive gates as well as town squares and houses reaching three stories. Wealthy inhabitants came to enjoy considerable comfort including barge parties.

© Victoria & Albert Museum, London/Art Resource, NY

RESTORATION OF AN ORDERED SOCIETY

The year 1000 was greeted at the time with anxiety. It was the first millennium since the birth of Jesus of Nazareth, and people thought that the end of the world was at hand. To historians looking back at the period from 1000 to 1150, however, the outlines of medieval society, government, culture, and the economy have become clear. Although rudimentary castles, the origins of feudalism (a type of patron-client relationship between lords and vassals), and the economic and social arrangement of manors and serfs for agriculture had begun in the Carolingian period, it is after the year 1000 that these characteristics of medieval society were fully formed. Feudalism permitted a new order for the society. The society that evolved in the Middle Ages was very hierarchical, with a small elite group of nobles and a large peasant population that supported it through agriculture. Rulers used feudal ties as a basis for establishing their governments and extending their power. The geographical and political states of Europe formed during this period, and the rulers' governmental innovations laid the groundwork for late medieval states. With a restoration of order and an increase in agricultural productivity, trade once again prospered. Surpluses of grain supported an urban population, and towns once again grew in Europe. Reformed monasticism and the fear of the millennium kindled the spark of popular piety that had begun in the tenth century. Taking advantage of the enthusiasm for religion and reform, the papacy underwent a period of major change and consolidation of power that is recognizable in the Roman Catholic Church today. Europeans began to look from the local scenes of their own estates and towns to the larger world. Through both warfare and long-distance trade, they expanded to the east into Slavic lands and into the eastern Mediterranean in a series of campaigns called the crusades.

Chapter 8. Restoration of an Ordered Society							
	Social Structure	Body Politic	Changes in the Organization of Production and in the Impact of Technology	Evolution of Family and Changing Gender Roles	War	Religion	Cultural Expression
I. Economic and Social Changes	●	●	●	●	●		●
II. Governments of Europe		●					
III. Reform of the Western Church		●				●	●
IV. The Crusades	●	●			●	●	

I. Economic and Social Changes

Historians use shorthand terms to refer to the period's major changes. *Manorialism* refers both to the economic organization of agricultural production and to the organization of the lives and labor of peasants who did the actual cultivating. Approximately 90 percent of the population were peasants. *Feudalism* refers to approximately the top 5 percent of the population. Feudalism governed relationships of the elite of society and consisted of a patron (lord) and clients (vassals). The lord offered his vassals protection and land in exchange for services from the vassals. Some historians favor the historical interpretation of Karl Marx and use *feudalism* to refer to both the social and economic organization of the manor and the personal, military, and governmental role of feudalism.

Europe experienced a period of growth and prosperity that began about 1050. A shift in weather to a warmer and dryer period, the release from the threat of external invasion, and the development of new agricultural practices discussed in chapter 6 all added to increased productivity. The new political order that feudalism began to offer brought at least a measure of peace and an expansion of trade. Economic and demographic growth led to a revival of cities and to internal and external colonization. The other roughly 5 percent of the population was made up of clergy and urban dwellers.

◆ FEUDALISM

The new stability in Europe altered the power structures and lives of the warrior class. Material comforts, housing, gender relations, and even the nature of warfare changed. But perhaps the most important factor for understanding the European Middle Ages was that the power relationships of the nobility to each other and to the monarch became more personal and private rather than being based on citizenship as in the Roman Empire.

Definition   Although historians debate the accuracy of using the term *feudalism* as shorthand for the personal bonds among the elite in the Middle Ages and as a descriptive term for the type of society and governments these bonds resulted in, the term is still a useful one. In its restricted meaning, *feudalism* refers to a patron/client relationship between two freemen (men who are not serfs), a lord and his vassal. *Vassal* derived from a Celtic word for servant, but in feudal terms *vassal* meant a free person who put himself under the protection of a lord and for whom he rendered loyal military aid. In practice, both lord and vassal came from the upper echelons of society, lay and clerical. Feudal arrangements did not include the serfs and the poorer freemen.

Historians have traced the development of feudalism to both the patron-client arrangements in the Roman Empire and to the chief-warrior relationship (*comitatus*) among the Germanic tribes. During the Carolingian period, changes in warfare made equipping and training warriors more expensive. The stirrup, unknown to the Romans, made it possible for a warrior to ride a horse without clasping it with his knees to stay in the saddle. The stirrup also permitted a more heavily armed warrior to fight, but this in turn required a bigger horse. Few warriors could afford the horse and new body armor, so the Carolingians began granting land to their warriors to support them. Charlemagne had a pyramidal plan for recruiting an army, with the king at the top, followed by counts and dukes, and under them the warriors. This simple plan proved unfeasible, and it took until about 1300 to work out the nuances of feudal relations.

The Feudal Milieu To understand the growth of feudalism, we must first recall the chaotic conditions that marked the Viking invasion and the decline of the Carolingian Empire. In a milieu in which the kings could not protect their realm from raids and could not rein in local counts and freebooters, individuals sought security through their own efforts. The freeman in search of protection had little recourse but to appeal to a neighbor stronger than himself. If the neighbor accepted, the two men entered into a close, quasi-familial relationship. Like the bonds between father and son, the feudal relationship between the strong "lord" and the weak freeman was initially more ethical and emotional than legally binding. As feudalism matured as a tool of government and social organization, oaths sealed the agreement and the lords gave vassals estates or fiefs to alleviate the cost of their service.

The true homeland of Western feudalism was the region between the Loire and Rhine rivers. The institutions that developed there were subsequently exported to England in the Norman Conquest and to southern Italy. Gradually, the organization of government and society in southern France, Spain, and the Kingdom of Jerusalem copied the feudal model. Many parts of Germany did not develop full feudalism because of the continued importance of free land tenure. The Celtic areas (Ireland, Scotland, Wales, Brittany) did not develop classical feudalism, because powerful clans traditionally extended such protection.

Perhaps because of the early importance of towns in Northern Italy, the use of feudal ties was stunted but not suppressed.

Vassalage Vassalage was an honorable personal bond between a lord and his man. An act of **homage** established the relationship. In this simple ceremony the prospective vassal placed his hands within those of his lord (sometimes they exchanged a kiss of peace) and swore to become his man. He might also swear **fealty** (swearing to be faithful to his oath of homage) on the Gospels or a saint's relic. The "joining of hands" was the central act in the ceremony of homage.

Vassalage imposed obligations on both the vassal and his lord. The vassal owed his lord material and military aid and counsel (advice). He had to perform military service in the lord's army and usually had to bring additional men in numbers proportionate to the wealth he derived from his land (fief). As military aid became more precisely defined, it was more a matter of contract than of emotional bonds. The contract could stipulate that the vassal serve, for example, forty days a year in a local war, less time if the lord intended to fight in foreign lands. The vassal could not refuse service, but if the lord asked for more than the customary time, the vassal could demand compensation or simply return home. The lord could demand other financial aids, such as paying the ransom if the lord was captured and paying for the ceremonies surrounding the knighting of his eldest son or the marriage of his eldest daughter.

The obligation of counsel required the vassal to give advice and to help the lord reach true judgments in legal cases that came before his court. Cases usually involved adjudication of disputes among the vassals and complaints brought by the lord against his men. By custom only a jury of his peers, that is, his fellow vassals, could judge a vassal.

The lord, in turn, owed his vassal protection and maintenance (military and material support). He had to come to his vassal's aid when requested, repel invaders from his vassal's land, and help a vassal being sued in another's court. In the formative period of feudalism, the lord's obligation of material support was provided in his own household, but as vassals became more

▲ Investiture Scene, Fresco, Ferrande Tower, Pernes-les-Fontaines, France, ca. 1270
Kneeling before his overlord the king, a vassal offers homage and receives in return investiture in a fief—the roll of parchment, which would have recorded the transaction in detail. As this thirteenth-century fresco from Pernes-les-Fontaines in France indicates, the ceremony takes place before witnesses.
Giraudon/Art Resource, NY

numerous and more distantly located and as great princes came to be included among them, sheer logistics prevented the lord from feeding all his men. Because a lord often had no cash revenues for making monetary compensations, he would distribute land as a form of payment for the vassal's allegiance.

Disloyalty on the part of the vassal, such as refusing military service, gave the lord the right to terminate the bonds of homage and take back any property that he had given to the vassal.

The Fief The lord's concession of land to his vassal was called a *fief* (rhymes with *leaf*). The granting of a fief superimposed on the personal relationship

of vassalage a second relationship, one involving property. The close union of personal and property ties was, in fact, the most characteristic feature of the Western feudal relationship.

The lord granted the fief to his vassal in a special ceremony called **investiture** (usually immediately following the act of homage). As a symbol of the land the vassal was receiving, the lord gave to his vassal a clod of earth or sprig of leaves. In a strict juridical sense the fief was a conditional, temporary, and nonhereditary grant of land or other income-producing property, such as an office, toll, or rent. At the vassal's death, disability, or refusal to serve his lord, the fief at once returned to the lord who granted it.

Although technically not inheritable, the fief gradually became hereditary. From the start, lords had found it convenient to grant a fief to the adult son of a deceased vassal, because the son could at once serve in his father's stead. The son had to make a special payment to the lord (the *relief*) to acquire the fief.

Women and Minors   Because women and young sons of vassals could not perform military service, their right to inherit initially was not guaranteed. But the advantages of orderly succession to valuable property led lords to recognize the right of a minor son to inherit. The lord retained the right of wardship, taking the heir and his property back into his hands or granting them to another noble until the heir reached the age of twenty-one.

Only reluctantly did feudal practice permit daughters to inherit a fief. Nevertheless, in most areas of Europe women could inherit. Their lord had the right to select their husbands for them, because their spouses assumed the obligations of service connected to the fief.

Subinfeudation   Initially, vassals were forbidden to sell the fief, grant it to the Church, or otherwise transfer it in whole or in part. Vassals, however, commonly sold or granted portions of their fiefs, but only with the lord's permission and usually accompanied by a money payment.

When lords regranted portions of their fiefs to other vassals, the process was called *subinfeudation.* Subinfeudation complicated the hierarchy that Charlemagne had initially envisioned. Instead of a neat pyramidal hierarchy, subinfeudation permitted vassals to have their own vassals. A vassal could acquire fiefs from several different lords, swearing homage and fealty to each. In case of conflict among his different lords, whom should he serve? To escape this dilemma, feudal custom required that the vassal select one of his lords as his *liege lord,* that is, the one whom he would serve against all others.

Castles   With the later invasions and breakdown of Carolingian government, those lords who could afford it invested in defensive fortress-homes, or castles. Initially these castles were a motte, a wooden tower built on a hill with an external courtyard, the bailey, surrounded by a wooden palisade. A castle-holder could offer weaker neighbors a place to shelter their animals and families in the event of attack. By the eleventh and twelfth centuries castles became more elaborate, with thick stone walls for the motte and larger stone-walled baileys that contained outbuildings such as stables, kitchens, and gardens. The moat, the ditch surrounding castles and sometimes filled with water, added to the defense. Castles were built throughout Europe and can still be seen today. The pace of castle building was rapid. In Florence and its surrounding countryside in Italy, for example, only two castles are mentioned in the sources before 900, 11 before 1000, 52 before 1050, 130 before 1100, and 205 before 1200.

The *castellan,* or owner of a castle, assumed many functions in addition to military ones. He acted as judge and tax collector and controlled the local church, including appointing the priest. The castellan was supported economically by a subject peasant population who cultivated the castle owner's land as well as giving him part of the crops they produced on their own plots. The castles with their lands constituted fairly stable, local governmental units.

Feudal Government   From about the year 1050, counts, dukes, and some kings were attempting to integrate these castles into centralized principalities, forcing the castellans to assume toward them the obligations of vassals and fief holders. The use of these feudal concepts and institutions to serve the interests of princely authority extended feudalism from bonds of personal loyalty and military service to a system of government.

In granting a fief, the lord gave his vassal all possible sources of revenue the land could produce. The primary source of wealth was from the work of the peasants, who were granted with the fief and cultivated the land. In addition, the lord gave the right to hold a manorial court and to profit from its fines and confiscations of livestock and goods. The manorial courts regulated the subject peasantry and were very lucrative. In addition, some vassals were granted the right to hear cases that were reserved for royal justice. This granting of royal judicial prerogatives contributed to another characteristic of feudal society, private justice (that is, the exercise of royal powers

The Terminology of Feudalism and Manorialism

FEUDALISM   An economic, political, and social organization of medieval Europe. Land was held by vassals from more powerful overlords in exchange for military and other services.

Vassal   A free warrior who places himself under a lord, accepting the terms of loyal service, fighting in time of war, and counsel in time of peace. As the system developed, women and minor sons also could become vassals, as could members of the clergy.

Aid   Aid was the military service that the vassal owed the lord.

Fief (sometimes called benefice)   Land given to a vassal from his lord in exchange for specified terms of service. A ceremonial presentation of a sheaf of grain often accompanied the grant of land.

Homage   An oath sworn by the vassal to the lord, acknowledging allegiance to the lord. The vassal took his oath by placing his hands within the hands of the lord.

Fealty   An oath, often accompanying the oath of homage, in which the vassal swears to uphold his homage. This oath was sworn on the Gospels or on a saint's relics.

Relief   An inheritance tax on the vassal at his death when the fief passed to his heir.

Subinfeudation   The grant of a fief by a vassal to a subordinate who becomes his vassal.

Liege Lord   That lord whom the vassal must serve even if he has conflicting oaths with subinfeudation.

MANORIALISM   An agricultural, legal, and social organization of land, including a nucleated village, large fields for agriculture, and serfs to work the land. The land and its inhabitants were called a manor and both belonged to the lord.

Manor   An estate held by the lord that included land, the people on the land, and a village, usually with a mill. A fief might contain a number of manors or sometimes just a part of one.

Open Fields   The agricultural area was divided up into three large fields (500 acres or more). The lord held land for his direct profit in these, and the serfs rented strips of land in all three fields for their profit and to pay their rent.

Manorial Court   The lord had the right to administer justice on his manor in order to regulate services and rents owed to him. Peasants also used manorial court for their own business and to keep peace within their village.

Serf or Villein   Peasant who was personally free, but bound to the lord of the manor and the land of the manor. Serfs rented land from the lord to cultivate to produce their own crops. In addition, they owed work for the lord and various gifts of produce.

Week Work   Work that the peasant owed to the lord every week.

Boon Work   Work that the peasant owed to the lord for special tasks such as plowing or harvesting.

Demesne Land   Land that the lord held for his own crops and profit. Serfs worked this land.

Glebe Land   Land held by the parish priest.

---

by private individuals as a right associated with their tenure of land). The idea that the king owned all the land and was the font of all justice did not disappear. In the twelfth and thirteenth centuries the kings began to use their position as pinnacle of the feudal hierarchy to assert the right to hear appeals from the courts of his chief vassals (as well as those "rear vassals" who stood lower on the feudal ladder). Monarchs also accepted directly cases that his vassals had traditionally heard. The exertion of these royal prerogatives brought about the gradual but unmistakable decline of private justice and led to the extension of royal justice throughout the realm.

◆ LIFE OF THE NOBILITY

Feudalism brought many changes to the elite's family arrangements, housing, fighting, and leisure activities. To proclaim their identity and distinctiveness from the rest of society, the nobles adopted family names, which usually recalled the name of the revered founder or of the ancestral castle. Other symbols also denoted elite status—coats of arms, mottoes, fanciful genealogies, and castles.

Noble Families   The appearance of a hereditary nobility in the eleventh and twelfth centuries

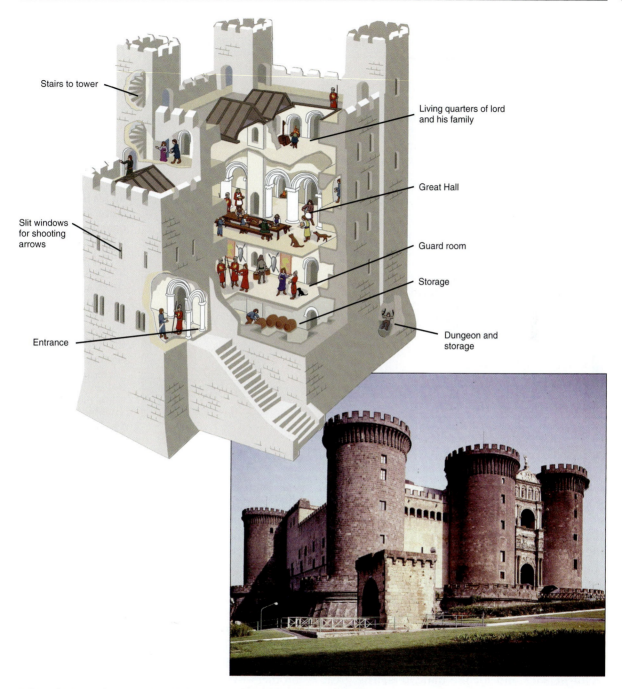

Stairs to tower

Living quarters of lord and his family

Great Hall

Slit windows for shooting arrows

Guard room

Storage

Entrance

Dungeon and storage

▲ Castel Nuovo (new castle), 13th century, with triumphal arch, Naples, Campania, Italy. Castles developed from mounds of earth with a stockade on top. A major development in the twelfth century was the elaborate square keep shown in the diagram above. The keep included areas for storage of large quantities of food in the event of siege, a guard room, the great hall where meals were served and the guard slept, and finally, on the top, quarters for the family. Square keeps were vulnerable to attack so round towers were developed to protect the corners of the castle as seen in the photograph.

Dagli Orti/The Art Archive

◄ A MEDIEVAL KNIGHT IN ARMOR The knight is fully armed with chain mail on his arms and steel plates on his shoulders and legs. He is equipped with spurs and a sword, and he is wearing a leather cap. His wife holds up his helmet and lance, and a daughter or court lady holds his shield. The surcoat he wears, the horse cover, and the shield represent his coat of arms. The illustration is from the fourteenth-century English *Lutteral Psalter.* By Permission of The British Library. Add. 42130. folio 202v

reflected a fundamental change in the structure of the elite families. In the Merovingian and Carolingian periods, families used partible inheritance; that is, all surviving sons inherited equally. In giving the fief, however, the lords endowed only one son and his immediate descendants. The custom came to be that the firstborn son would inherit the fief (primogeniture). If there were no sons, daughters inherited and the fief was divided equally among them.

Primogeniture had the advantage of keeping the estates intact, but it had implications for the younger sons and for the daughters. The great families provided their daughters with dowries, but otherwise excluded them from a full share in the inheritance. Anxious to attract a suitable husband for a daughter and settle her future early, noble fathers had to offer ever larger dowries and married their daughters off in their teens. Unmarried daughters usually became nuns. Younger sons had no lands unless they could win them in war or marry an affluent heiress. With no lands, they could not support a family. As a consequence, unattached young warriors abounded. Some entered the Church and rose to high offices. Others drifted from court to court as warriors for hire. Some found new opportunities in the aggressive expansion of Europe in Spain, eastern Europe, and the Holy Land.

Tancred de Hauteville's Sons   Among such aggressive young nobles were the sons of Tancred de Hauteville, a minor Norman vassal. Three of the brothers—William Iron-Arm, Humphrey, and Drogo—sought their fortunes as warriors, sometimes acting as mercenaries and sometimes as brigands. On their way to pilgrimage in Jerusalem, they found that Sicily and southern Italy were fine places to practice their skills of warfare. The Arab and Greek factions, who were fighting each other, were both willing to hire mercenaries. Soon the Hauteville brothers were carving out their own estates rather than working for the local rulers. William's half-brother, Robert Guiscard ("the Sly" or "the Fox") managed to conquer southern Italy and receive papal recognition for the territory. Robert's brother, Roger, captured Sicily and held it with papal approval in 1072. The brothers established a Norman kingdom in these two areas.

Knights and Armor   Improvements in fighting equipment, including chain mail, long swords, stirrups, and lances, meant that a long period of training was necessary to become a skilled warrior. The equipment was so expensive that only the elite could afford to buy and maintain it.

A warrior cult that grew up surrounding the training was transformed into knighthood. Young sons of the elite started at an early age to learn to ride and use the weapons of war. Vassals might send their sons to the lord's household at age seven or eight to act as pages, becoming squires in their teenage years. Twenty-one was the age of majority and was usually accompanied by knighthood, which gave the person the honorific title of "sir." Knights had to be skilled in arms, brave, loyal to a leader, and conventionally pious.

Song of Roland   The heroic poems, or *chansons de geste,* of the eleventh and twelfth centuries underscore the values fostered by knighthood and the lord-vassal relationship. The oldest and best known of these poems is the *Song of Roland,* which was probably composed in the last quarter of the eleventh century. The subject of the poem is the ambush of the rear guard of Charlemagne's army under the command of Roland by the Basques at Roncesvalles in 778, but poetic imagination (or perhaps older legend) transformed this minor Frankish setback into a major event in the war against Islam.

With fine psychological discernment, the poem examines the character of Roland. The qualities that make him a heroic knight—his dauntless courage and uncompromising pride—are at war with the qualities required of a good vassal—obedience, loyalty, cooperation, and common sense. Roland is in serious danger but refuses for reasons of personal dignity to sound his horn in time for Charlemagne to return and save him and his men. By the time Roland's pride relents and he does blow the horn, his troops' deaths are ensured. The

▲ MAKING COATS OF CHAIN MAIL
This depiction of a craftsman making chain mail suggests the high skills and hard labor that were needed to bend the metal into elaborate shapes. Armor made of chain mail allowed the knight far greater freedom of movement, but it could be penetrated by the sharp thrust of a sword or arrow. The expense of chain mail and of the other equipment associated with fighting, as well as the long training it took to become proficient in using the arms, meant that only the elite could afford the training and outfits for battle.
Stadtsbibliothek Nuremberg (Ms.) Amb. 317.2°, f. 10r

sensitive examination of the conflict between Roland's thoughtless if heroic individualism and the demands of the new feudal order gives this poem its stature as the first masterpiece of French letters.

Noblewomen   While the young sons in a noble family were being trained for the battlefield, their sisters were taught to live in or travel between castles. The fathers, if still alive—and if not then the lord—arranged the marriages of these young women to men they might never have seen and

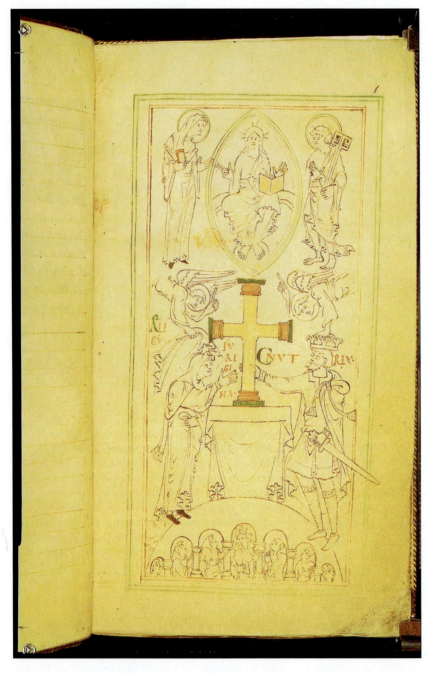

◄ MARRIAGE OF NOBLEWOMEN Noblewomen had little control over their marriages, because their fathers or lords used their marriages to cement political alliances or ensure the transfer of land. Here Emma (Aelfgyfu in the Anglo-Saxon text of the picture) is shown with her husband, King Cnut, presenting a Cross at Winchester. Cnut, a Norwegian, became king of England in 1016. To make his foreign origin more acceptable to the Anglo-Saxon population, he married the deceased king's widow. After the Norman Conquest in 1066 some Normans, to reinforce their claim to the territory, married the widows or daughters of the Anglo-Saxon nobles whose land they had confiscated.
© British Museum

who might have been much older or younger than themselves. Even as widows, these women's lord could arrange for their remarriage. Noble-women's chief functions were to cement alliances, transfer property, and produce children.

During periods of internal warfare in Europe and the Crusades, husband and wife often were separated for long periods of time. Noblewomen were called upon to administer the fief in their husbands' absence or to defend castles against siege.

Noblewomen were often knowledgeable in herbal cures, and they could care for the sick and wounded in their households. Like peasant women, they spun wool and flax. The elaborate embroideries for church vestments, wall and bed hangings, and personal adornment were often the work of noblewomen and their servants. Leisure activities included music, games, feasts, and stories.

Not all women who were married wanted to be; some would have preferred to become nuns. Christina of Markyate, daughter of a well-to-do family in England (d. after 1155) was forced into marriage by her parents but refused to consummate it. Her mother beat her and pulled her hair, and her father stripped her and threatened to force her out of the house. She fled and became a recluse, but finally became a nun. Some young women whose families forced them into nunneries were as miserable as those women forced into marriage. For a pious woman with a calling for monastic life, a nunnery offered an environment with educational opportunities, training in skilled crafts, and even the opportunity to administer nunnery property.

◆ MANORIALISM

Medieval Europe had a mix of cultivation strategies. Some areas were farmed by free peasants (those who owned their own land) who mixed cultivation with fishing or herding. Most of the grain, however, came from large manors with *serfs* (*villeins* was a term used in England and France) or unfree peasants working the land. As described in chapter 6, the major tool of agriculture was the heavy-wheeled plow with oxen or horses to draw it.

The manor, a community of serfs living under the authority of a lord, was the fundamental unit of economic, judicial, and social organization during the Middle Ages. The lord or his appointed officials regulated cultivation of the land as well as the rents, labor services, and fines that the peasants owed to the lord in return for the land they cultivated for themselves. Manors were characteristic of much of England, northern France, western Germany, and certain areas of the south, such as the Rhône and Po valleys. These areas were regions of fertile soil in which grains were cultivated intensively.

Division of Land The lands of most manors were divided into two or three large fields (see map 8.1). Within these fields, the land was further divided into strips for cultivation. The lord owned all the land but he rented strips of land in all three fields to the peasants, who also had a house and garden area. A peasant's strips were not contiguous, but were scattered in each of the three fields. The strips and housing plots were protected by custom, and the right to rent them was passed on through inheritance. Peasants did not have equal holdings; some might have as many as thirty acres and others as little as two acres. These pieces of land formed the peasants' own farms to support their families and pay their rent.

Interspersed with the peasants' land was the *demesne* (rhymes with reign) land, or land that the lord reserved for his own use and that the peasants cultivated for him. In addition, a manor might have land reserved for the parish priest, called *glebe* land, which the priest either worked himself or hired laborers to work for him.

Many manors had extensive meadows, forests, and wastelands, where the lord hunted and the peasants grazed their animals, collected firewood, and procured timber for their houses. Peasants paid fees to use the forests and wastelands that were part of the lord's demesne. Peasants often had their own common, a collectively owned meadow in which each resident had the right to graze a fixed number of animals. Peasants who had too little land to support themselves worked as agricultural laborers or had an additional occupation on the manor such as blacksmith, carpenter, or baker.

The Lord's Control The lord's control over his serfs was considerable. Serfs and their children were not chattel property, as were slaves, but they could not leave the manor without the lord's permission. The lord or his steward ran the manorial court, which was a way of regulating the serfs and an important source of profit from the manor. Peasants who did not pay their rent, who trespassed on the lord's property, or who otherwise broke the manorial rules paid fines in the court. The lord charged peasants for the use of his mill and winepress and required them to buy salt or iron from him. For many peasants, the manorial lord was the only government they ever directly confronted. Peasants paid to use the manorial court to settle their own disputes and to have a record kept of these transactions. The court also

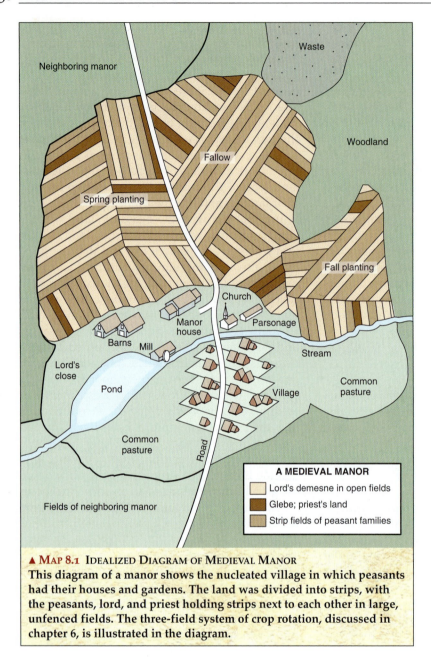

▲ **MAP 8.1 IDEALIZED DIAGRAM OF MEDIEVAL MANOR**
This diagram of a manor shows the nucleated village in which peasants
had their houses and gardens. The land was divided into strips, with
the peasants, lord, and priest holding strips next to each other in large,
unfenced fields. The three-field system of crop rotation, discussed in
chapter 6, is illustrated in the diagram.

regulated and punished disturbances of the peace
among villagers, including assaults, petty thefts,
and trespass.

Serfdom Most of the peasants inhabiting the
manor were serfs. Serfs were personally free, but
in addition to not having freedom of mobility,
they had to pay for the right to marry and had to
work for the lord a set number of days a week and
at intense periods of harvest and planting. Men
were usually obliged to work three days a week
on the lord's land, a service called **week work.**
The additional service at planting and harvest
was called **boon work.** The lord's fields had to be
plowed first and his crops brought in before those
of the serfs. The serfs also paid a yearly monetary
rent on their land. Lords received mandatory gifts
at holidays, such as eggs at Easter or a chicken at

Christmas—the origins of our holiday eating traditions. When a serf died and his farm passed to his son, or to a daughter if there were no sons, the family paid the lord an inheritance tax, either the best animal or money.

◆ PEASANT LIFE

While the life of the serf was one filled with heavy labor, the position had some security and advantages. Because serfs had a customary right to their land, they and their children could profit from the improvements they made on it. Moreover, the serfs' obligations and rents were traditional and fixed and could not be raised from year to year. Thus, in periods of economic prosperity, their rents remained fixed so that their profits increased.

Housing and Food Peasants lived in villages with large fields surrounding them. Housing varied from region to region. Where stone was plentiful, peasants built stone houses, often adding on to them so that parents, married children, and their children lived together as extended families in the same household. Other places had more rudimentary housing that resembled an A-frame of beams with the wall areas filled in with woven branches and covered with clay. These houses were cheap to build, and families living in them showed a preference for having only the conjugal couple and their children (in other words, the nuclear family) living in one house. Whatever the living arrangements, housing for the animals was connected to human housing, in part for warmth and in part because animals were the peasants' most valuable possessions.

◀ The peasant house contained one or two rooms with a fire in the center of the room in the early Middle Ages, or in a fireplace at the side of the room by the late Middle Ages, as this illustration indicates. Stables were attached to the houses to protect the livestock, which were the peasants' most valuable possessions. Pegs and poles held clothing. Furniture was sparse. The beehives lining the fence in the garden area provided honey, the only sweetener available to peasants. Grain was valuable; in this picture a stone tower protects the grain.
Giraudon/Art Resource, NY

▲ **Peasant Women's Work**
Women's work included a number of cottage crafts in addition to rearing children and helping out in the fields during harvest. Women did shearing, washing, and spinning of wool thread. They also wove rough cloth of both wool and linen.
Trinity College Library

Furnishings were rudimentary. They commonly included a straw pallet for a bed, a trestle table, benches, a cradle, sheets, towels, blankets, and pots and pans. Pegs held clothes, and rods suspended from the ceiling held hams, cheeses, and so on. Often the homes had a few luxury items, such as a piece of fine pottery or a crucifix.

Peasants largely ate a grain diet, with the addition of eggs, cheese, beans, and some meat for protein. Bread was made of a rough whole wheat or rye or a mixture of grains. Oats, peas, and beans were made into a gruel. For their ordinary drink, peasants made wine or beer, depending on the part of Europe in which they lived. Wine and olive oil were more typical of southern Europe, whereas beer and butter were more common in northern Europe.

Sex Roles Sex roles were strongly differentiated on the manors. Men did the plowing and heavy field work, cutting of firewood, carting, and construction. Women tended the domestic animals, milking them, making butter and cheese, and collecting eggs. Women also raised the children, did the brewing, cooked the simple meals, and made thread from wool and flax. They also spun rough cloth. Harvest, done in August and September, took everyone out to the fields to cut the grain and bind it into sheaves to take back to the village.

It would be a mistake to assume that peasant households were like American pioneer households in which most things were made at home. In the eleventh century even peasants had access to a market economy, selling their surplus grain and animals and buying ready-made goods in market towns. Clothing, metal pots, fine ceramics, animals, and luxury items were all bought at markets. Markets stimulated the growth of cottage industries, especially in the vicinity of towns. Peasants produced grain, livestock, fruit and vegetables, and various craft items to sell to urban dwellers. Market production was consistent with the sex roles on the manor: women producing thread, beer, and butter and cheese and men making various handicraft objects.

Popular Culture and Religion Popular entertainment included singing and dancing, wrestling and archery contests, and various ball games, including football. The peasant year, although filled with labor, was punctuated by festivals. Christmas celebrations lasted for twelve days, Mayday was a time for singing contests and maypoles, and Midsummer Eve was celebrated with bonfires.

Church councils repeatedly condemned dancing and singing in the churchyard, because they thought that such activities encouraged sin.

The rural church acquired new importance. Peasants contributed to building parish churches of stone. The parish priest was usually of peasant origin. Because he was frequently the only member of the community who could read, he aided the peasants in reading documents from merchants and government bureaucrats.

Free and Unfree Peasants Manors had both free and unfree peasants. Freedom did not bring a substantially better standard of living, but it meant that the free peasant did not have to do week work or boon work. Economic conditions could increase the number of free peasants. During the period of expansion to which this chapter is devoted, lords had to offer generous terms, frequently guaranteed in a written charter, to encourage peasants to clear forest lands for settlement or to move to newly conquered territories. The peasant who settled in these new lands paid only a small fixed rent for the lands he cleared and did not have to work for the landlord. He could leave the new village at will, selling his lands and the house he had built at their market value. A runaway serf who resided in a free village or a town for one year and one day without being claimed by his owner was thenceforth free.

As Europe became even more of a market economy during the twelfth and thirteenth centuries, lords used their demesne lands to produce cash crops. They found it easier to have their peasants pay a money rent for the land and to commute the customary labor services into a monetary payment. With this revenue, the lords hired laborers drawn from the increasing surplus peasant population to cultivate the demesne. The distinction between free and unfree peasants became less meaningful as peasants commuted their serfdom or intermarried with free peasants.

◆ EXPANSION OF EUROPE

Europe's population in the early Middle Ages, to about the year 1050, was small in absolute numbers and was not distributed evenly across the countryside. The end of invasions, the relative sta-

bility that feudalism was bringing to government, the increased agricultural productivity, and new economic opportunities encouraged growth in family size. For the first time since the fall of the western Roman Empire, Europe experienced a sustained and substantial population growth. Europe became too densely populated for its existing cultivated land and began to expand both internally and externally. The expansion of Europe involved the clearing of forest and marsh areas for cultivation and habitation. But Europe also expanded to the east into Slavic lands, into Spain, and even to the Holy Land during the crusades.

Internal Colonization In England, France, and Germany, the peasants cleared forests and drained marshes to expand agricultural space; in the Low Countries, they began building dikes and draining marshes by the sea. As we saw above, lords were willing to offer good terms to encourage peasants who would take up new land. This internal colonization can be seen in place names that indicate the home village, such as Great Horewood and the new settlement of Little Horewood. Other new settlements carry names such as Newcastle or Villenova (new town).

Conquest of Frontiers German nobles pushed eastward beyond the former borders of the Frankish empire (see map 8.2) into territories that were thinly inhabited by Slavs, Prussians, Letts, and Lithuanians. Some Germans settled just beyond the Elbe River and established the Principality of Brandenburg. Other Germans advanced along the shores of the Baltic Sea at the same time that Swedes began to move across Finland. The Russian prince of Novgorod, Alexander Nevsky, defeated the Swedes on the Neva River close to the Baltic Sea in 1240 and repulsed the Germans in another victory in 1242. Although these defeats halted further advances in northeastern Europe, the Germans and Swedes retained control of the shores of the Baltic Sea. The Germans had by then pushed through the middle Danube valley and founded another principality: Austria. Offering land and low rents, the nobles advertised in the West for peasants to migrate and settle the newly opened territories. By the early fifteenth century the *drang nach Osten* ("drive to the east") had clearly spent its strength, but it had tripled the

▲ MAP 8.2 GERMAN MIGRATION EASTWARD

European power swept over the sea as well as the land. The leaders were the maritime cities of Venice, Pisa, and Genoa. In 1015 and 1016 fleets from Pisa and Genoa freed Sardinia from Islamic rule.

◆ COMMERCIAL EXPANSION

The European economy remained predominantly agricultural, although new forms of economic endeavor were emerging. Trade, which had dwindled in the Carolingian age, became more vigorous. Most of the trade was local, between rural areas or between city and countryside, but a dramatic rebirth of trade also took place with regions beyond the European frontiers. Three trading zones developed, based on the Mediterranean Sea in the south, the Baltic Sea in the north, and the overland routes that linked the two seas (see map 8.3).

Mediterranean Trade   Venice, Pisa, and Genoa led this commercial expansion. In 998 and again in 1082 the Venetians received from the Byzantine emperors charters that gave them complete freedom of Byzantine waters. In the twelfth century Pisans and Genoese negotiated formal treaties with Islamic rulers that allowed them to establish commercial colonies in the Middle East and North Africa. Marseilles and Barcelona soon began to participate in the profitable eastern trade.

In this Mediterranean exchange, the East shipped condiments, medicines, perfumes, dyes, paper, ivories, porcelain, pearls, precious stones, and rare metals such as mercury—all of which were known in the West under the generic name of *spices*. Eastern traders also sent a variety of fine linens and cottons (damask, muslin, organdy) as well as brocades and silks. Western North Africa supplied animal skins, leather, cheese, ivory, and gold. Europe shipped wood and iron and products made from them (including entire ships), as well as grain, wine, and other agricultural commodities. By the year 1200 manufactured goods, especially woolen cloth woven in Flanders and finished in Italy, began to play an increasingly important role in the Mediterranean exchange. This cloth gave European merchants a product valued in the Eastern markets; with it they were able not only to pay for Eastern imports but also to generate a flow of precious metals into Europe.

area of German settlement over what it had been in Carolingian times (see map 8.2).

Settlers also moved into the Iberian Peninsula (present-day Spain and Portugal). In the mid-eleventh century the Christian kings, whose kingdoms were confined to the extreme north of the peninsula, began an offensive against the Muslims, who ruled most of Iberia. The Christians pushed south over two centuries until they held most of the peninsula. The battle of Las Navas de Tolosa (in 1212), between an allied Christian army and an invading Muslim army from North Africa, confirmed this domination. By 1275 only the emirate of Granada remained under Muslim rule. The Christian kings actively recruited Christian settlers for the territories they reconquered and gave them land under favorable terms. The reconquest and resettlement of the peninsula, known as the *Reconquista*, proved lasting achievements; the Iberian frontier remained almost unchanged for the next 280 years, during which time Castile, Aragon, Portugal, and other states developed and flourished.

In Italy the Hauteville brothers, as we have seen, succeeded in defeating the Muslims and Byzantines in southern Italy and Sicily and united the two regions into the Kingdom of Naples and Sicily. This victory opened new areas for European settlement.

▲ **MAP 8.3 MEDIEVAL TRADE ROUTES**
◆ www.mhhe.com/chambers8ch8maps

Baltic and Northern Trade Trade in northern Europe among the lands bordering the Baltic Sea linked the great ports of London, Bruges, Bergen, Cologne, Lübeck, and Novgorod with the many smaller maritime towns. The eastern Baltic regions sold grain, lumber and forest products, amber, and furs. Scandinavia supplied wood and fish. England provided raw wool and grains. Flanders, the great industrial area of the north, imported food stuffs and wool to support its cloth industry.

Overland Trade The northern and Mediterranean trading zones were joined by numerous overland routes. After 1100 the most active exchange between north and south was concentrated at six great fairs, held at various times of the year in the province of Champagne in France. Merchants from all over Europe could find at least one fair open no matter what time of year they came. Trade included local products, but the fairs' chief importance was as redistribution points for spices, fine cloth, and other luxury goods. The fairs guaranteed the merchants personal security, low tariffs, fair monetary exchange, and quick and impartial justice. For two centuries the fairs remained the greatest markets in Europe.

Milan became a center for overland trade that funneled the luxury goods from the Mediterranean trade to the north into Germany and products from that region back to Venice, Genoa, and Pisa.

◆ REBIRTH OF URBAN LIFE

Although the towns in Western Europe were increasing in size and social complexity, their growth was very slow even in this age of economic expansion. Before 1200 probably no town in Western Europe included more than 30,000 inhabitants. These small towns, however, were assuming new functions.

In the early Middle Ages the towns had been chiefly administrative centers, serving as the residence of bishops—or, much more rarely, of counts—and as fortified enclosures to which the surrounding rural population fled when under attack. (The original sense of the English word *borough* and of the German word *Burg* is "fortress.") As the revival of trade made many of these towns centers of local or international exchange, permanent colonies of merchants grew up around the older fortresses. These merchant quarters were sometimes called a *faubourg* ("outside the fortress"). Many European towns, especially in the north, still show these two phases of their early history in their central fortress and surrounding settlements (see map 8.4).

Urban Society Urban social organization was hierarchical, as was the rest of medieval society. At the top was a small elite group, usually referred to as *patricians*. In Italy the elite included nobles, merchants engaged in long-distance trade, and great landlords from the countryside, who lived for part or all of the year in the towns. In contrast, in Flanders and the rest of northern Europe the nobles and great landlords tended to keep to their rural estates, whence they viewed with disdain and fear the growing wealth of the towns. The powerful urban families in the north came chiefly from common origins, and most of them had founded their fortunes on commerce or the management of urban property. Social and cultural contrasts between town and countryside, then, were much sharper in the north than in Italy.

Below the patricians were shopkeepers and artisans. While the patricians had a single guild in most towns before 1200, after that date guilds multiplied, showing an ever greater diversifica-

tion in the commercial enterprises of the mercantile classes. Goldsmiths (also bankers), spice merchants, and those importing such items as salt fish and cloth, formed guilds. Artisans and less prominent merchants organized trade guilds to regulate their crafts, such as those of the shoemakers, bakers, saddlers, fishmongers, and so on. The craft guilds began disputing, often with violence and soon with some success, the political domination of the patricians. As urban economies became more developed in the thirteenth century and some industries, such as cloth making, became prominent, cities also supported a number of skilled laborers. Perhaps the most distinctive feature of urban society, even in the twelfth century, was the fluidity of class divisions. Vertical social mobility was easier in the city than in any other part of the medieval world, except possibly in the Church. The patrician class was always admitting new members, chiefly wealthy, recent immigrants from the countryside. The towns of the Middle Ages were more efficient than was rural society in recognizing, utilizing, and rewarding talent.

Urban Life The urban milieu provided entirely different living conditions than did that of the castle or the manor. The houses were close together and faced streets that could be narrow and smelly, because they served for general rubbish disposal. The houses were of stone and contained a cellar for storage, a ground floor for a shop or workplace, a hall and perhaps a loft above for living space. The area behind the house might contain a garden, a courtyard, and work space. In some towns the house completely surrounded the courtyard. Higher structures of three and four floors were characteristic of larger cities. Patricians had full houses to themselves, but many people rented portions of houses for business and suites of rooms for residences. The poorer people rented one room on the upper floors or even shared the rent for such spaces.

Rather than growing their own food, urban dwellers relied on the surrounding countryside to provide their sustenance. Small towns had one market square, but cities had separate markets for fish, meat, grain, bread, and so on. The diet varied very much by the wealth of the inhabitant, but an idea of the variety of foods available can be seen

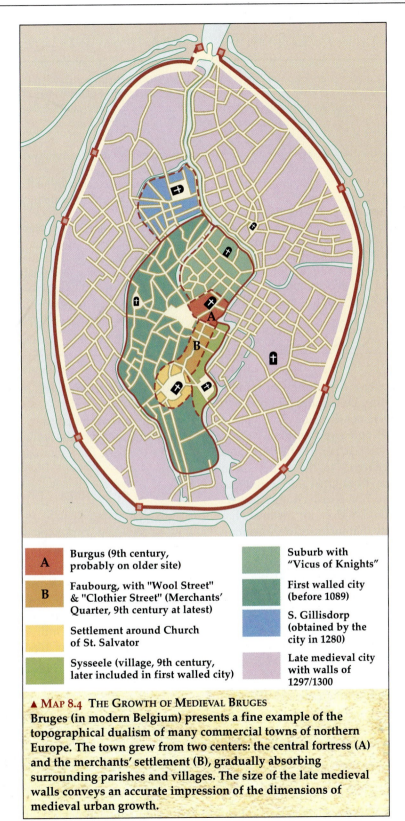

A	Burgus (9th century, probably on older site)
B	Faubourg, with "Wool Street" & "Clothier Street" (Merchants' Quarter, 9th century at latest)
	Settlement around Church of St. Salvator
	Sysseele (village, 9th century, later included in first walled city)
	Suburb with "Vicus of Knights"
	First walled city (before 1089)
	S. Gillisdorp (obtained by the city in 1280)
	Late medieval city with walls of 1297/1300

▲ MAP 8.4 THE GROWTH OF MEDIEVAL BRUGES

Bruges (in modern Belgium) presents a fine example of the topographical dualism of many commercial towns of northern Europe. The town grew from two centers: the central fortress (A) and the merchants' settlement (B), gradually absorbing surrounding parishes and villages. The size of the late medieval walls conveys an accurate impression of the dimensions of medieval urban growth.

A Twelfth-Century Description of London

◆

William Fitz Stephen introduced his biography of Thomas Beckett (written in 1183) with a description of his beloved city of London. He describes a busy commercial town with vendors of food catering to those on limited budgets as well as to nobles. Prepared food is available to take home or eat at a tavern. Peasants participate in the market economy by bringing livestock and other wares.

". . . there is in London upon the river's bank, amid the wine that is sold from ships and wine-cellars, a public cook shop. There daily, according to the season, you may find viands, dishes roast, fried and boiled, fish great and small, coarser flesh for the poor, the more delicate for the rich, such as venison and birds both big and little. If friends, weary with travel, should of a sudden come to any of the citizens, and it is not their pleasure to wait fasting till fresh food is bought and cooked and 'till servants bring water for hands and bread,' they hasten to the river bank, and there all things desirable are ready to their hand. However great the infinitude of knights or foreigners that enter the city or are about to leave it, at whatever hour of night or day, that the former may not fast too long nor the latter depart without their dinner, they turn aside thither . . . and refresh themselves. . . .

"In another place apart stand the wares of the country-folk, instruments of agriculture, long-flanked swine, cows with swollen udders and [sheep] 'woolly flocks.' Mares stand there, meet for plows, sledges and two-horsed carts."

From William Fitz Stephen, *Norman London* (Italica Press), pp. 52, 54.

---

in William Fitz Stephen's description of London (see "A Twelfth-Century Description of London").

Medieval cities were not the anonymous places that cities are now. People lived within a quarter of the city that provided them with their local courts and representatives to the larger urban government. Rich and poor lived side by side, often in the same house. The parish church served a very local population. London, for instance, had 104 churches for a city that included only a square mile of space within its walls.

Urban centers provided a rich variety of entertainment. Church feast days, civic celebrations, and visits of lords were all events calling for parades. Traveling entertainers—such as tumblers, animal trainers with their performing animals, players, and jugglers—offered diversion.

II. Governments of Europe 1000–1150

◆

The expansion of Europe, growth of towns, increased prosperity, and framework of feudalism permitted larger governmental units (see map 9.3 for political developments and boundaries). The establishment of institutions characteristic of the Middle Ages included the formation of monarchies and principalities as well as the reform and strengthening of the papacy. The feudal customs that established bonds between lord and vassal became the basis for revitalizing lay governments.

◆ NORMAN ENGLAND

We could use the history of any one of several principalities—the Duchy of Normandy, the County of Flanders, the Kingdom of Naples and Sicily, among others—to illustrate the political reorganization characteristic of feudal government. But England offers the best example of feudal concepts in the service of princes. The growth of feudalism in England was intimately connected with the Norman Conquest of 1066, so that we can look at feudalism as a system of government imposed on England by William the Conqueror.

The Norman Conquest Duke William of Normandy (1026–1087), the architect of the Conquest, is the epitome of the ambitious, energetic, and resourceful prince of the central Middle Ages. A bastard who had to fight 12 years to make good his claim over the Norman duchy, William early set his ambitions on the English crown. His claims were respectable, but not compelling. He was the first cousin of the last Saxon king, the childless Edward the Confessor, who allegedly had promised to make William heir to the throne. However, before his death, Edward selected the Saxon Harold Godwinson to succeed him, and his choice was supported by the Witan, the English royal council.

Edward died in 1066. William immediately recruited an army of vassals and adventurers to support his claim to the throne, but unfavorable winds kept his fleet bottled up in the Norman ports for six weeks. Meanwhile, Harold Hardrada, king of Norway, who also disputed Harold Godwinson's claim, invaded England with a Viking army, but the Saxons defeated his force near York on September 28, 1066. That same day, the channel winds shifted and William landed in England. Harold Godwinson foolishly rushed south to confront him. Although the Saxon army was not, as was once thought, technically inferior to the Norman army, it was tired and badly in need of rest and reinforcements after the victory over the Vikings. At the Battle of Hastings on October 14, fatigue seems eventually to have tipped the scales of an otherwise even struggle. The Normans carried the day and left Harold Godwinson dead upon the field. Duke William of Normandy had won his claim to be king of England.

Impact of the Conquest   The Norman Conquest provided areas of both continuity and change for the Anglo-Saxon population. Although local and central government remained similar, the society and economy underwent major reorientation.

The basic unit of local administration remained the shire, or county, under the supervision of the sheriff, who had primary responsibility for looking after the king's interests. The sheriff, chief official in the shire, administered the royal estates, collected the taxes, summoned and led contingents to the national militia, and presided over the shire court to enforce royal justice. William left all these institutions of local government intact.

The Conquest also brought major changes to Anglo-Saxon society. The Saxon *earls,* as the great nobles were called, and most of the lesser nobles, or *thanes,* lost their estates and fled. William redistributed the lands among his followers from the continent—his barons (a title of uncertain origin,

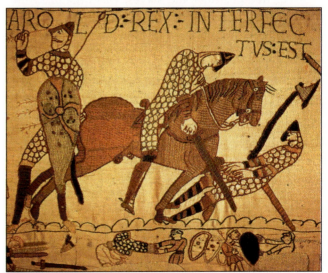

▲ **The Bayeux Tapestry**
More of an embroidery than a true tapestry, the Bayeux Tapestry is a strip of linen 231 feet long and 20 inches wide depicting the Norman Conquest of England in 1066. The story is laid out as a running narrative, like a cartoon strip. The tapestry was commissioned by Odo, Bishop of Bayeux and half brother of William, and was embroidered by women. In the portion shown here, William arrives at Pevensey (top); King Harold fights in the Battle of Hastings and is shot in the eye by an arrow, killing him (bottom). The tapestry was completed toward the end of the eleventh century and is now housed in a museum connected with the Cathedral of Bayeux in Normandy in France.
Erich Lessing/Art Resource, NY

now used to connote the immediate vassals of the king). He allotted land liberally but cautiously, creating each fief from several blocks of land in different parts of the island. This strategy gave his followers adequate support to serve him, but limited their autonomy and opportunity to rebel. William redefined the relations between the king and the great men of the realm on the basis of essentially feudal concepts. He now insisted that all English land be considered a fief held directly or indirectly (subinfeudated) from the king. The barons had to serve the king, and the knights had to serve the barons or risk losing their estates. In other words, he imposed a feudal hierarchy with the king as the recognized owner of all land and his vassals as recipients of fiefs from the king.

The peasant population, which had consisted of free peasants and slaves, was organized into manors on which most peasants became serfs.

Domesday Book In 1086 William conducted a comprehensive survey of the lands of England, the report of which became known as the *Domesday Book*. In line with William's policy of maintaining control over his land and assets, he sent out royal officers to every shire. Assembling a jury of six Englishmen and six Normans to swear to the validity of the testimony of the local population, the royal officers questioned a gathering of shire representatives about the number of manors, plow teams, meadows, forests, animals, and people on the land. The taxes, tolls, markets, mints, and services owed the king were all recorded. The survey shows a population of about 1.1 million people. *The Domesday Book* also shows that the chief resistance to the Normans was in the north, where before the Conquest the land had been thriving with agriculture but was now waste. The Normans had brutally killed or evicted the resisters and adopted a scorched earth policy. The survey gave William a clear record of his own holdings and those of his barons, and it enabled him to know how much service the land could support.

Curia Regis To maintain close contact with his barons and vassals, William adapted the Anglo-Saxon Witan to resemble the continental king's great council, or *curia regis*. Essentially, the great council was an assembly of bishops, abbots, and barons—in fact, anyone whom the king summoned. The council fulfilled the feudal functions of giving the king advice and serving as his principal court in reaching judgments. It was a much larger assembly than the Saxon Witan. Because the great council could not be kept permanently in session, a small council, consisting of those persons in permanent attendance at the court whom the king wished to invite, carried on the functions of the great council between its sessions. The development of the great and small councils had major importance for English constitutional history. The great council was the direct ancestor of Parliament, whereas the small council was the source of the administrative bureaus of the royal government.

Henry I William the Conqueror had three sons. The eldest became Duke of Normandy, the second, William Rufus, became king of England, and the youngest, Henry, was given a cash settlement. When William Rufus died of an arrow wound while hunting, Henry (r. 1100–1135) seized the royal treasure and became king. It was rumored at the time that Henry had a hand in his brother's death; the man who shot the arrow later received land grants from him. Henry I surrounded himself with able bishops who helped him organize the government. He also managed to take over the Duchy of Normandy when his eldest brother died, and once again united it with the kingdom of England.

Using the *curia regis* for settling feudal disputes, Henry began to make inroads in the autonomy of feudal lords by making his court one of appeal. He also began to reestablish the royal prerogative to try felonies, including homicide, robbery, arson, burglary, and larceny, which were offenses against the king's peace and punishable by death. The court business was profitable because the crown confiscated the goods from those convicted of crimes, but business was soon so brisk that the court was overwhelmed. The solution was to send itinerant justices, called *justices of eyre* (rhymes with tire), around to the counties to try cases in the shire courts and to investigate infringements of royal rights in the countryside.

Exchequer To make the *curia regis* more efficient, Henry created separate departments. The financial department became known as the Exchequer—a name derived from a tablecloth marked out in squares like a checkerboard on which accounts were audited. The tablecloth was really a large abacus on which pennies were in one column, shillings in the next, and pounds and their multiples in the other columns. The Chancellor who headed the Exchequer audited the sheriffs' accounts and kept track of other revenues. The Chancellor of the Exchequer is still the financial officer in the British cabinet today. Because wealth was the basis of power for any medieval king, Henry had established an efficient way to collect revenue owed him and to control his barons. With able administrators in charge of his government, he was free to spend more time in Normandy putting down rebellions of his own vassals and fighting off attempts by neighboring counts and dukes to acquire parts of Normandy.

◆ CAPETIAN FRANCE

In France the pattern of feudal development was much different from that of England. Central government all but disappeared in the turmoil following the age of Charlemagne. What governmental functions could still be performed amid the chaos were carried out by counts, castellans, and other lords of small territorial units. These factors alone would have made rebuilding an effective national monarchy considerably more difficult in France than in England; but, in addition, France was a much larger country, and its regions preserved considerable cultural diversity.

The evolution of larger units of feudal government, however, can be discerned in several compact and effectively governed principalities, especially in the north—the Duchy of Normandy, the counties of Flanders and Champagne, the royal lands of the Ile-de-France, and others. French kings sought with some success to establish a lord-vassal relation with the great dukes and counts who governed these principalities. The kings did not envision, and could not have achieved, the unification of the entire realm under their own direct authority. The goal of monarchical policy was rather a kind of federation of principalities bound together by a common fealty to the king on the part of distant dukes and counts. Again, the theory that the king was at the pinnacle of the feudal hierarchy served to give the king a basis for increasing his power over the whole of the realm of France.

The Capetians   In 987 the great nobles of France elected as their king Hugh Capet, whose descendants held the throne until 1792. Hugh was chosen primarily because his small possessions in the Ile-de-France, which included Paris and the surrounding region, made him no threat to the independence of the nobles. He and his successors for the next century made no dramatic efforts to enlarge their royal authority, but they carefully nursed what advantages they had: the central location of their lands; the title of king, which commanded a vague prestige; and a close association with the Church, which gave them an avenue of influence extending beyond their own territory. They also pursued a remarkably prudent policy of consolidating control over their own lands, and they had the good fortune to produce sons when the usual production of sons as heirs was only three generations. For three hundred years the kings crowned their sons during their own lifetime and thus built the tradition that the crown was theirs not by election but by hereditary right.

The Capetian policy first bore fruit under Louis VI, the Fat (r. 1108–1137). He achieved his goal of being master of his own possessions by successfully reducing to obedience the petty nobles and castellans who had been disturbing his lands and harassing travelers seeking to cross them (see "Louis VI Subdues a Violent Baron," p. 270). By the end of his reign, he had established effective control over the lands between the cities of Paris and Orléans. This move gave him a compact block of territory in the geographic heart of France. Louis VI promoted the colonization of forests and wastelands by establishing free villages, and he courted the support of the town communes. The king's encouragement of economic growth added to his own fiscal resources as he collected revenues from towns and trade.

◆ THE GERMAN EMPIRE

In the tenth and eleventh centuries the German lands east of the Rhine showed a pattern of political development very different from that of France or England. Whereas William forced central control over his territory in England by conquest and the Capetians established hereditary right to the French throne, Germany kept a strong tradition of elective kingship and a concentration of wealth and power in large territorial blocks—

LOUIS VI SUBDUES A VIOLENT BARON

◆

This selection describes the attempt of Louis VI (1108–1137), a strong monarch, to keep the peace in his realm. It comes from The Life of Louis VI, a chronicle by Suger, the head of a French monastery and a great admirer of the king. It is a good example of the chronicles that form one of the historian's basic sources for studying medieval history.

"A king is obliged by virtue of his office to crush with his strong right hand the impudence of tyrants. For such men freely provoke wars, take pleasure in plunder, oppress the poor, destroy the churches, and give themselves free reign to do whatsoever they wish. . . .

"One such wicked man was Thomas of Marle. For while King Louis was busy fighting in the wars which we mentioned earlier, Thomas ravaged the regions around Laon, Reims, and Amiens. . . . Thomas devastated the region with the fury of a wolf. No fear of ecclesiastical penalty persuaded him to spare the clergy; no feeling of humility convinced him to spare the people. Everyone was slaughtered, everything destroyed. He snatched two prize estates from the nuns of Saint-John of Laon. And treating the two castles of Crècy-sur-Serre and Nouvion-Catillon as his own, he transformed them into a dragon's lair and a den of thieves, exposing the nearby inhabitants to the miseries of fire and plunder.

"Fed up with the intolerable afflictions of this man, the churchmen of France met together (on December 6, 1114) at a great council at Beauvais. . . . The venerable papal legate Cuno, bishop of Praeneste, was particularly moved by the numerous pleas of the church and the cries of the orphans and the poor. He drew the sword of Saint Peter against Thomas of Marle, and with the unanimous assent of the council, declared him excommunicated, ripped from him in absentia the titles and honors of knighthood, branded him a criminal, and declared him unworthy of being called a Christian.

"Heeding the wishes of so great a council, King Louis moved quickly against Thomas. Accompanied by his army and the clergy, he turned at once against the heavily defended castle of Crècy. There, thanks to his men at arms, or should we say on account of divine aid, Louis achieved swift victory. He seized the new towers as if they were no more than the huts of peasants; he drove out the criminals; he piously slaughtered the impious; and as for those who had showed no pity, he in turn showed no pity towards them. . . . Flushed by the success of his decisive victory, the king moved quickly against the other illegally held castle, Nouvion."

From C. W. Hollister et al., *Medieval Europe: A Short Source Book* (New York: McGraw-Hill, 1992), pp. 207–208.

Saxony, Franconia, Swabia, and Bavaria. Originally districts of the Carolingian Empire, these territories became independent political entities under powerful dukes. Because these duchies were close to the hostile Eastern frontier, their inhabitants learned to appreciate the advantages of a unified leadership under territorial dukes. Paradoxically, the German populace also retained Charlemagne's Empire as the political ideal. The result of strong territorial allegiances and a desire for a larger political unit brought clashes between the nobles and their rulers throughout the Middle Ages.

Otto I, the Great The last direct descendant of Charlemagne in Germany, a feeble ruler known as Louis the Child, died in 911. Recognizing the need for a common leader, the German dukes in 919 elected as king one of their number, Henry of Saxony. His descendants held the German monarchy until 1024. The most powerful of this line of Saxon kings, and the true restorer of the German Empire, was Otto I, the Great (r. 936–973). Otto was primarily a warrior, and conquest was a principal foundation of his power. He routed the pagan Magyars near Augsburg in 955 and ended their menace to Christian Europe; he organized military provinces, or marches, along the Eastern frontier and actively promoted the work of German missionaries and settlers beyond the Elbe River; and in 951 he marched into Italy.

Restoration of the Empire The immediate rationale for Otto's entrance into Italy was the appeal

▲ CROWN OF THE GERMAN EMPIRE, TENTH AND
ELEVENTH CENTURIES
**The crown of the German Empire may originally
have been given to Otto I by Pope John, but
throughout the tenth and eleventh centuries various
pieces were added by different emperors. It eventually consisted of eight panels, decorated with cloi-
sonné enamels, which are hinged together with gold
filigree and surrounded with jewels and pearls.**
Art Resource, NY

Chronology

CHRONOLOGICAL CHART

Germany:	Otto I, the Great (**r. 936–973**)
	Otto II (**r. 973–983**)
	Henry III (**r. 1039–1056**)
	Henry IV (**r. 1056–1106**)
France:	Hugh Capet (**r. 987–996**)
	Louis VI, the Fat (**r. 1108–1137**)
	Council of Clermont and preaching of First Crusade (**1095**)
England:	Edward the Confessor (**r. 1042–1066**)
	Norman Conquest (**1066**)
	William I (**r. 1066–1087**)
	Domesday Book (**1086**)
	Henry I (**r. 1100–1135**)
Italy:	Pope Sylvester II (**999–1003**)
	College of Cardinals (**1059**)
	Pope Gregory VII (**1073–1085**)
	Canossa (**1077**)
	Roger de Hauteville (**d. 1101**) conquers Sicily (**1072**)
Crusades:	First Crusade (**1095–1099**)
	Second Crusade (**1147–1149**)
	Third Crusade (**1189–1192**)

of Adelaid, widow of one of the Italian kings, who
was about to be forced into an undesirable marriage. He rescued the queen and married her himself. Historians have debated the real reasons Otto
wished to secure power in Italy. Perhaps, like
Charlemagne, he hoped to rescue the papacy from
the clutches of the tumultuous Roman nobility, to
which it had once again fallen victim. Apparently,
Otto conceived of himself not just as a German
king, but as the leader of all Western Christians.
He could not allow Italy, especially Rome, to remain in chaos or permit another prince to achieve
a strong position there. In 962, during Otto's
second campaign in Italy, Pope John XII crowned
him "Roman Emperor," a title with more prestige
than power.

The coronation of 962 confirmed the close relations between Germany and Italy that lasted
through the Middle Ages. Although the German
emperors claimed to be the successors of the Caesars and of Charlemagne and thus the titular leaders of all Western Christendom, their effective
power never extended beyond Germany and Italy
and the small provinces contiguous to them—
Provence, Burgundy, and Bohemia.

Ecclesiastics as Administrators   Otto's problems
of governing his far-flung territories were more
formidable than the problems that confronted the
English and French kings. Hoping to keep control

over the powerful duchies, Otto distributed the territories among his relatives. They proved to be disloyal to him. He found, as had the Carolingians, that bishops and abbots were more reliable and loyal as administrators of his realm. Otto could appoint loyal, educated, and clever administrators and invest them with the fiefs associated with their office without being concerned about hereditary claims from these celibate priests. Because he claimed the right to appoint bishops and abbots as well as controlling their fiefs, the emperor established enclaves of power in the duchies and in Italy that no potential rival could match.

The Ottonian Renaissance The dynasty that Otto established fostered the revival of learning in Germany. The examples of two scholars indicate the intellectual activity that characterized the "Ottonian Renaissance."

Roswitha of Gandersheim (ca. 937–1004) came from a noble family of Saxony and was put into a Benedictine nunnery at an early age. A Saxon duke had founded Gandersheim in 852 with the intention that women of the Saxon dynasty would be its abbesses. Otto the Great's younger brother, a bishop, encouraged learning at the nunnery, and Roswitha had a series of learned nuns to teach her Latin. Her early writings were religious poetry, but, reading copies of Roman comedies that were in the nunnery library, she became fascinated by their language. Adapting the dramatic form, she wrote religious plays, the first plays to be written since Roman times. Toward the end of her life she wrote histories, including the *Deeds of Otto* about Otto the Great.

The other great figure was a monk, Gerbert of Aurillac in France (d. 1003). Gerbert came from a peasant family, but local monks recognized his genius and educated him. He was sent to Spain, where he came into contact with the great learning of Arab and Hebrew scholars in Barcelona. Although he studied with Christian scholars because he did not know Arabic, he learned something of Arab mathematics and astronomy. He had an abacus with Arabic numerals, but he did not use the zero as the Arabs did. His fame in France brought patronage from the Ottonians, who first made him tutor to the young Otto III and then appointed him pope in Rome, where

he served as Sylvester II. So great was his knowledge that people thought he was a necromancer or sorcerer. He was a man ahead of his time.

Artistic works flourished in the Ottonian period. The marriage of Otto II (r. 973–983) to a Byzantine princess formed an influential connection with Byzantine artistic expression. Otto III's ties were so close to Byzantium (his Greek mother acted as regent) that he learned Greek as a child. Soon German monastic workshops adapted the manuscript illuminations, ivory carving, and fine metal work of Byzantine craftsmen. The artistic style spread to the rest of Europe.

Salian House The Ottonian line ended when Henry II died in 1024. The German nobles selected as emperor Henry III (r. 1039–1056), from another branch of the Saxon line. Some historians consider him to have been one of the strongest early medieval German emperors. Continuing the policy that was now well established in Germany, he relied on bishops and abbots that he had appointed as his administrators. But he also had a sincere interest in Church reform. In 1046 he crossed the Alps and called councils of clergy to reform the Church. He succeeded in nominating a series of able and educated popes to carry out reform programs such as promoting clerical celibacy, forbidding the sale of Church offices (simony), and restoring the Benedictine Rule in monasteries.

Henry III left a six-year-old son, Henry IV (r. 1056–1106). During Henry IV's minority, he had time to observe the weaknesses of the German monarchy. His father had designated his mother as regent, but civil war broke out and Henry became a pawn in power shifts, living with first one faction and then another. This unsettling childhood made him a ruler adept at dealing with adversity, but less sure of himself in dealing with success. On becoming emperor, Henry IV realized that he needed to consolidate the royal demesne as the English and French kings were doing. He also had to suppress the overpowerful dukes. Because the largest block of demesne land was on the borders of Saxony, he encroached on the Duke of Saxony's borders. Exercising his feudal position as liege lord, Henry IV used a fight between one of his vassals and the Duke of Saxony as an excuse to depose the Duke. The move alienated the nobles, who feared for their own estates.

Wanting to extend his authority through officials he could trust, Henry IV raised a number of lower born men to the rank of *ministeriales* (bureaucrats and soldiers), equipping them with horses and armor. Again, he offended the nobility because he required them to take orders from these lowly soldiers and bureaucrats rather than from fellow nobles. Henry's nobles rebelled over these innovations. At this point, Henry turned to the pope for help, but encountered a pope—Gregory VII—who was a strict reformer. Their clash is called the *Investiture Controversy*, as will be explained shortly.

III. The Reform of the Western Church

The Church, like lay governments, was fundamentally transformed in the eleventh and twelfth centuries, acquiring characteristics that it was to retain in large measure to the present day. The reform of the Church resulted from a renewal of monastic discipline, an upsurge of popular piety among the laity, and a clerical revolt against the traditional system of lay domination over ecclesiastical offices and lands.

◆ THE CHURCH IN CRISIS

After the disintegration of the Carolingian Empire, a kind of moral chaos invaded the lives of the clergy. Since the fourth century, the Church had demanded that its clergy remain celibate, but this injunction was almost completely ignored in the post-Carolingian period. The sin of simony—the buying or selling of offices or sacraments—was also rampant. Many bishops and even some popes purchased their high positions, and parish priests frequently sold their sacramental services (baptisms, masses, absolutions of sins, marriages) to the people.

The traditional intervention of lay rulers in the affairs of the Church also led to the moral breakdown. On the highest level, the tradition of lay domination made the king or emperor effective head of the Church in their realms. At the local level, ecclesiastical offices and lands were largely under lay control. Landlords were considered to own churches and lands supporting them as their property. Thus, they could name the priests who served in those churches and profit from donations made to them, freely sell the offices they controlled, or distribute Church lands to their relatives and friends. The results were disastrous. The Church was flooded with unworthy men who were little concerned with their spiritual duties, and the pillaging of Church lands and revenues left many clerics without adequate livings.

Early Attempts at Reform   According to canon law, the bishops bore the chief responsibility for the clergy's moral conduct. A few reforming bishops in the tenth and eleventh centuries, some appointed by the German emperors, tried to suppress clerical marriage and the simony of their priests, but they could make little headway. The powers of a single bishop were perforce limited to his own diocese and to his own lifetime because he could not name his successor.

◆ MONASTIC REFORM

Cluniac Monasteries   Renewal of monastic discipline proved a more effective reform than the efforts of popes or bishops. The monastery of Cluny in Burgundy was the center of reform. Founded in 910, the monastery was placed directly under the pope (neither lay lords nor bishops could interfere in its affairs). The monastic community elected the abbot directly. He administered not only Cluny but also the many dependent monastic communities that his monks had founded or reformed. The abbot of Cluny could visit these communities at will and freely correct any abuses. The congregation of Cluny grew with extraordinary rapidity in the eleventh and twelfth centuries until it included no fewer than 1,184 houses, which were spread from the British Isles to Palestine.

The Cluniac monks advocated both a return to the strict observance of the Benedictine Rule (see chapter 6) and a new emphasis on the liturgy (services, songs, and prayers). The services were long, lasting most of the day and into the night. Rebuilding of the monastic church began around 1100. It became an example of a new architecture, Romanesque (discussed in chapter 9).

◆ PAPAL REFORM

The first of the reforming popes, Leo IX (r. 1049–1054), an appointee of the German emperor, traveled widely and presided at numerous councils, where he promulgated decrees ordering reforms in clerical marriage and simony, summoned bishops suspected of corruption, and deposed many of them. He was the first pope to make wide and regular use of papal *legates*, or emissaries, who, like Charlemagne's *missi dominici*, traveled through Europe, inspecting, reprimanding, and reforming. For the first time, lands distant from Rome were subject to the close supervision of the papacy.

Under Pope Nicholas II (r. 1058–1061) the movement toward ecclesiastical liberty took several forward strides. By allying himself with the Normans of southern Italy, Nicholas freed the papacy from military dependence on the German empire. He was the first pope who expressly, if vainly, condemned the practice of "lay investiture"—that is, receiving churches and Church offices from laymen. In 1059 a Roman council reformed papal elections and defined the principles and procedures by which popes to this day have been elected.

College of Cardinals Tradition required that the clergy and people of the diocese elect all bishops and, by extension, the pope as bishop of Rome. In practice, however, either the emperor named the pope, or in the emperor's absence the powerful noble families and factions of Rome did. The council of 1059, however, set up the election procedures for the pope, conferring this prerogative on the cardinals, the chief clergymen associated with the Church at Rome. This procedure ensured that the College of Cardinals, and the reformers who controlled it, could maintain continuity of papal policy. (Even today, all cardinals, no matter where they live in the world, hold a titular appointment to a church within the archdiocese of Rome.) The College of Cardinals simultaneously deprived both the emperor and the Roman nobility of one of their strongest powers, the appointment of the pope.

Gregory VII The climax of papal reform came with the pontificate of Pope Gregory VII (r. 1073–1085), a Cluniac monk named Hildebrand, who was instrumental in designing the College of Cardinals. Rather than being elected through the College of Cardinals, Gregory was proclaimed pope by the citizens and clergy of Rome. Gregory brought to the office a high regard for the papacy's powers and responsibilities and a burning desire for reform. With regard to Church matters, Gregory asserted that the pope wielded absolute authority—that he could, at will, overrule any local bishop in the exercise of his ordinary or usual jurisdiction.

Gregory's ideas on the relations of Church and state are less clear. According to some historians, he believed that all power on earth, including the imperial power, came from the papacy. According to others, Gregory held merely that the normal function of kings was far lower than the sacred authority of popes. This much at least is beyond dispute: Gregory believed that all Christian princes must answer to the pope in spiritual matters and that the pope himself had a weighty responsibility to guide those princes, including the rulers of the German Empire. Gregory's reforming ideals set up a direct conflict with the emperor Henry IV.

◆ INVESTITURE CONTROVERSY

As the name suggests, the principal issue in the Investiture Controversy was the practice of great laymen of "investing" bishops with their fiefs by using the spiritual symbols of office, the ring and staff (indicating their care of their flock of faithful), as secular indications of allegiance. At its root, the struggle revolved around the claims of these powerful laymen to dispose of ecclesiastical offices and revenues as fiefs by their authority as lords. Laymen felt that they had a right to select loyal churchmen as well as warriors for vassals. The giving of the ring and staff was, in their view, similar to giving a clod of earth in passing on the fief. For the German emperors, selecting the bishop meant selecting an imperial administrator. Kings and emperors also argued that they had a right to select and invest a bishop with his office because kings were anointed during their coronation ceremony, in imitation of David's coronation in the Old Testament, and consequently received spiritual and sacerdotal power. The pope, they argued, was not the only one with spiritual power.

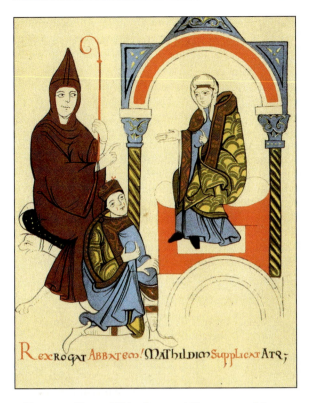

▲ Emperor Henry IV is shown at Canossa on his knees, begging Pope Gregory for readmission to the church. Countess Matilda of Tuscany, a powerful supporter of the pope, appears on the right.
AKG London

The Fight is Joined When Henry IV sent a letter in 1075 to Pope Gregory VII asking for help against his rebellious German nobles, Gregory, convinced that Henry was in a weak position, took advantage of the situation to condemn lay investiture and excommunicate some of Henry's advisers. Henry, who in the interval had defeated the rebellious nobles, reacted with fury; he summoned a meeting of loyal imperial bishops and declared Gregory not the true pope but a "false monk" (a reference to his elevation by acclamation rather than election in the College of Cardinals.) His letter continued: "descend and relinquish the apostolic throne which thou hast usurped. . . . I Henry, king by the grace of God, do say unto thee, together with all my bishops: Down, down, to be damned through all the ages." Not one to pause in what he thought to be the work of God, Gregory excommunicated Henry, thereby freeing Henry's subjects from allegiance to him. These acts struck at the fundamental

theory of the Christian empire, according to which the emperor was supreme head of the Christian people, responsible only to God.

Excommunication of Henry IV The excommunication broke the feudal vows of loyalty since fealty was sworn to a Christian lord, and excommunication placed a Christian outside the Church. Henry's enemies demanded that he be judged, with Pope Gregory presiding, before an assembly of lords and prelates. Gregory readily accepted the invitation to meet at Augsburg in February 1077. Henry resolved to fight spiritual weapons with spiritual weapons. He slipped across the Alps and intercepted Gregory, then on his way to Germany, at the Apennine castle of Canossa near Modena. Henry came in the sackcloth of a penitent, radiating contrition, pleading for absolution. Gregory, who doubted the sincerity of the emperor's repentance, refused for three days to receive him, while Henry waited in the snow. Finally, in the face of such persistence, Gregory the suspicious pope had to give way to Gregory the priest, who, like all priests, was obliged to absolve a sinner professing sorrow (see "Gregory VII's Letter to the German Nobility after Canossa").

The incident at Canossa is one of the most dramatic events of medieval history. Henry was the immediate victor. He had divided his opponents and stripped his German enemies of their excuse for rebelling. They named a rival emperor anyway, Rudolf of Swabia, but he was killed in battle in what seemed a divine judgment in Henry's favor. Gregory appears to have become unsure of himself after Canossa. He finally excommunicated Henry a second time in 1080 but was forced to flee Rome at the approach of Henry's army. Gregory died at Salerno in 1085, in apparent bitterness, avowing that his love of justice had brought him only death in exile. But the popes' claim of authority over kings and emperors was not dead.

Concordat of Worms After years of argument and struggle, the papacy and lay rulers settled the Investiture Controversy through the Concordat of Worms in 1122. They agreed that the lay rulers, including the emperor, would no longer invest prelates with the symbols of their spiritual office. The pope would allow the elections of imperial

GREGORY VII'S LETTER TO THE GERMAN NOBILITY AFTER CANOSSA

Henry intercepted Gregory at a castle in Canossa in January of 1077, dressed as a penitent. Gregory explains why he gave in to Henry's contrition and removed the excommunication.

"When, after long deferring . . . and holding frequent consultations, we had, through all the envoys who passed, severely taken him to task for his excesses: he came at length of his own accord, with a few followers, showing nothing of hostility or boldness. . . . And there, having laid aside all the belongings of royalty, wretchedly, with bare feet and clad in wool, he continued for three days to stand before the gate of the castle. Nor did he desist from imploring with many tears the aid and consolation of the apostolic mercy until he moved all those who were present there, and whom the report of it reached, to such pity and depth of compassion that, interceding for him with many prayers and tears, all wondered indeed at the unaccustomed hardness of our heart, while some actually cried out that we were exercising, not the gravity of apostolic severity, but the cruelty, as it were of a tyrannical ferocity.

"Finally, conquered by the persistence of his compunction and by the constant supplications of all those who were present, we loosed the chain of the anathema and at length received him into the favor of communion and into the lap of the holy mother church."

From Norman Downs, *Basic Documents in Medieval History* (Melborne, FL: Kreiger, 1959), pp. 64–65.

bishops and abbots to be held in the presence of the emperor or his representative, thus permitting the emperor to influence the outcome of elections. In addition, the emperor retained the right of investing prelates with their temporalities—that is, their imperial fiefs. Although a compromise, the Concordat was a real victory for the papacy because it gave the popes more control over their bishops throughout Europe than they had previously enjoyed. Ultimately, lay leaders accepted papal approval as essential to a valid choice of bishops.

◆ CONSOLIDATION OF PAPAL REFORM

In the twelfth century the popes continued to pursue and consolidate the Gregorian ideals of internal reform, freedom from lay domination, and centralization of papal authority over their bishops, abbots, and clergy. In their struggle to be free of lay authority, the reformers had insisted that members of the clergy, however minor their office, were to be tried in ecclesiastical courts, as were any cases touching on the sacraments and breaches of dogma: sacrilege, heresy, marriage, testaments, contracts, and the like. A complex system of ecclesiastical courts developed throughout Europe to try people. The ecclesiastical courts paralleled and at times rivaled the courts of the kings. Judicial decisions from the ecclesiastical courts could be appealed to Rome.

Canon Law Legal scholars at this time were compiling and clarifying the canons of the Church—the authoritative statements from the Bible, Church councils, Church fathers, and popes, which constituted the law of the Church. The compilation that was ultimately recognized as official and binding was the *Decretum*, put together by the Italian jurist Gratian in about 1142. With his systematic compilation came trained canon lawyers to comment on, interpret, and apply canon law.

Papal Curia Like the monarchs of Europe, the popes experimented with creating a stronger central bureaucracy in a papal *curia* (council). Among the most important branches was a centralized financial administration, the *camera* or chamber. It handled moneys coming into the papacy from estates the papacy directly held around Rome, from the proceeds of administering justice in ecclesiastical courts, and from money bishops paid to the papacy. A judicial branch of the curia dealt with appeals on matters of canon law. Like monarchs, popes also had a chancery for sending out official letters to their clergy, legates, rulers, and laymen.

The reform of the Church in the eleventh and twelfth centuries left an indelible mark on both religious and secular life in the West. The Church became a powerful force not only in people's spiritual lives but also in the politics of Europe. No longer could lay rulers easily dominate the papacy or its bishops. The leadership of the Church, reinforced by the wave of popular piety that resulted from the Cluniac movement, led to the preaching of the First Crusade.

IV. The Crusades

In the eleventh century Western Europeans launched a series of armed expeditions to the East in an effort to free the Holy Land from Islamic rule. Known as crusades, these expeditions stimulated trade, encouraged the growth of towns, and contributed to the establishment of a stable political order in the West. Seen from a different perspective, the crusades were costly failures: They drained resources for what proved to be a temporary foothold in Palestine; they worsened relations not only with the Muslims but also with Eastern Christians; and they set in motion one of Europe's grimmest traditions, in which crusading zeal stimulated dreadful riots and pogroms against those most accessible non-Christians, the Jews.

The appeal of the crusades was both religious and material. The Cluniac movement not only stimulated reform of the Church but also a revival of lay piety. The new prosperity and the expansion of trade had already opened markets in the East, and lay piety stimulated pilgrimage to the Holy Land and interest in freeing it from the Turks. As the growth of feudalism and the influence of more centralized governments became stronger, younger sons of nobles found fewer and fewer opportunities to carve out fiefs for themselves by conquest. The success of the Hautevilles in Sicily suggested the possibility of new lands to conquer. *The Song of Roland*, which was popular in Europe at the time, distorted the tenants of Islam and encouraged knights to fight the Muslims as infidels and polytheists.

◆ ORIGINS

The origins of the crusades must be sought in a double set of circumstances: social and religious movements in the West and the political situation in the East. Pilgrimage, a personal visit to a place made holy through the life of Christ or one of the saints or the presence of a sacred relic, was popular among Western Christians. Common since the fourth century, pilgrimages gained in popularity during the eleventh century. Bands of pilgrims, sometimes numbering in the thousands, set forth to visit sacred places; Palestine was the most holy.

The Turks The pilgrim traffic was threatened when the Seljuk Turks, Muslim nomads, overran much of the Middle East in the eleventh century. The Seljuks apparently did not consciously seek to prevent pilgrims from reaching Palestine, but they did impose numerous taxes and tolls on them, and many Christians became angry at the domination of the holy places of Palestine by a strong, aggressive Islamic power.

Even more daunting to the West was the possibility that the Turks would overrun the Christian empire of Byzantium. The Seljuks had crushed a Byzantine army at the Battle of Manzikert in 1071, and the road to Constantinople seemed wide open. The fall of Byzantium would remove the traditional barrier to Islamic advance toward the West and would be a major disaster for the Christian world. When, therefore, a delegation from the emperor of Byzantium requested the help of Pope Urban II in 1095, he resolved to appeal to the Western knights and princes to go to the aid of their fellow Christians in the East.

The Byzantine Empire Although severely threatened by the Turks, the Byzantine Empire was under able leadership once again with the Comnenus family. Alexius Comnenus (1081–1118) had some success against the Turks, but he needed mercenary soldiers to enlarge his army. Knowing of the Normans' successes in Sicily, he hoped to hire Norman mercenaries. When he wrote to Pope Urban II asking for assistance, he hoped to persuade the pope by suggesting that the schism between the Eastern and Western Churches, which had occurred in 1054, might be brought to an end.

◆ THE MOTIVES OF THE CRUSADERS

Religious Fervor   Christians viewed the crusades as acts of religious devotion. Even before Urban made his appeal, the idea had gained currency in the West that God would reward those who fought in a good cause, that is, that wars could be holy. The crusaders also shared the belief expressed in the movement for Church reform that the good ought not simply to endure the evils of the world but should attempt to correct them. This active, confident spirit contrasted strongly with the withdrawal from the world that most Christian writers recommended in the early Middle Ages.

Economic Motives for Expansion   Social and economic motivations also contributed to the expeditions. The age of mass pilgrimages and crusades, from about 1050 to 1250, corresponds to the period in medieval history during which the European population was growing rapidly. The crusades may be considered one further example of

▼ Christ Leading Crusaders
This fourteenth-century illustration from a manuscript on the Apocalypse captures an assumption that was common to all the crusaders— that their expedition was being led by Christ himself. On his magnificent charger, he leads into battle the troops carrying his symbol, the cross.
By Permission of The British Library, London. Royal 19BXV, pages:Fol 37 min

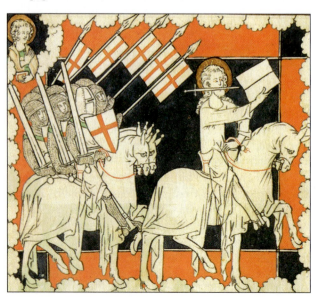

the expansion of Europe, similar in motivation and character to the Spanish *Reconquista* or the German *Drang nach Osten*. Of course, the crusades differed in at least one significant way from these other ventures. The crusades were almost exclusively military expeditions of Europe's warrior classes; peasants did not settle in Palestine in significant numbers as they did in the lands of Eastern Europe and in the Iberian Peninsula.

The Oversupply of Knights   The younger sons of European knights were particularly aware of the pressures created by an expanding population. Trained for war, they used their skills to fight each other for land and castles. Pope Urban apparently observed the effects of land shortage, for he is reported to have told the knights of France: "This land which you inhabit is too narrow for your large population; nor does it abound in wealth; and it provides hardly enough food for those who farm it. This is the reason that you murder and consume one another." Urban urged them not to fight fellow Christians, but to go to the traditional land of milk and honey and fight Muslims instead for land.

War against the Muslims thus offered constructive employment for Europe's surplus knights. In the twelfth century St. Bernard of Clairvaux, whose preaching inspired thousands to join the Second Crusade, frankly affirmed that all but a few of the knights on the crusades were "criminals and sinners, ravishers and the sacrilegious, murderers, perjurers, and adulterers." Bernard observed the double benefit of having them out of Europe: "Their departure makes their own people happy, and their arrival cheers those whom they are hastening to help. They aid both groups, not only by protecting the one but also by not oppressing the other." The crusades were, in one respect, a violent means of draining the violence from Western medieval life.

◆ THE FIRST CRUSADE

In November 1095, Pope Urban II preached a sermon at Clermont in southern France, calling on the nobility to undertake an expedition to the Holy Land. The pope's sermon was intended for the upper classes, but its plea had sensational results at all levels of Western society.

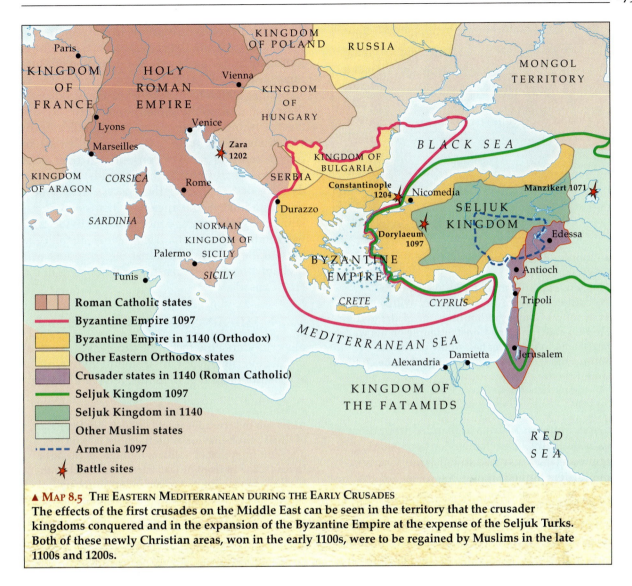

▲ **MAP 8.5** THE EASTERN MEDITERRANEAN DURING THE EARLY CRUSADES
The effects of the first crusades on the Middle East can be seen in the territory that the crusader kingdoms conquered and in the expansion of the Byzantine Empire at the expense of the Seljuk Turks. Both of these newly Christian areas, won in the early 1100s, were to be regained by Muslims in the late 1100s and 1200s.

The Popular Crusade In northern France and the Rhineland, influential preachers were soon rousing the people and organizing movements that historians now call the Popular Crusade. Bands of peasants and the poor (together with a few knights and clergy) set out for the East, miserably equipped and without competent leaders. They marched down the Rhine valley, attacking Jews as they went, and on through Hungary and Bulgaria to Constantinople. The emperor Alexius of Byzantium, who could only have been shocked at the sight of this hapless army, gave them transport across the Bosporus. The Turks at once cut them to pieces.

The Crusading Army Far better organized was the official First Crusade, which was led by nobles. Robert of Normandy, son of William the Conqueror, headed a northern French army; Godfrey of Bouillon, his brother Baldwin, and Robert of Flanders commanded an army of Lotharingians and Flemings; Raymond of Toulouse led the men of Languedoc; and Bohemund of Taranto and his nephew Tancred marshaled the Normans of southern Italy. These four armies moved by various overland and sea routes to Constantinople (see map 8.5) and arrived there in 1096 and 1097.

Although the leaders of the First Crusade had intended to conquer lands in the East in their own

▲ GODFREY APPROACHING THE GATE AT
CONSTANTINOPLE
**This miniature illustration of a history of the
expedition by one of its participants, William of
Tyre, shows Godfrey of Bouillon, the leader of the
First Crusade, entering Constantinople on his way to
Jerusalem. In the lower half of the picture he
approaches the city, and in the upper half he climbs a
ladder over the walls.**
Bibliothèque Nationale de France, Paris

name, Emperor Alexius demanded from them an
oath of fealty in exchange for provisioning the
armies as they marched to Palestine. Grudgingly,
the leaders agreed, promising to regard the emperor as the overlord of any lands they might reconquer from the Turks. Subsequently, both the
emperor and the Western leaders accused each
other of violating the terms of the oath. The failure
of the crusaders and the Byzantines to find a firm
basis for cooperating ultimately weakened, although it did not defeat, the enterprise. *The Alexiad*, written by Anna Comnena, daughter of
Alexius, reflects the Greek viewpoint: "there were
among the Latins such men as Bohemund and his
fellow counselors, who, eager to obtain the Roman Empire for themselves, had been looking
with avarice upon it for a long time."

Victories In 1097 the crusaders entered the
Seljuk Sultanate of Rum, achieving their first major victory at Dorylaeum. Baldwin then separated
his troops from the main body and conquered
Edessa, where he established the first crusader
state in the East. The decisive victory of the First
Crusade came in the battle for the port city of

Antioch. After that, the road to Jerusalem was
open. On July 15, 1099, the crusaders stormed
Jerusalem and slaughtered its population of Muslims, Jews, and Eastern Christians.

Besides a high level of organizational skill and
their own daring, the Westerners had the advantage of facing an enemy that was politically divided. The Seljuk Turks had only recently risen to
power and had not yet consolidated their rule.
They were still fighting the Fatimids, the ruling
dynasty of Egypt, over the possession of Palestine. In addition, the ancient schisms among Islamic religious sects continued to divide and
weaken the community. The Muslims' inability to
present a united front against the crusaders was
probably the decisive reason for the success of the
First Crusade.

◆ THE KINGDOM OF JERUSALEM

The crusaders now faced the problem of organizing a government for their conquered territory
and its population of Muslims, Jews, and Eastern

▼ THE PILLAGE OF JERUSALEM BY ANTIOCHUS
**Although the crusades were conducted in the name
of Christ, the behavior of their armies was no
different from that of soldiers throughout the ages.
In this scene in front of Jerusalem from a fifteenth-
century manuscript, the commander Antiochus
watches as his troops pile up the spoils they have
looted from the Holy City.**
Bibliothèque Nationale de France, Paris

▲ WOMEN ASSISTING KNIGHTS
This manuscript illustration makes it clear that women took part in battles alongside the male crusaders. Here they wield picks and axes and throw stones in a siege. Moreover, it is clear that the woman in the foreground, just behind the ladder, who does not cower behind a shield like the man on the ladder, is about to be killed by an arrow.
By Permission of The British Library, Ms Add. 15268 fol 101v

and Western Christians. They chose as ruler Godfrey of Bouillon, but he died in 1100, and his younger brother Baldwin, the conqueror of Edessa, succeeded him.

Baldwin organized his realm through the application of feudal concepts and institutions. He kept direct dominion over Jerusalem and its surroundings, including a stretch of coast extending from modern Gaza to Beirut. To the north, three fiefs—the County of Tripoli, the Principality of Antioch, and the County of Edessa—were made subject to his suzerainty (see map 8.6). Although King Baldwin and his successors were able to exert a respectable measure of authority over all these lands, profound weaknesses undermined their power. The kings were never able to push their frontiers to an easily defensible, strategic border, such as the Lebanese mountains. With only a small garrison, the Kingdom of Jerusalem depended on a constant influx of men and money from Europe. Many knights and pilgrims came, but relatively few stayed as permanent settlers. The Westerners constituted a foreign aristocracy, small in number and set over a people of largely different faith, culture, and sympathies. The wonder is not that the crusader states ultimately fell but that some of their outposts survived on the mainland of Asia Minor for nearly 200 years, until 1291 when the port of Acre fell at last.

◆ THE LATER CRUSADES

Although historians have traditionally assigned numbers to the later crusades, these expeditions were merely momentary swells in the steady current of Western people and treasures to and from the Middle East. The recapture of the city of

▲ CITIZENS OF EDESSA IN HOMAGE TO BALDWIN I
To emphasize the crusaders' triumph, this manuscript illustration shows Baldwin I, who captured Edessa in 1099, asserting his authority over the conquered Muslims. He sits on the left, with his knights next to him, and receives the homage and tribute of his new subjects.
Bibliothèque Nationale de France, Paris

Edessa by the Muslims in 1144 gave rise to the Second Crusade (1147–1149). Two armies, led by King Louis VII of France and the Emperor Conrad III of Germany, set out to capture Damascus to give the Kingdom of Jerusalem a more defensible frontier. They were soon forced to retreat ignominiously before superior Muslim forces.

The Third Crusade   The unification of the Muslims under Saladin prompted the Third Crusade (1189–1192). Saladin already controlled Egypt and was able to conquer Syria as well so that the Latin Kingdom was surrounded. His capture of Jerusalem threatened to eliminate the Latin Kingdom of Jerusalem entirely. Emperor Frederick Barbarossa and kings Philip II of France and Richard I, the Lion-Hearted, of England all marched to the East. (Frederick drowned while crossing through Asia Minor, and most of his forces turned back.) Philip II left the campaign early. Richard I fought on and the crusaders captured Acre. The Kingdom of Jerusalem remained limited to a narrow strip of the coast from Acre to Jaffa, but unarmed Christian pilgrims were given the right to visit Moslem-governed Jerusalem. These rights were paltry gains from so expensive a campaign.

The Fourth Crusade   Pope Innocent III preached the Fourth Crusade, but events soon took it out of his hands. The response was limited, so the leaders negotiated with Venice to take them by sea, rather than going overland, and to supply them with provisions for a year. In addition the Venetians were to provide their own troops and receive

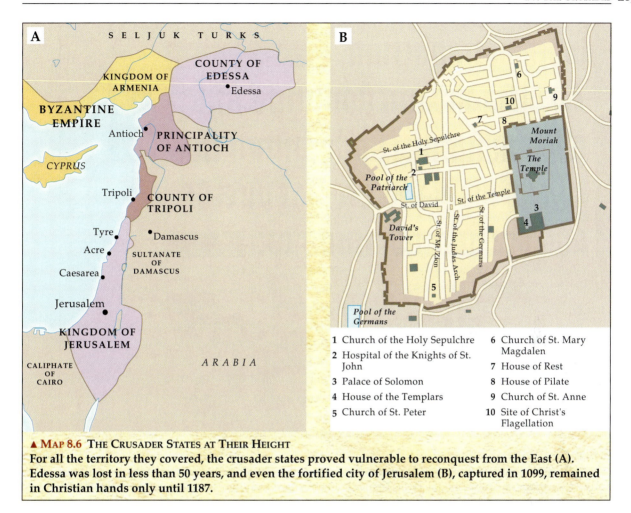

▲ MAP 8.6 THE CRUSADER STATES AT THEIR HEIGHT
For all the territory they covered, the crusader states proved vulnerable to reconquest from the East (A). Edessa was lost in less than 50 years, and even the fortified city of Jerusalem (B), captured in 1099, remained in Christian hands only until 1187.

Map A labels: SELJUK TURKS; COUNTY OF EDESSA; Edessa; KINGDOM OF ARMENIA; BYZANTINE EMPIRE; Antioch; PRINCIPALITY OF ANTIOCH; CYPRUS; Tripoli; COUNTY OF TRIPOLI; Tyre; Damascus; Acre; SULTANATE OF DAMASCUS; Caesarea; Jerusalem; KINGDOM OF JERUSALEM; CALIPHATE OF CAIRO; ARABIA

Map B labels: Mount Moriah; The Temple; St. of the Holy Sepulchre; Pool of the Patriarch; St. of David; St. of the Temple; David's Tower; St. of Mt. Zion; St. of the Judas Arch; St. of the Germans; Pool of the Germans

1 Church of the Holy Sepulchre
2 Hospital of the Knights of St. John
3 Palace of Solomon
4 House of the Templars
5 Church of St. Peter
6 Church of St. Mary Magdalen
7 House of Rest
8 House of Pilate
9 Church of St. Anne
10 Site of Christ's Flagellation

half the conquests. The Venetians proposed that the crusaders cancel their debt by aiding them in taking the trading port and Christian city of Zara, across the Adriatic from Venice. Although shocked at the proposal of attacking a Christian city, the crusaders were too far in debt to the Venetians to refuse. The Venetians and the crusade's leaders then persuaded the crusaders to attack Constantinople. The city, divided by factional strife, easily fell. Although Innocent III tried to stop the crusaders, they sacked the city and burned part of it. The Venetians and crusaders divided what remained of the Byzantine Empire into feudal principalities, but Western control lasted only until 1261.

Further Crusades With the Muslims of Egypt in control of Jerusalem, later crusaders tried new tactics. Emperor Frederick II married the heiress of the Latin Kingdom of Jerusalem and negotiated directly with the Muslim leaders to regain Jerusalem; the treaty did not long outlast him. King Louis IX of France tried two disastrous expeditions to North Africa (sometimes called the Sixth and Seventh Crusades), but neither succeeded and Louis died in the last attempt in Tunisia.

◆ MILITARY-RELIGIOUS ORDERS

Soon after the First Crusade, a new kind of institution, the military-religious order, was founded. The military-religious orders combined the dedication, discipline, and organizational experience of monasticism with the military purposes of the crusade. The orders offered armed

▲ KNIGHTS IN COMBAT
This contemporaneous manuscript illustration is a splendid depiction, full of motion and action, of two knights jousting. The figure on the left is thought to be Richard the Lion-Hearted, battling with Saladin himself.
By permission of the British Library (1007628.011)

escorts and safe lodgings to pilgrims on their way to Palestine. The orders became indispensable for the Latin Kingdom, assuming a major role in supplying the settlers with services, goods, defense, and means of communication back to Europe.

Templars The first of three great orders to emerge from the crusades was the Knights of the Temple, or Templars, founded sometime before 1120 by a group of French knights. The knights took the three monastic vows of poverty, chastity, and obedience and, like monks, lived together in their own convents or communities. The Templars assumed a major role in the maintenance of safe routes between Europe and the crusader states

and in the defense of the Kingdom of Jerusalem. The order also transported and guarded moneys in support of continued war, and thus became the most important banking institution of the age until its suppression by the pope in 1312.

Hospitalers The Knights of the Hospital of St. John of Jerusalem, or Hospitalers, founded about 1130, enjoyed an even longer history. Never as numerous or as wealthy as the Templars, they still made a major contribution to the defense of the Kingdom of Jerusalem. With the fall of Acre in 1291 the knights moved their headquarters to Cyprus, then to Rhodes, and finally to Malta. As the Knights of Malta, they ruled the island until 1798. This "sovereign order" of the Knights of

Malta survives today as an exclusively philanthropic confraternity.

Teutonic Knights   About 1190, German pilgrims organized the Teutonic Knights as a hospital order. Reorganized as a military order at the end of the twelfth-century, the Teutonic Knights

▼ HOSPITALERS IN RHODES

This fifteenth-century manuscript depiction of the capture of the island of Rhodes commemorates an event in 1306, when the Hospitaler knights attacked this fortress from the neighboring island of Cyprus. Wearing their distinctive tunic with its white cross, the Hospitalers swarmed through Rhodes, which they were to control until it was conquered by the Ottomans in 1522.

Bibliothèque Nationale de France, Paris

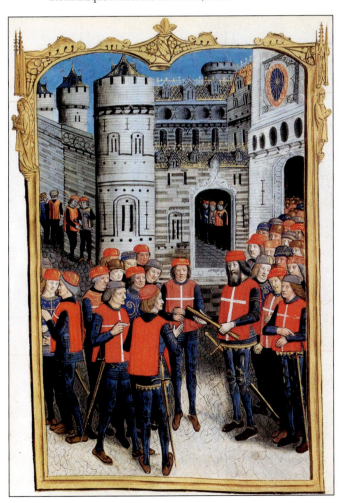

defended the eastern frontiers in Transylvania (in modern Romania) and, in 1229, in Prussia. There they became the armed vanguard of the German eastward expansion and conquered for themselves an extensive domain along the shores of the Baltic Sea. In 1525 the last grand master, Albert of Hohenzollern, adopted Lutheranism and secularized the order and its territories.

◆ RESULTS OF THE CRUSADES

Although the crusades did not produce a permanent Western political presence in Asia Minor, the whole experience of the campaigns and the contact with the East had a profound effect on Europe. When the Ottoman Turks, successors to the Seljuks, finally seized the islands of Cyprus and Crete, the Europeans had already found new routes to the Far East and were in the midst of a far broader overseas expansion.

Warfare   The crusades had a powerful influence on military technology. After their initial invasions, the crusaders waged a largely defensive war, becoming particularly skilled in the art of constructing castles. The numerous remains of crusader castles in nearly all the Eastern lands reflect these advances in such features as the overhanging tower parapets, from which oil or missiles could be rained down on attackers, and the angular castle entranceways that prevented the enemy from shooting directly at the gates. Islamic castles show a similar evolution toward a more advanced military design. Coincident with improvement of castle building was greater sophistication in siege engines to break down walls and gates. Battering rams, towers, mining under the walls (sapping), and catapults for throwing stones at walls all were used.

Economy   Historians still cannot draw up an exact balance sheet that registers accurately the economic gains and losses of the crusades. Although the campaigns were expensive, they also put a considerable amount of money in circulation by paying for weapons, provisions, shipping, and accommodations. Some of the money was drained to the East and only partially recovered in booty. Nevertheless, the crusades stimulated trade in sugar, spices, and similar products from the East and encouraged the production of luxury goods, such as silk cloth, in Europe itself.

Since expenses for the crusades exhausted traditional sources of revenue, popes and princes began to impose direct taxes on their own lands and subjects. To finance the Third Crusade in 1188, for example, the pope authorized, and the princes collected, the so-called Saladin tithe, a direct tax of 10 percent imposed on all clerical and lay revenues. (Previously, European governments had made little use of direct taxes, because they were difficult to assess and collect.) The imposition of the Saladin tithe and subsequent direct taxes required new institutional methods for assessments, collecting of moneys, and transferring funds to where they were most needed. The crusades, in other words, encouraged Western princes to develop taxation for government expense.

Explorations The crusades encouraged a curiosity about exotic cultures. Starting from the crusader principalities in the East, first missionaries and then merchants penetrated deep into central Asia, and by the early thirteenth century they had reached China. Their reports, especially the memoirs of the Venetian Marco Polo at the close of the thirteenth century, gave Europe abundant information about East Asia and helped inspire Western navigators in the late fifteenth and sixteenth centuries to seek new ways to trade with China directly. The desire to explore, conquer other cultures, and spread Christianity that was part of the crusades inspired later imperialism.

SUMMARY

The period from 1000 to 1150 was vigorously creative in every level of European life. Europe had changed substantially from what it was during the reign of Charlemagne. Its economy was more diversified and productive, its society more complex, its government more effective, its religion more organized. Europe had expanded its control into Spain, into the Slavic lands to the East, and even into Palestine. But the very innovations of the age posed severe problems for European society. How could the new forms of economic endeavor be reconciled with the older hostility and suspicion toward a life of buying and selling? How could the rising power of monarchs be reconciled with the self-consciousness and self-interest of the nobility, the reformed and independent Church, and the privileged towns? From about 1150 the West was trying to consolidate its recent advances and bring them into harmony with its older heritage. This effort at consolidation, reconciliation, and synthesis is the theme of Western history from 1150 to 1300.

QUESTIONS FOR FURTHER THOUGHT

1. It is said that the invasions of the Vikings, Magyars, and Muslims created the conditions that gave rise to feudalism. Do you agree with this statement, or would you point to other factors in the development of feudalism?

2. In a modern democracy, it is hard to imagine a strictly hierarchical society, but to understand the Middle Ages it is necessary to do so. How would you explain the medieval hierarchy to a fellow student?

3. What factors made the crusades possible? Do you think that the crusades would have been less violent if Western Christians had a greater understanding of Islam?

RECOMMENDED READING

◆

Sources

Alexiad of Anna Comnena. Elizabeth A. S. Dawes (tr.). 1978. A Greek version of the First Crusade.

*Benton, John F. (ed.). *Self and Society in Medieval France: The Memoirs of Abbot Guibert of Nogent (1064?–c. 1125).* 1970. An autobiography.

*Fitz Stephen, William. *Norman London,* with an essay by Sir Frank Stenton and introduction by F. Donald Logan. 1990. A description of London.

The Life of Christina of Markyate. C. H. Talbot (tr.). 1987.

Peters, Edward (ed.). *The First Crusade: The Chronicle of Fulcher of Chartres and Other Source Materials.* 1971. Sources that detail the First Crusade.

*Shinners, John (ed.). *Medieval Popular Religion, 1000–1500, A Reader.* 1997.

The Song of Roland. D. P. R. Owen (tr.). 1990. Many translations are available.

Stenton, Frank (ed.). *The Bayeux Tapestry.* 1957.

*Tierney, Brian (ed.). *The Crisis of Church and State, 1050–1300.* 1964. A selection of primary resources illustrating disputes between Church and state.

Whitelock, Dorothy (ed.). *The Anglo-Saxon Chronicle.* 1961.

Studies

*Arnold, Benjamin. *Medieval Germany, 500–1300: A Political Interpretation.* 1997.

Atiya, Azia S. *Crusade, Commerce, and Culture.* 1962. An evaluation of the results of the crusades in European history.

*Barraclough, Geoffrey. *The Origins of Modern Germany.* 1963. Classic interpretation of medieval German history.

*Bloch, Marc. *Feudal Society.* L. A. Manyon (tr.). 1961. A classic work on the social, economic, and cultural institutions in feudal society.

Chibnall, Marjorie. *Anglo-Norman England, 1066–1166.* 1987.

*Douglas, David C. *William the Conqueror: The Norman Impact upon England.* 1966. Outstanding among many biographies.

*Duby, Georges. *The Knight, the Lady, and the Priest: The Making of Modern Marriage in Medieval France.* 1983.

*———. *Rural Economy and Country Life in the Medieval West.* Cynthia Postan (tr.). 1968. A synthesis of rural life from 800 to 1400.

*Dunbabin, Jean. *France in the Making, 843–1100.* 1987. From Carolingian to Capetian France.

Ennen, Edith. *The Medieval Town.* Natalie Fryde (tr.). 1979. By a German historian; now the best introductory survey available in English.

*Ganshof, François. *Feudalism.* P. Grierson (tr.). 1961. Standard introduction to feudal institutions.

Gold, Penny Schine. *The Lady and the Virgin: Image, Attitude, and Experience in Twelfth-Century France.* 1985. A study based on literary and charter evidence exploring the role of women.

Green, Judith A. *The Government of England under Henry I.* 1986. Considers expansion of governmental institutions under Henry I.

*Herlihy, David. *Medieval Households.* 1985. Demography and family structure.

*Phillips, J. R. S. *The Medieval Expansion of Europe.* 1988. Crusades, but also other contacts with the Orient and the first explorations.

*Reuter, Timothy. *Germany in the Middle Ages, 800–1056.* 1991. This is a modern survey, brief and suited to students.

*Riley-Smith, Jonathan. *The First Crusade and the Idea of Crusading.* 1986. Examines the idea of the First Crusade and its reinterpretations.

*Southern, Richard W. *The Making of the Middle Ages.* 1955. Classic essay on twelfth-century culture.

*Swanson, R. N. *Religion and Devotion in Europe, c. 1215–c. 1515.* 1995. An emphasis on medieval religious experiences such as the mass and pilgrimages. Good book for students.

*Tellenbach, Gerd. *Church, State, and Christian Society at the Time of the Investiture Contest.* R. F. Bennett (tr.). 1970.

---

*Available in paperback.

▲ GOD AS ARCHITECT OF THE UNIVERSE
The notion of God creating the universe as an architect was common during the
Middle Ages. In this manuscript illumination, God is depicted holding a compass
and literally measuring the structure of the physical world.
Vienna, Austrian National Library

THE FLOWERING OF MEDIEVAL CIVILIZATION

The period from 1150 to the beginning of the thirteenth century was one of creativity in Western Europe. The refinements in living that the nobility were beginning to experience led to the creation of an elaborate court culture and a French vernacular literature that accompanied it. Women had a profound influence on the themes of that literature and on court behavior. Intellectual revival, which far outstripped the Carolingian and Ottonian renaissances, led to new sophistication in philosophy and theology and to the establishment of universities. University-educated men found careers in the Church, with the increasingly powerful monarchies, and in urban centers. A unifying theme of the flowering of medieval civilization was the strong sense of community and class identity that was developing in universities, guilds, villages, and among the nobility.

Monarchies expanded their control over their populations through bureaucracy and law. In pursuing the unification of their governments, they formalized feudal principles into governmental ones. The Church also continued to press forward its control over its bishops, abbots, and the religious beliefs of all Christians. Its claim was not unchallenged during this period, because the Church was faced with two widespread heresies. However, with the help of two new mendicant orders, the Franciscans and Dominicans, the Church was able to suppress the heresies. The continued religious enthusiasm and devotions of the laity are dramatically evident in the great Romanesque and Gothic churches that they gave their money to build.

	Social Structure	Body Politic	Changes in the Organization of Production and in the Impact of Technology	Evolution of Family and Changing Gender Roles	War	Religion	Cultural Expression
CHAPTER 9. THE FLOWERING OF MEDIEVAL CIVILIZATION							
I. CULTURAL DEVELOPMENTS	▨			▨		▨	▨
II. THE STATES OF EUROPE		▨			▨	▨	
III. THE CHURCH		▨				▨	▨

I. Cultural Developments

The changes that were going on in European society in the twelfth and early thirteenth centuries brought about an intellectual revival that revolutionized education. Universities developed that offered bachelor of arts degrees and advanced degrees in theology, law, medicine, and science. The increased bureaucratization of monarchies, the commercial transactions in cities, and the development of canon (Church) and civil law in general increased the demand for educated men with university degrees. As society became wealthier and more expansive, the austere Romanesque architecture inspired by the Cluniac reform gave way to Gothic architecture.

◆ THE RISE OF UNIVERSITIES

During the High Middle Ages, a new institution, the university, came to assume a role in intellectual life that it has not since relinquished. The university ranks as one of the most influential creations of the medieval world.

Monastic Schools Up to about 1050, monastic schools had dominated intellectual development in the West (see map 9.1). But the monastic devotion to prayer, self-denial, and mystical meditation was not especially favorable to original thought, while the isolation of monasteries restricted the experiences of the monastic scholar and made difficult the exchange of ideas that intellectual progress requires.

Cathedral Schools From about 1050 to 1200, the cathedral, or bishop's school, assumed the intellectual leadership in Europe. These schools were at first very fluid in their structure. The bishop's secretary, the chancellor, was usually in charge of the school and was responsible for inviting learned men, or "masters," to lecture to the students. Both students and masters roamed from town to town, seeking either the best teachers or the brightest (or best-paying) students and the most congenial atmosphere for their work. The

▲ **MAP 9.1 GREAT MONASTIC CENTERS OF LEARNING**

twelfth century was the age of the wandering scholars, who have left us charming traces of their spirit or at least that of their more frivolous members in the form of "goliardic" verses,[1] largely concerned with such unclerical subjects as the joys of wine, women, and song.

Townspeople frequently protested to the bishops or the king against the students, whom they resented because of their boisterous ways and because their clerical status—all students automatically took minor orders of clergy—gave them immunity from the local courts. Students for their part resented the high prices that townspeople charged for rooms, food, and drink. Riots involving town and gown (as clerics, students wore ecclesiastical dress) were violent and commonplace. To impose some order on this flux and to protect young students from incompetent or unorthodox teachers, the twelfth-century cathedral schools gradually insisted that masters possess a certification of their learning. The chancellor awarded this "license to teach," the ancestor of all modern academic degrees.

Universities   The throngs of masters and students, many of them strangers to the city in which they lectured and studied, eventually grouped themselves into guilds to protect their common interests. It was out of these spontaneously formed guilds of masters and students that the medieval university grew (*universitas* was a widely used Latin word for "guild," as discussed in Chapter 10). The masters in Paris, for example, formed a guild and received a royal charter in about 1200 and sanction from the Pope in 1231. These documents confirmed the guild's autonomy and authority to license teachers. By contrast, the University of Bologna had a guild of students who ran the university.

Italian Universities   Even in the early Middle Ages professional schools for the training of notaries, lawyers, and doctors survived in some Italian cities. The Italian schools enjoyed rapid

growth from the late eleventh century, which led to the formation of guilds. In Italy the students were older and professionally motivated, desiring degrees in canon law for a career in the church or in civil law (Justinian's *Corpus Juris Civilis*). Wishing to guarantee the quality of their training, the students rather than the professors constituted the dominant "university." At the oldest of these schools, the University of Bologna, the students established the fees to be paid to the professors and determined the hours and even the content of the lectures. Thomas Becket and Innocent III, who are discussed in this chapter, attended Bologna.

The University of Paris   The University of Paris became the model for northern Europe as professors founded schools at Oxford, Cambridge, Prague, and other cities throughout Europe (see map 9.2). These universities were run by the masters and granted the baccalaureate, or bachelor of arts degree. The curriculum was the *trivium* and *quadrivium* that Alcuin had developed in the Carolingian period (see p. 228). A master's degree involved further work and licensed the holder to teach. Higher degrees in theology, law, and medicine took five to seven years to complete. A candidate for a theology degree had to be thirty years old; the degree took seven years.

Students matriculated at a university in their early teens. They were expected to know Latin already and to have money for tuition and living expenses. At the University of Paris classes were in rented halls on the left bank of the river, and since the language of the lecturers was Latin, the area came to be—and still is—known as the Latin Quarter. Because the students were young, often poor, and undisciplined, Robert de Sorbonne founded a college, the first, in 1275 in Paris. Colleges provided meals, housing, and libraries for the students. Masters resided in the colleges and supervised student behavior. The system still exists at Oxford and Cambridge.

◆ SCHOLASTICISM

Scholasticism was both a way of reasoning and a body of writings: Scholastics applied dialectic to Christian dogma. Dialectic is the art of analyzing the logical relationships among propositions in a

---

[1]The exact etymology of the word *goliardic* remains unknown. It possibly derives from Goliath the Philistine, who was honored as a kind of antisaint by the boisterous students.

▲ **MAP 9.2 MEDIEVAL UNIVERSITIES**

dialogue or discourse. The method of presenting an argument was to state a proposition and then dispute its validity either orally or in writing. Scholasticism represented a shift from the humanistic studies of the early twelfth century. Cathedral schools such as Chartres emphasized familiarity with the classical authors, particularly Plato, and the ability to appreciate and write good Latin. But dialectic won out in the late twelfth century,

partly because Aristotle's complete logic became available to Western scholars.

Anselm of Canterbury   The first thinker to explore, although still not rigorously, the theological applications of dialectic was St. Anselm of Canterbury (1033–1109). Anselm defined his own intellectual interests as "faith seeking to understand"—in actuality, faith seeking to find logical

► The university as a community of scholars, teachers, and learners was a medieval innovation. Its structure was such that students exercised a degree of control that they rarely possess today. Since there were no salaries, professors relied on tuition fees for their daily bread, and students could starve out unpopular teachers merely by refusing to attend their classes. However, in other aspects, student life then was much the same as it is today. These scenes from a fifteenth-century manuscript show students gambling, opposing each other in disputations (class debates), and engaging in other activities of dormitory life.
University Library of Freiburg-im-Breisgau

consistency among its beliefs. He tried to show a necessary, logical connection between the traditional Judeo-Christian dogma that God is a perfect being and a logical proof that God exists. From the time of Anselm, Scholastic thought assumed that the human intellect was powerful enough to probe the logical and metaphysical patterns within which even God had to operate.

Abelard Peter Abelard (1079–1142) brought a new rigor and popularity to dialectical theology. We know a great deal about Peter Abelard because he wrote an autobiography later in his life called *Historia calamitatum* (*Story of My Calamities*). Eldest son of a petty noble from Brittany, Abelard was destined for warfare and lordship, but his intellectual interests overrode this career. As a wandering scholar, he came to Paris, entered into a decisive disputation with the leading theologian, and began to give lectures. His brilliance attracted the attention of a clergyman attached to Notre Dame Cathedral, who engaged Abelard to tutor his niece, Héloïse (ca. 1100–ca. 1163). Héloïse had a convent training and her uncle wanted to further her education by hiring the best instructor in Paris. Despite an age difference of twenty-four years, Abelard tells his readers, they fell in love and conceived a child. They had a clandestine marriage because Héloïse knew that it would ruin his career if he, as a member of the clergy, were married. He would have had to give up his lecturing, an activity only clergy could do. Her uncle, betrayed and angry, had thugs castrate Abelard to

▲ THE **Doorway of the Virgin at Chartres cathedral in France shows the seven liberal arts—arithmetic, astronomy, dialectic, geometry, grammar, music, and rhetoric—represented as female figures. These female figures each held a symbol of their discipline and they were used through Europe. The seven liberal arts formed the core subjects for the baccalaureate and the master's degrees.**
Mary Ann Sullivan

punish him. Abelard and Héloïse then entered separate monasteries.

The child of their marriage, Astrolabe, was born at Abelard's sister's home. Héloïse became a respected abbess, but in her letters to Abelard, it is apparent that she continued to care about him with undiminished love. Abelard's replies admonish her to pray and to administer the nunnery.

Abelard continued his writing, and in *Sic et Non* ("Yes and No") he used what became the standard Scholastic method of argumentation,

posing a formal question and citing authorities on both sides. Abelard assembled 150 theological questions and marshaled authorities from the Bible, Church councils, and Church fathers for arguments on either side. He made no effort to reconcile the discrepancies, but left the authorities standing in embarrassing juxtaposition (see "Abelard's *Sic et Non*," p. 295). *Sic et Non* implied that one must either enlist dialectic to reconcile the conflicts or concede that the faith was a tissue of contradictions. His book caused a furor of debate, and finally a Church council condemned it. To avoid charges of heresy, he was forced to throw it into the flames and submit to the Church. But the method of argument that he used, that of posing a question and then mustering arguments to support or refute it, became characteristic of medieval Scholasticism.

▼ HÉLOÏSE AND ABELARD, FROM ROMAN DE LA ROSE
Already a famous professor in Paris, Abelard began a secret relationship with Héloïse, and in revenge her relatives had him castrated. The two were then separated for decades, and their correspondence remains one of the most powerful human documents of medieval times. Despite the conventions of the day, Héloïse was clearly an equal partner in the relationship, as is indicated in this fifteenth-century depiction of the pair engaged in intense discussion.
Giraudon/Art Resource, NY

ABELARD'S *SIC ET NON*

Completed in 1138, Peter Abelard's Sic et Non ("Yes and No") explained the techniques for recon-ciling divergent opinions in theology and law. His approach reflects the ambition of Scholasticism to bolster faith through reason.

"Among the many words of the holy fathers some seem not only to differ from one another but even to contradict one another. . . . Why should it seem sur-prising if we, lacking the guidance of the holy spirit, fail to understand them?

"Our achievement of understanding is impeded especially by unusual modes of expression and by the different significances that can be attached to one and the same word. We must also take special care that we are not deceived by corruptions of the text or by false attributions when sayings of the [Church] fathers are quoted that seem to differ from the truth or to be contrary to it; for many apocryphal writings are set down under names of saints to enhance their authority, and even the texts of the divine scripture are corrupted by the errors of scribes. If, in scripture, anything seems absurd, you are not permitted to say, 'The author of this book did not hold the truth,' but rather that the book is defective or that the inter-preter erred or that you do not understand. But if anything seems contrary to truth in the works of later authors, the reader or auditor is free to judge, so that he may approve what is pleasing and reject what gives offense, unless the matter is established by certain reason or canonical authority.

"In view of these considerations we have under-taken to collect various sayings of the fathers that give rise to questioning because of their apparent contradictions. Assiduous and frequent questioning is indeed the first key to wisdom. For by doubting we come to inquiry; and through inquiring we per-ceive the truth."

From Brian Tierney, et al., *The Middle Ages: Sources of Medieval History*, 5th Ed. (McGraw-Hill Companies, 1992), pp. 172–175.

Reception of Aristotle   By the end of the twelfth century, dialectical argument was supreme in Paris and elsewhere. One reason it predominated was that, after the middle of the twelfth century, translators working chiefly in Spain and Sicily in-troduced European scholars to hitherto unknown works of Aristotle as well as to the great commen-tary that the Muslim Averroës had written on them. Christian thinkers now had at their disposal the full Aristotelian corpus, and it confronted them with a philosophical system based solely on observation and human reason. Aristotle's logic drove Western scholars to examine his works and their own faith through Aristotelian logic. The dif-ficult task of reconciling Aristotelian reason and nature with Christian revelation and divine grace remained the central philosophical problem of the thirteenth century.

Thomas Aquinas   The most gifted representative of Scholastic philosophy, and the greatest Christian theologian since Augustine, was St. Thomas Aquinas (1225?–1274), whose career well illus-trates the character of thirteenth-century intellec-tual life. At age seventeen Aquinas entered the new Dominican Order, perhaps attracted by its commit-ment to scholarship; he studied at Monte Cassino and Naples and later, as a Dominican, at Cologne and Paris (see map 9.2). His most influential teacher was another Dominican, Albertus Magnus, a German who wrote extensively on theology and natural science, especially biology. Aquinas was no intellectual recluse; he lectured at Paris and trav-eled widely across Europe. His was such an active mind that when he dined with King Louis IX of France, the king provided him with scribes to keep notes on his brilliant discourse.

Aquinas produced a prodigious amount of writing: commentaries on biblical books and Aristotelian works, short essays on philosophical problems, and the *Summa contra Gentiles*, which was probably intended for Dominican missionar-ies working to convert heretics and infidels. His most important work, however, was one he did not live to finish. Divided into three parts on God, Man, and Christ, the *Summa Theologica* was meant to provide a comprehensive introduction to Chris-tian theology and to present a systematic view of the universe that would do justice to all truth, natural and revealed, pagan and Christian.

Aquinas brought to his task a subtle and perceptive intellect, and his system rests on several fundamental, delicate compromises. In regard to faith and reason, he taught that both are roads to a single truth. Reason is based ultimately on sense experience, as Aristotle argued. It is a powerful instrument, but insufficient to teach people all that God wishes them to know. Nature is good, and humans can achieve some partial, temporary happiness in this life. But nature alone cannot carry them to ultimate understanding of matters such as the Trinity. These matters must be accepted on the basis of faith, not reason. In the final analysis, God's mind is infinite, while human beings' minds are finite.

Building his proof for the existence of God on Aristotelian logic, Aquinas used *a posteriori* arguments, or arguments based on empirical observation. For instance: All motion is caused; we can observe motion; but there cannot be an infinite regress of movers, therefore, there must be a prime mover who is God.

The *Summa* shows certain characteristic weaknesses of Scholasticism. Aquinas affirmed that natural truth is ultimately grounded in observation, but in fact, he observed very little. He borrowed from Aristotle rather than doing his own observation or experimentation. Many later thinkers found his system too speculative, too elaborate. Nonetheless, the *Summa* remains an unquestioned masterpiece of Western theology. It offers comment on an enormous range of theological, philosophical, and ethical problems, and consistently demonstrates openness, insight, and wisdom.

Duns Scotus   Aquinas' system fell under critical scrutiny in the generation following his death. Among his early critics, the most influential was a Scottish Franciscan, John Duns Scotus (1265?–1308). Drawing inspiration from St. Augustine, Duns Scotus affirmed that faith was logically prior to reason. His arguments were based on *a priori* reasoning, a Platonic rather than Aristotelian concept that deduced arguments from concepts already held in the mind. To Duns Scotus the proof of God's existence was not based, as

with Aquinas, on the perception of change in the universe, for he did not trust the accuracy of sense observation; rather, it derived from an exclusively intellectual analysis of the concept of God as a necessary being, an argument closer to Anselm before him and Descartes in the seventeenth century.

◆ SPIRITUAL APPROACHES TO KNOWLEDGE

Many people who thought deeply about the nature of God and religion argued that the dialectic approach was not the best way to achieve knowledge. They argued that a spiritual approach based on prayer and humility would bring about a greater understanding of God. They emphasized the human side of the religion by encouraging worship of Mary.

Worship of Mary   Mary, mother of Jesus, became an important figure in the dedication of churches and in popular worship. Her presence added a humanizing touch to the religion and invited prayers of intercession with Jesus and God. In the early Middle Ages, a stern, mature Jesus was depicted as a lawgiver in churches, but in the late twelfth century Mary with an infant Jesus on her hip came to dominate church dedications and sculpture.

Cistercians and St. Bernard   The Cistercians took their name from their first house at Cîteau. Although founded in 1098, their prominence came with the arrival of Bernard of Clairvaux (ca. 1090–1153) with thirty companions in 1112. St. Bernard played a major role in European politics, including the condemnation of Abelard's *Sic et Non*. He preached the Second Crusade and served as adviser to the monarchs of Europe.

The Cistercians advocated a greater simplicity than the Cluniacs. Their robes were made of white, undyed wool; for that reason they were called the "white monks." They avoided the grand churches and elaborate ceremonies of the Cluniacs. Their emphasis, instead, was on emotional devotion to Christ's and Mary's humility. All of their churches were dedicated to Mary.

St. Bernard praised the human, nurturing quality of Mary in hymns as well as in devotional practices.

The Cistercian order spread rapidly both within the older borders of Europe and into frontier lands in northern England, along the newly reclaimed wasteland of Flanders, and in the newly conquered Slavic lands to the east. The order became identified with the expansion of Europe and the spread of efficient estate management and agriculture.

Women's Spirituality   Women could not attend universities in the Middle Ages, so their intellectual life centered in the nunnery or court. Perhaps because of the new emphasis on the worship of Mary, women became more prominent in the spiritual life of the Church. Hildegard of Bingen (d. 1179) was an abbess, musician, and writer. She wrote in Latin on scientific questions and revelations and corresponded with emperors and popes.

Other women became well known for their piety and their mystical visions. Marie D'Oignies (d. 1213), whose life was recorded by Jacques de Vitry, was a founding mother of the Beguines, a group of religious women to be discussed in chapter 10. Withdrawing to a cell connected to a monastery, she had a reputation as a healer and an ascetic. Women throughout the Middle Ages became anchorites, or holy women living in cells connected to churches or monasteries. Women who pursued a rigorous, individual asceticism inspired other women and men to lead a spiritual life.

◆ ROMANESQUE ARCHITECTURE

The increased prosperity and the revival of popular piety in the Early Middle Ages produced two major new developments in architecture, sculpture, painting, and illustration. The austerity of the Cluniac period led to the sober Romanesque style—a style that took the Roman, rounded arch as its model. The Cistercian movement and the greater social, cultural, and technological exuberance of the mid-twelfth century expressed its piety with sunlit churches of the Gothic style (see illustration on p. 298).

The Romanesque Style   The architectural and artistic style of *Romanesque* (meaning "of Roman origins") took some elements from earlier models, but not exclusively; it also drew on other artistic traditions, such as Germanic, Byzantine, and Arab. Thus, Romanesque buildings in different parts of western Europe had distinctive design features.

The most impressive artistic monuments left to us from the Romanesque period include churches, monasteries, and castles. One objective in the Romanesque style was to roof churches in stone rather than wooden beams and thatch roofs that were vulnerable to burning. Around the year 1000, small stone-roofed churches began to appear, especially in southern Europe. At first the builders used the simple barrel, or tunnel, vault. Because of the weight of the masonry roof, walls had to be thick and the windows had to be small. Engineers then developed and mastered the use of the groin vault, which is formed by the intersection of two barrel vaults. The area of intersection is called the bay, and the roof over the bay is supported at four points, not by the entire length of the lateral walls. Bays could be built next to bays, an entire church could be roofed with stone, windows could be enlarged, and the monotony of tunnel vaulting would be avoided.

Romanesque Decoration   Romanesque churches were decorated on the exterior with stone sculpture. Romanesque statues, which exist by the thousands, show a marked quality of antirealism, a refusal to allow visual accuracy to dominate portrayals. The artists were striving to present a world as seen by faith. Christ, for example, had to be shown larger than the other figures, in keeping with his dignity. Demons and monsters, many drawn from the popular imagination, abound in Romanesque sculpture. While similar to Byzantine portrayals in its antirealism, Romanesque style, unlike the Byzantine, overflows with movement, tension, excitement, and the spirit of mystical exhilaration. Romanesque statuary documents the exuberant spirit of this age of reform, when people seemed convinced that God was actively at work among them, setting right the world.

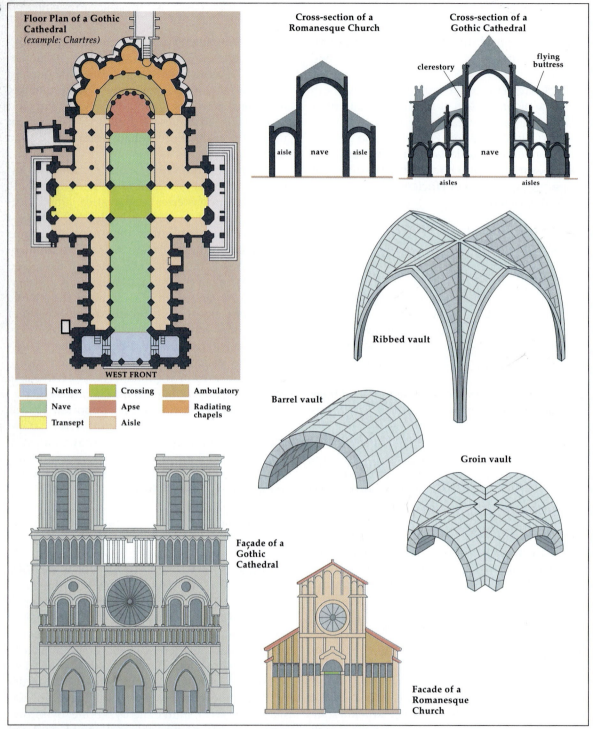

Floor Plan of a Gothic Cathedral
(example: Chartres)

WEST FRONT

Narthex	Crossing	Ambulatory
Nave	Apse	Radiating chapels
Transept	Aisle	

Cross-section of a Romanesque Church

aisle   nave   aisle

Cross-section of a Gothic Cathedral

clerestory

flying buttress

nave

aisles   aisles

Ribbed vault

Barrel vault

Groin vault

Façade of a Gothic Cathedral

Facade of a Romanesque Church

▲ The Romanesque cathedral shown in cross-section in the middle top and as a façade in the bottom shows the simple nave and isle construction of the cathedral. The roof was either a barrel vault or a groin vault. The Gothic cathedral shown in the floor plan and the façade could be a more elaborate structure because of the use of flying buttresses, shown upper right, which formed an external skeleton supporting the walls. The buttresses permitted the walls to have great expanses of windows since they were not bearing all the weight of the stone roof. The ribbed vault permitted greater height in the Gothic cathedral.

▲ PISA CATHEDRAL, CA. 1063–1272
One of the finest architectural ensembles in the new Romanesque styles of the eleventh and twelfth centuries is the cathedral and its surrounding buildings in Pisa, Italy. Although the famous leaning tower, which is now restored to nearly vertical, is the best known of these buildings, the huge marble-clad cathedral was in fact regarded as the supreme achievement of the Pisans and was widely influential in church building throughout Italy.
Casimir/eStock Photo

Other Characteristics of Romanesque Style
Nobles became consumers of art and architecture for building and furnishing their increasingly elaborate castles, but art remained, in most of its forms, the servant of the Church. The Cluniac monastic reform in the eleventh century brought with it a liturgical revival; the Cluniacs were especially devoted to (and occasionally criticized for) sumptuous religious services. Liturgical needs stimulated the art of metalwork (which produced chalices and other sacred vessels), glass making, and the weaving of fine fabrics for priests' vestments.

The Gregorian chant (named for Pope Gregory the Great, but in fact representing the traditional plainsong of the Church of Rome) was established as the common music of the Western Church in the Carolingian epoch. The eleventh and twelfth centuries witnessed the development of polyphonic music (part-singing). The coordination of the vocal parts in choral music also required systems of musical notation. A monk named Guido d'Arezzo is credited with giving the familiar names to the notes.

◆ THE GOTHIC STYLE

Artists as well as theologians were attempting to present a systematic view of the universe that was reflective of all truth. The artistic counterpart to the Scholastic *Summas* was the Gothic cathedral.

Gothic Architecture Sixteenth-century critics coined the word *Gothic* as an expression of contempt for these supposedly barbarous medieval buildings. In fact, the Goths had disappeared some 500 years before any Gothic churches were built. As used today, *Gothic* refers to the style of architecture and art that initially developed in the royal lands in France, including Paris and its surroundings, from about 1150. The abbey church of Saint-Denis near Paris, built by the Abbot Suger in 1144, is usually taken as the first authentic example of the Gothic style. In the thirteenth century

▲ TYMPANUM OF SOUTH PORTAL OF ST. PIERRE, MOISSAC, CA. 1115–1135
The revival of sculpture is one of the noteworthy achievements of Romanesque art. Integrating architecture and sculpture, this tympanum (the semicircular space above a church portal) shows the Second Coming of Christ, attended by symbols of the evangelists and the kings of the world seated in rows divided by stylized clouds.
Giraudon/Art Resource, NY

the Gothic style spread widely through Europe and found special application in the large churches built by two new thirteenth-century religious orders, the Franciscan and Dominican orders.

Technically, three engineering devices helped stamp the Gothic style: the pointed rather than rounded arch; ribbed vaulting, which concentrated support around the lines of thrust and gave the buildings a visibly delineated skeleton; and the flying buttress, an external support that allowed the walls to be made higher and lighter. The flying buttress also freed sections of the walls from the function of supporting the roof and therefore permitted the use of large areas for windows. The windows were filled with stained glass that depicted scenes from the Bible or from saints' lives. Romanesque architects had pioneered all three devices, but the Gothic engineers combined them and used them with unprecedented vigor and boldness.

The sculpture adorning buildings also represented innovation. Romanesque sculpture often conveyed great emotional power but did not reflect the natural world. Sculptors now wanted their works to emulate reality, or at least its handsomest parts (decorative foliage, for example, was carved with such accuracy that the botanical models can be identified). Their statues portray real and usually cheerful people, who subtly exert their own personalities without destroying the harmony of the whole.

The Gothic Spirit These magnificent churches with their hundreds of statues took decades to construct and decorate, and many were never

▲ ST. ETIENNE, CAEN, VAULTS, CA. 1115–1120
St. Etienne, Caen, was begun by William the Conqueror in 1067 and is considered a superb example of Norman Romanesque architecture. It was originally supposed to have a wooden roof, but it was vaulted in stone between 1115 and 1120. Each section of the roof is held up by six ribs that meet at the center and two arches, all of which rest on pillars at the side of the nave. The resultant pattern added to the sense of height and drew the eye ever upward toward heaven.
Foto Marburg/Art Resource, NY

completed. The builders intended that the churches provide a comprehensive view of the universe and instruction in its sacred history. One principal element of the Gothic aesthetic is a strong sense of order. The naked ribs and buttresses and the intricate vaulting constitute a

▲ AMIENS CATHEDRAL, CA. 1220–1236
Built between 1220 and 1236, Amiens Cathedral exemplifies the structure of a Gothic cathedral. The weight of the walls is supported by a system of buttresses and ribbed vaults, which allowed medieval builders to break up the walls with luminous areas of stained glass. The colored light that poured into these massive structures gave them an otherworldly majesty never before achieved.
Scala/Art Resource, NY

◄ In contrast to Romanesque sculpture, which overflows with great displays of emotion, Gothic sculpture evokes a sense of calm and orderly reality, as can be seen in the jamb figures on the central portal of Chartres Cathedral.
Foto Marburg/Art Resource, NY

spectacular geometry that instills in the viewer a vivid impression of intelligence and logical relationships. The churches, reflecting the structure of the universe, taught that God, the master builder, created and still governs the natural world with similar logic.

The most distinctive aspect of the Gothic style is its use of light in a manner unique in the history of architecture. Once within the church, the visitor has entered a realm defined and infused by a warm, colored glow. In Christian worship light is one of the most ancient, common, and versatile symbols. It suggests to the worshiper mystical illumination, spiritual beauty, grace, and divinity itself.

The thirteenth century was a great age of cathedral building. Gothic architecture reached its highest point with cathedrals in France, including those of Chartres, Paris, Amiens, and Rheims. England and Germany also produced fine Gothic cathedrals, such as Salisbury, Lincoln, and Cologne. As the style was perfected, more height and light could be added to the cathedrals. The most extreme example is Sainte-Chapelle in Paris, where the walls were replaced entirely with windows. Enhancing the style perfected in the thirteenth century, later additions came to be more elaborate, and by the fifteenth century the encrustation of the cathedrals with carvings and the height of the naves and towers have led historians to call them "wedding-cake Gothic."

◆ COURT CULTURE

At the same time that universities were being established and Gothic cathedrals were being built, the nobility was developing its own distinctive culture. Wealth, leisure, and refinements in living learned from the Arabs and Greeks influenced the culture. A new code of behavior that included

◄ SAINTE-CHAPELLE, PARIS, INTERIOR, 1243–1248
Sainte-Chapelle, the private chapel attached to the French royal palace in Paris, was built between 1243 and 1248 to house relics brought back from the crusades by Louis IX. The building was deliberately intended to resemble a reliquary, and the enormous jewel-colored stained-glass windows make up three-quarters of its wall surface.
Giraudon / Art Resource, NY

chivalry and courtly love became standard for all European nobility and was widely imitated by the urban elite as well.

Chivalry A new code of behavior refined the manners of knights. Added to bravery and loyalty, exemplified in *The Song of Roland* (see p. 255), were devotion to the Church, polite behavior, and rules for behavior at the table and in the lord's court. *Courtesy* means the manners appropriate to the noble court. The knight no longer was simply dubbed with a sword when he reached the age of twenty-one, but instead went through a religious ceremony that included a vigil and the blessing of his arms, a ritual cleansing, and an oath to protect women and the Church. In addition to using weapons, training for knighthood included learn-ing to sing or play an instrument, to carve a roast and serve it to a lord and lady, to dance, and to dress appropriately. The etiquette of tournaments was elaborately established and taught to knights when they were young.

Courtly Love Courtly love, or the polite relations between men and women, developed at the court of Eleanor of Aquitaine, of whom we shall speak presently. While married to Henry II of England, she and her sons and daughters spent much of their time at the seat of her duchy in Poitiers. One of the writers they patronized, Andreas Capellanus, updated Ovid's writings on love in a book called *The Art of Courtly Love*. The book instructs men on how to please and seduce women of different ranks, although when he refers to the love of a noble for a peasant he sanctions rape: "Do not hesitate to take what you seek and to embrace her by force." According to Andreas, Eleanor and her daughters set up a court to correct men who erred or to set tasks, such as fighting in a number of tournaments, for those wishing to win the love of a particular lady.

In an age of arranged marriages, in which love might or might not be present between the couples, courtly love permitted an atmosphere for flirtation. Historians debate whether adultery was widespread in these courts. Historians are also undecided about the influence courtly love had on the position of noblewomen in society: Did it trivialize them by making them mere objects of sexual desire, or did it make them more valued and respected?

▼ The most popular subject for courtly romance was the legends surrounding King Arthur. In the first picture, King Arthur is surrounded by his knights. His queen, Guinevere, is in the doorway. Below the induction of a knight to the Round Table is shown. The altar in the background indicates the religious nature of the knighting ceremony. Above is the romance of Tristan and below is the Holy Grail.
Musée Condé Chantilly/Dagli Orti/The Art Archive

Noblewomen As in the early Middle Ages, women in the twelfth century spent much of their time in and around their castles. The castles had become much more comfortable, with pleasant quarters attached to gardens reserved for the women. Although noblewomen still faced the tasks of household and estate management in the absence of their husbands, the new luxury goods available and courtly manners provided more entertainment for them in their leisure hours. For noblewomen, as for knights, acquiring skill in singing, dancing, and playing musical instruments was important. With luxurious silks more available since the crusades, dress became more elaborate and noblewomen undertook embroidery with silk as well as woolen thread. Noblewomen learned to read and write vernacular poetry and prose, which was undergoing a great vogue in the twelfth century.

Vernacular Literature Acting as patrons, the nobility encouraged the development of vernacular literature. Scholars believe that this literature, or some oral version of it, was appreciated well beyond aristocratic circles. Townspeople and even peasants seem to have delighted in hearing of the adventures of knights and ladies.

Of the vernacular literatures of Europe, only Anglo-Saxon possesses a substantial number of surviving writings that antedate the year 1000. In forming the literary tastes of Europe, the Romance tongues (the vernacular languages descended from Latin) achieved prominence, particularly French by the eleventh and twelfth centuries. Castilian was slightly later than French in producing an important literature in Spain, and Italian did not emerge as a major literary language until the late thirteenth century.

There were three principal genres of vernacular literature: the heroic epic, of which *The Song of Roland* is the best example; troubadour lyric poetry; and the courtly romance.

The Troubadours Very different from the heroic epic is troubadour lyric poetry. The novelty of this complex poetry is its celebration of women and of love, as opposed to heroic epics, which were written for the masculine society of the battle camp. The troubadours sang at courts, in which women exerted a powerful influence. In a mobile age, when knights and nobles would be away for long periods on crusades and wars, their mothers, wives, and daughters influenced the literature that was heard within the castle walls.

The troubadour usually addressed a lady of superior social station, almost always someone else's wife, whom he had little chance of winning. Courtly love (at least as the troubadours present it) was not a dalliance but quite literally a means of rescuing the lover from despondency and introducing him into an earthly paradise of his imagination. This discovery and intensive exploration of the emotion of love represents one of the most influential creations of the medieval mind.

The Courtly Romance The courtly romance, which entered its great age after 1150, combines traits of both heroic epics and troubadour lyric poetry. It is narrative in form, like the epic, but like lyrical love poetry, it allots a major role to women and love. Taking her stories from Celtic tales, Marie de France (d. 1210) wrote in the vernacular, composing *lais*, or brief romance narratives of love and adventure. Chrétien de Troyes wrote romances about King Arthur of Britain and his coterie of knights. Many of these tales are concerned with the tensions between adulterous love for a lord's wife and loyalty to the lord.

Popular Literature At a less elevated level were a range of ballads, songs, and stories. The goliardic poems of students have already been mentioned. The *fabliaux* were often stories of adulterous love in which the wife outsmarts the husband and sleeps with a student or a priest. The setting for these stories often reflects urban life in which the husband is a merchant absent on business. Fables, with animals as their protagonists, taught moral lessons, just as they did in the ancient world. And miracle stories, particularly miracles of the Virgin Mary, taught religious devotion.

II. The States of Europe

◆

Governments in the eleventh and early twelfth centuries had taken tentative steps toward expanding their control over their subjects and extending royal justice, as opposed to feudal justice,

to everyone. The growth of universities and the use of academically trained lawyers helped define governmental and legal procedures. The monarchs and their university-trained lawyers began the long process of implanting in the West the assumption that people should be governed by fixed and known procedures. Subjects valued the more uniform law that royal justice provided. It meant that merchants could travel from place to place under the rule of the same laws rather than the arbitrary administration of law that a feudal lord might apply. Lesser landholders appreciated a central court of appeal that could overcome the might of local overlords.

◆ ENGLAND

In England the kings were particularly aggressive in extending their control over the English countryside and their subjects by making royal justice the most important arbitrator in England. In doing so the kings clashed with the papacy and the English clergy, who claimed to be exempt from royal justice. Royal justice also undermined the prerogatives of the nobility and led to the rebellion that produced the *Magna Carta*.

Angevin Kingship Henry I had numerous bastard children, but the only legitimate child to survive him was a daughter, Matilda. Her first marriage was to the emperor of Germany, giving her the title of "Matilda Empress." Her second marriage was to the Count Geoffrey of Anjou. Rather than selecting a woman—and one who was married to a hostile and aggressive neighbor of the duchy of Normandy—the English nobility selected another descendent of William I's line, Stephen of Blois (r. 1135–1152), to be king. Civil war ensued, which was resolved with the compromise that the son of Matilda and the Count of Anjou would succeed to the throne at Stephen's death. In 1154 Henry of Anjou, grandson of Henry I, became the first Angevin king of England.

Henry II Through combined inheritances from his father and mother and his marriage to Eleanor of Aquitaine in 1152, Henry II ruled over a sprawling assemblage of territories that included, besides England, nearly the entire west of France from the English Channel to the Pyrenees Moun-

▲ **This enameled plate shows Count Geoffrey of Anjou, who died in 1151, holding a shield that depicts his family's new coat of arms.**
Giraudon/Art Resource, NY

tains (see map 9.3). A man of great energy who carried to completion many of the reforms of Henry I, Henry II ranks among the most gifted statesmen of the twelfth century and among the greatest kings of England.

Itinerant Justices Henry II left a permanent mark on English government and law. He resurrected the "justices in eyre" (that is, on journey, or itinerant), who were endowed with all the author-

ity of the king himself. The itinerant justice traveled regularly to the county courts, investigating and punishing crimes. Upon his arrival, the justice would impanel a jury of at least twelve "good men" and inquire of them under oath what crimes they had heard about since his last visit and whom they suspected of guilt. (This sworn inquest is the direct ancestor of the modern grand jury.) Those indicted by the twelve "good men" were still tried by the ancient ordeals of fire and water. After the Church condemned these procedures in 1215, a small, or petty (*petite* in French), jury was used, as it is today, to judge the guilt or innocence of the alleged felon.

The itinerant justices did not forcibly interfere in civil disputes, but they did offer the services of the royal court in settling them. Barons receiving fiefs from the king had also been given the right to hold a court and judge the disputes of their own knights and dependents. Normally, therefore, litigants in a civil dispute appeared before a baronial court. As a result of Henry's reforms, a litigant could purchase a royal writ, which ordered the sheriff to bring the case under the scrutiny of the royal court presided over by the justice in eyre. Sworn inquest juries were composed of "good men" from the neighborhood who were likely to know the facts at issue and were able to judge the truth or falsity of claims. They were put on oath to tell the truth of the case. While Henry made no effort to suppress baronial courts, the royal courts left them with a shrinking role in English justice.

Common Law In time the justices built up a considerable body of decisions, which then served as precedents in similar cases. The result was the development of "common law"—common in that it applied to the entire kingdom and was thus distinct from the local customs. It differed from Roman law in that it represented not the edict of an emperor but the principles, based on precedents set in earlier cases, that were followed in deciding similar ones. Precedent cases mark the beginning of the common law tradition under which most of the English-speaking world continues to live.

Thomas Becket The judicial reforms of Henry II led him into a bitter conflict with the English Church, which maintained its own ecclesiastical courts. Henry did not want a whole group of his

▲ ELEANOR OF AQUITAINE EFFIGY
Eleanor of Aquitaine bears comparison with other forceful female rulers of European history, such as Elizabeth I of England. Eleanor was a worthy consort for Henry II, one of the most powerful and innovative rulers of the Middle Ages, and is buried next to him. The site, a splendid French abbey, lies within the territories that Eleanor had inherited and added to the English kingdom. The crown and book in the effigy on her tomb are perfect symbols of the intelligence and power that characterized her life.
Giraudon/Art Resource, NY

subjects, members of the clergy, to fall outside his judicial system. Furthermore, the Church courts required only prayers or pilgrimages from those who committed felonies, while the king's court required hanging and confiscation of property. In 1164 Henry claimed the right to retry clerics accused of crime in his royal courts. The archbishop of Canterbury, Thomas Becket, rejected this claim. He argued that both the Bible and canon law forbade what we now call "double jeopardy"—that is, a second trial and punishment for one crime.

Becket had been a personal friend of Henry and had served him ably and faithfully as Chancellor of the Exchequer, the chief official of the realm. Royal friendship and favor had brought him his election as archbishop of Canterbury in 1162. After becoming archbishop, Becket seems to have undergone a conversion that made him devoted to the Church. When Henry tried to force Becket to agree to a document, the Constitutions of Clarendon, outlining the king's view of the relations of the church to the crown, Becket fled to France. He was reconciled with Henry once more

in 1170, but a few months later he excommunicated the bishops who had supported the king. Henry, then in France, demanded in fateful rhetoric, whether no man would free him of this pestilential priest. Four of the king's knights took the words to heart, journeyed to England, found Becket in his cathedral, and cut him down before the high altar on December 29, 1170. By popular acclaim Becket was regarded as a martyr and a saint. Canterbury became his shrine and a popular pilgrimage site. Henry had no choice but to revoke the objectionable reforms and perform an arduous personal penance for his unwise words, including a beating.

A compromise was reached in which clerics suspected of crimes were tried first in the royal courts and, if convicted, surrendered their wealth to the king. They were then tried in ecclesiastical court, in which punishment was a penance rather than hanging.

At the death of Henry II in 1189, the English monarchy wielded exceptional authority, but neither in practice nor in theory was it clearly established within what limits, if any, royal powers

▲ This depiction of the murder of Thomas Becket in Canterbury in 1170 was completed within a few years of the event. That it should have appeared as a wall painting in the church of Sts. Giovanni and Paolo in Spoleto, Italy, hundreds of miles away from Canterbury, suggests the intensity of the European reaction to the assassination.
André Held

should operate, or how, if at all, the great men of the realm might participate in government.

Richard I Henry's son and successor was Richard I, the Lion-Hearted. Growing up in Eleanor's court in Aquitaine, Richard acquired all the virtues of a model knight—boldness, military skill, stately bearing, even a flair for composing troubadour lyrics. He spent little time administering his realm, preferring fighting to ruling. In 1191 and 1192 he was fighting in the Holy Land on the Third Crusade. He died in 1199 from a neglected wound received while besieging a castle in a minor war in southern France. Richard spent less than ten months in England, but the English government continued to function efficiently even in

the absence of its king—testimony to its fundamental strength.

John I Richard was succeeded by his younger brother John, who, rightly or wrongly, is considered a wicked king. His reign is largely a record of humiliations suffered at the hands of the pope, King Philip II of France, and his own barons.

Early in his reign he married Isabelle of Angoulême, who was already engaged to a vassal of King Philip II of France. Philip, upholding his feudal obligation to defend his vassal, used the incident as a pretext to seize the duchy of Normandy. John's wars to recapture Normandy were expensive. To pay for them, John abused the feudal contract by demanding payments rather than military service, marrying off heiresses to the highest bidder, selling off wardships, and even extorting money from his subjects.

In 1206 John defied Pope Innocent III by rejecting Stephen Langton as archbishop of Canterbury. Innocent retaliated and put England under interdict in 1208. An interdict meant that the English clergy were not to baptize babies, marry couples, or bury the dead in public ceremony. When the interdict did not sway John, Innocent threatened to encourage Philip to invade. In 1213 John accepted Stephen Langton as archbishop of Canterbury.

Magna Carta   Already angry with John's abuses of the feudal contract and taxation, his enraged barons turned on him after a humiliating defeat at the Battle of Bouvines in 1214. Encouraged by Stephen Langton, they took to arms, and in June 1215 at Runnymede the barons forced John to grant them the "Great Charter." Archbishop Langton probably inspired, if not largely composed, the Magna Carta (so called because it was a large piece of parchment). The Magna Carta resembled oaths that English kings since Henry I had taken upon their coronation; it obligated the king to respect certain rights of his subjects. But no previous royal charter of liberties equaled it in length, explicitness, and influence (see "Excerpts from the Magna Carta," p. 312).

The Magna Carta disappoints most modern readers. Unlike the American Declaration of Independence, it offers no grand generalizations about human dignity and rights. Its sixty-three clauses, arranged without apparent order, are largely concerned with technical problems of feudal law—rights of inheritance, feudal relief, wardship, and widow's rights. But it did establish, more clearly than any previous document, that the king ought not to disturb the estates of the realm—Church, barons, and all free subjects—in the peaceful exercise of their customary liberties. It thus guaranteed to the clergy the freedom to elect bishops and to make appeals to Rome; it protected the barons against arbitrary exactions of traditional feudal dues; and it confirmed for the men of London and other towns "all their liberties and free customs." To all freemen it promised access to justice and judgment by known procedures. Finally, the king could impose new taxes only with the common consent of the realm. While these concessions were certainly significant, the Magna Carta addressed the concerns of only the elite. The rights of the unfree classes, the serfs and villeins who constituted 80 percent of the population at the time, are hardly mentioned.

The Magna Carta marked a major step toward government by recognized procedures that could be changed only with the consent of the realm. Of course, the barons and the bishops never anticipated that subjects other than themselves might be called on to give consent, but this limitation in no way compromises the importance of the principle established. Future generations of English were to interpret the provisions of the Magna Carta in a much broader sense than its authors had intended. The document is important not only for what it said but also for what it allowed future generations to believe about the traditional relationship in England between authority and liberty.

John immediately renounced the Magna Carta as an oath sworn under duress, and the pope upheld this position. Fighting continued, but John died suddenly, leaving his son Henry, a nine-year-old boy, as heir. The barons reissued the Magna Carta and formed a council to rule in Henry's name.

◆ FRANCE

In France the problems of consolidation were greater than they were in England. Unlike the English kings, who controlled the whole country, the Capetian kings of France held as their direct demesne (land they inherited) only the area around Paris (the Ile-de-France). Powerful dukes and counts controlled large provinces and were only nominally vassals to the kings of France. Marriage alliances and conquests seemed at first to be the only solution to unifying the territory that theoretically constituted France. Gradually, however, the French kings also used law as a means of making inroads into their powerful vassals' territory.

Louis VII   The able advisor to Louis VI, Abbot Suger (also patron of the first Gothic church), arranged the marriage of Louis VII (r. 1137–1180) to Eleanor of Aquitaine, heiress to the extensive lands of the Duchy of Aquitaine. This was Eleanor's first marriage; she later married Henry

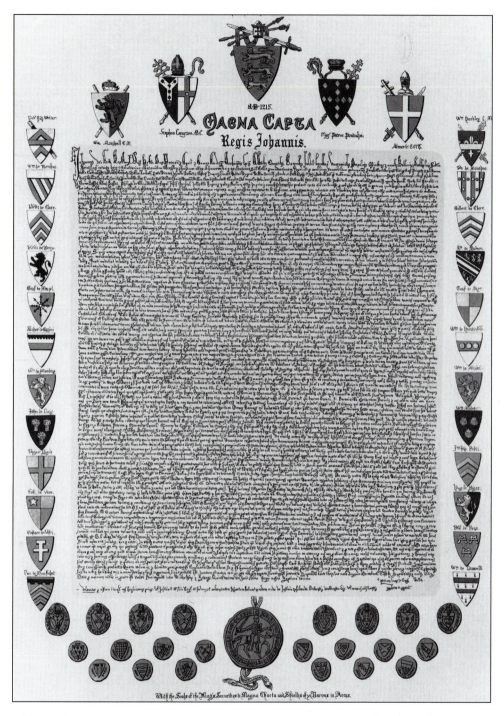

▲ MAGNA CARTA
Originally agreed to in 1215 by King John, the Magna Carta (or Great Charter) was intended to settle disputes over the rights and privileges of England's nobility. The document itself was issued in sealed copies and sent throughout England, but it was successively modified during the thirteenth century. This example, which is one of only four that have survived, dates from 1297, when the charter was confirmed in final form.
Corbis Bettmann

Excerpts from the "Magna Carta"

"John, by the grace of God, king of England, lord of Ireland, duke of Normandy and Aquitaine, and count of Anjou, to the archbishops, bishops, abbots, earls, barons, justiciars, foresters, sheriffs, stewards, servants, and to all his bailiffs and faithful subjects, greetings. Know that we, out of reverence for God and for the salvation of our soul and those of all our ancestors and heirs, for the honour of God and the exaltation of the holy church, and for the reform of our realm . . . :

"[6] Heirs may marry without disparagement; so nevertheless, that, before the marriage is contracted, it shall be announced to the relations by blood by the heir himself.

"[7] A widow, after the death of her husband, shall straightway, and without difficulty, have her marriage portion and her inheritance, nor shall she give anything in return for her dower, her marriage portion, or the inheritance which belonged to her. . . . And she may remain in the house of her husband, after his death, for forty days.

"[12] No scutage or aid shall be imposed in our kingdom unless by common counsel of our kingdom, except for ransoming our person, for making our eldest son a knight, and for once marrying our eldest daughter; and for these only a reasonable aid shall be levied. Be it done in like manner concerning aids from the city of London.

"[13] And the city of London shall have all its ancient liberties and free customs as well by land as by water. Furthermore, we will and grant that all other cities, boroughs, towns, and ports shall have all their liberties and free customs.

"[20] A free man shall not be amerced [fined] for a trivial offense except in accordance with the degree of the offense, and for a grave offense he shall be amerced in accordance with its gravity, yet saving his way of living; and a merchant in the same way, saving his stock-in-trade; and a villein shall be amerced in the same way, saving his means of livelihood—and none of the aforesaid amercements shall be imposed except by the oath of good men of the neighborhood.

"[21] Earls and barons shall not be amerced except by their peers, and only in accordance with the degree of the offense.

"[38] No bailiff shall in future put anyone to trial upon his own bare word, without reliable witnesses produced for this purpose.

"[39] No free man shall be arrested or imprisoned or disseised or outlawed or exiled or in any way victimized, neither will we attack him or send anyone to attack him, except by the lawful judgment of his peers or by the law of the land.

"[40] To no one will we sell, to no one will we refuse or delay right or justice.

"[52] If anyone has been disseised of or kept out of his lands, castles, franchises or his right by us without the legal judgment of his peers, we will immediately restore them to him: and if a dispute arises over this, then let it be decided by the judgment of the twenty-five barons who are mentioned below in the clause for securing the peace.

"[61] . . . the barons shall choose any twenty-five barons of the kingdom they wish, who must with all their might observe, hold and cause to be observed, the peace and liberties which we have granted and confirmed to them by this present charter of ours, so that if we, or our justiciar, or our bailiffs or any one of our servants offend in any way against anyone or transgress any of the articles of the peace or the security, and the offense be notified to four of the aforesaid twenty-five barons, those four barons shall come to us, or to our justiciar if we are out of the kingdom, and, laying the transgression before us, shall petition us to have that transgression corrected without delay. And if we do not correct the transgression . . . within forty days . . . , the aforesaid four barons shall refer that case to the rest of the twenty-five barons. And those twenty-five barons together with the community of the whole land shall distrain and distress us in every way they can . . . until, in their opinion, amends have been made; and when amends have been made, they shall obey us as they did before."

II of England. Her marriage to Louis more than doubled the lands under direct royal control, but the couple's incompatibility soon became clear. Louis had been raised for a career in the Church

and became king only when his older brother died. He retained a monkish character that clashed with Eleanor's upbringing in Aquitaine, where her grandfather had been one of the first to write troubadour poetry. Having failed to produce a male heir, Eleanor accompanied Louis on the Second Crusade hoping for better luck. She and her ladies dressed as Amazons and thoroughly enjoyed the jaunt. It was even rumored that she had an affair with her relative, Raymond of Antioch, while in the Holy Land. When the couple returned to France without a male heir, they agreed to have the Church annul their marriage on the grounds that they were too closely related. The dissolution of the marriage in 1152 meant that Eleanor resumed her duchy. In two months Henry II of England married her, although he was her junior by some ten years, and added the duchy of Aquitaine to his vast holdings in France (see map 9.3). Eleanor bore Henry four sons, two of whom (Richard and John) became kings of England.

Philip II Augustus   Louis VII's son by a later marriage, Philip II Augustus (r. 1180–1223), was not a great warrior, but he was an aggressive politician and an able administrator. Forced to go on the Third Crusade with Richard the Lion-Hearted and Frederick I Barbarossa, he left the battle to Richard and returned home to harass Richard's possessions in France. It was Philip's intervention on behalf of his vassal that permitted him to confiscate Normandy from John I (see map 9.3). The victory over King John at Bouvines confirmed England's loss of Normandy and brought new prestige to the Capetian throne.

Under Philip, royal influence began to penetrate to the south of France. In 1208 Pope Innocent III declared a crusade against the Albigensian heretics of the south (discussed later in this chapter), who enjoyed the protection of many powerful nobles. Philip's vassals flocked to the pope's call, overwhelmed the counts of Toulouse and other prominent nobles, and seized much of their lands. The defeat of the southern nobility left a vacuum of power that the king's authority soon filled.

Strengthening the Administration   In addition to increasing his lands, Philip strengthened the administration of his own properties, the royal demesne, although he still made no effort to interfere directly in the governments of the kingdom's fiefs. On the local level the representative of the king—the French counterpart of the English

Chronology
POLITICAL EVENTS

(d. 1106)	Henry VI of Germany
(1100–1135)	Henry I of England
(1108–1137)	Louis VI of France
(1137–1180)	Louis VII of France
(divorced 1152)	Eleanor of Aquitaine
(1154–1189)	Henry II of England
(married 1152)	Eleanor of Aquitaine
(1152–1190)	Frederick I Barbarossa
(1180–1223)	Philip II Augustus of France
(1189–1199)	Richard I of England
(1198–1216)	Pope Innocent III
(1199–1216)	John I of England
(1215)	Magna Carta
(1197–1250)	Frederick II Hohenstaufen of Sicily
(1227–1141)	Pope Gregory IX Inquisition
(1216–1172)	Henry III of England
(1226–1270)	Louis IX of France

sheriff—was the prévôt. About 1190, apparently in imitation of the English itinerant justices, Philip began to appoint a new official, the *bailli*, to oversee the work of the prévôt. The *bailli* supervised the collection of rents and taxes, the administration of justice, and all the king's interests within a certain prescribed circuit or area, but he never assumed the full range of functions and powers that the English justice in eyre had acquired. The baillinage system had some advantages, however, because the *bailli* was a paid official, increasingly university trained, and was moved from one place to another so that he could not build up local loyalties.

The central administration was also developing specialized bureaus, although less advanced than the English; the Chambre de Comptes, a special financial office, equivalent to the English Exchequer, gradually assumed responsibility for the royal finances.

SCOTLAND

WALES

ENGLAND

York ✦ Stamford Bridge 1066

DENMARK

Lübeck

POMERANIA

Bremen

FRISIA

Winchester
London

Canterbury

Bruges

Ghent

LOWER
LORRAINE

SAXONY

BRANDENBURG

MARCH OF
LUSATIA

POLAND

Hastings 1066 ✦

FLANDERS

Cologne

Aix-la-
Chapelle

THURINGIA

FRANCONIA

Bouvines 1214 ✦

Bayeux

Rouen

NORMANDY

Rennes

BRITTANY

MAINE

Paris

Reims

CHAMPAGNE

Trier

Mainz

Worms

Prague

BOHEMIA

MORAVIA

Nantes

ANJOU

Orléans

Troyes

UPPER
LORRAINE

Toul

Augsburg

Passau

AUSTRIA

TOURAINE

Dijon

Freiburg

SWABIA

POITOU

Poitiers

BURGUNDY

BAVARIA

Salzburg

Clermont

Cluny

Bordeaux

AQUITAINE

PÉRIGORD

AUVERGNE

KINGDOM
OF
BURGUNDY-
ARLES

LOMBARDY

Legnano 1176 ✦

Milan

HUNGARY

GASCONY

TOULOUSE

Pavia

Venice

NAVARRE

Toulouse

LANGUEDOC

Avignon

PROVENCE

Arles

Marseilles

Canossa

Bologna

REPUBLIC OF VENICE

ARAGON

Florence

Pisa

PATRIMONY
OF ST. PETER

Barcelona

TUSCANY

CASTILE

Rome

Naples

KINGDOM
OF THE
TWO SICILIES

French Royal Domain

987

987–1180

1180–1328

English holdings in France 1180

English holdings in France 1328

Holy Roman Empire ca. 1200

✦ Battle site

0   100   200 Miles

▲ **MAP 9.3** MEDIEVAL ENGLAND, FRANCE, AND GERMANY

◆ www.mhhe.com/chambers8ch9maps

◄ In this fourteenth-century manuscript illumination, St. Louis hears the pleas of his humble and defenseless subjects, chiefly women and a monk. Note the hanged felons in the left panel. The picture illustrates the abiding reputation for justice that St. Louis earned for the French monarchy.
New York Public Library

Philip Augustus' reign made the French monarchy the unquestioned master in the Ile-de-France, greatly enlarged the royal demesne, and began the process of extending royal justice into the feudal principalities.

St. Louis   The successor of Philip Augustus, Louis VIII, ruled for only three years (r. 1223–1226). At Louis' death in 1226 the throne passed to Louis IX, St. Louis (r. 1226–1270), one of the great figures of the thirteenth century. Even during his life, Louis was considered saintly. He attended at least two masses a day, was sternly abstemious in food and drink, often washed the feet of the poor and the wounds of lepers, and was scrupulously faithful to his wife, Margaret of Provence, who, like her husband, bore an aura of sanctity. His personal asceticism did not preclude a grand conception of royal authority. He added new pomp to court ceremonies and freely acted against the pope's wishes whenever the interests of the monarchy or his people seemed to require it.

Legal Reforms   In his own realm Louis made no attempt to extend the royal power at the expense of his nobles or to deprive them of their traditional powers and jurisdictions, but he did expect them to be good vassals. He forbade wars among them, arbitrated their disputes, and insisted that his ordinances be respected; he was the first king to legislate for the whole of France. Although Louis did not suppress the courts of the great nobles, he and his judges listened to appeals from their decisions, so that royal justice would be available to all his subjects. The king liked to sit in the open under a great oak at Vincennes near Paris to receive personally the petitions of the humble.

During Louis' reign, jurists began to clarify and codify the laws and customs of France. The most important of these compilations was the *Establishments of St. Louis*, drawn up before 1273. It contained, besides royal ordinances, the civil and feudal customs of several northern provinces and seems to have been intended for the guidance of judges and lawyers. It was not an authoritative code, but it and other compilations helped bring a new clarity and system to French law. Louis also confirmed the Parlement of Paris—a tribunal rather than a representative assembly like the English Parliament—as the highest court in France, a position it retained until 1789.

◆ THE IBERIAN KINGDOMS

The Christian *Reconquista* had achieved all but final victory by 1236, with only Granada still in Muslim hands. The principal challenge now was the consolidation of the earlier conquests under

▲ **Death of Louis IX**
Louis IX of France died of the plague in Tunis during his last Crusade. Attending his death bed in this manuscript illustration are his wife, Margaret of Provence, an unidentified bishop, and a mourner.
Master and Fellows of Corpus Christi College, Cambridge

Christian rule and the achievement of a stable governing order.

The three major Christian kingdoms that emerged from the Christian offensive were Portugal, Castile (including Leon), and Aragon (including Catalonia and Valencia), but they were not really united within their own territories. The Christian kings had purchased the support of both old and new subjects through generous concessions during the course of the *Reconquista*. Large communities of Jews and Muslims gained the right to live under their own laws and elect their own officials, and favored towns were granted special royal charters that permitted them to maintain their own court or forum. Barcelona and Valencia in the kingdom of Aragon and Burgos, Toledo, Valladolid, and Seville in the kingdom of Castile were virtually self-governing republics in the thirteenth century. Because women were scarce in the military society of the *Reconquista*, town laws gave them particular protection and property rights to encourage them to marry and have families. The military aristocracy, particularly in Castile, the largest of the Iberian kingdoms, held much of their lands not as fiefs but as properties in full, free title, which reinforced their independent spirit.

Strengthening the Monarchies   To hold all these elements together under a common government was a formidable task, but the kings also retained real advantages. The tradition of war against the Muslims gave kings a special prestige. And their rivals were too diverse and too eager to fight one another to be able to present a united challenge.

In order to impose a stronger, essentially feudal sovereignty over their subjects, the Iberian kings set about systematizing the laws and customs of their realms, thus clarifying both their own prerogatives and their subjects' obligations. Alfonso X of Castile (r. 1252–1284) issued an encyclopedia of legal institutions, meant to instruct lawyers and guide judges. This code, known as the *Siete Partidas* ("Seven Divisions"), was thoroughly imbued with the spirit of Roman law and presented the king as the source of all justice. The code did serve to educate the people to the high dignity of kingship, even if the kings could not enforce it. Even more than in England and France, feudal government in the Iberian kingdoms rested on a delicate compromise between royal authority and private privilege, and this apparently fragile system worked tolerably well.

Cortes Sooner than other Western monarchs, the Iberian kings recognized the practical value of securing the consent of their powerful subjects to major governmental decisions, particularly regarding taxes. By the end of the twelfth century the kings were frequently calling representative assemblies, called *Cortes*. Although they never achieved the constitutional position of the English Parliament because there were too many of them, the Cortes were the most powerful representative assemblies in Europe during the thirteenth century.

◆ GERMANY: THE HOLY ROMAN EMPIRE

For the German Empire, called the Holy Roman Empire in the late twelfth and early thirteenth centuries, the problems of unity as opposed to expansion remained unresolved. The lure of Italy and imperial aspirations diverted the attention of monarchs from unification of Germany. Meanwhile, the German dukes, unlike those of France, proceeded to establish independent authority. Unlike France with Paris or England with London, Germany did not have a capital city, nor did the German emperor have a unified demesne of his own. Furthermore, the German kingship remained elective for much of the Middle Ages, rather than being based on hereditary claim as was true in England and France.

Frederick I Barbarossa The ruler who came closest to building a lasting foundation for the German Empire was Frederick I (r. 1152–1190) of the House of Hohenstaufen. He was called *Barbarossa,* meaning "red beard." Large, handsome, gallant, and courageous, Frederick, like Charlemagne before him, gained a permanent place in the memories and myths of his people. He much resembles in his policies, if not quite in his achievements, the other great statesmen of the twelfth century— Henry II of England and Philip II of France. Frederick showed a broad eclecticism in his political philosophy. He claimed to be the special protector of the Church and therefore a holy figure. He called his empire the Holy Empire; the later title,

Holy Roman Empire, was used after 1254 and until Napoleon abolished this German Empire in 1806.

Frederick pursued three principal goals. First, he hoped to consolidate a strong imperial demesne consisting of Swabia, which he inherited; Burgundy, which he acquired by marriage; and Lombardy, which he hoped to subdue. These three contiguous territories would give him a central base of power that he could use for his second goal—to force the great German princes in the north and east to become his vassals. Finally, in Italy, he claimed, as successor of the Caesars, to enjoy the sovereignty that Roman law attributed to the emperors.

Italy and the Lombard League Frederick's Italian ambitions disturbed the popes and the town communes, which from about 1100 had become the chief powers in the northern half of the peninsula. Both feared that a strong emperor would cost them their independence. With active papal support, the northern Italian towns, led by Milan, formed a coalition known as the Lombard League that defeated the imperial forces at Legnano in 1176. The Battle of Legnano not only marked the failure of Frederick's efforts to establish full sovereignty over the Lombard cities but also was the first time in European history that an army of townsmen had bested the forces of an army under noble leadership. At the Peace of Constance in 1183, Frederick conceded to the towns almost full authority within their walls; the towns, in turn, recognized that their powers came from him, and they conceded to him sovereignty in the countryside. Frederick did not gain all that he had wished in Italy, but his position remained a strong one.

Germany Forced to turn his attention to Germany, Frederick made effective use of feudal custom to try his vassals, particularly Henry the Lion, who married a daughter of Henry II and Eleanor. Frederick summoned Henry in 1180 to face trial for refusing to fight in Italy. The court condemned Henry and confiscated his Saxon fief. With Henry humiliated and deprived of his lands, Frederick seemed to be the unchallenged master in Germany (see map 9.3).

Frederick now wanted to advance the empire's prestige in Europe and sought out a position of leadership in the Third Crusade. But the aged emperor **drowned** while trying to ford a small stream in Asia Minor, bringing to a pathetic end a crowded and brilliant career.

Henry VI (r. 1190–1197)   Barbarossa's son Henry VI married Constance, heiress to the Norman Kingdom of the Two Sicilies, so that their son would have a legal claim to southern Italy and to the German throne. The prospect of Italian unification under German auspices disturbed both the papacy and the free cities of Lombardy. The towns and the pope feared that the direct domination of the emperor would curtail their liberty. In his brief reign of seven years, however, Henry VI had little chance to unify Sicily, northern Italy, and Ger-

▼ FREDERICK II'S TREATISE ON FALCONRY
Frederick II was not only the dominant political leader of his age but also one of its most learned minds. He was an avid reader of classical texts and apparently used Aristotle's *Historia Animalium* as a guide in one of his favorite pursuits, a study of birds. Illustrated here is a page from his own copy of the treatise he wrote on falconry.
Città del Vaticano, Biblioteca Apostolica

many. He did come up with an unscrupulous way of raising money: by imprisoning Richard I on his way home from the Third Crusade and holding him for ransom.

Frederick II Hohenstaufen   Frederick II (r. 1212–1250), son of Henry and Constance, is one of the most fascinating personalities of the Middle Ages. A contemporary called him *stupor mundi* ("wonder of the world"). Later historians have hailed him as the first modern ruler, the prototype of the cold and calculating statesman. Frederick spoke six languages, loved learning, patronized poets and translators, founded a university, and, after a fashion, conducted scientific experiments. He also corrected Aristotle by writing on the margins of his works in several places, "It isn't so."

The pope crowned Frederick emperor in 1219 on the double promise that he would renounce his mother's inheritance of southern Italy and lead a crusade to Palestine. Frederick procrastinated on both agreements.

Fragmentation of Germany   Frederick's policy toward Germany was to take as much profit as he could and devote his attention to Italy. To stabilize the political situation in Germany, he established on the empire's eastern frontier a military-religious order, the Teutonic Knights, who eventually created the Prussian state; he recognized Bohemia as a hereditary kingdom and Lübeck as a free imperial city; and he issued the earliest charter of liberties to the Swiss cantons. (Later in the century, in 1291, the cantons entered into a "Perpetual Compact," or alliance, which marks the formal beginnings of the Swiss Confederation.) His most important policy, however, was to confer upon the German ecclesiastical princes and the lay nobles virtual sovereignty within their own territories. The emperor retained only the right to set the foreign policy of the empire, make war and peace, and adjudicate disputes between princes or subjects of different principalities. All other powers of government passed to the princes, and no later emperor could regain what Frederick gave away.

Attempt to Control Italy   In Italy Frederick pursued a much different policy. For the government of the Kingdom of the Two Sicilies, he relied on a trained lay bureaucracy. He rigorously centralized

▲ Emperor Frederick II, in the ship showing the imperial eagles, watches his soldiers assaulting prelates on their way to a council summoned by Pope Gregory IX in 1241. This contemporary illustration of the emperor's sacrilegious behavior, taken from a manuscript, is a good example of the war of propaganda by which both pope and emperor sought to win public sympathy.
The Granger Collection, New York

his administration, suppressed local privileges, imposed a universal tax in money on his subjects, recruited his army from all classes and from Muslims as well as Christians, and issued a constitution that, in the spirit of Roman law, interpreted all jurisdiction as stemming from the emperor. He encouraged trade and stabilized the currency, bringing prosperity to the port cities.

Frederick had to face the increasingly bitter opposition of the popes and the free cities of the north, because it was apparent he planned to pursue the old policies toward them. Pope Gregory IX excommunicated him in 1227 because of his failure to lead an Eastern crusade. Frederick then departed on the crusade, but he preferred to negotiate rather than fight and made a treaty with the Muslims that guaranteed unarmed Christian pilgrims access to Jerusalem. The more militant among the Western Christians believed that this treaty was dishonorable. Frederick returned to Italy in 1229 and came to terms with Pope Gregory a year later.

The Lombard towns remained fearful of his designs and finally formed a league against him. He defeated them in 1237, but his success once more awakened Gregory's fears of encirclement. Gregory again excommunicated Frederick. Both sides struggled to win the European public sympathy, but the tide of history began to turn against Frederick. To break the power of the Lombard towns, he unsuccessfully besieged Parma in 1248. In 1250 death cut short his efforts to unify Italy under imperial auspices.

Sicily and Germany after 1250 Frederick II had reinforced a political fragmentation in Germany that had become ever more pronounced since the eleventh century. Wishing to keep the fragmentation, Germany elected a weak emperor who would not interfere with the independent princes.

In southern Italy Frederick II had completed the constitutional reorganization that the Norman kings, his forebears, had begun. With Frederick dead, the pope saw an opportunity to remove

Sicily from German hands. With the pope's cooperation, in 1262 the brother of Louis IX, Charles of Anjou, defeated Manfred, Frederick's son, and won Sicily. Later, the native population rebelled in an incident known as the Sicilian Vespers. On Easter Monday 1282, while the church bells were ringing to call people for vespers, a massive insurrection occurred and the French were massacred. The forces loyal to Manfred's daughter had contacted her husband, the king of Aragon, and his fleet was already close at hand. The king of Aragon ousted the Angevins, but the continued war over the claims of Aragon and Anjou left the Kingdom of the Two Sicilies impoverished.

III. The Church

Since the time of the Gregorian reform of the eleventh century, the papacy had sought to build in Europe a unified Christian commonwealth, one based on faith and on obedience to the pope. In the early thirteenth century the Church came close to achieving this grand design, but it still had to face powerful challenges to both Christian unity and its own deficiencies in leadership. At the same time, the continued involvement of the papacy in political affairs, the moral laxity of the clergy, and the wealth of bishops, abbots, and popes offended the laity.

◆ THE GROWTH OF HERESY

The spread of heresy (adherence to religious views contrary to church dogma) in the eleventh and twelfth centuries can be traced to both discontent with the clergy and to new intellectual and spiritual demands on the part of the laity. The expansion of Europe meant that the population was more mobile and exposed to new ideas. Pilgrimage, crusade, and trade brought people into contact with the Greek church, with Islam, and with Eastern heretical groups. The movement into new territories, the growth of towns, the appearance of new trades and industries—all created strong psychological tensions, which often found an outlet in heretical movements. The Church's position was that the popes had the true interpretation of Christianity since their power derived from Peter through the Doctrine of the Petrine Succession (see chapter 6). The Church's charge

was to save all Christian souls; those who became heretics were, in the Church's view, condemned to damnation. Heretics must be returned to the doctrines of the Church.

Appeal of Heresies   Corruption in the Church played a role in the spread of heresy. Satirists poked fun at the money needed to get a case tried in ecclesiastical courts. Nobles envied the property and power of the Church; to them, heresy offered a justification for seizing the wealth of a corrupt Church for themselves.

Among the urban poor, heresy became a form of social protest against elite government. It held potential for rich townsmen, too, inasmuch as traditional Christianity had been highly suspicious of wealth, particularly when earned in the marketplace, and gave the rich merchant little assurance of reaching heaven.

Heresy had a particular appeal to women. Many women could not marry because of the large dowry demanded and could not enter a religious order because this also required a monetary contribution. The Church would not allow women to preach, to enter universities, or to have an active role in pastoral care. Church law upheld the legal subordination of women to men. Heretical groups welcomed women, teaching them to read the Scriptures and offering a spiritual equality that the established Church did not.

This was an age of spiritual and intellectual tension. Some laypersons wanted a more mystical and emotional reward from religion, and those with an education wanted a better educated clergy. Both wanted the Bible translated into vernacular languages so that they could read the word of God for themselves. The clergy resisted, maintaining that the laity would draw false conclusions from the Bible and that only trained readers should interpret it for the laity.

Waldensians   Around 1170 a rich merchant of Lyons, Peter Waldo, adopted a life of absolute poverty and began preaching. He soon attracted followers, who came to be known as "the poor men of Lyons," or Waldensians. The Waldensians attacked the moral laxness of the clergy and denounced the sacraments they administered. Women in the Waldensian movement could preach on a par with men. The group was declared heretical by the Lateran Council of 1215,

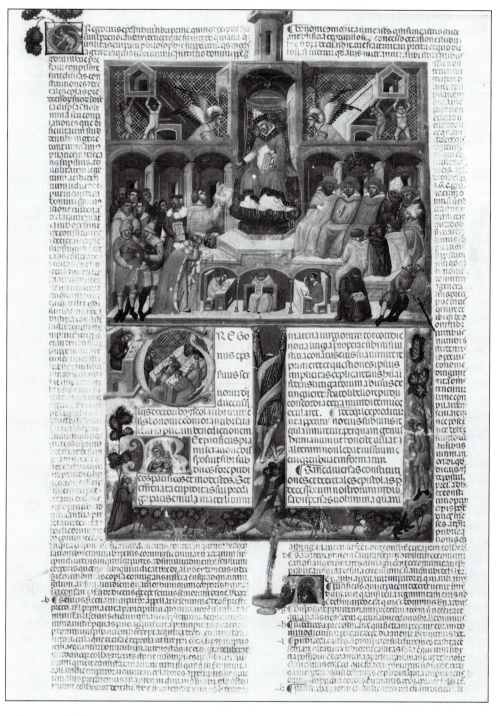

▲ **GREGORY IX DECRETALS**
One of the principal accomplishments of Pope Gregory IX was his sponsorship of an effort
to bring together and update the basic decisions and rulings of the Church. The resulting
collection is known as the decretals of Gregory IX, and it became the main source of canon
law. In this miniature from a fourteenth-century manuscript of the decretals, Gregory sits at
the center holding the book and surrounded by monks.
The Pierpont Morgan Library / Art Resource, NY

but the Church never succeeded in suppressing the movement.

Albigensians or Cathari   Far more powerful in their own day, though not destined to survive the Middle Ages, were the Cathari (Greek *katharos*, "pure"), or Albigensians, named for the town of Albi in Languedoc. The Albigensians' religious beliefs in purification of the body of material things developed from Manicheanism, an early dualist sect. The Albigensians, like the Manicheans, believed that two principles, or deities, a god of light and a god of darkness, were fighting for supremacy in the universe. They identified the god of darkness with the Old Testament and the creation of the material world, and the god of light with the New Testament and spiritual salvation. The good person must help the god of light vanquish the evil god of darkness, who had created and ruled the material world.

The true Albigensians led lives of rigorous asceticism. They abstained from sexual intercourse, since procreation replenished the earth, the domain of the god of darkness. Marriage they regarded as hypocrisy, and intercourse within it worse than any other sexual sin. They abstained from meat, since it was sexually reproduced. Because a sect that preached against marriage and procreation risked bringing about its own extinction, the Albigensians reached a practical compromise: Those who abided by these stringent regulations, both women and men, were the "Perfects" (they formed the priesthood); those who did not live by this stern code were the believers. Women who became Perfects had a higher sacerdotal status than did an abbess.

The Albigensians, like the Waldensians, denied all value to the sacraments and priesthood with the established Church. A person's affiliation to the sect rested on the agreement to accept the *consolamentum* before death. The Perfect came to the death bed and performed a laying on of hands as a spiritual baptism. The person then spent the last few days before death fasting to preserve the spiritual state for salvation. Many otherwise orthodox Christians found spiritual reassurance from the *consolamentum*, admired the Perfects, and appreciated the Albigensians' willingness to preach in the vernacular. The Albigensians developed a strong organization, with councils and a hierarchy of Perfects that resembled that of bishops.

◆ THE SUPPRESSION OF HERESY

The Church believed that the souls of Albigensians would be condemned to hell and that it was the responsibility of the Church, in its role as shepherd to its flock, to reclaim the Albigensians for the faith.

St. Dominic and the Mendicants   A priest from Castile named Dominic began to preach among the Albigensians of Languedoc in about 1205. Dominic insisted that his followers—whose mission was to preach—live in poverty and support themselves by begging; they thus constituted a *mendicant*, or begging, order. Mendicant orders were known as friars rather than monks, because they were to live with the laity rather than in the seclusion of the monastery and did not follow the Benedictine Rule. Dominic's instruction to his followers was: "The world henceforth is your home. . . . Go you therefore into the whole world and teach all nations."

The new Order of Preachers grew with amazing rapidity; the bishop of Toulouse approved the order in Toulouse in 1215 and papal approval followed shortly afterward. To prepare its members for their work, the Dominican Order stressed education. Their preachers were all university trained and many became masters at the universities. They became the intellectual arm of the medieval Church, counting among the order Albertus Magnus, Thomas Aquinas, and many other important religious thinkers of the thirteenth century. Dominicans responded to the demands of educated laity for intellectually stimulating sermons and to the needs of the Church for missionaries to the Turks and Mongols in the East.

Crusade against Albigensians   Reconversion through preaching, persuasion, and example remained a slow and uncertain process. While a bishop had the right to try a suspected heretic before his own court, a heretic who was protected by important men in the community was virtually immune to prosecution. Since the nobility of Toulouse, including the count of Toulouse, was sympathetic to the Albigensians, protection was easy to find.

By the early thirteenth century, the Church began to suppress the Albigensians by force. Pope Innocent III, of whom more will be said later, favored peaceful solutions to heresy until his legate, who had excommunicated the count of Toulouse

THE TECHNIQUES OF THE INQUISITION

◆

To combat heresy the Inquisition tried above all to get suspects to confess, repent, and thus save their souls. Bernard Gui, inquisitor at Toulouse in southern France between 1307 and 1323, left a vivid account of the psychological techniques used in interrogations.

"When a heretic is first brought up for examination, he assumes a confident air, as though secure in his innocence. I ask him why he has been brought before me. He replies, smiling and courteous, 'Sir, I would be glad to learn the cause from you.'

"I [Inquisitor]. You are accused as a heretic, and that you believe and teach otherwise than Holy Church believes.

"A [Answer]. (Raising his eyes to heaven, with an air of the greatest faith) Lord, thou knowest that I am innocent of this, and that I have never held any faith other than that of true Christianity. . . .

"I. I know your tricks. What the members of your sect believe you hold to be that which a Christian should believe. But we waste time in this fencing. Say simply, Do you believe in one God the Father, and the Son, and the Holy Ghost?

"A. I believe.

"I. Do you believe in Christ born of the Virgin, suffered, risen, and ascended to heaven?

"A. (Briskly) I believe.

"I. Do you believe the bread and wine in the mass performed by the priests to be changed into the body and blood of Christ by divine virtue?

"A. Ought I not to believe this?

"I. I don't ask if you ought to believe, but if you do believe.

"A. I believe whatever you and other good doctors order me to believe. . . .

"I. Will you then swear that you have never learned anything contrary to the faith which we hold to be true?

"A. (Growing pale) If I ought to swear, I will willingly swear.

"I. I don't ask you whether you ought, but whether you will swear.

"A. If you order me to swear, I will swear.

"I. I don't force you to swear, because as you believe oaths to be unlawful, you will transfer the sin to me who forced you; but if you will swear, I will hear it.

"A. Why should I swear if you do not order me to?

"I. So that you may remove the suspicion of being a heretic.

"A. Sir, I do not know how unless you teach me.

"I. If I had to swear, I would raise my hand and spread my fingers and say, 'So help me God, I have never learned heresy or believed what is contrary to the true faith.'

"Then trembling as if he cannot repeat the form, he will stumble along as though speaking for himself or for another, so that there is not an absolute form of oath, and yet he may be thought to have sworn. . . . Or he converts the oath into a form of prayer. . . . [And when further hard pressed he will appeal, saying] 'Sir, if I have done amiss in aught, I will willingly bear the penance, only help me to avoid the infamy of which I am accused.' But a vigorous inquisitor might not allow himself to be worked upon in this way, but proceed firmly until he makes these people confess their error, or at least publicly abjure heresy, so that if they are subsequently found to have sworn falsely, he can, without further hearing, abandon them to the secular arm."

H. C. Lea, *A History of the Inquisition of the Middle Ages*, Vol. 1 (1887), pp. 411–414.

for tolerating heresy, was murdered. Innocent proclaimed a crusade (1208–1229) against the Albigensians and the nobles who supported them. Knights from the north of France responded with zeal, but more out of greed for plunder than concern for orthodoxy. They defeated the nobles of Toulouse, but the problem of suppressing heresy remained.

Beginnings of Inquisition In 1231 Pope Gregory IX instituted a special papal court to investigate

and punish heresy. This was the famous papal *Inquisition*, which was to play a large and unhappy role in European history for the next several centuries. Like the English justices in eyre, the inquisitors were itinerant justices who visited the towns within their circuit at regular intervals. Strangers to the locale, they were not subject to pressures from the important men of the region. They accepted secret denunciations and, to protect the accusers, would not reveal their names to those denounced; at times they used evidence that was not even revealed to the accused. The accused had no right of counsel and could be tortured. The suspected heretics were, in fact, considered guilty before even being summoned to the Inquisition. They could confess and repent, with the likely consequence of a heavy penance and usually the confiscation of their property. But they had little chance to prove their innocence. As an ecclesiastical court, the Inquisition was forbidden to shed blood, but here too its procedures were novel: It delivered relapsed or unrepentant heretics to the secular authority with full knowledge that they would be put to death (see "The Techniques of the Inquisition," p. 323).

The weaknesses of the inquisitorial process soon became apparent. Secret procedures protected incompetent and even demented judges, who shocked and disgusted their contemporaries with their savage zeal. In addition, the Inquisition could function only where it had the close cooperation of the secular authority. It was never established in areas (for example, England) in which strong kings considered themselves fully competent to control heresy. (Kings characteristically equated religious and civil rebellion and considered heresy to be identical with treason.)

The number of heretics who were executed is not known exactly, but it was probably several hundred. Fines, confiscation of property, and imprisonment were the usual punishments for all but the most obstinate heretics. The Inquisition had a terrible effect upon the medieval Church because it associated the papacy with persecution and bloodshed.

◆ THE FRANCISCANS

Crusade and Inquisition could not alone preserve the unity of the medieval Church. A spiritual regeneration was needed; the Church had to reach lay people, especially those living in towns, and provide them with a spiritual message they could comprehend. The mendicant orders, or friars, met the needs of the laity. Dominicans spoke to those who wanted more intellectual content, while the Franciscans, the order founded by St. Francis of Assisi, responded to those who wanted a more spiritual, mystical approach.

Francis of Assisi Francis (1182?–1226) is probably the greatest saint of the Middle Ages and possibly the most sensitive poet of religious emotion. He succeeded in developing a style of piety that was both faithful to orthodoxy and abounding in new mystical insights. Since most of Francis' life is screened by legend, it is nearly impossible to reconstruct the exact course of his spiritual development. His father was a wealthy merchant in Assisi, but Francis as a young man fancied the life of a knight and the pleasures of courtly love and troubadour poetry. He tried the rowdy amusements of the city and the life of a knight. A severe illness after one of his nightlong parties led to a conversion. He turned to religion and adopted a life of poverty.

▼ **This fresco from the basilica of St. Francis at Assisi, traditionally attributed to the Florentine painter Giotto, shows the saint preaching to the birds. He congratulates them on their bright plumage and bids them sing in praise of God. The implication is that if people too recognize God's providence over them, they will respond with gratitude and joy.** Scala/Art Resource, NY

Franciscan Order Disciples began to gather almost at once around the "little poor man" of Assisi. In 1215 Francis obtained papal approval for a new religious order. The papacy had some hesitation, since Francis' order resembled Peter Waldo's Poor Men of Lyons, but Francis recognized papal authority and the Church now realized the need for this sort of spiritual mission. His Order of Friars Minor (Lesser Brothers) grew with extraordinary rapidity: within ten years it included some five thousand members and spread from Europe to Palestine; before the end of the century it was the largest order in the Church. Although the problems of administering a huge order did not command Francis' deepest interests, he did write a brief rule for the Friars in which he stressed the importance of poverty and simplicity.

The success of the Friars Minor was an authentic triumph for the Church. Giving themselves to poverty and preaching, the Friars Minor came to include not only a second order of nuns but a third order of lay people. Francis and his followers opened orthodox religion to delight in the natural world, to mystical and emotional experience, and to joy, which all people, they believed, including the ascetic and the pious, should be seeking.

◆ PAPAL GOVERNMENT

The papacy recognized that in a period of social change and religious crisis they would have to clean their own house as well as address the problems of heresy. The pope whose reign best illustrates the aspirations and the problems of the medieval Church is Innocent III (r. 1198–1216).

Innocent III Innocent was the product of the twelfth-century papacy. He had a liberal arts degree from Paris and studied canon law at Bologna. Entering the papal government, he became a cardinal at age twenty-nine. As pope he sought with vigor and with remarkable, if always partial, success to achieve three major goals: the eradication of heresy, the hegemony of the papacy over Europe, and the clarification of Christian discipline and belief.

Within Europe, heresy was the greatest threat to Christian unity, and though he ordered the crusade against the Albigensians, Innocent primarily looked to the new mendicant orders, the Domini-

cans and Franciscans, to counter the appeal of the heretics.

The pope sought to exert his leadership over the princes of Europe in all spiritually significant affairs. Some of his efforts to bend kings to his will have already been mentioned, such as his struggle with King John to install Stephen Langton as archbishop of Canterbury. He also excommunicated Philip II of France for discarding his queen in order to cohabit with another woman. Innocent had occasion to reprimand the kings of Aragon, Portugal, Poland, and Norway. No prior pope had scrutinized princely behavior with so keen an eye.

The Fourth Lateran Council Innocent realized that problems and ambiguities within the Church were partly responsible for the problems it faced with heresy and dissent. In 1215 he summoned some 1,500 prelates to attend the Fourth Lateran Council. The Council identified the sacraments as exactly seven and reaffirmed that they are essential to salvation; imposed an obligation of yearly confession and communion on the faithful; and defined the dogma of transubstantiation, according to which the priest, in uttering the words of consecration at Mass, transforms the substance of bread and wine into the body and blood of Christ. Transubstantiation unambiguously affirmed the Mass as miracle and thus conferred a unique power on the Catholic priesthood. The Council also pronounced on a wide variety of disciplinary matters: the qualifications for the priesthood, the nature of priestly education, the character of monastic life, the veneration of relics, and other devotional exercises.

The Council's actions had implications for the broader population of Europe. Since it forbade priests to officiate at ordeals and trials by battle, these judicial tools were no longer valid for determining guilt or innocence of a person accused of crime. England adapted by extending the jury system to a trial, or petty jury, and France established panels of magistrates to examine the evidence in imitation of the Inquisition.

With marriage established as a sacrament, it came under greater Church scrutiny. Previously, people had made private contracts of marriage. Now these private contracts were to be read at the church door and bans announced the three Sundays preceding marriage to be sure the parties had no prior marriages. The new rules also insisted that the couples must freely consent to the marriage. Historians have argued about the extent to which free consent made it easier for women to refuse undesirable, arranged marriages. Where property and titles were involved, free consent seems to have had little effect during the Middle Ages, but it did influence practice later. Clandestine marriages were still common and still binding on the couples.

SUMMARY

◆

The achievements in architecture and art, in intellectual life, in vernacular culture, in the improved standard of living, and in government have led historians to give the period of the twelfth and early thirteenth century the title of "The High Middle Ages." The growing consolidation of power by monarchs in France, England, and Germany, in addition to the strengthening of the papacy produced a demand for more educated men. Universities trained both theologians and those who would staff the growing bureaucracies of monarchies and the papacy. Urban governments developed along lines that are still familiar, and they too began to hire university-trained lawyers and notaries. The continued agricultural prosperity permitted the building of fine cathedrals throughout Europe. The Romanesque style that was typical of the Cluniac reform movement was replaced in the twelfth century with the Gothic style. The Gothic arches and the increased emphasis on windows were much in tune with the expansive feeling of the period. The Church, threatened by heresies, licensed two new orders, the Dominicans and Franciscans, who responded to the needs of the laity. The next hundred years, however, began to see an unraveling of the success of the papacy, while monarchies and ideas of governing lay society by a rule of law continued to develop.

QUESTIONS FOR FURTHER THOUGHT

◆

1. To what extent are contemporary universities similar to and different from medieval universities?

2. How did the Magna Carta reflect both continuity and change?

3. As you look at the buildings on your campus or in your town, what influences can you see of the Romanesque and Gothic architectural styles?

RECOMMENDED READING

◆

Sources

Aquinas, Thomas. *Basic Writings*. Anton C. Pegis (ed.). 1945.

Anselm of Canterbury. *Basic Writings: Proslogium, Monologium, Gaunilon's On Behalf of the Fool, Cur Deus Homo.* S. W. Deane (tr.). 1962.

*Brown, Raphael (ed. and tr.). *The Little Flowers of St. Francis*. 1971. Legends collected in the early fourteenth century exemplifying the style of Franciscan piety.

*Chrétien de Troyes. *Yvain, The Knight of the Lion.* Burton Raffel (tr.). 1987. Recent translation of a great French romance.

*De Villehardouin, Geoffrey, and Jean De Joinville. *Chronicles of the Crusades*. Margaret R. Shaw (tr.). 1963. The Fourth Crusade to Constantinople and the crusades of Louis IX.

*Frisch, Teresa G. *Gothic Art, 1140–1450: Sources and Documents.* 1987.

Goldin, Frederick. *Lyrics of the Troubadours and Trouvères: Original Texts, with Translations.* 1973. Troubadour works in both the original and translated versions.

*Marie de France. *The Lais of Marie de France.* Glyn S. Burgess and Keith Busby (trs.). 1986.

The Letters of Abelard and Héloïse. Betty Radice (tr.). 1974. A translation of their correspondence along with a short history of their lives.

*Otto of Freising. *The Deeds of Frederick Barbarossa.* Charles C. Mierow (tr.). 1953. Primary source regarding Frederick Barbarossa's life.

Paris, Matthew. *Chronicles: Monastic Life in the Thirteenth Century.* Richard Vaughan (ed.). 1984. Excerpts from an English chronicler with a superb perspective on medieval monastic mentalities.

*Peters, Edward (ed. and tr.). *Heresy and Authority in Medieval Europe.* 1980. Contains sources regarding medieval heresies and the response.

Studies

*Abulafia, David. *Frederick II: A Medieval Emperor.* 1988.

Barlow, Frank. *Thomas Becket.* 1986. Balanced biography of the martyred archbishop.

*Boswell, John. *Christianity, Social Tolerance, and Homosexuality in Western Europe from the Beginning of the Christian Era to the Fourteenth Century.* 1980. A learned survey of the treatment of homosexuals in medieval Europe.

Bouchard, Constance Brittain. *"Strong of Body, Brave and Noble": Chivalry and Society in Medieval France.* Cornell, 1998. Readable narrative of aristocracy aimed at general readers.

Calkins, Robert G. *Medieval Architecture in Western Europe: From A.D. 300 to 1500.* Oxford, 1998. Accompanied by an IBM-PC compatible CD-ROM. Calkins provides explanations of the transition from Romanesque buildings to Gothic.

Clanchy, M. T. *Abelard: A Medieval Life.* Blackwell, 1997. Abelard is placed within a medieval context with an emphasis on Héloïse's influence on him.

*Dillard, Heath. *Women of the Reconquest: Women in Castilian Town Society, 1100–1300.* 1984. Status of women on the Spanish frontier based on legal sources.

*Duby, Georges. *The Age of the Cathedrals: Art and Society, 980–1420.* Survey of the period, stressing the importance of artistic expression.

Fletcher, Richard. *Moorish Spain.* 1992. A concise survey of the Iberian Peninsula from the Muslim invasion to the fall of Granada.

*Furman, Horst. *Germany in the High Middle Ages, c. 1050–1200.* 1986. Readable survey of period.

Hallam, Elizabeth M. *Capetian France, 987–1328.* 1980. Survey of the period.

*Haskins, Charles H. *The Renaissance of the Twelfth Century.* 1927. A classic study.

———. *The Rise of Universities.* 1957.

*Holt, J. C. *Magna Carta.* 1965. Gives useful guidance to an extensive literature.

Lambert, Malcolm. *Medieval Heresy: Popular Movements from the Gregorian Reform to the Reformation.* 1992. Valuable summary of the heretical movements and the Church's response.

*LeRoy Ladurie, Emmanuel. *Montaillou: The Promised Land of Error.* Barbara Bray (tr.). 1978. Analysis of the inquisition records of one town's experience with Albigensianism. An engaging book.

*Moore, R. I. *The Formation of a Persecuting Society: Power and Deviance in Western Europe, 950–1250.* 1987. Examines the reasons for persecution in the Middle Ages.

*Morris, Colin. *The Discovery of the Individual, 1050–1200.* 1987. Looks not only at the intellectual movements of the twelfth century but also at the concept of the individual.

Munz, Peter. *Frederick Barbarossa: A Study in Medieval Politics.* 1969. A political biography.

*O'Callaghan, Joseph F. *A History of Medieval Spain.* 1975. Surveys medieval Spain.

*Panofsky, Erwin. *Gothic Architecture and Scholasticism.* 1951. Surveys the connections between Gothic architecture and Scholastic theory.

*Peters, Edward M. *Inquisition.* 1988. The Inquisition in fact and imagination.

*Sayers, Jane. *Innocent III: Leader of Europe 1198–1216.* 1994. Readable account of Innocent and his historical context.

*Southern, R. W. *The Making of the Middle Ages.* 1993. A standard book on medieval thought.

*Turner, Ralph V. *King John.* 1994. A political biography.

Wakefield, Walter L. *Heresy, Crusade, and Inquisition in Southern France, 1100–1250.* 1974. Narrative of events concerning the Albigensian crusade.

*Warren, William L. *Henry II.* 1973. Biography of this English king.

*Available in paperback.

▲ THE ENGLISH PARLIAMENT

A meeting of the English Parliament before Edward I. To the left are the bishops and to the right are the barons. The judges are seated on wool sacks between them. The wool sacks are an indication of the importance of England's export trade in wool. To further enhance Edward's position, his chief vassals — the king of Scotland and the Prince of Wales — sit on either side of him. The two archbishops are on the extreme right and left.

The Urban Economy and the Consolidation of States

*T*he period from roughly 1250 to the arrival of the Black Death in Europe in 1348 was one of urban development and intensified trade. New instruments of trade added a sophistication to business endeavors, and the demand for goods produced in cities brought prosperity to urban centers. Towns rebelled against the control of local lords and bishops, favoring instead self-government and charters of independence from the monarchs of Europe. Urban life entered into every aspect of medieval Europe: Major cathedrals were located in cities, middle-class urban dwellers made careers in government and represented the interests of their cities with the monarchs, urban bankers played an important role in international politics.

Monarchs in Europe continued to consolidate control over their subjects, but they began to do so in consultation with representatives of their subjects in such bodies as the Parliament in England, the Estates General in France, and the Cortes in Spain. But while Western monarchies flourished, Eastern Europe and the Byzantine Empire went through another grim period of invasions, this time from the Mongols of central Asia. Ultimately the Byzantine Empire revived, and Moscow became the center of a newly reconstituted state of Russia.

With their power on the rise, monarchs' conflicts with the papacy intensified. The papacy continued its policy of trying to control the actions of the monarchs, but increasingly it did not have the resources to compete with secular states. Corruption of the Church's fiscal policies resulted in the laity's increased criticism of the papacy. But the laity, particularly laywomen, found spiritual comfort and even distinction in society through individual spiritual journeys. The greatest synthesis of medieval culture, Dante's *Divine Comedy,* is itself a poem of personal spiritual exploration.

CHAPTER 10. THE URBAN ECONOMY AND THE CONSOLIDATION OF STATES							
	Social Structure	Body Politic	Changes in the Organization of Production and in the Impact of Technology	Evolution of Family and Changing Gender Roles	War	Religion	Cultural Expression
I. Cities, Trade, and Commerce	███	███	███	███			███
II. Monarchies and Representative Institutions	███	███			███	███	
III. Government in the East	███	███				███	
IV. Papacy and the Church				███		███	███
V. Learning and Literature							███

I. Cities, Trade, and Commerce

Urban development continued with the prosperity and population growth of the twelfth and thirteenth centuries. As urban centers became more populous and engaged in more sophisticated artisanal trades and long-distance import-export business, they increasingly wanted independence to govern their own affairs. People who flocked into urban centers were a free population who did not fit easily into the old social divisions: peasants, or those who tilled the soil; nobility, or those who fought; and clergy, or those who prayed. The urban population also worked with their hands, but many made money in banking and trade. Increasingly the urban population felt that nobles and bishops, who were their overlords, were a hindrance to economic prosperity. Townsmen needed laws of commerce and contract and freedom from taxes. Thus, urban dwellers encouraged the revival of Roman law, including the *Codex Justinianus*, and sent their sons to Bologna for at least a year or two of legal studies.

Major economic changes occurred in cities as large-scale production, extensive trade, complex commercial and banking institutions, and the amassing of great fortunes became commonplace features of cities. These urban centers show much of the spirit of modern business enterprises.

◆ URBAN GOVERNMENT

Town Independence   The route to independent town government could be peaceful or violent. Some lords were eager to establish free towns in order to bring in wealth. In St. Omer's charter, dating from 1127, the count of Flanders granted the town freedom from taxes and the right of self-government. London won a similar charter from Richard I when its citizens agreed to pay a substantial portion of his ransom from imprisonment in Germany. In France, Philip II Augustus found that granting royal charters to towns was a way of securing their loyalty to the crown rather than to the counts and dukes, thus extending royal authority into the provinces.

At other times towns resorted to violence to free themselves of bishops and feudal lords. One of the most famous revolts was in Laon, where the bishop was found hiding in a wine cask. The finder "lifting his battle ax brutally dashed out the brains of that sacred, though sinner's head." The mob cut off his legs and one man, seeing the bishop's ring on the dead man, cut the finger off and took the ring. Milan and the Lombard towns managed to free themselves of the local bishops, but they continually fought the German emperors to preserve their freedom.

Communes, Oligarchs, and Consuls   One instrument by which medieval townsmen sought to

▲ YPRES GUILD HALL, CA. 1260–1380
The Flemish towns were renowned for their textiles, and the economic importance of this manufacture is reflected by the size of the thirteenth-century cloth hall at Ypres (destroyed in World War I). Rows of arched windows and a central tower puncture the massive square edifice that functioned as the headquarters of the guild as well as the place in which goods were marketed.
© Collection Roger-Viollet/Getty Images

govern themselves was the *commune,* a permanent association created by the oath of its members and under the authority of several elected officials. Communes first appeared in the eleventh century in northern Italy and Flanders, the two most heavily urbanized areas of Europe.

Few towns kept a communal form of government. For the most part, the wealthier elements, the long-distance merchants and knights, took control of town offices. Although revolts continued, the type of government that gradually evolved in urban centers was the oligarchy, in which the elite men of the city controlled the city government and its offices.

In Milan in 1097 the city set up a government of consuls, drawn from the city elite. Their function was both political and judicial. In order to control Milan after defeating it, Frederick I placed a city manager in Milan. The new official was an outsider with no local ties and so proved to be more even-handed in justice than the consuls had

been. The institution became popular in northern Italy, and university-trained men entered the profession.

In northern Europe the model of a mayor and councilors or aldermen developed. The city wards elected them from the wealthier members of the city elite. They administered both the city and the judicial system.

Urban Population Everywhere the European urban population remained small compared to the rural population. In 1377 only 10 percent of the people in England lived in urban centers with a population greater than 3,200—a typical percentage for most of northern Europe—whereas in Tuscany and Flanders about a quarter of the population lived in urban centers.

The largest medieval city was Paris, with a population of perhaps 210,000 in 1328. Venice probably had 120,000 inhabitants in 1338. Few cities surpassed 40,000.

Urban Regulation Growing towns needed considerable organization to regulate their concentrated populations. The total area of London within its walls was only a square mile; therefore its population of 60,000 was densely settled, with people living in rented rooms in houses three to four stories high. The crowding in cities led to settlement outside the city walls in what became known as suburbs, from the Latin *sub urbs,* or "below or under the city."

One of the first concerns of mayors and their councils was the protection of the city. The walls of European cities protected them against possible external attack; the gates could be closed at night, keeping out undesirable criminal elements. Cities developed militias or at the least had guards to watch the gates and patrol the streets. To ensure order, many cities had curfews, rules about carrying weapons after dark, and ordinances on noise and nuisance (foul smells, obstruction of streets, and throwing slops out the window).

Sanitary measures included street cleaning, provision for public latrines, wells and conduits to provide clean water, and segregation of the most noisome businesses, such as butchering, to places that were not upwind of the city.

Civic pride motivated a number of urban amenities. Guilds and citizens contributed money to performances of plays, processions, and tournaments. Hospitals were a frequent charity, as were foundling homes, free grammar schools, gardens, and chapels. In addition to a cathedral or large church, cities built a guildhall (town hall) where city officials held urban courts, private citizens met to transact business, and archives preserved records of both official business and private contracts.

Moral Regulation Urban governments regulated the honesty and morality of their population. They maintained standard weights and measures and required those trading to use them. Prostitution was also regulated. While neither the Church nor urban governments condemned prostitution (they felt that it was better for men to seek sex with a prostitute than in adultery), they did not want its moral pollution in every part of the city. Some cities, such as London, limited the places that prostitutes could solicit. Other cities, such as Florence and Montpellier, set up official houses of prostitution, usually bathhouses, in which the city could regulate the trade and the health of the women practicing prostitution. People who used false weights, sold putrid food, or pimped or practiced prostitution outside the prescribed areas were fined and could be expelled from the cities for continuing offenses.

◆ THE ORGANIZATION OF CRAFTS

With the exception of mines, construction sites, and such enterprises as the arsenal in Venice, most work was performed in the home or in small shops. Increased efficiency was achieved through finely dividing the process of production and through developing highly specialized skills. A merchant or manufacturer acquired raw materials, gave (or "put") it out in sequence to specialized artisans, and then sold the finished product. Usually called the putting-out system, this method of production remained characteristic of the Western economy until the Industrial Revolution of the late eighteenth century.

Wool Cloth Production The making of woolen cloth, the largest industry of the medieval town, well illustrates the complex character of thirteenth-century manufacturing. The raw wool—often coming from England, Spain, or North Africa—was first prepared by sorters, beaters, and washers. The cleaned and graded wool was then carded, or combed.

The next task, the spinning, was usually done by women who worked in their own homes with a distaff, a small stick to hold the wool, and a spindle, a weight to spin and twist the strands into thread. The spinning wheel, apparently first invented in India, adopted by the Arabs, and brought to Italy in the late thirteenth century, added speed and better quality to thread making. Since antiquity, women had been the primary weavers in society, but the invention of a larger, more expensive loom meant that the investment was beyond that of ordinary households. The weavers established guilds, purchased looms for their shops, and trained men to do the heavy work of manipulating the looms and large cloths they produced.

▲ ITALIAN GRAIN MERCHANTS
This manuscript illustration shows Florentine grain merchants engaged in their trade and keeping their records in their shops. The manuscript itself noted the prices for grain between 1320 and 1335 that were set in the Or San Michele, the grain warehouse and market hall in Florence.
Scala/Art Resource, NY

Weavers worked on large looms in shops and wove the thread into broadcloths that were 30 yards in length. The cloth was then fulled—that is, washed and worked with special earths that caused the wool to mat. This was arduous work and was often done at a water-driven fulling mill. The giant cloth was then stretched on a frame to dry properly and shrink evenly. Next, the dry cloth was rubbed with teasels to raise the nap, and the nap was then carefully cut. Several times repeated, this last operation gave the cloth a smooth, almost silky finish, but it was extremely delicate work; one slip of the scissors could ruin the cloth and the large investment it represented.

At various stages in this process the wool could be dyed—whether as unspun wool, thread, or woven cloth. Medieval people loved bright colors, and dyers used a great variety of animal, vegetable, and mineral dyes and special earths, such as alum, to fix the colors.

The medieval woolen industry came to employ a large, diversified labor force, which worked materials brought from all corners of the known world. Capital and labor were sharply divided; a few great entrepreneurs controlled huge masses of capital. In Florence in about 1300, wool shops numbered between two hundred and three hundred; they produced between 80,000 and 100,000 big broadcloths with a value surpassing 1.2 million gold florins. More than thirty thousand persons earned their living from this industry.

People took their surnames from their occupations. In England, *Weber* denoted a weaver, *Fuller* the one who fulled the cloth, *Shearer* the one who cut the nap, and *Dyer* and *Tailor* the obvious.[1]

◆ THE GUILDS

To defend and promote their interests, the merchants and master artisans formed associations known as *guilds.* (In chapter 9 we saw that university masters and students had also formed guilds.) Merchant guilds appeared in European cities in about 1000. From the twelfth century both master artisans (weavers, bakers, shoemakers) and merchants in special trades (dealers in wool,

---

[1]Surnames gradually became fixed in the late Middle Ages, and many reflect occupations. *Brewster,* for instance, indicates a female brewer. Trade names as surnames were common, but so too were place names of towns or places in towns, such as *Townsend.* Physical characteristics also became surnames, such as *Squint* and *Blond.*

▲ CLOTH MARKET IN BOLOGNA
**The manufacture and marketing of textiles was one
of the main sources of wealth for the cities of
northern Italy. This scene, from a manuscript dated
1411, gives us a sense of what the cloth market in
Bologna must have been like as merchants examined,
bought, and sold various fabrics.**
Alinari/Art Resource, NY

production and examined the finished product to
maintain quality. To this end they restricted the
number of working hours and the number of employees that could be hired by any single master.
Guild members who produced bad quality goods
were fined and sometimes even publicly humiliated: A vintner who sold bad wine had to stand at
the public stocks, drink a gallon of his worst, and
have the rest poured over his head. The consuls
enforced the statutes, adjudicated disputes among
the members, administered the properties of the
guild, and supervised its expenditures. To protect
the members from external competition, cities required all those who practiced a trade or craft
within their walls to belong to the appropriate
guild. Guilds reserved the right to examine and
admit members (see "The Craft of Weavers of Silk
Kerchiefs at Paris," p. 335).

Guilds provided their members with a strong
sense of identity and fellowship. Often they aided
members who lost goods through fire or flood
and supported the widows and educated the or-
phaned children of deceased members. Banquets,
public processions, and religious ceremonies enriched the social life of the membership. Many
guilds were among the principal donors to charities and city beautification.

Apprenticeship One of the chief features of the
guilds was the apprenticeship system. Guilds
stipulated what the apprentices had to be taught
and what proof of skill they had to present to be
admitted into the guild, how long they had to
work and learn in the master's shop, and what the
master had to give them by way of lodging, food,
and pocket money. To enter an apprenticeship,
candidates or their family had to pay the master
and the guild an entrance fee; the training was,
therefore, not available to everyone. If, after finishing their training, they were too poor to open
their own shop, they worked as paid laborers, or
journeymen, in the shop of an established master.
Apprentices with family capital or loans from
their master could eventually become masters in a
guild and have a shop.

For boys, the age of entry into apprenticeship
ranged from about fourteen to eighteen years of
age. By the late Middle Ages masters required
apprentices to be able to read, write, and cast

spices, or silk) had organized their own independent guilds to ensure the quality of the goods they
produced and sold and to maintain a monopoly
over their craft or trade. A large industrial town
such as Florence had more than fifty professional
guilds.

Guild Functions Once a year the guild members
met to elect permanent officials, called consuls
or wardens. The consuls regulated methods of

THE CRAFT OF WEAVERS OF SILK KERCHIEFS AT PARIS
◆

In about 1270 Etienne de Goileau compiled a Book of Crafts recording guild regulations for Parisian guilds. Although the regulations here are for a woman's guild, the regulations were similar to those for other craft guilds.

"1. Any woman who wishes to weave silk kerchiefs in Paris may do so provided she knows how to practice the craft well and truly, according to the following usage and customs.

"2. First: it is ordered that no journeywoman of the craft may work on a feast day which the commune of the city celebrates and which is commanded by the Church.

"3. No one may work at night, because one cannot do as good work at night as during the day.

"4. It is ordered that no one may have more than one apprentice in the craft who is not related to her and one who is a relative; and she may not take an apprentice for fewer than seven years with a fee of twenty sous, or eight years without a fee. And if it happens that any mistress sells her apprentice for her need, she may not take another before her term is up; and if it happens that the apprentice buys her own freedom, the mistress may not take another

apprentice before the term of the one who bought her freedom is up.

"5. It is ordered that no mistress or journeywoman of the craft may buy silk from Jews, from spinsters or from any others, but only from the proper merchants.

"6. No woman may work on the premises of a man or woman if she does not know the craft.

"7. Whoever infringes any of these regulations, she must pay six sous as a fine for each time she is found at fault. . . .

"10. The aforesaid craft has three good women and true who will oversee the craft on behalf of the king, sworn and pledged at Chastelet, who will make known all the infringements against the craft, whenever they discover them."

From Emilie Amt, *Women's Lives in Medieval Europe: A Sourcebook* (Routledge, 1993), pp. 195–196.

---

accounts before becoming apprentices. Apprentices lived in the master's home, a relationship that could be quasi-familial or terribly abusive. The term of apprenticeship varied from seven to ten or more years; young men were in their twenties before they completed their training.

For girls, apprenticeship served different purposes, and their contracts were often shorter and not formally drawn up. Some girls entered into apprenticeships that would lead to independent careers, usually in dressmaking, embroidery, or silk working. Paris, for instance, had five guilds composed exclusively or predominantly of women. Many of the girls, however, learned a craft, such as gold thread making, that could be a useful supplement to their husbands and fathers in their labors. A young woman who had learned a trade would be a desirable marriage partner. Many widows continued in their own name the trade of their deceased husbands. Other widows remarried, bringing their skills and capital to establish another household.

◆ COMMERCIAL INSTITUTIONS

The growth of trade and manufacturing stimulated the development of sophisticated commercial institutions, though the pace of transactions and economic exchange was slow by our standards. The quickest a person or a letter could travel on land was between twenty and thirty miles per day: To get to Bruges by sea from Genoa took thirty days; from Venice, forty days.

Banks Since each monarch, independent city, bishop, and lord minted their own coinage, specialists were needed to assay coins for their precious metal content. Florence in 1252 began issuing gold florins—the first successful gold coinage in the West since ancient times. England maintained a stable silver currency, in contrast to Philip IV of France, who debased French currency so often that his subjects called him "the counterfeiter." Banks (from the Old French *banc*, or bench) set up at the great European trade fairs in St.

▲ COLLECTING SILKWORMS AND PREPARING SILK
One of the new industries that appeared in Europe in the fourteenth century was the raising of silkworms. Since the spinning of silk was a craft usually associated with women, this scene, from a fifteenth-century manuscript, shows a woman gathering silk cocoons from the mulberry bushes on which the worms lived, and from those cocoons the silk threads were unwound.
By Permission of The British Library, London. Ms. Royal. 16GV, Fol. 54v

Denis, Champagne, St. Ives, and elsewhere to assay money for a fee. Gradually bankers offered more sophisticated services. By the late 1300s "book transfers" had become commonplace; that is, a depositor could pay a debt without using coin by ordering the bank to transfer credit from his own account to his creditor's. At first the

depositor had to give the order orally, but by 1400 it was commonly written, making it an immediate ancestor of the modern check.

Loans and Usury   The Church condemned the practice of usury, which at the time meant any interest or profit on a loan, however tiny. In the Church's view, the only honest way to gain money was in exchange for work. Peasants and artisans worked with their hands, clergy prayed, and the nobility protected and governed society. Money could not make money, which is how the Church perceived the activity of bankers and merchants.

Because usury was prohibited, Christian merchants developed a variety of instruments of credit that disguised their profit. Most important for commercial purposes was the bill of exchange, in essence a loan, but one that required repayment at a specified time in another place with a higher valued currency. Thus, a Flemish merchant might borrow 100 pounds in Ghent and agree to repay the loan three months later in local money at a Champagne fair. He then bought goods in Ghent, sold them in Champagne, and repaid the bill in the highly valued florins. The rate of exchange thus concealed a substantial profit for the investor,

▼ EARLY BANKERS
This illustration from a printed Italian handbook, which gives instructions to merchants and is dated ca. 1496, shows the interior of a bank, or accounting house.
New York Public Library

who technically earned it for changing money, not for making the loan.

Partnerships Business was risky, especially that which relied on sea trade, because a boat and its cargo could sink. Partnerships and business associations were an important hedge against disaster. At Venice, Genoa, and Pisa, overseas ventures were most often financed through temporary partnerships, in which an investor gave a sum of money to a merchant traveling abroad in return for a share (usually three-quarters) of the eventual profits; the investor bore the entire loss if the ship sank or the venture failed.

In the inland Italian towns a more permanent kind of partnership developed, known as the *compagnia* (literally, "bread together," a sharing of bread). These earliest companies seem to have been partnerships among brothers. By the thirteenth century such companies commonly included as partners persons who were not blood relatives but who could contribute capital and services, and they also accepted deposits from nonpartners in return for fixed yearly payments of interest that were called "gifts," lest they be considered usurious.

These companies performed a wide variety of functions and grew in size. They traded in any product that promised a profit, wrote bills of exchange, and fulfilled other banking services. From the late twelfth century, they served the Roman curia as papal bankers. They were also drawn into the risky business of extending loans to princes for wars. In 1338 the Bardi and Peruzzi companies loaned a total of 1,500,000 florins to England; in 1342 the English king defaulted, leaving both companies bankrupt.

Medici Bank Merchant houses in the late fourteenth and fifteenth centuries were considerably smaller than those of the thirteenth century, but they were more flexible. The Medici bank of Florence, which functioned from 1397 until 1498, for example, was not a single monolithic structure; rather, it rested on separate partnerships, which established branches at Florence, Venice, Rome, Avignon, Bruges, and London. Central control and unified management were ensured by having the senior partners—members of the Medici family—

in all the contracts; but the branches had autonomy, and most important, the collapse of one did not threaten others. This system of interlocked partnerships resembled a modern holding company.

Jewish Lenders Jewish bankers, who were not under Church restrictions on usury, usually handled loans at high interest rates or rates above market value. Nobles going to war or paying a dowry for their daughters or financing the knighting of their sons mortgaged portions of their fiefs to Jews in return for loans. Since these loans were consumer rather than business loans and the nobles could not hope to raise the money to repay them, they lost the land to Jewish money lenders. Western European laws forbid Jews from actually having title to these lands, and the Jews sold the lands to other Christians at a profit. Some minor nobility overextended themselves on these loans and were ruined.

Accounting and Insurance Although double-entry bookkeeping was known in the ancient world, it was not widely practiced in the West until the 1300s. In single-entry bookkeeping, only the debts owed were recorded, so that a person did not know whether the year represented a profit or loss until all debts and receipts were tallied at the end of the year. Double-entry bookkeeping recorded both output in terms of goods and services and the profits that these outputs earned or lost. Thus, an individual, company, or government knew where it stood immediately with each transaction and any arithmetical mistakes were corrected with each entry.

Maritime insurance decreased the risk of losing everything if a ship went down. As early as 1318 insurance appeared in major Italian ports; a broker bought the ship and cargo at the port of embarkation and agreed to sell them back at a higher price once the ship reached its destination. If the ship sank, it was legally the broker's and he assumed the loss. By 1400 maritime insurance had become a regular item of the shipping business, and it was to play a major role in the opening of the Atlantic.

Insurance for land transport developed in the 1400s but was never common. The first life insurance contracts appeared in fifteenth-century Italy and were limited to particular periods (the duration of a voyage) or particular persons (a wife during pregnancy).

◆ SEA TRAFFIC

Ships Before about 1325 there was still no regular sea traffic between northern and southern Europe by way of the Atlantic, but it grew rapidly thereafter. New, bigger ships increased profits because they carried more cargo with relatively smaller crews. Large ships were safer at sea, they could sail in uncertain weather when smaller vessels had to stay in port, they could remain at sea longer, and they did not have to sail close to the coastline in order to replenish their supplies.

The larger vessels required more sophisticated means of steering and navigation. Before 1300, ships were turned by trailing an oar over the side. This method provided poor control. Sometime during the fourteenth century the stern rudder was developed, which enabled a captain to tack effectively against the wind and control the ship closely when entering or leaving ports. Voyages became quicker and safer, and the costs of maritime transport declined.

Navigational Instruments Ocean navigation also required a reliable means for estimating course and position, and here notable progress had been made in the late thirteenth century. Scholars at the court of King Alfonso X of Castile compiled the Alfonsine Tables, which showed with unprecedented accuracy the position and movements of the heavenly bodies. Using such tables, captains could take the elevation of the sun or stars with an astrolabe and calculate a ship's latitude, or position on a north-south coordinate. (They could not tell their longitude, or position on an east-west coordinate, until they could carry accurate clocks that could compare their time with that of a basic reference meridian, such as Greenwich in England. Until the 1700s, when the first accurate clocks immune to a ship's swaying were developed, navigators who sailed across the Atlantic could not tell how far they had traveled.)

The compass, whose origin is unclear, was common on Mediterranean ships by the thirteenth century. By 1300 Mediterranean navigators had remarkably accurate maps and port descrip-

▲ **VIEW OF VENICE**
This elaborate depiction of Venice in a fourteenth-century manuscript shows the buying and selling that was characteristic of the citizens of this commercial and maritime center. Particularly notable at the upper left are the four bronze horses that the Venetians brought back to the city after the capture and looting of Constantinople in 1204 during the Fourth Crusade. The horses were placed on the facade of the cathedral of St. Mark's, and they have remained there ever since.
The Bodleian Library, University of Oxford. MS. BODL. 264. fol., 218r.

tions that minutely described harbors, coastlines, and hazards. All these technical developments gave European mariners a mastery of Atlantic coastal waters and helped prepare the way for the voyages of discovery in the fifteenth century.

◆ URBAN LIFE

Life in an urban environment was quite different from life in a village or a castle. Housing could be palatial, as evidenced by the surviving grand houses of Venice and Florence, but most people lived in cramped and overcrowded quarters. Without space to cook or relax, many people bought their food from street vendors (the fast food of the Middle Ages) or in taverns. Because so many people crowded into urban centers, cities

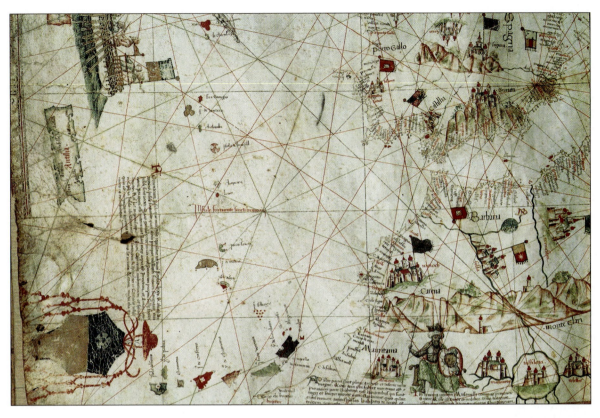

▲ AN EARLY MAP OF THE WESTERN MEDITERRANEAN
**Cartography benefited as sea voyages multiplied, as Europeans gained increased knowledge of the world, and
as they improved their skill in illustration. This map by the Italian cartographer Giovanni Benincasa
describes in great detail the coasts of Portugal, Spain, and North Africa.**
Scala/Art Resource, NY

were dirty and their populations prone to disease.
Medieval and early modern urban populations
did not replace themselves, but had to be augmented with immigration from the countryside.
Thus, cities had to assimilate fresh groups of
young people who came from the hinterland to be
servants or apprentices.

Marital and Household Customs Cities were
populous, but urban households tended to be
small and unstable. The average household size in
Florence in 1427 was only 3.8 persons, and in
some other cities it was even smaller. The low
numbers reflected the numerous deaths in a time
of plagues, but marital customs also had an effect.
Urban males who practiced crafts or were merchants were generally older than their brides. Because these men went through apprenticeships

and started a business to accumulate capital, they
postponed marriage. When they married, they
tended to marry younger women: Florentine
women were, on the average, less than eighteen
years old when they married for the first time;
women in London were more likely to be in their
early twenties. Many young people, both men
and women, came to the cities as servants and returned to their rural homes when they had
enough money to marry. These young people did
not form marriages in the urban centers at all.

Marriage customs varied in European cities. In
northern Europe the marriage contract included
dowry (the gift of the wife to the husband at marriage) and dower (a portion of the husband's
property set aside for the widow's life use). Since
women tended to outlive their husbands, they
usually collected their dowers. Custom varied

from town to town and from rural village to village, but widows usually had a third to half of their former husband's property for their lifetime. Widows were attractive marriage partners because the new husband could use the property as long as he returned it to the heirs when his wife died. Since widows frequently had family agricultural lands or businesses as well as young children, they preferred to remarry so that their new husbands could take over the farm or the trade.

▼ Woman Selling Poultry

Women worked at many trades during the Middle Ages. They contributed significantly to luxury crafts such as silk spinning and weaving, but they were also a major presence in the marketplace, selling such items as bread, beer, and poultry.
Bibliothèque Nationale de France, Paris

In Italy the dower had been abolished, and the dowry took on an increased importance in the formation of marriage. Florentine husbands typically tried to discourage their spouses from remarrying because widows, once remarried, might neglect the offspring of earlier unions and take their dowries to a new family. Thus, the wills of Florentine husbands often gave their widows special concessions that would be lost on remarriage: use of the family home, the right to serve as guardians over their children, sometimes a pension. In 1427 more than one-half of Florence's female population over forty were widows.

Urban wives had considerable influence within their families. Merchants relied on their wives to run both the household and business in their absence. Artisans' wives helped with their craft. Some wives had occupations or businesses that they could do along with running the house and rearing children. Silk weaving, running an inn or tavern, selling prepared foods, dressmaking, and other such occupations added considerably to family incomes or could support a single woman who chose not to marry.

II. Monarchies and the Development of Representative Institutions

Monarchs in England and France in the late thirteenth century tried to concentrate more power and control over their subjects. The continual warfare between the two countries, however, was very expensive, and the kings could not finance these wars without their subjects' financial and moral support. In trying to raise money to achieve their goals, monarchs enlisted the cooperation of the nobles, knights, and urban dwellers through representative institutions. In England, after the Magna Carta, these representatives often saw their role as a check on the monarchy. In France the monarch saw the representative institutions as bodies he could manipulate to achieve his own ends. The spread of royal justice and monarchical power meant increased bureaucracy. Middle-class, university-trained lawyers became justices and filled royal administrative posts.

▲ **Map 10.1 Europe, ca. 1250**
◆ www.mhhe.com/chambers8ch10maps

◆ ENGLAND AND THE DEVELOPMENT OF PARLIAMENT

The death of John I so soon after the signing of the Magna Carta and the long minority of his son, Henry III, increased the power of the nobles and the free population of England and their demand for a role in government. In the late thirteenth century, their protests resulted in the development of Parliament. The kings of the fourteenth century had such heavy expenditures for warfare in Wales, Scotland, and France that they continued to rely on Parliament to provide taxes to support their wars.

Origins of Parliament Henry III (r. 1216–1272) had an uneasy relationship with his barons from the beginning. During his minority, the barons

forced him to reissue the Magna Carta and appointed a regent who was to act on his behalf in consultation with a select council of barons.

Even after his majority in 1227, Henry III could only raise taxes through a grant from the Great Council of the barons and clergy. The meetings of the Great Council came to be called *parliaments.* (The word means "conversation" and, derivatively, an assembly in which discussion occurs.) Henry continued his father's policies of trying to regain Normandy. His wars and diplomatic efforts were expensive and unsuccessful, leading the barons to revolt against him under the leadership of Simon de Montfort (1208–1265). Simon de Montfort was the son of a French nobleman who came to England to pursue a claim to his English grandmother's estate. Henry befriended him, and de Montfort married Eleanor, Henry's sister. Like the other barons, however, de Montfort found Henry's ineptitude and expenditures too great. In 1258 the barons took control of the government, but dissensions within their own ranks rendered them unable to administer the realm. Henry regained power, but the barons under the leadership of de Montfort defeated him in 1264 at the battle of Lewes.

Because of continued divisions within the baronial ranks, Simon de Montfort sought to enlarge his power base by calling on the other constituents who had been at the signing of the Magna Carta, the knights and townsmen. In 1265 he summoned a parliament that included two knights elected from every shire and two townsmen from every town as well as the more powerful nobles, bishops, and abbots. Simon did not call the enlarged Great Council or a parliament to advise him, but rather sought to secure the loyalty of the countryside and the towns for his policies. The representatives were to go back to their shires and towns and inform the population of the baronial policies. De Montfort was slain in battle in 1265, but kings continued to call parliaments. In 1295, Henry III's son and successor, Edward I (r. 1272–1307), called the "Model Parliament," in which the two knights of the shire and two representatives from the towns became the customary practice.

Two Houses of Parliament Historians cannot assign an exact date for the division of Parliament into separate houses: the House of Lords included the tenants-in-chief (the immediate vassals of the king, the upper-rank nobility), bishops, and the most powerful abbots, while the House of Commons was composed of two knights from each shire and two representatives of the towns. The meetings were officially called "Parliaments." Two unique features of the English Parliament helped enhance the influence of Commons. First, the knights and lower-ranked nobility sat with the burgesses and learned to act together in their mutual interests. Second, though the bishops continued to sit in the House of Lords, they gradually became less interested in using Parliament as a vehicle for political representation. The bishops preferred to hold their own convocations to discuss Church affairs and to approve grants of money to

the king. The functions of the House of Lords were thus reduced, a fact that benefited the House of Commons.

Representation Parliament's role in levying taxes led to the development of a true system of representation. Feudal custom, the Magna Carta, and prudence had required that the English king seek the consent of his subjects for new taxes. He could not ask all freeholders of the realm individually. He might seek the consent of the separate shires and the towns, but this process was slow and awkward. Edward I ingeniously simplified the procedure of consent. Through special writs, he ordered the shires and the towns to elect representatives and to grant them "full power" to allow him to tax. These representatives, gathered in Parliament, thus had authority to consent to taxes that would be applicable to members of their shire and town. Paradoxically, the unique powers of the English king laid the basis for the eventual, unique powers of Parliament.

Parliament as a Judicial Court As the supreme feudal council, Parliament was also England's highest court (an honor the House of Lords retains today). The members attending its sessions would carry petitions or appeals from decisions made in lower courts. At the shire level, a sheriff might have been subject to local intimidation, but Parliament, as a countrywide body, would not be. By welcoming petitions, the king thus made his justice better known and respected throughout the realm. As with the U.S. Supreme Court, the decisions of Parliament determined the future policies of all English courts. The decisions were thus nearly the equivalent of legislation, and from them there was no appeal.

Edward I Henry III's son Edward I (r. 1272–1307) took over governing the realm even before the death of his father. Edward was the sort of king that the English nobility respected. He was a bold fighter, a crusader, and a success in wars. His interest in effective administration left a strong mark on English law and institutions. In 1284 he defeated the Welsh, killed their king, and later gave their land as an appanage (a province intended to provide "bread," or support) to his eldest son. (Since 1301 the heir presumptive to the English throne has borne the title Prince of Wales.) He also pursued a war with Scotland in an effort to control the entire island. His victory was short lived; Scotland regained independence under his son Edward II. He pursued a costly diplomatic war with France, which led to a breach with the Church and the growth of importance of Parliament.

Legal Reforms The powers and procedures of the royal government received a still clearer definition under Edward I. Edward produced no systematic codification of English law, like Justinian, but he sought to correct, codify, and enlarge the common law in certain critical areas and to give the system a new flexibility. He issued the first *Statutes of the Realm,* thereby setting a precedent for changing law only by legislation rather than by administrative decision. Edward's statutes required the barons to show by what warrant, or royal license, they exercised jurisdiction in their own courts, marking an important step in the decline of baronial justice. While he did not eliminate their courts, Edward kept the courts from growing and changing. They became increasingly obsolete. His laws limited Church courts as well. Religious houses could not acquire more land without royal permission, nor could they send money to Rome. The statutes were especially important in determining the property law of England, regulating inheritance, and defining the rights of lords, vassals, and the king when land changed hands through inheritance or purchase. Edward laid the foundations upon which the English (and eventually American) law of real estate rested for centuries. In enacting these statutes and in governing the kingdom, Edward also placed a new emphasis on securing the consent of his subjects through Parliament.

At Edward's death in 1307 the English constitution had acquired certain distinctive features. The constitution was not contained in a single written document, but was defined by both custom and statute law. The king was the chief of the state, but it was recognized that the nobility and the representatives from the shires and towns should have some participation in the decision-making processes, especially regarding taxes. The

extraordinary continuity of these arrangements over centuries to come is testimony to the sound construction that the medieval English kings, lords, and commoners gave to their government.

◆ FRANCE AND THE CONSOLIDATION OF RULE

In France as well as England, representative institutions became a tool in the aid of royal government. As the French kings extended their power over the various provinces, meetings of representatives of their free subjects became valuable venues in which to announce policies. The turbulent struggles with England and with the papacy dominated Capetian policy in the late thirteenth and fourteenth centuries.

Philip IV Louis IX's successors preserved the strength, but not the serenity, of his reign. His grandson Philip IV, the Fair (r. 1285–1314), is perhaps the most enigmatic of the medieval French kings; neither contemporaries nor later historians have agreed on his abilities. To some, Philip has seemed capable and cunning; to others, phlegmatic and uninterested, content to leave the business of government almost entirely to his ministers. If Philip lacked the personal ability to rule, he at least had the capacity to select strong ministers as his principal advisers. They were usually laymen trained in Roman law and possessing a high opinion of royal authority. They considered the king to be not merely a feudal monarch who ruled in agreement with the magnates of his realm but rather an "emperor in his own land" whose authority was free from all restrictions (the root sense of an absolute monarch) and subject to no higher power on earth.

The greatest obstacle to the advance of Philip's power was Edward I of England, master of the extensive fief of Aquitaine. Philip's resolve to drive England from the continent resulted in intermittent wars from 1294 to 1302. The woolen cloth weavers of the French county of Flanders relied on English wool. When Philip tried to block the importation of English wool into Flanders in order to hurt the English economy, the Flemish towns revolted against him. Philip's military campaign against them ended when the

Chronology

POLITICAL EVENTS

1198–1250	Frederick II of Germany and Sicily
r. 1226–1270	Louis IX of France
1216–1272	Henry III of England
r. 1264–1265	Baronial wars of Simon de Montfort
r. 1272–1307	Edward I of England
r. 1273–1291	Rudolf of Habsburg, Germany
r. 1261–1282	Michael VIII Palaeologus, Byzantine Empire
1259–1294	Mongols
r. 1285–1314	Philip IV of France
1291	Origin of Swiss Confederation
r. 1294–1303	Boniface VIII
r. 1305–1314	Pope Clement V
1346–1378	Beginning of Avignon papacy
	Charles IV
	Luxemburg of Germany
1356	Golden Bull

Flemish towns' militias defeated him at Courtrai in 1302.

These costly wars had placed a heavy burden on the royal finances. Philip pursued a number of unscrupulous tactics to replenish the treasury. Following the lead of Edward I, who had confiscated Jewish property in England and expelled the Jews in 1290, Philip confiscated Jewish property in France and expelled them in 1306. He imprisoned foreign merchants to extort money from them. And he encouraged the pope to declare the wealthy Knights Templars heretics so that he could confiscate their property and treasure in France. Finally, Philip insisted on his right to demand from the Church "free gifts," which were actually taxes. The issue led to a protracted dispute with Pope Boniface VIII (see later in this chapter). In seeking to dominate these international powers—the Knights Templars and the Church itself—Philip showed his determination to become truly sovereign in his own lands.

Estates General   Seeking funds in his struggle against England and the pope, Philip used his royal bureaucrats to meet with provincial representative councils, the *estates*, to grant taxation. The estates were composed of three houses: representatives of the nobility (including the upper and lower nobility), of the clergy, and of the commoners (mostly urban middle class). The provincial estates usually granted the taxes and did not dispute the king's policies.

Philip called the first meeting of the *Estates General*, with representatives of nobility, clergy, and commoners from all provinces, in 1302 and again in 1308. He used these meetings very much as Edward I used the Parliament. He informed delegates about the insults that he and France had

▼ **BATTLE OF THE GOLDEN SPURS**
In 1302, Flemish peasants, who had rebelled because Philip IV of France attempted to block the importation of wool from England, defeated the king at the battle of Courtrai. It was said that after the battle, seven hundred pairs of spurs were collected and displayed in the local cathedral. Some sense of the brutality of the fighting is conveyed by this illustration, with King Philip brandishing his sword at the center and the pile of bodies at the lower right. Chroniques de France, fol. 333r. Copyright Bibliothèque royale Albert 1er, Bruxelles.

suffered at the hands of Pope Boniface VIII and his reasons for confiscating the property of the Templars. The Estates General met for Philip's propaganda purposes, not to deliberate on his policies.

In trying to achieve a powerful, centralized monarchy, Philip left France in a deeply disturbed condition. The Flemish towns remained defiant, and the king of England threatened to go to war. With the outbreak of the Hundred Years' War in the mid-fourteenth century, France under Philip's successors entered one of the darkest periods of its history.

◆ THE HOLY ROMAN EMPIRE AND THE FRAGMENTATION OF RULE

Frederick II's policy of granting away imperial rights in Germany left the vast territory a conglomeration of independent cities, bishoprics, dukedoms, and principalities. The king of Aragon's conquest of Sicily separated it from imperial ambitions. The German territory went through a period of interregnum until 1273, when the German nobles met and elected Rudolph Habsburg (r. 1273–1291) emperor. In the late Middle Ages the locus of power of the Holy Roman Empire shifted to the east, away from the Rhine and into central Europe.

The Habsburgs   Rudolph Habsburg was selected in part because he was a minor noble with isolated lands near the Alps and into Alsace. He took some initiatives that limited the outlawry of minor knights who were acting as tyrants over their territory, but he could not take on the more powerful nobles. He managed to take Austria by conquest from the king of Bohemia and add this territory to the family estates. The Habsburg's successes in acquiring territory alarmed the German nobles and bishops. In 1308 the German nobles and bishops elected a member of the house of Luxemburg in place of the Habsburgs.

The Luxemburgs   Like the Habsburgs, the Luxemburgs used the position of emperor to increase their personal holdings. Charles IV (r. 1346–1378) centered his power in Bohemia, a new acquisition

of the Luxemburgs. To stabilize the process of electing the emperor, Charles promulgated the so-called Golden Bull of 1356, which fixed the number of electors at seven. The choice represented a balance of traditional parties: Three were ecclesiastics (the archbishops of Mainz, Trier, and Cologne) and four were powerful nobles (the king of Bohemia, the count palatine of the Rhine, the duke of Saxony, and the margrave of Brandenburg). The electors were to meet a month after the death of the king and elect a new one. The plan eliminated the papacy from the deliberations and future emperors broke the custom of having the pope bestow the imperial title. The Habsburgs once again gained control with the extinction of the Luxemburg line in 1437, thus joining Bohemia and Hungary with Austria and the Tyrol, which were already under Habsburg control.

Swiss Cantons   While Rudolph Habsburg was successfully adding to his territories, he lost three of the Swiss cantons that were part of his original patrimony. The cantons argued that they were granted independence under Frederick II. It was not until 1315 that the Habsburgs, with a large feudal force, tried to retake them. Swiss patriots rolled stones and tree trunks down on them as they marched through a mountain pass and then descended on them with their axes. Their success led other cantons to join them in a loose federation of independent cantons. The Swiss confederation was a new form of government for Europe—neither a monarchy nor a feudal principality. While retaining independence, they formed militias that cooperated in defending their territory.

III. Government in the East

While the West was secure from external invasions and able to continue its political, economic, and cultural development, the East was threatened by invasion from Asia once again. The East's defense against the new invaders meant that the West was sheltered, once again, from attack. The new threat came from the Mongols in the thirteenth century, followed by the Ottoman Turks in the fourteenth century.

◆ THE BYZANTINE EMPIRE

When Greece and Constantinople fell in the Fourth Crusade in 1204, the Greeks rallied under descendants from the imperial line and established several principalities in Asia Minor and along the southern shore of the Black Sea. But it was the territory in Asia Minor, with its capital in Nicaea, that eventually dominated the political scene.

Michael VIII Palaeologus   Under the leadership of Michael VIII Palaeologus (r. 1261–1282), the Nicaean empire managed to recapture Constantinople. By this time the Western attempt to establish an empire at Constantinople collapsed: The Venetians had taken the major trading islands and ports; the Western nobility had divided the Balkans into independent feudalities; and the Western emperors proved to be short lived and weak. Michael's general found the city unprotected and plundered of many of its treasures, which the crusaders had shipped back to Europe. The Greek population welcomed the return of Greek rule.

Michael VIII was an adept player in international politics and diplomacy. He needed to subdue a strong Bulgarian empire and the remaining Western feudal principalities in Greece and negotiate with the rising Serb state.

The Balkans   In the twentieth century we used the term "Balkanization" to refer to the splintering of a territory into a number of different states. Although the Byzantine emperors had settled various tribes in the Balkans, after the Fourth Crusade fights among these peoples became irreversible and are the root of modern tensions in the Balkans. The Bulgarians, taking advantage of the chaos after the Fourth Crusade, had established an empire (their leaders had taken the title of czar in imitation of the Roman "caesar") and threatened to invade Constantinople. Michael VIII managed to neutralize them through warfare and marriage with his female relatives. The Serbs had converted to Eastern Christianity in 1219. By Michael VIII's reign, they were beginning an ascendancy in the Balkans that allowed them to push into Byzantine territory.

Michael VIII left an empire that was again the Byzantine Empire, but warfare and taxation to defend the borders left it weak. Weakened as it was, it was still a major player, and the Palaeologus dynasty remained on the throne to the final fall in 1453.

◆ THE MONGOLS

The Mongols (of Turkic origin and sometimes called Tartars in medieval sources) threatened Europe much as other groups from central Asia, such as the Huns, had. They were composed of nomadic tribes organized under a chief, who took

▼ COURT OF A MONGOL KING
The courts of the Mongol kings, as this illustration from a Persian manuscript suggests, were dazzlingly opulent. When Louis IX of France sent presents of liturgical objects (chalices and books), the Mongol king rejected the gift and suggested that a tribute of gold and silver would be more appropriate.
Bibliothèque Nationale de France, Paris

the title of Genghis Khan, "Inflexible Emperor," in 1206. He turned eastward and took Beijing in 1216. Leaving his trusted lieutenants to subdue the rest of China, Genghis Khan turned his attention to the west and amassed the largest empire the world has ever known. Meeting little resistance from the Turks, his empire had expanded by 1225 to include central Asia, parts of Afghanistan, Persia, and the Caucasus.

The Golden Horde   In 1223 a Mongol army penetrated Eastern Europe in what seems to have been a reconnoitering expedition. The Mongols defeated the allied princes of Rus, and from 1237 to 1241 a Mongol army under the leadership of Batu, grandson of Genghis Khan, conducted raids throughout Eastern Europe, including Russia, Poland, and Hungary. The Mongols abandoned Poland and Hungary, but established the capital of a division of the Mongol empire, called "the Golden Horde," at Sarai, on the lower Volga River.

The khans, or rulers, of the Golden Horde maintained suzerainty over the lands of what are now Ukraine and Belarus until the mid-1300s and over eastern Russia until the mid-1400s. The princes who were subject to the Golden Horde had to pay tribute to the khans, but otherwise they could rule their own people. As a result, despite the power they exercised over the East Slavs for centuries, the Mongols' influence on Slavic languages and cultures remained relatively slight.

Resettlement of the East Slavs   The devastation of the Mongol invasions and the formation of the Golden Horde led a chronicler to lament that Kiev, once proudly known as the "mother of Rus cities," had only two hundred houses left standing in the 1200s. Rus population dispersed. Some colonists moved west into the upper Dniester River and became the ancestors of the modern Ukrainians and the Belorussians, or White Russians. After a short period of submission to the Mongols, these colonies fell under the political domination first of the grand dukes of Lithuania and then of the Polish kings. With a large Ukrainian population, these people developed their own literary languages and cultural traditions and remained under Polish or Austrian rule until 1944.

Other colonists moved north into a region ruled by the city of Novgorod, but it was too poor to either attract the Mongols or to support a dense population. The lands between the upper Volga and Oka rivers, the Russian "Mesopotamia," became the most important sites of Slavic resettlement, as the dense forests offered both relative security from the nomads and a productive soil. The Novgorod and Russian Mesopotamia immigrants were the ancestors of the modern Russians, forming the largest group of East Slavic peoples.

◆ MUSCOVITE RUSSIA

Historians call the period between the twelfth and fifteenth centuries the age of feudal Russia—the time during which Russia was divided into many princely domains. Nearly all the small towns within Russian Mesopotamia had their own princes, their own citadels, or *kremlins*, and their own territories. All the princes were subject to the khan of the Golden Horde.

Moscow gained preeminence primarily through the talents of its early princes. Abandoning the Kievan practice of dividing lands among surviving male heirs, the princes pursued a policy of primogeniture. They acquired new territories through wars, marriages, and purchases, and they sought to make Moscow the symbol and embodiment of Russian unity. Unlike Western Christians, they early on established a distinct Russian national and cultural identity.

Ivan I of Muscovy   Ivan I (r. 1328–1341) was the first Muscovite prince to raise Moscow to prominence. He extended his possessions along the entire course of the Moskva River and won enclaves of territory north of the Volga River. Ivan courted the favor of the still-powerful Mongol khan of the Golden Horde. In return for his loyalty and gifts, the khan made Ivan the chief representative of Mongol authority in Russia (the "grand duke"), with the right to collect the Mongol tribute from all Russian lands. Ivan increased his own treasury while collecting tribute for the Mongols.

With Ivan's encouragement the primate (or chief bishop) of the Russian Church often visited Moscow, finally making the city his permanent

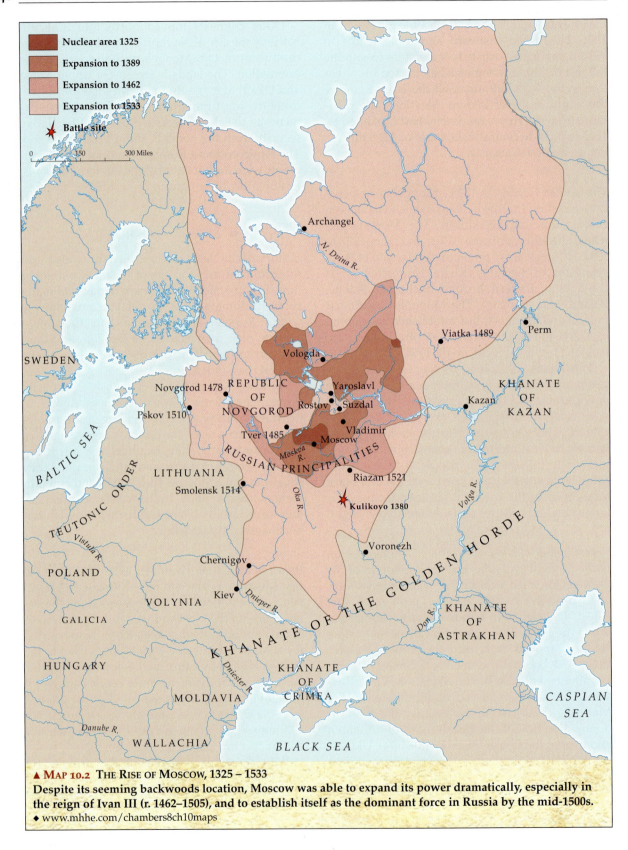

Nuclear area 1325

Expansion to 1389

Expansion to 1462

Expansion to 1533

★ **Battle site**

▲ **MAP 10.2** THE RISE OF MOSCOW, 1325 – 1533
Despite its seeming backwoods location, Moscow was able to expand its power dramatically, especially in the reign of Ivan III (r. 1462–1505), and to establish itself as the dominant force in Russia by the mid-1500s.
◆ www.mhhe.com/chambers8ch10maps

residence. This move made Moscow the head-quarters of the Russian Church even before it became the capital of the Russian people.

By the late 1300s the Mongols' power was declining, largely because of internal dissension. With the Mongols weakened, the princes of Moscow began to present themselves as leaders of the growing national opposition to Mongol rule.

Ivan III   Ivan III (r. 1462–1505) completed the unification of Russian land and laid the constitutional foundations for modern Russia. He acquired the prosperous city of Novgorod, which had developed strong trading and cultural links with Western Europe. The Novgorod merchant oligarchy favored its neighboring Catholic Lithuanians, but the populace was Orthodox in religion and preferred the prince of Moscow. Ivan demanded and received the submission of the city and incorporated Novgorod and its territories into the Muscovite state in 1478. Continuing his territorial expansion, he eventually ended two centuries of Mongol rule of Russia at the Oka River in 1480. No battle occurred, because neither side dared cross the river that separated them.

Tsar   Seeking to depict himself as the successor of the Byzantine emperors (Constantinople had fallen to the Ottoman Turks in 1453), Ivan adopted the title *tsar,* the Slavic equivalent of the Latin term *caesar.* Married to Sophia Palaeologus, who was the niece of the last Byzantine emperor and had been educated in Italy, Ivan added elaborate Byzantine pomp and etiquette to his court and adopted the Byzantine double-headed eagle as the seal and symbol of the new Russian empire. Under the influence of his wife, he invited Italian artists and architects to Moscow to help rebuild the Kremlin and make the city an impressive capital. In imitation of the Byzantine emperors, in 1497, Ivan promulgated a new code of laws known as the *Sudebnik.*

The Third Rome   The new strength and splendor of the tsar inspired several monastic scholars to propose the idea that Moscow was the third Rome. The first Rome, they said, had fallen into heresy, and the second, Constantinople, had been taken by the infidel. Moscow alone, the capital of the one Orthodox ruler, preserved the true religion.

Ivan's reforms were not completed until the reign of his grandson, Ivan IV, the Terrible (r. 1530–1584)—a tsar who brutally destroyed the old nobility of *boyars* (hereditary nobility) and imposed on all landowners the status of servant to the tsar. Nonetheless, Ivan III can be seen as the founder of the Russian state. He finished the task of unifying the Russian land and its people, and he declared himself to be the autocrat of Russia. Ivan III bequeathed to his successors one of the most characteristic institutions of modern Russia: its centralized, autocratic government.

IV. The Papacy and the Church

◆

While the monarchs of France and England were continuing to consolidate their rule over their subjects and while Russia was beginning to form a national identity around Moscow, papal administration also continued to expand. Often desperate for funds to carry on their ambitious political involvement in European affairs, the popes by the late thirteenth century exploited their spiritual powers to raise money for their political endeavors. In the past centuries new or reformed monastic orders had brought the Church back to its spiritual mission, but no new orders developed and existing ones had become increasingly corrupt.

◆ THE PAPACY

Boniface VIII   The papal curia and the college of cardinals were aware that the papacy was losing its prestige, and they sought to remedy the situation by electing as pope a famous hermit, who took the name Celestine V (1294). They assumed that he would be a pious figurehead and that they could carry on business as usual. Celestine, however, observed the corruption and feared that his soul would be endangered if he continued as pope; he resigned in five months. His successor, Boniface VIII (r. 1294–1303), was rumored to have rigged up a speaking tube to the papal sleeping chamber through which he intoned that it was the will of God that Celestine resign.

Clash with Philip IV of France   By the late thirteenth century the papacy was facing a rising

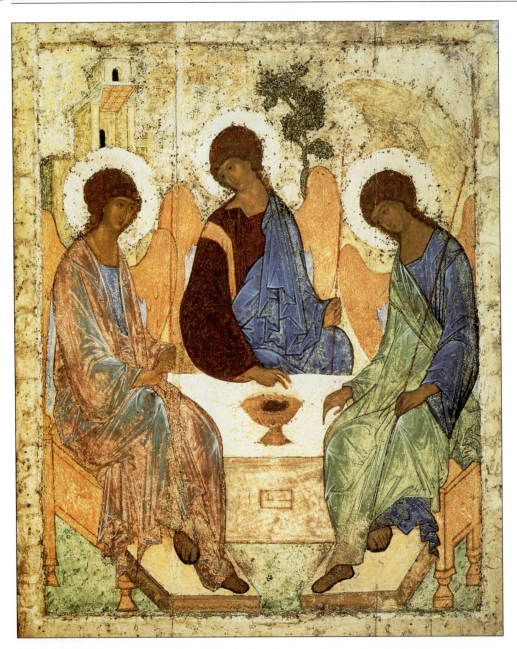

▲ **Andrei Rublev Old Testament Trinity, 1410–1420**
Andrei Rublev, one of the most influential Russian artists of the fifteenth century, worked within a Byzantine tradition of wall painting. His *Old Testament Trinity*, originally from a monastery, shows a reinterpretation of the standard Christian iconography: The three angels positioned around a dish represent God the Father, the Son, and the Holy Ghost.
Scala/Art Resource, NY

challenge from lay lords, who sought to tax the clergy within their own territories. Both Philip IV of France and Edward I of England had been taxing the clergy through the fiction of asking for, and always receiving, gifts or money for specific royal enterprises. In 1296, in the bull *Clericis laicos* (all solemn papal letters were called *bulls* because they were closed with a lead seal, or *bulla,* and they are usually identified by their first two words), Boniface forbade all clergy to make

▲ **Onion Domes at Kizhi**
Constructed entirely of wood, the remarkable churches of northern Russia, such as this eighteenth-century example from Kizhi, were made into magnificently elaborate structures even though they often served only small settlements. The onion domes were the characteristic symbol of the Russian Orthodox Church, and they were multiplied across the roofs of Russian churches.
Magnum Photos, Inc.

payments without papal permission. Such a restriction would have given the pope a powerful, if not controlling, voice in royal finances that no king could tolerate. The English simply ignored the order, but Philip retaliated by forbidding all exports of coin from his realm to Rome. Boniface issued another bull condemning Philip directly. Philip called a meeting of the Estates General in 1302 (the first such meeting) and presented the three estates with an exaggerated description of Boniface's insults to the French king and people and revived the rumors surrounding the resignation of Celestine.

With both his personal character and the papal authority threatened, Boniface issued the bull *Unam Sanctam,* which declared that Philip must submit to his authority or risk the damnation of his immortal soul (see *"Unam Sanctam,"* p. 352). Philip accused the pope of shocking crimes and demanded his arrest and trial at a general church council. To enforce his accusations, Philip sent one of his principal advisers to Italy. With the aid of a small army of Boniface's enemies, the French adviser broke into the papal palace at Anagni and arrested the pope in 1303. The citizens of Anagni rescued Boniface shortly afterward, but he died in Rome only a few months later.

Origin of the Avignon Papacy Succeeding popes capitulated to the French king and revoked *Unam Sanctam.* Philip's victory was complete when a Frenchman, Clement V, was elected pope in 1305. Clement V postponed going to Rome, preferring instead to settle in 1309 in the French-speaking

UNAM SANCTAM

◆

This statement of papal monarchy was issued by Pope Boniface VIII in 1302 to combat assertions of royal power by the kings of England and France against the authority of the universal Church. It did little, however, to deter the claims of such rulers to a growing sphere of authority.

"That there is one holy, Catholic and apostolic Church we are bound to believe and to hold, our faith urging us, and this we do firmly believe and simply confess; and that outside this Church there is no salvation or remission of sins. . . .

"We are taught by the words of the Gospel that in this Church and in her power there are two swords, a spiritual one and a temporal one. For when the apostles said 'Here are two swords' (Luke 22:38), meaning in the Church since it was the apostles who spoke, the Lord did not reply that it was too many but enough. Certainly anyone who denies that the temporal sword is in the power of Peter has not paid heed to the words of the Lord when he said, 'Put up thy sword into its sheath' (Matthew 26:52). Both then are in the power of the Church, the material sword and the spiritual. But the one is exercised for the Church, the other by the Church, the one by the hand of the priest, the other by the hand of kings and soldiers, though at the will and sufferance of the priest. One sword ought to be under the other and the temporal authority subject to the spiritual power. For, while the apostle says, 'There is no power but from God and those that are ordained of God'

(Romans 13:1), they would not be ordained unless one sword was under the other and, being inferior, was led by the other to the highest things. . . . But that the spiritual power excels any earthly one in dignity and nobility we ought the more openly to confess in proportion as spiritual things excel temporal ones. Moreover we clearly perceive this from the giving of tithes, from benediction and sanctification, from the acceptance of this power and from the very government of things. For the truth bearing witness, the spiritual power has to institute the earthly power and to judge if it has not been good. . . .

"Therefore, if the earthly power errs, it shall be judged by the spiritual power, if a lesser spiritual power errs it shall be judged by its superior, but if the supreme spiritual power errs it can be judged only by God not by man. . . . Therefore we declare, state, define and pronounce that it is altogether necessary to salvation for every human creature to be subject to the Roman Pontiff."

From Warren Hollister et al., *Medieval Europe: A Short Sourcebook* (McGraw-Hill Companies, 1992), pp. 215–216.

---

city of Avignon (the city was in Burgundy, a German, not French, territory). Selecting a series of French cardinals, Clement V and his successors found Avignon congenial. For the next sixty-eight years the popes lived within the shadow of the French monarchy, executing its policies. In Rome revenues from the papal estates fell into the hands of competing factions of nobility. These nobles were so hostile to the French popes that return became impossible.

Papal Corruption   Separated from the normal income derived from papal estates around Rome, the popes sought to finance their extravagant living in Avignon and the extensive church bureaucracy from other sources. The popes sold bishoprics (simony) and then extracted substantial payments from the first year that the bishop

held his office; they imposed tithes (a tenth of income) on the clergy; and they sold to laypersons and clergy exemptions and dispensations from the regulations of canon law. Divorce or penances for sins could be purchased from the pope's representatives for a fee. The Dominicans and Franciscans, wandering through the world as they did, proved to be ideal agents for selling release from the strictures of canon law.

Monastic Orders   In the past when the papacy had faced criticism and spiritual crisis, reforming monastic orders had come to its rescue. In the late thirteenth and fourteenth centuries, however, the monastic orders contributed to the Church's poor image. The Dominicans had become deeply implicated with the Inquisition, a role that cost them the trust of the laity. Rather than maintain their mendicant roots, both the Franciscans and Dominicans had become wealthy monastic orders. Within the Franciscans, a bitter fight developed between the Spiritual Franciscans, who wanted to return to the order as St. Francis had founded it, and the Conventual Franciscans, who favored monasteries and continued involvement in Church politics. The Conventuals won the fight, and the pope renounced the Spiritual Franciscans.

◆ LAY RELIGIOUS OBSERVANCE

Whatever their discontent with the papacy, the laity were devoted to the Christian religion and found renewed spiritual commitments in their parish churches, their individual salvation, and in lay organizations centered around religious observance.

Beguines and Beghars Already in the twelfth century, pious groups of laity had formed quasi-monastic groups. The Beguines and their male counterparts, the Beghards, were popular in northern European cities. They lived together in houses or with families. While Beguines did not take vows of chastity and did not live by orders, they lived pious lives devoted to simple tasks such as spinning and caring for the sick, the old, and the bodies of the dead (see "The Benguinage of Saint Elizabeth in Ghent [1328]," p. 354). They might spend their whole lives in this work or they might eventually marry. They were regarded with general suspicion by the Church, who tried to force them to become extensions of the Dominican order. The Franciscans and Dominicans had associated other laypersons, called the Third Order, or tertiaries to their orders. Tertiaries included widows or married people who worked in the world but spent time and money on charity and pious works. Many women found the tertiaries a refuge from household cares and an outlet for their spiritual drive.

Parish Guilds and Religious Practice Married laypersons formed social-religious guilds within their parishes. The guilds celebrated the feast of their patron saint, helped maintain the parish church and perhaps even built a chapel within the church for their own use, provided candles for worship, and performed religious plays. In the early fourteenth century, a new theological emphasis on purgatory (the state in which the soul remained until it expiated the sins committed during life) encouraged the growth of guilds. The guild members prayed for the souls of dead brethren and sisters to release their souls from purgatory into heaven. Guilds also provided fellowship, including feasts, burial processions for members, and charity for those who had suffered illness.

Another theological and liturgical change influenced the practice of lay piety in the later Middle Ages. The emphasis of the Fourth Lateran Council on transubstantiation (the miraculous conversion of the bread and wine to the body and blood of Christ) and the requirement that the laity take Holy Communion (Eucharist) at least once a year, elevated the importance of this liturgical practice. To aid the laity in understanding the importance of the Eucharist, a special day was set aside, Corpus Christi Day, on which the communion wafer, in a special box, was carried by the priest in religious procession. The procession won lay devotion, and popular religious plays were performed on Corpus Christi Day.

Antisemitism Many of the Corpus Christi plays represented Jews dishonoring the Communion wafer by boiling it or nailing it to a piece of wood and being subsequently converted. Thus, an unintended result of the emphasis on the Eucharist was increased antisemitism in thirteenth-century Europe. The Fourth Lateran Council had also mandated that Jews wear special signs, the Star of David, on their dress to indicate their religion. While these rules were not immediately enforced, they gradually became part of urban law. The participation of Jews in money lending led to feelings of competition and hostility on the part of the urban Christian population and the nobles and monasteries who had mortgaged their lands to borrow money from Jews. The hostility led to sporadic pogroms throughout Europe, such as the massacre of the Jews in London in 1264. The growing antisemitism in the thirteenth century was in marked contrast to the twelfth century, when Jewish and Christian scholars exchanged their theological ideas. The increased suspicion and hatred explains why Edward I and Philip IV

THE BEGUINAGE OF SAINT ELIZABETH IN GHENT (1328)

The Beguines were religious women who chose to live not in nunneries but in communities such as that of Saint Elizabeth or in homes of their own family or others. They supported themselves with manual labor and tended to the poor and sick. Some became preachers, writers, and mystics.

"The Beguinage of Saint Elizabeth . . . is encircled by ditches and walls. In the middle of it is a church, and next to the church a cemetery and a hospital, which the aforesaid ladies endowed for the weak and infirm of that same Beguinage. Many houses were also built there for habitation of the said women, each of whom has her own garden, separated from the next by ditches or hedges; and two chaplains were established in this place by the same ladies.

"In these houses, indeed, many dwell together communally and are very poor, having nothing but their clothing, a bed and a chest, nor are they a burden to anyone, but by manual work, washing the wool and cleaning the pieces of cloth sent to them from the town, they earn enough money daily that, making thereby a simple living, they also pay their dues to the church and give a modest amount in alms. And in each convent there is one who is called the mistress of work, whose duty is to supervise the work and the workers, so that all things are faithfully carried through according to God's will.

"We shall not say much of their abstinence from food and drink but this: that many of them are satisfied for the whole day with the coarse bread and pottage which they have in common in each convent, and with a drink of cold water they lessen their thirst rather than increase their appetite. And many among them are accustomed to fast frequently on bread and water, and many of them do not wear linen on their bodies, and they use straw pallets instead of beds."

From Emilie Amt, *Women's Lives in Medieval Europe: A Sourcebook* (Routledge, 1993), pp. 264–265.

---

were able to expel the Jews without public condemnation.

Individual Spiritualism A combination of the emphasis on the Eucharist and the Franciscans' encouragement of spiritual exercises that involved imaginative participation in scenes such as the Crucifixion led to individual quests for spiritual satisfaction. Women in particular took to this form of religious experience, imagining that they were at the Crucifixion and that the wounds of Christ could nourish them. These pious women might be nuns or Beguines, but many were laywomen who were wives, mothers, and daughters. They led lives of extreme abstinence, giving their food to the poor and refusing to eat themselves or trying to live only on the Communion wafers. In addition to fasting, some women performed extreme asceticism, beating themselves with whips and wearing hair shirts. Some became saints, and some died from starvation.

The most famous among the saints was Catherine of Siena (1347–1380), the daughter of a wool-dyer and his wife. She began fasting early in life and refused to marry. Her good works took her among the sick, where she tried to drink puss from the ulcers of a cancerous woman. Her biographer says that he saw her stuff twigs down her throat to bring up food, but he says that even when she seemed emaciated, she would rise up if there was work to be done among the poor. Although closely associated with the Dominicans all her life, she remained a laywoman.

While men dominated the ecclesiastical institutions of the Church, women were able to gain prestige through their individual spirituality, visions, and work among the poor. Much of their spiritual prestige came through manipulating food. Women were closely associated with preparing and serving food, and the shared meal was the basis of much of medieval life. When a daughter defied her parents by fasting or giving away their food to the poor, she defied basic assumptions about female behavior and could often use this advantage to manipulate her family into canceling marriage plans. Many clergymen found the women's fasting and asceticism a valuable tool for instructing both the laity and other clergy on the strength of these women's devotion. Women could overcome the constraints society put on

▲ WOMEN MYSTICS
During the fourteenth and fifteenth centuries, individuals sought salvation through meditation. Women were among the most famous mystics. Birgitta of Sweden (ca. 1302–1373) came from a noble family, married, and served in the royal household. Widowed in 1344, she retreated to a house near a Cistercian monastery and led a life of prayer and penance. She experienced a series of revelations, one of which is pictured here, which she recorded in Swedish. She was famous throughout Europe for her writings.
The Pierpont Morgan Library/Art Resource, NY

them, both as participants in family and Church, through their own spiritual quests.

V. Learning and Literature
◆

The thirteenth- and early fourteenth-century developments in learning and literature brought new trends in Scholasticism. Just as the Franciscans profoundly influenced individual spirituality, so too they influenced philosophy. Although some of the radical new philosophers had their works condemned in their lifetimes, their think-

ing laid the foundation for modern scientific inquiry. In vernacular literature, Dante (1265–1321) made the greatest syntheses of medieval culture in *The Divine Comedy*, in which he included Scholasticism, courtly romance, spiritual journey, classical learning, and contemporary politics.

◆ PHILOSOPHY

St. Bonaventure (1221–1274) Born in central Italy, Bonaventure was cured of a childhood illness through the intercession of St. Francis of Assisi. He went on to become a leading member of the Franciscan order and a contemporary of Thomas Aquinas at the University of Paris. Rather than advocating the rigorous logic for proof of the existence of God that Aquinas advocated, Bonaventure's proof was based on intuited principles (as was Duns Scotus'). To help humans understand the existence of God, Bonaventure emphasized spiritual exercises that began with looking at God's creations on Earth and seeing God in them. Contemplation would lead the believer to the revelation of God's existence. Bonaventure's theology and personal beliefs made him one of the great medieval mystics.

English Scholastics   Under the influence of two English Franciscans, Roger Bacon (1214–1294) and William of Ockham (ca. 1285–ca. 1349), philosophy began to investigate problems of natural laws. Both men were attracted to the emphasis in Aristotle's logic on empirical observation, and both are often considered the founders of Western scientific writing. Bacon's writings are in the medieval intellectual and Franciscan traditions, in that he emphasized revelation and the interior illumination of the soul through seven states of "internal experience." The new element in his writing is his argument that knowledge can only be verified through "experimental science," that is, he suggested establishing empirical hypotheses and developing ways of testing them. He did not specify whether he was advocating a new methodology for approaching knowledge or just a special subject matter that was different from established sciences and authorities. He was imprisoned for his unorthodox views in 1278.

William of Ockham did not attack Thomas Aquinas, but he did point out Aquinas' limitations. He argued that the articles of Christian faith could not be proved with logic and that they should be left to belief. Observation could be applied to nature, including the heavenly bodies and Earth. His guiding principle in logical argument is called Ockham's razor: "What can be explained on fewer principles is explained needlessly by more." Simplicity, or elegance of argument, became the basis for scientific explanation to the present day.

Medieval Science   Bacon and Ockham were medieval thinkers, but their students began to take their lessons to levels that we consider to be the beginnings of scientific thinking. Nicholas of Oresme (1320–1382), a student of Ockham, suggested that the movement of the planets could be better explained if Earth was in motion, like the planets, rather than stationary, which was the accepted view of the day. John Buridan (ca. 1300–ca. 1358) argued, following Ockham's razor, that there was no reason to assume that the celestial bodies were composed of a matter different from Earth. The work of Oresme later influenced Galileo's description of the uniform acceleration of falling bodies and Descartes' development of analytical geometry.

◆ DANTE

Literary output in most vernacular languages was abundant during the thirteenth century except in English, which was retarded in its development by the continued dominance of a French-speaking aristocracy. The masterpiece that best summarizes the culture of the age is the *Comedy* of Dante Alighieri.

Dante was born in Florence in 1265. Little is known of his education, but he seems to have been immersed in scholarship. The *Comedy* is one of the most learned, and hence most difficult, poems of world literature.

Two experiences in Dante's life profoundly influenced his attitudes and are reflected in his works. In 1274, when he was only nine years old, he fell deeply in love with a young girl named Beatrice. Much mystery surrounds her, but she seems to have been Beatrice Portinari, who later married into a prominent family and died in 1290. Dante could have seen her only rarely; we do not know if she ever returned his love. Still, in his youthful adoration of Beatrice he seems to have attained that sense of harmony and joy that the troubadours considered to be the great reward of lovers.

In 1302 an experience of a much different sort shattered his life. For political reasons Dante was exiled from Florence. He spent the remaining years of his life wandering from city to city, a disillusioned, even bitter man. He died in 1321 and was buried at Ravenna.

The Comedy   Dante composed his masterpiece from 1313 to 1321. He called it a *commedia* in conformity with the classical notion that a happy

el uamo tutta fua cou guizaua.
torcenco in fu la uenenofa forcha.
cha guifa di fcorpion la punta armaua
Lo duca diffe or connuen che fi torcha.
la noftra uia un poco in fina quella.
beftia maluagia che colla fi torcha.
Pero fcentcemmo a la teftra mamella.
e diece paffi femmo in fu loftremo.
perben ceffar la rena ela fiamella.

▲ A detail from a fourteenth-century manuscript copy of Dante's *Divine Comedy* illustrates the section of hell reserved for usurers. The Church regarded usury as one of the many earthly sins that condemn people in the eyes of God. Dante appears three times in this scene, on two occasions accompanied by his bearded guide, Virgil.

By permission of the British Library

ending made any story, no matter how serious, a comedy; the adjective *divine* was added to its title only after his death. The poem is divided into three parts, which describe the poet's journey through hell, purgatory, and heaven.

The poem opens with Dante "in the middle of the way of this our life." An aging man, he has grown confused and disillusioned; he is lost in a "dark forest" of doubt, harassed by wild animals, symbols of his own untamed passions. The theme of the poem is Dante's rediscovery of a former sense of harmony and joy. Leading him back to his lost peace are two guides. The first, Virgil, who represents human reason, conducts Dante through hell and then up the seven-storied mountain of purgatory to the earthly paradise, the vanished Eden, at its summit. In hell Dante encounters people who have chosen as their supreme goal in life something other than the love of God—riches, pleasure, fame, or power. Virgil shows Dante that

the good life cannot be built on such selfish choices. Reason, in other words, can enable humans to avoid the pitfalls of egoistic, material existence. In fact, reason can accomplish even more than that, for as embodied by Virgil, it guides Dante through purgatory and shows him how to acquire the natural virtues that are the foundations of the earthly paradise—a full and peaceful earthly existence.

In the dignity and power given to Virgil, Dante shares the high regard for human reason characteristic of the thirteenth century. However, reason can take humans only so far. To enter heaven, Dante needs a new guide—Beatrice herself, representative of supernatural revelation and grace. She takes the poet through the heavenly spheres into the presence of God, "in Whom is our peace." The peace and joy of the heavenly court set the dominant mood at the poem's conclusion, in contrast to the confusion and violence of the dark forest with which it opens.

The poem reflects the great cultural issues that challenged Dante's contemporaries—the relations between reason and faith, nature and grace, human power and the divine will. Dante, like Aquinas, was trying to combine two opposed views of human nature and its ability to shape its own destiny. One, rooted in the optimism of the twelfth and thirteenth centuries and in the more distant classical heritage, affirmed that human beings were masters of themselves and the world. The other, grounded in the Judeo-Christian tradition, saw them, fundamentally, as lost children in a vale of tears. Dante's majestic panorama summarizes not only the medieval vision of the universe but also his estimation of what it meant to live a truly wise, truly happy, truly human life.

Summary

◆

Medieval civilization attained a new stability in the thirteenth and early fourteenth centuries. Large-scale woolen cloth production, long-range commercial exchanges, and sophisticated business practices gave the economy a dynamic aura. In political life, feudal governments consolidated and clarified their constitutional procedures, and parliaments and representative assemblies came to play a recognized role in the processes of government. Urban institutions and the middle class became part of the political, economic, and social life of medieval Europe. The papacy energetically sought to lead the Western monarchs as their guide and conscience, but secular entanglements and fiscal problems threatened and gradually diluted its moral authority. While the papacy went into a serious decline, as did the Dominican and Franciscan orders, the laity remained deeply pious and increasingly sought communal or individual routes to salvation. Philosophy began to turn its attention to empirical science, and literature developed a new sophistication with the *Comedy* of Dante. The East, by contrast, suffered continual warfare and a devastating new invasion by the Mongols. Out of the ashes of this conquest, however, emerged a new state of Russia centered on Moscow. The fourteenth and fifteenth centuries, however, brought radical new challenges to the stability achieved in the thirteenth century. Famines became common in the early fourteenth century, Philip IV and Edward I had sown the seeds of the Hundred Years' War, and the Byzantine Empire was so weakened by protracted warfare that the arrival of the Ottoman Turks would finally spell its doom.

Questions for Further Thought

◆

1. In many ways the development of Parliament was a direct outgrowth of the Magna Carta. Who were the chief beneficiaries of the Magna Carta and of Parliament? How do these beneficiaries indicate a shift in the social class structure?

2. If you think of Dante's *Divine Comedy* as having intellectual roots in both medieval thought and the new "humanistic" thought, what elements of his writing would you use to make an argument that he was a bridge between the two?

3. Commerce assumed a larger and larger role in the European economy. What factors contributed to the success of trade and commerce? Think back to the early development of towns as well as the current chapter.

RECOMMENDED READING

◆

Sources

*Alighieri, Dante. *The Divine Comedy.* Mark Musa (tr.). 1996.

*Amt, Emilie (ed.). *Women's Lives in Medieval Europe: A Sourcebook.* 1993.

The Chronicle of Novgorod. Robert Mitchell and Neville Forbes (trs.). 1914. Portrays social and political life of the principal commercial town of medieval Russia.

*Geary, Patrick J. (ed.). *Readings in Medieval History.* 1997. Collection of documents and texts covering the whole of the Middle Ages. Selections are long and representative of the writings of historical figures.

Howes, Robert Craig (ed. and tr.). *The Testaments of the Grand Princes of Moscow.* 1967.

*Shinners, John (ed.). *Medieval Popular Religion, 1000–1500.* 1997. Valuable collection with generous selections from texts.

Studies

Boase, T. S. R. *Boniface VIII.* 1933. Standard biography of the controversial pope.

*Bynum, Caroline Walker. *Holy Feast and Holy Fast: The Religious Significance of Food to Medieval Women.* 1987. Discussion of female mystics in the later Middle Ages and their abstinence.

*Duby, Georges. *William Marshal: The Flower of Chivalry.* 1985. Sensitive biography of an Anglo-Norman lord.

Durham, Thomas. *Serbia: The Rise and Fall of a Medieval Empire.* 1989.

Fernández-Armesto, Felipe. *Before Columbus: Exploration and Colonization from the Mediterranean to the Atlantic, 1229–1492.* 1987. Discusses medieval exploration before Columbus, illustrating that later exploration grew out of the earlier tradition of navigating along the Atlantic coast.

*Geremek, Bronislaw. *The Margins of Society in Late Medieval Paris.* 1987. Examines the Parisian underworld.

*Hanawalt, Barbara. *Growing Up in Medieval London: The Experience of Childhood in History.* 1993. Childhood and adolescence in medieval London.

*Herlihy, David. *Opera Muliebria: Women and Work in Medieval Europe.* 1990. A survey of women's work with very good information on Paris.

*Jones, W. T. *A History of Western Philosophy: The Medieval Mind.* 1969. Very good survey with selections from the writings of major thinkers.

*Klapisch-Zuber, Christiane. *Women, Family, and Ritual in Renaissance Italy.* 1985. Collection of essays by Klapisch-Zuber concerning her work on women and the family.

Leuschner, Joachim. *Germany in the Late Middle Ages.* 1980. Survey of the period.

*Martin, Janet. *Medieval Russia 980–1584.* 1995. An accessible account of the development of medieval Russia.

*Miskimin, Harry A. *The Economy of Early Renaissance Europe, 1300–1460.* 1975. Synthesis of economic situation in Europe during this period.

Morgan, David. *The Mongols.* 1986. Emphasizes the impact of the Mongol conquests and empire on Eastern Europe.

Otis, Leah. *Prostitution in Medieval Society: The History of an Urban Institution in Languedoc.* 1985. Examination of prostitution in southern France.

Ozment, Steven. *The Age of Reform, 1250–1550: An Intellectual and Religious History of Late Medieval and Reformation Europe.* 1980. Survey of intellectual history for the period.

Strayer, Joseph R. *The Reign of Philip the Fair.* 1980. Biography of Philip with emphasis on his administration.

*Ward, Jennifer. *English Noble Women in the Later Middle Ages.* 1992. A valuable study of noble households and women in them.

*Wood, Charles T. *Philip the Fair and Boniface VIII: State vs. Papacy.* 2d ed. 1971. Presents historiography of this conflict.

*Available in paperback.

▲ **King Henry V of England crosses the Somme while French Marshal
Bouciquaut holds the ford at Blanchetaque before the Battle of Agincourt.**
Bibliothèque Nationale Paris/The Art Archive

Breakdown and Renewal in an Age of Plague

The vigorous expansion that marked European history from the eleventh to the thirteenth centuries came to an end in the 1300s. Plague, famine, and recurrent wars decimated populations and snuffed out former prosperity. At the same time, feudal governments as well as the papacy struggled against mounting institutional chaos. But for all the signs of crisis, the fourteenth and fifteenth centuries were not merely an age of breakdown. The failures of the medieval economy and its governments drove the Western peoples to repair their institutions. By the late fifteenth century the outlines of a new equilibrium were emerging. In 1500 Europeans were fewer in number than they had been in 1300, but they had developed a more productive economy and a more powerful technology than they had possessed two hundred years before. These achievements were to equip them for their great expansion throughout the world in the early modern period.

Some historians refer to the fourteenth and fifteenth centuries as the "autumn of the Middle Ages," emphasizing the decline and death of a formerly great civilization. People living at the time tended to think in terms of the Biblical passage in Revelations referring to the Four Horsemen of the Apocalypse—famine, disease, war, and the white horse of salvation. Constantinople, the last remnant of the Byzantine Empire, fell to the Ottoman Turks, providing a powerful symbol of decay. But the study of any past epoch requires an effort to balance the work of death and renewal. In few periods of history do death and renewal confront each other so dramatically as in the years between 1300 and 1500.

CHAPTER 11. BREAKDOWN AND RENEWAL IN AN AGE OF PLAGUE							
	Social Structure	Body Politic	Changes in the Organization of Production and in the Impact of Technology	Evolution of Family and Changing Gender Roles	War	Religion	Cultural Expression
I. POPULATION CATASTROPHES	▓			▓			
II. ECONOMIC DEPRESSION AND RECOVERY	▓	▓	▓	▓	▓		▓
III. POPULAR UNREST	▓	▓			▓		
IV. GOVERNMENTS OF EUROPE	▓	▓	▓	▓	▓	▓	
V. FALL OF BYZANTIUM AND THE OTTOMAN EMPIRE		▓			▓	▓	

I. Population Catastrophes

◆

The famines and plagues that struck European society in the fourteenth and fifteenth centuries profoundly affected economic life. Initially, they disrupted the established patterns of producing and exchanging goods and led directly to widespread hardship. As Europeans recovered and reorganized the economy to greatly changed demographic conditions, they were able to significantly increase the efficiency of economic production. To understand this paradox, we must see how the disasters affected the population of Europe.

◆ DEMOGRAPHIC DECLINE

A few censuses and other statistical records give us an insight into the size and structure of the European population in the 1300s. Nearly all these records were drawn up for purposes of taxation, and usually they survey only limited geographical areas—a city or a province. They are rarely complete even in limited areas and give us no reliable totals, but they still enable us to perceive with some confidence how the population was changing.

Population Losses   Almost every region of Europe from which we possess records shows an appalling decline of population between approxi-

mately 1300 and 1450. In Provence in southern France, the population seems to have shrunk after 1310 from between 350,000 and 400,000 to roughly one-third, or at most one-half, of its earlier size; only after 1470 did it again begin to increase. The city and countryside of Pistoia, near Florence, fell from about 43,000 people in the mid-thirteenth century to 14,000 by the early fifteenth. The nearby city and countryside of San Gimignano has not regained to this day the approximately 13,000 residents it had in 1332.

For the larger kingdoms of Europe, the figures are less reliable, but they show a similar pattern. England had a population of about 3.7 million in 1347 and 2.2 million by 1377. By 1550 it had no more people than it had had in the thirteenth century. France by 1328 may have reached 15 million; it, too, was not again to attain this size for two hundred years. In Germany, of some 170,000 inhabited localities named in sources before 1300, about 40,000 disappeared during the 1300s and 1400s. Since many of the surviving towns were also shrinking in size, the population loss was greater.

Certain favored regions of Europe—the fertile lands surrounding Paris and the Po valley in Italy—did continue to attract settlers and maintain fairly stable populations, but they owed their good fortune more to immigration than to high birthrates or immunity from disease. It can safely be estimated that all of Europe in 1450 had no more than one-half, and probably only one-third, of the population it had had around 1300. Population did not begin to recover until the end of the fifteenth century.

Famine and Hunger The first demographic catastrophe in late medieval Europe was famine and general food scarcities. In 1315, 1316, and 1317 a severe famine swept the north of Europe. Chroniclers described the incessant rainfall that rotted crops in the fields and prevented harvests; they spoke of people dying in the city streets and country lanes; cannibalism is another theme. In 1339 and 1340 a famine struck southern Europe. During famines, the starving people ate not only their reserves of grain but also most of the seed they had set aside for planting. Medieval Europe lacked a system that could handle such massive crop failures. When harvests failed, the monasteries and charitable institutions also lost their crops and could not aid the starving. The king of England tried to import several shiploads of grain for distribution in those years, but these loads fell into the hands of pirates before they reached England.

Why was hunger so widespread in the early fourteenth century? Some historians see the root of trouble in the sheer number of people the lands had to support by 1300. The medieval population had been growing rapidly since about 1000, and by 1300 Europe, so this analysis suggests, was becoming the victim of its own success. Parts of the continent were crowded, even glutted, with people. Some areas of Normandy, for example, had a population in the early fourteenth century not much below what they supported six hundred years later. Thousands, millions even, had to be fed without chemical fertilizers, power tools, and fast transport. Masses of people had come to depend for their livelihood on infertile soils, and even in good years they were surviving on the margins of existence.

Although hunger did not always result in starvation, malnutrition raised the death rate from respiratory infections and intestinal ailments, which also reached epidemic proportions in the fourteenth century. While some parts of Europe returned to prosperity and good diets before the next disaster—plague—the experience of others demonstrated the dual impact of famine and plague. Barceleona and its province of Catalonia experienced famine in 1333; plague in 1347–1351;

famine in 1358–1359; and plague in 1362–1363, 1371, and 1397.

◆ PLAGUE

The great plague of the fourteenth century, known as the Black Death, provides a dramatic, but not a complete, explanation for the huge human losses. Plague is endemic (always present) in several parts of the world, including southwestern United States, and occasionally spreads to become a pandemic. In the mid-fourteenth century it spread along caravan routes of central Asia and arrived at the Black Sea ports. Europe's active trade in luxury items from the East gave plague a route to Europe. In 1347 a merchant ship sailing from Caffa in the Crimea to Messina in Sicily seems to have carried rats infected with the plague. A plague broke out at Messina, and from there it spread rapidly throughout Europe (see map 11.1).

Nature of the Disease The plague took several forms in Europe. The most identifiable one—the one that contemporary sources describe (see "Boccaccio on the Black Death," p. 365)—is the bubonic form. The pathogenic agent (not discovered until the late nineteenth century) is *Bacillus pestis*. While normally a disease of rodents, particularly house rats, it can spread to humans by fleas that carry the infection from rodents to humans through a flea bite. Bubonic plague has an incubation period of about two to ten days; its symptoms are chills, high fever, headache, and vomiting. The next symptoms are swellings (bubos) in lymph nodes of the groin and clotting blood under the skin, hence the name "Black Death." Death is likely in 90 percent of the cases. Plague also spreads through a pneumonic variety in which the droplets containing the infection can spread directly from human to human. Infection is very rapid and bubos may not form before the bacillus travels through the bloodstream to the lungs, causing pneumonia and death within three or four days. The real killer in the 1300s seems to have been pneumonic plague; it probably was spread through coughing and was almost always fatal.

In spite of the virulence of pneumonic plague, it is hard to believe that medical factors alone explain the awesome mortality. Europeans had maintained close contact with the East, where the

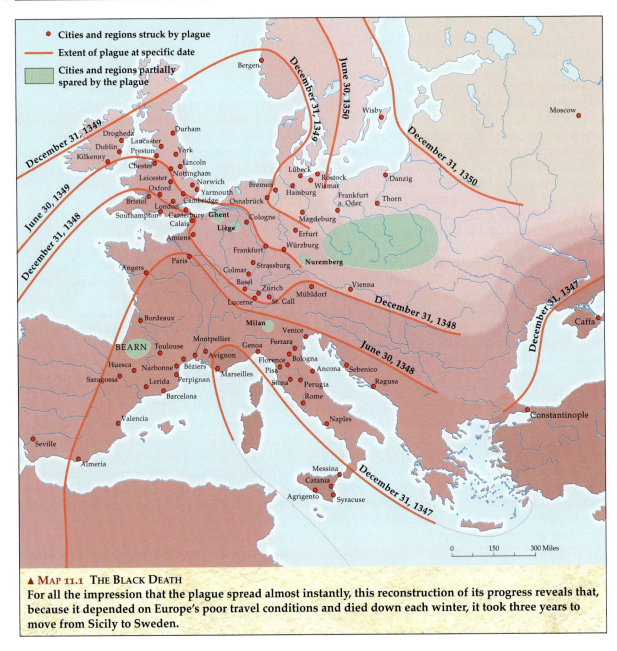

▲ MAP 11.1 THE BLACK DEATH
For all the impression that the plague spread almost instantly, this reconstruction of its progress reveals that, because it depended on Europe's poor travel conditions and died down each winter, it took three years to move from Sicily to Sweden.

plague had been endemic, since the eleventh century, but not until 1347 and 1348 did it make serious inroads in Europe. In addition, pneumonic plague is a disease of the winter months, but the plagues of the 1300s characteristically raged during the summer and declined in the cooler weather of autumn. Some scholars think the weather, which had become colder and wetter, brought famines and created a favorable environment for plague.

What made plague so much more terrifying than famine was that it struck the rich and poor; young and old, women and men; urban dwellers, nobles, peasants, monks, and clergy. Not knowing the cause of plague, physicians could do no more than lance the bubos to bring comfort, and many refused to treat plague patients at all. Those members of the clergy who went among the dying usually became infected themselves. Not knowing the true cause of the disease, people blamed the Jews

Boccaccio on the Black Death

◆

The following eyewitness description of the ravages of the Black Death in Florence was written by one of its most famous citizens, the writer Giovanni Boccaccio. This passage comes from his masterpiece, The Decameron, *written during the three years following the plague.*

"In the year of our Lord 1348, there happened at Florence a most terrible plague, which had broken out some years before in the Levant, and after making incredible havoc all the way, had now reached the west. There, in spite of all the means that art and human foresight could suggest, such as keeping the city clear from filth and the publication of copious instructions for preservation of health, it began to show itself in the spring. Unlike what had been seen in the east, where bleeding from the nose is the fatal prognostic, here there appeared certain tumors in the groin or under the arm-pits, some as big as a small apple, others as an egg, and afterwards purple spots in most parts of the body—messengers of death. To the cure of this malady neither medical knowledge nor the power of drugs was of any effect; whether because the disease was in its own nature mortal, or that the physicians (the number of whom, taking quacks and women pretenders into account, was grown very great) could form no just idea of the cause. Whichever was the reason, few escaped; but nearly all died the third day from the first appearance of the symptoms, some sooner, some later, without any fever or other symptoms. What gave the more virulence to this plague was that it spread daily, like fire when it comes in contact with combustibles. Nor was it caught only by coming near the sick, but even by touching their clothes. One instance of this kind I took particular notice of: the rags of a poor man just dead had been thrown into the street. Two hogs came up, and after rooting amongst the rags, in less than an hour they both turned around and died on the spot."

From Warren Hollister et al., *Medieval Europe: A Short Source Book* (McGraw-Hill Companies, 1992), pp. 248–249.

for poisoning the wells; others (the Flagelants) thought it was the wrath of God and walked in procession beating themselves. Eventually, cities formed a contagion theory of the disease and refused admittance within their walls of anyone who came from a city in which the plague was prevalent.

Pandemic The Black Death was not so much an epidemic as a pandemic (universal disease), striking an entire continent. The plague was the same one that had visited the Mediterranean and Western Europe in 542, during the reign of Justinian (see chapter 7). The plague struck not just once but repeatedly, until the last great outbreak in 1665, the Great Plague in London. A city was lucky if more than ten years went by without an onslaught; the plague was raging in some part of Europe almost every year.

Some of the horror of the plague can be glimpsed in this account by an anonymous cleric who visited the French city of Avignon in 1348: "To put the matter shortly, one-half, or more than a half, of the people at Avignon are already dead.

Within the walls of the city there are now more than 7,000 houses shut up; in these no one is living, and all who have inhabited them are departed. . . . On account of this great mortality there is such a fear of death that people do not dare even to speak with anyone whose relative has died, because it is frequently remarked that in a family where one dies nearly all the relations follow him."[1]

II. Economic Depression and Recovery

◆

A continent does not lose a third to a half of its population without feeling the effects immediately. After burying the dead, often in mass graves outside city walls, the survivors took stock of their economic position. According to contemporaries, survivors of the plague often gave up toiling in

[1]*Breve Chronicon clerici anonymi,* quoted in Francis Aidan Gasquet, *The Black Death of 1348 and 1349,* 1908, p. 46.

◀ THE *TRIUMPH OF DEATH*
The great social disaster of the Black Death left few traces in the visual arts; perhaps people did not wish to be reminded of its horrors. One exception was the *Triumph of Death*, a mural painted shortly after 1348 in the Camposanto (cemetery) of Pisa in Italy. In this detail of the mural, an elegant party of hunters happens upon corpses prepared for burial. Note the rider who holds a handkerchief — scented, undoubtedly — to his nose, to ward off the foul odors.
Art Resource, NY

the fields or looking after their shops; presumably, they saw no point in working for the future when it was so uncertain. But in the long run Europeans adapted to the new conditions. In agriculture, for example, the contraction of the population enabled the survivors to concentrate their efforts on better soils. In both agriculture and industry, the shortage of laborers was a challenge to landlords and entrepreneurs to save costs either by adopting productive measures that were less labor intensive or by increasing investment in labor-saving devices. Thus, the decline in population eventually encouraged Europeans to find better techniques for making the most of available resources.

◆ AGRICULTURAL SPECIALIZATION

Perhaps the best indication of the changes in the European economy comes from the history of prices. This evidence is scattered and rarely precise, but it does reveal roughly similar patterns in prices all over Europe. The cost of most agricultural products—cereals, wine, beer, oil, and meat—shot up immediately after the Black Death and stayed high until approximately 1375 in the north and 1395 in Italy. High food prices in a time

of declining population suggests that production was falling even more rapidly than the number of consumers. But high food prices mask the shift in agricultural production that led to greater specialization and improved diets.

Impact on the Peasantry   Some historians have called the period following the depletion of population a golden age for peasantry. Conditions did change for the peasants, but these changes were not uniformly for the better across Europe. The peasantry quickly realized that with labor in short supply they could demand higher wages for their labor, and that they could even break the bonds of their serfdom and move around the countryside to follow higher wages. The nobles and landlords were swift in their reaction to such gains.

In England the peasants had, as elsewhere in Europe, enjoyed a period of relative freedom from the labor demands of serfdom, but in the late thirteenth century landlords reimposed serfdom to take advantage of the money they could make from their crops in the period of high population and high demand for grain. With the sudden drop in population and demand for higher wages, Parliament passed the Statute of Laborers in 1351, which fixed prices and wages at what they were in 1347, the year before the plague. Like any law against supply and demand, the statute was hard to enforce, and during the course of the fifteenth century serfdom gradually disappeared in England, as the population moved away from the old manors or simply refused to pay any dues other than their rent.

Serfdom Revisited England's experience of a gradual decline in serfdom was by no means the pattern for Europe as a whole. In some parts of Europe, serfdom was reimposed or newly imposed in response to the decrease in laborers. In the eleventh and twelfth centuries, lords in the newly opened lands of Prussia and Poland offered peasants freedom to come and settle. By the late fifteenth century peasants began to lose their freedom in Poland, and by the early sixteenth century peasants in Hungary, Bohemia, Silesia, and Poland were serfs. By the early thirteenth century serfdom had almost disappeared in France, Italy, and western Germany. Following the Black Death, however, lords moved to reinstate it, and vestiges of it were to remain in those countries through the eighteenth century. In Catalonia, the thirteenth century saw a rise in serfdom and it was not until the late fifteenth century that serfs were freed.

Agricultural Specialization One branch of agriculture that enjoyed a remarkable period of growth in the fifteenth century was sheep raising. Since the prices for wool, skins, mutton, and cheese remained high, English landlords sought to take advantage of the market by fencing large fields and converting them from plowland into sheep pastures and expelling the peasants or small herders who had formerly lived there. This process, called enclosure, continued for centuries and played an important role in English economic and social history. Other countries as well began to have agricultural specialization. Netherlands did cheese and dairy while Spain developed Merino wool.

By the middle of the fifteenth century, agricultural prices stabilized, suggesting that production had become more dependable. Farms enjoyed the advantages of larger size, better location on more profitable soil, and increased capital investments in tools and animals. Agriculture was now more diversified, which benefited the soil, lowered the risk of famine from the failure of a single staple crop, and provided more nourishment for the people.

Gentry The specialized agriculture brought prosperity to the land-owning nobility, but also to a new rural middle class. The middle-class urban dwellers, lawyers, bureaucrats, and wealthy peasants began to invest in land in the countryside. With capital to invest in either the purchase or lease of land, these people made considerable profits. New fortunes gave rise to a country middle class called the gentry.

◆ PROTECTIONISM

The movement of prices created serious problems for employers in cities. As the labor force contracted, wages in most towns surged to levels as much as four times higher than they had been before 1348. Although the prices of manufactured goods also increased, they did not rise as much as wages, and this trend reduced profit margins. To offset these unfavorable tendencies, the employers sought government intervention. Between 1349 and 1351, England, France, Aragon, Castile, and other governments tried to fix prices and wages at levels favorable to employers. The typical policy was to forbid employers to pay more than customary wages and to require laborers to accept jobs at those wages. Such early experiments in a controlled economy failed.

Guilds on the Defensive A related problem for businesses was that competition grew as population fell and markets contracted. Traders tried to protect themselves by creating restricted markets and establishing monopolies. Guilds limited their membership, and some admitted only the sons of established masters. To keep prices high, some guilds prohibited their members from hiring any women as workers because their wages were low. Only wives and daughters of the household could work in the shops.

The Hanseatic League Probably the best example of the monopolizing trend is the association of northern European trading cities, the Hanseatic League. Formed in the late thirteenth century as a defensive association, by the early fourteenth

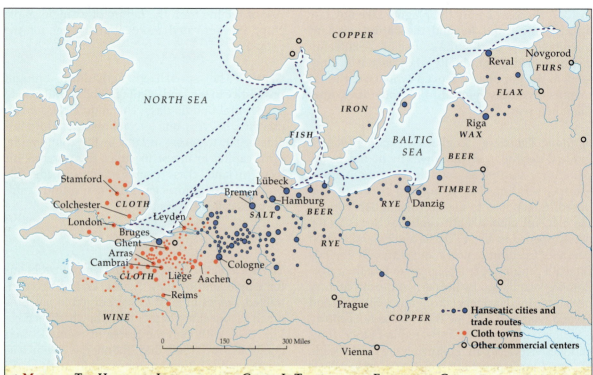

▲ **Map 11.2** The Hanseatic League and the Goods It Traded in the Fourteenth Century
Even in the age of the Black Death, international trade remained vigorous in northern Europe. Its leaders were the cities of the Hanseatic League, which shipped a variety of commodities across the continent, though the most sought-after commodity was the cloth produced in England, the Netherlands, and northern France.

century it imposed a monopoly on cities trading in the Baltic and North seas. It excluded foreigners from the Baltic trade and could expel member cities who broke trade agreements. At its height, the Hanseatic League included seventy or eighty cities, stretching from Bruges to Novgorod and led by Bremen, Cologne, Hamburg, and especially Lübeck (see map 11.2). Maintaining its own treasury and fleet, the league supervised commercial exchange, policed the waters of the Baltic Sea, and negotiated with foreign princes. By the late fifteenth century, however, it began to decline and was unable to meet growing competition from the Dutch in northern commerce. Never formally abolished, the Hanseatic League continued to meet—at lengthening intervals—until 1669.

◆ TECHNOLOGICAL ADVANCES

Attempts to raise the efficiency of workers proved to be far more effective than wage and price regulation in laying the basis for recovery. Employers were able to counteract high wages by adopting more rational methods of production and substituting capital for labor—that is, providing workers with better tools. Although hard times and labor shortages inspired most technical advances of the 1300s and 1400s, increased efficiency helped to make Europe a richer community.

Metallurgy Mining and metallurgy benefited from a series of inventions after 1460 that lowered the cost of metals and extended their use. Better techniques of digging, shoring, ventilating, and draining allowed mine shafts to be sunk several hundred feet into the earth, permitting the large-scale exploitation of the deep, rich mineral deposits of central Europe. Some historians estimate that the output from the mines of Hungary, the Tyrol, Bohemia, and Saxony grew as much as five times between 1460 and 1530. During this period, miners in Saxony discovered a method for extracting pure silver from the lead alloy in which it was often found—an invention that was of major

▲ Mining, 1389

One does not normally associate miners with elegant decoration, but in this fourteenth-century manuscript, a miner provides the subject for the ornamentation of the capital *M* that starts the word *metalla* (metals). That the artist even considered such a subject is an indication of the growing importance of the industry in this period.
Index, © Giancarlo Costa

importance for the later massive development of silver mines in America. Larger furnaces came into use, and huge bellows and trip-hammers, driven by waterpower, aided the smelting and working of metals. Simultaneously, the masters of the trade were acquiring a new precision in the difficult art of casting.

By the late fifteenth century, European mines were providing an abundance of silver bullion for coinage. Money became more plentiful, which stimulated the economy. Exploitation also began in the rich coal deposits of northern Europe. Expanding iron production meant more and stronger pumps, gears and machine parts, tools, and iron wares; such products found wide application in construction work and shipbuilding. Skill in metalworking contributed to two other inventions: firearms and movable metal type.

Firearms and Weapons Europeans were constantly trying to improve the arts of war in the Middle Ages. The crossbow was cranked up and shot with a trigger; it was so powerful that it could penetrate conventional armor. The long bow came into widespread use during the Welsh wars of Edward I. It was light, accurate, and could be shot rapidly. In response to these two weapons, armor became more elaborate, with exaggerated convex surfaces designed to deflect arrows from the chest, arms, and knees.

Siege weapons that hurled projectiles with great force and accuracy were also important. Adapting a Chinese invention for fireworks consisting of an explosive mixture of carbon, sulfur, and saltpeter, the Europeans developed gunpowder and cannons to hurl boulders at an enemy. Firearms are first mentioned in 1328, and cannons were used in the early battles of the Hundred Years' War. At first, their effect was chiefly psychological: The thunderous roar, merely by frightening the enemy's horses, did far more damage than the usually inaccurate shots. Still, a breakthrough had been made, and cannons gained in military importance. They played a major role in the fall of Constantinople in 1453. Their development depended primarily on stronger, more precise casting, on proper granulation of the powder to ensure that the charge burned at the right speed and put its full force behind the projectile, and on an understanding of the trajectory of the cannon ball when fired. With firearms, fewer soldiers could fight more effectively; capital, in the form of an efficient though expensive tool, was being substituted for labor.

Military Engineering Medieval architects and artists had long been interested in military engineering as well as building. Konrad Kyeser wrote and illustrated a book of weapons of war between 1395 and 1405. His work included cannons, siphons and wheels for raising water, pontoon bridges, hot-air balloons, and a device to pull horses across streams. He also made drawings of multiple guns arranged like a revolver. A Bohemian engineer's sketchbook shows the

▲ The *English Siege of Orléans* (1428–1429) shows the English soldiers behind a siege wall (left) firing cannons across the Loire River. The cannons at this stage were more frightening for their noise than for their destructive power because of design problems. The siege of Orléans was brought to an end by a French relief force led by Joan of Arc.
Bibliothèque Nationale de France, Paris

development of the use of cannon over fifty years; his book also has drawings of a primitive tank and a diving suit complete with a tube for getting air. Iacopo Mariano of Siena drew all sorts of mechanical counterbalances, that helped to operate cranes, bridges, and wells.

Mechanical Clocks Telling time in the Middle Ages was imprecise, based as it was on the position of the sun and the canonical hours for prayer at about three-hour intervals during the day. Times of meetings, for instance, were set within vague parameters of "at vesper," "at sunrise," or even within a few days. But in 1360 Henry De Vick designed the first mechanical clock with an hour hand for King Charles V of France, which

was placed in the royal palace in Paris. Other clocks had been alluded to in sources, but De Vick's marked the start of mechanical clocks in municipal buildings and large churches. Large astronomical clocks that showed the signs of the zodiac were the precursors of clocks that kept time and tolled the hours. Milan had a clock that struck a bell at every hour of the day. The regular ringing of the hours brought a new regularity to life, work, and markets and gave time itself a new value. Even if the clocks were inaccurate, they gave a focus to time and to the possibility of hours kept distinct from the seasonal position of the sun. Pocket watches, although cumbersome, had appeared by 1550 with the invention of the spring for running clocks.

▲ The mechanical clock, a medieval invention, was installed in major buildings. The Wells Cathedral clock was built in England. The face was decorated with the four winds and angels. The clock told the hours twenty-four hours a day and told the days in the lunar month. Bells tolled the hours.
(Top) Derek Bayes/Aspect Picture Library Ltd.
(Bottom) Science Museum, London

Printing The extension of literacy among laypeople and the greater reliance of governments and businesses on records created a demand for a cheap method of reproducing the written word. The introduction of paper from the East was a major step in reducing costs, for paper is far cheaper than parchment to produce. A substitute for the time-consuming labor of writing by hand was also necessary: Scribes and copiers were skilled artisans who commanded high salaries. To cut costs, printers first tried to press woodcuts—inked blocks with letters or designs carved on them—onto paper or parchment. But these "block books" represented only a small advance over handwriting, since a separate woodcut had to be carved for each page, and they tended to split after being pressed a number of times.

By the middle of the fifteenth century several masters were on the verge of perfecting the technique of printing with movable metal type. The first to prove this practicable was Johannes Gutenberg of Mainz, a former jeweler and stonecutter. Gutenberg devised an alloy of lead, tin, and antimony that would melt at a low temperature, cast well in the die, and be durable in the press; this alloy is still the basis of the printer's art. His Bible, printed in 1455, is the first major work reproduced through printing.

The technique spread rapidly. By 1500 some 250 European cities had presses. German masters held an early leadership, but Italians soon challenged their preeminence. The Venetian printer Aldus Manutius and his fellow Italians rejected the elaborate Gothic typeface used in the north and developed their own *italic* type, modeled on the clear script they found in old manuscripts. They believed this was the style of writing used in ancient Rome, but in fact they were imitating the Carolingian minuscule script.

The Information Revolution The immediate effect of the printing press was to multiply the output and cut the costs of books (see map 11.3). It made information available to a much broader segment of the population, and libraries could store more information at lower cost. Printing helped disseminate and preserve knowledge in standardized form—a major contribution to the advance of technology and scholarship. Printing produced a revolution in what we would call information

◄ Gutenberg's Bible
A page from Johannes Gutenberg's Bible marks one of the most significant technical and cultural advances of the fifteenth century: printing with movable type, a process that made possible a wider dissemination of literature and thought.
E. Harold Hugo

technology, and indeed it resembles in many ways the profound changes that computers are making in our own lives. Finally, printing could spread new ideas with unprecedented speed—a fact that was not fully appreciated, however, until the 1500s, when print became essential to the propaganda of religious reformers in the Protestant Reformation.

◆ THE STANDARD OF LIVING

For those who survived the famine, plagues, and wars, the standard of living became better as the economy began to grow again in the late fifteenth century; but the pall of death and disease hung over the survivors.

▲ MAP 11.3 THE SPREAD OF PRINTING BEFORE 1500
After its invention in the Rhineland, printing first spread along the rivers that were Europe's main highways. By 1500 it was concentrated mainly in southern Germany, the Netherlands, and northern Italy.

Reduced Life Expectancy The family memoirs of Florentine merchants, which recorded births and deaths, suggest that life expectancy from birth for these relatively affluent persons was forty years in about 1300, dropping to only eighteen years in the generation of the Black Death, and rising to thirty years in the fifteenth century as the plagues declined in virulence. (Today in the United States a newborn may be expected to survive for more than 76 years.) The principal victims were the very young. In many periods, between a half and a third of the babies born never reached age fifteen. Society swarmed with little children, but their deaths were common occurrences in almost every family.

The plague took a greater toll among young adults than among the aged. In effect, a person who survived one or more major epidemics had a good chance of living through the next onslaught. A mild attack of plague brought immunity rather than death as the population built up resistance to the disease; a favored few thus did reach extreme old age. The young adults always faced high risks of dying, perhaps because of their first exposure to plague or from other diseases. Friars who entered the convent of Sta. Maria Novella at Florence in the last half of the fourteenth century, for example, lived an average of only twenty years after entering their order (which they usually did in their late teens). The death toll of people in their child-bearing years slowed the demographic recovery.

Female Survival   Women seemed to be more robust than men in resisting or recovering from plague and the other diseases, and they became a

disproportionately larger part of the population. Historians have interpreted this fact in a number of ways. Some have argued that women took a greater role in urban and rural life and that this was a golden age for women. As historians find more evidence about women during this period, however, it appears that while more women found employment in urban centers, their roles were limited to household servants and unskilled labor. Women did not move into positions of power in government or guilds. Indeed, female guilds that had women as guild officers were forced to elect men.

Misogyny or the Debate over Women's Nature
Witchcraft charges against women were rare in the Middle Ages, but some historians have argued that the greater preponderance of women in the population contributed to the witch hunts of the sixteenth centuries. By the Late Middle Ages the intellectual debate about women's nature had become more pointed (see chapter 16). Both the ancient and the medieval world had relegated women to inferior positions, and some of the ancient and Christian authors had added strong negative invectives against women. The Church offered two images of women—Eve, the sinner who led Adam astray in the Garden of Eden, and the Virgin Mary, mother of Jesus. Neither image fit ordinary women's lives very well. As we saw in the last chapter, some very pious women commanded the respect of the Church through their asceticism.

The debate over women's nature came to the forefront early in the fourteenth century when Jean de Meun, an educated layman, revised a thirteenth-century poem, *The Romance of the Rose.* His additions became a satire on human follies, particularly those of the clergy and of women. Relying on ancient authors, theologians, and contemporary folklore, de Meun outlined the depravity, vanity, fickleness, and weaknesses of women.

A number of famous authors replied to his poem in the late fourteenth century, including Christine de Pisan. Christine's father was an Italian who had come to France as court astronomer to the French king. Her father oversaw her education in Latin and French. She married a French

▼ CHRISTINE DE PISAN PRESENTS POEMS TO ISABEAU OF BAVARIA
Christine de Pisan (1364–1439) was the author of several important historical and literary works including a biography of King Charles V of France and *The Book of the Three Virtues*, a manual for the education of women. She is here depicted presenting a volume of her poems to the queen of France, who is surrounded by ladies-in-waiting and the symbol of the French royal family, the fleur-de-lis. It is significant that there were such scenes of elegance and intellectual life even amidst the chaos and destruction of the Hundred Years' War.
By Permission of The British Library. Harly Ms. 4431 fol 3

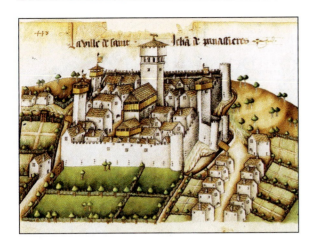

▲ View of Panissières, from a Fifteenth-Century Armorial

As the population of Europe began to recover from the Black Death, signs of expansion and prosperity became evident in its most fertile regions. This fifteenth-century view of the town of Panissières, in the rich Loire valley in France, indicates that houses were again springing up and fields were being cultivated outside the walls of the fortified heart of the town.

Bibliothèque Nationale de France, Paris

nobleman, but when he died, leaving her a widow with young children, she turned to writing and translating to make a living. Among her books was *The City of Ladies*, a refutation of Jean de Meun. She pointed to all the heroic women in history as examples of women's superior qualities, describing virtue in the most trying circumstances, heroism, self-sacrifice, wisdom, and leadership (see "The Status of Women in the Middle Ages: Historiographical Debate," p. 376).

Knowledge of the Human Body

During the Late Middle Ages, some modest advances were made in medicine. Eyeglasses, invented in the thirteenth century, were perfected in the fourteenth century. For the most part they were designed for reading rather than distance vision.

Until the later part of the Middle Ages, religious prohibitions against dissecting the human cadaver meant that medicine had not advanced much beyond the Hellenistic and Arabic contributions. By the end of the thirteenth century, a teacher of medicine at the University of Bologna wrote a textbook on dissections with illustrations of human anatomy. With a superior knowledge of the human body, physicians' ability to diagnose ills advanced, but their knowledge of cures did not. Surgery remained the practice of barber-surgeons, guildsmen whose sharp knives could shave beards and perform surgery and whose supply of leeches could draw blood. Such men remained more important for immediate cures than did university-trained physicians.

Housing and Diets

The revitalized economy brought improvements in housing, dress, and diet and increased spending on art and decorative objects. Housing was generally improving for most people in the Late Middle Ages. The increasing use of brick and tile meant that buildings were more substantial and more spacious. Changes in warfare meant that only kings could afford to build castles that would withstand a siege of cannons. The nobility, gentry, and wealthy urban dwellers built large town houses and country houses with gardens and large windows rather than defensive walls. The fireplace on the wall replaced the hearth in the center of the room even in peasant houses.

The European diet had been largely based on cereal products, and when population was dense, all land had to be devoted to raising grain, even if the land was not particularly well suited for it. Reduced population meant that land could be devoted to other crops or to animal rearing. Diet generally improved, with more meat, cheese, oil, butter, fruit, wine, and beer.

Courtesy and Dress

Refinements in living brought a new emphasis on polite behavior, particularly at the table. Guild ordinances began to include instructions about manners at the annual feast, and books of advice for young people moving up in social station proliferated in every language. Silver forks replaced fingers as a tool for polite dining among the upper class.

Dress for the upper classes became very grand, with the tall pointed caps and the long pointed shoes that we associate with medieval Europe. That the fine dress was not limited to the upper classes is obvious from the sumptuary legislation that cities and kingdoms passed, which tried to

THE STATUS OF WOMEN IN THE MIDDLE AGES: HISTORIOGRAPHICAL DEBATE

◆

The study of medieval women has become a major area of historical research in the past thirty years. Scholars have raised a number of unresolved questions about women's lives and their experiences. The questions discussed here suggest ongoing areas of research.

1. Does the periodization of political history apply to women's history or to the history of ordinary people? Historians have used watersheds in political history such as the Battle of Bosworth Field in 1485 to define the end of medieval England and the beginning of early modern England. But did women or peasants wake up after the battle and declare that a new era had begun and life was going to change for them? Intellectual movements, since they largely involved men, may have had little influence on women's lives, as Joan Kelly asked in her famous essay, "Did Women Have a Renaissance?"*

2. To what extent did the Church's misogyny influence the way women lived? In Church writings, women were either saintly like the Virgin Mary or sinners like Eve. The Church blessed women's roles only as virgins or as wives and mothers. The general misogyny was also prevalent in medieval lay society and appeared in jokes, in literary pieces such as the *Romance of the Rose,* and in various regulations regarding women. But did women consciously take these strictures to heart when they lived their everyday lives? Some women did move into positions of power as regents and queens; powerful female saints and mystics became a part of late medieval religious life; women joined the tertiaries and the Beguinages. Individual peasant and urban women farmed their plots or ran their own businesses. Many other women moved into business and administrative capacities when their husbands were away or when they became widows. But women who took these initiatives generally worked within a framework of acceptable female behavior. Joan of Arc, on the other hand, offended the Church perhaps more because she adopted male dress and role than because of the heresy and witchcraft charges the Inquisitors brought.

3. Understanding the role of patriarchy is important for understanding women's freedom in marriage and widowhood. Customs varied greatly depending on the availability of women for marriage, on local laws covering dower and dowry, and on economic necessity. Some marriage arrangements, particularly among the peasantry, assumed that the household was the unit of economic production and that the sex roles were equally important for the survival of the family. In urban Florence the age differences between spouses seemed to preclude a strong voice for a young bride. Other studies will, no doubt, show other patterns.

4. Women's participation in intellectual and political life continues to be researched. Women could not attend universities, be ordained as priests, or participate in legal and magisterial roles. On the other hand, nunneries, courts, and individual experiences did permit them to write, engage in intellectual debate, and contribute to the cultural enrichment of the Middle Ages. Much women's writing and artistic work has been lost, but enough survives to indicate the ways women participated in the cultural life of the Middle Ages. Christine de Pisan is an example of a writer who was so well-known that Richard II of England offered to be her patron.

*Joan Kelly, *Women, History, and Theory: The Essays of Joan Kelly* (University of Chicago Press, 1984), pp. 19–50.

regulate who was allowed to wear fine cloth with furs and who was prohibited from doing so.

Art for the Lay Consumer Consumption of art for domestic residences changed. In the past the chief patrons of the arts had been churches and nobility, and the major artistic themes had been religious. With more disposable wealth and a larger middle class, consumption patterns changed. While laypeople still gave heavily to the Church, they tended to give for the building of parish churches rather than cathedrals. But they also bought fine silver and gold objects, jewelry, furniture, and paintings, including portraits of themselves and their families. Oil paint was the favored new medium for pictures.

▲ **Dress became very elaborate, with tall headdresses for women and pointed shoes and tights for men. The most elaborate court was that of the Duke of Burgundy, which is pictured here with courtiers dancing.**
Bibliothèque Nationale de France, Paris

III. Popular Unrest

The demographic collapse and economic troubles of the fourteenth century deeply disturbed the social peace of Europe. European society had been remarkably stable and mostly peaceful from the Early Middle Ages until around 1300, and there is little evidence of uprisings or social warfare. The fourteenth and fifteenth centuries, however, witnessed numerous revolts of peasants and artisans against what they believed to be the oppression of the propertied classes.

◆ RURAL REVOLTS

One of the most spectacular fourteenth-century rural uprisings was the English Peasants' Revolt of 1381. This revolt originated in popular resentment against both the policies of the royal government and the practices of the great landlords. Although the Statute of Laborers (1351), which

tried to fix prices and wages at the preplague level, had little practical success, the mere effort to implement it aggravated social tensions, especially in the countryside, where it would have reimposed serfdom on the peasants. Concurrent attempts to collect poll taxes (a flat tax on each member of the population), which by their nature demanded less from the prosperous than the humble, crystallized resentment against the government.

Under leaders of uncertain background—Wat Tyler, Jack Straw, and a priest named John Ball—peasant bands, enraged by the latest poll tax, marched on London in 1381. They called for the abolition of serfdom, labor services, and tithes and demanded an end to the poll taxes. The workers of London, St. Albans, York, and other cities who had similar grievances rose in support of the peasants. After mobs killed the king's advisers and burned the houses of prominent lawyers and royal officials, King Richard II, then age fifteen, bravely met with the peasants in person at Mile End, outside the walls of London. One of his followers killed Wat Tyler as he negotiated with the king. Thinking quickly, Richard told the peasants that he was their leader and promised to give them charters of freedom. But as the peasants dispersed, the great landlords reorganized their forces and violently suppressed the last vestiges of unrest in the countryside; the young king also reneged on his promises and declared the charters invalid.

The peasant uprising in England was only one of many rural disturbances between 1350 and 1450, including revolts near Paris, called the Jacquerie, and in Languedoc, Catalonia, and Sweden. Germany also experienced such disturbances in the fifteenth century and a major peasant revolt in 1524, which was to feed into the tensions of the early days of the Protestant Reformation.

◆ URBAN REVOLTS

The causes of social unrest within the cities were similar to those in the countryside—wages and taxes. In the 1300s and early 1400s, Strasburg, Metz, Ghent, Liège, and Paris were all scenes of riots. Though not entirely typical, one of the most interesting of these urban revolts was the Ciompi uprising at Florence in 1378.

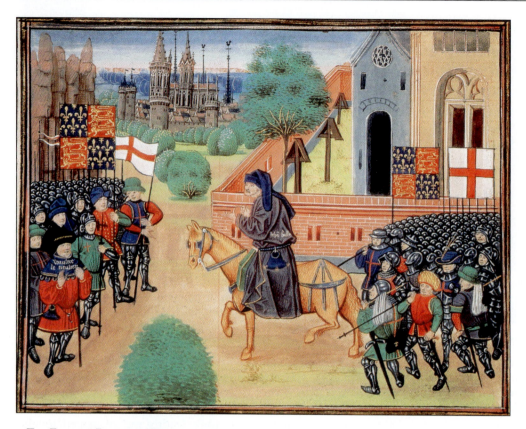

▲ The English Peasants' Revolt of 1381
One of the leaders of the peasant revolt was a preacher, John Ball, who is shown on the horse. One of his messages was a simple egalitarian rhyme: "When Adam delved and Eve span, where then were all the gentlemen?" Wat Tyler, another leader, is in the foreground holding a banner with the English coat of arms. Rather than a rabble with pitchforks, many peasants had trained in the militia that defended the English coast against French raids. Loyal to the king, the peasants did not want to kill him, but rather to get rid of his bad advisers.
British Library, London/Bridgeman Art Library

The Ciompi   Florence was one of the wool manufacturing centers of Europe; the industry employed probably one-third of the working population of the city, which shortly before the Black Death may have risen to 120,000 people. The wool industry, like most, entered bad times immediately after the plague. To protect themselves, employers cut production, thereby spreading unemployment. Since many of the employers were also members of the ruling oligarchy, they passed laws limiting wages and manipulating taxation and monetary policy to benefit the rich. The poorest workers were denied their own guild and had no collective voice that could influence the government. In all disputes they were subject to the employers' laws and judges.

The poorest workers—mainly the wool carders, known as *Ciompi*—rose in revolt. They demanded, and for a short time got, several reforms: The employers would produce at least enough cloth to ensure work, they would refrain from monetary manipulations considered harmful to the workers, and they would allow the workers their own guild and representation in communal government. These concessions did not offer any power for the workers, but they were nevertheless intolerable to the ruling oligarchy. Because the Ciompi did not have the leaders to maintain a steady influence on government policy, the great families regained full authority in the city by 1382 and quickly ended the democratic concessions. Although the Ciompi revolt was short-lived and ultimately unsuccessful, the incident is one of the first signs of the urban class tensions that would be a regular disturbance in future centuries.

◆ THE SEEDS OF DISCONTENT

While local and unique circumstances shaped each of the social disturbances of the 1300s and 1400s, the social movements had common elements. With the standard of living generally rising after the Black Death, misery was not the main cause of unrest. Rather, the peasants and workers, now reduced in number, were better able to bargain for lower rents, higher wages, and a fairer distribution of social benefits.

With the possible exception of the Ciompi, the people who revolted were rarely the desperately poor. In England, for example, the centers of the peasant uprising of 1381 were in the lower Thames valley—a region with more fertility, more prosperity, less oppression, and less serfdom than other parts of the kingdom had. Also, the immediate provocation for the revolt was the imposition of a poll tax, and poll taxes (or any taxes) do not alarm the truly destitute who cannot be forced to pay what they do not have, but they do anger people who have recently made financial gains and are anxious to hold on to them.

The principal goad to revolt in both town and country, therefore, seems to have been the effort of the propertied classes to retain their old advantages and deny the workers their new ones. Peasants and workers felt that their improving social and economic status was being threatened.

The impulse to revolt also drew strength from the psychological tensions of this age of devastating plagues, famines, and wars. The nervous temper of the times predisposed people to take action against real or imagined enemies. When needed, justifications for revolt could be found in Christian belief, for the Christian fathers had taught that neither the concept of private property nor social inequality had been intended by God. In John Ball's words: "When Adam delved and Eve span, where then were all the gentlemen?" The emotional climate of the period turned many of these uprisings into efforts to attain the millennium, to reach that age of justice and equality that Christ-

ian belief saw in the past, expected in the future, and put off for the present.

IV. Challenges to the Governments of Europe

◆

War, the third horseman of the Apocalypse, joined famine and disease. War was frequent throughout the Middle Ages but was never so widespread or long lasting as in the conflicts of the 1300s and 1400s. The Hundred Years' War between England and France is the most famous of these struggles, but there was fighting in every corner of Europe. The inbred violence of the age indicated a partial breakdown in governmental systems, which failed to maintain stability at home and peace with foreign powers.

The governmental systems of Europe were founded on multiple partnerships: feudal ties with vassals, relations with the Church, representative institutions, and subjects in general. The king enjoyed supreme dignity and even a recognized sacred character, but he was far from being an absolute ruler. In return for loyalty and service, he conceded a large share of the responsibility for government to a wide range of privileged persons and institutions: the great secular and ecclesiastical princes, the nobles, religious congregations, free cities or communes, and even favored guilds such as the universities. Out of the crises of the fourteenth and fifteenth centuries many of the new governments that came to dominate the European political scene in the late 1400s conceded far more power to a king, prince, despot, or oligarchy.

◆ ROOTS OF POLITICAL UNREST

Dynastic Instability   In a period of demographic instability, dynasties suffered, as did the population as a whole. The Hundred Years' War, or at least the excuse for it, arose from the failure of the Capetian kings of France, for the first time since the tenth century, to produce a male heir. The English War of the Roses resulted from the uncertain succession to the crown of England and the claims of the two rival houses of Lancaster and York. In Portugal, Castile, France, England, Naples,

Hungary, Poland, and the Scandinavian countries, the reigning monarchs of 1450 were not the direct, male, legitimate descendants of those reigning in 1300. Most of the founders of new lines had to fight for their positions.

Changes in Warfare   The same powerful economic forces that were creating new patterns of agriculture and trade were also reshaping the fiscal policies and financial machinery of feudal governments. War grew more expensive as well as more frequent. Better-trained armies were needed to fight for longer periods of time and with more complex weaponry. Above all, the increasing use of firearms added to the costs of war. To replace the traditional, undisciplined, unpaid, and poorly equipped feudal armies, governments came to rely on mercenaries, who were better trained and better armed than the vassals who fought to fulfill their feudal obligations. The major battles of the Hundred Years' War—those of Crécy, Poitiers, and Agincourt—showed the advantage of well-trained foot soldiers over knights. Many mercenaries were organized into associations known as companies of adventure, whose leaders were both good commanders and good businessmen. They took their enterprise where the market was most favorable, sold their services to the highest bidder, and turned substantial profits. Money increasingly determined who could hire mercenaries and thereby win battles.

Seeking Revenue   While war went up in price, the traditional revenues on which governments depended sank. Until the fourteenth century, the king or prince met most of the expenses of government from ordinary revenues, chiefly rents from his properties; but his rents, like everyone else's, were falling in the late Middle Ages. Governments of all types—monarchies, the papacy, cities—desperately sought to develop new sources of revenue. For example, the Avignon papacy, because it could not rely on the meager receipts from its lands, built a huge financial apparatus that sold ecclesiastical appointments, favors, and dispensations from normal canonical requirements; imposed tithes on ecclesiastical revenues; and sold remissions of sin known as indulgences. In France the monarchy established a monopoly over the sale of salt. In England the

king at various times imposed taxes on movable goods and on individuals (the poll tax), plus a host of smaller levies. The Italian cities taxed a whole range of items from windows to prostitutes. Under acute fiscal pressures, governments scrutinized the necessities, pleasures, and sins of society to find sources of revenue. Surviving fiscal records indicate that governments managed to increase their incomes hugely through taxes. For example, the English monarchy never collected or spent more than £30,000 per year before 1336; thereafter, the budget rarely sank below £100,000 and at times reached £250,000 in the late fourteenth century.

Representative Institutions   This new reliance on extraordinary taxes had important political consequences. The most lucrative taxes were not limited to the ruler's own lands but extended over all of the realm. Since he had no established right to these demands, the king had to seek the consent of his subjects. Therefore, he had to summon territorial or national assemblies of estates, such as Parliament in England or the Estates General in France, to grant new taxes. But these assemblies, in turn, often balked at the demands or offered taxes only in return for political concessions. Even in the Church, many reformers maintained that a general council should have ultimate control over papal finances. The extraordinary expansion of governmental revenues thus raised profound constitutional questions in both secular and ecclesiastical governments.

◆ THE NOBILITY AND FACTIONAL STRIFE

The Nobility   The nobility that had developed nearly everywhere in Europe also entered a period of instability in the Late Middle Ages. Birth was the main means of access to this class, and membership offered legal and social privileges such as exemption from most taxes, immunity from certain juridical procedures (such as torture), and hunting privileges. The nobles saw themselves as the chief counselors of the king and his principal partners in the conduct of government.

By the 1300s, however, the nobles began to experience economic instability. Their wealth was chiefly in land, and they, like all landlords, faced

▲ Family Towers at Lucca
This fourteenth-century view of the Italian city of Lucca testifies to the violence of factional conflict within these cities. Each major family and its leading supporters built a defensible structure, topped by an identifiable tower. Here, in a large building that surrounded a central courtyard and had its own chapel, they could find refuge from rival families and factions.
Scala/Art Resource, NY

the problem of declining rents. Unlike the gentry, they often lacked the funds needed for the new agricultural investments, and they continued to have the problem of finding income and careers for their younger sons. In short, the nobles were not immune from the acute economic dislocations of the times, and their class included men who lived on the brink of poverty as well as holders of enormous estates.

Factional Politics   To maintain their position, some of the nobles joined the mercenary companies. Others hoped to buttress their sinking fortunes through marriage or by winning offices, lands, pensions, or other favors from governments. But as the social uncertainties intensified, the nobles tended to coalesce into factions that disputed with one another over the control of government and the distribution of its favors. From England to Italy, factional warfare constantly disturbed the peace. A divided and grasping nobility added to the tensions of the age and to its violence.

Characteristically, a faction was led by a great noble house and included people of varying social station—great nobles in alliance with the leading royal house, poor knights, retainers, servants, sometimes even artisans and peasants. Some of the factions encompassed scores of families and hundreds of men and could almost be considered little states within a state, with their own small armies, loyalties, and symbols of allegiance in the colors or distinctive costumes (livery) worn by their members.

The Pastons   A good example of liveried retainers of these great nobles are the Pastons of England. The family originated from wealthy peasant stock who prospered in the agricultural opportunities of the fifteenth century. The founder of the family fortune, William, managed to marry up socially, taking a knight's daughter as wife. He educated his sons in law because land could be gained by legal maneuverings as well as through advantageous marriages. He was also careful about the local patronage system and placed his eldest son, John, in the Duke of Norfolk's household. John was part of the duke's retinue on ceremonial occasions. Sir John Fastolf, a soldier who made a fortune in the Hundred Years' War and was the model for Shakespeare's Falstaff, relied on John for legal advice and eventually made him his heir. The Pastons continually defended their lands either in court or in actual sieges. At one point John's wife, Margaret, organized the defense of one of their manors from armed attack. The people trying to obtain their property had the support of other great lords in the district, particularly the Duke of Suffolk. The family managed to survive the War of the Roses to emerge in the sixteenth century as nobility.

◆ ENGLAND, FRANCE, AND THE HUNDRED YEARS' WAR

All the factors that upset the equilibrium of feudal governments—dynastic instability, fiscal pressures, and factional rivalries—helped to provoke the greatest struggle of the epoch, the Hundred Years' War. The war had distinctive characteristics. It was not fought continually for one hundred years, but in different phases. The great battles were of less significance for determining the outcome than was the war of attrition against the population. Economic embargo and interruption of trade became weapons of states in winning wars.

Causes   The issue that is alleged to have started the Hundred Years' War was a dispute over the French royal succession. While most noble families had direct father-to-son succession for only three generations, the Capetians had produced male heirs for three hundred years. The last three Capetian kings (the sons of Philip IV, the Fair), all died without male heirs. In 1328, when the last Capetian died, the nearest surviving male relative was King Edward III of England, son of Philip's daughter Isabella. The Parlement of Paris—the supreme court of France—discovered that the laws of the Salian Franks precluded women from inheriting or transmitting a claim to the crown. Philip of Valois, a first cousin of the previous kings, became king. Edward did not at first dispute this decision, and, as holder of the French fiefs of Aquitaine and Ponthieu, he did homage to Philip VI.

More important than the dynastic issue was the clash of French and English interests in Flanders, an area whose cloth-making industry relied on

▼ *Ambrogio Lorenzetti*
THE *PEACEFUL CITY* (DETAIL FROM *GOOD GOVERNMENT*), 1338–1341
The effects of good government, seen in this idealized representation of the *Peaceful City* by Ambrogio Lorenzetti, include flourishing commerce, dancing maidens, and lavish residences, as opposed to the protective towers of feudal warfare. This fresco in the city hall of Siena was a constant reminder to the citizens of the advantages of living in their city.
Scala/Art Resource, NY

England for wool. In 1302 the Flemings had rebelled against their count, a vassal of the French king, and had remained virtually independent until 1328, when Philip VI defeated their troops and restored the count. At Philip's insistence, the count ordered the arrest of all English merchants in Flanders; Edward retaliated by cutting off the export of wool, which spread unemployment in the Flemish towns. The Flemings revolted once more and drove out the count. To give legal sanction to their revolt, they persuaded Edward to assert his claim to the French crown, which held suzerainty over Flanders.

The most serious point of friction, however, was the status of Aquitaine and Ponthieu. Edward had willingly performed ordinary homage for them, but Philip then insisted on liege homage, which would have obligated Edward to support Philip against all enemies. Edward did not believe that, as a king, he could undertake the obligations of liege homage to any man, and refused. Philip began harassing the frontiers of Aquitaine and declared Edward's fiefs forfeit in 1337. The attack on Aquitaine pushed Edward into supporting the Flemish revolt and was thus the main provocation for the Hundred Years' War.

Economic maneuvers by both sides aggravated tensions. The French king encouraged French pirates and shippers to interfere with the wine trade from English Gascony. Edward began to tax wool leaving England and encouraged the Flemish weavers to come to England under his special protection to set up workshops with their superior craftsmanship. Incidentally, this move was the beginning of the woolen cloth weaving tradition in England.

◆ THE TIDES OF BATTLE

The French seemed to have a decisive superiority over the English at the outset of the war. The population of France was perhaps 15 million; England had between 4 and 7 million. But the war was hardly ever a national confrontation, because French subjects (Flemings, Gascons, Burgundians) fought alongside the English against other French subjects. The confused struggle may, however, be divided into three periods: initial English victories from 1338 to 1360; French resurgence, then stalemate, from 1369 to 1415; and a wild denouement

with tides rapidly shifting from 1415 to 1453 (see map 11.4).

First Period   The English never fully exploited their early victories, nor did the French ever manage to undo them. An English naval victory at Sluys in 1340 ensured English communications across the channel and determined that France would be the scene of the fighting. Six years later Edward landed in France on what was more a marauding expedition than a campaign of conquest. Philip pursued the English and finally overtook them at Crécy. The English were on a hill, and Edward positioned his troops so that the longbowmen could shoot into the advancing French line. The French knights had arrived after a long journey, but decided to attack without waiting for their crossbowmen, who were coming on foot. Charging up the hill, the French knights met a rain of arrows that cut their horses from under them. The English knights came down to finish the fight. The victory ensured the English possession of Calais, which they took in 1347.

The scenario was repeated in 1356 at Poitiers when John II, who had succeeded Philip, attacked an English army led by Edward's son, the Black Prince, and suffered an even more crushing defeat. John was captured and died, unransomed by his son and vassals. English victories, the Black Death, and mutual exhaustion led to the Peace of Brétigny in 1360. The English were granted Calais and an enlarged Aquitaine, and Edward, in turn, renounced his claim to the French crown.

Second Period   The French were not willing to allow so large a part of their kingdom to remain in English hands. In 1369, under John's successor, Charles V, the French opened a second phase of the war. Their strategy was to avoid full-scale battles and instead wear down the English forces, and they succeeded. By 1380 they had pushed the English nearly into the sea, confining them to Calais and a narrow strip of the Atlantic coast from Bordeaux to Bayonne. Fighting was sporadic from 1380 until 1415, with both sides content with a stalemate. During this war of attrition, mercenaries on both sides devastated the countryside, plundering villages, ruining crops and vineyards, and driving the population to seek refuge. It was

▲ MAP 11.4 THE HUNDRED YEARS' WAR

Because of their closeness to the continent and their naval power, the English were able to dominate northern France, the area that traditionally had been that kingdom's heartland. As a result, Joan of Arc's decisive victory came not in Paris but in Orléans on the Loire River — which proved to be a crucial boundary between the two sides.

◆ www.mhhe.com/chambers8ch11maps

Chronology

THE HUNDRED YEARS' WAR

1328 Charles IV, last Capetian king in direct line, dies; Philip of Valois is elected king of France as Philip VI; Philip defeats Flemings at Cassel; unrest continues in Flemish towns.

1329 Edward III of England does simple homage to Philip for continental possessions but refuses liege homage.

1336 Edward embargoes wool exports to Flanders.

1338 Philip's troops harass English Guienne; Edward, urged on by the Flemings, claims French crown; war begins.

1346 Major English victory at Crécy.

1347–1351 Black Death ravages Europe.

1356 Black Prince defeats French at Poitiers.

1358 Peasants' uprising near Paris.

1360 Peace of Brétigny; English gain major territorial concessions but abandon claim to French crown.

1369 Fighting renewed in France.

1370 Bertrand du Guesclin, constable of France, leads French resurgence.

1381 Peasants' Revolt in England.

1392 Charles VI of France suffers first attack of insanity; Burgundians and Armagnacs contend for power over king; fighting wanes as both sides are exhausted.

1399 Henry IV of Lancaster takes English throne, deposing Richard II.

1415 Henry V wins major victory at Agincourt.

1420 Treaty of Troyes; Charles VI recognizes Henry V as legitimate heir to French crown; high-water mark of English fortunes.

1429 Joan of Arc relieves Orléans from English siege; Dauphin is crowned king at Reims as Charles VII.

1431 Joan is burned at the stake at Rouen.

1435 Peace of Arras; Burgundy abandons English side.

1436 Charles retakes Paris.

1453 Bordeaux falls to French; English retain only Calais on continent; effective end of war, though no treaty is signed.

a type of warfare that reappeared in the Thirty Years' War and in World War II.

Third Period The last period of the war, from 1415 to 1453, was one of high drama and rapidly shifting fortunes. Henry V of England invaded France and shattered the French army at Agincourt in 1415. The battle was a replay of Crécy and Poitiers. The English longbowmen shot at the French knights in full armor as they charged downhill into a marshy area. Henry's success was confirmed by the Treaty of Troyes in 1420, an almost total French capitulation. King Charles VI of France declared his son the Dauphin (the future Charles VII) illegitimate, named Henry his successor and regent of France, and gave him direct rule over all French lands as far south as the Loire River (see map 11.4). Charles also gave Henry his daughter Catherine in marriage, with the agreement that their son would become the next king of France.

The Dauphin could not accept this forced abdication, and from his capital at Bourges he led an expedition across the Loire River. The English drove his forces back and systematically took the towns and fortresses north of the river that were loyal to him. In 1428 they finally laid siege to Orléans, a city whose fall would have given them a commanding position in the Loire valley and would have made the Dauphin's cause desperate.

Joan of Arc The intervention of a young peasant girl, Joan of Arc, saved the Valois dynasty. Convinced that heavenly voices were ordering her to rescue France, Joan persuaded several royal officials, and finally the Dauphin himself, of the authenticity of her mission and was given command of an army. In 1429 she marched to Orléans and forced the English to raise the siege. She then escorted the Dauphin to Reims, the historic coronation city of France, where his coronation

▲ Joan of Arc, 1484

Surrounded by the clerics who had condemned her, Joan of Arc is bound to the stake in this scene from a manuscript that was prepared half a century after she was executed in 1431. Despite Joan's own preference for short hair and manly costume, she is shown here as a conventionally idealized female figure.
Bibliothèque Nationale de France, Paris

confirmed his legitimacy and won him broad support as the embodiment of French royalist sentiment. The tide had turned.

Joan passed from history as quickly and as dramatically as she had arrived. The Burgundians, allies of the English, captured her in 1430 and sold her to the English, who put her on trial for witchcraft and heresy (see "The Trial of Joan of Arc," p. 387). She was burned at the stake at Rouen in 1431. Yet Joan's commitment was one sign of an increasingly powerful feeling among the people. They had grown impatient with continuing destruction and had come to identify their own security with the expulsion of the English and the establishment of a strong Valois monarchy. This growing loyalty to the king finally saved France from its long agony. A series of French successes followed Joan's death, and by 1453 only Calais was left in English hands. No formal treaty ended the war, but both sides accepted the outcome: England was no longer a continental power.

◆ THE EFFECTS OF THE HUNDRED YEARS' WAR

Like all the disasters of the era, the Hundred Years' War accelerated change. It stimulated the development of firearms and the technologies needed to manufacture them, and it helped establish the infantry—armed with longbow, crossbow, pike, or gun—as superior in battle to mounted knights. It also introduced wars of attrition in which the countryside was devastated in an effort to bring the enemy to submission. The war had a major effect on government institutions in England and France.

Parliament The expense of fighting forced the English king to request more revenue through taxation. In England the king willingly gave Parliament a larger political role in return for grants of new taxes. The tradition became firmly established that Parliament had the right to grant or refuse new taxes, to agree to legislation, to channel appeals to the king, and to offer advice on important decisions such as peace and war. The House of Commons gained the right to introduce all tax legislation, since the Commons, unlike the Lords, were representatives of shires and boroughs. Parliament also named a committee to audit tax records and supervise payments. Equally important, the Commons could impeach high royal officials, a crucial step in establishing the principle that a king's ministers were responsible to Parliament as well as to their royal master. By the end of the Hundred Years' War, Parliament had been notably strengthened at the expense of royal power.

French Government The need for new taxes had a rather different outcome in France, where it enhanced the power of the monarchs while weakening the Estates General, the national representative assembly. In 1343 Philip VI established a monopoly over the sale of salt, fixing in many areas of France its cost and the amount each family could have to consume. The tax on salt, called the *gabelle*, was to be essential to French royal finance until 1789. In gaining support for this and other taxes, Philip and his successors sought the agreement of regional assemblies of estates as well as the national Estates General. The kings' reliance on the local estates hindered the rise of a centralized assembly that could speak for the entire kingdom. By the reign of Charles VII, during the last stages of the war, the monarchy obtained the right to impose national taxes (notably the *taille,* a direct tax from which nobles and clerics were exempt) without the consent of the Estates General. By

THE TRIAL OF JOAN OF ARC

◆

The records of the trial of Joan of Arc in Rouen in 1431 give us a rare opportunity to hear her directly, or at least the words a secretary heard. Whether recorded accurately or not, her testimony does give us a glimpse of her extraordinary spirit and determination.

"When she had taken the oath the said Jeanne was questioned by us about her name and her surname. To which she replied that in her own country she was called Jeannette. She was questioned about the district from which she came.

"She said she was born in the village of Dom-rémy. Asked if in her youth she had learned any craft, she says yes, to sew and spin; and in sewing and spinning she feared no woman in Rouen.

"Afterwards she declared that at the age of 13 she had a voice from God to help her and guide her. And the first time she was much afraid. And this voice came towards noon, in summer, in her father's garden. Asked what instruction this voice gave her for the salvation of her soul, she said it taught her to be good and to go to church often; and the voice told her that she should raise the siege of the city of Orléans.

"Asked whether, when she saw the voice coming to her, there was a light, she answered that there was a great deal of light on all sides. She added to the examiner that not all the light came to him alone!

"Asked whether she thought she had committed a sin when she left her father and mother, she answered that since God commanded, it was right to do so. She added that since God commanded, if she had had a hundred parents, she would have gone nevertheless.

"Jeanne was admonished to speak the truth. Many of the points were read and explained to her, and she was told that if she did not confess them truthfully she would be put to the torture, the instruments of which were shown to her.

"To which Jeanne answered in this manner: 'Truly if you were to tear me limb from limb and separate my soul from my body, I would not tell you anything more; and if I did say anything, I should afterwards declare that you had compelled me to say it by force.'"

From G. G. Coulton and Eileen Power (eds.), *The Trial of Jeanne d' Arc*, W. P. Barrett (trans.) (Routledge, 1931).

then, too, the royal government was served by a standing professional army—the first in any European country since the fall of the Roman Empire.

The War of the Roses Both England and France experienced internal dissension during the Hundred Years' War. Both countries experienced a brutalization of life, with groups of former fighters and thugs pillaging the countryside. After the death of Edward III in 1377, England faced more than a century of turmoil, with nobles striving to maintain their economic fortunes through factional conflicts. The powerful magnates and their liveried followers used law and brute force to gain lands of competitors, as we have seen in the case of the Pastons. The son of Henry V and Catherine of France, Henry VI, went through periods of insanity, which led to a civil war for succession to the throne. Two factions, the Lancastrians and the Yorkists, laid claim to the throne, and the English nobles aligned themselves on one side or the other. The civil war that followed is known to his-

torians as the War of the Roses (the Lancastrians' emblem was a red rose, the Yorkists' a white rose).

The civil war lasted some thirty-five years. While not bloody for the population as a whole, the war did decimate the ranks of the nobility. It also gave rise to the allegations that Richard III, a Yorkist, killed his two young nephews in the Tower of London because they had a clearer title to the kingship than he had. Finally, the Lancastrian Henry Tudor defeated Richard III at Bosworth Field in 1485. Henry VII married Elizabeth of York to heal the breech between the factions. By the end of the fifteenth century, prosperity had relieved the pressures on the English nobles, and the people in general, weary of war, welcomed the strong and orderly regime that Henry established.

Burgundy In France, too, the power of the monarchy was threatened by rival factions of nobles, the Armagnacs and the Burgundians. The Armagnacs wanted the war with England vigorously pursued, while the Burgundians favored accommodation. The territorial ambitions of the Burgundians also posed a threat to the French monarchy. King John II of France had granted the huge Duchy of Burgundy to his younger son, Philip the Bold, in 1363. Philip and his successors greatly enlarged their possessions in eastern France, the Rhône and Rhine valleys, and the Low Countries (see map 11.3). They were generous patrons of literature and the arts, and they made their court at Dijon the most brilliant in Europe.

The dukes seem to have sought to establish a Burgundian "middle kingdom" between France and the Holy Roman Empire; such a state would have affected the political geography of Europe permanently and undermined the position of the French monarch. But the threat vanished in 1477 when the last duke, Charles the Bold, was killed in battle with the Swiss at Nancy. His daughter and heir, Mary of Burgundy, could not hold her scattered inheritance together, and a large part of it came under French control.

The English and French States With the loss of most of its continental possessions, England emerged from the war geographically more consolidated. It was also homogeneous in its language (English gradually replaced French and Latin as the language of the law courts and administration) and more conscious of its cultural distinctiveness and national identity. Although the French had made some incursions in coastal areas, England had not been invaded, and the woolen industry began to be very profitable. Freed from its continental entanglements, England was ready for its expansion beyond the seas and for a surge in national pride and self-consciousness.

France did not immediately achieve quite the territorial consolidation of England, but the expulsion of the English from French lands and the disintegration of the Duchy of Burgundy left the French king without a major rival among his feudal princes. The monarchy emerged from the war with a permanent army, a rich tax system, and no clear constitutional restrictions on its exercise of power. Most significantly, the war gave the French king high prestige and confirmed him as the chief protector and patron of the people. Although rav-

aged by warfare, the land was so rich that, when the peasants returned and began cultivating, the French economy quickly recovered.

In both France and England, government at the end of the Middle Ages was still decentralized and "feudal," meaning here that certain privileged persons and institutions (nobles, the Church, towns, and the like) continued to hold and to exercise some form of private jurisdiction. They retained, for example, their own courts. But the king had unmistakably emerged as the dominant partner in the feudal relationship. Moreover, he was prepared to press his advantages in the sixteenth century.

◆ THE STATES OF ITALY

Free cities, or communes, dominated the political life of central and northern Italy in the early fourteenth century. The Holy Roman Empire claimed a loose sovereignty over much of the peninsula north of Rome, and the papacy governed the area around Rome; but most of the principal cities, and many small ones too, had gained the status of self-governing city-states.

The new economic and social conditions of the 1300s, however, worked against the survival of the smaller communes. Economic contraction made it increasingly difficult for industries and merchant houses in the smaller cities to compete with their rivals in the larger ones. And the rising costs of war made it hard for small communes to defend their independence. Factional strife made political order difficult in both small and large towns leading to despotisms. Regional states, dominated politically and economically by a single metropolis, replaced the numerous, free, and highly competitive communes.

Milan Perhaps the most effective Italian despot was the ruler of Milan, Gian Galeazzo Visconti (r. 1378–1402), who set about enlarging the Visconti inheritance of twenty-one cities in the Po valley. Through shrewd negotiations and opportune attacks, he secured the submission of cities to his east, which gave him an outlet to the Adriatic Sea. He then seized Bologna, purchased Pisa, and through a variety of methods was accepted as ruler of Siena, Perugia, Spoleto, Nocera, and Assisi. In the course of this advance deep into

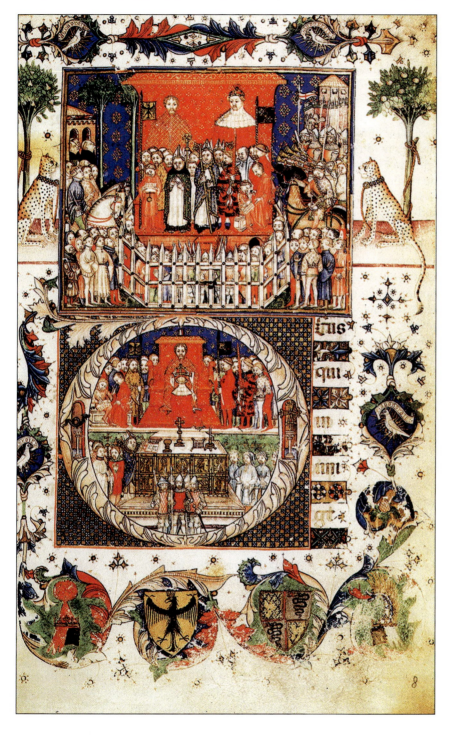

◄ INVESTITURE OF GIAN GALEAZZO VISCONTI, CA. 1395 This contemporary depiction of the investiture of Gian Galeazzo Visconti as duke of Milan is from a manuscript he commissioned to commemorate the occasion. The picture on top shows Visconti in a white cape seated next to the emperor's representative, who in the picture below places the diadem on the kneeling Visconti's head. The spectators, coming from all walks of life, include bishops and soldiers carrying cannons, but the ceremony itself takes place in front of an altar. The margins contain such Visconti family symbols as the eagle, the cheetah, and various fruit trees, and the entire manuscript leaf is a rich and colorful glorification of a central event in Visconti's life.
Index, © Giancarlo Costa

central Italy, Gian Galeazzo kept his chief enemies, the Florentines and the Venetians, divided, and he seemed ready to create a united Italian kingdom.

To establish a legal basis for his power, Gian Galeazzo secured from the emperor an appointment as imperial vicar in 1380 and then as hereditary duke in 1395. This move made him the only duke in all Italy, which seemed a step closer to a royal title. He revised the laws of Milan, but the chief administrative foundation of his success was his ability to wring enormous tax revenues from his subjects. Gian Galeazzo was also a generous patron of the new learning of his day; with his conquests, wealth, and brilliance, he seemed to be awaiting only the submission of the Florentines before adopting the title of king. But he died unexpectedly in 1402, leaving two minor sons who were incapable of defending their inheritance.

Florence   Florence by the mid-1300s was the principal banking center in Europe and one of the most important producers of luxury goods. Its silks, textiles, fine leather, and silver and gold objects were much prized, and the training its guilds offered in design and craftsmanship was a major reason for the high skills of its artists. The florin, the city's gold coin, had international standing as one of the most reliable currencies of the time, and the broad contacts of its merchants gave Florence a cosmopolitan air.

By the 1300s Florence had been a self-governing commune for two centuries, but it had rarely enjoyed political stability. It was ruled by a series of councils, whose members were drawn from the leading families. From time to time, however, as movements for wider representation arose, such as the Ciompi revolt of 1378, seats on the councils were opened to a broader segment of the citizenry—at times, as many as 20 percent of adult males may have been eligible for office.

The volatile fortunes of the different groups did not give way to a more stable regime until the rich Medici banking family gained control of the city's government in 1434 and made sure that only people they favored were defined as eligible for government positions. While retaining a facade of republican government, Cosimo de Medici established a form of boss rule over the city. His tax policies favored the lower and middle classes, and he also gained the support of the middle classes by appointments to office and other forms of political patronage. He secured peace for Florence and started his family's brilliant tradition of patronage of learning and the arts.

This tradition was enhanced by Cosimo's grandson, Lorenzo the Magnificent (r. 1469–1492), who beat back the plots of other powerful Florentine families and strengthened centralized control over the city. Lorenzo's Florence came to set the style for Italy, and eventually for Europe, in the splendor of its festivals, the elegance of its social life, the beauty of its buildings, and the lavish support it extended to scholars and artists.

Venice   Already independent for more than five hundred years, the city of Venice by 1400 controlled a far-flung empire in northern Italy and the eastern Mediterranean and kept a large army and navy. Venice's wealth came from its dominance of the import of goods from Asia, notably spices like black pepper and cloves, which were probably the most expensive commodities, per ounce, sold in Europe. Its wealthiest citizens also controlled its government; unlike Florence, Venice was ruled by a cohesive, rather than faction-ridden, oligarchy of some 150 families who inherited this dominance from generation to generation. From among their number they elected the *doge,* the head of the government, who held that position for life. (To increase turnover, older men were usually elected.)

Venice enjoyed remarkable political stability. There were occasional outbursts of discontent, but usually the patricians—who stayed united, relied on informers, made decisions in secret, and were ready to punish troublemakers severely—were able to maintain an image of orderliness and justice in government. They were also careful to show a concern for public welfare. The chief support of the navy, for instance—an essential asset for a city that, though containing more than 100,000 people, was built on a collection of islands in a lagoon—was a unique ship-building and arms manufacturing facility, the Arsenal. This gigantic complex, which employed more than 5 percent of the city's adult population, was not only the largest industrial enterprise in Europe but also a crucial source of employment. The Arsenal could build a fully equipped warship, starting from scratch, in just one day, and the skills it required helped maintain Venice's reputation as a haven for the finest artisans of the day. Not only men but entire families came to work there; one visitor described a "hall where about fifty women were making sails for ships" and another where one hundred women were "spinning and making ropes and doing other work related to ropes."

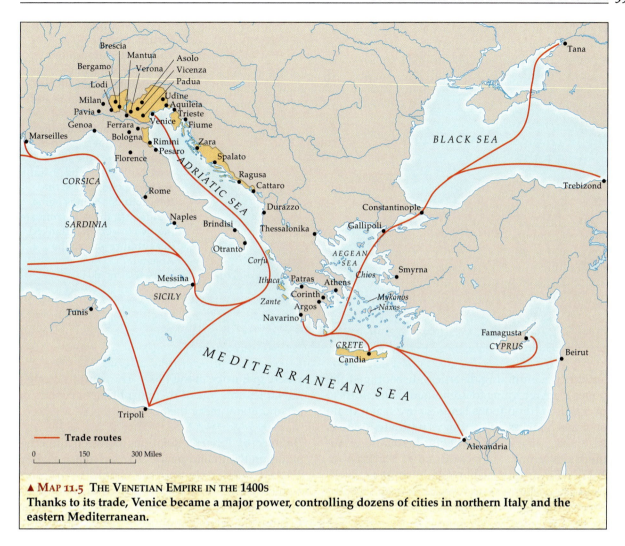

▲ **Map 11.5** The Venetian Empire in the 1400s
Thanks to its trade, Venice became a major power, controlling dozens of cities in northern Italy and the eastern Mediterranean.

An institution like the Arsenal promoted economic and social stability by offering so many jobs and also helped improve the craftsmanship and skills of the city's artisans. In addition, because of its location and its easy openness to all who wished to trade, Venice was a meeting ground for Slavs, Turks, Germans, Jews, Muslims, Greeks, and other Italians. It was a favorite tourist spot for travelers and for pilgrims on the way to the Holy Land, a major center for the new international art of printing, and famous for its shops and entertainments. By the mid-1400s, its coin, the ducat, was replacing the florin as a standard for all Europe; and its patrons, often interested in more earthy themes than the Florentines, were promoting a flowering of literature, learning, and the arts that made Venice a focus of Renaissance culture.

From the early fifteenth century onward, Venice initiated a policy of territorial expansion on the mainland. By 1405, Padua, Verona, and Vicenza had become Venetian dependencies (see map 11.5).

Papal States   The popes, like the leaders of the city-states, worked to consolidate their rule over their possessions in central Italy, but they faced formidable obstacles because the papacy was now located in Avignon in southern France. The difficult terrain of the Italian Papal States—dotted with castles and fortified towns—enabled communes, petty lords, and brigands to defy papal

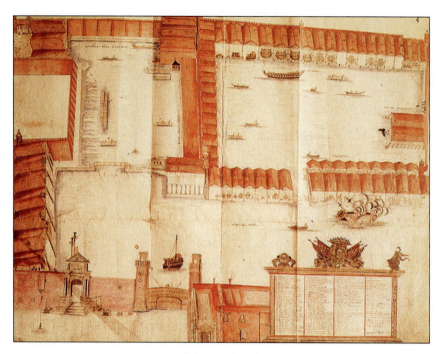

◀ *Antonio Natale*
Venice Arsenal
This eighteenth-century depiction of the huge complex that made up the Arsenal in Venice indicates some of the specialized buildings that formed the production line around the pools in which the ships were built. At the back, hulls are being laid, and in the foreground, a ship is being scuttled. At the very front are the two towers that flanked the entrance gate to the Arsenal.
Index, © Giancarlo Costa

authority. Continuing disorders discouraged the popes from returning to Rome, and their efforts to pacify their tumultuous lands were a major drain on papal finances. Even after its return to Rome in 1378, the papacy had difficulty maintaining authority. Not until the pontificate of Martin V (r. 1417–1431) was a stable administration established, and Martin's successors still faced frequent revolts throughout the fifteenth century.

Kingdom of Naples and Sicily The political situation was equally confused in the Kingdom of Naples and Sicily. Following the Sicilian Vespers in 1282, Sicily and Naples became a battleground for the competing ambitions of the Aragonese and the Angevins (descendants of Charles of Anjou). In 1435 the king of Aragon, Alfonso V, the Magnanimous, reunited Sicily and southern Italy and made the kingdom the center of an Aragonese empire in the Mediterranean. Alfonso sought to suppress the factions of lawless nobles and to reform taxes and strengthen administration. His efforts were not completely successful, for southern Italy and Sicily were rugged, poor lands and difficult to subdue; but he was at least able to overcome the chaos that had prevailed earlier. Alfonso thus extended to the Mediterranean the strengthening of central governments that took place else-

where in Europe in the 1400s. The court he created at Naples was one of the most brilliant centers of art and literature of the age.

Balance of Power Relations between the city-states on the Italian peninsula were tense as they clashed over trade and the acquisition of surrounding territory. The Peace of Lodi in 1454 ended a war among Milan, Florence, and Venice. Cosimo de Medici sought to make the peace a lasting one by creating an alliance system between Milan, Naples, and Florence on one side and Venice and the Papal States on the other (see map 11.6). During the next forty years, until the French invaded the peninsula in 1494, the balance was occasionally rocked but never overturned. This system represents one of the earliest appearances in European history of a diplomatic balance of power for maintaining peace.

V. The Fall of Byzantium and the Ottoman Empire

◆

Although the Byzantine Empire revived under Michael VIII Palaeologus, by the mid-fifteenth century the empire's control was effective only in

Republic of Florence
Duchy of Milan
Kingdom of Naples
Papal states
Venetian Republic

Aosta

DUCHY
OF SAVOY

Turin

Bergamo
Trent

Milan

Padua
MANTUA   Venice
Parma
Genoa   Ferrara
GENOA   Modena
Bologna

Lucca   Pistoia
Pisa   Urbino
Livorno   Florence
Siena
SIENA   Perugia
Assisi
ELBA
Orvieto

CORSICA   Rome

ADRIATIC
SEA

Pontecorvo
Barletta

Naples
Taranto

SARDINIA

TYRRHENIAN SEA

Cosenza

Palermo
Reggio

SICILY

Syracuse

| 0 | 50 | 100 Miles |

▲ MAP 11.6   THE ITALIAN STATES IN 1454
**Five major states dominated Italy after the Peace of Lodi in 1454. For the next 40 years they maintained a
balance of power among themselves, dominating the few independent areas—such as Siena, Genoa, and
Savoy—and a number of principalities too tiny to be shown on this map.**
◆ www.mhhe.com/chambers8ch11maps

Greece, the Aegean, and the area around Constantinople. The Ottoman Turks eventually fell heir to Byzantium's former power and influence, and by the early sixteenth century they were the unquestioned masters of southeast Europe and the Middle East.

◆ THE FALL OF CONSTANTINOPLE

The Rising Threat Turkish peoples had been assuming a large military and political role in the Middle East since the late tenth century. The Seljuk Turks dominated western Asia Minor since the late 1000s. Although Turks survived the attacks of Western crusaders, they were defeated by the Mongols in the thirteenth century. The Ottoman Turks, who had converted to Islam, followed the Mongol invasions and took over Asia Minor. They took their name from Osman, or Othman (r. 1290–1326), who founded a dynasty of sultans that survived for six centuries.

Establishing themselves at Gallipoli on the European side of the Straits in 1354, the Ottomans completely surrounded the Byzantine territory. The Byzantine emperors, fearing the worst for their small and isolated realm, tried desperately but unsuccessfully to persuade the West to send military help. At the council of Florence in 1439, Emperor John VII even accepted reunion with Rome, largely on Roman terms, in return for aid, but he had no power to impose the reunion of the churches on his people; in fact, many Eastern Christians preferred Turkish rule to submission to the hated Westerners.

The Capture of the City The Ottomans were unable to mount a major campaign against Constantinople until 1453, when Sultan Mehmet II, the Conqueror, finally attacked by land and water. The city fell after a heroic resistance, and Emperor Constantine XI Palaeologus, whose imperial lineage stretched back more than 1,400 years to Augustus Caesar, died in this final agony of the Byzantine Empire.

The fall of Constantinople had little military or economic effect on Europe and the Middle East. The Byzantine Empire had not been an effective barrier to Ottoman expansion for years, and Constantinople had dwindled commercially as well as politically. The shift to Turkish dominion did not,

as historians once believed, substantially affect the flow of trade between the East and West. Nor did the Turkish conquest of the city provoke an exodus of Byzantine scholars and manuscripts to Italy. Scholars from the East, recognizing the decline and seemingly inevitable fall of the Byzantine Empire, had been emigrating to Italy since the late fourteenth century; the revival of Greek letters was well under way in the West by 1453.

The End of an Era The impact of the fall was largely psychological; although hardly unexpected, it shocked the Christian world. The end of the Byzantine Empire had great symbolic importance for contemporaries and, perhaps even more, for later historians. In selecting Byzantium as his capital in 324, Constantine had founded a Christian Roman empire that could be considered the first authentically medieval state. For more than 1,000 years this Christian Roman empire played a major political and cultural role in the history of both Eastern and Western peoples. In some respects, the years of its existence mark the span of the Middle Ages, and its passing symbolizes the end of an era.

◆ THE OTTOMAN EMPIRE

Expansion Under Mehmet II (r. 1451–1481), who from the start of his reign committed his government to a policy of conquest, the Ottomans began a century of expansion (see "The Sultan Mehmet II," p. 395). After the fall of Constantinople, which became his capital under the name of Istanbul (though the name was not officially adopted until 1930), Mehmet subjugated Morea, Serbia, Bosnia, and parts of Herzegovina. He drove the Genoese from their Black Sea colonies, forced the khan of the Crimea to become his vassal, and fought a lengthy naval war with the Venetians. At his death the Ottomans were a power on land and sea, and the Black Sea had become a Turkish lake (see map 11. 7).

Early in the following century Turkish domination was extended over the heart of the Arab lands through the conquest of Syria, Egypt, and the western coast of the Arabian peninsula. (The Arabs did not again enjoy autonomy until the twentieth century.) With the conquest of the sacred cities of Mecca and Medina, the sultan

THE SULTAN MEHMET II

One of the first histories of the Ottomans by a Westerner was written by an English schoolmaster named Richard Knolles and published in 1603. It is obvious that a great deal of research went into his work, which is marked by vivid portraits such as this one of the Sultan Mehmet II, known as the Conqueror because of his capture of Constantinople, who had lived a century before Knolles wrote.

"He was of stature but low, square set, and strongly limbed; his complexion sallow and melancholy; his look and countenance stern, with his eyes piercing, and his nose so high and crooked that it almost touched his upper lip. He was of a very sharp and apprehending wit, learned especially in astronomy, and could speak the Greek, Latin, Arabic, Chaldee, and Persian tongues. He delighted much in reading of histories, and the lives of worthy men, especially the lives of Alexander the Great and Julius Caesar, whom he proposed to himself as examples to follow. He was of an exceeding courage, and a severe punisher of injustice. Men that excelled in any quality, he greatly favored and honorably entertained, as he did Gentile Bellini, a painter of Venice, whom he purposely caused to come from thence to Constantinople, to draw the lively counterfeit of himself for which he most bountifully rewarded him. He so severely punished theft, as that in his time all the ways were safe. He was altogether irreligious, and most perfidious, ambitious above measure, and in nothing more delighted than in blood: insomuch that he was responsible for the death of 800,000 men; craft, covetousness and dissimulation were in him accounted tolerable, in comparison of his greater vices. In his love was no assurance, and his least displeasure was death; so that he lived feared of all men, and died lamented of none."

From Richard Knolles, in John J. Saunders (ed.), *The Muslim World on the Eve of Europe's Expansion* (Prentice-Hall, 1966), adapted by T. K. Rabb.

▼ *Gentile Bellini*
MEHMET II
Mehmet II, here shown in a painting attributed to the Venetian artist Gentile Bellini, was the conqueror of Constantinople in 1453.
The Granger Collection, New York

assumed the title of caliph, "successor of the Prophet," claiming to be Islam's supreme religious head as well as its mightiest sword.

Suleiman II Suleiman II, the Magnificent (r. 1520–1566), brought the Ottoman Empire to its height of power. In 1521 he took the citadel of Belgrade, which had hitherto blocked Turkish advance up the Balkan Peninsula toward Hungary, and the next year he forced the Hospitalers, after a six-month siege, to surrender the island of Rhodes, a loss that was a crippling blow to Western naval strength in the eastern Mediterranean. Suleiman achieved his greatest victory in 1526 with the defeat of the king of Hungary's army at Mohacs and the occupation of Hungary. He then launched his most ambitious campaign, directed against Austria, the Christian state that now assumed chief responsibility for defending Europe's eastern frontiers. This effort, the high-water mark of Ottoman expansion into Europe, failed when Suleiman was unable to capture Vienna in 1529. The frustrated sultan returned home and turned his attention toward the East. His armies overran Mesopotamia and completed the conquest of

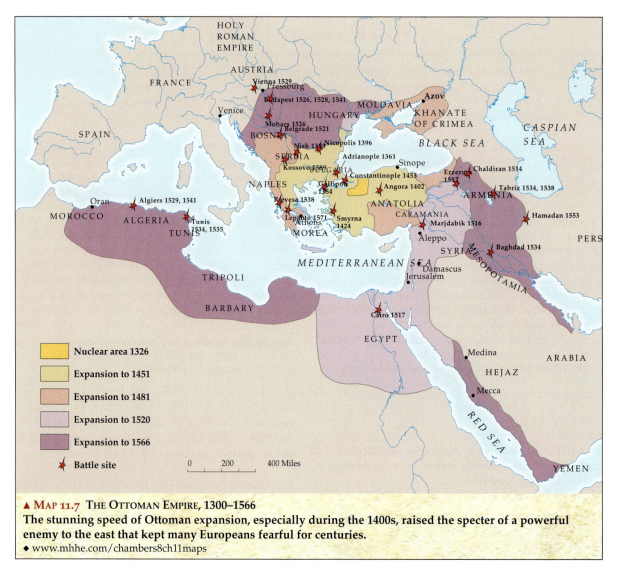

▲ **MAP 11.7 THE OTTOMAN EMPIRE, 1300–1566**
The stunning speed of Ottoman expansion, especially during the 1400s, raised the specter of a powerful enemy to the east that kept many Europeans fearful for centuries.
◆ www.mhhe.com/chambers8ch11maps

southern Arabia, and for the next two centuries the Ottoman Empire included all of southeastern Europe as well as the Middle East, Egypt, and Arabia.

Reasons for Success   The intense rivalries among the Christian faiths facilitated Ottoman expansion. Some Balkan Christians accepted papal supremacy, others adhered to the Eastern Orthodox traditions, and still others were regarded as heretics by both the Roman Catholics and the Orthodox. Often a Christian sect preferred the rule of the tolerant Ottomans to that of a rival Christian sect. In preserving peace among these dissident Christians, the Ottomans could serve as

impartial referees, while Christians obviously could not.

The Ottomans gained the loyalty of subject populations by allowing them to live by their own laws under their own officials, requiring them only to pay taxes and supply men for the Ottoman army and administration. Trade, for example, which remained vigorous in the Black Sea and the eastern Mediterranean Sea, was still largely in the hands of Greeks, Armenians, and Jews. The Ottomans themselves remained aloof from commercial undertakings and confined their careers to government service and the army.

Set on the frontier between the Islamic and Christian worlds, the Ottomans became a power in the political struggles of both Europe and the Middle East and were able to take advantage of favorable opportunities in both regions, even enlisting allies in one area to wage war in the other.

Power of the Sultan Influenced by Byzantine views of imperial authority, the sultan united in

▼ SULEIMAN
This portrait of Suleiman the Magnificent from a sixteenth-century Turkish manuscript suggests the ornate splendor that was associated with the awesome figure of the sultan. His court was famous for its lavish festivities and splendid costumes and decorations.
By Permission of The British Library. Ms. Add. 7880 fol. 53v

his own person supreme civil, military, and religious authority. Court ceremony contributed to the aura of sanctity that surrounded him as it had the emperor. Still more influential were Islamic traditions concerning governmental power, particularly the notion that the sultan was the successor of Muhammad, the legitimate ruler of all true believers. In a strict sense, the sultan could not be an absolute ruler, for he was, like every member of the Islamic community, subject to the sacred law. But he was also the supreme judge of that law; only revolution could challenge his authority.

The early sultans devised a striking solution to a problem common to most medieval states: the peaceful transfer of power from a ruler to his successor. From the fifteenth to the seventeenth century, the Ottomans followed what has come to be called the law of fratricide. The sultan cohabited with numerous slave girls of the harem, and usually he fathered numerous progeny. He then picked one of the boys to be his successor. At the sultan's death, the designated heir had the right and obligation to put his brothers and half-brothers to death. (They were strangled with a silken bowstring to avoid the shedding of their imperial blood.) The religious judges allowed such massacres because an uncontested succession was essential to the welfare of the empire.

The Sultan's Advisers Like all other medieval rulers, the sultan originally governed with the aid of a council of chosen advisers, which was called the *divan.* The function of presiding over the meetings of the divan fell to the grand *vizier,* who became the chief administrative official of the Ottoman state. The divan administered the civil and the military branches, including the collection of taxes and tribute, the conscription of soldiers, and the conduct of foreign affairs. It acted as a court of justice except in religious affairs, which were handled by judges trained in Islamic law.

The Sultan's Army The army had two principal divisions: unpaid holders of fiefs granted by the sultan in exchange for military service; and paid soldiers, technically considered slaves, who remained permanently in the sultan's service. As in the West, the fief holder was required to provide the military with armed men, the number being set in strict proportion to the revenue deriving from his estates. Among the paid soldiers, the most important were those belonging to the highly trained, thoroughly professional, but legally unfree corps of the *Janissaries*, meaning "new troops."

Slave armies had been common in Islamic states, but the Ottomans did not adopt the practice until the fifteenth century. According to the accounts of the earliest chronicles, Sultan Murad learned from a theologian in about 1430 that the Koran assigned him one-fifth of the booty captured by his army, including prisoners. Murad decided to convert his prisoners to Islam, teach them Turkish, and train them as a tough, well-disciplined military contingent, the Janissaries. The Ottomans continued to demand a tribute of young boys from the Christian parts of their vast empire as slaves for their elite corps. The Janissaries, dedicated to Islam, soon became a powerful force in Ottoman politics.

SUMMARY

◆

While the fall of Constantinople had a strong psychological effect on Europe, the threat of the Ottoman invasion initially meant little except to the Austrians, Hungarians, Balkan states, and the Knights Hospitalers. The West was preoccupied with the reality of the Four Horsemen of the Apocalypse. Early fourteenth-century famines, recurrent plague, and wars, including the Hundred Years' War, diverted their attention. By the end of the fifteenth century, peace was generally restored. England emerged as a government that would come to be described as a constitutional monarchy, the French king was on his way to a control over his subjects that would be called absolutism, and Italy had established a balance-of-power politics. The economy was strengthened by new inventions, such as the printing press, that would change the way people spread and received information to the present day. Europe was on the verge of new expansions. The explorations of the late fifteenth century introduced new concepts of power and wealth to the competing countries; the problems of the Church intensified with major splits; and the economy, although plagued with problems of overpopulation once again, was expanding in new directions and with new products from the conquests in America.

QUESTIONS FOR FURTHER THOUGHT

◆

1. What made the Hundred Years' War different from the other wars that you have studied in the Middle Ages?

2. Compare Europe in 800 to Europe in 1450. What new political boundaries had been established? How had society changed? How was the economy different?

3. What influence has epidemic disease and famine had on the history of Europe and the world in general?

RECOMMENDED READING

◆

Sources

*Brucker, Gene A. (ed.) *The Society of Renaissance Florence: A Documentary Study.* 1971. Collection of primary sources.

*Dobson, R. B. (ed.). *The Peasant's Revolt of 1381.* 1983. Primary sources related to the revolt.

*Froissart, Jean. *The Chronicles of England, France, Spain and Other Places Adjoining.* 1961. Chronicles of the Hundred Years' War.

*Horrox, Rosemary. *The Black Death.* 1994. Primary sources on the Black Death.

The Pastons: The Letters of a Family in the War of the Roses. Richard Barber (ed.). 1981.

Pernoud, Régine (ed.). *Joan of Arc: By Herself and Her Witnesses.* 1966. Documents relating to Joan's life and trial.

*Pizan, Christine de. *The Book of the City of Ladies.* Earl Jeffrey Richards (tr.). 1982. The author was a court writer who wrote this book on women's virtues in response to the debate of the time on women.

Studies

*Allmand, Christopher. *The Hundred Years' War: England and France at War, c. 1300–1450.* 1988. An account of the military aspects.

*Bennett, Judith M. *Women in the Medieval English Countryside.* 1987. An assessment of peasant women's status.

*Brucker, Gene A. *Giovanni and Lusanna: Love and Marriage in Renaissance Florence.* 1986.

Eisenstein, Elizabeth L. *The Printing Press as an Agent of Change in Early-Modern Europe.* 2 vols. 1979. Provocative interpretation of the place of printing in European history.

*Erler, Mary, and Maryanne Kowaleski (eds.). *Women and Power in the Middle Ages.* 1988. A collection of essays on women's access to and use of power.

Gillingham, John. *The Wars of the Roses: Peace and Conflict in Fifteenth-Century England.* 1981. Readable political and military history.

Gimpel, Jean. *The Medieval Machine.* Penguin, 1976. Useful analysis of mechanical innovations in the Middle Ages.

*Hanawalt, Barbara. *The Ties That Bound: Peasant Families in Medieval England.* 1986. Peasant life in England sympathetically viewed.

*——— (ed.). *Women and Work in Preindustrial Europe.* 1986. Collection of essays covering the issues of working women in Europe.

Harvey, L. P. *Islamic Spain 1250–1500.* 1990. A survey of the one non-Christian territory in Western Europe and its steady decline.

*Hilton, Rodney. *Bond Men Made Free.* 1979. A study of peasant unrest in the Late Middle Ages.

Kaeuper, Richard W. *War, Justice, and Public Order: England and France in the Late Middle Ages.* 1988. Assessment of the intersection of war and justice in two countries.

Martin, Henri-Jean, and Lucien Febvre. *The Coming of the Book: The Impact of Printing 1450–1800.* 1976. Survey.

Merriman, Roger B. *Suleiman the Magnificent, 1520–1566.* 1966.

Oakley, Francis. *The Western Church in the Later Middle Ages.* 1979.

*Perroy, Edouard. *The Hundred Years' War.* 1965. Classic; excellent survey.

Richmond, Colin. *The Paston Family in the Fifteenth Century: The First Phase.* 1990. The experiences of one family as seen through their letters during the War of the Roses.

Unger, Richard W. *The Ship in the Medieval Economy.* 1980. The evolution of medieval ship design.

Warner, Marina. *Joan of Arc: The Image of Female Heroism.* 1981. Examination of Joan's life and legend.

Wittek, Paul. *The Rise of the Ottoman Empire.* 1971.

*Ziegler, Philip. *The Black Death.* 1970. Synthesis of plague studies.

*Available in paperback.

▲ *Jan Van Eyck*

Portrait of Giovanni Arnolfini and His Wife, 1434

The symbolism that permeates this depiction of a husband and wife has led to the suggestion that it is a wedding picture. The bed and seeming pregnancy are symbols of marriage, and the husband blesses his wife as he bestows the sacrament of marriage (for which the Church did not yet require a priest). On the back wall, the mirror reflects the witnesses attending the wedding. Van Eyck's use of the new medium of oil paint allowed him to reproduce vividly the texture of the fur-edged robe and the glimmer of the mirror's glass.

TRADITION AND CHANGE IN EUROPEAN CULTURE, 1300–1500

By 1300 the civilization of Europe appeared to have settled into stable and self-assured patterns. Society as a whole shared assumptions about religious beliefs, about the appropriate way to integrate faith with the heritage of the ancient world, about the purposes of scholarship, and about the forms of literature and art. These shared assumptions have led historians to describe the outlook of the age as "the medieval synthesis." But such moments of apparent stability rarely last long. Within a few generations, profound doubts had arisen on such fundamental questions as the nature of religious faith, the authority of the Church, the aims of scholarship, the source of moral ideals, and the standards of beauty in the arts. As challenges to old ideas arose, especially in the worlds of religion and cultural expression, there was an outpouring of creativity that has dazzled us ever since. Because those who sought new answers tended to look for guidance to what they considered a better past—the ancient world, or the early days of Christianity—and sought to revive long-lost values, their efforts, and the times in which they lived, have been called an age of rebirth, or Renaissance.[1]

---

[1]The creator of the modern view of the Renaissance as one of the formative periods of Western history, and the single most influential historian of the subject, was Jacob Burckhardt (see Recommended Reading).

CHAPTER 12. TRADITION AND CHANGE IN EUROPEAN CULTURE							
	Social Structure	Body Politic	Changes in the Organization of Production and in the Impact of Technology	Evolution of Family and Changing Gender Roles	War	Religion	Cultural Expression
I. THE NEW LEARNING							
II. ART AND ARTISTS IN THE ITALIAN RENAISSANCE							
III. THE CULTURE OF THE NORTH							
IV. SCHOLASTIC PHILOSOPHY, RELIGIOUS THOUGHT, AND PIETY							
THE STATE OF CHRISTENDOM							

I. The New Learning

◆

Although traditional forms of learning remained vital in the fourteenth and fifteenth centuries, medieval Scholasticism, with its highly refined forms of reasoning, had little to offer Europe's small but important literate lay population. The curriculum was designed mainly to train teachers and theologians, whereas the demand was increasingly for practical and useful training, especially in the arts of persuasion and communication: good speaking and good writing. For many, the Scholastics also failed to offer moral guidance. As Petrarch emphasized, education was meant to help people lead a wise, pious, and happy life. A central aim of the Renaissance was to develop new models of virtue and a system of education that would do exactly that.

◆ THE FOUNDING OF HUMANISM

One minor branch of the medieval educational curriculum, rhetoric, was concerned with the art of good speaking and writing. More and more, its practitioners in Italy began to turn to the Latin classics for models of good writing. Their interest in the Classical authors was helped by the close relationship between the Italian language and Latin, by the availability of manuscripts, and by the presence in Italy of countless Classical monuments. It was rhetoricians who first began to argue, in the late thirteenth century, that education should be reformed to give more attention to the classics and to help people lead more moral lives.

These rhetoricians were to found an intellectual movement known as Humanism. The term *Humanism* was not coined until the nineteenth century. In fifteenth-century Italy, *humanista* signified a professor of humane studies or a Classical scholar, but eventually *Humanism* came to mean Classical scholarship—the ability to read, understand, and appreciate the writings of the ancient world. Humanist education helped its students master the classics, so they could learn both the wisdom they needed to choose the right way in life and the eloquence that could persuade others to follow that same way. The modern use of the word *humanism* to denote a secular philosophy that denies an afterlife has no basis in the Renaissance. Most Renaissance humanists read the Church fathers as avidly as they read pagan authors and believed that the highest virtues were rooted in piety. Humanism sought far more to enrich than to undermine traditional religious attitudes.

Petrarch The most influential early advocate of Humanism was Francesco Petrarca, known as Petrarch (1304–1374). He was a lawyer and cleric who practiced neither of those professions but rather devoted his life to writing poetry, scholarly and moral treatises, and letters. He became famous for his Italian verse—his sonnets inspired poets for centuries—but he sought above all to emulate Virgil by writing a Latin epic poem. A master of self-promotion, he used that work as the occasion for reviving the ancient title of "poet laureate" and having himself crowned in Rome in 1341. But he was also capable of profound self-examination. In a remarkable work, which he called *My Secret*—a dialogue with one of his heroes, St. Augustine—he laid bare his struggles to achieve spiritual peace despite the temptations of fame and love. Increasingly, he became concerned that nowhere in the world around him could he find a model of virtuous behavior that he could respect. The leaders of the Church he considered poor examples, for they seemed worldly and materialistic. Convinced that no guide from his own times or the immediate past would serve, Petrarch concluded that he had to turn to the Church fathers and the ancient Romans to find worthy examples of the moral life (see "Petrarch on Ancient Rome," p. 404).

How could one be a good person? By imitating figures from antiquity, such as Cicero and Augustine, who knew what proper values were and pursued them in their own lives, despite temptations and the distractions of public affairs. The period between their time and his own—which Petrarch regarded as the "middle" ages—he considered contemptible. His own world, he felt, would improve only if it tried to emulate the ancients, and he believed that education ought to teach what they had done and said. In particular, like the good rhetorician he was, he believed that only by restoring the mastery of the written and spoken word that had distinguished the great Romans—an imitation of their style, of the way they had conveyed their ideas—could his contemporaries learn to behave like the ancients.

Boccaccio The program Petrarch laid out soon caught fire in Florence, the city from which his family had come and in which he found influential friends and disciples. The most important

was the poet and writer Giovanni Boccaccio (1313–1375). He became famous in Florence for a collection of short stories known as *The Decameron*, written between 1348 and 1351. It recounts how a group of young Florentines—seven women and three men—fled during the Black Death of 1348 to a secluded villa, where for ten days each told a story. The first prose masterpiece in Italian, *The Decameron*'s frank treatment of sex and its vivid creation of ordinary characters make it one of the first major works in Western letters intended to divert and amuse rather than edify. But in his later years Boccaccio grew increasingly concerned with the teaching of moral values, and he became a powerful supporter of Petrarch's ideas.

The Spread of Humanism In the generation after Petrarch and Boccaccio, Humanism became a rallying cry for the intellectual leaders of Florence. They argued that, by associating their city with the revival of antiquity, Florentines would be identified with a distinctive vision that would become the envy of their rivals elsewhere in Italy. And that was indeed what happened. The campaign for a return to the classics started a revolution in education that soon took hold throughout Italy; the writing and speaking skills the humanists emphasized came to be in demand at every princely court (including that of the papacy); and the crusade to study and imitate the ancients transformed art, literature, and even political and social values.

Led by the chancellor of Florence, Coluccio Salutati (whose position, as the official who prepared the city's official communications, required training in rhetoric), a group of humanists began to collect ancient manuscripts and form libraries, so as to make accessible virtually all the surviving writings of Classical Latin authors. These Florentines also wanted to regain command of the Greek language, and in 1396 they invited a Byzantine scholar to lecture at the University of Florence. In the following decades—troubled years for the Byzantine Empire—other Eastern scholars joined the exodus to the West, and they and Western visitors returning from the East brought with them hundreds of Greek manuscripts. By the middle of the fifteenth century, Western scholars had both the philological skill and the manuscripts to

Petrarch on Ancient Rome

◆

Petrarch was so determined to relive the experience of antiquity that he wrote letters to famous Roman authors as if they were acquaintances. In one letter, he even described Cicero coming to visit him. While he was passing through Padua in February 1350, he recalled that the city was the birthplace of the Roman historian Livy, and he promptly wrote to him.

"I only wish, either that I had been born in your time or you in ours. If the latter, our age would have benefited; if the former, I myself would have been the better for it. I would surely have visited you. As it is, I can merely see you reflected in your works. It is over those works that I labor whenever I want to forget the places, times, and customs around me. I am often filled with anger at today's morals, when people value only gold and silver, and want nothing but physical pleasures.

"I have to thank you for many things, but especially because you have so often helped me forget the evils of today, and have transported me to happier times. As I read you, I seem to be living with Scipio, Brutus, Cato, and many others. It is with

them that I live, and not with the ruffians of today, among whom an evil star had me born. Oh, the great names that comfort me in my wretchedness, and make me forget this wicked age! Please greet for me those older historians like Polybius, and those younger than you like Pliny.

"Farewell forever, you unequalled historian!

"Written in the land of the living, in that part of Italy where you were born and buried, in sight of your own tombstone, on the 22nd of February in the 1350th year after the birth of Him whom you would have seen had you lived longer."

Petrarch, *Epistolae Familiares*, 24.8. Passages selected and translated by Theodore K. Rabb.

establish direct contact with the most original minds of the Classical world, and they were making numerous Latin and Italian translations of Greek works. Histories, tragedies, lyric poetry, the dialogues of Plato, many mathematical treatises, and the most important works of the Greek fathers of the Church fully entered Western culture for the first time.

Civic Humanism Salutati and his contemporaries and successors in Florence are often called civic humanists because they stressed that participation in public affairs is essential for full human development. Petrarch had wondered whether individuals should cut themselves off from the larger world, with its corruptions and compromises, and focus only on what he called the contemplative life, or try to improve that world through an active life. Petrarch's models had offered no clear answer. Cicero had suggested the need for both lives, but Augustine had been fearful of outside temptations. In the generations following Petrarch, however, the doubts declined, and the humanists argued that only by participating in public life, seeking higher ends for one's so-

ciety as well as oneself, could an individual be truly virtuous. Republican government was the best form, they argued, because unless educated citizens made use of their wisdom for the benefit of all, their moral understanding would not benefit their societies. These were lessons exemplified by the ancient classics, and thus in one connected argument the civic humanists defended the necessity of studying the ancients, the superiority of the active life, and the value of Florentine republican institutions.

◆ HUMANISM IN THE FIFTEENTH CENTURY

As the humanist movement gained in prestige, it captured all of Italy. Pope Nicholas V (1447–1455), for example, founded a library in the Vatican that was to become the greatest repository of ancient manuscripts in Italy. And princely courts, such as those of the Gonzaga family at Mantua and the Montefeltro family at Urbino, gained fame because of their patronage of humanists. Moreover, the influence of antiquity was felt in all areas of learning and writing. Literature was profoundly influenced by the ancients, as a new interest in Classical models reshaped the form and content of both poetry and drama, from the epic to the bawdy comedy. Purely secular themes, without religious purpose, became more common. And works of history grew increasingly analytic, openly acknowledging inspiration from ancient writers such as Livy.

Education   Perhaps the most direct effect was on education itself. Two scholars from the north of Italy, Guarino da Verona and Vittorino da Feltre, succeeded in turning the diffuse educational ideas of the humanists into a practical curriculum. Guarino argued for a reform of traditional methods of education, and Vittorino brought the new methods to their fullest development in the various schools he founded, especially his Casa Giocosa ("Happy House") at Mantua. The pupils included boys and girls, both rich and poor (the latter on scholarships). All the students learned Latin and Greek, mathematics, music, and philosophy; in addition—because Vittorino believed that education should aid physical, moral, and social development—they were taught social graces, such as dancing and courteous manners, and received instruction in physical exercises like riding and fencing. Vittorino's school attracted pupils from all over Italy, and his methods were widely imitated.

Ultimately, a humanist education was to give the elite throughout Europe a new way of measuring social distinction. It soon became apparent that the ability to quote Virgil or some other ancient writer was not so much a sign of moral seriousness as a badge of superiority. What differentiated people was whether they could use or recognize the quotations, and that was why the new curriculum was so popular—even though it seemed to consist, more and more, of endless memorizations and repetitions of Latin texts.

New Standards of Behavior   The growing admiration for the humanists and their teachings also gave an important boost to the patronage of arts and letters. In the age of gunpowder, it was no longer easy to claim that physical bravery was the supreme quality of noblemen. Instead, nobles began to set themselves apart not just by seeking a humanist education but also by pa-

▲ *Raphael*
BALDASSARE CASTIGLIONE
Raphael painted this portrait of his friend, the count Baldassare Castiglione, around 1514. Castiglione's solemn pose and thoughtful expression exude the dignity and cultivation that were described as essential attributes of the courtier in Castiglione's famous book on courtly behavior.
Giraudon/Art Resource, NY

tronizing artists and writers whose praise made them famous. Thus, a new image of fine behavior, which included the qualities that Guarino fostered—a commitment to taste and elegance as well as to courage—became widely accepted. This new lifestyle was promoted in a book, *The Courtier,* written in 1516 by Baldassare Castiglione, which took the form of a conversation among the sophisticated men and women at the court of Duke Federigo Montefeltro of Urbino, Castiglione's patron. *The Courtier* became a manual of proper behavior for gentlemen and ladies for centuries.

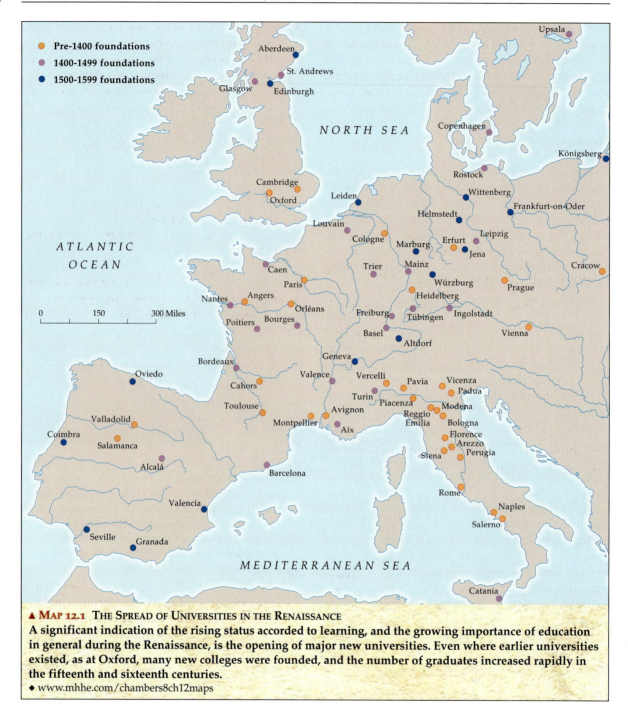

▲ **MAP 12.1** THE SPREAD OF UNIVERSITIES IN THE RENAISSANCE

A significant indication of the rising status accorded to learning, and the growing importance of education in general during the Renaissance, is the opening of major new universities. Even where earlier universities existed, as at Oxford, many new colleges were founded, and the number of graduates increased rapidly in the fifteenth and sixteenth centuries.

◆ www.mhhe.com/chambers8ch12maps

Humanism Triumphant By the mid-1400s Humanism dominated intellectual life in much of Italy, and by 1500 it was sweeping all of Europe, transmitted by its devotees and also by a recent invention, printing, which made the texts of both humanists and ancients far more easily available. Dozens of new schools and universities were founded, and no court of any significance was without its roster of artists and writers familiar with the latest ideas. Even legal systems were affected, as the principles of Roman law (which tended to endorse the power of the ruler) were adopted in many countries. But in the late fifteenth century the revival of antiquity took a direction that modified the commitment to the active life that had been the mark of the civic humanists. A new movement, Neoplatonism, emphasized the interest in spiritual values that was the heart of the contemplative life.

◆ THE FLORENTINE NEOPLATONISTS

The turn away from the practical concerns of the civic humanists toward a renewed exploration of grand ideals of truth and perfection was a result of the growing interest in Greek as well as Roman antiquity—especially the works of Plato. A group of Florentine philosophers, active in the last decades of the fifteenth century and equally at home in Greek and Latin, led the way. They were known as "Neoplatonists," or "new" followers of Plato.

Ficino   The most gifted of these Neoplatonists was the physician Marsilio Ficino. His career is a tribute to the cultural patronage of the Medici family, which spotted his talents as a child and gave him the use of a villa and library near Florence. In this lovely setting, a group of scholars and statesmen met frequently to discuss philosophical questions. Drawn to the idealism of Plato, Ficino and his colleagues argued that Platonic ideas demonstrated the dignity and immortality of the human soul. To spread these views among a larger audience, Ficino translated into Latin all of Plato's dialogues and the writings of Plato's chief followers. In his *Theologica Platonica* (1469), he made an ambitious effort to reconcile Platonic philosophy and the Christian religion.

Pico   Another member of the group was Count Giovanni Pico della Mirandola, who thought he could reconcile all philosophies in order to show that there was a single truth that lay behind every quest for the ideal. In 1486 Pico sought to defend publicly, in Rome, some nine hundred theses that would show the essential unity of all philosophies. The pope, fearful that the theses contained several heretical propositions, forbade the disputation, but Pico's introductory "Oration on the Dignity of Man" remains one of the supreme examples of the humanists' optimism about the potential of the individual.

The Philosophy of Neoplatonism   Both Ficino and Pico started from two essential assumptions. First, the entire universe is arranged in a hierarchy of excellence, with God at the summit. Second, each being in the universe, with the exception only of God, is impelled by "natural appetite" to seek perfection; one is impelled, in other words, to achieve—or at least to contemplate—the beautiful. As Pico expressed it, humans are unique in that they are placed in the middle of the universe, linked with both the spiritual world above and the material world below. Their free will enables them to seek perfection in either direction; they are free to become all things. A clear ethic emerges from this scheme: The good life should be an effort to achieve personal perfection, and the highest human value is the contemplation of the beautiful.

These writers believed that Plato had been divinely illumined and, therefore, that Platonic philosophy and Christian belief were two wholly reconcilable faces of a single truth. Because of this synthesis, and also its passionate idealism, Neoplatonic philosophy was to be a major influence on artists and thinkers for the next two centuries.

◆ THE HERITAGE OF THE NEW LEARNING

Although its scholarship was often arid and difficult, fifteenth-century Italian Humanism left a deep imprint on European thought and education. The humanists greatly improved the command of Latin; they restored a large part of the Greek cultural inheritance to Western civilization; their investigations led to a mastery of other languages associated with great cultural traditions, most notably Hebrew; and they laid the basis of modern textual criticism. They also developed new ways of examining the ancient world—through archaeology, numismatics (the study of coins), and epigraphy (the study of inscriptions on buildings, statues, and the like), as well as through the study of literary texts. As for the study of history, while medieval chroniclers had looked to the past for evidence of God's providence, the humanists used the past to illustrate human behavior and provide moral examples. They also helped standardize spelling and grammar in vernacular languages; and the Classical ideals of simplicity, restraint, and elegance of style that they promoted helped reshape Western literature.

No less important was the role of the humanists as educational reformers. The curriculum they devised spread throughout Europe in the sixteenth century, and until the twentieth century it continued to define the standards by which the lay leaders of Western society were trained. The fact that men and women throughout Europe came to be steeped in the same classics meant that they thought and communicated in similar ways. Despite Europe's divisions and conflicts, this common humanistic education helped preserve the fundamental cultural unity of the West.

II. Art and Artists in the Italian Renaissance

The most visible effect of Humanism and its admiration for the ancients was on the arts. Because the movement first took hold in Florence, it is not surprising that its first artistic disciples appeared among the Florentines. They had other advantages. First, the city was already famous throughout Italy for its art, because the greatest painters of the late 1200s and 1300s, Cimabue (1240–1302) and his pupil Giotto (1276–1336), were identified with Florence. Giotto, in particular, had decorated buildings from Padua to Naples and thus gained a wide audience for the sense of realism, powerful emotion, and immediacy that he created (in contrast to the formal, restrained styles of earlier artists). Second, Florence's newly wealthy citizens were ready to patronize art; and third, the city had a tradition of excellence in the design of luxury goods such as silks and gold objects. Many leading artists of the 1400s and 1500s started their careers as apprentices to goldsmiths, in whose workshops they mastered creative techniques as well as aesthetic principles that informed their painting, sculpture, and architecture.

◆ THREE FRIENDS

The revolution in these three disciplines was started by three friends, who were united by a determination to apply the humanists' lessons to art. They wanted to break with the styles of the immediate past and create paintings, statues, and buildings that would not merely imitate the glories of Rome but actually bring them back to life. All three went to Rome in the 1420s, hoping by direct observation and study of ancient masterpieces to

▲ *Giotto*
LAMENTATION
The Florentine Giotto di Bondone (1267?–1337) was the most celebrated painter of his age. He painted fresco cycles in a number of Italian cities, and this segment from one of them indicates the qualities that made him famous: the solid bodies, the expression of human emotion, and the suggestion of landscape, all of which created an impact that was without precedent in medieval art.
Alinari/Art Resource, NY

re-create their qualities and thus fulfill the humanists' goal of reviving the spirit of Classical times. The locals thought the three very strange, for they went around measuring, taking notes, and calculating sizes and proportions. But the lessons they learned enabled them to transform the styles and purposes of art.

Masaccio   Among the three friends, the painter Masaccio (1401–1428) used the inspiration of the ancients to put a new emphasis on nature, on three-dimensional human bodies, and on perspective. In showing Adam and Eve, he not only depicted the first nudes since antiquity but showed them coming through a rounded arch that was the mark of Roman architecture, as opposed to the pointed arch of the Middle Ages. The chapel he

▲ *Masaccio*
THE EXPULSION OF ADAM AND EVE, CA. 1425
Masaccio shows Adam and Eve expelled from paradise through a rounded archway that recalls ancient architecture. Also indicative of the influence of Roman art is the attempt to create what we would consider realistic (rather than stylized) human beings and to portray them nude, displaying powerful, recognizable emotions. This was one of the paintings that made the Brancacci Chapel an inspiration to generations of artists.
Erich Lessing / Art Resource, NY

decorated in a Florentine church, the Carmine, became a place of pilgrimage for painters, because here the values of ancient art—especially its emphasis on the individual human figure—were reborn.

Donatello Masaccio's friend Donatello (1386–1466) was primarily a sculptor, and his three-dimensional figures had the same qualities as Masaccio's in paint. Once again the focus was

▲ *Donatello*
DAVID, CA. 1430–1432
Like Masaccio, Donatello imitated the Romans by creating idealized nude bodies. His David has just killed and decapitated Goliath, whose head lies at his feet. Goliath's helmet recalls those worn by Florence's enemies, which makes this sculpture a work of patriotism as well as art. It happens also to have been the first life-size bronze figure cast since antiquity.
Alinari / Art Resource, NY

on the beauty of the body itself, because that had been a notable and distinctive concern of the ancients. The interest in the nude, accurately displayed, transformed the very purpose of art, for it led to an idealized representation of the human form that had not been seen in centuries. Because the biblical David—shown by Donatello in contemplation after his triumph over Goliath—symbolized vigor, youth, and the weak defeating the strong, he became a favorite hero for the Florentines.

Brunelleschi   The most spectacular of these three pioneers was the architect Brunelleschi (1377?–1446). For decades, his fellow citizens had been building a new cathedral, which, as a sign of their artistic superiority, was going to be the largest in Italy. Seen from above, it was shaped—as was traditional—like a cross. The basic structure was in place, but the huge space at which the horizontal and vertical met, the crossing, had not

yet been covered. In response to a competition for a design to complete the building, Brunelleschi, inspired by what he had learned in Rome, proposed covering the crossing with the largest dome built in Europe since antiquity. Although the first reaction was that it was impossible, eventually he got the commission. In an extraordinary feat of engineering, which required that he build the dome in rings, without using scaffolding, he erected a structure that became not only a fitting climax to the cathedral but also the hallmark of Renaissance Florence and an inspiration for all architects. The symmetrical simplicity of his other buildings shaped a new aesthetic of harmony and balance that matched what Masaccio and Donatello accomplished in painting and sculpture. In all three, the imitation of ancient Rome inspired subjects and styles that broke decisively with their immediate medieval past.

New Creativity   During the remaining years of the 1400s, a succession of artists, not just in Florence but increasingly in other parts of Italy as well, built on the achievements of the pioneer generation. They experimented with perspective and the modeling of bodies and drapery, so as to recapture the ancients' mastery of depth, and they made close observations of nature. Sculptors created monumental figures, some on horseback, in imitation of Roman models. And architects perfected the use of the rounded arches and symmetrical forms they saw in antique buildings. Subject matter also changed, as artists produced increasing numbers of portraits of their contemporaries and depicted stories out of Roman and Greek myths as well as traditional religious scenes. By the end of the 1400s, the leading Florentine painter of the day, Botticelli (1444?–1510), was presenting ancient subjects like the *Birth of Venus,* goddess of love, in exactly the way a Roman might have fashioned them.

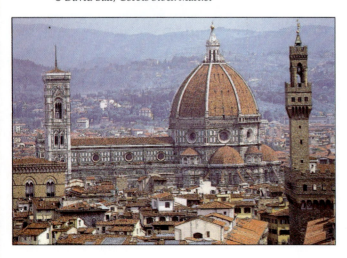

▼ *Brunelleschi*
Dome of Florence Cathedral, 1420–1436
Brunelleschi's famous dome—the first built in Italy since the fall of the Roman Empire—embodied the revival of classical forms in architecture. The contrast with the bell tower designed a century earlier by Giotto, with its suggestion of pointed Gothic arches, is unmistakable. The dome was a feat of engineering as well as design: Its 135-foot diameter was spanned without scaffolding, and Brunelleschi himself invented the machines that made the construction possible.
© David Ball/Corbis Stock Market

◆ THE HIGH RENAISSANCE

The artists at work in the early years of the 1500s are often referred to as the generation of the High Renaissance. Four, in particular—Leonardo, Raphael, Michelangelo, and Titian—are thought of as bringing the new movement that had begun a hundred years before to a climax.

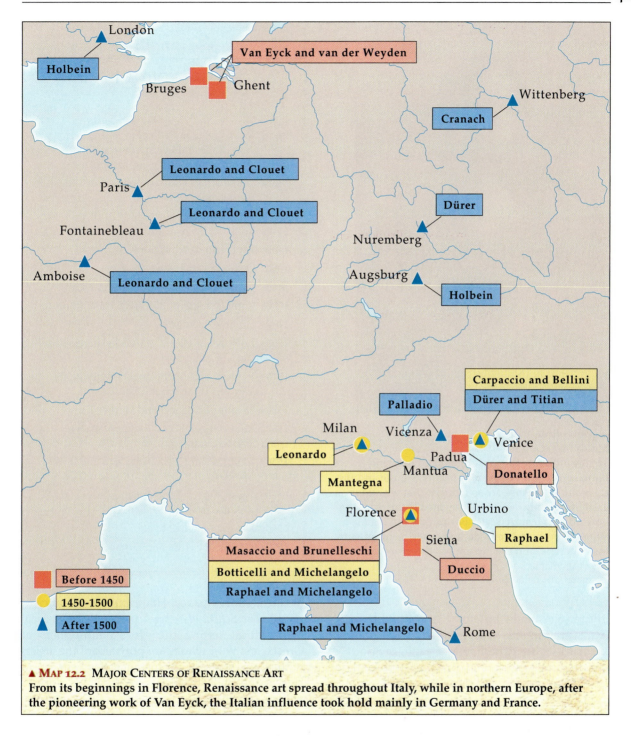

▲ **MAP 12.2** MAJOR CENTERS OF RENAISSANCE ART
From its beginnings in Florence, Renaissance art spread throughout Italy, while in northern Europe, after the pioneering work of Van Eyck, the Italian influence took hold mainly in Germany and France.

Leonardo The oldest, Leonardo (1452–1519), was the epitome of the experimental tradition. Always seeking new ways of doing things, whether in observing anatomy or designing fortifications, he was unable to resist the challenge of solving practical problems, even in his paintings. They are marvels of technical virtuosity, which make difficult angles, tricks of perspective, and bizarre geological formations look easy. His portrait of the *Mona Lisa*, for example, is famous not only for her

▲ *Leonardo da Vinci*
MONA LISA, CA. 1503–1505
This is probably the most celebrated image in Renaissance art. The famous hint of a smile and the calm and solid pose are so familiar that we all too easily forget how striking it seemed at the time and how often it inspired later portraits. As in his *Last Supper*, however, Leonardo was experimenting with his materials, and the picture has therefore faded over the years.
Giraudon/Art Resource, NY

Chronology

A CENTURY AND A HALF OF RENAISSANCE ART

1420s Masaccio, Donatello, and Brunelleschi visit Rome and begin transforming painting, sculpture, and architecture

1430s Donatello's *David;* completion of Brunelleschi's dome; Van Eyck's *Arnolfini Marriage*

1440s Botticelli born; death of Brunelleschi

1450s Leonardo da Vinci born

1460s Death of Donatello

1470s Dürer, Michelangelo, and Titian born

1480s Raphael born; Botticelli's *Birth of Venus*

1490s Dürer's *Apocalypse*

1500s Leonardo's *Mona Lisa;* Michelangelo's *David;* Cellini born

1510s Raphael and Michelangelo decorate the Vatican; Titian's *Bacchanal*

1520s Deaths of Raphael and Dürer

1530s Michelangelo's *Last Judgement* in the Sistine Chapel

1540s Cellini's *Salt Cellar;* Titian's *Charles V at Mühlberg*

1550s Vasari begins publishing his *Lives of the Artists*

1560s Death of Michelangelo

1570s Deaths of Cellini and Titian

---

mysterious smile but for the incredible rocky landscape in the background. Unfortunately, Leonardo also experimented with methods of painting; as a result, one of his masterpieces, the *Last Supper*, has almost completely disintegrated.

Raphael By contrast, Raphael (1483–1520) used the mastery of perspective and ancient styles that had been achieved in the 1400s to produce works of perfect harmony, beauty, and serenity. His paintings give an impression of utter relaxation, of an artist in complete command of his materials and therefore able to create sunny scenes that are balanced and at peace. His tribute to the ancient world, *The School of Athens*, places in a Classical architectural setting the great philosophers of Greece, many of whom are portraits of the artists of the day: Aristotle, for instance, has Leonardo's face. If the philosophers were the chief glory of Athens, Raphael seems to be saying, then the artists are the crowning glory of the Renaissance.

Michelangelo For Michelangelo (1475–1564), painting was but one means of expression. Equally at home in poetry, architecture, and sculpture, he often seems the ultimate embodiment of the achievements of his age. Constantly seeking

▲ *Raphael*
School of Athens
Painted in 1510 and 1511, this fresco celebrating the glories of Greek philosophy represents the triumph of the Renaissance campaign to revive antiquity. That the classical setting and theme could have been accepted as appropriate for a wall of the Vatican suggests how completely humanism had captured intellectual life. A number of the figures are portraits of artists whom Raphael knew: Plato, pointing to heaven at the back, has the face of Leonardo, and the notoriously moody Michelangelo broods, with his head on his arm, at the front.
Scala/Art Resource, NY

new effects, he once said that no two of the thousands of figures he depicted were the same, and one might add that just about every one of them conveys the sense of latent strength, of striving, that was Michelangelo's signature. In *The Creation of Man* Adam, shown at the moment of his creation, has not yet received the gift of life from God, but he already displays the vigor that Michelangelo gave to every human body. The same is true of Michelangelo's version of David, seemingly tranquil but showing his potential power in his massive, oversized hand. The human being is shown in full majesty, as an independent and potent individual.

Titian   In Venice, developments in art took a slightly different form. This was also a rich trading city, sophisticated, with broad international connections. But here Humanism was not so central, and the art—as befitted this most down-to-earth and cosmopolitan of Europe's cities—was more sensuous. The most famous Venetian painter, Titian (1482?–1576), depicted rich velvets, lush nudes, stormy skies, and dogs with wagging

◄ *Michelangelo*
THE CREATION OF MAN

Michelangelo worked on the ceiling of the Sistine Chapel in the Vatican from 1508 to 1512 and painted hundreds of figures. None has come to symbolize the rebirth associated with the Renaissance and the power of creative genius so forcefully as the portrayal of God extending a finger to bring the vigorous body of Adam to life. Tucked under God's other arm is the figure of Eve, ready to join Adam in giving birth to humankind.
Scala/Art Resource, NY

◄ *Titian*
BACCHANAL, CA. 1518

The earthy realism of Venice contrasted sharply with the idealization common in Florentine art. The setting and even the sky seem more tangible, and Titian's lush nude in the foreground (who was to be much copied) is the essence of sensuality. It has been suggested that the painting represents the different stages of life, from the incontinent child through the vigorous youths and adults to the old man who has collapsed in the back.
Scala/Art Resource, NY

tails with a directness and immediacy that enable the viewer almost to feel them. His friend Aretino said of one of his pictures: "I can say nothing of the crimson of the garment nor of its lynx lining, for in comparison real crimson and real lynx seem painted, and these seem real." Titian was Europe's most sought-after portraitist, and to this day we can recognize the leading figures of his time, and sense their character, because of the mastery of his depictions.

◆ STATUS AND PERCEPTION

Art as Craft To the generation of Masaccio, a painter was merely one of the many people engaged in a craft, not inherently more admired than a skilled leather finisher or mason. Like them, he was a member of a guild, he had to pass a carefully regulated apprenticeship, and he was subject to the rules that controlled his trade. Both Donatello and Brunelleschi were trained as goldsmiths, and the latter was even briefly imprisoned by his guild for not paying his dues while he was working on the cathedral dome—as an independent person, so he thought, and thus outside the guild structure. Given the Florentines' interest in gaining fame by beautifying their city, it was not surprising that the work of these artists should have attracted considerable attention. But it rarely occurred to anyone in the early 1400s—as Brunelleschi discovered from his guild—that they might deserve special respect or be considered more elevated than tradesmen. It was true that some of them were becoming famous throughout Italy, but would that lead to a change in their social status?

Humanism and the Change in Status The answer was that it did, and again the impetus came from the humanist movement. Three consequences of the revival of antiquity, in particular, began to alter the position of the artist. First was the recognition that the most vivid and convincing re-creations of the achievements of the ancient world were being produced in the visual arts. No letter written like Cicero's could compare with a painting, a statue, or a building as a means of bringing Rome back to life for all to see—as an open and public display of the virtues of Classical times.

A second influence was the humanists' new interest in personal fame. This had been an acceptable aspiration in antiquity, but during the Middle Ages spiritual concerns encouraged a disdain for worldly matters. It was still a problem for Petrarch to admit that, like the ancients he admired, he wanted to be famous. Among later humanists, the doubts receded, and the princes who valued their ideas eagerly accepted the notion that they should devote their lives to attaining fame. That was what nobles previously had won as warriors, but now there was a more reliable way to ensure that one's name lived forever.

The New Patrons That way was provided by the third of the humanists' lessons: that the truly moral person had to combine the contemplative with the active life. A prince, therefore, ought to cultivate the fine as well as the martial arts. No

▲ *Joos van Wassenhove and Pedro Berruguete*
FEDERIGO DA MONTEFELTRO
This remarkable painting embodies the new ideal of the gentleman that emerged in the Renaissance. Federigo da Montefeltro was both one of the most notable warriors and one of the most distinguished patrons of learning of the age, and this portrait captures both sides of his princely image. Sitting in his study with his richly clothed son, Guidobaldo, Duke Federigo is reading a book but is also dressed in armor.
Scala/Art Resource, NY

aristocratic court could be complete without its poets and painters, who sang their patron's praises while fashioning the masterpieces that not only brought prestige but also endured forever. As a result, if an aristocrat wanted immortality, it was no longer enough to be a famous warrior; now it became essential to build a splendid new palace or have one's portrait done by a famous painter. To be most like the virtuous heroes of Rome who were the society's ideal, vigorous leadership had to be linked to patronage of culture, and this outlook was not confined to noblemen. Noblewomen, whose chief role had long been to offer an idealized object of chivalric devotion and who continued to struggle to gain access to education, occasionally won that struggle, and the result was a refined patronage that could be crucial in fashioning a princely image. Without Isabella d'Este, for example, the court in Mantua would not have achieved its fame as a center of painting, architecture, and music. That both Leonardo and Titian did her portrait was a reflection not of her husband's importance but of her own independent contribution to the arts. Her rooms, surrounding a lovely garden, remain one of the wonders of the palace at Mantua and a worthy testimony to her fame as a patroness (see box, p. 417).

The effect of this new attitude was to transform the status of artists. They became highly prized at the courts of aristocrats, who saw them as extraordinarily effective image makers. Perhaps the most famous family of patrons in Italy, the Medici of Florence, were envied throughout Europe mainly because, for generations, they seemed always to be surrounded by the finest painters, sculptors, and architects of the age. And soon the richest princes in Italy, the popes, followed suit. The Church had been the main sponsor of art in the Middle Ages, but now it was the papacy in particular that promoted and inspired artistic production. In their determination to rebuild and beautify Rome as a worthy capital of Christendom, the popes gave such artists as Raphael and Michelangelo their most famous commissions—notably Michelangelo's Sistine Chapel within the Vatican. It was thus as a result of shifting patterns in the commissioning and buying of art that, as honored members of papal as well as princely courts, Renaissance artists created both a new aesthetic and a new social identity.

ISABELLA D'ESTE'S QUEST FOR ART

◆

As the passion for art took hold, the great patrons of the Renaissance became relentless in their search for new works. None was more avid than Isabella d'Este (1474–1539), who became the wife of the Gonzaga prince of Mantua at the age of sixteen and made her private suite of rooms (which she called her studio) a gathering place for artists, musicians, and poets for nearly fifty years. Her passion for art shines through her letters; in these extracts, she is pursuing both the Venetian painter Bellini and Leonardo da Vinci.

"To an agent, 1502: 'You may remember that many months ago we gave Giovanni Bellini a commission to paint a picture for the decoration of our studio, and when it ought to have been finished we found it was not yet begun. We told him to abandon the work, and give you back the 25 ducats, but now he begs us to leave him the work and promises to finish it soon. As till now he has given us nothing but words, tell him that we no longer care to have the picture, but if instead he would paint a Nativity, we should be well content, as long as he does not keep us waiting any longer.'

"Two months later: 'As Bellini is resolved on doing a picture of the Madonna and Child and St. John the Baptist in place of the Nativity scene, I should be glad if he would also include a St. Jerome; and about the price of 50 ducats we are content, but above all urge him to serve us quickly and well.'

"Three years later, to Bellini himself: 'You will remember very well how great our desire was for a picture painted by your hand, to put in our studio. We appealed to you for this in the past, but you could not do it on account of your many other commitments. (We recently heard you might be free,) but we have been ill with fever and unable to attend to such things. Now that we are feeling better it has occurred to us to write begging you to consent to painting a picture, and we will leave the poetic invention for you to make up if you do not want us to give it to you. As well as the proper payment, we shall be under an eternal obligation to you. When we hear of your agreement, we will send you the measurements of the canvas and an initial payment.'

"In the meantime, in May 1504, she wrote to Leonardo da Vinci: 'Hearing that you are staying in Florence, we have conceived the hope that something we have long desired might come true: to have something by your hand. When you were here and drew our portrait in charcoal, you promised one day to do it in color. Since it would be inconvenient for you to move here, we beg you to keep your good faith with us by substituting for our portrait a youthful Christ of about twelve years old, executed with that sweetness and soft ethereal charm which is the peculiar excellence of your art.'

"Five months later she wrote again: 'Some months ago we wrote to you that we wanted to have a young Christ, about twelve years old, by your hand. You replied that you would do this gladly, but owing to the many commissioned works you have on your hands, we doubt whether you remembered ours. Wherefore it has occurred to us to send you these few lines, begging you that you will turn to doing this little figure for us by way of recreation, which will be doing us a very gracious service and of benefit to yourself.'"

From D. S. Chambers (ed.), *Patrons and Artists in the Italian Renaissance* (London: Macmillan, 1970), pp. 128–130 and 147–148.

Vasari   In the mid-1500s, a leading protégé of the Medici, an architect and painter named Giorgio Vasari (1511–1574), sought to figure out how and why he and other artists were being showered with privileges. He himself had designed, built, and decorated a large new government office building in the center of the city—in Italian, *Uffizi* (now the main museum of Renaissance art in Florence). He had been knighted for his services, and to understand his good fortune, he looked to the past and wrote the first major work of what became a new field of study: the history of art.

Vasari suggested that certain artists were filled with a special spirit, which he called genius, that set them apart from—and above—other people. The status that artists had achieved was, in Vasari's account, richly deserved. Their genius and fame entitled them to high status, and it was appropriate that Titian, for example, lived in splendor, like the finest families of Venice. The

▲ *Sandro Botticelli*
Birth of Venus, ca. 1480
Sandro Botticelli was a member of the intellectual circle of Lorenzo de Medici, and this painting is evidence of the growing interest in Neoplatonism at the Medici court. The wistful, ethereal look on Venus' face reflects the otherworldliness that was emphasized by the Neoplatonists; moreover, their belief in the analogies that link all ideas suggests that Botticelli may have been implying that Venus resembled the Virgin Mary as a source of divine love. In depicting an ancient myth as ancient painters would have shown it, Botticelli represents the triumph of Renaissance ambitions, and the idealized beauty of his work helped shape an aesthetic standard that has been admired ever since.
Erich Lessing/Art Resource, NY

acceptance of artists into the uppermost levels of society was one of the most remarkable transformations produced by the Italian Renaissance.

III. The Culture of the North

North of the Alps the transformations of the 1300s and 1400s were not as dramatic as in Italy, but they had consequences after 1500 that were no less dramatic than the effects of Humanism, Neoplatonism, and the other changes in the south. This area of Europe did not have the many large cities and the high percentages of urban dwellers that were crucial to the humanist movement in Italy. Nor did the physical monuments and lan-

guages of northern Europe offer ready reminders of the Classical heritage. Humanism and the revival of classical learning—with its literate, trained laity—did not come to the north until the last decade of the fifteenth century. But in these territories, where cultural life was dominated by the princely court rather than the city, and by the knight rather than the merchant, there were other vital shifts in outlook.

◆ CHIVALRY AND DECAY

In 1919 a Dutch historian, Johan Huizinga, described northern European culture in the 1400s and 1500s not as a renaissance but as the decline of medieval civilization. His stimulating book, *The*

▲ *Benozzo Gozzoli*
PROCESSION OF THE THREE KINGS TO BETHLEHEM (DETAIL)
This enormous fresco in the Medici palace in Florence, completed in 1459, gives place of honor in the biblical scene of the procession of the Magi to the future ruler of Florence, the ten-year-old Lorenzo de Medici, riding a white horse, and to his grandfather Cosimo de Medici, the founder of the dynasty's power, who is behind Lorenzo, also on a white horse.
Erich Lessing/Art Resource, NY

Waning of the Middle Ages, focused primarily on the court of the dukes of Burgundy, who were among the wealthiest and most powerful princes of the north. Huizinga found tension and frequent violence in this society, with little of the serenity that had marked the thirteenth century. Writers and artists seemed to have little grasp on reality and displayed deep emotional instability. Although Huizinga's interpretation may have been exaggerated, his analysis did contain much that is accurate.

A good example of the poor grasp of reality was the extravagant cultivation of the notion of chivalry. Militarily, the knight was becoming less important than the foot soldier armed with longbow, pike, or firearms. But the noble classes of the north continued to pretend that knightly virtues governed all questions of state and society; they discounted such lowly considerations as money, arms, recruitment, supplies, and the total resources of countries in deciding the outcome of wars. For example, before the Battle of Agincourt, one knight told the French King Charles that he should not use contingents from the Parisian townsfolk because that would give his army an unfair numerical advantage; the

▲ *Benvenuto Cellini*
SALT CELLAR FOR FRANCIS I
**Benvenuto Cellini, a Florentine goldsmith who
challenged Giorgio Vasari's distinction between
artisan and artist in his lively *Autobiography* (1562),
executed this work for the French king Francis I in
1543. Juxtaposing allegorical images of the Earth and
the Sea, which he presented as opposing forces,
Cellini created figures as elegant as any sculpture
and set them on a fantastic base of gold and enamel.
His extraordinary skills indicate why so many
Renaissance artists began their careers in goldsmiths'
workshops.**
Erich Lessing/Art Resource, NY

battle should be decided strictly on the basis of
chivalrous valor.

Bravery and Display This was the age of the
perfect knight and the "grand gesture." King John
of Bohemia insisted that his soldiers lead him to
the front rank of battle, so that he could strike at
the enemy even though he was blind. The feats of
renowned knights won the admiration of chroniclers but hardly affected the outcome of battle.
And the reason for the foundation of new orders
of chivalry—notably the Knights of the Garter in
England and the Burgundian Knights of the
Golden Fleece—was that these orders would reform the world by cultivating knightly virtues.

Princes rivaled one another in the sheer glitter
of their arms and the splendor of their tournaments. They waged wars of dazzlement, seeking
to confound rivals with spectacular displays of
gold, silks, and tapestries. Court ceremony was

marked by excess, as were the chivalric arts of
love. A special order was founded for the defense
of women, and knights frequently took lunatic
oaths to honor their ladies, such as keeping one
eye closed for weeks. Obviously, people rarely
made love or war in this artificial way. But they
still drew satisfaction in dreaming about the possibilities for love and war if this sad world were
only a perfect place.

The Cult of Decay Huizinga called the extravagant lifestyle of the northern courts the "cult of
the sublime," or the impossibly beautiful. But he
also noted that both knights and commoners
showed a morbid fascination with death and its
ravages. Reminders of the ultimate victory of
death and treatments of decay are frequent in
both literature and art. One popular artistic motif
was the *danse macabre*, or dance of death, depicting people from all walks of life—rich and poor,
clergy and laity, good and bad—dancing with a
skeleton. Another melancholy theme favored by
artists across Europe was the *Pietà*—the Virgin
weeping over her dead son.

This morbid interest in death and decay in an
age of plague was not the result of lofty religious
sentiment. The obsession with the fleetingness of
material beauty in fact indicated how attached
people were to earthly pleasures; it was a kind of
inverse materialism. Above all, the gloom reflected a growing religious dissatisfaction. In the
1200s Francis of Assisi addressed death as a sister;
in the fourteenth and fifteenth centuries people
apparently regarded it as a ravaging, indomitable
fiend. Clearly (as Petrarch, too, had noted) the
Church was failing to provide consolation to
many of its members, and a religion that fails to
console is a religion in crisis.

Devils and Witches Still another sign of the unsettled religious spirit of the age was a fascination
with the devil, demonology, and witchcraft. The
most enlightened scholars of the day wondered
whether witches could ride through the air on
sticks. One of the more notable witch trials of
Western history was held at Arras in 1460, when
scores of people were accused of participating in
a witches' sabbath, giving homage to the devil,
and having sexual intercourse with him. In 1486
two inquisitors who had been authorized by the

pope to prosecute witches published the *Malleus Maleficarum* ("hammer of witches"), which defined witchcraft as heresy and became the standard handbook for prosecutors. Linked to the fear of the devil was a fear of women. They were the most frequent victims of witchcraft accusations, easy scapegoats in an age of social upheaval. Any hint of change in their traditional subordination to men, such as learning to read, combined with their vulnerability to make them targets of denunciation.

Relics   There was also a growing fascination with concrete religious images. The need to have immediate, physical contact with the objects of religious devotion added to the popularity of pilgrimages and stimulated the obsession with the relics of saints. These were usually fake, but they became a major commodity in international trade. Some princes accumulated collections of relics numbering in the tens of thousands.

Huizinga saw these aspects of northern culture as signaling the disintegration of the cultural synthesis of the Middle Ages. Without a disciplined and unified view of the world, attitudes toward war, love, and religion lost balance, and disordered behavior followed. The culture was not young and vigorous but old and dying. Yet the concept of decadence must be used with caution. Certainly this was a psychologically disturbed world that had lost the self-confidence of the thirteenth century; but these supposedly decadent people, though dissatisfied, were also passionately anxious to find solutions to the tensions that unsettled them. We need to recall that passion when trying to understand the appeal and the power behind other cultural movements—lay piety and efforts of religious reform.

◆ CONTEMPORARY VIEWS OF NORTHERN SOCIETY

Froissart and Langland   Huizinga wrote about chivalric society from the perspective of the twentieth century. Among contemporary observers was Jean Froissart (1333?–1400?) of Flanders, who traveled widely across England and the continent, recording the exploits of valiant men. His chronicles have no equal for colorful, dramatic narration, but he seemed overly preoccupied with

chivalric society, treating peasants and townspeople with contempt or indifference. His contemporary, a poet known as William Langland, offered the viewpoint of the humbler classes. His *Vision of Piers Plowman*, a poem describing eleven visions, probably written about 1360, is one of the most remarkable works of the age. Each vision is crowded with allegorical figures and filled with spirited comment about the various classes of people, the impact of plague and war on society, and the failings of the Church.

Chaucer   The greatest work of imaginative literature of the late fourteenth century was written by the son of a London vintner, Geoffrey Chaucer (1340?–1400), who was a soldier, diplomat, and government official. His *Canterbury Tales*, written in the 1390s, recounts the pilgrimage of some thirty men and women to the tomb of St. Thomas Becket at Canterbury. For entertainment on the road, each pilgrim agrees to tell two stories. Chaucer's lively portraits are a rich tapestry of English society, especially in its middle ranges. The stories also sum up the moral and social ills of the day. His robust monk, for example, ignores the Benedictine rule; his friar is more interested in donations than in the cure of souls; his pardoner knowingly hawks fraudulent relics; and the wife of Bath complains of prejudice against women. But Chaucer's picture remains good humored; he also praises the student of Oxford, who would gladly learn and gladly teach, and the rural parson, who cares for his flock while others neglect the faithful. Apart from the grace of his poetry, Chaucer had the ability to delineate character and spin a lively narrative. The *Canterbury Tales* is a masterly portrayal of human personalities and human behavior that can delight readers in any age.

◆ ART AND MUSIC

The leaders of the transformation in both the style and the status of artists in the 1400s were mainly Italians. But there were also major advances in northern Europe. Indeed, oil painting—on wood or canvas—was invented in the Netherlands, and its first great exponent, Jan Van Eyck, a contemporary of Donatello, revealed both the similarities and the differences between north and south. Van

Eyck was less interested in idealization than were the Florentines and more fascinated with the details of the physical world. One sees almost every thread in a carpet. But his portrait of an Italian couple, the Arnolfinis, is shot through with religious symbolism as well as a sly sense of humor about sex and marriage. The dog is a sign of fidelity, and the carving on the bedpost is of St. Margaret, the patron saint of childbirth; but the single candle is what newlyweds are supposed to keep burning on their wedding night, and the grinning carved figures behind their clasped hands are a wry comment on their marriage. The picture displays a combination of earthiness and piety that places it in a tradition unlike any in the Italy of this time (see p. 400).

Dürer The leading northern artist of the period of the High Renaissance was a German, Albrecht Dürer, who deliberately sought to blend southern and northern styles. He made two trips to Venice, and the results were clear in a self-portrait that shows him as a fine gentleman, painted in the Italian style. But he continued, especially in the engravings that made him famous, to emphasize the detailed depiction of nature and the religious purposes that were characteristic of northern art.

Dürer refused to break completely with the craft origins of his vocation. He knew, from his visits to Venice, that Italian painters could live like lords, and he was invited by the Holy Roman Emperor to join his court. But he preferred to remain in his home city of Nuremberg, earning his living more through the sale of his prints than from the stipends he was offered by patrons. Eventually he became a highly successful entrepreneur, creating different kinds of prints for different markets—the elite liked elegant and expensive copper engravings, while others preferred cruder but cheaper woodcuts—and producing a best seller in a book of illustrations of the Apocalypse. His wife was a highly effective seller of his prints, and she preferred running her stall in the marketplace to fine entertainments by city fathers. Indeed, the couple can be seen as pioneers in the business of art.

Developments in Music The process that was at work in the visual arts had similar effects in music, which again had developed primarily for liturgical purposes in the Middle Ages. In the Renaissance,

▲ *Albrecht Dürer*
THE FOUR HORSEMEN OF THE APOCALYPSE
The bestseller that Dürer published in 1498, *The Apocalypse*, has the text of the biblical account of the apocalypse on one side and full-page woodcuts on the other. The four horsemen who will wreak vengeance on the damned during the final Day of Judgment are Conquest holding a bow, War holding a sword, Famine, or Justice, holding scales, and Death, or Plague, riding a pale horse and trampling a bishop.
A. Dürer, "The Riders on the Four Horses from the Apocalypse," c. 1496. Woodcut. The Metropolitan Museum of Art, Gift of Junius S. Morgan, 1919. (19.73.209). Photograph © 2002 The Metropolitan Museum of Art, New York

musicians became as prized as artists at princely courts, and their growing professionalism was demonstrated by the organists and choir singers hired by churches, the trumpeters employed by cities for official occasions, and the composers and performers who joined the households of the wealthy. Musical notation became standardized, and instruments became more diverse as old ones were improved and new ones—such as the viol, the oboe, and the clavichord—were invented. Moreover, unlike the practice of art, which usually required apprenticeship to guilds that were closed to women, musical performance, whose patron saint was St. Cecilia, relied on the talents of both men and women.

Unlike the visual arts, the chief musical center of Europe around 1500 was in the Low Countries, not Italy. The choirmasters of cathedral towns like Bruges employed professional singers who brought to new levels the traditional choral form of four-part polyphony (that is, four different lines playing against one another). This complex vocal harmony had no need of instrumental accompaniment; as a result, freed from their usual subservience to the voice, instruments could be developed in new ways. The greatest masters of the time, Guillaume Dufay and Josquin des Prez, excelled in secular as well as religious music, and theirs was one field of creativity in which new techniques and ideas flowed mainly from the north to Italy, not the other way around.

IV. Scholastic Philosophy and Religious Thought

In theology, Scholasticism retained its hold even as Humanism swept the literary world. But it was not the thirteenth-century Scholasticism of Thomas Aquinas, which asserted that human reason could fashion a universal philosophy that embraced all truths and reconciled all apparent conflicts. Nor did the traditional acceptance of ecclesiastical law continue, with its definition of the Christian life in terms of precise rules of behavior rather than interior spirit. The style of thinking changed as the Scholastics of the 1400s and 1500s were drawn to analysis (breaking apart) rather than synthesis (putting together) as they examined philosophical and theological statements. Many of them no longer shared Aquinas' confidence in human reason, and they hoped to repair his synthesis or to replace it with new systems that, though less comprehensive, could at least be more easily defended in an age growing doubtful

about reason. Discussions of faith changed too, as more and more Christian leaders sought ways to deepen the interior, sometimes mystical, experience of God.

◆ THE "MODERN WAY"

The followers of Aquinas remained active in the schools, but the most original of the Scholastics in the fourteenth century took a different approach to their studies. They were known as nominalists, because they focused on the way we describe the world—the names (in Latin, *nomina*) that we give to things—rather than on its reality. The nominalists denied the existence, or at least the knowability, of the universal forms that make up the world—"manness," "dogness," and the like. The greatest among them was the English Franciscan William of Ockham (1300?–1349?), and his fundamental principle came to be called Ockham's razor. It can be stated in various ways, but essentially it says that, between alternative explanations for the same phenomenon, the simpler is always to be preferred.

Ockham On the basis of this "principle of parsimony," Ockham attacked the traditional focus of philosophy on the universal, ideal forms. These concepts had led Aquinas to argue, for instance, that all individual beings must be understood as reflections of their universal forms. By contrast, Ockham argued that the simplest way to explain the existence of any specific object is just to say it exists. The mind can find resemblances among objects and make generalizations about them, which can then be examined in coherent and logical ways. But these offer no certainty of the actual existence of Aquinas' ideal forms—the universal principles like "manness" that all beings and objects reflect.

The area of reality that the mind can grasp is thus severely limited. The universe, as far as human reason can detect, is a collection of separate beings and objects, not a hierarchy of ideal forms. The proper way to deal with this universe is by direct experience, not by speculating about abstract natures. Such a theology, based on observation and reason, was obviously rather limited. Ockham believed that one could still prove the existence of some necessary principles in the universe, but he thought human beings could know very little about the ultimate necessary principle, God.

Nominalist Theology

Ockham and many of his contemporaries insisted on the total power of God and humanity's absolute dependence on him. If he chose, God could reward vice, punish virtue, and act erratically; which raised the question, how could there be a stable system of theology or ethics? The nominalists' answer was that, instead of using his absolute power, God relied on his ordained power: through a covenant, or agreement, God assures people that he will act in consistent and predictable ways. Thus, theology becomes the study not of metaphysics but of God's will and covenant with the human race.

Nominalists rejected Aquinas' high assessment of human powers and his confident belief in the ordered and knowable structure of the natural world. Living in a disturbed, pessimistic age, they reflected the crisis of confidence in natural reason and human capability that is a major feature of the cultural history of the north in these years. Nominalists were popular in the universities, and Ockhamite philosophy, in particular, came to be known as the *via moderna* ("modern way"). Although nominalists and humanists were frequently at odds, they did share a dissatisfaction with aspects of the medieval intellectual tradition, especially the speculative abstractions of medieval thought; and both advocated approaches to reality that concentrated on the concrete and the present and demanded a strict awareness of method.

◆ SOCIAL AND SCIENTIFIC THOUGHT

Marsilius

The belief of the nominalists that reality was to be found not in abstract forms but in concrete objects had important implications for social thought. The most remarkable of these social thinkers was Marsilius of Padua, an Italian lawyer who served at the French royal court. In 1324 he wrote a book, *Defender of Peace*, which attacked papal authority and supported lay sovereignty within the Church. His purpose was obviously to endorse the independent authority of his patron, the king of France, who pursued a running battle with the pope. But his work had wider impli-

cations. Using nominalist principles, Marsilius argued that the reality of the Christian community, like the reality of the universe, consists of the sum of all its parts. The sovereignty of the Church thus belongs to its members, who alone can define the collective will of the community.

Marsilius was one of the first theorists of the modern concept of sovereignty. Emphasizing secular authority, he maintained that only regulations supported by force are true law and that, therefore, the enactments of the Church do not bind because they are not supported by coercive force. The Church has no right to power or to property and is entirely subject to the sovereign will of the state, which is indivisible, absolute, and unlimited. *Defender of Peace* is noteworthy not only for its radical ideas but also for its reflection of deep dissatisfactions. Marsilius and others revealed a hostile impatience with the papal and clerical domination of Western political life. They wanted laypersons to guide the Church and the Christian community. In this respect at least, the book was a prophecy of things to come.

New Explanations of Nature

In studies of nature, a few nominalists at Paris and Oxford in the fourteenth century took the first hesitant steps toward a criticism of the Aristotelian world system that had dominated European studies of physics since antiquity. At the University of Paris, for example, Jean Buridan proposed an important revision in Aristotle's theory of motion. If, as Aristotle had said, all objects are at rest in their natural state, what keeps an arrow flying after it leaves the bow? Aristotle had reasoned rather lamely that the arrow disturbs the air through which it passes and that it is this disturbance that keeps pushing the arrow forward. Buridan suggested, instead, that the movement of the bow lends the arrow a special quality of motion, an "impetus," that stays with it permanently unless removed by the resistance of the air. In addition, Buridan and other fourteenth-century nominalists theorized about the acceleration of falling objects and made some attempt to describe this phenomenon in mathematical terms. Although they were often inadequate or inaccurate, these attempts at new explanations started the shift away from an unquestioned acceptance of ancient systems (such as

Aristotle's) that was to climax, three hundred years later, in the scientific revolution.

Humanism and Science Humanists also helped prepare the way for scientific advance. They rediscovered important ancient writers whose works had been forgotten, and their skills in textual and literary criticism taught people to look with greater precision at works inherited from the past. As more of the classics became available, it became apparent that ancient authors did not always agree. Could they, therefore, always be correct? Furthermore, the idealism of Plato and the number mysticism of Pythagoras suggested that unifying forms and harmonies lay behind the disparate data of experience and observation. Once this assumption took hold, it was soon being argued that perhaps the cosmic harmonies might be described in mathematical terms.

V. The State of Christendom

The Church as an institution also experienced major transformations in the 1300s and 1400s. It continued to seek a peaceful Christendom united in faith and obedience to Rome. But the international Christian community was in fact beset by powerful forces (reflected by Marsilius) that undermined its cohesiveness and weakened papal authority and influence. Although the culmination of these disruptions did not come until the Reformation in the 1500s, the history of the previous two centuries made it clear that the institution was profoundly troubled.

The Avignon Exile The humiliation of Pope Boniface VIII by the agents of Philip IV of France at Anagni in 1303 opened the doors to French influence at the Curia. In 1305 the College of Cardinals elected a French pope, Clement V, who because of the political disorders in the Papal States eventually settled at Avignon (1309). Though technically a part of the Holy Roman Empire, Avignon was in language and culture a French city. The popes who followed Clement hoped to return to Rome but remained at Avignon, claiming that the continuing turmoil of central Italy would not permit papal government to function effectively. These popes were skilled administrators who expanded the papal bureaucracy enormously—especially its fiscal machinery—but the long absence from Rome clearly harmed papal prestige.

Fiscal Crisis Like many secular governments, the papacy at Avignon faced an acute fiscal crisis. But unlike the major powers of Europe, its territorial base could not supply it with the funds it needed, because controlling the Papal States usually cost more money than they produced. As a result, the papacy was drawn into the unfortunate practice of exploiting its ecclesiastical powers for financial gain. Thus, the popes insisted that candidates appointed to high ecclesiastical offices pay a special tax, which usually amounted to a third or a half of the first year's revenues. The popes also claimed the income from vacant offices and even sold future appointments to office when the incumbents were still alive. Dispensations, which were also sold, released a petitioner from the normal requirements of canon law. A monastery or religious house, for example, might purchase an exemption from visitation and inspection by the local bishop. The pope received in tithes one-tenth of the revenues of ecclesiastical benefices or offices throughout Christendom. And the Church offered indulgences, remissions of the temporal punishment for sin, in return for monetary contributions to the papacy.

These fiscal practices enlarged the popes' revenues, but they had deplorable results. Prelates who paid huge sums to Avignon tended to pass on the costs to the lower clergy. Parish priests, hardly able to live from their incomes, were more easily tempted to lower their moral standards. The flow of money to Avignon angered rulers and prompted demands for a halt to such payments and even for the confiscation of Church property. Dispensations gravely injured the authority of the bishops, since an exempt person or house all but escaped their supervision. The bishops were frequently too weak, and the pope too distant, to deal effectively with abuses on the local level. The fiscal measures thus helped sow chaos in many parts of the Western Church.

The Great Schism The end of the seventy-year Avignon exile led to a controversy that almost split the Western Church. In 1377 Pope Gregory XI returned reluctantly to Rome and died there a short time later. The Roman people, fearing that Gregory's successor would once more remove the court to Avignon and thereby deprive Rome of desperately needed revenues, agitated for the election of an Italian pope. Responding to this pressure, the College of Cardinals found a compromise candidate who satisfied both French and Italian interests, but the new pope, Urban VI (1378–1389), soon antagonized the French cardinals by trying to limit their privileges and by threatening to pack the College with his own appointments. Seven months after choosing Urban, a majority of the cardinals declared that his election had taken place under duress and was invalid; they then named a new pope, who returned to Avignon. Thus began the Great Schism of the West (1378–1417), the period when two, and later three, popes fought over the rule of the Church.

Christendom now had two pretenders to the throne of Peter, one in Rome and one in Avignon. Princes and peoples quickly took sides (see map 12.3), and the troubles of the papacy multiplied. Each pope had his own court and needed yet more funds, both to meet ordinary expenses and to pay for policies that he hoped would defeat his rival. And since each pope excommunicated the other and those who supported him, everyone in Christendom was at least technically excommunicated.

The Conciliar Movement   Theologians and jurists had long speculated on who should rule the Church if the pope were to become heretical or incompetent; some concluded that it should be the College of Cardinals or a general council of Church officials. Since the College of Cardinals had split into two factions, each backing one of the rival popes, many prominent thinkers supported the theory that a general council should rule the Church. These conciliarists, as they were called, went further. They wanted the Church to have a new constitution to confirm the supremacy of a general council. Such a step would have reduced the pope's role to that of a limited monarch, but the need to correct numerous abuses strengthened the idea that a general council should rule and reform the Church.

Pisa and Constance   The first test of the conciliarists' position was the Council of Pisa (1409), convened by cardinals of both Rome and Avignon. This council asserted its supremacy within the Church by deposing the two popes and electing another. But this act merely added to the confusion, for it left Christendom with three rivals claiming to be the lawful pope. A second council finally resolved the situation. Some four hundred ecclesiastics assembled at the Council of Constance (1414–1418), the greatest international gathering of the Middle Ages. The council was organized in a new way, with the delegates voting as nations to offset the power of the Italians, who made up nearly half the attendance. This procedure reflected the new importance of national and territorial churches. It enabled the delegates to depose both the Pisan pope and the Avignon pope and persuade the Roman pope to resign. In his stead they elected a Roman cardinal, who took the name Martin V. Thus, the Great Schism was ended, and the Western Church was once again united under a single pope.

As the meetings continued, the views of the conciliarists prevailed. The delegates formally declared that a general council was supreme within the Church. To ensure continuity in Church government, they also directed that new councils be summoned periodically.

◆ THE REVIVAL OF THE PAPACY

In spite of this assertion of supremacy, the council made little headway in reforming the Church. The delegates, mostly great prelates, were the chief beneficiaries of the fiscal system and were reluctant to touch their own privileges and advantages. The real victims of the fiscal abuses, the lower clergy, were poorly represented. As a result, the council could not agree on a general program of reform, because it was too large, too cumbersome, and too divided to maintain effective ecclesiastical government. The restored papacy soon reclaimed its position as supreme head of the Western Church.

The practical weaknesses of the conciliar movement were revealed at the Council of Basel (1431–1449). Because disputes broke out almost at once with the pope, the council deposed him and elected another, Felix V. The conciliar movement,

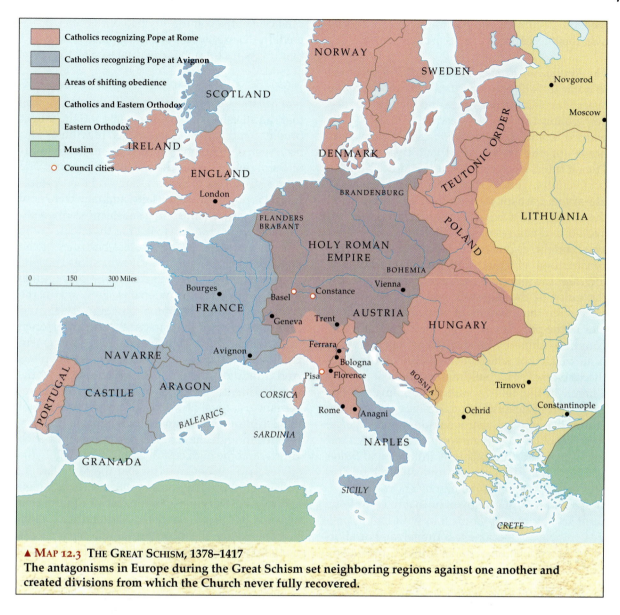

Catholics recognizing Pope at Rome
Catholics recognizing Pope at Avignon
Areas of shifting obedience
Catholics and Eastern Orthodox
Eastern Orthodox
Muslim
○ Council cities

NORWAY
SWEDEN
SCOTLAND
IRELAND
ENGLAND
London
DENMARK
BRANDENBURG
FLANDERS
BRABANT
HOLY ROMAN
EMPIRE
BOHEMIA
TEUTONIC ORDER
POLAND
LITHUANIA
Novgorod
Moscow
Bourges
Basel   Constance
Vienna
FRANCE
Geneva   Trent   AUSTRIA
HUNGARY
Ferrara
Avignon   Bologna
Pisa   Florence
BOSNIA
NAVARRE
CASTILE   ARAGON   CORSICA
Tirnovo
Rome   Anagni
Ochrid   Constantinople
PORTUGAL
BALEARICS
SARDINIA
NAPLES
GRANADA
SICILY
CRETE

0   150   300 Miles

▲ MAP 12.3 THE GREAT SCHISM, 1378–1417
The antagonisms in Europe during the Great Schism set neighboring regions against one another and created divisions from which the Church never fully recovered.

designed to heal the schism, now seemed responsible for renewing it. Recognizing the futility of its actions, the council tried to rescue its dignity when Felix died by endorsing the cardinals' election of a new pope, Nicholas V, in 1449 and then disbanding. This action ended efforts to give supreme authority to councils. But the idea of government by representation that they advanced was to have an important influence on later political developments in Europe.

Territorial Independence   Although the popes remained suspicious of councils, they had much more serious rivals to their authority in the powerful lay princes, who were exerting ever tighter control over territorial churches. Both England and France issued decrees that limited papal powers within their kingdoms, and this policy was soon imitated in Spain and the stronger principalities of the Holy Roman Empire. Although such decrees did not establish national or territorial churches, they do document the decline of papal control over the international Christian community.

The Revival of Rome   When Martin V returned to Rome in 1417, the popes faced the monumental task of rebuilding their office and their prestige as both political and cultural leaders of Europe. They wanted Rome to be a major capital, a worthy home for the papacy, and not dependent on French rulers or culture, as they had been for the past century. To this end, they adopted the new literary and artistic ideas of the Renaissance, and the result was a huge rebuilding program that symbolized the restored authority of the popes. They sought, as one contemporary put it, "by the construction of grand and lasting buildings to increase the honor of the Roman Church and the glory of the Apostolic see, and widen and strengthen the devotion of all Christian people." One of the popes even proclaimed that if any city "ought to shine by its cleanliness and beauty, it is above all that which bears the title of capital of the universe." The building of a new St. Peter's Church in the 1400s was but the climax of this campaign of beautification, designed to assert a cultural supremacy that went along with the supremacy of the Pope's authority. At the same time, vigorous military campaigns in the Papal States subdued that difficult territory and established the papacy as a major Italian power.

It could be argued, however, that in identifying itself so closely with Rome and with Italian politics, the papacy became less universal. For all its splendor and its renewed control over the institution of the Church, it was failing to retain the spiritual allegiance of Europe, especially in the north. The popes may have succeeded in reshaping the Church into a powerful and centralized body, and in making Rome once again a cultural capital of the Western world, but the new cultural and intellectual forces that were at work in the 1400s ultimately undermined the centrality of the papacy to the life of Europe.

◆ STYLES OF PIETY

Partly in response to the disorder of the Church as an institution, new forms of piety and religious practice began to appear. Whereas praying for the salvation of the community had once been considered the clergy's responsibility, many now felt that it was up to each individual to seek the favor of God.

Lay Mysticism and Piety   One consequence was that mysticism—an interior sense of the direct presence and love of God—which previously had been seen only in monastic life, began to move out of the monasteries in the thirteenth century. The prime mission of the Franciscans and the Dominicans was preaching to the laity, and they were now communicating some of the satisfactions of mystical religion. Laypersons wishing to remain in the outside world could join special branches of the Franciscans or Dominicans known as third orders. Confraternities, which were religious guilds founded largely for laypersons, grew up in the cities and, through common religious services and programs of charitable activities, tried to deepen the spiritual lives of their members. Humanism had strong overtones of a movement for lay piety. And hundreds of devotional and mystical works were written to teach laypersons how to feel repentance, not just how to define it. Translations of the Scriptures into vernacular languages also appeared, though the Church disapproved of such efforts, and the high cost of manuscripts before the age of printing severely limited their circulation.

This growth of lay piety was, in essence, an effort to give everyone access to forms of faith that hitherto had been restricted to a spiritual elite. Frightened by the disasters of the age, people hungered for emotional reassurance, for evidence of God's love and redeeming grace within themselves. Also, the spread of education among the laity, at least in the cities, made people discontented with empty forms of religious ritual.

Female Piety   The commitment to personal piety among the laity was particularly apparent among women. It is significant that in the years between 1000 and 1150 male saints outnumbered females by 12 to 1, but in the years 1348 to 1500 the ratio dropped to 2.74 to 1. Moreover, the typical female saints of the later Middle Ages were no longer queens, princesses, and abbesses. They were mystics and visionaries, ordinary yet charismatic people who gained the attention of the Church and the world by the power of their message and the force of their own personalities. Catherine of Siena (1347–1380), for example, was the youngest of the twenty-five children of a humble Italian dyer. Her reputation for holiness attracted a company of followers from as far away as England, and she wrote (or dictated, for she probably couldn't write) devotional tracts that are monuments of Italian literature. Similar charismatic qualities made a simple Englishwoman, Margery Kempe, famous for her visions and her piety.

Women who out of poverty or preference lived a religious life outside convents became numerous, especially in towns. Some lived with their families, and others eked out a living on the margins of society. Still others lived in spontaneously organized religious houses—called *Beguines* in northern Europe—where they shared all tasks and property. The Church was suspicious of these women professing a religious life outside convents, without an approved rule. But the movement was too large for the Church to suppress or control. And many of them came to be particularly identified with one of the most powerful forms of lay piety in this period, mysticism.

The Mystics Among the most active centers of the new lay piety was the Rhine valley, a region that was especially noted for its remarkable mystics. The most famous was the Dominican Meister Eckhart (1260?–1327?), a spellbinding preacher and a devoted student of Aquinas, who sought to bring his largely lay listeners into a mystical confrontation with God. Believers, he maintained, should cultivate the "divine spark" that is in every soul. To achieve this, they had to banish all thought from their minds and seek to attain a state of pure passivity. If they succeeded, God would come and dwell within them. Eckhart stressed the futility of dogma and, implicitly, traditional acts of piety. God is too great for such categories, he taught, and cannot be moved by conventional piety.

Brethren of the Common Life Just as the nominalists argued for philosophical reasons that God is unknowable, so the mystics dismissed the value of formal knowledge and stressed the need for love and an emotional commitment to God and

▲ *Pisan Artist of XIV Century*
THE MYSTIC MARRIAGE OF CATHERINE OF SIENA
Catherine of Siena was a nun who was known for her efforts to return the papacy to Rome. Part of the reason for her sainthood was that, like Joan of Arc, she experienced visions from an early age. She is shown here with her symbol, the lily, in a scene from one of her visions. About to enter into a mystic marriage with Christ, she is accepting the wedding ring directly from him. Note that in the Renaissance, wedding rings were often placed on the middle finger of the right hand.
Soprintendenza B.A.A.A.S., Pisa, Museo Nazionale di S. Matteo

his attributes. Perhaps the most influential of the mystics was Gerhard Groote of Holland. Groote wrote sparingly, exerting his influence over his followers largely through his personality. After his death in 1384, his disciples formed a religious congregation known as the Brethren of the Common Life. Taking education as their principal task, they founded schools in Germany and the Low Countries that imparted a style of lay piety known as the *devotio moderna* ("modern devotion"). Later reformers, such as Erasmus of Rotterdam and Martin Luther, were to be among their pupils.

Thomas à Kempis The richest statement of the *devotio moderna* appeared about 1425 in *The Imitation of Christ*, a small devotional manual attributed to Thomas à Kempis, a member of the Brethren of the Common Life. *The Imitation of Christ* says almost nothing about fasting, pilgrimages, or other traditional acts of private piety. Instead, it emphasizes interior experience as essential to religious life. The believer, it argued, needed only to emulate the life of Jesus. The book's ethical and social consciousness is also unusual. Powerful interior faith leads not to extreme acts of personal expiation but to highly ethical behavior: "First, keep yourself in peace, and then you shall be able to bring peace to others."

Features of Lay Piety The new lay piety was by no means a revolutionary break with the medieval Church, but it implicitly discounted the importance of many traditional institutions and practices. In this personal approach to God, there was no special value in the monastic vocation. As Erasmus would later argue, what was good in monasticism should be practiced by every Christian. Stressing simplicity and humility, the new lay piety was reacting against the pomp and splendor that had come to surround popes and prelates and to mark religious ceremonies. Likewise, the detailed rules for fasts, abstinences, and devotional exercises; the cult of the saints and their relics; and the traffic in indulgences and pardons all seemed peripheral to true religious needs. Without the proper state of soul, these traditional acts of piety were meaningless; with the proper state, every act was worship. This new lay piety, emerging as it did out of medieval religious traditions, was clearly a preparation for the reformations of faith that took place in the sixteenth century among both Protestants and Catholics. It helped produce a more penetrating faith at a time when the formal beliefs of the Middle Ages, for all their grandeur and logical intricacies, no longer fully satisfied the religious spirit and were leaving hollows in the human heart.

Although the *devotio moderna* was a religious movement with little regard for humanist learning, it shared the humanists' distaste for the abstractions and intellectual arrogance of Scholasticism, and their belief that a wise and good person will cultivate humility and will maintain a "learned ignorance" toward the profound questions of religion. Moreover, both movements directed their message primarily to laypersons, in order to help them lead a higher moral life. The humanists, of course, drew their chief inspiration from the works of pagan and Christian antiquity, whereas the advocates of the new lay piety looked almost exclusively to Scripture. But the resemblances were close enough for scholars like Erasmus and Thomas More, writing in the early 1500s, to combine elements from both in the movement known as Christian Humanism.

◆ MOVEMENTS OF DOCTRINAL REFORM

The effort to reform the traditions of medieval Christianity also led to open attacks on the religious establishment—fueled, of course, by antagonism toward the papacy and Church corruption and by the larger tensions of this troubled epoch. Above all, these attacks gained support because the Church remained reluctant to adapt its organization and teachings to the demands of a changing world. In two prominent cases, moreover, the critiques arose at a university, where the basic method of instruction, the disputation, encouraged the discussion of unorthodox ideas. At disputations, students learned by listening to arguments for and against standard views. It was not impossible for someone taking the "wrong" side in such a debate to be carried away and cross the line between a theoretical discussion and open dissent.

Wycliffe Whatever its origins, the most prominent of the assaults of the 1300s was launched by an Englishman, John Wycliffe (1320?–1384), who taught at Oxford University. Wycliffe argued that the Church had become too remote from the people, and he wanted its doctrines simplified. To this end, he sought less power for priests and a more direct reliance on the Bible, which he hoped would be translated into English to make it easier to understand. Beyond his unease over the Church's remoteness from ordinary believers, he may have had political reasons (and thus support) for his stand. He was close to members of the royal court, who were increasingly resistant to papal demands and who were troubled that, in the midst of England's war with France, the papacy should have come under French influence when it moved from Rome to Avignon. In 1365 Wycliffe denounced the payment of Peter's pence, the annual tax given by English people to the papacy, and shortly thereafter he publicly denounced the papal Curia, monks, and friars for their vices.

Wycliffe argued that the Scriptures alone declared the will of God and that neither the pope and the cardinals nor the Scholastic theologians could tell Christians what they should believe. In particular, he questioned one of the central dogmas of the Church that emphasized the special power of the priest: transubstantiation, which asserts that priests at the Mass work a miracle when they change the substance of bread and wine into the substance of Christ's body and blood. Besides attacking the exalted position and privileges of the priesthood in such rites as transubstantiation, Wycliffe denied the authority of the pope and the hierarchy to exercise jurisdiction or to hold property. He claimed that the true Church was that of the predestined—that is, those whom God would save and were thus in a state of grace. Only these elect could rule the elect; therefore, popes and bishops who had no grace could have their properties removed and had no right to rule. Responsibility for ecclesiastical reform rested with the prince, and the pope could exercise only as much authority as the prince allowed.

The Lollards Many of Wycliffe's views were branded heretical, but even though he was forced to leave Oxford when he offended his protectors at the royal court, they did keep him unharmed until he died. His followers, mostly ordinary people known as Lollards—a name apparently derived from *lollar* ("idler")—were not so lucky. They managed to survive as an underground movement in the countryside until the Protestant Reformation exploded more than a century later, but they were constantly hounded, and in 1428 the Church had Wycliffe's remains dug up, burned, and thrown into a river.

Hus An even harsher fate awaited Wycliffe's most famous admirer, a Bohemian priest named Jan Hus (1369–1415), who started a broad and even more defiant movement in his homeland. Hus was a distinguished churchman and scholar. He served as rector (the equivalent of president) of the Charles University in Prague, one of Europe's best-known institutions, and he was the main preacher at a fashionable chapel in Prague. Like Wycliffe, whose ideas he had first heard expounded at a disputation, he argued that priests were not a holy and privileged group, set apart from laypersons, but that the Church was made up of all the faithful. To emphasize this equality, he rejected the division that allowed the congregation at a Mass to consume the wafer that symbolized Christ's body but not the wine that symbolized his blood, which only the priest could drink. In a dramatic gesture, Hus shared the cup of wine with all worshipers, thus reducing the distinctiveness of the priest. His followers adopted a chalice, or cup, as the symbol of their movement.

Hus was not hesitant about defying the leadership of the Church. Denounced for the positions he had taken, he replied by questioning the authority of the pope himself: "If a Pope is wicked, then like Judas he is a devil and a son of perdition and not the head of the Church militant. If he lives in a manner contrary to Christ, he has entered the papacy by another way than through Christ." In 1415 Hus was summoned to defend his views before the Church Council at Constance. Although he had been guaranteed safe passage if he came to answer accusations of heresy, the promise was broken. He was condemned, handed over to the secular authorities, and executed (see "Hus at Constance," p. 432). But his followers, unlike the Lollards who stayed out of sight in England, refused to retreat in the face of persecution.

The Hussites A new leader, Jan Žižka, known as John of the Chalice, raised an army and led a successful campaign against the emperor, who was also king of Bohemia and the head of the crusade that was now mounted against the Hussites. The resistance lasted twenty years, outliving Žižka, but sustained by Bohemian nobles, and eventually the Hussites were allowed to establish a special church, the Utraquist Church, in which both cup and wafer were shared by all worshipers at Mass. But Hus's other demands, such as the

HUS AT CONSTANCE

◆

A few weeks before he was executed, Jan Hus wrote to his Czech followers to tell them how he had responded to his accusers at the Council of Constance:

"Master Jan Hus, in hope a servant of God, to all faithful Czechs who love God: I call to your attention that the proud and avaricious Council, full of all abomination, condemned my Czech books having neither heard nor seen them; even if it had heard them, it would not have understood them. O, had you seen that Council which calls itself the most holy, and that cannot err, you would have seen the greatest abomination! I have heard it commonly said that Constance would not for thirty years rid itself of the sins which that Council has committed. That Council has done more harm than good.

"Therefore, faithful Christians, do not allow yourselves to be terrified by their decrees, which will profit them nothing. They will fly away like butterflies, and their decrees will turn into a spiderweb.

They wanted to frighten me, but could not overcome God's power in me. They did not dare to oppose me with Scripture.

"I am writing this to you that you may know that they did not defeat me by any Scripture or any proof, but that they sought to seduce me by deceits and threats to recant and abjure. But the merciful Lord God, whose law I have extolled, has been and is with me, and I hope that He will be with me to the end and will preserve me in His grace until death.

"This letter was written in chains, in the expectation of death."

From Matthew Spinka (ed.), *The Letters of John Hus* (Manchester: University Press, 1972), pp. 195–197.

---

surrender of all personal possessions by the clergy (an echo of St. Francis), were rejected. Those who tried to fight on for these causes were defeated in battle, and after a long struggle the resistance came to an end, having made only a minor dent in the unity of the Church.

SUMMARY

◆

The popular appeal of Wycliffe and Hus reflected widespread dissatisfaction with official teachings in the late 1300s and 1400s—a dissatisfaction that Petrarch, too, had shared, though he did not challenge traditional doctrine but simply looked elsewhere for moral guidance. The movement that he launched, Humanism, transformed education and the arts, but others were determined to bring change to Europe's spiritual leadership as well. When, in pursuit of this ideal, Wycliffe and Hus chose to risk open confrontation, they demonstrated that reform ideas, advanced by charismatic leaders, could find a following among those who resented the authoritarian and materialistic outlook of the Church. At the same time, however, it became clear that such dissent could not survive without support from nobles, princes, or other leaders of society. Even with such help, the Hussites had to limit their demands; without it, they would have gained nothing. It was one hundred years after Hus's death before a new reformer arose who had learned these lessons, and he was to transform Western Christianity beyond recognition.

QUESTIONS FOR FURTHER THOUGHT

1. Why is it, when we think of the "golden ages" of history, that it is not just new ideas, but great art, that makes them seem such special times?

2. How do dominant cultural institutions like the medieval Church lose their hold over peoples' loyalty and respect?

RECOMMENDED READING

Sources

*Brucker, Gene A. (ed.). The Society of Renaissance Florence: A Documentary Study. 1971.

*Cassirer, Ernst, P. O. Kristeller, and J. H. Randall, Jr. (eds.). The Renaissance Philosophy of Man. 1953. Selections from Petrarch, Ficino, Pico, and others.

*Chambers, David, and Brian Pullan (eds.). Venice: A Documentary History, 1450–1630. 1992.

Kempe, Margery. The Book of Margery Kempe (1436). B. A. Windeatt (tr.). 1985. The autobiography of an extraordinary woman.

*Kohl, Benjamin G., and Ronald G. Witt (eds.). The Earthly Republic: Italian Humanists on Government and Society. 1978.

*Marsilius of Padua. Defender of Peace. Alan Gerwith (tr.). 1986.

Studies

*Baron, Hans. The Crisis of the Early Italian Renaissance: Civic Humanism and Republican Liberty in the Age of Classicism and Tyranny. 1966. Fundamental analysis of Florentine "civic humanism."

*Berenson, Bernard. The Italian Painters of the Renaissance. 1968. Classic essays on the history of art.

*Burckhardt, Jacob. The Civilization of the Renaissance in Italy. 1958. One of the pioneering works of European history, first published in 1860.

Cole, Bruce. The Renaissance Artist at Work: From Pisano to Titian. 1983.

*Hale, John. The Civilization of Europe in the Renaissance. 1993. The best overview.

*Hollingsworth, Mary. Patronage in Renaissance Italy from 1400 to the Early Sixteenth Century. 1994.

*Huizinga, Johan. The Waning of the Middle Ages. 1954.

Klapisch-Zuber, Christiane. Women, Family, and Ritual in Renaissance Italy. 1985. Collected essays.

*Kristeller, Paul O. Renaissance Thought and Its Sources. 1979. By a leading historian of Renaissance thought.

*Rabb, Theodore K. Renaissance Lives. 1993.

Web Sites

http://www.kfki.hu/%7Earthp/artist/html

http://www.hermitagemuseum.org

http://www.learner.org/exhibits/renaissance

http://www.mega.it/eng/egui/hogui.htm

*Available in paperback.

▲ *Lucas Cranach the Elder*
LUTHER IN THE VINEYARD
This work of propaganda uses the biblical image of Christians toiling in the vineyard of the Lord to contrast the seriousness and fruitfulness of the Protestants on the left with the greed and destructiveness of the Catholics on the right. Luther himself rakes in the center, while Melanchthon at the far left goes to the source (the Bible) and draws from the well; meanwhile, on the right, bishops and monks ruin the crops, burn the wood, and fill the well with stones.
AKG London

REFORMATIONS IN RELIGION

lthough it may have seemed monolithic and all-powerful, the Roman Church in the fifteenth century was neither a unified nor an unchallenged institution. It had long permitted considerable variety in individual beliefs, from the analytic investigations of canon lawyers to the emotional outpourings of mystics. There were local saints, some of whom were recognized as holy only by a few villages; and for many Europeans the papacy remained a distant and barely comprehensible authority. To assume that its theological pronouncements were understood by the average illiterate Christian is to misrepresent the loose, fragmentary nature of the medieval Church. Moreover, the political disputes and reform movements of the fourteenth and fifteenth centuries had raised doubts about the central structure and doctrines of the Church. That the papacy had weathered these storms by 1500 indicated both how flexible and how powerful it was. What was to be remarkable in the years that followed was the sudden revelation of the Church's fragility, as a protest by a single monk snowballed into a movement that shattered the thousand-year unity of Western Christendom.

CHAPTER 13. REFORMATIONS IN RELIGION							
	Social Structure	Body Politic	Changes in the Organization of Production and in the Impact of Technology	Evolution of Family and Changing Gender Roles	War	Religion	Cultural Expression
I. PIETY AND DISSENT							
II. THE LUTHERAN REFORMATION							
III. THE SPREAD OF PROTESTANTISM							
IV. THE CATHOLIC REVIVAL							

I. Piety and Dissent

◆

The Roman Church may have held sway throughout Western Europe in 1500, but it was proving less and less able to meet the increasingly varied needs of the faithful. Different ideas about the ways an individual might achieve salvation were spreading, and some were turning into criticisms that the Church hierarchy could neither refute nor silence.

◆ DOCTRINE AND REFORM

Two Traditions　A fundamental question that all Christians face is: How can sinful human beings gain salvation? In 1500, the standard official answer was that the Church was an essential intermediary. Only through participation in its rituals, and particularly through the seven sacraments its priests administered—baptism, confirmation, matrimony, the eucharist, ordination, penance, and extreme unction—did the believer have access to the grace that God offered as an antidote to sin. But there was another answer, identified with distinguished Church fathers such as St. Augustine: People can be saved by their faith in God and love of him. This view emphasized inward and personal belief and focused on God as the source of grace.

The two traditions were not incompatible; for centuries they had coexisted without difficulty. Yet the absence of precise definition in many areas of doctrine was a major problem for theologians,

because it was often difficult to tell where orthodoxy ended and heresy began. The position taken by the papacy, however, had grown less inclusive and adaptable over the years; by 1500 it seemed to be stressing the outward and institutional far more than the inward and personal route to salvation. Reformers for over a century had tried to reverse this trend, and it was unclear whether change would come from within or would require a revolution and split in the Church.

The Quest for Reform　The root of the demand for change, as Hus had known, was the need of many laypersons for a way to express their piety that was more personal than official practices allowed. Church rituals meant little, they felt, unless believers could cultivate an interior sense of the love and presence of God. Rejecting the theological subtleties of Scholasticism, they sought divine guidance in the Bible and the writings of the early Church fathers, especially St. Augustine. Lay religious fraternities dedicated to private forms of worship and charitable works proliferated in the cities, especially in Germany and Italy. The most widespread in Germany, the Brotherhood of the Eleven Thousand Virgins, consisted of laypeople who gathered together, usually in a church, to sing hymns. In the mid-fifteenth century, more than one hundred such groups had been established in Hamburg, a city of slightly more than ten thousand inhabitants. Church leaders, unhappy about a development over which they had no control, had tried to suppress them, to no avail.

▲ *Anonymous*
THE MARTYRDOM OF SAVONAROLA, CA. **1500**
This painting still hangs in the monastery of San Marco where Savonarola lived during his years of power. It shows the city's central square—a setting that remains recognizable to anyone who visits Florence today—where the bonfire of the "vanities" had been held in 1496, and where Savonarola was executed in 1498. The execution is depicted here as an event that the ordinary citizens of Florence virtually ignore as they go about their daily routines.
Erich Lessing/Art Resource, NY

Savonarola   The most spectacular outburst of popular piety around 1500 occurred in seemingly materialist Florence, which embraced Girolamo Savonarola, a zealous friar who wanted to banish the irreligion and materialism he saw everywhere about him. The climax of his influence came in 1496, when he arranged a tremendous bonfire in which the Florentines burned cosmetics, light literature, dice, and other such frivolities. Savonarola embodied the desire for personal renewal that had long been a part of Western Christianity but seemed to be gaining intensity in the 1400s. His attempts at reform eventually brought him into conflict with the papacy, which rightly saw him as a threat to its authority. The Church therefore denounced him and gave its support to those who resented his power in Florence. His opponents had him arrested in 1498 and then executed on a trumped-up charge of treason.

Reform in Spain   The widespread search for a more intense devotional life was a sign of spiritual vitality. But Church leaders in the age of

Savonarola gave little encouragement to ecclesiastical reform and the evangelization of the laity. Only in Spain were serious efforts launched to eradicate abuses and encourage religious fervor, and they were led not by Rome but by Queen Isabella herself and by the head of the Spanish Church, Cardinal Ximenes de Cisneros. In other countries the hierarchy reacted harshly when such movements threatened its authority.

◆ CAUSES OF DISCONTENT

Although its power over the Church had been restored by 1500, the papacy was still struggling to assert spiritual authority in the wake of the blows it had received in the previous two centuries. The move to Avignon, the Great Schism, and the conciliar movement had challenged its aura of moral and doctrinal superiority, and now its troubles multiplied.

Secular Interests   Of major concern to many Christians were the papacy's secular interests. Increasingly, popes conducted themselves like princes. With skillful diplomacy and military action, they had consolidated their control over the papal lands in the Italian peninsula; Julius II (1503–1513) was even known as the Warrior Pope. An elaborate court arose in Rome, famous for its lavish patronage of the arts and symptomatic of a commitment to political power and grandeur that seemed to eclipse religious duties. Matters had reached such a point that some popes used their spiritual powers to raise funds for their secular activities. The fiscal measures developed at Avignon had expanded the papacy's income, but the enlarged revenues led to widespread abuses. High ecclesiastical offices were bought and sold, and men (usually sons of nobles) were attracted to these positions by the opportunities they provided for wealth and power, not by a religious vocation.

Abuse was widespread at lower levels in the Church as well. Some prelates held several offices at a time and could not give adequate attention to any of them. The ignorance and moral laxity of the parish and monastic clergy also aroused antagonism. Even more damaging was the widespread impression that the Church was failing to

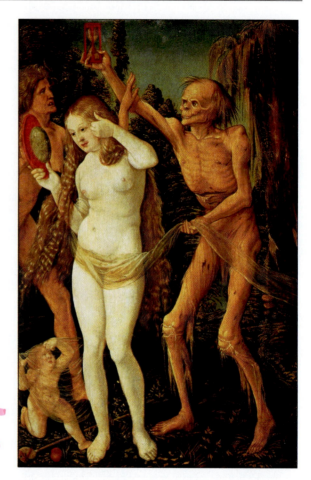

▲ *Hans Baldung Grien*
THE THREE AGES OF WOMAN AND DEATH, CA. 1510
The preoccupation with the transitoriness of life and the vanity of earthly things took many forms in the sixteenth century. Here the point is hammered home unmistakably, as the central figure—a young woman at the height of her beauty between infancy and old age—is reminded of the passage of time (the hourglass) and the omnipresence of death even as she admires herself in a convex mirror.
Erich Lessing / Art Resource, NY

meet individual spiritual needs because of its remoteness from the day-to-day needs of the average believer, its elaborate and incomprehensible system of canon law and theology, and its formal ceremonials. Above all, there was a general perception that priests, monks, and nuns were profiting from their positions, exploiting the people, and offering minimal moral leadership or religious guidance in return.

Anticlericalism These concerns provoked anticlericalism (hostility to the clergy) and calls for reform, which went unheeded except in the Spain of Cardinal Ximenes. For increasing numbers of deeply pious people, the growing emphasis on ritual and standardized practices seemed irrelevant to their personal quest for salvation. And their reaction was symptomatic of the broad commitment to genuine piety that was apparent not only in the followers of Wycliffe, Hus, and Savonarola but in many segments of European society in the early 1500s.

◆ POPULAR RELIGION

The Spread of Ideas It was not only the educated elite and the city dwellers (a minority of Europe's inhabitants) who sought to express their faith in personal terms. The yearning for religious devotion among ordinary villagers, the majority of the population, was apparent even when the local priest—who was often hardly better educated than his parishioners—did little to inspire spiritual commitments. People would listen avidly to news of distant places brought by travelers who stopped at taverns and inns (a major source of information and ideas), and increasingly the tales they told were of religious upheaval. In addition, itinerant preachers roamed some regions, notably Central Europe, in considerable numbers, and they drew crowds when they started speaking—on street corners in towns or out in the fields—and described the power of faith. They usually urged direct communication between believers and God, free from ritual and complex doctrine. To the vast crowds they often

▼ *Hans Sebald Beham*
CHURCH FESTIVAL, WOODCUT, 1535
The celebration of the anniversary of a church's consecration was one of the most important holidays in a village. Not everyone, however, used this opportunity for spiritual ends, like the couple getting married in front of the church. Some overindulged at the tavern (lower right); some had a tooth extracted (center left); and some, as the chickens in the center and various couples in the scene suggest, used the occasion for pleasure alone.
Hans Sebald Beham, German, 1500–1550. *"Large Peasant Holiday."* Woodcut, 1535. 36.2×114.2 cm. (Sections 1 and 2). Potter Palmer Collection, 1967.491. Photograph ©1998, The Art Institute of Chicago. All Rights Reserved.

drew, many of them seemed to echo the words of St. Augustine: "God and the soul I want to recognize, nothing else."

Equally important as a means of learning about and discussing the latest religious issues were the gatherings that regularly brought villagers together. Throughout the year, they would assemble to celebrate holidays—not only the landmarks of the Christian calendar like Christmas and Easter but also local festivals. Religion was always essential to these occasions. When, for example, the planting season arrived, the local priest would lead a procession into the countryside to bless the fields and pray for good crops. Family events, too, from birth to death, had important religious elements.

The Veillèe The most common occasion when the community's traditional beliefs and assumptions, however, was the evening gathering—generally referred to by its French name, *veillèe,* which means staying up in the evening. Between spring and autumn, when the weather was not too cold, a good part of the village came together at a central location after each day's work was done. There was little point in staying in one's own home after dark, because making a light with candles or oil was too expensive. Instead, sitting around a communal fire, people could sew clothes, repair tools, feed babies, resolve (or start) disputes, and discuss news. It was one of the few times when women were of no lesser status than men; the views they expressed were as important

▼ *Peter Brueghel*
THE PEASANT DANCE, CA. 1567
The most vivid images of life in the village during the sixteenth century were created by the Flemish artist Peter Brueghel. The different human types, and the earthiness of country life, are captured in scenes that show the villagers both at work and, as here, at ease and relaxed.
Erich Lessing/Art Resource, NY

as any in shaping the common outlook of the villagers.

A favorite occupation at the *veillèe* was listening to stories. Every village had its storytellers, who recounted wondrous tales of local history, of magical adventures, or of moral dilemmas, as the mood required. Biblical tales and the exploits of Christian heroes like the Crusaders had always drawn an attentive audience. Now, however, in addition to entertainment and general moral uplift, peddlers and travelers who attended the *veillèe* brought news of challenges to religious traditions. They told of attacks on the pope and Church practices and of arguments for a simpler and more easily understood faith. In this way the ideas of religious reformers spread and those with unorthodox views like the Lollards keep their faith alive. In some cases, the beliefs that were described made converts of those who heard them, and traveling preachers came to regard the gatherings at the *veillèes* as ready-made congregations. They were usually far more knowledgeable, better trained, and more effective than local priests.

The Role of the Priest   The response of the traditional Church to this challenge, after decades of indifference, was to insist that the local priest be better educated and more aware of what was at stake in the religious struggles of the day. As long as he had the support of the local authorities, he could make sure that his views dominated the *veillèe* and that contrary beliefs were not expressed. Whichever way the discussions at these communal gatherings went, however, they demonstrated the power of popular piety in the tens of thousands of villages that dotted the European countryside.

The Impact of Printing   The expression of this piety received unexpected assistance from technology: the invention of a printing press with movable type in the mid-1400s. At least a hundred years earlier, Europeans had known that by carving words and pictures into a wood block, inking them, and pressing the block onto paper, they could make an image that could be repeated on many sheets of paper. We do not know exactly when they discovered that they could speed up this cumbersome process, and therefore change the text from page to page, if they used individual

Der Buchdrücker.

▲ *Jost Amman*
"THE PRINTER" FROM *DAS STÄNDEBUCH (THE BOOK OF TRADES)*, **1568**
This illustration is the first detailed depiction of a printer's shop, showing assistants taking type from large wooden holders in the back, the press on the right, the pages being prepared and inked in the foreground, and finally the sheets of paper before and after they are printed.

letters and put them together within a frame. We do know, however, that a printer named Johannes Gutenberg, who lived in the city of Mainz on the Rhine, was producing books this way by the 1450s. The technique spread rapidly (see table on next page) and made reading material available to a much broader segment of the population.

It has been estimated that some nine million books had been printed by 1500. As a result, new ideas could travel with unprecedented speed. Perhaps a third of the trading and upper classes—townspeople, the educated, and the

▼ **The Spread of Printing through 1500**
Number of towns in which a printing press was established for the first time, by period and country

Period	German-Speaking Areas	Italian-	French-	Spain	England*	Netherlands	Other	Total
Before 1471	8	4	1	1	—	—	—	14
1471–1480	22	36	9	6	3	12	5	93
1481–1490	17	13	21	12	—	5	4	72
1491–1500	9	5	11	6	—	2	8	41
Total by 1500	56	58	42	25	3	19	17	220

*In an attempt to try to control the printers, the English government ordered that they work only in London and at Oxford and Cambridge universities.

Adapted from Lucien Febvre and Henri-Jean Martin, *The Coming of the Book: The Impact of Printing 1450–1800*, David Gerald (tr.) (London, NLB, 1976), pp. 178–179, 184–185.

nobility—could read, but books could reach a much wider audience, because peddlers began to sell printed materials throughout Europe. They were bought everywhere and became favorite material for reading out loud at *veillèes*. Thus, people who had had little contact with written literature in the days of manuscripts now gained access to the latest ideas of the time.

Printing and Religion   Printers were not slow to take advantage of the popular interest in books by publishing almanacs filled with home-spun advice about the weather and nature that were written specifically for simple rural folk. Even the almanacs, however, carried religious advice; and more importantly, translations of the Bible made it available to ordinary people in a language that, for the first time, they could understand. Books thus became powerful weapons in the religious conflicts of the day. Devotional tracts, lives of the saints, and the Bible were the most popular titles—often running to editions of around one thousand copies. They became means of spreading new ideas, and the ready markets they found reflected the general interest of the age in spiritual matters.

Printing lessened the dependence of ordinary people on the clergy; whereas traditionally the priest had read and interpreted the Scriptures for his congregation, now people could consult their own copies. By 1522, eighteen translations of the Bible had been published. Some fourteen thousand copies had been printed in German alone,

enough to make it easy to buy in most German-speaking regions. The Church frowned on these efforts, and governments tried to regulate the numbers and locations of presses; but in the end it proved impossible to control the effects of printing.

◆ **PIETY AND PROTEST IN LITERATURE AND ART**

Rabelais   The printing press broke the Church's monopoly over the dissemination of religious teachings. It thus became possible for the most gifted satirist of the sixteenth century, the French humanist François Rabelais, to ridicule openly the clergy and the morality of his day. Rabelais was a monk (as well as a doctor), and he was deeply unhappy that traditional religious practices had diverged so far from the ideals of Jesus. He was most famous for his earthy bawdiness, but again and again he returned to clerical targets, as in this passage from his *Gargantua* (1533):

"Don't monks pray to God for us?" "They do nothing of the kind," said Gargantua. "All they do is keep the whole neighborhood awake by jangling their bells. . . . They mumble over a lot of legends and psalms, which they don't in the least understand; and they say a great many paternosters . . . without thinking or caring about what they are saying. And all that I call a mockery of God, not prayer."

Broadsides Scurrilous broadsides no less stinging in tone became very popular during the religious disputes of the 1500s. These single sheets often contained vicious attacks on religious opponents and were usually illustrated by cartoons with obscene imagery. The broadsides were examples of partisan hostility, but their broader significance should not be ignored. Even the most lowly of hack writers could share with a serious author like Rabelais a sense of outrage at indifference in high places and find an audience for attacks on the inadequate spiritual leadership of the time.

Piety in Art The emphasis on religious belief, so evident in European literature, also permeated the work of northern artists (see plates on p. 400 and p. 422). The gruesome paintings of Hieronymus Bosch, for example, depicted the fears of devils and of hell that his contemporaries felt endangered them at all times. He put on canvas the demons, the temptations, the terrible punishments for sin that people considered as real as their tangible surroundings. Bosch's younger contemporary Matthias Grünewald conveyed the same mixture of terror and devotion. Like Bosch, he painted a frightening *Temptation of St. Anthony*, showing the travails of the saint who steadfastly resisted horrible attacks by the devil. These artists explored the darker side of faith, taking their inspiration from the fear of damnation and the hope for salvation—the first seen in the demons, the second in the redeeming Christ.

The depth of piety conveyed by these artists reflected the temper of Europe. In art and literature, as in lay organizations and the continuing popularity of itinerant preachers, people showed their concern for individual spiritual values and their

◄ *Matthias Grünewald*
The Temptation of St. Anthony, ca. 1510
This detail from a series of scenes Grünewald painted for the Isenheim Altar suggests the power that the devil held over the imagination of sixteenth-century Europeans. The gentle, bearded St. Anthony is not seated in contemplation, as in Dürer's portrayal (see plate on p. 444). Instead, he is surrounded by the monsters the devil has sent to frighten him out of his faith. This fear was a favorite subject of the period and provided artists like Bosch and Grünewald the opportunity to make vivid and terrifying the ordinary Christian's fear of sin.
Erich Lessing/Art Resource, NY

dissatisfaction with a Church that was not meeting their needs.

◆ CHRISTIAN HUMANISM

No segment of society expressed the strivings and yearnings of the age more eloquently than the northern humanists. The salient features of the humanist movement in Italy—its theory of education, its emphasis on eloquence, its reverence for the ancients, and its endorsement of active participation in affairs of state—began to win wide acceptance north of the Alps in the late 1400s. But the northerners added a significant religious dimension to the movement by devoting consider-

able attention to early Christian literature: the Bible and the writings of the Church fathers. As a result, they have been called *Christian humanists.*

The Northern Humanists By the end of the fifteenth century the influence of humanism, carried by the printing press, was Europe-wide. The northern humanists were particularly determined to probe early Christianity for the light it could throw on the origins and accuracy of current religious teachings. Indeed, northern humanism's broad examination of religious issues in the early 1500s helped create an atmosphere in which much more serious criticism of the Church could flourish.

▼ *Albrecht Dürer*
St. Anthony, Engraving, 1519
The ease and mastery that Dürer brought to the art of engraving made it as powerful and flexible a form as painting. Here the massive figure of the saint, deep in study, is placed in front of a marvelously observed city. The buildings display Dürer's virtuosity—their shapes echo the bulk and solidity of the figure—and they may have symbolized the temptations of city life for a saint who was revered for his solitary piety in the desert.
Victoria & Albert Museum, London/Art Resource, NY

The Christian humanists did not abandon the interest in classical authors or the methods for analyzing ancient texts, language, and style that had been developed by Italian humanism. But they put these methods to a new use: analysis of the Bible in order to explain more clearly the message of Jesus and his apostles, and thus to provide a better guide to true piety and morality. This deeply religious undertaking dominated the writings of the two most famous Christian humanists, one English and one Dutch.

More   Sir Thomas More (1478–1535), a lawyer and statesman, was the central figure of English humanism. His reputation as a writer rests primarily on a short work, *Utopia,* published in Latin in 1516, which describes an ideal society on an imaginary island. In it, More condemned war, poverty, intolerance, and other evils of his day and defined the general principles of morality that he felt should underlie human society. The first book of *Utopia* returns to the conflict between the active life and the contemplative life that Petrarch had emphasized, and asks whether a learned person should withdraw from the world to avoid the corruptions of politics or actively participate in affairs of state so as to guide policy. In his own career, More chose the latter path, with fatal results. The second, more famous, book of *Utopia* leaves such practical issues aside and describes what an ideal commonwealth might be like. Utopia's politics and society are carefully regulated, an almost monastic community that has succeeded in abolishing private property, greed, and pride—and thus has freed its inhabitants from some of the worst sins of More's day. The Utopians have accomplished all this without Christianity, and More implies that a society based on Christian principles can attain even greater good. Well-designed institutions, education, and discipline are his answer to the fall of Adam and Eve: Weak human nature can be led to virtuousness only if severely curbed.

Deeply devout and firmly attached to the traditional Church, More entered public life as a member of Parliament in 1504. He rose high in government service, but eventually he gave his life for remaining loyal to the pope and refusing to recognize the decision of his king, Henry VIII, to reject papal authority and become head of the English Church. When Henry had him beheaded for treason. More's last words revealed his unflinching adherence to the Christian principles he pursued throughout his life: "I die the King's good servant, but God's first."

Erasmus   The supreme representative of Christian humanism was the Dutchman Desiderius Erasmus (1466?–1536). Erasmus early acquired a

▼ *Hans Holbein the Younger*
PORTRAIT OF ERASMUS, **1523**
The leading portraitist of the age, Hans Holbein, painted his friend Erasmus a number of times. Here he shows the great scholar at work, possibly writing one of the many elegantly constructed letters that he sent to colleagues throughout Europe. The richness of the scene bears noting: the gold ring, the fine coat with a fur collar, and the splendid tapestry hanging over the paneled wall.
Scala/Art Resource, NY

taste for ancient writers, and he determined to devote himself to classical studies. For the greater part of his life, he wandered through Europe, writing, visiting friends, and occasionally working for important patrons. He always retained his independence, however, for unlike More, he answered the question of whether a scholar should enter public life by avoiding the compromises that would be necessary in the service of a ruler.

Erasmus was so famous for his learning and his literary skills that he dominated the world of letters of his time. Constantly consulted by scholars and admirers, he wrote magnificently composed letters that reflected every aspect of the culture of his age. He became known throughout Europe, however, as a result of a little book, *The Praise of Folly* (1509), which was one of the first best-sellers created by the printing press. Some of it is gay, lighthearted banter that pokes fun at the author himself, his friends, and the follies of everyday life and suggests that a little folly is essential to human existence. The book also points out that Christianity itself is a kind of folly, a belief in "things not seen." In many passages, though, Erasmus launches sharply satirical attacks against monks, the pope, meaningless ceremonies, and the many lapses from what he perceived to be the true Christian spirit.

The Philosophy of Christ   At the heart of Erasmus' work was the message that he called the "philosophy of Christ." He believed that the life of Jesus and, especially, his teachings in the Sermon on the Mount should be models for Christian piety and morality. For the Church's ceremonies and for rigid discipline he had only censure: Too often, he said, they served as substitutes for genuine spiritual concerns. People lit candles, for instance, but forgot that what counted was the spirit of religious devotion, not the form. By simply following the precepts of Jesus, he argued, a Christian could lead a life guided by sincere faith. Because of his insistence on ethical behavior, Erasmus could admire a truly moral people even if they were pagans. "I could almost say, 'Pray for me, St. Socrates!'" he once wrote.

Erasmus believed that the Church had lost sight of its original mission. In the course of fifteen centuries, traditions and practices had developed that obscured the intentions of its founder,

and purity could be restored only by studying the Scriptures and the writings of the early Church fathers. Here, the literary and analytic tools of the humanists became vitally important because they enabled scholars to understand the meaning and intention of ancient manuscripts. Practicing what he preached, Erasmus spent ten years preparing a new edition of the Greek text of the New Testament so as to correct errors in the Latin Vulgate, which was the standard version, and he revised it repeatedly for another twenty years. But the calm, scholarly, and tolerant moderation Erasmus prized was soon left behind by events. The rising intensity of religious reformers and their opponents destroyed the effort he had led to cure the ills of the Church quietly, from within. Erasmus wanted a revival of purer faith, but he would never have dreamed of rejecting the traditional authority of the Church. As Europe entered an age of confrontation, he found it impossible to preserve a middle course between the two sides, and he was swept aside by revolutionary forces that he himself had helped build but that Martin Luther was to unleash.

II. The Lutheran Reformation

The disputes over doctrine and the yearning for piety helped undermine the authority of the Roman Church. But it took a charismatic individual of extraordinary determination to break apart an institution that had survived for a thousand years. And without political support, even he could not have succeeded.

◆ THE CONDITIONS FOR CHANGE

That a major religious conflict should have erupted in the Holy Roman Empire is not surprising. In this territory of fragmented government, with hundreds of independent local princes, popular piety was noticeably strong. Yet anyone who was unhappy with Church leadership had all the more reason to resent the power of bishops, because in the empire they were often also princes—such as the aristocratic bishop who ruled the important city of Cologne on the Rhine. There were few strong secular princes who could protect the people from the fiscal demands of the Church, and the popes therefore regarded the empire as their surest source of revenue.

This situation was made more volatile by the ambitions of the secular princes. Their ostensible overlord, the emperor, had no real power over them, and they worked tirelessly to strengthen their control over their subjects and to assert their independence from all outside authority. A number of them were, in fact, to see the religious upheavals of the 1500s as a means of advancing their own political purposes. Their ambitions help explain why a determined reformer, Martin Luther, won such swift and widespread support.

◆ MARTIN LUTHER

Martin Luther (1483–1546) was born into a miner's family in Saxony in central Germany. The household was dominated by the father, whose powerful presence some modern commentators have seen reflected in his son's vision of an omnipotent God. The boy received a good education and decided to become a lawyer, a profession that would have given him many opportunities for advancement. But in his early twenties, shortly after starting his legal studies, he had an experience that changed his life. Crossing a field during a thunderstorm, he was thrown to the ground by a bolt of lightning, and in his terror he cried out to St. Anne that he would enter a monastery.

Luther in the Monastery Although the decision may well have been that sudden, it is clear that there was more to Luther's change of direction than this one incident, however traumatic. A highly sensitive, energetic, and troubled young man, he had become obsessed with his own sinfulness, and he joined a monastery as an Augustinian friar in the hope that a penitential life would help him overcome his sense of guilt. Once in the monastery, he pursued every possible opportunity to earn worthiness in the sight of God. He overlooked no means of discipline or act of contrition or self-denial, and for added merit he endured austerities, such as self-flagellation, that went far beyond normal requirements. But it was all useless: When officiating at his first Mass after his ordination in 1507, he was so terrified at the idea of a sinner like himself administering the sacrament of the Eucharist—that is, transforming

the wafer and wine into the body and blood of Christ—that he almost failed to complete the ritual.

Fortunately for Luther, his superiors took more notice of his intellectual gifts than his self-doubts and in 1508 they assigned him to the faculty of a new university in Wittenberg, the capital of Saxony. It was from his scholarship, which was excellent, and especially from his study of the Bible, that he was able at last to draw comfort and spiritual peace.

Justification by Faith This second crucial change in Luther's life, as important as the entry into the monastery, happened while he was preparing his university lectures. Until this point, which is known as "the experience in the tower," Luther could see no way that he, a despicable mortal, could receive anything but the fiercest punishments from a God of absolute justice. Now, however, he had an insight that led him to understand that he needed only to rely on God's mercy, a quality as great as divine justice (see "Luther's 'Experience in the Tower'"). The many advances in Luther's thinking thereafter came from this insight: that justification—which removes sin and bestows righteousness through a gift of grace—is achieved by faith alone.

◆ THE BREAK WITH ROME

In 1517 an event occurred that was ultimately to lead Luther to an irrevocable break with the Church. In the spring, a friar, Johann Tetzel, began to peddle indulgences a few miles from Wittenberg as part of a huge fund-raising effort to pay for the new Church of St. Peter in Rome. Originally, an indulgence had been granted to anyone going on a crusade. It was then extended to those who, though unable to join a crusade, gave enough money for a poor crusader to be able to reach the Holy Land. Indulgences released sinners from a certain period of punishment in purgatory before they went on to heaven; the theory was that they drew on a sort of credit from the treasury of merit built up by Jesus and the saints. But neither the theory nor the connection with money had been fully defined, and clerics had taken advantage of this vagueness simply to sell indulgences. Tetzel, an expert peddler, was offering

LUTHER'S "EXPERIENCE IN THE TOWER"

◆

The following passage was written by Luther in 1545, at least twenty-five years after the experience it described. As a result, scholars have been unable to decide (a) whether the breakthrough was in fact as sudden as Luther suggests; (b) when it took place—possibly as early as 1512, five years before the indulgence dispute, or as late as 1519, when Luther was already under attack for his views; or (c) how it should be interpreted—as a scholar's insight, as a revelation from God, or as Luther's later crystallization into a single event of a process that had taken many years.

"I wanted very much to understand Paul's Epistle to the Romans, but despite my determination to do so I kept being stopped by the one word, 'the righteousness of God.' I hated that word, because I had been taught to understand it as the active righteousness by which a just God punishes unjust sinners. The trouble was that, although I may have been an impeccable monk, I felt myself to be a sinner before God. As a result, not only was I unable to love, but I actually hated this just God, who punishes all sinners. And so I raged, yet I still longed to understand St. Paul.

"At last, as I grappled with the words day and night, God had mercy on me, and I saw the connection between the words 'the righteousness of God' and 'The righteous shall live by faith' (Romans 1:17). I understood that the righteousness of God refers to the gift by which God enables the just to live—that is, by faith. A merciful God justifies us by faith, as it is written: 'The righteous shall live by faith.' At that point, I felt as if I had been reborn and had passed through open doors into paradise. The whole of Scripture took on new meaning. As I had previously hated the phrase, 'the righteousness of God,' so now I lovingly praised it."

Translation from the Latin by Theodore K. Rabb of Luther's preface to the 1545 edition of his writings, in Otto Scheel (ed.), *Dokumente zu Luthers Entwicklung* (Tübingen: Mohr, 1929), pp. 191–192.

complete releases from purgatory without bothering to mention the repentance that, according to Church teachings, was essential if a sinner was to be forgiven or absolved.

The Ninety-Five Theses The people of Wittenberg were soon flocking to Tetzel to buy this easy guarantee of salvation. For Luther, a man groping toward an evangelical solution of his own doubts, it was unforgivable that people should be deprived of their hard-earned money for worthless promises. On October 31, 1517, he published in Wittenberg ninety-five theses, or statements, on indulgences that he offered to debate with experts in Christian doctrine.

This was no revolutionary document. It merely described, in Latin, what Luther believed to be correct teachings on indulgences: that the pope could remit only the penalties that he himself or canon law imposed; that, therefore, the promise of a general pardon was damnable; and that every true believer shared in the treasury of merit left by Jesus and the saints, whether or not he or she

obtained an indulgence. Within a few weeks, the story was all over the empire that a monk had challenged the sale of indulgences. The proceeds of Tetzel's mission began to drop off; and other members of his order, the Dominicans, rallied to their brother by attacking his presumptuous critic, Luther, of the rival order of the Augustinians.

Luther Elaborates The controversy soon drew attention in Rome. At first, Pope Leo X regarded the affair as merely a monks' quarrel. But, in time, Luther's responses to the Dominicans' attacks began to deviate radically from Church doctrine, and by 1520 he had gone so far as to challenge the authority of the papacy itself in three pamphlets outlining his fundamental position.

In *An Address to the Christian Nobility of the German Nation*, Luther made a frankly patriotic appeal to his fellow Germans to reject the foreign pope's authority. The Church, he said, consisted of all Christians, including the laity; hence, the nobles were as much its governors as the clergy, and they had a responsibility to remedy its defects.

▲ *Jörg Breu*
Engraving Depicting the Sale of Indulgences, ca. **1530**
This scene would have been a familiar one in Europe until Luther's attacks brought it to an end. The clerics on their fine horses on the right bring a cross and the papal bull, which is authenticated by the elaborate seals and ribbons that hang from it. The faithful put money in the barrel in the middle or hand it to the dispenser of certificates on the left, who sits near the large locked chest that will hold the revenues from the sales.
Bildarchiv Preussischer Kulturbesitz, Berlin

Indeed, Emperor Charles V had an obligation to call a council to end abuses. In *The Babylonian Captivity,* the most radical of the three works, Luther attacked the belief that the seven sacraments, the basis of the Church's authority, were the only means of attaining grace—the blessed state that was God's gift and was essential to salvation. He accepted only two, baptism and the eucharist, which had visible signs in the holy water, the wine, and the wafer; and he insisted that justification was by faith alone. In *The Liberty of the Christian Man* he explained his doctrine of faith and justification: though he did not reject good works, he insisted that only the individual believer's faith could bring salvation from an all-powerful, just, and merciful God. These three pamphlets had an overwhelming impact on Luther's fellow Germans. His appeal to their resentment of Church power and their wish for a more personal faith made him, almost overnight, the embodiment of a widespread yearning for religious reform.

The Diet of Worms There could no longer be any doubt that Luther was breaking with the Church, and in 1520 Pope Leo X issued a bull excommunicating him. Luther publicly tossed the document into a bonfire, defending his action by calling the pope an Antichrist. In 1521 Emperor Charles V, who was officially the papacy's secular representative, summoned the celebrated monk to offer his defense against the papal decree at a Diet of the Empire (a meeting of princes, city leaders, and churchmen) at Worms, a city on the Rhine.

The journey across Germany was a triumphant progress for Luther, who now seemed a heroic figure. Appearing before the magnificent assembly dressed in his simple friar's robe, he offered a striking contrast to the display of imperial and princely grandeur. First in German and then in Latin, he made the famous declaration that closed the last door behind him: "I cannot and will not recant anything, since it is unsafe and wrong to go against my conscience. Here I stand. I cannot do otherwise. God help me. Amen." On the following day the emperor gave his reply: "A single friar who goes counter to all Christianity for a thousand years must be wrong."

Luther Protected   Charles added legality to the papal bull by issuing an imperial edict calling for Luther's arrest and the burning of his works. At this point, however, the independent power of the German princes and their resentment of foreign ecclesiastical interference came to the reformer's aid. The Elector Frederick III of Saxony, who had never met Luther and who was never to break with the traditional Church, nonetheless determined to protect the rebel who lived in his territory. A fake kidnapping brought Luther to the Wartburg castle, one of Frederick's strongholds, and here Luther remained for almost a year, safe from his enemies.

◆ LUTHERAN DOCTRINE AND PRACTICE

While at the Wartburg castle, Luther, together with his friend Philipp Melanchthon, developed his ideas and shaped them into a formal set of beliefs that influenced most of the subsequent variations of Protestant Christianity. Codified in 1530 in a document known as the Augsburg Confession, these doctrines have remained the basis of Lutheranism ever since.

Luther's Debt to Nominalism   It is important to realize that some of Luther's positions had roots in nominalism, the most influential philosophical and theological movement of the fourteenth and fifteenth centuries, which had flourished at his old monastery. First, in opposition to Thomas Aquinas and the thirteenth-century attempts to unite reason and faith, the nominalists stressed the primacy of faith, the inadequacy of reason, and the unknowableness of God. Second, as a natural corollary to God's mystery, they emphasized his overwhelming power and majesty. Both of these beliefs were to reappear frequently in the reformers' writings.

Faith and the Bible   The influence of nominalism is apparent in the two fundamental assertions of Luther's teachings. First, faith alone—not good works or the receiving of the sacraments—justifies the believer in the eyes of God and wins redemption. People themselves are helpless and unworthy sinners who can do nothing to cooperate in their own salvation; God bestows faith on those he chooses to save. Second, the Bible is the sole source of religious authority. It alone carries the word of God, and Christians must reject all other supposed channels of divine inspiration: Church tradition, commentaries on the Bible, or the pronouncements of popes and Church councils.

These two doctrines had far-reaching implications. According to Luther, all people are equally capable of understanding God's word as expressed in the Bible and can gain salvation without the help of intermediaries; they do not need a priest endowed with special powers or an interceding church. Luther thus saw God's faithful as a "priesthood of all believers," a concept totally foreign to the traditional Church, which insisted on the distinction between clergy and laity. The distinction disappeared in Luther's doctrines, because all the faithful shared the responsibilities formerly reserved for priests.

Sacraments and the Mass   True to his reliance on biblical authority, Luther denied the efficacy of five of the sacraments. Only baptism and the eucharist remained as means by which God distributes grace. Moreover, the ceremony of the eucharist was now called *communion* (literally, "sharing") to emphasize that all worshipers, including the officiating clergy, were equal; all shared both wafer and wine. Luther also reduced the distinctiveness of priests by abolishing the sacrament of confession and by giving them the right to marry.

Luther's teachings on the sacraments transformed the Mass, the ceremony that surrounds the eucharist, which had caused him such trouble when he entered the monastery. According to

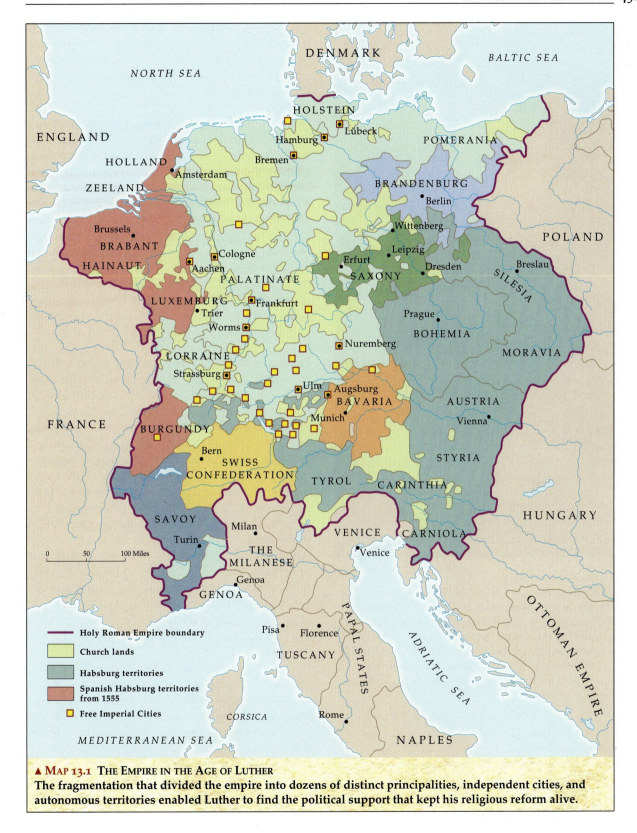

NORTH SEA

DENMARK

BALTIC SEA

ENGLAND

HOLLAND

ZEELAND

Amsterdam

HOLSTEIN

Lübeck

Hamburg

Bremen

POMERANIA

BRANDENBURG

Berlin

POLAND

Brussels

BRABANT

HAINAUT

Cologne

Aachen

PALATINATE

Wittenberg

Leipzig

Erfurt

SAXONY

Dresden

Breslau

SILESIA

LUXEMBURG

Trier

Frankfurt

Worms

Prague

BOHEMIA

MORAVIA

LORRAINE

Strassburg

Nuremberg

Ulm

Augsburg

BAVARIA

Munich

AUSTRIA

Vienna

STYRIA

FRANCE

BURGUNDY

Bern

SWISS
CONFEDERATION

TYROL

CARINTHIA

CARNIOLA

HUNGARY

SAVOY

Milan

Turin

THE
MILANESE

Genoa

GENOA

VENICE

Venice

OTTOMAN EMPIRE

Pisa

Florence

TUSCANY

PAPAL
STATES

ADRIATIC SEA

CORSICA

Rome

MEDITERRANEAN SEA

NAPLES

0   50   100 Miles

— Holy Roman Empire boundary

☐ Church lands

☐ Habsburg territories

☐ Spanish Habsburg territories
from 1555

☐ Free Imperial Cities

▲ MAP 13.1 THE EMPIRE IN THE AGE OF LUTHER
**The fragmentation that divided the empire into dozens of distinct principalities, independent cities, and
autonomous territories enabled Luther to find the political support that kept his religious reform alive.**

▲ *Lucas Cranach the Elder*
PORTRAIT OF MARTIN LUTHER, 1525
One of the first faces made familiar by portraits, but not belonging to a nobleman, was Luther's. Cranach painted the reformer a number of times, so we can see what he looked like at various periods of his life. Luther here is in his early forties, a determined figure who four years earlier had made his stand at the Diet of Worms.
Scala/Art Resource, NY

traditional dogma, when the priest raises the wafer, the host, during the Mass and recites the words *Hoc est corpus meum* ("This is my body"), the sacrifice of Jesus on the cross is reenacted. The wafer and the wine retain their outward appear-

ance, their "accidents," but their substance is transformed into the body and blood of Christ—in other words, transubstantiation takes place.

Luther asserted that the wafer and wine retain their substance as well as their accidents at the moment the priest says, "This is my body." The real presence of Christ and the natural substance coexist within the wafer and wine. Nothing suddenly happens; there is no miraculous moment. Instead, the believer is simply made aware of the real presence of God, who is everywhere at all times. Again, it is the faith of the individual, not the ceremony itself, that counts. Moreover, by allowing the congregation to drink the wine—as Hus had demanded—Luther further reduced the mystery of the Lord's Supper and undermined the position of the priest. And by abolishing the use of Latin, processions, incense, and votive candles, he simplified services and gave ordinary people a greater role in worship.

Translation of the Bible   With the priest reduced in stature, it was vital to make God's word more readily available to the faithful, so that they could read or hear the Bible for themselves. To this end, Luther began the long task of translating the Bible. He completed the work in 1534, creating a text that is a milestone in the history of the German language. Families were encouraged to read Scripture on their own, and the reformed faith stimulated rising literacy among women as well as men. This was Luther's last major contribution to the religious changes of the sixteenth century. Although he lived until 1546, henceforth the progress of the revolution he had launched would rely on outside forces: its popular appeal and the actions of political leaders.

◆ THE SPREAD OF LUTHERANISM

It is usually said that Lutheranism spread from above, advancing only when princes and rulers helped it along. Although this view has some merit, it does not adequately explain the growth of the movement. The response to Luther's stand was immediate and widespread. Even before the Diet of Worms, preachers critical of the Church were drawing audiences in many parts of the Holy Roman Empire, and in 1521 there were waves of image smashing, reports of priests marrying, and efforts to reform and simplify the sacraments.

Soon there were congregations following Luther's teachings throughout the empire and neighboring countries. Broadsides and pamphlets fresh from the printing presses disseminated the reformer's message with breathtaking speed, and they stimulated an immediate response from thousands who welcomed the opportunity to renew their faith.

Radical Preachers   As long as his own doctrines remained unaltered, Luther was naturally delighted to see his teachings spread. But from the start, people drew inferences that he could not tolerate. Early in 1522, for example, three men from the nearby town of Zwickau appeared in Wittenberg claiming to be prophets who enjoyed direct communication with God. Their ideas were, in Luther's eyes, damnable. When he returned from Wartburg castle, therefore, he preached eight sermons to expose their errors—a futile effort, because the movement to reform the Church was now too dispersed to control. Capitalizing on mass discontent, radical preachers incited disturbances in the name of faith, and soon social as well as religious protest exploded, posing a new challenge for Luther as he struggled to keep his protest under control.

Social and Religious Protest   The first trouble arose in the summer of 1522, started by the weakest independent group in the empire, the imperial knights. The knights occupied a precarious position in the social hierarchy because their holdings rarely consisted of more than a single castle. They accepted no authority but the emperor himself, and they resented the growing power of cities and princes (rulers of large territories) in the empire. Calling themselves true representatives of the

▼ Cartoon from Lutheran Woodcut Broadside
Vicious cartoons were a favorite device of religious propaganda during the Age of Religious Reformation. They were especially popular for an illiterate audience, which had to get the message from pictures. The more vivid the image, the easier it was to understand. Here the Protestants show the enemies of Luther as vicious animals. One theologian is a cat eating a mouse; another is a dog holding a bone. The Pope is in the middle, reaching out to Eck.
Germanisches Nationalmuseum Nürnberg

imperial system—that is, loyal supporters of the emperor's authority, in contrast to the cities and princes who wanted to be more independent— and using Lutheranism as further justification, the knights launched an attack on one of the leading ecclesiastical rulers, the archbishop of Trier. They were crushed within a year, but the Lutherans' opponents could now suggest that the new religious teachings undermined law and order.

Peasant Revolt   The banner of the new faith rose over popular revolts as well. A peasant uprising began in Swabia in 1524 and quickly engulfed the southern and central parts of the empire. Citing Luther's inspiration, and especially his teaching that faith was all the individual needed, the peasants published a list of twelve demands in 1525. Admittedly, ten of their grievances concerned social, not religious, injustices: They wanted an end to serfdom, tithes, and the restrictions and burdens imposed by their overlords, including prohibitions on hunting and fishing, excessive rents and services, and unlawful punishments. But they also had two religious aims: They wanted the right to choose their own pastors, and they refused to accept any authority other than Scripture to determine whether their demands were justified.

Luther sympathized with the last two claims, and at first he considered the peasants' demands reasonable. But when it became apparent that they were challenging all authority, he ignored the oppressions they had suffered and wrote a vicious pamphlet, *Against the Rapacious and Murdering Peasants*, calling on the nobility to cut them down without mercy so as to restore peace. A few months later the rebels were defeated in battle, and thereafter Luther threw his support unreservedly on the side of the princes and the established political and social order. He also grew more virulent in his attacks on Catholics and Jews and became as insistent as the Roman Church he was defying that his doctrines were not to be questioned.

◆ LUTHERANISM ESTABLISHED

The advance of Lutheranism thus far had depended largely on its appeal to the ordinary believer, and it continued to enjoy wide support. But when Luther was forced to choose between the demands of his humblest followers and the authority of the princes who had protected him, he opted for the princes. It was a decision that enabled his movement to survive and may well have saved him from the fate of Hus at the stake a century before. Had Luther not condemned the disorders, he would doubtless have been abandoned by the princes, and without their backing he and his followers could not have stood up to the traditional Church or been safe from the power of Charles V.

Luther's Conservatism   One of the reasons the new set of beliefs could attract these princes was its conservatism. Any person who accepted the basic doctrines of justification by faith alone and Scripture as the sole authority could be accepted as a Lutheran. Consequently, the new congregations could retain much from the old religion: most of the liturgy, the sacred music, and, particularly important, a structured church that, though less hierarchical than before, was still organized to provide order and authority.

The Lutheran Princes   Some rulers were swept up by the same emotions that moved their subjects, but others were moved by more material interests. Since the Church lost all its property when reform was introduced, princes could confiscate the rich and extensive ecclesiastical holdings in their domains. Furthermore, they now had added reason for flaunting their independence from Emperor Charles V, an unwavering upholder of orthodoxy. It was risky to adopt this policy, for Charles could strip a prince of his title. And if a prince promised to remain loyal to the Church, he could blackmail the pope into offering him almost as many riches as he could win by confiscation.

Nevertheless, the appeal of the new faith eventually tipped the balance for enough princes to create a formidable party capable of resisting Charles's power. While they were attending an imperial Diet at Speyer in 1529, they signed a declaration "protesting" the Diet's decree that no religious innovations were to be introduced in the empire. Thereafter, all who accepted religious reform, including the Lutherans, were known as Protestants; and adherents of the traditional Church, led from Rome, which continued to claim

▲ ENGRAVING OF THE *DIET OF AUGSBURG*, 1530
At the Diet—the meeting of the princes and cities of the Holy Roman Empire—in Augsburg in 1530, the Lutherans presented to the emperor, Charles V, a statement, or "confession," of their faith. This "Confession of Augsburg" became the founding doctrine of the Lutheran church. It was rejected as heretical by Charles, but he could not suppress it. One of the Lutheran princes told him in 1530 that he would rather have his head cut off than attend a Catholic mass. Charles was unable to crush such defiance.
Bibliothèque Nationale de France, Paris

that it was universal (or catholic), came to be known as Roman Catholics.

The following year, at another imperial Diet, the Lutheran princes announced their support of the Augsburg Confession, the official statement of Lutheran doctrines that had been prepared by Melanchthon and Luther. Charles V now threatened to use military force to crush the heresy, and in the face of this danger, the Lutherans formed a defensive league in 1531 at the small Saxon town of Schmalkalden. Throughout the 1530s this alliance consolidated Protestant gains, brought new princes into the cause, and, in general, amassed sufficient strength to deter Charles, who was re-peatedly distracted by foreign wars, from decisive military action.

War over Religion   The reform party became so solidly established that it negotiated with the Catholics on equal terms about the possibility of reconciliation in 1541, but the talks collapsed, and the chances for a reunification of Christendom evaporated. Not until 1546, the year of Luther's death, however, did open war begin. Then, after a brief campaign, Charles won a crushing victory over the Lutherans in 1547. But matters had advanced too far for their movement to collapse merely because of a single defeat on the battlefield. The new faith had won the devotion of a large part of the German people, particularly in the north and the east, farthest away from the center of imperial power. Some of the great cities of the south, such as Nuremberg, which had been centers of humanism, had also come over to the Lutheran side. By the 1550s Lutheranism had captured about half the population of the Empire.

The Catholic princes also played a part in ensuring the survival of the new faith. Fearful of Charles V's new power, they refused to cooperate in his attempt to establish his authority throughout the empire, and he had to rely on Spanish troops, who further alienated him from his subjects. The Lutherans regrouped after their 1547 defeat, and in 1555 the imperial Diet at Augsburg drew up a compromise settlement that exposed the decline of the emperor's power. Henceforth, each prince was allowed to determine the religion of his own territory, Lutheran or Catholic, and his subjects could leave (a major concession) if they were of the other faith. Religious uniformity was at an end, and the future of Lutheranism was secure.

The Heritage of Lutheranism   The influence that this first Protestant Church was to exert on all of European life was immense. The idea that all believers were equal in the eyes of God inspired revolutionary changes in thought and society. It justified antimonarchical constitutional theories, it allowed people to feel that all occupations were equally worthy and that there was nothing wrong with the life of the merchant or even the money-lender, and it undermined the hierarchic view of the universe. One can easily overstate the notion that Lutheranism made people more self-reliant, because independent and pioneering behavior was far from new. Nevertheless, there is no question that, by condemning the traditional reliance on priests and the Church and by making individuals responsible for their own salvation, Luther did encourage his followers to act on their own. Yet the new faith had its most immediate effect on religious life itself: Before the century was out, the dissent started by Luther inspired a multitude of sects and a ferment of ideas without precedent in the history of Europe.

III. The Spread of Protestantism

Hardly had Luther made his protest in 1517 when religious dissent in many different forms suddenly appeared. It was as if no more was needed than one opening shot before a volley of discontent broke out—testimony to the deep and widespread desire for individual piety of the times.

◆ ZWINGLI AND THE RADICALS

Zwingli's Reforms   The most influential of the new initiatives began in the Swiss city of Zurich, where reform was led by Ulrich Zwingli (1484–1531), a priest, humanist, and disciple of Erasmus. The doctrines he began to develop between 1519 and 1522 were similar to Luther's in that Zwingli based his ideas entirely on Scripture and emphasized faith alone. Suspicious of any reliance on Church rituals, Zwingli, even more than Luther, wanted to simplify religious belief and practice. In his view, none of the sacraments bestowed grace; they were merely signs of grace already given. Thus, baptism is symbolic, not a ceremony that regenerates the recipient; and communion is no more than a memorial and thanksgiving for the grace given by God, who is present only symbolically—not in actuality, as Luther believed.

Despite his obvious debt to Luther, Zwingli diverged significantly from the German. His new form of Protestantism was more thoroughly dependent on the individual believer and more devoid of mystery and ritual than anything Luther could accept. Zwingli saw a need for constant correction if people were to lead godly lives, and he established a tribunal of clergy and secular officials to enforce discipline among the faithful. They supervised all moral issues, from compulsory church attendance to the public behavior of amorous couples. They could excommunicate flagrant transgressors, and they maintained constant surveillance—through a network of informers—to keep the faithful moral and godly. Because Zwingli considered education vital for discipline, he founded a theological school and authorized a new translation of the Bible. He also insisted on lengthy sermons at each service. Worship was stripped bare, as were the churches, and preaching began to assume tremendous importance as a means of instructing believers and strengthening their faith. Zwingli also revived the ancient Christian practice of public confession of sin—yet another reinforcement of discipline.

Zwingli's Church   Zwingli's ideas spread rapidly in the Swiss Confederation, helped by the virtual autonomy of each canton, or region. By 1529 a number of cantons had accepted Zwinglianism. As a result, two camps formed in the country, and a war broke out in 1531 in which Zwingli himself was killed. Thereafter the Swiss Confederation remained split between Catholics and reformers. Zwinglianism never grew into a major religion, but it had a considerable effect on later forms of Protestantism, particularly Calvinism.

The Anabaptists   Both Luther and Zwingli wanted to retain church authority, and both therefore insisted that infant baptism was the moment of entry into the church, even though this belief had no scriptural sanction. Some radical reformers, however, insisted on taking the Bible literally and argued that, as in biblical times, baptism should be administered only to mature adults who could make a conscious choice to receive grace, not to infants who could not understand what was happening. Soon these reformers were being called *Anabaptists* ("rebaptizers") by their enemies. The term is often applied to all radicals, though in fact it described only one conspicuous group.

Radical Sects   Diversity was inevitable among the radical reformers, most of whom refused to recognize church organization, rejected priests, and gave individual belief free rein, sometimes to the point of recognizing only personal communication with God and disregarding Scripture. Many groups of like-minded radicals formed small sects—voluntary associations that rarely included more than one hundred or so adults—in an effort to achieve complete separation from the world and avoid compromising their ideals. They wanted to set an example for others by adhering fervently to the truth as they saw it, regardless of the consequences. Some sects established little utopian communities, holding everything in common, including property and spouses. Others disdained all worldly things and lived only for the supreme ecstasy of a trance in which they made direct contact with God himself. Many, believing in the imminent coming of the Messiah, prepared themselves for the end of the world and the Day of Judgment.

◆ PERSECUTION OF THE RADICALS

Such variety in the name of a personal search for God was intolerable to major reformers like Luther and Zwingli, who believed that their own doctrines were the only means of salvation. Once these branches of Protestantism were firmly entrenched, they, like the Catholic Church, became deeply committed to the status quo and to their own hierarchies and traditions. The established reformers thus regarded the radicals' refusal to conform as an unmistakable sign of damnation; Heinrich Bullinger, Zwingli's successor, put it bluntly when he wrote that individual interpretation of the Bible allowed each man to carve his own path to hell. Indeed, Lutherans were just as ready as Catholics to persecute those who rejected their particular brand of salvation.

Münster and the Melchiorites   The assault on the radicals began in the mid-1520s and soon spread through most of Europe. The imperial Diet in 1529 called for the death penalty against all Anabaptists, and indeed, most members of a group of more than thirty Anabaptist leaders who met to discuss their ideas in 1533 eventually died violently. Finally, in the northwest German city of Münster, a particularly fiery sect, inspired by a "prophet" named Melchior and known as Melchiorites, provoked a reaction that signaled doom even for less radical dissenters.

The Melchiorites had managed to gain considerable influence over the ordinary workers of Münster and over the craft guilds to which many belonged. They gained political control of the city early in 1534 and began to establish their "heavenly Jerusalem" on earth. They burned all books except the Bible, abolished private property, introduced polygamy, and in an atmosphere of abandon and chaos, dug in to await the coming of the Messiah. Here was a threat to society sufficient to force Protestants and Catholics into an alliance, and they captured the city and brutally massacred the Melchiorites. Thereafter, the radicals were savagely persecuted throughout the empire. To survive, many fled, first to Poland, then to the Low Countries and England, and eventually to the New World.

◆ JOHN CALVIN

During the 1530s, Protestantism began to fragment. Neither Lutherans nor Zwinglians expanded much beyond the areas in which their reforms had begun; sects multiplied but gained few followers; and it might have seemed that the original energy had left the movement. In the early 1540s, however, a new dynamism and also a more elaborate and systematic body of doctrine were brought to Protestantism by a second-generation reformer, John Calvin (1509–1564). Born in Noyon, a small town in northern France, Calvin studied both law and the humanities at the University of Paris. In his early twenties he apparently had a shattering spiritual experience that he later called his "sudden conversion," an event about which he would say almost nothing else. Yet from that moment on, all his energy was devoted to religious reform.

In November 1533 Calvin was indicted by French Church authorities for holding heretical views, and after more than a year in hiding, he took refuge in the Swiss city of Basel. There, in 1536 he published a little treatise, *Institutes of the Christian Religion,* outlining the principles of a

▼ ENGRAVING OF THE ARMY FROM BERN INVADING A NEIGHBORING PROVINCE IN 1536, FROM JOHANNES *STUMPF'S CHRONICLE,* 1548
These soldiers helped Geneva win its independence from the bishop who was the city's ruler. The Bernese also encouraged the acceptance of Protestantism, which John Calvin was soon to help establish in Geneva.
Bibliothèque Publique et Universitaire, Geneva.

new system of belief. He would revise and expand the *Institutes* for the remainder of his life, and it was to become the basis of Calvinism, the most vigorous branch of Protestantism in the sixteenth century.

Geneva   Later in 1536, Calvin settled in Geneva, where, except for a brief period, he was to remain until his death and where he was to create a new church in the 1540s. The citizens of this prosperous market center had just overthrown their prince, a Catholic bishop. In achieving their independence, they had allied with other Swiss cities, notably Bern, a recent convert to Zwinglianism. Rebels who, with the help of Protestants, had just freed themselves from an ecclesiastical overlord were understandably receptive to new religious teachings, though Calvin's beliefs were also supported by persecution and intolerance.

◆ CALVINISM

Outwardly, Calvinism seemed to have much in common with Lutheranism. Both emphasized people's sinfulness, lack of free will, and helplessness; both rejected good works as a means of salvation; both accepted only two sacraments, baptism and communion; both regarded all occupations as equally worthy in the sight of God; both strongly upheld established political and social authority; and both leaned heavily on St. Paul and St. Augustine in their views of faith, people's weaknesses, and God's omnipotence. But the emphases in Calvinism were very different.

Predestination   In arguing for justification by faith alone, Luther assumed that God can predestine a person to be saved but rejected the idea that damnation can also be preordained. Calvin's faith was much sterner. He recognized no such distinction: If people are damned, they should praise God's justice, because their sins certainly merit such a judgment; if people are saved, they should praise God's mercy, because their salvation is not a result of their own merits. Either way, the outcome is predestined, and nothing can be done to affect an individual's fate. It is up to God to save a person; he then perseveres in his mercy despite the person's sins; and finally, he alone decides whether to receive the sinner into the small band

of saints, or elect, whom he brings into heaven. Calvin's was a grim but powerful answer to the age-old Christian question: How can sinful human beings gain salvation?

Calvin believed that our behavior here on earth, whether good or bad, is no indication of our fate. He did suggest that someone who is to be saved by God is likely to be upright and moral, but such conduct is not necessarily a sign of salvation. However, because we should try to please God at all times, and because our communities ought to be fitting places for the elect to live, we must make every effort to lead lives worthy of one of the elect.

Morality and Discipline   Calvin therefore developed a strict moral code for the true believer that banned frivolous activities, like dancing, in favor of constant self-examination, austerity, and sober study of the Bible. To help the faithful observe such regulation, he reestablished public confessions, as Zwingli had, and required daily preaching. He made services starkly simple: Stripped of ornaments, worship concentrated on uplifting sermons and the celebration of communion. His doctrine of communion occupied a middle ground between Luther's and Zwingli's. He rejected Zwingli's interpretation, saying instead that Christ's body and blood were actually and not just symbolically present. But unlike Luther, he held that they were present only in spirit and were consumed only spiritually, by faith.

To supervise the morals of the faithful and ensure that the community was worthy of the elect, Calvin gave his church a strict hierarchical structure. It was controlled by church officials called deacons and by lay elders, who were able to function even in the hostile territories where many Calvinists found themselves. A body of lay elders called the *consistory* served as the chief ecclesiastical authority. These elders enforced discipline and had the power of excommunication, though local officials imposed the actual punishments—most notoriously in 1553, when a radical who denied the Trinity, Michael Servetus, was invited to Geneva and then executed for heresy.

Church Organization   Calvin's system produced a cohesiveness and organization achieved by no other Protestant church. The *Institutes* spelled out every point of faith and practice in detail—an enormous advantage for Calvin's followers at a time when new religious doctrines were still fluid. The believer's duties and obligations were absolutely clear, as was his or her position in the carefully organized hierarchy of the church. In France, for example, there was a small community (or cell) in each town, a governing synod (or council) in each local area, a provincial synod in each province, and a national synod at the top of the pyramid. Tight discipline controlled the entire system, with the result that Calvinists believed they were setting a moral and religious example that the entire world would eventually have to follow. They were part of a privileged community from whom the elect would be drawn. Thus, they could be oppressive when they had power, yet holy rebels when they were a minority. After all, since they were freed of responsibility for their own salvation, they were acting selflessly at all times. Like the children of Israel, they had a mission to live for God, and this sense of destiny was to be one of Calvinism's greatest strengths.

Preachers from Geneva traveled through Europe to win adherents and organize the faithful wherever they could. In 1559 the city opened a university for the purpose of training preachers, because Calvin regarded education as an essential means of instilling faith. From Geneva flowed a stream of pamphlets and books, which strengthened the faith of all believers and made sure that none who wished to learn would lack the opportunity. A special target was Calvin's homeland, France, where his preachers had their first successes, especially in the cities. Calvinism also won important support in the nobility, notably among women aristocrats, who often influenced their families to adopt the new beliefs.

By 1564, when Calvin died, his church was well established: more than a million adherents in France, where they were called Huguenots; the Palatinate converted; Scotland won by his fiery disciple, John Knox; and considerable groups of followers in England, the Low Countries, and Hungary. Despite its severity, Calvin's coherent and comprehensive body of doctrine proved to have wide appeal in an age of piety that yearned for clear religious answers.

The Appeal of Calvinism When those who adopted the new faith explained their conver-

sion, they usually did so in terms of a slow or sudden revelation—God had finally shown them the truth. But historians have noted that there were certain groups who seemed especially open to Protestant, and particularly Calvinist, teachings. All the reformed faiths did particularly well in cities, and it has been suggested that the long history of independence among townspeople made them more inclined to challenge traditional authorities. In addition, they tended to be more literate, and thus were drawn to beliefs that emphasized reading the Bible for oneself. And Calvinism put an emphasis on sobriety, discipline, and communal responsibility that would have appealed strongly to the increasingly self-confident merchants and artisans of the cities. That the Calvinists were also successful in the areas of southern France farthest away from central authority in Paris only reinforces the connection with an inclination toward independence and self-reliance. Geneva itself became a determinedly independent place—morals were strictly supervised, and there was an aura of public discipline that all visitors noted. Gradually in the seventeenth century the atmosphere of austerity softened, but the city continued to be seen as a model community for all Calvinists.

Women and Reform Cities were not the only centers of religious reform. In some parts of Europe, such as Scotland, new beliefs flourished outside towns because they won political support. But in all areas, the importance of women to the spread of Protestantism was unmistakable. Calvin's earliest significant converts were aristocratic women, whose patronage helped his faith take root at the highest levels of society. Like the literate women of the cities, they saw in its message an opportunity to express themselves and to work for others in ways that had not been possible before. They were often the main readers of the Bible in family gatherings; they took the lead in demanding broader access to education, especially for girls; and they were regularly prominent in radical movements.

One theologian who despaired at the results of Luther's translation of the New Testament reserved his most bitter complaints for the women who were studying the Bible for themselves. And the results were apparent not only

THE TRIAL OF ELIZABETH DIRKS

◆

In radical groups, women often occupied central roles they never achieved in the larger churches. Since the most important attributes of a believer in these groups were faith, commitment, and the presence of the holy spirit, there was frequently an egalitarianism not found elsewhere in sixteenth-century society. Thus it was that the radical "teacher" (or leader) whom the Inquisition in the Netherlands interrogated in January 1549 was a woman named Elizabeth Dirks. Her replies give us a vivid sense of the beliefs the Reformation was stimulating among ordinary people—though in this case they were put forward with a clarity and a conviction that would lead to Elizabeth's execution two months later.

"Examiner: We understand you are a teacher and have led many astray. Who are your friends?

"Elizabeth: Do not press me on this point. Ask me about my faith and I will answer you gladly.

"Examiner: Do you not consider our Church to be the house of the Lord?

"Elizabeth: I do not. For it is written that God said 'I will dwell with you.'

"Examiner: What do you think of our mass?

"Elizabeth: I have no faith in your mass, but only in the word of God.

"Examiner: What do you believe about the Holy Sacrament of the Eucharist?

"Elizabeth: I never in my life read in Scripture about a Holy Sacrament, but only of the Supper of the Lord.

"Examiner: You speak with a haughty tongue.

"Elizabeth: No. I speak with a free tongue.

"Examiner: Do you not believe that you are saved by baptism?

"Elizabeth: No: all the water in the sea cannot save me. My salvation is in Christ, who commanded me to love my God and my neighbor as myself.

"Examiner: Do priests have the power to forgive sins?

"Elizabeth: How should I believe that? Christ is the only priest through whom sins are forgiven.

"As torture was applied:

"Examiner: You can recant everything you have said.

"Elizabeth: No, I will not, but I will seal it with my blood."

Adapted from Thieleman von Bracht, *The Bloody Theater or Martyr's Mirror,* Daniel Rupp (trans.) (Lancaster, Pa.: David Miller, 1837), pp. 409–410.

---

among the literate. The records of the Inquisition, the Catholic tribunal charged with rooting out heresy, are full of the trials and executions of women who were martyrs for their beliefs and who died defending doctrines they had learned from preachers or other women. Again and again, they rejected the authority of priests and asserted their right to individual faith. It was determination like this that enabled the Reformation to establish itself and to spread until it posed a major challenge to the traditional Church (see "The Trial of Elizabeth Dirks"). Yet the encouragement of female piety by the major reformers should not be overdrawn, for (unlike the radicals) they insisted that women remain silent in services. Moreover, the abolition of nunneries, of the veneration of the Virgin, and of prayers to female saints narrowed the opportunities for spiritual expression among all Protestant women and reduced their roles in their faiths.

◆ THE ANGLICAN CHURCH

In England, which created its own version of the Protestant church, the role of the prince was crucial. There was a local tradition of dissent, represented by the Lollards, but it was severely repressed in the early days of the Reformation. King Henry VIII even wrote an attack on Luther that persuaded the pope to grant him the title "Defender of the Faith" that British monarchs still use. But by the late 1520s this loyalty was in peril, because Henry's wife was clearly not going to produce the male heir he needed to continue his dynasty, and the traditional solution—to have the pope annul the marriage—was unavailable. The result was another advance for the Reformation.

The King's Divorce The case Henry made to the pope was that he had married his brother's widow, Catherine of Aragon, under a special papal dispensation from the biblical law that prohibited a union between such close relatives. He argued that the lack of an heir proved the dispensation to have been sinful, and the marriage no marriage. Henry did not mention the fact that he had become infatuated with a young lady at court, Anne Boleyn, but under normal circumstances the papacy would not have hesitated to comply. At this very moment, however, the pope was in the power of the Emperor Charles V, who had invaded Italy. Charles, it happened, was Catherine's nephew, and he refused to allow this blot on her honor.

Stymied by Rome, Henry summoned England's Parliament in 1529 and gave it free rein to express bitter anticlerical sentiments. He sought opinions in European universities in favor of the divorce, and he even extracted a vague recognition from England's clergy of his position as "supreme lord" of the Church. Finally, one of his ministers, Thomas Cromwell, suggested a radical but simple solution: that Henry break with the pope, declare himself head of the Church, and divorce Catherine on his own authority. The king agreed, and in 1534 Parliament declared him supreme head of the newly independent Church of England. By joining Europe's Protestants in opposition to Rome, Henry gave his subjects a cause that was increasingly to stimulate their patriotic pride.

The English Church   The Reformation gave the monarchy a huge financial boost. Henry took over the ecclesiastical fees that the pope had collected, and he confiscated the immensely valuable property of all monasteries. When a revolt erupted against the Reformation in 1536, he crushed it easily. But in doctrine and the structure of the Church, Henry was deeply conservative; he allowed few changes in dogma or liturgy and seems to have hoped that he could continue the old ways, changing only the person at the head of the institution. He even tried to restrain the spread of Reformation beliefs, brought to England from the continent by travelers and books, and he persecuted heresy.

But it proved impossible to stop the momentum. Although many English men and women clung to tradition, others were drawn to the new religious ideas, and they pressured Henry to accept Protestant doctrines. Lollards had kept Wycliffe's ideas alive, and they now joined forces with Protestants inspired by continental reformers to demand services in English and easier access to Scripture. New translations of the Bible appeared in the 1530s, as did echoes of the opposition to clerical privilege that had swept Protestant areas on the continent. Perhaps realizing that the pressure would only grow, Henry had his son, Edward, tutored by a committed reformer. Edward VI ruled for only six years (1547–1553). He was followed by a committed Catholic, Mary, the daughter of Catherine of Aragon, but her attempt to turn back the clock failed. When her five-year reign ended, the English Church became firmly Protestant under the rule of Elizabeth I, the child Henry had with Anne Boleyn after the divorce (see chapter 15).

IV. The Catholic Revival

Those with Protestant sympathies usually refer to the Catholic revival that started in the 1530s as the Counter Reformation, implying that the Roman Church acted only as a result of criticisms by Luther and others. Catholic historians call it the Catholic Reformation, implying that the movement began within the Church and was not merely a reaction to Protestantism. There is justification for both views. Certainly the papacy was aware of its loss of control over millions of Christians, but a great deal of the effort to put the Church's house in order was a result of strong faith and a determination to purify the institution for its own sake.

◆ STRENGTHS AND WEAKNESSES

Although the institution faced serious problems of doctrine and organization, and a major reform effort was certainly needed, it is important to remember that the Church had a vast reserve of loyalty and affection. In the long run, many more Europeans remained Catholic than converted to Protestantism. They took comfort from tradition and from priests who, rather than demanding that believers achieve salvation on their own, offered the Church's mediation, beautiful ceremonies, and rituals to help people overcome their sins. Catholicism had a long history of charity for the poor, which it strengthened during the sixteenth century. For ordinary Christians, the familiarity, support, and grandeur they found in the Church were often reason enough to resist the reformers.

Losses and Difficulties   Yet there was no doubt that the first half of the sixteenth century was the lowest point in the history of the Catholic Church and that few could have expected the recovery that followed. By 1550 many areas of Europe had been lost to the Protestants, and even in regions that were still loyal the papacy was able to exercise little control. The French Church, for example, had a well-established tradition of autonomy, exemplified by the right France's kings had held since 1516 to make ecclesiastical appointments. In Spain, too, the monarchy retained its independence and even had its own Inquisition. In the Holy Roman Empire, those states that had rejected Protestantism gave the pope no more than token allegiance.

Moreover, there was still no comprehensive definition of Catholic doctrine on justification, salvation, and the sacraments. Worse yet, the Church's leadership was far from effective. Although one pope, Leo X, had attempted to correct notorious abuses such as simony, the sale of church offices, in the early sixteenth century, Rome simply did not have the spiritual authority to make reform a vital force in the Catholic Church.

Paul III   The situation changed with the pope elected in 1534: Paul III, a man not renowned for saintliness but a genius at making the right decisions for the Church. By the end of his reign, in 1549, the Catholic revival was under way.

◀ *Titian*
POPE PAUL III AND HIS NEPHEWS, ALESSANDRO AND OTTAVIO FARNESE, **1546**
The psychological tension Titian created in this family portrait is extraordinary. The shrewd seventy-seven-year-old pope who had launched the Church's vigorous response to Protestantism looks benignly on Ottavio, whose seemingly calculated gesture of deference hints at the aggressiveness that was soon to cause a major family quarrel over land and money. And Cardinal Alessandro, standing apart, was already a famous patron of art with little concern for Church affairs. Perhaps because of its revelation of character, the painting was never finished.
Erich Lessing/Art Resource, NY

The heart of Paul's strategy was his determination to assert papal responsibility throughout the Church. Realizing that uncertainties in Catholic doctrine could be resolved only by reexamining traditional theology, he decided within a few months of taking office to call a Church council for that purpose, despite the danger of rekindling the conciliar movement. It took ten years to overcome resistance to the idea, but in the meantime Paul attacked abuses throughout the Church, disregarding both vested interests and tradition. He aimed his campaign at all levels of the hierarchy, undeterred by powerful bishops and cardinals long used to a lax and corrupt regime. In addition, he founded a Roman Inquisition, a decision that reflected the era's growing reliance on persecution as a means of destroying dissent.

Paul realized that, in the long run, the revival of Catholicism would depend on whether his successors maintained his efforts. During his fifteen-year reign, therefore, he made a series of superb appointments to the College of Cardinals (the body that elects the popes); the result was the creation of possibly the most illustrious College in history. Many of its members were famous for their piety, others for their learning. They came from all over Europe, united by their devotion to the Church and their resolve to see it once again command admiration and reverence. The result of Paul's farsighted policy was to be a succession of popes through the early seventeenth century who would fully restore the atmosphere of spirituality and morality that had long been missing from the papacy.

◆ THE COUNCIL OF TRENT

The ecumenical, or general, council of Church leaders called by Paul finally assembled at Trent, a northern Italian city, in 1545, and met irregularly until the delegates managed to complete their work in 1563. The council's history was one of stormy battles between various national factions. The non-Italians pressed for decentralization of religious authority; the Italians, closely tied to the papacy, advocated a consolidation of power. For both sides, the divisions were political as well as ecclesiastical, because at issue was the independence not only of bishops but also of local

princes and kings. A large majority of the delegates were Italians, however, and their conclusions almost always reinforced the dominance of the pope. The threat of a revival of conciliarism never materialized.

Defining Doctrine In keeping with Paul's instructions, the Council of Trent gave more of its time to the basic issue of Church doctrine than to the problem of reform. Nearly all its decisions were intended to establish clear definitions of practice and belief and to end long-standing theological uncertainties or differences of opinion. The main sources for these decisions were the interpretations put forward by Thomas Aquinas, who now became the central theologian of the Catholic Church. At the same time, Trent's decrees were designed to affirm precisely those teachings that the Protestants had rejected. Catholicism from then on would be committed primarily to the outward, sacramental heritage of Christianity. In this view, the Bible is not the exclusive authority for the believer: Church tradition holds an equal place in establishing religious truth. Human will is free, good works as well as faith are a means of salvation, all seven sacraments are channels of grace, and Christ's sacrifice is reenacted in every Mass. The Council of Trent endorsed the special position of the priest and insisted that God be worshiped with appropriately elaborate ceremonies and rites.

These were the main decisions at Trent, but many minor matters were also settled: For the first time, the priest's presence became essential at the sacrament of marriage, a further reinforcement of his importance; the Vulgate, the Latin translation of the Bible prepared chiefly by St. Jerome, was decreed to be a holy text, a decision which rebutted humanists and other scholars who had found mistranslations of Greek and Hebrew in Jerome's work; and in direct contrast to the Protestants, gorgeous ritual was heavily stressed, which encouraged artists to beautify church buildings and ceremonies.

Restoring the Church The achievement of the council was to adjust the Church to the world. Many ordinary people, troubled by the stern

▲ *Titian*
THE COUNCIL OF TRENT, CA. **1564**
The splendor of the gathering of representatives of the Catholic Church from all of Europe is conveyed by this scene, attributed to Titian. The ranks of bishops in their miters, listening to one of their number address the assembly from the pulpit on the right, visibly embodied a Church putting itself in order as it faced the challenge of Protestantism.
Giraudon/Art Resource, NY

self-denial and predestination taught by most Protestant churches and sects, preferred the traditional comfort, ceremony, and support Catholicism had long offered. They were ready to champion their old faith as soon as its leadership restored its sense of purpose by removing abuses and defining doctrines. And the new discipline of the Church was apparent in the council's effort to deal with morality as thoroughly as with belief. When it gave its approval to the Inquisition and to the "Index of Forbidden Books," which informed all Catholics of the heretical works they were not allowed to read, the council signaled the determination of the Church to recover the ground it had lost.

◆ THE AFTERMATH OF TRENT

The new atmosphere of dedication swept through the Catholic Church, inspiring thinkers and artists throughout Europe to lend their talents to the cause. Painters, architects, and musicians caught up by the new moral fervor in Catholicism expressed their faith in brilliant and dramatic portrayals of religious subjects and in churches that were designed to dazzle the observer in a way that most Protestants could not allow. This artistic outpouring was, of course, far more than a reflection of the decisions of a few hundred prelates assembled in a council. It was also one of many indicators of the new vigor of Catholicism. In

France, for example, a new generation of Church leaders appeared in the late sixteenth century who were distinguished for their austerity, learning, and observance of duties.

Women in the Church Moreover, the crucial contribution of women to Protestantism was echoed in the revival of Catholicism. There was a remarkable flowering of new religious orders for women in the sixteenth and seventeenth centuries, many of which became identified with charitable works. Since one of the most important ways the Church set about winning back the faithful was by expanding its philanthropic activities—through new hospitals and expanded assistance to the poor, to orphans, and to other unfortunates—its female orders played an essential role in the Counter Reformation. And nowhere was their devout spirituality more apparent than in Spain, the most fiercely Catholic of all European countries.

The Spaniards expressed their religious passion in many ways—by insisting on converting the native peoples they conquered overseas, by giving great power to the Inquisition that guarded orthodoxy from large Muslim and Jewish communities at home, by encouraging lay as well as clerical piety, and by founding the most famous new order of the age, the Jesuits (see below). But no indication of their devotion was as distinctive as the great flowering of mysticism, which was most famously represented by St. Teresa (1515–1582).

St. Teresa The mystic seeks to worship God directly and immediately, in an encounter that usually takes place in a trance and without the intervention of a priest. Because this religious experience is entirely personal and does not require the mediation of the Church, it has always been looked on with suspicion by the authorities. St. Teresa was no exception. As a rich and spoiled young girl, she had led a rather loose life, and her concerned father had sent her to a convent to instill some discipline. Perhaps because the family had only recently converted from Judaism, considerable attention was also given to Teresa's religious education. She later recalled a time when, after reading the lives of saints, she decided to become a martyr for Christ. She set out with her

brother for North Africa, where she was determined to die fighting Muslims, but she was caught by an uncle. Of more lasting effect were the visions of God she began to have, which gradually convinced her that she had a special religious mission (see "St. Teresa's Visions," p. 467).

Church authorities became worried when, after becoming a nun, Teresa began to attract a following as a spiritual adviser to a number of women in her native city of Avila. Some churchmen suggested that her visions were the work of the devil, not God. After many examinations, however—and finally an interview with the king of Spain himself, who was deeply impressed by her holiness—the doubts evaporated. Teresa founded a strict new order of nuns and traveled all over Spain establishing convents. She soon became a legendary figure and was made a saint only forty years after her death. To Spaniards she has remained a heroine, the subject of many affectionate stories. Once, when her carriage got stuck in the mud, she looked heavenward and said, "If this is the way you treat your friends, God, no wonder you have so few of them." Above all, she came to embody the religious devoutness of Spain.

The Revitalized Papacy The most conspicuous embodiments of the new energy of the Church, however, were the popes themselves. Paul III's successors used their personal authority and pontifical resources not to adorn their palaces but to continue the enormous cleansing operation within the Church and to lead the counterattack against Protestantism. If a king or prince refused to help, the popes would try to persuade one of his leading subjects (for example, the Guise family in France or the dukes of Bavaria in the empire) to organize the struggle. Their diplomats and agents (often friars) were everywhere, urging Catholics to stamp out Protestantism. And the pontiffs insisted on strict personal morality so as to restore their reputation for piety and set a proper example to the faithful.

With the leaders of the Church thus bent on reform, the restoration of the faith and the reconquest of lost souls could proceed with maximum effect. And the popes had at their disposal a religious order established by Ignatius Loyola in 1540 specifically for these purposes: the Society of Jesus.

ST. TERESA'S VISIONS

These two passages are among the most famous from the autobiography that St. Teresa began writing in 1562, when she was forty-seven years old. The book is essentially the story of a spiritual journey, as a restless young woman gains purpose and strength through mystical visions and unwavering faith. Her account of a mystical transport in the second passage quoted here was the inspiration for a famous sculpture by Gian Lorenzo Bernini, The Ecstasy of St. Teresa, *in the seventeenth century.*

"I: One day, when I was at prayer, the Lord was pleased to reveal to me nothing but His hands, whose beauty was so great as to be indescribable. This made me very fearful. A few days later I also saw the Divine face. On St. Paul's Day, I saw a complete representation of his sacred Humanity. If there were nothing else in Heaven to delight the eyes but the extreme beauty of the glorified bodies there, that alone would be the greatest bliss. If I were to spend years and years imagining how to invent anything so beautiful, I could not do it. In its whiteness and radiance, it exceeds all we can imagine. It is a soft whiteness which, without wearying the eyes, causes them the greatest delight. By comparison with it, the brightness of our sun seems quite dim."

"II: It pleased the Lord that I sometimes saw beside me an angel in bodily form. He was not tall, but short, and very beautiful, his face aflame. In his hands I saw a long golden spear, and at the end of the iron tip I seemed to see a point of fire. With this he seemed to pierce my heart several times. When he drew it out, he left me completely afire with a great love for God. During the days when this continued, I went about as if in a stupor."

From E. Allison Peers, *The Life of Teresa of Jesus* (London: Sheed & Ward, 1944; New York: Doubleday, 1960), pp. 258–260, 273–274.

◆ IGNATIUS LOYOLA

The third of the great religious innovators of the sixteenth century, after Luther and Calvin, was Ignatius Loyola (1491–1556); unlike his predecessors, however, he sought to reform the Catholic Church from within. Loyola was the son of a Basque nobleman, raised in the chivalric and intensely religious atmosphere of Spain, and he was often at the royal court. In his teens he entered the army, but when he was thirty, a leg wound ended his military career. While convalescing, he was deeply impressed by a number of popular lives of the saints he read, and soon his religious interests began to take shape in chivalric and military terms. He visualized Mary as his lady, the inspiration of a Christian quest in which the forces of God and the devil fight in mighty battle. This was a faith seen from the perspective of the knight, and though the direct parallel lessened as Loyola's thought developed, it left an unmistakable stamp on his future work.

In 1522 Loyola gave up his knightly garb and swore to go on a pilgrimage to Jerusalem. He retired to a monastery for ten months to absolve himself of the guilt of a sinful life and to prepare spiritually for the journey to the Holy Land. At the monastery he had a momentous experience that, like Luther's and Calvin's, dominated the rest of his life. According to tradition, he had a vision lasting eight days, during which he saw in detail the outline of a book, the *Spiritual Exercises,* and a new religious order, the Society of Jesus.

The Spiritual Exercises The first version of the *Spiritual Exercises* certainly dated from this period, but like Calvin's *Institutes,* it was to be thoroughly revised many times. The book deals not with doctrines or theology but with the discipline and training necessary for a God-fearing life. Believers must undertake four weeks of contemplation and self-examination that culminate in a feeling of union with God, when they surrender their minds and wills to Christ. If successful, they are then ready to submit completely to the call of God and to pursue the Church's commands without question.

The manual was the heart of the organization of the Society of Jesus, and it gave those who followed its precepts (known as Jesuits) a dedication

▲ *Peter Paul Rubens*
THE MIRACLE OF ST. IGNATIUS, **1619**
Loyola quickly became one of the major heroes of the Catholic revival. Within less than sixty years of his death (1556), he was to become a saint of the Church. He was one of the heroes of Baroque art, as is apparent in this painting by Peter Paul Rubens, which creates a powerful image of Loyola at the moment when he cures a man and a woman who have been possessed by the devil.
Erich Lessing/Art Resource, NY

and determination that made them seem the Church's answer to the Calvinists. But while the end might be similar to Luther's and Calvin's—the personal attainment of grace—the method, with its emphasis on individual effort and concentration, could not have been more different. For the *Spiritual Exercises* emphasize that believers can act for themselves; they do not have to depend on faith alone to gain salvation, as Protestants assert. One can prepare for grace through a tremendous act of will and not rely solely on a gift from God. Loyola makes immense demands precisely because he insists that the will is free and that good works are efficacious.

Loyola's Followers   During the sixteen years after he left the monastery, Ignatius led a life of poverty and study. Though lame, he traveled to Jerusalem and back barefoot in 1523–1524, and two years later he found his way to the University of Alcala, where he attracted his first disciples, three fellow students. Suspected by the Inquisition of being rather too independent in their beliefs, the little band walked to Paris, where six more disciples joined them. Ignatius now decided to return to the Holy Land, but war prevented the companions from traveling beyond Venice. Instead, they preached in the streets, visited the poor and the sick, urged all who would listen to rededicate themselves to piety and faith, and in 1537 achieved ordination as priests. Their activities were beginning to take definite shape, and so they decided to seek the pope's blessing for their work. They saw Paul III in 1538, and two years later, despite opposition from those who saw it as a threat to the authority of local bishops, the pope approved a plan Ignatius submitted for a new religious order that would be supervised directly by the papacy.

◆ THE JESUITS

Jesuit Activities   The Society, or Company, of Jesus had four principal functions: preaching, hearing confessions, teaching, and missionary work. The first two were the Jesuits' means of strengthening the beliefs of individual Catholics or converting Protestants. The third became one of their most effective weapons. The Christian humanists he encountered convinced Loyola of the tremendous power of education. The Jesuits therefore set about organizing the best schools in Europe and were so successful that some Protestants sent their children to the Society's schools despite the certainty that the pupils would become committed Catholics. The instructors followed humanist principles and taught the latest ideas, including the most recent advances in science. The Jesuits' final activity, missionary work, brought them their most spectacular successes among both non-Christians and Protestants.

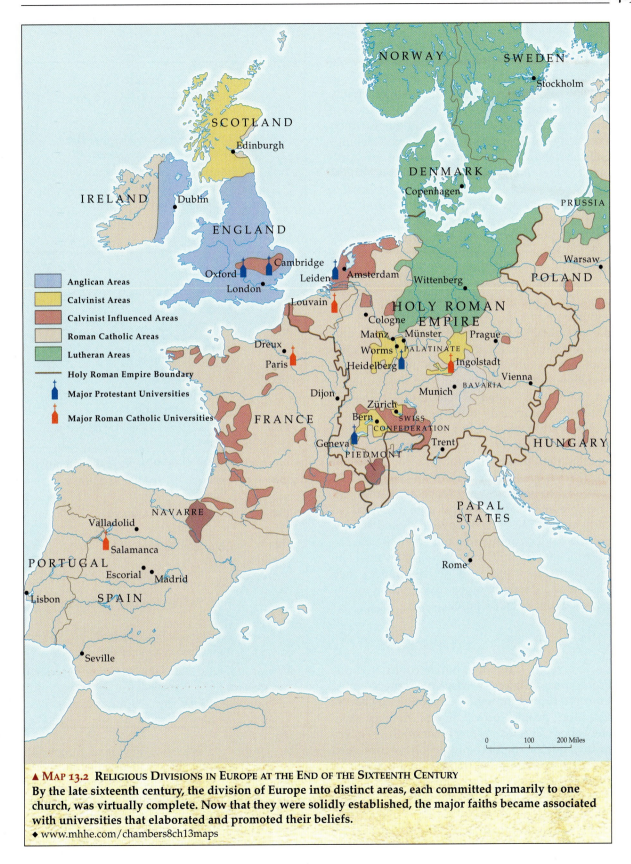

Anglican Areas

Calvinist Areas

Calvinist Influenced Areas

Roman Catholic Areas

Lutheran Areas

Holy Roman Empire Boundary

Major Protestant Universities

Major Roman Catholic Universities

▲ **MAP 13.2** RELIGIOUS DIVISIONS IN EUROPE AT THE END OF THE SIXTEENTH CENTURY
By the late sixteenth century, the division of Europe into distinct areas, each committed primarily to one church, was virtually complete. Now that they were solidly established, the major faiths became associated with universities that elaborated and promoted their beliefs.
◆ www.mhhe.com/chambers8ch13maps

Jesuit Campaigns   A number of qualities combined to make the Jesuits extraordinarily effective in winning converts and turning Catholics into militant activists. First, the order demanded high intellectual abilities. It selected recruits carefully (rejecting many applicants) and gave them a superb education. Jesuits were famous for their knowledge of Scripture and traditional teachings and their ability to out-argue opponents. In addition, they were highly effective preachers and excellent educators. Their discipline, determination, and awareness of the contemporary world soon won them a fearsome reputation. They had no equal in the forcefulness with which they advanced the aims of the Council of Trent and the papacy.

The Jesuits can be regarded as the striking arm of the Counter Reformation; indeed, their organization was to some extent modeled on the medieval military orders. A Jesuit at a royal court was often the chief inspiration for a ruler's militant support of the faith, and in many areas the Society was the main conqueror of rival beliefs— for example in Poland, where Jesuits in the late sixteenth century led a campaign that eradicated widespread Protestantism and created a devoted Catholic country. Yet it must be noted that in an age that took persecution for granted, the Jesuits always opposed execution for heresy; they far preferred to win a convert than to kill a heretic. Their presence was soon felt all over the world: As early as the 1540s, one of Loyola's first disciples, Francis Xavier, conducted a mission to Japan. Despite the many enmities they aroused by their single-mindedness and their self-assurance, their unswerving devotion was a major reason for the revival of the Roman Church.

◆ RELIGION AND POLITICS

As a revived Catholic Church confronted the Protestants, religious warfare of unprecedented ferocity erupted throughout Europe (see chapter 15). More people seemed to feel more passionately about faith than at any other time in Western history. But the conflict would not have continued as long as it did without the armies and resources provided by princes and monarchs. Both sides drew crucial support from rulers who were determined either to suppress any sign of heresy (that is, any faith other than their own) in their territo-

ries or to overthrow heretical regimes in neighboring lands. For these rulers, the struggle over religion was a means of establishing their authority in their own realms and a justification for aggression abroad.

Chronology

THE REFORMATION AND COUNTER REFORMATION

1517	Luther's protest begins: the ninety-five theses on indulgences.
1521	Diet of Worms: Luther condemned by Emperor Charles V.
1524–1525	Peasants' Revolt in Germany.
	Zürich adopts Zwingli's Reformation.
1531	Protestant League of Schmalkalden formed in Germany.
	Death of Zwingli.
	King Henry VIII proclaims himself head of the Church of England.
1534	Paul III becomes pope.
	Anabaptists take over the city of Münster in Germany.
1535	Thomas More executed for not accepting Henry VIII as head of the Church of England.
1536	Calvin comes to Geneva; first edition of his *Institutes*.
	Death of Erasmus.
1540	Pope Paul III approves the Jesuit Order.
1541	Calvin settles in Geneva permanently.
1545	Council of Trent begins.
1546	Death of Luther.
1556	Death of Loyola.
1559	First "Index of Forbidden Books" published.
	Execution of Protestants after Inquisition trials in Spain.
1564	Publication of the Decrees of the Council of Trent.
	Death of Calvin.

SUMMARY

◆

The strong connection between politics and belief, and its dire consequences, was the result of a transformation that was almost as far-reaching as the Reformation itself. Just as Western Christianity was changed forever in the sixteenth century, so too were the power and the ambition of the territorial state. At the same time as a handful of reformers, building on powerful social and intellectual forces, reshaped religious structures and practices, a handful of political leaders—building on no less powerful military, social, and economic forces—created armies, systems of taxation, and bureaucratic organizations that reshaped the structures and practices of central governments throughout Europe.

QUESTIONS FOR FURTHER THOUGHT

◆

1. If spiritual yearning has often changed individuals, why are outside forces such as politics necessary before large-scale changes in faith can take hold?

2. Is religious belief best understood as personal or as communal?

RECOMMENDED READING

◆

Sources

*Calvin, John. On God and Political Duty. J. T. McNeill (ed.). 1950.

*Erasmus, Desiderius. Essential Works of Erasmus. W. T. H. Jackson (ed.). 1965.

Loyola, Ignatius. The Spiritual Exercises of St. Ignatius. R. W. Gleason (ed.). 1964.

*Luther, Martin. Martin Luther: Selections from His Writings. John Dillenberger (ed.). 1961.

Studies

*Bossy, John. Christianity in the West, 1400–1700. 1985. An overview of the religious history of Europe by one of the leading historians of Catholic thought and practice.

*Bouwsma, William J. John Calvin: A Sixteenth-Century Portrait. 1988. The standard biography.

*Davis, Natalie Zemon. Society and Culture in Early Modern France. 1975. A collection of essays about popular beliefs and attitudes, particularly on religious matters, during the sixteenth century.

*Huizinga, Johan. Erasmus and the Age of Reformation. 1957. A warm and sympathetic biography, beautifully written.

Jones, M. D. W. The Counter Reformation. 1995.

*Kenny, Anthony. Thomas More. 1983. An excellent brief introduction to More's life and work.

Kittelson, James M. Luther the Reformer: The Story of the Man and His Career. 1986. The best introduction to Luther's life and thought.

O'Malley, John. The First Jesuits. 1993.

Scribner, Robert. For the Sake of Simple Folk: Popular Propaganda for the German Reformation. 1981. A pathbreaking analysis of how the Reformation was spread.

Tracy, James. Europe's Reformations, 1450–1650. 1999. A recent overview.

Wiesner, Merry. Women and Gender in Early Modern Europe. 1993.

Williams, George H. The Radical Reformation. 1962. The most comprehensive account of the sects and their founders.

Web Sites

http://history.hanover.edu/early/prot.html

http://history.hanover.edu/early/trent.html

http://www.fordham.edu/halsall/sbook1y.html

http://www.fordham.edu/halsall/mod/awdsbook02.html

http://www.ic.net.org/pub/resources/text/Wittenberg/Wittenberg-Luther.html

*Available in paperback.

▲ CENSUS AT BETHLEHEM

Although ostensibly a religious scene, the *Census at Bethlehem* gives us a glimpse of the growing intrusion into daily life of expanding governments. In their hardest season, winter, the people of this Flemish village have to line up in front of the bureaucrat at the table, who takes his fee even as he records the names of the villagers.

Art Resource, NY

♦

ECONOMIC EXPANSION AND A NEW POLITICS

E urope in 1400 was a poor, technologically backward, and politically disorganized area compared to the realms of the Indian moguls or Chinese emperors.
And yet within little more than a century, Europeans were expanding aggressively into Asia and the Americas. Their numbers were growing, their economy was booming, their technological advances were making possible the creation of new markets and
new empires, and their political leaders were developing structures of government and authority more elaborate than any that had been seen since the fall of the Roman Empire. The
emergence of this new world power was one of the most astonishing transformations in
Western history, and historians have long debated its causes. Their suggestions have ranged
from the initiatives of specific kings or explorers to such forces as demographic change or
climatic warming. Like the fall of the Roman Empire, however, this was so profound a reshaping of Europe's economy and politics that no definitive explanation seems possible. Yet
a survey of the main individual changes can help explain how far the reordering had progressed by the late sixteenth century.

CHAPTER 14. ECONOMIC EXPANSION AND A NEW POLITICS							
	Social Structure	Body Politic	Changes in the Organization of Production and in the Impact of Technology	Evolution of Family and Changing Gender Roles	War	Religion	Cultural Expression
I. EXPANSION AT HOME	�©		�©				
II. EXPANSION OVERSEAS	�©		�©				
III. THE CENTRALIZATION OF POLITICAL POWER		�©			�©	�©	
IV. THE SPLINTERED STATES	�©				�©		
V. THE NEW STATECRAFT	�©						�©

I. Expansion at Home

During the last third of the fifteenth century, even before Luther's rupture of Western Christendom, signs of change appeared in the demographic, economic, and political history of Europe. Some argue that the causes were political: that trade quickened and populations grew because of rising confidence as assertive regimes restored order and authority in a number of states. Others regard either economic or demographic advance as the source of change. In fact, though, all three were connected and all three reinforced one another. What is unmistakable is the increase in the number of Europeans after more than one hundred years of decline and the social and economic consequences of that increase.

◆ POPULATION INCREASE

Exact measurements are not possible, but it seems likely that the loss of population that began with the Black Death in the 1340s had run its course by the 1460s. Plagues, though recurrent, began to take less of a toll (perhaps because immunities developed); bad harvests became less frequent (perhaps because of a warming climate); and families were thus able to produce more surviving children. As a result, Europe's population rose by some 50 percent between 1470 and 1620. And cities expanded even faster: London had fewer than 50,000 inhabitants in the early sixteenth century but over 200,000 a hundred years later. There was also extensive reoccupation of marginal farmland, which had been abandoned in the fourteenth and fifteenth centuries because a shrinking population had provided no market for its produce. Now there were more mouths to feed, and the extra acres again became profitable.

Consequences of the Increase The rise in population was followed by a staggering jump in food prices. By the early 1600s wheat cost approximately five times more than in the late 1400s, an increase that far outpaced the movement of prices in general. It is not surprising, therefore, that this period witnessed the first wave of enclosures in England: Major landowners put up fences around common tilling or grazing ground, traditionally open to all the animals of the locality, and reserved it for their own crops or their sheep, whose wool was also in increasing demand. By 1600 about one-eighth of England's arable land had been enclosed. The only answer, when changes like these made a village incapable of supporting its growing population, was for people to move to towns and cities.

◆ ECONOMIC GROWTH

As markets began to grow in response to population pressures, the volume of trade also shot upward; commercial profits thus kept pace with those of agriculture. Customs receipts rose steadily, as did the yield of tolls from ships entering the Baltic Sea, one of the main routes of European trade. In many areas, too, shipbuilding boomed. This was the heyday of the English cloth trade and the great Spanish sheep farms, of the central German linen industry and the northern Italian silk industry. Printing became a widespread occupation, and gun making and glassmaking also expanded rapidly. Glassmaking had a major effect on European society because the increasing use of windows allowed builders to divide houses into small rooms, thus giving many people a little privacy for the first time.

The Growth of Banking Leading financiers who invested in the growing volume of trade accumulated large fortunes. For centuries the Italians had led economic advance, but in the sixteenth century firms of other nations were achieving international prominence. The most successful of the new enterprises was run by a family descended from a fourteenth-century weaver, Johannes Fugger of Augsburg. The sixteenth-century Fuggers financed the Spanish King Charles I's quest for the throne of the Holy Roman Empire and his later wars after he became the Emperor Charles V. Great bankers were thus often closely allied with monarchs, and like all merchants, they gained from the growing power of central governments. Rulers encouraged commerce in the hope of larger revenues from customs duties and taxes, and they gave leading entrepreneurs valuable privileges. Such alliances were eventually the undoing of some firms, which were ruined when kings went bankrupt, but until the late sixteenth century, Italian and German bankers controlled Europe's finances.

New Kinds of Businesses Almost every level of commercial activity offered opportunities for advancement. The guild system expanded in the sixteenth century to incorporate many new trades, and the structure of merchant enterprises became more elaborate. The idea took hold that a business firm was an impersonal entity—larger than the person who owned it—with an identity, legal status, permanence, and even profits that were not the same as those of its members. Here was yet another indication of major economic change.

Inflation The surest sign of growth, however, was the slow inflation of prices, which began around 1500 after some one hundred fifty years of either stagnant or falling prices. By modern standards, the increase was tiny—1 or 2 percent a year, totaling 75 percent in Spain by 1600 and slightly less elsewhere in Europe—but it prompted bitter protests from those who thought a loaf of bread had a "just" price and that any increase was mere exploitation by the baker. In general, however, the modest inflation was an indication that demand was rising, and it not only boosted profits but also reduced people's debts (because the amount that had been borrowed was worth less each year).

Silver Imports A major reason for the inflation was the growth of the population, but it was also propelled by the huge quantities of silver the Spaniards imported from the New World, which made money more readily available (see accompanying table). Most of the silver passed from Spain to the Italian and German merchants who financed Spanish wars and controlled the American trade, and thus it affected all of Europe. Other sources of supply, notably silver mines in Austria, were appearing at this time; but the flow of New World silver was the main reason for the end of the crippling shortage of precious metals and coins that had plagued Europe for centuries. By the middle of the seventeenth century, the continent's holdings in gold had increased by one-fifth

▼ **IMPORTS OF TREASURE TO SPAIN FROM THE NEW WORLD, 1511–1600**

Decade	Total Value*
1511–1520	2,626,000
1521–1530	1,407,000
1531–1540	6,706,000
1541–1550	12,555,000
1551–1560	21,437,000
1561–1570	30,418,000
1571–1580	34,990,000
1581–1590	63,849,000
1591–1600	85,536,000

*In ducats.

Source: Adapted from J. H. Elliott, *Imperial Spain, 1469–1716* (New York, 1964), p. 175.

▲ *Anonymous French Miniature*
MERCHANTS CLEARING ACCOUNTS
This sixteenth-century depiction of a group of people in a fine house calculating accounts gives a sense of the increasingly complicated exchanges that became necessary as commerce expanded. Books had to be checked and money counted. It is noteworthy that the transactions involve the monk on the left and the woman holding her purse on the right.
Corbis

and, more important, its stock of silver had tripled.

With money circulating more freely and markets growing, the profits of traders and financiers improved dramatically. They could invest more widely (for example, in overseas ventures) and thus achieve new levels of wealth.

The Commercial Revolution As the volume of trade rose, new mechanisms for organizing large-scale economic activity were put in place—a process that has been called Europe's commercial revolution. Bookkeepers devised new, standardized principles for keeping track of a firm's accounts, bankers created elaborate systems of agents and letters of credit to transfer funds across large distances, merchants developed more effective means of forming broad partnerships that were capable of major investments and of ensuring against losses, and governments gave increased support to new ventures and to the financial community in general. Essential to these activities was an attitude and a way of conducting business that is known as *capitalism.*

Capitalism Capitalism was both a product of economic change and a stimulus to further change. It is often thought of as a system, but it refers primarily to the distinct outlook and kinds of behavior displayed by certain people as they make, buy, and sell goods. At its root, capitalism means the accumulation of capital—that is, tangible wealth—for its own sake. In practice, this requires taking risks and also reinvesting whatever one earns so as to enlarge one's profits. Those who undertook long-distance trade had many capitalist traits: They took great risks, and they were prepared to wait months and even years in order to make as large a financial gain as possible. Similarly, bankers were prepared to lend their capital, despite the danger that the loan might not be repaid, in the hope of profit; and if they succeeded, they continually plowed their earnings back into their businesses to make them ever larger. The fortunes that these capitalists accumulated, and the desire for worldly riches that they displayed, became an essential stimulus to economic growth. Far from the rural world where food was grown primarily for survival, not for profit, they were forging a new way of thinking about money and wealth. Although their outlook had existed before, only in the sixteenth century did it come to dominate Europe's economy. As a result, traditional religious prohibitions on the charging of interest began to weaken, and materialist ambitions became more open and accepted.

Unease over this new outlook did not disappear. Shakespeare's play *The Merchant of Venice,* written in the 1590s, attacked the values that capitalism was coming to represent. He contrasted

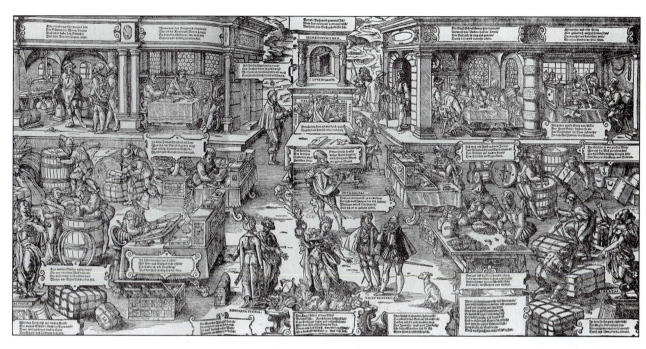

▲ *Jost Amman*
ALLEGORY OF TRADE, WOODCUT
This late-sixteenth-century celebration of the world of the merchant shows, around the sides, the shipping of goods, the keeping of accounts, and the exchange of money that were transforming economic life. In the center, the virtues of the merchant are symbolized: integrity (a man looking over his shoulder), taciturnity (two men on his right), and a knowledge of languages (two men in turbans) in front of judiciousness on a throne and a book representing invention.

unfavorably the quest for profit with more traditional commitments, such as charity and mercy. And his choice of Venice as a setting was appropriate because the large empire this city built in the eastern Mediterranean was mainly the result of a single-minded pursuit of trade. But criticism had no effect on the relentless spread of capitalism.

◆ SOCIAL CHANGE

Unequal Impacts in the Countryside Not everyone shared in the new prosperity of the sixteenth century. Landowners, food producers, artisans, and merchants benefited most from the rising population and could amass fortunes. Tenants who were able to harvest a surplus beyond their own needs did well, because for a while rents did not keep pace with food prices. But the wages of ordinary laborers lagged miserably. By the early 1600s, a laborer's annual income had about half the purchasing power it had had at the end of the

1400s, a decline that had its most drastic impact in Eastern Europe, where serfdom reappeared.

In the West, the large numbers of peasants who were forced off the land as the population rose turned to begging and wandering across country, often ending up in towns, where crime became a serious problem. Peasant uprisings directed at tax collectors, nobles, or food suppliers were almost annual affairs in one region or another of France after the mid-sixteenth century, and in England the unending stream of vagrants gave rise to a belief that the country was overpopulated. The extreme poverty was universally deplored, particularly as it promoted crime and disorder.

Relief of Distress Nobody could understand, much less control, the forces that were transforming society. Some governments tried to relieve the economic distress, but their efforts were not always consistent. English legislation in the sixteenth century, for example, treated beggars

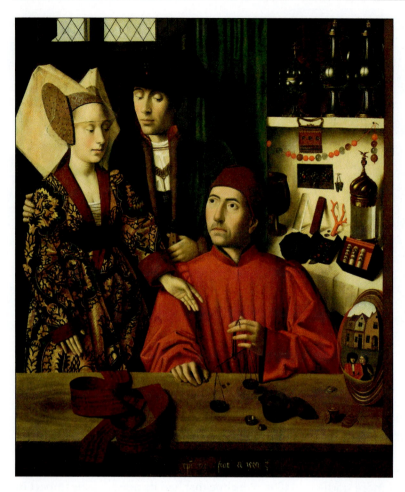

◄ *Petrus Christus*
St. Eligius as a Goldsmith, **1449**
Goldsmiths played a vital financial role in the early days of capitalism. Because of the value of the merchandise they made and sold, their shops—like the one here, with customers looking in the window, reflected in the convex mirror on the right—were sources of capital as well as goods. In addition to providing such items as the ring he is handing to the young woman, the goldsmith might well have provided investments for the traders in his city.
Petrus Christus, *St. Eligius.* 1449. Oil on Wood. 39 × 33⁷⁄₁₆″. The Metropolitan Museum of Art, Robert Lehman Collection, 1975. (1975.1.110) Photography © 1993 The Metropolitan Museum of Art

sometimes as shirkers who should be punished and at other times as unfortunates who needed to be helped. Not until the enactment of the English Poor Law of 1601, which provided work for the poor, did the more compassionate view begin to prevail. In the years that followed, governments in a number of countries began to create institutions that offered basic welfare benefits.

The traditional source of food for the hungry and care for the ill, the monastery, had lost its importance because of the Reformation and because governments were now considered responsible for the needy. Among the remedies governments offered were the workhouses established by the English Poor Law where, although conditions could be horrible, the destitute could at least find work, food, and shelter. Other governments founded hospitals, often staffed by nuns, which were especially important as places

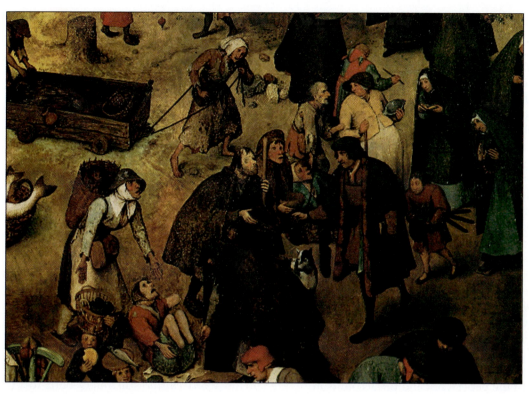

▲ *Pieter Brueghel the Elder*
CARNIVAL AND LENT, **1559**
**This detail from a huge scene shows one of the customary practices during the season of Lent: giving alms
to the poor. Beggars were a common subject for Brueghel, who used them to convey a vivid sense of the
appearance and behavior of the unfortunate as well as the more comfortable members of his society.**
Erich Lessing/Art Resource, NY

that looked after abandoned women or children.
But these institutions were few and far between,
and it was exceptional for a poor person to find
such relief. The conditions were especially harsh
for women forced off the land, because few

◄ *QUENTIN METSYS THE MONEY CHANGER AND
HIS WIFE* **1514**
**That people engaged in this business could be the
subject of a respectful portrait by a leading artist is
an indication that money lending and currency
dealing had come to be taken for granted in
European cities. It was a family enterprise, with the
wife helping her husband, and it is worth noting that
in business circles a literate woman—she has here
interrupted the reading of a book—was not that
unusual.**
Louvre

trades were open to them even if they got to a
town; their choice might be either continued vagrancy or prostitution.

The Hazards of Life in the Town Vagrancy was
only one of the signs that Europeans were wit-
nessing the beginnings of modern urbanization
with all its dislocations. Major differences also developed between life in the country and life in the
town. Rural workers may have led a strenuous
existence, but they escaped the worst hazards of
their urban counterparts. Whole sections of most
large cities were controlled by the sixteenth-
century equivalent of the underworld, which offered sanctuary to criminals and danger to most
citizens. Plagues were much more serious in
towns—the upper classes soon learned to flee to
the country at the first sign of disease—and
famines more devastating because of the far

poorer sanitation in urban areas and their remoteness from food supplies.

New Opportunities Nevertheless, it was in towns and cities that the economic advances of the age were most visible. As cities grew, they stimulated construction, not only of houses but also of public buildings and city walls. Anyone skilled in bricklaying, in carpentry, or even in carrying heavy loads found ready employment. Townsfolk needed endless services, from sign painting to the transportation of books, which created jobs at all levels. Given the demand for skills, guilds increasingly allowed the widows of members to take over their husbands' trades, and women shopkeepers were not uncommon. Nobody would have been taken aback, for example, to see an artisan's daughter or wife (like Agnes Dürer, the wife of the famous German artist) take charge of a market stall or a shop. In some trades, such as oil making and baking, women were often essential to production as well as sales, and there is also evidence of their growing importance as the keepers of the paperwork and the accounts in family businesses. The expansion of opportunity in the cities, in other words, had social as well as economic consequences.

At the top levels of society—at princely courts and in royal administrations, in the law, among the leaders of the burgeoning cities, and in growing empires overseas—the economic expansion enabled ambitious families to win fortunes and titles and to found new aristocratic dynasties. The means of advancement varied. Once a family had become rich through commerce, it could buy the lands that, in Protestant countries, rulers had confiscated from the Church, or the offices that many governments sold to raise revenue and build bureaucracies. In addition, the New World offered the possibility of acquiring vast estates. Since the possession of land or high office was the key to noble status, the newly rich were soon able to enter the ranks of the nobility. The long boom in commerce thus encouraged broad social change. By the 1620s, when the growth in the economy came to an end, a new aristocracy had been born that was destined to dominate Europe for centuries.

Daily Life The expanding resources changed many aspects of daily life. The availability (and affordability) of books, for example, helped promote literacy. Evidence is scarce, but the ability to sign documents, for example, tripled in many areas during the two centuries following the early 1500s. And many more could read than could write, though on both counts women lagged far behind. In Molière's play *The School for Wives* (1661), the lead character hopes his new wife can read, so that she can study the "Rules for Marriage" that he has written, but he is mortified when he discovers she can also write. With money, too, came broadening access to such consumer goods as household utensils, which transformed behavior at the table: by the seventeenth century, meals in polite society required individual place settings, with plates, napkins, knives, and forks.

At the same time, an enormous boom in house building, and the dividing off of rooms within these houses, created new atmospheres in the homes of the well-to-do. Private spaces were created whose names reflected their purposes: thus, the place where one studied became the study; in French the word *cuisine* still refers both to the kitchen and to the food that is cooked there. People began to collect souvenirs for decoration, to spend significant sums on furnishings, and to make the bedroom a special place. By the mid-1600s the dressing-gown was a popular item of clothing, and the room in which it might be worn could have suggestive overtones. When the English diarist Samuel Pepys came home one day, his wife was taking a dancing lesson in her room, and he feared the worst when the noise of her practicing stopped. But he had no compunction in making his wife jealous, even when she threatened him with a hot poker in their bedroom after one of his affairs. Such tribulations reflected a leisured class, forging new lives with the growing wealth of the time. Pepys himself was a naval administrator, a beneficiary of the new wealth Europeans had found at sea.

II. Expansion Overseas

Long before Europe's demographic and economic recovery began in the late 1400s, pioneer explorers had taken the first steps that led to the creation of huge empires overseas. Taking farther the voyages beyond Europe of the crusaders and such travelers as Marco Polo, sailors had been inching around Africa seeking a route to the Far East. Gradually, they moved farther afield and began conquering territory and peoples. The riches in goods and lands they eventually found would help fuel the boom of the sixteenth century.

◆ THE PORTUGUESE

Henry the Navigator Among the Portuguese, who began these voyages in the 1410s, there was little expectation of world-shattering consequences. The Portuguese lived in an inhospitable land whose seafarers had always been essential to the country's economy. The need for better agricultural opportunities had long turned their eyes toward Atlantic islands like the Canaries and the territories held by the Muslims (Moors) in North Africa. But this ambition had to be organized into a sustained effort if it was to achieve results, and in the early fifteenth century Prince Henry the Navigator, a younger son of the king, undertook that task.

Henry participated in the capture of the North African port of Ceuta from the Muslims in 1415, a crusading expedition that only whetted his ap-

petite for more such victories. At Ceuta he probably heard stories about lost Christians and mines of gold somewhere in the interior of Africa. A mixture of motives—profit, religion, and curiosity—spurred him on; and in 1419 he began patronizing sailors, mapmakers, astronomers (for their help in celestial navigation), shipbuilders, and instrument makers who were interested in discovery. They were mainly Italians, and their aim was not merely to make contact with Africans but to find an alternative route to India and the Far East around Africa (in order to avoid the Ottoman Empire, which was coming to dominate the eastern Mediterranean). The early adventurers did not succeed, but during their gradual advance down the West African coast, they opened a rich new trade in ivory, gold, and slaves.

To India and Beyond Then, in 1488, a Portuguese captain, Bartholomeu Dias, returned to Lisbon after making a landfall on the east coast of Africa, beyond the Cape of Good Hope, which previously no one had been able to pass. The way to India now seemed open, but before the Portuguese sent out their first expedition, the news arrived that a sailor employed by the Spaniards,

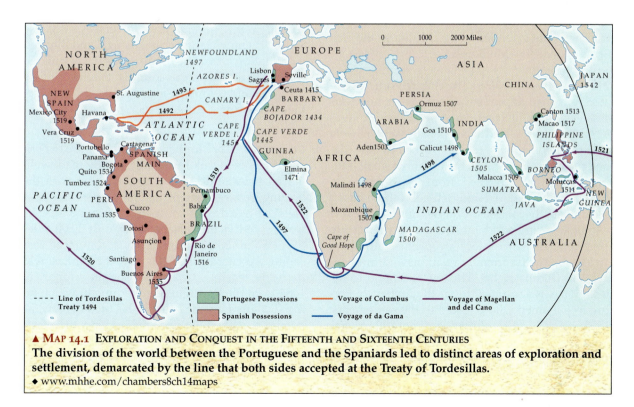

▲ **MAP 14.1** EXPLORATION AND CONQUEST IN THE FIFTEENTH AND SIXTEENTH CENTURIES
The division of the world between the Portuguese and the Spaniards led to distinct areas of exploration and settlement, demarcated by the line that both sides accepted at the Treaty of Tordesillas.
◆ www.mhhe.com/chambers8ch14maps

one Christopher Columbus, had apparently reached India by sailing west. To avoid conflicting claims that might interfere with their trade, Portugal and Spain signed the Treaty of Tordesillas in 1494. This gave Portugal possession of all the lands to the east of an imaginary line about 300 miles west of the Azores, and Spain a monopoly of everything to the west. Portugal thus kept the only practical route to India (as well as the rights to Brazil, which one of her sailors may already have discovered). Three years later Vasco da Gama took the first Portuguese fleet across the Indian Ocean.

At first, he found it hard to trade, because the Arabs, who had controlled these waters for centuries, tried to keep out all rivals. Within fourteen years, however, the Portuguese merchants had established themselves. The key to their success was naval power. In addition to improving the design of sails to increase speed and maneuverability, the Portuguese were the first to emphasize fire power, realizing that cannon, not soldiers, won battles at sea. In addition, they deployed their ships in squadrons rather than individually, a tactic that further increased their superiority. The result was overwhelming military success. A series of victories reduced Arab naval strength, and bombardments quieted stubborn cities. By 1513 Portugal's trading posts extended beyond India to the rich Spice Islands, the Moluccas.

The Portuguese Empire The empire Portugal created remained dependent on sea power, not overseas colonies. Except in Brazil, which was virtually unpopulated and where the settlers were able to establish huge estates worked by slave labor, the Portuguese relied on a chain of small trading bases that stretched from West Africa to China. They supplied and defended these bases, which usually consisted of little more than a few warehouses and a fort, by sea; and they tended to keep contacts with the local people to a minimum, so as to maintain friendly relations and missionary and trading rights. The one exception to the isolation was a result of the small numbers of Portuguese women who traveled to the settlements: In these early years there were more marriages with local women than there were in other European empires. But even though their effort remained relatively small-scale, the Portuguese

soon began to profit from their explorations. Between 1442 and 1446 almost one thousand slaves were brought home from Africa, and in the 1500s their wealth grew as they became major importers of luxuries from the East, such as spices, which were in great demand as medicines, preservatives, and tasty delicacies.

By dominating commerce with Eastern civilizations, which were not only richer but also more sophisticated than their own, Portugal's merchants controlled Europe's most valuable trade. But their dominance was to last less than a century, for their success spurred a competition for empire that was to stimulate new waves of overseas expansion. First, Spain determined to emulate her neighbor; and later, the Dutch, English, and French sought to outdo their predecessors and one another. This competition gave the Europeans the crucial stimulus that other peoples lacked, and it projected them into a dominance over the rest of the globe that would last for more than 450 years.

◆ THE SPANIARDS

Inspired by the same centuries-old crusading ambitions as the Portuguese, the Spaniards rode the second wave of expansion overseas. Because Spain was much larger than Portugal and directed its attention toward a more sparsely populated continent, the Spaniards founded their empire on conquest and colonization, not trade. But they got their start from a stroke of luck.

Columbus Christopher Columbus—an experienced Genoese sailor who was widely read, well-versed in Atlantic sailing, and familiar with the leading geographers of his day—seems to have believed (we do not know for certain, because he was a secretive man) that Asia lay only 3,500 miles beyond the Canary Islands. Thus, convinced that sailing west across the Atlantic to the Far East was perfectly feasible, Columbus sought support in 1484 from the Portuguese government, which refused. With a mystic belief in his own destiny, he persisted, gained the financial backing and blessing of Ferdinand V and Isabella I of Spain, and set sail in 1492. He was an excellent navigator (one of his discoveries on the voyage was the difference

▲ Woodcut of *Columbus Landing*
This picture, by a contemporary, shows King Ferdinand, back in Spain, pointing to Columbus' three ships and the natives greeting the explorer in the New World.
New York Public Library

accompanied the Europeans, was to undermine their ancient civilizations.

The Limits of Westward Voyages   By the end of Columbus' life in 1506, it was becoming apparent that he had found islands close by a new continent, not Asia. When, in 1513, the Spaniard Vasco de Balboa saw the Pacific Ocean from Central America, some thought that an easy westward passage to the riches of East Asia might still be found. But the last hope of a quick journey was dashed in 1522, when the one surviving ship from a fleet of five that had set out under Ferdinand Magellan three years before returned to Spain after the ordeal of having sailed around the world.

Magellan's 98-day crossing of the Pacific was the supreme accomplishment of seamanship in the age of discovery. But the voyage persuaded the Spaniards that Portugal had the fastest route to the East, and in 1529 they renounced all attempts to trade with the Spice Islands. Spain could now concentrate on the Americas, those unexpected continents that were to become not an obstacle on the way to the Spice Islands but possessions of unbelievable richness.

The Conquistador   Volunteers for empire building were amply available. When the last Muslim kingdom in southern Spain was conquered by the Castilians in 1492, soldiers with long experience of military service found themselves at loose ends. Many were the younger sons of noble families, who were often kept from inheriting land because Spanish law usually allowed only the eldest son to inherit. The prospect of unlimited land and military adventure across the Atlantic appealed to them, as it did to ambitious members of Castile's lower classes, and thus the *conquistador*, or conqueror, was born. There were not many of them—fewer than one thousand—but they overran much of the Americas in search of wealth and glory.

The first and most dramatic of these leaders was Hernando Cortés, who in 1519 landed on the Mexican coast and set out to overcome the rich Aztec civilization in the high plateau of central Mexico. His army consisted of only six hundred troops, but in two years, with a few reinforcements, he had won a complete victory. Guns alone made no important difference, because Cortés had only thirteen muskets and some unwieldy

between true and magnetic north), and he kept his men going despite their horror of being so long at sea without sight of land. After thirty-three days, he reached the Bahamas. He was disappointed that he found no Chinese or Japanese as he investigated Cuba and the west coast of Hispaniola (today's Haiti), but he was certain that he had reached Asia, even though the few natives he saw did not resemble those whom travelers such as Marco Polo had described.

Columbus crossed the Atlantic Ocean three more times, but he made no other significant discoveries. Yet he did also start the tradition of violence against local people that was to characterize the European conquest of the New World. During his first stay in the Caribbean, his men killed some of the natives they encountered. From the very beginning, therefore, it became clear that the building of empires in the Americas would be a process of destruction as well as creation, of cruelty as well as achievement (see "Two Views of Columbus"). For the victims, the effect of the brutality, soon intensified by the devastating diseases that

Two Views of Columbus

The following two passages suggest the enormous differences that have arisen in interpretations of the career of Christopher Columbus. The first, by Samuel Eliot Morison, a historian and a noted sailor, represents the traditional view of the explorer's achievements that held sway until recent years. The second, by Kirkpatrick Sale, a writer and environmentalist, indicates how radically the understanding of the effects of exploration has changed in recent years.

1. "Columbus had a Hellenic sense of wonder at the new and strange, combined with an artist's appreciation of natural beauty. Moreover, Columbus had a deep conviction of the sovereignty and the infinite wisdom of God, which enhanced all his triumphs. One only wishes that the Admiral might have been afforded the sense of fulfillment that would have come from foreseeing all that flowed from his discoveries. The whole history of the Americas stems from the Four Voyages of Columbus, and as the Greek city-states looked back to the deathless gods as their founders, so today a score of independent nations unite in homage to Christopher the stouthearted son of Genoa, who carried Christian civilization across the Ocean Sea."

From S. E. Morison, *Admiral of the Ocean Sea: A Life of Christopher Columbus* (Boston: Little, Brown, 1942), pp. 670–671.

2. "For all his navigational skill, about which the salty types make such a fuss, and all his fortuitous headings, Admiral Colón [Christopher Columbus]

could be a wretched mariner. The four voyages, properly seen, quite apart from bravery, are replete with lubberly mistakes, misconceived sailing plans, foolish disregard of elementary maintenance, and stubborn neglect of basic safety—all characterized by the assertion of human superiority over the natural realm. Almost every time Colón went wrong, it was because he had refused to bend to the inevitabilities of tide and wind and reef or, more arrogantly still, had not bothered to learn about them.

"Many of those who know well the cultures that once existed in the New World have reason to be less than enthusiastic about [the 1992 celebrations of] the event that led to the destruction of much of that heritage and the greater part of the people who produced it; others are planning to protest the entire goings-on as a wrongful commemoration of an act steeped in bloodshed, slavery, and genocide."

From Kirkpatrick Sale, *The Conquest of Paradise: Christopher Columbus and the Columbian Legacy* (New York: Knopf, 1990), pp. 209–210, 362.

cannon. More effective were his horses, his manipulation of the Aztecs' beliefs (especially after he murdered their ruler) to make them regard him as more powerful than he was, and the unshakable determination of his followers. The conquest of the Mexican Mayas also began under Cortés, while the Incas of Peru fell to Francisco Pizarro. Other conquistadors repeated these successes throughout Central and South America. By 1550 the conquest was over, and the military leaders gave way to administrators who began organizing the huge empire they had won.

◆ THE FIRST COLONIAL EMPIRE

The Spanish government established in the New World the same pattern of political administration that it was setting up in its European territories.

Representatives of the throne, viceroys, were sent to administer each territory and to impose centralized control. They were advised by the local *audiencia*, a kind of miniature council that also acted as a court of law, but the ultimate authority remained in Spain.

Real growth did not begin, however, until women pioneers came out to the settlements. In this empire, unlike Portugal's, intermarriage was strongly discouraged. Indeed, the indigenous peoples were treated with a brutality and disdain that set a dismal model for overseas empires. Their labor was cruelly exploited on farms and especially in silver mines that the Spaniards discovered, where working conditions were dreadful. Families were split apart so that men could be put to work, and local beliefs and traditions were actively suppressed (though many survived despite the oppression). Over the years, intermarriage between Europeans and natives increased, and a more united society evolved, but this transformation took centuries to achieve. In the meantime, Spain's colonies were an object of envy because of their mineral wealth. In 1545 Spaniards discovered a major vein of silver at Potosí, in Bolivia, and from those mines came the treasure that made fortunes for the colonists, sustained Spain's many wars, and ultimately enriched much of Europe. For the balance of the sixteenth century, however, despite the efforts of other countries, Portugal and Spain remained the only conspicuous participants in Europe's overseas expansion.

The Perilous Life of the Settlers It took a great deal of determination to board one of the ships that set off across the oceans from Europe. Life at sea offered discomfort and peril: horrible overcrowding, inadequate and often rotting food, disease, dangerous storms, poor navigation, and threats from enemy ships. One cannot determine numbers precisely, but it has been estimated that in some decades of the sixteenth and seventeenth centuries, fewer than two-thirds of those who embarked reached their destination. And their troubles did not end when they came off the ships. Unfamiliar countries, famine, illness, and attacks by natives and European rivals made life precarious at best. Although five thousand people sailed for Virginia between 1619 and 1624, for instance, disease and massacre kept the colony the same size at the end of that period—about one thousand inhabitants—as it had been at the beginning. And yet, despite the difficulties and dangers, people found reasons to keep coming.

The Aims of the Colonists For a few leaders, like the Spanish minor nobles known as *hidalgos* who commanded most of Spain's first missions, the attraction was partly adventure, partly the chance to command a military expedition of conquest, and partly the hope of making a fortune that seemed unlikely at home. For another fairly small group, the clergy, the aim was to bring the word of God to people who had never encountered Christianity before. And government officials and traders hoped they might advance more rapidly than in their native lands. For these middle and upper levels of society, however, survival was

rarely an issue: They might die in battle or from illness, and life may not have been as comfortable as it would have been at home, but the opportunities to exercise power or to make a fortune were far greater. The outlook was very different for the vast majority of the new settlers.

Finding Ordinary Settlers For most of them, leaving Europe was a fairly desperate act, an indication that almost any alternative seemed preferable to the bleak prospects in their homeland. If it had not been for the growth of population in the sixteenth century—and the many thousands it made homeless, unable to remain in their villages or make a living in towns—it is unlikely that enough emigrants would have been found to do the work in ports and on the land that was crucial to building empires in Asia and America. It is significant that fewer people moved from a rich country like France than from the less prosperous Spain and Portugal. Despite the pressures that persuaded thousands of people to leave their homelands, therefore, additional means had to be found to populate the empires.

Long before the English colonized Australia with convicts in the eighteenth century, for example, they were taking people out of prison to send overseas to places desperate for settlers. Another tactic was to offer land to anyone who was willing to work for others for seven years. The English, and to a lesser extent the French, permitted religious minorities who feared persecution at home to start a new and more independent existence in America. In general, powerful inducements like poverty or persecution were needed to drive Europeans to accept the hazards of the journey and the subsequent struggles of the pioneer. Some, such as the religious refugees, set out as families, but usually many more men than women made the voyage. In pioneer communities all labor was essential and difficult, but there is no question that women, not only more vulnerable to violence but also regarded as subordinate to males, had far more to risk by emigrating; the chronic imbalance between genders thus became yet another hardship of life overseas.

Exploitation of Settlers and Natives When even distress at home provided too few volunteers, the colonizers relied on force to obtain the workers

▲ *Slave Ship*
This picture, made aboard a slave ship, shows the dangerously crowded conditions in which Africans were brought to the New World. It is small wonder that so many died of disease even before the end of this miserable voyage.
National Maritime Museum, Greenwich, London

they needed. Just as captains often kidnapped men for a ship's crew, so, too, did the suppliers of settlers. Many persons woke up at sea surprised to find where they were. And once in the colonies, wage earners could expect their employment to be harsh. Indigenous populations, however, faced the most ruthless treatment: In Central and South America millions died (estimates vary between 25 and 90 percent of the native peoples, with the worst devastations in Mexico) as a result mainly of the new diseases the Europeans brought, though their susceptibility may have been heightened by the terrible forced labor to which they were subjected. Even exploitation, however, was not enough to feed the insatiable need for miners, laborers, servants, and farmhands.

The Commerce in Slaves   The solution the colonizers found was slavery, familiar since ancient times but virtually nonexistent among Europeans by 1500. To find the slaves, ships began visiting the west coast of Africa, where the local inhabitants were either captured or purchased from local rulers and then transported to the New World under the most ghastly conditions. They were thrown together in cramped, filthy quarters, often bound, barely fed, and beaten at the slightest provocation. Nor was there much improvement for those—often fewer than half—who survived the crossing. The slaves sustained the empires and made it possible for their white masters to profit from the silver, tobacco, cotton, and other goods they produced; but the grim conditions of their

NEWFOUNDLAND
(fishing settlements)

NORTH AMERICA

Jamestown
(1607) VIRGINIA

ATLANTIC OCEAN

St. Augustine

GULF OF MEXICO

Havana

Mexico City

San Juan de Ulúa

Vera Cruz

Santo Domingo

CARIBBEAN SEA

Cartagena

Portobello

Panama

Bogota

Quito

Tumbez

SOUTH AMERICA

Pernambuco

Lima

Cuzco

Bahia

PACIFIC OCEAN

Potosi

PORTUGUESE

SPANISH

Asuncion

Rio de Janeiro

Santiago

Buenos Aires

(Treaty of Tordesillas 1494)

Line of Demarcation

Spanish

Portuguese

English

▲ MAP 14.2 EMPIRE AND SETTLEMENT IN THE AMERICAS, 1493–1610
The leadership of the Spaniards in expanding into the New World during the century following the voyages of Columbus is apparent from the territories they dominated. The much smaller area controlled by the Portuguese, the tentative activities of the English in Virginia, and the occasional settlements of fishermen in Newfoundland paled by comparison with the Spanish empire.

lives, and their high rates of mortality, would have wiped them out if there had not been a constant stream of slaves from Africa to replenish their numbers.

Long-Term Effects For those settlers who reaped rewards from the mines and the agricultural products of America, or from the trade with Europe that enriched all the colonies, the hardships did not last long. They created flourishing cities and universities and made huge fortunes. Their commercial networks began to link the entire world together for the first time in history. But for the many who struggled to expand these empires, life on the frontier, despite the promise of new opportunities, remained hard and dangerous for centuries. And for the slaves, there was not the slightest improvement in conditions or even hope of improvement, until revolts and civil wars finally abolished slavery in the nineteenth century. This was the context in which European institutions and culture came to dominate the rest of the world, though the encounter was by no means a one-way process.

One historian has described the interaction that followed Columbus as the Columbian Exchange, because ideas, people, microbes, plants, and animals flowed in both directions between the Old and New Worlds. Although the Spaniards saw themselves as converting natives from paganism to Catholicism, local cultures often tailored Western ideas to their own needs and managed to retain ancient practices and attitudes. In India, both the Portuguese and the English adopted customs and language from the local population, thus confirming what the Frenchman Michel de Montaigne had said as early as the 1580s, when he had compared the greed and violence of the Europeans unfavorably with the simplicity and harmonious lives of those whom they had conquered. And a Spanish friar, Bartolomé de las Casas, published a book in 1542, *The Destruction of the Indies*, that was a remarkable first-hand account of the cruelties and destruction his countrymen had inflicted on innocent people and their paradisiacal land. For all that they learned, however, there is no question that the Europeans saw themselves mainly as teachers: their military and technological might entitled them, so they believed, to bring their "civilization" to the rest of the world.

III. The Centralization of Political Power

The economic and social transformations that began around 1500 gained important support from the actions of central governments. Especially in England, France, and Spain, rulers gave vital encouragement to the growth of trade, overseas expansion, and attempts to relieve social distress. At the same time, the growing prosperity of the age enhanced the tax revenues that were essential to their power. Both of these mutually reinforcing developments had long-term effects, but it could be argued that the creation of well-organized states, built around strong central governments, was even more decisive than the economic boom in shaping the future of Western Europe.

The rulers of England, France, and Spain in the late fifteenth and early sixteenth centuries were especially successful in accumulating and centralizing power, and historians have therefore called them "new monarchs." The reigns of Henry VII, Louis XI, and Ferdinand and Isabella, in particular, have come to be regarded as marking the end of more than a century of political fragmentation. They set in motion a revival of royal authority that eventually weakened all rivals to the crown and created the bureaucracies characteristic of the modern state.

◆ TUDOR ENGLAND

The English monarchs had relied for centuries on local cooperation to run their kingdom. Unlike other European countries, England contained only fifty or sixty families who were legally nobles out of a population of perhaps 2.5 million. But many other families, though not technically members of the nobility, had large estates and were dominant figures at the parish, county, and even national levels. They were known as gentry, and it was from their ranks that the crown appointed the local officers who administered the realm—notably the justices of the peace (usually referred to as JPs). These voluntary unpaid officials served as the principal public servants in the more than forty counties of the land.

For reasons of status as well as a feeling of responsibility, the gentry had always sought such appointments. From the crown's point of view, the great advantage of the system was its efficiency: Enforcement was in the hands of those who could enforce. As a "great man" in his neighborhood, the JP rarely had trouble exerting his authority. Thus, the king had at his disposal an administrative structure without rival in Europe because, unlike other rulers, he could count on the cooperation of the leaders of each locality. Since the gentry had so much responsibility, they developed a strong sense of duty over the centuries, and the king increasingly sought their advice.

Parliament and Common Law   In the sixteenth century an institution that had developed from this relationship, Parliament, began to take on a general importance as the chief representative of the country's wishes; it was increasingly considered the only body that could give a ruler's actions a broad stamp of approval. Although Parliament remained subordinate to the crown for a long time, England's kings already realized that without parliamentary consent they could not take measures such as raising extraordinary taxes.

Just as Parliament served to unify the country, so too did another ancient institution: the common law. This was a system of justice based on precedent and tradition that was the same, or "common," throughout England. In contrast to the Roman law that prevailed on the continent, common law grew out of the interpretations of precedent made by individual judges and the decisions of juries. A court could be dominated by local leaders, but in general this was a system of justice, administered by judges who traveled from area to area, that helped bind England together. Like Parliament, the common law would eventually be regarded by opponents of royal power as an independent source of authority with which the crown could not interfere. In the late 1400s, however, it was an important help to a king who was trying to overcome England's political fragmentation and forge a more unified realm.

Henry VII and the Revival of Royal Power
Henry VII (1485–1509), who founded the Tudor dynasty, came to the throne as a usurper in the aftermath of more than thirty years of civil conflict, the Wars of the Roses. England's nobles had caused chaos in these wars, and they had consistently ignored the wishes of the monarchy. The situation hardly looked promising for a reasser-

tion of royal power. Yet Henry both extended the authority of the crown and restored order with extraordinary speed.

His first concern was finance, because he knew that unless he had sufficient funds to run his government, his ability to control the nobles would remain uncertain. At the same time, he was aware that extra taxes were the surest way to alienate subjects who expected a king to "live of his own," that is, from the income his lands provided, from customs duties, and from the contributions he received at special times, such as the marriage of his daughter. It is a testimony to the care with which Henry nurtured his revenues, increased the profits of legal fees and fines, and tightened the administration of his resources, that by the end of his reign he had paid off the crown's debts and accumulated a substantial reserve. With careful management, and avoidance of foreign entanglements, he was able to "live of his own."

Restoring Order   Where domestic order was concerned, the revival of royal authority was largely due to the energy of the king and his chief servants. Henry increased the powers of the JPs, thus striking at the independence leading nobles had won during the previous two centuries. Under his leadership, too, the royal Council became a far more active and influential body. Leading officials not only exercised executive powers but also resumed hearing legal appeals—a policy that further undermined the independence of gentry and nobles, who could dominate proceedings in local courts. When the royal councillors sat as a court (known as Star Chamber from the decorations on the ceiling of the room where they met), there was no jury, local lords had no influence, and decisions were quick and fair. Eventually, Star Chamber and other royal courts that derived their jurisdiction from the authority of the king himself came to be seen as threats to England's traditional common law. Under the Tudors, however, they were accepted as highly effective means of restoring order and asserting the power of the central government.

Henry VIII and his Successors   The first Tudor was a conservative, building up his authority and finances by applying vigorously the traditional methods and institutions that were available to a king. The young man who followed him on the

HENRY VIII CLAIMS INDEPENDENCE FROM THE POPE

◆

One of the crucial acts of Parliament through which Henry VIII made the Church of England independent of Rome was the so-called Act in Restraint of Appeals, which became law in 1533. This law forbade English subjects from appealing court decisions to Rome, which they had been allowed to do when the pope was accepted as the supreme authority. To justify this action, the preamble of the act made a claim for the independence of England and the authority of the king that was typical of the new monarchs of the age.

"Where by divers sundry old authentic histories and chronicles it is manifestly declared that this realm of England is an empire, governed by one supreme head and king, having the dignity and royal estate of the imperial crown of the same, unto whom a body politic be bound and owe next to God a natural and humble obedience; he being also furnished by the goodness of Almighty God with whole and entire power, preeminence, authority, prerogative and jurisdiction to render justice and final determination in all causes, debates and contentions, without restraint to any foreign princes, [and] without the intermeddling of any exterior person, to declare and deter-

mine all such doubts. In consideration whereof the King's Highness, his Nobles and Commons, enact, establish and ordain that all causes, already commenced or hereafter coming into contention within this realm or within any of the King's dominions, whether they concern the King our sovereign lord or any other subject, shall be from henceforth heard, examined, discussed, finally and definitely adjudged and determined within the King's jurisdiction and authority and not elsewhere."

From 24 Henry VIII, c. 12, as printed in *Statutes of the Realm,* 11 vols. (London, 1810–1828), vol. 3, pp. 427–429.

---

throne, Henry VIII (1509–1547), was an arrogant, dazzling figure, a strong contrast to his careful father. In 1513 he removed a long-standing threat from England's north by inflicting a shattering defeat on an invading Scots army at Flodden. With his prestige thus enhanced, he spent the next fifteen years taking little part in European affairs and consolidating royal power at home.

The Transformation of Parliament The turning point in the reign came when Henry decided to break with the Roman Church (see chapter 13). The creation of an independent English Church had major political consequences, notably its strengthening of the institution of Parliament. The Reformation Parliament, summoned in 1529, remained in existence for seven years, and acted on more matters of importance than a Parliament had ever considered before. The laws it passed gave it new responsibilities, and the length of its sessions also enhanced its stature.

Previously, election to Parliament had been considered a chore by the townsmen and landed gentry in the House of Commons, who found the expense of unpaid attendance and the time it took

more irksome than did the wealthy nobles in the House of Lords. But this attitude changed in the 1530s as members of the Commons met again and again; they came to know one another and to regard themselves as guardians of Parliament's traditions and privileges. Eventually, they were to make the Commons the dominant house in Parliament.

Royal Power After guiding Henry through the break with Rome, Thomas Cromwell became the king's chief minister. He was a tireless bureaucrat who reorganized the administration of the country and used the newly created Privy Council, consisting of the king's principal advisers, to coordinate and direct royal government. The principal beneficiary of these events was the crown. Royal income rose markedly with the appropriation of Church fees and possessions, many of which were sold, making fortunes for speculators and new families of landowners. For all the stimulus he gave to parliamentary power and the landed class, Henry now had a much larger, wealthier, and more sophisticated administration at his disposal; and no one doubted where ultimate authority lay. He did not establish a standing army, as some of the continental kings did, because he could crush all opposition without it. And this strong central administration even survived the eleven years of uncertainty that followed Henry's death in 1547.

Edward VI and Mary I During the reign of Edward VI (1547–1553), who died while still a minor, the nobility attempted to regain control of the government. There was a relaxation of central authority, and the Reformation advanced rapidly. But even when Edward's half-sister, Mary I (1553–1558), reestablished Roman Catholicism, forced many of her subjects into exile, and pro-

voked two major revolts, royal power was strong enough to survive both nobles' ambitions and revolts. The revival of the nobles was short-lived, and Mary's death brought an end to the reversal of religions. The next monarch, Henry VIII's last surviving child, Elizabeth, demonstrated that the growth of the monarchy's authority had hardly been interrupted under Edward and Mary.

◆ VALOIS FRANCE

The rulers of France in the fifteenth century, members of the Valois family, were unlike the English kings in that they lacked a well-formed organization for local government. Aristocrats dominated

▼ *Unknown Artist*
Edward VI and the Pope
The anti-Catholic feelings that began to grow in England during the reign of Edward VI are expressed in this painting. The young king sits on his throne. His father, Henry VIII, who started the Reformation in England, points to him as the victor over Catholicism. The crushing of the old faith is symbolized by Christ's conquering of the pope and monks (below) and the destruction of Roman churches and images (through the window).
By Courtesy of The National Portrait Gallery, London (NPG4165)

many regions, particularly those farthest from Paris, and great nobles had become virtually independent rulers. With their own administrations and often their own courts and taxation, they left the crown little say in their affairs. The size of the kingdom also limited royal power; it took more than a week to travel from Paris to the remoter parts of the realm—almost double the time for the equivalent English journey. The monarchy had tried to resolve the problem of ruling distant provinces by granting to close relatives large blocs of territory that the crown seized or inherited. Theoretically, these relatives would execute royal wishes more effectively than the king could from Paris. In practice, however, an ambitious family member often became just as difficult to handle as any powerful noble. After 1469 the crown kept control over such acquisitions—an indication that it now had the resources to exercise authority even in areas far from the capital.

Royal Administration The administrative center of the government was the royal council in Paris. The greatest court of law in the land was the Parlement of Paris, which had remained a judicial body, unlike the English Parliament, and whose members were appointed by the crown. As the central administration grew in the fifteenth and early sixteenth centuries, various provinces received their own parlements, a recognition of the continuing strength of the demand for local autonomy. But there was a countervailing force: the dominance of Roman law, which (unlike England's common law) was based on royal decree and which allowed the monarch to govern by issuing ordinances and edicts. These had to be registered by the parlements in order to take effect, but usually that was a formality.

Estates and Finance Representative assemblies, known as *Estates,* also limited the power of the throne. A number of provinces had such Estates, and they had to approve the level of taxation and other royal policies. Negotiations with these bodies were essential for the support of the king's income and his army. But France's chief representative body, the Estates General—consisting of clergy, nobles, and townsmen from every region—never attained the prestige of the English Parliament and was never able to bind the coun-

try together or function as a vital organ of government. The French kings thus had a degree of independence that English monarchs did not achieve, particularly in the area of finance. For centuries they had supplemented their main sources of income, from lands and customs duties, with a sales tax (*aide*), a hearth tax (*taille*), and a salt tax (*gabelle*). In earlier days the consent of the localities had been required for such levies, but after 1451 the taxes could be collected on the king's authority alone, though he still had to negotiate the exact rate with provincial Estates and be careful not to go beyond what would seem reasonable to his subjects.

The Standing Army The most decisive source of power available to the French king (unlike the English king) was his standing army. The upkeep of the troops accounted for more than half the royal expenditures in Louis XI's reign, mainly because their numbers grew as revenues increased. In the 1480s a force of at least fifteen thousand men, chiefly professional mercenaries and military-minded nobles, was kept in readiness every campaigning season from spring to fall. Because of the rising costs associated with the development of gunpowder weapons, only the central government could afford to maintain such an army. And the troops had to be billeted in various provinces, with support from the local Estates. As a result, the entire French population eventually bore the indirect burden of heavier taxation, while many regions of France had direct contact with royal soldiers. Although frequently short of pay, the troops were firmly under royal control and hence a vital device—rarely used, but always a threat—in the strengthening of royal authority.

◆ LOUIS XI AND CHARLES VIII

When Louis XI (1461–1483) began his reign, he faced a situation as unpromising as that of Henry VII at his succession, for the country had just emerged from the Hundred Years' War and royal authority was generally ignored. English troops, which had been in France for most of the war, had finally departed in the 1450s; but a new and equally dangerous menace had arisen in the east: the conglomeration of territories assembled by successive dukes of Burgundy.

Legend:

— Holy Roman Empire boundary

- - - Ile de France boundary

Royal domain in 1461

Areas added to 1483

Areas added to 1498

Areas added to 1515

Areas added to 1547

Areas added to 1559

Areas added 1463–1493, and after 1659

Burgundian areas in 1477:
those in the Holy Roman Empire to be inherited
by the Habsburgs; those to the West by France.

Semi-independent areas

▲ **MAP 14.3** FRANCE IN THE FIFTEENTH AND SIXTEENTH CENTURIES
This map shows in detail the successive stages whereby the monarchy extended its control throughout France.

The Capture of Burgundy   By the 1460s the duke of Burgundy was among the most powerful lords in Western Europe. He ruled a loosely organized dominion that stretched from the Low Countries to the Swiss Confederation, and his capital, Dijon, had become a major cultural and political center. In 1474 Louis XI put together a coalition against Charles the Bold, Duke of Burgundy, who had been at war with him for some seven years, and in 1477 Charles was killed in battle with the French king's Swiss allies. Louis then reannexed the duchy of Burgundy itself; but Mary, the duke's daughter, retained the Low Countries, which would later form part of the inheritance of her grandson, the Holy Roman Emperor Charles V.

Diplomacy   The Burgundian lands added considerably to Louis' sphere of authority. His masterly maneuvering in the tortuous diplomacy of his day soon won him other territories; he was appropriately nicknamed "the Spider" because the prizes he caught in his web were the result of waiting or negotiation rather than victories on the battlefield. Simple luck enlarged his realm as well: In 1481 he inherited the three large provinces of Anjou, Maine, and Provence. The result was that by the end of his reign royal power had penetrated into massive areas where previously it had been unknown.

The Invasion of Italy   Louis XI's son and successor, Charles VIII (1483–1498), was only thirteen years old when his father died; his sister, Anne de Beaujeu, was named Regent and was at once challenged by a nobles' rebellion. Charles was fortunate, though, that Anne was a tough-minded woman whose troops defeated the rebels on the battlefield and who then called an Estates General that confirmed her rule. When he came of age, Charles determined to expand his dynasty's territory, and in 1494 he led an army into Italy at the request of the duke of Milan, who was afraid of being attacked by Florence and Naples. After some successes, the French settled into a prolonged struggle with the Habsburgs for control of the rich Italian peninsula. The conflicts lasted for sixty-five years, ending in defeat for the French. Although the Italian wars failed to satisfy the monarchy's territorial ambitions, they provided an outlet and distraction for the restless French nobility and gave the kings, as commanders in time of war, an opportunity to consolidate royal power at home.

◆ THE GROWTH OF GOVERNMENT POWER

After Charles VIII's reign, France's financial and administrative machinery grew in both size and effectiveness, largely because of the demands of the Italian wars. There was rarely enough money to support the adventure; the kings, therefore, relied heavily on loans from bankers, who sometimes shaped France's financial policies. At the same time, the crown made a determined effort to increase traditional royal revenues.

Raising Taxes   France was a rich country of 15 million people with the most fertile land in Europe; yet the financial needs of the monarch always outstripped his subjects' ability to pay. With exemptions from the *taille* and the *gabelle* for nobles, many towns, royal officeholders, and the clergy, the bulk of the taxes had to be raised from the very classes that had the least to give. Other means of raising revenue were therefore needed, and one solution was the sale of offices. Positions were sold in the administration, the parlements, and every branch of the bureaucracy to purchasers eager to obtain both the tax exemption and the considerable status (sometimes a title of nobility) that the offices bestowed. From modest and uncertain beginnings under Louis XII (1498–1515), the system widened steadily; by the end of the sixteenth century, the sale of offices provided the crown with one-twelfth of its revenues.

Many other rulers were adopting this device, and everywhere it had similar effects: It stimulated social mobility, creating dynasties of noble officeholders and a new administrative class; it caused a dramatic expansion of bureaucracies; and it encouraged corruption. The system spread most rapidly and the effects were most noticeable in France, where the reign of Francis I (1515–1547) witnessed a major increase in the government's power as its servants multiplied. Francis tried hard to continue expanding royal control by launching expeditions into Italy, but in fact, he contributed more to the development of the crown's authority by his actions at home.

Control of the Church   One of the most remarkable of Francis' accomplishments was the power he gained over the Church. He was highly successful in his Italian campaigns early in his reign, and he used the power he won in Italy to persuade the pope in 1516 to give the crown the right to appoint all of France's bishops and abbots. According to this agreement, the income a bishop earned during his first year in office still went to the Vatican, but in effect, Francis now controlled the French Church. Its enormous patronage was at his disposal, and he could use it to reward servants or raise money. By making an agreement with the pope, he did not need to break with Rome in order to obtain authority over the clergy, as did Henry VIII in England.

The Advance of Centralization   In the 1520s Francis also began a major reorganization of the government. He legalized the sale of offices and formed an inner council, more manageable than the large royal council, to act as the chief executive body of the realm. As part of this streamlining, he centralized all tax-gathering and accounting responsibilities in one agency in 1523. Against the parlements, meanwhile, the king invoked the *lit de justice,* a prerogative that allowed him to appear in person before an assembly that was delaying the registration of any of his edicts or ordinances and declare them registered and therefore law. As for the Estates General, they did not meet once between 1484 and 1560.

By the end of Francis' reign, royal power was stronger than ever before; but signs of disunity had appeared that would intensify in the years to come. The Reformation was under way, and one of its movements, Calvinism, soon caused religious divisions and social unrest in France. As the reign of Francis' son Henry II (1547–1559) came to a close, the Italian wars finally ended in a French defeat, badly damaging royal prestige. The civil wars that followed came perilously close to destroying all that France's kings had achieved during the previous one hundred years.

◆ UNITED SPAIN

The Iberian Peninsula in the mid-fifteenth century was divided into three very different kingdoms. Portugal on the west, with some 1.5 million in-

▲ *Anonymous* Miniature
Francis I and His Court, from the Manuscript of Antoine Macault's Translation of Diodorus Siculus, ca. 1532
The splendor and the patronage of learning for which the new monarchs were known are evoked by this tiny painting of the French king. He sits at a table with his three sons, surrounded by his courtiers and listening to the author reading the very manuscript (a translation of an ancient Greek historian) that this picture illustrates.
Giraudon/Art Resource, NY

habitants, looked overseas. Castile, in the center, with a population of more than 8 million, was the largest and richest area. Sheep farming was the basis of its prosperity, and its countryside was dominated by powerful nobles. Castile was the last kingdom still fighting Muslims on its southern frontier, and in this ceaseless crusade the nobles played a leading part. They had built up both a great chivalric tradition and considerable political strength as a result of their exploits, and their status was enhanced by the religious fervor that the long struggle had inspired. To the east, Aragon, slightly larger than Portugal, consisted of three areas: Catalonia, the heart of the kingdom and a great commercial region centered on the city of Barcelona; Aragon itself, which was little more than a barren hinterland to Catalonia; and Valencia, a farming and fishing region south of Catalonia along the Mediterranean coast.

In October 1469, Isabella, future queen of Castile, married Ferdinand, future king of Sicily and heir to the throne of Aragon. Realizing that the marriage would strengthen the crown, the Castilian nobles opposed the union, precipitating a ten-year civil war. But the two monarchs emerged victorious, and they created a new political entity: the Kingdom of Spain. They and their successors were to be as effective as the kings of England and France in centralizing power and establishing royal control over their realms.

Ferdinand and Isabella   When Ferdinand and Isabella jointly assumed the thrones of Castile in 1474 and Aragon five years later, they made no attempt to create a monolithic state. Aragon remained a federation of territories, administered by viceroys who were appointed by the king but who allowed local customs to remain virtually intact. The traditions of governing by consent and preserving the subjects' rights were particularly strong in this kingdom, where each province had its own representative assembly, known as the *Cortes*. In Castile, however, the two monarchs were determined to assert their superiority over all possible rivals to their authority. Their immediate aims were to restore the order in the countryside that had been destroyed by civil war, much as it had been in England and France, and to reduce the power of the nobility.

The first objective was accomplished with the help of the Cortes of Castile, an assembly dominated by urban representatives who shared the wish for order because peace benefited trade. The Cortes established special tribunals to pursue and try criminals, and by the 1490s it had succeeded in ending the widespread lawlessness in the kingdom.

The Centralization of Power   To reinforce their authority, Ferdinand and Isabella sharply reduced the number of great nobles in the royal council and overhauled the entire administration, particularly the financial agencies, applying the principle that ability, rather than social status, should determine appointments. As the bureaucracy spread, the *hidalgo,* a lesser aristocrat who depended heavily on royal favor, became increasingly important in government. Unlike the great nobles, whose enormous wealth was little affected by reforms that reduced their political role, the hidalgos were hurt when they lost their tax exemptions. The new livelihood they found was in serving the crown, and they became essential figures in the centralization of power in Castile as well as in the overseas territories.

The monarchs achieved greater leverage over their nobles in the 1480s and 1490s, when they gained control of the aristocracy's rich and powerful military orders. These wealthy organizations, run by Castile's most important aristocratic families, gave allegiance primarily to their own elected leaders. To take over their leadership required assertiveness and determination, especially by Isabella, Castile's ruler. At one point she rode on horseback for three straight days in order to get to one of the order's elections and control the outcome. The great nobles could not be subdued completely; nor did the monarchs seek to destroy their power, for they were essential servants of the crown in the army and the higher levels of government. But like the kings of England and France, Ferdinand and Isabella wanted to reduce the nobles' autonomy to a level that did not threaten central authority, and it was thus crucial that they overcame the independence of the military orders by 1500.

Independence of the Church   They also succeeded in weakening Spain's bishops and abbots, who were as strong and wealthy as leading nobles. When Ferdinand and Isabella finally destroyed the power of the Muslims in southern Castile in 1492, the pope granted the monarchy the right to make major ecclesiastical appointments in the newly won territory, and this right was extended to the New World shortly thereafter. During the reign of Ferdinand and Isabella's successor, Charles I, the monarchy gained complete control over Church appointments, making Spain more independent of Rome than any other Catholic state.

Royal Administration   Mastery over the towns and the Cortes of Castile proved easy to achieve. Where local rule was concerned, a minor royal official, the *corregidor,* was given new powers and a position of responsibility within the administrative hierarchy. He was usually a hidalgo, and he became the chief executive and judicial officer in his region, rather like the justice of the peace in England; he also supervised town affairs. The Cortes did not seriously restrict the crown because Spanish taxes, like French, could be raised without consent. The Castilian assembly met frequently and even provided additional funds for foreign wars, but it never challenged royal supremacy during this reign.

The justice system the monarchs supervised directly, hearing cases personally once a week. As in most Roman law systems, all law was considered to come from the throne, and the monarchs had full power to overrule the decisions of local courts, often run by nobles. Centralized judicial machinery began to appear, and in a few decades Castilian law was organized into a uniform code—always a landmark in the stabilization of a state. The code remained in effect for centuries and was a tribute to the determination and effectiveness with which the crown had centralized its dominions.

The Increase in Revenues   Considering the anarchy at the start of their reign and the absence of central institutions, Ferdinand and Isabella performed greater wonders in establishing royal power than any of the other new monarchs. Thanks to their takeover of the military orders and their growing bureaucracy, their finances soon improved. After the main administrative reforms were completed in the 1490s, the yield of the sales tax (the *alcabala*), the mainstay of royal income, rose dramatically. Total annual revenue is estimated to have soared from 80,000 ducats in 1474 to 2.3 million by 1504, the year Isabella died.

Religious Zeal   Religious affairs, too, helped the consolidation of royal authority. After the civil wars in Castile ended in 1479, the two monarchs sought to drive the Muslims from southern Castile. The reasons for the aggressive policy were clear: First, it complemented the drive for centralized power; second, war was a traditional interest for ambitious rulers, and it helped keep restless nobles occupied; and finally, the crusade stimulated the country's religious fervor, which in turn promoted enthusiasm for its rulers.

The religious zeal aroused by the fight with the Muslims intensified Spaniards' loyalty toward their rulers, and it is not surprising that the monarchy sought religious uniformity as a means of strengthening political uniformity. Nor did the campaign come to an end when the last Muslim stronghold in the south, Granada, capitulated in 1492. Later that year, all Jews were expelled from Spain. Some 150,000 of the country's most enterprising people—including prominent physicians, government officials, and other leaders of economic and cultural life—were given four months to leave. Targeting a visible and often persecuted minority was a popular move, and it also fed a religious passion that indirectly enhanced the crown's authority.

The Inquisition   The same drive to consolidate their strength had prompted Ferdinand and Isabella to obtain permission from the pope in 1478 to establish their own Inquisition. Since 1483 this body had been run by a royal council and given a mandate to root out those *Conversos* and *Moriscos*—converted Jews and former Muslims—who were suspected of practicing their old beliefs in secret. After the fall of Granada, the Church tried to convert the conquered Muslims, and in 1502 those who had not accepted Christianity were expelled from the country. Eventually, in 1609, the Moriscos too were exiled from Spain. The persecution helped foster a religious unity that only enhanced the political centralization that the monarchy had achieved.

Military and Diplomatic Achievements   The fall of Granada extended Spain's dominion southward, but there were also lands to be captured to the north and east. This venture was Ferdinand's responsibility, because men took command in war, and he focused on foreign affairs during the twelve years he ruled on his own after Isabella's death in 1504. He regained two provinces on the

French border, and then, worried by France's Italian invasion, Ferdinand entered the war in Italy.

His achievements in the next two decades were due to a combination of military and diplomatic skills unusual even among the highly capable rulers of the age. A reorganization of Spain's standing army made it the most effective in Europe, and it soon dominated Italy: By 1504 it had conquered Naples, and Spain had become a major power in the peninsula. Ferdinand also founded the finest diplomatic service of the sixteenth century, centered on five permanent embassies: at Rome, Venice, London, Brussels, and the Habsburg court. The ambassadors' reports and activities made him the best-informed and most effective maneuverer in the international politics of his reign. By the time of his death in 1516, the united Spain that he and Isabella created had gained both territory and authority at home and international power abroad. The successor to the throne inherited a monarchy fully as dynamic and as triumphant over its rivals as those of England and France.

◆ CHARLES V, HOLY ROMAN EMPEROR

To bolster their dynasty, Ferdinand and Isabella had married their children to members of the leading families of Europe. Their daughter Joanna became the wife of the Habsburg Archduke Philip of Austria, and her son Charles became heir to the royal throne of Spain as well as the Habsburg dukedom.

The Revolt of the Communes Early in his reign as King of Spain, however, Charles (1516–1556) had to withstand a major onslaught on the crown's position. Educated in Flanders, he spoke no Castilian, and when he arrived in Spain late in 1517, he soon aroused the resentment of the local nobility, particularly when members of the large Flemish entourage he brought with him were given positions in the government. The young king stayed for two and a half years, during which time he was elected emperor of the Holy Roman Empire (1519). This enhanced his prestige, but it also intensified his subjects' fears that he would become an absentee ruler with little interest in their affairs. The Cortes, in particular, showed open hostility when Charles requested

additional tax funds so that he could leave the country with Spanish troops to pursue his Europe-wide ambitions. As soon as he left in 1520, revolts began to break out in Spain's towns, and the risings of these communes racked the country for two years. The troubles Charles now endured were among the first of many major clashes during the next 150 years between the traditional dynastic aims of the leading European monarchs and the jealous sense of distinctiveness felt by their subjects.

Fortunately for the crown, the communes lacked clear aims; their resentments and hopes were deep but vague. They wanted to reverse the growth of royal power and restore their traditional autonomy—a grievance central governments were bound to encounter as they extended their authority. To this end, the communes asked for the removal of Flemish royal officials and a reduction in taxation, and at first they had the strong sympathy of the Spanish nobles, who particularly disliked the foreign ruler. But the movement soon revealed other aims, with social overtones: The communes launched attacks on the privileged orders of society, especially the nobility, and this lost the revolt its only chance for success. For the nobles then turned against the communes and defeated them in battle even before Charles returned to Spain.

Imperial Ambitions The king took warning from the uprisings and made sure that his administration was now kept entirely Spanish. As calm returned, his subjects could channel their energies into imperial missions overseas, where the conquest of Mexico was under way, and against the Ottoman Turks in the Mediterranean. The large empire the Spaniards established in Central and South America was the most notable extension of royal power during Charles's reign. Closer to home, however, there was little that gave him or his Spanish subjects cause for pleasure. As Holy Roman Emperor, Charles was the official ruler of almost all of continental Europe west of Poland and the Balkans, with the major exception of France; and although his real power in the Empire was limited, he was almost ceaselessly at war defending his territories. In the Spaniards' view, most of the wars helped Charles's ambitions as emperor and were thus irrelevant to Spain. As far as they were concerned, aside from the widening acquisitions in the New World, Charles did little to further the expansion started by Ferdinand and Isabella.

Royal Government The recurrent crises and wars kept Charles away from Spain for more than two-thirds of his forty-year reign. He relied, during these absences, on a highly talented administrator, Francisco de los Cobos, who shaped and clarified the government's policies. De los Cobos confirmed the supremacy of the crown by enlarging the bureaucracy and elaborating a system of councils that Ferdinand and Isabella had begun. In the 1520s this structure, which was to survive for centuries, received its final form. There were two types of council, one for each department of government—finance, war, the Inquisition, and so on—the other for each territory the crown ruled: Aragon, Castile, Italy, the Indies, and (later in the

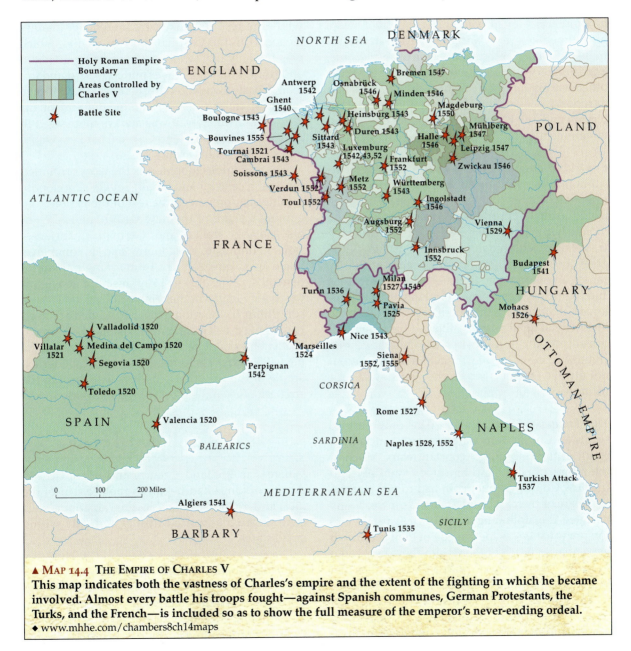

▲ MAP 14.4 THE EMPIRE OF CHARLES V
This map indicates both the vastness of Charles's empire and the extent of the fighting in which he became involved. Almost every battle his troops fought—against Spanish communes, German Protestants, the Turks, and the French—is included so as to show the full measure of the emperor's never-ending ordeal.
◆ www.mhhe.com/chambers8ch14maps

century) the Low Countries. At the head of this system was the Council of State, the principal advisory group, consisting of leading officials from the lower councils. All councils reported to the king or to his chief ministers, but since they all controlled their own bureaucracies, they were perfectly capable of running the empire in the monarch's absence.

What emerged was a vast federation, with Castile at its heart but with the parts, though directed from the center, allowed considerable autonomy. A viceroy in every major area (there were nine altogether, from Naples to Peru) ran the administration under the supervision of an *audiencia,* a territorial council, and while on the whole these officials were left to do as they wished, they had to report to Castile in minute detail at regular intervals and refer major decisions to the central government.

Control through the Bureaucracy   Although corruption was widespread and communications slow (it took over eight months to send a message from Castile to Peru), the centralization gave the monarch considerable power. The bureaucracy was staffed with hidalgos and townsmen, while great nobles—gaining prestige and authority through government service—held viceroyalties and high army posts. Some local initiative was allowed, if allied with the nobility, but basically the hierarchy of loyal servants allowed the crown full control. As a result, Spain's administrative machine was one of the most remarkably detailed (if not always efficient) structures ever devised for ruling so vast an empire.

The Financial Toll of War   The only serious strain on Charles's monarchy was financial, the result of the Habsburgs' constant wars. Much of the money for the fighting came from Italy and the Low Countries, but Spain had to pay a growing share of the costs, and Spaniards increasingly resented the siphoning away of their funds into foreign wars. It was the tragedy of their century of glory that so much of the wealth they discovered in South America was exported for hostilities that brought them little benefit.

The burden was by no means equally distributed. The more independent Cortes of Aragon was able to prevent substantial increases in taxation, which meant that Castile had to assume the brunt of the payments. To some extent this was balanced by a monopoly of trade with the New World that was granted to the inhabitants of Castile, but in the next century the basic inequality among different Spanish regions would lead to civil war.

New World Trade   Charles's finances were saved from disaster only by the influx of treasure—mainly silver—from America. Approximately 40 percent of the bullion went into the royal coffers, while the rest was taken by merchants (mainly Genoese) in the Castilian port of Seville, which was the only city where ships carrying goods to and from America were permitted to load and unload. Charles was receiving some 800,000 ducats' worth of treasure each year by the end of his reign. Unfortunately, it was always mortgaged in advance to the Italian and German bankers whose loans sustained his armies.

The difficulties mounted as the wars continued for over a century and a half. Seville's monopoly on shipping prevented the rest of the nation from gaining a share of the new wealth, and foreigners—notably Italian and German financiers—came to dominate its economy and its commerce. Spain was squeezed dry by the king's financial demands, yet he only just kept his head above water. In 1557, early in the reign of Charles's successor, Philip II, the monarchy had to declare itself bankrupt, a self-defeating evasion of its mammoth debts that it had to repeat seven times in the next 125 years. There has never been a better example of the way that ceaseless war can sap the strength of even the most formidable nation.

IV. The Splintered States

Whereas in England, France, and Spain the authority of kings had begun to replace that of the local lord, to the east of these three kingdoms such centralization advanced fitfully and only within small states.

The Holy Roman Empire   In the largest of these territories, the Holy Roman Empire, weak institutions prevented the emergence of a strong central government. Members of the leading family of Central Europe, the Habsburgs, had been elected to the imperial throne since the thirteenth century, but they lacked the authority and machinery to halt the fragmentation of this large territory; indeed, except for their own personal domain in the southeast of the empire, they ruled most areas and princes in name only. In addition to about two thousand imperial knights, some of whom owned no more than four or five acres, there were fifty ecclesiastical and thirty secular princes, more than one hundred counts, some seventy prelates, and sixty-six cities—all virtually independent politically, though officially subordinate to the emperor.

Local Independence   The princes, whose territories comprised most of the area of the Holy Roman Empire, rarely had any trouble resisting the emperor's claims; their main concern was to in-crease their own power at the expense of their subjects, other princes, and the cities. The cities themselves also refused to remain subordinate to a central government. In 1500, fifty of them contained more than two thousand inhabitants—a sizable number for this time—and twenty had over ten thousand. Their wealth was substantial because many were situated along a densely traveled trade artery, the Rhine River, and many were also political powers. But their fierce independence meant that the emperor could rarely tap their wealth or the services of their inhabitants. The only central institution alongside the emperor was the Diet, which consisted of three assemblies: representatives of the cities, the princes, and the seven electors who elected each new emperor.

▼ *Hartmann Schedel*
The Nuremberg Chronicle, **1493**
This lavishly illustrated book, a history of the world since the creation, is one of the earliest masterpieces of the printer's art. It took about four years to produce and contains dozens of elaborate woodcuts, most of which are recognizable views of European cities. This one depicts the proud and independent German city in which the book was printed, Nuremberg, a major center of art and craft work.
Rare Books and Manuscripts Division, New York Public Library, Astor, Lenox and Tilden Foundations

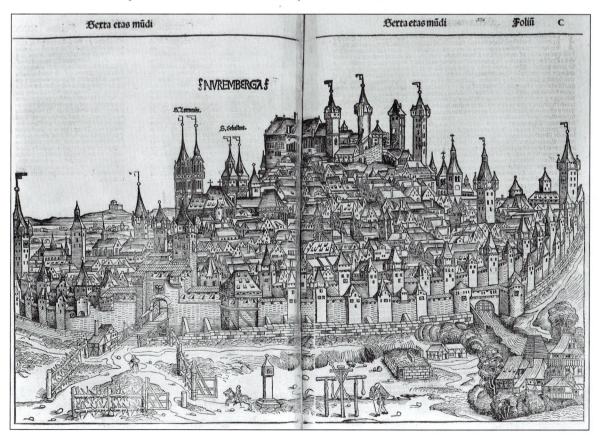

Given this makeup, the Diet became in effect the instrument of the princes; with its legislation they secured their position against the cities and the lesser nobility within their domains.

By the late fifteenth century, most princes had gained considerable control over their own territories. Their success paralleled the achievements of monarchs in England, France, and Spain except that the units were much smaller. Although the Habsburgs tried to develop strong central authority, they exercised significant control only over their personal domain, which in 1500 consisted of Austria, the Low Countries, and Franche-Comté.

Attempts at Centralization   Nevertheless, the need for effective central institutions was recognized, especially in the west and southwest of the Empire. In 1495 the emperor created a tribunal to settle disputes among local powers. Controlled and financed by the princes, the chief beneficiaries of its work, it made considerable headway toward ending the lawlessness that had marked the fifteenth century—an achievement similar to the restoration of order in France, Spain, and England at the same time. The tribunal's use of Roman law had a wide influence on legislation and justice throughout the empire, but again only to the advantage of the princes, who interpreted its endorsement of a leader's authority as referring only to themselves.

Other attempts at administrative reform had little effect, as ecclesiastical and secular princes tightened their hold on the many individual territories within the empire. The religious dissensions of the Reformation worsened the rivalries, dividing the princes and making Charles V no more than the leader of one party, incapable of asserting his authority over his opponents. The sheer

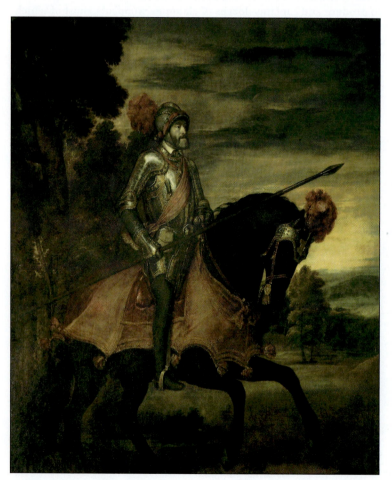

◀ *Titian*
Charles V at the Battle of Mühlberg,
1548
Because a statue of an ancient Roman emperor showed him in this pose, it was thought in the sixteenth century that a ruler appeared at his most magnificent on a horse and in full armor. Remarkable equestrian sculptures appeared in the fifteenth century, but this is the most famous such painting.
Erich Lessing/Art Resource, NY

number of Charles's commitments repeatedly diverted him, but even when he won decisive military victories, he could not break the long tradition of local independence. His dream had been to revive the imperial grandeur of an Augustus or a Charlemagne, and his failure brought to an end the thousand-year ambition to restore in Europe the power of ancient Rome.

Power and Decline in Hungary   In the late fifteenth century, the dominant force in Eastern and Central Europe was the Kingdom of Hungary, ruled by Matthias Corvinus (1458–1490). He was in the mold of the other new monarchs of the day: He restrained the great nobles, expanded and centralized his administration, dramatically increased the yield of taxation, and established a standing army. The king's power grew spectacularly both at home and abroad: He gained Bohemia and German and Austrian lands, and he made Vienna his capital in 1485.

Immediately after Matthias' death, however, royal authority collapsed. To gain Habsburg recognition of his right to the throne, his successor, Ladislas II (1490–1516), gave up the conquests of Austrian and German lands and married his children to Habsburgs. This retreat provided the nobles of Hungary with the excuse to reassert their position. They refused the king essential financial support and forced him to dissolve the standing army. Then, after a major peasant revolt against increasing repression by landowners, the nobles imposed serfdom on all peasants in 1514 at a meeting of the Hungarian Diet, which they controlled. Finally, they became the major beneficiaries of the conquest of Hungary by the Ottoman Empire over the next thirty years. That empire always supported leaders who promised allegiance to Constantinople; declaring loyalty to their new masters, the nobles were able to strengthen their power at the expense of both the old monarchy and the peasantry. By the mid-sixteenth century, a revival of central authority had become impossible.

The Fragmentation of Poland   Royal power in Poland began to decline in the 1490s, when the king was forced to rely on the lesser nobles to help him against the greater nobility. In return, he issued a statute in 1496 that strengthened the lower aristocrats against those below them, the

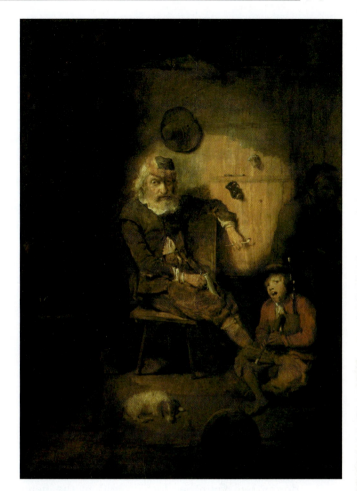

▲ *Christoph Paudiss*
Peasants in a Hut
The sadness in the eyes of these two figures, even in a relaxed moment—the old man smoking a pipe, the boy playing the bagpipes—reflects the hardships of the peasants who were at the lowest level of European society and in Eastern Europe were bound to the land as serfs.
Kunsthistorisches Museum, Vienna

townsmen and the peasants. The latter became virtual serfs, forbidden to buy land and deprived of freedom of movement. Once that was accomplished, the nobles united against the king. In 1505 the national Diet, consisting only of nobles, was made the supreme body of the land, and shortly thereafter it established serfdom officially. Since no law could now be passed without the Diet's consent, the crown's central authority was severely limited.

Royal and noble patronage produced a great cultural flowering around 1500 in Poland, which became an active center of Renaissance humanism and scholarship, most famously represented by the astronomer Nicolaus Copernicus. Yet the monarchy was losing influence steadily, as was apparent from the failure of its attempts to found a standing army. At the end of Sigismund II's reign (1548–1572), his kingdom was the largest in Europe; but his death ended the Jagellon dynasty, which had ruled for centuries. The Diet then made sure that succession to the crown, which had always been elective and controlled by nobles, would depend entirely on their approval—thus confirming the aristocracy's dominance and the ineffectiveness of royal authority.

Aristocracies   The political and social processes at work in Eastern and Central Europe thus contrasted starkly with developments in England, France, and Spain in this period. Nevertheless, although the trend was toward fragmentation in the East, one class, the aristocracy, did share the vigor and organizational ability that in the West was displayed by kings and queens. To that extent, therefore, the sense of renewed vitality in Europe during these years, spurred by economic and demographic growth, was also visible outside the borders of the new monarchies. But where nobles dominated, countries lost ground in the fierce competition of international affairs.

The Ottoman Empire   Only in one state in Eastern Europe was strong central authority maintained in the sixteenth century: the Ottoman Empire. From his capital in Constantinople, the sultan exercised unparalleled powers throughout the eastern Mediterranean and North Africa. He had a crack army of more than twenty-five thousand men, who stood ready to serve him at all times, and within his domains his supremacy was unquestioned. He was both spiritual and temporal head of his empire, completely free to appoint all officers, issue laws, and raise taxes. But these powers, geared to military conquest and extending over enormous territories, never became a focus of cohesion among the disparate races of the Balkans, the Middle East, and North Africa, because the sultan left authority in the hands of local

nobles and princes as long as his ultimate sovereignty was recognized. Whenever questions of loyalty arose (as they did sporadically in the Balkans), they revealed that the authority of the central government rested on its military might. That was more than enough, though, to prevent any serious challenges to the power of the Ottomans until they began to lose ground to the Habsburgs in the eighteenth century.

The first signs of weakening at the center began to appear after the death in 1566 of the sultan whose conquests brought the empire to its largest size, Suleiman the Great. Suleiman had gained control of the Balkans with a victory at Mohacs in 1526, and he had even briefly laid siege to Vienna in 1529. Under his successors, the determined exercise of authority that had marked his rule began to decline; harem intrigues, corruption at court, and the loosening of military discipline became increasingly serious. Yet the Ottomans remained an object of fear and hostility throughout the West—a constant threat to Central Europe from the Balkans and, despite naval setbacks, a formidable force in the eastern Mediterranean.

Republics in Italy   Italy, the cultural and economic leader of Europe, had developed a unique political structure during the Renaissance. In the fifteenth century the five major states—Naples, the Papal States, Milan, Florence, and Venice—established a balance among themselves that was preserved without serious disruption from the 1450s to the 1490s. This long period of peace was broken in 1494, when Milan, abandoning a long tradition of the Italians settling problems among themselves, asked Charles VIII of France to help protect it against Florence and Naples. Thus began the Italian wars, which soon revealed that these relatively small territories were totally incapable of resisting the force that newly assertive monarchies could bring to bear.

Venice and Florence had long been regarded by Europeans as model republics—reincarnations of Classical city-states and centers of freedom governed with the consent of their citizens. In truth, Venice was controlled by a small oligarchy and Florence by the Medici family, but the image of republican virtue was still widely accepted. Indeed, the political stability Venice had maintained for

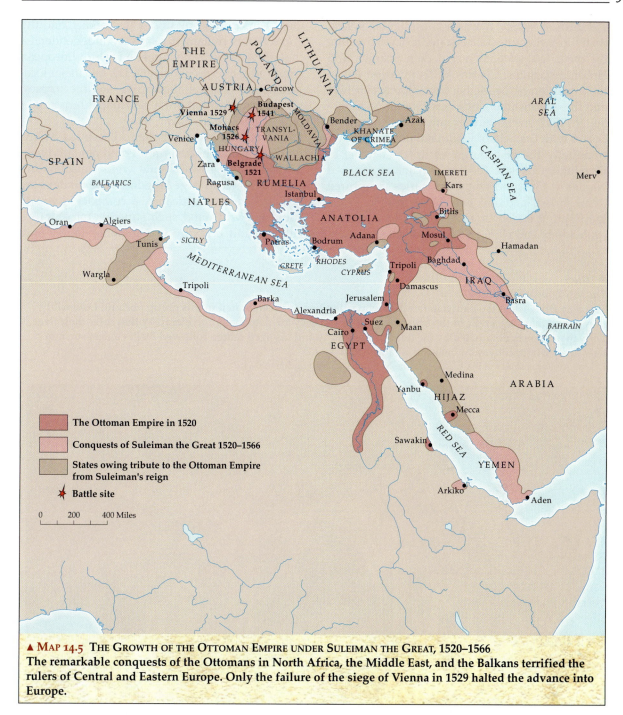

▲ MAP 14.5 THE GROWTH OF THE OTTOMAN EMPIRE UNDER SULEIMAN THE GREAT, 1520–1566
The remarkable conquests of the Ottomans in North Africa, the Middle East, and the Balkans terrified the rulers of Central and Eastern Europe. Only the failure of the siege of Vienna in 1529 halted the advance into Europe.

centuries was the envy of Europe. Tourists came not only to enjoy its many relaxations and entertainments but also to marvel at the institutions that kept the city calm, powerful, and rich. Venice's leaders, elegant patricians who patron-ized some of the most sought-after artists of the sixteenth century, such as Titian, were thought of as the heirs of Roman senators. Throughout Europe, the Italians were regarded as masters not only of politics but also of culture and manners.

The Italian Wars   It was a considerable shock, therefore, when the Italian states crumbled before the onslaught of French and then Spanish and Habsburg armies. Charles VIII's invasion led to the expulsion of the Medici from Florence in 1494 and the establishment of a new Florentine republic. In 1512 the family engineered a return to power with the help of Ferdinand of Aragon, and eventually the Habsburgs set up the Medici as hereditary dukes of Tuscany. Ferdinand annexed Naples in 1504, and Emperor Charles V captured Rome in 1527 and took over Milan in 1535. When the fighting ended in 1559, the Habsburgs controlled Italy and would do so for the next century.

Only Venice, Tuscany under the Medici, and the Papal States remained relatively independent—though Venice was no longer a force in European affairs after a series of defeats. The one major local beneficiary of the Italian wars was the papacy, whose army carved out a new papal territory in central and eastern Italy.

The critical lesson of these disastrous events was that small political units could not survive in an age when governments were consolidating their authority in large kingdoms. No matter how brilliant and sophisticated, a compact city-state could not withstand such superior force. Italy's cultural and economic prominence faded only

▼ *Titian*

THE VENDRAMIN FAMILY, **1547**
The magnificence of the patrician families who ruled Venice is celebrated in this group portrait. Ostensibly, they are worshiping a relic of the true cross, but in fact they are displaying the hierarchy that rules their lives. Only men appear, dominated by the head of the family and his aged father, followed by his eldest son and heir, all of whom convey an image of wealth and power.
Reproduced by courtesy of the Trustees, © The National Gallery, London (NG4452)

slowly, but by the mid-sixteenth century, except for the papacy, the international standing of its states was fading.

V. The New Statecraft

◆

The Italian states of the fifteenth century, in their intense political struggles and competition with one another, developed various new ways of pursuing foreign policy. During the Italian wars, these techniques spread throughout Europe and caused a revolution in diplomacy. Any state hoping to play a prominent role in international affairs worked under a serious disadvantage if it did not conform. And two Italians, Machiavelli and Guicciardini, suggested radically new ways of understanding the nature of politics and diplomacy.

◆ NEW INTERNATIONAL RELATIONS

The Italians' essential innovation was the resident ambassador. Previously, rulers had dispatched ambassadors to other states only for specific missions, such as to arrange an alliance, declare war, or deliver a message; but from the sixteenth century on, important states maintained representatives in every major capital or court at all times. The permanent ambassador could keep the home government informed of the latest local and international developments and could also move without delay to protect his country's interests. The Venetians, in particular, were masters of the new diplomacy. Leading patricians served as ambassadors, and they sent home brilliant political analyses that have remained crucial sources for historians ever since.

The New Diplomacy As states established embassies, procedures and organization became more sophisticated: A primitive system of diplomatic immunities (including freedom from prosecution for ambassadors and their households) evolved, formal protocol developed, and embassy officials were assigned different levels of responsibility and importance. Many advances were still to come, but by 1550 the outlines of the new diplomacy were already visible—yet another reflection of the growing powers and ambitions of central governments.

The dividing line between older arrangements and the new diplomacy was the Italian wars, a Europe-wide crisis that involved rulers as distant as the English King Henry VIII, and the Ottoman Sultan Suleiman the Great. Gradually, all states recognized that it was in everybody's interest not to allow one power to dominate the rest. In later years this prevention of excessive aggression was to be known as the balance of power, but by the mid-sixteenth century the idea was already affecting alliances and peace treaties.

◆ MACHIAVELLI AND GUICCIARDINI

As the Italian wars unfolded, political commentators began to seek theoretical explanations for the new authority and aggressiveness of rulers and the collapse of the Italian city-states. Turning from arguments based on divine will or contractual law, they treated effective government as an end in itself. The first full expression of these views came from the Italians, the pioneers of the methods and attitudes that were revolutionizing politics. When their small states proved unable to resist the superior forces of France and Spain, just as the ancient Greek city-states had succumbed to Macedonia and then to Rome, the Italians naturally wanted to find out why. The most disturbing answer was given by an experienced diplomat, Niccolò Machiavelli, who was exiled when the Medici took control of Florence in 1512. Barred from politics and bitter over the collapse of Italy, he set about analyzing exactly how power is won, exercised, and lost.

Machiavelli The result, *The Prince*, is one of the few radically original books in history. To move from his predecessors to Machiavelli is to see legal and moral thought transformed. Machiavelli swept away conventions as he attempted, in an age of collapsing regimes, to understand how states function and how they affect their subjects. If he came out of any tradition, it was the Renaissance fascination with method that had produced manuals on cooking, dancing, fencing, and manners. But he wrote about method in an area that had never previously been analyzed in this way: power. Machiavelli showed not why power does or should exist, but how it works. In the form of

▲ *Hans Holbein the Younger*
THE AMBASSADORS, **1533**
**Hans Holbein the Younger's *The Ambassadors* shows the worldliness that was expected of diplomats
(many of whom were also soldiers) in the sixteenth century. The two men are surrounded by symbols
of the skills, knowledge, and refinement their job required—geography, mathematics, literature, and
music. But despite this emphasis on material concerns, Holbein reminds us (in the optically distorted
skull across the bottom of the painting) that death and spiritual needs cannot be forgotten.**
Reproduced by courtesy of the Trustees, © The National Gallery, London (NG1314)

advice to a prince and without reference to divine,
legal, or natural justification, the book explains
what a ruler needs to do to win and maintain
complete control over his subjects. Machiavelli
did not deny the force of religion or law; what
concerned him was how they ought to be used in
the tactics of governing—religion for molding
unity and contentment, and devotion to law for

building the ruler's reputation as a fair-minded
person. *The Prince* outlines the methods to be used
to deal with insurrection and the many other
problems that rulers encounter. Fear and respect
are the bases of their authority, and they must exercise care at all times not to relax their control
over potential troublemakers or over their image
among the people.

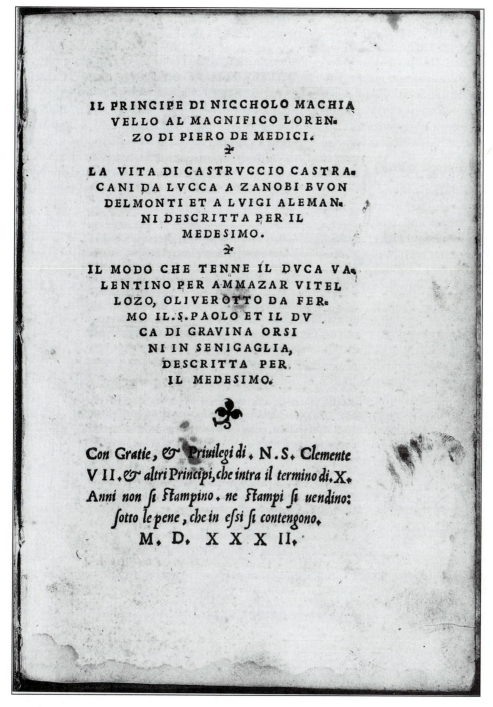

IL PRINCIPE DI NICCHOLO MACHIA
VELLO AL MAGNIFICO LOREN.
ZO DI PIERO DE MEDICI.

LA VITA DI CASTRVCCIO CASTRA.
CANI DA LVCCA A ZANOBI BVON
DELMONTI ET A LVIGI ALEMAN.
NI DESCRITTA PER IL
MEDESIMO.

IL MODO CHE TENNE IL DVCA VA.
LENTINO PER AMMAZAR VITEL
LOZO, OLIVEROTTO DA FER.
MO IL.S.PAOLO ET IL DV
CA DI GRAVINA ORSI
NI IN SENIGAGLIA,
DESCRITTA PER
IL MEDESIMO.

Con Gratie, & Priuilegi di. N.S. Clemente
VII.& altri Principi, che intra il termino di.X.
Anni non si Stampino. ne Stampi si uendino:
sotto le pene, che in essi si contengono.
M. D. XXXII.

▲ Title Page of the First Edition of Niccolo Machiavelli's *The Prince*, 1532
This deceptively simple and elegant title page begins the brief but revolutionary book by which Machiavelli is usually remembered. It remained unpublished for nearly twenty years after it was written (and for five years after its author's death), probably because of concern over the stir it would cause. And indeed, within twenty-five years of appearing in print, *The Prince* was deemed sufficiently ungodly to be added to the index of books that Catholics were forbidden to read.

Few contemporaries of Machiavelli dared openly to accept so harsh a view of politics, but he did not hesitate to expand his analysis in his other masterpiece, the *Discourses*. This book developed a cyclical theory of every government moving inexorably from tyranny to democracy and back again. His conclusion, drawn mainly from a study of Roman history, is that healthy government can be preserved only by the active participation of all citizens in the life of the state. And the state in turn, he suggested, is the force that keeps people civilized. As he put it in the *Discourses*, "Men act rightly only when compelled. The law makes men good." But there were better and worse states. Machiavelli took the Roman Republic as his ideal, and it was this model, together with his Italian patriotism (not his cynicism), that largely accounted for his long-lasting influence on European political thought.

Guicciardini The *History of Italy*, written in the 1530s by another Florentine, Francesco Guicciardini, was the first major work of history to rely heavily on original documents rather than secondhand accounts. If the conclusions he reached seem dauntingly cynical—he attributed even less to underlying historical forces than did Machiavelli, and like Thucydides, he argued dispassionately that fate determines everything—the reasons for his pessimism are not far to seek. The actions of rulers during his generation left little room for optimism; for shrewd observers like Machiavelli and Guicciardini, it must have been hard to avoid pessimism about public events.

Summary

It was appropriate that the political theorists of the sixteenth century should have emphasized the obsession with power that dominated the age in which they lived. The relentless pragmatism and ambition of kings and princes as they extended their authority both at home and abroad reshaped institutions and governments throughout Europe. Given the assertiveness of these rulers and the rising fanaticism generated by religious dispute, it is not surprising that there should have begun in the mid-sixteenth century a series of wars of a ferocity and destructiveness that Europe had never before seen.

Questions for Further Thought

1. Is there some reason that major economic changes and major political changes always seem to go hand in hand?

2. Is it inevitable that rapid economic advance will have both favorable and unfavorable effects on ordinary people?

RECOMMENDED READING

◆

Sources

*Guicciardini, Francesco. *The History of Italy and Other Selected Writings.* Cecil Grayson (tr.). 1964.

*Machiavelli, Niccolò. *The Prince and the Discourses.* Luigi Ricci (tr.). 1950.

*Parry, J. H. (ed.). *The European Reconnaissance: Selected Documents.* 1968.

Studies

*Bonney, Richard. *The European Dynastic States, 1494–1660.* 1991. An excellent overview.

*Crosby, Alfred W. *The Columbian Exchange: Biological and Cultural Consequences of 1492.* 1972. A fascinating study of plants, diseases, and other exchanges between the Old World and the New World.

Dewald, Jonathan. *The European Nobility, 1400–1800.* 1996.

*Elliott, J. H. *The Old World and the New, 1492–1650.* 1970. A survey of the impact on Europe of the overseas discoveries.

*Jeannin, Pierre. *Merchants of the Sixteenth Century.* Paul Fittingoff (tr.). 1972. A lucid introduction to sixteenth-century economic life.

*Mattingly, Garrett. *Renaissance Diplomacy.* 1971. An elegant account of the changes that began in international relations during the fifteenth century.

*Rady, Martin. *The Emperor Charles V.* 1988. An excellent overview, with illustrative documents, of the reign of the most powerful ruler in Europe.

*Rice, Eugene F., Jr. *The Foundations of Early Modern Europe, 1460–1559.* 1970. One of the best short surveys of the period, with three pages of suggested readings.

Scammell, G. V. *The First Imperial Age: European Overseas Expansion c. 1400–1715.* 1989. The best recent survey.

*Skinner, Quentin. *Machiavelli..* 1981. An excellent brief introduction to the man and his thought.

Wilford, John Noble. *The Mysterious History of Columbus: An Exploration of the Man, the Myth, the Legacy.* 1991. A judicious account, both of Columbus' career and of the ways it has been interpreted.

*Wrigley, E. A. *Population and History.* 1969. An introduction to the methods and findings of historical demography by one of the pioneers of the field.

*Available in paperback.

▲ *Francois Dubois*
THE MASSACRE OF ST. BARTHOLOMEW'S DAY
Although it makes no attempt to depict the massacre realistically, this painting by a Protestant does convey the horrors of religious war. As the victims are hanged, disemboweled, decapitated, tossed from windows, bludgeoned, shot, or drowned, their bodies and homes are looted. Dubois may have intended the figure dressed in widow's black and pointing at a pile of corpses near the river at the back to be a portrait of Catherine de Medici, who many thought inspired the massacre.
Musée Cantonal Des Beaux-Arts, Lausanne

WAR AND CRISIS

In the wake of the rapid and bewildering changes of the early sixteenth century—the Reformation, the rises in population and prices, the overseas discoveries, and the dislocations caused by the activities of the new monarchs—Europe entered a period of fierce upheaval. So many radical alterations were taking place that conflict became inevitable. There were revolts against monarchs, often led by nobles who saw their power dwindling. The poor launched hopeless rebellions against their social superiors. And the two religious camps struggled relentlessly to destroy each other. From Scotland to Russia, the century following the Reformation, from about 1560 to 1660, was dominated by warfare; and the constant military activity had widespread effects on politics, economics, society, and thought. The fighting, in fact, helped bring to an end the long process whereby Europe came to terms with the revolutions that had begun about 1500. As we will see, two distinct periods of ever more destructive warfare—the age of Philip II from the 1550s to the 1590s, and the age of the Thirty Years' War from the 1610s to the 1640s, with a decade of uneasy peace in between—led to a vast crisis of authority throughout Europe in the mid-1600s. From the struggles of that crisis there emerged fundamental economic, political, social, and religious changes, as troubled Europeans at last found ways to accept their altered circumstances.

CHAPTER 15. WAR AND CRISIS							
	Social Structure	Body Politic	Changes in the Organization of Production and in the Impact of Technology	Evolution of Family and Changing Gender Roles	War	Religion	Cultural Expression
I. RIVALRY AND WAR IN THE AGE OF PHILIP II							
II. FROM UNBOUNDED WAR TO INTERNATIONAL CRISIS							
III. THE MILITARY REVOLUTION							
IV. REVOLUTION IN ENGLAND							
V. REVOLTS IN FRANCE AND SPAIN							
VI. POLITICAL CHANGE IN AN AGE OF CRISIS							

I. Rivalry and War in the Age of Philip II

◆

The wars that plagued Europe from the 1560s to the 1650s involved many issues, but religion was the burning motivation, the one that inspired fanatical devotion and the most vicious hatred. A deep conviction that heresy was dangerous to society and hateful to God made Protestants and Catholics treat one another brutally. Even the dead were not spared: Corpses were sometimes mutilated to emphasize how dreadful their sins had been. These emotions, which began to dominate politics in this period, whose first decades were dominated by Philip II, gave the fighting a brutality unprecedented in European history.

◆ PHILIP II OF SPAIN

During the second half of the sixteenth century, international warfare was ignited by the leader of the Catholics, Philip II of Spain (r. 1556–1598), the most powerful monarch in Europe. A stern defender of the Catholic faith, who is looked back on by Spaniards as a model of prudence, self-discipline, and devotion, he was also a tireless administrator, building up and supervising a vast and complex bureaucracy. It was needed, he felt, because of the far-spreading territories he ruled: the Iberian Peninsula, much of Italy, the Netherlands, and a huge overseas empire. Yet his main concern was to overcome the two enemies of his church, the Muslims and the Protestants.

Against the Muslims in the Mediterranean area, Philip's campaigns seemed to justify the financial strains they caused. In particular, his naval victory over the Ottomans at Lepanto, off the Greek coast, in 1571 made him a Christian hero at the same time that it reduced Muslim power. Although the Ottomans remained a considerable force in the eastern half of the Mediterranean, Philip was unchallenged in the western half. He dominated the rich Italian peninsula; in 1580 he inherited the kingdom of Portugal; and his overseas wealth, passing through Seville, made this the fastest-growing city in Europe. The sixteenth century was the last age in which the Mediterranean was the heart of the European economy, but its prosperity was still the chief pillar of Philip's power.

▲ *El Greco*
THE DREAM OF PHILIP II, **1578**
Characteristic of the mystical vision of El Greco is this portrayal of the devout, black-clad figure of Philip II. Kneeling alongside the doge of Venice and the pope, his allies in the victory of Lepanto over the Turks, Philip adores the blazing name of Jesus that is surrounded by angels in heaven, and he turns his back on the gaping mouth to hell.
Reproduced by courtesy of the Trustees, © The National Gallery, London (NG6260)

Further north, Philip fared less well. He tried to prevent a Protestant, Henry IV, from inheriting the French crown and continued to back the losing side in France's civil wars even though Henry converted to Catholicism. Philip's policy toward England and the Netherlands was similarly ineffective. After the Protestant Queen Elizabeth I came to the English throne in 1558, Philip remained uneasily cordial toward her for about ten years. But relations deteriorated as England's sailors and explorers threatened Philip's wealthy New World possessions. Worse, in 1585 Elizabeth began to help the Protestant Dutch, who were rebelling against Spanish rule. Though their countries were smaller than Spain, the English and Dutch were able to inflict on Philip the two chief setbacks of his reign; and in the years after his death they were to wrest the leadership of Europe's economy away from the Mediterranean.

◆ ELIZABETH I OF ENGLAND

In a struggle with Spain, England may have seemed an unlikely victor: a relatively poor kingdom that had lost its continental possessions and for some time had played a secondary role in European affairs. Yet its people were united by such common bonds as the institution of Parliament and a commitment to the international Protestant cause that was carefully promoted by Queen Elizabeth I (r. 1558–1603).

Elizabeth is an appealing figure because she combined shrewd hardheadedness and a sense of the possible with a disarming appearance of frailty. Her qualities were many: her dedication to the task of government; her astute choice of advisers; her civilizing influence at court, where she encouraged elegant manners and the arts; her tolerance of religious dissent as long as it posed no political threat; and her ability to feel the mood of her people, to catch their spirit, to inspire their enthusiasm. Although social, legal, and economic practices usually subordinated women to men in this age, inheritance was respected; thus, a determined woman with a recognized claim to authority could win complete acceptance. Elizabeth was the most widely admired and most successful queen of her time, but she was by no means alone; female rulers also shaped the histories of France,

▲ *William Segar* (attrib.)
PORTRAIT OF ELIZABETH I, **1585**
Elizabeth I was strongly aware of the power of propaganda, and she used it to foster a dazzling public image. Legends about her arose in literature. And in art she had herself portrayed in the most elaborate finery imaginable. Here, she is every inch the queen, with her magnificent dress, the trappings of monarchy, and the symbol of virginity, the ermine.
By Courtesy of The Marquess of Salisbury

Sweden, and the southern Netherlands in the sixteenth and seventeenth centuries.

Royal Policy   Elizabeth could be indecisive, notably where the succession was concerned. Her refusal to marry caused serious uncertainties, and it was only the shrewd planning of her chief minister, Robert Cecil, that enabled the king of Scotland, James Stuart, to succeed her without incident in 1603. Similar dangers arose from her indecisive treatment of England's remaining Catholics. They hoped that Mary Queen of Scots,

a Catholic, would inherit the throne; and since she was next in line, they were not above plotting against Elizabeth's life. Eventually, in 1587, Elizabeth had Mary executed and the plots died away. Despite her reluctance to take firm positions, Elizabeth showed great skill in balancing policy alternatives, and her adroit maneuvering assured her of her ministers' loyalty at all times. She also inspired the devotion of her subjects by traveling throughout England to make public appearances; by brilliant speeches (see "Queen Elizabeth's Armada Speech"); and by shaping her own image, even regulating how she was to be depicted in portraits. She thus retained her subjects' allegiance despite the profound social changes that were eroding traditional patterns of deference and order. England's nobility, for instance, no longer dominated the military and the government; nearly all Elizabeth's ministers were new in national life; and the House of Commons was beginning to exert more political influence within Parliament than the House of Lords. All groups in English society, however, shared a resentment of Spanish power, and Elizabeth cultivated this sentiment astutely as a patriotic and Protestant cause.

◆ THE DUTCH REVOLT

The same cause united the people living in the provinces in the Netherlands that Philip inherited from his father, the Emperor Charles V. Here his single-minded promotion of Catholicism and royal power provoked a fierce reaction that grew into a successful struggle for independence: the first major victory in Western Europe by subjects resisting royal authority.

Causes of Revolt   The original focus of opposition was Philip's reorganization of the ecclesiastical structure so as to gain control over the country's Catholic Church, a change that deprived the aristocracy of important patronage. At the same time, the billeting of troops aroused the resentment of ordinary citizens. In this situation, the local nobles, led by William of Orange, warned of mass disorder, but Philip kept up the pressure: He put the Inquisition to work against the Calvinists, who had begun to appear in the Netherlands, and also summoned the Jesuits to combat the heretics. These moves were disastrous because they further

QUEEN ELIZABETH'S ARMADA SPEECH

Elizabeth's ability to move her subjects was exemplified by the speech she gave to her troops as they awaited the fight with the Spanish Armada. She understood that they might have doubts about a woman leading them in war, but she turned that issue to her own advantage in a stirring cry to battle that enhanced her popularity at the time and her legendary image thereafter.

"My loving People: We have been persuaded by some that are careful of our safety, to take heed how we commit ourselves to armed multitudes, for fear of treachery; but I assure you, I do not desire to live to distrust my faithful and loving people.

"Let tyrants fear; I have always so behaved myself, that, under God, I have placed my chiefest strength and safeguard in the loyal hearts and good will of my subjects, and therefore I am come amongst you, as you see, at this time, not for my recreation . . . but being resolved in the midst and heat of the battle, to live or die amongst you all, to lay down for my God, and for my kingdoms, and for my people, my honour and my blood, even in the dust.

"I know I have the body of a weak and feeble woman; but I have the heart and stomach of a king, and of a king of England too; and think foul scorn that . . . Spain, or any prince of Europe should dare to invade the borders of my realm; to which rather than any dishonour shall grow by me, I myself will take up arms, I myself will be your general, judge, and rewarder of every one of your virtues in the field. . . . By your concord in the camp, and your valour in the field, we shall shortly have a famous victory over those enemies of my God, of my kingdoms, and of my people."

Walter Scott (ed.), *A Collection of Scarce and Valuable Tracts, on the Most Interesting and Entertaining Subjects: But Chiefly Such as Relate to the History and Constitution of These Kingdoms*, vol. 1 (London, 1809), pp. 429–430.

◀ *Anonymous*
ENGRAVING OF THE SPANIARDS IN HAARLEM **This engraving was published to arouse horror at Spanish atrocities during the Dutch revolt. As the caption indicates, after the Spanish troops (on the right) captured the city of Haarlem, there was a great bloodbath (*ein gross bluit batt*). Blessed by priests, the Haarlemites were decapitated or hung, and then tossed in a river so that the city would be cleansed of them. The caption states that even women and children were not spared.** New York Public Library

undermined local autonomy and made the Protestants bitter enemies of the king.

Philip's aggressiveness provoked violence in 1566. Although the Protestants were still a tiny minority, they formed mobs in a number of cities, assaulted Catholics, and sacked churches. In response, Philip tightened the pressure, appointing as governor the ruthless duke of Alba, who used his Spanish troops to suppress opposition. Protestants were hanged in public, rebel groups were hunted down, and two nobles who had been guilty of nothing worse than demanding that Philip change his policy were executed.

Full-Scale Rebellion Organized revolt broke out in 1572, when a small group of Dutch sailors flying the flag of William of Orange seized the fishing village of Brill, on the North Sea. The success of these "sea beggars," as the Spaniards called them, stimulated uprisings in towns throughout the Low Countries. The banner of William of Orange became the symbol of resistance, and under his leadership full-scale rebellion erupted. By 1576, when Philip's troops mutinied and rioted in Antwerp, sixteen of the seventeen provinces in the Netherlands had united behind William. The next year, however, Philip offered a compromise

▼ *Pieter Brueghel the Elder*
THE MASSACRE OF THE INNOCENTS, CA. **1560**
Probably to avoid trouble, Brueghel hid his critique of the Spanish rulers of the Netherlands in this supposed portrayal of a biblical event. It would have been clear to anyone who saw it, however, that this was a scene of Spanish cruelty toward the local inhabitants in the harsh days of winter, as soldiers tear babies from their mothers and kill them.
Erich Lessing/Art Resource, NY

to the Catholic nobles, and the ten southern provinces returned to Spanish rule.

The United Provinces In 1579 the remaining seven provinces formed the independent United Provinces. Despite the assassination of William in 1584, they managed to resist Spain's army for decades, mainly because they could open dikes, flood their country, and thus drive the invaders back. Moreover, Philip was often diverted by other wars and, in any case, never placed total confidence in his commanders. The Calvinists formed the heart of the resistance; though still a minority, they had the most to lose, because they sought freedom for their religion as well as their

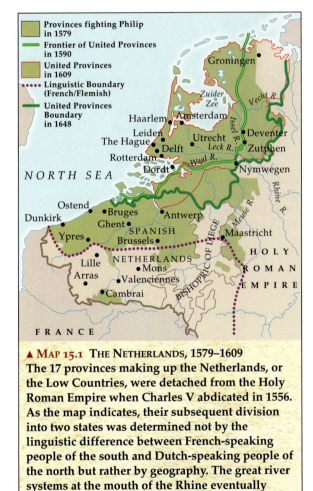

▲ Map 15.1 The Netherlands, 1579–1609
The 17 provinces making up the Netherlands, or the Low Countries, were detached from the Holy Roman Empire when Charles V abdicated in 1556. As the map indicates, their subsequent division into two states was determined not by the linguistic difference between French-speaking people of the south and Dutch-speaking people of the north but rather by geography. The great river systems at the mouth of the Rhine eventually proved to be the barriers beyond which the Spaniards could not penetrate.

country. William never showed strong religious commitments, but his son, Maurice of Nassau, a brilliant military commander who won a series of victories in the 1590s, embraced Calvinism and helped make it the country's official religion. Unable to make any progress, the Spaniards agreed to a twelve-year truce in 1609, but they did not recognize the independence of the United Provinces until the Peace of Westphalia in 1648.

The Armada Sixty years earlier, Philip had tried to end his troubles in northern Europe with one mighty blow. Furious that the English were interfering with his New World empire (their traders and raiders had been intruding into Spain's American colonies for decades) and that Elizabeth was helping Dutch Protestants, he sent a mammoth fleet—the Armada—to the Low Countries in 1588. Its task was to pick up a Spanish army, invade England, and thus undermine Protestant resistance. By this time, however, English mariners were among the best in the world, and their ships had greater maneuverability and firepower than did the Spaniards'. After several skirmishes in the Channel, the English set fire to a few of their own vessels with loaded cannons aboard and sent them drifting toward the Spanish ships, anchored off Calais. The Spaniards had to raise anchor in a hurry, and some of the fleet was lost. The next day the remaining Spanish ships retreated up the North Sea. The only way home was around Ireland; and wind, storms, and the pursuing English ensured that less than half the fleet returned safely to Spain. This shattering reversal was comparable in scale and unexpectedness only to Xerxes' disaster at Salamis more than two thousand years earlier. More than any other single event, it doomed Philip's ambitions in England, the Netherlands, and France and signaled a northward shift in power in Europe.

◆ CIVIL WAR IN FRANCE

The other major power of Western Europe, France, was rent apart by religious war in this period, but it too felt the effects of the Armada's defeat. By the 1550s Calvinism was gaining strength among French peasants and in the towns of the south and southwest, and its leaders had virtually

▲ *Anonymous*
THE ARMADA
This depiction suggests the sheer splendor of the scene as Philip II's fleet sailed through the Channel on its way to invading England. The opposing ships were never this close, but the colorful flags (red cross English, yellow cross Spanish) and the elaborate coats of arms must have been dazzling. The firing cannon and the sinking ship remind us that, amidst the display, there was also death and destruction.
National Maritime Museum, Greenwich, London

The Kings of France in the Sixteenth Century

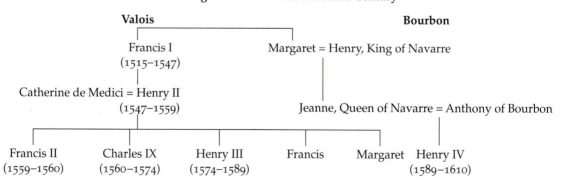

created a small semi-independent state. To meet this threat, a great noble family, the Guises, assumed the leadership of the Catholics; in response, the Bourbons, another noble family, championed the Calvinists, about a twelfth of the population. Their struggle split the country apart.

It was ominous that in 1559—the year that Henry II, France's last strong king for a generation, died—the Calvinists (known in France as Huguenots) organized their first national synod, an indication of impressive strength. During the next thirty years, the throne was occupied by Henry's three ineffectual sons. The power behind the crown was Henry's widow, Catherine de Medici (see "The Kings of France in the Sixteenth Century," p. 520), who tried desperately to preserve royal authority. But she was often helpless because the religious conflict intensified the factional struggle for power between the Guises and the Bourbons, both of whom were closely related to the monarchy and hoped one day to inherit the throne.

The Wars   Fighting started in 1562 and lasted for thirty-six years, interrupted only by short-lived peace agreements. Catherine switched sides whenever one party became too powerful; and she may have approved the notorious massacre of St. Bartholomew's Day—August 24, 1572—which started in Paris, spread through France, and destroyed the Huguenots' leadership. Henry of Navarre, a Bourbon, was the only major figure who escaped. When Catherine switched sides again and made peace with the Huguenots in 1576, the Guises formed the Catholic League, which for several years dominated the eastern half of the country. In 1584 the league allied with Spain's Philip II to attack heresy in France and deny the Bourbon Henry's legal right to inherit the throne.

The defeat of the Armada in 1588 proved to be the turning point in the French civil wars, for Spain could not continue helping the duke of Guise, who was soon assassinated, and within a few months Henry of Navarre inherited the throne as Henry IV (r. 1589–1610). He had few advantages as he began to reassert royal authority, because the Huguenots and Catholics ran almost

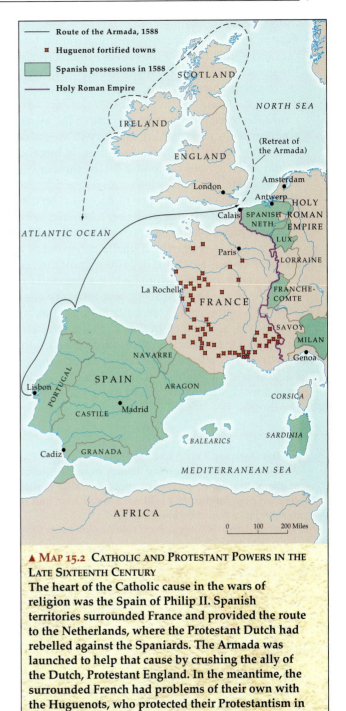

▲ **MAP 15.2   CATHOLIC AND PROTESTANT POWERS IN THE LATE SIXTEENTH CENTURY**
The heart of the Catholic cause in the wars of religion was the Spain of Philip II. Spanish territories surrounded France and provided the route to the Netherlands, where the Protestant Dutch had rebelled against the Spaniards. The Armada was launched to help that cause by crushing the ally of the Dutch, Protestant England. In the meantime, the surrounded French had problems of their own with the Huguenots, who protected their Protestantism in a network of fortified towns.
◆ www.mhhe.com/chambers8ch15maps

independent governments in large sections of France. In addition, the royal administration was in a sorry state because the crown's oldest rivals, the great nobles, could now resist all outside interference in their domains.

Peace Restored   Yet largely because of the assassination of the duke of Guise, Henry IV was able to restore order. The duke had been a forceful leader and a serious contender for the throne. His replacement was a Spanish candidate for the crown who had little chance of success. The distaste for a possible foreign ruler, combined with war weariness, destroyed much of the support for the Catholic League, which finally collapsed as a result of revolts against it in eastern France in the 1590s. These uprisings, founded on a demand for peace, increased in frequency and intensity after Henry IV renounced Protestantism in 1593 in order to win acceptance by his Catholic subjects. The following year Henry had himself officially crowned, and all of France rallied to the king as he beat back a Spanish invasion—Spain's final, rather weak, attempt to put its own candidate on the throne.

When Spain finally withdrew and signed a peace treaty in 1598, the fighting came to an end. To complete the reconciliation, Henry issued (also in 1598) the Edict of Nantes, which granted limited toleration to the Huguenots. Although it did not create complete religious liberty, the edict made Calvinist worship legal, protected the rights of the minority, and opened public office to Huguenots.

II. From Unbounded War to International Crisis

During the half century after Philip II's death, warfare spread throughout Europe. There was a brief lull in the early 1600s, but then the slaughter and the devastations began to multiply. For a while it seemed that nothing could bring the fighting to an end, and a feeling of irresolvable crisis descended on international affairs. Not until an entirely new form of peacemaking was devised, in the 1640s, was the fighting brought under control.

▼ "THE HANGING TREE," ENGRAVING FROM JACQUES CALLOT'S *MISERIES OF WAR,* 1633
An indication of the growing dismay over the brutality of the Thirty Years' War was the collection of sixteen prints produced by the French engraver Callot depicting the life of the soldier and the effects of armies on civilian populations. His soldiers destroy, loot, and rape, and only a few of them receive the punishments they deserve, like this mass hanging.
Anne S. K. Brown Military Collection, Brown University Library

◆ THE THIRTY YEARS' WAR

The new arena in which the warfare erupted was the Holy Roman Empire. Here religious hatreds were especially disruptive because the empire lacked a central authority and unifying institutions. Small-scale fighting broke out repeatedly after the 1550s, always inspired by religion. Although elsewhere the first years of the seventeenth century were a time of relative peace that seemed to signal a decline of conflict over faith, in the empire the stage was being set for the bloodiest of all the wars fired by religion.

Known as the Thirty Years' War, this ferocious struggle began in the Kingdom of Bohemia in 1618 and continued until 1648. The principal battleground, the empire, was ravaged by the fighting, which eventually involved every major ruler in Europe. At first it was a renewed struggle between local Protestants and Catholics, but eventually it became a fight among political rivals who were eager to take advantage of the fragmentation of the empire to advance their own ambitions. As the devastation spread, international relations seemed to be sinking into total chaos; but the chief victims were the Germans, who, like the Italians in the sixteenth century, found themselves at the mercy of well-organized states that used another country as a place to settle their quarrels.

The First Phase, 1618–1621   The immediate problem was typical of the situation in the empire. In 1609 the Habsburg Emperor Rudolf II promised toleration for Protestants in Bohemia, one of his own domains. When his cousin Ferdinand, a pious Catholic, succeeded to the Bohemian throne in 1617, he refused to honor Rudolf's promise, and the Bohemians rebelled in 1618. Since the crown was elective, they declared Ferdinand deposed, replacing him with the leading Calvinist of the empire, Frederick II of the Palatinate. Frederick accepted the crown, an act of defiance whose only possible outcome was war.

The first decade or so of the war was a time of victories for the Catholics, and in particular the Habsburg Emperor. When Ferdinand became emperor (r. 1619–1637), the powerful Catholic Maximilian of Bavaria put an army at his disposal. Within a year, the imperial troops won a stunning victory over the Bohemians. Leading rebels were

▲ **"HEADS OF THE BOHEMIAN REBELS," ENGRAVING FROM MATHAUS MERIAN,** *THEATRUM EUROPAEUM,* **CA. 1630**
Since the scene had not changed when the engraving was made, this illustration is probably a fairly accurate representation of the punishment in 1621 of the leaders of the Bohemian rebellion. Twenty-four rebels were executed, and the heads of twelve of them were displayed on long poles at the top of the tower (still standing today) on the bridge over Prague's river. The heads were kept there for ten years.

executed or exiled, and Ferdinand II confiscated all of Frederick's lands. Maximilian received half as a reward for his army, and the remainder went to the Spaniards, who occupied it as a valuable base for their struggle with the Dutch. In this first round, the Catholic and imperial cause had triumphed.

The Second Phase, 1621–1630   When the truce between the Spaniards and the Dutch expired in 1621, and warfare resumed in Germany as well as in the Netherlands, the Protestants made no progress for ten years. A new imperial army was raised by Albrecht von Wallenstein, a minor Bohemian nobleman and remarkable opportunist who had become one of the richest men in the empire. In 1624 Wallenstein, realizing that the emperor remained weak because he lacked his own army, offered to raise a force if he could billet it and raise its supplies wherever it happened to be stationed. Ferdinand agreed, and by 1627 Wallenstein's army had begun to conquer the northern region of the empire, the last major center of Protestant strength. To emphasize his supremacy, Ferdinand issued the Edict of Restitution in 1629, ordering the restoration to Catholics of all the territories they had lost to Protestants since 1552.

But these Habsburg successes were more apparent than real, because it was only the extreme disorganization of the empire that permitted a mercenary captain like Wallenstein to achieve such immense military power. Once the princes realized the danger he posed to their independence, they united (Catholic as well as Protestant) against the Habsburgs, and in 1630 they forced the dismissal of Wallenstein by threatening to keep Ferdinand's son from the imperial

▼ *Jan Asselyn*
THE BATTLE OF LÜTZEN
Although it is not an accurate rendition of the scene, this painting of Gustavus Adolphus (the horseman in a brown coat with sword raised) shot by a gunman in red does give the flavor of seventeenth-century battle. Because of the chaos, the smoke, and the poor visibility that often obscured what was happening, Gustavus' escort did not notice when Gustavus was in fact hit by a musket shot that shattered his left arm and caused his horse to bolt. Further shots killed him, and not until hours after the battle was his seminaked body found, stripped of its finery.
Herzog Anton Ulrich-Museum, Braunschweig. Museum photo, B. P. Keiser

succession. This concession proved fatal to the emperor's cause, for Sweden and France were preparing to unleash new aggressions against the Habsburgs, and Wallenstein was the one military leader who might have been able to resist the onslaught.

The Third Phase, 1630–1632 The year 1630 marked the beginning of a change in fortune for the Protestants and also a drift toward the purely political aim (of resisting the Habsburgs) that was coming to dominate the war. Although France's king was a Catholic, he was ready to join with Protestants against other Catholics so as to undermine Habsburg power. Early in 1630 the French attacked the duke of Savoy, a Habsburg ally, and occupied his lands. Then, in 1631, they allied with Gustavus Adolphus of Sweden, who, dismayed by Ferdinand's treatment of Protestants and fearing a Habsburg threat to Swedish lands around the Baltic Sea, had invaded the empire in 1630. The following year Gustavus destroyed an imperial army in a decisive battle that turned the tide against the Habsburgs.

Ferdinand hastily recalled Wallenstein, whose troops met the Swedes in battle at Lützen in 1632. Although Gustavus' soldiers won the day, he himself was killed, and his death saved the Habsburg dynasty. Nothing, however, could restore Ferdinand's former position. The emperor was forced by the princes to turn against Wallenstein once more; a few months later Ferdinand had Wallenstein assassinated. The removal of the great general marked the end of an era, because Wallenstein was the last leader for more than two centuries who was capable of establishing unified authority in what is now Germany.

The Fourth Phase, 1632–1648 Gustavus' success opened the final phase of the war, as political ambitions—the quest of the empire's princes for independence and the struggle between the Habsburgs and their enemies—almost completely replaced religious aims. The Protestant princes began to raise new armies, and by 1635 Ferdinand had to make peace with them. In return for their promise of assistance in driving out the Swedes, Ferdinand agreed to suspend the Edict of Restitution and to grant amnesty to all but Frederick of the Palatinate and a few Bohemian rebels. Ferdi-

nand was renouncing most of his ambitions, and it seemed that peace might return at last.

But the French could not let matters rest. In 1635 they finally declared war on Ferdinand. For the next thirteen years, the French and Swedes rained unmitigated disaster on Germany. Peace negotiations began in 1641, but not until 1648 did the combatants agree to lay down arms and sign the treaties of Westphalia. Even thereafter the war between France and Spain, pursued mainly in the Spanish Netherlands, continued for another eleven years; and hostilities around the Baltic among Sweden, Denmark, Poland, and Russia, which had started in 1611, did not end until 1661.

The Effect of War The wars and their effects (such as the diseases spread by armies) killed off more than a third of Germany's population. The conflict caused serious economic dislocation because a number of princes—already in serious financial straits—sharply debased their coinage. Their actions worsened the continentwide trade depression that had begun around 1620 and had brought the great sixteenth-century boom to an end, causing the first drop in prices since 1500. Few contemporaries perceived the connection between war and economic trouble, but nobody could ignore the drain on men and resources, the crisis in international relations, or the widespread destruction caused by the conflict.

◆ THE PEACE OF WESTPHALIA

By the 1630s it was becoming apparent that the fighting was getting out of hand and that it would not be easy to bring the conflicts to an end. There had never been such widespread or devastating warfare, and many diplomats felt that the settlement had to be of far greater scope than any negotiated before. And they were right. When at last the treaties were signed in 1648, after seven years of negotiation in the German province of Westphalia, a landmark in international relations was passed—remarkable not only because it brought an anarchic situation under control but because it created a new system for dealing with wars.

The most important innovation was the gathering at the peace conference of all the participants in the Thirty Years' War, rather than the usual practice of bringing only two or three belligerents together. The presence of ambassadors from Bavaria, Brandenburg, Denmark, France, the Holy Roman Empire, Saxony, Spain, Sweden, Switzerland, and the United Provinces made possible, for the first time in European history, a series of all-embracing treaties that dealt with nearly every major international issue at one stroke. Visible at the meetings was the emergence of a state system. These independent states recognized that they were creating a mechanism for controlling their relations with one another. Although some fighting continued, the Peace of Westphalia in 1648 became the first comprehensive rearrangement of the map of Europe in modern times.

Peace Terms The principal beneficiaries were France and Sweden, the chief aggressors during the last decade of the war. France gained the provinces of Alsace and Lorraine, and Sweden obtained extensive territories in the Holy Roman Empire. The main loser was the House of Habsburg, since both the United Provinces and the Swiss Confederation were recognized as independent states, and the German princes, who agreed not to join an alliance against the emperor, were otherwise given almost complete independence.

The princes' autonomy was formally established in 1657, when they elected as emperor Leopold I, the head of the House of Habsburg, in return for two promises. First, Leopold would

▼ *Gerard Terborch*
The Peace of Westphalia, **1648**
The artist was an eyewitness to this scene, the formal signing of peace between the United Provinces and Spain in Münster on May 15, 1648. The two leaders of the Spanish delegation on the right put their hands on a Bible as they swear to uphold the terms of the treaty, and the Dutch on the left all raise their hands as they declare "So help me God." Terborch himself, dressed in brown, is looking out at the viewer on the far left.
Reproduced by courtesy of the Trustees, © The National Gallery, London (NG896)

▲ **MAP 15.3** TERRITORIAL CHANGES, 1648 – 1661
This map shows the territorial changes that took place after the Thirty Years' War. The treaties of Westphalia (1648) and the Pyrenees (1659) arranged the principal transfers, but the settlements in the Baltic were not confirmed until the treaties of Copenhagen, Oliva (both 1660), and Kardis (1661).
◆ www.mhhe.com/chambers8ch15maps

give no help to his cousins, the rulers of Spain; and second, the empire would be a state of princes, in which each ruler would be free from imperial interference. This freedom permitted the rise of Brandenburg-Prussia and the growth of absolutism—the belief that the political authority of the ruler was unlimited—within the major principalities. Moreover, the Habsburgs' capitulation

prepared the way for their reorientation toward the east along the Danube River—the beginnings of the Austro-Hungarian Empire.

The Effects of Westphalia For more than a century, the settlement reached at Westphalia was regarded as the basis for all international negotiations. Even major new accords, such as the one that ended yet another series of wars in 1713, were seen mainly as adjustments of the decisions of 1648. In practice, of course, multinational conferences were no more effective than brief, limited negotiations in reducing tensions among states. Wars continued to break out, and armies grew in size and skill. But diplomats did believe that international affairs were under better control and that the chaos of the Thirty Years' War had been replaced by something more stable and more clearly defined.

This confidence was reinforced as it became clear after 1648 that armies were trying to improve discipline and avoid the excesses of the previous thirty years. As religious passions waned, combat became less vicious and the treatment of civilians became more orderly. On battlefields, better discipline reduced the casualty rate from one death per three soldiers in the 1630s to one death in seven, or even one in twenty, during the early 1700s. The aims of war also changed significantly.

Changed International Relations   The most obvious differences after the Peace of Westphalia were that France replaced Spain as the continent's dominant power and that northern countries—especially England and the Netherlands, where growth in population and in commerce resumed more quickly than elsewhere—took over Europe's economic leadership. But behind this outward shift a more fundamental transformation was taking place. What had become apparent in the later stages of the Thirty Years' War was that Europe's states were prepared to fight only for economic, territorial, or political advantages. Dynastic aims were still important, but supranational goals like religious causes could no longer determine a state's foreign policy.

The Thirty Years' War was the last major international conflict in Europe in which two religious camps organized their forces as blocs. After 1648 such connections gave way to purely national interests; it is no surprise that the papacy denounced the peace vehemently. For this shift marked the decisive stage of a process that had been under way since the Late Middle Ages: the emergence of the state as the basic unit and object of loyalty in Western civilization. That it had

taken a major crisis, a descent into international anarchy, to bring about so momentous a change is an indication of how profoundly the upheavals of the mid-seventeenth century affected European history. Indeed, the reshaping of the relations among Europe's states for centuries to come that was achieved at Westphalia is but one example of the multiple military and political consequences of this age of crisis.

III. The Military Revolution

The constant warfare of the sixteenth and seventeenth centuries brought about dramatic changes in the ways that battles were fought and armies were organized.

◆ WEAPONS AND TACTICS

The Use of Gunpowder   Since the 1330s, gunpowder had been used occasionally and to little effect. Now it came to occupy a central place in warfare. The result was not only the creation of a new type of industry, cannon and gun manufacture, but also a transformation of tactics. Individual castles could no longer be defended against explosives; even towns had to build heavy and elaborate fortifications if they were to resist the new firepower. Sieges became expensive, complex operations whose purpose was to bring explosives right up to a town wall so that it could be blown up. This process required an intricate system of trenches, because walls were built in star shapes so as to multiply angles of fire and make any approach dangerous. Although they became increasingly costly, sieges remained essential to the strategy of warfare until the eighteenth century.

New Tactics   In open battles, the effects of gunpowder were equally expensive. The new tactics that appeared around 1500, perfected by the Spaniards, relied on massed ranks of infantry, organized in huge squares, that made the traditional cavalry charge obsolete. Interspersed with the gunners were soldiers carrying pikes. They fended off horses or opposing infantry while the men with guns tried to mow the enemy down.

The squares with the best discipline usually won, and for more than a century after the reign of Ferdinand of Aragon, the Spaniards had the best army in Europe. Each square had about three thousand troops, and to maintain enough squares at full strength to fight all of Spain's battles required an army numbering approximately forty thousand. The cost of keeping that many men clothed, fed, and housed, let alone equipped and paid, was enormous. But worse was to come: New tactics emerged in the early seventeenth century that required even more soldiers.

Since nobody could outdo the Spaniards at their own methods, a different approach was developed by their rivals. The first advance was made by Maurice of Nassau, who led the Dutch revolt against Spain from the 1580s. He relied not on sheer weight and power but on flexibility and mobility. Then Sweden's Gustavus Adolphus, one of the geniuses of the history of warfare, found a way to achieve mobility on the field without losing power. His main invention was the salvo: Instead of having his musketeers fire one row at a time, like the Spaniards, he had them all fire at once. What he lost in continuity of shot he gained in a fearsome blast that, if properly timed, could shatter enemy ranks. Huge, slow-moving squares were simply no match for smaller, faster units that riddled them with well-coordinated salvos.

◆ THE ORGANIZATION AND SUPPORT OF ARMIES

These tactical changes brought about steady increases in the size of armies, because the more units there were, the better they could be placed on the battlefield. Although the Spanish army hardly grew between 1560 and 1640, remaining at 40,000 to 60,000 men, the Swedes had 150,000 by 1632; and at the end of the century, Louis XIV considered a force of 400,000 essential to maintain his dominant position in Europe.

This growth had far-reaching consequences. One was the need for conscription, which Gustavus introduced in the late 1620s. At least half his army consisted of his own subjects, who were easier to control than foreign mercenaries. Because it also made sense not to disband such huge forces each autumn, when the campaigning season ended, most armies were kept permanently ready. The need to maintain so many soldiers the year round caused a rapid expansion of supporting administrative personnel. Taxation mushroomed. All levels of society felt the impact, but especially the lower classes, who paid the bulk of the taxes and provided most of the recruits. Rulers made military service as attractive as possible so as to tempt the many who had to struggle to find

▼ *Anonymous Engraving after Jacques de Gheyn*
WAFFENHANDLUNG
The expansion of armies and the professionalization of war in the seventeenth century were reflected in the founding of military academies and in the growing acceptance of the notion that warfare was a science. There was now a market for published manuals, especially if they had illustrations like this one, which shows how a pikeman was supposed to crouch and hold his weapons (stabilizing his pike against his foot) when facing a cavalry charge.
Deutsches Historisches Museum, Berlin, Germany

regular meals, clothing, housing, and wages. Social distinctions were reduced; an able young man could rise high in the officer corps, though the top ranks were still reserved for nobles. Even the lower echelons were given important responsibilities because the new system of small, flexible units gave considerable initiative to the junior officers who led them.

New Ranks   Other changes followed. Maneuverability on the field demanded tighter discipline, which was achieved by introducing drilling and combat training. The order of command was clarified, and many ranks familiar today—major, colonel, and the various levels of general—appeared in the seventeenth century. The distinctions were reinforced by uniforms, which became standard equipment. These developments created a sense of corporate spirit among military officers, an international phenomenon that was to occupy an important place in European society for three centuries.

◆ THE LIFE OF THE SOLDIER

For the average soldier, who was now a common sight in Europe, life in the army began with recruitment. Some genuinely wanted to join up. They had heard stories of adventure, booty, and comradeship, and they were tempted by free food and clothing. But in many cases the "volunteers" did not want to go, for they had also heard of the hardship and danger. Unfortunately for them, recruiting officers had quotas, and villages had to provide the numbers demanded of them. Community pressure, bribery, enlistment of drunken men, and even outright kidnapping helped fill the ranks.

Joining an army did not necessarily mean cutting oneself off from friends or family. Men from a particular area enlisted together, and in some cases, wives and even children came along. There were dozens of jobs to do aside from fighting, because soldiers needed cooks, launderers, peddlers, and other tradespeople to sustain them. On the battlefield, too, menial tasks like carrying gunpowder to the artillerymen could be performed by noncombatants—this particular job was often done by boys. An army in the field often needed five people for every soldier. The large majority of the troops, though, were on their own. For companionship, they looked to camp followers or to the women of the town they were occupying. Few barracks had been built, and therefore, unless they were on the march or out in the open on a battlefield, they were housed (or billeted) with ordinary citizens. Since soldiers almost never received their wages on time—delays could be as long as a year or more—they rarely could pay for their food and housing. Local civilians, therefore, had to supply their needs or risk the thievery that was universal. It was no wonder that the approach of an army was a terrifying event.

Military Justice   Officially, there were severe penalties for misbehavior—imprisonment, flogging, or, for crimes like desertion, execution. Yet discipline, though harsh, was only occasionally enforced, because men were needed for combat and it was easy to slip away from an army. Troops had their own law and courts, but the main goal of their officers was to maintain an effective fighting force. Disputes with civilians rarely ended in a judgment against a soldier. Punishments were uncommon even for corruption at an army's upper levels (for instance, when officers who were paid to raise troops listed phantom recruits and kept their wages).

Discomforts of Military Life   The relatively light legal restrictions did not mean that military life was easy. Soldiers suffered constant discomfort. A garrison might be able to settle into a town in reasonable conditions for a long stretch, but if it was besieged, it became hungry, fearful, and vulnerable. Days spent on the march could be grim, exhausting, and uncertain; even in camps soldiers were often filthy and wet. Real danger was not common, though it was intense during battles and occasionally during sieges. Even a simple wound could be fatal, because medical care was generally appalling. Yet the most persistent discomfort for the soldier was boredom. Sieges dragged, and even the hard labor of digging trenches or moving cannons must have been a relief from the tedious waiting. Despite traditional recreations—drink,

▲ *Sebastian Vrancx*
A MILITARY CAMP
Vrancx was himself a soldier, and the many military scenes he painted during the Thirty Years' War give us a sense of the life of the soldier during the long months when there were no campaigns or battles. Conditions could be grim, but there were many hours during which a soldier could simply nap, chat, or play dice.
Co Elke Wilford, Hamburg/Hamburger/Kunsthalle

gambling, and the brawls common among soldiers—the attractions were limited; most military men had few regrets when they returned to civilian life.

IV. Revolution in England

◆

In the 1640s and 1650s the growing burdens of war and taxation, and the mounting assertiveness of governments, sparked upheavals throughout Europe that were the equivalent in domestic politics of the crisis in international relations. In country after country, people rose up in vain attempts to restore the individual and regional autonomies that were being eroded by powerful central governments. Only in England, however, did the revolt become a revolution—an attempt to overturn the social and political system and create a new structure for society.

◆ PRESSURES FOR CHANGE

The Gentry The central figures in the drama were the gentry, a social group immediately below the nobles at the head of society. They ranged from people considered great in a parish or other small locality to courtiers considered great throughout the land. Although in Elizabeth's

▲ MAP 15.4 AREAS OF FIGHTING, 1618–1660
The endemic fighting of this age of crisis engulfed most of central Europe and involved soldiers from every country.

reign there were never more than sixty nobles, the gentry numbered close to twenty thousand. Most of the gentry were doing well economically, profiting from agricultural holdings and crown offices. A number also became involved in industrial activity, and hundreds invested in new overseas trading and colonial ventures. The gentry's participation in commerce made them unique among the landed classes of Europe, whose members were traditionally contemptuous of business affairs, and it testified to the enterprise and vigor of England's social leaders. Long important in local administration, they flocked to the House of Commons to express their views of public matters (often elbowing aside the traditional nobility in the process). Their ambitions eventually posed a serious threat to the monarchy, especially when linked with the effects of rapid economic change.

Economic Advance   In Elizabeth's reign, thanks to a general boom in trade, England's merchants, aided by leading courtiers, had begun to transform the country's economy. They opened commercial links throughout Europe and parts of Asia and promoted significant industrial development at home. Mining and manufacture developed rapidly, and shipbuilding became a major industry. The production of coal increased fourteen-fold between 1540 and 1680, creating fortunes and an expertise in industrial techniques that took England far ahead of its neighbors.

The economic vigor and growth that ensued gave the classes that benefited most—gentry and merchants—a cohesion and a sense of purpose that made it dangerous to oppose them when they felt their rights infringed. They were coming to see themselves as leaders of the nation, almost alongside the nobility. They wanted respect for their wishes, and they bitterly resented the economic interference and political high-handedness of Elizabeth's successors.

The Puritans   Heightening this unease was the sympathy that many of the gentry felt toward a small but vociferous group of religious reformers, the Puritans. Puritans believed that the Protestant Anglican Church established by Elizabeth was still too close to Roman Catholicism, and they wanted further reductions in ritual and hierarchy. Elizabeth refused, and although she tried to avoid a confrontation, in the last years of her reign she had to silence the most outspoken of her critics. As a result, the Puritans became a disgruntled minority. By the 1630s, when the government tried to repress religious dissent more vigorously, many people in England, non-Puritan as well as Puritan, felt that the monarchy was leading the country astray and was ignoring the wishes of its subjects. Leading parliamentarians in particular soon came to believe that major changes were needed to restore good government in England.

◆ PARLIAMENT AND THE LAW

The place where the gentry made their views known was Parliament, the nation's supreme legislative body. Three-quarters of the House of Commons consisted of gentry. They were better educated than ever before, and nearly half of them had legal training. Since the Commons had to approve all taxation, the gentry had the leverage to pursue their grievances.

The monarchy was still the dominant force in the country when Elizabeth died in 1603, but Parliament's demand to be heard was gathering momentum. Although the queen had been careful with money, in the last twenty years of her reign her resources had been overtaxed by war with Spain and an economic depression. Thus, she bequeathed to her successor, Scotland's James Stuart, a huge debt—£400,000, the equal of a year's royal revenue; his struggle to pay it off gave the Commons the means to seek changes in royal policy.

James I's Difficulties   Trouble began during the reign of James I (r. 1603–1625), who had a far more exalted view of his own powers than Elizabeth and who did not hesitate to tell his subjects that he considered his authority almost unlimited. In response, gentry opposed to royal policies dominated parliamentary proceedings, and they engaged in a running battle with the king. They blocked the union of England with Scotland that James sought. They drew up an "Apology" explaining his mistakes and his ignorance, as a Scotsman, of English traditions. They forced two of his ministers to resign in disgrace. And they wrung repeated concessions from him, including the unprecedented right for Parliament to discuss foreign policy.

Conflict over the Law   The Commons used the law to justify their resistance to royal power. The basic legal system of the country was the common law—justice administered on the basis of precedents and parliamentary statutes and relying on the opinions of juries. This system stood in contrast to Roman law, prevalent on the continent, where royal edicts could make law and decisions were reached by judges without juries. Such practices existed in England only in a few royal courts of law, such as Star Chamber, which, because it was directly under the crown, came to be seen as an instrument of repression.

The common lawyers, whose leaders were also prominent in the Commons, resented the growing business of the royal courts and attacked them in Parliament. Both James and his successor were accused of pressuring judges, particularly after they won a series of famous cases involving a subject's right to criticize the monarch. Thus, the crown could be portrayed as disregarding not only the desires of the people but the law itself. The king still had broad powers, but when he exercised them contrary to Parliament's wishes, his actions seemed to many to be taking on the appearance of tyranny.

◆ RISING ANTAGONISMS

The confrontation between Parliament and king grew worse during the 1620s, especially in the reign of James's son, Charles I (r. 1625–1649). At the Parliament of 1628–1629, the open challenge to the crown reached a climax in the Petition of Right, which has become a landmark in constitutional history. The petition demanded an end to imprisonment without cause shown, to taxation without the consent of Parliament, to martial law in peacetime, and to the billeting of troops among civilians. Charles agreed, in the hope of gaining much-needed subsidies, but then broke his word. To many, this betrayal seemed to threaten Parliament's essential role in government alongside the

king. Seeking to end discussion of these issues in the Commons, Charles ordered Parliament dissolved. With great daring, two members denied the king even this hallowed right by holding the speaker of the House in his chair while they passed a final angry resolution denouncing Charles' actions.

Resentful subjects were clearly on the brink of openly defying their king. Puritans, common lawyers, and disenchanted country gentry had taken over the House of Commons; Charles avoided further trouble only by refusing to call another session of Parliament. This he managed to do for eleven years, all the while increasing the repression of Puritanism and using extraordinary measures (such as reviving crown rights to special taxes that had not been demanded for a long time) to raise revenues that did not require parliamentary consent. But in 1639, the Calvinist Scots took up arms rather than accept the Anglican prayer book, and the parliamentarians had their chance. To pay for an army to fight the Scots, Charles had to turn to Parliament, which demanded that he first redress its grievances. When he resisted, civil war followed.

◆ CIVIL WAR

The Parliament that met in early 1640 did not last long, because Charles refused to change his policies, the Commons refused to grant a subsidy, and the king angrily dissolved the session. But Charles had no way to pay for an army without taxes. By the summer of 1640, the Scots occupied most of northern England, and Charles had to summon a new Parliament. This one sat for thirteen years, earning the appropriate name of the Long Parliament.

In its first year, the House of Commons abolished the royal courts, such as Star Chamber, and made mandatory the writ of habeas corpus (which prevented imprisonment without cause shown); it declared taxation without parliamentary consent illegal; and it ruled that Parliament had to meet at least once every three years. Meanwhile, the Puritans in the Commons prepared to reform the church. Oliver Cromwell, one of their leaders, demanded abolition of the Anglican Book of Common Prayer and strongly attacked the authority and very existence of bishops. The climactic vote came the next year, when the Commons passed a Grand Remonstrance, which outlined for the king all the legislation they had passed and asked that bishops be deprived of votes in the House of Lords.

The Two Sides This demand was the prelude to a more revolutionary Puritan assault on the structure of the Church, but in fact the Grand Remonstrance passed by only eleven votes. A moderate group was detaching itself from the Puritans, and it was to become the nucleus of a royalist party. The nation's chief grievances had been redressed, and there was no longer a uniform desire for change. Still, Charles misjudged the situation and tried to arrest five leaders of the Commons, supposedly for plotting treason with the Scots. But Parliament resisted, and the citizens of London, openly hostile to Charles, sheltered the five. England now began to split in two. By late 1642 both the royalists and the antiroyalists had assembled armies, and the Civil War was under way.

What made so many people overcome their habitual loyalty to the monarchy? We know that the royalists in Parliament were considerably younger than their opponents, which suggests that it was long experience with the Stuarts and nostalgia for Elizabeth that created revolutionaries. Another clear divide was regional. The south and east of England were primarily antiroyalist, while the north and west were mostly royalist. These divisions indicated that the more cosmopolitan areas, closer to the continent and also centers of Puritanism, were largely on Parliament's side. The decision was often a personal matter: A prominent family and its locality chose one side because its rival, a nearby family, had chosen the other. The Puritans were certainly antiroyalist, but they were a minority in the country and influential in the House of Commons only because they were so vociferous and determined. Like all revolutions, this one was animated by a small group of radicals (in this case, Puritans) who alone kept the momentum going.

Independents and Presbyterians As the fighting began, a group among the Puritans known as Independents urged that the Anglican Church be replaced by a congregational system in which each local congregation, free of all central authority, would decide its own form of worship. The most important leader of the Independents in Parliament was Oliver Cromwell. Opposed to them, but also considered Puritans, were the Presbyterians, who wanted to establish a strictly organized Calvinist system, like the one in Scotland in which local congregations were subject to centralized authority, though laypersons did participate in church government. Since both the Scots, whose alliance was vital in the war, and a majority of the Puritans in the Commons were Presbyterians, Cromwell agreed to give way, but only for the moment. The two sides also quarreled over the goals of the war, because the antiroyalists were unsure whether they ought to defeat Charles completely. This dispute crossed religious lines, though the Independents were in general more determined to force Charles into total submission, and eventually they had their way.

As the fighting continued, Cromwell persuaded the Commons to allow him to reorganize the antiroyalist troops. His New Model Army—whipped to fervor by sermons, prayers, and the singing of psalms—became unbeatable. At Naseby in 1645, it won a major victory, and a year later Charles surrendered. The next two years were chaotic. The Presbyterians and Independents quarreled over what to do with the king, and finally civil war resumed. This time the Presbyterians and Scots backed Charles against the Independents. But even with this alliance the royalists were no match for the New Model Army; Cromwell soon defeated his opponents and captured the king.

The King's Fate At the same time, in 1647, the Independents abolished the House of Lords and removed all Presbyterians from the House of Commons. This "Rump" Parliament tried to negotiate with Charles but discovered that he continued to plot a return to power. With Cromwell's approval, the Commons decided that their monarch, untrustworthy and a troublemaker, would have to die. A trial of dubious legality was held, and though many of the participants refused to sign the death warrant, the "holy, anointed" king was executed by his subjects in January 1649, to the horror of all Europe and most of England.

▲ *Anonymous*
ENGRAVING OF *THE EXECUTION OF CHARLES I*
This contemporary Dutch engraving of the execution of Charles I shows the scaffold in front of the Banqueting House in Whitehall—a building that still can be seen in London. On the far right of the scaffold, the executioner displays the severed head for the crowd.
The Granger Collection, New York

◆ ENGLAND UNDER CROMWELL

Oliver Cromwell was now master of England. The republic established after Charles's execution was officially ruled by the Rump Parliament, but a Council of State led by Cromwell controlled policy with the backing of the army. And they had to contend with a ferment of political and social ideas. One group, known as the Levellers, demanded the vote for nearly all adult males and parliamentary elections every other year. The men of property among the Puritans, notably Cromwell himself, were disturbed by the egalitarianism of these proposals and insisted that only men with an "interest" in England—that is, land—should be qualified to vote.

Radical Ideas   Even more radical were the Diggers, a communistic sect that sought to implement

the spirit of primitive Christianity by abolishing personal property; the Society of Friends, which stressed personal inspiration as the source of faith and all action; and the Fifth Monarchists, a messianic group who believed that the "saints"—themselves—should rule because the Day of Judgment was at hand. People of great ability, such as the famous poet John Milton, contributed to the fantastic flood of pamphlets and suggestions for reform that poured forth in these years, and their ideas inspired future revolutionaries. But at the time, they merely put Cromwell on the defensive, forcing him to maintain control at all costs.

Cromwell's Aims   Cromwell himself fought for two overriding causes: religious freedom (except for the Anglican and Catholic churches) and

Oliver Cromwell's Aims

◆

When Parliament in late 1656 offered to make Oliver Cromwell the king of England as a way of restoring political stability, he hesitated before his deepest principles. When he finally came to Parliament with his reply on April 13, 1657, he turned down the offer of a crown and explained in a long speech—from which a passage follows—why he felt it would be wrong to reestablish a monarchy in England.

"I do think you ought to attend to the settling of the peace and liberties of this Nation. Otherwise the Nation will fall in pieces. And in that, so far as I can, I am ready to serve not as a King, but as a Constable. For truly I have, before God, often thought that I could not tell what my business was, save comparing myself to a good Constable set to keep the peace of the parish. And truly this hath been my content and satisfaction in the troubles I have undergone . . . I was a person who, from my first employment, was suddenly lifted up from lesser trusts to greater. . . . The Providence of God hath laid aside this Title of King; and that not by sudden humor, but by issue of

ten or twelve years Civil War, wherein much blood hath been shed. I will not dispute the justice of it when it was done. But God in His severity hath eradicated a whole Family, and thrust them out of the land. And God hath seemed providential not only in striking at the family but at the Name [of king]. It is blotted out. God blasted the very Title. I will not seek to set up that which Providence hath destroyed, and laid in the dust: I would not build Jericho again."

From Thomas Carlyle (ed.), *Oliver Cromwell's Letters and Speeches*, vol. 3 (London, 1908), pp. 230, 231, and 235.

---

constitutional government. But he achieved neither, and he grew increasingly unhappy at the Rump Parliament's refusal to enact reforms. When the assembly tried to prolong its own existence, he dissolved it in 1653 (the final end of the Long Parliament), and during the remaining five years of his life he tried desperately to lay down a new constitutional structure for his government. Cromwell always hoped that Parliament itself would establish the perfect political system for England, but he refused to influence its proceedings. The result was that he ignored the realities of politics and could never put his ideals into practice.

Cromwell was driven by noble aspirations, but in the end he had to rule by military dictatorship. From 1653 on he was called lord protector and ruled through eleven major generals, each responsible for a different district of England and supported by a tax on the estates of royalists. To quell dissent, he banned newspapers; to prevent disorder, he took such measures as enlisting innkeepers as government spies. Cromwell was always a reluctant revolutionary; he hated power and sought only limited ends. Some revolutionaries, like

Lenin, have a good idea of where they would like to be carried by events; others, like Cromwell, move painfully, hesitantly, and uncertainly to the extremes they finally reach. It was because he sought England's benefit so urgently and because he considered the nation too precious to abandon to irreligion or tyranny that Cromwell remained determinedly in command to the end of his life.

The End of the Revolution Gradually, more traditional political forms reappeared. The Parliament of 1656 offered Cromwell the crown, and, though he refused, he took the title of "His Highness" and ensured that the succession would go to his son. Cromwell was monarch in all but name, yet only his presence ensured stability (see box: "Oliver Cromwell's Aims"). After he died, his quiet, retiring son Richard proved no match for the scheming generals of the army, who created political turmoil. To bring an end to the uncertainty, General George Monck, the commander of a well-disciplined force in Scotland, marched south in 1660, assumed control, and invited the son of Charles I, Charles II, to return from exile and restore the monarchy.

Results of the Revolution Only the actions taken during the first months of the Long Parliament—the abolition of royal courts, the prohibition of taxation without parliamentary consent, and the establishment of the writ of habeas corpus—persisted beyond the revolution. Otherwise, everything seemed much the same as before: Bishops and lords were reinstated, religious dissent was again repressed, and Parliament was called and dissolved by the monarch. But the tone and balance of political relations had changed for good.

Henceforth, the gentry could no longer be denied a decisive voice in politics. In essence, this had been their revolution, and they had succeeded. When in the 1680s a king again tried to impose his wishes on the country without reference to Parliament, there was no need for another major upheaval. A quiet, bloodless coup reaffirmed the new role of the gentry and Parliament. The crisis of authority that had arisen from a long period of growing unease and open conflict had been resolved, and the English could settle into a system of rule that with only gradual modification remained in force for some two centuries.

V. Revolts in France and Spain

♦

The fact that political upheaval took place not only in England but in much of Europe in the 1640s and 1650s is the main reason that historians have come to speak of a "general crisis" during this period. Political institutions and political authority were being challenged in many countries, and although only England went through a revolution, the disruptions and conflicts were also significant in the two other major states of the age, France and Spain.

♦ THE FRANCE OF HENRY IV

In the 1590s Henry IV resumed the strengthening of royal power, which had been interrupted by the civil wars that had begun in the 1560s. He mollified the traditional landed aristocracy, known as

▼ *Anonymous*

THE SEINE FROM THE PONT NEUF, CA. 1635

Henry IV of France, celebrated in the equestrian statue overlooking the Seine that stands in Paris to this day, saw the physical reshaping of his capital as part of the effort to restore order after decades of civil war. He laid out the first squares in any European city, and under the shadow of his palace, the Louvre, he built the Pont Neuf (on the right)—the first open bridge (without houses on it) across the Seine.
Giraudon/Art Resource, NY

the nobility of the sword, with places on his Council of Affairs and with large financial settlements. The principal bureaucrats, known as the nobility of the robe, controlled the country's administration, and Henry made sure to turn their interests to his benefit. Because all crown offices had to be bought, he used the system both to raise revenues and to guarantee the loyalty of the bureaucrats. He not only accelerated the sales of offices but also invented a new device, an annual fee known as the *paulette,* which ensured that an officeholder's job would remain in his family when he died. This increased royal profits (by the end of Henry's reign in 1610, receipts from the sales accounted for one-twelfth of crown revenues) and also reduced the flow of newcomers and thus strengthened the commitment of existing officeholders to the crown.

By 1610 Henry had imposed his will throughout France, and he was secure enough to plan an invasion of the Holy Roman Empire. Although he was assassinated before he could join his army, and the invasion was called off, his heritage, especially in economic affairs, long outlived him. France's rich agriculture may have had one unfortunate effect—successful merchants abandoned commerce as soon as they could afford to move to the country and buy a title of nobility (and thus gain exemption from taxes)—but it did ensure a solid basis for the French economy. Indeed, agriculture suffered little during the civil wars, though the violence and the rising taxes did cause uprisings of peasants (the main victims of the tax system) almost every year from the 1590s to the 1670s.

Mercantilism By restoring political stability, Henry ended the worst economic disruptions, but his main legacy was the notion that his increasingly powerful government was responsible for the health of the country's economy. This view was justified by a theory developed mainly in France: mercantilism, which became an essential ingredient of absolutism. Mercantilism was more a set of attitudes than a systematic economic theory. Its basic premise—an erroneous one—was that the world contained a fixed amount of wealth and that each nation could enrich itself only at the expense of others. To some

thinkers, this theory meant hoarding bullion (gold and silver); to others, it required a favorable balance of trade—more exports than imports. All mercantilists, however, agreed that state regulation of economic affairs was necessary for the welfare of a country. Only a strong, centralized government could encourage native industries, control production, set quality standards, allocate resources, establish tariffs, and take other measures to promote prosperity and improve trade. Thus, mercantilism was as much about politics as economics and fit perfectly with Henry's restoration of royal power. In line with their advocacy of activist policies, the mercantilists also approved of war. Even economic advance was linked to warfare in this violent age.

◆ LOUIS XIII

Unrest reappeared when Henry's death left the throne to his nine-year-old son, Louis XIII (r. 1610–1643). The widowed queen, Marie de Medici, served as regent and soon faced revolts by Calvinists and disgruntled nobles. In the face of these troubles, Marie summoned the Estates General in 1614. This was their last meeting for 175 years, until the eve of the French Revolution; and the weakness they displayed, as various groups within the Estates fought one another over plans for political reform, demonstrated that the monarchy was the only institution that could unite the nation. The session revealed the impotence of those who opposed royal policies, and Marie brought criticism to an end by declaring her son to be of age and the regency dissolved. In this absolutist state, further protest could be defined as treason.

Richelieu For a decade, the monarchy lacked energetic direction; but in 1624, one of Marie's favorites, Armand du Plessis de Richelieu, a churchman who rose to be a cardinal through her favor, became chief minister and took control of the government. Over the next eighteen years, this ambitious and determined leader resumed Henry IV's assertion of royal authority (see "Richelieu on Diplomacy").

The monarchy had to manage a number of vested interests as it concentrated its power, and

RICHELIEU ON DIPLOMACY

◆

The following passages are taken from a collection of the writings of Cardinal Richelieu that was put together after his death and published in 1688 under the title Political Testament. *The book is presented as a work of advice to the king and summarizes what Richelieu learned of politics and diplomacy as one of Europe's leading statesmen during the Thirty Years' War.*

"One cannot imagine how many advantages States gain from continued negotiations, if conducted wisely, unless one has experienced it oneself. I admit I did not realize this truth for five or six years after first being employed in the management of policy. But I am now so sure of it that I say boldly that to negotiate everywhere without cease, openly and secretly, even though one makes no immediate gains and future gains seem unlikely, is absolutely necessary for the good of the State. . . . He who negotiates all the time will find at last the right moment to achieve his aims, and even if he does not find it, at least it is true that he can lose nothing, and that through his negotiations he knows what is happening in the world, which is of no small consequence

for the good of the State. . . . Important negotiations must not be interrupted for a moment. . . . One must not be disheartened by an unfortunate turn of events, because sometimes it happens that what is undertaken with good reason is achieved with little good fortune. . . . It is difficult to fight often and always win. . . . It is often because negotiations are so innocent that one can gain great advantages from them without ever faring badly. . . . In matters of State one must find an advantage in everything; that which can be useful must never be neglected."

From Louis Andrè (ed.), *Testament Politique* (Editions Robert Laffont, 1947), pp. 347–348 and 352; translated by T. K. Rabb.

Richelieu's achievement was that he kept them under control. The strongest was the bureaucracy, whose ranks had been swollen by the sale of offices. Richelieu always paid close attention to the views of the bureaucrats, and one reason he had such influence over the king was that he acted as the head and representative of this army of royal servants. He also reduced the independence of traditional nobles by giving them positions in the regime as diplomats, soldiers, and officials without significant administrative responsibility. Finally, he took on the Huguenots in a military campaign. After he defeated them, he abolished most of the guarantees in the Edict of Nantes and ended the Huguenots' political independence.

Royal Administration   Under Richelieu the sale of offices broke all bounds: By 1633 it accounted for approximately one-half of royal revenues. Ten years later more than three-quarters of the crown's direct taxation was needed to pay the salaries of the officeholders. It was a vicious circle, and the only solution was to increase the taxes on

the lower classes. As this financial burden grew, Richelieu had to improve the government's control over the realm to obtain the revenue he needed. He increased the power of the *intendants*, the government's chief agents in the localities, and established them (instead of the nobles) as the principal representatives of the monarchy in each province of France. Unlike the nobles, the *intendants* depended entirely on royal favor for their position; consequently, they enthusiastically recruited for the army, arranged billeting, supervised the raising of taxes, and enforced the king's decrees. They soon came to be hated figures, both because of the rising taxes and because they threatened the power of the nobles. The result was a succession of peasant uprisings, often led by local notables who resented the rise of the *intendants* and of royal power.

◆ POLITICAL AND SOCIAL CRISIS

France's foreign wars made the discontent worse, and it was clear that eventually the opponents of the central government would reassert themselves. But the centralization of power by the crown had been so successful that when trouble erupted, in a series of revolts known as the *Fronde* (or "tempest"), there was no serious effort to reshape the social order or the political system. The principal actors in the Fronde came from the upper levels of society: nobles, townsmen, and members of the regional courts and legislatures known as parlements. Only rarely were these groups joined by peasants, resentful of taxes and other government demands and vulnerable to starvation when harvests failed. For the Fronde never raised issues that linked up with the peasants' uprisings. These focused on issues like food scarcities, which often brought women into prominent roles, especially since soldiers were reluctant to shoot them. But without noble support, such disorders remained fairly low-scale; they never reached the level of disruption that was to overtake France in the Revolution.

Mazarin The death of Louis XIII in 1643, followed by a regency because Louis XIV was only five years old, offered an opportunity to those who wanted to reverse the rise of absolutism. Louis XIII's widow, Anne of Austria, took over the government and placed all the power in the hands of an Italian, Cardinal Giulio Mazarin. He used his position to amass a huge fortune, and he was therefore a perfect target for the anger caused by the encroachment of central government on local authority.

Early in 1648 Mazarin sought to gain a respite from the monarch's perennial financial trouble by withholding payment of the salaries of some royal officials for four years. In response, the members of various institutions in Paris, including the Parlement, drew up a charter of demands. They wanted the office of *intendant* abolished, no new offices created, power to approve taxes, and enactment of a habeas corpus law.

The Fronde Mazarin reacted by arresting the Paris Parlement's leaders, thus sparking a popular rebellion in the city that forced him and the royal family to flee from the capital—an experience the young Louis XIV never forgot. In 1649 Mazarin promised to redress the *parlementaires'* grievances,

and he was allowed to return to Paris. But the trouble was far from over; during that summer, uprisings spread throughout France, particularly among peasants and in the old Huguenot stronghold, the southwest.

The next three years were marked by political chaos, mainly as a result of intrigues and shifting alliances among the nobility. As it became clear that the perpetual unrest was producing no results, Mazarin was able to take advantage of disillusionment among nobles and *parlementaires* to reassert the position of the monarchy. He used military force and threats of force to subdue Paris and most of the rebels in the countryside, and he brought the regency to an end by declaring the fourteen-year-old Louis of age in 1652. Although the nobles were not finally subdued until the following year, and peasants continued their occasional regional uprisings for many years to come, the crown now established its authority as the basis for order in the realm. As surely as England, France had surmounted its crisis and found a stable solution for long-standing conflicts.

◆ SOURCES OF DISCONTENT IN SPAIN

For Spain the crisis that swept much of Europe in the mid-seventeenth century—with revolt in England and France and war in the empire—meant the end of the country's international power. Yet the difficulties the monarchy faced had their roots in the sixteenth century. Philip II had already found it difficult to hold his sprawling empire together despite his elaborate bureaucracy. Obsessively suspicious, he maintained close control over all administrative decisions, and government action was, therefore, agonizingly slow. Moreover, the bureaucracy was run by Castilian nobles, who were resented as outsiders in other regions of the empire. And the standing army, though essential to royal power, was a terrible financial drain.

Philip did gain wide admiration in Spain for his devoutness. He persecuted heresy, and for a while was even suspicious of the great flowering of Spanish mysticism led by St. Teresa. Philip's commitment to religion undoubtedly promoted political cohesion, but the economic strains caused by relentless religious warfare eventually undermined Spanish power.

INQVISITION

▲ *Anonymous*
ENGRAVING OF *THE SPANISH INQUISITION*, 1560
The burning of heretics was a major public event in sixteenth-century Spain. Aimed mainly at people who practiced Judaism or Islam secretly and in a few cases at Protestants, the Inquisition's investigations usually led to imprisonment or lesser punishments. The occasional executions of those who determinedly refused to accept Catholic teachings, even after torture, were carried out by secular authorities, and they attracted huge crowds.
Bibliothèque Nationale de France, Paris

Economic Difficulties Spain was a rich country in Philip's reign, but the most profitable activities were monopolized by limited groups. Because royal policy valued convenience above social benefit, the city of Seville (dominated by foreign bankers) received a monopoly over shipping to and from the New World; other lucrative pursuits, such as wool and wine production, were also controlled by a small coterie of insiders. The only important economic activities that involved large numbers of Spaniards were shipping and the prosperous Mediterranean trade, centered in Barcelona, which brought wealth to much of Catalonia. Thus, the influx of silver into Spain was not profitably invested within the country. Drastically overextended in foreign commitments, Philip had to declare himself bankrupt three times. For a while it seemed that the problems might ease because there was peace during the reign of Philip's son, Philip III (r. 1598–1621). But in fact, Philip III's government was incompetent and corrupt, capable neither of dealing with the serious consequences of the spending on war nor of broadening the country's exports beyond wool and wine. And when the flow of treasure from the New World began to dwindle after 1600, the crown was deprived of a major source of income that it was unable to replace (see table: "Imports

▼ IMPORTS OF TREASURE TO SPAIN FROM THE NEW WORLD, 1591–1660

Decade	Total Value*
1591–1600	85,536,000
1601–1610	66,970,000
1611–1620	65,568,000
1621–1630	62,358,000
1631–1640	40,110,000
1641–1650	30,651,000
1651–1660	12,785,000

*In ducats.

Adapted from J. H. Elliott, *Imperial Spain, 1469–1716* (Edward Arnold, The Hodder Neadling PLC Group, 1964), p. 175.

of Treasure to Spain"). The decline was caused partly by a growing use of precious metals in the New World colonies but also by depletion of the mines.

In the meantime, tax returns at home were shrinking. The most significant cause of this decrease was a series of severe plagues, which reduced the population of Castile and Aragon from 10 million in 1590 to 6 million in 1700. No other country in Europe suffered a demographic reversal of this proportion during the seventeenth century. In addition, sheep farming took over huge tracts of arable land, and Spain had to rely increasingly on imports of expensive foodstuffs to feed its people. When Spain resumed large-scale fighting against the Dutch and French under Philip IV (r. 1621–1665), the burdens became too much to bear. The effort to maintain the commitment to war despite totally inadequate finances was to bring the greatest state in Europe to its knees.

◆ REVOLT AND SECESSION

The final crisis was brought about by the policies of Philip IV's chief minister, the count of Olivares. His aim was to unite the realm so that all the territories shared equally the burden of maintaining Spanish power. Although Castile would no longer dominate the government, it would also not have to provide the bulk of the taxes and army. Olivares' program was called the Union of Arms, and while it seemed eminently reasonable, it caused a series of revolts in the 1640s that split Spain apart.

The reason was that Castile's dominance had made the other provinces feel that local independence was being undermined by a centralized regime. They saw the Union of Arms, imposed by Olivares, as the last straw. Moreover, the plan appeared at a time when Spain's military and economic fortunes were in decline. France had declared war on the Habsburgs in 1635, the funds to support an army were becoming harder to raise, and in desperation Olivares pressed more vigorously for the Union of Arms. But all he accomplished was to provoke revolts against Castile in the 1640s by Catalonia, Portugal, Naples, and Sicily. By 1641 Catalonia and Portugal had declared themselves independent republics and placed themselves under French protection. Plots began to appear against Olivares, and Philip dismissed the one minister who had understood Spain's problems but who, in trying to solve them, had made them worse.

The Revolts The Catalonian rebellion continued for another eleven years, and it was thwarted in the end only because the peasants and town mobs transformed the resistance to the central government into an attack on the privileged and wealthy classes. When this happened, the Catalan nobility abandoned the cause and joined the government side. About the same time, the Fronde forced the withdrawal of French troops from Catalonia. When the last major holdout, Barcelona, fell to a royal army in 1652, the Catalan nobles could regain their rights and powers, and the revolt was over.

The Portuguese had no social upheaval; as a result, though not officially granted independence from Spain until 1668, they defended their autonomy easily and even invaded Castile in the 1640s. But the revolts that the people of Sicily and Naples directed at their Castilian rulers in 1647 took on social overtones. In Naples the unrest developed into a tremendous mob uprising led by a local fisherman. The poor turned against all representatives of government and wealth they could find, and chaos ensued until the leader of the revolt was killed. The violence in Sicily, the result of soaring taxes, was aimed primarily at government officials. But in both Naples and Sicily the government was able to reassert its authority by force within a few months.

Consequences   The effect of this unrest was to end the Spanish government's international ambitions and, thus, the worst of its economic difficulties. Like England and France, Spain found a new way of life after its crisis: It became a stable second-level state, heavily agricultural, run by its nobility.

VI. Political Change in an Age of Crisis

Although the level of violence was highest in England and Spain, almost all of Europe's countries experienced the political upheavals of this era of "general crisis." In some cases—for instance, Sweden—the conflict was minor and did little to disturb the peace of the land. But everywhere the basic issue—Who should hold political authority?—caused some degree of strife. And each state had to find its own solutions to the competing demands of governments and their subjects.

◆ THE UNITED PROVINCES

The Dutch did not escape the struggles against the power of centralized governments that created an atmosphere of crisis in much of Europe during the middle decades of the seventeenth century. Despite the remarkable fluidity of their society, the Dutch, too, became embroiled in a confrontation between a ruling family seeking to extend its authority and citizens defending the autonomy of their local regions. The outcome determined the structure of their government for more than a century.

The United Provinces were unique in a number of ways. Other republics existed in Europe, but they were controlled by small oligarchies; the Dutch, who had a long tradition of a strong repre-

sentative assembly, the Estates General, had created a nation in which many citizens participated in government through elected delegates. Although powerful merchants and a few aristocrats close to the House of Orange did create a small elite, the social differentiation was less than elsewhere in Europe. The resulting openness and homogeneity underlay the economic mastery and cultural brilliance of the United Provinces.

Commerce and Tolerance   The most striking accomplishment of the Dutch was their rise to supremacy in the world of commerce. Amsterdam displaced Antwerp as the continent's financial capital and gained control of the trade of the world's richest markets. In addition, the Dutch rapidly emerged as the cheapest international shippers. As a result, by the middle of the seventeenth century they had become the chief carriers of European commerce.

The openness of Dutch society permitted the freest exchange of ideas of the time. The new state gave refuge to believers of all kinds, whether extreme Protestant radicals or Catholics who wore their faith lightly, and Amsterdam became the center of a brilliant Jewish community. This freedom attracted some of the greatest minds in Europe and fostered remarkable artistic creativity. The energy that produced this outpouring reflected the pride of a tiny nation that was winning its independence from Spain.

Two Political Parties   Yet there was a basic split within the United Provinces. The two most urbanized and commercial provinces, Holland and Zeeland, dominated the Estates General because they supplied a majority of its taxes. Their representatives formed a mercantile party, which advocated peace abroad so that their trade could flourish unhampered, government by the Estates General so that they could make their influence felt, and religious toleration so that their cities could attract enterprising people of all faiths. In opposition to this mercantile interest was the House of Orange: the descendants of William of Orange, who sought to establish their family's leadership of the Dutch. They were supported by the more rural provinces and stood for war be-

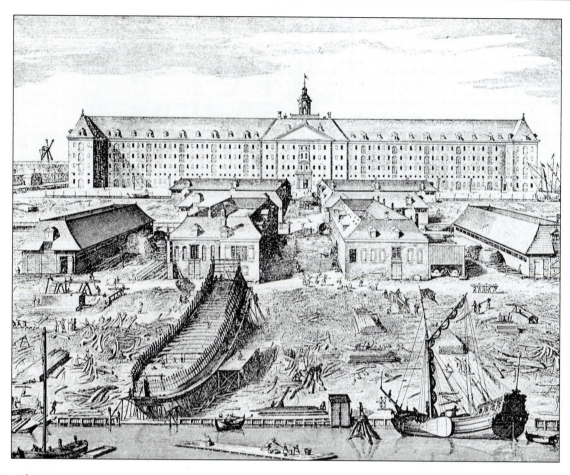

▲ *Anonymous*
ENGRAVING OF *A DUTCH SHIPYARD*
The Dutch became the best shipbuilders in Europe in the seventeenth century; the efficiency of their ships, which could be manned by fewer sailors than those of other countries, was a major reason for their successes in trade and commerce.
The Granger Collection, New York

cause their authority and popularity derived from their command of the army, for centralized power to enhance the position of the family, and for the strict Calvinism that was upheld in the rural provinces.

The differences between the two factions led Maurice of Nassau to use religion as a pretext to execute his chief opponent, Jan van Oldenbarneveldt, the representative of the province of Holland, in 1618. Oldenbarneveldt was against war with Spain, and his removal left the House of Orange in control of the country. Maurice resumed

the war in 1621, and for more than twenty years, his family remained in command, unassailable because it led the army in wartime. Not until 1648—when a new leader, William II, tried to prolong the fighting—did the mercantile party reassert itself by insisting on peace. As a result, the Dutch signed the Treaty of Westphalia, which recognized the independence of the United Provinces. It now seemed that Holland and Zeeland had gained the upper hand. But their struggle with the House of Orange continued (there was even a threat by Orange troops to besiege Amsterdam) until William

II suddenly died in 1650, leaving as his successor a baby son, William III.

Jan De Witt The mercantile interest now assumed full power, and Jan De Witt, the representative of the province of Holland, took over the government in 1653. De Witt's aims were to leave as much authority as possible in the hands of the provinces, particularly Holland; to weaken the executive and prevent a revival of the House of Orange; to pursue trading advantage; and to maintain peace so that the economic supremacy of the Dutch would not be endangered. For nearly twenty years he guided the country in its golden age. But in 1672 French armies overran the southern provinces, and De Witt lacked the military instinct to fight a dangerous enemy. The Dutch at once turned to the family that had led them to independence; a mob murdered De Witt; and the House of Orange, under William III, resumed the centralization that henceforth was to characterize the political structure of the United Provinces. The country had not experienced a midcentury upheaval as severe as those of its neighbors, but it had nevertheless been forced to endure unrest and violence before the form of its government was securely established.

◆ SWEDEN

The Swedes, too, settled their political system in the mid-seventeenth century. In 1600 Sweden, a Lutheran country of a million people, was one of the backwaters of Europe. A feudal nobility dominated the countryside, a barter economy made money almost unknown, and both trade and towns were virtually nonexistent. Moreover, the country lacked a capital, central institutions, and government machinery. The royal administration consisted of the king and a few courtiers; other officials were appointed only to deal with specific problems as they arose.

Gustavus Adolphus (r. 1611–1632) transformed this situation. He won over the nobles by giving them dominant positions in a newly expanded bureaucracy, and he reorganized his army. Thus equipped both to govern and to fight, Gustavus embarked on a remarkable series of conquests abroad. By 1629 he had made Sweden the most

Chronology

AN AGE OF CRISIS, 1618–1660

1618 Revolt in Bohemia, beginning of Thirty Years' War.

1621 Resumption of war between Spanish and Dutch.

1629 Edict of Restitution—high point of Habsburg power.

1630 Sweden enters war against Habsburgs.

1635 France declares war on Habsburgs.

1639 Scots invade England.

1640 Revolts in Catalonia and Portugal against Spanish government.

1642 Civil War in England.

1647 Revolts in Sicily and Naples against Spanish government.

1648 Peace of Westphalia ends Thirty Years' War. Outbreak of Fronde in France. Coup by nobles in Denmark. Revolt of Ukraine against Poland. Riots in Russian cities.

1650 Constitutional crisis in Sweden. Confrontation between William of Orange and Amsterdam in Netherlands.

1652 End of Catalan revolt.

1653 End of Fronde.

1655 War in Baltic region.

1659 Peace of the Pyrenees between France and Spain.

1660 End of English revolution. Treaties end war in Baltic.

powerful state in the Baltic area. He then entered the Thirty Years' War, advancing victoriously through the Holy Roman Empire until his death, in 1632, during the showdown battle with Wallenstein. Without their great general, the Swedes could do little more than hang on to their gains, but they were now a force to be reckoned with in international affairs.

Government and Economy The highly efficient system of government established by Gustavus and his chief adviser, Axel Oxenstierna, was to be the envy of other countries until the twentieth century. At the heart of the system were five administrative departments, each led by a nobleman, with the most important—the Chancellery, for diplomacy and internal affairs—run by Oxenstierna. An administrative center emerged in Stockholm, and the new bureaucracy proved that it could run the nation, supply the army, and implement policy even during the last twelve years of Gustavus' reign, when the king himself was almost always abroad.

A major cause of Sweden's amazing rise was the development of the domestic economy, stimulated by the opening up of copper mines and the development of a major iron industry. The country's traditional tar and timber exports were also stepped up, and a fleet was built. By 1700 Stockholm had become an important trading and financial center, growing in the course of the century from fewer than five thousand to more than fifty thousand inhabitants.

The Nobles   The one source of tension amidst this remarkable progress was the position of the nobles. After Gustavus died, they openly challenged the monarchy for control of government and society. Between 1611 and 1652 they more than doubled the proportion of land they owned in Sweden, and much of this growth was at the expense of the crown, which granted away or sold lands to help the war effort abroad. Both peasants and townspeople viewed these developments with alarm, because the nobility usually pursued its own rather than public interests. The concern intensified when, in 1648, the nobles in neighboring Denmark took advantage of the death of a strong king to gain control of their government. Two years later the showdown came in Sweden.

Political Confrontation   The monarch now was Gustavus' daughter Christina, an able but erratic young queen who usually allowed Oxenstierna to run the government. For some time, she had hoped to abdicate her throne, become a Catholic, and leave Sweden—an ambition she fulfilled in 1654. She wanted her cousin Charles recognized

as her successor, but the nobles threatened to create a republic if she abdicated. The queen, therefore, summoned the Riksdag, Sweden's usually weak representative assembly, in 1650; she encouraged the townspeople and peasants to raise their grievances and allowed them to attack the aristocracy. Soon these groups were demanding the return of nobles' lands to the crown, freedom of speech, and real power; under this pressure, the nobility gave way and recognized Charles X as successor to the throne.

The political upheaval of 1650 was short-lived. Once Christina had her way, she turned against the Riksdag and rejected the lower estates' demands. Only gradually did power shift away from the great nobles toward a broader elite of lesser nobles and bureaucrats, but the turning point in Sweden, as elsewhere, was during the crisis years of the mid-seventeenth century.

◆ EASTERN EUROPE AND THE CRISIS

In Eastern Europe, too, long-term patterns became clear in this period. The limits of Ottoman rule were reconfirmed when an attack on Vienna failed in 1683. Although the Ottomans' control of the Balkans did not immediately waver, their government was increasingly beset by internal problems, and their retreat from Hungary was under way by 1700. Further north, Poland's weak central government lost all claim to real authority in 1648 when it proved unable to stop a group of nobles in the rich province of the Ukraine from switching allegiance from the king of Poland to the tsar in Moscow. And in Russia, following a period of disorder known as the Time of Troubles (1584–1613), the new Romanov dynasty began consolidating its power. The nobility was won over, the last possibilities for escaping serfdom were closed, the legal system was codified, the church came under the tsar's control, and the revolts that erupted against these changes between 1648 and 1672 were brutally suppressed. As elsewhere in Europe, long-standing conflicts between centralizing regimes and their opponents were resolved, and a new political system, supported by the government's military power, was established for centuries to come.

Summary

◆

Because these struggles were so widespread, historians have called the midcentury period an age of "general crisis." In country after country, people tried to resist the growing ambitions of central governments. These confrontations reached crisis proportions in almost all cases during the 1640s and 1650s and then subsided at the very time that the anarchy of warfare and international relations was resolved by the Peace of Westphalia. As a result, the sense of settlement after 1660 contrasted sharply with the turmoil of the preceding decades. Moreover, the progression in politics from turbulence to calm had its analogs in the cultural and social developments of the sixteenth and seventeenth centuries.

Questions for Further Thought

◆

1. **Are the social benefits of warfare so minimal, compared to its destructive effects, that one can dismiss them as unimportant?**

2. **Why are there differences in the ways warfare changes domestic politics?**

Recommended Reading

◆

Sources

Bodin, Jean. *On Sovereignty*. Julian H. Franklin (ed. and tr.). 1992. An abridgment of Bodin's *Six Books of the Republic*.

Kossmann, E. H., and A. E. Mellink. *Texts Concerning the Revolt of the Netherlands*. 1974. A collection of Spanish and Dutch documents that reveal the different political and religious goals of the two sides.

Studies

*Aston, Trevor (ed.). *Crisis in Europe, 1560–1660: Essays from Past and Present*. 1965. This is a collection of the essays in which the "general crisis" interpretation was initially put forward and discussed.

Braudel, Fernand. *The Mediterranean and the Mediterranean World in the Age of Philip II*. S. Reynolds (tr.). 2 vols. 1972 and 1973. A pioneering and far-ranging work of social history.

*Duplessis, Robert R. *Transitions to Capitalism in Early Modern Europe*. 1997.

*Elliott, J. H. *Richelieu and Olivares*. 1984. A comparative study of the two statesmen who dominated Europe in the 1620s and 1630s; also analyzes the changing nature of political authority.

*Hale, J. R. *War and Society in Renaissance Europe, 1450–1620*. 1985. A vivid account of what it meant to be a soldier.

Hirst, Derek. *Authority and Conflict: England, 1603–1658*. 1986. The most recent survey of the revolution and its origins.

MacCaffrey, Wallace. *Elizabeth I*. 1994.

*Mattingly, Garrett. *The Armada*. 1959. This beautifully written book, which was a best seller when it first appeared, is a gripping account of a major international crisis.

Moote, A. Lloyd. *The Revolt of the Judges: The Parlement of Paris and the Fronde, 1643–1652*. 1971. The most detailed account of the causes of the Fronde and its failures.

Parker, Geoffrey. *The Dutch Revolt*. 1977. This brief book gives a good introduction to the revolt of the Netherlands and the nature of Dutch society in the seventeenth century.

———. *The Military Revolution: Military Innovation and the Rise of the West, 1500–1800*. 1988. The most recent history of the transformation of warfare in this period.

———. *The Thirty Years' War.* 1984. The most up-to-date history of the war.

Pierson, Peter. *Philip II of Spain.* 1975. A clear and lively biography of the dominant figure of the second half of the sixteenth century.

*Rabb, Theodore K. *The Struggle for Stability in Early Modern Europe.* 1975. An assessment of the "crisis" interpretation, including extensive bibliographic references.

---

*Available in paperback.

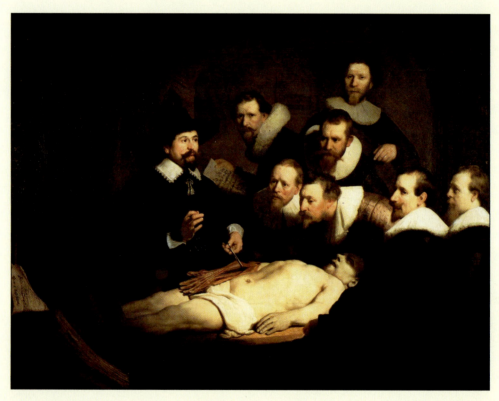

▲ *Rembrandt van Rijn*
THE ANATOMY LESSON OF DR. NICOLAAS TULP, **1632**
**Among the many representations of the public anatomy lessons so popular in
seventeenth-century Holland, the most famous is one of Rembrandt's greatest paintings,**
The Anatomy Lesson of Dr. Nicolaas Tulp.
Mauritshuis, The Hague

CULTURE AND SOCIETY IN THE AGE OF THE SCIENTIFIC REVOLUTION

Of all the many changes of the sixteenth and seventeenth centuries, none had a more far-reaching impact than the scientific revolution. By creating a new way of understanding how nature worked—and by solving long-standing problems in physics, astronomy, and anatomy—the theorists and experimenters of this period gave Europeans a new sense of confidence and certainty. Although the revolution began with disturbing questions, but few clear answers, about the physical world, it ended by offering a promise of knowledge and truth that was eagerly embraced by a society racked by decades of religious and political turmoil and uncertainty. Indeed, it is remarkable how closely intellectual and cultural patterns paralleled the progression from struggle and doubt to stable resolution that marked the political developments of these years. In the mid-seventeenth century, just as Europe's states were able to create more settled conditions following a major crisis, so in the realms of philosophy and the study of nature a long period of searching, anxiety, and dispute was resolved by scientists whose discoveries and self-assurance helped restore a sense of order in intellectual life. And in literature, the arts, and social relations, a time of insecurity and doubt also gave way to an atmosphere of confidence and calm.

	Social Structure	Body Politic	Changes in the Organization of Production and in the Impact of Technology	Evolution of Family and Changing Gender Roles	War	Religion	Cultural Expression
CHAPTER 16. CULTURE AND SOCIETY IN THE AGE OF THE SCIENTIFIC REVOLUTION							
I. SCIENTIFIC ADVANCE FROM COPERNICUS TO NEWTON							▨
II. THE EFFECTS OF THE DISCOVERIES	▨						▨
III. THE ARTS AND LITERATURE							▨
IV. SOCIAL PATTERNS AND POPULAR CULTURE	▨		▨	▨		▨	▨

I. Scientific Advance from Copernicus to Newton

◆

Fundamental to the transformation of Europe in the seventeenth century were advances in the knowledge of how nature worked. At first the new discoveries added to the uncertainties of the age, but eventually the scientists were seen as models of orderly thought, who had at last solved ancient problems in convincing fashion.

◆ ORIGINS OF THE SCIENTIFIC REVOLUTION

The Importance of Antiquity   Until the sixteenth century, the study of nature in Europe was inspired by the ancient Greeks. Their work shaped subsequent research in three main fields: Aristotle in physics, Ptolemy in astronomy, and Galen in medicine. The most dramatic advances during the scientific revolution came in these fields, to some extent because it was becoming evident that the ancient theories could not account for new observations without highly complicated adjustments. For instance, Aristotle's belief that all objects in their natural state are at rest created a number of problems, such as explaining why an arrow kept on flying after it left a bow. Similarly, Ptolemy's picture of the heavens, in which all motion was circular around a central earth, did not readily ex-

plain the peculiar motion that observers noticed in some planets, which at times seemed to be moving backward. And dissections often showed Galen's anatomical theories to be wrong.

Despite these problems, scientists (who in the sixteenth and seventeenth centuries were still known as "natural philosophers" or seekers of wisdom about nature) preferred making adjustments rather than beginning anew. And it is unlikely they would have abandoned their cherished theories if it had not been for other influences at work in this period. One such stimulus to rethinking was the humanists' rediscovery of a number of previously unknown ancient scientists, who had not always agreed with the theories of Aristotle or Ptolemy. A particularly important rediscovery was the work of Archimedes, whose writings on dynamics helped inspire new ideas in physics.

The Influence of "Magical" Beliefs   Another influence was a growing interest in what we now dismiss as "magic," but which at the time was regarded as a serious intellectual enterprise. There were various avenues of magical inquiry. Alchemy was the belief that matter could be understood and transformed by mixing substances and using secret formulas. A famous sixteenth-century alchemist, Paracelsus, suggested that metals as well as plants might have medicinal properties, and he helped demonstrate that mercury (if carefully used) could cure syphilis.

at the same time. One of the latter, derived from a system of Jewish thought known as *cabala,* suggested that the universe might be built around magical arrangements of numbers. The ancient Greek mathematician Pythagoras had also suggested that numerical patterns might connect all of nature, and his ideas now gained new attention. For all its irrational elements, it was precisely this interest in new and simple solutions for long-standing problems that made natural philosophers capable, for the first time, of discarding the honored theories they had inherited from antiquity, trying different ones, paying greater attention to mathematics, and eventually creating an intellectual revolution.

Observations, Experiments, and Instruments
Two other influences deserve mention. The first was Europe's fascination with technological invention. The architects, navigators, engineers, and weapons experts of the Renaissance were important pioneers of a new reliance on measurement and observation that affected not only how domes were built or heavy cannons were moved but also how problems in physics were addressed. A second, and related, influence was the growing interest in experiment among anatomists. In particular, the medical school at the University of Padua became famous for its dissections and direct observations of nature; many leading figures in the scientific revolution were trained there.

It was not too surprising, therefore, that during the sixteenth and seventeenth centuries important new instruments were invented, which helped make scientific discovery possible: the telescope, the vacuum pump, the thermometer, the barometer, and the microscope. These instruments encouraged the development of a scientific approach that was entirely new in the seventeenth century: It did not go back to the ancients, to the practitioners of magic, or to the engineers. This approach rested on the belief that in order to make nature reveal its secrets, it had to be made to do things it did not do normally. What this meant was that one did not simply observe phenomena that occurred normally in nature—for instance, the way a stick seems to bend when it is placed in a glass of water—but created conditions that were not normal. With the telescope, one saw secrets

▲ *Peter Brueghel*
The Alchemist, Engraving
This down-to-earth portrayal, typical of Brueghel's art, shows the alchemist as an undisciplined figure. He is surrounded by a chaos of instruments and half-finished experiments, and his helpers resemble witches. Like Brueghel, most people thought it unlikely that this disorganized figure would make a major contribution to the understanding of nature. Giraudon/Art Resource, NY

Another favorite study was astrology, which suggested that natural phenomena could be predicted if planetary movements were properly interpreted.

What linked these "magical" beliefs was the conviction that the world could be understood through simple, comprehensive keys to nature. The theories of Neoplatonism—an influential school of thought during the Renaissance, based on Plato's belief that truth lay in essential but hidden "forms"—supported this conviction, as did some of the mystical ideas that attracted attention

hidden to the naked eye; with the vacuum pump, one could understand the properties of air.

◆ THE BREAKTHROUGHS

Vesalius   The earliest scientific advances came in anatomy and astronomy, and by coincidence they were announced in two books published in 1543, which was also the year when the earliest printed edition of Archimedes appeared. The first book, *The Structure of the Human Body* by Andreas Vesalius (1514–1564), a member of the Padua faculty, pointed out errors in the work of Galen, the chief authority in medical practice for over a thousand years. Using dissections, Vesalius produced anatomical descriptions that opened a new era of careful observation and experimentation in studies of the body.

Copernicus   The second book, *On the Revolutions of the Heavenly Spheres* by Nicolaus Copernicus (1473–1543), a Polish cleric who had studied at Padua, had far greater consequences. A first-rate mathematician, Copernicus believed that the calculations of planetary movements under Ptolemy's system had grown too complex. In Ptolemaic astronomy, the planets and the sun, attached to transparent, crystalline spheres, revolved around the earth. All motion was circular, and irregularities were accounted for by epicycles—movement around small revolving spheres that were attached to the larger spheres. Influenced by Neoplatonic ideas, Copernicus believed that a simpler picture would reflect more accurately the true structure of the universe. In sound Neoplatonic fashion, he argued that the sun, as the most splendid of celestial bodies, ought rightfully to be at the center of an orderly and harmonious universe. The earth, no longer immobile, would thus circle the sun.

Copernicus' system was, in fact, scarcely simpler than Ptolemy's—the spheres and epicycles were just as complex—and he had no way of demonstrating the superiority of his theory. But he was such a fine mathematician that his successors found his calculations of planetary motions indispensable. His ideas thus became part of intellectual discussion, drawn on when Pope Gregory XIII decided to reform the calendar in 1582. The

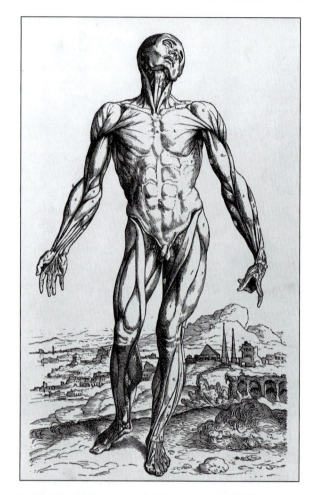

▲ *Titian* (attrib.)
Engraving Illustrating *The Structure of the Human Body* by Andreas Vesalius, 1543
Almost as remarkable as the findings themselves were these illustrations of the results of Vesalius' dissections. Traditionally, professors of anatomy read from textbooks to their students while lowly barber-surgeons cut up a cadaver and displayed the parts being discussed. Vesalius did his dissections himself and thus could observe directly such structures as the musculature. Here his illustrator displays the muscles on a gesturing figure and places it in a stretch of countryside near Padua, where Vesalius taught.

Julian calendar, in use since Roman times, counted century years as leap years, thus adding extra days that caused Easter—whose date is determined by the position of the sun—to drift farther and farther away from its normal occurrence in late March. The reform produced the Gregorian calendar, which we still use. Ten days were simply dropped: October 5, 1582, became October 15; and since then only one out of every four century years has been counted as a leap year (1900 had no February 29, but 2000 did). The need for calendar reform had been one of the motives for Copernicus' studies, which thus proved useful even though his theories remained controversial.

Theories in Conflict For more than half a century, the effect of *Revolutions* was to cause growing uncertainty, as the scholarly community argued over the validity of the new ideas and the need to abandon the old ones. The leading astronomer of the period, the Dane Tycho Brahe (1546–1601), produced the most remarkable observations of the heavens before the invention of the telescope by plotting the paths of the moon and planets every night for decades. But the only theory he could come up with was an uneasy compromise between the Ptolemaic and Copernican systems. There was similar indecision among anatomists, who admired Vesalius but were not ready to discard Galen.

◆ KEPLER AND GALILEO ADDRESS THE UNCERTAINTIES

As late as 1600, it seemed that scientists were creating more problems than solutions. But then two brilliant discoverers—Johannes Kepler (1571–1630), a German disciple of Brahe, and Galileo Galilei, an Italian professor of mathematics—made major advances on the work of Copernicus and helped resolve the uncertainties that had arisen in the field of astronomy.

Kepler and the Laws of Planetary Motion Like Copernicus, Kepler believed that only the language of mathematics could describe the movements of the heavens. He was a famous astrologer and an advocate of magical theories, but he was also convinced that Copernicus was right. He threw himself into the task of confirming the sun-centered (heliocentric) theory, and by studying Brahe's observations, he discovered three laws of

---

Chronology
◆
THE SCIENTIFIC REVOLUTION

1543 Publication of Copernicus' *On the Revolutions of the Heavenly Spheres*

Publication of Vesalius' *The Structure of the Human Body*

First printing of the work of Archimedes

1582 Pope Gregory XIII reforms the calendar

1609 Publication of Kepler's first two laws of planetary motion

1610 Publication of Galileo's *Starry Messenger*

1619 Publication of Kepler's third law of planetary motion

1627 Publication of Bacon's *New Atlantis*

1628 Publication of Harvey's *On the Motion of the Heart*

1632 Publication of Galileo's *Dialogue on the Two Great World Systems*

1633 Condemnation of Galileo by the Inquisition

1637 Publication of Descartes' *Discourse on Method*

1639 Pascal's theorem concerning conic sections

1660 Founding of the Royal Society of London for Improving Natural Knowledge

1666 Founding of the French Royal Academy of Sciences

1687 Publication of Newton's *Mathematical Principles of Natural Philosophy*

---

planetary motion (published in 1609 and 1619) that opened a new era in astronomy. Kepler was able to prove that the orbits of the planets are ellipses and that there is a regularity, based on their distance from the sun, which determines the movements of all planets. So revolutionary were these laws that few astronomers accepted them until Isaac Newton used them fifty years later as the basis for a new system of the heavens.

Galileo and a New Physics A contemporary of Kepler's, the Italian Galileo Galilei (1564–1642), took these advances a stage further when he became the first to perceive the connection between planetary motion and motion on earth. His studies revealed the importance to astronomy not only of observation and mathematics but also of physics. Moreover, he was the first to bring the new understanding of the universe to the attention of a reading public beyond the scholarly world. Galileo's self-consciousness about technique, argument, and evidence marks him as one of the first investigators of nature to approach his work in essentially the same way as a modern scientist.

The study of motion inspired Galileo's most fundamental scientific contributions. When he began his investigations, the Aristotelian view that a body is naturally at rest and needs to be pushed constantly to keep moving dominated the study of dynamics. Galileo broke with this tradition, developing instead a new type of physical explanation that was perfected by Isaac Newton half a century later. Much of Galileo's work was based on observation. From watching how workers at the Arsenal in Venice used pulleys and other devices to lift huge weights, he gained insights into physics; adapting a Dutch lens maker's invention, he built a primitive telescope that was essential to his studies of the heavens; and his seemingly mundane experiments, such as swinging a pendulum or rolling balls down inclined planes, were crucial means of testing his theories. Indeed, it was by moving from observations to abstraction that Galileo arrived at the first wholly new way of understanding motion since Aristotle: the principle of inertia.

This breakthrough could not have been made by observation alone. For the discovery of inertia depended on mathematical abstraction, the ability to imagine a situation that cannot be created experimentally: the motion of a perfectly smooth ball across a perfectly smooth plane, free of any outside forces, such as friction. Galileo's conclusion was that "any velocity once imparted to a moving body will be rigidly maintained as long as external causes of acceleration and retardation are removed. . . . If the velocity is uniform, it will not be diminished or slackened, much less destroyed." This insight overturned the Aristotelian view. Galileo had demonstrated that only mathe-

matical language could describe the underlying principles of nature.

A New Astronomy Galileo's most celebrated work was in astronomy. He first became famous in 1610, when he published his discoveries, made with the telescope, that Jupiter has satellites and the moon has mountains. Both these revelations were further blows to traditional beliefs, which held that the earth is changing and imperfect while the heavens are immutable and unblemished. Now, however, it seemed that other planets had satellites, just like the earth, and that these satellites might have the same rough surface as the earth. This was startling enough, but Galileo also argued that the principles of terrestrial physics could be used to explain phenomena in the heavens. He calculated the height of the mountains on the moon by using the geometric

▼ *Galileo Galilei*
THE MOON, 1610
This sketch of the moon's surface appeared in Galileo's *Starry Messenger* (1610). It shows what he had observed through the telescope and had interpreted as proof that the moon had a rugged surface because the lighted area within the dark section had to be mountains. These caught the light of the setting sun longer than surrounding lower terrain and revealed, for example, a large cavity in the lower center of the sketch.

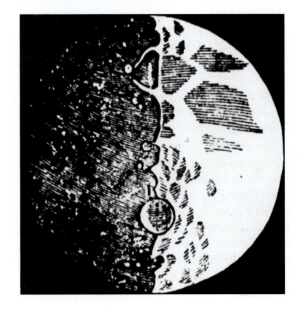

GALILEO AND KEPLER ON COPERNICUS

◆

In 1597 Kepler sent Galileo a copy of his New Astronomy, *which argued for the Copernican theory of the heavens, and asked the Italian for his opinion. The exchange of letters that followed, with Galileo cautious and Kepler urging him on, reflects an age when the new ideas were not yet proved and also gives a hint, in Kepler's last comments, of the troubles that lay ahead.*

Galileo to Kepler: "Like you, I accepted the Copernican position several years ago. I have written up many reasons on the subject, but have not dared until now to bring them into the open. I would dare publish my thoughts if there were many like you; but, since there are not, I shall forbear."

Kepler's Reply: "I could only have wished that you, who have so profound an insight, would choose another way. You advise us to retreat before the general ignorance and not to expose ourselves to the violent attacks of the mob of scholars. But after a tremendous task has been begun in our time, first by Copernicus and then by many very learned mathematicians, and when the assertion that the Earth moves can no longer be considered something new, would it not be much better to pull the wagon to its goal by our joint efforts, now that we have got it under way, and gradually, with powerful voices, to shout down the common herd? Be of good cheer, Galileo, and come out publicly! If I judge correctly, there are only a few of the distinguished mathematicians of Europe who would part company with us, so great is the power of truth. If Italy seems a less favorable place for your publication, perhaps Germany will allow us this freedom."

From Giorgio de Santillana, *The Crime of Galileo* (Chicago: University of Chicago Press, 1955), pp. 11 and 14–15.

---

techniques of surveyors, and he described the moon's secondary light—seen while it is a crescent—as a reflection of sunlight from the earth. Galileo was treating his own planet simply as one part of a uniform universe. Every physical law, he was saying, is equally applicable on earth and in the heavens, including the laws of motion. As early as 1597 Galileo had admitted (in a letter to Kepler) that some of his discoveries in physics could be explained only if the earth were moving, and during the next thirty years he became the most famous advocate of Copernicanism in Europe (see "Galileo and Kepler on Copernicus").

Galileo made a powerful case. Why, he asked, was it necessary to say that the entire universe revolved around the earth when all celestial motions could be explained by the rotation of a single planet, the earth? When academic and religious critics pointed out that we would feel the earth moving or that the Bible said Joshua made the sun stand still, he reacted with scorn. In response to religious objections, he asserted that "in discussions of physical problems we ought to begin not from the authority of scriptural passages, but from sense experience and necessary demonstrations."

Conflict with the Church For all the brilliance of his arguments, Galileo was now on dangerous ground. Although traditionally the Catholic Church had not concerned itself with investigations of nature, in the early seventeenth century the situation was changing. The Church was deep in the struggle with Protestantism, and it responded to the challenge to its authority by trying to control potentially questionable views. And Galileo's biting sarcasm toward other scientists antagonized Jesuit and Dominican astronomers. These two orders were the chief upholders of orthodoxy in the Church. They referred Galileo's views to the Inquisition and then guided the attack on Copernicanism by seeking to condemn the brilliant advocate who had made the theory famous throughout Europe.

The Book and the Trial In 1616 the Inquisition forbade Galileo, within certain limits, to teach the heretical doctrine that the earth moves. When one of his friends was elected pope in 1623, however, Galileo thought he would be safe in writing a major work on astronomy, as long as he remained within the limits set in 1616. The result was

Galileo's *Dialogue on the Two Great World Systems,* published in 1632 (with the approval, probably accidental, of the Church). A marvelously witty, elegant book, the *Dialogue* is one of the few monuments in the history of science that the layperson can read with pleasure. And so it was intended. Galileo wrote it in Italian, not the Latin that had always been used for scholarly works, because he wanted it to reach the widest possible audience.

In April 1633 he was brought before the Inquisition for having defied the order not to teach Copernicanism. To establish their case, his accusers used a forged document that suggested the 1616 limits were stricter than they were. In a trial that has caused controversy ever since, the aged astronomer, under threat of torture, abjured the "errors and heresies" of believing that the earth moved. But he did not remain docile for the remainder of his life, though he was kept under house arrest and progressively lost his eyesight. Many of his letters ridiculed his opponents, and in 1638 he published (in tolerant Holland) his principal work on physics, the *Two New Sciences.*

Galileo's Legacy   The condemnation of Galileo discouraged further scientific activity by his compatriots. Italy had been a leader of the new investigations, but now major further advances were made by the English, Dutch, and French. Yet this shift showed merely that the rise of science, once begun, could not be halted for long. By the late 1630s, no self-respecting astronomer could deny the correctness of the Copernican theory.

Assurance Spreads   The new studies of nature may have caused tremendous bewilderment at first, as scientists struggled with the ideas of pioneers like Copernicus and Vesalius. But in the end these investigations created a renewed sense of certainty about the physical world, which was to have a far-reaching influence. This was true not only in physics and astronomy but also in anatomy, where, in 1628, another genius of the scientific revolution, the English doctor William Harvey, revolutionized the understanding of the human body when he identified the function of the heart and proved that the blood circulates.

◆ THE CLIMAX OF THE SCIENTIFIC REVOLUTION: ISAAC NEWTON

The culmination of the scientific revolution was the work of Isaac Newton (1642–1727), who made decisive contributions to mathematics, physics, astronomy, and optics and brought to a climax the changes that had begun with Copernicus. He united physics and astronomy into a single system to explain all motion, he helped transform mathematics by developing the calculus, and he established some of the basic laws of modern physics.

Part of the explanation of his versatility lies in the workings of the scientific community at the time. Newton was a retiring man who nevertheless got into fierce arguments with prominent contemporaries, such as the learned German scholar and scientist Wilhelm von Leibniz, who was working on the calculus. If not for his active participation in meetings of scientists at the recently founded Royal Society of London (see p. 562) and the effort he had to make to demonstrate his views to his colleagues, Newton might never have pursued his researches to their conclusion. He disliked the give-and-take of these discussions, but he felt forced in self-justification to prepare some of his most important papers for the Royal Society. Such institutions were now being established throughout Europe to promote the advance of science, and their creation indicates how far the scientific community had come since the days of Copernicus, who had worked largely in isolation.

The Principia   Newton's masterpiece, *The Mathematical Principles of Natural Philosophy* (1687)— usually referred to by the first word of its Latin title, the *Principia*—was the last widely influential book to be written in Latin, the traditional language of scholarship. Latin was still useful to Newton, who wanted as many experts as possible to read the book, because he was seeking to refute the approach to science associated with the widely admired French philosopher and mathematician René Descartes (see p. 560). In contrast to Descartes, who emphasized the powers of the mind and pure reason in investigating nature, Newton believed that mere hypotheses, constructions of logic and words, were not the tools of a true scientist. As he put it in a celebrated phrase, "Hypotheses non fingo" ("I do not posit hypotheses"), because everything he said was proved by experiment or by mathematics.

The most dramatic of Newton's findings was the solution to the ancient problem of motion. Building on Galileo's advances and overturning Aristotle's theories once and for all, Newton defined his system in three laws: first, in the absence of force, motion continues in a straight line; second, the rate of change of the motion is determined by the forces acting on it (such as friction); and third, action and reaction between two bodies are equal and opposite. To arrive at these laws, he defined the concepts of mass, inertia, and force in relation to velocity and acceleration as we know them today.

Newton extended these principles to the entire universe by demonstrating that his laws govern the motions of the moon and planets too. Using the concept of gravity, he provided the explanation of the movement of objects in space that is the foundation for current space travel. There is a balance, he said, between the earth's pull on the moon and the forward motion of the satellite, which would continue in a straight line were it not for the earth's gravity. Consequently, the moon moves in an elliptical orbit in which neither gravity nor inertia gains control. The same pattern is followed by the planets around the sun (as Kepler had shown).

The Influence of Newton Largely on the basis of the uniformity and the systematic impersonal forces that Newton described, the view of the universe as a vast machine gained ground. According to this theory, all motion is a result of precise, unvarying, and demonstrable forces. There is a celestial mechanics just like the mechanics that operates on earth. It was nor far from this view to the belief that God is a great watchmaker who started the marvelous mechanism going but intervenes only when something goes wrong and needs repair. The general philosophical implication that the world was stable and orderly was as important as the specific discoveries in making Newton one of the idols of his own and the next centuries. The educated applauded Newton's achievements, and he was the first scientist to receive a knighthood in

England. Only a few decades after the appearance of the *Principia*, the poet Alexander Pope summed up the public feeling:

> Nature and nature's law lay hid in night;
> God said, "Let Newton be!" and all was light.

So overpowering was Newton's stature that in physics and astronomy the remarkable advances of 150 years slowed down for more than half a century after the publication of the *Principia*. There was a general impression that somehow Newton had done it all, that no important problems remained. There were other reasons for the slowdown—changing patterns in education, an inevitable lessening of momentum—but none was so powerful as the reverence for Newton, who became the intellectual symbol of his own and succeeding ages.

II. The Effects of the Discoveries

◆

The scientists' discoveries about the physical universe made them famous. But it was the *way* they proved their case that made them so influential. The success of their reasoning encouraged a new level of confidence in human powers that helped end the doubts and uncertainties of the previous age.

◆ A NEW EPISTEMOLOGY

Galileo had stressed that his discoveries rested on a way of thinking that had an independent value, and he refused to allow traditional considerations, such as common sense or theological teachings, to interfere with his conclusions. Scientists were now moving toward a new epistemology, a new theory of how to obtain and verify knowledge. They stressed experience, reason, and doubt; they rejected all unsubstantiated authority; and they developed a revolutionary way of determining what was a true description of physical reality.

Scientific Method The process the scientists said they followed, after they had formulated a hypothesis, consisted of three parts: first, observations; second, a generalization induced from the observations; and third, tests of the generalization by experiments whose outcome could be predicted by the generalization. A generalization remained valid only as long as it was not contradicted by experiments specifically designed to test it. The scientist used no data except the results of strict observation—such as the time it took balls to roll down Galileo's inclined planes, or the path Kepler saw the planets following—and scientific reasoning uncovered the laws, principles, or patterns that emerged from the observations. Since measurement was the key to the data, the observations had a numerical, not a subjective, value. Thus, the language of science naturally came to be mathematics.

In fact, scientists rarely reach conclusions in the exact way this idealized scheme suggests. Galileo's perfectly smooth balls and planes, for instance, did not exist, but Galileo understood the relevant physical theory so well that he knew what would happen if one rolled across the other, and he used this "experiment" to demonstrate the principle of inertia. In other words, experiments as well as hypotheses can occur in the mind; the essence of scientific method is a special way of looking at and understanding nature.

◆ THE WIDER INFLUENCE OF SCIENTIFIC THOUGHT

The principles of scientific inquiry received attention throughout the intellectual community only gradually; it took time for the power of the scientists' method to be recognized. If the new methods were to be accepted, their effectiveness would have to be demonstrated to more than a few specialists. This wider understanding was eventually achieved by mid-century as much through the efforts of ardent propagandizers like Francis Bacon as through the writings of the great innovators themselves. Gradually, they were able to convince a broad, educated public that science, after first causing doubts by challenging ancient truths, now offered a promise of certainty that was not to be found anywhere else in an age of general crisis.

◆ BACON AND DESCARTES

Bacon's Vision of Science   Although he was not an important scientist himself, Francis Bacon was the greatest of science's propagandists, and he in-

spired a whole generation with his vision of what it could accomplish for humanity. His description of an ideal society in the *New Atlantis*—published in 1627, the year after his death—is a vision of science as the savior of the human race. It predicts a time when those doing research at the highest levels will be regarded as the most important people in the state and will work on vast government-supported projects to gather all known facts about the physical universe. By a process of gradual induction, this information will lead to universal laws that, in turn, will enable people to improve their lot on earth. Bacon's view of research as a collective enterprise inspired a number of later scientists, particularly the founders of the Royal Society of London, and by the mid-seventeenth century, his ideas had entered the mainstream of European thought.

Descartes and the Principle of Doubt   The Frenchman René Descartes (1596–1650) made the first concentrated attempt to apply the new methods of science to theories of knowledge, and, in so doing, he laid the foundations for modern philosophy. The impulse behind his work was his realization that, for all the importance of observation and experiment, people can be deceived by their senses. In order to find some solid truth, therefore, he decided to apply to all knowledge the principle of doubt—the refusal to accept any authority without strict verification. He began with the assumption that he could know unquestionably only one thing: that he was doubting. This assumption allowed him to proceed to the observation "I think, therefore I am," because the act of doubting proved he was thinking, and thinking, in turn, demonstrated his existence.

From the proof of his own existence he derived a crucial statement: That whatever is clearly and distinctly thought must be true. This assertion in turn enabled him to construct a proof of God's existence. We cannot fail to realize that we are imperfect, he argued, and we must therefore have an idea of perfection against which we may be measured. If we have a clear idea of what perfection is, then it must exist; hence, there must be a God.

The Discourse on Method   Descartes' proof may have served primarily to show that the principle

▲ **Frans Hals Portrait of Descartes, 1649 (Royal Museum of Fine Arts, Copenhagen) The increasingly common portraits of scientists in the seventeenth century testify to their growing fame. In this case, Descartes sat for one of the Netherlands' most renowned artists, and because the painting was copied in a number of engravings, his face became as well known as that of many kings and princes.**
Erich Lessing/Art Resource, NY

of doubt did not contradict religious belief, but it also reflected the emphasis on the power of the mind in his major work, *Discourse on the Method of Rightly Conducting the Reason and Seeking Truth in the Sciences* (1637). Thought is a pure and unmistakable guide, he said, and only by relying on its operations can people hope to advance their understanding of the world. Descartes developed this view into a fundamental proposition about the nature of the world—a proposition that philosophers have been wrestling with ever since.

He stated that there is an essential divide between thought and extension (tangible objects) or, put another way, between spirit and matter. Bacon and Galileo had insisted that science, the study of nature, is separate from and unaffected by faith or theology, the study of God. But Descartes turned this distinction into a far-reaching principle, dividing not only science from faith but even the reality of the world from our perception of that reality. There is a difference, in other words, between a chair and how we think of it as a chair.

The Influence of Descartes Descartes' emphasis on the operations of the mind gave a new direction to epistemological discussions. A hypothesis gained credibility not so much from external proofs as from the logical tightness of the arguments used to support it. The decisive test was how lucid and irrefutable a statement appeared to be to the thinking mind, not whether it could be demonstrated by experiments. Descartes thus applied what he considered the methods of science to all of knowledge. Not only the phenomena of nature but all truth had to be investigated according to the methods of the scientist. At the same time, his insistence on strict definitions of cause and effect helped create a general scientific and intellectual theory known as *mechanism*. In its simplest form, mechanism holds that the entire universe, including human beings, can be regarded as a complicated machine and thus subject to strict physical principles. The arm is like a lever, the elbow is like a hinge, and so on. Even an emotion is no more than a simple response to a definable stimulus. This view was to influence philosophers for generations.

Descartes' contributions to the scientific research of his day were theoretical rather than experimental. In physics, he was the first to perceive the distinction between mass and weight; and in mathematics, he was the first to apply algebraic notations and methods to geometry, thus founding analytic geometry. Above all, his emphasis on the principle of doubt undermined forever traditional assumptions such as the belief in the hierarchical organization of the universe. And the admiration he inspired indicated how completely his methods had captured his contemporaries' imagination.

◆ PASCAL'S PROTEST AGAINST THE NEW SCIENCE

At midcentury only one important voice still protested against the new science and, in particular, against the materialism of Descartes. It belonged to a Frenchman, Blaise Pascal, a brilliant mathematician and experimenter. Pascal's investigations of probability in games of chance produced the theorem that still bears his name, and his research in conic sections helped lay the foundations for integral calculus. He also helped discover barometric pressure and invented a calculating machine. In his late twenties, however, Pascal became increasingly dissatisfied with scientific research, and he began to wonder whether his life was being properly spent. Moved by a growing concern with faith, Pascal had a mystical experience in November 1654 that made him resolve to devote his life to the salvation of his soul.

The Pensées During the few remaining years of his life, Pascal wrote a collection of reflections—some only a few words long, some many pages—that were gathered together after his death and published as the *Pensées* (or "reflections"). These writings revealed not only the beliefs of a deeply religious man but also the anxieties of a scientist who feared the growing influence of science. He did not wish to put an end to research; he merely wanted people to realize that the truths uncovered by science were limited and not as important as the truths perceived by faith. As he put it in one of his more memorable *pensées*, "The heart has its reasons that reason cannot know."

Pascal's protest was unique, but the fact that it was put forward at all indicates how high the status of the scientist and his methods had risen by the 1650s. Just a quarter-century earlier, such a dramatic change in fortune would have been hard to predict. But now the new epistemology, after its initial disturbing assault on ancient views, was offering one of the few promises of certainty in an age of upheaval and general crisis. In intellectual matters as in politics, turmoil was gradually giving way to assurance.

◆ SCIENCE INSTITUTIONALIZED

Many besides Bacon realized that scientific work should be a cooperative endeavor and that information should be exchanged among all its practitioners. A scientific society founded in Rome in 1603 made the first major effort to apply this view, and it was soon followed up in France, where in the early seventeenth century a friar named Marin Mersenne became the center of an international network of correspondents interested in scientific work. He also spread news by bringing scientists together for discussions and experiments. Contacts that were developed at these meetings led eventually to a more permanent and systematic organization of scientific activity.

The Royal Society In England, the first steps toward such organization were taken at Oxford during the Civil War in the 1640s, when the revolutionaries captured the city and replaced those at the university who taught traditional natural philosophy. A few of the newcomers formed what they called the Invisible College, a group that met to exchange information and discuss each other's work. The group included only one first-class scientist, the chemist Robert Boyle; but in 1660 he and eleven others formed an official organization, the Royal Society of London for Improving Natural Knowledge, with headquarters in the capital. In 1662 it was granted a charter by Charles II—the first sign of a link with political authority that not only boosted science but also indicated the growing presence of central governments in all areas of society.

The Royal Society's purposes were openly Baconian. Its aim for a few years—until everyone realized it was impossible—was to gather all knowledge about nature, particularly if it had practical uses. For a long time the members offered their services for the public good, helping in one instance to develop for the government the science of social statistics ("political arithmetic," as it was called). Soon, however, it became clear that the society's principal function was to serve as a headquarters and clearing center for research. Its secretaries maintained an enormous correspondence to encourage English and foreign scholars to send in news of their discoveries. And in 1665 the society began the regular publication of *Philosophical Transactions*, the first professional scientific journal.

Other Scientific Societies Imitators soon followed. In 1666 Louis XIV gave his blessing to the

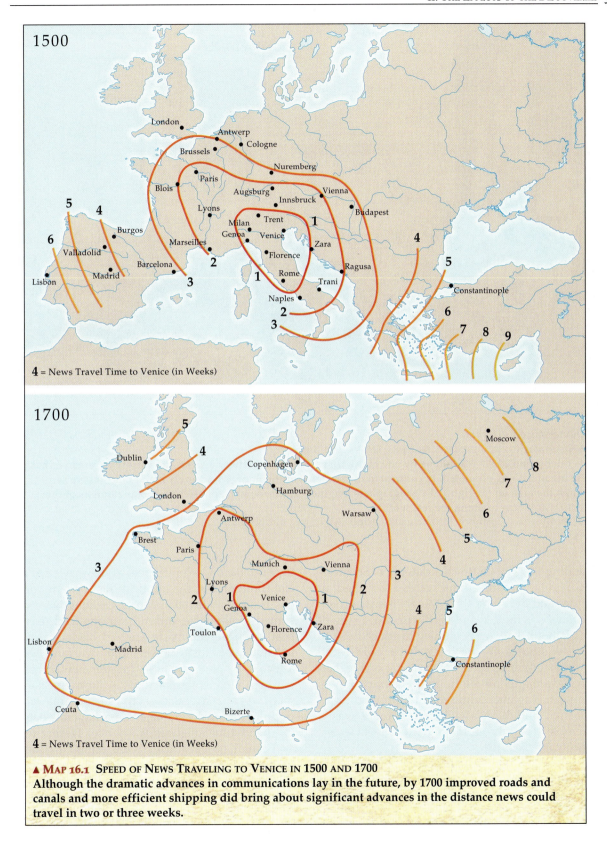

1500

5   4

6

Valladolid

Lisbon   Madrid   Burgos

Barcelona   Marseilles   Lyons   Blois   Paris   Brussels   London   Antwerp   Cologne

Nuremberg

Augsburg   Vienna

Innsbruck   Budapest

Trent

Milan   Genoa   Venice

Florence

Rome   Zara   Ragusa

Naples   Trani

Constantinople

4   5   6   7   8   9

1   2   3

4 = News Travel Time to Venice (in Weeks)

1700

5   4

Dublin

London   Brest

Lisbon

Paris   Antwerp   Copenhagen   Hamburg   Warsaw   Moscow

Munich   Vienna

Lyons

Madrid   Toulon   Genoa   Venice   Florence   Zara

Rome

Ceuta   Bizerte   Constantinople

3   2   1   1   2   3   4   5   6   7   8

4 = News Travel Time to Venice (in Weeks)

▲ **Map 16.1** Speed of News Traveling to Venice in 1500 and 1700
Although the dramatic advances in communications lay in the future, by 1700 improved roads and
canals and more efficient shipping did bring about significant advances in the distance news could
travel in two or three weeks.

▲ *Charles-Nicolas Cochin*
The Académie Royale des Sciences, Paris, Engraving, **1698**
This celebration of the work done by one of the first scientific societies suggests the variety of research that these organizations promoted. In contrast to the students of theology, who merely read books (as we see through the arch on the right), the geographers, engineers, astronomers, physicists, and anatomists of the scientific academy examine the real world.
© British Museum, Department of Prints and Drawings ([C292] Neg # N/N R8-85)

founding of a French Royal Academy of Sciences, and similar organizations were established in Naples and Berlin by 1700. Membership in these societies was limited and highly prized, a sign of the glamour that was beginning to attach itself to the new studies. By the 1660s there could be no doubt that science, secure in royal patronage, had become a model for all thought. Its practitioners were extravagantly admired, and throughout intellectual and high social circles, there was a scramble to apply its methods to almost every conceivable activity.

The Wider Appeal of Science Descartes had applied the ideas of science to philosophy in general; Bacon had put them at the service of social thought. But the applications were not only on these high levels. Formal gardens were designed to show the order, harmony, and reason that science had made such prized qualities. Methods of fortification and warfare were affected by the principles of the new investigations, such as the need for accurate measurement. As the scientists' activities became more popular and fashionable, even aristocrats began to spend time playing at science. Herbariums and small observatories were added to country estates, and parties featured an evening of star gazing. Science also fascinated the general populace. Among the most eagerly anticipated occasions in seventeenth-century Holland was the public anatomy lesson. The body of a criminal would be brought to an enormous hall that was packed with students and a fascinated public. A famous surgeon would dissect the cadaver, announcing and displaying each organ as he removed it.

On the whole, the reverence for science and its methods did not develop from an understanding of its actual accomplishments or its potential consequences. Rather, it was caused by the fame of the spectacular discoveries that had offered new and convincing solutions to centuries-old problems in astronomy, physics, and anatomy. Here was a promise of certainty and order in a world that otherwise was bedeviled by conflict and doubt. As a result, the protests of Pascal could be ignored, and the new discipline could be given unblemished admiration. The entire world was coming to be viewed through the scientist's eyes—a striking achievement for a recently minor member of the intellectual community—and the qualities of regularity and harmony associated with science began to appear in the work of artists and writers.

III. The Arts and Literature

We have seen that in the mid-seventeenth century a more settled Europe emerged from the political turbulence and crisis of the late 1500s and early 1600s. And we have seen that the development of science followed a similar pattern—with decades of uncertainty as old truths were challenged, followed by a new sense of assurance in the mid-seventeenth century. Not surprisingly, so too did the concerns of the arts and literature.

◆ UNSETTLING ART

Mannerism One response that was provoked by the upheavals of the sixteenth century was the attempt to escape reality, an effort that was echoed by some of the painters of the age, known as *Mannerists*. The Mannerists and their patrons reacted against the serenity and idealization of the High Renaissance by cultivating artificial and esoteric images of the world; they undermined

perspective, distorted human figures, and devised unnatural colors and lighting to create startling effects.

El Greco Mannerism was embodied in El Greco (1541–1614), a Greek who was trained in Italy and settled in Spain. His compelling and almost mystic canvases created an otherworldly alternative (reminiscent of St. Teresa's visions) to the troubles of his time. El Greco's cool colors, eerie lighting, and elongated and often agonized human beings make him one of the most distinctive painters in the history of art (see p. 515). After 1600, though, painters increasingly rejected the Mannerists' flight from reality; eventually the arts, too, reflected the sense of settlement that descended over European civilization in the mid-seventeenth century.

◆ UNSETTLING WRITERS

Michel de Montaigne In the world of literature, the concerns of the age were most vividly expressed by the Frenchman Michel de Montaigne (1533–1592). Obsessed by the death he saw all around him and determined to overcome his fears, he retired in 1570 to his country home in order to "essay," or test, his innermost feelings by writing short pieces of prose even about subjects he did not fully comprehend. In the process he created a new literary form, the essay, that also helped shape the modern French language. But his chief influence was philosophical: He has inspired the search for self-knowledge ever since.

At first Montaigne's anxieties led him to the radical doubt about the possibility of finding truth that is known as *Skepticism;* this preoccupation inspired the total uncertainty of his motto, "Que sais-je?" ("What do I know?"). Eventually, however, Montaigne struggled toward a more confident view, taking as his model the ancient saying "Know thyself." By looking into one's own person, one can find values that hold true at least for oneself, and these will reflect the values of all humanity. Montaigne came close to a morality without theology, because good and self-determination were more important to him than doctrine, and he saw everywhere religious people committing inhuman acts. Trying to be an angel is wrong, he said; being good is enough.

Neostoicism A more general application of some of these ideas was a theory known as *Neostoicism*, inspired by the ancient Stoics' emphasis on self-knowledge and a calm acceptance of the world. The most influential of the Neostoics, a Dutch writer named Justus Lipsius, argued that public leaders ought to be guided by profound self-examination. Lipsius urged rulers to be restrained and self-disciplined, and he was much admired by the kings and royal ministers of the seventeenth century.

Cervantes In Spain the disillusionment that accompanied the political and economic decline of Europe's most powerful state was perfectly captured by Miguel de Cervantes (1547–1616). Cervantes saw the wide gap between the hopes and the realities of his day—in religion, in social institutions, in human behavior—and made the dichotomy the basis of scathing social satire in his novel *Don Quixote*.

At one level, Cervantes was ridiculing the excessive chivalry of the Spanish nobility in his portrayal of a knight who was ready to tilt at windmills, though he obviously admired the sincerity of his well-meaning hero and sympathized with him as a perennial loser. On another level, the author brought to life the Europe of the time— the ordinary people and their hypocrisies and intolerances—with a liveliness rarely matched in literature. His view of that society, however, was far from cheery. "Justice, but not for my house," says Don Quixote. Cervantes avoided politics, but he was clearly directing many of his sharpest barbs at the brutality and disregard for human values that were characteristic of his fanatical times. And in England another towering figure was grappling with similar problems.

Shakespeare For the English-speaking world, the most brilliant writer of this and all other periods was William Shakespeare (1564–1616), whose characters bring to life almost every conceivable mood: searing grief, airy romance, rousing nationalism, uproarious humor. Despite his modest edu- cation, his imagery shows a familiarity with subjects ranging from astronomy to seamanship, from alchemy to warfare. It is not surprising, therefore, that some have doubted that one man could have produced this amazing body of work. During most of his writing career, Shakespeare was involved with a theatrical company, where he often had to produce plays on short notice. He thus had the best of all possible tests—audience reactions—as he gained mastery of theatrical techniques.

Shakespeare's plays made timeless statements about human behavior: love, hatred, violence, sin. Of particular interest to the historian, however, is what he tells us about attitudes that belong especially to his own era. Again and again, legality and stability are shown as fundamental virtues amidst turbulent times. Shakespeare's expressions of patriotism are particularly intense; when in *Richard II* the king's uncle, John of Gaunt, lies dying, he pours out his love for his country in words that have moved the English ever since:

> This royal throne of kings, this scepter'd isle,
> This earth of majesty, this seat of Mars,
> This other Eden, demi-paradise, . . .
> This happy breed of men, this little world,
> This precious stone set in the silver sea, . . .
> This blessed plot, this earth,
> This realm, this England.

> RICHARD II, ACT 2, SCENE 1

As in so much of the art and writing of the time, instability is a central concern of Shakespeare's plays. His four most famous tragedies— *Hamlet, King Lear, Macbeth,* and *Othello*—end in disillusionment: The heroes are ruined by irresoluteness, pride, ambition, or jealousy. Shakespeare was exploring a theme that had absorbed playwrights since Euripides—the fatal flaws that destroy the great—and producing dramas of revenge that were popular in his day; but the plays also demonstrate his deep understanding of human nature. Whatever one's hopes, one cannot forget human weakness, the inevitability of decay, and the constant threat of disaster. The contrast appears with compelling clarity in a speech delivered by Hamlet:

What a piece of work is man! How noble in reason! how infinite in faculties! in form and moving how express and admirable! in action how like an angel! in apprehension how like a god! the beauty of the world, the paragon of animals! And yet to me what is this quintessence of dust? Man delights not me.

HAMLET, ACT 2, SCENE 2

Despite such pessimism, despite the deep sense of human inadequacy, the basic impression Shakespeare gives is of immense vigor, of a restlessness and confidence that recall the many achievements of the sixteenth century. Yet a sense of decay is never far absent. Repeatedly, people seem utterly helpless, overtaken by events they cannot control. Nothing remains constant or dependable, and everything that seems solid or reassuring, be it the love of a daughter or the crown of England, is challenged. In this atmosphere of ceaseless change, where landmarks easily disappear, Shakespeare conveys the tensions of his time.

◆ THE RETURN OF ASSURANCE IN THE ARTS

The Baroque   After 1600, the arts began to move toward the assurance and sense of settlement that was descending over other areas of European civilization. A new style, the Baroque, sought to drown the uneasiness of Mannerism in a blaze of grandeur. Passion, drama, mystery, and awe were the qualities of the Baroque: Every art form—from music to literature, from architecture to opera— had to involve, arouse, and uplift its audience.

The Baroque style was closely associated with the Counter Reformation's emphasis on gorgeous display in Catholic ritual. The patronage of leading Church figures made Rome a magnet for the major painters of the period. Elsewhere, the Baroque flourished primarily at the leading Catholic courts of the seventeenth century, most notably the Habsburg courts in Madrid, Prague, and Brussels, and remained influential well into the eighteenth century in such Catholic areas as the Spanish Empire. Few styles have conveyed so strong a sense of grandeur, theatricality, and ornateness.

Caravaggio   The artist who first shaped the new aesthetic, Caravaggio (1571–1610), lived most of his life in Rome. Although he received commissions from high Church figures and spent time in a cardinal's household, he was equally at home among the beggars and petty criminals of Rome's dark back streets. These ordinary people served as Caravaggio's models, which shocked those who believed it inappropriate for such humble characters to represent the holy figures of biblical scenes. Yet the power of Caravaggio's paintings—their depiction of highly emotional moments, and the drama created by their sharp contrasts of light and dark—made his work much prized. He had to flee Rome after he killed someone in a brawl, but he left behind an outpouring of work that influenced an entire generation of painters.

Rubens   Among those who came to Rome to study Caravaggio's art was Peter Paul Rubens (1577–1640), the principal ornament of the brilliant Habsburg court at Brussels. His major themes typified the grandeur that came to be the hallmark of Baroque style: glorifications of great rulers and also of the ceremony and mystery of Catholicism. Rubens' secular paintings convey enormous strength; his religious works overwhelm the viewer with the majesty of the Church and excite the believer's piety by stressing the power of the faith.

Velázquez   Other artists glorified rulers through idealized portraiture. The greatest court painter of the age was Diego Velázquez (1599–1660). His portraits of members of the Spanish court depict rulers and their surroundings in the stately atmosphere appropriate to the theme. Yet occasionally Velázquez hinted at the weakness of an ineffective monarch in his rendering of the face, even though the basic purpose of his work was always to exalt royal power. And his celebration of a notable Habsburg victory, *The Surrender of Breda*, managed to suggest the sadness and emptiness as much as the glory of war.

Bernini   GianLorenzo Bernini (1598–1680) brought to sculpture and architecture the qualities that Rubens brought to painting, and like Rubens

▲ *Caravaggio*
The Supper at Emmaus, ca. 1597
By choosing moments of high drama and using sharp contrasts of light, Caravaggio created an immediacy that came to be one of the hallmarks of Baroque painting. Here he shows the moment during the supper at Emmaus when his disciples suddenly recognized the resurrected Christ. The force of their emotions and their almost theatrical gestures convey the intensity of the moment, but many at the time objected to the craggy, tattered appearance of the disciples. These were not idealized figures, as was expected, but ordinary people at a humble table.
Reproduced by courtesy of the Trustees, © The National Gallery, London (NG172)

he was closely associated with the Counter Reformation. Pope Urban VIII commissioned him in 1629 to complete both the inside and the outer setting of the basilica of St. Peter's in Rome. For the interior Bernini designed a splendid papal throne that seems to float on clouds beneath a burst of sunlight, and for the exterior he created an enormous plaza, surrounded by a double colonnade, that is the largest such plaza in Europe. Similarly, his dramatic religious works reflect the desire of the Counter Reformation popes to electrify the

faithful. The sensual and overpowering altarpiece dedicated to the Spanish mystic St. Teresa makes a direct appeal to the emotions of the beholder that is the epitome of the excitement and confidence of the Baroque.

New Dimensions in Music   The seventeenth century was significant, too, as a decisive time in the history of music. New instruments, notably in the keyboard and string families, enabled composers to create richer effects than had been possible

▲ *Artemisia Gentileschi*
JUDITH SLAYING HOLOFERNES, CA. **1620**
Women artists were rare in the seventeenth century because they were not allowed to become apprentices. But Artemisia (1593–1652) was the daughter of a painter who happened to be a friend of Caravaggio, and she had the opportunity to become a gifted exponent of Baroque style. Known throughout Europe for her vivid portrayals of dramatic scenes (she painted the murder of Holofernes by the biblical heroine Judith at least five times), she practiced her chosen profession with considerable success, despite the trauma of being raped at age seventeen by a friend of her father's—an act of violence that may be reflected (and avenged) in this painting.
Scala/Art Resource, NY

▲ *Peter Paul Rubens*
The Descent from the Cross, 1612
This huge altarpiece was one of the first pictures Rubens painted upon returning to his native
Antwerp after spending most of his twenties developing his art in Italy. The ambitious scale, the
strong emotions, the vivid lighting, and the dramatic action showed the artist's commitment to
the Baroque style that had recently evolved in Italy, and the powerful impact of the altarpiece
helped make him one of the most sought-after painters of the day.
Scala/Art Resource, NY

▲ *Diego Velázquez*
THE SURRENDER OF BREDA, **1635**
The contrasting postures of victory and defeat are masterfully captured by Diego Velázquez in *The Surrender of Breda*. The Dutch soldiers droop their heads and lances, but the victorious Spaniards hardly show triumph, and the gesture of the victorious general, Ambrogio Spinola, is one of consolation and understanding.
Oroñoz

before. Particularly in Italy, which in the sixteenth and seventeenth centuries was the chief center of new ideas in music, musicians began to explore the potential of a form that first emerged in these years: the opera. Drawing on the resources of the theater, painting, architecture, music, and dance, an operatic production could achieve splendors that were beyond the reach of any one of these arts on its own. The form was perfectly attuned to the courtly culture of the age, to the love of

display among the princes of Europe, and to the Baroque determination to overwhelm one's audience.

The dominant figure in seventeenth-century music was the Italian Claudio Monteverdi (1567–1643), one of the most innovative composers of all time. He has been called with some justification the creator of both the operatic form and the orchestra. His masterpiece, *Orfeo* (1607), was a tremendous success, and in the course of

▲ *GianLorenzo Bernini*
St. Peter's Square and Church, Rome
The magnificent circular double colonnade that Bernini created in front of St. Peter's is one of the triumphs of Baroque architecture. The church itself was already the largest in Christendom (markers in the floor still indicate how far other famous churches would reach if placed inside St. Peter's), and it was topped by the huge dome Michelangelo had designed. The vast enclosed space that Bernini built reinforced the grandeur of a church that was the pope's own.
Joachim Messerschmidt/The Stock Market

▲ *GianLorenzo Bernini*
THE ECSTASY OF ST. TERESA, **1652**
**Bernini's sculpture is as dramatic an example of
Baroque art as the paintings of Caravaggio. The
moment that St. Teresa described in her
autobiography at which she attained mystic ecstasy,
as an angel repeatedly pierced her heart with a dart,
became in Bernini's hands the centerpiece of a
theatrical tableau. He placed the patrons who had
commissioned the work on two walls of the chapel
that houses this altarpiece, sitting in what seem to be
boxes and looking at the stage on which the drama
unfolds.**
Scala/Art Resource, NY

the next century operas gained in richness and
complexity, attracting composers, as well as audiences, in ever-increasing numbers.

◆ STABILITY AND RESTRAINT IN THE ARTS

Classicism   Classicism, the other major style of
the seventeenth century, attempted to recapture
(though on a much larger scale than Renaissance
imitations of antiquity) the aesthetic values and
the strict forms that had been favored in ancient
Greece and Rome. Like the Baroque, Classicism
aimed for grandiose effects, but unlike the
Baroque, it achieved them through restraint and
discipline within a formal structure. The gradual
rise of the Classical style in the seventeenth century echoed the trend toward stability that was
taking place in other areas of intellectual life and
in politics. In the arts, the age of striving and unrest was coming to an end.

Poussin   The epitome of disciplined expression
and conscious imitation of Classical antiquity is
the work of Nicolas Poussin (1594–1665), a French
artist who spent much of his career in Rome.
Poussin was no less interested than his contemporaries in momentous and dramatic subjects, but
the atmosphere is always more subdued than in
the work of Velázquez or Rubens. The colors are
muted, the figures are restrained, and the settings
are serene. Peaceful landscapes, men and women
in togas, and ruins of Classical buildings are features of his art.

The Dutch Style   In the United Provinces different forces were at work, and they led to a style
that was much more intimate than the grandiose
outpourings of a Rubens or a Velázquez. Two aspects of Dutch society, Protestantism and republicanism, had a particular influence on its painters.
The Reformed Church frowned on religious art,
which reduced the demand for paintings of biblical scenes. Religious works, therefore, tended to
express personal faith. And the absence of a court
meant that the chief patrons of art were sober
merchants, who were far more interested in precise, dignified portraits than in ornate displays.
The result, notably in the profound and moving

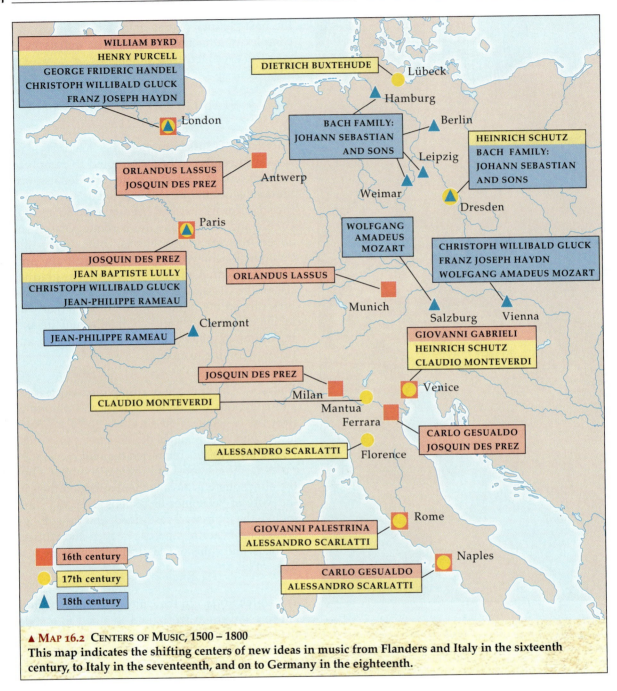

WILLIAM BYRD
HENRY PURCELL
GEORGE FRIDERIC HANDEL
CHRISTOPH WILLIBALD GLUCK
FRANZ JOSEPH HAYDN

London

DIETRICH BUXTEHUDE

Lübeck

Hamburg

Berlin

BACH FAMILY:
JOHANN SEBASTIAN
AND SONS

Leipzig

HEINRICH SCHUTZ
BACH FAMILY:
JOHANN SEBASTIAN
AND SONS

ORLANDUS LASSUS
JOSQUIN DES PREZ

Antwerp

Weimar

Dresden

Paris

WOLFGANG
AMADEUS
MOZART

CHRISTOPH WILLIBALD GLUCK
FRANZ JOSEPH HAYDN
WOLFGANG AMADEUS MOZART

JOSQUIN DES PREZ
JEAN BAPTISTE LULLY
CHRISTOPH WILLIBALD GLUCK
JEAN-PHILIPPE RAMEAU

ORLANDUS LASSUS

Munich

Salzburg

Vienna

Clermont

JEAN-PHILIPPE RAMEAU

GIOVANNI GABRIELI
HEINRICH SCHUTZ
CLAUDIO MONTEVERDI

JOSQUIN DES PREZ

Milan

Venice

CLAUDIO MONTEVERDI

Mantua
Ferrara

CARLO GESUALDO
JOSQUIN DES PREZ

ALESSANDRO SCARLATTI

Florence

Rome

16th century

17th century

18th century

GIOVANNI PALESTRINA
ALESSANDRO SCARLATTI

Naples

CARLO GESUALDO
ALESSANDRO SCARLATTI

▲ MAP 16.2 CENTERS OF MUSIC, 1500 – 1800
This map indicates the shifting centers of new ideas in music from Flanders and Italy in the sixteenth century, to Italy in the seventeenth, and on to Germany in the eighteenth.

works of Rembrandt, was a compelling art whose beauty lies in its calmness and restraint.

Rembrandt Rembrandt van Rijn (1606–1669) explored an amazing range of themes, but he was particularly fascinated by human character, emotion, and self-revelation. Whether children or old people, simple servant girls or rich burghers, his subjects are presented without elaboration or idealization; always the personality speaks for itself. Rembrandt's most remarkable achievement in portraiture—and one of the most moving series of canvases in the history of art—is his depiction of the changes in his own face over his lifetime. The

▲ *Nicolas Poussin*
The Inspiration of the Epic Poet, ca. 1628
Whereas Baroque art emphasized emotion, the classical style sought to embody reason. Poussin, the leading Classical artist of his time, believed that painting, like poetry, had to elevate the minds of its audience. The poet was thus a particularly apt subject for him—a noble and serious theme that could be presented as a scene from antiquity, with formal figures, muted colors, and ancient symbols like the laurel wreath. Poussin's views became the official doctrine of the academy of art founded in France with royal approval, and they influenced generations of painters.
Scala/Art Resource, NY

brash youth turns into the confident, successful, middle-aged man, one of the most sought-after painters in Holland. But in his late thirties the sorrows mounted: He lost his beloved wife, and commissions began to diminish. Sadness fills the eyes in these pictures. The last portraits move from despair to a final, quiet resignation as his sight slowly failed. Taken together, these paintings bear

comparison with Montaigne's essays as monuments to the exploration of one's own spirit—a searching appraisal that brings all who see it to a deeper understanding of human nature.

One could argue that Rembrandt cannot be fitted into either of the dominant styles of his time. Except for his powerful use of light, his work is far more introspective than most of the Baroque.

Nor did he adopt the forms of antiquity, as did Poussin and other Classical painters. Yet, like the advocates of Classicism, Rembrandt in his restraint seemed to anticipate the art of the next generation. After his death in 1669, serenity, calm, and elegance became the watchwords of European painting. An age of repose and grace was succeeding a time of upheaval as surely in the arts as in other spheres of life.

▼ *Rembrandt*
Self-Portrait with Palette, 1660
More than sixty self-portraits by Rembrandt have survived; though all are penetrating explorations of human character, those from his last years are especially moving. We see him here in his mid-fifties with the tools of his trade. Adapting Caravaggio's interest in light, he uses different shades of brown and the illumination of the face to create a somber and reflective mood. The very act of thinking is captured in this canvas, not to mention the full life that is etched in Rembrandt's wrinkles.
Scala/Art Resource, NY

Classicism in Drama   By the middle of the seventeenth century, the formalism of the Classical style was also being extended to literature, especially drama. This change was most noticeable in France, but it soon moved through Western Europe, as leading critics insisted that new plays conform to the structure laid down by the ancients. In particular, they wanted the three Classical unities observed: unity of place, which required that all scenes take place without change of location; unity of time, which demanded that the events in the play occur within a twenty-four-hour period; and unity of action, which dictated simplicity and purity of plot.

Corneille   The work of Pierre Corneille (1606–1684), the dominant figure in the French theater during the midcentury years, reflects the rise of Classicism. His early plays were complex and involved, and even after he came into contact with the Classical tradition, he did not accept its rules easily. His masterpiece, *Le Cid* (1636), based on the legends of a medieval Spanish hero, technically observed the three unities, but only by compressing an entire tragic love affair, a military campaign, and many other events into one day. The play won immediate popular success, but the critics, urged on by the royal minister Cardinal Richelieu, who admired the regularity and order of Classical style, condemned Corneille for imperfect observance of the three unities. Thereafter, he adhered to the Classical forms, though he was never entirely at ease with their restraints.

Passion was not absent from the Classical play; the works of Jean Racine (1639–1699), the model Classical dramatist, generate some of the most intense emotion ever seen on the stage. But the exuberance of earlier drama was disappearing. Nobody summed up the values of Classicism better than Racine in his eulogy of Corneille:

> You know in what a condition the stage was when he began to write. . . . All the rules of art, and even those of decency and decorum, broken everywhere. . . . Corneille, after having for some time sought the right path and struggled against the bad taste of his

day, inspired by extraordinary genius and helped by the study of the ancients, at last brought reason upon the stage.

Paul Mesnard (ed.), *Oeuvres de J. Racine*, vol. 4 (1886), p. 366, translated by T. K. Rabb.

This was exactly the progression—from turbulence to calm—that was apparent throughout European culture in this period.

IV. Social Patterns and Popular Culture

◆

The new sense of orderliness, of upheaval subdued, was visible throughout European society in the last years of the seventeenth century. After decades of political and religious conflict, of expressions of uneasiness in philosophy, literature, and the arts, stability and confidence were on the rise. Similarly, the end of population decline, the restoration of social order, and the suppression of disruptive forces like witchcraft indicated that the tensions were easing at all levels of society.

◆ POPULATION TRENDS

The sixteenth-century rise in Europe's population was succeeded by a period of decline that in most areas lasted long after the political and intellectual upheavals subsided. The rise had been fragile, because throughout these centuries only one child in two reached adulthood. Each couple had to give birth to four children merely to replace themselves, and since they had to wait un-

til they were financially independent to marry— usually in their mid-twenties—they rarely had the chance to produce a big family. Before improvements in nutrition in the nineteenth century, women could bear children only until their late thirties; on average, therefore, a woman had some twelve years in which to give birth to four children to maintain the population. Because lactation delayed ovulation, the mean interval between births was almost two and a half years, which meant that most couples were capable of raising only two children to adulthood. As soon as there was outside pressure—such as plague, famine, or war—population growth became impossible.

The worst of these outside pressures in the seventeenth century was the Thirty Years' War, which alone caused the death of more than 5 million people. It also helped plunge Europe into a debilitating economic depression, which, in turn, decreased the means of relieving the regular famines that afflicted all areas. Disasters like these were not easily absorbed, despite government efforts to distribute food and take other measures to combat natural calamities. Only when better times returned could population increase resume. Because England and the Netherlands led in economic recovery, they experienced a demographic revival long before their neighbors; indeed, the rise in their numbers, which began in the 1660s, accounted for most of the slight population increase the whole of Europe was able to achieve in this difficult century. By 1700, though, prosperity and population were again on the rise—both a reflection and a cause of Europe's newfound assurance and stability.

▼ Europe's Population, 1600–1700, by Regions			
Region	*1600**	*1700*	*Percentage Change*
Spain, Portugal, Italy	23.6	22.7	−4
France, Switzerland, Germany	35.0	36.2	+3
British Isles, Low Countries, Scandinavia	12.0	16.1	+34
Total	70.6	75.0	+6

*All figures are in millions.

Source: Jan de Vries, *The Economy of Europe in an Age of Crisis, 1600–1750* (Cambridge, 1976), p. 5.

◆ SOCIAL STATUS

The determinants of status in modern times—wealth, education, and family background—were viewed rather differently in the seventeenth century. Wealth was significant chiefly to merchants, education was important mainly among professionals, and background was vital primarily to the nobility. But in this period the significance of these three social indicators began to shift. Wealth became a more general source of status, as ever-larger numbers of successful merchants bought offices, lands, and titles that allowed them to enter the nobility. Education was also becoming more highly prized; throughout Europe attendance at institutions of higher learning soared after 1550, bringing to universities the sons of artisans as well as nobles. And although background was being scrutinized ever more defensively by old-line nobles, who regarded family lineage as the only criterion for acceptance into their ranks, their resistance to change was futile as the "new" aristocrats multiplied.

In general, it was assumed that everyone occupied a fixed place in the social hierarchy and that it was against the order of nature for someone to move to another level. The growing social importance of wealth and education, however, indicates that mobility was possible. Thanks to the expansion of bureaucracies, it became easier to move to new levels, either by winning favor at court or by buying an office. High status conferred important privileges: Great landowners could demand services and fees from their tenants; nobles, bureaucrats, and those with political rights in cities were often exempt from taxes; and courtiers controlled portions of the vast patronage that the government disbursed.

Contradictions in the Status of Women   At each level of society, women were usually treated as subordinate by the legal system: In many countries, even the widows of aristocrats could not inherit their husbands' estates; an abbess could never become prominent in Church government; and the few women allowed to practice a trade were excluded from the leadership of their guild. Yet there were notable businesswomen and female artists, writers, and even scientists among the growing numbers of successful self-made people

in this period. Widows often inherited their husbands' businesses and pursued thriving careers in their own right, from publishing to innkeeping. One of Caravaggio's most distinguished disciples was Artemisia Gentileschi; the Englishwoman Aphra Behn was a widely known playwright; and some of the leading patrons of intellectual life were the women aristocrats who ran literary circles, particularly in Paris. In fiction and drama, female characters often appeared as the equals of males, despite the legal restrictions of the time and the warnings against such equality in sermons and moral treatises.

◆ MOBILITY AND CRIME

The Peasants' Plight   The remarkable economic advances of the sixteenth century helped change attitudes toward wealth, but they brought few benefits to the lower levels of society. Peasants throughout Europe were, in fact, entering a time of increasing difficulty at the end of the sixteenth century. Their taxes were rising rapidly, but the prices they got for the food they grew were stabilizing. Moreover, landowners were starting what has been called the "seigneurial reaction"—making additional demands on their tenants, raising rents, and squeezing as much as they could out of the lands they owned. The effects of famine and war were also more severe at this level of society. The only escapes were to cities or armies, both of which grew rapidly in the seventeenth century. Many of those who fled their villages, however, remained on the road, part of the huge bodies of vagrants and beggars who were a common sight throughout Europe.

A few of those who settled in a town or city improved their lot, but for the large majority, poverty in cities was even more miserable and hungry than poverty on the land. Few could become apprentices, and day laborers were poorly paid and usually out of work. As for military careers, armies were carriers of disease, frequently ill fed, and subject to constant hardship.

Crime and Punishment   For many, therefore, the only alternative to starvation was crime. One area of London in the seventeenth century was totally controlled by the underworld. It offered refuge to fugitives and was never entered by respectable citizens. Robbery and violence—committed equally by desperate men, women, and even children—were common in most cities. As a result, social events like dinners and outings, or visits to the theater, took place during the daytime because the streets were unsafe at night.

If caught, Europe's criminals were treated harshly. In an age before regular police forces, however, catching them was difficult. Crime was usually the responsibility of local authorities, who depended on part-time officials (known in England as constables) for law enforcement. Only in response to major outbreaks, such as a gang of robbers preying on travelers, would the authorities recruit a more substantial armed band (rather like a posse in the American West) to pursue criminals. If such efforts succeeded in bringing offenders to justice, the defendants found they had few rights, especially if they were poor, and punishments were severe. Torture was a common means of extracting confessions; various forms of maiming, such as chopping off a hand or an ear, were considered acceptable penalties; and repeated thefts could lead to execution. Society's hierarchical instincts were apparent even in civil disputes, where nobles were usually immune from prosecution and women often could not start a case. If a woman was raped, for example, she had to find a man to bring suit. In one famous case in Italy, a girl's father sued the rapist because it was his honor that had been damaged by the attack.

◆ CHANGE IN THE VILLAGES AND CITIES

Loss of Village Cohesiveness Over three-quarters of Europe's population still lived in small village communities, but their structure was changing. In eastern Europe, peasants were being reduced to serfdom; in the west—our principal concern—familiar relationships and institutions were changing.

The essence of the traditional village had been its isolation. Cut off from frequent contact with the world beyond its immediate region, it had been self-sufficient and closely knit. Everyone knew everyone else, and mutual help was vital for survival. There might be distinctions among villagers—some more prosperous, others less so— but the sense of cohesiveness was powerful. It ex-

tended even to the main "outsiders" in the village, the priest and the local lord. The priest was often indistinguishable from his parishioners: almost as poor and sometimes hardly more literate. He adapted to local customs and beliefs, frequently taking part in semi-pagan rituals so as to keep his authority with his flock. The lord could be exploitative and demanding; but he considered the village his livelihood, and he therefore kept in close touch with its affairs and did all he could to ensure its safety, orderliness, and well-being.

Forces of Change The main intrusions onto this scene were economic and demographic. As a result of the boom in agricultural prices during the sixteenth century, followed by the economic difficulties of the seventeenth, differences in the wealth of the villagers became more marked. The richer peasants began to set themselves apart from their poorer neighbors, and the feeling of village unity began to break down. These divisions were exacerbated by the rise in population during the sixteenth century—which strained resources and forced the less fortunate to leave in search of better opportunities in cities—and by the pressures of taxation, exploitation, plague, and famine during the more difficult times of the seventeenth century.

Another intrusion that undermined the traditional cohesion of the community was the increased presence of royal officials. For centuries, elected councils, drawn from every part of the population, had run village affairs throughout Europe. In the late seventeenth century, however, these councils began to disappear as outside forces—in some cases a nearby lord, but more often government officials—asserted their control over the localities. Tax gatherers and army recruiters were now familiar figures throughout Europe. Although they were often the target of peasant rebellions, they were also welcomed when, for example, they distributed food during a famine. Their long-term influence, however, was the creation of a new layer of outside authority in the village, which was another cause of the division and fragmentation that led many to flee to the city.

As these outside intrusions multiplied, the interests of the local lord, who traditionally had defended the village's autonomy and had offered help in times of need, also changed. Nobles were beginning to look more and more to royal courts and capital cities, rather than to their local holdings, for position and power. The natural corollary was the "seigneurial reaction," with lords treating the villages they dominated as sources of income and increasingly distancing themselves from the inhabitants. Their commitment to charitable works declined, and they tended more and more to leave the welfare of the local population to church or government officials.

City Life As village life changed, the inhabitants who felt forced to leave headed for the city—an impersonal place where, instead of joining a cohesive population, they found themselves part of a mingling of peoples that was breaking down the isolation of local areas. The growing cities needed ever wider regions to provide them with food and goods, and they attracted the many who could not make ends meet in the countryside. Long-distance communications became more common, especially as localities were linked into national market and trade networks, and in the cities the new immigrants met others from distant villages.

A city was a far more chaotic place than a rural community. Urban society in general was fragmentary and disorganized, even if an individual area, such as a parish, seemed distinct and cohesive—some parishes, for example, were associated with a single trade. A city's craft guilds gave structure to artisans and shopkeepers, regulating their lives and providing welfare, but less than half the population could join a guild. The rest did odd jobs or turned to crime. The chief attraction of cities was the wide variety of economic opportunity: for women, in such areas as selling goods and processing food; for men, in construction, on the docks, and in delivery services. But employment was unpredictable, and citizens did not have community support to fall back on in hard times as they did in the village. Even forms of recreation and enjoyment were different in the city.

Popular Culture in the City One major difference between country and town was the level of literacy. Only in urban areas were there significant numbers of people who could read: It has been estimated that in cities perhaps a third of adult males were literate by 1700. Not only was reading

necessary for commerce but it had been strongly encouraged by the Reformation, with its insistence that the faithful read the Bible for themselves. This stimulus ensured that literacy also rose among women, who increasingly became pupils at the growing number of schools in Europe (although they were still not admitted to universities). As many as 25 percent of the adult women in cities may have been able to read.

These changes had a notable effect on urban life. There was now a readership for newspapers, which became common by the mid-seventeenth century, as did the coffeehouses in which they were often read. Although newspaper stories were regularly inaccurate or untrue, and their writers (relying on informants at courts) could find themselves prosecuted for showing the authorities in a bad light, they were avidly consumed, and they made politics for the first time a subject of wide interest and discussion. Theater and opera also became popular entertainments, with women for the first time taking stage roles and obtaining performances for plays they had written. When the English royal official Samuel Pepys hired a new servant in the 1660s, he made sure she could play an instrument so that she could take part in the family's musical evenings. Sales of books surged, often because they had a popular audience, and they gave broad circulation to traditional favorites, such as travel stories and lives of saints, as well as to the latest ideas of science.

◆ BELIEF IN MAGIC AND RITUALS

Although in the countryside cultural patterns looked different—with lower literacy, simpler recreations, and more visible religiosity—there was one area of popular culture in which the outlook of the city and the village was remarkably similar: the belief in magic. The townspeople may have seemed more sophisticated, but the basic assumption they shared with their country cousins was that mysterious forces controlled nature and their own lives, and there was little they could do to ensure their own well-being. The world was full of spirits, and all one could do was encourage the good, defend oneself against the evil, and hope that the good would win. Nothing that happened—a calf dying, lightning striking a house—was accidental. Everything had a purpose. Any unusual event was an omen, part of a larger plan, or the action of some unseen force.

Charivari To strengthen themselves against trouble, people used whatever help they could find. They organized special processions and holidays to celebrate good times such as harvests, to lament misfortunes, to complain about oppression, or to poke fun at scandalous behavior. These occasions, known as "rough music" in England and *charivari* in France, often used the theme of "the world turned upside down" to make their point. In the set pieces in a procession, a fool might be dressed up as a king, a woman might be shown beating her husband, or a tax collector might appear hanging from a tree. Whether ridiculing a dominating wife or lamenting the

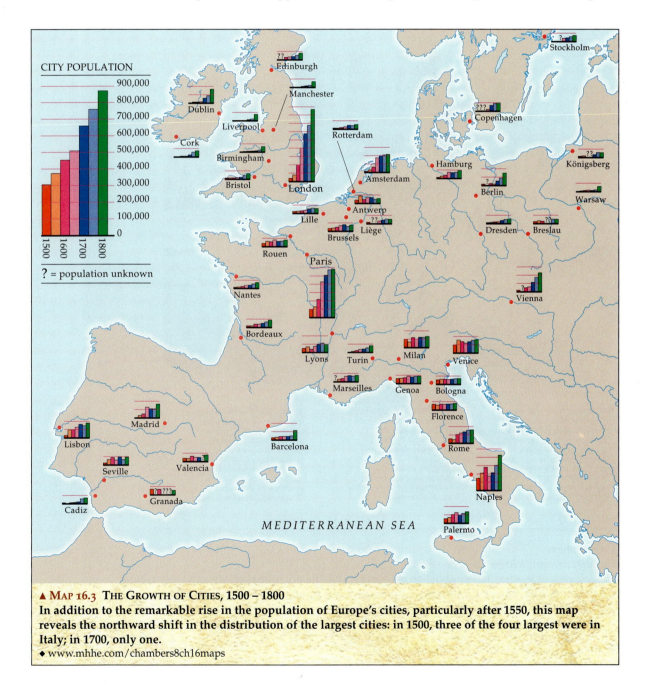

▲ **Map 16.3** **The Growth of Cities, 1500 – 1800**
In addition to the remarkable rise in the population of Europe's cities, particularly after 1550, this map reveals the northward shift in the distribution of the largest cities: in 1500, three of the four largest were in Italy; in 1700, only one.
◆ www.mhhe.com/chambers8ch16maps

▲ *Anonymous*
THE NEWSVENDOR, WOODCUT
The ancestor of the regularly published newspaper was the occasional single sheet describing the latest news or rumors. Printers would produce a few hundred copies and have them sold by street vendors whenever they had an event of some importance to describe: a battle, the death of a ruler, or some fantastic occurrence like the birth of a baby with two heads. As cities and the potential readership grew, the news sheets expanded; by the seventeenth century they had distinctive names and began to appear every week.
Bibliothèque Nationale de France, Paris

lack of bread, the community was expressing its solidarity in the face of difficulty or distasteful behavior through these rituals. They were a form of public opinion, enabling people to let off steam and express themselves.

The potential for violence was always present at such gatherings, especially when religious or social differences became entangled with other resentments. The viciousness of ordinary Protestants and Catholics toward one another revealed a frustration and aggressiveness that was not far below the surface—it was not uncommon, for example, for one side to mutilate the dead bodies of the other. When food was scarce or new impositions had been ordered by their rulers, peasants and townspeople needed little excuse to show their anger openly. Women took the lead, not only because they had firsthand experience of the difficulty of feeding a family but also because troops were more reluctant to attack them. This tradition was still alive in 1789, in the early days of the French Revolution, when a band made up primarily of women marched from Paris to the royal court at Versailles to demand bread.

Other Magical Remedies Ordinary people also had other outlets for their frustrations. Recognizing their powerlessness in the face of outside forces, they resorted to their version of the magic that the literate were finding so fashionable at this very time. Whereas the sophisticated patronized astrologers, paying handsomely for horoscopes and advice about how to live their lives, the peasants and the poor consulted popular almanacs or sought out "cunning men" and wise women for secret spells, potions, and other remedies for their anxieties. Even religious ceremonies were thought of as being related to the rituals of the magical world, in which so-called white witches—the friendly kind—gave assistance when a ring was lost, when a new bride could not become pregnant, or when the butter would not form out of the milk.

Witches and Witch-Hunts Misfortunes, in other words, were never just plain bad luck; rather, there was intent behind everything that happened. Events were willed, and if they turned out badly, they must have been willed by the good witch's opposite, the evil witch. Such beliefs often led to cruel persecutions of innocent victims—

usually helpless old women, able to do nothing but mutter curses when taunted by neighbors, and easy targets if someone had to be blamed for unfortunate happenings.

This quest for scapegoats naturally focused on the most vulnerable members of society, such as Jews or, in the case of witches, women. Accusations were often directed at a woman who was old and alone, with nobody to defend her. She was feared because she seemed to be an outsider, or not sufficiently deferential to her supposed betters. It was believed that witches read strange books and knew magic spells, an indication of what many regarded as inappropriate and dangerous levels of literacy and learning for a woman.

In the sixteenth and seventeenth centuries, the hunt for witches intensified to levels never previously reached. This period has been called the era of the "great witch craze," and for good reason. There were outbursts in every part of Europe, and tens of thousands of the accused were executed. Dozens of men, most of them clerics, made witch-hunting a full-time profession and persuaded civic and other government authorities to devote their resources to stamping out this threat to social and religious stability. Suspects were almost always tortured, and it is not too surprising that they usually "confessed" and implicated others as servants of the devil. The practices that were uncovered varied—in some areas witches were said to dance with the devil, in others to fly on broomsticks, in others to be possessed by evil spirits who could induce dreadful (and possibly psychosomatic) symptoms—but the punishment was usually the same: burning at the stake. And the hysteria was infectious. One accusation could trigger dozens more until entire regions were swept with fear and hatred.

◆ FORCES OF RESTRAINT

By the middle of the seventeenth century, the wave of assaults on witches was beginning to recede (see box: "A Witness Analyzes the Witch Craze"). Social and political leaders came to realize that the campaigns against witches could endanger authority, especially when accusations were turned against the rich and privileged classes. Increasingly, therefore, cases were not brought to trial, and when they were, lawyers and

▲ *Hans Baldung Grien*
Witches, Woodcut
This woodcut by the German artist Grien shows the popular image of witches in early modern Europe. One carries a potion while flying on a goat. The others put together the ingredients for a magic potion in a jar inscribed with mystical symbols. The fact that witches were thought to be learned women who could understand magic was another reason they were feared by a Europe that expected women to be uneducated.
Private Collection

A WITNESS ANALYZES THE WITCH CRAZE

◆

Although for most Europeans around 1600 witchcraft was real—a religious problem caused by the devil—there were a few observers who were beginning to think more analytically about the reasons for the rapid spread of accusations. One such observer was a clergyman named Linden, who was attached to the cathedral of the great city of Trier in western Germany. His description of a witch-hunt in the Trier region ignored the standard religious explanations.

"Inasmuch as it was popularly believed that the continued sterility of many years was caused by witches, the whole area rose to exterminate the witches. This movement was promoted by many in office, who hoped to gain wealth from the persecution. And so special accusers, inquisitors, notaries, judges, and constables dragged to trial and torture human beings of both sexes and burned them in great numbers. Scarcely any of those who were accused escaped punishment. So far did the madness of the furious populace and the courts go in this thirst for blood and booty that there was scarcely anybody who was not smirched by some suspicion of this crime. Meanwhile, notaries, copyists and innkeepers grew rich. The executioner rode a fine horse, like a noble of the court, and dressed in gold and silver; his wife competed with noble dames in the richness of her array. A direr pestilence or a more ruthless invader could hardly have ravaged the territory than this inquisition and persecution without bounds. Many were the reasons for doubting that all were really guilty. At last, though the flames were still unsated, the people grew poor, rules were made and enforced restricting the fees and costs of examinations, and suddenly, as when in war funds fail, the zeal of the persecutors died out."

From George L. Burr (ed.), "The Witch Persecutions," *Translations and Reprints from the Original Sources of European History,* vol. 3 (Philadelphia: University of Pennsylvania, 1902), pp. 13–14.

doctors (who approached the subject from a different point of view from the clergy) cast doubt on the validity of the testimony. Gradually, excesses were restrained and control was reestablished; by 1700 there was only a trickle of new incidents.

The decline in accusations of witchcraft reflected not only the more general quieting down of conflict and upheaval in the late seventeenth century but also the growing proportion of Europe's population that was living in cities. Here, less reliant on the luck of good weather, people could feel themselves more in control of their own fates. If there were unexpected fires, there were fire brigades; if a house burned down, there might even be insurance—a new protection for individuals that was spreading in the late 1600s. A process that has been called the "disenchantment" of the world—growing skepticism about spirits and mysterious forces, and greater self-reliance— was under way.

Religious Discipline The churches played an important part in suppressing the traditional reliance on magic. In Catholic countries the Counter Reformation produced better-educated priests who were trained to impose official doctrine instead of tolerating unusual local customs. Among Protestants, ministers were similarly well educated and denounced magical practices as idolatrous or superstitious. And both camps treated passion and enthusiasm with suspicion. Habits did not change overnight, but gradually ordinary people were being persuaded to abandon old fears and beliefs. There were still major scares in mid-century. An eclipse in 1654 prompted panic throughout Europe; comets still inspired prophecies of the end of the world; and in the 1660s a self-proclaimed messiah named Shabtai Zvi attracted a massive following among the Jews of Europe and the Middle East. Increasingly, though, such visions of doom or the end of time were becoming fringe beliefs, dismissed by authorities and most elements of society. Eclipses and comets now had scientific explanations, and the messiah came to be regarded as a spiritual, not an immediate, promise.

SUMMARY

◆

Even at the level of popular culture, therefore, Europeans had reason to feel, by the late seventeenth century, that a time of upheaval and uncertainty was over. A sense of confidence and orderliness was returning, and in intellectual circles the optimism seemed justified by the achievements of science. In fact, there arose a scholarly dispute around 1700, known as the "battle of the books," in which one side claimed, for the first time, that the "moderns" had outshone the "ancients." Using the scientists as their chief example, the advocates of the "moderns" argued—in a remarkable break with the reverence for the past that had dominated medieval and Renaissance culture—that advances in thought were possible and that one did not always have to accept the superiority of antiquity. Such self-confidence made it clear that, in the world of ideas as surely as in the world of politics, a period of turbulence had given way to an era of renewed assurance and stability.

QUESTIONS FOR FURTHER THOUGHT

◆

1. **Are there similarities in the creativity that marks the scientist and the artist?**

2. **Is it fair to ask whether popular beliefs and rituals do more harm than good?**

RECOMMENDED READING

◆

Sources

*Drake, Stillman (tr. and ed.). *Discoveries and Opinions of Galileo.* 1957. The complete texts of some of Galileo's most important works.

*Hall, Marie Boas (ed.). *Nature and Nature's Laws: Documents of the Scientific Revolution.* 1970. A good collection of documents by and about the pioneers of modern science.

Studies

Biagioli, Mario. *Galileo, Courtier: The Practice of Science in the Culture of Absolutism.* 1993. A fascinating study of the political forces at work in Galileo's career.

Braudel, Fernand. *Capitalism and Material Life, 1400–1800.* Miriam Kochan (tr.). 1973. A classic, pioneering study of the structure of daily life in early modern Europe.

Brink, Jean, Alison Coudert, and Maryanne Horowitz (eds.). *The Politics of Gender in Early Modern Europe.* 1989.

*Burke, Peter. *Popular Culture in Early Modern Europe.* 1978. A lively introduction to the many forms of expression and belief among the ordinary people of Europe.

*Gutmann, Myron P. *Toward the Modern Economy: Early Industry in Europe, 1500–1800.* 1988. A clear survey of recent work on economic development in this period.

*Kuhn, Thomas S. *The Structure of Scientific Revolutions.* 1962. A suggestive interpretation of the reasons the scientific revolution developed and took hold.

*Ladurie, Emmanuel Le Roy. *The Peasants of Languedoc.* John Day (tr.). 1966. A brilliant evocation of peasant life in France in the sixteenth and seventeenth centuries.

*Levack, Brian P. *The Witch-Hunt in Early Modern Europe.* 1987. An excellent survey of the belief in witchcraft and its consequences.

*Popkin, Richard H. *The History of Scepticism from Erasmus to Descartes.* 1964. Taking one strand in European thought as its subject, this lively study places both Montaigne and Descartes in a new perspective.

Rabb, Theodore K. *Renaissance Lives.* 1993. Brief biographies of fifteen people, both famous and obscure, who lived just before and during this period.

*Shapin, S. *The Scientific Revolution.* 1996.

*Shearman, John. *Mannerism.* 1968. The best short introduction to a difficult artistic style.

*Thomas, Keith. *Religion and the Decline of Magic.* 1976. The most thorough account of popular culture yet published, this enormous book, while dealing mainly with England, treats at length such subjects as witchcraft, astrology, and ghosts in a most readable style.

*Available in paperback.

▲ *Louis XIV and His Family*

Louis XIV (seated) is shown here in full regal splendor surrounded by three of his heirs. On his right is his eldest son, on his left is his eldest grandson, and, reaching out his hand, is his eldest great-grandson, held by his governess. All three of these heirs died before Louis, and thus they never became kings of France.

THE EMERGENCE OF THE EUROPEAN STATE SYSTEM

The acceptance of strong central governments that emerged out of the crisis of the mid-seventeenth century was a victory not merely for kings but for an entire way of organizing political structures. As a result of huge increases in the scale of warfare and taxation, bureaucracies had mushroomed, and their presence was felt throughout Europe. Yet no central administration, however powerful, could function without the support of the nobles who ruled the countryside. Regional loyalties had dominated European society for centuries, and only a regime that drew on those loyalties could hope to maintain the support of its subjects. The political structures that developed during the century following the 1650s were, therefore, the work not only of ambitious princes but also of a nobility long accustomed to exercising authority and now prepared to find new ways of exerting its influence. There were conflicts between monarchs and their subjects, to be sure, but to the leaders of society during the century following the crisis of the 1640s and 1650s, it was clear that state building required a common effort to establish stronger political, social, military, financial, and religious structures that would support effective government. The institutions and practices they created have remained essential to the modern state ever since.

	Social Structure	Body Politic	Changes in the Organization of Production and in the Impact of Technology	Evolution of Family and Changing Gender Roles	War	Religion	Cultural Expression
I. Absolutism in France	�_	▊			▊		
II. Other Patterns of Absolutism	▊	▊			▊		
III. Alternatives to Absolutism	▊	▊	▊				▊
IV. The International System	▊	▊			▊		

Chapter 17. The Emergence of the European State System

I. Absolutism in France

One way of creating a strong, centralized state was the political system known as absolutism, the belief that the monarch was absolute—that all power emanated from his unlimited authority. Absolutism was based on a widely held theory known as the divine right of kings. This theory arose from the fact that kings were anointed with holy oil at their coronations; it asserted that the monarch was God's representative on earth.

◆ THE RULE OF LOUIS XIV

The most famous example of absolutism was the kingdom of France, which became the most powerful and also the most imitated regime in Europe. Taken to an extreme, as it was by Louis XIV (1643–1715), this view justified absolute power and treated treason as blasphemy. The leading advocate of the theory, Bishop Bossuet, called Louis God's lieutenant and argued that the Bible itself endorsed absolutism. In reality, the king worked in close partnership with the nobles to maintain order, and he often (though not always) felt obliged to defend their local authority as a reinforcement of his own power. Nevertheless, the very notion that the king not only was supreme but could assert his will with armies and bureaucracies of unprecedented size gave absolutism both an image and a reality that set it apart from previous systems of monarchical rule. Here at last was a force that could hold together

and control the increasingly complex interactions of regions and interest groups that made up a state.

Versailles The setting in which a central government operated often reflected its power and its methods. Philip II in the late 1500s had created, at the Escorial outside Madrid, the first isolated palace that controlled a large realm. A hundred years later, Louis XIV created at Versailles, near Paris, a far more elaborate court as the center of an even larger and more intrusive bureaucracy than Philip's. The isolation of government and the exercise of vast personal power seemed to go hand in hand.

The king moved the court in the 1680s to Versailles, 12 miles from Paris, where, at a cost of half a year's royal income, he transformed a small château his father had built into the largest building in Europe. There, far from Parisian mobs, he enjoyed the splendor and the ceremonies, centered on himself, which exalted his majesty. His self-aggrandizing image as "Sun King" was symbolized by coins that showed the sun's rays falling first on Louis and then by reflection onto his subjects, who thus owed life and warmth to their monarch. Every French nobleman of any significance spent time each year at Versailles, not only to maintain access to royal patronage and governmental affairs but also to demonstrate the wide support for Louis' system of rule. Historians have called this process the domestication of the aristocracy, as great lords who had once drawn their

▲ *THE PALACE OF VERSAILLES IN 1668*
This painting shows Versailles not long before Louis decided to move there; he was soon to begin an enormous expansion into the gardens at the back that more than doubled the size of the buildings. In this scene, the royal coach, with its entourage, is just about to enter the château.
Giraudon/Art Resource, NY

status from their lineage or lands came to regard service to the throne as the best route to power. But the benefits cut both ways. The king gained the services of influential administrators, and they gained privileges and rewards without the uncertainties that had accompanied their traditional resistance to central control.

Court Life The visible symbol of Louis' absolutism was Versailles. Here the leaders of France assembled, and around them swirled the most envied social circles of the time. From the court emanated the policies and directives that increasingly affected the lives of the king's subjects and also determined France's relations with other states.

At Versailles, too, French culture was shaped by the king's patronage of those artists and writers who appealed to the royal taste. For serious drama and history, Louis turned to the playwright and writer Racine (1639–1699); for comedy, to the theatrical producer and playwright Molière (1622–1673); and for opera and the first performances of what we now call ballet, to the composer Lully (1632–1687). Moreover, all artistic expression, from poetry to painting, was regulated by royal academies that were founded in the 1600s; backed by the king's authority, these academies laid down rules for what was acceptable in such areas as verse forms or architectural style. For example, when the famous Italian sculptor and architect Bernini came to Paris to design part of a royal palace and fashion a sculpture of the king, both works were rejected as overly ornate. Official taste was what counted. The dazzling displays at Versailles had to observe strict rules of dignity and gravity that were considered the only means of exalting the king. Yet everything was done on a scale and with a magnificence that no other European ruler could match, though many tried.

Paris and Versailles   The one alternative to Versailles as a center of society and culture was Paris, and indeed the split between court and capital was one of the divisions between government and people that eventually was to lead to the French Revolution. A particularly notable difference was in the role of women. Versailles was overwhelmingly a male society. Women achieved prominence only as royal mistresses in Louis' early years, or as the creators of a rigidly pious atmosphere in his last years. They were also essential to the highly elaborate rituals of civility and manners that developed at Versailles. But they were allowed no independent initiative in social or cultural matters. In Paris, by contrast, women established and dominated the salons that promoted easy conversation, a mixture of social backgrounds, and forms of expression—political discussion and ribald humor, for example—that were not acceptable at the staid and sober court. Yet the contrasts were not merely between the formal palace and the relaxed salon. Even before Louis moved to Versailles, he banned as improper one of Molière's comedies, *Tartuffe,* which mocked excessive religious devoutness. It took five years of reworking by Molière before Louis allowed the play to be performed (1669), and it then became a major hit in Paris, but it was never a favorite at court.

◆ GOVERNMENT

Absolutism was more than a device to satisfy royal whims, for Louis was a gifted administrator and politician who used his power for state building. By creating and reorganizing government institutions, he strengthened his authority at home and increased his ascendancy over his neighbors. The longest-lasting result of his absolutism was

that the French state won control over three crucial activities: the use of armed force, the formulation and execution of laws, and the collection and expenditure of revenue. These functions, in turn, depended on a centrally controlled bureaucracy responsive to royal orders and efficient enough to carry them out in distant provinces over the objections of local groups.

Nobody could suppress all vested interests and local loyalties, but the bureaucracy was supposed to be insulated from outside pressure by the absolute monarch's power to remove and transfer appointees. This independence was also promoted by training programs, improved administrative methods, and the use of experts wherever possible—both in the central bureaucracy and in provincial offices. Yet the system could not have functioned without the cooperation of local aristocrats, who were encouraged to use the power and income they derived from official positions to strengthen central authority.

The King's Dual Functions   At the head of this structure, Louis XIV carried off successfully a dual function that few monarchs had the talent to sustain: He was both king in council and king in court. Louis the administrator coexisted with Louis the courtier, who hunted, cultivated the arts, and indulged in huge banquets. In his view, the two roles went together, and he held them in balance. Among his numerous imitators, however, the easier side of absolutism, court life, consumed an excessive share of a state's resources and became an end in itself. The effect was to give prestige to the leisure pursuits of the upper classes while sapping the energies of influential figures. Louis was one of the few who avoided sacrificing affairs of state to regal pomp.

Like court life, government policy under Louis XIV was tailored to the aim of state building. As he was to discover, there were limits to his absolutism; the resources and powers at his disposal were not endless. But until the last years of his reign, they served his many purposes extremely well (see "Louis XIV on Kingship," see p. 594). Moreover, Louis had superb support at the highest levels of his administration—ministers whose viewpoints differed but whose skills were carefully blended by their ruler.

▲ *Antoine Watteau*
FÊTE IN THE PARK, **1718**
The luxurious life of the nobility during the eighteenth century is captured in this scene of men and women in fine silks, enjoying a picnic in a lovely park setting.
Reproduced by Permission of the Trustees of the Wallace Collection, London

Competing Ministers Until the late 1680s the king's two leading advisers were Jean-Baptiste Colbert and the marquis of Louvois. Colbert was a financial wizard who regarded a mercantilist policy as the key to state building. He believed that the government should give priority to increasing France's wealth. As a result, he believed that the chief danger to the country's well-being was the United Provinces, Europe's great trader state, and that royal resources should be poured into the navy, manufacturing, and shipping. By contrast, Louvois, the son of a military administrator, consistently emphasized the army as the foundation of France's power. He believed that the country was threatened primarily by land— by the Holy Roman Empire on its flat, vulnerable northeast frontier—and thus that resources should be allocated to the army and to border fortifications.

◆ FOREIGN POLICY

Louis tried to balance these goals within his overall aims—to expand France's frontiers and to assert his superiority over other European states. Like the magnificence of his court, his power on the international scene served to demonstrate *la gloire* (the glory) of France. But his effort to expand that power prompted his neighbors to form coalitions and alliances of common defense, designed to keep him in check. From this response was to emerge the concept of a state system and

LOUIS XIV ON KINGSHIP

◆

From time to time, Louis XIV put on paper brief accounts of his actions: For example, he wrote some brief memoirs in the late 1660s. These reflections about his role as king were intended as a guide for his son and indicate both his high view of kingship and the seriousness with which he approached his duties. The following are extracts from his memoirs and other writings.

"Homage is due to kings, and they do whatever they like. It certainly must be agreed that, however bad a prince may be, it is always a heinous crime for his subjects to rebel against him. He who gave men kings willed that they should be respected as His lieutenants, and reserved to Himself the right to question their conduct. It is His will that everyone who is born a subject should obey without qualification. This law, as clear as it is universal, was not made only for the sake of princes: it is also for the good of the people themselves. It is therefore the duty of kings to sustain by their own example the religion upon which they rely; and they must realize that, if their subjects see them plunged in vice or violence, they can hardly render to their person the respect due to their office, or recognize in them the living image of Him who is all-holy as well as almighty.

"It is a fine thing, a noble and enjoyable thing, to be a king. But it is not without its pains, its fatigues, and its troubles. One must work hard to reign. In working for the state, a king is working for himself. The good of the one is the glory of the other. When the state is prosperous, famous, and powerful, the king who is the cause of it is glorious; and he ought in consequence to have a larger share than others do of all that is most agreeable in life."

From J. M. Thompson, *Lectures on Foreign History, 1494–1789* (Oxford: Blackwell, 1956), pp. 172–174.

---

the notion of a balance of power among the states of Europe.

In his early years Louis relied heavily on Colbert, who moved gradually toward war with the Dutch when he was unable to undermine their control of French maritime trade. But the war (1672–1678) was a failure, and so the pendulum swung toward Louvois' priorities. In the early 1680s Louis adopted the marquis's aims and claimed a succession of territories on France's northeast border. No one claim seemed large enough to provoke his neighbors to fight, especially since the Holy Roman Emperor, Leopold I, was distracted by a resumption in 1682 of war with the Turks in the east. The result was that France was able to annex large segments of territory until, in 1686, a league of other European states was formed to restrain Louis' growing power (see Map 17.1).

Louis versus Europe   The leaders of the league were William III of the United Provinces and Emperor Leopold. Leopold was prepared to join the struggle because, even though his war with the Turks was to continue until 1699, the fighting turned in his favor after 1683, when his troops broke a Turkish siege of Vienna. And six years later William became a far more formidable foe when he gained the English throne. In 1688 the league finally went to war to put an end to French expansion. When Louis began to lose the territories he had gained in the 1680s, he decided to seek peace and remove Louvois from power in 1690, though the war did not end until 1697. But the respite did not last long. Four years later France became involved in a bitter war that brought famine, wretched poverty, and humiliation. This was a war to gain the Spanish throne for Louis' family, regardless of the terrible consequences of the fighting. This final, ruinous enterprise revealed both the new power of France and its limits. By launching an all-out attempt to establish his own and his country's supremacy in Europe, Louis showed that he felt capable of taking on the whole of the continent; but by then he no longer had the economic and military base at home or the weak opposition abroad to ensure success.

Economic strains had begun to appear in the 1690s, when shattering famines throughout France reduced tax revenues and the size of the workforce, even as enemies began to unite abroad. Louis had the most formidable army in Europe—400,000 men by the end of his reign—but both William and Leopold believed he could be defeated by a combined assault, and they led the attack in the final showdown when the Habsburg king of Spain, Charles II, died without an heir in 1700.

The War of Spanish Succession   There were various claimants to the Spanish throne, and Charles himself had changed his mind a number of times, but at his death his choice was Philip, Louis XIV's grandson (see genealogical table below). Had Louis been willing to agree not to unite the thrones of France and Spain and to allow the Spanish empire to be opened (for the first time) to foreign traders, Charles's wish might have been respected. But Louis refused to compromise, and in 1701 William and Leopold created the so-called Grand Alliance, which declared war on France the following year. The French now had to fight virtually all of Europe in a war over the Spanish succession, not only at home but also overseas, in India, Canada, and the Caribbean.

Led by two brilliant generals—the Englishman John Churchill, duke of Marlborough, and the Austrian Prince Eugène—the Grand Alliance won a series of smashing victories. France's hardships were increased by a terrible famine in 1709. Although the criticism of his policies became fierce, and dangerous rebellions erupted, the Sun King retained his hold over his subjects. Despite military disaster, he was able to keep his nation's borders intact and the Spanish throne for his grandson (though he had to give up the possibility

THE SPANISH SUCCESSION, 1700

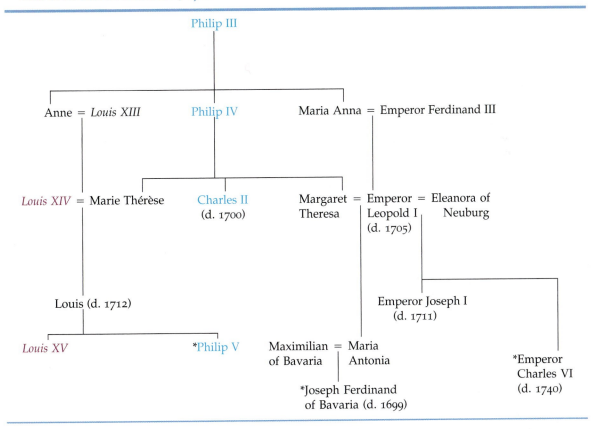

Note: Names in blue = Kings of Spain; names in red = Kings of France.

*People designated at various times as heirs of Charles II.

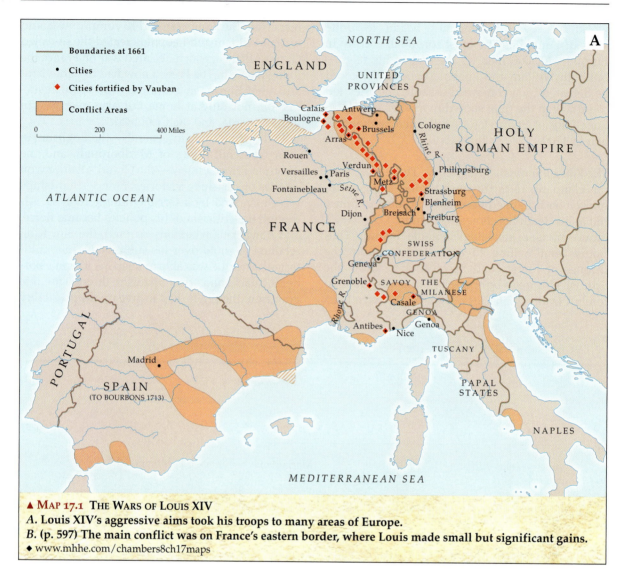

▲ MAP 17.1 THE WARS OF LOUIS XIV
A. Louis XIV's aggressive aims took his troops to many areas of Europe.
B. (p. 597) The main conflict was on France's eastern border, where Louis made small but significant gains.
◆ www.mhhe.com/chambers8ch17maps

of union with France and end the restrictions on trade in the Spanish empire) when peace treaties were signed at Utrecht in 1713 and 1714. When it was all over, Louis' great task of state building, both at home and abroad, had withstood the severest of tests: defeat on the battlefield.

◆ DOMESTIC POLICY

Control and Reform The assertion of royal supremacy at home was almost complete by the time Louis came to power, but he extended centralized control to religion and social institutions. Both the Protestant Huguenots and the Catholic Jansenists interfered with the religious uniformity

that Louis considered essential in an absolutist state. As a result, pressures against these groups mounted steadily. In 1685 Louis revoked the Edict of Nantes, now almost a century old, which had granted Protestants limited toleration, and he forced France's 1 million Huguenots either to leave the country (four-fifths did) or to convert to Catholicism. This was a political rather than a religious step, taken to promote unity despite the economic consequences that followed the departure of a vigorous, productive, and entrepreneurial minority.

Jansenism was more elusive. It had far fewer followers, and it was a movement that emphasized spiritual values within Catholicism. But the

France in 1661

French gains by 1713

Boundary of the greatest gains of Louis XIV

UNITED PROVINCES

Calais

Antwerp

Boulogne

Brussels

SPANISH NETHERLANDS

Cologne

Arras

Rhine R.

Verdun

Philippsburg

Paris

Seine R.

Metz

LORRAINE

Strassburg

ALSACE

Blenheim

Breisach

Dijon

Freiburg

FRANCHE-COMTE

FRANCE

SWISS CONFEDERATION

Geneva

SAVOY

Grenoble

Rhone R.

Casale

GENOA

Antibes   Nice

0   100   200 Miles

MEDITERRANEAN SEA

came law. The Parlement of Paris was the only governmental institution that offered Louis any real resistance. The issues over which it caused trouble were usually religious, and the link between *parlementaire* independence and Jansenism gave Louis more than enough reason for displeasure. He razed the Jansenists' headquarters, the Abbey of Port-Royal, and persuaded the pope to issue a bull condemning Jansenism. He was prevented from implementing the bull—over *parlementaire* opposition—only by his death in 1715.

The drive toward uniformity that prompted these actions was reflected in all of domestic policy. Louis kept in check what little protest arose in the parlements and either forbade or overruled their efforts to block his decrees; major uprisings by peasants in central France in the 1690s and 1700s were ruthlessly suppressed, as were all disturbances; Parisian publishers came under bureaucratic supervision; and the *intendants*, the government's chief provincial officers, were given increased authority, especially to supply the ever-growing money and recruitment needs of the army.

At the outset of his rule, Louis used his power to improve France's economy. In this, he followed a pattern familiar from earlier monarchs' reigns: an initial burst of reform measures designed to cure the country's economic ills, which were gradually forgotten because foreign policy demanded instant funds. In the early years, under Colbert's ministry, major efforts were made to stimulate manufacturing, agriculture, and home and foreign trade. Some industries, notably those involving luxuries, like the silk production of Lyons, received considerable help and owed their prosperity to royal patronage. Colbert also tried, not entirely effectively, to reduce the crippling effects of France's countless internal tolls. These were usually nobles' perquisites, and they could multiply the cost of shipped goods. The government divided the country into a number of districts, within which shipments were to be toll-free, but the system never removed the worst abuses. Louis also tried to boost foreign trade, at first by financing new overseas trading companies and later by founding new port cities as naval and commercial centers. He achieved notable success only in the West Indies, where sugar plantations became a source of great wealth.

very fact that it challenged the official Church emphasis on ritual and was condemned by Rome made it a source of unrest. Even more unsettling was its success in gaining support among the magistrate class—the royal officers in the parlements, who had to register all royal edicts before they be-

◆ THE END OF AN ERA

Louis' success in state building was remarkable, and France became the envy of Europe. Yet ever since the Sun King's reign, historians have recalled the famines and wars of his last years and have contrasted his glittering court with the misery of most French people. Taxes and rents rose remorselessly, and in many regions the hardships were made worse by significant declines in the population. Particularly after the famines of the 1690s and 1709, many contemporaries remarked on the dreadful condition of France's peasants.

The reign of Louis XIV can thus be regarded as the end of an era in the life of the lower classes. By pushing his need for resources to its limits, he inflicted a level of suffering that was not to recur, because governments increasingly came to realize that state building depended on the welfare and support of their people. In the eighteenth century, although there was still much suffering to come, the terrible subsistence crises, with their cycles of famine and plague, came to an end, largely because of official efforts to distribute food in starving areas and to isolate and suppress outbreaks of plague. Thus, although the hand of the central government was heavier in 1715 than a hundred years before, it was becoming more obviously a beneficent as well as a burdensome force. The Counter Reformation Church, growing in strength since the Council of Trent, also had a more salutary influence as religious struggles died away, for it brought into local parishes better-educated and more dedicated priests who, as part of their new commitment to service, exerted themselves to calm the outbreaks of witchcraft and irrational fear that had swept the countryside for centuries. Despite the strains Louis had caused, therefore, his absolutist authority was now firmly in place and could ensure a dominant European role for a united and powerful France.

◆ FRANCE AFTER LOUIS XIV

The Sun King had created a model for absolutism in partnership with his nobility, but the traditional ambitions of the nobles reasserted themselves after he died in 1715, leaving a child as his heir. The duke of Orléans, Louis XIV's nephew, who became regent until 1723, was committed to giving authority to the aristocracy. He also restored the parlements to political power and replaced royal bureaucrats with councils composed of leading members of the nobility. The scheme was a failure because the councils were unable to govern effectively. The parlements, however, would never again surrender their power to veto royal legislation. They became a rallying point for those who opposed centralization and wished to limit the king's powers.

Finance was also a serious problem for the government, because of the debts left by Louis XIV's wars. A brilliant Scottish financier, John Law, suggested an answer: a government-sponsored central bank that would issue paper notes, expand credit, and encourage investment in a new trading company for the French colonies. By tying the bank to this company, the Company of the Occident, a venture that promised subscribers vast profits from the Louisiana territory in North America, Law set off an investment boom. But the public's greed soon pushed prices for the company's stock to insanely high levels. A bust was inevitable, and when it came, in 1720, the entire scheme of bank notes and credit collapsed.

Louis XV and Fleury   The same political and financial problems were to plague France, in different forms, throughout the eighteenth century, until the leaders of the French Revolution sought radical ways to solve them in the 1790s. Yet the uncertainties of the regency did give way to a long period of stability after 1726, when Louis XV gave almost unlimited authority to his aging tutor and adviser, Cardinal Fleury. Cautious, dedicated to the monarchy, and surrounded by talented subordinates, Fleury made absolutism function quietly and effectively and enabled France to recover from the setbacks that had marked the end of Louis XIV's reign. Fleury's tenure coincided with abundant harvests, slowly rising population, and increased commercial activity.

Political Problems   Fleury contained the ambitions of the governing class, but when he died in 1743 at the age of 90, the pressures exploded. War hawks plunged France into the first of several unsuccessful wars with its neighbors that strained French credit to the breaking point. At home royal authority also deteriorated. Having no one to

TWO VIEWS OF LOUIS XIV

Implicit in any assessment of the reign of Louis XIV in France is a judgment about the nature of absolutism and the kind of government the continental European monarchies created in the late seventeenth and eighteenth centuries. From the perspective of Frenchman Albert Sorel, a historian of the French Revolution writing at the end of the nineteenth century, the Revolution had been necessary to save France from Louis' heritage. For the American John Rule, a historian who concerned himself primarily with the development of political institutions during the seventeenth century, the marks of Louis XIV's rule were caution, bureaucracy, and order.

Sorel: "The edifice of the state enjoyed incomparable brilliance and splendor, but it resembled a Gothic cathedral in which the height of the nave and the arches had been pushed beyond all reason, weakening the walls as they were raised ever higher. Louis XIV carried the principle of monarchy to its utmost limit, and abused it in all respects to the point of excess. He left the nation crushed by war, mutilated by banishments, and impatient of the yoke which it felt to be ruinous. Men were worn-out, the treasury empty, all relationships strained by the violence of tension, and in the immense framework of the state there remained no institution except the accidental appearance of genius. Things had reached a point where, if a great king did not appear, there would be a great revolution."

From Albert Sorel, *L'Europe et la révolution française,* 3rd ed., vol. 1, (Paris, 1893), p. 199, as translated in William F. Church, ed., *The Greatness of Louis XIV: Myth or Reality?* (Boston: D. C. Heath, 1959), p. 63.

Rule: "As Louis XIV himself said of the tasks of kingship, they were at once great, noble, and delightful. Yet Louis' enjoyment of his craft was tempered by political prudence. At an early age he learned to listen attentively to his advisers, to speak when spoken to, to ponder evidence, to avoid confrontations, to dissemble, to wait. He believed that time and tact would conquer. Despite all the evidence provided him by his ministers and his servants, Louis often hesitated before making a decision; he brooded, and in some instances put off decisions altogether. As he grew older, the king tended to hide his person and his office. Even his officials seldom saw the king for more than a brief interview. And as decision-making became centralized in the hands of the ministers, [so] the municipalities, the judges, the local estates, the guilds and at times the peasantry contested royal encroachments on their rights. Yet to many in the kingdom, Louis represented a modern king, an agent of stability whose struggle was their struggle and whose goal was to contain the crises of the age."

From John C. Rule, "Louis XIV, *Roi-Bureaucrate,*" in Rule (ed.), *Louis XIV and the Craft of Kingship* (Columbus: Ohio State University Press, 1969), pp. 91–92.

replace Fleury as chief minister, Louis XV put his confidence in a succession of advisers, some capable, some mediocre. But he did not back them when attacks from court factions became troublesome. Uninterested in government, he avoided confrontation, neglected affairs of state, and devoted himself instead to hunting and to court ceremony.

Although Louis XV provided weak leadership, France's difficulties were structural as well as personal. The main problems—special privileges, political power, and finance—posed almost impossible challenges. Governments that levy new taxes arbitrarily seem despotic, even if the need for them is clear and the distribution equitable. One of France's soundest taxes was the *vingtième,* or twentieth, which was supposed to tap the income of all parts of French society roughly equally. But the nobility and clergy evaded most of the tax. Naturally, aggressive royal ministers wanted to remedy that situation. In the 1750s, for example, an effort was made to put teeth into the *vingtième's* bite on the clergy's huge wealth. But the effort merely ruined the career of the capable royal official who devised it. The clergy resisted furiously; and the parlements joined the attack

▲ *P. D. Martin*
PROCESSION AFTER LOUIS XV'S CORONATION AT RHEIMS, **1722**
This magnificent scene, in front of the cathedral in which French kings traditionally were crowned, provides a sense of the throngs who came to celebrate the day in 1722 when Louis XV officially came of age and received his crown. Paintings depicting royal virtue were erected around the cathedral, and Louis himself (in red on a white horse just to the right of center) was preceded by a flag covered with his symbol, the fleur-de-lis. The other flags remind us that this event was an occasion for international pageantry.
Giraudon/Art Resource, NY

against the "despotism" of a crown that taxed its subjects arbitrarily. Thus, the privileged groups not only blocked reforms but also made the monarch's position more difficult by their opposition and rhetoric of liberty as they fought to limit royal absolutism.

The Long Term Despite these special interests, the 1700s were a time of notable advance for Europe's most populous and wealthy state. France in this period experienced remarkable expansion in population, in the rural economy, in commerce, and in empire building. No one knew at the time that the failures of reforming royal ministers in

the mid-1700s foretold a stalemate that would help bring the old regime crashing down.

II. Other Patterns of Absolutism
◆

Four other monarchies pursued state building through absolutist regimes in this period, often in imitation of the French model. The governments they created in Vienna, Berlin, Madrid, and St. Petersburg differed in their strengths and weaknesses, but all were attempts to centralize power around a formidable ruler.

◆ THE HABSBURGS AT VIENNA

The closest imitation of Versailles was the court of the Habsburg Leopold I, the Holy Roman Emperor (1658–1705). Heir to a reduced inheritance that gave him control over only Bohemia, Austria, and a small part of Hungary, Leopold still maintained a splendid establishment. His plans for a new palace, Schönbrunn, that was supposed to outshine Versailles were modified only because of a lack of funds. And his promotion of the court as the center of all political and social life turned Vienna into what it had never been before: a city for nobles as well as small-time traders.

Nevertheless, Leopold did not display the pretensions of the Sun King. He was a younger son and had come to the throne only because of the death of his brother. Indecisive, retiring, and deeply religious, he had no fondness for the bravado Louis XIV enjoyed. He was a composer of some talent, and his patronage laid the foundation for the great musical culture that was to be one of Vienna's chief glories. But he did inherit considerable royal authority, which he sought to expand—though unlike Louis XIV he relied on a small group of leading nobles to devise policy and run his government.

Government Policy The Thirty Years' War that ended in 1648 had revealed that the elected head of the Holy Roman Empire could no longer control the princes who nominally owed him allegiance. In his own domains, however, he could maintain his control with the cooperation of his nobility. The Privy Council, which in effect ran Leopold's government, was filled largely with members of aristocratic families, and his chief advisers were always prominent nobles. To make policy, he consulted each of his ministers and then, even when all agreed, came to decisions with agonizing slowness.

Unlike the other courts of Europe, Schönbrunn did not favor only native-born aristocrats. The leader of Austria's armies during the Turks' siege of Vienna in 1683 was Charles, duke of Lorraine, whose duchy had been taken over by the French. His predecessor as field marshal had been an Italian, and his successor was to be one of the most brilliant soldiers of the age, Prince Eugène of Savoy. They became members of the Austrian no-

bility only when Leopold gave them titles within his own dominions, but they all fitted easily into the aristocratic circles that controlled the government and the army.

Eugène and Austria's Military Success Prince Eugène (1663–1736) was a spectacular symbol of the aristocracy's continuing dominance of politics and society. A member of one of Europe's most distinguished families, he had been raised in France but found himself passed over when Louis XIV awarded army commissions, perhaps because he had been intended for the Church. Yet he was determined to have a military career, and he volunteered to serve the Austrians in the war with the Turks that, following the siege of Vienna, was to expand Habsburg territory in the Balkans by the time peace was signed in 1699 (see Map 17.2). Eugène's talents quickly became evident: He was field marshal of Austria's troops by the time he was 30. Over the next forty years, as intermittent war with the Turks continued, he became a decisive influence in Habsburg affairs. Though foreign-born, he was the minister primarily responsible for the transformation of Vienna's policies from defensive to aggressive.

Until the siege of Vienna by the Turks in 1683, Leopold's cautiousness kept Austria simply holding the line, both against Louis XIV and against the Turks. In the 1690s, however, at Eugène's urging, he tried a bolder course and in the process laid the foundations for a new Habsburg empire along the Danube River: Austria-Hungary. He helped create the coalition that defeated Louis in the 1700s, he intervened in Italy so that his landlocked domains could gain an outlet to the sea, and he began the long process of pushing the Turks out of the Balkans. Although Leopold did not live to see the advance completed, by the time of Eugène's death, the Austrians' progress against the Turks had brought them within a hundred miles of the Black Sea.

The Power of the Nobility Yet the local power of the nobility tempered the centralization of Leopold's dominions. Unlike Louis XIV, who supported his nobles only if they worked for him, Leopold gave them influence in the government without first establishing control over all his lands. The nobles did not cause the Habsburgs as

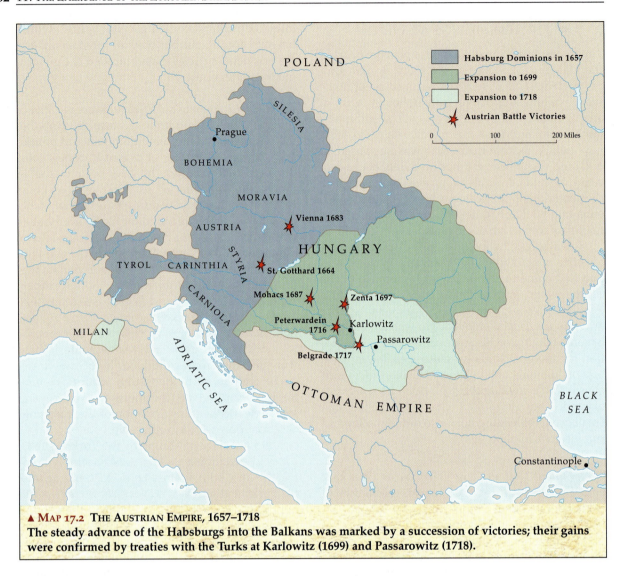

▲ **Map 17.2   The Austrian Empire, 1657–1718**
The steady advance of the Habsburgs into the Balkans was marked by a succession of victories; their gains were confirmed by treaties with the Turks at Karlowitz (1699) and Passarowitz (1718).

much trouble as they had during the Thirty Years' War, but Leopold had to limit his centralization outside Austria. Moreover, as Austrians came increasingly to dominate the court, the nobles of Hungary and Bohemia reacted by clinging stubbornly to their local rights. Thus, compared to France, Leopold's was an absolutism under which the nobility retained far more autonomous power—and a far firmer base of local support.

◆ THE HOHENZOLLERNS AT BERLIN

The one new power that emerged to prominence during the age of Louis XIV was Brandenburg-Prussia, and here again state building was made

possible by a close alliance between a powerful ruler and his nobles. Frederick William of Hohenzollern (r. 1640–1688), known as the "great elector," ruled scattered territories that stretched seven hundred miles from Cleves, on the Rhine, to a part of Prussia on the Baltic. That so fragmented and disconnected a set of lands could be shaped into a major European power was a testimony to the political abilities of the Hohenzollerns. The process began when, taking advantage of the uncertainties that followed the Thirty Years' War, Frederick William made his territories the dominant principality in northern Germany and at the same time strengthened his power over his subjects.

Foreign Policy His first task was in foreign affairs, because when he became elector, the troops of the various states that were fighting the Thirty Years' War swarmed over his possessions at will. Frederick William realized that by determination and intelligent planning, even a minor prince could emerge from these disasters in a good position if he had an army. With some military force at his disposal, he could become a useful ally for the big powers, who could then help him against his neighbors; while at home he would have the strength to crush his opponents.

By 1648 Frederick William had eight thousand troops, and he was backed by both the Dutch and the French in the Westphalia negotiations that year as a possible restraint on Sweden in northern Europe. Without having done much to earn new territory, he did very well in the peace settlement, and he then took advantage of wars around the Baltic in the 1650s to confirm his gains by switching sides at crucial moments. In the process, his army grew to twenty-two thousand men, and he began to use it to impose his will on his own lands. The fact that the army was essential to Frederick William's success—at home and abroad—was to influence much of Prussia's and thus also Germany's subsequent history.

Domestic Policy The role of the military in establishing the elector's supremacy was apparent throughout Brandenburg-Prussia's society. In 1653 the Diet of Brandenburg met for the last time, sealing its own fate by giving Frederick William the right to raise taxes without its consent. The War Chest, the office in charge of financing the army, took over the functions of a treasury department and collected government revenue even when the state was at peace. The implementation of policies in the localities was placed in the hands of war commissars—who originally were responsible for military recruitment, billeting, and supply in each district of Brandenburg-Prussia, but now became the principal agents of all government departments.

Apart from the representative assemblies, Frederick William faced real resistance only from the long-independent cities of his realm. Accustomed to going their own way because authority had been fragmented in the empire for centuries, and especially during the Thirty Years' War, city leaders were dismayed when the elector began to in-

tervene in their affairs. Yet once again sheer intimidation overcame opposition. The last determined effort to dispute his authority arose in the rich city of Königsberg, which allied with the Estates General of Prussia to refuse to pay taxes. But this resistance was crushed in 1662, when Frederick William marched into the city with a few thousand troops. Similar pressure brought the towns of Cleves into submission after centuries of proud independence.

The Junkers The main supporters and beneficiaries of the elector's state building were the Prussian nobles, known as Junkers (from the German for "young lord," *jung herr*). In fact, it was an alliance between the nobility and Frederick William that undermined the Diet, the cities, and the representative assemblies. The leading Junker families saw their best opportunities for the future in cooperation with the central government, and both in the representative assemblies and in the localities, they worked to establish absolutist power—that is, to remove all restraints on the elector. The most significant indicator of the Junkers' success was that by the end of the century, two tax rates had been devised, one for cities and one for the countryside, to the great advantage of the latter.

As the nobles staffed the upper levels of the elector's army and bureaucracy, they also won new prosperity for themselves. Particularly in Prussia, the support of the elector enabled them to reimpose serfdom and consolidate their land holdings into vast, highly profitable estates. This area was a major grain producer, and the Junkers made the most of its economic potential. To maximize profits, they eliminated intermediaries by growing and also distributing their produce. Efficiency became their hallmark, and their wealth was soon famous throughout the Holy Roman Empire. These Prussian entrepreneurs were probably the most successful group of European aristocrats in pursuing economic and political power.

Frederick III Unlike Louis in France, Frederick William had little interest in court life. The Berlin court became the focus of society only under his son, Elector Frederick III, who ruled from 1688. The great elector himself was more interested in organizing his administration, increasing tax returns, building his army, and imposing his authority at home and abroad. He began the development of his capital, Berlin, into a cultural center—he founded what was to become one of the finest libraries in the world, the Prussian State Library—but this was never among his prime concerns. His son, by contrast, had little interest in state building, but he did enjoy princely pomp and encouraged the arts with enthusiasm.

Frederick III lacked only one attribute of royalty: a crown. When Emperor Leopold I, who still had the right to confer titles in the empire, needed Prussia's troops during the War of the Spanish Succession, he gave Frederick, in return, the right to call himself "king in Prussia," and the title soon became "king of Prussia." At a splendid coronation in 1701, Elector Frederick III of Brandenburg was crowned King Frederick I, and thereafter his court could feel itself the equal of the other monarchical settings of Europe.

Frederick determinedly promoted social and cultural glitter. He made his palace a center of art and polite society to compete, he hoped, with Versailles. A construction program beautified Berlin with new churches and huge public buildings. He also established an Academy of Sciences and persuaded the most famous German scientist and philosopher of the day, Gottfried Wilhelm von Leibniz, to become its first president. All these activities obtained generous support from state revenues, as did the universities of Brandenburg and Prussia. By the end of his reign in 1713, Frederick had given his realm a throne, celebrated artistic and intellectual activity, and an elegant aristocracy at the head of social and political life.

◆ RIVALRY AND STATE BUILDING

Europe's increasingly self-confident states were in constant rivalry with their neighbors during the eighteenth century. The competition intensified their state building, because the conflicts compelled rulers to expand their revenues, armies, and bureaucracies. The counter-example was Poland, which failed to centralize and was partitioned three times by Russia, Austria, and Prussia, until in 1795 it ceased to exist as a sovereign state. Political consolidation, by putting a premium on military and economic power, shaped both the map of modern Europe and the centralization of the major states.

The relationship between international rivalry and internal development is well illustrated by Prussia and Austria. In the mid-eighteenth century these two powers were vying to dominate central Europe, and they instituted reforms so as to wage their struggle more effectively. Each was governed by an absolute ruler who built the state by increasing the size of the army, collecting larger revenues, and developing bureaucracies for the war effort. It did not seem to matter whether the ruler was a modern pragmatist like Frederick II of Prussia or a pious traditionalist like Maria Theresa of Austria. In their own way, both understood the demands of the state system.

◆ THE PRUSSIA OF FREDERICK WILLIAM I

Prussia's Frederick William I (r. 1713–1740) was relentless in his pursuit of a strengthened absolutism at home and Europe-wide influence abroad. Strikingly different from his refined father, this spartan ruler approached affairs of state as all business and little pleasure. He disdained court life, dismissed numerous courtiers, and cut the salaries of those who remained. Uncluttered by royal ceremonies, his days were strictly regulated as he attempted to supervise all government activities personally.

Emphasis on the Military   It has been said that Frederick William I organized his state to serve his military power. During his reign the army grew from 38,000 to 83,000, making it the fourth largest in Europe, behind France, Russia, and Austria. While still relying on foreign mercenaries for one-third of his troops, he also instituted a form of conscription. And all his soldiers had to undergo intensive drilling and wear standardized uniforms. Determined to build an effective cadre of professionals, he forbade his subjects to serve in foreign armies and compelled the sons of nobles to attend cadet schools to learn martial skills and attitudes. In this military state, Frederick William I was a colorful commander in chief; he maintained a personal regiment of towering grenadiers and always wore a uniform, declaring that he would be buried in it. But he did not intend to die in battle. For all his involvement with military life, he

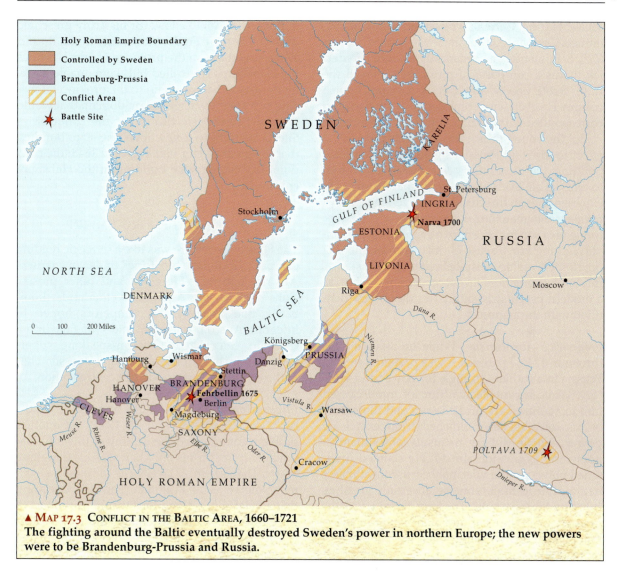

▲ **MAP 17.3** CONFLICT IN THE BALTIC AREA, 1660–1721
The fighting around the Baltic eventually destroyed Sweden's power in northern Europe; the new powers were to be Brandenburg-Prussia and Russia.

avoided committing his army to battle, and was able to pass it on intact to his son.

Centralization kept pace with the growth of the army. In 1723 the General Directory of Finance, War, and Domains took over all government functions except justice, education, and religion. A super-agency, it collected revenues and oversaw expenditures (mostly military) and local administration. Even education was seen merely as a way to encourage people to serve the state. Frederick made education compulsory for all children, ordering local communities to set up schools where there were none, though he never enforced these decrees. The promotion of education was thus

theoretical, not practical, and had few social consequences. Many teachers, for example, were clergy who taught as a sideline. Uninterested in intellectual pursuits for their own sake, the king allowed the universities to decline; they did not fit his relentless vision of how to build his state.

◆ FREDERICK THE GREAT

Frederick William I's most notable triumph, perhaps, was the grooming of his successor. This was no mean task. Frederick II (r. 1740–1786) seemed opposite in temperament to his father and little inclined to follow in his footsteps. The father was a God-fearing German Protestant. The son disdained German culture and was a deist (see p. 670). Sentimental and artistically inclined, Frederick II was a composer of music who played the flute, wrote poetry, and greatly admired French culture. He even wrote philosophical treatises and corresponded with leading European intellectuals.

But the young prince was not exempt from the effort to draw all Prussians into the task of state building. On the contrary: His father forced him to work at all levels of the state apparatus so as to experience them directly, from shoveling hay on a royal farm to marching with the troops. The father trained his son for kingship, reshaping his personality, giving him a sense of duty, and toughening him for leadership. Despite Frederick's resistance, this hard apprenticeship succeeded. In the end, as a modern psychiatrist might say, the prince identified with the aggressor.

Frederick's Absolutism   When he assumed the throne in 1740, Frederick II was prepared to lead Prussia in a ruthless struggle for power and territory. While his intellectual turn of mind caused him to agonize over moral issues and the nature of his role, he never flinched from exercising power. But he did try to justify absolutism at home and aggression abroad. He claimed undivided power for the ruler, not because the dynasty had a divine mission but because only absolute rule could bring results. The king, he said, was the first servant of the state, and in the long run an enlightened monarch might lead his people to a more rational and moral existence. Some of his objectives, such as religious toleration and judicial reform, he could reach at once, and by putting them into effect Frederick gained a reputation as an "enlightened" absolutist.

But these were minor matters. The paramount issue, security, provided the best justification for absolutism. Success here required Prussia to improve its vulnerable geographic position by acquiring more territory, stronger borders, and the power to face other European states as an equal. Until that was achieved, Frederick would not consider the domestic reforms that might disrupt the flow of taxes or men into the army, or provoke his nobility. The capture of territory was his most singular contribution to the rise of Prussia and what earned him his title of Frederick the Great. As it

happened, a suitable task for his army presented itself in the year Frederick II came to the throne, 1748—an attack on the province of Silesia, which the Habsburgs controlled but were unable to defend. Prussia had no claim to the province; it was simply a wealthy neighboring domain that would expand Prussia's territory. Yet the conquest of Silesia brought to a new level the state building that the great elector had begun in 1648; the reaction also shaped state building in the Habsburg empire.

◆ THE HABSBURG EMPIRE

The Habsburg empire was like a dynastic holding company of diverse territories under one crown: Austria, Bohemia, Hungary, and other possessions such as the Austrian Netherlands, Lombardy, and Tuscany. The emperors hoped to integrate Austria, Bohemia, and Hungary into a Catholic, centralized, German-speaking superstate. But the traditional representative assemblies in these provinces resisted such centralization.

International Rivalry   In the reign of Leopold's successor, Charles VI (r. 1711–1740), yet another problem complicated the destiny of this multinational empire, for his only heir was his daughter, Maria Theresa. In 1713 Charles drafted a document known as the Pragmatic Sanction, declaring that all Habsburg dominions would pass intact to the eldest heir, male or female; and for the next twenty-five years he sought recognition of the Pragmatic Sanction from the European powers. By making all kinds of concessions and promises, he won this recognition on paper. But when he died in 1740, his daughter found that the commitments were worthless: The succession was challenged by force from several sides. Concentrating on diplomacy alone, Charles had neglected the work of state building, leaving an empty treasury, an inadequately trained army, and an ineffective bureaucracy.

In contrast to Austria, Prussia had a full treasury, a powerful army, and a confident ruler, Frederick II, who seized the Habsburg province of Silesia without qualm. His justification was simply "reasons of state," combined with the Habsburgs' faltering fortunes. And Maria Theresa had her hands more than full, because the French

▲ *E. F. Cunningham*
THE RETURN OF FREDERICK II FROM A MANEUVRE, 1787
Were it not for the richly embroidered saddle cover and the fine white horse, Frederick the Great would be hard to spot among his officers. Nor is there anything to indicate that the two men on the black and brown horses behind him are his nephew and grandnephew. This sober evocation of a king as a professional soldier contrasts strikingly with earlier glorifications (see plate, p. 502).
Staatliche Schlösser und Garten, Schlöss Charlottenburg, Potsdam

declared war on her to support their ally Bavaria's claim to the Habsburg throne. Meanwhile, Spain hoped to win back control of Austria's Italian possessions. Worse yet, Maria Theresa faced a rebellion by the Czech nobles in Bohemia. Her position would probably have been hopeless if Hungary's Magyar nobles had followed suit. But Maria Theresa promised them autonomy within the Habsburg empire, and they offered her the troops she needed to resist the invaders.

The War of Austrian Succession In the War of Austrian Succession (1740–1748) that followed, Maria Theresa learned the elements of state build-

ing. With her Hungarian troops and with financial help from her one ally, Britain, she fought her opponents to a stalemate. Frederick's conquest of Silesia proved to be the only significant territorial change produced by the war. Even for England and France, who fought the war mainly in overseas colonies, it was a standoff. But Maria Theresa was now determined to recover Silesia and humiliate Prussia, and this required a determined effort of state building.

Maria Theresa The woman whose authority was established not by her father's negotiations but by force of arms was a marked contrast to her archenemy, Frederick. The Prussian king was practical and irreligious; Maria Theresa was moralistic and pious. While Frederick barely tolerated a loveless marriage, the Habsburg ruler enjoyed a happy domestic life, bearing numerous children and taking great personal interest in their upbringing. Her personality and her ruling style were deceptively traditional, for she was a shrewd innovator in the business of building and reasserting the power of her state.

Unlike Frederick, or for that matter her own son and successor, Joseph II, Maria Theresa had a strong regard for her dynasty. In this respect, being a woman made no difference to the policies or government of the empire. She believed in the divine mission of the Habsburgs and conscientiously attended to the practical needs of her realm.

Reform in Church and State It was because she put the state's interests first that this most pious of Catholic sovereigns—who disdained religious toleration and loathed atheists—felt obliged to reform the Church. Responding to waste and self-interest in her monasteries, she forbade the founding of new establishments. She also abolished the clergy's exemptions from taxes, something the French king found impossible to do.

A new bureaucratic apparatus was constructed on the models of French and Prussian absolutism. In Vienna, reorganized central ministries recruited staffs of experts. In the provinces, new agents were appointed who were largely free of local interests, though some concession did have to be made to the regional traditions of the Habsburg realm. The core domains (excluding Hungary and the Italian possessions) were reorganized into ten provinces, each subdivided into districts directed by royal officials. With the help of these officials, the central government could wrest new taxes from the local diets. Meanwhile, Maria Theresa brought important nobles from all her domains to Vienna to participate in its social and administrative life. She also reformed the military, improving the training of troops and establishing academies to produce a more professional officer corps. Thus did international needs help shape domestic political reforms.

◆ HABSBURGS AND BOURBONS AT MADRID

In Spain the Habsburgs had little success in state building either at home or abroad. The king who followed Philip IV, Charles II (r. 1665–1700), was a sickly man, incapable of having children; and the War of the Spanish Succession seriously reduced the inheritance he left. Both the southern Netherlands and most of Italy passed to the Austrian Habsburgs, and Spain's overseas possessions often paid little notice to the homeland.

The Spanish nobility was even more successful than the Austrian in turning absolutism to its advantage. In 1650 the crown had been able to recapture Catalonia's loyalty only by granting the province's aristocracy virtual autonomy, and this pattern recurred throughout Spain's territories. Parasitic, unproductive nobles controlled the regime, often for personal gain. The country fell into economic and cultural stagnation, subservient to a group of powerful families, with its former glory visible mainly in its strong navy.

Bourbon Spain Yet Spain and its vast overseas possessions remained a force in eighteenth-century affairs. When the Bourbons gained the crown, following the War of Spanish Succession, they ended the traditional independence of Aragon, Catalonia, and Valencia and integrated these provinces into the kind of united Spain Olivares had sought eighty years earlier. They imported the position of *intendant* from France to administer the provinces, and although the nobles remained far more independent, the Bourbons did begin to impose uniform procedures on the country. In mid-century the ideas of Enlightened Absolutism that were visible elsewhere in Europe had their effect, largely because of a liberal reformer, Count Pedro de Campomanes. The most remarkable change concerned the religious order that had been identified with Spain since the days of its founder, Loyola: the Jesuits. They had become too powerful and too opposed to reform, and so they were expelled from Spanish territory in 1767.

In a sense, though, the Jesuits were to have their revenge. Spain's colonies in America were flourishing in the eighteenth century: Their trade

▲ *M. van Meytens*
MARIA THERESA AND HER FAMILY, **1750**
Although the setting is just as splendid, the portrayal of Maria Theresa with her husband and thirteen of her
sixteen children suggests a domesticity that is absent from Louis XIV's family portrait of half a century before
(see plate, p. 588).
Scala/Art Resource, NY

with Europe was booming; they were attracting new settlers; and by 1800 they had over 14 million inhabitants. But they were still subject to the same absolutist control as the homeland. It was largely under the inspiration of disgruntled Jesuits that the idea of breaking free from Spain took hold in the Empire, an idea that led to the independence movements of the 1800s.

◆ PETER THE GREAT AT ST. PETERSBURG

One of the reasons the new absolutist regimes of the late seventeenth and eighteenth centuries seemed so different from their predecessors was that many of them consciously created new settings for themselves. Versailles, Schönbrunn, and Berlin were all either new or totally transformed

sites for royal courts. But only one of the autocrats of the period went so far as to build an entirely new capital: Tsar Peter I (the Great) of Russia (1682–1725), who named the new city St. Petersburg after his patron saint.

Peter's Fierce Absolutism None of the state-building rulers of the period had Peter's terrifying energy or ruthless determination to exercise absolute control. He was only nine when he was chosen tsar, and in his early years, when his sister and his mother were the effective rulers, he witnessed ghastly massacres of members of his family and their associates by soldiers in Moscow. Like little Louis XIV, endangered by Paris mobs during the Fronde, Peter determined to leave his capital city. Soon after he assumed full powers in 1696, therefore, he shifted his

▼ *PETER THE GREAT AT ST. PETERSBURG*
In the eighteenth century Peter the Great of Russia outstripped the grandeur of other monarchs of the period by erecting an entirely new city for his capital. St. Petersburg was built by forced labor of the peasants under Peter's orders; they are shown here laying the foundations for the city.
Tass/Sovfoto

court to St. Petersburg, despite thousands of deaths among the peasants who were forced to build the city in a cold and inhospitable swamp. Well over six feet tall—a giant by the standards of the time—Peter terrorized those around him, especially during his many drunken rages. His only son, Alexis, a weak and retiring figure, became the focus of opposition to the tsar, and Peter had him put in prison, where Alexis mysteriously died. Peter refused even to attend his funeral.

Western Models Early in his reign, Peter suffered a humiliating military defeat at the hands of the Swedes. This merely confirmed his view that, in order to compete with Europe's powers, he had to bring to Russia some of the advances the Western nations had recently made. To observe these achievements firsthand, Peter traveled incognito through France, England, and the Netherlands in 1697 and 1698, paying special attention to economic, administrative, and military practices (such as the functioning of a Dutch shipyard). Many of his initiatives were to derive from this journey, including his importation of Western court rituals, his founding of an Academy of Sciences in 1725, and his encouragement of the first Russian newspaper.

Italian artists were brought to Russia, along with Scandinavian army officers, German engineers, and Dutch shipbuilders, not only to apply their skills but also to teach them to the Russians. St. Petersburg, the finest eighteenth-century city built in Classical style, is mainly the work of Italians. But gradually Russians took over their own institutions—military academies produced native officers, for example—and by the end of Peter's reign they had little need of foreign experts.

Bureaucratization In ruling Russia, Peter virtually ignored the Duma, the traditional advisory council, and concentrated instead on his bureaucracy. He carried out countless changes until he had created an administrative apparatus much larger than the one he had inherited. Here again he copied Western models—notably Prussia, where nobles ran the bureaucracy and the army, and Sweden, where a complex system of government departments had been created. Peter organized his administration into similar departments:

Each had either a specialized function, such as finance, or responsibility for a geographic area, such as Siberia. The result was an elaborate but unified hierarchy of authority, rising from local agents of the government through provincial officials up to the staffs and governors of eleven large administrative units and finally to the leaders of the regime in the capital. Peter began the saturating bureaucratization that characterized Russia from that time on.

The Imposition of Social Order The tsar's policies laid the foundations for a two-class society that persisted until the twentieth century. Previously, a number of ranks had existed within both the nobility and the peasantry, and a group in the middle was seen sometimes as the lowest nobles and sometimes as the highest peasants. Under Peter such mingling disappeared. All peasants were reduced to one level, subject to a new poll tax, military conscription, and forced public work, such as the building of St. Petersburg. Below them were serfs, whose numbers were increased by legislation restricting their movement. Peasants had a few advantages over serfs, such as the freedom to move, but their living conditions were often equally dreadful. Serfdom itself spread throughout all areas of Peter's dominions and became essential to his state building because, on royal lands as well as the estates of the nobles, serfs worked and ran the agricultural enterprise that was Russia's economic base.

At the same time, Peter created a single class of nobles by substituting status within the bureaucracy for status within the traditional hierarchy of titles. In 1722 he issued a table of bureaucratic ranks that gave everyone a place according to the office he held. Differentiations still existed, but they were no longer unbridgeable, as they had been when family was the decisive determinant of status. The result was a more controlled social order and greater uniformity than in France or Brandenburg-Prussia. The Russian aristocracy was the bureaucracy, and the bureaucracy the aristocracy.

The Subjugation of the Nobility This was not a voluntary alliance between nobles and government, such as existed in the West; in return for his support and his total subjection of the peasantry, Peter required the nobles to provide officials for his bureaucracy and officers for his army. When he began the construction of St. Petersburg, he also demanded that the leading families build splendid mansions in his new capital. In effect, the tsar offered privilege and wealth in exchange for conscription into public service. Thus, there was hardly any sense of partnership between nobility and throne: The tsar often had to use coercion to ensure that his wishes were followed. On the other hand, Peter helped build up the nobles' fortunes and their control of the countryside. It has been estimated that by 1710 he had put under the supervision of great landowners more than forty thousand peasant and serf households that had formerly been under the crown. And he was liberal in conferring new titles—some of them, such as count and baron, copies of German examples.

Control of the Church   Peter's determination to stamp his authority on Russia was also apparent in his destruction of ecclesiastical independence. He accomplished this with one blow: He simply did not replace the patriarch of the Russian Church who died in 1700. Peter took over the monasteries and their vast income for his own purposes and appointed a procurator (at first an army officer) to supervise religious affairs. The church was, in effect, made a branch of government.

Military Expansion   The purpose of all these radical changes was to assert the tsar's power both at home and abroad. Peter established a huge standing army, more than three hundred thousand strong by the 1720s, and imported the latest military techniques from the West. One of Peter's most cherished projects, the creation of a navy, had limited success, but there could be no doubt that he transformed Russia's capacity for war and its position among European states. He extended Russia's frontier to the south and west, and, at the battle of Poltava in 1709, reversed his early defeat by the Swedes. This victory began the dismantling of Sweden's empire, for it was followed by more than a decade of Russian advance into Estonia, Livonia, and Poland. The very vastness of his realm justified Peter's drive for absolute control, and by the time of his death he had made Russia the dominant power in the Baltic and a major influence in European affairs.

III. Alternatives to Absolutism

The absolutist regimes offered one model of political and social organization, but an alternative model—equally committed to uniformity, order, and state building—was also created in the late seventeenth century: governments dominated by aristocrats or merchants. The contrast between the two was noted by contemporary political theorists, especially opponents of absolutism. And yet the differences were often less sharp than the theorists suggested, mainly because the position of the aristocracy was similar throughout Europe.

◆ ARISTOCRACY IN THE UNITED PROVINCES, SWEDEN, AND POLAND

In the Dutch republic, the succession of William III to the office of Stadholder in 1672 seemed to be a move toward absolutism. As he led the successful resistance to Louis XIV in war (1672–1678), he increasingly concentrated government in his own hands. Soon, however, the power of merchants and provincial leaders in the Estates General reasserted itself. William did not want to sign a peace treaty with Louis when the French invasion failed. He wanted instead to take the war into France and reinforce his own authority by keeping the position of commander in chief. But the Estates General, led by the province of Holland, ended the war.

A decade later William sought the English crown, but he did so only with the approval of the Estates General, and he had to leave separate the representative assemblies that governed the two countries. When William died without an heir, his policies were continued by his close friend Antonius Heinsius, who held the same position of grand pensionary of Holland that Jan de Witt had once occupied; but the government was in effect controlled by the Estates General. This representative assembly now had to preside over the decline of a great power. In finance and trade, the Dutch were gradually overtaken by the English, while in the war against Louis XIV, they had to support the crippling burden of maintaining a land force, only to hand over command to England. Within half a century Frederick II of Prussia was to call the republic "a dinghy boat trailing the English man-of-war."

Dutch Society The aristocrats of the United Provinces differed from the usual European pattern. Instead of ancient families and bureaucratic dynasties, they boasted merchants and mayors. The prominent citizens of the leading cities were the backbone of the Dutch upper classes. Moreover, social distinctions were less prominent than in any other country of Europe. The elite was composed of hard-working financiers and traders, richer and more powerful but not essentially more privileged or leisured than those farther down the social ladder. The inequality described in much eighteenth-century political writing—the special place nobles had, often including some immunity from the law—was far less noticeable in the United Provinces. There was no glittering court,

▲ **MAP 17.4** THE EXPANSION OF RUSSIA AND THE PARTITION OF POLAND
All three of the powers in Eastern Europe—Prussia, Russia, and Austria—gained territory from the dismemberment of Poland. At the same time, Russia was expanding to the south and east.

and although here as elsewhere a small group controlled the country, it did so for largely economic ends and in different style.

Sweden   The Swedes created yet another nonabsolutist model of state building. After a long struggle with the king, the nobles emerged as the country's dominant political force. During the reign of Charles XI (1660–1697), the monarchy was able to force the great lords to return to the state the huge tracts of land they had received as rewards for loyalty earlier in the century. Since Charles stayed out of Europe's wars, he was able to conserve his resources and avoid relying on the nobility as he strengthened the smoothly running bureaucracy he had inherited from Gustavus Adolphus.

His successor, Charles XII (r. 1697–1718), however, revived Sweden's tradition of military conquest. He won land from Peter the Great, but then made the fatal decision to invade Russia. Defeated at the battle of Poltava in 1709, Charles had to retreat and watch helplessly as the Swedish empire was dismembered. By the time he was killed in battle nine years later, his neighbors had begun to overrun his lands, and, in treaties signed from 1719 to 1721, Sweden reverted to roughly the territory it had had a century before.

Naturally, the nobles took advantage of Charles XII's frequent absences to reassert their authority. They ran Sweden's highly efficient government while he was campaigning and forced his successor, Queen Ulrika, to accept a constitution that gave the Riksdag effective control over the country. The new structure, modeled on England's political system, gave the nobility the role of the English gentry—leaders of society and the shapers of its politics. A splendid court arose, and Stockholm became one of the more elegant and cultured aristocratic centers in Europe.

Poland   Warsaw fared less well. In fact, the strongest contrast to the French political and social model in the late seventeenth century was Poland. The sheer chaos and disunity that plagued Poland until it ceased to exist as a state in the late eighteenth century were the direct result of continued dominance by the old landed aristocracy, which blocked all attempts to centralize the government. There were highly capable kings in this period—

notably John III, who achieved Europe-wide fame by relieving Vienna from the Turkish siege in 1683. These monarchs could quite easily gather an army to fight, and fight well, against Poland's many foes: Germans, Swedes, Russians, and Turks. But once a battle was over, the ruler could exercise no more than nominal leadership. Each king was elected by the assembly of nobles and had to agree not to interfere with the independence of the great lords, who were growing rich from serf labor on fertile lands. The crown had neither revenue nor bureaucracy to speak of, and so the country continued to resemble a feudal kingdom, where power remained in the localities.

◆ THE TRIUMPH OF THE GENTRY IN ENGLAND

The model for a nonabsolutist regime was England, even though King Charles II (r. 1660–1685) seemed to have powers similar to those of his ill-fated father, Charles I. He still summoned and dissolved Parliament, made all appointments in the bureaucracy, and signed every law. But he no longer had prerogative courts like Star Chamber, he could not arrest a member of Parliament, and he could not create a new seat in the Commons. Even two ancient prerogatives, the king's right to dispense with an act of Parliament for a specific individual or group and his right to suspend an act completely, proved empty when Charles II tried to exercise them. Nor could he raise money without Parliament; instead, he was given a fixed annual income, financed by a tax on beer.

The Gentry and Parliament   The real control of the country's affairs had by this time passed to the group of substantial landowners known as the gentry. In a country of some 5 million people, perhaps fifteen to twenty thousand families were considered gentry—local leaders throughout England, despite having neither titles of nobility nor special privileges. Their percentage, 2 percent of the population, was probably about the same as the percentage of titled nobles in other states. Yet the gentry differed from these other nobles in that they had won the right to determine national policy through Parliament. Whereas in France, Austria, Brandenburg-Prussia, and Russia, nobles depended on monarchs for power and were sub-

◀ ENGRAVING FROM *THE WESTMINSTER MAGAZINE*, 1774
Political cartoons were standard fare in eighteenth-century newspapers and magazines. This one shows a weeping king of Poland and an angry Turk (who made no gains) after Poland was carved up in 1772 by Frederick the Great, the Austrian emperor, and the Russian empress. Louis XV sits by without helping his ally Poland, and all are urged on by the devil under the table.

servient to their rulers, the English revolution had made the gentry an independent force. Their authority was now hallowed by custom, upheld by law, and maintained by the House of Commons, a representative assembly that was both the supreme legislature and the body to which the executive government was ultimately responsible.

Not all the gentry took a continuing interest in affairs of state, and only a few of their number sat in the roughly five-hundred-member House of Commons. Even the Commons did not exercise a constant influence over the government; nevertheless, the ministers of the king had to be prominent representatives of the gentry, and they had to be able to win the support of a majority of the members of the Commons. Policy

was still set by the king and his ministers, but the Commons had to be persuaded that the policies were correct; without parliamentary approval, a minister could not long survive.

The Succession   Despite occasional conflicts, this structure worked relatively smoothly throughout Charles II's reign. But the gentry feared that Charles's brother, James, next in line for the succession and an open Catholic, might try to restore Catholicism in England. To prevent this, they attempted in 1680 to force Charles to exclude James from the throne. But in the end the traditional respect for legitimacy, combined with some shrewd maneuvering by Charles, ensured that there would be no tampering with the succession.

▲ *Sir Joshua Reynolds*

LADY SMITH AND HER CHILDREN

The quiet serenity and assurance of England's gentry in the eighteenth century is apparent in all their portraits, whether the head of the household is present or, as in this case, we see only his wife and children.

Lady Smith (Charles Delaval) and her Children (George Henry, Louisa, and Charlotte") Oil on canvas. 55⅜ × 44⅛".
The Metropolitan Museum of Art, Bequest of Collis P. Huntington, 1900 (25.110.10), Photograph ©1987
The Metropolitan Museum of Art

Soon, however, the reign of James II (r. 1685–1688) turned into a disaster. Elated by his acceptance as king, James rashly offered Catholics the very encouragement the gentry feared. This was a direct challenge to the gentry's newly won power, and in 1688 seven of their leaders, including members of England's most prominent families, invited the Protestant ruler of the United Provinces, William III, to invade and take over the throne. Though William landed with an army half the size of the king's, James, uncertain of his support, decided not to risk battle and fled to exile in France. Because the transfer of the monarchy was bloodless and confirmed the supremacy of Parliament, it came to be called the Glorious Revolution.

William and Mary The new king gained what little title he had to the crown through his wife,

Mary (see the genealogical table below), and Parliament proclaimed the couple joint monarchs early in 1689. The Dutch ruler took the throne primarily to bring England into his relentless struggles against Louis XIV, and he willingly accepted a settlement that confirmed the essential role of Parliament in the government. A Bill of Rights determined the succession to the throne, defined Parliament's powers, and established basic civil rights. An Act of Toleration put an end to all religious persecution, though members of the official Church of England were still the only people allowed to vote, sit in Parliament, hold a government office, or attend a university. In 1694 a statute declared that Parliament had to meet and new elections had to be held at least once every three years.

Despite the restrictions on his authority, William exercised strong leadership. He guided

THE ENGLISH SUCCESSION FROM THE STUARTS TO THE HANOVERIANS

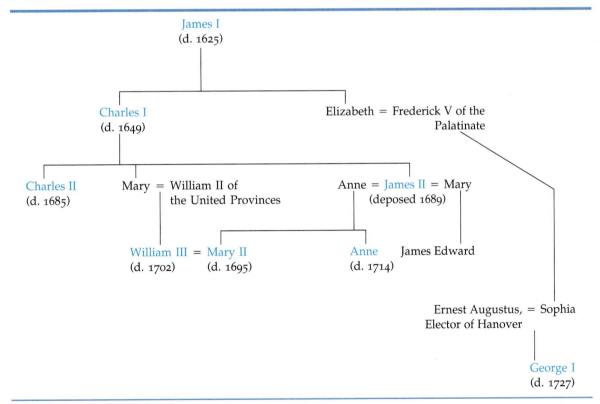

Note: Names in blue = Monarchs of England.

England into an aggressive foreign policy, picked ministers favorable to his aims, and never let Parliament sit when he was out of the country to pursue the war or to oversee Dutch affairs. In his reign, too, the central government grew considerably, gaining new powers and positions, and thus new opportunities for political patronage. But unlike James, William recognized his limits. He tried to have the Bill of Rights reversed and a standing army established, but he gave up when these efforts provoked major opposition. By and large, therefore, the gentry were content to let the king rule as he saw fit, for they had shown by their intervention in 1688 that ultimately they controlled the country.

◆ POLITICS AND PROSPERITY

The political system in England now reflected the social system: A small elite controlled both the country's policy and its institutions. This group was far from united, however, as was apparent when a party system began to appear in Parliament during Charles II's reign. On one side were the Whigs, who opposed royal prerogatives and Catholicism and were largely responsible for the attempt to exclude James II from the throne. Their rivals, the Tories, stood for the independence and authority of the crown and favored a ceremonial and traditional Anglicanism.

Party Conflict   Because the Whigs had been the main advocates of the removal of James II, they controlled the government for most of William III's reign. They supported his war against Louis XIV (1689–1697), because France harbored both James and his followers (the romantic but ill-fated Jacobites, who kept trying to restore James's line to the throne). This was a fairly nonpartisan issue, but the Tories and Whigs still competed fiercely for voters. Because the qualification for voting—owning land worth forty shillings a year in rent—had become less restrictive as a result of inflation (which made forty shillings a fairly modest sum) and was not to be raised to a higher minimum until the late 1700s, England now had what would be its largest electorate before the 1860s. Almost 5 percent of the population (more than 15 percent of adult males) could vote, and although results

were usually determined by powerful local magnates, fierce politicking was common. And in the election of 1700 there was a major upset: The Tories won by opposing renewal of war with Louis XIV, who had seemed restrained since the end of the previous war in 1697.

Within two years, however, and despite William's death in 1702, England was again at war with France, this time over the Spanish succession; and soon the Whigs were again in control of the government. The identification of the parties with their attitude toward war continued until 1710, when weariness over the fighting brought the Tories back into power. They persuaded Queen Anne, William's successor, to make peace with France at Utrecht in 1713; and they lost power only because they made the mistake of negotiating with the rebel Jacobites after Anne died in 1714 without an heir. Anne's successor was a German prince, the elector of Hanover, who founded the new Hanoverian dynasty as George I (1714–1727). Since they firmly supported his succession, the Whigs regained control of the government when George came to the throne. They then entrenched themselves for almost a century.

The Sea and the Economy   At the same time, England was winning for itself unprecedented prosperity and laying the foundations of its world power. The English navy was the premier force on the sea, the decisive victor over France during the worldwide struggle of the early eighteenth century. Overseas, England founded new colonies and steadily expanded the empire. When England and Scotland joined into one kingdom in 1707, the union created a Great Britain ready to exercise a worldwide influence.

The economic advances were equally remarkable. A notable achievement was the establishment of the Bank of England in 1694. The bank gained permission to raise money from the public and then lend it to the government at a favorable 8 percent interest. Within 12 days its founders raised more than a million pounds, demonstrating not only the financial stability of England's government but also the commitment of the elite to the country's political structure. London was becoming the financial capital of the world, with her merchants gaining control of maritime trade

▲ *William Hogarth*
THE POLLING, **1754**
Despite the high reputation of the polling day as the central moment in the system of representative government, Hogarth's depiction of it in this scene suggests how corrupt and disheveled the process of voting was. The sick and the foolish are among the mob of voters; the central figure looks bewildered as he is told what to do; on the right a bloated official cannot decide whether a voter should be allowed to take his oath on the Bible with a wooden hand; and all ignore the distress of Britannia, the symbol of Britain, in her coach on the left.
By Courtesy of the Trustees of Sir John Soane's Museum, London

from east Asia to North America. And the benefits of the boom also helped the lower levels of society.

English Society With the possible exception of the Dutch, ordinary English people were better off than their equivalents elsewhere in Europe. Compared with the sixteenth century, there was little starvation. The system of poor relief may often have been inhumane in forcing the unfortunate to

work in horrifying workhouses, but it did provide them with the shelter and food they had long lacked. It is true that thousands still found themselves unable to make a living in their home villages each year and were forced by poverty to take to the roads. And the many who ended up in London hardly improved their situation. The stream of immigrants was driving the capital's population toward half a million, and the city contained frightful slums and miserable crime-ridden

▲ *New Gallows at the Old Bailey,* Engraving
It was an indication of the severity of English criminal justice that the gallows erected near the chief court in London, the Old Bailey, in the mid-eighteenth century were specially constructed so that ten condemned criminals, both men and women, could be executed at once.
© British Museum

sections. Even a terrible fire in London in 1666 did little to improve the appallingly crowded living conditions, because the city was rebuilt much as before, the only notable additions being a series of splendid churches. But the grimness should not be overdrawn.

After more than a century of inflation, the laborer could once again make a decent living, and artisans were enjoying a growing demand for their work. Higher in the social scale, more men had a say in the political process than before, and more found opportunities for advancement in the rising economy—in trade overseas, in the bureaucracy, or in the expanding market for luxury goods. It has been estimated that in 1730 there were about sixty thousand adult males in what we would call the professions. England also had better roads than any other European country and a more impartial judicial system. Yet none of these gains could compare with those that the gentry made. In fact, many of the improvements, such as fair administration of justice, were indi-

rect results of what the upper classes had won for themselves. The fruits of progress clearly belonged primarily to the gentry.

◆ THE GROWTH OF STABILITY

Like the absolutist regimes, the British government in the 1700s was able to advance state-building—to expand its authority and its international power. This was the work not so much of a monarch as of the "political nation": the landowners and leading townsmen who elected almost all the members of Parliament. Their control of the nation was visible in the distribution of the 558 seats in the House of Commons, which bore little relation to the size of constituencies. In 1793, for example, fifty-one English and Welsh boroughs, with fewer than fifteen hundred voters, elected one hundred members of Parliament, nearly a fifth of the Commons. Many districts were safely in the pocket of a prominent local family; and elsewhere elections were often determined by bribery, influence, and intimidation. On the national level, loose party alignments pitted Whigs, who wanted a strong Parliament and usually preferred commercial to agricultural interests, against Tories, who tended to support the king and policies that favored large landholders. But the realities of politics were shaped by small factions within these larger groups, and alliances revolved around the control of patronage and office.

War and Taxes As the financial and military needs and capabilities of the government expanded, Parliament now created a thoroughly bureaucratized state. Britain had always prided itself on having a smaller government and lower taxes than its neighbors, largely because, as an island, it had avoided the need for a standing army. All that now came to an end. Starting with the struggle against Louis XIV, wars required constant increases in resources, troops, and administrators. A steadily expanding navy had to be supported, as did an army that reached almost two hundred thousand men by the 1770s. Before the 1690s, public expenditures rarely amounted to £2 million a year; by the 1770s, they were almost £30 million, and most of that was spent on the military. In this period, as a result, Britain's fiscal bureaucracy more than tripled in size. The recruiting officer became a regular sight, and so too did the treasury men who were imposing increasingly heavy tax burdens.

Unlike their counterparts on the continent, however, the wealthier classes in Britain paid considerable taxes to support this state building, and they maintained more fluid relations with other classes. The landed gentry and the commercial class, in particular, were often linked by marriage and by financial or political associations. Even great aristocrats sometimes had close ties with the business leaders of London. The lower levels of society, however, found the barriers as high as they had ever been. For all of Britain's prosperity, the lower third of society remained poor and often desperate. As a result, despite a severe system of justice and frequent capital punishment, crime

▼ *Samuel Scott*
THE BUILDING OF WESTMINSTER BRIDGE, CA. **1742**
The elegance, but not the squalor, of city life in the eighteenth century is suggested by this view of Westminster.
The Building of Westminster Bridge. Oil on Canvas. 24×44 ⅜″. The Metropolitan Museum of Art, Purchase, Charles B. Curtis Fund and Joseph Pulitzer Bequest, 1944. (44.56) Photograph ©1993 The Metropolitan Museum of Art

was endemic in both country and town. The eighteenth century was the heyday of that romantic but violent figure, the highwayman.

The Age of Walpole The first two rulers of the Hanoverian dynasty, George I (r. 1714–1727) and George II (r. 1727–1760), could not speak English fluently. The language barrier and their concern for their German territory of Hanover left them often uninterested in British politics, and this helped Parliament grow in authority. Its dominant figure for over twenty years was Sir Robert Walpole, who rose to prominence because of his skillful handling of fiscal policy during the panic following the collapse of an overseas trading company in 1720. This crash, known as the South Sea Bubble, resembled the failure of John Law's similar scheme in France, but it had less effect on government finances. Thereafter, Walpole controlled British politics until 1742, mainly by dispensing patronage liberally and staying at peace.

Many historians have called Walpole the first prime minister, though the title was not official. He insisted that all ministers inform and consult with the House of Commons as well as with the king, and he continued to sit in Parliament in order to recruit support for his decisions. Not until the next century was it accepted that the Commons could force a minister to resign. But Walpole took a first step toward ministerial responsibility, and to the notion that the ministers as a body or "cabinet" had a common task, and he thus shaped the future structure of British government.

Commercial Interests In Great Britain as in France, the economic expansion of the eighteenth century increased the wealth and the social and political weight of the commercial and financial middle class. Although Londoners remained around 11 percent of the population, the proportion of the English who lived in other sizable towns doubled in the 1700s; and by 1800 some 30 percent of the country's inhabitants were urbanized. Walpole's policy of peace pleased the large landlords but angered this growing body of merchants and businesspeople, who feared the growth of French commerce and colonial settlements. They found their champion in William Pitt, later earl of Chatham, the grandson of a man who had made a fortune in India. Eloquent, self-confi-

dent, and infused with a vision of Britain's imperial destiny, Pitt began his parliamentary career in 1738 by attacking the government's timid policies and demanding that France be driven from the seas. Though Walpole's policies continued even after his resignation in 1742, Pitt's moment finally came in 1758, when Britain became involved in a European war (see pp. 625–627). that was to confirm her importance in continental affairs.

◆ CONTRASTS IN POLITICAL THOUGHT

The intensive development of both absolutist and antiabsolutist forms in the seventeenth century stimulated an outpouring of ideas about the nature and purposes of government. Two Englishmen, in particular, developed theories about the basis of political authority that have been influential ever since.

Hobbes A story has it that Thomas Hobbes, a brilliant scholar from a poor family who earned his livelihood as the tutor to aristocrats' sons, once picked up a copy of Euclid's *Elements* and opened the book in the middle. The theorem on that page seemed totally without foundation, but it rested on a proof in the preceding theorem. Working his way backward, Hobbes discovered himself finally having to accept no more than the proposition that the shortest distance between two points is a straight line. He thereupon resolved to use the same approach to analyze political behavior. The story is probably apocryphal because as a young man Hobbes was secretary to Francis Bacon, who doubtless gave him a taste for science. Yet it does capture the essence of his masterpiece, *Leviathan* (1651), which began with a few premises about human nature from which Hobbes deduced major conclusions about political forms.

Leviathan Hobbes's premises, drawn from his observation of the strife-ridden Europe of the 1640s and 1650s, were stark and uncompromising. People, he asserted, are selfish and ambitious; consequently, unless restrained, they fight a perpetual war with their fellows. The weak are more cunning and the strong more stupid. Given these unsavory characteristics, the state of nature—which precedes the existence of society—is a state of war, in which life is "solitary, poor, nasty,

▲ *PORTRAIT OF THOMAS HOBBES*
This depiction of the famous philosopher shows him with a twinkle in the eye and a smile that might seem surprising, given the pessimism about human nature in his *Leviathan.*
New York Public Library / Art Resource, NY

brutish, and short." Hobbes concluded that the only way to restrain this instinctive aggressiveness is to erect an absolute and sovereign power that will maintain peace. Everyone should submit to the sovereign because the alternative is the anarchy of the state of nature. The moment of submission is the moment of the birth of orderly society.

In a startling innovation, Hobbes suggested that the transition from nature to society is accomplished by a contract that is implicitly accepted by all who wish to end the chaos. The unprecedented feature of the contract is that it is not between ruler and ruled; it is binding only on the ruled. They agree among themselves to submit to the sovereign; the sovereign is thus not a party to the contract and is not limited in any way. A government that is totally free to do whatever it wishes is

best equipped to keep the peace, and peace is always better than the previous turmoil. The power of Hobbes's logic, and the endorsement he seemed to give to absolutism, made his views enormously influential. But his approach also aroused hostility. Although later political theorists were deeply affected by his ideas, many of Hobbes's successors denounced him as godless, immoral, cynical, and unfeeling. It was dislike of his message, not weaknesses in his analysis, that made many people unwilling to accept his views.

Locke   John Locke, a quiet Oxford professor who admired Hobbes but sought to soften his conclusions, based his political analysis on a general theory of knowledge. Locke believed that at birth a person's mind is a *tabula rasa*, a clean slate; nothing, he said, is inborn or preordained. As human beings grow, they observe and experience the world. Once they have gathered enough data through their senses, their minds begin to work on the data. Then, with the help of reason, they perceive patterns, discovering the order and harmony that permeate the universe. Locke was convinced that this underlying order exists and that every person, regardless of individual experiences, must reach the same conclusions about its nature and structure.

When Locke turned his attention to political thought, he put into systematic form the views of the English gentry and other antiabsolutists throughout Europe. The *Second Treatise of Civil Government*, published in 1690, was deeply influenced by Hobbes. From his great predecessor, Locke took the notions that a state of nature is a state of war and that only a contract among the people can end the anarchy that precedes the establishment of civil society. But his conclusions were decidedly different.

Of Civil Government   Using the principles of his theory of knowledge, Locke asserted that, applying reason to politics, one can prove the inalienability of three rights of an individual: life, liberty, and property. Like Hobbes, he believed that there must be a sovereign power, but he argued that it has no power over these three natural rights of its subjects without their consent. And this consent—for taxes, for example—must come from a representative assembly of men of property, such as

LOCKE ON THE ORIGINS OF GOVERNMENT

The heart of John Locke's Second Treatise of Civil Government, *written in the mid-1680s before England's Glorious Revolution but published in 1690, is its optimism about human nature—as opposed to Hobbes's pessimism. In this passage Locke explains why, in his view, people create political systems.*

"If man in the state of nature be so free, if he be absolute lord of his own person and possessions, equal to the greatest, and subject to nobody, why will he part with his freedom, and subject himself to the dominion and control of any other power? To which it is obvious to answer, that though in the state of nature he hath such a right, yet the enjoyment of it is very uncertain, and constantly exposed to the invasions of others. This makes him willing to quit this condition, which, however free, is full of fears and continual dangers; and it is not without reason that he seeks out and is willing to join in society with others, who have a mind to unite, for the mutual preservation of their lives, liberties, and estates, which I call by the general name, property. The great and chief end, therefore, of men's putting themselves under government, is the preservation of their property.

"But though men when they enter into society give up the equality, liberty, and power they had in the state of nature into the hands of society; yet it being only with an intention in every one the better to preserve himself, his liberty, and property, the power of the society can never be supposed to extend further than the common good. And all this to be directed to no other end but the peace, safety, and public good of the people."

From John Locke, *The Second Treatise of Civil Government,* Thomas P. Peardon (ed.) (Indianapolis: Bobbs-Merrill, 1952), chapter 9, pp. 70–73.

Parliament. The affirmation of property as one of the three natural rights (it became "the pursuit of happiness" in the more egalitarian American Declaration of Independence) is significant. Here Locke revealed himself as the voice of the gentry. Only those with a tangible stake in their country have a right to control its destiny, and that stake must be protected as surely as their life and liberty. The concept of liberty remained vague, but it was taken to imply the sorts of freedom, such as freedom from arbitrary arrest, that appeared in the English Bill of Rights. Hobbes allowed a person to protect only his or her life. Locke permitted the overthrow of the sovereign power if it infringed on the subjects' rights—a course the English followed with James II and the Americans with George III.

Locke's prime concern was to defend the individual against the state, a concern that has remained essential to liberal thought ever since (see "Locke on the Origins of Government"). But it is important to realize that his emphasis on property served the elite better than the mass of society. With Locke to reassure them, the upper classes

put their stamp on eighteenth-century European civilization.

IV. The International System

While rulers built up their states by enlarging bureaucracies, strengthening governmental institutions, and expanding resources, they also had to consider how best to deal with their neighbors. In an age that emphasized reasoned and practical solutions to problems, there was hope that an orderly system could be devised for international relations. If the reality fell short of the ideal, there were nevertheless many who thought they were creating a more systematic and organized structure for diplomacy and warfare.

◆ DIPLOMACY AND WARFARE

One obstacle to the creation of impersonal international relations was the continuing influence of traditional dynastic interests. Princes and their ministers tried to preserve a family's succession, and they arranged marriages to gain new titles or alliances. Part of the reason that those perennial rivals, Britain and France, remained at peace for nearly thirty years until 1740 was that the rulers in both countries felt insecure on their thrones and thus had personal motives for not wanting to risk aggressive foreign policies.

Gradually, however, dynastic interests gave way to policies based on a more impersonal conception of the state. Leaders like Frederick II of Prussia and William Pitt of Britain tried to shape their diplomacy to what they considered the needs of their states. "Reasons of state" centered on security, which could be guaranteed only by force. Thus, the search for defensible borders and the weakening of rivals became obvious goals. Eighteenth-century leaders believed that the end (security and prosperity) justified the means (the use of power). Chasing the impossible goal of complete invulnerability, leaders felt justified in using the crudest tactics in dealing with their neighbors.

"Balance of Power" and the Diplomatic System
If there was any broad, commonly accepted principle at work, it was that hegemony, or domination by one state, had to be resisted because it threatened international security. The concern aroused by Louis XIV's ambitions showed the principle at work, when those whom he sought to dominate joined together to frustrate his designs. The aim was to establish equilibrium in Europe by a balance of power, with no single state achieving hegemony. From the War of Spanish Succession until the rise of Napoleon, that balance was maintained, though the means could be unsavory.

The diplomats guided by "reasons of state" and the balance of power knew there were times when they had to deceive. They might fabricate a claim to a province or a princely title, and it was known that ambassadors were spies by vocation. They offered the bribes that were a part of foreign policy and negotiated treaties that they sometimes expected their prince to violate.

Yet diplomacy also could stabilize: In the eighteenth century it grew as a serious profession, paralleling the rationalization of the state itself. Foreign ministries were staffed with experts and clerks, who kept extensive archives, while the heads of the diplomatic machine, the ambas-sadors, were stationed in permanent embassies abroad. This routinized management of foreign relations helped foster a sense of collective identity among Europe's states despite their endless struggles. Linguistically and socially, diplomats gave a sugar coating to international relations. French was now the common language of diplomacy; by 1774 even a treaty between Turks and Russians was drafted in that language. And socially the diplomats were cosmopolitan aristocrats, who saw themselves as members of the same fraternity, even if the great powers dominated international agreements, usually at the expense of the smaller states. For example, Prussia, Austria, and Russia satisfied their territorial ambitions by partitioning Poland among themselves. Ignoring the Poles, they declared in 1772 that "whatever the limits of the respective claims, the acquisitions which result must be exactly equal." Resolving disputes by negotiation could be as amoral as war.

◆ ARMIES AND NAVIES

Despite the settlement of some conflicts by diplomacy, others led to war. Whereas Britain emphasized its navy, on the continent the focus of bureaucratic innovation and monetary expenditure was the standing army, whose growth was striking. France set the pace. After 1680 the size of its forces never fell below 200,000. In Prussia the army increased in size from 39,000 to 200,000 men between 1713 and 1786. But the cost, technology, and tactics of armies and navies served to limit the devastation of eighteenth-century warfare. The expenses led rulers to conserve men, equipment, and ships carefully. Princes were quick to declare war but slow to commit armies or navies to battle. Casualties also became less numerous as discipline improved and the ferocity that had been caused by religious passions died away.

Tactics and Discipline On land, the building and besieging of fortresses continued to preoccupy military planners, even though the impregnable defenses built by the French engineer Sebastian Vauban to protect France's northeastern border were simply bypassed by the English general Marlborough when he pursued the French army in the War of the Spanish Succession. The

▲ *L. N. van Blarenberghe*
THE BATTLE OF FONTENOY, **1745**
This panorama shows the English and Dutch assaulting the French position in a battle in present-day Belgium. The French lines form a huge semicircle from the distant town to the wood on the left. The main attacking force in the center, surrounded by gunfire, eventually retreated, and news of the victory was brought to Louis XV, in red on the right, by a horseman in blue who is doffing his hat.
Giraudon/Art Resource, NY

decisive encounter was still the battle between armies, where the majority of the troops—the infantry—used their training to maneuver and fire in carefully controlled line formations. The aim of strategy was not to annihilate but to nudge an opposing army into abandoning a position in the face of superior maneuvers. Improved organization also reduced brutality. Better supplied by a system of magazines, more tightly disciplined by constant drilling, troops were less likely to desert or plunder than they had been during the Thirty Years' War. At sea, the British achieved superiority by maneuvering carefully controlled lines of ships and seeking to outnumber or outflank the enemy.

As these practices took hold, some encounters were fought as if they were taking place on a parade ground or in a naval strategy room. Pitched battles were increasingly avoided, for even important victories might be nullified if a winning army or navy returned to its home bases for the winter. And no victor ever demanded unconditional surrender; in almost all cases, a commander would hesitate to pursue a defeated company or squadron.

Officers   The officer corps were generally the preserve of Europe's nobility, though they also served as channels of upward social mobility for wealthy sons of middle-class families who purchased commissions. In either case, the officer ranks tended to be filled by men who lacked the professional training for effective leadership. Officers were likely to be long on martial spirit but short on technical skills. The branches of service

▲ ENGRAVING OF A MILITARY ACADEMY, FROM H. F. VON FLEMING, *VOLKOMMENE TEUTSCHE SOLDAT,* 1726
This scene, of young men studying fortifications and tactics in a German academy, would have been familiar to the sons of nobles throughout Europe who trained for a military career in the eighteenth century.

that showed the most progress were the artillery and the engineers, in which competent middle-class officers played an unusually large role.

Weak Alliances A final limit on the scale of war in the eighteenth century was the inherent weakness of coalitions, which formed whenever a general war erupted. On paper these alliances looked formidable. On battlefields, however, they were hampered by primitive communications and lack of mobility even at the peak of cooperation. Moreover, the partnerships rarely lasted very long. The competitiveness of the state system bred distrust among allies as well as enemies. Sudden abandonment of coalitions and the negotiation of separate peace treaties mark the history of almost every major war.

◆ THE SEVEN YEARS' WAR

The pressures created by the competition of states and dynasties finally exploded in a major war, the Seven Years' War (1756–1763). Its roots lay in a realignment of diplomatic alliances prompted by Austria. Previously, the Bourbon-Habsburg rivalry had been the cornerstone of European diplomacy. But by the 1750s two other antagonisms had taken over: French competition with the British in the New World and Austria's vendetta against Prussia over Silesia. For Austria, the rivalry with Bourbon France was no longer important. Its position in the Holy Roman Empire depended now on humbling Prussia. French hostility toward Austria had also lessened, and thus Austria was free to lead a turnabout in alliances—

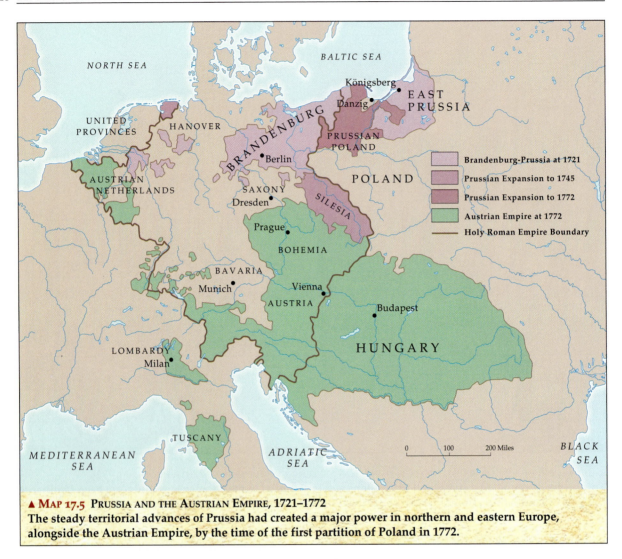

▲ **MAP 17.5** PRUSSIA AND THE AUSTRIAN EMPIRE, 1721–1772
The steady territorial advances of Prussia had created a major power in northern and eastern Europe, alongside the Austrian Empire, by the time of the first partition of Poland in 1772.

a diplomatic revolution—so as to forge an anti-Prussian coalition with France and Russia. Russia was crucial. The pious Empress Elizabeth of Russia loathed Frederick II and saw him as an obstacle to Russian ambitions in eastern Europe. Geographical vulnerability also made Prussia an inviting target, and so the stage was set for war.

Prussia tried actively to compensate for its vulnerability. But its countermoves only alienated the other powers. Frederick sought to stay out of the Anglo-French rivalry by coming to terms with both these states. He had been France's ally in the past, but he now sought a treaty with England, and in January 1756 the English, hoping to protect the royal territory of Hanover, signed a neutrality accord with Prussia, the Convention of Westminster. Frederick had no wish to repudiate his friendship with France, but the French, who had not been informed of the negotiations in advance, saw the Convention as an insult, if not a betrayal: the act of an untrustworthy ally. France overreacted, turned against Prussia, and thus fell into Austria's design (see "Maria Theresa in a Vehement Mood"). Russia too considered the Convention of Westminster a betrayal by its supposed ally England. English bribes and diplomacy were unable to keep Russia from actively joining Austria to plan Prussia's dismemberment.

Maria Theresa in Vehement Mood

◆

The animosities and ambitions that shaped international relations in the eighteenth century were exemplified by the Empress Maria Theresa. Her furious reaction to the event that destroyed Europe's old diplomatic system—England's signing of the Convention of Westminster with Maria Theresa's archenemy, Frederick the Great—suggests how deep were the feelings that brought about the mid-century conflagration. After learning the news and deciding (in response) to ally herself with France, she told the British ambassador on May 13, 1756, exactly where she stood.

"I have not abandoned the old system, but Great Britain has abandoned me and the system, by concluding the Prussian treaty, the first intelligence of which struck me like a fit of apoplexy. I and the king of Prussia are incompatible; and no consideration on earth will ever induce me to enter into any engagement to which he is a party. Why should you be surprised if, following your example in concluding a treaty with Prussia, I should now enter into an engagement with France?

"I am far from being French in my disposition, and do not deny that the court of Versailles has been my bitterest enemy; but I have little to fear from France, and I have no other recourse than to form such arrangements as will secure what remains to me. My principal aim is to secure my hereditary possessions. I have truly but two enemies whom I really dread, the king of Prussia and the Turks; and while I and Russia continue on the same good terms as now exist between us, we shall, I trust, be able to convince Europe, that we are in a condition to defend ourselves against those adversaries, however formidable."

From William Coxe, *History of the House of Austria*, vol. 3 (London: Bohn, 1847), pp. 363–364.

The Course of War   Fearing encirclement, Frederick gambled on a preventive war through Saxony in 1756. Although he conquered the duchy, his plan backfired, for it activated the coalition that he dreaded. Russia and France met their commitments to Austria, and the three began a combined offensive against Prussia. For a time Frederick's genius as a general brought him success. His forces won a spectacular victory at Rossbach in late 1757 over a much larger French-Austrian army. Skillful tactics and daring surprise movements would bring other victories, but strategically the Prussian position was shaky. Frederick had to dash in all directions across his provinces to repel invading armies whose combined strength far exceeded his own. Each successive year of the war, he faced the prospect of Russian attacks on Brandenburg in the north and Austrian thrusts from the south through Silesia and Saxony. Disaster was avoided mainly because the Russian army returned east for winter quarters regardless of its gains, but even so, the Russians occupied Berlin.

On the verge of exhaustion, Prussia at best seemed to face a stalemate with a considerable loss of territory; at worst, the war would continue and bring about a total Prussian collapse. But the other powers were also war-weary, and Frederick's enemies were becoming increasingly distrustful of one another. In the end, Prussia was saved by one of those sudden changes of reign that could cause dramatic reversals of policy in Europe. In January 1762 Empress Elizabeth died and was replaced temporarily by Tsar Peter III, a passionate admirer of Frederick. He quickly pulled Russia out of the war and returned Frederick's conquered eastern domains of Prussia and Pomerania. In Britain, meanwhile, William Pitt was replaced by the more pacific earl of Bute, who brought about a reconciliation with France; both countries then ended their insistence on punishing Prussia. Austria's coalition collapsed.

Peace   The terms of the Peace of Hubertusburg (1763), settling the continental phase of the Seven Years' War, were therefore surprisingly favorable to Prussia. Prussia returned Saxony to Austria but paid no compensation for the devastation of the duchy, and the Austrians recognized Silesia as Prussian. In short, the status quo was restored.

Frederick could return to Berlin, his dominion preserved partly by his army but mainly by luck and the continuing fragility of international alliances.

SUMMARY

If, amidst the state building of the eighteenth century, Europe's regimes were ready to sustain a major war even if it brought about few territorial changes, that was not simply because of the expansion of government and the disciplining of armies. It was also the result of remarkable economic advances and the availability of new resources that were flowing into Europe from the development of overseas empires. In politics, this was primarily an age of consolidation; in economics, it was a time of profound transformation.

QUESTIONS FOR FURTHER THOUGHT

1. Although Americans naturally prefer regimes that provide for representation and citizen participation in government, are there times when it is advantageous for a state to have an authoritarian or absolutist regime?

2. How important is the development of a capital city or a center of government in the process of state-building?

RECOMMENDED READING

Sources

*Hobbes, Thomas. *Leviathan.* 1651. Any modern edition.

*Locke, John. *Second Treatise of Civil Government.* 1690. Any modern edition.

Luvvas, J. (ed.). *Frederick the Great on the Art of War.* 1966.

Studies

*Behrens, C. B. A. *Society, Government, and the Enlightenment: The Experience of Eighteenth-Century France and Prussia.* 1985.

Brewer, John. *The Sinews of Power: War, Money, and the English State, 1688–1783.* 1989. The work that demonstrated the importance of the military and the growth of bureaucracy in eighteenth-century England.

*Hatton, R. N. *Europe in the Age of Louis XIV.* 1969. A beautifully illustrated and vividly interpretive history of the period that Louis dominated.

*Holmes, Geoffrey. *The Making of a Great Power: Late Stuart and Early Georgian Britain, 1660–1722;* and *The Age of Oligarchy: Pre-industrial Britain, 1722–1783.* 1993. The best detailed survey.

Lossky, Andrew. *Louis XIV and the French Monarchy.* 1994.

Mettam, Roger. *Power and Faction in Louis XIV's France.* 1988. An analysis of government and power under absolutist rule.

Oresko, Robert, G. C. Gibbs, and H. M. Scott (eds.). *Royal and Republican Sovereignty in Early Modern Europe.* 1997.

*Plumb, J. H. *The Growth of Political Stability in England, 1675–1725.* 1969. A brief, lucid survey of the development of parliamentary democracy.

Raeff, Marc. *The Well-Ordered Police State: Social and Institutional Change through Law in the Germanies and Russia, 1600–1800.* 1983.

*Sumner, B. H. *Peter the Great and the Emergence of Russia*. 1950. The best short introduction to Russian history in this period.

*Tuck, Richard. *Hobbes*. 1989. A clear introduction to Hobbes's thought.

Weigley, R. F. *The Age of Battles: The Quest for Decisive Warfare from Breitenfeld to Waterloo*. 1991. The best military history of the age.

*Available in paperback.

▲ **The docks of Marseilles in southern France.**
Musée de la Marine. © Photo RMN / Art Resource, NY

THE WEALTH OF NATIONS

*I*n the early eighteenth century the great majority of Europe's people still lived directly off the land. With a few regional exceptions, the agrarian economy remained immobile: It seemed to have no capacity for dramatic growth. Technology, social arrangements, and management techniques offered little prospect of improvement in production. Several new developments, however, were about to touch off a remarkable surge of economic advance. The first sign, and a growing stimulus for this new situation, was the sustained growth of Europe's population. This depended in turn on an expanding and surer food supply. While changes in agrarian output on the continent were modest but significant, in England innovations in the control and use of land dramatically increased food production and changed the very structure of rural society.

The exploitation of overseas colonies provided another critical stimulus for European economic growth. Colonial trade in slaves, sugar, tobacco, and other raw materials radiated from port cities like London and Bristol in England and Bordeaux and Nantes in France. An infrastructure of supportive trades and processing facilities developed around these ports and fed trade networks for the reexport across Europe of finished colonial products. The colonies, in turn, offered new markets for goods manufactured in Europe, such as cotton fabrics. Undergirding most of this commerce was the Atlantic slave trade and plantation slavery in the New World.

In one small corner of the economy, the growing demand for cotton cloth at home and abroad touched off a quest among English textile merchants for changes in the organization and technology of production. Dramatic structural change in English cotton manufacturing heralded the remarkable economic transformation known as industrialization. By the early nineteenth century, fundamental changes in the methods of raising food and producing goods were under way in Britain and were spreading to the continent. This chapter explores the character of economic development, the impediments to that process, the nature of eighteenth-century innovations in agriculture, manufacturing, and trade, and some of the social consequences of these economic transformations.

CHAPTER 18. THE WEALTH OF NATIONS							
	Social Structure	Body Politic	Changes in the Organization of Production and in the Impact of Technology	Evolution of Family and Changing Gender Roles	War	Religion	Cultural Expression
I. Demographic and Economic Growth	▓		▓	▓			
II. The New Shape of Industry			▓				▓
III. Innovation and Tradition in Agriculture	▓		▓	▓			
IV. Eighteenth-Century Empires	▓	▓			▓		

I. Demographic and Economic Growth

◆

Perhaps the most basic, long-term historical variable is the movement of population. Historical demographers deal with the migrations of existing populations, from country to city, across national borders or even oceans. More fundamentally, they study the trends over time within populations and chart death rates, birth rates, and the growth or decline of population. Similarly, economic historians analyze macroeconomic trends in production and prices, which in turn can reinforce population growth or deter it. In this section we will consider certain trends in the demography and economy of eighteenth-century Europe, which combined to support economic growth.

◆ A NEW DEMOGRAPHIC ERA

In the relationship between people and the land, between demography and agriculture, European life before the eighteenth century showed little change. Levels of population seemed to flow like the tides, in cyclical or wavelike patterns. Population might increase substantially over several generations, but eventually crop failures or the ravages of plague and other contagious diseases would drive the level of population down once again. In extreme cases, a lack of able-bodied workers led to the abandonment of land, and entire villages disappeared altogether. Such dramatic population

losses had last occurred in seventeenth-century Germany, Poland, and Mediterranean Europe (the southern parts of Italy, Spain, and France).

For centuries Europe's population had been vulnerable to subsistence crises. Successions of poor harvests or crop failures might leave the population without adequate food and would drive up the price of grain and flour beyond what the poorest people could afford. If actual starvation did not carry them off, undernourishment made people more vulnerable than usual to disease. Such crises could also set off a chain of side effects, from unemployment to pessimism, that made people postpone marriage and childbearing. Thus, subsistence crises could drive down the birthrate as well as drive up the death rate, causing in combination a substantial loss in population.

Population Growth   Although barely perceived by most Europeans at the time, a new era in Europe's demography began around 1730, and by 1800 Europe's population had grown by at least 50 percent. (Since the first censuses were not taken until the early nineteenth century, all population figures prior to that time are only estimates.) During the eighteenth century (which is considered, demographically, to have begun around 1730), Europe's estimated population jumped from about 120 million to about 180 or 190 million. Europe had probably never before experienced so rapid and substantial an increase in the number of its people. Prussia and Sweden may have doubled their populations, while

Spain's grew from 7.5 million to about 11.5 million. Even higher growth rates in England and Wales raised the population there from an estimated 5 million people in 1700 to more than 9 million in 1801, the date of the first British census. The French, according to the best estimates, numbered about 19 million at the death of Louis XIV in 1715 and probably about 26 million in 1789. France was the most densely populated large nation in Europe in the late eighteenth century and, with the exception of the vast Russian Empire, the most populous state, which no doubt helps to explain its remarkable military preponderance in the revolutionary and Napoleonic eras.

Europe's population growth of the eighteenth century continued and indeed accelerated during the nineteenth century, thus breaking once and for all the tidelike cycles and immobility of Europe's demography. What caused this fundamental transformation in the underlying structure of European history?

Falling Death Rates   There are two possible explanations for rapid population growth: a fall in death rates or a rise in birthrates. The consensus among historians is that a decline in mortality rates, rather than a rise in birthrates, accounts for most of the population growth in the eighteenth century, although England seems to have been an exception. Declines in the death rate did not occur because of improvements in medical science or hygiene, which became important factors in

▼ In these two French parishes, the seventeenth century came to a close with severe food shortages and sharp surges of mortality. In a more favorable economic climate, by contrast, the later eighteenth century brought an almost consistent annual surplus of births over deaths.

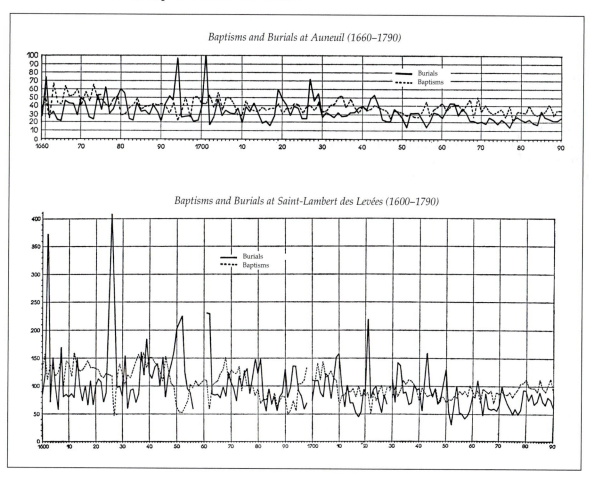

driving down mortality only in the later nineteenth century. Instead, Europe was beginning to enjoy a stabler and better food supply, perhaps owing to a mild improvement in average climate compared with that of the seventeenth century, which some historians regard as a "little ice age" of unusually cold and wet weather. The opening of new agricultural land in Poland, Hungary, and Russia helped increase Europe's food supplies, as did incremental advances in transportation networks (which made it easier to move regional grain surpluses to where they were most needed) and agrarian changes in England (to be discussed later in this chapter).

Europe's population remained extremely vulnerable to disease. Endemic diseases such as tuberculosis, typhoid, and malaria still ravaged the populations of many regions. Periodic epidemics of dysentery (which attacked the digestive system), influenza (lethal to the respiratory systems of the elderly), typhus (a lice-borne disease that flourished in the conditions of poverty), and smallpox (which assaulted rich and poor alike) continued to take their toll. But a better-nourished population could perhaps stand up to those assaults with greater success.

With the exception of England, birthrates in most regions of Europe do not seem to have increased in the eighteenth century. A high average age at marriage, with women typically well into their twenties and men in their mid to late twenties, served to check population growth. Since the birth of illegitimate children remained relatively rare, late marriages kept women from becoming pregnant during some of their most fecund years; they therefore had fewer babies altogether. In England, however, where greater geographic mobility and economic opportunities may have encouraged young couples to start families earlier, the average age at marriage came down and birthrates increased, helping to explain Britain's explosive population growth.

◆ PROFIT INFLATION: THE MOVEMENT OF PRICES

The population grew in eighteenth-century Europe in tandem with an increasing pace and scale of economic activity. Europe's overall wealth expanded, though not steadily and consistently. While the economy experienced periods of fluctu-

ation, of growth and decline, the long-term, or secular, trend was positive, compared with the stagnation and economic difficulty that prevailed (outside of England) during the "long seventeenth century," until roughly 1730. Scholars have made particularly rigorous studies of the economic cycles in France as revealed through the history of prices, and there is reason to believe that economies elsewhere in Europe behaved comparably to France's.

During the first decades of the eighteenth century, prices generally remained stable, perpetuating the long depression of the seventeenth century and no doubt reflecting the exhaustion of the European states from the War of the Spanish Succession. As with Europe's demographic growth, significant economic growth began around 1730 and lasted up until the peace settlements that followed the Napoleonic wars in 1815. Gradual inflation in prices dominated the era. Since French money was kept stable after 1726, the upward movement of prices must be attributed to other causes. Primarily, the rise in prices reflected the stimulus and pressures of a growing population in France and a growing demand for food, land, goods, and employment.

Gently rising prices and gradual, mild inflation usually stimulate the economy—unlike sharp spikes of inflation that create hard times. This nearly century-long cycle of "profit inflation" generated economic growth. There were, of course, periodic reversals or countercyclical trends. In France, for example, prosperity leveled off around 1770, ushering in two decades of falling profits, unemployment, and hard times. The difficulties were compounded by a succession of crop failures and sharply rising grain prices in 1788 and 1789, coincident with the outbreak of the French Revolution. After the 1790s, however, profit inflation resumed until the end of the Napoleonic era.

The Impact of Inflation   Over the long term, the inflation did not affect all products, all sectors of the economy, or all segments of society equally. Prices in France between 1726 and 1789 increased by an average of about 65 percent. The cost of grains, the basic food for the poor, rose slightly more than the average and considerably more than other agricultural products, such as wine and meat. Rents rose sharply, suggesting a shortage of available land; in relation to averages for the decade of the 1730s, money rents had grown by 98 percent in the 1780s. Real wages, on the other hand, increased by a meager 22 percent in the same period, which points to a glut of workers competing for employment and to hard times for many wage earners.

These differentials had important social and economic effects. High rents in the countryside and low wages in the city took wealth from the poor and delivered it to the landlord and employer. Inflation helped drive many tenants from the soil, to the advantage of their better-off neighbors, who were eager to expand their holdings. In the city, inflation enabled merchants and manufacturers to sell goods for more and pay workers relatively less. Finally, inflation hurt the French government because its revenues did not grow as fast as its expenditures. Since a portion of French lands owned by the nobles and the Church was exempt from the land tax, the government relied heavily on sales and excise taxes that weighed on ordinary consumers. This inadequate and regressive tax base eventually contributed to a financial crisis for the French monarchy in the 1780s.

◆ PROTOINDUSTRIALIZATION

Agriculture alone could not ensure economic growth in a heavily populated country like England, France, or the Netherlands. The excess of people to land in such countries meant that many rural people could not actually earn their

▼ In contrast to textile work, common artisanal trades such as shoemaking, tailoring, dressmaking, furniture making, and food services would continue to be conducted in small workshops down through the nineteenth century.
Bulloz/© Photo RMN/Art Resource, NY

livelihood in agriculture. One solution for needy families was domestic manufacturing. Traditionally, artisans in urban guilds manufactured the cloth fabrics used by Europeans. But textiles could also be produced through the putting-out system, whereby merchants distributed raw materials like wool or flax to rural households. Men and women would spin the raw material into yarn on hand-powered spinning machines; rural weavers working on looms in their cottages would then weave the yarn into cloth.

Protoindustrialization is the name historians give to a type of economic development that occurred before the rise of the factory system in the late eighteenth century. In this phase, the volume of rural manufacturing increased under the putting-out system, as more rural families devoted more time to industrial work—primarily spinning, weaving, or finishing textiles. This trend was particularly noticeable in certain regions of the Netherlands, Belgium, the Rhineland, France, and England, where the towns remained sources of capital, materials, and marketing services but where merchants employed labor in the countryside.

Protoindustrialization had important economic, social, and demographic repercussions. Economically, it strengthened marketing networks, spurred capital accumulation that could be reinvested in production, generated additional revenue for needy rural families, and thereby increased their demand for products and services. Socially, it familiarized rural inhabitants with industrial processes and cash relationships. Demographically, it may have loosened restraints on marriages and births, which in turn might have led to increased immigration into the cities and thus to urban growth. On the other hand, protoindustrialization did not lead to significant technological improvements or to marked advances in productivity; it could not sustain continuous economic growth.

II. The New Shape of Industry

While most economic activity continued in traditional fashion, dramatic change began during the late eighteenth century in a few corners of the English economy, especially in the manufacture of cotton cloth. Structural economic transformation hinged on increasing the productivity of labor, through two kinds of innovation: the development of more efficient tools and machines, and the exploitation of new sources of energy to drive those machines. These innovations in turn led to a reorganization of labor in a new kind of site called the factory.

Such changes in production, however, did not arise out of thin air. They were rooted in a host of favorable preconditions in English society. The legal system regulating property rights, efficient financial institutions, market structures, growing consumer demand, even a new mode of economic analysis—the free-market doctrines of Adam Smith—provided a favorable environment for the innovations in textile manufacturing toward the end of the century. As such changes spread and visibly changed the landscape, critics would later describe them as an "industrial revolution." That term no doubt overstates the case—since it took decades for such changes to take hold more widely—but it is safe to say that the European economy would never be the same.

◆ TOWARD A NEW ECONOMIC ORDER

In analyzing any economic system—traditional or modern, capitalist or socialist—economists distinguish between performance and structure. *Performance* is measured by output: the total, or gross, product and the amount produced per individual in the community. This per capita productivity is generally the best measure of an economy's performance. A distinctive feature of an industrial economy is its capacity for sustained growth in per capita production. *Structure* refers to all those characteristics of a society that support or affect performance. Economic, legal, and political institutions; tax policies; technology; demographic movements; even culture and ideology all make up the structure underlying the economy.

Industrialization required innovations in technology, which dramatically raised per capita productivity, but these innovations alone do not entirely explain the advent of industrialism. Social structure itself influences technological development in any age. To ask why dramatic change occurred in industry is thus to pose two deeper questions: What were the structural obstacles to technological innovation and entrepreneurship in traditional European society? And what changes in that society, from the late eighteenth century onward, promoted and rewarded innovation?

Impediments to Economic Innovation   One major obstacle to innovation was the small size of most European markets, which were cut off from one another by physical barriers, political frontiers, tariff walls, and different laws, moneys, and units of measurement. Small markets slowed the growth of specialized manufacture and limited the mobility of capital and labor. Similarly, the highly skewed distribution of wealth typical of many European communities distorted the structure of demand. In many countries, a narrow aristocracy absorbed most disposable income, and the economy organized itself largely to serve the wealthy few. Catering to the desires of the rich, the economy produced expensive luxury goods, often exquisite in quality and workmanship but always in relatively small quantities. Such small markets and skewed demand dampened the incentive to manufacture an abundance of relatively inexpensive goods.

Also crucial to the industrializing process was the question of property rights and privileges—whether they would encourage a high rate of return on innovation or impede it. In the towns, the guilds presented a major obstacle to economic innovation. Guild regulations, or government regulation of the economy enforced by the guilds, prescribed the techniques to be used in production and often dictated the terms and conditions under which goods could be sold, apprentices taken on, or workers hired. Out of simple self-interest, given their stake in existing arrangements, the guilds favored traditional technology and managerial techniques.

Governments, too, helped sustain these restrictive practices, principally by exploiting them for their own fiscal benefit. The French government, for example, collected substantial fees from guilds and could turn to them for loans as well. Governments also restricted economic activity by licensing monopoly companies with exclusive rights to trade in certain regions, such as the East Indies, or to manufacture certain products, such as fine porcelain. With assured markets and profits, these companies were not likely to assume the risks of new ventures, and they blocked others from do-

ing so. Cultural attitudes may also have discouraged entrepreneurial efforts. Many persons, particularly in the aristocratic classes, still regarded money made in trade or manufacture as somehow tainted. The highest aspiration of successful French business families seems often to have been the purchase of a noble title.

Adam Smith   Although these institutions and attitudes still marked European life in the eighteenth century, they were subject to ever sharper criticisms. From midcentury on, certain French social thinkers denounced guild control of production in the towns and economic privilege and monopoly in all forms. But the seminal work in this new school of economic thought was *An Inquiry into the Nature and Causes of the Wealth of Nations* (1776) by the Scottish philosopher Adam Smith. Smith argued that money in and of itself did not constitute wealth but was merely its marker. Wealth derived from the added value in manufactured items produced by the combination of invested capital and labor. Smith believed that economic progress required that each individual be allowed to pursue his or her own self-interest freely, without restriction by guilds, the state, or tradition. He argued that on all levels of economic activity—from manufacturing to the flow of international trade—a natural division of labor should be encouraged. High tariffs, guild restrictions, and mercantilist restraints on free trade all artificially obstructed economic activity. Smith became a founding father of *laissez-faire* economic theory, meaning, in effect: Let individuals freely pursue their own economic interests. In the aggregate, free individual enterprise would create more wealth than any artificial regulation could encourage (see "Laissez-Faire Ideology," p. 640).

Laissez-faire became a battle cry taken up by British businesspeople and factory owners in the early nineteenth century. Such arguments slowly affected policy. In 1786 France and Britain signed a free-trade treaty, lowering protective tariffs on imported textiles. Guilds were already growing weaker in most towns and were relatively powerless in towns of recent growth, like Manchester and Birmingham in England, where new industries such as cotton manufacturing escaped guild supervision altogether. This trend reached its culmination when the government of revolutionary

LAISSEZ-FAIRE IDEOLOGY

At the heart of Adam Smith's laissez-faire ideology was a belief that individual self-interest is the motor of economic progress, a notion epitomized in this selection by Smith's reference to the "invisible hand." By the same token, each region or country should pursue what it does best, an argument against protective tariffs for domestic industry.

"Every individual is continually exerting himself to find out the most advantageous employment for whatever capital he can command. . . . But it is only for the sake of profit that any man employs a capital in the support of industry; and he will always, therefore, endeavor to employ it in the support of that industry of which the produce is likely to be of the greatest value, or to exchange for the greatest quantity either of money or of other goods. . . . [In so doing] he generally neither intends to promote the public interest, nor knows how much he is promoting it . . . he intends only his own security; and by directing that industry in such a manner as its produce may be of the greatest value, he intends only his own gain. [But] he is in this, as in many other cases, led by an invisible hand to promote an end which was not part of his intention. By pursuing his own interest he frequently promotes that of the society more effectually than when he really intends to promote it.

"What is the species of domestic industry which his capital can employ, and of which the produce is likely to be of the greatest value, every individual, it is evident, can, in his local situation, judge much better than any statesman or lawgiver can do for him. . . . To give the monopoly of the home market to the produce of domestic industry, in any particular art or manufacture, is in some measure to direct private people in what manner they ought to employ their capitals, and must, in almost all cases, be either a useless or hurtful regulation. If the produce of domestic can be brought there as cheaply as that of foreign industry, the regulation is evidently useless. If it cannot, it must generally be hurtful. . . . If a foreign country can supply us with a commodity cheaper than we ourselves can make it, better buy it from them with some part of the produce of our own industry."

A. Smith, *An Inquiry into the Nature and Causes of the Wealth of Nations* (1776), book 4, ch. 2.

France permanently dissolved all guilds and restrictive trade associations in 1791. Similarly, the British Parliament revoked the laws regulating apprenticeships in the 1790s. Legally and socially, the entrepreneur was winning greater freedom.

◆ THE ROOTS OF ECONOMIC TRANSFORMATION IN ENGLAND

Of all the nations of Europe, England was the first to develop a social structure strongly supportive of innovation and economic growth. England's advantages were many, some of them deeply rooted in geography and history. This comparatively small realm contained an excellent balance of resources. The plain to the south and east, where traditional centers of English settlement concentrated, was fertile and productive. The uplands to the north and west possessed rich deposits of coal and iron, and their streams had powered flour mills since the Middle Ages.

Proximity to the sea was another natural advantage. No part of the island kingdom was distant from the coast. At a time when water transport offered the sole economical means for moving bulky commodities, the sea brought coal close to iron, raw materials close to factories, and products close to markets. Above all, the sea gave Britain's merchants access to the much wider world beyond their shores.

Efficiency of transport was critical in setting the size of markets. During the eighteenth century, Britain witnessed a boom in the building of canals and turnpikes by private individuals or syndicates. By 1815 the country possessed some 2,600 miles of canals linking rivers, ports, and other towns. In addition, few institutional obstructions to the movement of goods existed. United under a strong monarchy, Britain was free of internal tariff barriers, unlike prerevolutionary France, Germany, or Italy. Merchants everywhere counted in the same money, measured their goods by the same standards, and conducted their affairs under the protection of the common law. By contrast, in France differences in provincial legal codes and in weights and measures complicated and slowed exchange. As the writer Voltaire sarcastically remarked, the traveler crossing France by coach changed laws as frequently as horses.

The English probably had the highest standard of living in Europe and generated strong consumer demand for manufactured goods. English society was less stratified than that on the continent, the aristocracy powerful but much smaller. Primogeniture (with the family's land going to the eldest son) was the rule among both the peers (the titled members of the House of Lords) and the country gentlemen or squires. Left without lands, younger sons had to seek careers in other walks of life, and some turned toward commerce. They frequently recruited capital for their ventures from their landed fathers and elder brothers. English religious dissenters, chiefly Calvinists and Quak-

ers, formed another pool of potential entrepreneurs; denied careers in government because of their religion, many turned their energies to business enterprises.

British Financial Management   A high rate of reinvestment is critical to industrialization; reinvestment, in turn, depends on the skillful management of money by both individuals and public institutions. Here again, Britain enjoyed advantages. Early industrial enterprises could rely on Britain's growing banking system to meet their capital needs. In the seventeenth century, the goldsmiths of London had assumed the functions of bankers. They accepted and guarded deposits, extended loans, transferred upon request credits from one account to another, and changed money. In the eighteenth century, banking services became available beyond London; the number of country banks rose from three hundred in 1780 to more than seven hundred by 1810. English

▼ Incremental improvements in road and water transportation facilitated economic growth in the eighteenth century. In France the government enlisted peasants periodically to work on the upkeep of major highways under a system of forced labor known as the royal *corvée.*
Giraudon/Art Resource, NY

businesspeople were familiar with banknotes and other forms of commercial papers, and their confidence in paper facilitated the recruitment and flow of capital.

The founding of the Bank of England in 1694 marked an epoch in the history of European finance. The bank took responsibility for managing England's public debt, sold shares to the public, and faithfully met the interest payments due to the shareholders, with the help of government revenue (such as the customs duties efficiently collected on Britain's extensive foreign trade). When the government needed to borrow, it could turn to the Bank of England for assistance. This stability in government finances ensured a measure of stability for the entire money market and, most important, held down interest rates in both the public and private sectors. In general, since the Glorious Revolution of 1688, England's government had been sensitive to the interests of the business classes, who in turn had confidence in the government. Such close ties between money and power facilitated economic investment.

In contrast, France lacked a sound central bank, and extensive government borrowing drove up interest rates in the private sector as well. On balance, although limited capital and conservative management held back French business enterprises, they dampened but did not suppress the expansion of the economy. France remained a leader in producing wool and linen cloth as well as iron, but it seemed more inclined to produce luxury items or very cheap, low-quality goods. On the other hand, England (with its higher standard of living and strong domestic demand) seemed more adept at producing standardized products of reasonably good quality.

◆ COTTON: THE BEGINNING OF INDUSTRIALIZATION

The process of early industrialization in England was extremely complex and remains difficult to explain. What seems certain is that a strong demand for cheap goods was growing at home and abroad in the eighteenth century, and a small but important segment of the English community perceived this opportunity and responded to it.

Specifically, the market for cotton goods became the most propulsive force for change in industrial production. Thanks to slave labor in plantation colonies, the supply of raw cotton was rising dramatically. On the demand side, lightweight cotton goods were durable, washable, versatile, and cheaper than woolen or linen cloth. Cotton, therefore, had a bright future as an item of mass consumption. But traditional textile manufacturing centers in England (the regions of protoindustrialization such as East Anglia and the Yorkshire districts) could not satisfy the growing demand. The organization and technology of the putting-out system had reached its limits. For one thing, the merchant was limited to the labor supply in his own district; the farther he went to find cottage workers, the longer it took and the more cumbersome it became to pass the materials back and forth. Second, he could not adequately control his workers. Clothiers were bedeviled with embezzlement of raw materials, poor workmanship, and lateness in finishing assigned work. English clothiers were therefore on the lookout for technological or organizational innovations to help them meet a growing demand for textiles.

Machines and Factories   Weavers could turn out large amounts of cloth thanks to the invention of the fly shuttle in the 1730s, which permitted the construction of larger and faster handlooms. But traditional methods of spinning the yarn caused a bottleneck in the production process. Responding to this problem, inventors built new kinds of spinning machines that could be grouped in large factories or mills. Richard Arkwright's water frame drew cotton fibers through rollers and twisted them into thread. Not simply an inventor but an entrepreneur (one who combined the various factors of production into a profitable enterprise), Arkwright initially housed his machines in a large factory sited near a river so that his machines could be propelled by waterpower.

At around the same time, James Watt had been perfecting the technology of steam engines—machinery originally used to power suction pumps that would evacuate water from the pits of coal mines. The earliest steam engine had produced a simple up-and-down motion. Watt not only redesigned it to make it far more efficient

▲ Richard Arkwright not only invented this power-driven machine to spin cotton yarn but also proved to be a highly successful entrepreneur with the factory he constructed at Cromford in the Lancashire region.
The Science Museum, London

and powerful but also developed a system of gears to harness the engine's energy into rotary motion that could drive other types of machines. In 1785 Arkwright became one of Watt's first customers when he switched from waterpower to steam engines as the means of driving the spinning machines in his new cotton factory. With Arkwright (who became a millionaire) and Watt, the modern factory system was launched (see "Richard Arkwright's Achievement," p. 644).

Spinning factories, however, disrupted the equilibrium between spinning and weaving in the other direction: Yarn was now abundant, but handloom weavers could not keep up with the pace. This disequilibrium created a brief golden age for the weavers, but merchants were eager to break the new bottleneck. In 1784 Edmund Cartwright designed a power-driven loom. Small

technical flaws and the violent opposition of handloom weavers retarded the widescale adoption of power looms until the early nineteenth century, but then both spinning and weaving were totally transformed. Power-driven machinery boosted the output of yarn and cloth astronomically, while merchants were able to assemble their workers in factories and scrutinize their every move to maximize production. In a factory, one small boy could watch over two mechanized looms whose output was fifteen times greater than that of a skilled hand loom weaver.

In 1760 Britain imported only 2.5 million pounds of raw cotton; by 1830 it was importing 366 million pounds. Cotton textiles had become the single most important industrial product in terms of output, capital investment, and number of workers. Its production was almost exclusively organized in factories using power-driven machinery at all stages. In the process, the price of cotton yarn fell to about one-twentieth of what it had been in the 1760s. Lancashire, with its abundant waterways and coal deposits to fuel steam engines, became the center of a booming cotton cloth industry, and Manchester, its leading city, became the cotton capital of the world.

III. Innovation and Tradition in Agriculture

In England around 1700, an estimated 80 percent of the population lived directly from agriculture; a century later that proportion had fallen to approximately 40 percent. This shift of labor from agriculture would have been inconceivable had English farming not become far more productive during that period. English farmers introduced significant improvements in their methods of cultivation, including the techniques of convertible husbandry and the enclosure of large compact farms. These enabled English agriculture to supply the growing towns with food as well as excess labor and capital. On the continent, however, whether bound to the land as serfs in Eastern Europe or legally free in the West, peasants generally clung to traditional agrarian ways. Time-worn survival strategies provided the best hope for

RICHARD ARKWRIGHT'S ACHIEVEMENT

◆

This celebration of British industrialization, the factory system, and entrepreneurship begins by extolling Richard Arkwright's accomplishments in the 1780s.

"When the first water frames for spinning cotton were erected at Cromford, about sixty years ago, mankind were little aware of the mighty revolution which the new system of labour was destined by Providence to achieve, not only in the structure of British society, but in the fortunes of the world at large. Arkwright alone had the sagacity to discern, and the boldness to predict in glowing language, how vastly productive human industry would become, when no longer proportioned in its results to muscular effort, which is by its nature fitful and capricious, but when made to consist in the task of guiding the work of mechanical fingers and arms, regularly impelled with great velocity by some indefatigable physical power [such as a steam engine].

"The main difficulty did not lie so much in the invention of a proper self-acting mechanism for drawing out and twisting cotton into a continuous thread, as in the distribution of different members of the apparatus into one co-operative body . . . and above all, in training human beings to renounce their desultory habits of work, and to identify themselves with the unvarying regularity of the complex automaton. To devise and administer a successful code of factory discipline, suited to the necessities of factory diligence, was the Herculean enterprise, the noble achievement of Arkwright. . . . It required, in fact, a man of Napoleonic nerve and ambition to subdue the refractory tempers of work-people accustomed to irregular paroxysms of diligence, and to urge on his multifarious and intricate constructions in the face of prejudice, passion, and envy."

Andrew Ure, *The Philosophy of Manufactures* (1835).

▼ **The engineering firm of Bolton & Watt became famous for its steam engines, whose complex mechanisms of cams, gears, and levers could harness the power of steam to a variety of uses in industry and transportation.**
The Science Museum, London

security but also assured a climate hostile to untested innovations.

◆ CONVERTIBLE HUSBANDRY

A central problem in any agricultural system is that repeated harvests on the same land eventually rob the soil of its fertility. Since the Early Middle Ages, the usual method of restoring a field's fertility involved letting the land lie fallow for a season (that is, resting it by planting nothing) every second or third year. This fallowing allowed bacteria in the soil to take needed nitrogen from the air. A quicker and better method, heavy manuring, could not be used widely because most farmers were unable to support sufficient livestock to produce the manure. Feeding farm animals, particularly with fodder during the winter, was beyond the means of most peasants.

But fallowing was an extremely inefficient and wasteful method of restoring the soil's fertility. One key to improving agricultural productivity, therefore, lay in eliminating the fallow periods, which in turn required that more animals be raised to provide fertilizer. In a given year, instead of being taken out of cultivation, a field could be planted not with grain but with turnips or with nitrogen-fixing grasses that could supply fodder for livestock. The grazing livestock would in turn deposit abundant quantities of manure on those fields. Thus, by the end of that season the soil's fertility would be greater, and next year's grain crop was likely to produce a higher yield than it would have if the field had simply been left fallow the year before.

In the 1730s Charles Townshend (known as "Turnip Townshend") showed the value of planting turnips and other fodder crops in such a rotation system instead of letting the land lie fallow. One of the first British landlords to adopt this approach on a broad scale was Jethro Tull, an agriculturist and inventor. Tull's zeal in conducting his experiments and advocating new farming methods proved infectious. By the late eighteenth century, Norfolk, in the east of England, had achieved particular prominence for such techniques, known as *convertible husbandry*.

Improving Landlords With convertible husbandry, innovative or "improving" landlords never let their land lie fallow but always put it to

some productive use. They also experimented with techniques designed to enhance the texture of the soil. If soil was normally too thin to retain water effectively, farmers added clays or marl to help bind the soil. In those regions in which the soil had the opposite problem of clumping too rigidly after rainfalls, they lightened the soil by adding chalk and lime to inhibit the clotting.

Eighteenth-century agrarian innovators also experimented with the selective breeding of animals. Some improved the quality of pigs, while others developed new breeds of sheep and dramatically increased the weight of marketed cattle. Soil management and livestock breeding did not depend on any high-tech knowledge or machinery but simply on a willingness to experiment in land management and to invest capital to achieve higher yields.

◆ THE ENCLOSURE MOVEMENT IN BRITAIN

To make use of new agricultural methods, farmers had to be free to manage the land as they saw fit. This land management was all but impossible under the open-field system that had dominated the countryside in Europe since the Middle Ages. Under the open-field system, even the largest landlords usually held their property in numerous elongated strips that were mixed in with and open to the land of their neighbors. Owners of contiguous strips had to follow the same routines of cultivation. One farmer could not raise grasses to graze cattle when another was raising wheat or leaving the land fallow. The village as a whole determined what routines should be followed and thus effectively managed each holding. The village also decided such matters as how many cattle each member could graze on common meadows and how much wood each could take from the forest. The open-field system froze the technology of cultivation at the levels of the Middle Ages.

Landowners who wished to form compact farms and apply new methods could do so only by enclosing their own properties. Both common law and cost considerations, however, worked against fencing the numerous narrow strips unless the property of the entire village could be rearranged, which required the agreement of all the community. Such voluntary enclosures

◀ Livestock and people could range freely over the land in open-field villages after the crops were harvested. The regrouping of scattered parcels and the enclosure of those consolidated properties would put an end to an entire rural way of life.

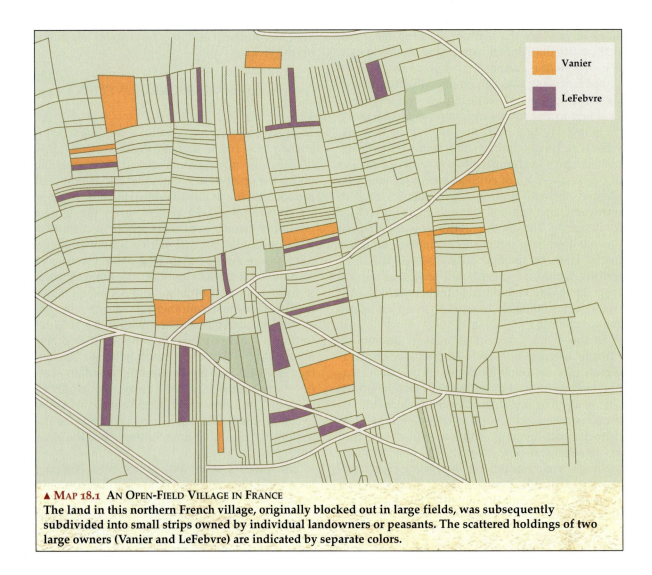

Vanier

LeFebvre

▲ Map 18.1 An Open-Field Village in France
The land in this northern French village, originally blocked out in large fields, was subsequently subdivided into small strips owned by individual landowners or peasants. The scattered holdings of two large owners (Vanier and LeFebvre) are indicated by separate colors.

were nearly impossible to organize. In England, however, there was an alternative: An act of Parliament, usually passed in response to a petition by large landowners, could order the enclosure of all agrarian property in a village even against the opposition of some of its inhabitants. Then large landowners could fence in their land and manage it at their discretion.

Enclosing properties in a village was difficult and expensive. The lands of the village had to be surveyed and redistributed, in compact blocks, among the members in proportion to their former holdings. But over the course of the eighteenth century, the high rents and returns that could be earned with the new farming methods made enclosures very desirable investments. Numerous acts authorizing enclosure in a village had been passed by Parliament in earlier periods, but a new wave of such acts began to mount around the middle of the eighteenth century. Parliament passed 156 individual acts of enclosure in the decade of the 1750s; from 1800 to 1810 it passed 906 acts. Cumulatively, the enclosure movement all but eradicated the traditional open-field village from the British countryside.

The Impact of Enclosure While enclosure was clearly rational from an economic standpoint, it brought much human misery in its wake. The redistribution of the land deprived the poor of their traditional rights to the village's common land (which was usually divided among the villagers as well) and often left them with tiny, unprofitable plots. Frequently, they were forced to sell their holdings to their richer neighbors and seek employment as laborers or urban workers. However, no massive rural depopulation occurred in the wake of enclosures. For one thing, the actual work of fencing the fields required a good deal of labor, and some of the new husbandry techniques were also labor-intensive. In fact, the new industrial labor force drew as much on small-town artisans and casual laborers as on the dislodged rural poor.

The enclosure movement transformed the English countryside physically and socially, giving it the appearance it retains today of large verdant fields, neatly defined by hedges and fences. Enclosures in Britain led to the domination of rural society by great landlords and their prosperous tenant farmers, who usually held their farms under long leases. Conversely, enclosures resulted in the near disappearance in England of the small peasant-type cultivators still typical of Western Europe. If enclosures did not abruptly push people to the towns, neither did they encourage growth in rural settlements. Enclosures were, therefore, a major factor in the steady shift of Britain's population from countryside to city and in the emergence of the first urban, industrial economy in the nineteenth century.

◆ SERFS AND PEASANTS ON THE CONTINENT

On the continent, peasants continued to work their small plots of land—whether owned or rented—in the village of their ancestors. In Eastern Europe, however, the peasants' status was still defined by a system of serfdom similar to that which prevailed in Western Europe during the Middle Ages.

Lords and Serfs in Eastern Europe In most of Central and Eastern Europe, nobles retained a near monopoly on the ownership of land and peasants remained serfs, their personal freedom severely limited by the lord's supervision. Serfs could not marry, move away, or enter a trade without their lord's permission. This personal servitude ensured that peasants would be available to provide the labor that the lord required. In return the peasants received access to plots of land (which they did not actually own) and perhaps some rudimentary capital, such as seed for their crops. Much of their time, however, was spent in providing unpaid labor on their lord's domain, the amount of labor service determined by custom rather than by law. Labor service often took up three days a week, and even more during harvest time. In Russia it was said that the peasants worked half the year for their master and only half for themselves (see "The Condition of the Serfs in Russia," p. 648)

The degree of exploitation in European serfdom naturally varied. In Russia, Poland, Hungary, and certain small German states, the status

The Condition of the Serfs in Russia

◆

For publishing this unprecedented critique of the miseries and injustices of serfdom, the author was imprisoned by Catherine II.

"A certain man left the capital, acquired a small village of one or two hundred souls [i.e., serfs], and determined to make his living by agriculture. . . . To this end he thought it the surest method to make his peasants resemble tools that have neither will nor impulse; and to a certain extent he actually made them like the soldiers of the present time who are commanded in a mass, who move to battle in a mass, and who count for nothing when acting singly. To attain this end he took away from his peasants the small allotment of plough land and the hay meadows which noblemen usually give them for their bare maintenance, as a recompense for all the forced labor which they demand from them. In a word, this nobleman forced all his peasants and their wives and children to work every day of the year for him. Lest they should starve, he doled out to them a definite quantity of bread. . . . If there was any real meat, it was only in Easter Week.

"These serfs also received clothing befitting their condition. . . . Naturally these serfs had no cows, horses, ewes, or rams. Their master did not withhold from these serfs the permission, but rather the means to have them. Whoever was a little better off and ate sparingly, kept a few chickens, which the master sometimes took for himself, paying for them as he pleased.

"In a short time he added to his two hundred souls another two hundred as victims of his greed, and proceeding with them just as with the first, he increased his holdings year after year, thus multiplying the number of those groaning in his fields. Now he counts them by the thousands and is praised as a famous agriculturalist.

"Barbarian! What good does it do the country that every year a few thousand more bushels of grain are grown, if those who produce it are valued on a par with the ox whose job it is to break the heavy furrow? Or do we think our citizens happy because our granaries are full and their stomachs empty?"

Alexander Radischev, *A Journey from St. Petersburg to Moscow* (1790).

---

of the serf scarcely differed from that of a slave. Russian and Polish serfs were in effect chattels who could be sold or traded at their lords' discretion, independent of the land they lived on or their family ties. In Russia the state itself owned many peasants and could assign them to work in the mines and factories of the Ural Mountains. Russian and Polish lords could inflict severe corporal punishment on their serfs, up to forty lashes or six months in prison. Peasants had no right of appeal to the state against such punishments.

Serfdom was not as severe in Prussia or the Habsburg monarchy, and the state did assure peasants of certain basic legal rights. In theory, peasants could not be expelled from their plots so long as they paid all their dues and rendered all the services they owed, although in practice the lords could usually remove them if they wished to. Since it was increasingly profitable for the lords to farm large domains directly, many felt an incentive to oust peasants from their tenures or to increase peasant labor services beyond customary limits.[1]

Lords and Peasants in Western Europe In Western Europe, by contrast, serfdom had waned. Most peasants were personally free and were free to buy land if they could afford it. Peasants were not necessarily secure or prosperous, however. There was not enough land to satisfy the needs of all peasant families, and lack of real independence was the rule. Moreover, most French, German, Spanish, and Italian peasants still lived under the authority of a local noble in a system called *seigneurialism*. The peasants owed these lords

---

[1]In certain regions of Spain and southern Italy, this situation had existed for centuries; noble lords monopolized the ownership of land in vast estates, or *latifundia,* on which their nominally free peasants provided the labor.

▲ In Poland and Russia rural lords had direct control over their serfs without intervention by the state. Their powers included the right to inflict corporal punishment.
© Corbis

various dues and obligations on their land, even if the peasants otherwise owned it. Seigneurial fees and charges (for example, a proportion of the harvest, somewhere between 5 and 15 percent) could be a considerable source of income for the lord and an oppressive burden to the already hard-pressed peasant. In addition, the lords administered petty justice in both civil and criminal matters; enjoyed the exclusive privilege of hunting rights across the lands of the village, no matter who owned them; and profited from monopolies on food-processing operations such as flour mills, bread ovens, and wine presses.

Concerned as they were with securing their basic livelihood, few peasants worried about trying to increase productivity with new farming methods. Satisfied with time-tested methods of cultivation, they could not risk the hazards of novel techniques. Along with growing grain for their own consumption, peasant households had to meet several obligations as well: royal taxes, rents, seigneurial dues, the tithe to the local church, and interest payments on their debts. In short, most peasant households in Western Europe were extremely insecure and relied on custom and tradition as their surest guides.

Peasant Survival Strategies Every peasant household in Western Europe hoped to control enough land to ensure its subsistence and meet its obligations. Ideally, it would own this land. But most peasants did not own as much land as they needed and were obliged to rent additional plots or enter into sharecropping arrangements. Peasants therefore hated to see the consolidation of small plots into large farms, for this meant that the small plots that they might one day afford to buy or lease were becoming scarcer. The lords and the most prosperous peasants, on the other hand, were interested in extending their holdings, just like the "improving" landlords across the English Channel.

When the land that small peasants owned and rented did not meet their needs, they employed other survival strategies. Peasants could hire out as laborers on larger farms or migrate for a few months to other regions to help with grain or wine harvests. They might practice a simple rural handicraft or weave cloth for merchants on the putting-out system. Some peasants engaged in illegal activities such as poaching game on restricted land or smuggling salt in avoidance of royal taxes. When all else failed, a destitute peasant family might be forced to take to the road as beggars.

The Family Economy   In their precarious situation, peasants depended on strong family bonds. A peasant holding was a partnership between husband and wife, who usually waited until they had accumulated enough resources, including the bride's dowry, to establish their own household. Men looked for physical vigor and domestic skills in their prospective brides. ("When a girl knows how to knead and bake bread, she is fit to wed," went a French proverb.) In peasant households the wife's domain was inside the cottage, where she cooked, repaired clothing, and perhaps spent her evenings spinning yarn. Wives were also responsible for the small vegetable gardens or the precious hens and chickens that peasants maintained to raise cash for their obligations. The husband's work was outside: gathering fuel, caring for draft animals (if the family owned any), plowing the land, planting the fields, and nurturing the crops. But at harvest time everyone worked in the fields.

Peasants also drew strength from community solidarity. Many villages possessed common lands open to all residents. Poorer peasants could forage there for fuel and building materials, and could inexpensively graze whatever livestock they owned. Since villagers generally planted the same crops at the same times, after the harvest livestock was allowed to roam over the arable fields and graze on the stubble of the open fields, a practice known as vacant pasture. All in all, insecurity and the scarcity of land in continental villages made it risky and improbable that peasants would adopt innovative methods or agree to the division of common land.

The Limits of Agrarian Change on the Continent
Change, therefore, came more slowly to the continental countryside than it did to England. The Netherlands, the Paris basin and the northeast of France, the Rhineland in Germany, and the Po valley of Italy experienced the most active development—all areas of dense settlement in which high food prices encouraged landlords with large farms to invest in agricultural improvements and to adopt innovative methods.

Like their English counterparts, innovating continental farmers waged a battle for managerial freedom, though the changes they sought were not as sweeping as the English enclosure movement. Most French villages worked the land under an open-field system in which peasants followed the same rhythms and routines of cultivation as their neighbors, with the village also determining the rights of its members on common lands. From the middle of the century on, the governing institutions of several provinces banned obligatory vacant pasture and allowed individual owners to enclose their land; some authorized the division of communal lands as well. But the French monarchy did not adopt enclosure as national policy, and after the 1760s provincial authorities proved reluctant to enforce enclosure ordinances against the vigorous opposition of peasants. Traces of the medieval village thus lasted longer in France and Western Europe than in England.

In France in 1789, on the eve of the Revolution, probably 35 percent of the land was owned by the peasants who worked it. In this regard, the French peasants were more favored than those of most other European countries. But this society of small

▲ **In contrast to England as well as Russia, the small-holding peasant remained the most typical social type in France. In the peasant "family economy," husband and wife each made vital contributions to the household's productivity.**
Musée du Louvre. Photo ©R.M.N./Art Resource, NY

peasant farms was vulnerable to population pressures and was threatened by sharp movements in prices—two major characteristics of eighteenth-century economic history, as we have seen. The pattern of land distribution in France and the character of rural society, superficially favorable to the peasant, thus also caused acute tension in the countryside.

In the regions close to the Mediterranean Sea, such as southern Italy, difficult geographical and climatic conditions—the often rugged terrain, thin soil, and dearth of summer rain—did not readily allow the introduction of new techniques either, although many peasants improved their income by planting market crops such as grapes for wine or olives for oil instead of grains for their own consumption. Still, most peasants continued to work their lands much as they had in the Late Middle Ages and for the same poor reward. Fertile areas near the Baltic Sea, such as east Prussia, benefited from the growing demand for grains in Western countries, but on the whole, Eastern Europe did not experience structural agrarian change until the next century.

IV. Eighteenth-Century Empires

◆

The economic dynamism of the eighteenth-century derived not simply from growing population and consumer demand, or from English innovations in agriculture and textile manufacturing. Europe's favorable position as a generator of wealth owed as much to its mercantile empires across the seas. Colonial trade became an engine of economic growth in Britain and France. Plantation economies in the Atlantic world, fueled by the West African slave trade, provided sugar, tobacco, and cotton for an ever-expanding consumer demand. In the East spices, fine cloths, tea, and luxury goods similarly enriched European merchants. But behind the merchants and trading companies stood the military and naval muscle of the British and French states. Their rivalry finally erupted in a "Great War for Empire"—the global dimension of the Seven Year's War on the continent. Here British victories came not only in North America and the Caribbean, but also in South Asia, where they ousted the French from their foothold in India. This left the British free to extend their sway in the nineteenth century over India, which became "the jewel in the crown" of British imperial dominion.

◆ MERCANTILE AND NAVAL COMPETITION

After 1715 a new era began in the saga of European colonial development. The three pioneers in overseas expansion had by now grown passive, content to defend domains already conquered. Portugal, whose dominion over Brazil was recognized at the Peace of Utrecht in 1715, retired from active contention. Likewise, the Dutch could scarcely compete for new footholds overseas and now protected their interests through cautious neutrality. Although Spain continued its efforts to exclude outsiders from trade with its vast empire in the New World, it did not pose much of a threat to others. The stage of active competition was left to the two other Atlantic powers, France and Britain.

The Decline of the Dutch   The case of Dutch decline is an instructive counterexample to the rise of French and British fortunes. In the seventeenth century the United Provinces, or Dutch Netherlands, had been Europe's greatest maritime power. But this federated state emerged from the wars of Louis XIV in a much weakened position. The country had survived intact, but it now suffered from demographic and political stagnation. The population of 2.5 million failed to rise during the eighteenth century, thus setting the Dutch apart from their French and British rivals. As a federation of loosely joined provinces, whose seven provincial oligarchies rarely acted in concert, the Netherlands could barely ensure the common defense of the realm.

The Dutch economy suffered when French and English merchants sought to eliminate them as the middlemen of maritime commerce and when their industry failed to compete effectively. Heavy indirect taxes on manufactured goods and the high wages demanded by Dutch artisans forced up the price of Dutch products. What kept the nation from slipping completely out of Europe's economic life was its financial institutions. Dutch merchants shifted their activity away from actual trading ventures into the safer, lucrative areas of credit and finance. Their country was the first to perfect the uses of paper currency, a stock market, and a central bank. Amsterdam's merchant-bankers loaned large amounts of money to private borrowers and foreign governments, as the Dutch became financial instead of trading brokers.

The British and French Commercial Empires
Great Britain, a nation that had barely been able to hold its own against the Dutch in the seventeenth century, now began its rise to domination of the seas. Its one serious competitor was France, the only state in Europe to maintain both a large army and a large navy. Their rivalry played itself out in four regions. The West Indies, where both France and Britain had colonized several sugar-producing islands, constituted the fulcrum of both empires. The West Indian plantation economy, in turn, depended on slave-producing West Africa. The third area of colonial expansion was the North American continent, where Britain's thirteen colonies became centers of settlement whereas New France remained primarily a trading area. Finally, both nations sponsored powerful companies for trade with India and other Asian lands. These compa-

nies were supposed to compete for markets without establishing colonies.

The two colonial systems had obvious differences and important similarities. French absolutism fostered a centralized structure of control for its colonies, with intendants and military governors ruling across the seas as they did in the provinces at home. Britain's North American colonies, by contrast, remained independent from each other and to a degree escaped direct control from the home government, although Crown and Parliament both claimed jurisdiction over them.

British colonies each had a royal governor but also a local legislature of sorts, and most developed traditions of self-government. Nonetheless, the French and British faced similar problems and achieved generally similar results. Both applied mercantilist principles to the regulation of colonial trade, and both strengthened their navies to protect it.

Mercantilism Mercantilist doctrine supported the regulation of trade by the state in order to increase the state's power against its neighbors (see

▼ **Commerce increased dramatically in the Atlantic ports of England and France as ships embarked for Africa, the Caribbean, North America, and Spanish America as well as other parts of Europe. Businesses that supplied those ships or that processed colonial products brought back to Europe grew apace. Shown here, the port of Bristol in England.**
City of Bristol Museum and Art Gallery, Avon, UK/Bridgeman Art Library, London/New York

chapter 15). Mercantilism was not limited to the Atlantic colonial powers. Prussia was guided by mercantilism as much as were Britain and France, for all regarded the economic activities of their subjects as subordinate to the interests of the state.

Mercantilist theory advocated a favorable balance of trade as signified by a net inflow of gold and silver, and it assumed that a state's share of bullion could increase only at its neighbor's expense. Colonies could promote a favorable balance of trade by producing valuable raw materials or staple crops for the parent country and by providing protected markets for the parent country's manufactured goods. Foreign states were to be excluded from these benefits as much as possible. By tariffs, elaborate regulations, bounties, or prohibitions, each government sought to channel trade between its colonies and itself. Spain, for example, restricted trade with its New World colonies exclusively to Spanish merchant vessels, although smugglers and pirates made a mockery of this policy.

Europe's governments sought to exploit overseas colonies for the benefit of the parent country and not simply for the profit of those who invested or settled abroad. But most of the parties to this commerce prospered. The large West Indian planters made fortunes, as did the most successful merchants, manufacturers, and shipowners at home who were involved in colonial trade. Illicit trade also brought rewards to colonial merchants; John Hancock took the risk of smuggling food supplies from Boston to French West Indian planters in exchange for handsome profits.

"Empire" generally meant "trade," but this seaborne commerce depended on naval power: Merchant ships had to be protected, trading rivals excluded, and regulations enforced. This reciprocal relationship between the expansion of trade and the deployment of naval forces added to the competitive nature of colonial expansion. Naval vessels needed stopping places for reprovisioning and refitting, which meant that ports had to be secured in strategic locations such as Africa, India, and the Caribbean and denied to rivals whenever possible.

◆ THE PROFITS OF EMPIRE

The call of colonial markets invigorated European economic life. Colonial commerce provided new

products, like sugar, and stimulated new consumer demand, which in turn created an impetus for manufacturing at home. It is estimated that the value of French commerce quadrupled during the eighteenth century. By the 1770s commerce with their colonies accounted for almost one-third of the total volume of both British and French foreign trade. The West Indies trade (mainly in sugar) bulked the largest, and its expansion was truly spectacular. The value of French imports from the West Indies increased more than tenfold between 1716 and 1788, from 16 million to 185 million livres.

The West Indies seemed to be ideal colonies. By virtue of their tropical climate and isolation from European society, which made slavery possible, the islands produced valuable crops difficult to raise elsewhere: tobacco, cotton, indigo, and especially sugar, a luxury that popular European taste soon turned into a necessity. Moreover, the islands could produce little else and therefore depended on exports from Europe. They could not raise an adequate supply of food animals or grain to feed the vast slave population, they could not cut enough lumber for building, and they certainly could not manufacture the luxury goods demanded by the planter class.

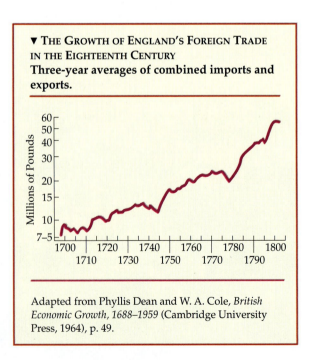

▼ THE GROWTH OF ENGLAND'S FOREIGN TRADE IN THE EIGHTEENTH CENTURY
Three-year averages of combined imports and exports.

Adapted from Phyllis Dean and W. A. Cole, *British Economic Growth, 1688–1959* (Cambridge University Press, 1964), p. 49.

Triangular Trade   Numerous variations of "triangular trade" (between the home country and two colonial areas) revolved around the West Indies. One pattern began with a ship departing from a British port with a cargo of manufactured products—paper, knives, pots, blankets, and the like—destined for the shopkeepers of North America. Landing at Marblehead, Massachusetts, or Philadelphia, the ship might exchange its goods for New England fish oil, fish, beef, and timber. These products would then be transported to Jamaica or Barbados to be traded for sugar that would be turned over to British refineries many months later. Another variation might see a ship set out from Newport, Rhode Island (the chief slaving port in North America), with a cargo of New England rum. Landing in West Africa, the ship would acquire slaves in exchange for the rum and then sail to the Indies to sell the slaves for bills of exchange or for molasses, from which more rum could be distilled. French and British manufacturers in the port cities made fortunes by refining or finishing colonial products such as sugar, indigo, tobacco, and furs and reexporting them to other European markets. Colonial commerce was superimposed on a complex pattern of European trade in which the Atlantic states carried off the lion's share of the profits.

◆ SLAVERY, THE FOUNDATION OF EMPIRE

Much of this dynamic global trade rested on slavery. Endless, backbreaking labor transformed a favorable climate and the investment of speculators into harvested plantation crops (see "A British Defense of Slavery and the Plantation Economy," p. 656). A publication of the chamber of commerce of Nantes, France's chief slaving port, publicly argued that without slavery there would be no French colonial commerce at all. At the height of the Atlantic slave traffic, about 88,000 blacks were removed from Africa annually—half in British ships, a quarter in French, and the rest in Dutch, Portuguese, Danish, and American ships (see "Magnitude of the Slave Trade"). More than 600,000 slaves were imported into the island of Jamaica in the eighteenth century. The population of Saint-Domingue around 1790 comprised about

---

▼ **MAGNITUDE OF THE SLAVE TRADE**
The following figures represent the best current estimate of the number of persons removed from Africa and transported as slaves to the New World during the entire period of the Atlantic slave trade.

British Caribbean	1,665,000
British North America (to 1786)	275,000
United States (after 1786)	124,000
French Caribbean	1,600,000
Dutch Caribbean	500,000
Brazil	3,646,000
Spanish America	1,552,000

From Philip D. Curtain, *The Atlantic Slave Trade: A Census* (University of Wisconsin Press, 1969).

---

half a million slaves compared with 35,000 whites of all nationalities and 28,000 mulattoes and free blacks.

Trafficking in slaves was competitive and risky but highly profitable. The demand for slaves in the West Indies, Brazil, Venezuela, and the southern colonies of North America kept rising, pushing up prices. In both Britain and France, chartered companies holding exclusive rights from the Crown originally monopolized the slave trade. They did not actually colonize or conquer African territory but instead established forts, or "factories," on the West African coast for the coordination and defense of their slaving expeditions. Gradually, the monopolies were challenged by other merchants and investors who combined to launch their own ships on slaving voyages. The West Indian planters, who needed more slaves, welcomed all additional sources. The independent traders clustered in port cities like Bristol and Liverpool in England, and by the 1730s they had broken the monopoly on the slave trade.

The Ordeal of Enslavement   Europeans alone did not condemn black Africans to slavery. In this period, Europeans scarcely penetrated the interior of the continent; the forbidding topography and the resistance of the natives confined them to coastal areas. The actual enslavement took place in the interior at the hands of aggressive local groups

A British Defense of Slavery
and the Plantation Economy

"The most approved judges of the commercial interests of these Kingdoms have ever been of the opinion that our West Indies and African Trades are the most nationally beneficial of any we carry on. It is also allowed on all hands that the Trade to Africa is the branch which renders our American Colonies and Plantations so advantageous to Great Britain; that traffic only affording our plantations a constant supply of Negroe servants [slaves] for the culture of their lands in the produce of *sugars, tobacco, rice, rum, cotton, pimento,* and all others our plantations produce. So that the extensive employment of our shipping in, to, and from America, the great brood of seamen consequent thereupon, and the daily bread of the most considerable part of our British Manufacturers, are owing primarily to the labor of Negroes; who, as they were the first happy instrument of raising our Plantations, so their labor only can support and preserve them, and render them still more and more profitable to their Mother Kingdom.

"The Negroe Trade therefore, and the natural consequences resulting from it, may be justly esteemed an inexhaustible fund of Wealth and Naval Power to this Nation. And by the overplus of Negroes above what have served our own Plantations, we have drawn likewise no inconsiderable quantities of treasure from the Spaniards. . . . What renders the Negroe Trade still more estimable and important is that near nine tenths of those Negroes are paid for in Africa with British produce and manufactures only. We send no specie of bullion to pay for the products of Africa. . . . And it may be worth consideration, that while our Plantations depend only on planting by Negroes, they will neither depopulate our own Country, become independent of her Dominion, or any way interfere [i.e., compete] with the interests of the British Manufacturer, Merchant, or Landed Gentleman."

Malachy Postlethwayt, *The National and Private Advantages of the African Trade Considered* (London, 1746).

---

whose chiefs became the intermediaries of this commerce. The competition among European traders for the slaves tended to drive up the prices that African middlemen could command in hardware, cloth, liquor, or guns. In response, some traders ventured into new areas in which the Africans might be more eager to come to terms. Increasing demand, rising prices, and competitiveness spread the slave trade and further marred the future of West African society.

Many blacks failed to survive the process of enslavement at all. Some perished on the forced marches from the interior to the coast or on the nightmarish "middle passage" across the Atlantic, which has been compared to the transit in freight cars of Jewish prisoners to Nazi extermination camps in World War II. Because the risks of slaving ventures were high and the time lag between investment and return somewhere from one to two years, the traders sought to maximize their profits by jamming as many captives as possible

onto the ships. Medium-sized ships carried as many as five hundred slaves on a voyage, all packed below deck in only enough space for each person to lie at full length pressed against neighboring bodies, and with only enough headroom to crawl, not to stand. Food and provisions were held to a minimum. The mortality rate that resulted from these conditions was a staggering 10 percent or more on average, and in extreme cases exceeded 50 percent.

Agitation against slavery by Quakers and other reformers in Britain and France focused initially on the practices of the slave trade rather than on slavery itself. After the 1780s, participation in the Atlantic slave trade tapered off, and the supply of slaves was replenished mainly from children born to slaves already in the New World. A dismal chapter in Europe's relations with the outside world dwindled to an end, although the final suppression of slaving voyages did not come for several more decades.

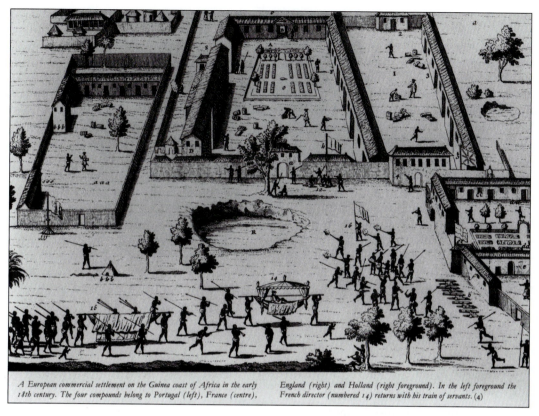

A European commercial settlement on the Guinea coast of Africa in the early 18th century. The four compounds belong to Portugal (left), France (centre), England (right) and Holland (right foreground). In the left foreground the French director (numbered 14) returns with his train of servants. (4)

▲ An early eighteenth-century European commercial settlement on the west coast of Africa consisted of four national compounds: Portuguese, French, English, and Dutch.

▼ This diagram of "tight packing" below deck conveys the horror of the trans-Atlantic slaving voyages, known as the "middle passage." The drawing was circulated by British antislavery reformers.
Courtesy of the New-York Historical Society

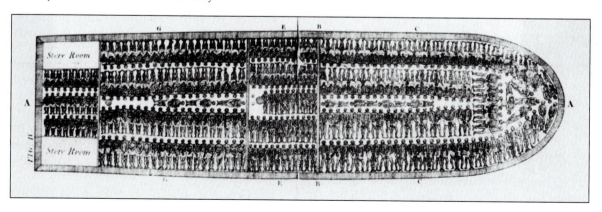

◆ MOUNTING COLONIAL CONFLICTS

In the New World, the population of Britain's North American colonies reached about 1.5 million by midcentury. Some colonists pushed the frontier westward, while others clustered around the original settlements, a few of which—like Boston, New York, and Philadelphia—could now be called cities. The westward extension of the frontier and the growth of towns gave a vitality to the British colonial world that New France appeared to lack. Since there was little enthusiasm among the French for emigration to the Louisiana Territory or Canada, the French remained thinly spread in their vast dominions. Yet France's colonies were well organized and profitable, and French West Indian planters underpriced the sugar of their British competitors.

As French fishermen and fur traders prospered in Canada, French soldiers established a series of strongholds to support them, including the bastion of Fort Louisbourg at the entrance to the Gulf of St. Lawrence and a string of forts near the Great Lakes (see map 18.2), which served as bridgeheads for French fur traders and as a security buffer for Quebec province. In Louisiana, at the other end of the continent, New Orleans guarded the terminus of the Mississippi River. On their side, the British established their first large military base in North America at Halifax, Nova Scotia, contesting French penetration of the fishing grounds and waterways of the St. Lawrence Gulf.

Conflict on the Frontier   The unsettled Ohio valley was a second focus of colonial rivalry in North America. Pushing south from their Great Lakes trading forts and north from their posts on the Mississippi, the French began to assume control over that wilderness. A new string of forts formed pivots for potential French domination of the whole area between the Appalachian Mountains and the Mississippi—territory claimed and coveted by British subjects in the thirteen colonies. The threat grew that the French might completely cut off the westward expansion of these colonies. On their side, the French feared that British penetration of the Ohio valley would lead to encroachments on their Canadian territory.

In jockeying for position, both sides sought the allegiance of the American Indians, and in this respect the French gradually gained the upper hand. Because they were traders only, not settlers, the French did not force the Native Americans from their traditional hunting grounds as the British had done repeatedly. Hence, the American Indians were willing to cooperate with the French in sealing off the Ohio valley. A large land investment company, the Ohio Company of Virginia, faced ruin with that prospect, and in 1745 it attempted to break the French and Indian hold on the Ohio valley by sending an expedition against Fort Duquesne. Led by a young militiaman named George Washington, the raid failed.

Contrary to a British tradition of letting settled colonies pay for themselves, the home government eventually shouldered the burden of colonial defense. An expedition of British army regulars was sent to do the job that the colonial militia could not accomplish. Limited skirmishes were about to give way to a full-scale war as each side began to reinforce its garrisons and naval squadrons. In May 1756, after several years of unofficial hostilities, Britain and France formally declared war.

◆ THE GREAT WAR FOR EMPIRE

The pressures created by the competition of states, dynasties, and colonial empires in the eighteenth century exploded in midcentury in Europe's last large-scale war before the French Revolution. Its continental phase, known as the Seven Years' War, centered on the bitter rivalry between Austria and Prussia, but enmeshed Russia, France, and Britain as well. As we saw in chapter 17, this protracted war ended in 1763 with a peace treaty that essentially restored the status quo. The other phase of this midcentury conflagration revolved around Anglo-French competition for empire in North America, the West Indies, and India. Historians call it the Great War for Empire, and its North American sector was known as the French and Indian War. It was this great global confrontation that produced the most striking changes when the smoke cleared.

The Great War for Empire was one of Britain's high moments in history, the stuff of patriotic legends. The conflict started, however, in quite another fashion. Jumping to the initiative on several fronts, the better-coordinated French struck the

▲ **MAP 18.2** ANGLO-FRENCH RIVALRY IN NORTH AMERICA AND THE CARIBBEAN AS OF 1756

first blows. The Mediterranean island of Minorca and several key British forts on the Great Lakes fell to the French. At the same time, Britain's expeditionary force to the continent, fighting in alliance with Prussia, suffered humiliating defeats. Yet the French had disadvantages that would show in the long run. Spread so thinly in North America, they would be hard put to follow their early success in the French and Indian War. More important, France depended on naval support to reinforce, supply, and move its troops; unfortunately for France, a fairly even naval matchup in the 1740s had turned into clear British naval superiority by the 1750s. British ships of the line outnumbered French ships almost two to one.

Pitt's Strategy When William Pitt became Britain's prime minister in 1758, the tide was about to turn in the Great War for Empire. Pitt, later the Earl of Chatham, was the grandson of a man who had made a fortune in India. Eloquent, supremely self-confident, infused with a vision of Britain's imperial destiny, Pitt had begun his career in Parliament in 1738 by denouncing the timid policies of the government and demanding that France be driven from the seas. Now he had his chance to lead Britain in the battle against its archrival. Pitt brought single-mindedness and vigor to his task. Although he honored Britain's commitment to Prussia, he attached highest priority to defeating France in the colonial world. His strategy involved an immediate series of offensives and an imaginative use of the British navy. He assigned the largest segment of the British fleet to cover the French home fleet, and he waited.

The French hoped to invade the British Isles as the surest method of bringing the enemy to the

▼ **British naval power is shown here laying siege to the French stronghold of Louisbourg in July 1758.**
New Brunswick Museum, Saint John, N.B.

peace table, and the French fleet was ordered to prepare the way. In 1759 major battles were joined between French squadrons from Brest and Toulon and the British ships assigned to cover them. The British decimated the French fleet in these naval battles and thus decided the fate of colonial empires. Henceforth, the British had an almost free hand at sea and could prevent France from deploying its superior military forces in the colonial world. Unable to transport men and supplies to its colonies, France could no longer reinforce its garrisons or repel amphibious landings by the British. In every theater of the war, French colonial possessions fell to the British, thanks to Britain's naval supremacy.

In the French and Indian War, for example, Britain's forces defeated France in the battle of Quebec in September 1759. Had the French been able to reinforce Montreal, which they still held, they could have launched a counterattack against Britain's overextended lines. But Pitt's successful naval strategy had made it impossible for the French to reinforce their overseas garrisons. By September 1760 this last outpost of French power in North America capitulated to the British, who had already ousted the French from the Ohio valley and the Great Lakes area. In the West Indies the long duel between the two powers also turned into a rout. One by one Britain seized the French islands.

The Treaty of Paris   In the peace negotiations that followed (concluded by the Treaty of Paris in 1763), Britain did not insist on retaining all its conquests. A war-weary British government was prepared to return certain colonies to France in exchange for an end to the fighting. Since British West Indian planters feared competition from the inclusion of the French islands in the British trading system, the British government returned several of those sugar-producing islands. But France did surrender Canada, which Britain chose to retain, perhaps unwisely; the British occupation of Canada removed the threat of French power, which had helped keep the restive colonists of North America loyal to Britain. (On that front, France would soon have its revenge when it came to the aid of the rebellious thirteen colonies in the War for American Independence.) In the long run, a relatively minor matter in the Treaty of Paris,

which excluded French troops from India, proved to be supremely important.

◆ THE BRITISH FOOTHOLD IN INDIA

A Decaying Empire   Like England and France in the Late Middle Ages or like fifteenth-century Italy, the Indian subcontinent was in a state of political disintegration by the eighteenth century. The decline of the once mighty Mughal Empire stemmed from ethnic strife, dynastic instability and factionalism, greed, and incompetence in the ruling circles. As yet the decline had little to do with European incursions. In 1739, for example, it was a Persian army that fought its way to Delhi and sacked that ancient capital of the Mughal Empire.

Trading for the spices, tea, and textiles produced in India, British and French merchants had quietly prospered on the fringes of the subcontinent. Britain administered its political and commercial interests in India through the London East India Company—a private corporation established in the seventeenth century to compete with the Dutch in the Far East. The company's commercial depots in India formed a tripod pattern at Bombay, Calcutta, and Madras. Initially, neither the English nor the French sought to establish colonies in India. They used small armed forces merely to defend their commercial interests and property and depended on the good will of the native *nawabs* (provincial governors), who encouraged European traders in order to fill their own coffers with tribute payments.

As their struggle for supremacy around the globe heated up, however, the French and British began to maneuver more aggressively by force and diplomacy among native groups in India, much as they were doing in the Ohio valley and the Great Lakes regions of North America. While the French initially got the better of this game, taking Madras from the British briefly in the 1740s, the British were learning fast how to maximize their military and diplomatic assets to outmaneuver both the French and any natives who rose to challenge them. When the *nawab* of Bengal tilted toward the French in 1756 and decided to teach the British a lesson after they had fortified their positions without his permission, he set in motion a catastrophic change in the subcontinent's balance of power.

From Trade to Conquest   Young Robert Clive, who had sailed to India as a lowly and ill-paid clerk of the East India Company in the 1740s, was by now in charge of the nine hundred Europeans and fifteen hundred *sepoys,* or native soldiers, employed by the company. The company directed Clive to oust the French and to suppress any native opposition to British influence in the huge and populous province of Bengal. Clive faced an army of almost 50,000 men fielded by the *nawab,* but he undercut its effectiveness by bribing a general who coveted the *nawab*'s position for himself. After the decisive battle of Plassey (June 1757), as the body of the *nawab* floated downriver, Clive escorted his successor to the throne.

After Plassey the *nawabs* became figureheads. Real power lay in the East India Company's hands, in an arrangement known as "dual government." The East India Company exercised the most oppressive kind of domination in Bengal: unchecked power without responsibility. The company collected taxes, controlled trade, and increased its military control. Greedy company officials siphoned off much of the treasure into their own pockets. Men like Clive who had sailed to India poor later returned with fortunes to England, where they were known as "nabobs" (a sarcastic play on the term *nawab*).

Britain thus won primacy in Bengal, the economic heartland of India, by exploiting Indian rivalries in the chaos of the tottering Mughal Empire, at first ruling indirectly through native puppets. A number of civil wars made it easier for the British to dominate much of India. The company's muskets, cannons, and discipline defeated the last serious attack mounted against it in 1764. In the process the British ousted the French from any influence in the subcontinent, as agreed in the Treaty of Paris. Thus, on the verge of losing one empire in North America, the British were laying the foundations for another in South Asia.

When Parliament passed the India Act of 1784, the British government effectively replaced the company as the ultimate authority and named a new ruling official, the governor-general of India. Ironically, the first to fill that office was Lord Cornwallis, who had brought the American War

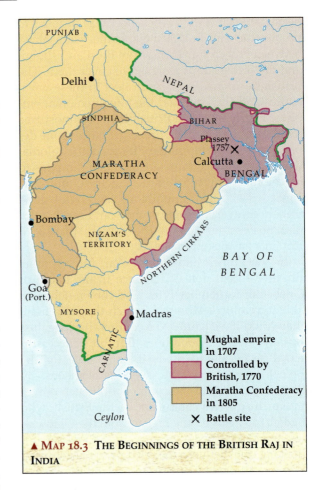

▲ MAP 18.3   THE BEGINNINGS OF THE BRITISH RAJ IN INDIA

of Independence to a close by surrendering to the rebels at Yorktown in 1781.

The British Raj   To create a class loyal to British rule, or *raj*, Cornwallis turned India's rural gentry into landlords by giving them title deeds. Traditionally, the gentry had collected rents from their peasants, but could not remove them from the land. Now, as owners in the new Western sense, they could evict the peasants and do with the land whatever they wished. The governor-general reserved the highest positions in the army and civil bureaucracy for whites, however. In each district he appointed two British magistrates, one combining the functions of police superintendent and tax collector and the other responsible for administering justice. They were assisted by a horde of Indian clerks, runners, and translators. In addition the British monopolized the commerce in salt and opium. The salt monopoly extracted money from

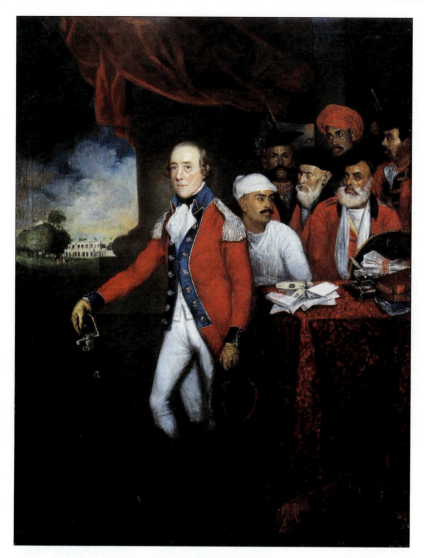

◄ **This painting depicts a British district officer in 1799 in Madras, one of the regions of the Indian subcontinent in which the British began to exercise control after they ousted the French and defeated native forces that challenged them. The official's main function was to supervise the collection of taxes, which he did with the cooperation of local Indian princes and merchants.** Courtesy of the National Gallery of Ireland

the Indian population, while the opium was exported to China in exchange for Chinese tea to satisfy consumer demand back in Britain.

Later in the nineteenth century, behind the British soldiers, tax collectors, and magistrates, came educators and reformers with a novel sense of mission. As one of them put it, "we hope to create a class of persons Indian in blood and color, but English in taste, in opinion, in morals and intellect." By the 1830s, in other words, the British were not simply extracting wealth or strategic advantage from India but considered India as their own dominion in which they were duty bound to impose their own values on the Indian people.

SUMMARY

◆

French and English merchants capitalized aggressively on the commercial opportunities afforded by overseas colonies, plantation economies, and slavery, but these traders required backing by their states in the form of naval power. The growth of the British and French empires thus reflected the dynamics of the competitive European state system. Those empires propelled the growth of a global maritime economy and thus became major factors in the economic dynamism of the eighteenth century. It is well to remember, however, that two totally disenfranchised groups supported the entire structure of state power and mercantile profit: the slaves in the colonies and the serfs, peasants, or agricultural laborers in Europe. Their toil produced the food supplies, staple commodities, and revenues that sustained the merchants, landowners, rulers, armies, and navies of the great powers. The economic future, however, lay not with plantation slavery, serfdom, or seigneurialism but with innovations in agriculture and industrial production that would yield sustained economic growth and whose roots in England we have sketched. Along with the intellectual and cultural transformations to be discussed in the next chapter, these agricultural and industrial innovations heralded the dawn of the modern era.

QUESTIONS FOR FURTHER THOUGHT

1. How can one best understand the economic transformations observable in late eighteenth-century England? What particular advantages did English society have in fostering innovation?

2. What are the principal characteristics of a traditional peasant society? How significant were the differences between peasant society in Eastern and Western Europe, and what accounts for the differences?

3. In what ways can demographic trends affect economic and social development?

RECOMMENDED READING

Sources

Forster, Robert, and Elborg Forster (eds.). *European Society in the Eighteenth Century.* 1969. A varied and suggestive anthology.

Radischev, Alexander. *A Journey from St. Petersburg to Moscow* [1790]. 1958. The first major exposé of the miseries of Russian serfdom.

*Smith, Adam. *An Inquiry into the Nature and Causes of the Wealth of Nations* [1776]. 1961. The seminal work in the liberal economic tradition.

*Young, Arthur. *Travels in France during the Years 1787, 1788, 1789.* 1972. A critical view of French agriculture by an English expert.

Studies

*Ashton, T. S. *The Industrial Revolution, 1760–1830.* 1962. A brief, classic account of early industrialization in Britain.

*Berg, Maxine. *The Age of Manufactures: Industry, Innovation, and Work in Britain, 1700–1820.* 1986. An important revisionist view, emphasizing the persistence of domestic and workshop manufacturing, alongside the new factory system.

*Blum, Jerome. *The End of the Old Order in Rural Europe.* 1976. A valuable trove of information on rural conditions, particularly in the regions of serfdom.

Brewer, John, N. McKendrick, and J. H. Plumb. *Birth of a Consumer Society: The Commercialization of Eighteenth Century England.* 1982. A pioneering book on the development of consumer demand.

Chambers, J. D., and G. E. Mingay. *The Agricultural Revolution, 1750–1880.* 1966. A reliable overview and interpretation.

Craton, Michael. *Sinews of Empire: A Short History of British Slavery.* 1974. An excellent synthesis.

*Davis, David B. *The Problem of Slavery in Western Culture.* 1966. And *The Problem of Slavery in the Age of Revolutions.* 1975. A comparative history of Western attitudes toward slavery from ancient times to the nineteenth century.

*De Vries, Jan. *The Economy of Europe in an Age of Crisis, 1600–1750.* 1976. A reliable survey of the European economy before the industrial revolution.

*Flinn, M. W. *The European Demographic System, 1500–1820.* 1981. A concise overview of the historical demography of early modern Europe.

*Gutmann, Myron. *Toward the Modern Economy: Early Industry in Europe.* 1988. Another fine synthesis illustrating the complexity of the European economy.

Hufton, Olwen. *The Poor of Eighteenth-Century France.* 1974. A luminous study of the survival strategies of the indigent and of the institutions that aided or repressed them.

Link, Edith M. *The Emancipation of the Austrian Peasantry, 1740–1789.* 1949. Traces the efforts and frustration of Habsburg agrarian reformers.

*Mathias, Peter. *The First Industrial Nation: An Economic History of Britain, 1700–1914.* 2d ed. 1976. A reliable survey combining quantitative and descriptive analysis.

North, Douglass C. *Structure and Change in Economic History.* 1981. Stresses the importance of supportive legal institutions in the coming of industrialism.

*Parry, J. H. *Trade and Dominion: The European Overseas Empires in the Eighteenth Century.* 1971. A panoramic overview.

Post, John D. *Food Shortage, Climatic Variability, and Epidemic Disease in Pre-industrial Europe: The Mortality Peak in the Early 1740s.* 1985.

Reiley, James. *International Government Finance and the Amsterdam Capital Market, 1740–1815.* 1980. The Dutch success in shifting from commerce to finance.

Sheridan, Richard. *Sugar and Slavery: An Economic History of the British West Indies, 1623–1755.* 1974.

*Valenze, Deborah. *The First Industrial Woman.* 1995. A rich synthesis on women workers before and during early industrialization in Britain.

Wilson, Charles. *England's Apprenticeship, 1603–1767.* 1965. An economic history of England before the agricultural and industrial revolutions began.

*Wrigley, E. A. *Population and History.* 1969. A fascinating introduction to the field of historical demography.

*Available in paperback.

▲ An evening of socializing with Queen Marie-Antoinette of France.

THE AGE OF ENLIGHTENMENT

Sharp breaks have been rare in Europe's intellectual and religious life—two of the defining themes in the Western experience—but we are about to witness one. During the eighteenth century, the great scientific and philosophical innovations of the previous century evolved into a naturalistic worldview divorced from religion. Scientific knowledge and religious skepticism, previously the concerns of an extremely narrow group of learned people, entered the consciousness of Europe's elites in a way that would have startled Descartes or Newton. Displacing the authority of religion with that of reason, the new outlook offered an optimistic vision of future progress in human affairs. Known as the Enlightenment, this movement formed the intellectual foundation for a new sense of modernity.

Never since pagan times, certainly not during the Renaissance, was religious belief so directly challenged. Many important eighteenth-century intellectuals no longer believed in Christianity and wished to reduce its influence in society. They argued that there was no divine standard of morality, no afterlife to divert humanity from worldly concerns. These writers developed a strong, sometimes arrogant, sense of their own capacity to ignore traditional authority and guide society toward change.

The evolution of cultural institutions and the media of the day gave these writers an increasingly wide forum. While aristocratic patronage and classical culture remained influential, a new kind of middle-class culture was developing alongside a much wider reading public and an expanding sphere of public discussion.

Yet, as we turn to consider the Enlightenment within the varied cultural environments of the eighteenth century, we should not exaggerate. Although they were critics of their society, most eighteenth-century intellectuals lived comfortably amid Europe's high culture. They had scant interest in or understanding of the vibrant popular culture around them. On the contrary, their growing belief in "public opinion" referred solely to the educated elites of the aristocracy and the middle classes.

CHAPTER 19. THE AGE OF ENLIGHTENMENT							
	Social Structure	Body Politic	Changes in the Organization of Production and in the Impact of Technology	Evolution of Family and Changing Gender Roles	War	Religion	Cultural Expression
I. THE ENLIGHTENMENT							
II. EIGHTEENTH-CENTURY ELITE CULTURE							
III. POPULAR CULTURE							

I. The Enlightenment

◆

Building on seventeenth-century science, on skepticism in matters of religion, and on a heightened appreciation for the culture of classical antiquity, eighteenth-century intellectuals approached their calling in a new spirit. They believed that human behavior and institutions could be studied rationally, like Newton's universe, and that their faults could be corrected. They saw themselves as participants in a movement—which they called the Enlightenment—that could make educated men and women more rational, tolerant, and virtuous. While the Enlightenment had creative adherents across the Western world, its capital was undoubtedly in Paris, where an ideology of progress and freedom gradually took shape. Renowned writers such as Voltaire, Diderot, and Rousseau produced a steady flow of remarkable works across a wide range of subjects, which governmental censorship could not suppress, try as it might.

◆ THE BROADENING REVERBERATIONS OF SCIENCE

It is hard to think of two men less revolutionary in temperament than the seventeenth century's René Descartes and Isaac Newton. Both were conservative on matters outside the confines of science, had relatively little concern for social institutions, remained practicing Christians, and wrote only for small learned audiences. Yet their legacy of insight into the world of nature produced in succeeding generations what has been described as "a permanent intellectual insurrection," which unfolded in a spirit undreamed of by either man.

The Popularization of Science   While eighteenth-century scientists pondered the cosmologies of Descartes and Newton, nonscientists in England and on the continent applied the methodologies of Descartes, Newton, and the philosopher John Locke to other realms of human thought. They fused the notion of methodical doubt and naturalistic explanations of phenomena into a scientific or mathematical spirit, which at bottom simply meant confidence in reason and a skeptical attitude toward accepted dogmas. They attempted to popularize scientific method, with the aim of transforming the values of Western civilization. Writers translated the discoveries of scientists into clear and even amusing general reading. The literary talents of these enthusiasts helped make household words of Newton and Descartes among educated Europeans.

A more calculating and ambitious propagandist of the scientific spirit was the Frenchman François-Marie Arouet, who wrote under the pen name of Voltaire and is virtually synonymous with the Enlightenment. While his chief talents lay in literature and criticism, Voltaire also spent some time studying Newton's work. In 1738 he published a widely read popularization called *Elements of the Philosophy of Newton*. However dry the study of physics, Voltaire argued, it frees the mind from dogma, and its experimental methods provide a model for the liberation of human thought. Moreover, Voltaire related Newton's achievement to the environment of a liberal

England that also produced Francis Bacon and John Locke, the three of whom Voltaire adopted as his personal Trinity. In his *Philosophical Letters on the English* (1734)—a celebration of English toleration and an indirect attack on religious bigotry, censorship, and social snobbery in France—Voltaire had already noted the respect enjoyed in England by its writers and scientists. He saw this recognition of talent as a crucial component of a free society and as a condition for the achievements of a man like Newton.

Popularizations of scientific method stimulated public interest in science, as mathematicians, cartographers, and astronomers made notable advances in their fields. But further scientific progress was far from automatic. In chemistry, for example, the traditions of alchemy persisted, and phenomena such as fire long escaped objective analysis. At the end of the century, however, a major breakthrough occurred when the Englishman Joseph Priestley isolated oxygen and the Frenchman Antoine Lavoisier analyzed the components of air and water and came close to explaining the process of combustion.

The vogue for science also had a dubious side, apparent, for example, in the great popularity of mesmerism. This pseudoscience of magnetic fields purported to offer its wealthy devotees relief from a variety of ailments by the use of special "electrical" baths and treatments. Although repeatedly condemned by the Academy of Sciences in Paris, mesmerism continued to attract educated followers.

Natural History The most widely followed scientific enterprise in the eighteenth century was natural history, the science of the earth's development—a combination of geology, zoology, and botany. This field of study was easy for the nonscientist to appreciate. Its foremost practitioner was G. L. Buffon, keeper of the French Botanical Gardens—a patronage position that allowed him to produce a multivolume *Natural History of the Earth* between 1749 and 1778. Drawing on a vast knowledge of phenomena such as fossils, Buffon went beyond previous attempts to classify the data of nature and provided both a description and a theory of the earth's development.

Although he was a nonbeliever, Buffon did not explicitly attack religious versions of such events as the Creation; he simply ignored them, an omission of obvious significance to his readers. Similarly, while he did not specifically contend that human beings have evolved from beasts, he implied it. "It is possible," he wrote, "to descend by almost insensible degrees from the most perfect creature to the most formless matter." Buffon's earth did not derive from a singular act of divine creation that would explain the origins of human beings. The readers of his *Natural History* or its

◄ **French chemist Lavoisier conducts an experiment in his laboratory to study the composition of air during the process of respiration.**
© Corbis

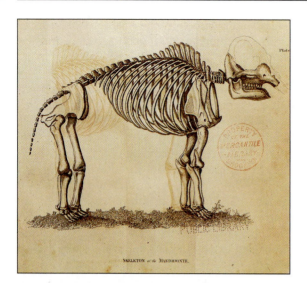

▲ **An image of a mastadon from the section on fossil remains in Buffon's** *Natural History.*
Courtesy Brooklyn Public Library

numerous popularizations in several languages thus encountered a universe that had developed through evolution.

◆ BEYOND CHRISTIANITY

The erosion of biblical revelation as a source of authority is one hallmark of the Enlightenment. This shift derived some of its impetus from seventeenth-century scientists and liberal theologians who were themselves believing Christians but who opposed religious superstition or "enthusiasm," as they called it. They had hoped to accommodate religion to new philosophical standards and scientific formulations by eliminating the superstitious imagery that could make religion seem ridiculous and by treating the world of nature as a form of revelation in which God's majesty could be seen. The devil, for example, could be considered as a category of moral evil rather than as a specific horned creature with a pitchfork. They hoped to bolster the Christian religion by deemphasizing miracles and focusing on reverence for the Creator and on the moral teachings of the Bible. Their approach did indeed help educated people adhere to Christianity during the eighteenth century. In the final analysis, however, this

kind of thinking diminished the authority of religion in society.

Toleration   One current of thought that encouraged a more secular outlook was the idea of toleration, as propounded by the respected French critic Pierre Bayle. Consciously applying methodical doubt to subjects that Descartes had excluded from such treatment, Bayle's *Critical and Historical Dictionary* (1697) put the claims of religion to the test of critical reason. Certain Christian traditions emerged from this scrutiny as the equivalent of myth and fairy tale, and the history of Christianity appeared as a record of fanaticism and persecution. Bayle's chief target was Christianity's attempts to impose orthodoxy at any cost (for example, the Spanish Inquisition and Louis XIV's revocation of the Edict of Nantes and persecution of French Protestants). Though a devout Calvinist himself, Bayle advocated complete toleration, which would allow any person to practice any religion or none at all. An individual's moral behavior rather than his or her creed is what mattered, according to Bayle. Ethics, he argued, do not depend on the Bible; a Muslim, a Confucian, a Jew, even an atheist can be moral.

The most striking success of the eighteenth-century campaign for toleration came with the Edict of Toleration issued by the Habsburg emperor Joseph II on his ascendancy to the throne in 1781. For the first time, a Catholic Habsburg ruler recognized the right of Protestants and Jews in his realm to worship freely and to hold property and public office (see "Joseph II on Religious Toleration," p. 671). Joseph also tried to reduce the influence of the Catholic Church by ordering the dissolution of numerous monasteries on the grounds that they were useless and corrupt. Part of their confiscated wealth was used to support the medical school at the University of Vienna.

Deism   Voltaire became the Enlightenment's most vigorous antireligious polemicist. This prolific writer was one of the century's most brilliant literary stylists, historians, and poets. Those talents alone would have assured his fame. But Voltaire was also a dedicated antagonist of Christianity. For tactical reasons, much of his attack against *l'infame* ("the infamous thing"), as he

JOSEPH II ON RELIGIOUS TOLERATION

◆

Between 1765 and 1781 Joseph II was joint ruler of the Habsburg Empire with his pious mother, Empress Maria Theresa. Joseph advocated a utilitarian approach to religious toleration (Document I) but made little headway against Maria Theresa's traditional insistence that the state must actively combat religious dissent. Soon after Maria Theresa's death, Joseph promulgated a series of decrees on religion, including a landmark Toleration Edict for Protestants (Document II) and even a special, if somewhat less sweeping, edict of toleration for the Jews of his domains.

(I) LETTER TO MARIA THERESA, JULY 1777

"The word *toleration* has caused misunderstanding. . . . God preserve me from thinking it a matter of indifference whether the citizens turn Protestant or remain Catholics. . . . I would give all I possess if all the Protestants of your States would go over to Catholicism. The word *toleration* as I understand it, means only that I would employ any persons, without distinction of religion, in purely temporal matters, allow them to own property, practice trades, be citizens if they were qualified and if this would be of advantage to the State and its industry. . . . The undisturbed practice of their religion makes them far better subjects and causes them to avoid irreligion, which is a far greater danger to our Catholics."

(II) TOLERATION EDICT OF OCTOBER 1781

"We have found Ourselves moved to grant to the adherents of the Lutheran and Calvinist religions, and also to the non Uniat Greek religion, everywhere, the appropriate private practice of their faith. . . . The Catholic religion alone shall continue to enjoy the prerogative of the public practice of its faith. . . . Non-Catholics are in future admitted under dispensation to buy houses and real property, to acquire municipal domicile and practice as master craftsmen, to take up academic appointments and posts in the public service, and are not to be required to take the oath in any form contrary to their religious tenets. . . . In all choices or appointments to official posts . . . difference of religion is to be disregarded."

From C. A. Macartney (ed.), *The Habsburg and Hohenzollern Dynasties in the 17th and 18th Centuries* (HarperCollins, 1970), pp. 151 and 155–157.

---

called Christianity, targeted such practices as monasticism or the behavior of priests. His ultimate target, though, was Christianity itself, which, he declared, "every sensible man, every honorable man must hold in horror."

Voltaire's masterpiece, a best-seller called *The Philosophical Dictionary* (1764), had to be published anonymously and was burned by the authorities in Switzerland, France, and the Netherlands. Modeled after Bayle's dictionary, it was far blunter. Of theology, he wrote, "We find man's insanity in all its plenitude." Organized religion is not simply false but pernicious, he argued. Voltaire believed that religious superstition inevitably bred fanaticism and predictably resulted in bloody episodes like the Saint Bartholomew's Day Massacre.

Voltaire hoped that educated Europeans would abandon Christianity in favor of deism, a belief that recognized God as the Creator but held that the world, once created, functions according to natural laws without interference by God. Humanity thus lives essentially on its own in an ordered universe, without hope or fear of divine intervention and without the threat of damnation or the hope of eternal salvation. For deists, religion should be a matter of private contemplation rather than public worship and mythic creeds. Although certain figures in the Enlightenment went beyond deism to a philosophical atheism, which rejected any concept of God as unprovable, Voltaire's mild deism remained a characteristic view of eighteenth-century writers. At bottom, however, this form of spirituality was essentially secular. Broad-minded clergy could accept many of the arguments of eighteenth-century science and philosophy, but they could not accept deism.

▲ In 1745 the Habsburg monarchy expelled an estimated seventy thousand Jews from Prague to appease anti-semitic sentiment.

◆ THE PHILOSOPHES

Science and secularism became the rallying points of a group of French intellectuals known as the *philosophes*. Their traditionalist opponents employed this term to mock the group's pretensions, but the philosophes themselves used that label with pride. They saw themselves as a vanguard, the men who raised the Enlightenment to the status of a self-conscious movement. The leaders of this influential coterie of writers were Voltaire and Denis Diderot. Its ranks included mathematicians Jean d'Alembert and the Marquis de Condorcet, the magistrate Baron de Montesquieu, the government official Jacques Turgot, and the atheist philosopher Baron d'Holbach. Thus, the French philosophes came from both the aristocracy and the middle class. Outside of France their kinship extended to a group of brilliant Scottish philosophers, including David Hume and Adam Smith; to the German playwright Gotthold Lessing and the philosopher Immanuel Kant; to the Italian economist and penal reformer the Marquis of Beccaria; and to such founders of the American Philosophical Society as Benjamin Franklin and Thomas Jefferson.

Intellectual Freedom The philosophes shared above all else a critical spirit, the desire to reexamine the assumptions and institutions of their societies and expose them to the tests of reason, experience, and utility. Today this might sound banal, but it was not so at a time when almost everywhere religion permeated society. Asserting the primacy of reason meant turning away from faith, the essence of religion. It meant a decisive break with the Christian worldview, which placed religious doctrine at the center of society's values. The philosophes invoked the paganism of ancient Greece and Rome, where the spirit of rational inquiry prevailed among educated people. They ridiculed the Middle Ages as the "Dark Ages" and contrasted the religious spirit of that era to their

WHAT IS ENLIGHTENMENT?

◆

The most concise formulation of the Enlightenment's spirit is conveyed in an essay of the 1780s by the German philosopher Immanuel Kant. As Kant makes clear, intellectual freedom and the role of public opinion refer not so much to the average person in the street as to the educated classes—serious writers (whom he calls "scholars") and their public. Note that in drawing the distinction between the public realm (where freedom is vital) and the private realm (where obedience is rightly expected), Kant reverses the labels that we would likely assign to the two realms today.

"Enlightenment is man's emergence from his self-imposed nonage. Nonage is the inability to use one's own understanding without another's guidance. This nonage is self-imposed if its cause lies not in lack of understanding but in indecision and lack of courage to use one's own mind without another's guidance. Dare to know. (*Sapere aude*). 'Have the courage to use your own understanding,' is therefore the motto of the Enlightenment.

"Laziness and cowardice are the reasons why such a large part of mankind gladly remain minors all their lives, long after nature has freed them from external guidance. They are the reasons why it is so easy for others to set themselves up as guardians. It is so comfortable to be a minor. If I have a book that thinks for me, a pastor who acts as my conscience, then I have no need to exert myself. . . .

"This enlightenment requires nothing but freedom: freedom to make public use of one's reason in all matters. . . . On the other hand, the private use of reason may frequently be narrowly restricted without especially hindering the progress of enlightenment. By 'public use of reason' I mean that use which man, as a scholar, makes of it before the reading public. I call 'private use' that use which a man makes of his reason in a civic post that has been entrusted to him . . . and where arguing is not permitted: one must obey. . . . Thus it would be very unfortunate if an officer on duty and under orders from his superiors should want to criticize the appropriateness or utility of his orders. He must obey. But as a scholar he could not rightfully be prevented from taking notice of the mistakes in the military service and from submitting his views to his public for its judgement."

own sense of liberation and modernity. In *The Decline and Fall of the Roman Empire* (1776–1788), the historian Edward Gibbon declared that Christianity had eclipsed a Roman civilization that had sought to live according to reason rather than myths.

The inspiration of antiquity was matched by the stimulus of modern science and philosophy. The philosophes laid claim to Newton, who made the universe intelligible without the aid of revelation, and Locke, who uncovered the workings of the human mind. From Locke they went on to argue that human personality is malleable: Its nature is not fixed, let alone corrupted by original sin. People are, therefore, ultimately responsible to themselves for what they do with their lives. Existing arrangements are no more nor less sacred than experience has proved them to be. As the humanists had several centuries before, the philosophes placed human beings at the center

of thought. Unlike most humanists, however, philosophes placed thought in the service of change and launched a noisy public movement.

Persecution and Triumph   Philosophes appeared clamorous to their contemporaries because they had to battle entrenched authority. Religious traditionalists and the apparatus of censorship in almost all countries threatened the intellectual freedom demanded by the philosophes. They often had to publish their works clandestinely and anonymously. Sometimes they were pressured into withholding manuscripts from publication altogether or into making humiliating public apologies for controversial books. Even with such caution, almost all philosophes saw some of their publications confiscated and burned. A few were forced into exile or sent to jail: Voltaire spent several decades across the French border in Switzerland, and Voltaire and Diderot both spent time in prison. Although the notoriety produced by these persecutions stimulated the sale of their works, the anxiety took its toll.

By the 1770s, however, the philosophes had survived their running war with the authorities. Some of them lived to see their ideas widely accepted and their works acclaimed. Thus, even if they had contributed little else to the Western experience, their struggle for freedom of expression would merit them a significant place in its history.

Pioneering in the Social Sciences   But the philosophes achieved far more. In their scholarly and polemical writings, they investigated a wide range of subjects and pioneered in several new disciplines. Some philosophes—Voltaire, for example—were pathbreaking historians. Moving beyond traditional chronicles of battles and rulers' biographies, they studied culture, social institutions, and government structures in an effort to understand past societies as well as describe major events. Practically inventing the notion of social science, they investigated the theoretical foundations of social organization (sociology) and the workings of the human mind (psychology). On a more practical level, they proposed

▼ **In 1778, the last year of his life, Voltaire returned triumphantly to Paris. When he attended a performance of one of his plays at the national theater (known as the *Comédie Française*), the audience greeted him with tumultuous enthusiasm. To this day a statue of Voltaire holds pride of place in that renowned theater, where he first made his reputation.**
Giraudon/Art Resource, NY

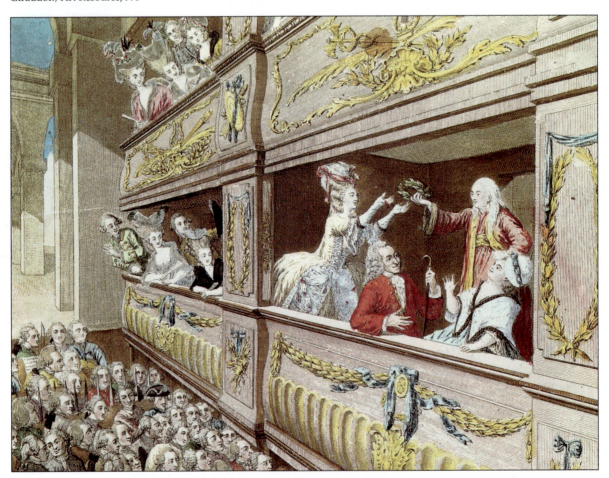

fundamental reforms in such areas as the penal system and education.

The philosophes embedded their study of social science in questions of morality and the study of ethics. Enlightenment ethics were generally utilitarian. Such philosophers as David Hume tried to define good and evil in pragmatic terms; they argued that social utility should become the standard for public morality. This approach to moral philosophy in turn raised the question of whether any human values were absolute and eternal. Among the philosophers who grappled with this challenge, Kant tried to harmonize the notion of absolute moral values with practical reason.

Political Liberty   The most influential work of social science produced by the Enlightenment was probably *The Spirit of the Laws* (1748) by the French magistrate Montesquieu. The book offered a comparative study of governments and societies. On the one hand, Montesquieu introduced the perspective of relativism: He tried to analyze the institutions of government in relation to the special customs, climate, religion, and commerce of various countries. He thus argued that no single, ideal model of government existed. On the other hand, he deeply admired his own idealized version of the British system of government; he thereby implied that all societies could learn from the British about liberty.

Montesquieu's sections on liberty won a wide readership in Europe and in America, where the book was influential among the drafters of the U.S. Constitution. Political liberty, said Montesquieu, requires checks on those who hold power in a state, whether that power is exercised by a king, an aristocracy, or the people. Liberty can thrive only with a balance of powers, preferably by the separation of the executive, the legislative, and the judicial branches of government. Montesquieu ascribed a central role to aristocracies as checks on royal despotism. Indeed, many eighteenth-century writers on politics considered strong privileged groups, independent from both the crown and the people, as the only effective bulwarks against tyranny. To put it another way, Montesquieu's followers thought that the price for a society free from despotism was privilege for some of its members.

Liberal Economics   French and British thinkers of the Enlightenment transformed economic theory with attacks against mercantilism and government regulation. We noted in chapter 18 Adam Smith's critique of artificial restraints on individual economic initiative. In France, the Physiocrats similarly argued that economic progress depended on freeing agriculture and trade from restrictions. Since in their view land was the only real source of wealth, they also called for reforms in the tax structure with a uniform and equitable land tax. In opposition to a traditional popular insistence on government intervention to maintain supplies of grain and flour at fair prices, the Physiocrats advocated freedom for the grain trade to operate according to the dictates of supply and demand. The incentive of higher prices would encourage growers to expand productivity, they believed, and in this way the grain shortages that plagued Europe could eventually be eliminated, although at the cost of temporary hardship for most consumers.

◆ DIDEROT AND THE *ENCYCLOPEDIA*

The Enlightenment thus produced not only a new intellectual spirit but also a wide range of critical writings on various subjects. In addition, the French philosophes collectively generated a single work that exemplified their notion of how knowledge could be useful: Diderot's *Encyclopédie* (*Encyclopedia*).

Diderot   Denis Diderot never achieved the celebrity of his friend Voltaire, but his career proved equally central to the Enlightenment. The son of a provincial knife maker, Diderot was educated in Jesuit schools, but at the first opportunity he headed for Paris. Continuing to educate himself while living a bohemian existence, Diderot developed an unshakable sense of purpose: to make himself into an independent and influential intellectual.

Within a few years, he had published a remarkable succession of writings—novels and plays, mathematical treatises, an attack on inept medical practices, and several works on religion and moral philosophy. His most original writings examined the role of passion in human personality and in any system of values derived from an understanding of human nature. Specifically, Diderot affirmed the role of sexuality, arguing against artificial taboos and repression. As an advocate of what was sometimes called "the natural man," Diderot belies the charge leveled against the philosophes that they overemphasized reason to the neglect of feeling. The thread of religious criticism in these works was also notable. Starting from a position of mild skepticism, Diderot soon passed to deism and ended up in the atheist camp.

Diderot's unusual boldness in getting his works published brought him a considerable reputation but also some real trouble. Two of his books were condemned by the authorities as contrary to religion, the state, and morals. In 1749 he spent one hundred days in prison and was released only after making a humiliating apology. At about that time, Diderot was approached by a publisher to translate a British encyclopedic reference work into French. After a number of false starts, he persuaded the publisher to sponsor instead an entirely new and more comprehensive work that would reflect the interests of the philosophes.

The Encyclopedia   The *Encyclopedia, or Classified Dictionary of the Sciences, Arts, and Occupations*, an inventory of all fields of knowledge from the most theoretical to the most mundane, constituted an arsenal of critical concepts. As the preface stated: "Our Encyclopedia is a work that could only be carried out in a philosophic century. . . . All things must be examined without sparing anyone's sensibilities. . . . The arts and sciences must regain their freedom." The ultimate purpose of the *Encyclopedia*, wrote its editors, was "to change the general way of thinking." Written in this spirit by an array of talented collaborators, the expensive twenty-eight-volume *Encyclopedia* (1752–1772) fulfilled the fondest hopes of its editors and four thousand initial subscribers.

In such a work, religion could scarcely be ignored, but neither could it be openly attacked. Instead, the editors treated religion with artful satire or else relegated it to a philosophical or historical

▼ Diderot's *Encyclopedia* focused much of its attention on technology. Illustrations of mechanical processes, such as the one shown here for making plate glass, filled eleven folio volumes.

plane. Demystified and subordinated, religion was probed and questioned like any other subject, much to the discomfort of learned but orthodox critics.

Science stood at the core of the *Encyclopedia*, but the editors emphasized the technological or practical side of science with numerous articles and plates illustrating machines, tools, and manufacturing processes. They praised the roles of mechanics, engineers, and artisans in society and stressed the benefits of efficient production in the advance of civilization. Such emphasis implied that technology and artisanal skills constituted valuable realms of knowledge comparable to theoretical sciences such as physics and mathematics.

On economic topics the encyclopedists tended to echo the Physiocratic crusade against restrictions on trade and agriculture. But the opinions and aspirations expressed were those of the elites, whose prerogatives, especially in matters of property, were not being threatened. Articles that might reflect the concerns of the popular masses on such issues as wages or affordable food prices were notably absent. Nor did the *Encyclopedia* take a novel line on questions of government. The authors generally endorsed absolute monarchy, provided it was reasonably efficient and just. The major political concerns of the editors were civil rights, freedom of expression, and the rule of law.

The* Encyclopedia's *Impact In retrospect, after the French Revolution, the *Encyclopedia* does not seem very revolutionary. Yet in the context of the times, it assuredly was. The revolution that Diderot sought was intellectual. As he wrote in a letter to a friend, the encyclopedists were promoting "a revolution in the minds of men to free them from prejudice." Judging by the reaction of religious and government authorities, they were eminently successful. "Up till now," commented one French bishop, "hell has vomited its venom drop by drop." Now, he concluded, it could be found assembled between the *Encyclopedia*'s covers.

After allowing the first three volumes to appear, the French government banned the *Encyclopedia* in 1759 and revoked the bookseller's license to issue the remaining volumes. As the attorney general of France put it: "There is a project formed, a society organized to propagate materialism, to destroy religion, to inspire a spirit of independence, and to nourish the corruption of morals." Most of the *Encyclopedia*'s contributors prudently withdrew from the project, but Diderot went underground and continued the herculean task until the subscribers received every promised volume, including eleven magnificent folios of illustrations. By the time these appeared, the persecutions had receded. Indeed, the *Encyclopedia* was reprinted in cheaper editions (both legal and pirated) that sold out rapidly, earning fortunes for their publishers. This turn of events ensured the status of Diderot's project as the landmark of its age.

◆ JEAN-JACQUES ROUSSEAU

Arguably the most original and influential eighteenth-century thinker, Jean-Jacques Rousseau stood close to but self-consciously outside the coterie of the philosophes, for Rousseau provided in his life and writing a critique not only of the status quo but of the Enlightenment itself. Obsessed with the issue of moral freedom, Rousseau found society far more oppressive than most philosophes would admit, and he considered the philosophes themselves to be part of the problem.

Young Rousseau won instant fame when he submitted a prize-winning essay in a contest sponsored by a provincial academy on the topic, "Has the restoration of the arts and sciences had a purifying effect upon morals?" Unlike most respondents, Rousseau answered that it had not. He argued that the lustrous cultural and scientific achievements of recent decades were producing pretension, conformity, and useless luxury. Most scientific pursuits, he wrote, "are the effect of idleness which generate idleness in their turn." The system of rewards in the arts produces "a servile and deceptive conformity . . . the dissolution of morals . . . and the corruption of taste." Against the decadence of high culture, he advocated a return "to the simplicity which prevailed in earliest times"—manly physical pastimes, self-reliance, independent citizens instead of fawning courtiers.

Rousseau's Moral Vision Rousseau had no wish to return to a state of nature, a condition of anarchy in which force ruled and people were slaves of appetite. But the basis of morality, he argued, was conscience, not reason. "Virtue, sublime science of simple minds: are not your principles graven on every heart?" This became one of his basic themes in two popular works of fiction, *Julie, or the New Héloise* (1761), and *Emile, or Treatise on Education* (1762).

In the first novel, Julie is educated in virtue by her tutor St. Preux but allows herself to fall in love with and be seduced by him. In the second half of the novel, Julie breaks away from St. Preux and marries Monsieur de Wolmar, her father's wealthy friend. She maintains a distant friendship with her old lover and rears her children in exemplary fashion, overseeing their education. In the end she overcomes her past moral lapse and sacrifices her own life to save one of her children. Wolmar then brings in the chastened St. Preux to continue the children's education. This tale of love, virtue, and motherhood won an adoring audience of male and female readers who identified with the characters, shed tears over their moral dilemmas, and applauded Rousseau for this superb lesson in the new sensibility.

Emile recounts the story of a young boy raised to be a moral adult by a tutor who emphasized experience over book learning and who considered education a matter of individual self-development. This new kind of man of course required a comparably sensitive wife, attuned to practical matters and without vain aristocratic pretenses. Sophie, the girl in question, received a very different type of education, however, one concerned with virtue but far more limited in its scope. Rousseau depicted men and women liberating themselves from stultifying traditional values, yet in the new relationships he portrayed in these novels, women held a decidedly subordinate position. Their virtues were to be exclusively domestic in character, while the men would be prepared for public roles—a distinction that deeply troubled feminist thinkers in the future (see "Mary Wollstonecraft on the Education of Women," p. 679).

The Rebel as Cultural Hero Rousseau himself was by no means a saint. His personal weaknesses—including the illegitimate child that he fathered and abandoned—doubtless contributed to his preoccupation with morality and conscience. Nonetheless, his rebellious life as well as his writings greatly impressed the generation of readers

and writers coming of age in the 1770s and 1780s. Not only did he quarrel with the repressive authorities of Church and state—who repeatedly banned his books—but he also attacked the pretensions of his fellow philosophes, whom he considered arrogant, cynical, and lacking in spirituality.

By the 1770s the commanding figures of the Enlightenment, such as Voltaire and Diderot, had won their battles and had become masters of the most prestigious academies and channels of patronage. In a sense, they had themselves become

▼ **The French revolutionaries acclaimed both Voltaire and Rousseau and transferred their remains to a new Pantheon. But Rousseau was the man considered by many French people to be the Revolution's spiritual father, as suggested by his position in this allegorical painting of 1793, filled with the new symbolism of liberty and equality.** Giraudon/Art Resource, NY

Mary Wollstonecraft on the Education of Women

◆

The sharpest challenge to Rousseau's widely shared attitude toward women came only in 1792, with the publication of Mary Wollstonecraft's A Vindication of the Rights of Woman. *Inspired by the French Revolution's doctrine of natural rights, this spirited writer deplored the fact that society kept women (in her words) frivolous, artificial, weak, and in a perpetual state of childhood. While men praised women for their beauty and grace, they hypocritically condemned them for a concern with vanity, fashion, and trivial matters, yet refused to treat them as rational human beings who could contribute to society as much as men. Her book emphasized the need for educational reform that would allow women to develop agile bodies and strong minds. Along the way Wollstonecraft took particular aim at Rousseau's* Emile.

"The conduct and manners of women, in fact, evidently prove that their minds are not in a healthy state; for, like the flowers which are planted in too rich a soil, strength and usefulness are sacrificed to beauty. . . . One cause of this barren blooming I attribute to a false system of education, gathered from the books written on this subject by men who, considering females rather as women than human creatures, have been more anxious to make them alluring mistresses than affectionate wives and rational mothers. The understanding of the sex has been so bubbled by this specious homage, that the civilized women of the present century, with a few exceptions, are only anxious to inspire love, when they ought to cherish a nobler ambition, and by their abilities and virtues exact respect.

"[T]he most perfect education, in my opinion, is such an exercise of the understanding as is best calculated to strengthen the body and form the heart.

Or, in other words, to enable the individual to attain such habits of virtue as will render it independent. In fact, it is a farce to call any being virtuous whose virtues do not result from the exercise of its own reason. This was Rousseau's opinion respecting men: I extend it to women, and confidently assert that they have been drawn out of their sphere by false refinement, and not by an endeavor to acquire masculine qualities. Still the regal homage which they receive is so intoxicating, that till the manners of the times are changed, and formed on more reasonable principles, it may be impossible to convince them that the illegitimate power, which they obtain by degrading themselves, is a curse, and that they must return to nature and equality."

From Sandra M. Gilbert and Susan Gubar (eds.), *The Norton Anthology of Literature by Women: The Tradition in English* (W. W. Norton Co, 1985).

---

the establishment. For younger writers frustrated by the existing distribution of influence and patronage, Rousseau became the inspiration.

Rousseau's Concept of Freedom   What proved to be Rousseau's most enduring work, *The Social Contract*, published in 1762, became famous only after the French Revolution dramatized the issues that the book had raised. (The Revolution, it could be said, did more for the book than Rousseau did for the Revolution, which he neither prophesied nor advocated.) *The Social Contract* was not meant as a blueprint for revolution but rather as an ideal standard against which readers might measure their own society. Rousseau did not expect that this standard could be achieved in practice, since

existing states were too large and complex to allow the kind of participation that he considered essential.

For Rousseau, a government distinct from the individuals over whom it claims to exercise authority has no validity. Rousseau denied the almost universal idea that some people are meant to govern and others to obey. In the ideal polity, Rousseau said, individuals have a role in making the law to which they submit. By obeying it, they are thus obeying themselves as well as their fellow citizens. For this reason, they are free from arbitrary power. To found such an ideal society, each citizen would have to take part in creating a social contract laying out the society's ground rules. By doing so, these citizens would establish

ROUSSEAU'S CONCEPT OF THE GENERAL WILL

"The essence of the social compact reduces itself to the following terms: Each of us puts his person and all his power in common under the supreme direction of the general will, and, in our collective capacity, we receive each member as an indivisible part of the whole. . . .

"In fact, each individual, as a man, may have a particular will contrary or dissimilar to the general will which he has as a citizen. His particular interest may speak to him quite differently from the common interest: his absolute and naturally independent existence may make him look upon what he owes to the common cause as a gratuitous contribution, the loss of which will do less harm to others than the payment of it is burdensome to himself. . . . He may wish to enjoy the rights of citizenship without being ready to fulfill the duties of a subject. The continuance of such an injustice could not but prove the undoing of the body politic.

"In order then that the social compact may not be an empty formula, it tacitly includes the undertaking, which alone can give force to the rest, that whoever refuses to obey the general will shall be compelled to do so by the whole body. This means nothing less than that he will be forced to be free; for this is the condition which, by giving each citizen to his country, secures him against all personal dependence. In this lies the key to the working of the political machine."

From Jean-Jacques Rousseau, *The Social Contract*, Book 1 (David Campbell Publishers).

themselves as "the sovereign." This sovereign—the people—then creates a government that will carry on the day-to-day business of applying the laws.

Rousseau was not advocating simple majority rule but rather a quest for consensus as to the best interests of all citizens. Even if it *appears* contrary to the welfare of some or even many citizens, Rousseau believed, the best interest of the community must be every individual's best interest as well, since that individual is a member of the community. Rousseau called this difficult concept "the general will." Deferring to the general will means that an individual ultimately must do what one *ought*, not simply what one *wants*. This commitment derives from conscience, which must do battle within the individual against passion, appetite, and mere self-interest. Under the social contract, to use Rousseau's most striking phrase, the individual "will be forced to be free" (see "Rousseau's Concept of the General Will"). Thus, for Rousseau, individual freedom depends on a political framework involving consent and participation as well as subordination of individual self-interest to the commonweal. More than any of the philosophes, Rousseau argued that individual freedom depends on the arrangements governing the collectivity.

II. Eighteenth-Century Elite Culture

The Enlightenment was merely one dimension of Europe's vibrant cultural life in the eighteenth century. An explosive increase in publishing activity, legal and underground, served diverse audiences. New cultural forums and institutions, such as salons and freemasons lodges, combined with new media to create a kind of "public sphere" for the uninhibited exchange of ideas. Meanwhile, the realm of literature saw remarkable innovation, including the rise of the novel. Royal courts and aristocracies still dominated most activity in music and the fine arts through their patronage, but here too the presence of a growing middle-class audience made itself felt and offered new opportunities of recognition for composers and artists.

◆ COSMOPOLITAN HIGH CULTURE

As the expansive, cosmopolitan aspects of European high culture are described here, it must be remembered that the mass of Europe's peasants and workers remained virtually untouched by these developments, insulated within their local environments and traditions. But the educated and wealthy, the numerically small and influential elites, enjoyed a sense of belonging to a common European civilization. French was the international language of this culture; even King Frederick II of Prussia favored French over German. Whatever the effects of Frederick's attitude might have been—the German dramatist Lessing, for one, considered it a deplorable cultural prejudice—the widespread knowledge of French meant that ideas and literature could circulate easily past language barriers.

The Appeal of Travel Europeans sharpened their sense of common identity through travel literature and by their appetite for visiting foreign places. Although transportation was slow and uncomfortable, many embarked on a "grand tour," whose highlights included visits to Europe's large cities (such as London, Paris, Rome, and Vienna) and to the ruins of antiquity—to the glories of the modern and the ancient worlds.

Kings, princes, and municipal authorities were embellishing their towns with plazas, public gardens, theaters, and opera houses. Toward the end of the century, amenities such as street lighting and public transportation began to appear in a few cities, with London leading the way. From the private sector came two notable additions to the urban scene: the coffeehouse and the storefront window display. Coffeehouses, where customers could chat or read, and enticing shop windows, which added to the pleasures of city walking (and stimulated consumer demand), enhanced the rhythms of urban life for tourists and residents alike. When a man is tired of London, Samuel Johnson remarked, he is tired of life.

Travelers on tour invariably passed from the attractions of bustling city life to the silent monuments of antiquity. As the philosophes recalled the virtues of pagan philosophers like Cicero, interest grew in surviving examples of Greek and Roman architecture and sculpture. Many would have agreed with the German art historian Johann Winckelmann that Greek sculpture was the most worthy standard of aesthetic beauty in all the world.

The Republic of Letters Among writers, intellectuals, and scientists, the sense of a cosmopolitan

European culture devolved into the concept of a "republic of letters." The phrase, introduced by sixteenth-century French humanists, was popularized by Pierre Bayle (noted earlier as a proponent of religious toleration), who published a critical journal that he called *News of the Republic of Letters*. The title implied that the realm of culture and ideas stretched across Europe's political borders. In one sense, it was an exclusive republic, limited to the educated; but it was also an open society to which people of talent could belong regardless of their social origins. For this reason, European intellectuals felt that their republic of letters was a model for a public sphere in which political and social issues could be debated freely as well.

Aside from the medium of the printed word, the republic of letters was organized around the salons and the academies. Both institutions encouraged social interchange by bringing together socially prominent men and women with talented writers. The philosophes themselves exemplified this social mixture, for their "family" was composed in almost equal measures of nobles (Montesquieu, Holbach, Condorcet) and commoners (Voltaire, Diderot, d'Alembert). Voltaire, while insisting that he was as good as any aristocrat, had no desire to topple the aristocracy from its position; rather, he sought amalgamation. As d'Alembert put it, talent on the one hand and birth and eminence on the other both deserve recognition.

The Salons Usually organized and led by women of wealthy bourgeois or noble families, the salons sought to bring together important writers with the influential persons they needed for favors and patronage. The salon of Madame Tencin, for example, helped launch Montesquieu's *Spirit of the Laws* in the 1740s, while the salon of Madame du Deffand in the 1760s became a forum in which the philosophes could test their ideas (see figure, p. 682). The salons also helped to enlarge the audience and contacts of the philosophes by introducing them to a flow of foreign visitors, ranging from German princes to Benjamin Franklin. Private newsletters kept interested foreigners and provincials abreast of activities in the Parisian salons when they could not attend personally, but salons also operated in Vienna, London, and Berlin.

The salons placed a premium on elegant conversation and wit. The women who ran them insisted that intellectuals make their ideas lucid and comprehensible to laypeople, which increased the likelihood that their thought and writings would have some impact. The salons were also a forum in which men learned to take women seriously, and they constituted a unique cultural space for women between the domestic and public spheres. But the salons' emphasis on style over substance led Rousseau to denounce them as artificial rituals that prevented the display of genuine feeling and sincerity.

Freemasonry   Throughout Europe, freemasonry was another important form of cultural sociability that often crossed the lines of class and (less commonly) of gender. Operating in an aura of secre-

tiveness and symbolism, the masonic lodges fostered a curious mixture of spirituality and rationalism. Originating as clubs or fraternities dedicated to humane values, they attracted a wide range of educated nobles, commoners, and liberal clergy, while some lodges accepted women as well. But toward the end of the century, freemasonry was torn by sectarian controversies and its influence seemed to be diminishing.

The Learned Academies   As important for the dissemination of ideas in the eighteenth century as the salons were the learned academies. These ranged from the Lunar Society in Birmingham, a forum for innovative British industrialists and engineers, to state-sponsored academies in almost every capital of southern and central Europe, which served as conduits for advanced scientific

▼ **This 1814 painting of Mme. Geoffrin's Salon in 1755 reflects the artist Lemonnier's imagination rather than historical reality. His canvas depicts an assemblage of all the major philosophes and their patrons that never actually took place. Yet it does accurately convey the social atmosphere and serious purpose of the Parisian salons. At the center is a bust of Voltaire, who lived in exile at the time.**
Giraudon/Art Resource, NY

and philosophical ideas coming from Western Europe. In France, moreover, academies were established in more than thirty provincial cities, most of which became strongholds of advanced thinking outside the capital.

These provincial academies were founded after the death of Louis XIV in 1715, as if in testimony to the liberating effect of his demise. Most began as literary institutes, concerned with upholding traditional values such as purity of literary style. A few academies adhered to such goals well into midcentury, but most gradually shifted their interests from literary matters to scientific and practical questions in such areas as commerce, agriculture, and local administration. They became offshoots, so to speak, of the *Encyclopedia*'s spirit. Indeed, when a Jesuit launched an attack against the *Encyclopedia* in the Lyons Academy, many members threatened to resign unless he retracted his remarks.

By the 1770s the essay contests sponsored by the provincial academies and the papers published by their members had turned to such topics as population growth, capital punishment and penology, education, poverty and welfare, the grain trade, the guilds, and the origins of sovereignty. A parallel shift in membership occurred. The local academies began as privileged corporations, dominated by the nobility of the region. Associate membership was extended to commoners from the ranks of civil servants, doctors, and professionals. Gradually, the distinction between regular and associate participants crumbled. The academies admitted more commoners to full membership, and a fragile social fusion took place.

◆ PUBLISHING AND READING

The eighteenth century saw a notable rise in publishing that was geared to several kinds of readers. Traveling circulating libraries originated in England around 1740 and opened untapped markets for reading material; by the end of the century almost one thousand traveling libraries had been established. "Booksellers," or publishers—the intermediary between author and reader—combined the functions of a modern editor, printer, salesperson, and (if need be) smuggler. Their judgment and marketing techniques helped create as well as fill the demand for books, since they conceived and financed a variety of works. The *Encyclopedia* originated as a bookseller's project; so, too, did such enduring masterpieces as Samuel Johnson's *Dictionary*, a monumental lexicon that helped purify and standardize the English language. Booksellers commissioned talented stylists to write popular versions of serious scientific, historical, and philosophical works. Recognizing a specialized demand among women readers, they increased the output of fictional romances and fashion magazines and also began to publish more fiction and poetry by women. In general, the entertainment and instruction of a diverse but educated audience became the focus of most publishers.

Journals and Newspapers Eighteenth-century publishing was notable for the proliferation of periodicals. In England, which pioneered in this domain, the number of periodicals increased from 25 to 158 between 1700 and 1780. In one successful model, Addison and Steele's *Spectator* (1711), each issue consisted of a single essay that sought in elegant but clear prose to raise the reader's standards of morality and taste. Their goal was "to enliven Morality with Wit, and to temper Wit with Morality. . . . To bring Philosophy . . . to dwell in clubs and assemblies, at tea-tables and coffeehouses." Eliza Haywood adapted this format in her journal, *The Female Spectator* (1744–1756), in which she advocated improvement in the treatment of women and greater "opportunities of enlarging our minds." (A comparable periodical in France, the *Journal des Dames*, which appeared in 1759, propagated the writings of the Enlightenment but also raised the question of women's place in society.) Another type of journal published extracts and summaries of books and covered current events and entertainment; one such journal, the *Gentleman's Magazine*, reached the impressive circulation of fifteen thousand in 1740. More learned periodicals specialized in book reviews and serious articles on science and philosophy.

Most important for the future of reading habits in Europe was the daily newspaper, which originated in England. Papers like the *London Chronicle* at first provided family entertainment and then took on classified advertisements (thereby

A

DICTIONARY

OF THE

ENGLISH LANGUAGE:

IN WHICH

The WORDS are deduced from their ORIGINALS,

AND

ILLUSTRATED in their DIFFERENT SIGNIFICATIONS

BY

EXAMPLES from the best WRITERS.

TO WHICH ARE PREFIXED,

A HISTORY of the LANGUAGE,

AND

AN ENGLISH GRAMMAR.

BY SAMUEL JOHNSON, A. M.

IN TWO VOLUMES.

VOL. I.

Cum tabulis animum censoris sumet honesti :
Audebit quaecunque parum splendoris habebunt,
Et sine pondere erunt, et honore indigna ferentur,
Verba movere loco ; quamvis invita recedant,
Et versentur adhuc intra penetralia Vestae :
Obscurata diu populo bonus eruet, atque
Proferet in lucem speciosa vocabula rerum,
Quae priscis memorata Catonibus atque Cethegis,
Nunc situs informis premit et deserta vetustas.   HOR.

-

LONDON

Printed by W. STRAHAN,

For J. and P. KNAPTON; T. and T. LONGMAN; C. HITCH and L. HAWES;
A. MILLAR· and R. and J. DODSLEY.

MDCCLV.

▲ The title page of Samuel Johnson's pioneering *Dictionary of the English Language* (1755 edition), one of the masterpieces of eighteenth-century literature.
Mary Evans Picture Library

spurring consumerism and the notion of fashion). English newspapers of course published news of current events, but only after strenuous battles for permission from a reluctant government did they win the right to report directly on parliamentary debates. In France, a handful of major Parisian newspapers enjoyed privileged monopolies in exchange for full compliance with government censorship. This arrangement severely restricted their ability to discuss government and politics,

although other periodicals published outside France's borders helped satisfy the demand for such coverage in France. With the Revolution of 1789, however, a politically aroused French citizenry provided unimagined opportunities for the growth of political journalism.

"Bad Books"   The demand for books and the dynamism of the publishing industry created new employment opportunities for men and women. Although the number of would-be writers swelled, relatively few could develop their talents without constraint or achieve financial independence without patronage. Many remained poverty-stricken and frustrated.

Publishers thus could hire legions of otherwise unemployed writers to turn out the kinds of books for which they sensed a great demand: potboilers, romances, salacious pamphlets, and gossip sheets, which pandered to low tastes. Paid for quantity and speed rather than quality, these hack writers led a precarious, humiliating existence. Booksellers and desperate writers saw money to be made in sensational pamphlets assailing the character of notorious aristocrats, in partisan pamphlets attacking a particular faction in court politics, and in pornography. Sometimes they combined character assassination and pornography in pamphlets dwelling on the alleged perversions of rulers or courtiers. For all its wild exaggeration, such material helped "desacralize" monarchy and created a vivid image of a decadent aristocracy.

To satisfy the public's demand for gossip, character assassination, and pornography in violation of laws regulating the book trade in France, publishers located just across the French border marketed such books and pamphlets clandestinely. They smuggled this material into France, along with banned books by writers like Voltaire and Rousseau, using networks of couriers and distributors. In their sales lists of what they called Philosophic Books, the clandestine publishers lumped together banned books by serious writers along with such illicit publications as *The Scandalous Chronicles, The Private Life of Louis XV,* and *Venus in the Cloister* (a pornographic account of the alleged perversions of the clergy). The police made the same judgment. In attempting to stop the flow of "bad books," they scarcely distinguished between a banned work by Voltaire assaulting religious bigotry and a libelous pamphlet depicting the queen as a corrupt pervert.

◆ LITERATURE, MUSIC, AND ART

Unlike the artistic style of the seventeenth century, generally classified as baroque, the artistic style of the eighteenth century cannot be given a single stylistic label. The nature of the audience and the sources of support for writers and composers also varied considerably. But several trends proved to be of lasting importance: the rise of the novel in England, the birth of romantic poetry, the development of the symphony in Austria, and the changing social context of French painting late in the century.

The Rise of the Novel   The modern novel had its strongest development in England, where writers and booksellers cultivated a growing middle-class reading public. The acknowledged pioneer of this new genre was Samuel Richardson, a bookseller as well as a writer. With a series of letters telling the story, Richardson's *Pamela, or Virtue Rewarded* (1740) recounted the trials and tribulations of an honest if somewhat hypocritical servant girl. Pamela's sexual virtue is repeatedly challenged but never conquered by her wealthy employer, Mr. B., who finally agrees to marry her. An instant success, this melodrama broke from the standard forms and heroic subjects of most narrative fiction. Richardson dealt with recognizable types of people.

Pamela's apparent hypocrisy, however, prompted a playwright and lawyer named Henry Fielding to pen a short satire called *Shamela*, which he followed with his own novel *Joseph Andrews*. Here comedy and adventure replaced melodrama; Fielding prefaced *Joseph Andrews* with a manifesto claiming that the novel was to be "a comic epic in prose." Fielding realized the full potential of his bold experimentation with literary forms in *Tom Jones* (1749), a colorful, robust, comic panorama of English society featuring a gallery of brilliantly developed characters and vivid depictions of varied social environments.

The novel was thus emerging as a form of fiction that told its story and treated the development of personality in a realistic social context. It seemed to mirror its times better than other forms of fiction, and like the dramas that filled the stage in the second half of the century, most novels focused on family life and everyday problems of love, marriage, and social relations. Novelists could use broad comedy, or they could be totally serious; they could experiment endlessly with forms and techniques and could deal with a wide range of social settings.

Fanny Burney   In *Evelina, or A Young Lady's Entrance into the World* (1778), the writer Fanny Burney used the flexibility of the novel to give a woman's perspective on eighteenth-century

▼ One of the leading French portrait painters, and the most successful female artist of the era anywhere, was Élisabeth Vigée-Lebrun, who enjoyed the patronage of Queen Marie Antoinette. Shown here is one of several portraits that Vigée-Lebrun painted of the French queen.
Giraudon/Art Resource, NY

English social life. In the form of letters, like *Pamela* and Rousseau's *Julie*, *Evelina* traces a provincial girl's adventures in London as she discovers her true father and finds a suitable husband. While falling back on conventional melodrama, in which marriage is the only happy ending for a young woman, Burney also uses social satire to suggest how society restricts, and even endangers, an independent woman's life. If Burney was ambivalent about the possibilities for female independence in the social world, her own writing, together with that of other women writers of the period, demonstrated the opportunities for female artistic achievement.

Satire Meanwhile, writers with more didactic objectives perfected a satiric genre called the philosophical tale, as exemplified by the great Irish satirist Jonathan Swift in his *Gulliver's Travels* (1726). The French philosophes favored this form of satire because it allowed them to criticize their society covertly and avoid open clashes with the censors. Thus, Montesquieu created a range of mythical foreign settings and travelers from the Levant to ridicule contemporary European morality in *The Persian Letters* (1721). Voltaire similarly achieved great success in his tale *Candide* (1759), a critique of the notion that this was the best of all possible worlds. His exotic characters and incidents disguised an Enlightenment tract against the idiocy and cruelty that he saw in European society.

The Birth of Romantic Poetry During most of this century of innovation in prose fiction, poetry retained its traditional qualities. Still the most prized form of literary expression, poetry followed unchanging rules on what made good literature. Each poetic form had its particular essence and rules, but in all types of poems diction was supposed to be elegant and the sentiments refined. Poets were expected to transform the raw materials of emotion into delicate language and references that only the highly educated could appreciate. In this neoclassical tradition, art was meant to echo eternal standards of truth and beauty. Poets were not permitted to unburden their souls or hold forth on their own experiences. The audience for poetry was the narrowest segment of the reading public—"the wealthy few," in the phrase of William Wordsworth, who criticized eighteenth-century poets for pandering exclusively to that group.

By the end of the century, however, the restraints of neoclassicism finally provoked rebellion in the ranks of English and German poets. Men like Friedrich von Schiller and Wordsworth defiantly raised the celebration of individual feeling and inner passion to the level of a creed, which came to be known as romanticism. These young poets generally prized Rousseau's writings, seeing the Genevan rebel as someone who had forged a personal idiom of expression and who valued inner feeling, moral passion, and the wonders of nature. Hoping to appeal to a much broader audience, these poets decisively changed the nature of poetic composition and made this literary form, like the novel, a flexible and more accessible vehicle of artistic expression.

Goethe The writer who came to embody the new ambitions of poets, novelists, and dramatists was Johann von Goethe, whose long life (1749–1832) spanned the beginnings and the high point of the romantic movement. A friend of Schiller and many of the German writers and philosophers of the day, he soon came to tower over all of them. Goethe first inspired a literary movement known as *Sturm und Drang* (Storm and Stress), which emphasized strong artistic emotions and gave early intimations of the romantic temperament. The best-known work of Sturm und Drang was young Goethe's *The Sorrows of Young Werther* (1774), a novel about a young man driven to despair and suicide by an impossible love.

Courted by many of the princes and monarchs of Germany, Goethe soon joined the circle of the duke who ruled the small city-state of Weimar, where he remained for the rest of his life. There flowed from his pen an astonishing stream of works—lyrical love poetry, powerful dramas, art and literary criticism, translations, philosophic reflections, an account of his travels in Italy, and studies of optics, botany, anatomy, and mathematics. Even though he held official posts in the duke's court, Goethe's literary output never flagged. His masterpiece, *Faust*, occupied him for nearly fifty years and revealed the progress of his art. The first part (published in 1808) imbued with romantic longing the somewhat autobiographical story of a man who yearns to master all of knowledge and who makes a pact with the devil to achieve his goal. But the second part (1831) emphasized the renunciation and determination that came to be Goethe's credo. The final lines are:

> He only earns his freedom and existence
> Who daily conquers them anew.

What had begun in the youthful exuberance and energy of romanticism ended in an almost classical mood of discipline. No wonder that Goethe seemed to his contemporaries to be the last "universal man," the embodiment of conflicting cultural values and Western civilization's struggle to resolve them.

The Symphony For Europe's elites, music offered the supreme form of entertainment, and the development of the symphony in music paralleled the rise of the novel in literature. It must be noted at once, however, that a great deal of eighteenth-century music was routine and undistinguished. For much of the century, composers still served under royal, ecclesiastical, or aristocratic patronage. They were bound by rigid formulas of composition and by prevailing tastes tyrannically insistent on conventions. Most listeners wanted little more than pleasant melodies in familiar forms; instrumental music was often commissioned as background fare for balls or other social occasions.

The heartland of Europe's music tradition shifted during the eighteenth century from Italy and France to Austria. Here a trio of geniuses transformed the routines of eighteenth-century composition into original and enduring masterpieces. True, the early symphonies of Franz Joseph Haydn and young Wolfgang Amadeus Mozart were conventional exercises. As light and tuneful as its audience could wish, their early music had little emotional impact. By the end of their careers, however, these two composers had altered the symphonic form from three to four movements, had achieved extraordinary harmonic virtuosity, and had brought a deep if restrained emotionalism to their music. Haydn and Mozart had changed the symphony radically from the elegant trifles of earlier years.

Beethoven Ludwig van Beethoven consummated this development and ensured that the symphony, like the novel and romantic poetry, would be an adaptable vehicle for the expression of creative genius. In each of his nine symphonies, as well as in his five piano concertos, Beethoven progressively modified the standard formulas, enlarged the orchestra, and wrote movements of increasing intricacy. His last symphony burst the bonds of the form altogether. Beethoven introduced a large chorus singing one of Schiller's odes to conclude his *Ninth Symphony* (1824), making it a celebration in music of freedom and human kinship. Laden with passion, the music is nevertheless recognizable as an advanced form of the classical symphony. Thus, it provides a bridge between the music of two periods: eighteenth-century classicism and nineteenth-century romanticism.

Aristocratic and court patronage remained the surest foundation for a career in music during the eighteenth century. Haydn, for example, worked with mutual satisfaction as the court composer for one prince from 1761 to 1790. At the end of his long life, however, Haydn moved out on his own, having won enough international recognition to sign a lucrative contract with a London music publisher who underwrote performances of his last twelve symphonies. In contrast, Mozart had an unhappy experience trying to earn his living by composing. After a few miserable years as court composer for the Archbishop of Salzburg, Mozart escaped to Vienna but could not find a permanent employer. He was obliged to eke out an inadequate living by teaching, filling private commissions, and giving public concerts. Beethoven did much better at freeing himself from dependence on a single patron through individual commissions and public concerts.

The Social Context of Art Unlike the situation in literature and music, there were no notable innovations in the field of painting during most of the eighteenth century. With the exception of the Frenchman Jacques-Louis David, eighteenth-century painters were overshadowed by their

◄ *Jean-Baptiste Greuze*
THE FATHER'S CURSE
Instead of the aristocrats or classical figures that most artists chose for their subjects, Jean-Baptiste Greuze painted ordinary French people. His portraits and dramatic scenes (such as *The Father's Curse*) seemed to echo Rousseau's call for honest, "natural" feeling.
Giraudon/Arts Resource, NY

predecessors. Neoclassicism remained a popular style in the late eighteenth century, with its themes inspired by antiquity and its timeless conceptions of form and beauty, comparable to the rules of neoclassical poetry.

The social context of painting, however, was changing. Most commissions and patronage still depended on aristocrats and princes, but the public was beginning to claim a role as the judge of talent in the visual arts. Public opinion found its voice in a new breed of art critics, unaffiliated with official sources of patronage, who reached their new audience through the press in the second half of the century. The Royal Academy of Art in France created the opening for this new voice

► *J.-H. Fragonard*
THE SWING (1767)
The kind of art held in high esteem in eighteenth-century France included the sensuous and ornate scenes of aristocratic life in the so-called rococo style painted by Jean-Honoré Fragonard, such as shown here (detail).
The Wallace Collection, London/The Bridgeman Art Library, London

◄ *Jacques-Louis David* THE OATH OF THE HORATII **The greatest innovation in French painting came in reaction to the artificiality of the rococo style and subject matter, with a return to favor of "noble simplicity and calm grandeur." This neoclassical style found its supreme expression in the work of Jacques-Louis David. Such history paintings as** *The Oath of the Horatii* **evoked the ideal of civic virtue in ancient Greek and Roman civilization.**
Scala/Art Resource, NY

by sponsoring an annual public exhibition, or "salon," starting in 1737. People could view the canvases chosen by the Academy for these exhibitions and could reach their own judgments about the painters. In this way a public sphere of cultural discourse came into being, where once the official word of the Academy had determined the matter of taste and reputation in painting.

David and Greuze David, a brilliant painter in the neoclassical style, won the greatest renown in this arena of public opinion during the 1780s. He skillfully celebrated the values of the ancient world in such historical paintings as *The Oath of the Horatii* (see figure, above), *The Death of Socrates,* and *Brutus.* Discarding many of the standard conventions for history painting (and thereby drawing criticism from the Academy), David overwhelmed the public with his vivid imagery and the emotional force of his compositions. His paintings of the 1780s unmistakably conveyed a yearning for civic virtue and patriotism that had yet to find its political outlet in France. Not surprisingly, David became the most engaged and triumphant painter of the French Revolution.

In an entirely different vein, a few eighteenth-century artists chose more mundane and "realistic" subjects or themes for their canvases, parallel in some respects to what novelists and playwrights were doing. Jean-Baptiste Greuze, for example, made a hit in the Parisian exhibitions of the 1770s with his sentimentalized paintings of ordinary people in family settings caught in a dramatic situation, such as the death of a father or the banishment of a disobedient son. William Hogarth, a superb London engraver who worked through the medium of prints and book illustrations, went further down the social pyramid with his remarkable scenes of life among the working classes and the poor.

III. Popular Culture

◆

While the cultural world of aristocratic and middle-class elites has been extensively studied, the culture of artisans, peasants, and the urban poor remains more dimly known. In those sectors of society, culture primarily meant recreation, and it was essentially public and collective. Despite traditions of elementary schooling in certain regions and the spread of literacy among some groups, literacy rates remained generally low. Popular culture did have its written forms, but these were less prevalent than the oral traditions embodied in songs, folktales, and proverbs. Despite the rare firsthand traces of popular culture in the historical record, it is possible to suggest the rich variety of sociability and recreational practice among working people in traditional society.

◆ POPULAR LITERATURE

Far removed from the markets for Voltaire and the *Gentleman's Magazine* existed a distinct world of popular literature—the reading matter consumed by journeymen and peasants, the poor and the almost poor, those who could barely read and those who could not read at all. From the seventeenth through the early nineteenth century, but particularly in the eighteenth century, publishers produced for this audience small booklets written anonymously, printed on cheap paper, and costing only a few pennies. These brochures were sold by itinerant peddlers who knew the tastes of their customers; presumably the booklets were often read aloud by those who could read to those who could not.

This popular literature took three major forms. Religious material included devotional tracts, saints' lives, catechisms, manuals of penitence, and Bible stories, all written simply and generously laced with miracles. Readers who were preoccupied with fears of death and damnation

▼ **A page from an English almanac of 1769 on the month of July includes saints' days, information about likely weather patterns, and advice about agricultural matters and health care.**
General Research Division, New York Public Library, Astor, Lenox, and Tilden Foundations

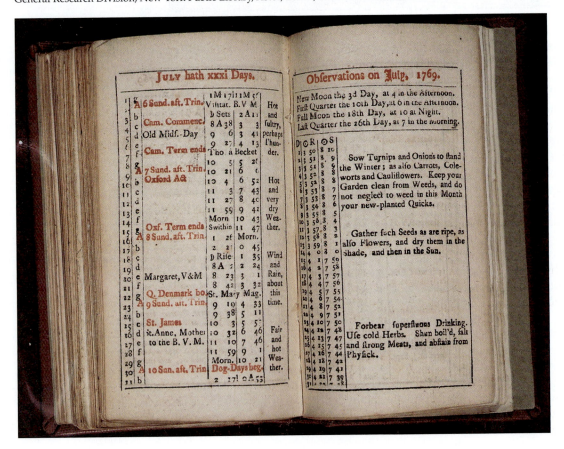

sought reassurance in these works that a virtuous life would end in salvation. Almanacs constituted a second type of popular literature, which appealed to the readers' concern for getting along in this life. Almanacs and how-to-live-successfully pamphlets discussed things like the kinds of potions to take for illnesses and featured astrology—how to read the stars and other signs for clues about the future. The third type of popular literature provided entertainment: tales and fables, burlesques and crude satires, mixtures of fiction and history in which miraculous events frequently helped bring the story to a satisfactory conclusion.

Although useful information may have trickled down through these booklets, most of them were escapist. The religiosity and supernatural events of popular literature separate it from the growing rationalism and secularism of elite culture. Moreover, it could be argued that by ignoring such problems as food shortages, high taxes, and material insecurity, popular writings fostered submissiveness, a fatalistic acceptance of a dismal status quo. Glimpsing the content of this popular literature helps us understand why Voltaire had no hope of extending his ideas on religion to the masses.

Oral Tradition Almanacs and pamphlets for working people were produced by outsiders, printers and writers who were themselves well educated. Oral tradition encompassed more authentic forms of popular culture: folktales told at the fireside on long winter nights, songs passed on from generation to generation, sayings that embodied the conventional wisdom of the people.

Themes touching on hunger, sex, or oppression were more likely to turn up in songs or oral tales than in booklets. Songs and tales expressed the joyful bawdiness of ordinary men and women but also the ever-present hardships and dangers of daily life: the endless drudgery of work in the fields, the gnawing ache of an empty stomach, the cruelty of parental neglect or mean stepparents, the desperation of beggars on the road. The most fantastic tales evoked a threatening world in which strangers might turn out to be princes or good fairies but might just as well turn into wolves or witches. Oral tradition also celebrated

the shrewdness and cunning of ordinary people struggling for survival, in the spirit of the saying: "Better a knave than a fool." Often rendered in local dialects, these tales or songs would have been incomprehensible to an educated Parisian, Londoner, or Viennese.

◆ LITERACY AND PRIMARY SCHOOLING

The Wars of Religion had spurred the spread of literacy and elementary schooling in Europe. Protestantism explicitly promoted literacy so that Christians could read their Bibles directly; strongly Protestant societies such as Scotland, Switzerland, and Sweden had unusually high rates of literacy by the eighteenth century. The Catholic Church, as well, believed that the spread of literacy would serve its cause in the battle against heresy. While teaching reading, Catholic schoolmasters could provide religious instruction and could socialize children into the beliefs and behavior of a Catholic way of life.

A unique study of literacy in France carried out in the late nineteenth century, based on signatures versus Xs on parish marriage registers all across the country, indicates a national literacy rate (meaning the ability to read) in 1686 of about 21 percent, which reached 37 percent a century later. These national averages, however, conceal striking regional and social disparities. The south of France had much lower rates than the north/northeast, and rural literacy rates lagged significantly behind those of the towns. While agricultural laborers rarely could read, urban artisans were generally literate. The widest gap of all, however, separated men from women, the rates in 1786 being 47 and 27 percent, respectively. Similarly, estimates for England suggest a male literacy rate of slightly under 60 percent and a female rate of about 40 percent.

Primary Education Schooling was not intended to transform society or lift the mass of people out of the situations into which they were born. On the contrary, it was supposed to maintain the social order and reinforce the family in promoting piety and decent behavior among the young. Many among the elites (including Voltaire) were

▲ **Most eighteenth-century elementary school teachers used the extremely inefficient individual method of instruction, in which pupils read to the teacher from whatever book they happened to bring from home, while the other pupils occupied themselves as best they could.**
© Tallandier, Bibliothèque des Art Decoratif, Paris. Photo Jean-Loup Charmet.

skeptical about the value of education for peasants and laborers. Might it not confuse them, or make it more difficult for them to accept the drudgery to which they seemed destined? Peasant or laboring parents might well have shared such skepticism about educating their young. Education could seem a waste of time when their children could be contributing to the family's livelihood; they might especially begrudge spending the money on tuition that most elementary schooling required.

A village usually hired a schoolmaster in consultation with the pastor or priest; schools usually straddled community and church, since the schoolmaster often served as the pastor's aide. Except in towns that had charitable endowments to support schooling, the parents, the village, or some combination of the two paid the schoolmaster, and for that reason numerous villages did

without any schooling. Even a modest tuition could deter impoverished parents from hiring a master, enrolling their children, or keeping them in school for a sufficient time. Since schoolmasters taught reading first and writing separately and later, many pupils, especially girls, were not kept in school long enough to learn how to write anything but their names. Schooling, in other words, was largely demand-driven, the product of a community's level of wealth and interest. When a region achieved a critical mass of literacy, however, interest in schooling generally became more widespread and gradually reached lower down the social scale.

Schooling in Central Europe While England and France left primary schooling entirely to the chance of local initiative, the Habsburg monarchy seriously promoted primary education and thereby became the first Catholic realm to do so. The Habsburg General School Ordinance of 1774 authorized state subsidies, in combination with local funds, for the support of a school in almost every parish. Attendance was supposed to be compulsory, though the state had no way to enforce it. The state also intended to train future teachers at institutions called normal schools. A similar two-pronged strategy was adopted in Prussia under Frederick II at about the same time, although little was done to implement it.

In Prussia, as in most of Europe, schoolmasters remained barely competent and poorly paid. Frederick II indeed had a limiting vision of popular education: "It is enough for the country people to learn only a little reading and writing. . . . Instruction must be planned so that they receive only what is most essential for them but which is designed to keep them in the villages and not influence them to leave." As elsewhere in Europe, the goals of elementary schooling were to inculcate religion and morality, propagate the virtues of hard work, and promote sobriety and deference to one's superiors.

◆ SOCIABILITY AND RECREATION

If the educated elites had their salons, masonic lodges, and learned academies, the common people also formed organized cultural groups. Many artisans, for example, belonged to secret societies that combined fraternal and trade-union functions. Young unmarried artisans frequently traveled the country, stopping periodically to work with comrades in other towns in order to hone their skills. Artisans also relied on their associations for camaraderie and ritual celebrations. Rivalries among federations of artisan associations occasionally led to pitched battles, however—a far cry from the nineteenth-century ideal of labor solidarity. Married artisans often joined religious confraternities, which honored a patron saint and ensured a dignified funeral when they died, or mutual aid societies to which they contributed small monthly dues to pay for assistance if illness or accident should strike.

Taverns and Festivals Corresponding to the coffeehouses of the urban middle classes were the taverns in working-class neighborhoods. These noisy, crowded places catered to a poor clientele, especially on Sunday and on Monday, which working people often took as a day off, honoring (as they put it) "Saint Monday." The urban common people were first beginning to consume wine in the eighteenth century, still something of a luxury except in its cheapest watered form. In England gin was the poor person's drink, cheap and plentiful until the government levied a hefty excise tax after realizing that too many people were drinking themselves into disability and death—a concern depicted in Hogarth's etchings, p. 694.

More commonly, drinking was not done in morbid fashion but as part of a healthy and vibrant outdoor life. In England, before the spread of industrialization changed the cultural as well as physical landscape, popular pastimes followed a calendar of holidays that provided occasions for group merrymaking, eating, drinking, dressing-up, contests, and games. Local festivals were particularly comfortable settings for single young men and women to meet each other. The highlight of a country year usually came in early autumn after the summer harvest was in, when most villages held a public feast that lasted several days. In Catholic countries similar festivities were often linked with church rituals. Popular observances included the commemoration of local patron saints, pilgrimages to holy places, and the period of Carnival before Lent.

Sports A growing "commercialization of leisure" in the eighteenth century supported new spectator sports, such as horse racing and boxing matches. Blood sports constituted a more prevalent popular recreation. Bullbaiting, for example, involved setting loose a pack of dogs on a tethered steer. These events were usually collaborations between a butcher (who provided the steer, its meat to be sold later) and an innkeeper (whose yard served as the arena and who sold refreshments to the spectators). Cockfighting, similar in its gory results, attracted gentlemen and commoners alike, who enjoyed wagering on the outcome.

In early modern Europe, gentlefolk and commoners had been accustomed to mixing in recreational and religious settings: fairs and markets,

▲ In his *Gin Lane* etching of 1750, Hogarth depicted the results of excessive gin drinking by the English common people as death, apathy, and moral decay. A cheerful companion piece called *Beer Street*, however, suggested that drinking in moderation was an acceptable practice.

Hogarth, *Gin Lane*. The Metropolitan Museum of Art, Harris Brisbane Dick Fund, 1932. Photography © 2002 The Metropolitan Museum of Art, New York.

Hogarth, *Beer Street*. The Metropolitan Museum of Art, Harris Brisbane Dick Fund, 1932. [32.35 (123)]. Photograph © 2002 The Metropolitan Museum of Art, New York.

sporting events, village or town festivals, Carnival in Catholic countries. But in the eighteenth century, as aristocrats and bourgeois alike became more concerned with good manners and refinement, these elite groups began to distance themselves from the bawdy and vulgar behavior of ordinary people. With growing intolerance, they censured popular recreational culture in the hope of "reforming" the people into a more sober and orderly lifestyle. Social status was based on birth or wealth, but cultural taste was becoming its behavioral marker.

SUMMARY

◆

The philosophes, celebrated members of Europe's cultural establishment by the 1770s, hoped that their society would gradually reform itself under their inspiration. Although these writers criticized their society, they were not its subverters. Distrustful of the uneducated masses and afraid of popular emotion, superstition, and disorder, the philosophes were anything but democrats. Nonetheless, the Enlightenment challenged basic traditional values of European society: from Voltaire's polemics against Christianity through the sober social science of Diderot's *Encyclopedia* to the impassioned writings of Rousseau. Along with a flood of "bad books"—the pornography and scandal sheets of the clandestine publishers—booksellers, writers, and journalists disseminated critical ideas among Europe's educated men and women. The philosophes challenged the automatic respect for convention and authority, promoted the habit of independent reflection, and implanted the conviction that the reform of institutions was both necessary and possible. They promoted a climate that put the status quo on the defensive and in which revolution—when provoked under particular circumstances— would not be unthinkable.

QUESTIONS FOR FURTHER THOUGHT

◆

1. What were the core values of the Enlightenment and how would you assess their strengths and weaknesses? What might have produced a backlash against Enlightenment values in subsequent periods? How might one defend them today?

2. How does the music, painting, and literature of the eighteenth century compare to the high culture of earlier periods you have studied, such as the Renaissance or the seventeenth century? Has the social or political context of cultural life changed? Were there comparable changes in the realm of popular culture? Why, or why not?

3. What do you make of Jean-Jacques Rousseau?

RECOMMENDED READING

◆

Sources

Gay, Peter (ed.). *The Enlightenment: a Comprehensive Anthology*. 1973.

Gendzier, Stephen (ed.). *Denis Diderot: The Encyclopedia: Selections*. 1967.

*Jacob, Margaret C. *The Enlightenment: A Brief History with Documents*. 2001.

Mohl, Mary R., and Helene Koon (eds.). *The Female Spectator: English Women Writers Before 1800*. 1977.

Vigée-Lebrun, Marie-Louise . . . Élisabeth. *Memoirs*. S. Evans (ed.). 1989. Memoirs of the most notable female painter in eighteenth-century France.

*Voltaire. *The Portable Voltaire*. 1977.

Studies

*Brewer, John. *The Pleasures of the Imagination: English Culture in the Eighteenth Century*. 1997. A lively, panoramic survey of the production and consumption of high culture in all its forms.

Bruford, W. H. *Germany in the Eighteenth Century: The Social Background of the Literary Revival*. 1952. A useful survey.

Capp, Bernard. *English Almanacs, 1500–1800: Astrology and the Popular Press*. 1979. A probing study of the most important genre of popular literature.

*Chartier, Roger. *The Cultural Origins of the French Revolution*. 1991. A synthesis of recent research on publishing, the public sphere, and the emergence of new political attitudes.

Cranston, Maurice. *Jean-Jacques, The Noble Savage,* and *The Solitary Self*. 1982, 1991, and 1995. A three-volume study of the life and work of Rousseau, critical but sympathetic.

*Crow, Thomas. *Painters and Public Life in Eighteenth-Century Paris*. 1985. A pioneering work on the development of a public sphere of critical discourse about art.

*Darnton, Robert. *The Forbidden Best Sellers of Pre-Revolutionary France*. 1995. A pathbreaking work on the circulation, content, and impact of banned books.

*Gay, Peter. *The Enlightenment: An Interpretation*. 2 vols. 1966 and 1969. A masterly, full-bodied exposition of Enlightenment thought.

*Goodman, Dena. *The Republic of Letters: a Cultural History of the French Enlightenment*. 1994. Focuses on the salons and the roles of women in cultural and intellectual life.

*Hampson, Norman. *A Cultural History of the Enlightenment*. 1969. A good general introduction to Enlightenment ideas.

*Isherwood, Robert. *Farce and Fantasy: Popular Entertainment in Eighteenth-Century Paris*. 1986. A cultural and institutional history of fairs and popular theater.

Malcolmson, R. W. *Popular Recreations in English Society, 1700–1850*. 1973. A good survey of a neglected subject.

*Maza, Sarah. *Private Lives and Public Affairs: the Causes Célèbres of Pre-Revolutionary France*. 1993. An original analysis of scandals and lawsuits that raised social consciousness in the later eighteenth century.

McClellan, James. *Science Reorganized: Scientific Societies in the Eighteenth Century*. 1985.

Melton, James Van Horn. *Absolutism and the Eighteenth-Century Origins of Compulsory Schooling in Prussia and Austria*. 1988. An excellent comparative study.

Munck, Thomas. *The Enlightenment: A Comparative Social History*. 2000.

Palmer, Robert R. *Catholics and Unbelievers in Eighteenth-Century France*. 1939. The response of Catholic intellectuals to the century's philosophic thought.

Payne, Harry. *The Philosophes and the People*. 1976. An analysis of the Enlightenment's liberal elitism.

Porter, Roy, and Mikulas Teich (eds.). *The Enlightenment in National Context*. 1981. A comprehensive geographic overview.

*Roche, Daniel. *The People of Paris: An Essay on Popular Culture in the Eighteenth Century*. 1987. On the material culture and aspirations of ordinary Parisians.

*Spencer, Samia (ed.). *French Women and the Age of Enlightenment.* 1984. A pioneering collection of essays on a variety of literary and historical themes.

Venturi, Franco. *Italy and the Enlightenment.* 1972. Essays on important Italian philosophes by a leading historian.

*Watt, Ian. *The Rise of the Novel: Studies of Defoe, Richardson, and Fielding.* 1957. The view from England.

Wilson, Arthur. *Diderot.* 1972. An exhaustive, reliable biography of the consummate French philosophe.

*Available in paperback.

▲ *THE STORMING OF THE BASTILLE.*
Bulloz/© Photo RMN/Art Resource, NY

THE FRENCH REVOLUTION

Well into the eighteenth century, the long-standing social structures and political institutions of Europe were securely entrenched. Most monarchs still claimed to hold their authority directly from God. In cooperation with their aristocracies, they presided over realms composed of distinct orders of citizens, or *estates* as they were sometimes known. Each order had its particular rights, privileges, and obligations. But pressures for change were building during the century. In France, the force of public opinion grew increasingly potent by the 1780s. A financial or political crisis that could normally be managed by the monarchy threatened to snowball in this new environment. This vulnerability was less evident in Austria, Prussia, and Russia, however, where strong monarchs instituted reforms to streamline their governments. Similarly, in Britain the political system proved resilient despite explosions of discontent at home and across the Atlantic.

Unquestionably, then, the French Revolution constituted the pivotal event of European history in the late eighteenth century. From its outbreak in 1789, the Revolution transformed the nature of sovereignty and law in France. Under its impetus, civic and social institutions were renewed, from local government and schooling to family relations and assistance for the poor. Soon its ideals of liberty, equality, and fraternity resonated across the borders of other European states, especially after war broke out in 1792 and French armies took the offensive.

The French Revolution's innovations defined the foundations of a liberal society and polity. Both at home and abroad, however, the new regime faced formidable opposition, and its struggle for survival propelled it in unanticipated directions. Some unforeseen turns, such as democracy and republicanism, became durable precedents for the future even if they soon aborted. Other developments, such as the Reign of Terror, seemed to nullify the original liberal values of 1789. The bloody struggles of the Revolution thus cast a shadow over this transformative event as they dramatized the brutal dilemma of means versus ends.

CHAPTER 20. THE FRENCH REVOLUTION							
	Social Structure	Body Politic	Changes in the Organization of Production and in the Impact of Technology	Evolution of Family and Changing Gender Roles	War	Religion	Cultural Expression
I. Reform and Political Crisis		�			▪		
II. 1789: The French Revolution	▪	▪					▪
III. The Reconstruction of France	▪	▪		▪		▪	
IV. The Second Revolution	▪	▪		▪	▪	▪	

I. Reform and Political Crisis

To put the French Revolution into perspective, it helps to compare political tensions and conflicts elsewhere in Europe. Strong monarchs with reputations for being "enlightened" reigned in Prussia, Austria, Spain, and even Russia. Their stature seemingly contrasts with the mediocrity of Louis XV and Louis XVI, who ruled in France. Yet the former did not get far in reforming their realms or granting rights and freedom to their subjects. The limits of "enlightened absolutism," therefore, should be kept in mind when considering the crisis that confronted France. In the Low Countries, meanwhile, conflicts between princes, oligarchies, and popular forces erupted into failed revolutions, while in Britain energetic movements for political reform ran into determined opposition. This rigidity had a particular impact across the Atlantic, where Britain's thirteen colonies in North America were driven to rebellion and a revolutionary war for independence.

◆ "ENLIGHTENED ABSOLUTISM" IN CENTRAL AND EASTERN EUROPE

During the late nineteenth century, German historians invented the concept of "enlightened absolutism" to describe the Prussian and Habsburg monarchies of the eighteenth century. Critical of the ineptitude and weakness of French monarchs in that period, these historians argued that the strength of an enlightened ruler had been the surest basis for progress in early modern Europe. A king who ruled in his subjects' interest, they implied, avoided violent conflicts like those of the French Revolution. Earlier strong monarchs, such as Philip II of Spain and France's Louis XIV (who had once declared: "I am the state"), had been irresponsible; in contrast, these German historians argued, Frederick II of Prussia symbolized the enlightened phase of absolutism with his comment that the ruler is merely the "first servant of the state."

Previous chapters, however, have demonstrated that monarchs dealt with the same fundamental issues during all stages of absolutism. They always strove to assert their authority over their subjects and to maximize the power of their state in relation to other realms, principally by means of territorial expansion. Any notion that Enlightenment thinking caused monarchs to desist from these efforts is misleading. Still, several eighteenth-century monarchs did initiate reforms from above and did modify their styles of ruling in order to appear more modern or enlightened. Frederick II of Prussia and Catherine II of Russia, for example, lavished praise on Voltaire and Diderot, and those philosophes returned the compliment. These rulers may simply have been engaging in public relations. Yet the fact that they seemed supportive of such controversial writers suggests that absolutism had indeed adopted a new image.

Catherine the Great (r. 1762–1796) played this game to its limit. In 1767 she announced a new experiment in the direction of representative government—a policy hailed as a landmark by her philosophe admirers, who were too remote from St. Petersburg to see its insincerity. Catherine convened a Legislative Commission, a body of delegates from various strata of Russian society who were invited to present grievances, propose reforms, and then debate the proposals. In the end, however, she sent the delegates home under the pretext of having to turn her attention to a war with Turkey. Little came of the Legislative Commission except some good publicity for Catherine. In fact, she later promulgated a Charter of the Nobility, which, instead of limiting the nobility's privileges, strengthened their corporate status and increased their control over their serfs in exchange for their loyalty to the throne.

Conceptions of Enlightened Rule in Germany In justification of absolute monarchy, eighteenth-century German writers depicted the state as a machine and the ruler as its mainspring. Progress came from sound administration, through an enlightened monarch and well-trained officials. In keeping with this notion, German universities began to train government bureaucrats, and professors offered courses in the science of public finance and administration called *cameralism*. Before long, the governments of Prussia and Austria introduced the rudiments of a civil service system.

The orders for the bureaucracy came from the monarchs, who were expected to dedicate themselves to the welfare of their subjects in return for their subjects' obedience. The framework for this command-obedience chain was to be a coherent body of public law, fairly administered by state officials. According to its advocates, this system would produce the rule of law, a *Rechtsstaat*, without the need for a written constitution or a representative parliament. The ruler and his or her officials, following their sense of public responsibility and rational analysis, would ensure the citizens' rights and well-being.

◆ JOSEPH II AND THE LIMITS OF ABSOLUTISM

Joseph II, coruler of the Habsburg Empire with his mother, Maria Theresa, from 1765 and sole ruler in the 1780s, vigorously promoted reform from above. Unlike Frederick or Catherine, he did not openly identify with the philosophes, and he maintained his own Catholic faith. But Joseph proved to be the most innovative of the century's major rulers as well as one of its most autocratic personalities. It was a problematic combination.

Sound rule for Emperor Joseph involved far more than the customary administrative and financial modernization necessary for survival in the competitive state system. With startling boldness he implemented several reforms long advocated by Enlightenment thinkers: freedom of expression, religious toleration, greater state control over the Catholic Church, and legal reform. A new criminal code, for example, reduced the use of the death penalty, ended judicial torture, and allowed for no class differences in the application of the laws. By greatly reducing royal censorship, Joseph made it possible for Vienna to become a major center of literary activity. And we have already noted Joseph's remarkable Edicts of Religious Toleration for Protestants and for Jews. But Joseph's religious policies did not stop there. To make the Catholic Church serve its parishioners better, Joseph forced the clergy to modernize its rituals and services. Most of his Catholic subjects, however, preferred their traditional ways to Joseph's streamlined brand of Catholicism. These "reforms" proved extremely unpopular.

Agrarian Reform Joseph's most ambitious policies aimed to transform the economic and social position of the peasants. In this respect the Habsburg emperor acted far more boldly than any other eighteenth-century sovereign. Agrarian reform was generally the weak side of "enlightened absolutism," since Frederick II and Catherine II did little to improve the lot of the peasants or serfs in their realms. Joseph, however, set out to eradicate serfdom and to convert Habsburg peasants into free individuals in command of their persons and of the land they cultivated.

By royal decree, Joseph abolished personal servitude and gave peasants the right to move, marry, and enter any trade they wished. He then promulgated laws to secure peasants' control over the land they worked. Finally and most remarkably, he sought to limit the financial obligations of peasant tenants to their lords and to the state. All land was to be surveyed and subject to a uniform

▲ **Joseph II, shown here visiting a peasant's field, actually promulgated his momentous agrarian reform edicts without any significant consultation with the peasants before or after the fact.**
Austrian Press & Information Service

tax. Twelve percent of the land's annual yield would go to the state and a maximum of 18 percent would go to the lord. This tax replaced previous seigneurial obligations in which peasants owed service to their lord that could consume more than one hundred days of labor a year.

Joseph ordered these reforms in an authoritarian fashion, with little consultation and no consent from any quarter. Predictably, these reforms provoked fierce opposition among the landowning nobles. But they also perplexed most peasants, who already distrusted the government because of its arbitrary religious policies. Joseph made no effort to build support among the peasants by carefully explaining the reforms, let alone by modifying their details after getting feedback from the grass roots. As a sympathetic chronicler of Joseph's reign observed, "He brought in his beneficial measures in an arbitrary manner."

His arbitrary manner, however, was not incidental. Joseph acknowledged no other way of doing things, no limitation on his own sovereignty. In reaction to the opposition that his reforms aroused, he moved to suppress dissent in the

firmest possible way. Not only did he restore censorship in his last years, but he elevated the police department to the status of an imperial ministry and gave it unprecedented powers. By the time he died, in 1790, Joseph was a disillusioned man. His realm resembled less a *Rechtsstaat* than a police state, and his successors quickly restored serfdom.

◆ CONSTITUTIONAL CRISES IN THE WEST

While "enlightened absolutists" reigned in Austria, Prussia, and Russia, political tension and spirited debate over the institutions of government erupted in several Western European countries. To understand these crises, we must recall the role of estates in European history. The term is both a social and a political signifier. Socially, every person belonged to one legally distinct order or another. The clergy usually constituted the First Estate of the realm, the nobles formed the Second Estate, and both maintained a common aristocratic viewpoint. The remainder of the population constituted the Third Estate. In the past the estates had sent representatives to national and provincial assemblies or diets, which shared in making government decisions. But absolutism had drastically curtailed the political role of the estates, as we have seen in previous chapters. It was the Third Estate's new bid for prominence and power in several countries at the expense of the dominant aristocratic orders that made the late eighteenth century, as historian R. R. Palmer calls it, "the age of the democratic revolution."

Monarchs and Aristocrats On one level monarchs and the privileged orders were perennial and natural rivals. The rights and privileges of various groups reduced the fiscal resources of kings and princes and hampered their ability to pursue internal reform. Eighteenth-century struggles over political power often began when rulers initiated changes in traditional political or economic arrangements. While monarchs might wish to allocate a smaller place to nobles in the business of government, nobles would not willingly cede the privileges they held and might demand an even larger share in the exercise of power.

Aristocracies all over Europe thus sought to advance their fortunes and consolidate their roles in their country's traditional or unwritten constitutions. In the last decades of the century, the nobility continued to enjoy a near monopoly over high offices in the state, the army, and the Church. In 1781, for example, officers' commissions in the French army were limited almost exclusively to those who could prove descent from four generations of nobility. Aristocrats in several countries demanded that local assemblies of estates, which they expected to dominate, be granted a larger share of political power.

Upheavals over such issues erupted in the Austrian Netherlands (Belgium) and in the Dutch Netherlands, where provincial oligarchies rebelled against the centralizing reforms of their princes: Joseph II in Belgium and the Prince of Orange in the Dutch Netherlands. In each case a more democratic element of unprivileged commoners, including urban artisans, turned these conflicts into triangular struggles as they took up arms to oppose both princely tyranny and oligarchic privilege. To a certain extent, these Dutch and Belgian "patriots," as they called themselves,

provided a foretaste of the French Revolution. Their suppression, in turn, suggested that counterrevolution was a force to be reckoned with.

◆ UPHEAVALS IN THE BRITISH EMPIRE

An aggressive monarch, George III, helped ignite political unrest in Great Britain. He was intent on advancing royal authority, but rather than bypass Parliament altogether, he simply tried, as Whig ministers had before him, to control its members through patronage and influence. The Whig aristocrats saw this operation as a threat to their own traditional power. Not only did they oppose the king and his ministers in Parliament, but they enlisted the support of citizens' groups outside of Parliament as well. These organizations were calling for political reform, including representation in Parliament proportionate to population, stricter laws against political corruption, and greater freedom of the press.

"Wilkes and Liberty" John Wilkes, a member of Parliament and a journalist, became the center of this rising storm. Wilkes viciously attacked the king's prime minister, and by implication the king himself, over the terms of the Treaty of Paris, which ended the Seven Years' War in 1763. The government arrested him for seditious libel on a general warrant. When the courts quashed the indictment, the government then accused Wilkes of having authored a libelous pornographic poem, and this time he fled to France to avoid prison. He stayed in France for four years; but in 1768, still under indictment, he returned to stand once more for Parliament. Three times he was reelected, and three times the House of Commons refused to seat him. With the ardent support of radicals and to the acclaim of crowds in London, who marched to the chant of "Wilkes and Liberty," Wilkes finally took his seat in 1774.

Agitation for parliamentary reform drew support primarily from shopkeepers, artisans, and property owners, who had the franchise in a few districts but were denied it in most others. Thus, even without a right to vote, English citizens could engage in politics and mobilize the power of public opinion, in this case by rallying to Wilkes. Most radicals called only for political reform, not for the overthrow of the British political system. They retained a measure of respect for the nation's political traditions, which ideally guaranteed the rights of "freeborn Englishmen."

Rebellion in America   Great Britain did face revolutionary action in the thirteen North American colonies. George III and his prime minister, Lord North, attempted to force the colonies to pay the costs, past and present, of their own defense. The policy would have meant an increase in taxes and a centralization of authority in the governance of the British empire. Colonial landowners, merchants, and artisans of the eastern seaboard organized petitions and boycotts in opposition to the proposed fiscal and constitutional changes.

The resistance in North America differed fundamentally from comparable movements in Europe. American political leaders did not appeal to a body of privileges that the actions of the monarchy were allegedly violating. Instead, they appealed to traditional rights supposedly enjoyed by all British subjects, regardless of status, and to theories of popular sovereignty and natural rights advanced by John Locke and other English libertarian writers. When conciliation and compromise with the British government failed, the American Declaration of Independence in 1776 gave eloquent expression to those concepts. The lack of a rigid system of estates and hereditary privileges in American society, the fluid boundaries that separated the social strata, and the traditions of local

▼ **The committee that drafted the American Declaration of Independence included John Adams, Thomas Jefferson, and Benjamin Franklin, all shown here standing at the desk.**
Yale University Art Gallery, Trumball Collection

government in the colonies—from town meetings in New England to the elected legislatures that had advised colonial governors—blunted the kinds of conflicts between aristocrats and commoners that derailed incipient revolutionary movements in Ireland, Belgium, and the Dutch Netherlands.

These differences help to explain the unique character of the American rebellion, which was simultaneously a war for independence and a political revolution. The theories that supported the rebellion, and the continuing alliance between social strata, made it the most democratic revolution of the eighteenth century before 1789. The American Revolution created the first state governments, and ultimately a national government, in which the exercise of power was grounded not on royal sovereignty or traditional privilege but on the participation and consent of male citizens (apart from the numerous black slaves, whose status did not change). Even more important as a historical precedent, perhaps, it was the first successful rebellion by overseas colonies against their European masters.

II. 1789: The French Revolution

Although the rebellion in America stirred sympathy and interest across the Atlantic, it seemed remote from the realities of Europe. The French Revolution of 1789 proved to be the turning point in European history. Its sheer radicalism, creativity, and claims of universalism made it unique. Its ultimate slogan—"Liberty, Equality, Fraternity"—expressed social and civic ideals that became the foundations of modern Western civilization. In the name of individual liberty, French revolutionaries swept away the institutionalized constraints of the old regime: seigneurial charges upon the land, vestiges of feudalism, tax privileges, guild monopolies on commerce, and even (in 1794) black slavery overseas. The revolutionaries held that legitimate governments required written constitutions, elections, and powerful legislatures. They demanded equality before the law for all persons and uniformity of institutions for all regions of the country, denying the claims to special treatment of privileged groups, provinces, towns,

or religions. The term *fraternity* expressed a different kind of revolutionary goal. Rousseauist in inspiration, it meant that all citizens regardless of social class or region shared a common fate in society and that the nation's well-being could override the interests of individual citizens.

◆ ORIGINS OF THE REVOLUTION

Those who made the Revolution believed they were rising against despotic government, in which citizens had no voice, and against inequality and privilege. Yet the government of France at that time was no more tyrannical or unjust than it had been in the past. On the contrary, a process of modest reform had been under way for several decades. What, then, set off the revolutionary upheaval? What had failed in France's long-standing political system?

An easy answer would be to point to the incompetence of King Louis XVI (r. 1774–1792) and his queen, Marie Antoinette. Louis was good-natured but weak and indecisive, a man of limited intelligence who lacked self-confidence and who preferred hunting deer to supervising the business of government. By no stretch of the imagination was he an enlightened absolutist. Worse yet, his young queen, a Habsburg princess, was frivolous, meddlesome, and tactless. But even the most capable French ruler could not have escaped challenge and unrest in the 1780s. It is the roots of the political crisis, not its mismanagement, that claim the historian's attention.

The Cultural Climate In eighteenth-century France, as we have seen, intellectual ferment preceded political revolt. For decades the philosophes had questioned accepted political and religious beliefs. They undermined confidence that traditional ways were the best ways. But the philosophes harbored deep-seated fears of the uneducated masses and did not question the notion that educated and propertied elites should rule society; they wished only that the elites should be more enlightened and more open to new ideas. Indeed, the Enlightenment had become respectable by the 1770s, a kind of intellectual establishment. Rousseau damned that establishment and wrote of the need for simplicity, sincerity, and virtue, but the word *revolution* never flowed from his pen either.

More subversive perhaps than the writings of Enlightenment intellectuals were several sensational lawsuits centered on the scandalous doings of high aristocrats. The melodramatic legal briefs published by the lawyers in such cases were eagerly snatched up by the reading public along with the prohibited "bad books"—the clandestine gossip sheets, libels, exposés, and pornography—discussed earlier. All this material indirectly, at least, portrayed the French aristocracy as decadent and the monarchy as a ridiculous despotism. Royal officials and philosophes alike regarded the authors of this material as "the excrement of literature," as Voltaire put it. And writers forced to earn their living by turning out such stuff were no doubt embittered at being stuck on the bottom rung in the world of letters. Their resentment would explode once the Revolution began in 1789, and many became radical journalists either for or against the new regime. In itself, however, the "literary underground" of the old regime did not advocate, foresee, or directly cause the Revolution.

Class Conflict? Did the structure of French society, then, provoke the Revolution? Karl Marx, and the many historians inspired by him, certainly believed so. Marx saw the French Revolution as the necessary break marking the transition from the aristocratic feudalism of the Middle Ages to the era of middle-class capitalism. In this view, the French bourgeoisie, or middle classes, had been gaining in wealth during the eighteenth century and resented the privileges of the nobility, which placed obstacles in the path of their ambition. Though they framed their ideology in universal terms in 1789, the middle classes led the Revolution in order to change the political and social systems in their own interests.

Three decades of research have rendered this theory of the Revolution's origins untenable. Whether a sizable and coherent capitalist middle class actually existed in eighteenth-century France is questionable. In any case, the leaders of the Revolution in 1789 were lawyers, administrators, and liberal nobles, and rarely merchants or industrialists. Moreover, the barrier between the nobility of the Second Estate and the wealthy and educated members of the Third Estate was porous, the lines of social division frequently (though not always) blurred. Many members of the middle class identified themselves on official documents as "living nobly," as substantial property owners who did not work for a living. Conversely, wealthy nobles often invested in mining, overseas trade, and finance—activities usually associated with the middle classes. Even more important, the gap between the nobility and the middle classes was nothing compared with the gulf that separated both from the working people of town and country. In this revisionist historiography, the bourgeoisie did not make the Revolution so much as the Revolution made the bourgeoisie (see "On the Origins of the French Revolution").

Yet numerous disruptive pressures were at work in French society. A growing population left large numbers of young people in town and country struggling to attain a stable place in society. New images and attitudes rippled through the media of the day, despite the state's efforts to censor material it deemed subversive. The nobility, long since banished by Louis XIV from an independent role in monarchical government, chafed at its exclusion, while the prosperous middle classes too aspired to a more active role. The monarchy struggled to contain these forces within the established social and political systems. Until the 1780s it succeeded, but then its troubles began in earnest.

◆ FISCAL CRISIS AND POLITICAL DEADLOCK

When he took the throne in 1774, Louis XVI tried to conciliate elite opinion by recalling the Parlements, or sovereign law courts, that his grandfather had banished in 1770 for opposing his policies. This concession to France's traditional "unwritten constitution" did not suffice to smooth the new sovereign's road. Louis' new controller-general of finances, Jacques Turgot, encountered a storm of opposition from privileged groups to the reforms he proposed.

The Failure of Reform Turgot, an ally of the philosophes and an experienced administrator, hoped to encourage economic growth by a policy

ON THE ORIGINS OF THE FRENCH REVOLUTION

◆

A long-held view of the French Revolution's origins attributed the starring role to the middle class, "the rising bourgeoisie." Liberal historians of the nineteenth century regarded the middle class as the carrier of liberal ideals—individual freedom, civil equality, representative government—that finally came to fruition in the French Revolution. Marxists considered the triumph of capitalism to be the pivotal issue in modern history and linked it to the political ascendancy of the middle class in the French Revolution. In a sense, both versions of this "social interpretation" of the French Revolution read its causes back from its results. In his classic synthesis of 1939 embodying the social interpretation, for example, Georges Lefebvre begins with these observations:

"The ultimate cause of the French Revolution of 1789 goes deep into the history of France and of the western world. At the end of the eighteenth century the social structure of France was aristocratic. It showed the traces of having originated at a time when land was almost the only form of wealth, and when the possessors of land were the masters of those who needed it to work and to live. It is true that in the course of age-old struggles the king had been able gradually to deprive the lords of their political powers and subject nobles and clergy to his authority. But he had left them the first place in the social hierarchy.

"Meanwhile the growth of commerce and industry had created, step by step, a new form of wealth, mobile or commercial wealth, and a new class, called in France the bourgeoisie. . . . In the eighteenth century commerce, industry and finance occupied an increasingly important place in the national economy. It was the bourgeoisie that rescued the royal treasury in moments of crisis. . . . The role of the nobility had correspondingly declined; and the clergy, as the ideal which it proclaimed lost prestige, found its authority growing weaker. These groups preserved the highest rank in the legal structure of the country, but in reality economic power, personal abilities and confidence in the future had passed largely to the bourgeoisie. Such a discrepancy never lasts forever. The Revolution of 1789 restored the harmony between fact and law."

From Georges Lefebvre, *The Coming of the French Revolution*, R. R. Palmer (trans.) (Princeton University Press, 1989).

Since the 1950s, revisionist historians have challenged this "social interpretation" of the French Revolution. In his new synthesis, William Doyle summarizes some of their research and arguments.

"Money, not privilege, was the key to pre-revolutionary society in France. Wealth transcended all social barriers and bound great nobles and upper bourgeois together into an upper class unified by money. . . . Eighteenth-century capitalism was far from a bourgeois monopoly. One of its basic features was the heavy involvement of nobles. . . . [On the other hand,] the wealth of all social groups in pre-revolutionary France was overwhelmingly non-capitalist in nature. Capitalism had not become the dominant mode of production in the French economy before 1789. . . . there was between most of the nobility and the proprietary sectors of the middle class, a continuity of investment forms and socio-economic values that made them, economically, a single group.

"If the nobility and the bourgeoisie had so much in common, why did they become such implacable enemies in 1789? [Since] the Revolution could not be explained in economic terms as a clash of opposed interests. . . . it was time to revert to a political explanation of the Revolution's outbreak. The radical reforms of 1789 were products of a political crisis, and not the outcome of long-maturing social and economic trends. [As historian George Taylor concluded:] 'It was essentially a political revolution with social consequences and not a social revolution with political consequences.'"

From William Doyle, *Origins of the French Revolution* (Oxford University Press, 1988).

of nonintervention, or laissez-faire, that would give free play to economic markets and allow individuals maximum freedom to pursue their own economic interests. He proposed to remove all restrictions on commerce in grain and to abolish the guilds. In addition, he tried to cut down on expenses at court and to replace the obligation of peasants to work on the royal roads (the *corvée*) with a small new tax on all landholders. Privately, he also considered establishing elected advisory assemblies of landowners to assist in local administration. Vested interests, however, viewed Turgot as a dangerous innovator. When agitation against him mounted in the king's court at Versailles and in the Paris Parlement, Louis took the easy way out and dismissed his contentious minister. With Turgot went perhaps the last hope for significant reform in France under royal leadership.

Deficit Financing The king then turned to Jacques Necker, a banker from Geneva who had a reputation for financial wizardry. Necker had a shrewd sense of public relations. To finance the heavy costs of France's aid to the rebellious British colonies in North America, Necker avoided new taxes and instead floated a series of large loans at exorbitant interest rates as high as 10 percent. (England, through sound management of its public finances and public confidence in the government, financed its war effort with loans at only 3 or 4 percent interest.)

By the 1780s royal finances hovered in a state of permanent crisis. Direct taxes on land, borne mainly by the peasants, were extremely high but were levied inequitably. The great variations in taxation from province to province and the numerous exemptions for privileged groups were regarded by those who benefited from them as traditional liberties. Any attempt to revoke these privileges therefore appeared to be tyrannical. Meanwhile, indirect taxes on commercial activity (customs duties, excise or sales taxes, and royal monopolies on salt and tobacco) hit regressively at consumers, especially in the towns. Any tax increases or new taxes imposed by the monarchy at this point would be bitterly resented. At the same time, the cycle of borrowing—the alternative to increased taxes—had reached its limits. New loans would only raise the huge interest payments

already being paid out. By the 1780s those payments accounted for about half the royal budget and created additional budget deficits each year.

Calonne and the Assembly of Notables When the king's new controller-general, Charles Calonne, pieced all this information together in 1787, he warned that, contrary to Necker's rosy projections, the monarchy was facing outright bankruptcy. Though no way had yet been found to win public confidence and forge a consensus for fiscal reform, the monarchy had to act and could no longer rely on old expedients. Calonne accordingly proposed to establish a new tax, called the *territorial subvention*, to be levied on the yield of all landed property without exemptions. At the same time, he proposed to convene *provincial assemblies* elected by large landowners to advise royal officials on the collection and allocation of revenues.

Certain that the Parlements would reject this scheme, Calonne convinced the king to convene an Assembly of Notables, comprising about 150 influential men, mainly but not exclusively from the aristocracy, who might more easily be persuaded to support the reforms. To Calonne's shock, the Assembly of Notables refused to endorse the proposed decrees. Instead, they denounced the lavish spending of the court and insisted on auditing the monarchy's financial accounts. To save the day, Louis dismissed Calonne and appointed one of the notables, Archbishop Brienne, in his place. Brienne now submitted Calonne's proposals to the Parlement, which not only rejected them but also demanded that Louis convene the Estates General, a body representing the clergy, nobility, and Third Estate, which had not met since 1614. Louis responded by sending the members of the Parlements into exile. But a huge outcry in Paris and in the provinces against this arbitrary act forced the king to back down: After all, the whole purpose of Calonne's proposals had been to build public confidence in the government.

Facing bankruptcy and unable to float new loans in this atmosphere, the King recalled the Parlements, reappointed Necker, and agreed to convene the Estates General in May 1789. In the opinion of the English writer Arthur Young, who was visiting France, the kingdom was "on the verge of a revolution, but one likely to add to the scale of the nobility and clergy." The aristocracy's determined opposition was putting an end to absolutism in France. But it was not clear what would take its place.

◆ FROM THE ESTATES GENERAL TO THE NATIONAL ASSEMBLY

The calling of the Estates General in 1789 created extraordinary excitement across the land. The king invited his subjects to express their opinions about this great event, and thousands did so in pamphlet form. Here the "patriot," or liberal, ideology first took shape. Self-styled patriots came from the ranks of the nobility and clergy as well as from the middle classes; they opposed traditionalists, whom they labeled as "aristocrats." Their top priority was the method of voting to be used in the Estates General. While the king accorded the Third Estate twice as many delegates as the two higher orders, he refused to promise that the deputies would all vote together (by head) rather than separately in three chambers (by order). Voting by order would mean that the two upper chambers would outweigh the Third Estate no matter how many deputies it had. Patriots had hoped that the lines dividing the nobility from the middle class would crumble in a common effort by France's elites at reform. Instead, it appeared as if the Estates General might sharpen the lines of separation between the orders.

The Critique of Privilege   It did not matter that the nobility had led the fight against absolutism. Even if they endorsed new constitutional checks on absolutism and accepted equality in the allocation of taxes, nobles would still hold vastly disproportionate powers if the Estates General voted by order. In the most influential pamphlet about the Estates General, Emmanuel Sieyès posed the question, "What is the Third Estate?" and answered flatly, "Everything." "And what has it been until now in the political order?" he asked. Answer: "Nothing." The nobility, he claimed, monopolized all the lucrative positions in society while doing little of its productive work. In the manifestos of Sieyès and other patriots, the enemy was no longer simply absolutism but privilege as well.

Unlike reformers in England or the Belgian rebels against Joseph II or even the American revolutionaries of 1776, the French patriots did not simply claim that the king had violated historic traditions of liberty. Rather, they contemplated a complete break with a discredited past. As a basis for reform, they would substitute reason for tradition. It is this frame of mind that made the French Revolution so radical.

Cahiers and Elections   For the moment, however, the patriot spokesmen stood far in advance of opinion at the grass roots. The king had invited all citizens to meet in their local parishes to elect delegates to district electoral assemblies and to draft grievance petitions (*cahiers*) setting forth their views. The great majority of rural cahiers were highly traditional in tone and complained only of particular local ills or high taxes, expressing confidence that the king would redress them. Only a few cahiers from cities like Paris invoked concepts of natural rights and popular sovereignty or demanded that France must have a written constitution, that sovereignty belonged to the nation, or that feudalism and regional privileges should be abolished. It is impossible, in other words, to read in the cahiers the future course of the Revolution. Still, these gatherings of citizens promoted reflection on France's problems and encouraged expectations for change. They thereby helped raise the nation's political consciousness.

▼ **Suddenly free of traditional restrictions, hawkers sold a cascade of new pamphlets and journals in 1789.**
Bibliothèque Nationale de France, Paris

▲ **Thousands of pamphlets were published to discuss the calling of the Estates General in 1789, but the grievances and claims of the Third Estate translated most readily into vivid imagery and caricature; this print was titled "The Awakening of the Third Estate."**
Roger-Viollet/Bibliothèque Nationale de France, Paris

So too did the local elections, whose royal ground rules were remarkably democratic. Virtually every adult male taxpayer was eligible to vote for electors, who, in turn, met in district assemblies to choose representatives of the Third Estate to the Estates General. The electoral assemblies were a kind of political seminar, where articulate local leaders emerged to be sent by their fellow citizens as deputies to Versailles. Most of these deputies were lawyers or officials, without a single peasant or artisan among them. In the elections for the First Estate, meanwhile, parish priests rather than Church notables formed a majority of the deputies. And in the elections for the Second Estate, about one-third of the deputies could be described as liberal nobles or patriots, the rest traditionalists.

Deadlock and Revolution   Popular expectation that the monarchy would provide leadership in reform proved to be ill-founded. When the deputies to the Estates General met on May 5, Necker and Louis XVI spoke to them only in generalities and left unsettled whether the estates would vote by order or by head. The upper two estates proceeded to organize their own chambers, but the deputies of the Third Estate balked. Vainly inviting the others to join them, the Third Estate took a decisive revolutionary step on June 17 by proclaiming that it formed a "National Assembly." A few days later more than a third of the deputies from the clergy joined them. The king, on the other hand, decided to cast his lot with the nobility and locked the Third Estate out of its meeting hall until he could present his own

▲ When the king opened the meeting of the Estates General, the deputies for each estate were directed to sit in three separate sections of the hall.
Bulloz/© Photo RMN/Art Resource, NY

program. But the deputies moved to an indoor tennis court and swore that they would not separate until they had given France a constitution.

The king ignored this act of defiance and addressed the delegates of all three orders on June 23. He promised equality in taxation, civil liberties, and regular meetings of the Estates General at which, however, voting would be by order. France would be provided with a constitution, he pledged, "but the ancient distinction of the three orders will be conserved in its entirety." He then ordered the three estates to retire to their individual meeting halls, but the Third Estate refused to move. "The assembled nation cannot receive orders," declared its spokesman. Startled by the determination of the patriots, the king backed down. For the time being, he recognized the National Assembly and ordered deputies from all three estates to join it.

Thus, the French Revolution began as a nonviolent, "legal" revolution. By their own will, delegates elected by France's three estates to represent their own districts to the king became instead the representatives of the entire nation. As such, they claimed to be the sovereign power in France—a claim that the king now seemed powerless to contest. In fact, however, he was merely biding his time until he could deploy his army to subdue the capital and overwhelm the deputies at Versailles. Twenty thousand royal troops were ordered into the Paris region, due to arrive sometime in July.

◆ THE CONVERGENCE OF REVOLUTIONS

The political struggle at Versailles was not occurring in isolation. The mass of French citizens, politically aroused by elections to the Estates General, was also mobilizing over subsistence issues. The winter and spring of 1788–1789 had brought severe economic difficulties, as crop

▲ Jacques-Louis David's depiction of the Tennis Court Oath, one of the great historical paintings, captures the deputies' sense of idealism and purpose.
Giraudon/Art Resource, NY

failures and grain shortages almost doubled the price of flour and bread on which the population depended for subsistence. Unemployed vagrants filled the roads, angry consumers stormed grain convoys and marketplaces, and relations between town and country grew tense. Economic anxieties merged with rage over the obstructive behavior of aristocrats in Versailles. Parisians believed that food shortages and royal troops would be used to intimidate the people into submission. They feared an "aristocratic plot" against the National Assembly and the patriot cause.

The Fall of the Bastille   When the King dismissed the popular Necker on July 11, Parisians correctly assumed that a counterrevolution was about to begin. They prepared to resist, and most of the king's military units pulled back. On July 14 Parisian crowds searching for weapons and am-

munition laid siege to the Bastille, an old fortress that had served as a royal prison and in which gunpowder was stored. The small garrison resisted, and a fierce firefight erupted. Although the troops soon capitulated, dozens of citizens were hit, providing the first martyrs of the Revolution, and the infuriated crowd massacred several soldiers as they left the fortress. Meanwhile, patriot electors ousted royal officials of the Paris city government, replaced them with a revolutionary municipality, and organized a citizens' militia to patrol the city. Similar municipal revolutions occurred in twenty-six of the thirty largest French cities, thus ensuring that the defiance in the capital would not be an isolated act.

The Parisian insurrection of July 14 not only saved the National Assembly but altered the Revolution's course by giving it a far more popular dimension. Again the king capitulated. He

▲ The fall of the Bastille was understood at the time to be a great turning point in history, and July 14 eventually became the French national holiday. Numerous prints and paintings evoke the daunting qualities of the fortress, the determination of the besieging crowd, and the heroism of individuals in that crowd.
Bulloz/© Photo RMN/Art Resource, NY

traveled to Paris on July 17 and, to please the people, donned a ribbon bearing three colors: white for the monarchy and blue and red for the capital. This *tricolor* would become the emblem of the new regime.

Peasant Revolts and the August 4 Decree   These events did not pacify the anxious and hungry people of the countryside. Peasants had numerous and long-standing grievances. Population growth and the parceling of holdings reduced the margin of subsistence for many families, while the purchase of land by rich townspeople further shrank their opportunities for economic advance-

ment. Seigneurial dues and church tithes weighed heavily on many peasants. Now, in addition, suspicions were rampant that nobles were hoarding grain in order to stymie the patriotic cause. In July peasants in several regions sacked the castles of the nobles and burned the documents that recorded their seigneurial obligations.

This peasant insurgency blended into a vast movement known to historians as "the Great Fear." Rumors abounded that the vagrants who swarmed through the countryside were actually "brigands" in the pay of nobles, who were marching on villages to destroy the new harvest and cow the peasants into submission. The fear was baseless, but it stirred up the peasants' hatred and suspicion of the nobles, prompted armed mobilizations in hundreds of villages, and set off new attacks on manor houses.

Peasant revolts worried the deputies of the National Assembly, but they decided to appease the peasants rather than simply denounce their violence. On the night of August 4, therefore, certain deputies of the nobility and clergy dramatically renounced their ancient privileges. This action set the stage for the Assembly to decree "the abolition of feudalism" as well as the end of the church tithe, the sale of royal offices, regional tax privileges, and social privilege of all kinds. Later, it is true, the Assembly clarified the August 4 decree to ensure that property rights were maintained. While personal servitudes such as hunting rights, manorial justice, and labor services were suppressed outright, the Assembly decreed that most seigneurial dues would end only after the peasants had paid compensation to their lords. Peasants resented this onerous requirement, and most simply refused to pay the dues; pressure built until all seigneurial dues were finally abolished without compensation by a more radical government in 1793.

III. The Reconstruction of France

The summer of 1789 had seen a remarkable sequence of unprecedented events. A bloodless, juridical revolution from above (engineered by the patriot deputies to the Estates General) combined with popular mobilization from below in town and country made the French Revolution seem irresistible. After the clearing operations of August 4, the National Assembly set out not simply to enact reforms but to reconstruct French institutions on entirely new principles. With sovereignty wrested from the king and vested in the people's deputies, no aspect of France's social or political system was immune to scrutiny, not even slavery in the colonies. First, the Assembly adopted a set of general principles known as the Declaration of the Rights of Man and Citizen. Then it proceeded to draft a constitution, settle the question of voting rights (where the issue of women's citizenship first came up), reorganize the structures of public life, and determine the

future of the Catholic clergy. None of this occurred without intense disagreement, especially over the religious issue and the role of the king. Moreover, Austria and Prussia eventually decided on armed intervention against revolutionary France. In 1792 war broke out, which led directly to the fall of the monarchy and to a new, violent turn in the Revolution.

◆ THE DECLARATION OF THE RIGHTS OF MAN AND CITIZEN

By sweeping away the old web of privileges, the August 4 decree permitted the Assembly to construct a new regime. Since it would take months to draft a constitution, the Assembly drew up a Declaration of the Rights of Man and Citizen to indicate its intentions (see "Two Views of the Rights of Man," p. 715). The Declaration was the death certificate of the old regime and a rallying point for the future. It affirmed individual liberties but also set forth the basic obligation of citizenship: obedience to legitimate law. The Declaration enumerated natural rights, such as freedom of expression and freedom of religious conscience, but (unlike the America Bill of Rights) stipulated that even these rights could be circumscribed by law. It proclaimed the sovereignty of the nation and sketched the basic criteria for a legitimate government, such as representation and the separation of powers. The Declaration's concept of natural rights meant that the new regime would be based on the principles of reason rather than history or tradition.

In his *Reflections on the Revolution in France,* published in 1790, the Anglo-Irish statesman Edmund Burke condemned this attitude, as well as the violence of 1789. In this influential counterrevolutionary tract, Burke argued that France had passed from despotism to anarchy in the name of misguided, abstract principles. Burke distrusted the simplicity of reason that the Assembly celebrated. In his view, the complexity of traditional institutions served the public interest. Burke attacked the belief in natural rights that guided the revolutionaries; something was natural, he believed, only if it resulted from long historical development and habit. Trying to wipe the slate of history clean was a grievous error, he wrote, since society "is a contract between the dead, the living,

Two Views of the Rights of Man

◆

The radical theoretical and practical implications of French revolutionary ideology are suggested in a comparison of two essentially contemporaneous documents. The Prussian General Code, a codification initiated by Frederick the Great and issued in its final form in 1791 after his death, reinforced the traditional prerogatives of the nobility under an umbrella of public law. The French National Assembly's Declaration of the Rights of Man and Citizen (1789) established the principle of civil equality alongside the doctrines of national sovereignty, representation, and the rule of law. While the Prussian General Code exemplifies the old order against which French revolutionary ideology took aim, the Declaration became a foundational document of the liberal tradition.

EXCERPTS FROM THE PRUSSIAN GENERAL CODE, 1791

- This general code contains the provisions by which the rights and obligations of inhabitants of the state, so far as they are not determined by particular laws, are to be judged.
- The rights of a man arise from his birth, from his estate, and from actions and arrangements with which the laws have associated a certain determinate effect.
- The general rights of man are grounded on the natural liberty to seek and further his own welfare, without injury to the rights of another.
- Persons to whom, by their birth, destination or principal occupation, equal rights are ascribed in civil society, make up together an *estate* of the state.
- The nobility, as the first estate in the state, most especially bears the obligation, by its distinctive destination, to maintain the defense of the state. . . .
- The nobleman has an especial right to places of honor in the state for which he has made himself fit.
- Only the nobleman has the right to possess noble property.
- Persons of the burgher [middle-class] estate cannot own noble property except by permission of the sovereign.
- Noblemen shall normally engage in no burgher livelihood or occupation.

From R. R. Palmer (trans.), *The Age of Democratic Revolution* (Princeton University Press, 1959), pp. 510–511.

EXCERPTS FROM THE FRENCH DECLARATION OF THE RIGHTS OF MAN AND CITIZEN, 1789

1. Men are born and remain free and equal in rights. Social distinctions may be based only on common utility.

3. The principle of all sovereignty rests essentially in the nation. No body and no individual may exercise authority which does not emanate expressly from the nation.

4. Liberty consists in the ability to do whatever does not harm another; hence the exercise of the natural rights of each man has no limits except those which assure to other members of society the enjoyment of the same rights. These limits can only be determined by law.

6. Law is the expression of the general will. All citizens have the right to take part, in person or by their representatives, in its formation. It must be the same for all whether it protects or penalizes. All citizens being equal in its eyes are equally admissible to all public dignities, offices and employments, according to their capacity, and with no other distinction than that of their virtues and talents.

13. For maintenance of public forces and for expenses of administration common taxation is necessary. It should be apportioned equally among all citizens according to their capacity to pay.

14. All citizens have the right, by themselves or through their representatives, to have demonstrated to them the necessity of public taxes, to consent to them freely, to follow the use made of the proceeds, and to determine the shares to be paid, the means of assessment and collection and the duration.

---

and the unborn." Society's main right, in Burke's view, was the right to be well-governed by its rulers. Naturally this argument did not go unchallenged, even in England. Mary Wollstonecraft countered with *A Vindication of the Rights of Man*, followed shortly by her seminal *Vindication of the Rights of Woman*, while Thomas Paine published *The Rights of Man* in 1792 to refute Burke.

◆ THE NEW CONSTITUTION

Representative Government From 1789 to 1791, the National Assembly acted as a Constituent Assembly to produce a constitution for France. While proclaiming equal civil rights for all French citizens, it effectively transferred political power from the monarchy and the privileged estates to the body of propertied citizens; in 1790 nobles lost their titles and became indistinguishable from other citizens. The new constitution created a limited monarchy with a clear separation of powers. Sovereignty effectively resided in the representatives of the people, a single-house legislature to be elected by a system of indirect voting. The king was to name and dismiss his ministers, but he was given only a suspensive or delaying veto over legislation; if a bill passed the Assembly in three successive years, it would become law even without royal approval.

Under the French Constitution of 1791, every adult male of settled domicile who satisfied minimal tax-paying requirements (roughly two-thirds of all adult males) gained the right to vote, with a higher qualification needed to serve as an elector. Although it favored the propertied, France's new political system was vastly more democratic than Britain's. Still, the National Assembly considered the vote to be a civic function rather than a natural right. "Those who contribute nothing to the public establishment should have no direct influence on government," declared Sieyès. In the same frame of mind the Assembly excluded all women from voting.

Women in the Revolution That the Assembly even debated political rights for women testifies to the potential universalism of the Revolution's principles. A brief but spirited drive for women's suffrage advanced through pamphlets, petitions, and deputations to the Assembly—most notably the "Declaration of the Rights of Women" (1791) drafted by the playwright Olympe de Gouges. But the notion of gender difference and separate spheres, popularized by Rousseau, easily prevailed. The great majority of deputies believed women to be emotional and frivolous. Too easily influenced to be independent, they must be excluded from the new public sphere—the more so because of the deputies' belief that elite women had used their sexual powers nefariously behind the scenes during the old regime to influence public policy. Now public life would be virtuous and transparent, uninfluenced by feminine wiles. Instead, women would devote themselves to their crucial nurturing and maternal roles in the domestic sphere.

This type of discourse has prompted some feminist scholars to claim that the revolutionary public sphere "was constructed not merely without women but against them." Balanced against this argument, however, is an offsetting consideration. Male revolutionaries may have distrusted women, and some were overt misogynists, yet their own ideology and political culture created unprecedented public space for women. True, women could not vote or hold office, but otherwise *citoyennes* had extensive opportunity for political participation. Women actively engaged in local conflicts over the Assembly's religious policy (discussed later in this chapter). In the towns they agitated over food prices, and in October 1789 Parisian women led a mass demonstration to Versailles that forcibly returned the king and queen to Paris (see p. 717). Combining traditional concerns over food scarcities with antiaristocratic revolutionary ideology, women frequently goaded authorities like the national guard into action.

In unprecedented numbers women also took up the pen to publish pamphlets and journals. Their physical presence in public spaces was even more important. Women helped fill the galleries of the Assembly, of the Paris Jacobin Club, and later of the Revolutionary Tribunal—shouting approval or disapproval and in general monitoring their officials. In at least sixty towns women formed auxiliaries to the local Jacobin club, where they read newspapers, debated political issues, and participated in revolutionary festivals.

Nor did Rousseauian antifeminism prevent the revolutionaries from enacting dramatic advances in the civil status of women. Legislation between 1789 and 1794 created a more equitable family life by curbing paternal powers over children, lowering the age of majority, and equalizing the status of husbands and wives in regard to property. Viewing marriage as a contract between a free man and a free woman, the revolutionaries provided the right of divorce to either spouse should the marriage go sour. A remarkably egalitarian inheritance

▲ In October 1789 Parisian women were furious over the high cost of bread and suspicious of the king and queen. In concert with the National Guard, they set out on an armed march to confront the royal couple in Versailles. To appease the menacing crowd, Louis XVI agreed to return to Paris and to cooperate with revolutionary authorities.
Giraudon/Art Resource, NY

law stipulated that daughters as well as sons were entitled to an equal share of a family's estate. Finally, in the domain of education—central to the feminist vision of Mary Wollstonecraft that the French Revolution had crystalized—an unprecedented system of universal and free primary schooling in 1794 extended to girls as well as boys and provided for state-salaried teachers of both sexes.

Race and Slavery As the Assembly excluded women from voting citizenship without much debate, other groups posed challenges on how to apply "the rights of man" to French society. In eastern France, where most of France's forty thousand Jews resided amid discrimination, public opinion scorned them as an alien race not entitled to citizenship. Eventually, however, the Assembly rejected that argument and extended civil and political equality to Jews. A similar debate raged over the status of the free Negroes and mulattoes in France's Caribbean colonies. White planters, in

alliance with the merchants who traded with the islands, were intent on preserving slavery and demanded local control over the islands' racial policy as their best defense. The planters argued that they could not maintain slavery, which was manifestly based on race, unless free people of color were disenfranchised.

When the Assembly accepted this view, the mulattoes rebelled. But their abortive uprising had the unintended consequence of helping ignite a slave rebellion. Led by Toussaint-L'Ouverture, the blacks turned violently on their white masters and proclaimed the independence of the colony, which became known as Haiti. In 1794 the French revolutionary government belatedly abolished slavery in all French colonies.

Unifying the Nation Within France the Assembly obliterated the political identities of the country's historic provinces and instead divided the nation's territory into eighty-three departments of roughly equal size (see map 20.1). Unlike the old

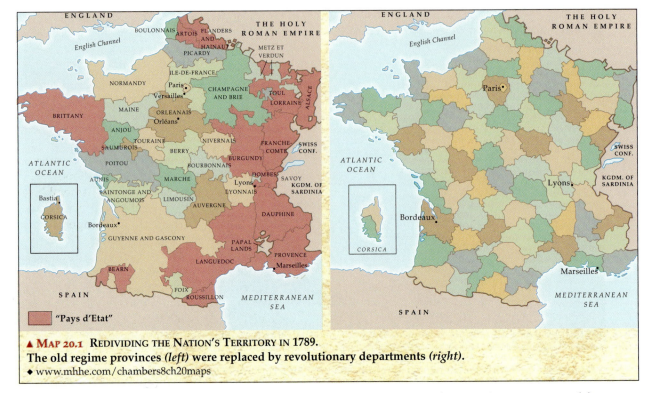

▲ **MAP 20.1**   REDIVIDING THE NATION'S TERRITORY IN 1789.
The old regime provinces *(left)* **were replaced by revolutionary departments** *(right).*
◆ www.mhhe.com/chambers8ch20maps

provinces, each new department was to have exactly the same institutions. The departments were,
in turn, subdivided into districts, cantons, and
communes (the common designation for a village
or town). On the one hand, this administrative
transformation promoted local autonomy: The citizens of each department, district, and commune
elected their own local officials, and in that sense
political power was decentralized. On the other
hand, these local governments were subordinated
to the national legislature in Paris and became instruments for promoting national integration and
uniformity.

The new administrative map also created the
boundaries for a new judicial system. Sweeping
away the parlements and law courts of the old
regime, the revolutionaries established a justice of
the peace in each canton, a civil court in each district, and a criminal court in each department. The
judges on all tribunals were to be elected. The Assembly rejected the use of juries in civil cases but
decreed that felonies would be tried by juries;
also, criminal defendants for the first time gained
the right to counsel. In civil law, the Assembly encouraged arbitration and mediation to avoid the

time-consuming and expensive processes of formal litigation. In general, the revolutionaries
hoped to make the administration of justice faster
and more accessible.

Economic Individualism   The Assembly's clearing operations extended to economic institutions
as well. Guided by the dogmas of laissez-faire theory and by its uncompromising hostility to privileged corporations, the Assembly sought to open
up economic life to individual initiative, much as
Turgot had attempted in the 1770s. Besides dismantling internal tariffs and chartered trading
monopolies, it abolished merchants' and artisans'
guilds and proclaimed the right of every citizen to
enter any trade and conduct it freely. The government would no longer concern itself with regulating wages or the quality of goods. The Assembly
also insisted that workers bargain in the economic
marketplace as individuals, and it therefore
banned workers' associations and strikes. The
precepts of economic individualism extended to
the countryside as well. At least in theory, peasants and landlords were free to cultivate their
fields as they saw fit, regardless of traditional

collective practices. In fact, those deep-rooted communal restraints proved to be extremely resistant to change.

◆ THE REVOLUTION AND THE CHURCH

To address the state's financial problems, the National Assembly acted in a way that the monarchy had never dared contemplate. Under revolutionary ideology, the French Catholic Church could no longer exist as an independent corporation—as a separate estate within the state. The Assembly, therefore, nationalized Church property (about 10 percent of the land in France), placing it "at the disposition of the nation," and made the state responsible for the upkeep of the Church. It then issued paper notes called *assignats,* which were backed by the value of these "national lands." The property was to be sold by auction at the district capitals to the highest bidders. This plan favored the bourgeois and rich peasants with ready capital and made it difficult for needy peasants to acquire the land, though some pooled their resources to do so.

The sale of Church lands and the issuance of assignats had several consequences. In the short run, they eliminated the need for new borrowing. Second, the hundreds of thousands of purchasers gained a strong vested interest in the Revolution, since a successful counterrevolution was likely to reclaim their properties for the Church. Finally, after war broke out with an Austrian-Prussian coalition in 1792, the government made the assignats a national currency and printed a volume of assignats way beyond their underlying value in land, thereby touching off severe inflation and new political turmoil.

Religious Schism The issue of church reform produced the Revolution's first and most fateful crisis. The Assembly intended to rid the Church of inequities that enriched the aristocratic prelates of the old regime. Many Catholics looked forward to such healthy changes that might bring the clergy closer to the people. In the Civil Constitution of the Clergy (1790), the Assembly reduced the number of bishops from 130 to 83 and reshaped diocesan boundaries to conform exactly with those of the new departments. Bishops and parish priests were to be chosen by the electoral assemblies in the departments and districts and were to be paid according to a uniform salary scale that favored those currently at the lower end. Like all other public officials, the clergy was to take an oath of loyalty to the constitution.

The clergy generally opposed the Civil Constitution because it had been dictated to them by the National Assembly; they argued that such questions as the selection of bishops and priests should be negotiated either with the Pope or with a National Church Council. But the Assembly asserted that it had the sovereign power to order such reforms, since they affected temporal rather than spiritual matters. In November 1790 the Assembly demanded that all clergy take the loyalty oath forthwith; those who refused would lose their positions and be pensioned off. In all of France only seven bishops and about 54 percent of the parish clergy swore the oath; but in the west of France only 15 percent of the priests complied. A schism tore through French Catholicism, since the laity had to take a position as well: Should parishioners remain loyal to their priests who had refused to take the oath (the nonjuring, or refractory, clergy) and thus be at odds with the state? Or should they accept the unfamiliar "constitutional clergy" designated by the districts to replace their own priests?

The Assembly's effort to impose reform in defiance of religious sensibilities and Church autonomy was a grave tactical error. The oath crisis polarized the nation. It seemed to link the Revolution with impiety and the Church with counterrevolution. In local communities, refractory clergy began to preach against the entire Revolution. Local officials fought back by arresting them and demanding repressive laws. Civil strife rocked hundreds of communities.

◆ COUNTERREVOLUTION, RADICALISM, AND WAR

Opposition to the Revolution had actually begun much earlier. After July 14 some of the king's relatives had left the country in disgust, thus becoming the first émigrés, or political exiles, of the Revolution. During the next three years, thousands of nobles, including two-thirds of the royal army's officer corps, joined the emigration. Across the Rhine River in Coblenz, émigrés formed an army that threatened to overthrow the new regime at the first opportunity. The king himself publicly submitted to the Revolution, but privately he smoldered in resentment. Finally, in June 1791, Louis and his family fled in secret from Paris, hoping to cross the Belgian frontier and enlist the aid of Austria. But Louis was stopped at the French village of Varennes and was forcibly returned to Paris.

Moderates hoped that this aborted escape would finally end the king's opposition to the Revolution. The Assembly, after all, needed his cooperation to make its constitutional monarchy viable. It did not wish to open the door to a republic or to further unrest. Radicals such as the journalist Jean-Paul Marat, on the other hand, had long thundered against the treachery of the king and the émigrés and against the Assembly itself for not acting vigorously against aristocrats and counterrevolutionaries. But the Assembly was determined to maintain the status quo and adopted the fiction that the king had been kidnapped. The Assembly reaffirmed the king's place in the new regime, but Louis' treasonous flight to Varennes ensured that radical agitation would continue.

The Outbreak of War When the newly elected Legislative Assembly convened on October 1, 1791, the questions of counterrevolution at home and the prospect of war abroad dominated its stormy sessions. Both the right and the left saw advantages to be gained in a war between France and Austria. The king and his court hoped that a military defeat would discredit the new regime and restore full power to the monarchy. Most members of the Jacobin Club—the leading radical

▼ The assault on the Tuileries of August 10, 1792 led to a brief battle with numerous casualties among the besiegers and infuriated reprisals against the garrison after it surrendered. The event brought an end to the constitutional monarchy and led directly to the founding of the first French Republic.
Giraudon/Art Resource, NY

political club in Paris—wanted war to strike down the foreign supporters of the émigrés and domestic counterrevolutionaries.

When Francis II ascended the throne of the Habsburg monarchy in March 1792, the stage was set for war. Unlike his father, Leopold, who had rejected intervention in France's affairs, Francis fell under the influence of émigrés and bellicose advisers. He was determined to assist the French queen, his aunt, and he also expected to make territorial gains. With both sides thus eager for battle, France went to war in April 1792 against a coalition of Austria, Prussia, and the émigrés.

Each camp expected rapid victory, but both were deceived. The French offensive quickly faltered, and invading armies soon crossed France's borders. The Legislative Assembly ordered the arrest of refractory clergy and called for a special corps of twenty thousand national guardsmen to protect Paris. Louis vetoed both measures and held to his decisions in spite of demonstrations against them in the capital. For all practical purposes, these vetoes were his last acts as king. The legislature also called for one hundred thousand volunteers to bolster the French army and defend the homeland.

The Fall of the Monarchy As Prussian forces began a drive toward Paris, their commander, the Duke of Brunswick, rashly threatened to level the city if it resisted or if it harmed the royal family. When Louis XVI published this Brunswick Manifesto, it seemed proof that he was in league with the enemy. Far from intimidating the revolutionaries, the threat drove them forward. Since a divided Legislative Assembly refused to act decisively in the face of royal obstructionism, Parisian militants, spurred on by the Jacobin Club, organized an insurrection.

On August 10, 1792, a crowd of armed Parisians stormed the royal palace at the Tuileries, literally driving the king from the throne. The Assembly then had no choice but to declare Louis XVI suspended. That night more than half the Assembly's members themselves fled Paris, making it clear that the Assembly too had lost its legitimacy. The deputies who remained ordered elections for a National Convention to decide the king's fate, to draft a republican constitution, and to govern France during the current emergency.

What the events of 1789 in Versailles and Paris had begun, the insurrection of August 10, 1792 completed. The old regime in France had truly been destroyed.

IV. The Second Revolution

By 1792—just three years after the fall of the Bastille—the Revolution had profoundly altered the foundations of government and society in France. The National Assembly introduced constitutional government, legislative representation, and a degree of local self-government. It repudiated absolutism, as well as aristocratic and group privilege; established civil equality and uniform institutions across the country; freed peasants from much of the seigneurial system, and religious minorities from persecution. Yet the Revolution was far from over, for these changes had been won only against intense opposition, and the old order was far from vanquished. European monarchs and aristocrats encouraged refractory priests, émigrés, and royalists in France to resist.

The patriots, threatened in 1792 by military defeat and counterrevolution, were themselves divided. Some became radicalized, while others grew alienated from the Revolution's increasingly radical course. But each increment of opposition stiffened the resolve of the Revolution's strongest partisans. The dominant Jacobins forged an alliance with Parisian militants known as the *sans-culottes* (literally, men who wore trousers rather than fashionable knee breeches). Together they propelled France into a second revolution: a democratic republic that espoused a broadening notion of equality. At the same time, however, the Jacobin government instituted an improvised revolutionary dictatorship and a reign of terror against "the enemies of the people." Thus, the second revolution was distorted, as the ideals of equality became confused with the impulse to repress any opposition by the most drastic means.

◆ THE NATIONAL CONVENTION

The insurrection of August 10, 1792, created a vacuum of authority until the election of a National Convention was completed. A revolutionary Paris

▲ **Beset by invasion jitters and fearing a plot to force open the capital's overcrowded jails, mobs of Parisians invaded the prisons and over the course of three days in September 1792 slaughtered more than two thousand prisoners.**
Bulloz/© Photo RMN/Art Resource, NY

Commune, or city government, became one power center, but that bastion of radicalism could not control events even within its own domain. As thousands of volunteers left for the battlefront, Parisians nervously eyed the capital's jails, which overflowed with political prisoners and common criminals. Radical journalists like Marat saw these prisoners as a counterrevolutionary striking force and feared a plot to open the prisons. A growing sense of alarm finally exploded early in September. For three days groups of Parisians invaded the prisons, set up "popular tribunals," and slaughtered more than two thousand prisoners. No official dared intervene to stop the carnage, known since as the September massacres.

The sense of panic eased, however, with the success of the French armies. Bolstered by units of volunteers, the army finally halted the invaders at the Battle of Valmy on September 20. Two months later it defeated the allies at Jemappes in the Austrian Netherlands, which the French now occu-

pied. Meanwhile, the Convention convened and promptly declared France a republic.

Settling Louis XVI's fate proved to be extremely contentious. While the deputies unanimously found the former king guilty of treason, they divided sharply over the question of his punishment. Some argued for clemency, while others insisted that his execution was a necessary symbolic gesture as well as a fitting punishment for his betrayal. Finally, by a vote of 387 to 334, the Convention sentenced Louis to death and voted down efforts to reprieve this sentence or delay it for a popular referendum. On January 21, 1793, Louis was guillotined, put to death like an ordinary citizen. The deputies to the Convention had become regicides (king killers) and would make no compromise with the counterrevolution.

Factional Conflict   From the Convention's opening day, two bitterly hostile groups of deputies vied for leadership and almost immobilized it

▲ After the National Convention concluded its trial of former King Louis XVI and voted to impose the death penalty without reprieve, "Louis Capet" was guillotined and the leaders of the Republic became regicides, king killers.
Bulloz/© Photo RMN/Art Resource, NY

with their rancorous conflict. One group became known as the *Girondins,* since several of its spokesmen were elected as deputies from the Gironde department. The Girondins were fiery orators and ambitious politicians who advocated provincial liberty and laissez-faire economics. They reacted hostilely to the growing radicalism of Paris and broke with or were expelled by the Jacobin Club, to which some had originally belonged. Meanwhile Parisian electors chose as their deputies leading members of the Jacobin Club, such as Danton, Robespierre, and Marat. The Parisian deputation to the Convention became the nucleus of a group known as the *Mountain,* so-called because it occupied the upper benches of the Convention's hall. The Mountain attracted the more militant provincial deputies and attacked the Girondins as treacherous compromisers unwilling to adopt bold measures in the face of crisis. The Girondins, in turn, denounced the

Mountain as would-be tyrants and captives of Parisian radicalism and held them responsible for the September prison massacres.

Several hundred deputies stood between these two factions. These centrists (known as the *Plain*) were committed to the Revolution but were uncertain which path to follow. The Plain detested popular agitation, but they were reluctant to turn against the sans-culottes, who so fervently supported the Revolution.

◆ THE REVOLUTIONARY CRISIS

By the spring of 1793 the National Convention faced a perilous convergence of invasion, civil war, and economic crises that demanded imaginative responses. Austria and Prussia had mounted a new offensive in 1793, their alliance strengthened by the addition of Spain, Piedmont, and Britain. Between March and September, military reversals occurred on every front. The Convention reacted by introducing a military draft, which in turn touched off a rebellion in western France by peasants and rural weavers, who had long resented the patriot middle class in the towns for monopolizing local political power and for persecuting their priests. In the isolated towns of the Vendée region, south of the Loire River, the rebels attacked the Republic's supporters. Priests and nobles offered leadership to the insurgents, who first organized into guerrilla bands and finally into a "Catholic and Royalist Army." The Vendée rebels briefly occupied several towns, massacred local patriots, and even threatened the port of Nantes, where British troops could have landed.

Meanwhile, economic troubles were provoking the Parisian sans-culottes. By early 1793 the Revolution's paper money, the assignat, had declined to 50 percent of its face value. Inflation was compounded by a poor harvest, food shortages, hoarding, and profiteering. Municipal authorities fixed the price of bread but could not always secure adequate supplies. Under these conditions the government could not even supply its armies.

The Purge of the Girondins Spokesmen for the sans-culottes demanded that the Convention purge the Girondins and adopt a program of "public safety," including price controls for basic commodities, execution of hoarders and speculators, and forced requisitions of grain. Behind these demands lay the threat of armed insurrection. This pressure from the sans-culottes aided the Mountain in their struggle against the Girondins, but it could easily have degenerated into anarchy. In a sense, all elements of the revolutionary crisis hinged on one problem: the lack of an effective government that would not simply respond to popular pressures but would organize and master them. When the sans-culottes mounted a massive armed demonstration for a purge of the Girondins on June 2, centrist deputies reluctantly agreed to go along. The Convention expelled twenty-three Girondin deputies, who were subsequently tried and executed for treason.

Factionalism in the Convention reflected conflict in the provinces. Moderate republicans in several cities struggled with local Jacobin radicals and sympathized with the Girondin deputies in

▲ **MAP 20.2** **CONFLICTS IN REVOLUTIONARY FRANCE**
◆ www.mhhe.com/chambers8ch20maps

their campaign against the Parisian sans-culottes. In the south, local Jacobins lost control of Marseilles, Bordeaux, and Lyons to their rivals, who then repudiated the Convention. As in the Vendée revolt, royalists soon took over the resistance in Lyons, France's second largest city. This act was an intolerable challenge to the Convention. Labeling the anti-Jacobin rebels in Lyons and elsewhere as "federalists," the Convention dispatched armed forces to suppress them (see map 20.2). In the eyes of the Jacobins, to defy the Convention's authority was to betray France itself.

◆ THE JACOBIN DICTATORSHIP

Popular radicalism in Paris had helped bring the Mountain to power in the Convention. The question now was: Which side of this coalition between the Mountain and the sans-culottes would dominate the other? The sans-culottes seemed to believe that the sovereign people could dictate

▲ **Bitter fighting in the Vendée between counterrevolutionaries and republicans caused a profound split in the loyalties of western France, which endured for at least the next hundred years. Each side cultivated its own memories of the event and honored its own martyrs.**
Giraudon/Art Resource, NY

their will to the Convention. Popular agitation peaked on September 5, when a mass demonstration in Paris demanded new policies to ensure food supplies. To give force to the law, urged the sans-culottes, "Let terror be placed on the order of the day." The Convention responded with the Law of the Maximum, which imposed general price controls, and with the Law of Suspects, which empowered local revolutionary committees to imprison citizens whose loyalty they suspected.

Revolutionary Government In June the triumphant Mountain had drafted a new democratic constitution for the French Republic and had submitted it to an unprecedented referendum, in which almost 2 million citizens had overwhelmingly voted yes. But the Convention formally laid the constitution aside and proclaimed the government "revolutionary until the peace." Elections, local self-government, and guarantees of individual liberty were to be suspended until the Republic had defeated its enemies within and without. The Convention placed responsibility for military, economic, and political policy, as well as control over local officials, in the hands of a twelve-man Committee of Public Safety. Spontaneous popular action was about to give way to revolutionary centralization.

Maximilien Robespierre emerged as the Committee's leading personality and tactician. An austere bachelor in his mid-thirties, Robespierre had

▲ **The Paris Jacobin Club began as a caucus for a group of liberal deputies to the National Assembly. During the Convention it became a bastion of democratic deputies and middle-class Parisian radicals while continuing to serve as a "mother club" for affiliated clubs in the provinces.**
Giraudon/Art Resource, NY

been a provincial lawyer before the Revolution. As a deputy to the National Assembly he had ardently advocated greater democracy. His main political forum was the Paris Jacobin Club, which by 1793 he more or less dominated. In the Convention, Robespierre was inflexible and self-righteous in his dedication to the Revolution. He sought to appease the sans-culottes but also to control them, for he placed the Revolution's survival above any one viewpoint (see "Robespierre's Justification of the Terror").

Local political clubs (numbering more than five thousand by 1794) formed crucial links in the chain of revolutionary government. The clubs nominated citizens for posts on local revolutionary institutions, exercised surveillance over those officials, and served as "arsenals of public opinion." The clubs fostered the egalitarian ideals of the second revolution and supported the war effort. They also saw it as their civic duty to de-

nounce fellow citizens for unpatriotic behavior and thereby sowed fear and recrimination across the land.

For the Jacobins tolerated no serious dissent. The government's demand for unity during the emergency nullified the right to freedom of expression. Among those to fall were a group of ultrarevolutionaries led by Jacques-René Hébert, a leading radical journalist and Paris official. The extremists were accused of a plot against the Republic and were guillotined. In reality, Hébert had questioned what he deemed the Convention's leniency toward "enemies of the people." Next came the so-called indulgents. Headed by Georges-Jacques Danton, a leading member of the Jacobin Club, they publicly argued for a relaxation of rigorous measures. For this dissent they were indicted on trumped-up charges of treason and were sentenced to death by the revolutionary tribunal. This succession of purges, which started

ROBESPIERRE'S JUSTIFICATION OF THE TERROR

◆

"If the spring of popular government in time of peace is virtue, the springs of popular government in revolution are at once *virtue and terror:* virtue, without which terror is fatal; terror, without which virtue is powerless. Terror is nothing other than justice, prompt, severe, inflexible; it is therefore an emanation of virtue. . . . It is a consequence of the general principle of democracy applied to our country's most urgent needs.

"It has been said that terror is the principle of despotic government. Does your government therefore resemble despotism? Yes, as the sword that gleams in the hands of the heroes of liberty resembles that with which the henchman of tyranny are armed. Let the despot govern his brutalized subjects by terror; he is right, as a despot. Subdue by terror the enemies of liberty, and you will be right, as founders of the Republic. The government of the revolution is liberty's despotism against tyranny. Is force made only to protect crime?

"Society owes protection only to peaceable citizens; the only citizens in the Republic are the republicans. For it, the royalists, the conspirators are only strangers or, rather, enemies. This terrible war waged by liberty against tyranny—is it not indivisible? Are the enemies within not the allies of the enemies without? The assassins who tear our country apart, the intriguers who buy the consciences that hold the people's mandate; the traitors who sell them; the mercenary pamphleteers hired to dishonor the people's cause, to kill public virtue, to stir up the fire of civil discord, and to prepare political counter-revolution—are all those men less guilty or less dangerous than the tyrants [abroad] whom they serve?

"We try to control revolutions with the quibbles of the courtroom; we treat conspiracies against the Republic like lawsuits between individuals. Tyranny kills, and liberty argues."

From Robespierre's speech to the Convention on "The Moral and Political Principles of Domestic Policy," February 1794.

with the Girondins and later ended with Robespierre himself, suggested, as one victim put it, that "revolutions devour their own children."

The Reign of Terror Most of those devoured by the French Revolution, however, were not its own children but a variety of armed rebels, counterrevolutionaries, and unfortunate citizens swept into the vortex of war and internal strife. As an official policy, the Reign of Terror sought to organize repression so as to avoid anarchic violence like the September massacres. It reflected a state of mind that saw threats and plots everywhere (some real, most imagined). The laws of the Terror struck most directly at the people perceived to be enemies of the Revolution: Refractory priests and èmigrès, for instance, were banned from the Republic upon threat of death. But the Law of Suspects also led to the incarceration of as many as 300,000 ordinary citizens for their opinions, past behavior, or social status.

The Terror produced its own atrocities: the brutal drowning of imprisoned priests at Nantes; the execution of thousands of noncombatants during the military campaigns of the Vendée; and the summary executions of about two thousand citizens of Lyons, more than two-thirds of them from the wealthy classes. ("Lyons has made war against liberty," declared the Convention, "thus Lyons no longer exists.") But except in the two zones of intense civil war—western France and the area of "federalist" rebellion in the south (see map 20.2)—the Terror struck by examples, not by the execution of large groups.

◆ THE SANS-CULOTTES: REVOLUTION FROM BELOW

The Parisian sans-culottes formed the crowds and demonstrations that produced the Revolution's dramatic turning points (see chronology), but they also threw themselves into a daily routine of political activism during the second revolution of 1792–1794. The sans-culottes were mainly artisans, shopkeepers, and workers—building

Chronology ♦

TURNING POINTS IN THE FRENCH REVOLUTION

June 17, 1789	Third Estate declares itself a National Assembly.
July 14, 1789	Storming of the Bastille and triumph of the patriots.
August 10, 1792	Storming of the Tuileries and the end of the monarchy (followed by the September prison massacres).
January 21, 1793	Execution of Louis XVI.
March 1793	Vendée rebellion begins.
June 2, 1793	*Sans-culottes* intimidate the Convention into purging the Girondin deputies. "Federalist" rebellion begins in Lyons.
September 5, 1793	*Sans-culottes* demonstrate for the enactment of economic controls and Terror.
October 1793	The Jacobin dictatorship and the Terror begin: The Convention declares that "the government is revolutionary until the peace."
9 Thermidor year II (July 27, 1794)	Fall of Robespierre.
1–2 Prairial year III (May 20–21, 1795)	Failed insurrection by Parisian *sans-culottes* for "Bread and the Constitution of 1793."
18 Brumaire year VIII (November 9, 1799)	Coup d'état by General Bonaparte and the "revisionists."

contractors, carpenters, shoemakers, wine sellers, clerks, tailors, cafe keepers. Many owned their own businesses; others were wage earners. But they shared a strong sense of local community in the capital's varied neighborhoods.

Popular Attitudes The supply and price of bread obsessed the sans-culottes. As consumers, they faced inflation and scarcities with fear and rage and demanded forceful government intervention to ensure the basic necessities of life. Sans-culotte militants believed in property rights, but they insisted that people did not have the right to misuse property by hoarding food or speculating. As one petition put it, "What is the meaning of freedom, when one class of men can starve another? What is the meaning of equality, when the rich, by their monopolies, can exercise the right of life and death over their equals?" The sans-culotte call for price controls clashed dramatically with the dogma of laissez-faire. By 1793, however, the Jacobins had acknowledged "the right to subsistence" in their new constitution and had instituted price controls under the Law of the Maximum to regulate the economy during the emergency.

Bitterly antiaristocratic, the sans-culottes displayed their social attitudes in everyday behavior. They advocated simplicity in dress and manners and attacked opulence and pretension wherever they found or imagined them to be. Under the sans-culottes' disapproving eye, high society and fancy dress generally disappeared from view. Vices like prostitution and gambling were attributed to aristocrats and were denounced in the virtuous society of the Revolution; drinking, the common people's vice, was tolerated.

The revolutionaries symbolized their break with the past by changing the names of streets and public places to eliminate signs of royalism, religion, or aristocracy. The Palais Royal thus became the Palais d'Egalité (Equality Palace). Some citizens exchanged their Christian names for the names of secular heroes from antiquity, like Brutus. And all citizens were expected to drop honorifics like *monsieur* and *madame* in favor of the simple, uniform designation of *citizen*. Even the measurement of time changed when the Convention decreed a new republican calendar that renamed the months and replaced the seven-day

▲ At the height of the "dechristianization" movement (which lasted for about eight months in 1793 – 1794), more than eighteen thousand priests renounced their vocations. About a third were also pressured into marrying as a way of proving the sincerity of their resignations. ("They shave me in the morning and have me married by evening.")
Bibliothèque Nationale de France, Paris

week with a symmetrical ten-day *décadi*. The Year I dated from the establishment of the Republic in 1792.

Popular Politics The Convention believed in representative democracy with an active political life at the grass roots, but during the emergency it decreed a centralized revolutionary dictatorship. The sans-culottes preferred a more decentralized style of participatory democracy. They believed that the local assembly of citizens was the ultimate sovereign body. At the beginning of the year II (1793–1794), the forty-eight sections of Paris functioned almost as autonomous republics in which local activists ran their own affairs. Political life in Paris and elsewhere had a naive, breathless quality and made thousands of ordinary citizens feel that they held real political power (see "A Portrait of the Parisian Sans-Culotte," p. 730).

Within this upsurge of activism, the Society of Revolutionary-Republican Women, founded in Paris in the spring of 1793, constituted a vanguard of female radicals. The members of this club were undeterred by their exclusion from the vote, which did not much concern them at this point. Even without voting rights, women considered themselves citizens in revolutionary France.

In agitating for severe enforcement of price controls and the compulsory use of republican symbols, however, these women irritated the revolutionary government. Before long the ruling Jacobins perceived them as part of an irresponsible ultra-left opposition, whom they denounced as *enragés*, rabid ones. In October the government arrested the most prominent *enragés*, male and female, closed down the Society of Revolutionary-Republican Women, and forbade the formation of female political clubs in the future. The

A PORTRAIT OF THE PARISIAN SANS-CULOTTE

"A Sans-Culotte is a man who goes everywhere on his own two feet, who has none of the millions you're all after, no mansions, no lackeys to wait on him, and who lives quite simply with his wife and children, if he has any, on the fourth or fifth floor. He is useful, because he knows how to plough a field, handle a forge, a saw, or a file, how to cover a roof or how to make shoes and to shed his blood to the last drop to save the Republic. And since he is a working man, you will never find him in the Cafe de Chartres where they plot and gamble. . . . In the evening, he is at his Section, not powdered and perfumed and all dolled up to catch the eyes of the *citoyennes* in the galleries, but to support sound resolutions with all his power and to pulverize the vile faction [of moderates]. For the rest, a Sans-Culotte always keeps his sword with a sharp edge, to clip the ears of the malevolent. Sometimes he carries his pike and at the first roll of the drum, off he goes to the Vendée, to the Army of the Alps or the Army of the North."

From a pamphlet attributed to the Parisian militant Vingternier: "A Reply to the Impertinent Question: But What Is a Sans-Culotte?" (1794).

▲ The radical activists of the Paris sections — the sans-culottes and their female counterparts — made a point of their plebeian forms of dress, their freedom to bear arms, and their egalitarian insignias, such as the red liberty cap.
Bulloz/© Photo RMN/Art Resource, NY

government's spokesman derided these activists as "denatured women," viragos who neglected their maternal duties. Behind this bitter antifeminist rhetoric can be discerned a sense of anxiety. In the virile and punitive world of radical republicanism (see the illustration of Hercules on p. 731), the Jacobins yearned for an offsetting feminine virtue to soften the severity required in the public sphere.

To Robespierre, in any case, the notion of direct democracy appeared unworkable and akin to anarchy. The Convention watched the sans-culottes with concern, supportive of their democratic egalitarianism but fearful of the unpredictability, disorder, and inefficiency of this popular movement. The Mountain attempted to encourage civic participation yet control it. From the forty-eight sections of Paris, however, came an endless stream of petitions, denunciations, and veiled threats to the government. In the spring of 1794 the Convention finally curbed the power of the sections by drastically restricting their rights and activities. But in forcibly cooling down the ardor of the sans-culottes, the revolutionary government necessarily weakened its own base of support.

◆ THE REVOLUTIONARY WARS

Ultimately, the Revolution's fate rested in the hands of its armies, although no one had thought in such terms in 1789. France's revolutionary ideology had initially posed no direct threat to the

▲ Amidst elaborate arrays of symbolism, revolutionary iconography generally used the figure of a woman to represent its ideals. Briefly in the period 1793–1794, however, the Jacobins introduced the more aggressive masculine figure of Hercules to represent the Republic.
(left) Bulloz/© Photo RMN/Art Resource, NY (right) © Collection Roger-Viollet/Getty Images

European state system. Indeed, the orators of the National Assembly had argued that the best foreign policy for a free society was peace, neutrality, and isolation from the diplomatic intrigues of monarchs. But peaceful intentions did not imply pacifism. When counterrevolution at home coalesced with threats from abroad, the revolutionaries vigorously confronted both. As in most major wars, however, the initial objectives were soon forgotten. As the war expanded, it brought revolution to other states.

The revolutionary wars involved standard considerations of international relations as well as new and explosive purposes. On the one hand, France pursued the traditional aim of extending and rounding off its frontiers. On the other hand,

France now espoused revolutionary principles such as the right of a people to self-determination. As early as September 1791, the National Assembly had declared that "the rights of peoples are not determined by the treaties of princes."

Foreign Revolutionaries and French Armies
Even before 1789 "patriots" in Geneva, the Dutch Netherlands, and the Austrian Netherlands (Belgium) had unsuccessfully challenged the traditional arrangements that governed their societies, and the French Revolution rekindled those rebellious sentiments. Foreign revolutionaries were eager to challenge their governments again, and they looked to revolutionary France for assistance. Refugees from these struggles had fled to France

▲ To bolster the professional troops of the line army in 1791 and again in 1792 after the war began, the government called for volunteers, one of whom is shown in this sentimental and patriotic portrait bidding farewell to his family. By 1793, the National Convention had to go further and draft all able-bodied young, single men.
Musée Carnavalet, Paris, France/Giraudon/Bridgeman Art Library

and now formed pressure groups to lobby French leaders for help in liberating their own countries during France's war against Austria and Prussia. Some revolutionaries from areas contiguous to France (Belgium, Savoy, and the Rhineland) hoped that the French Republic might simply annex those territories. Elsewhere—in the Dutch Netherlands, Lombardy, Ireland, and the Swiss Confederation—insurgents hoped that France would help establish independent republics by overthrowing the ruling princes or oligarchies.

Few French leaders were interested in leading a European crusade for liberty, but practical considerations led them to intervene. As the war spilled over into Belgium and the Rhineland, the French sought to establish support abroad by incorporating the principles of the Revolution into their foreign policy. Thus, in December 1792 the Convention decided that feudal practices and hereditary privileges would be abolished wherever French armies prevailed. The people thus liberated, however, would have to pay for their liberation with special taxes and requisitions of supplies for French troops. By 1794 France had a permanent foothold in Belgium and soon annexed that territory to the Republic. Yet Robespierre was dubious about foreign entanglements; he believed that liberty had to be secured in France before it could be exported abroad. The Committee of Public Safety thus declined to support a distant Polish revolutionary movement, refused to invade Holland, and attempted to avoid any involvements in Italy.

Citizen-Soldiers The fighting men who defended France and carried its revolution abroad were a far different body from the old royal army. The National Assembly of 1789 retained the notion of a professional army but opened officers' careers to ordinary soldiers, especially after most of the royal officer corps emigrated or resigned. At the same time, the concept of the citizen-soldier was introduced in the newly organized national guard, which had elected officers. When the war against the coalition began in 1792, the government enrolled more than 100,000 volunteers for short-term service at the front. But when the coalition launched its second offensive in 1793, the inadequacy of the French army demanded drastic innovations.

The Convention responded with the mass levy of August 1793 (*levée en masse*). All able-bodied unmarried men between the ages of eighteen and twenty-five were drafted for military service, without the option of buying themselves a replacement. About 300,000 new recruits poured into the armies, while perhaps 200,000 draftees fled to avoid service. By the end of 1794 the French had almost 750,000 men under arms. With elected officers at their head, the citizen-soldiers marched off to the front under banners that read "The French people risen against the tyrants." The Convention merged these recruits with the regulars of the line army into units called demibrigades, so that the professionals could impart their military skills to the new troops.

Revolutionary Warfare   Military tactics in the field reflected a combination of revolutionary spirit and pragmatism. The new demibrigades did not have the training to be deployed in the well-drilled line formations of old-regime armies. Commanders instead favored mass columns that could move quickly without much drilling. Mass and mobility characterized the armies of the French Revolution. The Committee of Public Safety advised its commanders, "Act offensively and in masses. Use the bayonet at every opportunity. Fight great battles and pursue the enemy until he is destroyed."

The revolutionary government fostered new attitudes toward military life. The military was under civilian control. Discipline applied equally to officers and men, and wounded soldiers received generous veterans benefits. The Convention insisted that generals show not only military talent but the will to win. Many young officers rose quickly to command positions, but some generals fared badly. The commander of the defeated Rhine army in early 1793, for example, was branded a traitor, tried, and guillotined. Meanwhile, economic mobilization at home produced the weapons, ammunition, clothing, and food necessary to support this mass army.

In late 1793 and early 1794 the armies of the Republic won a string of victories, culminating in the Battle of Fleurus in June 1794, which liberated Belgium for the second time. French armies also triumphed at the Pyrénées and the Rhine and forced their enemies one by one to the peace table—first Spain and Prussia, then Piedmont. An army crippled at the outset by treason and desertion, defeat, lack of training and discipline, and collapsing morale had been forged into a potent force in less than two years. Militarily, at least, the revolutionary government had succeeded brilliantly.

SUMMARY

To its most dedicated supporters, the revolutionary government had two major purposes: first, to surmount a crisis and steer the Republic to victory; and second, to democratize France's political and social fabric. Only the first objective, however, won widespread adherence. The National Convention held a polarized nation together, consolidated the Republic, and defeated its foreign enemies, but only at enormous and questionable costs. Moderates and ultrarevolutionaries alike resented the stifling political conformity imposed by the revolutionary government. Wealthy peasants and businesspeople chafed under the economic regimentation, and Catholics bitterly resented local "dechristianization" campaigns. The Jacobins increasingly isolated themselves, making enemies on every side. It is not surprising, then, that the security provided by the military victories of 1793–1794 would permit the Convention to end the Jacobin dictatorship and abandon its rhetoric of radical egalitarianism. But the question remained: What would take its place?

QUESTIONS FOR FURTHER THOUGHT

◆

1. How do you explain the onset of the French Revolution? Was it an accident, so to speak, or did it have long-term causes that made it in some sense inevitable?

2. How do you see the relationship between the liberal phase of the French Revolution (1789–1792) and its radical phase (1792–1794)? Why do revolutions often "devour their own children"?

3. The slogan of the French Revolution eventually became "Liberty, Equality, Fraternity." What was meant by fraternity? Are liberty and equality inherently in tension or are they complementary and mutually reinforcing?

RECOMMENDED READING

◆

Sources

*Beik, Paul H. (ed.). *The French Revolution*. 1971. A comprehensive anthology.

*Hunt, Lynn (ed.). *The French Revolution and Human Rights: A Brief Documentary History*. 1996. Excerpts from revolutionary debates on the rights of the poor, free blacks and slaves, Jews, and women.

*Levy, Darlene, H. Applewhite, and M. Johnson (eds.). *Women in Revolutionary Paris, 1789–1795*. 1979. A documentary history of women activists.

Stewart, J. H. *A Documentary Survey of the French Revolution*. 1951. A compendium of important official documents.

*Walzer, Michael (ed.). *Regicide and Revolution: Speeches at the Trial of Louis XVI*. 1992. Documents and penetrating analysis.

Studies

*Blanning, T. C. W. *The French Revolutionary Wars, 1787–1802*. 1996. A brief but comprehensive synthesis.

———. *Joseph II and Enlightened Despotism*. 1970. A convenient synthesis on a fundamental subject.

*Christie, Ian. *Wars and Revolutions: Britain, 1760–1815*. 1982. Focuses on British government policy in the age of revolutions.

Cobb, Richard. *The French and Their Revolution: Selected Writings*. D. Gilmour (ed.). 1998. An anthology of writings by a great historian of ordinary people caught up in the French Revolution. Should be compared to Soboul's account of the popular movement.

*De Tocqueville, Alexis. *The Old Regime and the French Revolution*. Stuart Gilbert (tr.). 1955. A classic interpretation of the Revolution's genesis, first published in the 1850s.

*Doyle, William. *Origins of the French Revolution*. 1988. A reliable synthesis of revisionist historiography. Should be compared to Lefebvre's interpretation.

*———. *The Oxford History of the French Revolution*. 1989. A readable, detailed narrative.

*Forrest, Alan. *Soldiers of the French Revolution*. 1990. A deft synthesis of recent research.

Furet, Francois, and Mona Ozouf (eds.). *A Critical Dictionary of the French Revolution*. 1989. A collection of essays, some brilliant and some idiosyncratic, on selected events, actors, institutions, ideas, and historians of the French Revolution.

Godineau, Dominique. *The Women of Paris and Their French Revolution*. 1998. The best account of ordinary Parisian women's participation in the French Revolution—a story of citizenship without voting rights.

Hufton, Olwen. *Women and the Limits of Citizenship in the French Revolution*. 1992. A critical view of the subject.

*Hunt, Lynn. *Politics, Culture, and Class in the French Revolution*. 1984. A pioneering analysis of the imagery and sociology of revolutionary politics.

*Jones, Peter. *The Peasantry in the French Revolution.* 1988. A comprehensive study of the impact of the Revolution on rural society.

*Kennedy, Emmet. *A Cultural History of the French Revolution.* 1989. The Revolution's impact on cultural institutions and artistic activity.

McManners, John. *The French Revolution and the Church.* 1970. A superb synthesis on a major issue.

*Middlekauff, Robert. *The Glorious Cause: the American Revolution 1763–1789.* 1982. A comprehensive and balanced synthesis.

*Palmer, Robert R. *The Age of the Democratic Revolution: A Political History of Europe and America, 1760–1800.* 2 vols. 1959 and 1962. A magisterial comparative survey of the origins and course of revolutionary movements in the eighteenth century, from America to Poland.

*———. *Twelve Who Ruled: The Year of the Terror in the French Revolution.* 1941. A modern classic, by far the best book on the subject.

*Popkin, Jeremy. *Revolutionary News: The Press in France 1789–1799.* 1990. An excellent analysis of journalism and the impact of journalists in the revolutionary decade.

Scott, H. M. (ed.). *Enlightened Absolutism: Reforms and Reformers in Later Eighteenth-Century Europe.* 1990. A comprehensive assessment.

*Soboul, Albert. *The Parisian Sans-Culottes and the French Revolution.* 1964. An abridgement of a landmark French thesis; should be compared to Cobb's study.

*Sutherland, Donald. *France 1789–1815: Revolution and Counter-revolution.* 1985. A fine general history of the period.

Tackett, Timothy. *Becoming a Revolutionary: The Deputies of the French National Assembly and the Emergence of a Revolutionary Culture (1789-1790).* 1996. A sensitive collective biography and interpretation of the Revolution's initial course.

*Woloch, Isser. *The New Regime: Transformations of the French Civic Order, 1789–1820s.* 1994. A thematic study of new civic institutions and how they fared, from the beginning of the Revolution to the Restoration of the Bourbons.

*Available in paperback.

▲ *Jacques Louis David*
NAPOLEON BONAPARTE
General Bonaparte, in an uncompleted portrait by Jacques-Louis David.
Giraudon/Art Resource, NY

THE AGE OF NAPOLEON

The second phase of the French Revolution (1792–1794) left a stark legacy of contradictions. On the one hand, the National Convention moved for the first time since ancient Athens to institute a democratic republic: a government without kings, based on universal male suffrage and affirming such popular rights as the right to subsistence and to education for all. On the other hand, the Convention responded to foreign military threats, internal rebellion, and intense factionalism by establishing a revolutionary dictatorship. Individual liberties disappeared, and terror against "enemies of the people" became the order of the day. With the crisis finally surmounted by repression and military victories in 1794, most members of the Convention wearied of those repressive policies and wished to terminate the Revolution as quickly as possible.

Ending the Terror while preserving the Revolution's positive gains, however, proved extremely difficult. By 1794 too much blood had been spilled, too much social hatred and recrimination had accumulated. The new regime could not easily be steered toward the safe harbor of republican liberty in such a polarized atmosphere. In the end General Napoleon Bonaparte replaced the Republic with a personal dictatorship—an outcome that the men of 1789 (schooled in the history of the Roman Republic) had feared from the start.

Would Bonaparte betray the Revolution or consolidate it, as he transformed the Republic's political institutions and social policies? And, since the struggle for and against revolution had long since spilled across France's borders, what would be the consequences for Europe of Napoleon's ascendancy? After 1800 the public life of both France and Europe hinged to an unparalleled degree on the will of a single man. Gradually his designs became clear: a strong centralized state ruled from the top down in France, and an imperial reorganization of Europe totally dominated by France. Undergirding both developments was arguably the most significant priority of Napoleon: the implementation of mass conscription and the consequent militarization of European society. On a vast new scale, war had once again become the central motif of the Western experience.

	Social Structure	Body Politic	Changes in the Organization of Production and in the Impact of Technology	Evolution of Family and Changing Gender Roles	War	Religion	Cultural Expression
CHAPTER 21. THE AGE OF NAPOLEON							
I. FROM ROBESPIERRE TO BONAPARTE		▓			▓		
II. THE NAPOLEONIC SETTLEMENT	▓	▓		▓		▓	
III. NAPOLEONIC HEGEMONY IN EUROPE		▓	▓		▓		
IV. OPPOSITION TO NAPOLEON		▓			▓		▓

I. From Robespierre to Bonaparte

Relatively secure after the military victories of 1793–1794, the National Convention repudiated the Terror and struck at the leading terrorists in a turnabout known as the Thermidorian reaction. Jacobinism, however, was now a permanent part of French political experience, along with antirevolutionary royalism. The political spectrum of modern European history was beginning to emerge. Most revolutionaries now attempted to establish a moderate or centrist position, but they proved unequal to the task. During the four unsteady years of the Directory regime (1795–1799), meanwhile, French armies helped bring revolution to other parts of Western Europe, only to provoke a second anti-French coalition. This new challenge brought the weaknesses of the Republic to a head and allowed an ambitious general and hero of the Republic to seize power. With the backing of disillusioned civilian politicians, Napoleon Bonaparte emerged as the head of the French state.

◆ THE THERMIDORIAN REACTION (1794–1795)

When the military victories over the coalition and the Vendée rebels in the year II (1793–1794) eased the need for patriotic unity, long-standing clashes

over personalities and policies exploded in the Convention. Robespierre prepared to denounce yet another group of unspecified intriguers, presumably to send them to the guillotine as he had Hébert and Danton. But his enemies made a preemptive strike and denounced Robespierre to the Convention as a tyrant. The Convention no longer needed Robespierre's uncompromising style of leadership. Moderate deputies now repudiated him along with his policies of terror. The Parisian sans-culottes might have intervened to keep Robespierre in power, but the Jacobins had alienated their one-time allies when they curbed the sans-culottes' political autonomy several months earlier. On July 27, 1794 (9 Thermidor year II in the revolutionary calendar), the Convention declared Robespierre an outlaw and he was guillotined the following day, along with several loyal associates.

Anti-Jacobinism Robespierre's fall broke the Revolution's momentum. As the Convention dismantled the apparatus of the Terror, suspects were released from jail, the revolutionary committees that had spearheaded the Terror were abolished, and some of their former members were arrested in turn. The Convention closed the Paris Jacobin Club, once the main forum for Robespierre's influence, while the political clubs in the provinces gradually withered away. The Convention also

▲ With its field of guillotines, this Thermidorian caricature *(Robespierre Guillotining the Executioner)* portrays Robespierre as a murderous tyrant who had depopulated France.
Giraudon/Art Resource, NY

arrests, assassinations, and, in the south of France, wholesale massacres.

The Thermidorian reaction also released France from the social austerity of the year II. The Jacobins' insistence on public virtue gave way to the toleration of luxury, fancy dress, and self-indulgence among the wealthy. The titles *monsieur* and *madame* reappeared, replacing the republican designation of *citizen*. In keeping with laissez-faire ideology, the Thermidorians rescinded economic controls. With the marketplace again ruled by supply and demand, skyrocketing inflation reignited. Worse yet, the harvest of 1795 proved mediocre, and many consumers suffered worse privations than those they had dreaded during the shortages of 1793. In near-famine conditions, mortality rates rose markedly; police reports spoke of little but popular misery.

The Last Revolutionary Uprising Former militants attempted to spark a political reversal and halt the Thermidorian reaction. In the spring of 1795 sans-culottes began to demonstrate in Paris with the slogan "Bread and the Constitution of 1793." The Thermidorians, however, were moving in the opposite direction. They viewed the Jacobin Constitution of 1793 as far too democratic and looked for an excuse to scrap it altogether. In May sans-culottes launched a poorly organized insurrection (the revolt of Prairial year III). In a grim and desperate gamble, they invaded the Convention's hall, where they won the sympathy of only a handful of deputies. Their hours were numbered. In two days of street fighting, government forces overwhelmed the insurgents. Afterward, thirty-six sans-culottes were executed, and twelve hundred more were imprisoned for their activism during the Terror. This event proved to be the last mobilization of the Parisian revolutionary crowd and the final eclipse of the egalitarian movement.

◆ THE DIRECTORY (1795–1799)

By the end of 1795, the remaining members of the Convention considered the Revolution over. The extremes had been vanquished, and the time for the "peaceable enjoyment of liberty" seemed at hand. The Thermidorians drafted a new constitution—the constitution of the year

extended an amnesty to the surviving Girondins and arrested a few leading deputies of the Mountain. Those who had taken responsibility for the Terror in the year II now found themselves under attack. The anti-Jacobin thirst for retribution eventually produced a "white terror" against the Jacobins and the sans-culottes that resulted in

◄ **The Parisian sans-culottes launched a futile rebellion in the spring of 1795 for "Bread and the Constitution of 1793" in response to hyperinflation and severe food shortages.**
Photothèque des Musées de la Ville de Paris, © Spadem 1995

III (1795)—proclaimed a general amnesty, and hoped to turn a new page. The revolutionary government, which had replaced the fallen constitutional monarchy in 1793, gave way to a constitutional republic, known as the Directory after its five-man executive.

The Directory's proponents declared that the Republic should "be governed by the best citizens, who are found among the property-owning class." The new constitution said little about the popular rights proclaimed by the Constitution of 1793, like the right to subsistence, public assistance, or free education. The constitution also abandoned the universal male suffrage promised in 1793 and restored the propertied franchise of 1791 and the system of indirect elections. The regime's two-house legislature was designed to moderate the political process, while its five-man executive was meant to prevent the rise of a dictator. The Directory also feared a royalist resurgence. Since genuinely free elections at this point might be carried by the antirepublicans of the right, the outgoing Convention decided to coopt two-thirds of its members into the new legislature, thereby ensuring a substantial degree of political continuity. Government troops led by an officer named Napoleon Bonaparte easily crushed a royalist revolt against this power grab.

The Directory wished to command the center of the political spectrum, which one historian has aptly called "the mirage of the moderates." To maintain themselves in power, however, the directorials violated the liberties pledged in their own constitution. They repeatedly purged elected officials and periodically suppressed political clubs and newspapers on the left and right. In general they refused to acknowledge the legitimacy of organized opposition of any kind. This attitude explains the succession of coups and purges that marked the Directory's four years. Although the repressive measures were mild compared with those of the Terror—deportation usually being the harshest punishment meted out—they ultimately undermined the regime's viability. In the end many moderate republicans walked away from their own creation.

The Political Spectrum For all its repressive qualities, however, the Directory regime was democratic enough to allow most shades of the political spectrum some visibility. The full range of opinions in France, obscured previously by the

Terror, was evident during the years of the Directory and would persist with some modifications into the twentieth century. The most important legacy of all, no doubt, was the apathy born of exhaustion or cynicism. Most citizens, especially peasants, had wearied of politics and distrusted all officials, whatever government they served. Participation in the Directory regime's annual elections was extremely low.

Within this context of massive apathy, politically conscious minorities showed fierce partisanship. On the right, ultraroyalists (including émigrés, refractory priests, and armed rebels in western France) hoped to overthrow the Republic altogether. Some worked with the exiled Bourbon

▼ *The Directory Falls between Two Stools* **is a caricature depicting the political dilemma of the Directory, which vainly sought a centrist position between the left and right.**
Bulloz/© Photo RMN/Art Resource, NY

princes and with British secret agents. More moderate royalists hoped to win control of the Republic's political institutions lawfully and then bring back the émigrés and refractory priests while stamping out the last vestiges of Jacobinism.

On the left of the spectrum stood the Neo-Jacobins—democrats in their own eyes, anarchists to their opponents. The Neo-Jacobins adhered to the moderate Republic of 1795 but identified positively with the experience of 1793. They did not advocate a return to the Terror or the use of force to regain power. Instead, the Neo-Jacobins promoted grassroots activism through local political clubs, petition drives, newspapers, and electoral campaigns to keep alive the egalitarian ideals of the year II, such as free public education and progressive taxation.

At the far end of the spectrum stood a tiny group of radicals whose significance would loom larger in the next century than it did in 1796. Their leader was François-Noël Babeuf, who had changed his name to Gracchus Babeuf in 1793. The Babeuvists viewed the revolutionary government of the year II as a promising stage that had to be followed by a final revolution in the name of the masses. The Babeuvists advocated a vaguely defined material equality, or communism, for all citizens—a "community of goods," as they called it. They also assigned a key role to a small revolutionary vanguard in carrying out this final revolution. Regarding the present Republic as simply a new form of oppression by the elites, they conspired to overthrow it.

The Elusive Center The Directory's adherents stood somewhere in the center of this broad spectrum, hostile to royalists and Neo-Jacobins alike and ready to shift their ground with any change in the political balance. Thus, although the Neo-Jacobins had spurned Babeuf's calls for insurrection, after Babeuf's plot was exposed the Directory joined forces with the right. But when the first regular elections in the year V (1797) produced a royalist victory, the Directory reversed field. Backed by influential generals, the government purged newly elected royalist deputies, suppressed royalist newspapers, and allowed the Neo-Jacobins to open new clubs.

After a few months, however, the Directory grew fearful of the revived left. During the elections of the year VI (1798), Neo-Jacobins and Directorial moderates vied for influence in what almost amounted to party rivalry. But in the end the Directory would not risk the results of free elections. Again it intervened: It closed down clubs and newspapers, manipulated electoral assemblies, and purged those Neo-Jacobins who were elected anyway. Interestingly, at almost the same moment that France's government was quashing its political rivals, leaders of the American republic were reluctantly coming to accept opposition parties as legitimate. In France, however, the Directory would not tolerate organized opposition, and that rigidity contributed to the Republic's demise.

◆ THE RISE OF BONAPARTE

Meanwhile, the Directory years provided unexpected impetus for revolutionary expansion in Europe, which brought into being a half-dozen "sister republics" (see map 21.1), including the Batavian Republic in the Netherlands and the Helvetic Republic in the Swiss Confederation. Revolutionary change also spread through the entire Italian peninsula, as French commanders in the field began to make their own diplomacy. Among them was a young brigadier general, Napoleon Bonaparte.

Bonaparte personifies the world-historic individual—the rare person whose life decisively dominates the course of historical events. Born in 1769 of an impoverished but well-connected family on the French-controlled island of Corsica, Napoleon scarcely seemed destined to play such a historic role. His youthful ambitions and fantasies involved little more than leading Corsica to independence from France. Sent to French military academies, he proved a diligent student, adept at mathematics. Aloof from his aristocratic classmates, whose pretensions he resented, self-reliant and energetic, Bonaparte became an expert on artillery.

After 1789 the young officer returned to Corsica, but his ambitions ran up against more conservative forces on the island. Eventually, local factional conflict drove him and his family off Corsica altogether. Bonaparte then moved onto a much larger stage. He rose steadily and rapidly through the military ranks, based in part on the luck of opportunities but equally on his ability to act decisively. While on leave in Paris in 1795, Bonaparte was assigned to the planning bureau of the war ministry. There he advocated a new strategy: opening a front in Italy to strike at Austrian forces and push into Germany from the south, while French armies on the Rhine pushed as usual from the west. The strategy was approved, and Bonaparte gained command of the Army of Italy in 1796.

The Making of a Hero   Austria's forces outnumbered the French in Italy, but Bonaparte moved his troops rapidly to achieve surprise and numerical superiority in specific encounters. The end result was a major victory that brought the French into the Habsburg domain of Lombardy and its capital, Milan. Bonaparte's overall plan almost miscarried, since the Army of the Rhine did not advance as planned. But this mishap made his own triumphs all the more important to the Directory. And Bonaparte ensured his popularity with the government by making his campaign self-supporting through organized levies on the Italians.

Bonaparte brought a great sense of excitement and drama to the French occupation of Lombardy. His personal magnetism and his talent in manipulating people attracted many Italians. The general encouraged the Italians to organize their own revolutionary movement; the liberation of northern Italy, he believed, would solidify support for his army and enhance his own reputation. This policy distressed the Directory, since it had intended to trade back conquests in Italy in exchange for security on the Rhine frontier. But in the end the Directory endorsed the Treaty of Campo Formio, in which Bonaparte personally negotiated a peace settlement with Austria in October 1797. Austria recognized a new, independent state in northern Italy, the Cisalpine Republic, and left the Rhine question to future negotiations. The Directory regime had found the hero it so desperately needed.

The French now focused their patriotic aspirations on defeating the last member of the first coalition: the hated British enemy. Bonaparte naturally yearned for the glory of accomplishing this feat, and he was authorized to prepare an

MAP 21.1 FRANCE AND ITS SISTER REPUBLICS, 1798

Map labels:

NORTH SEA

ENGLAND

PRUSSIA

BATAVIAN REPUBLIC 1798

Amsterdam

AUSTRIAN NETHERLANDS (BELGIUM) AND RHINELAND PROVINCES 1795

Paris

BAVARIA

ATLANTIC OCEAN

AUSTRIAN EMPIRE

FRANCE

Geneva

HELVETIC REPUBLIC 1798

SAVOY 1792

Bordeaux

Lyons

Turin

Milan

Campoformio

VENICE

Venice

PIEDMONT

CISALPINE REPUBLIC 1797

OTTOMAN EMPIRE

Marseilles

NICE 1792

Genoa

TUSCANY

ADRIATIC SEA

SPAIN

NAPOLEON'S INVASION OF EGYPT 1798

CORSICA

ROMAN REPUBLIC 1798

Rome

PARTHENOPIAN REPUBLIC 1799

SARDINIA

Naples

0   100   200 Miles

MEDITERRANEAN SEA

SICILY

Legend:

French Republic at 1792

Annexed to France 1792-1795

Sister Republics

invasion force. Previous seaborne landings directed at Ireland had failed, however, and Bonaparte too finally had to abandon the scheme because of France's insufficient naval force.

Instead, in the spring of 1798 Bonaparte launched an expedition to Egypt intended to strike at Britain's colonial interests, including the approaches to India. But British naval superiority, in the form of Admiral Horatio Nelson's fleet, turned the expedition into a debacle. The British destroyed the French fleet at the Battle of the Nile, thereby marooning a French army in North Africa. Worse yet, the French were beaten back in several engagements with Turkish forces. Only cynical news management prevented the full story of this defeat from reaching France; instead, the expedition's exotic details and scientific explorations held the attention of the French public. Bonaparte extricated himself from this mess by slipping off through the British blockade, in effect abandoning his army as he returned to France.

◆ THE BRUMAIRE COUP

While Bonaparte floundered in Egypt, the Directory was faltering under political pressures at home. Charges of tyranny and ineptitude accumulated against the directors. Further French expansion into Italy, which produced new sister republics centered in Rome and Naples, precipitated a new coalition against France, consisting of Britain, Russia, and Austria. In June 1799 ill-supplied French forces were driven out of most of Italy and Switzerland.

Widespread discontent with the Directory led to the defeat of many government-sponsored candidates in the spring elections of 1799. The legislature then ousted four of the five directors and named Sieyès, a respected leader of the patriots in 1789, among the replacements. Sieyès and his supporters secretly wished to alter the constitution itself, for they had lost confidence in the regime's institutions, especially its annual elections. These "revisionists" wanted to redesign the Republic along more oligarchic lines, as opposed to the Neo-Jacobins, who wished to democratize the Republic. The centrist position had virtually disappeared. The revisionists blocked emergency measures proposed by the Neo-Jacobins in reaction to the new war crisis and breathed a sigh of relief as French armies rallied and repulsed Anglo-Russian forces in the Batavian Republic and Switzerland. Most of Italy was lost for the time being, but the threat to France itself had passed. Sieyès and the revisionists moved against the Neo-Jacobins by closing their clubs and newspapers and prepared for a coup.

A General Comes to Power   Although no dire military threat remained to propel the country into the arms of a general, the revisionists wished to establish a more centralized, oligarchic republic, and they needed a general's support. Generals were the only national heroes in France, and only a general could organize the force necessary to ensure the coup's success. Bonaparte's return to France from Egypt thus seemed most timely. Bonaparte was not the revisionists' first choice, but he proved to be the best available one. On his trip up from the Mediterranean, people had cheered him warmly, since they knew little of the Egyptian fiasco and saw him in his role as victor of the Italian campaign.

Contrary to the intentions of Sieyès and his fellow conspirators, Bonaparte became the tail that wagged the dog. Once the coup began, he proved to be far more ambitious and energetic than the other conspirators and thrust himself into the most prominent position. Bonaparte addressed the legislature to denounce a mythical Jacobin plot and to demand emergency powers for a new provisional government. Along with two former directors, he was empowered to draft a new constitution; a cooperative rump of the legislature subsequently approved the new arrangements. Thus unfolded the coup of 18 Brumaire year VIII (November 9, 1799).

The Brumaire coup had not been intended to install a dictatorship, but that was its eventual result. In the maneuvering among the revisionists, Bonaparte's ideas and personality prevailed. The plotters agreed to eliminate meaningful elections, which they saw as promoting political instability. They agreed also to enshrine the social ideals of 1789, such as civil equality, and to bury those of the year II, such as popular democracy. The vague notion of popular sovereignty gave way to concentrated authority. The general came out of the coup as the regime's strongman, and Sieyès' elaborate plans for a republican oligarchy ended up in the wastebasket. On one other point, the plotters were particularly deceived. With General Bonaparte's leadership they hoped to achieve durable peace through military victory. Instead, the Napoleonic regime promoted unbounded expansion and endless warfare.

II. The Napoleonic Settlement in France

◆

Bonaparte's prime asset in his rapid takeover of France was the apathy of its citizens. Most French people were so weary politically that they saw in Bonaparte what they wished to see.[1] The Committee of Public Safety had won grudging submission through its terroristic policies; Bonaparte achieved the same result almost by default. As a brilliant propagandist for himself and a man of great personal appeal, he soothed a divided France. Ultraroyalists and dedicated Jacobins never warmed to his regime, but most citizens fell between those positions. They relished the prospect of a strong, reliable government, a return to order and stability, a codification of basic revolutionary gains, and settlement of the agonizing religious conflict.

◆ THE NAPOLEONIC STYLE

Napoleon Bonaparte was not a royalist or a Jacobin, not a conservative or a liberal, though his attitudes were flavored by a touch of each viewpoint. Authority, not ideology, was his great concern, and he justified his actions by their results. The revolutionaries of 1789 could consider Napoleon one of theirs because of his hostility toward the unjust and ineffective institutions of the old regime. He had little use for seigneurialism, the cumbersome institutions of Bourbon absolutism, or the congealed structures of aristocratic privilege, which the Revolution had destroyed. Napoleon valued the Revolution's commitment to equality of opportunity and continued to espouse that liberal premise. Other rights and liberties of 1789 he curtailed or disdained.

Ten years of upheaval had produced a grim paradox: The French Revolution had proceeded in the name of liberty, yet successive forms of repression had been mounted to defend it. Napoleon fit comfortably into this history; unlike the Directory, he made no pretense about it. The social gains of the Revolution would be preserved through political centralization and authoritarian control. Napoleon's field of action was in fact far greater than that of the most powerful eighteenth-century monarch, for no entrenched aristocracy existed to resist him. Thanks to the clearing operations of the Revolution, he could reconstruct at will.

Tragically, however, Napoleon drifted away from his own rational ideals. Increasingly absorbed in his personal power, he began to force domestic and foreign policies on France that were geared to his imperial ambitions. Increasingly he concentrated his government on raising men and money for his armies and turned his back on revolutionary liberties.

◆ POLITICAL AND RELIGIOUS SETTLEMENTS

Bonaparte gave France a constitution, approved in a plebiscite, that placed almost unchecked authority in the hands of a First Consul (himself) for ten years. Two later constitutional revisions, also approved overwhelmingly in plebiscites, increased executive power and diminished the legislative branch until it became simply a rubber stamp. The first revision, in 1802, converted the consulship into a lifetime post; the second, in 1804, proclaimed Napoleon hereditary emperor. The task of proposing new laws passed from elected representatives to appointed experts in the Council of State. This new body advised the ruler, drafted legislation under his direction, and monitored public officials. Such government by experts stood as an alternative to meaningful parliamentary democracy for the next century.

The system of local government established by Bonaparte in 1800 came ironically close to the kind of royal centralization that public opinion had roundly condemned in 1789. Bonaparte eliminated the local elections that the Revolution had emphasized. Instead, each department was now administered by a *prefect* appointed by the ruler. The four-hundred-odd subprefects on the district level as well as the forty thousand mayors of France's communes were likewise appointed. With minor changes, the unquestionably efficient prefectorial system survived in France for 150 years, severely limiting local autonomy and self-government.

---

[1]It is customary to refer to him as Bonaparte until 1804, when the general crowned himself Emperor Napoleon I.

▲ **Napoleon Bonaparte as First Consul, at the height of his popularity, painted by his admirer J.-B. Gros.**
Bulloz/© Photo RMN/Art Resource, NY

Police-state methods finished what constitutional change began: the suppression of independent political activity. From the legislature to the grass roots, France was depoliticized. The government permitted no organized opposition, reduced the number of newspapers drastically, and censored the remaining ones. The free journalism born in 1789 gave way to government press releases and news management. In 1811 only four newspapers remained in Paris, all hewing to the official line. Political clubs were prohibited, outspoken dissidents deported, and others placed under police surveillance. All these restrictions silenced liberal intellectuals as well as former political activists.

Chronology

NAPOLEON'S ASCENDANCY IN FRANCE

Nov. 1799	Coup d'etat of 18 Brumaire
Dec. 1799	Bonaparte becomes First Consul
Feb. 1800	Inauguration of prefectorial system
July 1801	Concordat with the Church
May 1802	Legion of Honor founded
Aug. 1802	Bonaparte becomes Life Consul
March 1804	Promulgation of Civil Code
May 1804	Napoleon becomes emperor
Aug. 1807	Suppression of the Tribunate
March 1808	Organization of the Imperial Nobility

The Concordat Napoleon's religious policies promoted tranquillity at home and a good image abroad. Before Brumaire the Republic tolerated Catholic worship in theory but severely restricted it in practice. Continued proscription of the refractory clergy; insistence on the republican calendar, with its ten-day weeks that made Sunday a workday; and a drive to keep religious instruction out of elementary schools curtailed the free and familiar exercise of Catholicism. These policies provoked wide resentment among the mass of citizens whose commitment to Catholicism remained intact throughout the Revolution.

Though not a believer himself, Napoleon judged that major concessions to Catholic sentiment were in order, provided that the Church remained under the control of the state. In 1801 he negotiated a Concordat, or agreement, with Pope Pius VII. It stipulated that Catholicism was the "preferred" religion of France but protected religious freedom for non-Catholics. The Church was again free to operate in full public view and to restore the refractory priests. Primary education would espouse Catholic values and use Catholic texts, as it had before the Revolution, and clerical salaries would be paid by the state. Though nominated by the ruler, bishops would again be consecrated by the pope. But as a major concession to

FAMILY AND GENDER ROLES UNDER THE NAPOLEONIC CIVIL CODE

◆

"Art. 148. The son who has not attained the full age of 25 years, the daughter who has not attained the full age of 21 years, cannot contract marriage without the consent of their father and mother; in case of disagreement, the consent of the father is sufficient.

"Art. 212. Married persons owe to each other fidelity, succor, assistance.

"Art. 213. The husband owes protection to his wife, the wife obedience to her husband.

"Art. 214. The wife is obliged to live with her husband, and to follow him to every place where he may judge it convenient to reside: the husband is obliged to receive her, and to furnish her with everything necessary for the wants of life, according to his means and station.

"Art. 215. The wife cannot plead [in court] in her own name, without the authority of her husband, even though she should be a public trader . . . or separate in property.

"Art. 217. A wife . . . cannot give, alienate, pledge, or acquire by free or chargeable title, without the concurrence of her husband in the act, or his consent in writing.

"Art. 219. If the husband refuses to authorize his wife to pass an act, the wife may cause her husband to be cited directly before the court of first instance . . . which may give or refuse its authority, after the husband shall have been heard, or duly summoned.

"Art. 229. The husband may demand a divorce on the ground of his wife's adultery.

"Art. 230. The wife may demand divorce on the ground of adultery in her husband, when he shall have brought his concubine into their common residence.

"Art. 231. The married parties may reciprocally demand divorce for outrageous conduct, ill-usage, or grievous injuries, exercised by one of them towards the other."

---

the Revolution, the Concordat stipulated that land confiscated from the Church and sold during the Revolution would be retained by its purchasers. On the other hand, the government dropped the ten-day week and restored the Gregorian calendar.

The balance of church-state relations tilted firmly in the state's favor, for Napoleon intended to use the clergy as a major prop of his regime. The pulpit and the primary school became instruments of social control, to be used, as a new catechism stated, "to bind the religious conscience of the people to the august person of the Emperor." As Napoleon put it, the clergy would be his "moral prefects." Devout Catholics came to resent this subordination of the Church. Eventually Pope Pius renounced the Concordat, to which Napoleon responded by removing the pontiff to France and placing him under house arrest.

◆ THE ERA OF THE NOTABLES

With civil equality established and feudalism abolished, Napoleon believed that the Revolution was complete. It remained to encourage an or-

derly hierarchical society to counteract what he regarded as the excessive individualism of revolutionary social policy. Napoleon intended to reassert the authority of the state, the elites, and, in family life, the father.

In the absence of electoral politics, Napoleon used the state's appointive powers to confer status on prominent local individuals, or notables, thus associating them with his regime. These local dignitaries were usually chosen from among the largest taxpayers: prosperous landowners, former nobles, businessmen, and professionals. Those who served the regime with distinction were honored by induction into the Legion of Honor, nine-tenths of whose members were military men. "It is with trinkets that mankind is governed," Napoleon once said. Legion of Honor awards and appointments to prestigious but powerless local bodies were precisely such trinkets, and they endured long after their creator was gone.

Napoleon offered more tangible rewards to the country's leading bankers when he chartered a national bank that enjoyed the credit power derived from official ties to the state. In education,

Napoleon created elite secondary schools, or *lycées*, to train future government officials, engineers, and officers. The *lycées* embodied the concept of careers open to talent and became part of a highly centralized French academic system called the *University*, which survived into the twentieth century.

The Civil Code Napoleon's most important legacy was a civil code regulating social relations and property rights. Baptized the Napoleonic Code, it was in some measure a revolutionary law code that progressives throughout Europe embraced. Wherever it was implemented, the Civil Code swept away feudal property relations and gave legal sanction to modern contractual notions of property. The code established the right to choose one's occupation, to receive equal treatment under the law, and to enjoy religious freedom. At the same time, it allowed employers to dominate their workers by prohibiting strikes and trade unions. Nor did the code match prop-erty rights with popular rights like the right to subsistence.

Revolutionary legislation had emancipated women and children by establishing their civil rights. Napoleon undid most of this by restoring the father's absolute authority in the family. "A wife owes obedience to her husband," said the code, which proceeded to deprive wives of property and juridical rights established during the 1790s and to curtail the right to divorce while establishing a kind of double standard in the dissolution of a marriage (see "Family and Gender Roles under the Napoleonic Civil Code," p. 747). The code also expanded the husband's options in disposing of his estate, although each child was still guaranteed a portion.

The prefectorial system of local government, the Civil Code, the Concordat, the University, the Legion of Honor, and the local bodies of notables all proved to be durable institutions. They fulfilled Napoleon's desire to create a series of "granite masses" on which to reconstruct French

▼ **Deputies from the Cisalpine Republic of Italy proclaim Napoleon Bonaparte their president in 1802.**
Giraudon/Art Resource, NY

▲ **Admiral Nelson's heavily armed three-decker ship of the line, which inflicted devastation on the French fleet at Trafalgar.**
National Maritime Museum, Greenwich, London (BHC1096)

society. His admirers emphasized that these institutions contributed to social stability amid France's chronic political unrest, arguing that they were skillful compromises between revolutionary liberalism and an older belief in hierarchy and central authority. Detractors point out that these institutions were class oriented and excessively patriarchal. Moreover, they fostered overcentralized, rigid structures that might have sapped the vitality of French institutions in succeeding generations. Whatever their merits or defects, these institutions took root, unlike Napoleon's attempt to dominate all of Europe.

III. Napoleonic Hegemony in Europe

After helping to give France a new government, Bonaparte turned to do battle against the second anti-French coalition in northern Italy. The outcome of his campaign against Austria would either solidify or destroy his regime. Within a few years, Napoleon's dictatorial tendencies became clear enough within France, but in the arena of international relations his ambitions lost all semblance of restraint. Bonaparte evolved from a winning general of the Republic to an imperial conqueror. After defeating his continental opponents on the battlefield in a series of ever more murderous campaigns, he still faced an implacable enemy in Britain. Unable to invade Britain, he resorted to economic warfare and blockade, but Britain withstood that assault as well. Meanwhile, the raw militarism of Napoleon's rule became evident in the relentless expansion of military conscription within the Empire.

◆ MILITARY SUPREMACY AND THE REORGANIZATION OF EUROPE

Bonaparte's strategy in 1800 called for a repeat of the 1797 campaign: He would strike through Italy while the Army of the Rhine pushed eastward against Vienna. Following French victories at Marengo in Lombardy and Hohenlinden in Germany, Austria sued for peace. The Treaty of Lunéville (February 1801) essentially restored France to the position it had held after Bonaparte's triumphs in Italy in 1797.

In Britain a war-weary government now stood alone against France and decided to negotiate. The Treaty of Amiens (March 1802) ended hostilities and reshuffled territorial holdings outside Europe, such as the Cape Colony in South Africa, which passed from the Dutch to the British. But this truce proved precarious since it did not settle the future of French influence in Europe or of commercial relations between the two great powers. Napoleon abided by the letter of the treaty but soon violated its spirit. Britain and Austria alike were dismayed by further expansion of French influence in Italy, Switzerland, and North America. Most important, perhaps, France seemed determined to exclude British trade rather than restore normal commercial relations. Historians agree that the Treaty of Amiens failed to keep the peace because neither side was ready to abandon its century-long struggle for predominance.

The Third Coalition A third anti-French coalition soon took shape, a replay of its predecessors. France ostensibly fought to preserve the new regime at home and its sister republics abroad. The coalition's objectives included the restoration of the Netherlands and Italy to "independence," the limitation of French influence elsewhere, and, if possible, a reduction of France to its prerevolutionary borders. Like most such alliances, the coalition would be dismembered piecemeal.

French hopes of settling the issue directly by invading Britain proved impossible once again. At the Battle of Trafalgar (October 1805), Admiral Nelson's fleet crushed the combined naval forces of France and its ally Spain. Nelson, an innovative tactician who broke rule-book procedures on the high seas just as French generals did on land, died of his wounds in the battle but ensured the security of the British Isles for the remainder of the Napoleonic era.

Napoleon meanwhile had turned against the Austro-Russian forces. Moving 200,000 French soldiers with unprecedented speed across the continent, he took his enemies by surprise and won a dazzling succession of victories. After occupying Vienna he proceeded against the coalition's main army in December. Feigning weakness and retreat at the moment of battle, he drew his numerically superior opponents into an exposed position, crushed the center of their lines, and inflicted a decisive defeat. This Battle of Austerlitz was Napoleon's most brilliant tactical achievement, and it forced the Habsburgs to the peace table. The resulting Treaty of Pressburg (December 1805), extremely harsh and humiliating for Austria, imposed a large indemnity and required the Habsburgs to cede their Venetian provinces.

France and Germany By now the French sphere of influence had increased dramatically to include most of southern Germany, which Napoleon reorganized into the Confederation of the Rhine, a client realm of France (see map 21.2). France had kept Prussia neutral during the war with Austria by skillful diplomacy. Only after Austria made peace did Prussia recognize its error in failing to join with Austria to halt Napoleon. Belatedly, Prussia mobilized its famous but antiquated army; it was rewarded with stinging defeats by France in a number of encounters culminating in the Battle of Jena (October 1806). With the collapse of Prussian military power, the conquerors settled in Berlin and watched the prestige of the Prussian ruling class crumble. Napoleon was now master of northern Germany as well as the south. For a while it appeared that he might obliterate Prussia entirely, but he restored its sovereignty—after amputating part of its territory and imposing a crushing indemnity.

Napoleon was free to reorganize central Europe as he pleased. After formally proclaiming the end of the Holy Roman Empire in 1806, he liquidated numerous small German states and merged them into two new ones: the Kingdom of Westphalia, with brother Jérôme on the throne, and the Grand Duchy of Berg, to be ruled by his brother-in-law Joachim Murat. His ally Saxony became a full-scale kingdom, while a new duchy of Warsaw was carved out of Prussian Poland. This "restoration" of Poland had propaganda value; it made the emperor appear as a champion of Polish aspirations, compared to the rulers of Prussia, Russia, and Austria, who had dismembered Poland in a series of partitions between

▲ **Napoleon amidst the carnage on the battlefield of Eylau, the bloodiest engagement to date of the revolutionary-Napoleonic era, where the French and Russians fought each other to a stalemate in 1807.** Giraudon/Art Resource, NY

1772 and 1795. Moreover, Napoleon could now enlist a Polish army and use Polish territory as a base of operations against his remaining continental foe, Russia.

France and Russia   In February 1807 Napoleon confronted the colossus of the east in the Battle of Eylau; the resulting carnage was horrifying but inconclusive. When spring came, only a dramatic victory could preserve his conquests in central Europe and vindicate the extraordinary commitments of the past two years. The Battle of Friedland in June was a French victory that demoralized Russia's Tsar Alexander I and persuaded him to negotiate.

Meeting at Tilsit, the two rulers buried their differences and agreed, in effect, to partition Europe into eastern and western spheres of influence. Each would support the other's conquests and mediate in behalf of the other's interests. The Treaty of Tilsit (July 1807) sanctioned new annexations of territory directly into France and the re-

organization of other conquered countries. The creation of new satellite kingdoms became the vehicle for Napoleon's domination of Europe. Like the French Republic, the sister republics became kingdoms between 1805 and 1807. And it happened that Napoleon had a large family of brothers ready to wear those new royal crowns.

The distorted shape of Napoleonic Europe is apparent on maps dating from 1808 to 1810 (see map 21.2). His chief satellites included the Kingdom of Holland, with brother Louis on the throne; the Kingdom of Italy, with Napoleon himself as king and his stepson Eugène de Beauharnais as viceroy; the Confederation of the Rhine, including brother Jérôme's Kingdom of Westphalia; the Kingdom of Naples, covering southern Italy, with brother Joseph the ruler until Napoleon transferred him to Spain and installed his brother-in-law Murat; and the Duchy of Warsaw. Belgium, the Rhineland, Tuscany, Piedmont, Genoa, and the Illyrian provinces had been annexed to France. Switzerland did not become a kingdom,

▲ MAP 21.2 EUROPE AROUND 1810

but the Helvetic Republic (as it was now called) received a new constitution dictated by France. In 1810, after yet another war with Austria, a marriage was arranged between the house of Bonaparte and the house of Habsburg. Having divorced Joséphine de Beauharnais, Napoleon married princess Marie Louise, daughter of Francis II, who bore him a male heir the following year.

◆ NAVAL WAR WITH BRITAIN

For a time it seemed that Britain alone stood between Napoleon and his dream of hegemony over Europe. Since Britain was invulnerable to invasion, Napoleon hoped to destroy its influence by means of economic warfare. Unable to blockade British ports directly, he could try to close off the continent: keep Britain from its markets, stop its exports, and thus ruin its trade and credit. Napoleon reasoned that if Britain had nowhere to sell its manufactured goods, no gold would come into the country and bankruptcy would eventually ensue. Meanwhile, overproduction would cause unemployment and labor unrest, which would turn the British people against their government and force the latter to make peace with France. At the same time, French advantages in continental markets would increase with the elimination of British competition.

The Continental System Napoleon therefore launched his "Continental System" to prohibit British trade with all French allies. Even neutral ships were banned from European ports if they carried goods coming from the British Isles. Britain responded in 1807 with the Orders in Council, which in effect reversed the blockade: It *required* all neutral ships to stop at British ports to procure trading licenses and pay tariffs. In other words, the British insisted on regulating all trade between neutral states and European ports. Ships that failed to obey would be stopped on the high seas and captured. In an angry response, Napoleon, in turn, threatened to seize any neutral ship that obeyed the Orders in Council by stopping at British ports.

Thus, a total naval war between France and Britain enveloped all neutral nations. Indeed, neutral immunity virtually disappeared, since every ship was obliged to violate one system or the other and thus run afoul of naval patrols or privateers. While the British captured only about forty French ships a year after 1807 (for few were left afloat), they seized almost three thousand neutral vessels a year, including many from the United States.

The Continental System did hurt British trade. British gold reserves dwindled, and 1811 saw widespread unemployment and rioting. France was affected, in turn, by Britain's counterblockade, which cut it off from certain raw materials necessary for industrial production. But the satellite states, as economic vassals of France, suffered the most. In Amsterdam, for example, shipping volume declined from 1,350 ships entering the port in 1806 to 310 in 1809, and commercial revenues dropped calamitously. Out of loyalty to the people whom he ruled, Holland's King Louis

▲ *J. A. D. Ingres*
Napoleon I Enthroned
Emperor Napoleon I on his imperial throne in 1806, by the great portrait painter Ingres. Note the dramatic contrast in appearance with the young, intense military hero of the Republic in David's portrait at the beginning of this chapter.
Giraudon/Art Resource, NY

Bonaparte tolerated smuggling. But this action so infuriated Napoleon that he ousted his brother from the throne and annexed the Kingdom of Holland directly to France. Smuggling was, in fact, the weak link in the system, for it created holes in Napoleon's wall of economic sanctions

Chronology

NAPOLEON AND EUROPE

June 1800	Battle of Marengo and defeat of the Second Coalition
Feb. 1801	Treaty of Lunéville with Austria
March 1802	Treaty of Amiens with Britain
Sept. 1802	Annexation of Piedmont
1805–1806	Third Coalition forms
Oct. 1805	Battle of Trafalgar and defeat of French fleet
Dec. 1805	Battle of Austerlitz; defeat of Austria
1806	Battle of Jena and humiliation of Prussia
1807	Stalemate with Russia; battles of Eylau and Friedland
July 1807	Treaty of Tilsit with Russia
	Consolidation of satellite kingdoms
1807	Launching of Continental System against British trade
Feb. 1808	Invasion of Spain
July 1809	Battle of Wagram; Austria defeated again
April 1810	Napoleon weds princess Marie Louise of Austria
Dec. 1810	Annexation of Holland
July 1812	Invasion of Russia
Oct. 1812	Retreat and destruction of Grand Army
Oct. 1813	Battle of Leipzig and formation of Fourth Coalition
March 1814	Battle of France and Napoleon's abdication

that constantly needed plugging. This problem drove the emperor to ever more drastic actions.

◆ THE NAPOLEONIC CONSCRIPTION MACHINE

One key to Napoleon's unrestrained ambitions in Europe was the creation of an efficient administrative state in France and its annexed territories.

State penetration of the countryside under Napoleon achieved its most dramatic impact by creating a veritable conscription machine, which continuously replenished the ranks of the imperial army.

The National Convention's mass levy of August 1793 had drafted all able-bodied unmarried men between the ages of eighteen and twenty-five. But this unprecedented mobilization had been meant as a one-time-only emergency measure, a temporary "requisition." There was no implication that subsequent cohorts of young men would face conscription into the army as part of their civic obligations. When the war resumed in 1798, however, the Directory passed a conscription law that made successive "classes" of young men (that is, those born in a particular year) subject to a military draft should the need arise. The Directory immediately implemented this law and called up three classes, but local officials reported massive draft evasion in most of the departments. Many French youths found the prospect of military service repugnant. From this shaky foundation, however, the Napoleonic regime developed a successful conscription system.

The Rules of the Game   After much trial and error with the details, timetables, and mechanisms, the system began to operate efficiently within a few years. The government assigned an annual quota of conscripts for each department. Using parish birth registers, the mayor of every community compiled a list of men reaching the age of nineteen that year. These youths were then led by their mayor to the cantonal seat on a specified day for a draft lottery. Panels of doctors at the departmental capitals later verified or rejected claims for medical exemptions. In all, about a third of French youths legally avoided military service because they were physically unfit—too short, lame, or deformed or suffering from poor eyesight, chronic diseases, or other infirmities.

In the draft lottery, youths picked numbers out of a box; marriage could no longer be used as an exemption, for obvious reasons. Those with high numbers were spared (for the time being), while those who drew low numbers filled the local induction quota. Two means of avoiding service remained: The wealthy could purchase a replacement, and the poor could flee. True, the regime

L'Ogre Dévorateur du Genre humain

▲ **Royalist caricatures often depicted Napoleon as an ogre whose conscription machine devoured the nation's young men.**
Bibliothèque Nationale de France, Paris

had a bad conscience about allowing draftees to hire replacements, because the practice made its rhetoric about the duties of citizenship sound hollow. But to placate wealthy notables and peasants with large holdings (who were sometimes desperate to keep their sons on the farm), the government permitted the hiring of a replacement under strict guidelines that made it difficult and expensive but not impossible. The proportion of replacements was somewhere between 5 and 10 percent of all draftees.

Draft Evasion For Napoleon's prefects, conscription levies were always the top priority among their duties, and draft evasion was the number one problem. Dogged persistence, bureaucratic routine, and various forms of coercion gradually overcame this chronic resistance. From time to time, columns of troops swept through areas in which evasion and desertion were most

common and arrested culprits by the hundreds. But draft evaders usually hid out in remote places—mountains, forests, marshes—so coercion had to be directed against their families as well. Heavy fines assessed against the parents did little good, since most were too poor to pay anything. A better tactic was to billet troops in the draft evaders' homes; if their families could not afford to feed the troops, then the community's wealthy taxpayers were required to do so. All these actions created pressure on the youths to turn themselves in. By 1811 the regime had broken the habit of draft evasion, and conscription was generally becoming accepted as a disagreeable civic obligation, much like taxes. In fact, just as draft calls were beginning to rise sharply, draft evasion fell dramatically. In 1812 prefects all over France reported that the year's levies were more successful than ever before.

Napoleon had begun by drafting 60,000 Frenchmen annually, but by 1810 the annual quotas had risen steadily to 120,000, and they continued to climb. Moreover, in 1810 the emperor ordered the first of many "supplementary levies," calling up men from earlier classes who had drawn high lottery numbers. In January 1813, to look ahead, Napoleon replenished his armies by calling up the class of 1814 a year early and by making repeated supplementary calls on earlier classes.

IV. Opposition to Napoleon

By 1808, with every major European power except Britain vanquished on the battlefield, Napoleon felt that nothing stood in his way. Since Spain and, later, Russia seemed unable or unwilling to stop smuggling from Britain, thus thwarting his strategy of economic warfare, the emperor decided to deal with each by force of arms. His calculations proved utterly mistaken, and in both places he ultimately suffered disastrous defeats. The emperor's confrontations with Spain and Russia proved that his reach had exceeded his grasp. More generally, Napoleon's intrusion into Italy, Germany, Spain, and Russia set in motion various responses and movements of resistance. French expansion sparked new forms of nationalism in some quarters, but also liberalism and reaction.

Finally, all his opponents coalesced, defeated Napoleon on the battlefield, and drove him from his throne.

◆ THE "SPANISH ULCER"

Spain and France shared a common interest in weakening British power in Europe and the colonial world. But the alliance they formed after making peace with each other in 1795 brought only troubles for Spain, including the loss of its Louisiana Territory in America and (at the Battle of Trafalgar) most of its naval fleet. The Spanish royal household, meanwhile, was mired in scandal. Prime Minister Manuel de Godoy, once a lover of the queen, was a corrupt opportunist and extremely unpopular with the people. Crown Prince Ferdinand despised Godoy and Godoy's protectors, the king and queen, while Ferdinand's parents actively returned their son's hostility.

Napoleon looked on at this farce with irritation. At the zenith of his power, he concluded that he must reorganize Spain himself to bring it solidly into the Continental System. As a pretext for military intervention, he set in motion a plan to invade Portugal, supposedly to partition it with Spain. Once the French army was well inside Spain, however, Napoleon intended to impose his own political solution to Spain's instability.

Napoleon brought the squabbling king and prince to France, where he threatened and bribed one and then the other into abdicating. The emperor then gathered a group of handpicked Spanish notables who followed Napoleon's scenario by petitioning him to provide a new sovereign, preferably his brother Joseph. Joseph was duly proclaimed king of Spain. With 100,000 French troops already positioned around Madrid, Joseph prepared to assume his new throne, eager to rule under a liberal constitution and to believe his

▼ Tricked and cajoled out of the Spanish throne by Napoleon, Ferdinand VII sits unhappily as a virtual prisoner in Bayonne, across the French border.
Bulloz/© Photo RMN/Resource, NY

brother's statement that "all the better Spanish people are on your side." As he took up the crown, however, an unanticipated drama erupted.

Popular Resistance Faced with military occupation, the disappearance of their royal family, and the crowning of a Frenchman, the Spanish people rose in rebellion. It began on May 2, 1808, when an angry crowd in Madrid rioted against French troops, who responded with firing squads and brutal reprisals. This bloody incident, known as the Dos de Mayo and captured in Goya's famous paintings, has remained a source of Spanish national pride, for it touched off a sustained uprising against the French. Local notables created com-

mittees, or *juntas,* to organize resistance, mainly by peasants and monks, and to coordinate campaigns by regular Spanish troops. These troops were generally ineffective against the French, but they did produce one early victory: A half-starved French army was cut off and forced to surrender at Bailén in July 1808. This defeat broke the aura of Napoleonic invincibility.

The British saw a great opportunity to attack Napoleon in concert with the rebellious Spanish people. Landing an army in Portugal, the British actually bore the brunt of anti-French military operations in Spain, in what they called the Peninsular War. In a grueling war of attrition, their forces drove the French out of Portugal, and after five

▼ **The great Spanish artist Francisco Goya memorably captured the brutality of French reprisals against the citizens of Madrid who dared to rebel against the Napoleonic occupation on May 2, 1808.**
Erich Lessing/Art Resource, NY

▲ In a relentlessly bleak series of drawings collectively entitled *The Horrors of War*, Goya went on to record the savagery and atrocities committed by both sides of the struggle in Spain.
The Norton Simon Art Foundation, Pasadena, CA

years of fighting and many reversals they pushed the French back across the Pyrénées in November 1813. The British commander, the Duke of Wellington, had grasped the French predicament when he said: "The more ground the French hold down in Spain, the weaker they will be at any given point."

About 30,000 Spanish guerilla fighters helped wear down the French and forced the occupiers to struggle for survival in hostile country. The guerillas drew French forces from the main battlefields, inflicted casualties, denied the French access to food, and punished Spanish collaborators. In short, the Spanish fighters established the model for modern guerilla warfare. Their harassment kept the invaders in a constant state of anxiety, which led the French to adopt harsh measures in reprisal. But these "pacification" tactics only escalated the war's brutality and further enraged the Spanish people.

Together, the juntas, the Spanish regulars, the guerillas, and the British expeditionary force kept a massive French army of up to 300,000 men pinned down in Spain. Napoleon referred to the war as his "Spanish ulcer," an open sore that would not heal. Though he held the rebel fighters in contempt, other Europeans were inspired by their example of armed resistance to France.

The Spanish Liberals The war, however, proved a disaster for Spanish liberals. Torn between loyalty to Joseph, who would have liked to be a liberal ruler, and nationalist rebels, liberals faced a difficult dilemma. Those who collaborated with Joseph hoped to spare the people from a brutal war and to institute reform from above in the tradition of Spanish enlightened absolutism. But they found that Joseph could not rule independently; Napoleon gave the orders in Spain and relied on his generals to implement them. The liberals who joined the rebellion organized a provisional government by reviving the ancient Spanish parliament, or Cortes, in the southern town of Cádiz. Like the French National Assembly of 1789, the Cortes of Cádiz drafted a liberal constitution in 1812 (see "Spanish Liberals Draft a Constitution, 1812," p. 761), which pleased the British and was therefore tolerated for the time being by the juntas.

In reality, most nationalist rebels despised the liberals. Most rebels were royalists who were fighting for the Catholic Church, the Spanish monarchy, and the old way of life. When in 1814 Wellington finally drove the French out of Spain and former crown prince Ferdinand VII took the throne, the joy of the Cádiz liberals quickly evaporated. As a royalist mob sacked the Cortes building, Ferdinand tore up the constitution of 1812, reinstated absolutism, restored the monasteries and the Inquisition, revived censorship, and arrested the leading liberals. Nationalist reactionaries emerged as the victors of the Spanish rebellion and the Peninsular War.

Independence in Spanish America The Creoles, descendants of Spanish settlers who were born in the New World, also profited from the upheaval in Spain. Spain had been cut off from its vast empire of American colonies in 1805, when the British navy won control of the Atlantic after the Battle of Trafalgar. In 1807 a British force attacked Buenos Aires in Spain's vice-royalty of the Río de la Plata (now Argentina). The Argentines—who raised excellent cattle on the *pampas*, or grassy plains—were eager to trade their beef and hides for British goods, but Spain's rigid mercantilism had always prevented such beneficial commerce. The Argentines welcomed the prospect of free trade, but not the prospect of British conquest. With Spain unable to defend them, the Creoles organized their own militia and drove off the invaders. Gaining confidence from this victory, they pushed aside the Spanish viceroy and his bureaucrats and took power into their own hands, though they still swore allegiance to the Spanish crown. The subsequent upheaval in Spain, however, led the Argentines to declare their independence. After Ferdinand regained the Spanish throne in 1814, he sent an army to reclaim the colony, but the Argentines, under General José de San Martín, drove it off, and Argentina made good on its claim to full independence.

Rebellion spread throughout Spanish America, led above all by Simón Bolívar, revered in the hemisphere as "The Liberator." After Napoleon removed the king of Spain in 1808, the Creoles in Spain's vice-royalty of New Granada (encompassing modern-day Venezuela, Colombia, and

LOUISIANA
French 1800–1803;
sold to U.S. 1803

UNITED STATES
(from 1783)

TEXAS

ATLANTIC OCEAN

New Orleans

**REPUBLIC OF
MEXICO**

1821 / 1821

FLORIDA
Spanish 1783–1819;
sold to U.S. 1819

Gulf of Mexico

Cuba

REPUBLIC
OF HAITI

1804

*VICEROYALTY
OF NEW SPAIN*

Caribbean Sea

**UNITED PROVINCES
OF CENTRAL AMERICA**

1821 / 1823

VENEZUELA

1830

BRITISH
GUYANA

DUTCH
GUIANA

FRENCH
GUIANA

*VICEROYALTY OF
NEW GRANADA*

**REPUBLIC OF
GREATER COLOMBIA**

1811 / 1830

ECUADOR
1830

*VICEROYALTY
OF PERU*

**EMPIRE OF
BRAZIL**

1822

PERU

1821 / 1821

PACIFIC OCEAN

BOLIVIA

1825

PARAGUAY
1811

*VICEROYALTY
OF LA PLATA*

**REMAINING COLONIAL
POSSESSIONS**

	Spanish Possessions
	Former borders of Spanish viceroyalties
PERU	Former names of Spanish viceroyalties
	British Possessions
	French Possessions
	Dutch Possessions

Date of
independence
from colonial
power

Date of
separation
from other
states

1821 / 1823

URUGUAY
1814 / 1828

Buenos Aires

CHILE

1810 / 1818

**ARGENTINE
CONFEDERATION**

1810

*Islas Malvinas/
Falkland Islands*
British 1765–1770;
Spanish 1770–1820

▲ MAP 21.3 SOUTH AMERICA AFTER INDEPENDENCE
◆ www.mhhe.com/chambers8ch21maps

SPANISH LIBERALS DRAFT A CONSTITUTION, 1812

◆

"The general and extraordinary Cortes of the Spanish nation, duly organized . . . in order duly to discharge the lofty objective of furthering the glory, prosperity and welfare of the Nation as a whole, decrees the following political Constitution to assure the well-being and upright administration of the State.

"Art. 1: The Spanish Nation is the union of all Spaniards from both hemispheres.

"Art. 3: Sovereignty resides primarily in the Nation and because of this the right to establish the fundamental laws belongs to it exclusively.

"Art. 4: The Nation is obligated to preserve and protect with wise and just laws civil liberty, property and the other legitimate rights of all the individuals belonging to it.

"Art. 12: The religion of the Spanish Nation is and always will be the Catholic, Apostolic, Roman and only true faith. The Nation protects it with wise and just laws and prohibits the exercise of any other.

"Art. 14: The Government of the Spanish Nation is an hereditary limited Monarchy.

"Art. 15: The power to make laws resides in the Cortes with the King.

"Art. 16: The power to enforce laws resides in the King.

"Art. 27: The Cortes is the union of all the deputies that represent the Nation, named by the citizens.

"Art. 34: To elect deputies to the Cortes, electoral meetings will be held in the parish, the district, and the province.

"Art. 59: The electoral meetings on the district level will be made up of the electors chosen at the parish level who will convene at the seat of every district in order to name the electors who will then converge on the provincial capital to elect the deputies to the Cortes.

"Art. 338: The Cortes will annually establish or confirm all taxes, be they direct or indirect, general, provincial or municipal. . . .

"Art. 339: Taxes will be apportioned among all Spaniards in proportion to their abilities [to pay], without exception to any privilege."

From *Political Constitution of the Spanish Monarchy,* proclaimed in Cadiz, March 19, 1812. (trans. James B. Tueller).

Ecuador) elected a congress, which declared independence from Spain. An arduous, protracted war with the Spanish garrisons followed, and by 1816 Spain had regained control of the region. But Bolívar resumed the struggle and gradually wore down the Spanish forces; in one campaign his army marched six hundred miles from the torrid Venezuelan lowlands over the snow-capped Andes Mountains to Colombia. Finally in 1819 the Spanish conceded defeat. Bolívar's dream of one unified, conservative republic of Gran Colombia soon disintegrated under regional pressures into several independent states, but not before Bolívar launched one final military campaign and liberated Peru, Spain's remaining colony in South America (see map 21.3, p. 760).

◆ THE RUSSIAN DEBACLE

Napoleon did not yet realize in 1811 that his entanglement in Spain would drain French military power and encourage resistance in central Europe. On the contrary, never were the emperor's schemes more grandiose. Surveying the crumbling state system of Europe, he imagined that it could be replaced with a vast empire, ruled from Paris and based on the Napoleonic Code. He mistakenly believed that the era of the balance of power among Europe's states was over and that nationalist sentiments need not constrain his actions.

Russia now loomed as the main obstacle to Napoleon's imperial reorganization and domination of Europe. Russia, a restive ally with ambitions of its own in Eastern Europe, resented the restrictions on its trade under the Continental System. British diplomats, anti-Napoleonic exiles such as Baron Stein of Prussia, and nationalist reactionaries at court all pressured the tsar to resist Napoleon. Russian court liberals, more concerned with domestic reforms, hoped on the contrary that Alexander would maintain peace with France, but by 1812 their influence on the tsar had waned. For

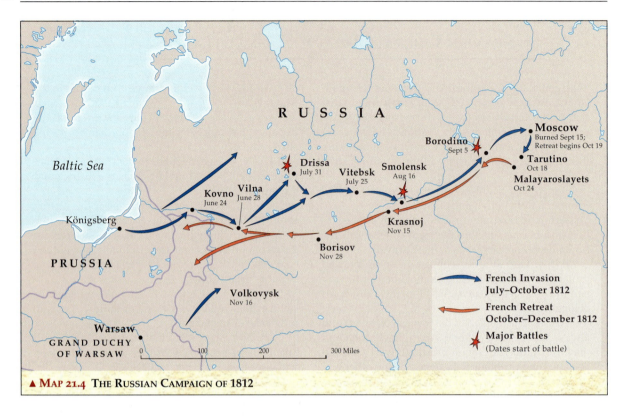

▲ **MAP 21.4** THE RUSSIAN CAMPAIGN OF 1812

his part, Napoleon wanted to enforce the Continental System and humble Russia. As he bluntly put it: "Let Alexander defeat the Persians, but don't let him meddle in the affairs of Europe." Once again two major powers faced each other with diminishing interest in maintaining peace.

Napoleon prepared for his most momentous military campaign. His objective was to annihilate Russia's army or, at the least, to conquer Moscow and chase the army to the point of disarray. To this end he marshaled a "Grand Army" of almost 600,000 men (half of them French, the remainder from his satellite states and allies) and moved them steadily by forced marches across central Europe into Russia. The Russians responded by retreating in orderly fashion and avoiding a fight. Many Russian nobles abandoned their estates and burned their crops to the ground, leaving the Grand Army to operate far from its supply bases in territory stripped of food. At Borodino the Russians finally made a stand and sustained a frightful 45,000 casualties, but the remaining Russian troops managed to withdraw in order (see map 21.4). Napoleon lost 35,000 men in that battle; but

far more men and horses were dying from hunger, thirst, fatigue, and disease in the march across Russia's unending, barren territory. The greatly depleted ranks of the Grand Army staggered into Moscow on September 14, 1812, but the Russian army was still intact and far from demoralized.

The Destruction of the Grand Army In fact, the condition of Moscow demoralized the French. They found the city deserted and bereft of badly needed supplies. The next night Moscow was mysteriously set ablaze, causing such extensive damage as to make it unfit to be the Grand Army's winter quarters. Realistic advisers warned the emperor that his situation was dangerous, while others told him what he wished to hear— that Russian resistance was crumbling. For weeks Napoleon hesitated. Logistically it was imperative that the French begin to retreat immediately, but that would constitute a political defeat. Only on October 19 did Napoleon finally order a retreat, but the order came too late.

The delay forced an utterly unrealistic pace on the bedraggled army as it headed west. Supplies

◄ Just as Goya's drawings captured the unique ferocity of the Spanish campaign, this illustration evokes the particular agonies of climate and logistics in the Russian debacle.
Photo Archive, Nationalbibliotek Austria

were gone, medical care for the thousands of wounded nonexistent, horses lacking. French officers were poorly prepared for the march, and the soldiers grew insubordinate. Food shortages compelled foraging parties to sweep far from the main body of troops, where these men often fell prey to Russian guerillas. And there was the weather—Russia's bitter cold and deep snow, in which no commander would wish to find himself leading a retreat of several hundred miles, laden with wounded and loot but without food, fuel, horses, or proper clothing. Napoleon's poor planning, the harsh weather, and the operation of Russian guerilla bands made the long retreat a nightmare of suffering for the Grand Army. No more than 100,000 troops survived the ordeal. Worse yet, the Prussian contingent took the occasion to desert Napoleon, opening the possibility of mass defections and the formation of a new anti-Napoleonic coalition.

◆ GERMAN RESISTANCE AND THE LAST COALITION

Napoleon was evidently impervious to the horror around him. On the sleigh ride out of Russia he was already planning how to raise new armies and set things aright. Other European statesmen, however, were ready to capitalize on Napoleon's defeat in Russia and demolish his empire once and for all. Provocative calls for a national uprising in the various German states to throw off the tyrant's yoke reinforced the efforts of diplomats like Prussia's Baron Stein and Austria's Klemens von Metternich to revive the anti-Napoleonic coalition.

Reform from Above in Prussia In Prussia after the defeat of 1806, the government had introduced reforms intended to improve the quality of the bureaucracy by offering nonnobles more access to high positions and by reducing some of the nobility's privileges. The monarchy hoped thereby to salvage the position of the nobility and the authority of the state. Prussian military reformers adopted new methods of recruitment to build up a trained reserve force that could be rapidly mobilized, along with a corps of reserve officers to take command of these units. Prussia, in other words, hoped to achieve French-style efficiency and military mobilization without resorting to new concepts of citizenship, constitutions, legislatures, or the abolition of seigneurialism. On the level of propaganda and the symbolic gesture, writers in Prussia and other German states called for a popular war of liberation under the slogan "With God for King and Fatherland."

Against this background of Prussian military preparation and growing nationalist sentiment, the diplomats maneuvered and waited. Finally, in March 1813, King Frederick William III of Prussia signed a treaty with Russia to form an offensive coalition against Napoleon. A great struggle for Germany ensued between the Russo-Prussian forces and Napoleon and his allies. Austria continued to claim neutrality and offered to mediate the dispute, but at a meeting in Prague, Napoleon rejected an offer of peace in exchange for restoring all French conquests since 1802.

In August, as Napoleon learned of new defeats in Spain, Habsburg Emperor Francis finally declared war on his son-in-law. Napoleon called up underage and overage conscripts and was able to field one last army, but his major southern German ally, Bavaria, finally changed sides. A great battle raged around Leipzig for three days in October, and when the smoke cleared, Napoleon was in full retreat. German states were free from Napoleon's domination, but Prussia's rulers were also free from the need to concede further reforms in the political and social order.

The Fall of Napoleon   In the belief that he could rely on his conscription machine, Napoleon had rebuffed offers by the allies to negotiate peace in 1813. In fact, however, he reached the end of the line in November 1813 with a desperate call for 300,000 more men to defend France against the allies. Difficulties were inevitable, wrote one prefect, "when the number of men required exceeds the number available." Another reported: "There

is scarcely a family that is not oppressed by conscription." Alongside sizable contingents of Italians, Germans, and other foreigners from the annexed territories and satellite states, nearly 2.5 million Frenchmen had been drafted by Napoleon. At least 1 million of those conscripts never returned.

With Napoleon driven back into France, British troops reinforced the coalition to ensure that it would not disintegrate once central Europe had been liberated. The coalition offered final terms to the emperor: He could retain his throne, but France would be reduced to her "normal frontiers." (The precise meaning of this term was left purposely vague.) Napoleon, still hoping for a dramatic reversal, chose to fight, and with some reluctance the allies invaded France. Napoleon led the remnants of his army skillfully but to no avail. The French had lost confidence in him, conscription had reached its limits, and no popular spirit of resistance to invasion developed as it had in 1792. Paris fell in March 1814. The price of this defeat was unconditional surrender and the emperor's abdication. Napoleon was transported to the island of Elba, between Corsica and Italy, over which he was granted sovereignty. After twenty-two years of exile, the Bourbon dynasty returned to France.

◆ THE NAPOLEONIC LEGEND

For Napoleon, imperial authority—originating with him in France and radiating throughout Europe—represented the principle of rational progress. In his view, the old notion of balance of power among European states merely served as an excuse for the British to pursue their selfish interests. While paying lip service to the notion of Italian, Spanish, and Polish nationhood, Napoleon generally scorned patriotic opposition to his domination as an outmoded, reactionary sentiment—exemplified by the "barbaric" guerillas in Spain fighting for king and religion. Modern-minded Europeans, he believed, would see beyond historic, parochial traditions to the prospect of a new European order. Indeed, Napoleon's credibility with some reformers in Europe was considerable. The Bavarian prime minister, for instance, justified his collaboration with France in 1810 in these words: "The spirit of the

NAPOLEON JUSTIFIES HIMSELF IN 1815

"I have cleansed the Revolution, ennobled the common people, and restored the authority of kings. I have stirred all men to competition, I have rewarded merit wherever I found it, I have pushed back the boundaries of greatness. Is there any point on which I could be attacked and on which a historian could not take up my defense? My despotism? He can prove that dictatorship was absolutely necessary. Will it be said that I restricted freedom? He will be able to prove that license, anarchy, and general disorder were still on our doorstep. Shall I be accused of having loved war too much? He will show that I was always on the defensive. That I wanted to set up a universal monarchy? He will explain that it was merely the fortuitous result of circumstances and that I was led to it step by step by our very enemies. My ambition? Ah, no doubt he will find that I had ambition, a great deal of it—but the grandest and noblest perhaps, that ever was: the ambition of establishing and consecrating at last the kingdom of reason and the full exercise, the complete enjoyment, of all human capabilities!"

From B. Las Cases (ed.), *Mémorial de Sainte-Hélène*.

new age is one of mobility, destruction, creativity. . . . The wars against France offer the [unfortunate] possibility of bringing back old constitutions, privileges, and property relations."

During his final exile, however, Napoleon came to recognize that nationalism was not necessarily reactionary—as one could plainly see in the nationalistic but liberal Cortes of Cádiz of 1812. Progressive thinking and nationalist aspirations could coexist. From exile Napoleon rewrote his life story to portray his career as a series of defensive wars against selfish adversaries (especially Britain) and as a battle in behalf of the nations of Europe against reactionary dynasties. In this way, Napoleon brilliantly (if falsely) put himself on the side of the future.

These memoirs and recollections from exile formed the basis of the Napoleonic legend, as potent a force historically, perhaps, as the reality of the Napoleonic experience. The image they projected emphasized how General Bonaparte had consolidated what was best about the French Revolution while pacifying a bitterly divided nation and saving it from chaos. They cast the imperial experience in a deceptively positive light, glossed over the tyranny and unending military slaughter, and aligned Napoleon with pragmatism, efficiency, and modernity (see "Napoleon Justifies Himself in 1815").

The Napoleonic legend also evoked a sense of grandeur and glory that moved ordinary people in years to come. Napoleon's dynamism and energy became his ultimate inspirational legacy to succeeding generations. In this way, the Napoleonic legend fed on the romantic movement in literature and the arts. Many young romantics (including the poet William Wordsworth and the composer Ludwig van Beethoven) saw in the French Revolution a release of creativity and a liberation of the individual spirit. Napoleon's tyranny eventually alienated most such creative people. But the Napoleonic legend, by emphasizing the bold creativity of his career, meshed nicely with the sense of individual possibility that the romantics cultivated. Napoleon's retrospective justifications of his reign may not be convincing, but one can only marvel at the irrepressible audacity of the man.

SUMMARY

In the confrontations between Napoleon and his European adversaries, France still embodied the specter of revolution. Even if the revolutionary legacy in France amounted by that time to little more than Napoleon's contempt for the inefficiency and outmoded institutions of the old regime, France after Brumaire remained a powerful challenge to the status quo. Napoleon intended to abolish feudalism, institute centralized administrations, and implant the French Civil Code in all of France's satellite states. But by 1808 his extravagant international ambitions relied on increasingly tyrannical and militaristic measures. These in turn provoked a range of responses, including nationalist rebellions. Britain and Russia, then Prussia and Austria, joined forces once more to bring the Napoleonic Empire down, to restore the balance of power in Europe, and to reinstall the Bourbons in France. But the clock could not really be set back from Europe's experience of revolution and Napoleonic transformation. The era of modern political and social conflicts had begun.

QUESTIONS FOR FURTHER THOUGHT

◆

1. Apart from Jesus, more books have probably been written about Napoleon than any other historical figure. What accounts for this enduring fascination? Compare Napoleon to dominant leaders of the past whom you have studied (e.g. Alexander the Great, Caesar, Philip II, and Louis XIV).

2. Was Napoleon a revolutionary? Did he consolidate or betray the French Revolution?

3. Using the boxed excerpt in which Napoleon justifies his conduct as a starting point, what is *your* assessment of his reign?

RECOMMENDED READING (SEE ALSO CHAPTER 20)

◆

Sources

De Caulaincourt, Armand. *With Napoleon in Russia.* 1935. A remarkable account of the diplomacy and warfare of the 1812 debacle by a man at Napoleon's side.

Herold, J. C. (ed.). *The Mind of Napoleon.* 1961.

Thompson, J. M. (ed.). *Napoleon Self-Revealed.* 1934.

*Walter, Jakob. *The Diary of a Napoleonic Foot Soldier.* M. Raeff (ed.). 1991. A vivid and appalling account of the Russian campaign.

Studies

*Bergeron, Louis. *France under Napoleon.* 1981. A fresh and insightful evaluation of the Napoleonic settlement in France.

*Broers, Michael. *Europe under Napoleon, 1799–1815.* 1996. An incisive and up-to-date synthesis on French expansion in Europe.

Chandler, David. *Napoleon's Marshals.* 1986. By a leading expert on Napoleonic military history.

*Connelley, Owen. *Blundering to Glory: Napoleon's Military Campaigns.* 1988. An irreverent but incisive account of Napoleon's military leadership.

———. *Napoleon's Satellite Kingdoms.* 1965. A study of the states conquered by France and ruled by the Bonaparte family.

*Ellis, Geoffrey. *Napoleon.* 1997. A concise profile.

Elting, John. *Swords around a Throne: Napoleon's Grande Armee.* 1988. An eminently readable military history.

Forrest, Alan. *Conscripts and Deserters: The Army and French Society during the Revolution and Empire.* 1988. A study of popular resistance to revolutionary and Napoleonic conscription.

Gates, David. *The Spanish Ulcer: A History of the Peninsular War.* 1986. On the Spanish rebellion, the French response, and Wellington's expeditionary force.

*Geyl, Pieter. *Napoleon, For and Against.* 1949. Napoleon and the historians, as reviewed by a Dutch scholar with no illusions.

*Herold, J. Christopher. *The Age of Napoleon.* 1963. A brilliant popular history of the era.

Lefebvre, Georges. *Napoleon.* 2 vols. 1959. A general history of the period by a master historian.

*Lynch, John. *The Spanish American Revolutions, 1808–1826.* 1973. A comprehensive account of the independence movements in Spanish America and their aftermath.

Lyons, Martyn. *France under the Directory.* 1975. A brief topical survey of the Revolution's later, unheroic phase.

*———. *Napoleon Bonaparte and the Legacy of the French Revolution.* 1994. A good recent textbook.

Marcus, G. J. *A Naval History of England, II: The Age of Nelson.* 1971. The standard history of British naval supremacy.

*Markham, Felix. *Napoleon.* 1966. Perhaps the best biography in English.

*Palmer, Robert R. *The World of the French Revolution.* 1971. Emphasizes the interplay of French power and revolutionary movements outside of France.

Rosenberg, Hans. *Bureaucracy, Aristocracy, and Autocracy: The Prussian Experience, 1660–1815.* 1958. On reform from above in Prussia that largely preserved the status quo.

Rothenberg, Gunther. *The Art of Warfare in the Age of Napoleon.* 1978. A good analysis of strategy and tactics.

*Sutherland, D. M. G. *France, 1789–1815: Revolution and Counter-revolution.* 1985. A fine general history of France in this period.

Tulard, Jean. *Napoleon: The Myth of the Savior.* 1984. A synthesis by the leading French expert on Napoleon.

*Woloch, Isser. *Napoleon and His Collaborators: The Making of a Dictatorship.* 2001.

Woolf, Stuart. *A History of Italy, 1700–1860.* 1979. An authoritative general history, with fine chapters on this period.

*Woronoff, Denis. *The Thermidorian Regime and the Directory.* 1984. A synthesis by a French historian on France between Robespierre and Bonaparte.

*Available in paperback.

▲ The contrast of new and old: The train from Vienna to Baden frightened the horses in this watercolor done in 1847 by Leander Russ.
AKG London

FOUNDATIONS OF THE NINETEENTH CENTURY: POLITICS AND SOCIAL CHANGE

fter twenty-five years of war, peace was a dramatic change. The first concern of the powers that had opposed Napoleon was to guarantee that no one state would be able to dominate the continent again. They began by redrawing the map, shifting boundaries to create an interlocking network of states that could resist aggression. They accomplished that at the peace conference in Vienna.

The wars against France had been about more, however, than territory or the balance of power. The allies had fought to preserve monarchy and social hierarchy, and they sought a peace that would prevent events like the French Revolution in the future. The first step was to impose regimes that would be safely conservative. For the most part, they restored the dynasties that had been overturned. These restored regimes were nonetheless new, and establishing them raised classical questions about the body politic—how power should be organized, what institutions should direct society, and who should participate in deciding policy. The possibility of revolution thus remained a fact of life, dreaded by some and hoped for by others, reinvoked in each country by the risings, acts of repression, and major reforms of the next thirty years.

The challenge to the restoration experiment was not just political. Enforced stability was expected to bring social peace and economic benefits. In some parts of Europe, however, industrialization was under way and beginning to transform society. The technologies that stimulated economic development and the changing economy's impact on social structure and family were also part of the political and social system of the restoration and are treated in this chapter. Coming after the French Revolution and Napoleon, these changes opened the way to a new era of passionate politics and pervasive social change. How Europeans dealt with the resulting tensions is the subject of chapter 23.

CHAPTER 22. FOUNDATIONS OF THE NINETEENTH CENTURY							
	Social Structure	Body Politic	Changes in the Organization of Production and in the Impact of Technology	Evolution of Family and Changing Gender Roles	War	Religion	Cultural Expression
I. THE POLITICS OF ORDER		▓					
II. THE PROGRESS OF INDUSTRIALIZATION		▓	▓		▓		
III. THE SOCIAL EFFECTS	▓			▓			

I. The Politics of Order

Allied leaders wanted to design a peace that would impose order across the continent. Once they settled the boundaries between states, they placed crowned heads on hereditary thrones and pressed these conservative monarchs to prevent disorder in their own lands. Internationally, they sought to establish an intricate balance of power that would make war unlikely and assure that the major powers would join in stamping out any future threat of revolution. But revolutions broke out in 1820–1821 and 1830, an early measure of the limited effectiveness of the experiment in international conservatism.

◆ THE CONGRESS OF VIENNA

To forge these arrangements, the great international conference known as the Congress of Vienna met in September 1814, an occasion for serious deliberations and elaborate pomp centered on the crowned heads of Austria, Prussia, Russia, and dozens of lesser states. Officials, expert advisers, princesses and countesses, dancers and artists, and the ambitious of every rank flocked to the Austrian capital. Their contrived gaiety and bewigged elegance made the Congress a symbol of aristocratic restoration. The business of the Congress remained the responsibility of the four great powers—Austria, Great Britain, Russia, and Prussia—an inner circle to which France was soon admitted. Prince Klemens von Metternich, who had led the Austrian

Empire to this triumph, conducted the affairs of the Congress with such skill that its provisions can be seen as largely his work. Handsome, elegant, and arrogant, Metternich was the epitome of an aristocrat, fluent in all the major European languages, a dandy who dabbled in science and

▼ In the tradition of aristocratic portraits, Prince Metternich is conveyed as a polished courtier; the medals, symbolic of his position and power, are also a reminder of the purpose of his policies.
Mansell/TimePix

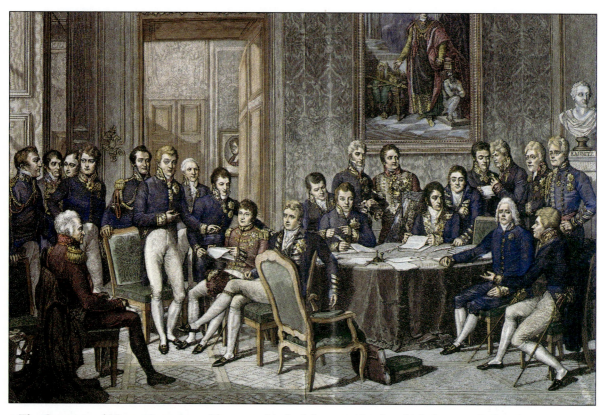

▲ **The Congress of Vienna is portrayed here as a kind of elegant salon in which the very clothes these statesmen wore mix the styles of the old regime and the new century.**
AKG London

shone in the ballroom. More consistently than any other single figure, he had understood the extent of Napoleon's ambitions and had welded the international alliance that defeated the French emperor. Metternich was named foreign minister of Austria in 1809 and would hold that position for nearly forty years, tying his vision of European order to Austria's interests. Metternich was generally supported by Lord Castlereagh, England's able foreign minister. Russia's Tsar Alexander I, who acted as his own chief diplomat, was more unpredictable. Educated in the ideas of enlightened despotism, Alexander was now more given to mysticism and conservative fear and was attracted to grandiose programs upsetting to the careful calculations of self-interest by which the Congress reached agreement.

The Peace Terms The most pressing issue these statesmen faced was the future of France. Most of the allies favored restoring some sort of monarchy, and the Treaty of Paris, signed in May 1814, had recognized as king Louis XVIII, a brother of the executed Bourbon, Louis XVI. The treaty also granted France its expanded frontiers gained by 1792. A settlement covering all the territory affected by the Napoleonic wars would take longer. Warily watching one another, the allies soon included Prince Talleyrand, the French representative, in their deliberations. A former bishop who had served the First Republic and then the Directory, he had helped Napoleon to power and been his foreign minister for eight years. Talleyrand was now the indispensable servant of Louis XVIII, using all his famous shrewdness to regain for France its former influence.

The concerns of these men focused on continental Europe, for only Great Britain among the victors had extensive interests overseas, and British designs on South Africa, Ceylon, and

Malta were modest enough to be accepted by the other European states. Europe was considered the sphere of the great powers; each closely weighed the claims of the others, and all especially watched Russia, with its mammoth armies, undefined ambitions, and quixotic tsar.

Conflicting interests kept Austria, Prussia, and Russia from dividing up Poland as they had in the eighteenth century, but neither did they want to risk creating an independent Poland. So Russia received most of Poland to be ruled as a separate kingdom, and Prussia took about half of Saxony—a triumph of old regime diplomacy in which each of the powers got something (see map 22.1). Prussia was also given greatly enlarged territories in the Rhineland, ensuring that formidable Prussian armies would stand along the French border. The former Austrian Netherlands were absorbed into a new, independent Kingdom of the Netherlands, which created another strong buffer against France and met the British desire that no major power control the Low Countries' important river ports across the channel from England. Austria, in return for ceding the southern Netherlands, acquired Venetia and recovered Lombardy, which greatly strengthened Austrian dominance of northern Italy. The other duchies of northern Italy went to dukes with close Austrian ties (in a touch of chivalry, Marie Louise, Napoleon's now throneless Austrian wife, was given Parma to rule).

The terms agreed on at Vienna constituted the most extensive European peace settlement since the treaty of Westphalia in 1648.[1] Each of the victors had gained territory, and France was surrounded by states capable of resisting any future French aggression. The final act was signed in June 1815 by the five great powers and by Sweden, Spain, and Portugal, a gracious recognition of their past importance.

Napoleon's Hundred Days The deliberations of the Congress were interrupted in March 1815 by the terrifying news of Napoleon's escape from exile. He had tried to make the best of ruling the

island of Elba and had even showed something of his old flair as he designed uniforms, held receptions, and inquired into the local economy. But the island principality was far too small to contain an emperor's ambition. Landing in the south of France, he was joined by units of the French army as he moved toward Paris. Louis XVIII waited for signs of resistance that did not develop, then climbed into his carriage and once again headed for the eastern border. Napoleon became the ruler of France without firing a shot. He then tried to negotiate with the powers allied against him, but they declared him an outlaw and quickly assembled their troops. After several minor battles, Napoleon was defeated for the last time at Waterloo on June 18 and surrendered to the British. They dispatched him to the more distant island of St. Helena, in the South Atlantic.

Napoleon's dashing venture lasted only a hundred days, but its effects were felt far longer. The terms of peace were altered, and the possibility of restoring a stable monarchy was called into question. Allied armies quickly defeated Napoleon; France was required to pay an indemnity, and its boundaries were reduced to those of 1789 (which entailed the loss of much of the Saar region to Prussia). The Bourbons again returned to the French throne, haunted by the specter of renewed revolution and permanently embarrassed by the ease with which Napoleon had retaken power. Napoleon had used his Hundred Days to soften the memory of his despotism with a series of liberal measures (including a ban on slave traffic in the French colonies) and the promise of a constitution. Even from St. Helena, he continued to propagandize for Bonapartism, redefining it as a system for achieving both national strength and social change. Allied statesmen, with power on their side, did not pay so much attention to popular opinion.

Principles of International Order The restorations of 1815 acknowledged many of the changes of the past twenty-five years. The Bourbons were restored in France but now governed with a constitution. In Germany, the Holy Roman Empire and hundreds of minor German principalities, all abolished by Napoleon, were not restored but were consolidated into thirty-nine states,

---

[1]The Kingdom of Sardinia would have liked Lombardy but got Genoa, the ancient Italian maritime republic. Russia took Finland from Sweden, which in turn got Norway from Denmark.

Legend:

— German Confederation boundary

Bavaria and Palatinate

Kingdom of Prussia

Austrian Empire

Kingdom of Sardinia

Italian States
PIEDMONT
PAPAL STATES
KINGDOM OF TWO
SICILIES
A PARMA
B MODENA
C LUCCA
D TUSCANY
E SAN MARINO

German States
PRUSSIA
1 HANOVER
2 OLDENBURG
3 MECKLENBURG-
SCHWERIN
4 NASSAU
5 HESSE-CASSEL
6 HESSE
7 SAXONY
8 BADEN
9 WURTTEMBERG
10 BAVARIA AND
PALATINATE
11 BRUNSWICK

▲ **MAP 22.1 EUROPE, 1815**

including Prussia and Austria, and joined in a loose confederation. The diplomats at Vienna were also innovative in their use of experts as advisers on technical matters of history and law. The Congress established the principle that navigation on international riverways should be open to all and set down rules of diplomatic conduct useful to this day. For the next hundred years Europe would be free of European war, due in part to the complicated arrangements negotiated at Vienna.

The Congress was less impressive in the realm of ideas. Recognizing the need to invoke some general principle to justify such far-reaching arrangements, Talleyrand suggested they were only restoring governments made legitimate by

METTERNICH ANALYZES THE THREAT TO TRANQUILLITY

◆

On December 15, 1820, Metternich wrote the Habsburg emperor from the international conference he had called to deal with the threat of revolution. Metternich argued that all monarchs must act together against the common threat, which he blamed on the middle class.

"Europe presents itself to the impartial observer under an aspect at the same time deplorable and peculiar. We find everywhere the people praying for the maintenance of peace and tranquillity, faithful to God and their Princes. . . . The governments, having lost their balance, are frightened, intimidated, and thrown into confusion by the cries of the intermediary class of society, which, placed between the Kings and their subjects, breaks the scepter of the monarch, and usurps the cry of the people—that class so often disowned by the people, and nevertheless too much listened to. . . .

"We see this intermediary class abandon itself with a blind fury and animosity. . . . to all the means which seem proper to assuage its thirst for power, applying itself to the task of persuading Kings that their rights are confined to sitting upon a throne, while those of the people are to govern, and to attack all that centuries have bequeathed as holy and worthy of man's respect—denying, in fact, the value of the past, and declaring themselves the masters of the future.

" . . . The evil is plain; the means used by the faction which causes these disorders are so blamable in principle, so criminal in their application, and expose the faction itself to so many dangers, that . . . we are convinced that society can no longer be saved without strong and vigorous resolutions on the part of the Governments. . . .

"By this course the monarchs will fulfill the duties imposed upon them by Him who, by entrusting them with power, has charged them to watch the maintenance of justice, and the rights of all, to avoid the paths of error. . . . and to show themselves as they are, fathers invested with the authority belonging by right to the heads of families, to prove that, in days of mourning, they know how to be just, wise, and therefore strong. . . .

"The Governments, in establishing the principle of stability, will in no wise exclude the development of what is good, for stability is not immobility. But it is for those who are burdened with the heavy task of government to augment the well-being of their people! It is for Governments to regulate it according to necessity and to suit the times. It is not by concessions, which the factious strive to force from legitimate power, . . . that wise reforms can be carried out. That all the good possible should be done is our most ardent wish; but . . . even real good should be done only by those who unite to the right of authority the means of enforcing it."

From Prince Richard Metternich (ed.), *Memoirs of Prince Metternich, 1815–1829*, Mrs. Alexander Napier (trans.) (Scribner's Sons Publishers, 1970).

---

tradition and public support; but that justification gave more weight to public opinion than his colleagues could accept. Aiming for something more stirring, Tsar Alexander proposed a Holy Alliance, an agreement that all states would conduct their affairs according to Christian teachings. The principle seemed vague enough; and though some were publicly skeptical, nearly all European governments signed. Three refused: The Ottoman sultan cared too little for Christian teachings, the pope cared too much, and Britain rejected any permanent commitments on the continent. Historians, too, have tended to dismiss the Holy Alliance as a meaningless expression of Alexander's

mysticism. Yet there was something modern, and maybe wise, in the tsar's recognition that the international order should make some moral appeal to public opinion.

Opposition to the Settlement Proponents of change—Europe's liberals, reformers, and nationalists—would later recall the Congress of Vienna as the occasion during which aristocrats danced while foisting reactionary regimes on the people of Europe. Such critics cited not its realistic compromises but the brutal shuffling of territory without regard to the claims of nationality or constitutions.

In fact, the new order was not so solid as it seemed. In 1820 and 1821 uprisings occurred in both Italy and Spain, led by young army officers who were influenced by memories of Napoleonic reforms and convinced that individual advancement and efficient government required a constitution. Metternich quickly called for a "concert of Europe" to snuff the flames of revolution by force,

▼ *Eugène Delacroix*
GREECE EXPIRING
The Greek revolution captured the imagination of many Europeans, and Delacroix's *Greece Expiring* has all the elements of that fascination. Greece is symbolized by an ordinary peasant girl who is also a classical figure of liberty, come alive. The Turk in the background, a colorful and exotic figure of oppression, evokes centuries of conflict. Romanticism, nationalism, and political liberty come together on the stones of Greek culture and the arm of a martyred freedom fighter.
Giraudon/Art Resource, NY

Chronology

CHALLENGES TO THE VIENNA SETTLEMENT

May 1814	Treaty of Paris
September 1814–June 1815	Congress of Vienna
March 1815–June 1815	Napoleon's 100 days
1817	German students at Wartburg
1820–1821	Revolts in Spain and Italy
1821–1829	Greek war of independence
1825	Decembrist rising in Russia
1830	Revolution in France, Belgium

but unanimity among the former allies was breaking down. Great Britain disapproved sending foreign troops to put down a constitutional government in Naples and did not attend the conference, which approved Austrian intervention in Naples and called on France to send troops against the revolution in Spain. French forces met little resistance in Spain, and their royal parade was welcomed by conservatives throughout Europe as evidence of the French monarchy's revived prestige.

The next step, some suggested, was to put down the revolts in Latin America, where leaders cited principles associated with the French and American revolutions. Movements for independence from Spain and Portugal, which had steadily gained ground from the time of Napoleon, burst forth anew with the 1820 revolution in Spain. But talk of intervention brought stern warnings from Britain and the proud announcement of the Monroe Doctrine from the United States, declaring the Americas outside the sphere of European power politics. Metternich's concept of a European concert to maintain order was being circumscribed.

The Concert of Europe was hardly invoked at all when Greeks revolted against Ottoman Turk rule in 1821. Cries for freedom from that home of ancient democracy excited liberals throughout Europe, an early demonstration of the power of nationalist movements that would be repeated throughout the century. Metternich restrained Russia from rushing to war against the Ottomans as it often had in the past, but he could not keep the British and French fleets from intervening in 1827, when the sultan seemed at last about to subdue the Greeks. Russia declared war a few months later. Greece was granted independence in 1829 on terms arranged by the European powers, stipulating that it must have a king but one who was not a member of the ruling family of a major power. With that policy, the leading European states altered the status quo after all. They did so partly in response to public opinion, but they also made sure that the Greek rising would go no further. In the name of Greek freedom, Britain, France, and Russia displayed a willingness to use force, a preoccupation with their own self-interest, and an eagerness to carve up the Ottoman Empire that foreshadowed the practice of imperialism later in the century.

◆ THE PILLARS OF THE RESTORATION: RUSSIA, AUSTRIA, PRUSSIA

Even the most reactionary rulers accepted some of the changes (and the potential for increased power) brought by revolution, war, and Napoleonic occupation. To maintain social order in the nineteenth century, the state would need to be more effective than before in order to sustain large armies and collect more taxes, support a better-trained bureaucracy, dispense justice more evenly, and provide more services. Because they would thus affect the lives of their subjects more directly, governments would have to be more concerned with popular sentiment. For these reasons, the organization of the state became an issue even in conservative Russia, Austria, and Prussia, the guardians of the European restoration.

The Russian Empire   By 1820 Tsar Alexander had abandoned his earlier enthusiasm for new ideas. As Metternich's staunchest ally, Alexander im-

posed harsh censorship, increased restrictions on universities, and made sure that the constitution granted to the newly organized Kingdom of Poland was largely ignored. On Alexander's death in 1825, a group of young army officers, the Decembrists, attempted a coup and called for a constitution in Russia. Like the leaders of the revolts in Naples and Spain a few years earlier, the Decembrists saw a constitution as an essential step toward a more efficient and progressive administration. Their poorly planned and isolated conspiracy was easily defeated, but it would be remembered by conservatives as an ever-present danger and by revolutionaries as part of Russia's radical tradition. Alexander's younger brother, Nicholas I, succeeded him, convinced that only a loyal army and his own decisiveness had prevented revolution. He turned Russia into Europe's strongest pillar of reaction by his example at home and his willingness to use force abroad. He was a diligent administrator who gave his closest attention to the army and the police and who established a more effective bureaucracy by making it more directly responsible to the state and less attached to the nobility.

Nevertheless, petty corruption, the arrogance of local officials, and fear of change continued to undermine the government's capacity to manage a vast land of varied peoples in which communication was poor and few had the means or the will to effect reform. Most thoughtful people, including the state's highest officials, agreed that serfdom had become a hindrance to Russia's development. The commissions ordered to study the matter gathered data and noted that hundreds of peasant uprisings had had to be suppressed by force, but they proposed no solution. Despite fears that education bred discontent, the government built schools; and among the literate minority, discussion of Russia's future became a compelling theme. The government even attempted to establish a kind of official philosophy based on the teachings of the Russian Orthodox Church. Intellectuals who expected Russia to develop along familiar European lines were known as Westernizers. Those who stressed the uniqueness of Russia were called Slavophiles, and they argued that Russia's religion, peasant communes, and traditional culture gave Russia a unique destiny.

Despite this urgent questioning about Russia's place in a changing world and despite loquacious exiles, bitter Poles, angry peasants, and its own immobility, the authority of the Russian state remained. Nicholas would watch with pride in 1848 as his empire escaped the revolutions that swept over most of the thrones of Europe.

The Habsburg Empire Habsburg rule over German, Italian, and Eastern European lands relied on a well-organized bureaucracy. Forged by Maria Theresa and Joseph II, that system of government had enabled Austria to survive the Napoleonic wars without dramatic transformation despite repeated defeat. Metternich and others recognized the need for domestic reform, but their projects for better fiscal planning, stronger local government, and recognition of the empire's diverse nationalities came to nothing. Habsburg rule remained locked in stalemate between an increasingly cautious central bureaucracy and a selfish local aristocracy.

Hungary proved particularly troublesome for the Habsburg empire, for the dominant Magyar aristocracy had a strong sense of their historical identity and a good deal of power, although they remained a minority in their own country. Emperor Francis I grudgingly acknowledged many of their claims, and by the 1840s Magyar had replaced German as the official language of administration and schooling in Hungary. More demands followed. The campaign for a more representative parliament and related reforms was led by Lajos Kossuth, who became Hungary's leading statesman, able through newspapers and public meetings to reach much of the nation. This widespread agitation, stimulated by the example of nationalist ferment in Italy, encouraged other groups subject to Habsburg rule to claim national rights of their own. Much of Polish Galicia rose in revolt in 1846; but weakened by the bitter antagonism between Polish peasants and their masters, the uprising was soon suppressed. In Croatia and Bohemia, too, angry peasants and nationalists often had different aims. The various national groups opposed to Habsburg rule, often hostile to each other, were also internally divided by class, religion, and language. Their divisions helped sustain Habsburg rule. Throughout the empire, however, growing nationalist movements sought to overcome these social divisions, giving broader appeal to criticisms of Habsburg rule that came mainly from merchants and lawyers. At the center, despite much good advice and many promising plans, inaction remained the safest compromise.

Prussia and the German Confederation Germans called the later battles against Napoleon (1813–1814) the Wars of Liberation, and after that common national experience, talk of "Germany" meant more than it had before. The Congress of Vienna acknowledged this awareness with the creation of the German Confederation. A cautious gesture toward national sentiment that preserved the position of the strongest local rulers while tacitly acknowledging the changes that French dominance had brought, a confederation required some coordination among Germany's many states. Any stronger union was prevented by the rivalry of Austria and Prussia, distaste for reform among restoration regimes, and the conflicting ambitions of German princes. The Confederation's diet, more a council of ambassadors from member states than a representative assembly, was permitted to legislate only on certain matters—characteristically, restriction of the press was one of them.

In practice, the German Confederation was important in German politics largely when Metternich wished to make it so. He used it, for example, to suppress agitation led by nationalist and reformist student groups in the universities. In 1817 some of these groups organized a celebration of the three hundredth anniversary of Luther's theses with a rally, the Wartburg Festival. Several hundred young people gathered to drink, listen to speeches full of mystical nationalist rhetoric, sing songs, and cheer as a corporal's cane and a Prussian military manual were tossed into a bonfire. Even such symbolic challenges to military authority alarmed governments in both Berlin and Vienna. When a well-known reactionary writer was assassinated, the Confederation was pressed into issuing the Carlsbad Decrees of 1819, which intensified censorship, proscribed dangerous professors and students, outlawed fraternities and political clubs, and required each state to

▲ German authorities worried greatly that university students would be a center of political agitation, and this print from a series on student life in the 1820s suggests why. Privileged, educated, and idle young men meeting to drink and smoke were all too likely to talk about politics, spread radical ideas, and maybe even hatch plots. AKG London

guarantee that its universities would be kept safely conservative (see "Policing Universities— The Carlsbad Decrees").

Despite these fears, there was less agitation within the German Confederation than in most of the rest of Europe. In fact, the cultural life of these largely rural lands thrived in complacent university and market towns that seemed to eschew politics on a larger scale. Meanwhile, Prussian influence increased. Its national educational system was capped by the new but prestigious University of Berlin, its administration and its army seemed models of modern efficiency, and its policies included measures that stimulated economic growth. In 1818 Prussia lowered tariffs, allowing raw materials free entry into both its eastern and western Prussian territories. The results were so impressive that within a decade the Prussian tariff

was adopted by many of the smaller states that were nearly surrounded by Prussian territory. By 1833 most German governments except Austria had joined Prussia's customs union, the *Zollverein*, which proved a further spur to commerce. One of the most important steps toward German unification under Prussia had been taken without clear nationalist intent. Prussia was finding ways to win the benefits of liberal institutions without liberal politics.

◆ THE TEST OF RESTORATION: SPAIN, ITALY, AND FRANCE

The durability of the conservative order that the Congress of Vienna sought to impose would depend less on the autocracies in Russia, Austria, and Prussia than on the new regimes imposed in

Policing Universities—The Carlsbad Decrees

◆

The Carlsbad Decrees, drafted by Metternich, were adopted by the Diet of the German Confederation in 1819 to be applied in all its member states.

"1. There shall be appointed for each university a special representative of the ruler of each state, the said representatives to have appropriate instructions and extended powers, and they shall have their place of residence where the university is located. . . .

"This representative shall enforce strictly the existing laws and disciplinary regulations, he shall observe with care the attitude shown by the university instructors in their public lectures and registered courses; and he shall, without directly interfering in scientific matters or in teaching methods, give a beneficial direction to the teaching, keeping in view the future attitude of the students. Finally, he shall give unceasing attention to everything that may promote morality . . . among the students. . . .

"2. The confederated governments mutually pledge themselves to eliminate from the universities or any other public educational institutions all instructors who shall have obviously proved their unfitness for the important work entrusted to them by openly deviating from their duties, or by going beyond the boundaries of their functions, or by abusing their legitimate influence over young minds, or by presenting harmful ideas hostile to public order or subverting existing governmental instructions. . . .

"Any instructor who has been removed in this manner becomes ineligible for a position in any other public institution of learning in another state of the Confederation.

"3. The laws that for some time have been directed against secret and unauthorized societies in the universities shall be strictly enforced. . . . The special representatives of the government are enjoined to exert great care in watching these organizations.

"The governments mutually agree that all individuals who shall be shown to have maintained their membership in secret or unauthorized associations, or shall have taken membership in such associations, shall not be eligible for any public office.

"4. No student who shall have been expelled from any university by virtue of a decision of the university senate ratified or initiated by the special representative of the government, shall be admitted by any other university. . . .

"As long as this edict remains in force, no publication which appears daily, or as a serial not exceeding twenty sheets of printed matter, shall be printed in any state of the Confederation without the prior knowledge and approval of the state officials. . . . "

Excerpt from Louis L. Snyder (ed.), *Documents of German History* (Rutgers University Press, 1958), pp. 158–159.

Spain, Italy, and France. There, the effects of revolution and Bonapartism had been woven into the fabric of public life. Intensely divided over questions of government—its form, powers, and policies—conservatives and liberals alike considered politics central to everything else.

Spain and Italy In Spain the Bourbon king Ferdinand VII regained his throne in 1814 when Napoleon's army was expelled. Strong enough to denounce the constitution he had promised, Ferdinand was too weak to do much more. He benefited from patriotic resentment against French rule, but his government found no solution for its own inefficiency or the nation's poverty. In

Spain's American colonies, the revolts led by José de San Martín and Simón Bolívar gained strength, and in 1820 the army that was assembled in Spain to reconquer the colonies mutinied instead and marched on Madrid. The king was then forced to grant a constitution after all, and for three years the constitutional regime struggled to cope with Spain's enormous problems, weakened by its own dissension and its uncooperative monarch. The regime's restrictions on religious orders raised powerful opposition from the Church, freedom of the press produced more devastating criticism, and a constitution in Spain was no help in reconquering the rebellious colonies. When a French army once again crossed into Spain in 1823, this time with the blessing of the Concert of Europe and in the name of order, the Spaniards who had fought French invasion so heroically just ten years earlier were strangely acquiescent. The constitution disappeared again, but the threat of revolution did not.

In Italy restoration meant the return to power of the aristocracies the French had ousted and reestablishment of the separate Italian states.[2] Yet the years of Napoleonic rule had established institutions (and hopes) that the new regimes could not ignore, and they promised constitutions, enlightened administration, peace, and lower taxes—even though their insecure rulers were hardly prepared to take such initiatives. Cautious, moderately repressive, and conveniently corrupt, these regimes provided the sleepy stability Metternich thought appropriate for Italians. Such an atmosphere bred some conspiracy and rumors of far more. Secret groups began to meet across Italy. Known collectively as the *Carbonari* (charcoal burners), they varied in membership and program. Most were middle class, although their name suggested a life of rural simplicity. Some talked of tyrannicide, some promised equality and justice, and some sought mild reform; they had in common the excitement of secret meetings, terrifying oaths, and ornate rituals.

By 1820 news of revolution in Spain was enough to prompt revolts in Italy. Young army officers led the demand for a constitution in Naples; but as the Neapolitan army turned to put down a rising in Sicily, an Austrian army was dispatched to Naples to remove the new constitutional regime. A similar revolt erupted in Piedmont, causing the king to abdicate in favor of his son, and Charles Albert, the prince regent, hastily granted a constitution. But when the new monarch arrived, the Austrian army was with him. Piedmont's constitution lasted two weeks. These revolutions, which left Italy's reactionary governments more rigid and Austrian influence more naked, demonstrated the inadequacy of romantic conspiracies but affirmed an Italian radical and patriotic tradition that would continue to grow.

The Bourbons Restored in France More than anything else, Europe's conservative order was meant to prevent France from again becoming the center of military aggression or revolutionary ideas, and the restoration there was an especially complex compromise. France was permitted a constitution called the Charter, presented as a gift from Louis XVIII and not as a right. It granted the legislature more authority than Napoleon had allowed but left the government largely in the hands of the king. The old estates were wisely forgotten, replaced by a Chamber of Peers with hereditary members and a Chamber of Deputies chosen by an electorate limited to prosperous landowners. Napoleon's centralized administration and effective system of taxation were willingly kept intact.

The regime's supporters, shaken by Napoleon's easy return during the Hundred Days, were determined to crush their enemies. A violent "white terror" broke out in parts of the countryside as those tainted with a revolutionary past were ousted from local office or even killed. Yet Louis XVIII resisted as best he could the more extreme demands of the reactionary ultraroyalists; land confiscated from the Church and from the émigré aristocracy during the Revolution was not returned to them, and most of those who had gained office or wealth since 1789 were allowed quietly to live out their lives. The king and his ministers, moderate and able men, pursued a course of administrative efficiency and political restraint. From 1816 to 1820 they governed well in a relatively peaceful and prosperous country, and Paris became again Europe's most brilliant center of science and the arts.

The Catholic Church, weakened in the intervening years by the loss of property and a decline in the number of new priests, revived remarkably. Missions of preachers toured the countryside calling for a return to the faith, praising the monarchy, and ceremonially planting crosses of repentance for the sins of revolution. The nobles, traditionally rather skeptical in matters of

---

[2] Italy was divided into three monarchies, four duchies, and a republic. The Kingdom of Sardinia (Sardinia and Piedmont), the Papal States, and the Kingdom of the Two Sicilies were monarchies. The Grand Duchy of Tuscany and the duchies of Lucca, Modena, and Parma were all tied to the Habsburgs, who annexed Lombardy and Venetia. The disappearance of the republics of Genoa (part of Piedmont) and Venice left tiny San Marino, safe on its mountaintop, the oldest republic in the world.

religion, were now more pious; and so, too, for the first time in more than a century, were France's leading writers. To the surprise of many Catholics, however, Napoleon's 1801 Concordat with the Church remained in effect, another of his institutional arrangements to prove remarkably lasting.

From Opposition to Revolution in France Despite its achievements, the regime remained insecure and uncertain, satisfying neither Catholics nor anticlericals, neither ultraroyalists nor liberals. The assassination of the duke of Berry in 1820

▼ **This official portrait of Charles X by François Gerard, in the up-to-date romantic style, echoes the portraits of Louis XIV and suggests the way a regime that looked to the past wanted to be seen.**
Chateau de Versailles, France/Giraudon/Bridgeman Art Library

reminded everyone how fragile the monarchy was. The duke was the son of Louis' younger brother and the last Bourbon likely to produce an heir. The royal line seemed doomed until the widowed duchess gave birth to a son eight months later. Louis XVIII reacted to the assassination by naming more conservative ministers, increasing restrictions on the press, and dismissing some leading professors. The air of reaction grew heavier in 1824 when his brother succeeded to the throne as Charles X. A leader of the ultraroyalists, Charles had himself crowned at Reims in medieval splendor, in a ceremony redolent with symbols of the divine right of kings and the alliance of throne and altar.

The new government gave the Church fuller control of education, declared sacrilege a capital crime, and granted a cash indemnity to those who had lost land in the Revolution. In reality, the law against sacrilege was never enforced, and the indemnity, which helped end one of the most dangerous issues left from the Revolution, was a limited one. France remained freer than most European countries, but Charles's subjects worried about the intentions of an ultraroyalist regime that disliked the compromises on which it rested. Public criticism increased, leading politicians joined the parliamentary opposition, and radical secret societies blossomed. Disturbed by liberal gains in the elections of 1827, Charles X dutifully tried a slightly more moderate ministry, but he could not conceal his distaste for it. By 1829 the king could stand no more. While political disputes grew more inflamed, he appointed a cabinet of ultraroyalists only to have the Chamber of Deputies reject them. He called new elections, but instead of regaining seats the ultraroyalists lost still more. Determined not to show the hesitancy of Louis XVI, Charles X reacted with firmness. In 1830 he and his ministers suddenly issued a set of secretly drafted decrees, the July Ordinances, which dissolved the new Chamber of Deputies even before it met, further restricted suffrage, and muzzled the press. Having shown his fiber, the king went hunting.

A shocked Paris slowly responded. Crowds began to mill about, some barricades went up, and stones were thrown at the house of the prime minister. Newspapers disregarded the ordinances and denounced the violation of the constitution, and the government responded with enough troops to raise tempers but too few to enforce order. Charles began to back down, but people were being killed (nearly seven hundred died in the three days of Paris fighting), some of the soldiers were mingling with the crowds, and liberal leaders were planning for a new regime. Once again, Paris was the scene of a popular uprising, and Charles X, victim of what he most detested, abdicated on August 2. For fifteen years, and for the only time in its history, France had been administered by its aristocracy, which had performed with probity and seriousness. The nation had prospered at home and enjoyed some success in foreign affairs, but the monarchy had been meant above all to provide political stability, which the Bourbon regime, the restoration's most important experiment, had failed to do.

II. The Progress of Industrialization

Political instability was one aspect of the larger process of change. In parts of Europe economic growth of a distinctive kind was creating a dynamic of continuing expansion in which the elements of growth—new inventions, demand for more capital, factory organization, more efficient transportation, and increased consumption—stimulated each other and thus led to further growth. Particular historical conditions had begun in the previous century to bring these factors together, but once the pattern of industrial development was clearly established in the nineteenth century, it began to spread, creating new challenges for government.

◆ THE TECHNOLOGY TO SUPPORT MACHINES

Industrialization required the efficient use of raw materials, beginning with cheap metals, such as iron, which could be formed into machines, and cheap fuel, such as coal. The increased importance of iron and coal gave England an important advantage, for it was well supplied with deposits of coal that lay conveniently close to its iron ore.

Coal, Iron, and Steam   The English had increasingly turned to the use of coal as the once-great forests were cut down, and miners had begun taking coal from deeper veins, often beneath the water table. The need for powerful pumps to remove the water stimulated experiments to harness steam. Coal was not useful in smelting iron, however, because its impurities combined with the iron, resulting in an inferior product. For high-quality wrought iron, ironmasters therefore traditionally used charcoal, which was expensive. This problem stimulated experiments by eighteenth-century engineers in smelting with coke prepared from coal to produce pig iron, which could be cast but not worked or machined. As demand for iron and steel increased, the search for new techniques continued, resulting in the 1780s in the puddling process, the first commercially feasible effort to purify iron

▼ The crucial resource of industrialization was coal, and coal mining was one of the earliest industrial activities, employing steam engines to pump water and creating large, polluting enterprises in which hundreds of workers labored as drones, as at this English mine in Northumberland.
Mary Evans Picture Library

using coke alone. It was a breakthrough that convinced ironmasters like John Wilkinson that iron would be the building material of a new age. His improved techniques for boring cylinders made it possible to make better cannons and steam engines, and he built the world's first iron bridge over the Severn River in 1779, experimented with iron rails, launched an iron boat, and at his death was buried in an iron coffin.

The development of steam power also had a long history. In the third century Hero of Alexandria had employed a jet of steam to spin a small wheel, and the account of his experiments, translated into English in 1575, suggested one means by which heat could be converted into motion. The first modern steam engines were based on another principle, however. In the seventeenth century several scientists proved that the atmosphere has weight, and Otto von Guericke in Germany used atmospheric pressure to push a piston through a cylinder, overcoming the efforts of twenty men to restrain it. Such sensational experiments encouraged construction of an "atmospheric engine," which required creating a partial vacuum, and before the end of the seventeenth century, atmospheric machines using the condensation of steam to create the needed vacuum were being designed both in England and on the continent.

The Steam Engine   The first commercially successful atmospheric engine was invented in England by Thomas Savery, who described it in a book published in 1702 and significantly entitled *The Miner's Friend.* Used as a pump, Savery's engine was woefully inefficient; but a decade later another Englishman, Thomas Newcomen, returned to the piston and cylinder design, which completely separated engine and pump and proved a third more efficient. Newcomen engines were soon being used not only in Great Britain but in France, Denmark, Austria, and Hungary.

The most fundamental step in the development of steam was the work of James Watt, a young mechanic and instrument maker working at the University of Glasgow. In the 1760s he made important improvements on the Newcomen engine, while still relying on atmospheric pressure pushing against a vacuum. But he also recognized the enormous potential in the direct pressure created when expanding steam pushed against a piston.

His work took years, for it required new levels of precision in machining cylinders and pistons, new designs for valves, and new knowledge of lubricants and the properties of steam itself. Patented in 1782, Watt's first practical model was nearly three times more efficient than the Newcomen engine. Once he added a system of gears for converting the piston's reciprocating motion to the rotary motion needed to drive most machines, the steam engine had become much more than a pump.

Getting these inventions into use required the business talents of Watt's partner, the Birmingham industrialist Matthew Boulton. He recognized that the demand for cheap power had become more critical with the new inventions in the textile industry (including Arkwright's water frame, Crompton's spinning mule, and Cartwright's power loom, discussed in chapter 18). From the 1780s on, the steam engine was being used in factories, and some five hundred were built before 1800. Even these early machines represented a remarkable improvement over traditional sources of power. They produced between six and twenty horsepower,[3] comparable to the largest windmills and water mills, and did so more reliably and wherever they were needed. An economy traditionally starved for sources of power had overcome that obstacle.

◆ THE ECONOMIC EFFECTS OF REVOLUTION AND WAR

Great Britain's lead over continental countries in goods produced, capital invested, and machinery employed had widened steadily from 1789 to 1815. Nonetheless, there had been economic growth on the continent, too, where the exploitation of resources became more systematic,

---

[3]The average man working hard can muster about one-tenth horsepower, or about seventy-five watts; the horse itself works continuously at a power output of only one-half horsepower. James Watt first defined the unit of horsepower as 33,000 foot-pounds per minute, but this could be achieved only by the strongest horses and only for short periods. The largest windmills in the eighteenth century could develop probably as much as fifty horsepower, but perhaps two-thirds of this was lost in friction. The best water mills seem to have produced ten horsepower, but most of them rarely surpassed five.

population increased, transportation generally improved, the means of mobilizing capital for investment expanded, and more and more political and business leaders were concerned with speeding industrial growth. In important respects the French Revolution and the Napoleonic era had cleared the way for future industrialization. In France, western Germany, northern Italy, and the Low Countries, land tenure was no longer the most pressing economic and social issue. Less constrained by custom and legal restrictions, landowners, including peasant proprietors, could more easily shift their production to meet the demands of a national market. The abolition of guilds and old commercial restrictions had eliminated some obstacles to the free movement of workers and the establishment of new enterprises. The Napoleonic Code and French commercial law not only favored free contracts and an open marketplace but also introduced the advantages of uniform and clear commercial regulations. The French government had exported a common and sensible standard of weights and measures, encouraged the establishment of technical schools (the Polytechnic School in Paris long remained the world's best), and honored inventors and inventions of every sort, from improved gunpowder to new techniques for raising sugar beets. Under Napoleon, Europe had benefited from improved highways and bridges and a large zone of free trade; and the Bank of France, as restructured in 1800, had become the European model of a bank of issue providing a reliable currency.

In the short run, however, the years of war had slowed and disrupted Europe's economic growth. Vast resources in material and men were destroyed or wastefully used up. When peace came, governments were burdened with heavy debts, and returning soldiers had to find ways to support themselves in a changed economy. The Continental System, which had initially swung production and trade in France's favor, had collapsed with Napoleon's fall, bringing down many of the enterprises that it had artificially sustained. Both political change and renewed British competition discouraged daring capital investment. During the war, Great Britain had found compensation in American markets for its exclusion from continental ones and had avoided the shock of military invasion; but it, too, suffered a severe slump in the postwar years when the anticipated continental demand for British goods failed to materialize and the transition to a peacetime economy proved difficult to achieve.

◆ PATTERNS OF INDUSTRIALIZATION

By the mid-1820s, however, British trade was reviving, and by 1830 its economy was being transformed. Although no single industry was yet fully mechanized, the pattern of industrialization was clear. Later, that pattern would be repeated in much of the world, but contemporaries attributed England's leadership to unique advantages. Cotton had become the most important industry, benefiting from a large consumer market as spinning cotton thread and then weaving the cloth were mechanized. Growth in one economic sector stimulated growth in others. Increased textile production, for example, accelerated the use of chemical dyes; greater iron production required more coal. A few factories in one place encouraged the growth of others in the same region, where they could take advantage of the available workforce and capital; this concentration of production in turn increased the demand for roads, canals, and, later, railways. All this growth required more capital, and on the cycle went. In continuity, range of industries affected, national scope, and rate of increase, Great Britain's industrial growth in the first half of the nineteenth century was the greatest humankind had yet experienced.

Railroads New inventions became whole industries and were integrated into the economy with dazzling speed. The steam engine's application to rail travel is a classic case. The first successful steam railway line was built in England in 1825; a few years later an improved engine impressed spectators by outracing a horse, and in 1830 the first passenger line took its riders the thirty-two miles from Liverpool to Manchester in an hour and a quarter. Just more than a decade later, there were 2,000 miles of such rail lines in Great Britain; by 1851 there were 7,000 (see "Gladstone Argues for Regulating Railroad Fares").

Railroads constituted a new industry that stimulated further industrialization. They bought huge quantities of iron and coal. They carried food and raw materials to cities, manufactured products to consumers, and building materials

GLADSTONE ARGUES FOR REGULATING RAILROAD FARES

◆

Sir Robert Peel supported his young colleague, William Gladstone, in trying to push a bill for the regulation of railroads through the English Parliament. Conflicting interests eventually forced Gladstone's plan to be watered down (there was great fear that the government would seek to purchase private railroad companies and considerable opposition to its regulating them very heavily); but Gladstone won his point, set forth in his speech on July 8, 1844, that Parliament should have a voice in setting rates as a matter of social policy.

"Of the forty Clauses of the Bill, twenty-four related to the provisions respecting purchase; those from the twenty-fifth to the twenty-eighth related to third-class passengers. He must say that he felt strongly that the case of the third-class passengers [on] those trains was becoming a national question of great importance, and though averse to any general interference by Government with the management of these Companies, he did think it was wise to make a provision while it could be done without any breach of public faith, whereby those persons—being, as they were frequently, the least able to bear exposure to the cold, and obliged to remove frequently in search of bread, from one part of the country to the other—might be able to transfer themselves at the charge of 1*d.* a mile, without such exposure to the severity of the weather as amounted in many cases to severe personal suffering. It was on that ground they had introduced Clauses which certainly, so far as they went, were of the nature of interference. There were other Clauses regarding the public service, access of

the public to the station and yards, conduct of inspectors, the prosecution of Railway Companies who exceeded the powers for which they were incorporated, contracts with Government, loan notes, and other matters so trivial that he need not mention them. . . .

" . . . With railways the Legislature were dealing with a new system producing new results, and likely to produce unforeseen effects. Was it not wise, then, to make provision for the future? Was it wise to trust themselves to all changes which the next ten or fifteen years might produce with regard to public communication by railway, without a thought for providing for the difficulties that might arise. Was it wise to place themselves in a position in which, whatever might be the exigency, they would be debarred from any interference."

From *Hansard's Parliamentary Debates:* 3d Series, Vol. 76 (1844).

▼ **Stephenson's North Star engine of 1837 was meant to be an object of beauty, combining technology and craftsmanship.**
Science Museum, London, UK/Bridgeman Art Library

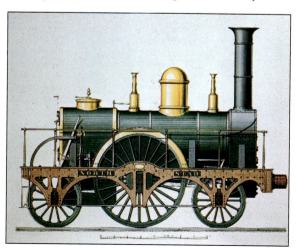

and fertilizers to the countryside. And they made it easier for the men and women who crowded into dirt-stained railway cars to travel in search of work. Similarly, the telegraph, developed by a generation of scientists working in many countries and quickly adopted as an adjunct of railroading, expanded to other uses, becoming a military necessity and a conveyor of news to the general public. The most impressive of the early long telegraph lines was Samuel F. B. Morse's from Philadelphia to Washington, opened in 1843. Less than a decade later, Britain laid 4,000 miles of telegraph lines, and a cable to the continent was in operation.

Yet the leap from new invention to industrialization was not necessarily direct or predictable. Often dozens of subsidiary inventions or improvements were necessary to make a new machine competitive. Everywhere, but more often on the continent than in Britain, small-scale manufacturing and crafts persisted alongside the new. Machines themselves were usually made of wood and were frequently still driven by wind, waterpower, or horses. But the water-driven mills, charcoal-fired smelters, and hand-powered looms that dotted the countryside would be gradually but relentlessly displaced, as would hundreds of thousands of skilled artisans and rural families working in their homes to make products in the old ways—a transformation that accounted for much of the human suffering occasioned by industrialization.

National Differences In 1815 many regions of the continent, including such traditional commercial centers as Barcelona and Naples, had seemed ready to follow the British example of industrial growth, but by the 1850s the zone of industrialization had narrowed to include only northeastern France, Belgium and the Netherlands, western Germany, and northern Italy. Industrial change in this zone was uneven but more extensive than outside it. Countries poorly endowed in coal and iron, such as Italy, faced formidable obstacles. Although Saxony in eastern Germany was an early industrial center, most of Germany remained an area of quiet villages in which commerce relied on peddlers and trade fairs, even though by midcentury the German states were crisscrossed by the continent's largest railway network. Except for pockets of industrial development, Eastern Europe remained a world of agricultural estates. The centuries-old triangular trade between Europe, the West Indies, and North America declined in importance, as did the European ports that had depended on commerce in sugar and raw materials, now overshadowed by the export of manufactured goods and the entrepreneurial activity of merchants on both sides of the ocean.

Belgium, which had prospered from its former connections with Holland, built on its tradition of technological skill, its geographical advantages as a trade center accessible by water, and its excellent supplies of coal to become the continent's first industrialized nation. Belgium extracted more coal than did France or Germany and was the first country to complete a railway network. The French railway system, on the other hand, was

▼ **Production in Belgium, France, and the United Kingdom**

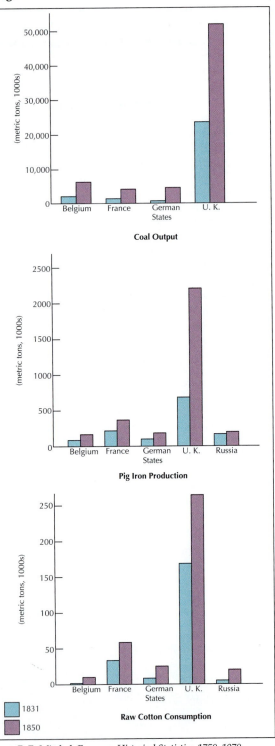

Coal Output

Pig Iron Production

Raw Cotton Consumption

1831
1850

From B. R. Mitchel, *European Historical Statistics, 1750–1970* (Columbia University Press, 1975), pp. 360–361, 428–429.

not finished until after Germany's, for it was slowed by political conflict despite early and ambitious plans. France's canals, considered good in 1815, had trebled by 1848; and its production of iron, coal, and textiles increased severalfold in the same period. This growth would have been impressive a generation earlier, but Britain's expansion in each of these sectors was several times greater. In iron production, for example, the two countries were about equal in 1800, but by 1850 Britain's output was six or seven times greater. Britain outstripped France still more in textiles and coal, producing by midcentury half the world total of these items.

Everywhere, increased production led to more commerce and closer international ties as capital, techniques, workers, and managers moved from Britain across the channel and spread from Belgium and France into the rest of Europe. Finance became so internationally linked that the Bank of France granted an emergency loan to the Bank of England in 1825, only a decade after Waterloo; and the domestic banking policies of the United States, in response to a financial panic in 1837, led to a wave of crises in the financial centers of Europe.

State Politics   Although many writers argued that the new prosperity followed from natural economic laws that worked best unimpeded by government, by midcentury the state was centrally involved in the process of economic growth. Railroads required franchises and the power of eminent domain before a spike was pounded. Inevitably, routes, rates, and even the gauge of the track became political matters to be settled by parliaments or special commissions. In Belgium and in most of Germany, railroads were owned as well as planned by the state.

Tariffs, the dominant issue in British politics in the 1840s, became a critical question in every country. In 1846, after a wrenching public campaign, Britain abolished the tariff on grain, known as the Corn Laws. In doing so, the nation expressed confidence in its position as the world's greatest center of manufacture and sided with those who favored trade and a lower price for bread rather than with the landowners who benefited from higher grain prices. Equally important to economic development was the role of govern-

ment in banking and currency. Just before the middle of the century, Parliament granted the Bank of England a monopoly on issuing money and required companies to register with the government and publish their annual budget as a guide to investors. Similar steps were taken across Europe. Before industries could effectively tap private wealth, investors needed assurance that they risked only the money they invested, without being liable (as in a partnership) for all a firm's debts. That assurance required new legislation establishing limited liability and encouraging the formation of corporations, and every major country passed such measures.

The Role of Government   The growth of cities and the benefits of new technology created additional social demands involving government. By the 1840s most cities had a public omnibus, some sidewalks, and gas lighting in certain areas. Such services, usually provided by private companies, had to be subsidized, regulated, and given legal protection by the government. As the cost and importance of these services increased, so did the state's participation in them, often extending to full ownership. The growing role of government was exemplified by the postal service, which most states had provided since the seventeenth and eighteenth centuries. These postal systems, which were with few exceptions graft-ridden and unreliable, proved inadequate for an industrial era. In Britain demands for improvement led a little-known inventor and radical to propose a solution that captured the thinking of the new age. He called for standard envelopes and payment in advance by means of an adhesive stamp. That, he said, using current arguments, would not only eliminate graft and reduce costs but the service would pay for itself because lower rates would increase volume. His reforms, denounced as dangerous and impractical, passed nevertheless in 1840; and within twenty years the volume of mail in Britain increased sixfold. By then, money orders, savings accounts, and the telegraph had been added to postal services. In France mail delivery was extended to rural areas, and by the 1850s every major government was adopting the new system, including the postage stamp, which quickly became the object of a fashionable middle-class hobby.

▲ By 1830 it was possible to conceive of life transformed by technology, as in this imagined view of what London's important White Chapel road might soon become, with traffic jams and smog but on an unpaved road with room for dogs.

National Railway Museum, York, UK/Bridgeman Art Library

Effective government, in short, was now expected to further economic development—by subsidizing ports, transportation, and new inventions; by registering patents and sponsoring education; by encouraging investment and enforcing contracts; and by maintaining order and preventing strikes. In the 1840s the leaders of Britain, France, and Belgium busily did these things—in Great Britain the number of government employees increased about fourfold in the first half of the century—and the desire in other countries to have governments that would similarly foster economic development was an important element in the revolutions of 1848 and the nationalist movements of the period that followed.

The Crystal Palace The British celebrated their position as the masters of industrialization in 1851 with the first international industrial exhibition. Prominent people from the aristocracy, business, and government joined in the planning, and a specially designed pavilion was built in London, a sort of giant greenhouse called the Crystal Palace, which proved to be an architectural milestone. Many governments feared that Britain risked revolution by attracting huge mobs to London, but the admiring crowds proved well behaved.

The exhibition provided a significant comparison of the relative economic development of the participating countries. Russia displayed primarily raw materials; Austria showed mainly luxury

▲ A glass cathedral enclosing trees, statues, and fountains, the Crystal Palace organized national exhibits as a kind of encyclopedia of world industry, with subcategories for different products, as in the Indian exhibit at the left.
Guildhall Library, London/Art Resource, NY

handicrafts. So did the German *Zollverein* and the Italian states, whose appearance as single economic units foretold the advantages of national unification. Although unable to fill all the space it had demanded, the United States impressed viewers with collections of fossils, cheap manufactured products for use in the home, mountains of dentifrice and soap, and a series of new inventions, including Colt revolvers, a sewing machine, McCormick's reaper, and a vacuum coffin. French machines, which ranged from a much-admired device for folding envelopes to a submarine, were generally considered the most elegant. But British machines surpassed everyone's in quantity, size, and variety. It is, explained London's *Morning Chronicle*, "to our wonderful industrial discipline—our consummately arranged organization

▼ British products dominated the machinery section of the Crystal Palace Exhibition. Here men and women marveled at Joseph Whitworth's lathe for forming railway wheels, a machine for making machines.
Guildhall Library, Corporation of London, UK/Bridgeman Art Library

of toil, and our habit of division of labour—that we owe all the triumph." By 1850 Great Britain was the wealthiest nation in history,[4] and over the next twenty years, it would continue to increase its lead in goods produced.

III. The Social Effects

Economic growth on such a scale was accompanied by far-reaching social change. Even in its early stages, industrialization impinged on all of society, from the state to the family, affecting governmental functions, the nature of work, women's roles, and childhood. Child labor, tyrannical foremen, teeming slums, and unemployment brought new social problems and required new social policies as the growing prosperity and security of the middle class contrasted all the more sharply with the destitution of the urban poor.

◆ THE DIVISION OF LABOR

The Factory The factory quickly became the symbol of the age. Well before industrialization, there had been workplaces in which hundreds of people labored under one roof; conversely, even in industrialized societies, most wage earners did not work in factories. But the factory symbolized a different kind of power—the power of steam and of technology, the power of capital to assemble machinery and laborers, the power of competition to drive down prices and wages, the power of markets to absorb ever more production and determine what would be produced. Above all, the factory symbolized the capacity of this whole system to change the landscape, to erect or transform cities, and to reshape the lives of masses of men, women, and children.

The factory model was most clearly triumphant in the production of textiles. Spinning and weaving had always been domestic tasks; even in Europe's most important textile centers,

▲ This Nasmyth steam hammer looms above the men who endure heat and noise to feed it—in every way the symbol of a new era.
Science Museum, London

where merchants collected the output from hundreds of looms, the actual work had been done primarily in the home, where it might involve all the family. The most successful weavers often employed other workers, so that the average domestic establishment contained about a half-dozen weavers. Pay and working conditions varied with the region, the season, and the ability of middlemen to control the prices of the thread they supplied and the cloth they purchased and resold. Textile factories, on the other hand, required an investment in buildings, machinery, and raw materials far beyond the reach of most weavers; and production per worker increased more than a thousandfold with the factory's efficient organization and power-driven machinery. By the 1830s cotton factories in Manchester, larger than most, averaged nearly three hundred employees.

These factories would slowly drive the older forms of textile production out of business, although the flexibility of domestic production (and the weavers' hatred of factories) long kept the older ways alive in some regions and for special products. Those who came to work in a factory might be former weavers, but they were likely to

---

[4]Although all estimates for this period are uncertain, it seems likely that by 1860 the per capita wealth of the French was about two-thirds and of the Germans about two-fifths that of the British.

be less skilled laborers (often migrants) driven by poverty. Most were women and children, hired to tend power looms, splice thread, or sweep the floor. Children were paid less than women and women less than men, who did the heaviest work and served as carpenters and mechanics. At first, children usually worked with their parents, even in the factories; but increased specialization meant that, like their mothers and fathers, children came to be employed and supervised without regard to family ties.

Factory Life The workday usually began at 5:30 or 6:00 in the morning and lasted for twelve hours of work plus whatever time was allotted for meals and for recesses (when belts were replaced and machinery fixed). The workroom, hot in summer and cold in winter, was usually kept moist so the taut thread would break less readily. Employers, concerned about keeping the expensive machinery running, found their workers too often lethargic and sullen, prone to drunkenness and indifference. To maintain the discipline that efficient production demanded, foremen used whips, curses, and most of all, fines (fines for lateness, for slacking off, for flawed work, for talking, and sometimes even for singing or whistling).

The best employers, like the middle-class reformers and the inspectors subsequently appointed as the result of factory legislation, were shocked by these conditions, and by the workers themselves, in whom they discovered foul language, filthiness, poor health, ignorance, and promiscuity. Factory owners could see no solution beyond more discipline, and nearly all employers opposed such measures as the law finally passed in England in 1847 that limited the workday to ten hours. Even that legislation was primarily an embarrassed response to the evils of child labor, which had been bitterly criticized by reformers and intellectuals, as in this excerpt from Elizabeth Barrett Browning's poem *The Cry of the Children*, published in 1843:

> And well may the children weep before you!
>   They are weary ere they run.
> They have never seen the sunshine, 'nor the glory,
>   Which is brighter than the sun.
> They know the grief of man, without his wisdom.
>   They sink in man's despair, without its calm;
> Are slaves, without the liberty in Christendom,

▼ **Under the foreman's close supervision, women kept the textile looms running.**
Alfred A. Knopf/Random House

> Are martyrs, by the pang without the palm,—
> Are worn, as if with age, yet unretrievingly
> The harvest of its memories cannot reap,—
> Are orphans of the earthly love and heavenly,
> Let them weep! Let them weep!

Many workers, especially those with established skills—hatters, masons, tanners, typesetters, bakers, and eventually, steam-engine makers—took the lead in forming labor organizations and agitating for political redress. Although skilled laborers tended to look down on factory workers, the latter were, in income at least, better off than about half of all laborers; and their lot improved a bit as legislation hesitantly restricted hours and set some standards of hygiene and safety.

Differentiation   The increased division of labor was not limited to the allocation of work within factories, and sociologists use the term *differentiation* to describe the spread of specialization among groups and institutions that was a characteristic of the nineteenth century. Just as factories separated work from family life, so money exchange and legal contracts differentiated economic from personal or social relationships. Business affairs and governmental functions became more specialized, matters determined by calculation or regulation rather than status or social connection. Maintaining the peace, collecting taxes, inspecting factories and schools, and administering welfare measures fell to separate agencies. In addition, social tasks (such as the registration of births and deaths and provisions for education and charity) that had once been performed more informally and largely through the churches, were now increasingly absorbed by the state—another reason for the importance of politics in this period. Just as each trade and each locality followed its own course of social change, so each nation differed in the pace and manner of institutional differentiation. Britain, more than continental states, left many public matters to local government and private groups; in France the role of the national government increased; and the German states tended to combine centralizing bureaucracies with considerable local autonomy. Whatever the pattern, the growth of differentiation brought increased professional-

ization and exposed tensions between government and established interests, between national policy and local custom.

◆ THE FAMILY

To a great many nineteenth-century observers, social change threatened to undermine the family, and moralists of every sort warned that the very institution most central to civilization was in danger. Recent research has suggested a different view. The heightened concern for the family was a response to real stress, but it was also an expression of a growing belief in the importance of the family, which would prove to be an extraordinarily adaptable institution.

Traditional Roles   Family life in Europe had always been related to social status. For the aristocracy, family encompassed a wide network of relatives, privilege, and power. Women played a critical but subordinate role as carriers of the dowries that joined estates, as managers of large domestic staffs, and as centers of the social circles in which aristocrats met. Among peasants, the family unit might include grandparents or, where plots were large enough, even in-laws, cousins, and nephews. Particularly in the Mediterranean regions, such extended families often shared housing in the village but worked in different nearby fields. When they could, however, a young couple generally set up a household of their own. In regions where peasants owned land, they had difficulty keeping it intact while giving something to all their children. Law and custom might require equal division of inheritance (as in France), primogeniture (inheritance by the eldest son, as in England), or other more complicated arrangements. But everywhere bitter disputes were frequent, for the elderly feared dispossession and the children feared that they would not get their share in time.

The family was the basic economic unit, pooling income from various sources and dividing labor in customary ways. Women usually handled household chores and the smaller animals, the men were responsible for the heavier work, and everyone worked together in critical periods of planting and harvest. Often the women had more

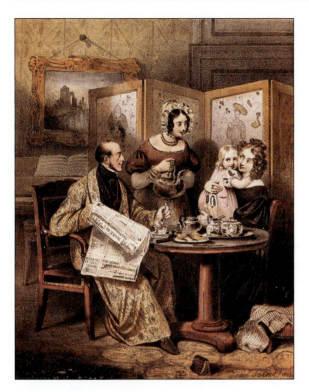

▲ The bourgeois family at breakfast: perfect domestic harmony, father looks up from the morning newspaper to enjoy the scene of an angelic child and adoring wife, a servant tends to them in front of the Chinese screen that sets off the eating space.
© Tallandier

access than the men to additional sources of income—piecework from a nearby mill or domestic service for the well-to-do—and they played a central role in marketing. Men, on the other hand, were more likely to travel considerable distances, especially in difficult times, in order to pick up a bit of work on roads or docks or at some great landlord's harvest. As population increased, the children were more often pushed out to seek employment in the nearest mills and towns.

The Impact of Industrialization   For artisans as well as peasants, the family was often the unit of production, although the division of tasks by sex was usually more explicit, and even small workshops had long tended to exclude women, at least from the better-paid tasks. Working-class women and children were accustomed to long hours of labor. The strain on the family in the industrial age came rather from the lack of housing, the conditions of work, and the need for cash, which was compounded by the risk of unemployment. Not only did women and children have to supplement the father's income, but they were less and less likely to work side by side; if taught a trade, children were less likely to learn it from their parents. Sometimes the father, with his preindustrial skills, remained unemployed and did housework while his wife and children earned wages, which the socialist Friedrich Engels believed was another source of "the righteous indignation of the workers at being virtually turned into eunuchs."

Adolescents in factory towns, hardened at an early age, were probably more likely to leave home when their pay allowed, and urban conditions made it more difficult for the family to support the aged and the sick. Such factors did weaken family ties, as did—at least in the eyes of the upper classes—the common practice for working men and women to live together without the trouble or expense of formal marriage rites. Yet among workers, too, the family survived, and the home remained a special place expected to provide protection for small children, a haven for wage earners, and temporary shelter for relatives come to seek a job.

Women's Roles   The fact that women worked for pay may also have slowly lessened their domestic subordination, even if it did not lead directly to the new and superior stage of family life that Karl Marx thought it might. In the lower-middle class, especially in France, women were as important as and frequently more visible than men in operating small shops. The life of the middle-class woman, however, contrasted greatly with that of her poorer sisters, and the role allotted to wife and mother became one of the most apparent and important indicators of social status. Women continued to be the organizers, patrons, critics, and ornaments of many of Europe's most cultivated circles; but the middle class isolated women from the harsh competition of business and politics. As the contemporary French historian Jules Michelet complained, "By a singular set of circumstances—social, economic, religious—man lives separated from woman." In

Victorian England gentlemen met in their clubs or withdrew from the ladies after dinner for their cigars and weighty talk.

Except for the well-to-do who had domestic (female) servants, wives of every class—no matter what their other burdens—were expected to prepare and serve the food, wash and mend clothes, and clean the home. Victorian discourse often made the ideal of femininity appear to be an idle and pallid creature, encased in corset or bustle, whose tendency to faint was a sign of delicacy. In reality women's roles were far more significant and varied, but the image may well have reflected values widely shared. Allowing a wife to be idle even if her husband worked hard was a kind of conspicuous consumption, a partial imitation of aristocratic elegance. There were signs, too, of an unconscious effort to sustain a sort of counterculture. If men must be competitive, hard, and practical, women should be tender, innocent, and gracious—the weak but pure upholders of morality and aesthetic sensibility. The middle-class woman with no estate to manage and few servants to direct was almost literally placed on a pedestal. Neither her needlework nor her piano playing was viewed as serious, but her role in maintaining the protective calm of the home and as exemplar of the moral virtues was.

Moral Seriousness Middle-class concern with the family also emphasized the special moral role of women within the home, conceived as a private citadel largely closed to the outside world. The liberal dream of combining individualism and social order found its model in the family, where the patriarchal father, devoted mother, and carefully trained children were meant to live in disciplined harmony. Childhood itself lasted longer in the middle class, for manners, education, and character required elaborate preparation. The mother was the core of this home; and books, newspapers, magazines, and sermons enthusiastically described the talents her role required. Motherhood was treated as an honored occupation, fondly depicted in novels and in the new women's magazines founded, like the Parisian *Journal des Femmes* of 1832, to make women "skilled in their duties as companions and mothers."

Clearly, these attitudes were related to the famous prudery of the age and the distrust of sexual passion. In 1818 Thomas Bowdler produced his *Family Shakespeare*, a "bowdlerized" version "in which . . . those words and phrases are omitted which cannot with propriety be read in a family," a strange sensitivity after two hundred years of admiration for Shakespeare's dramas. And "the anti-English pollution of the waltz . . . the most degenerating that the last or present century can see" was denounced in *The Ladies' Pocket Book of Etiquette* of 1840. The middle classes sought to maintain an orderly world through convention. At a time when prostitution and drunkenness were believed to have reached new heights, prudery was more than repression; it was an effort to bend society to the self-discipline on which

▼ **Ironsmiths at work in France in a characteristically small workshop: A master, young helper, and boy already learning the trade. Living quarters were probably overhead.**
Art Resource, NY

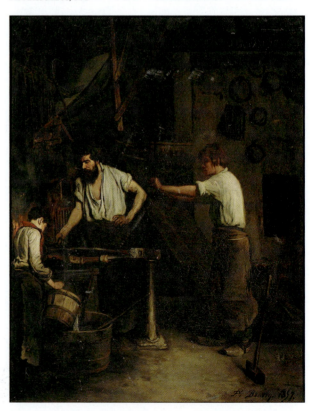

morality, a thriving commerce, the advancement of knowledge, and personal fulfillment were thought to rest.

◆ THE STANDARD OF LIVING

Historians agree more about the general pattern of social change in the first half of the nineteenth century than about its effects on the standard of living, particularly of the working class. For this period, England is the critical case; scholars agree that between 1790 and 1840 national wealth about doubled but that the upper classes were the principal beneficiaries. Did workers gain, too? Certainly they were poor, but poverty, even of the bleakest sort, was not new (and the growing protest against such destitution was in itself one of the important changes of the period). The poorest peasants of Sicily who lived in caves or those of Sweden or Ireland who lived in holes dug into the ground may have been victims of the social system; they were hardly victims of industrialization.

Living Conditions   What *was* new was the terrible crowding in industrial areas and the workers' helpless dependence on their employers. The conditions in which workers lived made poverty more miserable, more obvious to all, and more threatening to the general welfare. The crowding was partly the result of increased population, but it followed directly from the rapid growth of factory towns. There, hastily built housing may often have been drier and cleaner than peasant hovels that had served for centuries, but squeezing whole families into a single room and cramming hundreds and thousands of people into slums with little light, with a single source of insalubrious water, and with no means for disposing of sewage created problems so different in scale as to be different in kind (see "Reports on the Housing Crisis in France and Germany"). Industrialization also added the special hazards of lead and phosphorous poisoning; and the assault on the lungs of coal mining, cotton spinning, and machine grinding combined with poor nutrition to make tuberculosis ubiquitous. Everywhere in Europe members of the working class were recognizably thinner, shorter, and paler than other people.

The work available had always changed with the seasons, and laborers in many regions and trades were accustomed to migrating to follow harvests and other temporary opportunities for work. Industrialization, however, often brought a demoralizing dependence. Most new factories employed between 150 and 300 men, women, and children whose well-being was largely tied to a single employer. A high proportion of these people were new to the area in which they lived, starkly dependent on cash to pay their rent, to purchase rough cotton for clothes, to provide the bread that was the staple of their diet, and to buy some candles and coal. For millions, employment was never steady; for millions of others, unemployment was the norm. It was common for a third of the adult males of a town to be without work, especially in the winter, and pauperism was acknowledged to be the social disease of the century, a condition that included some 10 percent of the population in Britain and only slightly less in France. Workers, of course, suffered most in the periodic economic depressions that baffled even the most optimistic observers. The depression of 1846 was nearly universal, and that of 1857 extended from North America to Eastern Europe. Layoffs in the Lancashire cotton industry ran so high in the 1860s as a result of the American Civil War that at one time more than 250,000 workers, better than half the total, lived by what they could get on relief. The recipes for watery soup handed out by the charitable agencies of every city define the thinness of survival.[5]

Purchasing Power   Although most workers everywhere suffered from the changing conditions of employment, workers in some trades and

---

[5]The French chef of the Reform Club of London was much admired for his "good and nourishing" recipe: 1/4 lb. leg of beef, 2 oz. of drippings, 2 onions and other vegetables, 1/2 lb. flour, 1/2 lb. barley, 3 oz. salt, 1/2 oz. brown sugar–and 2 gallons of water! It was by no means the cheapest soup. Cited in Cecil Woodham-Smith, *The Great Hunger* (1964), p. 173.

Reports on the Housing Crisis in France and Germany

◆

The housing crisis was not limited to cities with a lot of new industry, as these two descriptions, expressing the shock of middle-class reformers, show. The first is from André Guépin, Nantes au XIXe siècle (Nantes, 1835); the second, giving Dr. Bluemner's impression of Breslau, is from Alexander Schneer, Über die Zuständer der arbeitenden Klassen in Breslau (Berlin, 1845).

"If you want to know how he [the poorer worker] lives, go—for example—to the Rue des Fumiers which is almost entirely inhabited by this class of worker. Pass through one of the drain-like openings, below street-level, that lead to these filthy dwellings, but remember to stoop as you enter. One must have gone down into these alleys where the atmosphere is as damp and cold as a cellar; one must have known what it is like to feel one's foot slip on the polluted ground and to fear a stumble into the filth: to realise the painful impression that one receives on entering the homes of these unfortunate workers. Below street-level on each side of the passage there is a large gloomy cold room. Foul water oozes out of the walls. Air reaches the room through a sort of semi-circular window which is two feet high at its greatest elevation. Go in—if the fetid smell that assails you does not make you recoil. Take care, for the floor is uneven, unpaved and untiled—or if there are tiles, they are covered with so much dirt that they cannot be seen. And then you will see two or three rickety beds fitted to one side because the cords that bind them to the worm-eaten legs have themselves decayed. Look at the contents of the bed—a mattress; a tattered blanket of rags (seldom washed since there is only one); sheets sometimes; and a pillow sometimes. No wardrobes are needed in these homes. Often a weaver's loom and a spinning wheel complete the furniture. There is no fire in the winter. No sunlight penetrates [by day], while at night a tallow candle is lit. Here men work for fourteen hours [a day]."

"*Question:* What is the condition of the living quarters of the class of factory workers, day labourers and journeymen?

Reply of the City Poor Doctor, Dr. Bluemner: "It is in the highest degree miserable. Many rooms are more like pigsties than quarters for human beings. The apartments in the city are, if possible, even worse than those in the suburbs. The former are, of course, always in the yard, if places in which you can hardly turn round can be called apartments. The so-called staircase is generally completely in the dark. It is also so decrepit that the whole building shakes with every firm footstep; the rooms themselves are small and so low that it is hardly possible to stand upright, the floor is on a slope, since usually part of the house has to be supported by struts. The windows close badly, the stoves are so bad that they hardly give any heat but plenty of smoke in the room. Water runs down the doors and walls. The ground-floor dwellings are usually half underground."

From Sidney Pollard and Colin Holmes (eds.), *Documents of European Economic History*, Vol. 1. (St. Martin's Press, 1968), pp. 494–495, 497–498.

places were distinctly better off; and overall, real wages—measured, that is, in terms of what they could buy—may have begun to increase somewhat even before the general rise in wages in the mid-1840s and notably again in the 1850s, though these gains meant less in new factory towns, where workers could be forced to buy shoddy goods at high prices in company stores. Alcoholism was so extensive that in many a factory town paydays were staggered in order to reduce the dangerous number of drunks, a sign of alienation that may also have reflected an increase in available money. Technology brought benefits as well. The spread of the use of soap and cotton underwear was an enormous boon to health, and by midcentury brick construction and iron pipes had improved housing even for many of the relatively poor. Luxuries such as sugar, tea, and meat were becoming available to the lower-middle class and to the more prosperous artisans.

▲ Hopelessness dominates J. Leonard's painting of the poor coming to the charitable doctor in an endless stream.
Musée des Beaux-Arts, Valenciennes/Giraudon/Bridgeman Art Library

The vigorous debate among historians over whether industrialization raised or lowered workers' standard of living in the first half of the century has become in large measure a judgment about the effects of capitalism. But historians generally agree that whatever improvements occurred reached the masses slowly and often could not compensate for the added burdens of industrial employment or the growing chasm between the destitute and the regularly employed. In industrial Europe the urban poor remained a subject of baffled concern. The more fortunate workers and the middle classes were unquestionably more prosperous than they had been in the recent past, which made the contrast with the poverty of those beneath them even more striking. A luxury restaurant in Paris (by 1830 Paris had more than three thousand restaurants of every type in contrast to only fifty or so before the Revolution) might charge twenty-five or thirty times an average worker's daily wage for a single meal; even modest restaurants charged twice a worker's daily wage—to a clientele that ate three or four times a day, in contrast to the two meals of many workers. From the top to the bottom of society, the gradations in status and wealth were subtle, but the differences between the comfortable minority and the poor majority were palpable in every aspect of daily life.

THE INDUSTRIAL REVOLUTION AND THE STANDARD OF LIVING

◆

Debates among historians about the impact of the industrial revolution in England on the standard of living of workers is likewise a debate about capitalism and social policy, but its evolution is also a result of increased historical knowledge and new methods. These excerpts show the diverse emphases and shifting conclusions but not the careful reasoning and the extraordinary range of the research that makes this literature still worth reading.

From John L. and Barbara Hammond, The Rise of Modern Industry *(M. S. G. Haskell House, 1925).**

"The apologies for child labour were precisely the same as the apologies for the slave trade. Cobbett put it in 1833 that the opponents of the Ten Hours Bill had discovered that England's manufacturing supremacy depended on 30,000 little girls. This was no travesty of their argument. The champions of the slave trade pointed to the £70,000,000 invested in the sugar plantations, to the dependence of our commerce on the slave trade. . . . The argument for child labour followed the same line. . . . Sir James Graham thought that the Ten Hours Bill would ruin the cotton industry and with it the trade of the country. . . . Our population, which had grown rapidly in the Industrial Revolution was no longer able to feed itself; the food it bought was paid for by its manufactures: those manufactures depended on capital: capital depended on profits: profits depended on the labour of the boys and girls who enabled the manufacturer to work his mills long enough at a time to repay the cost of the plant and to compete with foreign rivals. This was the circle in which the nation found its conscience mangled.

" . . . Thus England asked for profits and received profits. Everything turned to profit. The towns had their profitable dirt, their profitable smoke, their profitable slums, their profitable disorder, their profitable ignorance, their profitable despair. The curse of Midas was on this society: on its corporate life, on its common mind, on the decisive and impatient step it had taken from the peasant: to the industrial age. For the new town was not a home where man could find beauty, happiness, leisure, learning, religion, the influences that civilize outlook and habit, but a bare and desolate place, without colour, air or laughter, where man, woman and child worked, ate and slept. This was to be the lot of the mass of mankind: this the sullen rhythm of their lives. The new factories and the new furnaces were like the Pyramids, telling of man's enslavement, rather than of his power, casting their long shadow over the society that took such pride in them."

From Thomas S. Ashton, "The Standard of Life of the Workers in England, 1790–1830," Journal of Economic History, *Vol. 9, 1949.**

"Let me confess at the start that I am of those who believe that, all in all, conditions of labour were becoming better, at least after 1820, and that the spread of the factory played a not inconsiderable part in the improvement. . . . One of the merits of the factory system was that it offered, and required, regularity of employment and hence stability of consumption. During the period 1790–1830 factory production increased rapidly. A greater proportion of the people came to benefit both as producers and as consumers. The fall in the price of textiles reduced the

price of clothing. Government contracts for uniforms and army boots called into being new industries, and after the war the products of these found a market among the better-paid artisans. Boots began to take the place of clogs and hats replaced shawls, at least for wear on Sundays. Miscellaneous commodities, ranging from clocks to pocket handkerchiefs, began to enter into the scheme of expenditure, and after 1820 such things as tea and coffee and sugar fell in price substantially. The growth of trade-unions, friendly societies, savings banks, popular newspapers and pamphlets, schools, and nonconformist chapels—all give evidence of the existence of a large class raised well above the level of mere subsistence."

From Eric J. Hobsbawm, "The British Standard of Living, 1790–1850," Economic History Review *1957.**

"We may consider three types of evidence in favour of the pessimistic view: those bearing on (a) mortality and health, (b) unemployment and (c) consumption. . . . We must not forget that mortality rates did not improve drastically until very much later—say, until the 1870s or 1880s—and may therefore be less relevant to the movement of living standards than is sometimes supposed. . . . The rise in mortality rates in the period 1811–41 is clearly of *some* weight for the pessimistic case, all the more as modern work . . . tend[s] to link such rates much more directly to the amount of income and food consumption than to other social conditions.

" . . . It is too often forgotten that something like 'technological' unemployment was not confined to those workers who were actually replaced by new machines. It could affect almost all pre-industrial in-dustries and trades. . . . Doubtless the general expansion of the early industrial period (say 1780–1811) tended to diminish unemployment except during crises: doubtless the decades of difficulty and adjustment after the wars tended to make the problem more acute. From the later 1840s, the working classes began to adjust themselves to life under a new set of economic rules . . . but it is highly probable that the period 1811–42 saw abnormal problems and abnormal unemployment. . . . These notes on unemployment are sufficient to throw doubt upon the less critical statements of the optimistic view, but not to establish any alternative view. . . . Per capita consumption can hardly have risen. The discussion of food consumption thus throws considerable doubt on the optimistic view."

From Ronald M. Hartwell, "The Rising Standard of Living in England, 1800–1850," Economic History Review *1961.**

"People lived longer because they were better nourished and sheltered, and cleaner, and thus were less vulnerable to infections and other diseases (like consumption [tuberculosis]) that were particularly susceptible to improved living standards. Factory conditions also improved. . . . But increasing life expectation and increasing consumption are no measures of ultimate well-being, and to say that the standard of living for most workers was rising, is *not* to say that it was high, *nor* that there was no dire poverty, and cyclical fluctuations and technological unemployment of a most distressing character.

" . . . Thus much misunderstanding has arisen because of assumptions—mainly misconceptions—about England before the Industrial Revolution; assumptions, for example, that rural life was naturally better than town life, that working for oneself was better and more secure than working for an em-ployer, that child and female labour was something new, that the domestic system . . . was preferable to the factory system, that slums and food adulteration were peculiar products of industrialization, and so on. . . . The new attitude to social problems that emerged with the industrial revolution was that ills should be identified, examined, analysed, publicised and remedied, either by voluntary or legislative action. Thus evils that had long existed—child labour, for example—and had long been accepted as inevitable, were regarded as new ills to be remedied rather than as old ills to be endured. It was during the industrial revolution, moreover, and largely because of the economic opportunities it afforded to the working class women, that there was the beginning of the most important and most beneficial of all the social revolutions of the last two centuries, the emancipation of women."

From Theodore S. Hamerow, The Birth of a New Europe, State and Society in the Nineteenth Century. *University of North Carolina Press, 1983, pp. 140–141.*

"The debate goes on and on because the evidence is ambiguous, lending itself to a variety of interpretations. Yet taken as a whole, it does point to a few tentative conclusions. The first generation or two of workers under the industrial revolution experienced no major change in its standard of living as a result of the economic transformation of which it was a part. There were some members of the labor force, especially those in the textile trades, who undoubtedly suffered a decline, as skilled handicraftsmen found themselves unable to compete with machinery. On the other hand there were others, in metallurgy or engine building, for example, who improved their position as a result of the rationalization of production. For most of them, however, the coming of the industrial revolution made little difference with regard to income, workday, diet, or housing.

"This was especially true of those employed in agriculture, who still made up the great bulk of the labor force. Yet even those engaged in manufacture experienced only minor changes in their accustomed level of subsistence. The goods and services generated by early industrialization remained largely inaccessible to them. But the new hardships imposed on the working population by the rationalization of production were less the result of a long-term decline in income than of psychological disorientation. Millions of people who had grown up amid the certainties and traditions of the village or small town were suddenly thrown into an alien environment of factories, shops, tenements, and slums, where the values of rural society soon disintegrated before the hard realities of the urban experience. The outcome was a profound demoralization, which primarily reflected not a change in the standard of living but a change in the way of life.

"Such generalizations about the initial effect of the industrial revolution may be open to challenge, but there can be little doubt about what happened subsequently. Within fifty years the standard of living of the lower classes began to rise. The evidence on this point is incontrovertible."

*From Philip A. M. Taylor (ed.), *The Industrial Revolution in Britain: Triumph or Disaster?* (D. C. Heath, 1970).

SUMMARY

◆

The reorganization of Europe in 1815 had focused on politics as the key to social order. The system of international relations that the victors established proved reasonably effective, but the conservative domestic arrangements they favored were challenged from the start. In trying various combinations of repression and compromise, the restoration regimes acknowledged that they had not achieved the stability hoped for. At the same time, accelerating industrial growth made new demands of government and placed new strains on society. Not stability but change would be the central reality of the new century. While Europe's leaders chose different means for containing change, millions dealt with it in daily struggles over wages and housing, food and family.

QUESTIONS FOR FURTHER THOUGHT

◆

1. Following the French Revolution and Napoleon, Europe's leaders sought to create peace and lasting stability through international agreements and political firmness at home. Was that possible? Is it ever?

2. Do historical explanations as to why industrialization began when it did, spread from country to country, and became a self-perpetuating process of change indicate that economic growth will spread everywhere and continue forever?

3. Moralists then, like moralists now, worried that industrialization might destroy the family. Were their fears misplaced?

RECOMMENDED READING

◆

Sources

Memoirs of Prince Metternich. 5 vols. Published in the United States in the 1890s, this edition was reissued in 1970. The published memoirs and correspondence of diplomats are a wonderful source, and larger libraries will have editions of *The Memoirs and Correspondence of Viscount Castlereagh* (12 vols.) and the *Memoirs of the Prince of Talleyrand* (5 vols.). All of these books give a lively picture of the Congress of Vienna.

For the subsequent years, *France and the European Alliance, 1816–1821: The Private Correspondence between Metternich and Talleyrand,* 1948, is particularly useful.

Wilson, Charles, and Geoffrey Parker. *An Introduction to the Sources of European Economic History, 1500–1800.* 1977.

Studies

*Ashton, T. S. *The Industrial Revolution, 1760–1830.* 1998. This reissue of an older and optimistic classic includes a new introduction reviewing subsequent literature and an up-to-date bibliography.

*Carr, Raymond. *Spain, 1808–1975.* 1982. The most balanced and comprehensive account in any language.

*Cipolla, Carlo M. (ed.). *The Industrial Revolution, 1700–1914.* 1973. The essays collected here give a good sense of the range of factors and interpretations important for understanding industrialization.

Davies, Norman. *God's Playground: A History of Poland.* Vol. 2: *From 1789 to the Present.* 1981. Effectively studies the development of a nation without a national government.

*Frader, Laura L., and Sonya O. Rose. *Gender and Class in Modern Europe.* 1996. A collection of essays exploring the relationship between social change and conceptions of gender and class in several countries from 1800 to after World War I.

*Gash, Norman. *Aristocracy and People: Britain, 1815–1865.* 1979. An incisive and balanced account of how British politics adapted to social and economic change.

*Gideon, Siegfried. *Mechanization Takes Command.* 1948. This provocative analysis of the social and aesthetic implications of the machine age has become a classic.

Goodman, J., and K. Honeyman. *Gainful Pursuits: The Making of Industrial Europe, 1600–1914.* 1988. Attentive to the variety of interests that made industrialization a continuing process.

Hamerow, Theodore S. *The Birth of a New Europe: State and Society in the Nineteenth Century.* 1983. A systematic, informative consideration of the major social changes of the nineteenth century, noting their connection to industrialization and the role of the state.

*Henderson, W. O. *The Industrialization of Europe: 1780–1914.* 1969. A general study contrasting developments in England and on the continent.

*Hobsbawm, E. J. *The Age of Revolution: Europe 1789 to 1848.* 1970. A sparkling, influential Marxist assessment of the period.

*Kemp, Tom. *Industrialization in Nineteenth-Century Europe.* 2d ed. 1985. A useful comparative analysis of differences and similarities in the process of industrialization as it spread across Europe.

Kissinger, Henry A. *A World Restored: Metternich, Castlereagh, and the Problems of Peace, 1812–22.* 1957. The author's subsequent fame adds to the interest of this account, which is very sympathetic to Metternich.

Kossman, Ernst H. *The Low Countries, 1780–1940.* 1978. Valuable and balanced treatment of a region that was an important participant in all the trends of modern European history.

*Landes, David S. *The Unbound Prometheus: Technological Change and Development in Western Europe from 1750 to the Present Day.* 1969. Emphasizes the role of technology.

*Macartney, C. A. *The Habsburg Empire, 1790–1918.* 1968. Detailed and authoritative.

Magraw, Roger. *France, 1815–1914: The Bourgeois Century.* 1986. A clear general account attentive to social change.

*More, Charles. *Understanding the Industrial Revolution.* 2000. Applies modern theory to rethinking the origins, nature, and development of the industrial revolution.

Nibberdey, Thomas. *Germany from Napoleon to Bismarck, 1800–1866.* 1996. An invaluable modern synthesis.

*Nicolson, Harold. *The Congress of Vienna: A Study in Allied Unity, 1812–1822.* 1970. A lively account of the process of peacemaking by a British official who was at the Paris peace conference one hundred years later.

O'Brien, Patrick, and Caglar Keyder. *Economic Growth in Britain and France, 1780–1914.* 1978. A thorough examination of statistical methods and data for the period, focusing in particular on wages and productivity.

*Pollard, Sidney. *Peaceful Conquest: The Industrialization of Europe 1760–1970.* 1981. A provocative study that focuses on the importance of geographical regions and not political units.

Price, Roger. *An Economic History of Modern France, 1730–1914.* 1981. Underlines the importance of modes of communication and transportation in the development of the marketplace.

*Rémond, René. *Religion and Society in Modern Europe.* 1999. An impressive overview of a topic too often neglected.

*Rich, Norman. *Great Power Diplomacy, 1814–1914.* 1992. A classic kind of diplomatic history, in which the century is seen in terms of international relations; includes a very useful bibliography.

Seton-Watson, Hugh. *The Russian Empire, 1801–1917.* 1967. A solid, largely political survey.

*Smith, Bonnie G. *Changing Lives: Women in European History Since 1700.* 1989. Discussion of the major trends affecting all classes; excellent bibliographies.

*Tilly, Louise, and Joan Scott. *Women, Work, and Family.* 1978. Discusses the impact of industrialization on women and on the family economy.

*Trebilcock, Clive. *The Industrialization of the Continental Powers, 1780–1914.* 1981. A synthesis that uses modern research to emphasize the political implications of industrialization.

*Wandycz, Piotr S. *The Lands of Partitioned Poland, 1795–1918.* 1974. A standard, balanced account.

Woloch, Isser (ed.). *Revolution and the Meanings of Freedom in the Nineteenth Century.* 1996. Ten specialists assess the impact of revolutions in different European countries (and Latin America), from the memory of the French Revolution to the Russian Revolution, which closed out an era obsessed with the promise and dangers that revolution might bring.

*Available in paperback.

▲ Delacroix's painting presents the revolution of 1830 in France as the heroic rising of the
people, poor and middle class together, being led by Liberty into a new era.
Louvre, Paris, France/Peter Willi/Bridgeman Art Library

LEARNING TO LIVE WITH CHANGE

Everyone knew that after twenty-five years of revolution and war Europe was not the same as before, and even in 1814 it was clear to many that economic developments were bringing further change. Thus, change itself became the central preoccupation of philosophy and the arts as well as politics. And that was as true of those who decried what was lost from the past as of those who welcomed the prospects of a new kind of society. While intellectuals wrestled with these issues, the very structure of society (and the ways of describing it) continued to be transformed. Social relations based on custom were giving ways to ones seemingly controlled by the impersonal rules of law and economics. Populations were growing larger, and more people lived in cities, where lifestyles and social problems were different. Industrialization subjected millions to hardships for which neither individual charity nor government had adequate answers. These changes, experienced more intensely in cities than in the countryside and more in Western than in southern or Eastern Europe, raised explosive questions and in Western Europe led to new liberal regimes.

CHAPTER 23. LEARNING TO LIVE WITH CHANGE							
	Social Structure	Body Politic	Changes in the Organization of Production and in the Impact of Technology	Evolution of Family and Changing Gender Roles	War	Religion	Cultural Expression
I. IDEAS OF CHANGE							
II. THE STRUCTURE OF SOCIETY							
III. THE SPREAD OF LIBERAL GOVERNMENT							

I. Ideas of Change

Political ideas, social theories, and new movements in the arts were all closely interconnected in the early nineteenth century. They altered the way people painted pictures, wrote poetry, collected statistics, analyzed society, studied biology, and understood history. Several elements served to connect all this creative diversity and increase its impact. The writers, scientists, artists, and professors whose works were most influential increasingly saw themselves as having a special place in society because of their talents and knowledge. Primarily male and largely from the middle class, they depended less on patronage than on their connections to established institutions such as academies, universities, publishing houses, magazines, and newspapers. Through exhibitions, public lectures, and publications, they sought to reach others like themselves and then a broader audience. Their need to explain modern society, like their effort to comprehend the French Revolution, produced competing interpretations that were, in fact, debates about the nature of society and the sources of historical change.

◆ ROMANTICISM

Romanticism, a movement in philosophy and the arts, cannot be captured in any simple definition. Associated with the great burst of creativity in Germany in the latter part of the eighteenth century and with the ideas of Jean-Jacques Rousseau (see chapter 19), the romantic movement, initially strongest in Germany and England, rapidly spread across the continent and to North America. Romanticism affected every aspect of culture and in such a variety of ways that it is best understood as a set of attitudes and aesthetic preferences rather than as a defined doctrine. Although by midcentury other styles and concerns challenged romanticism, its influence continued well into the twentieth century.

Certain themes were characteristic: an emphasis on feeling, emotion, and direct experience more than on universal principles and abstract logic; a preoccupation with erotic love, often unrequited, and mortality; fascination with nature understood as an unconquerable power, raw and unpredictable; a search for the organic relatedness of all life that went beyond the cold analysis of cause and effect; a concern for spirituality, deep and mysterious, that tended to dismiss thinkers of the Enlightenment as shallow; interest in the momentary, the accidental, and the uniquely colorful in human affairs; and an admiration for imagination and originality that hailed the individual genius who was capable of experiences and feelings more profound than those of ordinary mortals. These preferences were revealed in matters of fashion as well as content. English gardens became the vogue. Carefully arranged to look natural, with great trees and hidden copses along a rolling terrain dappled with flowers of varied colors and heights, gardens in the English style replaced, or were added to, the geometrical plots and cropped hedges of the classical garden. Romantic artists and writers favored flamboyant dress that distinguished them from aristocrats or bourgeois and presented themselves as pensive and passionate.

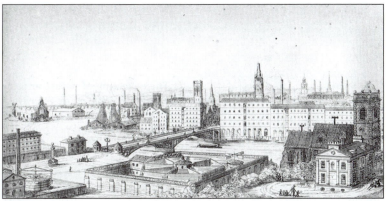

▲ **A convert to Catholicism and a leading student of Gothic architecture, Augustus Pugin was one of the architects of the Houses of Parliament. These illustrations, part of a book on *Contrasts* comparing Catholic and Protestant society, sum up the romantic and conservative critique of modern society for replacing church spires with smokestacks, cottages and artisanship with massive tenements and factories, and charities with prisons. (The new prison in the foreground is Jeremy Bentham's Panopticon, designed so that a single guard can see down all the cellblocks.)**
New York Public Library

Romantic Philosophy and Literature Romantic modes of thought flourished in conjunction with the revival of religion, the increased interest in history, and rising nationalism, all of which are discussed in the next chapter; but their core was philosophical. Romantic thinkers wrote about metaphysics, aesthetics, the philosophy of nature, and, in Germany and Scandinavia, even a romantic philosophy of science. While envisioned in terms of grand systems (F. W. J. Schelling's works were widely read in Germany despite their almost mystic complexity), romantic philosophies were often expressed piecemeal in poetry, aphorisms, meditations on death, and autobiographical accounts of youthful yearning and the quest for truth. In Germany August Wilhelm Schlegel and

in England Samuel Taylor Coleridge (heavily influenced by German philosophy) were among the most influential romantic thinkers, through intense personal friendships with other intellectuals as well as their published work. Both wrote poetry, drama, and essays on philosophy and theology. August's brother, August Wilhelm Schlegel, was a major critic and theoretician.

Coleridge's *Rime of the Ancient Mariner*, one of the great long poems in English, is a tale of guilt, redemption, and the supernatural. Full of evocative nautical lore, the poem tells of a seaman cursed to wear a dead albatross around his neck, a result of his violence against nature. He is released from that weight only in the end, as he comes to feel God's love. With William Wordsworth, his closest friend, Coleridge campaigned for a new kind of poetry, direct and emotive. Wordsworth's poems contrasted the beauty of nature with urban corruption, the clear-eyed and innocent responsiveness of youth with the jaded sadness of age. Like William Blake before him, he denounced the materialism of his age. Blake, whose drawings and poems were filled with religious mystery, also believed that poets had a special wisdom that society should heed; and many other romantics could have joined in Blake's cry:

> Hear the voice of the Bard,
> Who present, past, and future, sees
> The Holy Word
> That walk'd among the ancient trees.

The anguish, depression, and despair experienced in their personal lives became for romantic poets a sign of their own sensitivity and a summons to a higher vision of the meaning of life.

In France, where romanticism developed somewhat later, Madame Anne-Louise de Staël's essays on the German thinkers stimulated a whole generation of philosophers, historians, and novelists, ranging from the young Victor Hugo, whose plays and novels (*The Hunchback of Notre Dame* and *Les Misérables* are the best known) made him the towering figure of French letters through most of the century, to the swashbuckling stories of Alexander Dumas' *Three Musketeers*. Novelists and dramatists in Italy and Russia, as well as in England, France, and Germany, often set their tales in the distant past and tended to favor vivid description and singular settings appropriate to occurrences beyond rational understanding. Turning from the Enlightenment and its veneration for the Renaissance, they preferred the rougher, sprawling picture of human experience in seventeenth-century writers like Shakespeare and Cervantes (stimulating an important revival of interest in their work) and felt a kinship with the Middle Ages as an age of faith and spontaneity that produced such achievements as Dante's poetry and Gothic architecture.

The Wider Influence of Romanticism   The fairy tales of Hans Christian Andersen combined the romantic delight in folk culture and affection for childhood. Throughout the Western world there was a new taste for tales of ghostly spirits (Edgar Allen Poe was one of the first American writers to achieve international recognition) and paintings of

storms and ruins that evoked unseen powers, as in the landscapes of William Constable and J. M. W. Turner in England and Caspar David Friedrich in Germany (note the Turner painting below).

Literary and artistic works thus burst beyond classical forms. Romantic painters like Théodore Géricault in France emphasized vibrant color and swirling lines without the sharp outlines and balanced composition so important to their predecessors. Like Eugène Delacroix (note his paintings on pp. 775 and 804), they were drawn to exotic scenes from the past and from North Africa and the Middle East.

Romantic values came together with particular power in music, admired for its ability to communicate an ineffable understanding deeper than

▼ The evocation of nature and time, favorite romantic themes, made the ruins of Tintern Abbey the subject of a poem by Wordsworth and of this watercolor by J. M. W. Turner.
Victoria and Albert Museum, London/Art Resource, NY

WORDSWORTH ON THE ROLE OF THE POET

◆

Wordsworth was one of England's most popular poets, and the success of his Lyrical Ballads *may have encouraged him to write a preface to the second edition, explaining what he was up to. He points out that his poems differ from classical poetry with its greater formality and lofty themes, and he justifies his use of ordinary speech. In making his case, he touches on many of the themes characteristic of the romantic movement.*

"The principle object of these Poems was to choose incidents and situations from common life, and to relate or describe them, throughout, as far as was possible in a selection of language really used by men, and, at the same time, to throw over them a certain colouring of imagination, whereby ordinary things could be presented to the mind in an unusual aspect. . . . Humble and rustic life was generally chosen because, in that condition, the essential passions of the heart find a better soil in which they can attain their maturity, are less under restraint, and speak a plainer and more emphatic language; because in that condition of life our elementary feelings co-exist in a state of greater simplicity, and, consequently, may be more accurately contemplated and more forcibly communicated; because the manners of rural life germinate from those elementary feelings . . . ; and, lastly, because in that condition the passions of men are incorporated with the beautiful and permanent forms of nature. . . .

" . . . For all good poetry is the spontaneous overflow of powerful feelings: and though this be true, Poems to which any value can be attached were never

produced on any variety of subjects but by a man who, being possessed of more than usual organic sensibility, had also thought long and deeply. . . .

"The Man of science seeks truth as a remote and unknown benefactor; he cherishes and loves it in his solitude; the Poet, singing a song in which all human beings join with him, rejoices in the presence of truth as our visible friend and hourly companion. Poetry is the breath and finer spirit of all knowledge; it is the impassioned expression which is the countenance of all Science. Emphatically may it be said of the Poet, as Shakespeare hath said of man, 'that he looks before and after.' He is the rock of defence for human nature; an upholder and preserver, carrying everywhere with him relationship and love . . . ; the Poet binds together by passion and knowledge the vast empire of human society, as it is spread over the whole earth, and over all time."

From William Wordsworth, "Preface to the Second Edition of *Lyrical Ballads*" in *William Wordsworth: Selected Poems and Prefaces,* Jack Stillinger (ed.) (Houghton-Mifflin Co., 1965).

---

words. The response to the works of Beethoven had brought a self-conscious seriousness to music. Critics wrote of his symphonies and string quartets in terms of their philosophic profundity, and audiences listened in reverent silence, finding in that shared experience something akin to religion. Subsequent romantic composers appealed even more directly to the heart, emphasizing melody and using freer harmonies. When words and music were combined, as in the song cycles of Franz Schubert and Robert Schumann, or in grand opera (often hailed as the highest of the arts), it was the music that mattered most.

Both conservatives and radicals drew upon the romantic movement, for it was both a call for change and a response to it, attentive to politics as well as to philosophy and the arts. Conservatives found in romantic values powerful arguments for

rejecting the French Revolution and considered it the lamentable result of Enlightenment rationalism and of the universalism that ignored the local variety and tradition conservatives treasured. Stability, they argued, was possible only in a society organically connected, held together as it had been in the Middle Ages by respect for custom and religion. They contrasted their vision of an organic society with the competition and selfish individualism of modern capitalism.

Radicals, however, used romantic themes to argue that a new era required shattering old institutional constraints, much as creativity in the arts fostered the breaking of established art forms. Romantic thinkers tended to see folk culture and language as natural expressions of the nation. For conservatives these values validated rural life and custom; for radicals the promise of this culture would be realized when the people spontaneously arose to achieve new freedoms. In Germany and England many romantics had, like Wordsworth, initially welcomed the French Revolution only to turn away from it in disgust. Victor Hugo, on the other hand, turned from conservatism to become a lifelong advocate of radical change. A younger generation of English poets, led by Lord Byron, Percy Bysshe Shelley, and John Keats, were persistent critics of church and state drawn to the promise of revolution. In its aspirations and its tumultuousness romanticism expressed the preoccupation with change that marked the age.

◆ SOCIAL THOUGHT

Conservatism   Conservatism grew from opposition to the French Revolution to become what today would be called an ideology—a coherent view of human nature, social organization, political power, and the sources of change that generally justified the status quo. This conservatism was not mere nostalgia for the past. Rather, like the restoration regimes established in 1815, conservatives advocated changes when designed to strengthen the kind of society they favored.

Not that conservatives always agreed. But in arguing for social order, they tended to emphasize the limitations of human understanding, the wisdom of established customs, the value of hierarchy, and the social importance of religion. From those concerns, conservatives mounted a powerful critique not just of radical programs but of modern society itself as perilously inclined toward antisocial individualism, materialism, and immorality. More than a matter of temperament or interest, conservatism would remain a vigorous part of European intellectual life and political discourse throughout the nineteenth century.

From the late eighteenth century on, the powerful English prose of Edmund Burke (see discussion on p. 714) provided what was perhaps the most influential formulation of the conservative position. Society, he argued, exists through continuity. By granting special privileges to certain groups, it fulfills social needs in a way that sustains order, achieving a delicate arrangement in which rank is related to social function and in which differences of status, having evolved through time, are acceptable to all. This "natural" historical order, Burke argued, was far wiser than

▲ By George Cruikshank, the most famous English cartoonist of the day, this cartoon reflects the vitriolic quality of political debate in the early nineteenth century. A satanic figure of Reform (the Phrygian cap on a pike behind him was a symbol of the French Revolution) assaults Britannia, who relies on religion to save her. Sarcastically entitled, "Death or Liberty," the subtitle is more straightforward: "or Britannia and the Virtues of the Constitution in Danger of Violation from the Great Political Libertine, Radical Reform."
Private Collection/Bridgeman Art Library

the "artificial" plans of radicals, no matter how well intentioned. The Burkean view thus allowed for gradual change, at least in theory; in practice, such arguments could be used against any plan for general reform. This tendency was strengthened by a distrust of reason that rejected the ideas of the Enlightenment as dangerously abstract. No social schemes or written constitutions could reconstitute society, because it was a great interconnecting web, and slogans about rights or equality merely concealed selfish interests and encouraged false hopes.

Conservatives found in history the record of how painfully civilization had developed and how fragile it remained, and many saw evidence not only of human error but of divine will in events since the French Revolution. Christianity was the source of Europe's strength, and Christian fear a necessary restraint on humanity's selfish and prideful nature. Without it, society dissolved into revolution and anarchy. Political battles were part of a far larger millennial conflict.

Such views gave conservative thought both militancy and depth. Europeans were used to

MAISTRE'S OPPOSITION TO REFORM

◆

Over the course of the past twenty years, most European governments had adopted constitutions when Joseph de Maistre, writing from exile in Russia, set forth his objections to them in his Essay on the Generative Principle of Political Constitutions. *First published in Russia in 1810 and in Paris in 1814, the essay was reprinted many times.*

"Every thing brings us back to the general rule—*man cannot create a constitution; and no legitimate constitution can be written.* The collection of fundamental laws, which must essentially constitute a civil or religious society, never has been written, and never will be, *a priori.* It is only when society finds itself already constituted, without being able to say how, that it is possible to make known, or explain, in writing, certain special articles; but in almost every case these declarations or explanations are the effect of very great evils, and always cost the people more than they are worth.

" . . . Not only does it not belong to man to create institutions, but it does not appear that his power, *unassisted,* extends even to change for the better institutions already established. . . . *Nothing* [says the philosopher, Origen] . . . *can be changed for the better among men, without God.* All men have a conscious-

ness of this truth, without being in a state to explain it to themselves. Hence that instinctive aversion, in every good mind, to innovations. The word *reform,* in itself, and previous to all examinations, will be always suspected by wisdom, and the experience of every age justifies this sort of instinct.

" . . . To apply these maxims to a particular case . . . the great question of parliamentary reform, which has agitated minds in England so powerfully, and for so long a time, I still find myself constrained to believe, that this idea is pernicious, and that if the English yield themselves too readily to it, they will have occasion to repent."

From Scholars' Facsimiles & Reprints (New York: Delmar, 1977), reprinting of the edition of Joseph de Maistre, *Essay on the Generative Principle of Political Constitutions* (Boston: Little and Brown, 1847).

---

receiving radical ideas from France, and two of the most pungent exponents of conservatism were men who wrote in French, Joseph de Maistre and Louis de Bonald. Society's first task, they argued, is self-preservation. Only authority can check the selfish wills of individuals, and authority requires undivided sovereignty, social hierarchy, close links between church and state, and the vigilant suppression of dangerous ideas. These writers thus connected religion to politics and tied the Church to aristocracy and monarchy. Revolution, Maistre explained, is divine retribution for false ideas (see "Maistre's Opposition to Reform," above). This hard-headed conservatism, very different from Burke's, contained little that was humane or tolerant. With its praise of hangmen and censors, it spoke only to those who already shared its fears. Terrified of weakening the dikes that held back revolution, it left little room for compromise, divided while calling for unity, and relied on power while speaking of the social good. Nevertheless, as a way of understanding change, mobilizing opposition to liberal de-

mands, and criticizing modern life, conservatism would be a profoundly influential element in modern thought.

Liberalism   Liberalism, like conservatism, was not so much a compact doctrine as a set of attitudes. Whereas conservatism emphasized tradition and hierarchy, liberalism was associated with ideas of social progress, belief in economic development, and values associated with the middle class. Confident that their ideas would triumph, liberals generally welcomed change and looked forward to the future.

They appraised society primarily in terms of freedom for individual choice and opportunities for individual growth, an emphasis that gave some ethical dignity to the pain of industrialization and lent promise to the process of social change. They believed their principles were universally valid; yet, to the perpetual surprise of its adherents, liberalism proved a creed of limited appeal, forever subject to attack and internal division. Enthusiasm for limited constitutional reform produced disagreements over how limited it should be. In practice, reconciling liberty with order or equal rights with private property proved contentious and led to attacks on liberalism and divisions among liberals themselves. Some theorists reduced liberalism to little more than the narrow justification of individual success. Others expanded it until the demand for social justice overshadowed its founding principles of competition and individualism. In each country the temper of liberalism was different, shaped by a national history liberals never wholly dominated.

Political Liberalism Liberal political thought was rooted in the writings of John Locke and of the philosophes; and liberals in the nineteenth century believed that their programs would benefit individuals and society as a whole. A leading French liberal, Benjamin Constant, put the case succinctly: "The liberty of the individual is the object of all human association; on it rest public and private morality; on it are based the calculations of industry and commerce, and without it there is neither peace, dignity, nor happiness for men." By this creed, freedom would lead to morality, prosperity, and progress. The freedom that liberals sought was primarily political and legal, and they generally favored a constitution and representative institutions, freedom of the press and of assembly, an extension of the jury system, separation of church and state, public education, and administrative reform. Most liberals did not favor democracy—political wisdom, they thought, required the advantages of education and leisure and the restraint that came with owning property—but nearly all believed that giving ideas a free hearing and propertied voters a free voice would result in policies beneficial to all.

Economic Liberalism Although liberal politics and liberal economic theory were closely related, they were nevertheless separable. The advocates of one were not always committed to the other. Still, England's example of economic growth as well as political liberty made it the model of nineteenth-century liberalism. Adam Smith's argument that government intervention in the free play of the market restricted economic forces, which if left to themselves would increase productivity and prosperity, became a dogma of

liberalism. As systematically expounded by Englishman David Ricardo in his *Principles of Political Economy and Taxation* (1817), liberal theory became the keystone of modern economics. Ricardo, a financier who became wealthy during the Napoleonic wars and then retired from business, became an important public figure; but his great influence lay in his precise, flat prose that presented economics as a science.

The wealth of the community, Ricardo declared, comes from land, capital, and labor; and these three "classes" are compensated by rent, profit, and wages. A product's value results from the labor required to make it: This was the labor theory of value, which socialists would later use for very different purposes. For Ricardo, this theory led to principles of property similar to those of Locke and to an emphasis on labor saving as the source of profit, a view foreshadowed by Adam Smith. The value of land or of work was determined not by individual decisions but by economic laws. The poorest land in cultivation simply sustains those who work it; but the most fertile land produces more for the same labor, and that increment constitutes profit, paid to the landlord as rent. As population pressures bring more (and poorer) land into cultivation, rents rise because the difference between the best and worst land increases. Similarly, wages subtract from profit, but the rate of pay is set by an "iron law of wages" (Ricardo's phrase is characteristic). It decrees that when labor is plentiful, the workers tend to be paid at the subsistence level. Short-term fluctuations in prices are the natural regulator within this system, pushing people to activities for which demand is high. Ricardan economics thus extended the sphere of inexorable economic laws to social relations.

For Ricardo, both land and labor are commodities, their value quite unaffected by any sentimental talk about the virtues of rural life or artisanship, and society is a collection of competing interests. Legislation cannot raise wages or prevent the marketplace from working in its natural way; but if people acknowledge economic laws and act in their own best interest, a natural harmony and progress follow.

Ricardo called his subject *political economy*, and a powerful reform movement developed from it. Landed interests, liberals argued, had misused political power for their own benefit while harming the rest of society. Throughout Europe liberal economic theory thus added important weight to demands that special privilege be eliminated (as the French Revolution had done), that governments be responsive to their citizens (who best know their own interests), and above all that the state not try to regulate production and trade. As economic growth became more impressive, it was natural for liberals to add that politicians should adopt some of the openness, efficiency, and energy of the men of action who were transforming the economy.

Utilitarianism The call for political and social reform could also lead to renewed emphasis on the role of the state, as it did in the utilitarianism of another Englishman, Jeremy Bentham. Like the philosophes, Bentham believed he could rationally deduce practical programs from universal principles, and he was ready to write a constitution for Russia or codify the laws of Latin American republics. Bentham began his reform campaign by criticizing the legal system, and he remained all his life an opponent of the precedent-bound courts of England. Some of his most important writings before 1789 appeared first in French (the revolutionaries gave him French citizenship).

In contrast to most philosophes, he rejected the doctrine of natural rights as a meaningless abstraction. In his system utility replaced natural rights as the basis of public policy, and utility was measured by determining the greatest good for the greatest number. In the Enlightenment tradition, he combined plans of detailed reform with a theory of psychology. The good is that which avoids pain and gives pleasure—a calculation all people make for themselves anyway and that better education would enable them to make more wisely.[1] Thus, just as self-interest built great industry, so it could create a just and happy society. In contrast to Burke's emphasis on tradition and many liberals' preference for limited government, Bentham gave the state a central role. It should assign penalties for undesirable actions and rewards

for desirable ones, distributing pain and pleasure to induce socially beneficial behavior.

Bentham's followers, sober intellectuals who called themselves *philosophic radicals*, did not necessarily adopt all his doctrines, but they applied his principles in every sphere. By his death in 1832, they were among the most important reformers of Parliament, law, prisons, education, and welfare. A special group within a larger liberal movement, they shared and contributed to the tendency of liberals everywhere to press for humane reforms on grounds of common sense and natural harmony.

John Stuart Mill Its very malleability enabled liberalism to endure as a doctrine and a political force; and its broader meaning is best exemplified in John Stuart Mill, the most important liberal spokesperson of the nineteenth century. Mill's father was a leading Benthamite, and he raised his son in the strictest utilitarianism; but the younger

▼ **This photograph of John Stuart Mill shows a sensitive intellectual who is also distinctly middle class; compare the Ingres portrait on p. 827.**
The Granger Collection, New York

---

[1]Bentham called this the "felicific calculus," but his verbal pomposity was famous: After-dinner walks were "postprandial perambulations."

Mill gradually came with searching candor to modify received doctrine. Mill was extraordinarily learned—a philosopher, economist, and publicist—and he wrote some of the most influential classics of modern thought. Fearful of the intolerance and oppression of which any social class or political majority was capable, he made freedom of thought a first principle. He advocated universal suffrage as a necessary check on the elite and proportional representation as a means of protecting minorities. Influenced by Auguste Comte, the French social theorist who was one of the founders of sociology, Mill acknowledged the critical role of institutions in social organization, and he admitted that the institutions, even liberal ones, suited to one stage of historical development might not be appropriate for another.

To counterbalance the influence of the established elites, Mill favored a more open administration, organized interest groups, and workers' cooperatives. Moved by the problems of the industrial poor, he tried to distinguish between production (to which liberal economics could still apply) and distribution (in which the state might intervene in behalf of justice), and he came to see that collective action by the workers could enhance freedom rather than restrict it. He sought a place for aesthetic values within the colder utilitarian doctrine he inherited, and in later years Mill courageously advocated causes, such as the emancipation of women and the confiscation of excess profit, that seemed fearfully radical to most contemporaries (see "Mill Opposes the Subjection of Women"). His liberalism, thus modified and extended, remained firm; and his essay, *On Liberty*, published in 1859, stands as one of the important works of European political theory, a careful but heartfelt, balanced but unyielding declaration that society can have no higher interest than the freedom of each of its members.

◆ THE EARLY SOCIALISTS

Socialist thought offered a radical alternative to conservative and liberal ideologies, varied as each of those were. Among scores of socialist schemes, those of Saint-Simon, Fourier, and Owen, were notable for the attention they won among intellectuals and political leaders. All three men had lived through the French Revolution and had personal experience of burgeoning capitalism in the early stages of industrialization, and each of them founded a movement that disseminated telling criticisms of capitalism. Competition, they argued, is wasteful and cruel, induces hard-hearted indifference to suffering, misuses wealth, and leads to frequent economic crises. They offered instead scores of suggestions for organizing production differently and creating a harmonious, orderly, and truly free society.

Saint-Simon   As a young French officer, Claude Henri de Rouvroy, Comte de Saint-Simon, fought alongside George Washington at Yorktown. During the French Revolution, he abandoned his title, made and lost a fortune speculating in land, and then devoted himself to the difficult career of a seer. Injustice, social divisions, and inefficiency could be overcome, he believed, in a society directed by experts standing above the conflict: scientists, men of affairs (*industriels*), and artists. These specialists, chosen for their ability, would design plans to increase productivity and prosperity for the benefit of all. The integrated, organic quality of Greek city-states and of the Middle Ages could be recaptured in the industrial age with scientists and managers (who would have the authority once granted priests and soldiers) leading humanity to self-fulfillment and love.

Saint-Simon's theories won a significant following, especially among the bright engineers at France's . . . cole Polytechnique, and an extraordinary number of France's leading engineers and entrepreneurs in the next generation fondly recalled the Saint-Simonian enthusiasms of their youth. In their penchant for planning, in their grand economic projects, and in their schemes for social reform, they carried elements of his teaching into the world of affairs and respectable politics. There were important Saint-Simonian movements in every country, and later socialists would long sustain his respect for industrialization and the power of planning.

Fourier   François Marie Charles Fourier had been a traveling salesman before dedicating himself, at the same time as Saint-Simon, to a theory that he firmly believed would rank among the greatest discoveries ever made. His cantankerous yet shrewd writings on contemporary society

MILL OPPOSES THE SUBJECTION OF WOMEN

◆

John Stuart Mill published his essay The Subjection of Women *in 1869. His arguments were based on familiar ideas about individualism and modern progress, but their extension to women's rights and in such absolute terms went much further than most contemporary discussion.*

"The object of this Essay is to explain, as clearly as I am able, the grounds of an opinion which I have held from the very earliest period when I had formed any opinions at all on social or political matters, and which, instead of being weakened or modified, has been constantly growing stronger by the progress of reflection and the experience of life: That the principle which regulates the existing social relations between the two sexes—the legal subordination of one sex to the other—is wrong in itself, and now one of the chief hindrances to human improvement; and that it ought to be replaced by a principle of perfect equality, admitting no power or privilege on the one side, nor disability on the other.

" . . . The masters of all other slaves rely, for maintaining obedience, on fear; either fear of themselves, or religious fears. The masters of women wanted more than simple obedience, and they turned the whole force of education to effect their purpose. All women are brought up from the very earliest years in the belief that their ideal of character is the very opposite to that of men; not self-will, and government by self-control, but submission, and yielding to the control of others. All the moralities tell them that it is the duty of women, and all the current sentimentalities that it is their nature, to live for others; to make complete abnegation of themselves, and to have no life but in their affections.

" . . . So far as the whole course of human improvement up to this time, the whole stream of modern tendencies, warrants any inference on the subject, it is, that this relic of the past is discordant with the future, and must necessarily disappear.

"For what is the peculiar character of the modern world—the difference which chiefly distinguishes modern institutions, modern social ideas, modern life itself, from those of times long past? It is, that human beings are no longer born to their place in life, and chained down by an inexorable bond to the place they are born to, but are free to employ their faculties, and such favourable chances as offer, to achieve the lot which may appear to them most desirable.

"If this general principle of social and economical sciences is . . . true, we ought to act as if we believed it, and not to ordain that to be born a girl instead of a boy, any more than to be born black instead of white, or a commoner instead of a nobleman, shall decide the person's position through all life. . . .

"At present, in the more improved countries, the disabilities of women are the only case, save one, in which laws and institutions take persons at their birth, and ordain that they shall never in all their lives be allowed to compete for certain things. The one exception is that of royalty.

" . . . The social subordination of women thus stands out an isolated fact in modern social institutions; a solitary breach of what has become their fundamental law; a single relic of an old world of thought and practice exploded in everything else, but retained in the one thing of most universal interest."

From John Stuart Mill, "The Subjection of Women," *Three Essays* (Oxford: Oxford University Press, 1975).

---

were so copious that his manuscripts have still not all been printed, despite the devotion of generations of admirers. Largely self-taught, he committed to paper his fantasies of the strange beasts and incredible inventions that would abound in the future. His central concept, however, was an ideal community, the *phalanstery* (from *phalanx*). Once even one was created, the happiness and well-being of its members would inspire the establishment of others until all of society was converted.

A phalanstery should contain some sixteen hundred men, women, and children, representatives of all the types of personality identified in Fourier's elaborate psychology. He listed a dozen passions that move human beings and proposed to organize the phalanstery in such a way that individuals would accomplish the tasks society required simply by doing what they wanted. Each member would perform a variety of tasks, engaging in no one task for too long; pleasure and work would flow together. Largely self-sufficient, a phalanstery would produce some goods for export and pay its members according to the capital, labor, and talent that each contributed. Although no phalanstery was ever established exactly as Fourier planned (he even offered designs for the architecture), communities were founded on Fourierist principles from the United States to Romania; and if few of them survived for long, the vision endured of a society in which cooperation replaced compulsion and joy transformed drudgery.

Robert Owen   Robert Owen was one of the success stories of industrial capitalism: A self-made man, he rose from selling cloth to be the manager and part owner of a large textile mill in New Lanark, Scotland. Owen ran the mill in a way that transformed the whole town, and by the end of the Napoleonic wars, distinguished visitors were traveling from all over Europe to see the miracle he had wrought in New Lanark. The workday was shortened from seventeen to ten hours. New housing eventually allowed an employee's family several rooms; inspection committees maintained cleanliness; gardens were planted and sewers installed. In nursery schools with airy, pleasant rooms, children were given exercise, encouraged to sing and dance, taught without corporal punishment, and trained in the useful arts. Most promising of all, the subjects of this paternalistic kingdom developed a pride in their community, productivity rose, and profits increased.

Owen had, he felt, disproved Ricardo's dismal economic laws; and he set about establishing ideal communities elsewhere. Like Fourier's, they would be placed in a rural setting and would supply most of their own needs. Members would take meals and enjoy entertainment in common, and children would be raised communally. The young would be educated to the age of eight and then engage in productive labor until they were twenty-six; after five years in distributive or managerial jobs, adults would assume the tasks of government, cultivating the sciences and the arts in their increasing leisure time. The controlled environment would assure good character among community members, and the division of tasks would provide them with varied and interesting lives. Standardized production would offer more goods at lower cost (the snobbery that made luxuries attractive would disappear), and higher wages would increase sales (see "Owen Tells Congress about the Science of Socialism," p. 817).

Even after losing most of his wealth when the community of New Harmony, which he founded in Indiana, failed, Owen remained the single most important figure in the labor movement and in the workers' cooperatives that he helped spread across England in the 1830s and 1840s. But by the time of his death, in 1858, Owen, who had converted to spiritualism, was largely ignored by the world he had sought to remake.

The Socialist Critique   Although much in these socialist movements was easily ridiculed, the values they stressed echoed those of growing workers' movements everywhere. These early socialists sought to combine an older sense of community with the possibilities of a new era. They imagined a society enriched by new inventions and new means of production, in which new forms of social organization would foster cooperation and love. Their indictment of capitalism, their insights into the nature of productivity and exchange, and their attention to social planning and education had an impact far beyond their relatively small circles of believers. The dream of fraternity and of work that was fulfilling echoed through later socialist and anarchist movements; yet nearly everyone ultimately rejected their ideas as impractical and too radical. Bucolic isolation and artisanal production became increasingly unrealistic in the face of industrialization, and these theories were incredibly vague about problems of politics and power.

The nature of their radicalism, however, deserves a closer look. The criticisms of liberal society mounted by Saint-Simon, Fourier, and Owen were not so different overall from the conservative attack. With some restrictions (Saint-Simon, for example, insisted on the abolition of inheritance), they even allowed private property, and none of them was thoroughly democratic. What most shocked contemporaries were their views on the status of women, sexual mores, and Christianity. All rejected the place allotted women in bourgeois society, and Owen not only specified that

OWEN TELLS CONGRESS ABOUT THE SCIENCE OF SOCIALISM

◆

Robert Owen made a number of trips to the United States in connection with the Owenite community on the Wabash River at New Harmony, Indiana. His international fame was such that on one of these trips he was invited to give two addresses to the U.S. Congress. In the first he called on Congress to adopt his principles; and in the second—delivered on March 7, 1825—he set out in some detail his plan for a community of up to five thousand people on one or two thousand acres, with a square of large buildings at the center (each 1,000 feet long). These buildings would house the "school, academy, and university" as well as washrooms, kitchens, dining halls, dormitories for children over the age of two, and apartments. Owen described the arrangements for central heating and cooling, gardens, manufacturing, and farms and discussed how the community would be governed by an elected committee. But before entering into such specific matters, he presented the general principles of his program:

"Then it should be ever remembered, that the first principle of the science is derived from the knowledge of the facts, *that external circumstances may be so formed as to have an overwhelming and irresistible influence over every infant that comes into existence, either for good or evil . . . and thus, at pleasure, make any portion, or the whole, of the human race, poor, ignorant, vicious, and wretched; or affluent, intelligent, virtuous, and happy.*

"And thus, also, form man to understand and to practice pure and genuine religion, which never did nor ever will consist in unmeaning phrases, forms, and ceremonies; but in the daily, undeviating practice . . . of charity, benevolence, and kindness . . . [this] is the *universal religion* of human nature.

" . . . Having then discovered, as I believe I have, the science of the influence of circumstances, and a rational, and therefore, a pure and genuine religion, the next important consideration is, to ascertain in what manner the new science and the new religion can be applied to produce the promised practical results. I have been frequently urged to apply these principles to the present state of society, and not attempt to disturb it, but endeavor to make them unite harmoniously together. . . . The inventor of the Steam Engine might as well have been required to unite his new machinery with the inefficient and clumsy horse engine. . . . The fact is . . . the system which I propose now for the formation and government of society, is founded on principles, not only altogether different, but directly opposed to the system of society which has hitherto been taught and practised at all times, in all nations.

" . . . My conviction is, that, from necessity and inclination, the individual or old system of society would break up, and soon terminate; from necessity, because the new societies would undersell all individual producers, both of agricultural productions, and manufactured commodities. And from inclination, because it is scarcely to be supposed that anyone would continue to live under the miserable, anxious, individual system of opposition and counteraction, when they could with ease form themselves into, or become members of, one of these associations of union, intelligence, and kind feeling."

From Oakley C. Johnson (ed.), *Robert Owen in the United States* (Humanities Press, 1970).

women should share in governing but believed that their emancipation required lessening their family responsibilities. All wrote of sensual pleasure as good and of its repression as a characteristic European error. The Saint-Simonians publicly advocated free love, and Fourier carefully provided that neither young nor old should be deprived of the pleasures of the flesh. Owen was only slightly less outspoken in his contempt for Christian marriage. At the same time, all three stressed religion as the source of community feeling, brotherhood, and ethics. Their efforts to replace what they had eliminated therefore led to imitations of Christian ritual and foggy mysticism that provided an easy target for their opponents. By the end of the nineteenth century, these

▲ **A saintly father figure, Fourier instructs his disciples from a hill overlooking an idyllic setting and an imagined phalanstery, Fourier's orderly community for four hundred families.**
AKG London

thinkers would be remembered as "utopian socialists"; for by then, socialist thought would center on the more hard-headed and systematic theories of Karl Marx (see chapter 26).

II. The Structure of Society

Nineteenth-century politics, economies, and ideological conflict had to deal with fundamental changes in social organization. The abstract idea that society consists of distinct social classes flourished because it took into account the spreading effects of industrialization. Population growth and urbanization altered the way people lived and raised new challenges to which individuals, families, groups, and governments had to respond.

◆ SOCIAL CLASSES

Theories of change combined with everyday experience to alter the way nineteenth-century society was perceived. In the old regime, discussion of the "orders" or "ranks" in society had referred to an imaginary social pyramid rising from the lowliest peasant through all the ranks to the monarch. In this idealized picture, each person had an assigned place in that pyramid and social relations were governed by elaborate networks of reciprocal responsibilities. In the nineteenth century, society was most often described in terms of a few broad strata, called classes. A person was said to belong to a given social class less on the basis of connection to others than as an attribute of his, or her husband's, occupation. The source of income was assumed to imply something of the values held, the style of life led, and later, the political and social interests likely to be favored. This emphasis on class fit well with increased reference to the "middle" or "middling" class. Social relations were represented as matters of free contract between individuals, with middle-class mobility the model. Descriptive of an expanding, fluid, unequal, national society, the concept of class gained urgency with the sharpening contrast between the middle class and the urban poor.

The Aristocracy   The class most easily identified was the aristocracy. Recognized since the Middle Ages as a special group, it included all nobles (whose rank gave them a number of formal privileges) and their immediate relatives, whether they held noble titles or not; members of the upper gentry, who were large landholders and lived like nobles; and (in the ancient commercial cities of the Netherlands, northern Germany, and northern Italy) the established and wealthy patrician families, who dominated the cities though they might not bear titles.

In the nineteenth century, however, the aristocracy was on the defensive. It had been a principal target of the French Revolution, and its privileges and influence were subsequently challenged by new industrial wealth (which overshadowed the fortunes of large landholders), wider participation in politics, the growth of the state, and cultural change. The aristocracy's relative decline was so clear, in fact, that its continued importance is easily overlooked.

A member of France's parliament could rise in 1821 to ask, "What is the aristocracy?" and answer: "I am going to tell you: . . . it is the coalition of those who want to consume without producing, to live without working, to know everything without learning anything, to capture all the honors without having earned them, to occupy all the jobs without being able to fulfill them; that is the aristocracy."[2]

In most countries aristocrats continued to control most of the wealth, were closely allied to an established church, and dominated the upper levels of administration and the military. By training and tone the most international of social classes, aristocrats would remain the preeminent diplomats even in governments dominated by the middle class. Aristocrats also stimulated some of the most influential critiques of nineteenth-century society, denouncing the middle class for selfishness and materialism, proclaiming urban life morally inferior to rural, and lamenting the loss of gentlemanly honor. The efforts of the aristocracy to defend its position, the means used, and the success achieved provide an important measure of social and political development in each country.

National Differences in Aristocracies   In much of Europe, especially the south and east, the aristocracy held on to local power and tremendous wealth, a social pattern exemplified by the Kingdom of Naples and by Russia. In both states the nobility, constituting only about 1 percent of the population, in effect ruled over most of the peasant masses. Three-fifths of the people in southern Italy lived on baronial estates, and after the defeat of Napoleon the aristocracy there worked with king and church to reestablish its authority. In Russia a fraction of the nobility held one-third of the land, and most of the rest of the land, although owned by the state, was administered by nobles. Tyrants on their estates and dominant over local administration, Russia's aristocracy was a pillar of tsarist rule.

In countries in which the nobles made up a higher proportion of the population, the pattern was somewhat different. In Poland, Hungary, and Spain, many of the nobility were extremely poor, and they tended to alternate between desperate allegiance to an empty title and sympathy for radical change, thus becoming another important source of political instability. In some countries, however, aristocrats sought to strengthen their influence through representative government and decentralization, thereby cooperating with political and economic reformers. The confident Magyars took this position in Hungary, and so, even more open-mindedly, did the aristocrats of northern Italy, Belgium, and Great Britain. They were thus prominent during the revolutions of 1848 in

---

[2] Cited in Nicholas J. Richardson, *The French Prefectural Corps, 1814–1830* (Cambridge, 1966), p. 4.

Hungary and northern Italy and in the subsequent nationalist movements in those countries. The Belgian aristocracy cooperated with liberals in the revolution of 1830 and afterward, accepting an endless string of concessions and reforms. In England, above all, the aristocracy proved willing to accept liberal programs in exchange for keeping their political prominence. Of the one hundred men who served as cabinet ministers in Britain between the electoral reforms of 1832 and 1867, sixty-four were sons of nobles; and perhaps four-fifths of the members of Parliament were landholders or their representatives, closely tied to the aristocracy. On the other hand, younger sons and lesser aristocrats in England were more closely associated with the upper-middle class, which lessened the sharpness of social division.

In Prussia, the most influential aristocrats were the Junkers of east Prussia, owners of large estates, some of which included sizable villages. The Junkers maintained their traditional position even when the state became the instrument of dramatic and rapid change. Considered crude and ignorant by most of the aristocracies of Europe—which set great store by polished manners, elegant taste, and excellent French—the Junkers had a proud tradition of service to the state and loyalty to their king. In local government, in the bureaucracy, in the army, and at the court, their manners and their values—from rectitude to fondness for dueling, from arrogance to loyalty—set the tone of Prussian public life.

France is thus the European exception, for there the old aristocracy was reduced to a minor role in national politics after the revolution of 1830. Its members retained major influence in the Church, army, and foreign service, but those institutions were also on the defensive. Yet even in France, aristocrats maintained a strong voice in local affairs and were a major influence on manners and the arts. Everywhere, however, aristocrats were in danger of being isolated from important sources of political and economic power. Lineage was once of such importance that tracing family lines had been a matter of state; now, pride of family was becoming a private matter.

Peasants The overwhelming majority of all Europeans were peasants, a social class as firmly tied to the land and to tradition as the aristocracy.

Praised by conservatives for simple virtues and solid values, disparaged by progressives for their ignorance, peasants struggled to make ends meet in a changing world.

An important change occurred with the emancipation of peasants from traditional obligations to the lord whose land they worked. These "feudal" obligations typically might have required the peasant to give the lord a number of days of labor or to use the lord's grain mill at rates the lord set. The French Revolution abolished such requirements, a policy carried to much of Western Europe by Napoleon, decreed in Prussia as part of the reforms of 1806, and spread to most of Eastern Europe with the revolutions of 1848. These changes encouraged peasant producers to enter the commercial market; but they also deprived peasants of such traditional protections against hard times as the use of a common pasture, the right to glean what was left after the first harvest, and the practice of foraging for firewood in forests owned by others.

Similarly, the decline of the putting-out system and of local industries took away critical income, especially during the winter months. Gradually and with considerable local variation, peasants were becoming more dependent on the little piece of land to which they had some legal claim or on the wages that could be earned from labor. Agriculture became more commercial, its production increasingly intended for market rather than for mere subsistence or local consumption. Profits increased with the cultivation of one or two cash crops and with the use of improved fertilizers and machinery, but these changes were easier for those farmers with more capital and bigger holdings than most peasants enjoyed. Because larger farms were more likely to be profitable, landed nobles, bourgeois investors, and richer peasants sought to expand and consolidate their holdings, a trend encouraged by legislation in much of northern Europe. Although additional land was put under cultivation to meet rising demand, especially in the West, it was usually of poor quality and divided into small plots, and thus it did not greatly improve the peasant economy. As governments became more efficient, they reached more deeply into peasant society for taxes and conscripts, while population growth and competition from more distant markets added other pressures.

Peasant Activism   Peasants, however, were not just passive victims of outside forces. They tenaciously maintained old loyalties to their region, their priests, and their habitual ways; and they were the despair of reformers, who were often defeated by peasant suspicion of outsiders and opposition to change. But peasants also used elaborate ties of family and patronage to build effective social networks, and they were frequently shrewd judges of their interests, cooperating with measures that promised immediate benefits while resisting all others with the skepticism of experience.

Their hunger for land, resentment of taxes and military service, and sense of grievance against those above them could also become a major political force. Peasant involvement made a crucial difference in the early days of the French Revolution, in the Spanish resistance to Napoleon, in the wars of German liberation, and in the strength of nationalism in Germany and Italy. Rulers were kept on edge by eruptions of peasant violence in southern England in the 1820s; Ireland in the 1830s and 1840s; Wales, Silesia, and Galicia in the 1840s; and on a smaller scale in most other countries. The outbreaks of 1848 would topple the system of feudal service in the Austrian Empire and eastern Prussia, though rural indifference to constitutional claims and to workers' demands undermined the urban revolutions there.

The peasantry was deeply divided between those who owned land and those who were forced to sell their labor. Some of the former, especially in the West, grew relatively prosperous and joined the influential notables of their region. More of them survived on small plots by being as little dependent on cash as possible, vulnerable to the slightest change in weather or market, and by supplementing their income by whatever odd jobs family members could find. In most of Europe peasants were tenants who received only a part of the crops they raised, with the rest going to their landlords. Such arrangements could provide significant security, but they also tended to be inflexible, discouraging adaptation to changes in prices, markets, and technology. Rural laborers were the poorest and most insecure of all, the tinder of violence and the recruits for factory work.

Peasants and Social Change   A central problem for nineteenth-century European society was how to integrate the agricultural economy and the masses dependent on it into the developing commercial and industrial economy. By the 1850s the process had gone farthest in France and Great Britain but by opposite means. In Britain the

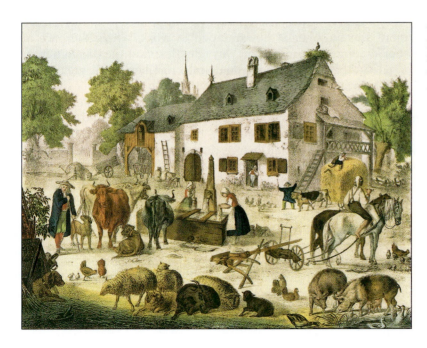

◄ **This idealized picture of prosperous peasants and bustling farmyard is a German lithograph of 1850.**
AKG London

peasantry was largely eliminated as the continuing enclosures of great estates reduced the rural poor to laborers, shifting from place to place and hiring out for the season or by the day. The concentration of landholding in Great Britain was one of the highest in Europe: Some 500 aristocratic families controlled half the land; and some 1,300 others, most of the rest. In France, on the other hand, peasants owned approximately one-third of the arable land and were gradually gaining more. They made the most of their situation by favoring crops that required intense cultivation, such as grapes and sugar beets, and by maintaining small-scale craft industries.

Patterns elsewhere lay between these two extremes. Small landholding persisted in western Germany, northern Italy, Switzerland, the Netherlands, Belgium, and Scandinavia alongside a trend toward the consolidation of larger farms that reduced millions to becoming day laborers. In Germany emancipation from personal obligations to the lord usually required peasants to pay for their freedom with part (often the best part) of the land they had previously cultivated. Recent historical research has also established that the size of land holdings and the situation of peasants varied greatly with local conditions—the quality of the soil, the favored crop, government policy, and legal custom.

The clear distinction remained, however, between these western and central regions and Eastern Europe, where peasants were more directly subject to the power of the lord, most of all under Russian serfdom. In the West, developments that increased agricultural productivity often made the life of peasants more precarious. In the East, the landowners' authority over their peasants included claims to their unpaid labor, which in Russia ranged from a month or so of work each year to several days a week. The disadvantages of such a system were many, and the eventual emancipation of Russian serfs in the 1860s proved necessary for economic growth and minimal military and administrative efficiency. As urbanization and industrialization advanced, many writers waxed nostalgic for the bucolic purity and sturdy independence of peasant life, but the social and economic problems of the peasantry were, in fact, some of the gravest and most intractable of European society.

Workers   Industrial workers attracted far more attention than did the peasantry; yet even in Britain industrial workers were a minority among paid laborers (there were more domestic servants than factory hands). Industrial workers, however, were taken to be indicative of the new age because of the environment in which they lived and worked and because of their absolute dependence on wages set by employers, who could fire them at will and who determined the tasks performed as well as the conditions of work and the length of the workday. To many, such workers seemed a social threat, and in the 1830s and 1840s, serious French analysts wrote of the "dangerous classes" crowding into Paris.

Most factory workers earned too little to sustain a family even when work was steady, and the employment of women and children became as necessary to the family's survival as it was advantageous to employers, who appreciated their greater dexterity and the lower wages they would accept. The largest factories were cotton mills, in which commonly half the laborers were women and a quarter, children. In coal mines, women and children, who were hired to push carts and work in the narrower shafts, made up a smaller proportion of the workforce. A class of men, women, and children was thereby formed of people dependent on cash for their subsistence and subject to the rigid discipline of their employers. Awakened before dawn by the factory bell, they tramped to work, where the pace of production was relentless and the dangers from machinery and irate foremen were great. Any lapse of attention during a workday of fourteen hours or more, even stopping to help a neighbor, brought a fine and a harsh reprimand. Children were frequently beaten, just as men had been beaten before fines proved more effective, and workers were spurred by the hated system of payment for tasks completed.

Industrial workers were thus set apart by the conditions of their labor, the slums in which they lived, and special restrictions such as the *livret*, or passport, that all French workers were required to present when applying for a job and on which previous employers recorded comments on the worker's conduct and performance. Life was still more precarious for the millions without regular employment, who simply did such tasks as they

▲ An etching of Dean Mills in 1851 shows cotton spinning as contemporaries liked to think of it: women working together with nimble industriousness under the watchful but gentle eye of a sturdy foreman, all in the iron grandeur of an immaculate, orderly, huge new factory.
Mansell/Time, Inc.

could find, hauling or digging for a few pence. Understandably, the powerful worried about the social volcano on which they lived, and the sensitive feared the effect of the immorality and degradation that accompanied industrial life.

Artisans and Skilled Workers The most independent workers were the artisans, who had been stripped of their tight guilds and formal apprenticeships by the French Revolution, by a series of laws passed in Britain in the years before the 1830s, and by a similar process in Germany that was completed by the revolutions of 1848. Nevertheless, artisans continued to ply their crafts in a hierarchy of masters, journeymen, and apprentices, working in small shops in which conditions varied as much according to the temper of the master as to the pressures of the market. Skilled workers, from carpenters and shoemakers to me-

chanics, moved in a less organized labor market but were distinctly better paid than the masses of the unskilled. Although they were vulnerable to competition from machines and new products and, above all, to unemployment during the frequent economic slumps, in general these skilled workers were among the beneficiaries of industrialization. Their real wages tended slowly to increase, and they could expect to earn enough to support their families in one or two bare rooms on a simple diet.

In contrast, uneducated and exhausted industrial workers, often strangers to one another, for the most part lacked the means necessary for effective concerted action to improve their lot. Their frequent outbursts of resentment and intermittent strikes usually ended in some bloodshed and sullen defeat. Sometimes riots, demonstrations, and strikes became local revolutions, spreading across the north of England in 1811 and 1812, breaking out in Lyons in 1831 and 1834, Bristol in 1831, Lancashire in 1841, and Silesia in 1844. Significantly, most of these outbursts were led by artisans, who felt most keenly the threat of economic change and held clearer visions of their rights and dignity. Although the authorities usually blamed such disturbances on the sinister plots of a few agitators, they were for the most part expressions of resentment and of a growing sense of a common interest.

Early Labor Movements Trade unions were banned everywhere except in England after 1824, and even there the laws against conspiracy restricted their activity; but various local organizations had developed since the eighteenth century to take the place of the declining or outlawed guilds. By midcentury more than 1.5 million British workers may have belonged to such groups, called friendly societies in England, which tended to form around a few of the more skilled workers and to meet in secret, often of necessity but also as a sign of brotherhood and trust. Although their members were fond of elaborate rituals and terrifying oaths, these societies served specific purposes that were tellingly modest, such as providing burial costs for members or assistance in times of illness. There were also

movements that aimed to increase the workers' control over their lives. Consumers' cooperatives were numerous by the 1830s in England, as were artisans' production cooperatives, often established with church support, in France and Italy. Such programs sometimes became associated with radical politics, a specter likely to rouse crushing opposition even from liberal governments. For the most part, however, these expressions of workers' insistence on their rights and dignity remained small in scale and local in influence.

The hundreds of strikes that occurred throughout Western Europe in the first half of the century suggested what unions might accomplish; but without funds, organizational experience, or effective means of communication, these labor movements usually petered out after a few years or sometimes a few months. Not even the Workingman's Association for Benefiting Politically, Socially, and Morally the Useful Classes, launched with some fanfare in England in 1836, managed to survive for long or bring off the general strike its more radical members dreamed of. Yet these organizations did influence Parliament to favor factory legislation. The meetings, torchlight parades, and special workers' newspapers and tracts all contributed to the growing sense of belonging to a distinctive class. So, above all, did the repression by police and courts that usually followed.

▼ **Le Creusot was a carefully planned and controlled company town that provided housing for the workers in its foundries.**
Roger-Viollet/Getty Images

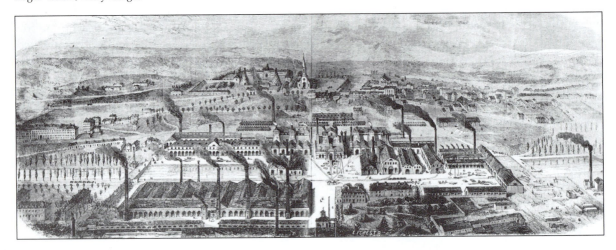

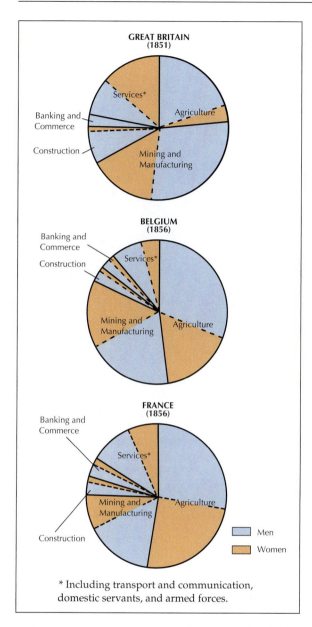

GREAT BRITAIN
(1851)

Services*

Banking and
Commerce

Construction

Agriculture

Mining and
Manufacturing

BELGIUM
(1856)

Banking and
Commerce

Construction

Services*

Mining and
Manufacturing

Agriculture

FRANCE
(1856)

Banking and
Commerce

Services*

Mining and
Manufacturing

Agriculture

Construction

☐ Men

☐ Women

* Including transport and communication,
domestic servants, and armed forces.

▲ THE WORKFORCE IN INDUSTRIAL NATIONS, MID-1850S
From P. Bairoch et al., *The Working Population and Its Structure*
(Gordon & Breach Science Publishers Inc., 1968).

By midcentury millions of workers in Britain, somewhat fewer perhaps in France, and smaller numbers elsewhere shared heroes and rituals, believed they faced a common enemy, and adopted organization as the prime means of defending themselves in a hostile world. In Britain the na-

tional trades unions of skilled workers formed in the 1830s and 1840s (with only some 100,000 members then) steadily increased their size and influence, reaching more than a million members a generation later.

The vast majority of the working class, however, remained essentially defenseless, possessing meager skills, dependent on unstable employment, and living in the isolation of poverty. Ideas of *fraternité* and *égalité,* of the rights of freeborn English people, and of simple patriotism, often expressed in Biblical prose, communicated a common sense of hope and outrage to the millions of men and women who attended rallies, met in dingy cafés, and read the working-class press (or listened as it was read to them). Newspapers and pamphlets intended for workers were numerous in England after 1815, less widespread in France in the 1830s and 1840s, and present everywhere in 1848. The common themes were people's natural rights, pride of work, and the claims of social justice.

The Middle Classes   Of all the social classes, the most confident and assertive was the middle class. At the top stood the great bankers, who in London and Paris were often closely connected to the liberal aristocracy and whose political influence after 1830 was considerable. Just below them in status, the great industrialists and the wealthiest merchants were more separate from and a little contemptuous of the traditional elites. The bottom of the middle class consisted of office clerks, schoolteachers, and small shopkeepers, often distinguishable from artisans only by their pretensions. This petite bourgeoisie constituted most of the middle class numerically, but the class was epitomized by those neither at the top nor bottom but in between: most merchants, managers, and upper bureaucrats and nearly all lawyers, doctors, engineers, and professors. The view that such disparate groups made up a social class resulted as much from ideas shared as from common interests. Opposed to aristocratic privilege, they saw themselves as the beneficiaries of social changes that allowed talented people to gain security and influence.

They were primarily an urban class and intimately connected with the commerce and politics of city life. In Paris they constituted nearly all of that part of the population (between one-fourth and one-fifth) that was prosperous enough to pay some taxes, have at least one maid, and leave an estate sufficient to cover the costs of private burial.[3] In other cities their proportion was probably somewhat smaller. Among nations, they were most numerous in Great Britain, a sizable fraction in France and Belgium, and a smaller minority elsewhere. The middle class was the only social class that it was possible to fall out of, and people established their membership in it by economic self-sufficiency, literacy, and respectability. Their manner, their dress, and their homes were thus symbols of their status and were meant to express values of probity, hard work, fortitude, prudence, and self-reliance. No matter how favored by birth or fortune, they tended to think of themselves as self-made.

Middle-Class Values While industrial centers were notoriously drab, the middle-class home became more ornate, packed with furnishings that boasted of elaborate craftsmanship. Women's fashions similarly featured ornamental frills, and shops translated Parisian elegance into forms available to more modest purses. Masculine garb, by contrast, grew plainer, a point of some pride in a practical age; and clerk and banker tended to dress alike. Those who forged great industries out of daring, foresight, and luck; those who invented or built; and those who taught or tended shop or wrote for newspapers came to share a certain pride in one another's achievements as proof that personal drive and social benefit were in harmony and as a harbinger of progress yet to come.

More than any other, the middle class was associated with an ideology; and the triumph of the middle class in this period—so heralded then and by historians since—related as much to constitutionalism and legal equality, individual rights, and economic opportunity as it did to any explicit transfer of power. The conquests of the middle class were measured not just by its rise in impor-

▲ Fashion magazines like *La Mode Illustré* kept middle-class women informed of the latest styles and elegant touches to which they might aspire.
Bulloz/© RMN/Art Resource, NY

tance but also by a more general adoption of values associated with it. Even being in the middle, between the extremes of luxury and power and of poverty and ignorance, was seen as an advantage, a kind of inherent moderation. Most of Europe's writers, scientists, doctors, lawyers, and businesspeople would have felt no need to blush on finding themselves called by a London paper in 1807 "those persons . . . always counted the most valuable, because the least corrupted, members of society," or on hearing John Stuart Mill speak a generation later of "the class which is universally described as the most wise and the most virtuous part of the community, the middle rank." Society was understood in terms of social class at a time when the hallmarks of the era—flourishing commerce, science, and technology; great works of art

---

[3]Perhaps the most detailed study yet made of the middle class in this period is Adeline Daumard's *La Bourgeoisie parisienne de 1815 . . . 1848* (1963).

▲ **Dominique Ingres portrayed the entrepreneur Louis Bertrand as the very epitome of the self-reliant, aggressive man of the industrial middle class.**
Giraudon/Art Resource, NY

and institutions of culture; triumphant movements of liberalism and nationalism—were seen as achievements of the middle class.

◆ THE CHANGING POPULATION

While Europeans grappled with political, economic, and social changes, they also faced the fact that there were more and more people—more people to feed, more seeking work, and more living in cities.

Demographic Growth The effects of population growth were particularly visible in areas in which industrialization was under way, and historians used to think that industrialization had stimulated a rising birthrate with new opportunities for employment, particularly of children. But demographic research has challenged that view, and current explanations emphasize a decline in

disease-carrying germs, an increase in the food supply, a lowering of the age at which people married, and, after 1870, some improvement in public sanitation.

Admittedly spotty data suggest that the world experienced a decline in some common diseases beginning in the eighteenth century. Microbes have cycles (like those of locusts but less regular), and remissions had undoubtedly occurred many times before. Now, however, better supplies of food allowed the larger number of babies surviving the perilous years of infancy to reach adulthood and form families of their own.

The food supply rose because of better transportation, more effective agricultural techniques, and the potato. Agricultural associations, usually led by enlightened aristocrats, campaigned for more scientific farming; and the humble potato, not common on the continent before 1750, was a staple of the peasant's diet in most of Europe by 1830.[4] Potatoes are easy to cultivate in a small space and can yield more calories per acre than any other crop. While infant mortality remained enormously high by modern standards, even a slight decline in death rates could make a great difference in the total number of people, so close to subsistence did most Europeans live.

Population and Society The reasons for the trend toward earlier marriage are less clear, but peasants freed from servile obligations apparently tended to marry and form new households at a younger age. Early marriage was facilitated by the spread of cottage industry, which preceded the new factories and enabled families to add to their income by spinning or weaving at home.

The increased number of people in a single generation—only a slight rise in a single decade or province—multiplied in the next generation and led to an enormous increase in the aggregate. As population grew, the proportion who were young and in the childbearing years grew still faster, which increased the ratio of births to the total population. The net result was that the 180 to

---

[4]William L. Langer made an effective case for the potato's importance in "Europe's Initial Population Explosion," *American Historical Review,* 1963, pp. 1–17.

190 million Europeans of 1800 had become 266 million by 1850 and 295 million by 1870.

The effects of a larger population were far-reaching. More people consumed more food, which necessitated more intensive cultivation and the use of land previously left fallow. An increasing population also meant an expanding market for goods other than food, an element of growth that would have stronger impact later in the century. More people meant a larger potential work-force readier to leave the countryside for industrial jobs; and this mobility became a social change of immeasurable importance, for it reduced the isolation of country folk and stimulated a pattern of migration to the Americas that would become a flood. Young people constituted a greater proportion of the population, which may have made for increased restiveness and a larger pool of potential radical leaders.[5] There was also a distinction in birthrates by social class, which demographers call *differential fertility*. On the whole, the higher a man stood on the social scale, the fewer the children in his family, which led some to interpret the lower classes' fertility as a lack of foresight and moral restraint and to worry that they would eventually overwhelm society.

The most influential analysis of population was Thomas R. Malthus' *An Essay on the Principle of Population as It Affects the Future Improvement of Society*, first published in 1798 and reissued in many revisions. Observing the Britain of his time, Malthus argued that human population, unless checked by death (through war, famine, or pestilence) or deliberate sexual continence, increases faster than the supply of food. A clergyman, he advocated continence; but he remained pessimistic that human beings were capable of such restraint. An economist as well, Malthus presented demography as a science closely attached to liberal economic theory, with the convenient

corollary that the misery of the poor resulted from their own improvidence.

Urbanization At the turn of the century, greater London reached 1 million in population. No European city since imperial Rome had ever approached this size. Paris, with about half that number, would reach 1 million a generation later. The third largest European city in 1800, Naples, had some 350,000 inhabitants; and in all Europe there were then only twenty-two cities with populations of more than 100,000. By midcentury there were forty-seven. Great Britain was the leader, with six cities over the 100,000 mark; London's population had surpassed 2.5 million by 1856, Liverpool had grown from 80,000 to almost 400,000, and Manchester and Glasgow each had more than 300,000 people. By the 1850s, half of Britain's population lived in towns or cities, making it the most urbanized society since the classical era.

On the continent most old cities increased by at least 50 percent in the first half of the century, and many a town became a city. The major capitals burgeoned. Paris reached a population of nearly 1.5 million by 1850; Berlin almost trebled, to 500,000; and a similar growth rate pushed Brussels to 250,000. St. Petersburg, Vienna, and Budapest all had populations between 400,000 and 500,000.

By the 1860s the English countryside was actually losing people, as were some sections of France. The tide of urbanization was overwhelming, and nearly all the subsequent increase in European population would end up in cities swelling with immigrants, as rural folk moved to nearby villages, villagers to towns, and town dwellers to cities. Clearly, the tide of urbanization was strongest where industry was great, but the growth of ports and national capitals demonstrated the importance of great commercial, financial, and political centers as well.

Urban Problems Society had neither the experience nor the means to cope very well with such an expansion. Urban conditions for all but the reasonably prosperous were unspeakable. Narrow alleys were littered with garbage and ordure that gave off an overpowering stench. The water supply in Paris, better than in most large cities,

---

[5]In 1789 perhaps 40 percent of France's population was between twenty and forty years old and another 36 percent under twenty, the highest proportion of the young that France has ever known. The nationalist organization Young Italy limited membership to those under forty, and probably most of the leaders of the revolutions of 1848 would have met that standard. The relation of youth to revolution is interestingly discussed in Herbert Moller, "Youth as a Force in the Modern World," *Comparative Studies in Society and History*, April 1968.

▲ **In this famous engraving of London by Gustave Doré, the rhythmic sameness and cramped efficiency of new housing suggest a machine for living appropriate to the age of the railroad.**
New York Public Library

offered access to safe water only at fountains that dotted the city (the affluent paid carriers by the bucket), and in London the private companies that provided water allowed it to flow only a few hours a day. In most cities the water supply came from dangerously polluted rivers. Sewage was an even more serious problem. A third of Manchester's houses used privies in the 1830s, and a decade later the ratio of inside toilets to population was 1 to 212. In London cesspools menaced health only slightly less than still more public means of disposal.

The most dramatic inadequacy, however, was in housing. A third of Liverpool's citizens lived crowded into dark, cold cellars, and conditions in

Lille were similar. In every city the poor of both sexes crowded into filthy, stuffy, unheated rooms; and over the cities, especially manufacturing and mining towns, chemical smog and coal smoke darkened the sky. It is hardly surprising that crime was rampant, that often more than a third of the births were illegitimate, and that the number of prostitutes soared (reaching perhaps 80,000 in London, where 9,000 were officially registered; 3,600 were registered in Paris).

Maintaining public order became a new kind of problem. Governments had used the police primarily as secret agents whose job was to ferret out real or potential enemies. But the protection of lives and property in great cities, the effective handling of crowds, and the enforcement of local ordinances required something other than spies or the military. London's police force was established by Sir Robert Peel in 1829,[6] and the Paris Municipal Guard was created under Guizot a few years later.

For all their misery, cities continued to grow; and through the century the worst conditions were slowly alleviated by housing codes, public sewers, and reliable water supplies. These improvements were made possible in part by industrialization, which gradually provided iron pipes, water closets, gas lighting, better heating, and sounder buildings. Urban life developed a style of its own, increasingly distinct from life in the countryside. Towns clustered around factories and railway stations, and cities teeming with the poor and indigent were also the thriving centers of communication, commerce, politics, and culture.

▲ The visitation of the poor by charitable members of the middle class was expected to bring a good example as well as food and clothes.
Jean-Loup Charmet

◆ SOCIAL WELFARE

Social questions were debated in hundreds of speeches and pamphlets and in newspaper articles that worried about public health and morals, class division, and pauperism. These discussions were filled with the appalling facts uncovered through parliamentary and private inquiries in Britain and scholarly investigations in France. Using the rational techniques that seemed to work brilliantly when applied to issues of profits and politics, these humanitarian attempts to improve the lot of the lower class had discouragingly modest results, although individual employers, especially in Britain and Alsace, improved conditions somewhat by building special housing for their workers, drab barracks that nonetheless seemed marvels of cleanliness and decency.

Charity   Middle-class radicals supported efforts like those of England's Society for the Diffusion of Useful Knowledge, founded in 1826 to carry enlightenment to the lower classes. They contributed to and gave lectures for workers at night schools, many of which were run by the Mechanics' Institutes (of which there were more than 700 in Great Britain by 1850) and by the Polytechnic

Association of France (which had more than 100,000 participants on the eve of the revolution of 1848). Thousands of middle-class people personally carried the lamp of truth to the poor in the form of Bibles, pious essays, moral stories, and informative descriptions of how machines worked. Ambitious members of the lower-middle class were, however, more likely than workers to take advantage of these opportunities.

For the truly poverty-stricken, charities were established at an astounding rate; more than 450 relief organizations were listed in London alone in 1853, and whole encyclopedias cataloging these undertakings were published in France. A revival of Christian zeal provided powerful impetus to such groups in Britain, and on the continent new Catholic religious orders, most with specific social missions, were founded by the hundreds. They sponsored lectures, organized wholesome recreation to compete with the temptations of the tavern, set up trade apprenticeships, provided expectant mothers with a clean sheet and a pamphlet on child care, opened savings banks that accepted even the tiniest deposit, campaigned for hygiene and temperance, gave away soup and bread, supported homes for abandoned children and fallen women, and ran nurseries, schools, and

---

[6]The role played by Sir Robert Peel led to the nickname "Bobbies," by which the police are still called.

hostels. These good works were preeminently the province of women. Catholic nuns and Protestant matrons in the middle class were expected to uplift the poor by example as well as charity. The Society of St. Vincent de Paul believed that pious men could have a similar effect. Organized in Paris in 1835, it soon spread to all of Catholic Europe, requiring thousands of educated and well-to-do men to visit the poor regularly so that they might teach thrift and give hope by their very presence. Although these heroic efforts were important for some lucky individuals and were a significant means of informing the comfortable about the plight of the poor, they were never adequate to the social challenge. Most of Europe's urban masses remained largely untouched by charity or religion.

Public Health In matters of public health, standards of housing, working conditions, and education, governments were forced to take a more active role. By modern standards the official measures were timid and hesitant, and the motives behind them were as mixed as they were in factory legislation, which was favored not only by humanitarians but by landed interests happy to restrict industrialists. Vaccination, enforced by progressive governments, made smallpox less threatening; but beyond that, advances in medicine contributed little to public health. The great work of immunization would come later in the century. The most important medical gain of the 1840s was probably the use of anesthesia in surgery, dentistry, and childbirth.

Serious epidemics broke out in every decade. Typhus, carried by lice, was a constant threat, accounting for one death in nine in Ireland between 1816 and 1819, and infected water spread typhoid fever in city after city. A cholera epidemic, which apparently began along the Ganges River in 1826, spread through East Asia, reaching Moscow and St. Petersburg by 1830; 100,000 people died of cholera in Russia in two years. From Russia it spread south and west, to Egypt and North Africa, to Poland, Austria, and into Germany, where it was reported in Hamburg in 1831. Despite efforts to put ports in quarantine (a move opposed by shipping interests), the disease reached northern England and then France in that same year and continued slowly to the south, tak-

ing a ninth of Palermo's population in the period from 1836 to 1837.

Reaction to the cholera epidemic in Britain, France, and Germany revealed much about social change. An official day of fasting, prayer, and humiliation in England and warnings of the archbishop of Paris that the cholera was divine retribution expressed the strength of traditional faith and revealed widespread distrust of an era of materialism and its claims to progress.

But governments were expected to act. Torn between two inaccurate theories of how the disease spread,[7] governments mobilized inspectors to enforce such sanitary regulations as existed (not infrequently the inspectors faced riots by a populace fearful of medical body snatchers eager to dissect corpses). In Paris and Lille tenements were whitewashed by the tens of thousands, foods inspected, streets and sewers cleaned by official order; similar steps were taken in the German states and in Britain, where the demonstrated inadequacy of local government prompted establishment of a national Public Health Commission with extraordinary powers over towns and individuals. Carefully collected statistics led to a new understanding of how disease spread and of the importance of social factors for public health. Over the years, doctors and inspectors reported with troubled consciences on the terrible conditions they had found among lower-class neighbors whose quarters they had never visited before. Another cholera epidemic followed in the 1840s and lesser ones thereafter, but the shock and uncertainty of what to do was never again so great. Gradually, hospitals, too, came under more direct state supervision as the cost and complexity of medical treatment increased. By midcentury housing and sanitary codes regulated most of urban construction throughout the West, and inspectors were empowered to enforce these rules.

The Irish Famine Liberalism showed its other face in England's handling of the terrible potato famine in Ireland. As the potato blight struck late in 1845, disaster for a population so dependent on a single crop was not hard to predict. By winter hundreds of thousands of families sold what little

---

[7]The cholera bacillus was finally identified by Robert Koch in 1883.

they had to survive, were forced off the land, and began to suffer the diseases that accompany famine. Hope rested on a good harvest the following year. In spring and summer the potato plants emerged promisingly; but when desperate peasants dug them up, there was only stinking rot. In 1846 the blight was nearly total; and in that year and the next millions died, about a quarter of the population—the exact number will never be known. Roads were lined with bodies, huts abandoned. For several years some of England's ablest officials struggled with bureaucratic earnestness to collect information, organize relief, and maintain order in a corpse-strewn land; yet they were so inhibited by respect for the rules of liberal economics and the rights of property that their efforts had limited effect. In England, even those public figures most concerned to provide help to the Irish tended to view the famine as a natural disaster rather than a failure of policy; and many blamed Irish laziness for the country's dependence on potatoes, an easy crop to grow.

Ireland did produce grain, but that brought a better price in Britain. The landowners, mainly English and absentee, followed market principles and continued to export most of their wheat to England even as famine spread. Most Irish farmers rented the tiny plots they worked and paid for them principally by selling the pig or two they could raise on the same potatoes that provided their subsistence. When that crop failed and they had no money for rent, landlords usually forced them off the land. The relief law that denied aid to anyone who farmed more than a quarter acre of land had a similar effect, forcing tenants to abandon farming so their families might have food. The Irish famine, which made migration to the United States a part of Irish life and stimulated increased hatred of English rule, also fostered debate about what the responsibilities of a liberal government should be.

Government Regulation   In the 1830s and 1840s governments also began reluctantly to regulate child labor, banning employment of those under nine years old in textile mills in Britain and factories in Prussia, under eight in factories in France, and under ten in mines in Britain. By the end of the 1840s, similar measures had been adopted in Bavaria, Baden, Piedmont, and Russia. Generally,

the laws variously held the workday to eight or nine hours for children under twelve or thirteen years old and to twelve hours for those under sixteen or eighteen. Britain and France included additional requirements that the very young be provided with a couple of hours of schooling each day. To be effective, such regulations required teams of inspectors, provided for only in Britain, where earnest disciples of Jeremy Bentham applied the laws diligently. This expansion of government authority had been vigorously opposed by industrialists and many liberals; but mounting evidence of the harmful effects of industrial work made the need apparent, and the ability to gather such evidence became one of government's most important functions.

The most bitterly controversial welfare measure of the period was Britain's Poor Law of 1834. The old system of relief required each county to supplement local wages up to a level of subsistence determined by the price of bread. The system, expensive and inadequate to changing needs, was attacked by liberal economists, who charged that it cost too much and discouraged workers from migrating to new jobs. An extensive campaign for reform led to the Poor Law of 1834, based on the Benthamite notion that unemployment had to be made unattractive. Those receiving relief were required to live in workhouses, where discipline was harsh, conditions were kept suitably mean, and the sexes were separated. The new law was resented as a cruel act of class conflict, and it proved unenforceable in much of the nation, though recent studies suggest that it was somewhat less harsh in either practice or intent than its critics charged. On the continent welfare measures kept more traditional forms while gradually shifting the responsibility for directing them from local and religious auspices to the state.

Education   Public education also became a matter of national policy. Prussia had declared local schooling compulsory in 1716, and efforts to enforce and regulate that requirement culminated in 1807 with the creation of a bureau of education. In the following decades the government, with the cooperation of the Lutheran clergy, established an efficient system of universal primary instruction with facilities to train the teachers now needed and to guarantee that the subject matter taught would remain rudimentary and politically safe. The network of secondary schools was also enlarged but kept quite separate, generally not admitting graduates of the ordinary primary schools. Most of the German states had similar arrangements, establishing nearly universal elementary education.

In France the French Revolution had provided the framework for a national system of public schools meant as a substitute for the extensive but more informal and largely religious schools of the old regime. Slowly that vision of a national system of public schools took effect. By 1833 every commune was required to support a public school, and schooling steadily expanded while the quality of teachers improved and the power of inspectors over tightfisted local authorities increased. By the revolution of 1848, three-fourths of France's school-age children were receiving some formal instruction.

In Britain conflict between the Church of England and other Protestant churches prevented creation of a state-controlled system of elementary schools, a lack welcomed by those conservatives who opposed educating the masses. Nevertheless, Parliament voted in 1833 to underwrite the construction of private schools, and subsidies for education gradually increased in amount and scope each year thereafter. From Spain to Russia, elementary schools were favored by every government and passionately demanded by liberals. The public schools of Europe, inadequate and impoverished, offered little chance of social advancement to those forced to attend them, but few doubted that they could be a major instrument for improving society as well as a force for social peace.

III. The Spread of Liberal Government

♦

These limited social programs were part of the great age of liberalism that began in 1830, made England its model, and spread to the continent with revolution in France and the revolt that created Belgium. With the establishment of liberal governments, these representative monarchies of the West stood in sharp contrast to the autocratic governments of Central and Eastern Europe.

♦ GREAT BRITAIN

Britain's withdrawal in the 1820s from Metternich's Concert of Europe represented more than insular habit. The world's leading example of liberalism, Britain was coming to favor liberal programs in other countries, too. But the triumph of liberalism at home had not come without serious conflict.

Pressure for Change The turmoil of the postwar years was heightened by the economic crisis that resulted from demobilization and the collapse of wartime markets, and popular meetings echoed with cries of class resentment. The issues were both social and political. The government's economic policies—removal of the wartime income tax and a higher tariff on grains, which made bread more expensive—favored the rich. To change policies required reform of the political system; and the agitation for that reform, which swept the country, was heated and sometimes violent.

The government at first responded with repression. Habeas corpus was suspended for the first time in English history in 1817. A mass meeting for reform at St. Peter's Field, Manchester, in 1819 so terrified the local magistrates that they called out troops. In the ensuing charge, hundreds of demonstrators, including women and children, were wounded, and several were killed. With bitter mockery people called it the Peterloo Massacre. Parliament responded by passing the Six Acts of 1819, which restricted public meetings, facilitated the prosecution of radicals, and imposed a stamp tax intended to cripple the radical press. In 1820 the discovery of a clumsy plot to blow up the cabinet at dinner added to the atmosphere of political danger. Support for the established order continued to ebb, and the scandal of George IV's personal life earned public contempt. Old restrictions on Protestant dissenters and Roman Catholics (they could not hold public office, for example) now brought rising criticism of the special privileges accorded the Church of England.

Even an unreformed Parliament could be sensitive to public opinion, however, and it began to support temperate compromises on some critical issues. Under the leadership of George Canning, the government gave a voice to people like

William Huskisson, a businessman well known for his belief in the new economics. It reduced some tariffs and repealed the Combination Acts that had banned unions, although an amendment effectively outlawing strikes was soon added. As the minister in charge of the Home Office, Sir Robert Peel ceased the prosecution of newspapers and the use of political spies, halved the list of capital crimes, and put domestic order in the hands of civil authority by creating a police force. The Tories, who opposed such measures, looked to the conservative Duke of Wellington, the prestigious victor over Napoleon at Waterloo, to resist further change; yet as prime minister even he saw the need to push through Parliament a measure he himself disliked, allowing Catholics and religious dissenters to vote and to hold public office. All of these issues—religious freedom, the legitimacy of labor unions, tariffs, restrictions on the press—led to agitation that from London to Ireland increasingly focused on the need to reform Parliament itself. Elections in 1830, required by the death of King George IV and the accession of William IV, only raised the political temperature. In the countryside, laborers set haystacks afire by night; by day, stern magistrates ordered laborers accused of seditious activity transported to Australia.

The Reform Bill of 1832   As public turmoil rose (and British leaders watched with concern the revolution of 1830 in France), a new cabinet pre-

▼ **Pre-reform leaders addressing plitical unions at New Hall Hill, Birminghan regarding the reform Bill, 1832.**
Mary Evans Picture Library

sented a bill to reform the electoral system. The measure was approved in the House only after a new election and was then rejected in the Lords until the king reluctantly threatened to create enough new peers to get it through. Each defeat made the public mood uglier, and the king's intervention came amid demonstrations, the burning of the town hall and the bishop's palace in Bristol, and much dark talk about the French example.

The bill itself offered a good deal less than the more outspoken radicals had wanted, but it marked a fundamental change in Britain's electoral system. Suffrage was increased, allowing some 800,000 well-to-do men to vote, based on the property they owned or the rents they paid.[8] More important than the increased suffrage was the elimination of local variation in favor of a uniform national standard which, as many Tories warned, could easily be broadened in the future. Before the Reform Bill was passed, many boroughs that sent representatives to Parliament were barely villages (the most notorious, Old Sarum, was uninhabited), and the bustling cities of Birmingham and Manchester had had no representatives at all. Perhaps a third of the members of Parliament owed their seats to the influence of some lord. Now representation was at least crudely related to population, and the voices of commerce and manufacturing were both more numerous and louder.

Although restricted suffrage and social tradition (and open voting) guaranteed the continued dominance of the upper classes, Parliament was ready after 1832 to turn to other reforms. Slavery was abolished in Britain's colonies in 1833, a victory for Protestant reformers and humanitarian radicals. The Factory Act, limiting the hours children worked,[9] soon followed, as did the Poor Law of 1834. A law granting all resident taxpayers the

---

[8]This electorate was considerably broader than that established in either France or Belgium in 1830, though Belgium, the only country to give elected representatives a salary, had in many respects Europe's most liberal constitution. About 1 Frenchman in 160 could vote in 1830; 1 Briton in 32, after the Reform Bill of 1832. About 1 Belgian in 95 could vote by 1840; and 1 in 20, by 1848. Universal male suffrage permits approximately one-fifth of the total population to go to the polls.

[9]The work week was limited to 48 hours for children between the ages of six and thirteen, and to 69 hours for those between ages fourteen and eighteen.

with petitions containing thousands of signatures (see "The Great Charter," p. 836). These petitions were summarily rejected, however, and by 1842 the movement was weakening. It failed, despite its size, to find a program that could for long mobilize the masses struggling for survival; and it failed, despite its emphasis on political rather than more threatening economic goals, to stir the consciences of those in power. Angry or desperate workers could riot here or there, but in England they were too isolated from one another and from other classes to gain their political, let alone their social, goals.

The other great popular movement, against the grain tariff, was victorious. The Anti-Corn Law League grew out of urban resentment over the high cost of bread resulting from grain tariffs—the Corn Laws—that benefited the landowning

right to vote in municipal elections challenged aristocratic influence even more directly than the Reform Bill of 1832. When young Victoria ascended the throne in 1837, representative government was stronger than ever. Her reign of more than six decades would rival that of Queen Elizabeth I as a period of British glory and power, but she would remain subordinate (often against her wishes) to an increasingly flexible political system.

Chartism and the Corn Laws Two great popular movements helped define the limits of that political system. Chartism was a huge, amorphous workers' movement, the central aim of which was political democracy, spelled out in what was called the People's Charter.[10] With articulate leaders and a working-class base, Chartists propagandized widely; held huge demonstrations in 1839, 1840, and 1848; and were accused of causing riots that ended with scores of deaths. Although treated by the state as dangerous revolutionaries, their principal tactic was to present Parliament

▼ **The British House of Commons sat in a new building of gothic splendor that made parliamentary liberty seem ancient and the two-party system inevitable.**
Houses of Parliament, Westminster, London, UK/Bridgeman Art Library

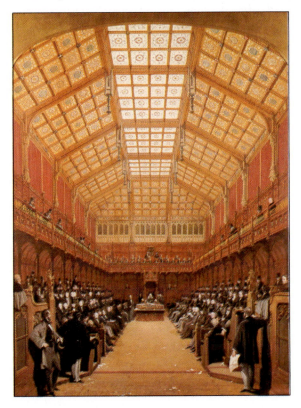

---

[10] The six points of the People's Charter were universal male suffrage, a written ballot, abolition of property qualifications for members of Parliament, payment of the members, constituencies of equal population, and annual elections. All but the last of these points had been adopted by 1918.

The Great Charter

♦

The Chartist movement reached its peak in 1842 with the presentation to the House of Commons of the Great Charter. There were more than 3 million signatures on this petition calling for universal male suffrage, annual parliaments, lower taxes, and greater attention to the needs of the poor.

TO THE HONOURABLE THE COMMONS OF GREAT BRITAIN AND IRELAND, IN PARLIAMENT ASSEMBLED.

"The petition of the undersigned people of the United Kingdom,

"Sheweth—That Government originated from, was designed to protect the freedom and promote the happiness of, and ought to be responsible to, the whole people.

"That the only authority on which any body of men can make laws, and govern society, is delegation from the people.

"That as Government was designed for the benefit and protection of, and must be obeyed and supported by all, therefore all should be equally represented.

"That any form of Government which fails to effect the purposes for which it was designed, and does not fully and completely represent the whole people, who are compelled to pay taxes to its support, and obey the laws resolved upon by it, is unconstitutional, tyrannical, and ought to be amended or resisted.

"That your honourable House, as at present constituted, has not been elected by, and acts irresponsibly of, the people; and hitherto has only represented parties, and benefited the few, regardless of the miseries, grievances, and petitions of the many. Your honourable House has enacted laws contrary to the expressed wishes of the people, and by unconstitutional means enforced obedience to them, thereby creating an unbearable despotism on the one hand, and degrading slavery on the other. . . .

"That the existing state of representation is not only extremely limited and unjust, but unequally divided, and gives preponderating influence to the landed, and monied interests, to the utter ruin of the small-trading and labouring classes.

"That bribery, intimidation, corruption, perjury, and riot, prevail at all parliamentary elections, to an extent best understood by the Members of your honourable House.

"That your petitioners complain that they are enormously taxed to pay the interest of what is termed the national debt, a debt amounting at present to £800,000,000, being only a portion of the enormous amount expended in cruel and expensive wars for the suppression of all liberty, by men not authorised by the people, and who, consequently, had no right to tax posterity for the outrages committed by them upon mankind. . . .

"That your petitioners would direct the attention of your honourable House to the great disparity existing between the wages of the producing millions, and the salaries of those whose comparative usefulness ought to be questioned, where riches and luxury prevail amongst the rulers, and poverty and starvation amongst the ruled.

"That your petitioners, with all due respect and loyalty, would compare the daily income of the Sovereign Majesty, with that of thousands of the working men of this nation; and whilst your petitioners have learned that her Majesty receives daily for her private use the sum of £164 17*s.* 10*d.*, they have also ascertained that many thousands of the families of the labourers are only in the receipt of 3 3/4*d.* per head per day. . . .

"That your petitioners believe all men have a right to worship God as may appear best to their consciences, and that no legislative enactments should interfere between man and his Creator.

"That your petitioners maintain that it is the inherent, indubitable, and constitutional right, founded upon the ancient practice of the realm of England, and supported by well approved statutes, of every male inhabitant of the United Kingdom, he being of age and of sound mind, non-convict of crime, and not confined under any judicial process, to exercise the elective franchise in the choice of Members to serve in the Commons House of Parliament."

classes. From Manchester the movement spread throughout the country, becoming a kind of crusade, an attack on the privileges of aristocracy in the name of the "productive orders" of society, the middle and working classes. The league's propaganda used the new techniques of popular politics: parades and rallies, songs and speeches, pamphlets and cartoons. Its slogans were printed on trinkets for children, ribbons for women, drinking cups for men. Two manufacturers, Richard

▲ Mass meetings had been one of the Chartists' most effective devices, and this one held on Kensington Common in London, April 10, 1848, was one of the most publicized. With revolution on the continent and famine in Ireland, radical hopes were as high as conservative fears. The twenty-thousand who attended this meeting had passed armed soldiers, policemen, and special constables. The expectation of violence explains the small number of women and children in this photograph. What might have been the beginning of a revolution in England was instead the Chartists' last national demonstration.
The Royal Archives © 2002 Her Majesty Queen Elizabeth II

Cobden and John Bright, proved effective spokesmen who became influential figures in public life, spreading the gospel of free trade across the land. To the upper classes, such activity seemed in terrible taste; and conservatives argued that the nation's greatness was rooted in its landed estates.

In the face of this sort of coalition of the middle and working classes, however, British politics proved responsive. Twice Sir Robert Peel's government lowered duties on a wide range of items, including grain, but the league demanded more. Finally, in 1845, Peel announced his support for outright repeal of the Corn Laws. The threat of famine in Ireland had decided the issue for him. Almost simultaneously, the Whig leader, Lord John Russell, affirmed his conversion to the principles of free trade. Yet neither man was eager to carry the fight through the houses of Parliament. Ultimately, Peel undertook the task, and in 1846 he shepherded the measure through both the Commons and the Lords. The grain tariff was

reduced to almost nothing, and nearly all duties were abolished or greatly lowered. As in 1832, the political system had bent when demands for reform gained widespread support among the middle class, but Peel's courage split his party and ended his ministry. He was jeered by angry Tories as a young newcomer, Benjamin Disraeli, rose to decry Peel's treachery to the aristocracy. The growing weight of public opinion and the liberal creed had triumphed; the sphere of political debate had expanded to include vexing social issues.

◆ THE REVOLUTIONS OF 1830

Uprisings across Europe   The cause of reform in Britain had benefited from fear of revolution, following a wave of revolutions on the continent in 1830. The first of these occurred in France. Brief and largely limited to Paris, it was a revolution nevertheless, and any uprising in France was a European event. Minor revolts stimulated by the

French example occurred in central Italy, Spain, Portugal, some of the German principalities, and Poland. Austria once again extinguished revolt in Italy, and the Russian army crushed Poland's rebels; elsewhere, the results were more lasting.

Belgium   In the southern Netherlands, Catholics and liberals took the occasion to rise against Dutch rule. This revolt was a direct challenge to the provisions of the Congress of Vienna. Britain opposed any intervention by the great powers, however, once convinced that France had no territorial designs on the Netherlands; and Britain led in arranging international guarantees for the independence of the southern Netherlands, which became Belgium. The British and French then pressured the Dutch to acquiesce.

The Belgian monarchy established in 1830 was one of the triumphs of liberal constitutionalism; and the new state, which owed its existence both to French restraint and British protection, took as its king Leopold I, who had lived long in England (he was an uncle of Queen Victoria) and who soon married the daughter of Louis Philippe. The constitution went further than France's in guaranteeing civil rights and the primacy of the Chamber of Deputies; and politics continued to revolve around a coalition—rare in Europe—of Catholics and liberals, aristocrats and members of the upper-middle class.

Rapidly becoming the most industrialized nation on the continent, Belgium was prosperous; and if its lower classes were more miserable and a greater proportion of them illiterate than in France, that very fact permitted the social isolation of its leaders. Self-confident and satisfied with the new order of things, they built on the administrative traditions left from earlier Austrian and French rule as well as that of the Dutch and proved themselves remarkably adept at planning railroads, reforming taxes and schools, and making timely political concessions.

Switzerland   Liberal institutions spread to Switzerland, too, as part of the international trend spurred by the revolutions of 1830. Beginning in 1828, some cantons adopted such liberal measures as representative government and freedom of the press, and ten cantons formed a league in 1832 to agitate for religious freedom and for a stronger, secular central government within the Swiss con-

federation. These policies were resisted by seven largely Catholic cantons, which were dominated by their aristocracies and soon formed an alliance, the Sonderbund. By 1847 the two leagues were at war. The Sonderbund looked for support from conservative and Catholic states, but none came (the papacy, Austria, and Piedmont had their hands full with revolts in Italy), and the liberal sympathies of Britain and France once again proved decisive. With the Sonderbund's defeat, Switzerland became a federal state with a new constitution, influenced by the example of the United States, that provided for universal male suffrage.

France's July Monarchy   In France, Charles X's abdication led not to the succession of his son, as the king had hoped, but to a provisional government. Organized largely in newspaper offices, it had a faintly republican coloration but soon settled for a liberal monarchy. Most of France was ready to accept that compromise when the Marquis de Lafayette, still a republican and a popular hero, stepped out on the balcony of the Hôtel de Ville to present Louis Philippe as the candidate for the throne. The symbols of revolution and moderation were neatly combined in France's new monarchy under the House of Orléans, the liberal branch of the royal line headed by Louis Philippe (his father had voted with the Jacobins for the death of Louis XVI).

Louis Philippe's posters proclaimed him citizen-king, and the Revolution's tricolor replaced the Bourbon flag. Known as the July Monarchy, the new regime began with a constitution presented as a contract the king swore to keep, not as a gift he granted. Similar to the one it replaced, the contract offered stronger guarantees of political freedom, lowered property requirements for voters (nearly doubling their number to some 170,000, safely restricted to men of means), and replaced the hereditary upper house with lifetime peers. Because most of the old aristocracy resigned their offices, never to return to public life, there was an important change in government personnel. Those who replaced the aristocracy, professional people and bearers of newer (often Napoleonic) titles, differed from their predecessors more in outlook than in social origin. In his appeal to the people of Paris, Louis Philippe sounded more radical than he was, and the new government hastened to assure Europe's other monarchs

▲ Jeanron's depiction of a Parisian barricade in 1830 (later used to illustrate Louis Blanc's socialist history of the period) presents a more realistic scene of the fighting than Delacroix's more famous version but a very similar heroic vision of workers and middle class together (see p. 804).
Roger-Viollet/Getty Images

that this French revolution would send no militants to sponsor or support revolution elsewhere.

The overriding political question of the 1830s in France was the July Monarchy itself, which was attacked from left and right. Louis Philippe presented himself as a good bourgeois, while the regime's opponents on both sides sought broader support. With strong Catholic support, legitimists (those in favor of the Bourbons) campaigned in the countryside and the newspapers. A mass held in Paris on the anniversary of the death of Charles X's son and heir, who had been assassinated in 1820, became a demonstration that in turn prompted an anticlerical crowd to sack and loot the archbishop's palace and a nearby church. In 1832 the duchess of Berry, whose infant son was now the legitimist claimant to the throne, tried to stage an uprising. Republicans were active, too, often in secret groups that had provocative names like the Society of the Rights of Man. When the silk workers of Lyons went on strike, it was viewed as a republican revolt and was suppressed with the bitterness of class hatred by the bourgeois National Guard. That politi-

cal climate encouraged another contender, the Bonapartist heir, Louis Napoleon, to attempt to stir an uprising in 1836 and again in 1840.

Limited Liberalism in France Yet all these attempts failed; and the July Monarchy presented itself as a center of stability and patriotism, even laying claim to the cult of Napoleon I by bringing the emperor's body back from St. Helena and placing it with nationalist pomp in the marble crypt of the Invalides. The government built on the administrative system that had been developed under the Revolution and Napoleon to promote public education, new if limited social services, and industrialization. With time (and restrictions on the press) opposition quieted, and many of the middle-class notables of France rallied to a government of cautious moderation that talked of progress.

A regime largely isolated from workers, peasants, and the old aristocracy had found in nationalism its most effective means of reaching a larger public. Yet it remained divided between those

◄ Carefully staged ceremonies marked the return of Napoleon's ashes from St. Helena for internment in Paris on December 15, 1840, as a national, patriotic event.
AKG London

who wanted further reform and wider suffrage and those, like the king himself, who believed the proper balance between liberty and order had been achieved. The former were led by Adolphe Thiers; the latter, by François Guizot. Both were journalists and historians of great talent; but their skillful verbal duels, often models of parliamentarism, failed to mobilize opinion in France as agitation over the Corn Laws had done in England. From 1840 to 1848 the government was dominated by Guizot. A Protestant in a Catholic country, an intellectual in politics, a man who held broad principles rigidly, Guizot had in excess failings common to many liberals of the nineteenth century. He spoke of liberty, progress, and law in eloquent terms that made his cautious practices seem hypocritical. In 1848 the whole regime fell as easily as incumbents losing an election.

The two freest and most prosperous of Europe's great nations had developed similarly since 1830. In both, liberal governments led by able men sought through reasonable compromise, the rule of law, and parliamentary politics to unify their nations and to make "progress" compatible with stability. Discontent and workers' misery, though frightening, were understood in the councils of government primarily as a threat to order. In England reform had to be wrung from a powerful aristocracy that was, in the end, secure enough to cede under pressure. In France the aristocracy

counted for little after 1830; but the government, fearful of the more radical hopes for democracy and social justice that it excluded, remained uncertain of its popular support.

Spain The victories of French and British liberalism seemed part of a general trend. In Spain the monarchy itself wooed liberals. When King Ferdinand VII died in 1833, he had carefully arranged for his three-year-old daughter, Isabella, to succeed him. But the king's brother, Don Carlos, denounced the arrangement as illegal[11] and began an uprising that lasted until 1839. The Carlists, who favored autocracy and the traditional claims of Spanish Catholicism, found their greatest support in rural areas and regions of the north that were resentful of rule from Madrid. Despite eventual defeat, Don Carlos won a place in Spanish legend as a dashing and chivalric hero, protector of old Spanish virtues; and Carlism would remain a conservative rallying cry in every subsequent Spanish revolution.

---

[11]Don Carlos cited the Salic law, dating from Merovingian times, which prohibited women from acceding to royal thrones. Generally followed on the continent, the law meant that in 1837 England's Queen Victoria could not also assume rule over Hanover as her father had. In Spain Ferdinand VII had abolished the Salic law in 1830 by what was known as a pragmatic sanction.

To win liberal support, the regency ruling in Isabella's name granted a constitution in 1834. Cautiously modeled on the French constitution of 1814, with narrow suffrage and protection of royal power, it established representative institutions as a lasting feature of Spanish politics. Even so modest a step placed Spain in the liberal camp, and Isabella's government relied on extensive support from Britain and France against threats from abroad, an alliance joined by Portugal after similar concessions there. Internal war brought generals into politics and conflict between two camps: the moderates (who supported the constitution of 1834 and admired Guizot's France) and the anticlerical progressives (who demanded a democratic constitution and the election of local officials). Only after a couple of military coups did moderates establish a regime in the 1840s strong enough to hold power for a decade. Everywhere, the changes and the aspirations that brought constitutions, limited suffrage, and circumscribed freedoms were based on a delicate balance that proved difficult to maintain.

SUMMARY

Clusters of ideas about the nature of historical change, about how to prevent revolutions or achieve them, and about the kind of future that industrialization might bring had grown into the ideologies that have divided Western social thought ever since. In the arts and philosophy, romanticism pointed nostalgically to the past but also toward the new, hailing individual genius yet yearning for community. Conservatives sustained standards critical of the new age; liberals gained strength from their confidence in the future; and socialists envisioned an alternative to capitalist industrialization. From 1815 on, a variety of political experiments, each claiming to be permanent, had been tried in Europe. The problem for conservative regimes was to increase their political effectiveness while preserving as much of the old social order as possible. Although liberal regimes fostered the benefits of uniform justice, legal equality, individual rights, and broader political participation, they faced the question of how far such principles could be taken without creating instability. They, like the conservative regimes they replaced, were a compromise. In fact, all available ideas, institutions, and policies were challenged by the social changes that accompanied industrialization, factory labor, demographic growth, and urbanization. Living with change had become a definition of modernity. There was an explosive mixture in these intellectual, social, and political trends; and they came together in the revolutions that swept across Europe in 1848 and in the increased emphasis on the importance of the state, especially a national state that could demand the loyalty of its citizens.

QUESTIONS FOR FURTHER THOUGHT

1. What explains the relevance, two centuries later, of political and cultural ideologies that took shape during the French Revolution and early years of industrialization?

2. How is it that society can still be described in terms of social classes despite all the social and political changes that have occurred?

3. What kinds of people are most likely to be drawn to liberalism or to reject its appeal? Does that change over time?

RECOMMENDED READING

◆

Sources

Engels, Friedrich. *The Condition of the Working Class in England*. Written in 1844 and available in many modern editions, this influential work by Karl Marx's friend and coauthor paints a dark picture of the working-class slum and conveys the moral outrage radicals felt.

Ure, Andrew. *The Philosophy of Manufactures*. 1835. An early and classic justification of liberal economics, emphasizing its promised benefits for all.

Novels are important sources for understanding nineteenth-century society. Elizabeth Gaskell (*Mary Barton* and *North and South*) and Charles Dickens (*Hard Times* and *Oliver Twist*) provided contemporaries with an influential picture of social conditions in England; Honoé de Balzac's *Père Goriot* set the tone for criticisms of the selfishness of the middle class.

Studies

*Bellamy, Richard. *Liberalism and Modern Society: A Historical Argument*. 1992. Treats the changes over time and the national differences in the meanings of liberalism.

Berdahl, Robert M. *The Politics of the Prussian Nobility: The Development of a Conservative Ideology*. 1988. Shows how political interests and social structure led to the formation of a conservatism that dominated much of German history.

*Briggs, Asa. *Victorian Cities*. 1970. Colorful studies of the urban politics and social life of individual cities.

Brock, Michael. *The Great Reform Act*. 1974. Analyzes the significance of the Reform Bill of 1832 through a close examination of the political and social forces that brought it about.

*Chevalier, Louis. *Laboring Classes and Dangerous Classes in Paris during the First Half of the Nineteenth Century*. Frank Jellinek (tr.). 1981. This detailed study of the Parisian poor also says much about French society in general during the early years of industrialization.

Church, Clive H. *Europe in 1830: Revolution and Political Change*. 1983. A study that emphasizes the significance of the revolutions of 1830 by noting their transnational connections and impact.

Coffin, Judith G. *The Politics of Women's Work: The Paris Garment Trades, 1750-1915*. 1996. The quintessential women's work was in the garment industry, and this study reveals the long evolution of women in the labor movement and of ideas about gender, issues that concerned all of society.

*Davidoff, Leonore, and Catherine Hall. *Family Fortunes: Men and Women of the English Middle Class, 1780–1850*. 1985. A wonderfully rich and concrete picture of the aspirations and concerns of middle-class life.

Dennis, Richard. *English Industrial Cities of the Nineteenth Century*. 1984. A comprehensive study of the special nature and problems of this new kind of city.

De Ruggiero, Guido. *The History of European Liberalism*. R. G. Collingswood (tr.). 1977. A classic comparison of the different concepts of liberalism that were dominant in each of the major European nations.

Franklin, S. H. *The European Peasantry: The Final Phase*. 1969. Taken together, these essays on different countries reveal not only the striking differences in peasants' lives but the importance of the peasantry for understanding the general history of European nations.

*Hamerow, Theodore S. *Restoration, Revolution, and Reaction: Economics and Politics in Germany, 1815–1871*. 1958. A complex analysis of the relationship of social classes and the state to economic change in this revolutionary period.

Harrison, J. F. C. *The Early Victorians, 1832–1851*. 1971. A lively account of the personalities and issues that marked the beginning of a new era.

*Heilbroner, Robert L. *The Worldly Philosophers*. 1972. A good introduction to the ideas of the economic liberals.

Himmelfarb, Gertrude. *On Liberty and Liberalism: The Case of John Stuart Mill*. 1974. Penetrating and controversial analysis of the still-controversial philosopher of liberalism.

Holmes, Stephen. *Benjamin Constant and the Making of Modern Liberalism*. 1984. The biographical focus offers a valuable insight into the evolution of liberalism on the continent.

*Hopkins, Eric. *Industrialisation and Society: A Social History, 1830–1951*. 2000. A wide-ranging discussion of the impact of industrialization on British society through the nineteenth century and on to the welfare state.

Johnson, Douglas. *Guizot: Aspects of French History*. 1963. Insightful essays focusing on the dominant figure of the July Monarchy and revealing the tensions between aspirations for a liberal society and conservative fear for order.

Katznelson, Ira, and Artistide R. Zolberg (eds.). *Working-Class Formation: Nineteenth-Century Patterns in Western Europe and the United States.* 1986. Significant interpretative essays by some leading scholars that take a fresh look at how working-class awareness was formed and at the values and attitudes associated with it.

*Lichtheim, George. *A Short History of Socialism.* 1975. Well-constructed treatment of the evolution of socialist ideas in their historical context.

*Lindemann, Albert S. *A History of European Socialism.* 1984. Establishes the line of continuity from the early socialists through labor movements and the eventual dominance of Marxism.

*Lukács, Georg. *The Historical Novel.* Hannah and Stanley Mitchell (trs.). 1962. Insightful and learned study of the social significance of the nineteenth-century novel by one of Europe's leading Marxist scholars.

*Manuel, Frank. *The Prophets of Paris.* 1965. An excellent discussion of French utopian thinkers.

Perkin, Harold. *The Origins of Modern English Society, 1780–1860.* 1969. Provides a clear picture of the diverse sectors of English society and how they adapted to the changes of the period.

Porter, Roy, and Mikul Teich (eds.). *Romanticism in National Context.* 1988. Particularly useful for the student because this volume of interpretive essays includes many on smaller European nations.

Price, Roger. *A Social History of Nineteenth-Century France.* 1987. A clear synthesis of recent research that provides an excellent introduction.

*Riasanovsky, Nicholas V. *The Emergence of Romanticism.* 1992. An excellent introduction to the origins of European romanticism that emphasizes its importance for rising nationalism.

*Rudé, George. *The Crowd in History, 1730–1884.* 1964. Argues that there was a fundamental change in the social composition and demands of crowds, and therefore of their significance, after industrialization.

Segalen, Martine. *Love and Power in the Peasant Family: Rural France in the Nineteenth Century.* J. C. Whitehouse and Sarah Mathews (trs.). 1983. Shows the active role of peasant society in the process of social change.

*Sewell, William H., Jr. *Work and Revolution in France: The Language of Labor from the Old Regime to 1848.* 1980. An important study that shows the radical potential and continuing strength of a preindustrial working-class culture in the industrial era.

*Shanin, Teodor (ed.). *Peasants and Peasant Society.* 1987. Essays treating the varied aspects of peasant society, reflecting important recent scholarship; especially useful on Eastern Europe.

Snell, K. D. M. *Annals of the Laboring Poor: Social Change and Agrarian England, 1660–1900.* 1985. A pioneering look at the position of the rural underclass in Britain and the transformation of their world in the nineteenth century.

*Stromberg, Roland N. *European Intellectual History since 1789.* 1975. A graceful and thorough presentation of the major trends.

*Thompson, Dorothy. *The Chartists: Popular Politics in the Industrial Revolution.* 1984. A lively and sympathetic account that relates working-class action to the larger social context.

*Thompson, Edward P. *The Making of the English Working Class.* 1964. A remarkable work of sympathetic insight and exhaustive research that continues to influence studies of the working class in all societies.

Valenze, Deborah. *The First Industrial Woman.* 1995. Establishes the connection between new modes of production, ideas of gender, and women's economic roles.

Walker, Mack. *German Home Towns: Community, State, and General Estate, 1648–1871.* 1971. Sensitive and original treatment of the response of small-town life to political and social change, showing the historical significance of the ambivalence felt toward the state, liberalism, and nationalism.

*Weiss, John. *Conservatism in Europe, 1770–1945: Traditionalism, Reaction, and Counter-Revolution.* 1977. Provides a valuable survey of the rich variety and social insight in conservative thought and of the political importance of conservative movements.

---

*Available in paperback.

Kaiser Wilhelm   Kaiserin Augusta

▲ Victory and the birth of a new Germany: The Halls of Versailles ring as Prussian officers hail the proclamation of Prussia's King Wilhelm as German Kaiser.
Bildarchiv Preussischer Kulturbesitz

Chapter 24

NATIONAL STATES AND NATIONAL CULTURES

In the spring of 1848 revolution swept across Europe from France to Hungary. Popular uprisings seemed to transform Europe in a few dramatic months; yet the revolutionary regimes were soon suppressed. They nevertheless demonstrated that revolution could erupt at any time, that demands for political freedom could win passionate support, that class conflict could be explosive, that military power could be decisive, and that nationalism could make the broadest appeal of all. In the next thirty years, two new national states, Italy and Germany, came into being and governments everywhere took increased responsibility for shaping public life. That included supporting a formal culture that was both an expression of national identity and a means of defining and propagating it.

	Social Structure	Body Politic	Changes in the Organization of Production and in the Impact of Technology	Evolution of Family and Changing Gender Roles	War	Religion	Cultural Expression
CHAPTER 24. NATIONAL STATES AND NATIONAL CULTURES							
I. THE REVOLUTIONS OF 1848	░░░	░░░			░░░		
II. THE POLITICS OF NATIONALISM	░░░	░░░			░░░		
III. NINETEENTH-CENTURY CULTURE						░░░	░░░

I. The Revolutions of 1848

◆

The revolutions of 1848 spread by a kind of spontaneous imitation from city to city, their causes, early successes, and ultimate defeat somewhat different in each case. Yet all of them went through comparable phases in which easy victory and initial euphoria was followed by rising social conflict and, ultimately, by the triumph of the forces of order.

Two years of poor harvests and industrial recession in most of Europe preceded these outbreaks, but economic crisis alone does not make a revolution. In Ireland more than a million people died from starvation during the famine years from 1846 to 1849; yet that tragedy did little more to shake British rule than the Chartist movement. In Switzerland, Belgium, and the Netherlands major liberalization occurred without a serious revolt. Revolutions occurred where governments were distrusted and where the fear and resentment fed by rising food prices and unemployment found focus in specific political demands.

◆ THE OPENING PHASE

France In France Guizot's government refused to widen the suffrage, and that led to the fall of the July Monarchy. The parliamentary opposition launched a protest movement that staged large banquets across the country. When a nervous government, aware of its unpopularity, banned the banquet scheduled for Paris in late February 1848, some members of the Chamber of Deputies an-

nounced they would attend anyway. Crowds gathered in the streets, and workers who could never have afforded banquet tickets started to build barricades. The rituals of revolution had begun. Louis Philippe, ever sensitive to middle-class opinion, held a review of his citizen militia, the National Guard. When they sullenly refused to cheer him, Louis Philippe knew his days were numbered. He abdicated in favor of his grandson and left for England, much as Charles X had done just eighteen years before. This time, too, the effort to preserve a dynasty was ignored, and a provisional government of men chosen by two rival newspapers appeared at the Hôtel de Ville and declared France a republic. The Paris crowds cheered, and political clubs organized. The new cabinet—led by Alphonse de Lamartine, a handsome and much-admired romantic poet—was dominated by moderates who at first cooperated with more radical members (including a socialist, Louis Blanc). They agreed that the republic should adopt universal male suffrage, a degree of democracy allowed in no other large nation, and that the citizen's right to work was a principle of government, establishing a commission to hold public hearings on problems of labor. Noting that each French revolution "owed it to the world to establish yet one more philosophic truth," the republic abolished the death penalty.

At the same time, the new regime was careful to demonstrate its restraint. It refused to intervene in behalf of revolutions in other countries, rejected proposals for adopting a red flag as the symbol of socialism and kept the familiar tricolor but with a red cockade or rosette of ribbon, and levied new

▲ **Lamartine persuades the crowd to reject the red flag and let the new French republic keep the tricolor.**
Musée du Petit Palais, Paris/Giraudon/Bridgeman Art Library

taxes to balance the budget. Relations with the Catholic Church were the best in a generation, and April elections for a constituent assembly took place in good order. Nearly 85 percent of the eligible electorate voted, giving moderate republicans an overwhelming majority. The Second Republic seemed solidly established.

Revolution Spreads As news of the events in France sped across Europe, a conservative nightmare became a reality. Nearly every capital had citizens who found exciting promise in words like *constitution, rights, liberty,* and *free press.* In Hungary the Diet cheered Lajos Kossuth, the Magyar leader, as he called on March 3 for representative government; and in the same week demonstrations with similar demands erupted in the cities of the Rhineland, soon giving way to revolution there and then in Vienna (March 12), Berlin (March 15), Milan (March 18), and Venice (March 22). Each of these revolutions followed a similar pattern. The news from France would attract excited crowds; groups of men—especially journalists, lawyers, and students—would meet in cafés to discuss rumors and newspaper reports. Governments that did not quickly grant constitutions

(as they had tended to do in Italy) would call out troops to maintain order; and with a kind of inevitability, some incident would occur—a shot fired by a soldier insulted once too often or by someone in the crowd with an unfamiliar gun.

Then barricades would rise in the style that came from Paris, constructed of paving stones, a passing coach ceremoniously overturned, nearby trees, and furniture. Barricades became the people's voice, threatening but vague, as workers and professional people, men, women, and children labored together. When blood was shed, the crowd had its martyrs. In Paris corpses were carried around on a cart as a spur to revolutionary determination; in Berlin the king, supporting his fainting queen, acceded to the crowd's demands and paid his respects, bareheaded, to the subjects his troops had killed. When new concessions were won, the atmosphere would grow festive. New flags would fly, often a tricolor, an echo of the French Revolution but with colors symbolizing some other nation. In the almost universal dedication to politics, newspapers and pamphlets appeared in floods (one hundred new newspapers in Vienna, nearly five hundred in Paris). Radicals would seek ever after to recapture the unanimity

▲ **In one of the early triumphs of the 1848 revolutions, the citizens of Milan forced the Austrian Army to leave the city. Everyone now knew how to build barricades, and the whole family helped, using whatever was available.**
Index, Milan, Museo del Risorgimento. Photo, © G. Costa

and joy of those early days of revolution. Others, and not just conservatives, would never forget fearsome mobs, fanatical faces, and ugly threats.

Central Europe   In the Austrian Empire, the Hungarian Diet had by mid-March established a free press and a national guard, abolished feudal obligations (with compensation to the lords), and required nobles to pay taxes. Everyone noticed the parallel to 1789. Reluctantly Vienna agreed that Hungary could levy its own taxes and direct its own army. The Hungarian example encouraged students in Vienna to demand representative government for Austria as well, and crowds soon clashed with the troops and formed specific demands. In rapid order Metternich resigned, censorship was abolished, a constitution was promised, and firearms were passed out to the students. When students rejected the proposal that all men except factory workers and servants be allowed to vote, universal male suffrage was conceded. Hungarian autonomy then brought similar demands from Czechs in Bohemia, Croatians in Croatia, and Romanians in Transylvania (these last two domains under Hungarian rule). The old Austrian Empire had all but collapsed.

When Frederick William IV of Prussia learned the incredible news of an uprising in Vienna and the fall of Metternich, he granted the concessions on which he had stalled for months, relaxing censorship and calling a meeting of the Landtag. Fighting broke out anyway, and Frederick William then agreed to remove his hated troops from Berlin, used the evocative word *Germany* in proclamations to "my dear Berliners," and wore the German national colors: black, gold, and red. A constituent assembly was elected in May by universal but indirect male suffrage, and when it met in Berlin, where a civic guard now kept order, revolution seemed to have triumphed in Prussia, too. Events in the rest of Germany confirmed that victory. In May, 830 delegates elected by universal male suffrage convened at Frankfurt to write a constitution for all of Germany. They were mostly from the smaller states of the more liberal west, and more than half of them were lawyers and professors. But there were also businessmen, members of the liberal gentry, and even nobles, suddenly awkward in such society. The great majority favored a monarchical German state with an almost democratic constitution as the brilliant, difficult, and noisy assembly set about to write a constitution for a united Germany.

The arrangements contrived in 1815 at the Congress of Vienna were under siege in Italy as well, where in the 1820s and 1830s the kingdoms of Piedmont in the north and Naples (including Sicily) in the south had barely weathered earlier revolts, which had also threatened the smaller duchies in between. A well-organized rising in Palermo against rule from Naples was actually the first of the revolutions in 1848; but it was news of the revolution in Paris that made it possible to demand constitutions in Naples, Tuscany, and Piedmont. Even the Papal States got a constitution, though it awkwardly preserved a veto for the pope and the College of Cardinals. Lombardy and Venetia had been ruled as part of the Habsburg Empire since 1815, but shortly after the revolution in Vienna, a revolt broke out in Milan against the Austrian forces there. The Austrians were forced to retreat, and the "Five Glorious Days of Milan" were added to the heroic legends of March. Then Venice rose up to reestablish the Venetian republic of old, and the possibility that the Italian peninsula might be

Chronology

THE OPENING PHASE,
1848

France	German States		Italian States
	Habsburg Empire	*Prussia*	

France

Feb. 22 Barricades in Paris.

Feb. 23 Louis Philippe abdicates; Republic proclaimed.

Apr. 23 French elections.

German States

Habsburg Empire

Mar. 3 Hungarian demands.

Mar. 12 Student risings in Vienna.

Mar. 13 Metternich resigns.

Mar. 15–31 Liberal legislation; Hungarian autonomy.

Apr. 8 Czechs promised a constituent assembly.

Apr. 25 Emperor proclaims constitution for Austria.

May 15 Vienna: Demonstrators demand democracy.

May 17 Emperor flees.

Prussia

Mar. 15 Berlin rising.

Mar. 18–21 Prussian king calls Landtag.

May 18 Frankfurt national assembly meets.

May 22 Prussian constituent assembly meets.

Italian States

Jan. 12 Palermo revolt.

Feb. 10 King in Naples grants constitution.

Feb. 17 Constitution granted in Tuscany.

Mar. 4 Constitution granted in Piedmont.

Mar. 14 Pope grants constitution.

Mar. 18–22 Milan revolt: Five Glorious Days.

Mar. 22 Venice declares republic.

May 30 Italian troops defeat Austrians.

---

freed from foreign rule stimulated a nationalist fervor that forced Piedmont to join the war against Austria.

◆ THE FATAL DISSENSIONS

Social Class Everywhere, however, the new freedom exposed divisions among those who had fought for it. In France these divisions were primarily social—between Paris and the countryside, between the middle class and the workers. Finding conditions little improved under a republic, workers agitated for a social program and pinned their hopes on the national workshops that had been established as an echo of ideas popularized by the socialist Louis Blanc. Imagined as cooperatives in which workers would work for themselves and share the profits, the workshops that the Republic established were in practice little

more than a program of temporary relief. Unemployed men from Paris and the countryside nevertheless enrolled by the tens of thousands. To moderate republicans the workshops represented a dangerous principle and outrageous waste. The government ordered them disbanded in June. To workers the workshops represented an explicit promise and the beginning of a new era. They responded by building barricades in the working-class sections of Paris. For three days the poor fought with the ferocity of hopelessness before the Republic's troops under General Cavaignac systematically crushed the threat to order.

More than a thousand people died; thousands more would be sent to prison or into exile. The June Days remained the very symbol of class conflict for socialists, and radicals never quite recaptured their faith that democracy alone would lead to social justice. Given almost dictatorial powers,

Cavaignac took steps to restrict the press, suppress radical societies, and discipline workers. Yet Cavaignac remained a convinced republican; and the assembly continued to write a constitution that maintained universal suffrage and provided for a president directly elected by popular vote. But after June there was something a little hollow about the Second Republic.

National Ambitions   In Germany and Austria, also, revolution uncovered latent conflicts between workers and the middle class and among artisans, peasants, and nobles; but the outcome was determined more by competing nationalisms and the fact that kings still had their armies. The Frankfurt parliament felt little sympathy for uprisings by other nationalities against German rule. Instead of protesting the repression of revolution, it congratulated the Austrian field marshal who bombarded Prague (where Czechs had staged a

▼ A silent street in Paris, its rubble, bodies, and blood — the emblems of revolution defeated in this painting by Ernest Meissonier.
Giraudon/Art Resource, NY

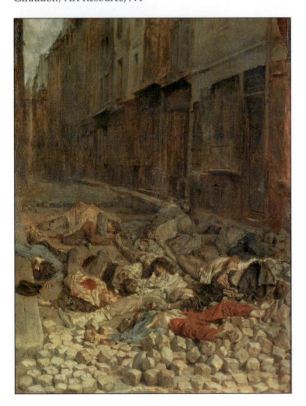

Pan-Slav conference) on his German victory; and it applauded the Austrian forces that regrouped in northern Italy and fought their way back into Milan. It called on the Prussian army to put down a Polish uprising in Posen and to fight against Denmark in Schleswig and Holstein. In September when riots broke out in Frankfurt itself, the assembly invited Austrian and Prussian troops to restore order. Conflicts among multiple nationalities were also strengthening the Habsburgs at home, as the emperor mobilized Croatians demanding autonomy from Hungary much as Hungary had from Austria. In parts of the empire, Austrian officials were also able to win peasant support by abolishing serfdom and by playing on their distrust of local revolutionaries.

The armies that soon moved on Frankfurt and Vienna confronted resistance that, like the June Days in Paris, revealed an even greater popular fury and more radical demands than the risings of February and March. Politics turned more radical in Rome, too, where the pope had proved not to be an Italian nationalist; economic conditions worsened, and a government that had promised much accomplished little. When his prime minister was assassinated, Pius IX slipped across the border into the Kingdom of Naples, and a representative assembly gave the eternal city its ancient title of Roman Republic. Venice and France were also republics, and assemblies were still busy drafting constitutions in Vienna, Berlin, and Frankfurt, but there could be no doubt that conservative forces were gaining ground.

◆ THE FINAL PHASE

New Leaders   In December, France elected a president, and the candidates who had been prominent in the new republic finished far behind Louis Napoleon Bonaparte, who won 70 percent of the votes. The ambitious nephew of Emperor Napoleon, he had campaigned as a republican. He had written more about social questions and workers' needs than any other candidate; and he was supported by the Catholic Church and the

▶ An engraving of the violence in Frankfurt in September 1848 contrasts the fighting styles of troops and the defenders of revolution.
The Granger Collection, New York

Chronology

◆

FATAL DISSENSIONS,

1848

France

June 23–26 June Days insurrection.

Nov. 4 Constitution.

German States

Habsburg Empire

June 12 Prague bombarded; Pan-Slav congress dissolved; military dictatorship.

June 22 Assembly in Vienna adopts constitution, peasants emancipated.

Sept. 17 Austrian army from Croatia invades Hungary.

Oct. 31 Vienna bombarded, occupied.

Prussia

June–Sept. Frankfurt assembly supports Prussia against Danes in Schleswig-Holstein.

Italy

July 24 Austrians defeat Italian army.

Nov. 25 Pope flees Rome.

Chronology

THE FINAL PHASE,
1848–1849

France	German States		Italy
	Habsburg Empire	*Prussia*	
Dec. 20 Louis Napoleon elected president.	**Dec. 2.** Francis Joseph, emperor.	**Dec. 5** Prussian assembly dissolved.	**Feb. 9** Roman Republic established.
	Jan. 5 Budapest occupied.	**Mar. 27** Frankfurt constitution completed; rejected by Prussia on Apr. 21.	**Mar. 23** Decisive defeat of Piedmont by Austria.
	Mar. 4 Austrian Reichstag dissolved; its constitution replaced.		**Apr. 24** French army lands in Papal States.
	Apr. 13 Hungary declares a republic.		**June 30** Rome falls to French.
	June 17 Russia invades Hungary.		**Aug. 28** Venice surrenders.
	Aug. 13 Hungary capitulates.		

monarchists, for want of anyone else, as a man of order. Above all, he had his name.[1] Austria, too, found a strong new leader in Prince Felix von Schwarzenberg, who filled the place Metternich left vacant; and in December he persuaded the emperor to abdicate in favor of his eighteen-year-old nephew, Franz Joseph I, who could promise a fresh start. In Prussia the king felt confident enough to dissolve the Landtag and promulgate a constitution of his own, one very similar to Piedmont's and Belgium's. Ten months of turmoil had led back to the arrangements of February.

Military Force One by one, the remaining revolutionary regimes were subdued. The Frankfurt Assembly, having completed its constitution for a unified Germany, in March 1849 elected the Prussian king as German emperor, only to have him reject a crown from the "gutter," declaring that the ones he recognized came by grace of God. The Frankfurt constitution—with its touching list of old abuses to be abolished, its universal male suffrage and promises of civil rights and education—would never be tested (see "The Frankfurt Constitution," p. 853). New revolutions broke out in the Rhineland, Saxony, and Bavaria, but all were quashed in June and July with the aid of Prussian troops. The Habsburgs' multinational armies bombarded the revolutionaries of Vienna into submission and soon turned on Hungary, where a republic had been declared because Schwarzenberg refused to permit Hungary to have a constitution. The Hungarians battled for months against the armies of Austria and against Croatians, several groups of Slavs, and Romanians until Russia intervened in June to seal the fate of the Hungarian republic.

In Italy, too, military force was decisive. Austria defeated Piedmont one more time, leaving it nothing to show for its support of Italian independence except an enormous debt, an unpopular

---

[1] On trial for his attempted coup in 1840, Louis Napoleon had concluded his defense with these words: "I represent before you a principle, a cause, and a defeat: the principle is sovereignty of the people; the cause, that of the Empire; the defeat, Waterloo. The principle you have recognized; the cause you have served; the defeat you want to avenge."

THE FRANKFURT CONSTITUTION

◆

The Frankfurt Parliament completed its work on a constitution for Germany in 1849. It was a long and detailed document, carefully proscribing the repressive acts that had been most common in the preceding years. Its proud assertions of German freedom remain significantly vague, however, about the enforcement of its provisions and what the boundaries of the German nation will be.

THE FUNDAMENTAL RIGHTS OF THE GERMAN PEOPLE

"Article 1

¶ 131. The German people consists of the citizens of the states, which make up the Reich.

¶ 132. Every German has the right of German Reich's citizenship. He can exercise this right in every German land. Reich's franchise legislation shall provide for the right of the individual to vote for members of the national assembly.

¶ 133. Every German has the right to live or reside in any part of the Reich's territory, to acquire and dispose of property of all kinds, to pursue his livelihood, and to win the right of communal citizenship.

The terms of living and residence shall be established by a law of settlement; trade regulations shall be established by regulations affecting trade and industry; both to be set by the Reich's administration for all of Germany.

¶ 134. No German state is permitted to make a distinction between its citizens and other Germans in civil, criminal, and litigation rights which relegates the latter to the position of foreigners.

¶ 135. Capital punishment for civil offenses shall not take place, and, in those cases where condemnation has already been made, shall not be carried out, in order not to infringe upon the hereby acquired civil law.

¶ 136. Freedom of emigration shall not be limited by any state; emigration levies shall not be established.

All matters of emigration remain under the protection and care of the Reich.

"Article 2

¶ 137. There are no class differences before the law. The rank of nobility is abolished.

All special class privileges are abolished.

All Germans are equal before the law.

All titles, insofar as they are not bound with an office, are abolished and never again shall be introduced.

No citizen shall accept a decoration from a foreign state.

Public office shall be open to all men on the basis of ability.

All citizens are subject equally to military service; there shall be no draft substitutions.

"Article 3

¶ 141. The confiscation of letters and papers, except at an arrest or house search, can take place with a legally executed warrant, which must be served on the arrested person at once or within the next twenty-four hours.

¶ 142. The secrecy of letters is inviolable.

Necessary exceptions in cases of criminal investigation and in the event of war shall be established by legislation.

"Article 4

¶ 143. Every German shall have the right freely to express his opinion through speech, writing, publication, and illustration.

The freedom of the press shall be suspended under no circumstances through preventive measures, namely, censorship, concessions, security orders, imposts, limitation of publication or bookselling, postal bans, or other restraints."

From Louis L. Snyder (ed.), *The Documents of German History* (Rutgers University Press, 1958).

---

government, a new ruler, a cautious constitution, and the red, white, and green flag of Italian nationalism. Ten years later the constitution and the flag would seem quite a lot; for the time being, Austrian power once again dominated the Italian peninsula. There was soon a further foreign presence in the center of Italy, for Louis Napoleon sent French armies to restore the pope and defeat the Roman Republic, which fought with heroic tenacity for three months before being overrun. The

Kingdom of Naples did not reconquer Sicily until May 1849 and only after a bombardment of the city of Messina that gave Ferdinand II the nickname King Bomba. The last of the revolutionary regimes to fall was the Venetian republic, defeated in August 1849 more by starvation and cholera than by the Austrian artillery that accomplished the unprecedented feat of lobbing shells three miles from the mainland into the island city.

The Results A famous liberal historian has called 1848 "the turning-point at which modern history failed to turn,"[2] and his epigram captures the sense of destiny thwarted that still colors the liberal view of 1848. Current historical analysis of the failures of 1848 generally makes five broad points. First, liberal constitutions, new economic policies, and increased civil rights failed to pull strong and lasting support from artisans, peasants, and workers, whose more immediate needs were neither met nor understood. Second, the revolutions of February and March were made primarily by the middle classes, strengthened by popular discontent; but when radicals sought more than representative government and legal equality, the middle classes worried about order and private property. Isolated from the masses, they were too weak to retain power except in France; and there order came only after repression of the urban poor and erosion of constitutional liberties. Third, the leaders of the revolutions, inexperienced in practical politics, often mistook parliaments for power and left intact the established authorities that would soon turn on them. Fourth, nationalism divided revolutionaries and prevented the cooperation that was essential for durable success. Fifth, no major nation was ready to intervene in behalf of change. Britain was sympathetic, France encouraging, and the United States (its consulates centers of republicanism) enthusiastic; but none of that sympathy matched the military assistance Russia gave the Austrian emperor or the formidable armies of Austria and Prussia.

The events of 1848 had significant effects nonetheless. Revolution so widespread measured the failures of restoration, displayed again the power of political ideas, and uncovered the effects of a generation of social change. Many of the gains won in that year endured: The peasants of eastern Prussia and the Austrian Empire were emancipated in 1848 and remained free of servile obligations; Piedmont and Prussia kept their new, limited constitutions. The monarchs triumphant in 1849 punished revolutionaries with execution, flogging, prison, and exile, but they also learned that they must pay more attention to winning some popular support. Liberals would never again depend so optimistically on the spontaneous power of the people, and advocates of social reform would be more skeptical of political liberalism. International power clearly constrained domestic policy, but political leaders of every hue now also recognized the potential force of nationalism.

II. The Politics of Nationalism

Why nationalism assumed such importance in the nineteenth century and has retained it to the present day remains one of the important questions of modern history. As an ideology, it represents itself as a natural, age-old sentiment arising spontaneously; yet nationalism is essentially a modern phenomenon and often seems to require persistent propaganda. Associated with liberalism in the first part of the nineteenth century, nationalism came to be embraced and used by both the left and the right. And it affected politics on every level: international relations; the unification of Italy and Germany, which changed the map of Europe; and domestic policies in every sort of government.

◆ THE ELEMENTS OF NATIONALISM

Nationalism's deepest roots lie in a shared sense of regional and cultural identity, especially as those roots are expressed in custom, language, and religion. This shared culture had been greatly affected, even shaped, by the development of the state, whose power and importance had increased since the state building of the seventeenth century. But it was the experience of the French Revolution that established nationalism as a political force capable of mobilizing popular enthusiasm, of

[2]George Macaulay Trevelyan, *British History in the Nineteenth Century and After*, 1937, p. 292.

reforming society, of creating seemingly irresistible political movements, and ultimately of greatly adding to the power of the state.

Liberation and Modernization   Napoleon I had appealed to national feeling in much of Europe, most notably Poland and Italy. In Germany the fight against Napoleon was called a national war of liberation, and the Allies had somewhat more timidly evoked national feeling to recruit opposition to the French in Spain and (less successfully) Italy. The association of liberation and nationalism had been particularly marked in the New World, where the American Revolution had fostered a fervent nationalism and where, as a result of their revolt against Spanish rule, elite groups had carved Central and South America into new states and claimed a national identity for each of them.

Nationalism was also a movement for self-conscious modernization, embraced by people who believed that their societies might equal the industrial wealth of England and acquire political systems as responsive and efficient as those of Britain and France. In the course of the nineteenth century, increased communication, literacy, and mobility further stimulated the sense of belonging to a larger but definable community. Nationalism was thus a response to social and economic change, one that promised to bring middle classes and masses together in support of common goals. Nationalists, like conservatives and socialists, stressed the values of community; like liberals, they tended to believe that change could bring progress.

National Identity   As an intellectual movement, nationalism was an international phenomenon, everywhere emphasizing the importance of culture; yet it was informed by cultural romanticism, with its rejection of the universalism of the Enlightenment. Thus, German intellectuals such as Johann Gottfried von Herder and Johann Gottlieb Fichte were characteristic in urging their countrymen to put aside values imported from France in favor of a uniquely German culture.

The exploration of ethnic origins took many forms. A group of German scholars made philology a science, and by the 1830s and 1840s an extraordinary revival of national languages had occurred across Europe. Gaelic was hailed as the national tongue of Ireland; in Finland the first public lecture in Finnish marked a break from the dominant Swedish culture; intellectuals in Bohemia began abandoning their customary German to write in Czech. More remarkable still was the number of languages consciously contrived out of local dialects and invented vocabularies. Norwegian became distinct from Danish, Serbian from other Slavic languages, and Slovak from Czech—all literary languages by the 1840s, each the work of a handful of scholars whose task of establishing a national language was made easier by widespread illiteracy.

This fascination with folk culture and a national past was reinforced by an emphasis on history as a popular but scholarly form of knowledge that revealed each nation's historic mission. Germans wrote of a special sense of freedom embodied in Germanic tribes, expanded in the Reformation, and now extended to the state. French historians wrote eloquently of France's call to carry reason and liberty across Europe, and Italian writers proclaimed that Italy was destined to lead Europe once again as it had as the home of Roman civilization and the center of Christianity. The poet Adam Mickiewicz, lecturing in Paris, inspired Polish nationalists with his descriptions of how Poland's history paralleled the life of Christ and had yet to achieve Resurrection. Francis Palacky pioneered in stressing the role of the Czechs as leaders of the Slavs. Such visions were repeated in poetry and drama, which now blossomed in the native tongue and justified resistance to alien rule. This cultural nationalism, which circulated among intellectuals, students, professional people, and journalists, served as a weapon of middle-class self-assertion, whereby people who felt cramped by their society's social hierarchy, unsympathetic bureaucracy, or stagnant economy could win broader support for their own dreams of progress.

Political Goals   In places subject to foreign rule, the political goal of nationalist movements was independence. Everywhere, economic issues were central. Campaigns for agricultural improvement, promoted by the liberal aristocracy, became nationalist programs in Hungary and Italy. In Germany Friedrich List, a leading liberal economist, argued that the American example proved the

▲ In 1844 Daniel O'Connell was released from prison after having served three months on the charge of attempting to repeal the Act of Union that subordinated Ireland to England. His release was the occasion of a great parade in Dublin. Ordinary people celebrated, too, as shown here in an illustration from *The Illustrated London News*, a picture that must have frightened many English readers.

Mary Evans Picture Library

need for tariffs to protect fledgling industries and made his analysis into a nationalist battle cry. Only a united Germany with a national tariff, he insisted, could create an internal area of free trade sufficient to develop the industry and vigorous middle class necessary for competitive strength and independence. Everywhere nationalist groups generally demanded public education, more political freedom, and efficient government. Strengthened by its promises of economic growth and its respect for native traditions, nationalism generated political movements of broad appeal, capable of mobilizing popular enthusiasm. Daniel O'Connell's inflammatory speeches won thousands to his Young Ireland organization and its demands for the end of union with Great Britain. In the 1830s and 40s, he led the largest such protest movement Europe had yet seen.

◆ A NEW REGIME: THE SECOND EMPIRE IN FRANCE

Elections in France had left the Second Republic ruled by a president, Louis Napoleon, who would eventually subvert it, and a Chamber of Deputies in which a majority were monarchists who had not wanted a republic at all.

From Republic to Empire Often at odds with the deputies, Napoleon continued to play to public opinion; and when, in the third year of his four-year term, the Chamber rejected a constitutional amendment that would have allowed him a second term, he struck. His coup d'état came on the eve of December 2, 1851—the anniversary of the first Napoleon's coronation as emperor in 1804 and of his victory at Austerlitz in 1805. Potential opponents, including two hundred deputies, were quickly taken into custody; troops occupied the streets and overran hastily built barricades. At the same time, Napoleon restored universal manhood suffrage, which the conservative Chamber had restricted.[3] Resistance was serious in many parts of France—hundreds were killed and more than 20,000 people arrested—but brief. Three weeks later Napoleon's actions were ratified by more than 90 percent of the voters in a national plebiscite. Exactly one year after this first coup, Napoleon had the Second Republic transformed into the Second Empire and became Emperor Napoleon III, a change even more overwhelmingly supported in another plebiscite. Citizens could do no more than vote yes or no, to accept changes already effected or risk whatever might follow from a negative vote.

The Second Empire claimed a democratic mandate but held authoritarian power. It was supported by most businessmen and the Catholic Church, accepted by most monarchists, local notables, and peasants. It sponsored programs for social welfare as well as economic growth and promised both peace and national glory. Napoleon III was influenced by Saint-Simonian socialism, attracted by liberal nationalism, and obsessed by belief in his own destiny—Napoleon the Little to his opponents, the Emperor to most of the French.

The economy boomed in the 1850s; and the French government fostered economic growth more systematically than any other government in Europe, using tax incentives to stimulate

---

[3]They did so by using a residence requirement that excluded "unstable" workers, that is, those who had recently moved.

▲ **Haussmann's rebuilding of Paris began with the demolition of buildings that had stood for centuries.**
Giraudon/Art Resource, NY

investment, making it easier to form companies with limited liability, and adding its own special investment funds (of which the Crédit Mobilier for industry was the most famous). Among its many programs of public works, the rebuilding of Paris was one of the most elaborate. A pioneering venture in city planning, the project typified the imperial style. Plans were reviewed by Napoleon III himself, who favored ostentatious structures of equal height, and directed by his extraordinarily able prefect Georges Haussmann. New parks were created and slums cleared, often with painful dislocation for their residents; wide boulevards, planned for their striking vistas and as an aid to traffic, incidentally made it hard to build barricades. Facades often received more attention than the buildings behind them, but the buildings were now served by a vast new sewer and water system. Such massive projects stimulated land speculation and profiteering; yet the result was a city healthier and more convenient, envied and

imitated throughout the world. The court of Napoleon and Empress Eugénie was brilliant, and French prestige in the arts and sciences (enhanced by the fame of Louis Pasteur's discoveries in biology) was never higher. The emperor presented himself as the patron of educational and social reform and, in the Napoleonic tradition, rewarded talent with honors and promotions, taking credit for France's prestige.

The Liberal Empire   By the 1860s, however, the empire's fortunes were changing, its policies at home and abroad subject to rising criticism. The coalition of interests that had supported Napoleon was breaking up. Foreign ventures intended to extend French influence and satisfy national pride had their political costs. Support of Italian unification antagonized French Catholics, and the attempt to gain imperial glory by intervention in Mexico ended in disaster. Steps toward free trade, including a major tariff agreement with

◄ The ladies and gentlemen of the court and diplomatic corps assembled in 1860 to watch Napoleon III take the imperial prince in a rowboat. The family scene with the emperor as father reflected the popular appeal that a modern ruler needed, especially if elected by plebiscite.
Roger-Viollet/Getty Images

Great Britain in 1860, appealed to liberal economists but upset many producers. At the same time, workers wanted more from the government than public works projects and support for mutual-aid societies. Restrictions of political freedom were increasingly resented, and opponents' criticisms became more intense.

Napoleon's response was a gradual liberalization that in 1860 enlarged the role of the legislature and by 1868 included freedom of the press and of assembly; a full-fledged parliamentary system was in place two years later. The government also encouraged workers' organizations and acknowledged the right to strike. Like the establishment of public secondary schools, which the Church opposed, these new measures alienated some old supporters without, however, mollifying an opposition that gained in each election. Republicans held nearly half the lower house in 1869, and a republican was prime minister the following year, which turned out to be the Second Empire's last.

The Second Empire had pioneered a new kind of regime, one that was authoritarian but played to public opinion, that imposed order but fostered social programs and economic growth, and that used national prestige to counter domestic division. Balancing those tensions became increasingly difficult.

◆ NATIONALISM AND INTERNATIONAL RELATIONS

The Politics of Patriotism The conflicts of 1848 and 1849 had suggested the political potential of nationalism, a lesson that Prussia, Austria, Britain, Piedmont, and France would all seek to apply. In 1849 Prussia still hoped to lead a confederation of North German states, finding the nationalist dreams of the Frankfurt assembly more attractive once the assembly itself had no voice. Austria promoted a competing solution. Eager to reassert Habsburg influence in Germany after revolution in Hungary had been quelled, Schwarzenberg shrewdly reconvoked the diet of the old German Confederation, putting the German states in the dangerous position of having to choose between Austrian and Prussian leadership. With the clear support of Russia, Austria then threatened Prussia with war; before so grave a challenge, Prussia backed down, abandoning its scheme for a German union. Habsburg hegemony over Germany seemed assured.

The British foreign secretary also exploited the nationalist appeal of an assertive policy. Henry John Temple, Viscount Palmerston, was a flamboyant aristocrat, frequently at odds with his cabinet colleagues, often indifferent to procedural niceties, but shrewdly alert to public opinion.

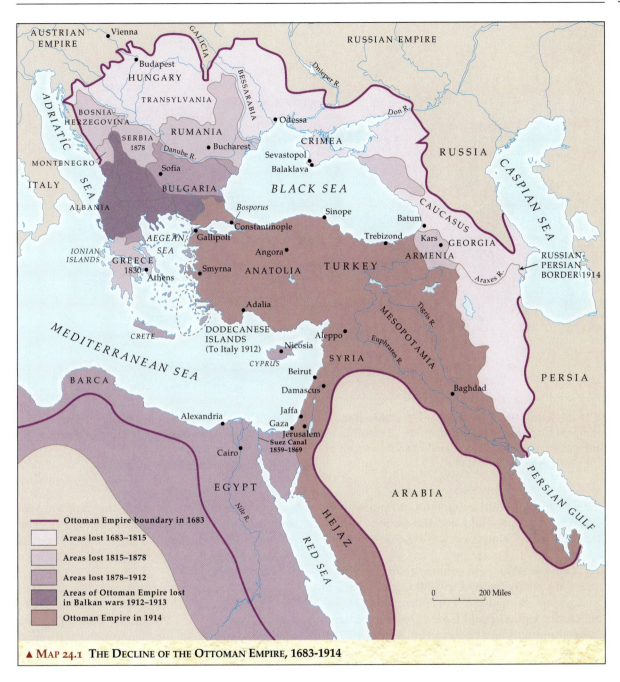

▲ MAP 24.1 THE DECLINE OF THE OTTOMAN EMPIRE, 1683-1914

Thus, he made an issue of national honor out of one British citizen's claims against the Greek government. An Athenian mob had burned the house of one Don Pacifico because he was a Portuguese Jew; but he had been born in Gibraltar and held British citizenship. Palmerston vigorously supported Pacifico's demands for compensation from the Greek government, sending notes, threats,

and finally the British fleet to Greece until an indemnity was paid. Palmerston defended his stand in the House of Commons. Dramatically, he recalled the pride of ancient Romans, who could say *"Civis Romanus sum"* ("I am a Roman citizen") and know themselves secure throughout their empire. A British subject, Palmerston declared, "in whatever land he may be, shall feel confident that

▲ The Crimean War generated considerable enthusiasm in Britain and France, with the help of colorful accounts from the front. This dramatic illustration from a British paper shows Florence Nightingale rushing to aid wounded soldiers, a service that made her and professional nurses famous.
The Granger Collection, New York

the watchful eye and strong arm of England will protect him against injustice and wrong." To the public at least, Palmerston was vindicated.

The Crimean War   The restless search for international prestige led France and Great Britain to war against Russia in 1854 over competing claims by Roman Catholic and Greek Orthodox monks to be the guardians of Jerusalem's holy places. France, citing traditions going back to the time of the crusades and the policies of Cardinal Richelieu several centuries later, supported the Latin monks. France pressed the Ottoman sultan, whose empire included Jerusalem, to grant them specific privileges. Russia, as defender of the Orthodox faith, demanded a protectorate over Orthodox churches within the Ottoman Empire and showed its determination by occupying Wallachia and Moldavia, Danubian lands under Ottoman suzerainty. This Russian expansion, part of

a long-term pattern, worried the English, who saw a threat to their own empire in any extension of Russian influence in the direction of Persia or Afghanistan. Britain encouraged the sultan to resist Russia's demands.

Negotiations repeatedly broke down; Britain and France sent their fleets into the Aegean Sea, and in October 1853 the sultan exuberantly declared war on Russia. Russian forces destroyed an Ottoman fleet, however, and Britain and France decided to fight Russia to preserve the balance of power in the Middle East. That announcement in March 1854 was greeted with patriotic enthusiasm in London and Paris. Six months after war was declared, not having found a more convenient battlefield, British and French forces landed in the Crimea, which juts into the Black Sea. The war was conducted with remarkable incompetence on both sides. Russia was unable to mobilize or effectively deploy the large armies

MAZZINI'S NATIONALISM

◆

"On the Duties of Man" *is one of Giuseppe Mazzini's most famous essays. It was first written in 1844 for Italian workers living in England, and the excerpts here are from the fifth chapter, which was added for a new edition in 1858. Despite the events of the intervening years, Mazzini's romantic faith had changed little. The essay's title was meant to contrast with the French Revolution's "Declaration of the Rights of Man," which Mazzini criticized for encouraging selfishness and materialism.*

"Your first duties—first as regards importance—are, as I have already told you, towards Humanity . . . If you do not embrace the whole human family in your affection, . . . if, wheresoever a fellow-creature suffers, or the dignity of human nature is violated by falsehood or tyranny—you are not ready, if able, to aid the unhappy, and do not feel called upon to combat, if able, for the redemption of the betrayed or oppressed—you violate your law of life, you comprehend not that Religion which will be the guide and blessing of the future.

"But what can each of you, singly, *do* for the moral improvement and progress of Humanity? . . . The watchword of the faith of the future is *Association,* and . . . [the] means was provided for you by God when he gave you a country; when, even as a wise overseer of labour distributes the various branches of employment according to the different capacities of the workmen, he divided Humanity into distinct groups or nuclei upon the face of the earth, thus creating the germ of Nationalities. Evil governments have disfigured the divine design. Nevertheless you may still trace it, distinctly marked out—at least as far as Europe is concerned—by the course of the great rivers, the direction of the higher mountains, and other geographical conditions. They have disfigured it by their conquests, their greed, and their jealousy even of the righteous power of others. . . .

"These governments did not, and do not, recognize any country save their own families or dynasty, the egotism of caste. But the Divine design will infallibly be realized. Natural divisions, and the spontaneous, innate tendencies of the peoples, will take the place of the arbitrary divisions sanctioned by evil governments. The map of Europe will be redrawn. The countries of the Peoples, defined by the vote of free men, will arise upon the ruins of the countries of kings and privileged castes. . . .

"O my brothers, love your Country! Our country is our Home, the house that God has given us, placing therein a numerous family that loves us, and whom we love. . . . Our country is our common workshop, whence the products of our activity are sent forth for the benefit of the whole world. . . . In labouring for our own country on the right principle, we labour for Humanity."

From Giuseppe Mazzini, *On the Duties of Man* (Greenwood Publishing Group).

---

that made it so feared, and Britain's supply system proved inadequate for hostilities at such a distance. In 1855 the allies welcomed the aid of little Piedmont and, a full year after invading the Crimea, finally took Sevastopol. Russia sued for peace and agreed to accept terms to be defined at a European congress in Paris.

Congress of Paris The Congress signified an important shift in the European balance. It met in Paris rather than Vienna and was preoccupied with issues of nationalism. In 1856 Russia counted for less than it had in 1815, and the conservative alliance of Austria, Prussia, and Russia that had dominated the continent for a generation had broken up over competing ambitions in the Balkans and Germany. The Congress required Russia to cede some territory at the mouth of the Danube River, to surrender its claims to any protectorate over Christians in the Ottoman Empire, and to accept a ban on warships in the Black Sea. Only this last point really rankled. The more troublesome issues all had to do with national claims. Britain and France did not want to give the Danubian principalities to either Russia or Austria. The issue was postponed because the obvious resolution—uniting the two territories and allowing them autonomy, a procedure that began a few years later—would create the basis for a Romanian national state, and Austria was learning to fear

▲ **In his portraits and in his personal life, Mazzini seemed as much a romantic poet as a revolutionary agitator.**
The Granger Collection, New York

nationalism as a threat to the Habsburg empire. Such fears prevented Napoleon III from putting the question of Polish independence on the agenda as he wanted to; but the Congress did discuss the rising discontent in Italy, the only concession Piedmont won for having helped the victors in the Crimea. Even that was enough to produce patriotic outbursts in Italy and to frighten Austria.

Almost 500,000 soldiers died in the Crimean War, the highest toll of any European conflict from the Napoleonic wars to World War I. Two-thirds of the casualties were Russian, and two-thirds of all losses resulted from sickness and bad care. Yet the outbreak of war produced a surge of enthusiasm no government could ignore. The public diplomacy that led to the war, the parades of magnificently uniformed soldiers, and the heroic stories reported by an aggressive journalism underscored its political importance. Under Western pressure, the Ottoman Empire began to adopt the

modernizing institutions of the West; and Russia, sobered by defeat, launched an era of fundamental reform unequaled since the days of Peter the Great. In Italy and Germany the way was opening for still more drastic changes.

◆ A NEW NATION: THE UNIFICATION OF ITALY

Giuseppe Mazzini   Across the Italian peninsula, all the revolutions of 1848 had declared an independent nation to be one of their primary goals; and in doing so they employed the ideas of Giuseppe Mazzini, one of Europe's most important revolutionaries (see "Mazzini's Nationalism," p. 861). For fifteen years, Mazzini had lived in exile, mainly in London, organizing conspiracies and writing passionate propaganda in pamphlets and thousands of letters. His nationalist movement, Young Italy, had stimulated similar efforts in Ireland, Switzerland, and Hungary. Until 1848, the conspiracies he fostered had resulted in tragic failures; yet like the clandestine committees, secret meetings, and smuggled newspapers that surrounded them, these plots, though unsuccessful, had disseminated the belief that once corrupt regimes were toppled, the people would rise in common cause. Revolutionary and democratic, Mazzini was also a moralist who criticized the French Revolution for stressing rights over moral duty and who rejected socialism as materialistic. In nationalism he saw the expression of natural communities, the basis for popular democracy and international brotherhood.

Italy renewed would lead the way. A man of letters steeped in romanticism, Mazzini nonetheless wrote tellingly about the specific grievances of peasants, artists, professionals, and intellectuals. His influence was especially strong in northern Italy, where in the 1830s and 1840s young lawyers, liberal landowners, and some members of the aristocracy began to find national implications in nearly everything they did. Annual congresses of Italian scientists became quiet demonstrations of patriotic aspirations; disputes over where railroad lines should be built became means of expressing discontent with Austrian rule. Literary journals and societies for agricultural improvement took up the nationalist theme.

For Mazzinians, 1848 was the great chance (Mazzini himself was one of the leaders of the Roman Republic), and the defeats that followed were an even greater blow to Mazzinianism than to Italian nationalism. As Austria regained dominance of the peninsula, Mazzini had returned to exile and Italian nationalists began to look elsewhere for leadership. The papacy, restored by French arms, was no longer sympathetic to Italian unity; Austria ruled Lombardy and Venetia repressively, and all the other Italian regimes except Piedmont were Austrian dependencies.

The Role of Piedmont   Although a small state, Piedmont held some promise for patriots. It had fought Austria, and its young king, Victor Emmanuel II, though no liberal, ruled with a parliament. The kingdom had a tradition of military strength and bureaucratic rectitude. More recently, its government had encouraged commerce and industry, and its efforts to win trade away from Austria through commercial treaties excited Italians elsewhere. These policies acquired firmer purpose in 1852, when Count Camillo Cavour became prime minister. Cavour was a gentleman-farmer who had traveled in France and England. He believed in economic and scientific progress, representative government with limited suffrage, the rule of law, and religious tolerance. Nationalism he understood primarily as an avenue to modernization, and he found in free trade, sound finances, and railroads a power that could remake Piedmont.

Cavour pursued his liberal goals with tactical brilliance, skillfully using newspapers and parliamentary debate to mold public opinion. He created a centrist parliamentary coalition with which he dominated both king and parliament from 1852 until his death in 1861. In that brief time he established himself as one of the outstanding statesmen of the century. Piedmont's internal strength was Cavour's first concern, but he also sought to make his state the center of Italy's resurgence, the Risorgimento.[4] He welcomed exiles from other parts of the peninsula, encouraged the nationalist press, and sought every opportunity for symbolic gestures of patriotism. He was aided in this goal by the Italian National Society, one of whose founders was the president of the Venetian republic in 1848. The National Society propagandized for Italian unity under Piedmont's king and established secret committees in most of the cities of Italy. Its members were predominantly liberal aristocrats, local lawyers, and professors; and in calling for Italian unity, the society combined Mazzinian rhetoric with hardheaded insistence on the need for international alliances and military force. Economic liberalism largely replaced more generous and vaguer social theories.

War against Austria   Most of all, Cavour depended on astute foreign policy. He had pushed for Piedmont's participation in the Crimean War and was rewarded with the discussion of the Italian question at the Congress of Paris. Using his state's enhanced international position, he argued that Italy repressed would remain a danger to European order. He appealed for liberal sympathy throughout Western Europe, and he courted Napoleon III. At last, in July 1858, Cavour and Napoleon III met secretly. It was easy to argue that war was inevitable, given Austria's resentment of Piedmont's growing prominence. If France would support Piedmont against Austria, Cavour promised to accept a complicated set of arrangements designed to benefit France and limit Piedmont's expansion. The plan, too delicately balanced to be practical, sought cautious ends through cynical daring.

Austria, watching young Lombards and Venetians escape conscription by streaming to Piedmont as volunteers, determined to end the nationalist threat once and for all. It sent Piedmont an ultimatum so strong that Cavour needed only to reply with cautious dignity in order to have his war. On April 29, 1859, Austria invaded Piedmont, and France went to the rescue of a small state attacked by her giant neighbor. The rapid movement of large French armies was impressive, but thereafter the war was fought with little tactical brilliance on either side. The Austrians suffered a serious defeat in June, but a larger battle three weeks later was as indecisive as it was

---

[4]*Risorgimento,* now the historian's label for the whole period of Italian unification, was a term meaning "resurgence," often used by nationalists and made the title of a liberal newspaper that Cavour helped to found and edit.

bloody. As the Austrians retreated to the fortresses controlling the Lombard plain, Napoleon suddenly lost his taste for war and unilaterally assented to a truce. The emperors of France and Austria agreed that Piedmont should have Lombardy but not Venetia and that the other Italian states should remain as before.

Formation of the Italian Kingdom   Those other Italian states, however, had not survived the excitement of a national war. Gentle revolutions accompanied the march of Piedmontese troops throughout northern Italy. When local patriots gathered in the streets, the dukes of Modena, Parma, and Tuscany simply fled, to be replaced by provisional governments led by members of the National Society. These governments quickly adopted Piedmontese laws and held elections to representative assemblies. The terms of the truce arranged by France and Austria could not be carried out; and after a few months, the provisional governments held plebiscites—a device Napoleon could hardly reject—on the question of annexation to Piedmont. Italians trooped to the polls with bands playing and flags waving, peasants behind their lords and workers with their guilds. The result was as one-sided as in the plebiscites in France. Piedmont's King Victor Emmanuel ruled from the Alps to Rimini on the Adriatic. The province of Savoy and the city of Nice were turned over to France.

Moderate liberals had united half of Italy. Sputtering revolts in Sicily gave more democratic nationalists a chance to lead a different sort of Risorgimento. Former Mazzinians, eager to promote a Sicilian uprising, gathered guns in Genoa and planned an expedition that Cavour dared neither support nor oppose. Its leader would be Giuseppe Garibaldi, Italy's most popular hero. Exiled for his Mazzinian activity in the 1830s, Garibaldi had spent ten years fighting for democratic causes in South America, returning to Italy in time to take part in the wars of 1848. He had directed the heroic defense of the Roman Republic in 1849 and led the most effective corps of volunteers in 1859. In his greatest exploit of all, he set sail for Sicily one night in May 1860, with a thousand men, mainly middle-class youths from Lombardy, Venetia, and the Romagna.

Garibaldi Goes South   No event in the nineteenth century so captured the popular imagination as that daring venture. The Expedition of the Thousand was like some ancient epic come to life in an industrial age: Untrained men, wearing the red shirts Garibaldi had adopted in South America, fought with bravery and discipline, enthusiastically supported in the Sicilian countryside. Garibaldi's tactics confused and defeated the Neapolitan generals, despite their far larger and better-equipped forces. In two weeks the Red Shirts occupied Palermo and within two months almost all of Sicily. Volunteers flocked from all over Italy to join Garibaldi, and money was raised in his behalf in all the towns of northern Italy and from New York to Stockholm.

The epic continued when, against all odds, Garibaldi sailed across the strait and landed on the Italian mainland. He declared his goal to be Rome itself and not just Naples. That worried Cavour, who considered Garibaldi irresponsible and believed that an attack on Rome might lead Austria and France to intervene on behalf of the pope. So Cavour encouraged uprisings in the

▼ **The handshake of Victor Emmanuel and Garibaldi, which sealed the unification of Italy as their armies met in 1860, became a favorite subject for illustrations of the Risorgimento. This engraving is English.**
Culver Pictures, Inc.

SWITZERLAND

SAVOY
(To France 1860)

AUSTRIA

Bolzano

TYROL
1919

Trent

Magenta
1859

LOMBARDY

Milan   Peschiera   Verona   Gorizia

Turin   Solferino   Villafranca   Trieste

FRANCE   Alessandria   Po R.   Mantua   Legnago   Fiume 1924

PIEDMONT   PARMA   Ferrara   VENETIA
1866

Venice

ISTRIA
1919

NICE
(To France 1860)   PARMA   Modena   Bologna

Genoa   MODENA   ROMAGNA   Rimini

LUCCA   Lucca   SAN MARINO

Pisa   Arno R.   Florence   Urbino   Zara
1920

TUSCANY   Perugia   Ancona

ELBA   Siena   YUGOSLAVIA

CORSICA
(French)   PAPAL   LISSA

Ajaccio   UMBRIA   LACOSTA
1920   ADRIATIC SEA

STATES

Civitavecchia   Tiber R.

CAPRERA   Rome   1870

Gaeta   Volturno R.   Bari

SARDINIA   Naples   Taranto   SASENO

TYRRHENIAN SEA   ALBANIA

CORFU

KINGDOM OF THE   GREECE
TWO SICILIES

MEDITERRANEAN SEA   Palermo   Messina

SICILY   Catania   0   50   100 Miles

PANTELLERIA   Syracuse

Annexed 1860   MEDITERRANEAN SEA

TUNISIA

PELAGIE I.   MALTA (British)

Legend:
- Kingdom of Sardinia at 1859
- Areas annexed in 1859
- Areas annexed in 1860
- Areas annexed in 1866
- Area annexed in 1870
- Areas annexed from 1919 to 1924
- Italian boundary at 1924
- ✖ Fortress

▲ MAP 24.2 THE UNIFICATION OF ITALY

Papal States and then sent Piedmontese troops to preserve order. Carefully skirting the area around Rome, they moved south to meet Garibaldi. On September 18, between lines of suspicious men, Giuseppe Garibaldi and Victor Emmanuel rode out to shake hands and unite Italy. Garibaldi added to his legend by thus giving way in the interests of union, and the Piedmontese took over. Plebiscites confirmed the union, and in March 1861 the Kingdom of Italy was proclaimed.

United Italy   The Kingdom of Italy included almost all of Italy except for Rome and Venetia. Catholics throughout the world opposed the annexation of Rome, which Napoleon III was

pledged to protect; and Austrian troops were massed in Venetia. Italy acquired Venetia in 1866 as a by-product of war between Austria and Prussia. Austria offered it in return for Italy's neutrality; Prussia had promised it to Italy if Prussia defeated Austria with Italy's support. Italy kept its prior pledge to Prussia, went to war, fought poorly, but got Venetia following Prussia's rapid victory. Rome was annexed when French troops withdrew during the Franco-Prussian War of 1870; the new nation finally had its ancient capital.

More lasting problems remained. To many Italians, especially in the south, unification felt like a foreign occupation, and Italy's leaders were appalled at the poverty and corruption they could not overcome. Pius IX forbade Catholics to take

▼ **A demonstration in Florence's historic Piazza della Signoria in 1866 for the annexation of Venetia to the new Kingdom of Italy.**
Scala/Art Resource, NY

part in national elections and rejected the indemnity and guarantees of protection the government offered. United Italy was poor and overwhelmingly agricultural. It had no coal or iron, and three-quarters of the population was illiterate. With liberal conviction the Italian government assumed the debts of all the former governments and struggled to balance the annual budget. Despite taxes that were among the highest in Europe, Italy continued to lag in schools, railways, and roads. The sale of Church lands failed to benefit peasants as much as hoped, and the lower Piedmontese tariffs brought instant distress to hundreds of small producers in the rest of the peninsula. It took years of sporadic fighting to enforce order in the south. For millions of artisans and peasants, few tangible benefits followed from replacing reactionary dukes with a liberal national state.

◆ A NEW NATION: THE UNIFICATION OF GERMANY

German cultural identity had grown throughout the first half of the nineteenth century, from the battles against Napoleon to the statements of the Frankfurt Parliament. It was strengthened by achievements in philosophy, science, literature, and music that were seen as German accomplishments no matter what German kingdom, principality, or free city they occurred in. The open question was what the political expression of that identity should be. The German Confederation was ineffectual; none of the schemes for unification in 1848 had been adopted, and Austria had blocked Prussian plans for leadership in 1850. Yet it was Prussia that created modern Germany.

The Dominance of Prussia Several factors account for Prussia's eventual dominance. One was economic. The *Zollverein*, the tariff union Prussia led, continued to prosper with industrialization in the Rhineland and Prussia, and by 1853 every German state except Austria had joined it. Another factor was Austria's multinational preoccupations, and its vulnerability to nationalisms was highlighted by the campaign for the unification of Italy. Most important of all was the dynamism of Prussia itself. It was the largest German state,

with a powerful army and an efficient administration, and Prussian politics began a new era in 1858 with the rule of William I.[5]

After a long period of reaction in which the press and public discussion were severely repressed, politics had become more open and livelier. Liberal nationalists, particularly in the Rhineland, campaigned for a more representative government; William sought to strengthen the army, and a constitutional crisis resulted. The Prussian constitution of 1850 allowed universal male suffrage but avoided democracy by dividing voters into three classes according to the taxes they paid. Each of the three classes elected an equal number of representatives, ensuring that those chosen by the two wealthier classes would be a majority. In addition, the king could veto any legislation and appoint the ministers of his choice.

Although designed to ensure conservative dominance, the three-class system had the unexpected effect of magnifying the voice of new industrial wealth, and the majority of the Landtag was now prepared to challenge the monarch. The military budget became their battleground. With William's support, General Albrecht von Roon, minister of war, and Helmuth von Moltke, his chief of staff, proposed to double the army and add to its equipment. Although the proposal was defeated, the government went ahead with its plan. Liberals, who distrusted Prussian militarism and an army dominated by the Junkers, insisted the government must be responsible to the legislature; and the opposition gained in the elections of 1862. Convinced that royal authority was at stake, William called on God and conscience, threatened abdication, and named Otto von Bismarck his chief minister.

Bismarck's Leadership Bismarck was a member of the Junker class, better educated than many. His pride of caste and reactionary views were resented by liberals, and most conservatives considered him to be as erratic and dangerous as Napoleon III. An experienced diplomat familiar with Europe's major capitals, he stood out by

[5]William I became regent in 1858—when his brother, Frederick William, was judged insane—and king on his brother's death in 1861.

reason of his cosmopolitan outlook as much as his enormous self-confidence. For thirty years officials and legislators would have to live with his stinging sarcasm, bruising contempt, and brilliance. Bismarck surprised conservatives with his appeal to nationalism, shrewdly used power wherever he found it, and made success in foreign policy his justification. He lectured the deputies: If Germans looked to Prussia, it was because of its powerful army, not because of any liberal institutions; and he added, in the most famous statement he ever uttered, that "the great questions of the day will not be settled by speeches and majority decisions—that was the mistake of 1848 and 1849—but by blood and iron."

Bismarck dissolved the parliament and used heavy government pressure in the subsequent elections but with little effect. So Bismarck ignored parliament whenever he could and encouraged divisions within the legislature whenever

possible. He closed opposition newspapers and manipulated the rest. Promotions in the civil service and judiciary went to those unquestionably loyal; and, once confident of his position, Bismarck spent funds and collected taxes without parliamentary authorization.

In return he offered a remarkable string of foreign triumphs. While blocking Austria's efforts to lead the German Confederation, he courted Russian friendship. When in 1863 Russia repressed a Polish uprising with such severity that Austria, France, and Britain joined in protest, Prussia supported the tsar. Bismarck used conflict over Schleswig and Holstein to assert leadership in German affairs. German nationalists were outraged at attempts by the king of Denmark to annex Schleswig and to extend his authority over Holstein, but Prussia overshadowed the German Diet by persuading Austria to join in war against Denmark in January 1864. Bismarck then foiled

▼ **Crowds cheer as Prussian troops parade through the Brandenburg Gate in Berlin in 1866, celebrating Prussia's victory over Austria and the formation of the North German Confederation.**
AKG London

international negotiations until the Danes were defeated. Schleswig was placed under Prussian administration and Holstein, surrounded by Prussian troops, under Austrian control, in an awkward arrangement sure to breed contention between Austria and Prussia.

The Austro-Prussian War, 1866
Friction with the Habsburg Empire increased almost daily, and Bismarck prepared for war while ensuring Austria's diplomatic isolation. He dangled visions of territory along the Rhine before Napoleon III, won Italy's support by promising it Venetia, and gained Russia's assurance of neutrality. Both Austria and Prussia were already mobilizing when Prussian troops found an excuse to march into Holstein in June 1866. Initially, Austria had the support of most of the German Confederation, but Hanover surrendered to Prussia within two weeks. Three Prussian armies swept into Bohemia, and at the Battle of Sadowa, Austria suffered overwhelming defeat. The Austro-Prussian War lasted just seven weeks. Experts had predicted a long fight, but Prussia, well equipped and ready, applied the lessons of the American Civil War, using railroads and telegraph to move with a speed for which Austria was unprepared.

Many Prussian conservatives had been shocked at Bismarck's disrespectful and belligerent treatment of Austria, but now they were eager to take advantage of Austria's defeat and looked forward to significant territorial gains. Instead, Bismarck insisted on leniency, against the wishes of his king and generals. Austria surrendered no territory, but Prussia's gains elsewhere changed the face of Europe. It annexed several states that had sided with Austria,[6] established a confederation of North German states under Prussian leadership, and got the South German states to accept a military alliance with Prussia.

The North German Confederation
The North German Confederation was a Bismarckian structure that seemed to protect local interests and to point toward democracy yet ensured the dominance of Prussia. It left member states free to regulate their local affairs but joined them through a common army under Prussian officers and a bi-

cameral federal parliament. The upper house, the Bundesrat, was composed of forty-three delegates sent in varying numbers from the separate states; Prussia's seventeen gave it more than the one-third necessary for a veto. The lower house, the Reichstag, was elected by universal male suffrage; but the king of Prussia appointed the chancellor, who was responsible to no one else.

After Prussia's victories, the Prussian Parliament retroactively legalized the taxes and expenditures Bismarck had imposed. No German nationalist believed Bismarck's federation to be a satisfactory or permanent solution. Germany's unification, like Italy's, would be achieved in stages and through war and diplomacy. North Germany, Protestant and more industrial than the south, offered a sound foundation for the kind of Germany Bismarck envisioned, as different from the largely agricultural and Catholic south as northern Italy was from Naples. With their own cultural traditions and ancient dynasties, Germany's southern states still looked to Vienna as their traditional center, admired Paris, and remained suspicious of Berlin.

The Franco-Prussian War, 1870
More than elections and trade were necessary if Germany was to be quickly united, and war with France filled the need. Historians once hotly disputed who was to blame for that war and whether it was "necessary." New research and changing perspectives have lessened the controversy. The war was wanted by Bismarck but first declared by France, on both sides the result more of nationalism than of long-range calculation. It was provoked by competition over influence in Spain. Queen Isabella II had been forced to abdicate in 1868, and the provisional government there, seeking a replacement, picked a Hohenzollern prince. He declined, under heavy French pressure; but a shaky French government, eager to curry popular favor at home, continued to press its case. In a famous interview at the western German spa of Ems, where William I was taking the baths, the French ambassador demanded a public guarantee that the Hohenzollern candidacy would not be put forward again. The king refused and telegraphed a report to Bismarck, who edited the Ems dispatch to make French demands seem more imperious and the king's refusal more abrupt, then released

---

[6]They were Hanover, Nassau, Electoral Hesse, and Frankfurt.

Map key:

- German Confederation boundary in 1815
- Prussia in 1815
- Annexed by Prussia by 1866
- Joined with Prussia in North German Confederation, 1867
- North German Confederation boundary in 1867
- States added to form German Empire in 1871
- Battle site
- Fortress

▲ MAP 24.3 THE UNIFICATION OF GERMANY

it to the press. Bismarck, Roon, and Moltke correctly assumed that war would follow. The French government responded to the patriotic fury it had helped ignite and declared war on Prussia in July 1870.

France hoped for support from Italy and Austria but had failed to establish formal agreements, and these states remained neutral. The French army, more formidable than Austria's had been, possessed modern equipment in some respects superior to that of the Germans, but the Germans were better prepared and far more decisively led. In rapid movements German armies pushed through Alsace and encircled the French army at

Metz. After heavy losses on both sides, another French force, attempting to relieve Metz, was defeated at Sedan in September. There Napoleon III surrendered and was taken prisoner. Major fighting was over, but French resistance continued. Paris, quickly surrounded by German troops, held out under a long siege, and a provisional French government kept an army in the field. An armistice came only at the end of January 1871, when Paris capitulated.

The brief war had profound effects. A German national state was created. In France the Second Empire fell to be succeeded by the Third Republic after bitter internal conflict. France was required to pay an indemnity of 5 billion francs and to cede Alsace and Lorraine, harsh terms that established enmity between France and Germany as a central fact of European affairs.

The German Reich The decision to annex Alsace-Lorraine was primarily a military one, intended to provide Germany with strong fortifications in case of future conflict with France. But it was also a response to the demands of German nationalists, whose support Bismarck still needed, for there were many Germans who did not welcome unification under Prussia. Well before the final French surrender, Bismarck began difficult negotiations with each of the South German states. They had joined in fighting France with a mixture of enthusiasm and fear, but it took threats, concessions, and secret funds to arrive at terms for a permanent union with North Germany. William I was then crowned German kaiser (emperor) in the Hall of Mirrors of the French palace of Versailles on January 18, 1871, the anniversary of the founding of the Prussian monarchy.

With modifications, the constitution of the North German Confederation was extended to all the new nation. Many domestic matters were reserved to the twenty-five states that made up the Reich. There was no doubt, however, that the great new nation would be dominated by Prussia. The Second Reich[7] was from its inception a powerful nation. Germany in 1871 was already more

---

[7]The old Holy Roman Empire was patriotically honored as having been the first Reich.

populous than France, and its rate of demographic growth was the fastest Europe had ever known. Germany's industrial production increased at an astounding rate. Because it had developed later than Great Britain and France, its industrial equipment was more modern, and the French indemnity added to the available capital. The German government made heavy investments in railroads and spurred industrialization with tax benefits, tariffs, and policies encouraging the formation of large combines, the famous German cartels. German universities led all others in the application of scientific methods to every discipline.

Such rapid growth fed tensions between powerful conservative circles, a growing but insecure middle class, and workers increasingly aware of their distinct interests. Nowhere were materialistic and urban values more intensely attacked than in industrial Germany. Bismarck, worried about internal threats to the new nation, chose to demonstrate the supremacy of the state by moving against two potential opponents: first the Catholic Church and then the socialist party.

Internal Conflict Rather grandiosely named the Kulturkampf ("Struggle for Civilization"), the conflict with the Catholic Church centered on the state's right to approve appointments, restrict religious orders, and supervise seminaries. Many of these measures were common in much of Europe, but there was a harshness in the new state's execution of them and in the rhetoric surrounding them. Intended to assure the "Germanization" of Alsace and the Polish parts of Prussia (both largely Catholic), the measures accentuated regional and ideological differences. Yet the Kulturkampf was not a success. It made martyrs of many a priest and nun, and Catholics rallied to their Church as a majority of bishops went into exile. The Catholic Center party steadily gained votes, and when the more flexible Leo XIII became pope in 1878, Bismarck sought an understanding with the Vatican. That battle of civilization subsided as Bismarck turned his sights on another growing movement.

Socialism did not offend Bismarck either in its criticism of laissez-faire economics or in its call for the state to be socially active, and he had gotten on well with the leading German socialist of the

BISMARCK'S SOCIAL PROGRAM

◆

Between 1883 and 1887 the German parliament passed three laws that created a new model for the role of the state in social legislation. Bismarck introduced the first of these (providing for sickness insurance) in April 1881 in a speech to the parliament that reflects the power of his personality as well as the clarity of his reasoning and of his prejudices.

"For the past fifty years we have been talking about the social question. Since the Socialist Law was passed, I have been repeatedly reminded, in high quarters as well as low, of the promise I then gave that something positive should be done to remove the causes of Socialism. . . . I do not believe that our sons, or even our grandsons, will be able finally to solve the question. Indeed, no political questions can ever be mathematically settled, as books are balanced in business; they crop up, have their time, and give way to other questions propounded by history. Organic development wills that it shall be so. I consider it my duty to take up these questions without party feeling or excitement, because I know not who is to do so, if not the imperial government.

"Deputy Richter has pointed out the responsibility of the state for what it is now doing. Well, Gentlemen, I feel that the state should also be responsible for what it leaves undone. I am not of the opinion that *laissez faire, laissez aller,* 'pure Manchester policy,' 'everybody takes care of himself,' 'the weakest must go the wall,' 'to him who hath shall be given, from him who hath not shall be taken even that which he hath,' can be practiced in a monarchically, patriarchically governed state. . . .

"An appropriate title for our enterprise would be 'practical Christianity,' but we do not want to feed poor people with figures of speech, but with something solid. Death costs nothing; but unless you will put your hands in your pockets and into the state Exchequer, you will not do much good. To saddle our industry with the whole affair—well, I don't know that it could bear the burden."

From Louis L. Snyder (ed.), *The Documents of German History* (New Brunswick: Rutgers University Press, 1958).

1860s, Ferdinand Lassalle. But as socialists sought a mass following and in 1875 established the Social Democratic party, their attacks on autocracy, the military, and nationalism seemed dangerous. Using as justification two attempts in 1878 to assassinate the kaiser (neither by a socialist), Bismarck demanded laws repressing socialism. The Reichstag refused, and the election of 1878 in which conservatives and the Center party made some gains was fought largely on that issue. Most socialist publications were banned and socialist meetings prohibited unless supervised by the police. The Social Democrats were, in effect, forced underground, although they were free to speak in the Reichstag, and their party gained support with every election.

The campaigns against Catholics and socialists were abandoned by the 1880s as no longer needed or effective, but they were part of a larger political realignment. The conservatives and Catholics who had resisted the new Germany came to accept it, while liberals, torn between Bismarck's accomplishments and their old principles, grew weaker. A more durable coalition was formed around the tariff of 1879. Its higher duties, a response to the economic problems caused by rapid growth and by a European agricultural depression, protected manufactured and agricultural goods, drawing together the most powerful interest groups in German society. Supported by Junker landlords, industrialists, the army and navy, and nationalists, the new tariff gave the conservative state and its powerful leaders their political base. In the 1880s Bismarck also established a system of national insurance to aid workers in times of illness and unemployment and to help provide for pensions upon retirement. Paid for by contributions from employers and workers, these measures became an influential model of modern social policy (see "Bismarck's Social Program" above). At home and abroad, Bismarck had mastered techniques for preserving conservative interests in a dynamic society.

◆ RESHAPING THE OLDER EMPIRES

In a Europe of industrial growth and national states, war more than ever stood as the ultimate test of the state's efficiency. The wars that made Italy and Germany were understood to require drastic political changes in the nations that lost— Russia in 1856, Austria in 1859 and 1866, and France in 1870.

Limited Reform in the Russian Empire Of the 74 million people in Russia, some 47 million were serfs. Their emancipation began in 1861 by the tsar's decree. Intellectuals had argued against serfdom for generations, and peasants spoke through frequent uprisings. Serfdom was constricting economic development, and any major political reforms required its abolition. Defeat in the Crimean War added urgency; and Tsar Alexander II, who had assumed the throne in 1855, announced his commitment to modernization. Quietly he pressed the nobles to lead the way; but while secret committees drafted proposals for ending serfdom, most nobles dragged their feet.

Emancipation was thus imposed by edict, a daring step cautiously framed. More than 22 million serfs gained legal rights and were promised title to the land they worked or its equivalent. If they accepted one-quarter of that, they would owe no payments; otherwise they contracted a long-term debt to the state, which compensated the lord. In practice, the lord usually kept the best land for himself and often got an inflated price for the land he lost. Former serfs on the whole found themselves with less land than they needed to support families and make their payments. Although they were required to fulfill other obligations to their former masters for only two more years, they often remained dependent on those nobles for pasture and water rights and for the wage labor that had become a necessity. A few years later the government liberated the nearly 25 million state peasants, who worked on government-owned estates, granting them somewhat more favorable terms. Russia's peasants nevertheless remained a caste distinguishable in

▲ In this 1861 photograph a Russian official is reading to peasants on a Moscow estate the "Regulations Concerning the Peasantry," the decree that abolished serfdom.
Novosti/Sovfoto

dress, speech, and customs, with special laws and punishments, including flogging, applicable only to them.

The law of 1861 also gave the *mir*, or village commune, new importance. It elected its own officials and held peasant land in common; the officials assigned plots to individuals, decided what would be planted, and assessed the taxes owed the state. The former serfs could not leave the commune or sell their land without permission. The *mir*, which came to be considered a characteristic Slavic institution, thus sustained traditional ways and served as the agent of the state at the same time that it provided peasants a voice in communal decisions. Other reforms followed. In 1864 district councils (*zemstvos*, elected through a three-class system like Prussia's) were made responsible for local primary schools, roads, and welfare. These steps were part of a process that—along with increased schooling, relaxed censorship, and reduced military service[8]—made Russia more like other European nations. Each reform, however, accomplished less than hoped for and uncovered yet more that needed to be done. Leaders remained fearful. Concessions in Poland were followed by revolution in 1863. It was harshly quelled, and Poland's separate status ended. Repression increased in Russia, too, as censorship and police surveillance tightened. While pan-Slavists stressed Russia's special destiny and disdained liberal parliamentarianism as alien, an isolated intelligentsia was drawn to more radical ideas, and conspirators plotted more drastic remedies. Yet when a bomb killed Alexander II in 1881, his son smoothly succeeded him as Alexander III; tsarist Russia could survive an assassination.

Compromise to Preserve the Austro-Hungarian Empire Following the revolutions of 1848, the Habsburg monarchy under the young Franz Joseph I had sought to create a modern, unitary state. For the first time in its history, the empire was subjected to uniform laws and taxes. But military defeats in Italy and then at the hands of Prussia plus mounting debts proved that more changes were needed. In 1860 Franz Joseph announced a new federal constitution, giving considerable authority to regional diets. Intended to reduce resentment against high-handed government, it was a failure from the start, opposed by liberals and bureaucrats alike while provoking dangerous arguments among the empire's diverse nationalities. So the emperor reversed himself the next year and established a bicameral parliament for the entire empire. Having stirred visions of local self-government and autonomous nationalities, he now wanted to subordinate local governments to rule from Vienna and to a parliament in which a lower house elected by a four-class system ensured the dominance of the German-speaking middle class.

Hungary in particular objected, led by the liberal nationalist Ferencz Deák, who had campaigned for Hungary's Constitution of 1848. Neither side was strong enough to have its way, and the war with Prussia finally brought a compromise. In 1867 Hungary became an autonomous state, joined to Austria only through the emperor, Franz Joseph, who became king of Hungary, and through common policies for defense and diplomacy. The emperor had kept his authority in foreign policy, which was what he cared about most, by conceding to one nationality what he denied to others. Within Hungary itself, domestic politics centered on conflict between the dominant Magyars and the non-Magyar majority and between the diverging interests of Austrian industry and Hungary's great landholders.

Within Austria's imperial parliament, the emperor turned for support first to the German liberals, who offended him by their anticlericalism, and then to the Czechs and Poles, who disturbed him with their nationalist demands. More fundamental reform proved difficult; and although ministers were now responsible to parliament, policy rested more on a conservative bureaucracy dominated by Germans. An awkward compromise, the Dual Monarchy, gave power to wealthy landlords and merchants, and it rested on the dominance of Magyars (over Romanians, Croatians, and Serbs) and of Germans in cooperation with Czechs and Poles (over Slovenes, Slovaks, and Ruthenians). It lasted for fifty years as one of Europe's great powers, an empire of diversified peoples and cultures, threatened by nationalism, changing even while resisting change, with more freedom in practice than in principle, and sustained at its center by the graceful civilization of Vienna.

III. Nineteenth-Century Culture

Europe's cultural life was as dynamic as its economy and politics. In the nineteenth century the arts were understood to be national and urban rather than centered in courts, salons, or villages (*provincial* had become a pejorative term); and

---

[8]The old military system, which required selected serfs to serve twenty-five years, was changed in 1874 to one of universal service, with generous exemptions and only six years of active duty. Those who completed primary school were liable for only four years of duty; those who finished secondary school, for two years; and those with university education, for just six months.

they were remarkable for quantity as well as quality. There were more writers, artists, musicians, and scholars than ever before; and they reached larger audiences through expanding cultural institutions and markets.

◆ THE ORGANIZATION OF CULTURE

Before the nineteenth century, most paintings and musical compositions were commissioned for a particular place or occasion. Now music moved from palaces, churches, and private salons to public concert halls; artists sold their paintings to any purchaser and, by midcentury, in galleries created for that purpose; and writers found themselves engaged in commercial activity. Theaters ranged from the new music halls to the great stages and opera houses built (usually by the state) to rank with parliament buildings as monuments of national or civic pride. Most major cities supported choirs, bands, and symphony orchestras, which grew larger and technically more proficient. Conservatories and museums became national public institutions, maintaining official taste and considerably increasing Europe's stock of highly trained artists, musicians, and scholars. Some of the greatest of these institutions—the British Museum in London, the Bibliothèque Nationale in Paris, the Hermitage in St. Petersburg, the Alte Pinakothek in Munich—opened to the public in the 1840s. Whether in palaces once private or in imposing new structures, cultural institutions were treated as civic and national monuments. Lending libraries, charging a few pence per volume, were common even in smaller cities. In Paris the Louvre became the model art museum that provided access to everyone and expressed the era's understanding of culture by displaying works of art by country of origin and in chronological order. This was an urban, bourgeois culture that sought to make the city itself a cultural statement.

Cultural life—associated with the state, tied to a market economy, and promulgating shared values and taste—helped to create national identity and to establish social status. The intended public was, for the most part, the same public that was active in politics, the professions, and business—or rather, such people and their wives. They bought tickets for concerts just as they frequented restaurants with famous chefs, enjoying in both cases pleasures once part of private society and now open to all who had the inclination and money. Participation in this exciting culture also set boundaries of decorum that distinguished the middle class from those below them and defined the distinctive roles thought appropriate to men and women. High culture was expected to sustain these public values, although individual artists and intellectuals often criticized that fact and attacked a system that left an artist's fate dependent either on administrators or what would sell to the public. The tension between creative expression and market, which sometimes in itself stimulated creativity, became a much lamented hallmark of modernity.

Reaching a Wider Public　This public culture encompassed an expanded range of activities. For those who sought self-improvement, there were public lectures on the sober implications of political economy or the wonders of steam power or newer marvels like photography, which was being enthusiastically applied to the needs of science and exploration, widely used for portraits, and recognized as the newest of the arts.[9] No cultural institution was more important than the press, and the newspaper became a major instrument of culture and politics. By 1830 there were more than two thousand European newspapers, and liberals everywhere fought the censorship, special taxes, and police measures with which governments sought to constrain so awesome a social force. The *Times* of London had a circulation of 5,000 in 1815 and of 50,000 by midcentury; two of the most popular French papers, the *Presse* and *Siècle*, reached a circulation of 70,000.

As newspapers came to rely more on advertising than on subscriptions for their revenue, they increased in size, they published articles on a wider range of topics (including items on fashion and domestic concerns aimed at women), and they attracted readers by serializing novels by

---

[9]Daguerre announced his photographic process to the French Academy in 1839, which persuaded the government to purchase his rights and give the new technique to the world, unencumbered by royalties.

▲ **In reporting on current events,** *The Illustrated London News* **held its audience with sensational images of disasters, like this one of an explosion in the room of a Neapolitan fortress where percussion caps were manufactured.**
The Illustrated London News, August 1855

writers as famous as Honoré de Balzac, the elder Alexandre Dumas, and Charles Dickens. Technology aided these changes. Press services such as the Agence Havas and Reuters quickly adopted the telegraph; and the *London Illustrated News,* which created the picture magazine in 1842, was immediately copied in every large country. Satirical magazines (*Punch* was founded in London in 1840, a few years after the *Caricature* and *Chiarivari* in Paris) made the cartoon a powerful political weapon, raised to art by Honoré Daumier's biting pictures of fat bankers and complacent bourgeois.

The Cultural Professions Professionalization affected the arts as well as other occupations. The violinist Niccolò Paganini, who transformed violin technique, commanded huge fees and enormous crowds wherever he played; the soprano Jenny Lind, "the Swedish Nightingale," was the rage of Europe as was Franz Liszt, piano virtuoso and composer. Many a young man announced that he was a painter and proudly starved, in Paris if possible, out of loyalty to his career (there were 354 registered artists in Paris in 1789, 2,159 in 1838). A few, among them England's great landscape painter J. M. W. Turner, became wealthy.

The most popular writers—Balzac, Sir Walter Scott, Victor Hugo, Dickens—were able to live by their pen alone, among the most honored figures of their age. There were also many women novelists. Expected to write light romances, they generally were not taken very seriously; and to escape that prejudice a number of women writers adopted masculine pen names. Still, the rising prestige of the professional writer enabled some extraordinary women, like George Eliot (Mary Evans Cross) and Elizabeth Gaskell in England and George Sand in France, to be recognized as influential thinkers. For a middle-class public faced with so much new work to choose from, critics became important; like professors, they were professional intellectuals who guided taste much as the popular books on etiquette and gastronomy taught manners to people of new means and prepared the bourgeois palate for haute cuisine.

◆ THE CONTENT OF CULTURE

Varied Forms The most admired artistic works were valued for a moral seriousness and formality that distinguished them from popular culture. In painting, great historical scenes were the most admired, ranked considerably above genre painting or portraits. Music was increasingly treated as a kind of spiritual essay, to be heard reverentially in concerts suitable to its distinctive forms—symphony, concerto, quartet, and sonata—all considered to have a social and intellectual importance. The novel's great popularity was related to the social panorama it presented. Balzac attempted in his novels to encompass all the "human comedy" (the phrase contrasted with Dante's divine concerns), showing the wealthy, the ambitious, and the poor in their roles as husbands, wives, soldiers, bankers, politicians, and writers. Novelists used social types to analyze society and challenge the public conscience, and no reformer was more influential than Dickens. Scott's swashbuckling stories of romance and chivalry in an earlier age probed the connection between personal character and social tension in a way that influenced writers throughout Europe. Theater and opera featured historical settings; and Hugo, Alexander Pushkin, and Alessandro Manzoni promulgated patriotism by connecting high ideals to the national past, painting in words (much as the most admired paintings put on canvas) monumental interpretations of historical events. The novel's most common theme, the conflict between personal feeling

◄ **Most European cities boasted elegant theaters like this one in Vienna.**
Mary Evans Picture Library

(especially romantic love) and social convention, explored critical contemporary issues of individualism and social change.

Conceptions of culture were also strongly gendered. Women were held to have qualities—including a natural sense of beauty and openness to emotion—that made them especially responsive to art. Women were thought to be the principal readers of novels, and novels presented women's lives in ways that underscored the inequities of their social subordination and ultimately enlarged the perception of women's abilities (as in Gustave Flaubert's *Madame Bovary* and Thomas Hardy's *Tess of the d'Urbervilles*). Women were especially associated with the intimate side of middle-class culture, the popularity of poetry, lithographs, watercolor paintings, and piano music[10]—all to be savored in the parlor with the woman of the house at the center.

Changing Styles   In culture as in philosophy there was also a strong desire for synthesis, for ideas and forms that would tie everything together. In the arts this urge gave lyric opera special resonance. Opera was first of all theater, combining popular appeal with aristocratic elegance, and performances were important civic events. Elaborate plots, often in historical settings, and flowery poetic texts were closely followed along with the varied, tuneful, and complex music, the whole further enriched by ballet, colorful sets, and special effects. The two leading operatic composers of the period were Giuseppe Verdi and his exact contemporary Richard Wagner. Verdi was an Italian national hero, whose compelling and often patriotic music explored human emotion and character in diverse contexts, often historical ones explicitly about politics. Wagner carried the search for an artistic synthesis still further. He wrote his own texts and increasingly used Germanic myths with nationalist intent. In his operas recurrent musical themes were identified with major ideas and characters to create a whole in which voices, instruments, words, and visual experience moved inseparably to a powerful climax.

By the 1840s rapidly changing and competing artistic styles had become a characteristic of modern culture, a response to social change and new audiences but also an expression of the creative artist's sense of self. Some artists adapted romanticism's emphasis on individual genius to claim that the merit of a piece of art was independent of any social or moral purpose and to adopt, therefore, the cry of art for art's sake. For others, the goal of the artist should be to capture the essence of "modernity," extracting "from fashion whatever element it may contain of poetry within history," in the words of Charles Baudelaire.[11] By midcentury, realism was becoming the dominant style, as writers and painters reemphasized close observation in a socially concerned effort to portray ordinary people, sometimes with shocking directness, as in Flaubert's acid account of a young middle-class wife's aimless existence in a small French town or Gustave Coubet's paintings of rural workers and villages. Innovation was often taken for a sign of genius, and the belief that artists must be in an avant-garde, ahead of their duller public, became a cliché. Often disturbing to their audiences, the arts were never more honored nor artists more critical of their own society than in the nineteenth century.

Religious Thought   Religion was regarded with comparable ambivalence. In some respects the nineteenth century was a very religious age, for thoughtful people cared greatly about religion. Protestant and Catholic missions campaigned with an intensity not seen since the seventeenth century, and the pious became more militant and turned to social action, preaching temperance, teaching reading, and establishing charities. This focus on the problems of modern life was connected, however, to the fear that religion was losing its social importance. Some intellectuals became bitter anticlericals, seeing in the church the barrier to progress. More typically, especially

---

[10]Industrial techniques had made the piano, with its iron frame, economical enough to be a common sight in middle-class homes.

[11]From his essay on the painter Constantin Guys in Charles Baudelaire, *The Painter of Modern Life and Other Essays*, Jonathan Mayne (tr. and ed.), 1965, p. 12.

▲ **Courbet, a leader in the shift toward social realism in painting, presents the artist in his studio in touch with all classes of men and women. Many of those portrayed here were well-known artists and radicals.**
Scala/Art Resource, NY

in England, stern morality and propriety were substituted for theology. Theological works nevertheless accounted for a high proportion of the titles publishers produced. Friedrich Schleiermacher's writings were as influential in German philosophy as in Protestant theology, and it made headlines when the Abbé Lamennais, once a powerful spokesman of Catholic renewal, broke with the Church in the 1830s when it rejected the connection he made between Christianity and democracy. The impact of historical research on religion created a sensation across Europe when the Protestant David Strauss published his *Life of Jesus* in 1835, for it cast erudite doubt on the accuracy of the Gospel, frightening many with the apparent need to choose between scholarship and Christ. In Denmark the writings of Søren Kierkegaard starkly explored ethical dilemmas in a passionate search for faith; and his intense, semiautobiographical essays that interweave biblical stories and personal symbols have continued to fascinate twentieth-century thinkers.

The Sense of History Nineteenth-century intellectual life emphasized historical thinking. A romantic respect for the past, nationalists' claims, explanations of revolution, economic theory, and preoccupation with change all underscored the importance of history. Its systematic study became an admired profession. In England, France, and Germany, national projects were launched for publishing historical documents and for training scholars to interpret them. Some historians were as widely read as novelists, among them Jules Michelet, for whom French history was a dramatic story of the people's fight for freedom, and Thomas B. Macaulay, for whom the history of England was a record of progressive change through moderation and compromise. In each country certain events and themes—in England, the Glorious Revolution of 1688; in France, the

Revolution; in Germany, the rise of Prussia—were favored as part of an intense search for national roots, heroes, and patterns of development significant for the present. Many a political leader first gained fame as a historian.

This preoccupation with history received its most powerful philosophic expression in the writings of Georg Wilhelm Friedrich Hegel, a German Rhinelander who watched with fascination the unfolding of the French Revolution and the spread of Napoleon's influence. Thoroughly trained in philosophy and Lutheran theology, Hegel set out to establish a philosophy as comprehensive as that of Thomas Aquinas or Aristotle. He was determined to reconcile contradictions between science and faith, Christianity and the state, the ideal and the real, the eternal and the temporal. The key, he believed, lay in the meaning of history and the nature of the historical process.

According to Hegel, that process is dialectical. Society in any era constitutes an implicit statement about life and values expressed through social structures and actions, which can be thought of as its thesis. That thesis, however, is never adequate to every need, and its incompleteness generates contrary views, institutions, and practices—the antithesis. Thus, every society gives rise to conflict between thesis and antithesis until from that dialectic a new synthesis is molded. This synthesis becomes, in turn, another thesis that generates a new antithesis. History thus moves by this dialectic in a steady unfolding of what Hegel called the World Spirit, and it always moves toward greater human freedom and self-awareness. In the ancient East, Hegel said, only one man was free; in Greece and Rome, some were free; in the Germanic Christian kingdoms after the Reformation, all were free. Since the French Revolution, people have consciously acted on history, knowing what they want and fulfilling the World Spirit at the same time. Thus, cosmic order and human reason ultimately work together; history has a religious meaning.

Hegel's important philosophy was—as he would have said it had to be—an important expression of his age. Like most nineteenth-century thinkers, he was determined to find eternal meaning in historical change and was convinced that his own nation was the highest articulation of that meaning. Hegel's influence increased after his death, in 1831. Philosophy and literary criticism both tended to become ever more historical, and historians looked more systematically for relationships among all aspects of culture. Following another wave of the revolutions he abhorred, some of his followers claimed to find humanity's highest ethical expression in the Prussian state at war, while others—led by Karl Marx, the most famous of the Hegelians—predicted the state's withering away. By then it was a European habit to approach any question of society, culture, or politics in terms of historical change.

SUMMARY

◆

In 1848 a wave of revolutions, the most spontaneous and widespread Europe had ever known, brought new governments to power. Defeated before they could complete their democratic and egalitarian programs, these revolutionary regimes left important legacies not only in measures passed but lessons learned. In the future, radicals would not rely on middle-class support and political reform, liberals would be more willing to sacrifice democracy for social order. In these circumstances the most effective governments of the 1850s were those that adopted parts of the revolutionaries' programs and some of their techniques for reaching a broader public while keeping the forces of order on their side. Thus, the Second Empire of Napoleon III was the principal guarantor of that social order and economic growth important to the propertied classes. Piedmont and Prussia, as the focus of nationalist movements, won significant followings and triumphed dramatically in creating national states in Italy and Germany. In this Europe of the modern national state, astute political leaders from England to Prussia found ways to undertake new social responsibilities, facilitate industrialization, and mobilize popular support without giving way to full democracy or radical programs. Closely associated with the nation, cultural institutions flourished, supporting a diverse and dynamic culture that was one of the great achievements of the age. By the 1870s, European nations had the means to generate unprecedented power and the will to spread their influence around the world.

QUESTIONS FOR FURTHER THOUGHT

◆

1. What is the historical significance of revolutions in which the revolutionaries are defeated?

2. Why did nationalism become so important in the nineteenth century?

3. Nationalist ideologies have much in common, but what accounts for the important differences among them?

4. When you look at art, listen to music, or read works written in the nineteenth century, what characteristics do you identify with the period in which they were created?

RECOMMENDED READING

◆

Sources

Marx, Karl. *The Class Struggles in France, 1848–1850* and *The Eighteenth Brumaire of Louis Napoleon.* Early and brilliant applications of Marx's ideas to contemporary political events, these essays on the revolution of 1848 in France and on Napoleon's coup d'état also show Marx's power as a polemicist.

Treitschke, Heinrick. *History of Germany in the Nineteenth Century.* Written shortly after German unification, this vast work exemplifies the importance of history as nationalist propaganda.

Trollope, Frances Milton. *Travels and Travellers.* 2 vols. 1846. A novelist well known for travel essays, Mrs. Trollope's chatty descriptions contain insightful comments on European society and the position of women on the eve of revolution.

Studies

*Agulhon, Maurice. *The Republican Experiment, 1848–1852.* Janel Lloyd (tr.). 1983. An authoritative study of politics and society during the Second French Republic, sensitive to popular attitudes and concerns.

*Alter, Peter. *Nationalism.* 1989. A valuable introduction to the history of European nationalism organized around an interesting classification of the different kinds of nationalism.

*Anderson, Benedict. *Imagined Communities: Reflections on the Origin and Spread of Nationalism.* 1983. An important and provocative analysis of modern nationalism around the world, stressing its origins in European culture and capitalism.

*Beales, Derek. *The Risorgimento and the Unification of Italy.* 1982. Concise, skeptical introduction to the history of Italian unification.

*Chadwick, Owen. *The Secularization of the European Mind.* 1975. Perceptive, careful introduction to changing patterns of thought affecting attitudes toward religion.

Freifel, Alice. *Nationalism and the Crowd in Liberal Hungary, 1848–1914.* 2000. Demonstrates the unique aspects of Hungarian nationalism.

*Gellner, Ernest. *Nations and Nationalism.* 1983. An effort to build a theory by analyzing the relation of industrialization to nationalism.

*Greenfield, Liah. *Nationalism: Five Roads to Modernity.* 1992. An ambitious comparison of nationalism and state-making in England, France, Russia, Germany, and the United States.

Greenfield, Kent R. *Economics and Liberalism in the Risorgimento: A Study of Nationalism in Lombardy, 1814–1848.* 1978. A classic study of the connection between economic change and nationalism.

*Hamerow, Theodore S. *The Social and Economic Foundations of German Unification, 1858–1871.* 2 vols. 1969 and 1972. The politics and ideas of unification placed in the context of a developing economy.

Hemmings, F. W. J. *Culture and Society in France, 1789–1848.* 1987. *Culture and Society in France, 1848–1898.* 1971. A literary scholar's provocative and comprehensive analysis of the relationship between cultural styles and social context.

*Howard, Michael. *The Franco-Prussian War.* 1969. Exemplary study of how war reflects (and tests) an entire society.

*Jelavich, Barbara. *History of the Balkans.* 2 vols. 1983. An impressively thorough survey of both society and politics, from the eighteenth century to the present.

*Mack Smith, Denis. *Cavour.* 1985. An expert and well-written assessment of the personalities and policies that created an Italian nation.

*McLeod, Hugh. *Religion and the People of Western Europe, 1789–1970.* 1981. A well-conceived interpretive survey of the impact of social change on religious practice.

*Mosse, George L. *The Nationalization of the Masses: Political Symbolism and Mass Movements in Germany from the Napoleonic Wars through the Third Reich.* 1975. One of the most recent and complete efforts to find the roots of Nazism in popular nationalism.

*Newman, Gerald. *The Rise of English Nationalism: A Cultural History, 1740–1830.* 1998. Shows, as older interpretations did not, the fundamental importance of rising nationalism in industrializing Britain.

Olsen, Donald J. *The City as a Work of Art: London, Paris, Vienna.* 1986. Combines an analysis of how ordinary people really lived with an appreciation of the aesthetics of the modern city and the economic and political realities behind it.

Pflanze, Otto. *Bismarck and the Development of Germany: The Period of Unification, 1815–1871.* 1963. A balanced assessment that places each of Bismarck's actions in its larger context.

*Pinkney, David. *Napoleon III and the Rebuilding of Paris.* 1958. Studies the political background to one of the most extensive, influential, and successful examples of urban policy.

*Plessis, Alain. *The Rise and Fall of the Second Empire, 1852–1871.* Jonathan Mandelbaum (tr.). 1985. A balanced assessment of this important political experiment, making good use of current scholarship.

*Poovey, Mary. *Making a Social Body: British Cultural Formation, 1830–1864.* This study of how the public was conceived in literature and politics exposes the ways in which public institutions helped construct categories of gender and class.

*Read, Donald. *England 1868–1914: The Age of Urban Democracy.* 1979. Political change presented in terms of economic and social conditions.

Reardon, B. M. G. *Religion in the Age of Romanticism: Studies in Early Nineteenth-Century Thought.* 1985. An excellent introduction to the formation of one of the most important intellectual traditions of the century.

Riasanovsky, Nicholas V. *Nicholas I and Official Nationality in Russia.* 1959. An important study of how a conservative regime sought to use nationalism to strengthen the state.

Rich, Norman. *Why the Crimean War? A Cautionary Tale.* 1985. A concise synthesis and engaging interpretation of the political and diplomatic problems involving the major powers.

Royle, Trevor. *Crimea: The Great Crimean War, 1854–1856.* 2000. A balanced military history incorporating the latest research that demonstrates the war's lasting influence.

Salvemini, Gaetano. *Mazzini.* 1957. Still the best introduction to Mazzini's thought and its relationship to his revolutionary activities.

Saville, John. 1848: *The British State and the Chartist Movement.* 1987. A careful study of why Chartism failed to win its aims at the moment revolution succeeded elsewhere.

*Sperber, Jonathan. *The European Revolutions, 1848–1851.* 1994. A fresh synthesis that pays attention to popular attitudes and symbolic actions as well as political and social conflict.

*Stearns, Peter N. 1848: *The Revolutionary Tide in Europe.* 1974. Assesses conflicting interpretations in bringing together accounts of these diverse revolutions.

Szporluk, Roman. *Communism and Nationalism: Karl Marx versus Friedrich List.* 1988. By drawing attention to the ideas of List, one of the most influential figures of his day, this study suggests that in Central and Eastern Europe nationalism and Marxism were, from the first, competing programs for modernization and economic development.

Wandycz, Piotyr S. *The Lands of Partitioned Poland, 1795–1918.* 1974. An excellent overview of the history of divided Poland.

*Williams, Roger L. *The French Revolution of 1870–1871.* 1969. An introduction to the long-standing controversies about the Paris Commune.

*Zeldin, T. *France: 1848–1945.* 2 vols. 1973–1977. Reissued in five paperback volumes, 1979–1981. Lively essays on an unusual array of topics that add up to an important look at French society and culture.

*Available in paperback.

▲ The Reverend John Williams was an English missionary who had extraordinary success converting native populations on the islands of the South Seas. He wrote codes of law for them and taught them European construction techniques before moving on to win more converts elsewhere. This painting depicts his arrival in November 1839 on an island in the New Hebrides, where on the following day the natives killed him.
Maidstone Museum and Art Galley, Kent, UK/Bridgeman Art Library

Chapter 25

EUROPEAN POWER: WEALTH, KNOWLEDGE, AND IMPERIALISM

In the second half of the nineteenth century, for the first time in history, economic growth became an expectation, seen as a natural development that could continue in a self-sustaining process. New technologies, large-scale industry, better communication, and greater capital investment made unprecedented productivity possible, and these gains were in turn a triumph of social organization and new knowledge. Clearly, economic growth, scientific discovery, and social change were interconnected; and there was a demand for social theories that could explain these developments and establish ways to direct them in the future, much as science uncovered the laws of nature. With its increasing trade, curiosity, and power, this expansive civilization also strengthened its contacts across the globe. Then, rather suddenly, more informal links and influence hardened into imperial rule and a competitive rush for empire. Imperialism gained support as the proud assertion of national power.

CHAPTER 25. EUROPEAN POWER: WEALTH, KNOWLEDGE, AND IMPERIALISM							
	Social Structure	Body Politic	Changes in the Organization of Production and in the Impact of Technology	Evolution of Family and Changing Gender Roles	War	Religion	Cultural Expression
I. THE ECONOMICS OF GROWTH	▓		▓	▓			
II. THE KNOWLEDGE OF NATURE AND SOCIETY							▓
III. EUROPE AND THE WORLD		▓	▓		▓	▓	▓
IV. MODERN IMPERIALISM	▓	▓	▓	▓	▓	▓	▓

I. The Economics of Growth

The dynamism of Europe's economy in the second half of the nineteenth century was unprecedented. As economic growth accelerated, it reached into sectors previously little affected and spread beyond Europe's industrial heartlands into most of the continent. While Europe's population grew more rapidly than ever before, the value of manufacturing went up three times as fast; most of society experienced some of its benefits. Factories, especially those that produced steel and chemicals, coupled large-scale production with new technologies, like those connected to electricity. The impact of these developments was so great that historians often speak of this as the second industrial revolution. Distribution and marketing operated on a larger scale, too, and department stores used new techniques of merchandising to entice a wider public to higher levels of consumption.

◆ THE SECOND INDUSTRIAL REVOLUTION

Industrial growth in this period benefited from new technology, production in large-scale factories, increased consumer spending, and more available capital.

New Technologies Exciting new inventions were adapted to commercial uses with striking speed. A whole new industry developed to produce and supply electricity. Thomas Edison's incandescent light bulb, developed in the 1870s, was quickly followed by central power stations to distribute power over a wide area, including public lighting

▼ **MAIL (MILLIONS OF PIECES)**
The volume of mail has been used by some scholars as an indicator of modernization, reflecting increased literacy, internal communication, and commercial activity. In these terms, then, the relative position of the several nations on this chart is suggestive of more than gross population, as are the points at which Germany surpasses first France and then the United Kingdom or at which Russia surpasses Italy and Austria-Hungary.

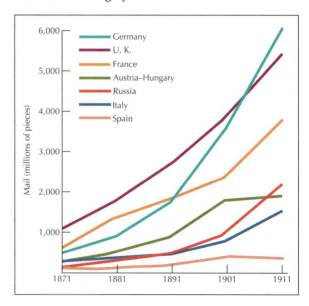

in New York and London in 1882 and in Berlin a few years later. The steam turbine, shown in the 1880s to be more efficient than the reciprocating engine, was soon widely employed in ships and factories, fueled by oil as well as coal. By 1900 the manufacture of generators, cables, and motors, an important new industry in itself, allowed greater and cheaper production in scores of other fields. The telephone, invented in 1876, became a business necessity and an established private convenience within a few decades. New chemical processes and synthetics led to improved products ranging from dyes, textiles, and paints to fertilizers and explosives

Home sewing machines spread rapidly, first in the United States and then across Europe, the most important of many new labor-saving devices that allowed women to increase their contribution to the home economy even when they also worked outside the home. The bicycle granted new mobility and independence to women as well as men. Inventions were now expected to change people's lives, and products created directly for the consumer market responded to the growing purchasing power of the masses. The automobile in the 1890s, the airplane in the 1900s, and the radio a decade later were all greeted with enthusiasm even before their commercial possibilities were established.

By 1890 Europe was producing even more steel than iron. The Bessemer converter developed in the 1860s permitted far higher temperatures in smelter furnaces, and subsequent discoveries made it profitable to use lower-grade ores. British,

▼ The Bessemer process of removing impurities from molten iron, which revolutionized the industry, was based on English and American patents; but the Krupp steelworks installed these massive converters in 1862 and continued to lead in steel production in both size and efficiency when this photograph was taken in 1880. Ullstein Bilderdienst

MAKING THE DEALS THAT CREATED A CARTEL

◆

Cartels, strongest in Germany, existed in other countries, too. Here the general manager of an iron rolling mill that made rails describes how in 1878 a cartel of rail producers came to be formed in Austria.

"In 1878 there were in Austria-Hungary nine rail rolling mills with an annual capacity of about 120,000 tons. A large part of these mills had been set up in the years 1869–73, that is to say in a period in which railway building flourished in Austria-Hungary as never before. . . . The picture changed in the course of 1873. The lines that had been started were being finished, but no new ones were being built. . . .

"I was then the general manager of one of these rail rolling mills. . . . If our works did not get an annual minimum quantity of orders of 10,000 tons, it would be faced with the impossibility of employing its work force. We should have had to close and face bankruptcy. . . . My task was therefore a simple one; to get orders at all costs.

"In 1878 . . . on the day when contracts were awarded [by the Kaiser Franz-Joseph Railway], the manager . . . told me: 'Yours was the lowest; but since two other works are also prepared to come down to our price, I shall divide the order into three parts. . . .' I tried to make representations; in vain, the decision stood. After I had left the office of the managing director, I met the managers of the other two works which had come down to my price. Because of the years of bitter competition, our personal relations had also suffered, but this time we shook hands, and the rail cartel, the first cartel in Austria, the model for other later cartels, also in Germany, was born. At the moment when it became clear that no works could succeed in getting sufficient orders to stay fully employed, each reached the conviction that there was nothing left but at last to attempt to get higher prices. The course of the tendering negotiations with the Franz-Joseph Railway had shown the way. We reached agreement to distribute the total demand according to certain ratios among all the works, and sought then to get the highest prices possible in the light of foreign competition, and the rates of freight and of customs duty."

From Karl Wittgensteing, "Kartelle in Österreich," in Gustav Schmoller (ed.), *Über wirtschaftliche, Kartelle in Deutschland und im Auslande* (Leipzig, 1894); as quoted in Carroll and Embree, *Readings in European History since 1814* (1930).

German, and French maritime shipping, which doubled between 1870 and 1914, depended on faster and larger steamships.

Germany's Economic Growth The German economy, especially, expanded spectacularly following unification. Already rich in natural resources, Germany acquired more raw materials as well as factories with the annexation of Alsace-Lorraine. Its system of railroads provided excellent communications; the famous educational system produced ample numbers of the administrators and engineers the commercial sector now required. The government, which had played an active role in every facet of industrialization, continued to cooperate with business interests. Military needs stimulated basic industry, and a growing population provided an eager domestic market.

German factories, being newer than those of Britain or France, employed the latest and most efficient equipment, obtaining the necessary capital through a modern banking structure. By 1900 those plants were far bigger than anyone else's, and firms engaged in the various stages of production often combined in huge cartels that dominated an entire sector of industry, from raw material to finished product, as Germany became preeminent in new fields such as chemicals and electricity (see "Making the Deals That Created a Cartel," above). German salespeople appeared all over the world with catalogs in local languages and products suited to local conditions, selling with a drive and optimism British merchants resented as bad manners.

Older Industrial Economies The older industrial economies of Great Britain, Belgium, and France continued to grow but more slowly. By 1900 France's industrial production, despite the loss of important textile and iron centers in Alsace, had reached the level of Great Britain's a generation earlier, when Britain had led the world. French iron production more than doubled in the first twenty-five years of the Third Republic, and new processes made the nation's ore output second only to that of the United States. In value of production per capita, a figure that suggests something of a nation's standard of living, France remained ahead of Germany, though behind England.

By the turn of the century, Great Britain, whose industrial superiority had seemed a fact of nature, was clearly being surpassed in some of the critical indexes of production by both Germany and the United States. Although the British economy did continue to grow, the fear that it was falling behind became a serious issue in English public life; economic historians remain fascinated by the question of why an economy once so dynamic was sluggish. Several factors stand out. British plants and equipment were old, and owners hesitated to undertake the cost of modernizing or replacing them. Well-established firms often made it hard for new companies to get a start. Without technical secondary schools like those of Germany and France, English schooling remained weak in technical subjects and provided less opportunity for social mobility than on the continent. Indeed, social attitudes, always difficult to analyze precisely, may explain more than strictly economic factors. British industrialists, slow to appreciate the value of specialists and resistant to new ways, became less venturesome and perhaps a little complacent. Even so, London remained the financial capital of the world.

The Spread of Industrialization   That world was increasingly industrialized. The industrial potential of the United States was apparent by the time of the Civil War, although few expected subsequent growth to be as dramatic as it was by the turn of the century. Rich in natural resources, America had a continent in which to expand, millions of immigrants eager to supply needed labor, schooling that sustained technological inventiveness, an openness and mobility that encouraged enterprise, and a democracy that pioneered in creating a consumer society.

But other nations were industrializing, too: Italy and Japan, which had very limited natural

▼ **Industrial Production**
(Thousands of Metric Tons)

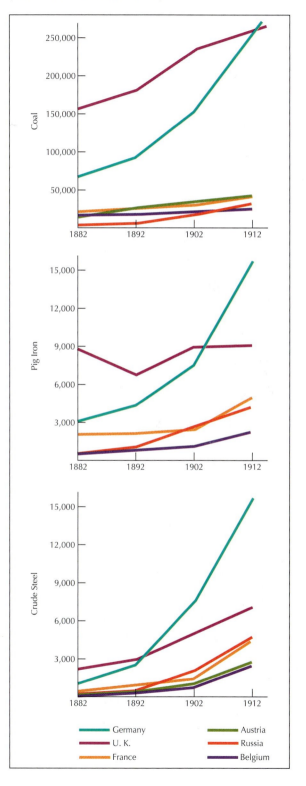

resources; and Russia and Sweden, which had appeared rural, poor, and backward compared to industrialized Western Europe. Assumptions that related industrial progress to European values, Protestantism, or Anglo-Saxon institutions were belied by the changes in the nature of industrialization itself. It no longer depended so directly on the possession of critical resources like coal and iron ore but could be accomplished with foreign investment and imported technology. Newly industrializing countries, reluctant to leave their fate to market forces and the interests of foreigners, expected government and investment banks to favor and protect new industries.

Agriculture Although greater prosperity and growing populations increased the demand for food, the percentage of the population that made its living in agriculture continued to decline, down to only 8 percent in Britain, 22 percent in Belgium, and 35 percent in Germany toward the end of the century. In France, which maintained a more balanced economy (as did the Netherlands and Sweden), 43 percent of the population lived off the land. But everywhere the wider use of machinery and chemical fertilizers increased the capital investment required for farming, and improved transportation intensified international competition. These factors encouraged much greater specialization. The most famous example is Denmark, where agriculture began to center on a highly capitalized and profitable dairy industry. But in France, too, wheat and sheep production declined in favor of wine grapes and sugar beets, which farmers could raise more profitably.

Global connections were increasingly important. Civil war in the United States, which cut off Europe's supply of cotton from the southern states, caused unemployment in England's mills and created a boom for Egyptian cotton. After 1865, cheaper grain from the Americas and Eastern Europe, especially Russia, poured into Europe on larger ships to be distributed on improved railroads, pushing prices down at a time when farmers needed cash for the improvements required to make farming profitable. Britain now imported almost all its grain, and Germany, a great deal. More young men abandoned the countryside, and landed interests pressed their governments for

help in the face of recurrent agricultural crises. The most common response was protective tariffs, which were raised in France, Germany, Austria, Russia, Italy, and Spain. Initially applied primarily to agriculture, the new tariffs were soon extended to manufactured goods as well, reversing the trend toward liberal policies that had favored free trade from the 1830s to the 1870s.

The Long Depression But the trade barriers did not stop the general decline in prices. Strangely, the second industrial revolution occurred in one of the longest and most severe periods of deflation in European history. From the 1870s to 1896, prices, interest rates, and profits fell, with far-reaching effects. This dynamism in which one part of the economy soared while another declined was socially disruptive. Handicraft industries, which had survived side by side with mechanized manufacturing throughout Europe, were forced out of business. So were numerous smaller and less efficient industrial firms. The great boom in railroad building ended, and governments had to save socially or politically important lines deserted by bankrupt companies.

As competition sharpened, many industrialists welcomed the support governments could give through tariffs, state spending, and colonial policies. Economic demands became a central theme of politics as more and more of economic life centered on great factories owned by large corporations (and closely tied to banks and government) that employed hundreds or even thousands of workers who, in turn, increasingly organized into industrial labor unions.

◆ THE DEMOGRAPHIC TRANSITION

Europe's population continued to grow during the second industrial revolution and did so at an increasing rate. The 295 million Europeans in 1870 had become nearly 450 million by 1914, and the age distribution or demographic profile had changed completely.

Declining Rates of Mortality and Fertility Population had increased despite the fact that in most of Europe birthrates had begun to decline, and it did so because mortality rates were falling still

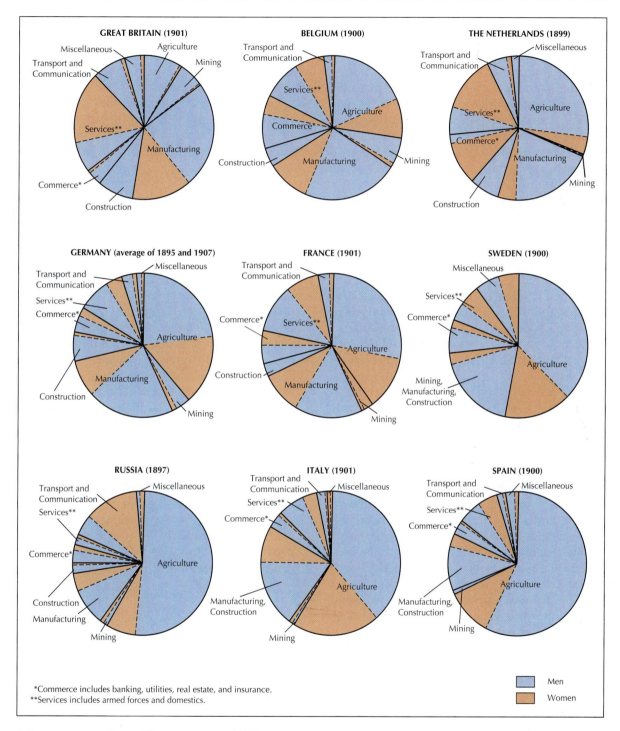

GREAT BRITAIN (1901)

Miscellaneous — Agriculture
Transport and Communication — Mining
Services** — Manufacturing
Commerce* — Construction

BELGIUM (1900)

Transport and Communication
Services**
Commerce* — Agriculture
Construction — Manufacturing — Mining

THE NETHERLANDS (1899)

Transport and Communication — Miscellaneous
Services** — Agriculture
Commerce* — Manufacturing
Construction — Mining

GERMANY (average of 1895 and 1907)

Transport and Communication — Miscellaneous
Services**
Commerce* — Agriculture
Construction — Manufacturing
Mining

FRANCE (1901)

Transport and Communication
Commerce* — Services**
Agriculture
Construction — Manufacturing — Mining

SWEDEN (1900)

Miscellaneous
Services**
Commerce* — Agriculture
Mining, Manufacturing, Construction

RUSSIA (1897)

Transport and Communication — Miscellaneous
Services**
Commerce* — Agriculture
Construction
Manufacturing — Mining

ITALY (1901)

Transport and Communication — Miscellaneous
Services**
Commerce* — Agriculture
Manufacturing, Construction — Mining

SPAIN (1900)

Transport and Communication — Miscellaneous
Services**
Commerce* — Agriculture
Manufacturing, Construction — Mining

*Commerce includes banking, utilities, real estate, and insurance.
**Services includes armed forces and domestics.

Men
Women

▲ **ECONOMICALLY ACTIVE POPULATION, CA. 1900**
From P. Bairoch et al., *The Working Population and Its Structure* (Gordon V. Breach, 1968), p. 119.

more steeply. This pattern of a declining birthrate accompanied by a more rapidly falling mortality rate, which is called the *demographic transition,* continues in our own time and has become one of the marks of modernity that spread from Europe to the rest of the world.

Death rates initially declined because of lower infant mortality rates, a result of improved sanitation, better diet, and the virtual elimination of diseases such as cholera and typhus. By the turn of the century, improvements in medical care lowered mortality rates among adults as well. Thus, the population grew despite the declining birthrate.

Lower mortality rates reflected the benefits of industrial prosperity, but the declining birthrates marked a subtler change.[1] The number of children in a family was becoming more a matter of choice, aided by the spread of contraception; where bourgeois values took root and child labor declined, workers followed the upper classes in the trend toward later marriage, fewer births, and smaller families.

The Social Impact Although the issues are complicated and the statistics uncertain, estimates of crude birthrates around 1910 suggest the social significance of this changing pattern: Birthrates were highest in Romania, Bulgaria, Portugal, Hungary, Italy, and Spain; they were lowest in Switzerland, Belgium, and France. Parents who were confident their children would live, who wanted them to inherit property and receive some education, chose to have fewer of them. Before 1850 population growth had been higher in Western than in Central and Eastern Europe. That pattern was now reversed, and the enormous increases in populations to their east gave the French added reason to fear Germany's larger and younger population and the Germans cause to worry in turn about the Russian giant to their east. Another outcome of population growth was a new mobility as the growing numbers of people in the countryside moved to towns and from towns to cities. Mainly the young and the poor,

they were responding to new ambitions as well as perennial misery. In doing so, they added to the sense of restless change within Europe. In most cities a majority of residents had been born elsewhere.

These economic, demographic, and social changes reached into the peasant hut and the urban slum. Meat and white bread became regular, although not daily, parts of the diet for most people in the industrialized countries. Commerce offered cheap products at fixed prices, and jobs in sales and distribution provided new opportunities for both men and women to rise into the lower-middle class. Although domestic service remained the primary occupation for young girls, those with some education could increasingly consider teaching, nursing, or clerical work. For most workers, however, there was little prospect of social mobility; but there were gains in wages and stable employment as the result of an improved economy and the pressure from growing working-class movements. Women still constituted about one-third of the workforce and remained concentrated in poorly paying jobs. Those with full-time jobs tended to be young, between the ages of fifteen and twenty-five, but most working-class women continued to supplement the family income with work as laundresses and seamstresses or as the makers of artificial flowers or matchboxes, usually with the aid of their small children. Male industrial workers, as they became better paid, were pleased to see their wives give up factory jobs, and unions argued for a "family wage" to make that possible. Ordinary people thus shared, more than they had in the past, in Europe's increased prosperity and dynamism.

II. The Knowledge of Nature and Society

Knowledge was expanding, too. Scientific discoveries underlay technological innovation far more directly than in the first industrial revolution, and science itself was becoming ever more organized into distinctive specialties pursued by professional researchers (the term *scientist* was first used in the 1830s). The educated public could understand the new scientific theories, and scientific

---

[1]*Birthrate* is used here as the more familiar term, but *fertility rate*—the ratio of the number of children born to the number of women of childbearing age—is the more precise term preferred by demographers.

ideas were an important part of the general discourse about religion, progress, and ethics. Establishing the laws of nature rekindled hope that laws of social development might similarly be discovered and beneficially applied; and the new inventions, discoveries, and theories that were hailed as evidence of modern advancement justified increased devotion to research.

◆ THE CONQUESTS OF SCIENCE

The clearest intellectual triumphs were in the natural sciences. Understood as contributions to general philosophy, new findings in the sciences were expected to affect learning in all spheres of study but also to have practical effects on the economy and ordinary life.

Physics and the Laws of Thermodynamics *Thermodynamics,* the study of the relationship between heat and mechanical energy, became the core of nineteenth-century physics. Building on theorems stated by Nicolas Sadi Carnot early in the century, the study of thermodynamics developed in many directions at once, addressing both fundamental properties of matter and the practical problems of steam engines. By midcentury, laws predicting the behavior of gases came to be applied to the field

▼ **Michael Faraday at work in his laboratory at the Royal Institution.**
Courtesy of the Director of the Royal Institution, London

of mechanics as well. The combined work of scientists in many countries culminated in the mathematical formulation of the two fundamental laws of thermodynamics. One states the principle of the conservation of energy: Energy can be transformed into heat or work but neither created nor destroyed, and heat or work can be transformed into energy. The other law declares that any closed physical system tends toward equilibrium, a system in which heat becomes uniformly distributed and which therefore cannot be used to produce work.[2] In practical terms, this second law means that heat can be made to do work only when connected through an engine to some cooler body. Philosophically, the law invited troubled speculation about the universe as a giant machine in which the level of energy must inexorably decline.

The study of magnetism advanced in a similar way from the work of Michael Faraday. He had shown in the 1830s and 1840s that lines of magnetic force are analogous to gravity and that electricity can induce magnetism (in reverse, the principle of the dynamo). In 1873 James Clerk Maxwell published equations that described the behavior of electricity, magnetism, and light in terms of a single, universal system. Thus, gravity, magnetism, electricity, and light were all related. By the end of the century, physics had established mathematical laws of theoretical beauty and practical power extending from the universe to the atom, which was then conceived of as a miniature solar system. Thermodynamics led to the development of more efficient sources of power. The investigations of electricity led to the telegraph by midcentury and to electric lights and motors for hundreds of uses a generation later.

New Developments in Chemistry and Biology
The fundamental generalizations of chemistry are contained in the periodic law and periodic table published by Dmitri Mendeleev in 1869. The distinction between compounds and elements had been clearly established for only half a century, and the difference between molecules and atoms came to be generally accepted only in 1860. Yet Mendeleev's table established a marvelous symmetry, so precise that the elements could all be charted by atomic weight, with similar elements occurring at regular intervals. This regularity even allowed for the prediction of unknown elements that would, when discovered, fill the gaps in the table. By the 1880s inorganic and organic chemistry were becoming two separate fields.

The recognition of germs and the realization that they were not spontaneously generated had immediate practical results, for in the 1860s the discoveries of Louis Pasteur in France led to the techniques for destroying germs called *pasteurization*, which were of crucial importance to the wine, dairy, and silk industries. As a result of his work in immunology, Pasteur also developed a preventive vaccine against rabies. In England Joseph Lister discovered that germs could be killed by carbolic acid, and the application of that knowledge made surgery a reasonable remedy rather than a desperate gamble. A decade later Robert Koch in Germany showed that different diseases were caused by distinct microbes, discovered the microorganism responsible for tuberculosis, and opened the way to new techniques in bacteriology and in the battle against communicable diseases. Advances such as these not only improved agriculture and medicine but also stimulated the drive to make sanitation and public health into systematic sciences.

Such achievements resulted from the efforts of hundreds of scientists freely exchanging ideas across national boundaries and working with precise methods and the logic of mathematics. Experiments admired in the 1820s seemed crude by the 1870s, and science became the province of carefully trained professionals rather than inspired amateurs. Research demanded even more systematic organization and larger and more expensive laboratories. The success of science stimulated a general expansion of secondary and higher education, and most of the academic disciplines that constitute the modern university achieved their separate identity in the late nineteenth century, establishing professional organizations and scholarly journals that created communities of specialists and fostered communication within them. Tangible evidence in the form of practical benefits as well as intellectual pride sustained the optimistic view that science progressed at an unprecedented pace for the benefit of all humankind.

---

[2]The measure of the energy unavailable for work is called *entropy*, a term coined by the physicist Rudolf Clausius in 1865.

◆ SOCIAL SCIENCE AND IDEAS OF PROGRESS

Auguste Comte The philosophy of Auguste Comte (1798–1857), enormously influential from midcentury on, was characteristic of much nineteenth-century thought. Clearly rooted in the ideas of the Enlightenment, his philosophy gave greater attention to the process of historical change. Like Hegel a few years earlier, Comte sought to erect a comprehensive philosophical system that would encompass all human knowledge. Hegel and Comte both believed that their era had opened a final stage in historical development. Comte was especially impressed, as were most contemporary intellectuals, by the social role of religion, the conquests of natural science, and the possibilities of human progress. For many years private secretary to Saint-Simon (see p. 814), Comte retained a confidence characteristic of the early socialists that society would soon be reorganized on rational principles.

He systematically elaborated his philosophy, which he called *positivism*, in ten volumes published between 1830 and 1845; these, with his other writings, established positivism as an international movement even before his death in 1857.[3] The key to civilization, he argued, is humanity's understanding of the world, which has developed through three historical stages. In the first, the theological stage, humankind interpreted everything in terms of gods who lived in nature. In the second, or metaphysical stage, people learned through Christianity to think in more abstract terms. In the third, or positive stage, now dawning, human understanding was becoming scientific through objective and precise observation followed by generalization in the form of scientific laws. Every science, he argued, has already passed through the first two stages and into the third—astronomy first, then physics, chemistry, and biology. Now a new science, *sociology* (Comte coined the term), must crown the progression.

While thus honoring the role of established religion, Comte announced its demise, substituting

a "religion of humanity" of his own invention. Some devoted followers accepted his complex scheme whole; many more would find inspiration in Comte's conviction that progress and social order led to, and required, the proper organization of society. More generally, Comte's ideas contributed greatly to widespread acceptance of the view that civilization progresses with increased knowledge discovered through the scientific method and that the great need now was for the scientific study of society and of humankind itself. This creed inspired and shaped much of the rapid development of the social sciences—economics, political science, anthropology, sociology, and psychology—later in the century.

Karl Marx No theory about society and history has proved more influential than the work of Karl Marx. Marx was born in 1818 into a middle-class Rhineland Jewish family that had prospered with the lifting of civil disabilities that accompanied the revolutionary armies from France. He was an able student and received an excellent education at the leading German universities. Too radical to be permitted an academic career, he turned to journalism and became editor of a famous liberal newspaper, the *Rheinische Zeitung*. But his attacks on censorship and his views on economics led the Prussian government to demand his removal, and in 1843 Marx left for Paris. There he met other exiles and leading French radicals, people to whom he would later give the dismissive and enduring label of "utopian" socialists, and there he established a friendship with Friedrich Engels that would become a lifetime's collaboration.

Trained in German philosophy, abreast of contemporary economics, and in touch with the currents of radical thought, Marx began in Paris the systematic development of his own ideas. He outlined his theory of history in a powerful, apocalyptic tone in the *Communist Manifesto*, written jointly with Engels, which was published just before the revolutions of 1848. Little noticed at first, it proved to be one of the greatest pieces of propaganda of all time, a specific program and a general call to action combined with a philosophy of history. Marx devoted the rest of his life—which he spent in poverty-stricken exile in London from 1849 to 1883—to the painstaking elaboration of his ideas in essays, letters, and the comprehensive

---

[3]Later, the term *positivism* came to refer not so much to Comte's specific theories as to a method he advocated: the construction of logical theories based on facts established through empirical research.

▲ **Something of the power of his personality shows through in this photograph of Karl Marx, bourgeois and scholar (with reading glass).**
The Granger Collection, New York

treatise *Das Kapital*, the first volume of which was published in 1867. Engels, who shared Marx's exile in Britain, edited the second and third volumes, which appeared in 1885 and 1894.

Marx's Theory of History Marx wrote with verve on contemporary affairs—his essays on the revolutions of 1848 and Louis Napoleon's coup d'état are classics—but fundamentally he wanted, like so many thinkers of his time, to build a comprehensive philosophical system. Later in the century his followers would compare him with Darwin as the "discoverer" of the "law" of history: dialectical materialism. The dialectic came from Hegel and his followers. Marx kept the idea

of a dialectic as the process of historical change, but rejected Hegel's idealism—the view that the dialectic works through ideas that constitute the spirit of the age—and insisted instead that any society rests fundamentally on the organization of its economy, on its mode of production.

Political systems, Marx said, grow from these material underpinnings, and in each system the dominant social class expresses the needs, values, and interests associated with a particular mode of production. The agricultural economy of the Middle Ages required the feudal system with its particular social values and laws, upheld by the landowning aristocracy. That system produced its antithesis in the middle class. But the industrial society of capitalism, dominated by the middle class, was now producing a new antithesis embodied in the rising working class, or *proletariat*. Class conflict is the mechanism of historical progress, and the triumph of the proletariat will bring a new synthesis, a classless society.

By its own inevitable laws, history would thus lead to a new era, one similar to the future envisioned by other socialists. In the classless society, people would no longer be forced into the inequality that capitalist production requires. At present, the primary purpose of the state was to protect property and enforce inequality, but in the new era the state would wither away, unneeded. Revolutions, in this analysis, mark the arrival to power of a new class. They are, however, more than mere transfers of power. A new class brings changes in law, religion, and customs, which it then maintains in its own interest. The middle class, in Marxist terms, had represented a great, progressive force. But capitalism, despite all the ideologies and social institutions designed to shore it up, will fail through its own internal contradictions.

Marx's Analysis of Capitalism Marx's detailed analysis of capitalism took much from the classical economists (at a time when they were beginning to be outmoded). The value of a product, he insisted somewhat obscurely, comes from the value of all the labor required to produce it, all the labor necessary to transform raw materials into manufactured goods. The capitalist makes a profit by keeping part of the value added by all this labor done by others, that is, by exploiting the working class. But capitalists must compete with each other, and to do so, they are forced to lower prices, which in turn reduces profits. This reduction in profits has two effects. First, the capitalist must exploit labor more harshly, cutting wages to the minimum required for subsistence. Second, the smaller producers will fail, which will lead to larger concentrations of capital and force more and more members of the middle class into the proletariat, the class of people who have nothing but their labor to sell. Thus, a shrinking capitalist class suffering from declining profits will face a growing proletariat. Capitalism, therefore, lays the basis for socialism by depriving all but a few of property. The contradictions will be resolved when the whole system fails.

Many of Marx's specific predictions now seem wrong. Although some of the rich have grown richer, the poor are not poorer as Marx predicted. Marx simply did not see much that is central to the modern economy—ever-expanding technology, mass consumption, and the spread of ownership through public sale of stocks. He did not anticipate the social effects of literacy, popular democracy, and mass communication. Marxist psychology is inadequate, with little acknowledgment of the loyalties and the irrationality so important in human personality. He sought to combine in one system Hegel's most difficult ideas, the economic theories of liberalism, the "scientific" method of positivism, and the moral vision of socialism—a combination awkward at best. Such critical terms as *class* and *state* remained ambiguous, and the concept of class struggle, applied elastically to a single event and to centuries of history, lost its analytic force. The goal of history, according to Karl Marx, is the classless society; yet he sketched that condition only vaguely and left unanswered fundamental questions about it and about the means of obtaining it.

The Appeal of Marxism Despite such weaknesses, and the theory's every flaw has been widely broadcast, Marxism has deeply affected all modern thought, shaped the policies of all sorts of governments, and provided a core for some of the most powerful political movements of the last hundred years. Such impact requires explanation, and perhaps four points can capture something of the answer.

First, Marxism not only sees society as a whole and explains historical change but demands systematic and detailed analyses of the interrelationship among social values, institutions, politics, and economic conditions. It also suggests methods for conducting such analyses. These qualities, plus the impressive body of important Marxist studies that have resulted, account for its continuing importance in all the social sciences.

Second, Marxism accepts and indeed hails industrialization as inevitable and beneficial even while accepting most criticism of industrial society. Many reformers dreamed of green gardens and simpler days; but Marx believed that the machine can free human beings from brute labor and that it can, through greater productivity, provide well-being for all. Industrialization could be made to provide solutions to the very problems it created. Thus, Marxism has had special appeal for societies eager to modernize.

Third, the theory is rich in moral judgments without having to defend any ethical system. Although social values are considered relative, and those of his opponents are denounced as hypocritical, Marx's own rage at injustice rings out in a compelling call to generous sentiments that rejects sentimentality.

Finally, Marxism not only claims the prestige of science but offers the security of determinism. Knowing where destiny leads, Marxists can accept the uneven flow of change, confident that any defeats are temporary. Opponents are to be recognized and fought less for what they say or do than for what they represent—for their "objective" role in the structure of capitalism. Their concessions do not alter their destiny, and the Marxist is free to adopt whatever tactics will further the inevitable movement of history toward the victory of the proletariat. Just as Marx believed that small (quantitative) changes may lead to sudden qualitative ones, so Marxists can favor short-term reforms as well as revolution. The variety inherent in Marx's system has been a source of bitter division as well as strength among socialists, but it helped keep Marxism more vigorous and coherent than any other of the grand theories spawned in the nineteenth century.

Charles Darwin A more concrete and more shocking theory of human progress emerged from

▲ With self-conscious art, the photographer of an elderly Charles Darwin suggested some timeless mystery.
New York Public Library

Charles Darwin's *On the Origin of Species*, a milestone in the history of science published in 1859.[4] With sober caution, Darwin had worked much as Comte said a scientist should. Born into a well-known family of clergy and doctors with ties to many of England's leading intellectuals, Darwin had difficulty in finding a suitable career. But his respect for facts led him to collect evidence about natural history from every available source—his own observations from travel in the South Seas, the work of others, the lore of farmers. He first formulated his concept of natural selection in 1838, but not until Alfred R. Wallace indepen-

---

[4]The full title of Darwin's work suggests its broad and provocative implications: *On the Origin of Species by Natural Selection, or the Preservation of Favoured Races in the Struggle for Life.* The first edition sold out on the day of publication.

dently developed a very similar theory could Darwin be persuaded to publish his findings.

Although Darwin's presentation was the more fully and carefully developed, the parallel theories of the two men suggest how much both owed to ideas already current. Biologists had shown in impressive detail the close relationship between biological forms and their functions in supporting life. Geologists had begun to analyze the earth in terms of the effect of natural forces over thousands of years, without recourse to sudden cataclysms or divine intervention. Classical economists, especially Malthus, had stressed the importance to social development of the cruel conflict for food, which Darwin made the essential key to natural selection.

Darwinian Evolution   Darwin established that the variety of species is potentially infinite—rejecting the classical and Christian ideas of immutable forms in nature—and argued that there is an almost constant modification of species, each tested in the universal struggle for existence. He not only presented detailed evidence for evolution but described its mechanism: Only those well adapted to their environment survived to reproduce, as their progeny would. Over millions of years, through the process of natural selection, more complex or "higher" forms of life emerged, each form proliferating as its environment permitted and as competition for food and survival dictated.

This scientific theory, expressed with caution and supported by massive evidence, almost instantly became the center of controversies that raged throughout Europe for a generation. Evolution, mutable species, survival determined by brute conflict rather than divine will—each of these theories challenged established assumptions in science and theology. Nor did Darwin hide his belief that the same laws apply to the development of human beings and beasts. This seemed to many a scandalous disregard of divine providence and Christian teaching. Nowadays, most theologians and scientists generally agree that there is no necessary conflict between the concept of evolving species and Christian doctrine, but such tolerance required a differentiation between the study of natural laws and religious tradition that few in the nineteenth century were willing to make.

Huxley's Social Darwinism

"Evolution and Ethics," a much reprinted lecture that T. H. Huxley gave at Oxford in 1893, was perhaps the most famous statement of what can be called the gentle interpretation of the social implication of Darwin's theories.

"Man, the animal, in fact, has worked his way to the headship of the sentient world, and has become the superb animal which he is, in virtue of his success in the struggle for existence. The conditions having been of a certain order, man's organization has adjusted itself to them better than that of his competitors in the cosmic strife. In the case of mankind, the self-assertion, the unscrupulous seizing upon all that can be grasped, the tenacious holding of all that can be kept, which constitute the essence of the struggle for existence, have answered. For his successful progress, throughout the savage state, man has been largely indebted to those qualities which he shares with the ape and the tiger; his exceptional physical organization; his cunning, his sociability, his curiosity, and his imitativeness; his ruthless and ferocious destructiveness when his anger is roused by opposition.

"But, in proportion as men have passed from anarchy to social organization, and in proportion as civilization has grown in worth, these deeply ingrained serviceable qualities have become defects. . . . In fact, civilized man brands all these ape and tiger promptings with the name of sins, he punishes many of the acts which flow from them as crimes; and, in extreme cases, he does his best to put an end to the survival of the fittest of former days by axe and rope.

" . . . The history of civilization details the steps by which men have succeeded in building up an artificial world within the cosmos. Fragile reed as he may be, man, as Pascal says, is a thinking reed: there lies within him a fund of energy operating intelligently and so far akin to that which pervades the universe, that it is competent to influence and modify the cosmic process.

" . . . Moreover, the cosmic nature born with us and, to a large extent, necessary for our maintenance, is the outcome of millions of years of severe training, and it would be folly to imagine that a few centuries will suffice to subdue its masterfulness to purely ethical ends. Ethical nature may count upon having to reckon with a tenacious and powerful enemy as long as the world lasts. But, on the other hand, I see no limit to the extent to which intelligence and will, guided by sound principles of investigation, and organized in common effort, may modify the conditions of existence, for a period longer than that now covered by history. And much may be done to change the nature of man himself."

From Thomas H. Huxley, *Evolution and Ethics and Other Essays* (New York: D. Appleton and Company, 1916).

Social Darwinism   People eager to apply science to society quickly extended Darwin's principles to more current concerns, a tendency that came to be called *social Darwinism*. Few of the claims of social Darwinism were logically necessary extensions of Darwin's views, but reference to his grand theories added universal meaning, scientific prestige, and a new vocabulary to contemporary debate. Social Darwinists tended to ignore the unimaginably long time span in which Darwinian theory operated and to extend the formal concept of species by loose analogy to groups, classes, nations, or civilizations. An invitingly tough-minded way to reason, Social Darwinism was used to argue for opposing policies. Thomas Hux-

ley, the greatest intellectual propagandist for Darwin's theories, battled clergy who rejected human evolution as contrary to the Bible, but his conception of social Darwinism held it to be consonant with the teachings of Indian philosophy, Buddhism, ancient Greece, and Christianity (see "Huxley's Social Darwinism," above).

Some writers in Great Britain and the United States used the vocabulary of social Darwinism to argue that better education and social welfare constitute a higher stage of evolution and that an environment thus improved would produce a superior species. But Darwinism was more commonly used to justify competition in the marketplace or between nations, as the mechanism of evolution in which the fittest triumph. At its most extreme, social Darwinism presented this law of the jungle as realistic, scientific, and beneficial.

Usually not so unmodulated, the assumptions of social Darwinism nevertheless infiltrated many aspects of late nineteenth-century social thought. Ideas of genetic determinism employing (often fallacious) theories of genetics were widespread; these ideas cropped up in loose talk about national characteristics and theories that ranked races as superior or inferior, in a science of eugenics that looked for ways to discourage the unfit from breeding, in the codification of traditional views about gender in which male dominance was said to be based on innate differences between men and women, in elaborate systems for identifying criminal types by physiology, and in the emergence of inherited characteristics as a literary theme in novels and drama.

Herbert Spencer   One of the grandest statements of the laws of progress was the *Synthetic Philosophy* of Herbert Spencer, published in a series of studies that first appeared in the 1850s and continued to 1896. Spencer's ideas were closely tied to those of Comte and Darwin, and his contemporaries (especially in Great Britain and the United States) ranked him among the major philosophers of all time. Spencer's central principle, which made progress "not an accident, but a necessity," was the evolution of all things from simplicity to complexity, from homogeneity to diversity. With heavy erudition, he traced this process in physics and biology, sociology and psychology, economics and ethics. Such comprehensiveness was part of his appeal, and he applied his theses to physical matter, to human understanding, and to social institutions. He was admired for his claim to be hardheaded and practical; but while he refused to worry about the metaphysical abstractions of traditional philosophy, he maintained the assumptions of a narrow and rigid liberalism.

Spencer argued that the marketplace is the true test of the fittest, and that it must be uninhibited by state intervention even in behalf of welfare or public education. When he died in 1903, much of his work was already outmoded. Strict laissez-faire had been abandoned even by most liberals, his sort of rationalism had come under heavy attack, and the disciplines of the social sciences had

moved toward subtler theories. His confidence that universal laws of development enshrined the values of middle-class English Protestants would soon seem quaint.

The Study of Other Societies   Interest in other societies had long been a significant current in European thought, shaped by centuries of conflict with Islam and admiration for Greek and Roman civilization. Curiosity about other ways of life had increased in the age of exploration, stimulated by the reports of missionaries and the experience of trade, conquest, and rule. Subsequently, Enlightenment thinkers had observed other societies as a way to study the effects of diverse environments, customs, and political forms. Attention to Chinese or Persian civilization was a way of criticizing European societies while searching for universal patterns in human behavior.

The nineteenth-century effort to establish a science of society was enriched by increased contact with other lands as well as by liberal economic theory, the experience of industrial change, and ideas of historical evolution. Much as Darwinian ideas were influenced by economic theory and discoveries in geology, so anthropology, which now became a distinctive field of study, bore the imprint of the new work in sociology and history and of new opportunities to study the Americas and Asia. Many distinguished scholars of ancient law and of linguistics developed their methods through the study of Indian civilization. And many of the leading advocates of reform in England formed their views from the experience of governing in India.

Confident of their own place on the evolutionary scale, Europeans tended to see other societies as recapitulating their own historic development, a view that encouraged both affectionate interest and disdain for cultures considered to be stuck in a distant past. At the same time, Europeans learned from non-European civilizations, most obviously in the social sciences but in many other fields as well. Asian and later African art influenced the arts in Europe, and European medical practice adopted herbs and drugs used elsewhere. On the whole, however, these growing global connections strengthened the sense that Europe's was a distinctive civilization superior to any other.

through economic exploitation, trade, political advice, Christian missions, humanitarian opposition to slavery, and conflicts with Native Americans. In the non-Western world, this European presence tended to be disruptive, for Europeans brought technology and wealth, expansive interests, and new ideas that challenged established ways. That (often unintentional) subversion of custom and authority helped prepare the way for the explosion of imperial conquest at the end of the century.

▲ *James McNeill Whistler*
THE PRINCESS FROM THE LAND OF PORCELAIN, **1864**
Increased familiarity with Chinese and Japanese art strongly influenced Western artists interested in new styles, including the impressionists or their friend, James McNeill Whistler, who painted this portrait in 1864.
Courtesy of the Freer Gallery of Art, Smithsonian Institution, Washington, D.C. 03.91

III. Europe and the World

◆

For most of the nineteenth century, European influence on other continents came primarily through cultural, economic, and political connections rather than conquest. The energy of Europe spilled across the world but did so mainly

◆ THE APPARENT DECLINE OF COLONIAL EMPIRES

Following the American and French revolutions, most liberals truly believed that the age of empire had passed. They associated empire politically with the old regime and economically with an outmoded mercantilism.

Independence Movements in Latin America
Latin American history seemed to prove the point. In the twenty years from 1804 to 1824, France lost control of Haiti, Portugal of Brazil, and Spain of all the rest of Latin America save Cuba and Puerto Rico. Deeply affected by the examples of the French and American revolutions, the independence movements of Latin America were in turn models of the kind of nationalism and state making that would soon sweep Europe. Although subsequent conflicts among the new states of Latin America created plenty of opportunities for British and French involvement, empire was not at issue.

Independence from European rule did not eliminate Europe's cultural influence or profitable trade. Garibaldi had been hailed as the hero of two worlds in 1848 when he returned to Italy from Latin America, because it was believed he fought on both continents for the same principles of freedom and national independence. Creoles, the descendants of Europeans who now ruled Latin America, maintained and strengthened their cultural ties to Spain and France. They followed the latest continental trends in music and literature, fashion and science; shared an intellectual life close to Europe's (positivism was especially strong in Latin America); adapted constitutions modeled on that of the United States; and purchased the goods brought by English merchants.

The Middle East In the Middle East, too, Europe's liberal governments tended to favor local efforts to throw off foreign domination as the Ottoman Empire declined in power. Britain and France had ensured the independence of Greece. Later, Mohammed Ali, the Ottoman governor in Egypt, formed an alliance with France when he set out on an independent course that led Egypt to fight a war against Turkey (1832–1833, 1839, and 1841) and to conquer the Sudan. Determined to create a more modern and efficient regime, Mohammed Ali also adopted institutions like those of the Napoleonic state, established French as the language of administration in Egypt, and opened the country to other European influences. As early as 1833, Saint-Simonian engineers arrived with plans for building a canal at Suez, a project that would eventually lead to European dominance in Egypt.

◆ EUROPE'S GROWING ENGAGEMENT OVERSEAS

A dynamic deeper than national policies underlay Europeans' expanding interest in the world outside Europe. Qualities admired in nineteenth-century society—scientific curiosity, religious values, the rule of law, individual initiative, economic growth—intersected with the realities of demographic change and international rivalry to multiply connections between Europe and the rest of the world.

Explorers No longer expected to reveal civilizations previously unknown to Europe, exploration continued to have scientific and practical importance (even when its primary goal was not met: The persistent search for a northwest passage across northern Canada incidentally benefited whaling). Most expeditions explored territory their governments did not claim (in contrast to Lewis and Clark's exploration of the newly purchased Louisiana Territory) as European geologists, botanists, and cartographers scrambled over mountains and along rivers and charted the seas in more detail than ever before. Nevertheless, published statistics, lists of flora and fauna, maps,

and descriptions of local peoples constituted a kind of intellectual dominion, an element of potential power assembled in the libraries and learned societies of European capitals.

Missionaries Christian campaigns for religious revival and reform at home easily spread elsewhere as well. Campaigns against the slave trade led to British intervention in parts of East Africa and to the French creation of Libreville in the Congo as a haven for freed slaves in 1847. Liberia, where the first American black colonists arrived in 1822, became an independent state in the same year. David Livingston made his way across central Africa in the 1850s, opposing the slave trade while stimulating interest in that vast continent among traders and statesmen. Foreign missions came to be among the best organized, most prominent, and widely supported of religious activities.

Missionaries brought their European language and customs, standards of morality, and conceptions of work and leisure. Their presence in Africa attracted other Europeans, and they looked to their home governments for support. Catholic and Protestant missionaries competed for influence in Madagascar, for example, and soon the British and French governments were engaged in a parallel competition for influence there. Christian missionaries were important in Asia, too, where they had been active for centuries. Increasingly, however, when missionaries were threatened by local populations, European governments tended to intervene.

Universal Values: Law and Money Europeans considered their laws and standards of conduct to be based on universal values, applicable everywhere, much like their religion. As thousands of resolute missionaries and avid traders poured across the globe, they became more extensively involved in unfamiliar societies; they tended to insist that social relations should be regulated according to their rules. Often, local rulers, impressed by the confidence and power of these Europeans, were won over. In the Middle East, Africa, and Asia many rulers recognized that self-protection and their own ambitions required that they try to deal with European traders, seek alliances with powerful foreign nations, and adopt

▲ After elaborate ceremonies, the opening of the Suez Canal in 1869 was marked by a parade of ships, including new steamships and a sailboat with the lateen sail characteristic of the Mediterranean. Both the empress Eugénie of France and the emperor Franz-Joseph of Austria attended the ceremonies for which the khedive of Egypt commissioned Verdi to write an opera, *Aida*, first performed two years later.
Mary Evans Picture Library

some European techniques and institutions. Such policies required money, which Europeans were ready to lend. As debts mounted, payments often fell into arrears, and that became a justification for more forceful European intervention.

Efforts at modernization in Egypt led to the completion of a railway from Alexandria to Cairo and the concession to Ferdinand de Lesseps of the rights to construct the Suez Canal. Those projects also entailed Egypt's first foreign loan in 1854. A serious burden by 1863, the debt grew to be thirty times larger in the following decade. In ten years more Egypt became a British protectorate. The Bey of Tunis was so badly in debt by 1869 that he accepted international (meaning European) control of Tunisian finances, and that led to French conquest a decade later. Mexico's suspension of debt payments in 1861 prompted a joint intervention by Britain, Spain, and France, which was followed by Louis Napoleon's disastrous efforts to establish a lasting influence there. He arranged the appointment of Archduke Maximilian of Austria as emperor of Mexico, but Maximilian's

regime was soon toppled, and he was executed in 1867.

Military Intervention In general Europeans were injected into the affairs of other continents less as the result of official plans than as an effect of burgeoning commerce, the advantages of European technology, and the ambitions of individual European diplomats, military officers, and merchants. However contacts began, they could culminate in military action. The English reformers who objected to slavery also opposed the opium trade between India and China, long a source of profit for English merchants. Yet Chinese efforts to restrict that trade resulted in a conflict with Britain that ended with China's cession of Hong Kong (1841) and a grant of special rights to foreigners.

Something similar but more devastating took place as a result of the Taiping Rebellion (1850–1864). A Chinese-led millenarian movement, which incorporated elements of Christian belief, gained strength from peasant discontent and the rising resentment of foreigners. The movement grew to the point that it seemed to threaten the stability of the Chinese empire itself. When its members attacked Europeans, their governments put new pressure on a Chinese government battling for survival. In 1860 British and French forces occupied Peking and burned the summer palace in retaliation for the seizure of their envoys, and Russia took Vladivostock—that loss was recognized by China's Department of Foreign Affairs, a ministry not needed before. China also granted extraterritorial rights, trading privileges, and protection of their missionaries to Britain, the United States, France, and Russia.

Elsewhere, too, conflicts that began as local issues often resulted in the further exercise of European political power. The persecution of Christians in Cochin China brought French and Spanish forces to the scene. They occupied Saigon in 1858, the beginning of an intrusion that in twenty years saw the eastern provinces of Cochin China transformed into French Indochina. The mistreatment of American castaways in Japan prompted the arrival of an American fleet with demands that went beyond that issue to include trading rights. The treaty Japan signed with the United States in 1854 was quickly followed by similar ones with the major European nations, ending Japan's centuries-old policy of isolation.

A process was underway that led to greater European domination without requiring conscious imperial designs, and the privileges that Europeans demanded usually did not include outright control. The growing European presence, upsetting to local institutions and customs, disrupted established society. When these disruptions undermined stability and threatened some European national or legal claim, European governments responded with a show of force and increased demands. Resistance to this pressure brought more European force and a more official European role.

Direct Rule   In those places already under direct imperial rule, there was also a pattern of resistance followed by tighter control. A revolt in Java against the Dutch (1825–1830) resulted in their taking firmer charge over the entire Dutch East Indies. In Algeria, invaded by France's Bourbon monarchy just before its fall in 1830, succeeding French administrations responded to guerrilla attacks or uncooperative local leaders by expanding the area under military control until all of Algeria had been conquered. With each subsequent uprising, the French brought in more troops and established firmer boundaries (resulting in conflict with Morocco). Finally, in 1869 Algeria was placed under French civilian rule.

In India, too, Britain's well-established position led to ever greater involvements. Protecting access to India stirred British interest in Afghanistan and led to wars in Burma and the opening of Siam to European trade in 1855. Within India itself, the East India Company, under charter from the British government, had long exercised authority through local princes. But empire building was already under way during the governor-generalship of Lord William Bentinck (1828–1835), who supervised affairs more closely. Maintaining order led to border skirmishes that subsided only as British forces gained command of more territory. Campaigns against bands of *thags* (the source of the English word *thugs*) resulted in more intensive British policing.

Many in England criticized corruption within the East India Company, and reformers demanded more humanitarian policies. The result was deeper British involvement in Indian affairs.

▲ **Although many criticized their government's practices in India, the British public continued to be thrilled by dramatic tales of heroic derring-do, as in this illustration from an account of a British attack following the 1857 revolt.**
Mary Evans Picture Library

The custom of *sati* (in which a widow placed herself on her husband's funeral pyre) was banned, trade opened to merchants not connected to the company, and the production of tea and coffee encouraged. The country's first railroad was built in 1853 and a school system established the following year. Administrative reforms made officials more responsible and more intrusive, and Thomas Macaulay, historian and reformer, was commissioned to design a law code for India. It extended British influence deeper into Indian society.

This British activity, which often ran counter to traditional practices and religious beliefs, provoked resistance and the shock of rebellion in

1857. It began with a revolt among the native troops whom the British employed in northern India and spread to popular risings eventually repressed but only after terrible atrocities on both sides. In Britain, public opinion was outraged at the ungrateful Indians but also at the brutality of English officials. The upshot was more reforms intended to make British administration more efficient and responsive, further annexations of Indian territories, and the promotion of the governor-general to viceroy. The British crown had established direct sovereignty over India.

Even where the authority of one European nation was contested by other European powers, the upshot was likely to be increased European influence. That had happened when Britain and France had opposed Russia's claims against the Ottoman Empire, which led to the Crimean War (see p. 860). It happened again when Russian pressure on Afghanistan and Persia brought British counterpressure. In these regions and later in Africa, a common pattern repeated itself. To resist pressure from one European state, local leaders turned for help to another; that help brought demands for special concessions, offers of military alliances, and the lasting presence of European military and political advisers.

Migration Missionaries, traders, and soldiers were not the only ones expanding European influence. Ordinary, usually poor, Europeans carried their languages and cultures around the world in the greatest voluntary movement of peoples in human history. This wave of migration continued a century-old trend but on an unprecedented scale, facilitated by rapidly growing populations, an established pattern of migration from rural areas to cities within Europe itself, and larger boats

▼ *C. J. Staniland*
The Emigrant Ship
Staniland's painting shows English men (mainly young) and some women crowding on board ship to start a new life overseas. By this time, toward the end of the century when emigration from Europe was at its height, the ships were larger and the voyage shorter and less dangerous than it had been a generation earlier.
Bradford Art Galleries and Museum, West Yorkshire, UK/Bridgeman Art Library

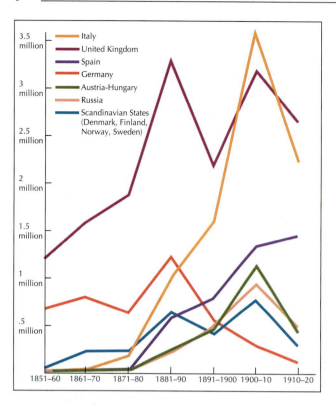

▲ **EMIGRATION FROM EUROPE**
From B. R. Mitchell, *European Historical Statistics*, 1750–1970 (Columbia University Press, 1979), p. 135.

charging cheaper fares. Unemployment in Europe, opportunities in the New World, and visions of a better life pushed Europe's poor to crowd into the steerage of ship after ship.

Between 1875 and 1914 some 26 million Europeans emigrated overseas, more than half of them to the United States, with Latin America the next most common destination. Smaller numbers sought their fortunes in Asia and Africa. More people left the United Kingdom than any other country, going to Australia, Canada, and South Africa as well as to the United States. Before 1890 the United Kingdom, the Scandinavian countries, and Germany sent migrants in highest proportion to their domestic population. After 1890 the leaders were the United Kingdom, Italy, Spain, and Portugal. Overall, the greatest exodus in proportion to population came from Ireland. But every nation except France (Europe's major receiver of immigrants) contributed significant numbers to the movement. Perhaps a third of those who left their homeland to go overseas eventually re-

turned, and they, too, added to the experiences and human networks that connected Europe to the world.

Most of these migrants were from rural areas, often members of peasant families who hoped to add to their family holdings with the money they could earn abroad. Some, like Scandinavians in the northern plains of the United States or Italians in California and parts of South America, were fortunate enough to find new land in climates similar to those they had left, where they could successfully employ farming techniques they already knew. When they could, migrants with special skills continued in the trades they knew. English and Polish miners were drawn to the coal fields of Pennsylvania and the mines of northern Michigan; Italian masons looked for work in the construction industry that flourished in expanding cities.

Cities offered the most opportunities, however, and cities are where most European migrants went, taking whatever jobs they could find, even when not in the trades they already knew as tailors, leather workers, or seamstresses. Their large numbers produced concentrations of ethnic groups that sustained much of their old culture and thereby enriched with their cuisine, music, tastes, and habits the cultural life of the places in which they settled: Eastern European Jews (escaping pogroms as well as poverty) in London and Paris as well as New York; Irish, Italians, and Eastern Europeans in cities across North America; Italians and Spaniards in South America. Because poor migrants had few political connections and most of them settled in lands not ruled from Europe, this great movement contributed little to the spread of European empire.

IV. Modern Imperialism

Quite suddenly in the last quarter of the nineteenth century, European nations asserted political authority over much of Africa and Asia. That seemed such a transformation that it came to be called the "new imperialism." Empire was not new; the change lay in the attitude toward empire and in the rapid, competitive expansion of the territories European nations claimed. Commentators then and historians since have recognized the need to explain this push for empire, and the explanations, which became a part of political debate, continue to affect our understanding of modern society.

◆ THE MEANINGS OF IMPERIALISM

Empire and, to a lesser extent, *imperialism* are terms that have been used throughout Western history, but the meanings have changed. For most of European history, ancient Rome stood as the model of empire, and that usage continued through most of the nineteenth century. Spain's empire and the British Empire were often compared to the Roman model; and Rome's grandeur was consciously evoked by the tsars of Russia, the Habsburg monarchs, and both Napoleons when they called themselves *emperors*.

Late Nineteenth-Century Usage This emphasis had shifted by the 1870s. When contemporaries spoke of imperialism then (and they spoke and wrote about it a great deal), they generally meant a European state's intervention in and continuing domination over non-European territory. The altered meaning reflected the striking new reality. In the single generation preceding World War I, European states suddenly spread their political dominion around the world. Most of the newly acquired lands had few European settlers (the primary means of exploiting local wealth in the past), and most of the new lands lay in tropical zones that Europeans had heretofore found unappealing and unhealthy. Dramatic evidence of Europe's dynamism, imperialism was justified as a necessary Darwinian struggle, as an agent of progress—carrying higher civilization and Christianity to backward lands—and as the expression of national interest. Imperialism became an ideology of expansionism, superiority based on race, international capitalist competition, and opposition to free trade.

Capitalism and Culture Since World War II, the term *imperialism* is often used to describe economic and cultural domination with or without direct political control. As such, imperialism is seen as part of the global expansion of capitalism, with Europe (mainly Western Europe and, by the end of the nineteenth century, the United States as

▲ **Bourdeax had been a major Atlantic port for centuries, but in the 1860s Éduoard Manet could still portray the harbor as a colorful clutter of fishing boats and vessels for coastal shipping.**
Buhrle Collection, Zurich, Switzerland/Bridgeman Art Library

well) its core and with the poor and distant lands of Africa, the Americas, and Asia its periphery. Modern studies of imperialism thus often focus on the unequal relations between core and periphery and trace the development of those relations with the spread of a world market, from the trade in luxuries and slaves during the seventeenth century to the multinational corporations of today.

Understood in this sense, modern European imperialism has existed over four centuries but clearly increased enormously in the nineteenth century, especially from the 1860s on. Trade expanded in value and geographical range. Wherever commerce took them, Europeans built docks and warehouses, established companies, and made new investments. Whether directed by business managers in Europe, by European settlers, or by non-European merchants in the periphery, these commercial enterprises adopted European techniques of management, accounting, and technology. Local businesses expanded by attracting European capital, and much of the profit they generated returned to European banks and investors.

These enterprises tied to foreign markets in turn transformed local economies through their purchases of local goods and services and their labor policies. This process expanded with improved communication. Steamships required better ports, more reliable and expensive provisions,

▲ By the end of the century shipping was associated with power and empire, as in this painting by Frederick Scarborough, which shows lighters ready to tend to the needs of the great steamships in the harbor of London, the world's greatest port.
Rowles Fine Art, Powis, Wales, UK/Bridgeman Art Library

and larger cargoes. Telegraph lines connected India to Europe in 1865, and a cable ran from Vladivostok to Shanghai, Hong Kong, and Singapore by 1871. By the 1880s rail lines operated on every continent; more were being built, all requiring European equipment, engineers, and investment. By the turn of the century, the automobile began to generate a demand not only for highways and bridges but also for a steady flow of petroleum, the basis for new international corporations.

Merchants and migrants, missionaries and officials, scientists and reporters continued to carry European languages, laws, and customs around the world, deeply affecting local cultures. In the second half of the nineteenth century, universities on the European model were established from Constantinople to India; students from China, Japan, India, and the Middle East became familiar figures in European and American centers of learning. These developments, which affected ordinary social life and challenged the position of traditional elites, point to the principle meaning of imperialism today as a process by which Western interests use their power to increase their wealth while disrupting and transforming non-Western societies.

◆ EXPLANATIONS OF IMPERIALISM

By the turn of the century, the opponents of imperialism had an explanation for the pervasive imperial fever.

J. A. Hobson   In 1902 J. A. Hobson, a British economist, published *Imperialism: A Study*, a critical tract that has been heavily attacked by subsequent scholars yet remains the starting point of modern analysis (see "The Interpretation of Imperialism," p. 909). Writing during the Boer War (discussed later in this chapter), Hobson was eager to show that imperialism offered little real benefit to restless Europeans or to commerce. Emigrants, he noted, preferred to go to the Americas, and Britain's trade with the European continent and the Americas was far greater and growing faster than its trade with its colonies.

Hobson found the economic explanation of imperialism to lie in the influence of speculators and financiers, a small number of people who controlled great wealth and looked for quick profits by investing outside Europe. Through their social and political connections, such people got their governments to protect their investments in undeveloped lands and made calculated use of the missionaries, soldiers, and patriotic dreamers who glorified empire. Imperialism thus stemmed from the manipulation of public opinion in the interest of certain capitalists.

V. I. Lenin   Hobson's analysis inspired the still more influential theory of V. I. Lenin. The leader of Russia's Marxist revolutionaries, Lenin provided a Marxist interpretation of a subject on which Marx had written little. In *Imperialism: The Last Stage of Capitalism* (1916), Lenin agreed with Hobson that the stimulus behind empire building was basically economic and that the essence of colonialism was exploitation. Lenin argued, however, that imperialist ventures grew not just from the policies of a few but from the very dynamics of capitalism itself.

Competition lowered profits and resulted in monopolies, forcing surplus capital to seek investments overseas. The alternative, to enlarge the domestic market by raising wages, would be uncompetitive and thus further reduce profit. Imperialism was, therefore, the last "stage" of capitalism, the product of its internal contradictions. Looking back on the outbreak of World War I, Lenin would add that imperial rivalries involved whole nations and led to wars that further hastened the end of capitalism. For many, *imperialist* became an epithet for a system considered decadent as well as immoral.

Current Views   Although influenced by these interpretations, most historians have remained uncomfortable with them. The emphasis on capitalism contributes little to an understanding of the actual process of imperial conquest, in which capitalists were often reluctant participants. It does not explain why imperialists called for political control beyond treaty rights or for the swift spread of European power into areas that offered small financial return. In fact, even British investment and trade remained much greater with other independent nations than with its own colonies. Nor do economic arguments tell us much about the role of the popular press, explorers, earnest missionaries, and ambitious soldiers in pressing hesitant politicians to back imperial conquest.

Many other factors are needed to help explain the sudden increase in the pace and importance of European imperialism in the late nineteenth century, although all analysts today would agree that economic interests, at least in the long run, played a major part. Even early in the century, the European economy had been closely tied to imports of raw materials such as cotton and timber and of commodities like tea and sugar. Policies that guaranteed those supplies were sure to win broad domestic support. A general increase in trade and the growing demand for rubber, oil, and rare metals stimulated interest in access to critical or profitable resources. Beyond these specific needs, the nineteenth-century experience of rapid economic growth made it easier to believe that new lands offered the chance to make a fortune.

Military commanders tended to favor imperial policies not only because they brought increased military budgets but also because properly placed telegraph posts and coaling stations, which enabled navies to remain far from home, acquired strategic as well as commercial importance. Nineteenth-century technology facilitated imperialism, providing the portable power of European arms and making communication with distant places easier. Dynamite lessened the difficulty of building roads, and modern medicine reduced the dangers of the tropics. Competition between nations made colonies seem more important, and competition in international commerce taught businesses to seek special protection for their colonial ventures from their home governments.

Class, Race, and Gender   Knowledge was important in another way, too, for imperialism selectively incorporated conceptions of race, civilization, the proper roles of men and women, and how society should be organized. That is why historians today often study imperialism for what it reveals about European society. In their empires, clusters of English, French, and Dutch officials and their families codified their own customs and social rules in explicit detail applied to every social encounter, from shopping to child rearing. Even when they created schools and systems of health care intended to improve the lot of natives, imperial authorities institutionalized their values and largely ignored local values and experience. European colonies tended to establish sharply defined class distinctions among themselves and to maintain elaborate racial

The Interpretation of Imperialism

◆

Debate on the interpretation of imperialism has not ceased since the publication of J. A. Hobson's Imperialism: A Study *in 1902. The work went through many editions and remains worth reading today. Hobson was a highly respected British economist and social scientist, and his study is filled with statistics and careful argument. His conclusions capture some of the essence, and polemic tone, of the case he made.*

"If Imperialism may no longer be regarded as a blind inevitable destiny, is it certain that imperial expansion as a deliberately chosen line of public policy can be stopped?

"We have seen that it is motivated, not by the interests of the nation as a whole, but by those of certain classes, who impose the policy upon the nation for their own advantage.... The essentially illicit nature of this use of the public resources of the nation to safeguard and improve private investments should be clearly recognized.

" . . . Analysis of Imperialism, with its natural supports, militarism, oligarchy, bureaucracy, protection, concentration of capital and violent trade fluctuations, has marked it out as the supreme danger of modern national States. The power of the imperialist forces within the nation to use the national resources for their private gain, by operating the instrument of the States, can only be overthrown by the establishment of a genuine democracy."

Joseph A. Schumpeter, who was born in Austria, achieved international fame with the publication of The Theory of Economic Development *in 1912, when he was twenty-nine years old. The famous essay titled "The Sociology of Imperialism," written a few years later, was an extension of his interest in economic growth under capitalism and was in part a rebuttal of economic explanations of imperialism, particularly those of Hobson and of Marxists from Lenin on. Imperialism, Schumpeter argued, was not a natural outgrowth of capitalism but rather a leftover from the precapitalist era centered in the policies of the aristocracy.*

"Here we find that we have penetrated to the historical as well as the sociological sources of modern imperialism. It does not *coincide* with nationalism and militarism, though it *fuses* with them by supporting them as it is supported by them. It too is—not only historically, but also sociologically—a heritage of the autocratic state, of its structural elements, organizational forms, interest alignments, and human attitudes, the outcome of precapitalist forces which the autocratic state has reorganized, in part by the methods of early capitalism. It would never have evolved by the 'inner logic' of capitalism itself. This is true even of mere export monopolism. It too has its sources in absolutist policy and the action habits of an essentially precapitalist environment. . . . But export monopolism, to go a step further, is not yet imperialism. And even if it had been able to arise without protective tariffs, it would never have developed into imperialism in the hands of an unwarlike bourgeoisie. If this did happen, it was only because the heritage included the war machine, to-gether with its socio-psychological aura and aggressive bent, but because a class oriented toward war maintained itself in a ruling position. This class clung to its domestic interest in war, and the pro-military interests among the bourgeoisie were able to ally themselves with it. This alliance kept alive war instincts and ideas of overlordship, male supremacy, and triumphant glory—ideas that would have otherwise long since died. It led to social conditions that, while they ultimately stem from the conditions of production, cannot be explained from capitalist production methods alone. And it often impresses its mark on present-day politics, threatening Europe with the constant danger of war.

"This diagnosis also bears the prognosis of imperialism. The precapitalist elements in our social life may still have great vitality; special circumstances in national life may revive them from time to time; but in the end the climate of the modern world must destroy them."

Hannah Arendt was an important political theorist steeped in German philosophy who came to the United States after escaping from Nazi Germany. One of her most important works was The Origins of Totalitarianism, *first published in 1951. In it she argued that the Nazi regime built on trends deeply embedded in European society, including imperialism.*

"Expansion as a permanent and supreme aim of politics is the central political idea of imperialism. Since it implies neither temporary looting nor the more lasting assimilation of conquest, it is an entirely new concept in the long history of political thought and action. The reason for this surprising originality—surprising because entirely new concepts are very rare in politics—is simply that this concept is not really political at all, but has its origin in the realm of business speculation, where expansion meant the permanent broadening of industrial production and economic transactions characteristic of the nineteenth century."

" . . . The historical truth of the matter is that race-thinking, with its roots deep in the eighteenth century, emerged simultaneously in all Western countries during the nineteenth century. Racism has been the powerful ideology of imperialistic policies since the turn of the century. It certainly has absorbed and revived all the old patterns of race opinions which, however, by themselves would hardly have been able to create or, for that matter, to degenerate into racism as a *Weltanschauung* or an ideology. In the middle of the last century race opinions were still judged by the yardstick of political reason: Tocqueville wrote to Gobineau [a French thinker who developed a theory of race in European history that was much admired in Germany] about the latter's doctrines, 'They are probably wrong and certainly pernicious.' Not until the end of the century were dignity and importance accorded to race-thinking as though it had been one of the major spiritual contributions of the Western world.

"Until the fateful days of the 'scramble for Africa,' race-thinking had been one of the many free opinions which, within the general framework of liberalism, argued and fought for each other to win the consent of public opinion. Only a few of them became full-fledged ideologies, . . . and only two have come out on top and essentially defeated all the others: the ideology which interprets history as an economic struggle of classes, and the other that interprets history as a natural fight of races."

Wolfgang Mommsen, a distinguished member of a family of famous historians, for years served as director of the German Historical Institute in London and as a professor of history at the University of Düsseldorf. His Theories of Imperialism *began as a series of lectures given at the University of Amsterdam in 1970, and it reflects the complexity and ambiguities of current interpretations.*

"The broad lines of a possible interpretation of imperialism were already laid down by such classic theorists as Hobson, Hilferding, Schumpeter and Lenin; later writers have endeavored, on the basis of these studies, to produce more differentiated models taking into account recent research and developments in the world situation. An important new light is cast by recent British research, which on the one hand has developed the idea of 'informal imperialism' and thus widened the scope of the enquiry in general, and on the other has drawn attention to the independent role of the 'periphery,' especially the indigenous ruling classes, which have often had much to do with the character, timing and direction of imperial expansion.

"It must be said that the older theories of imperialism have lost much of their usefulness because they are too Eurocentric and also tend to reduce the whole phenomenon to a single cause. A modern theory which gives due weight to the periphery, while recognizing that its so-called crises were themselves the result of informal European penetration, is better able to comprehend the phenomenon of third-world underdevelopment without necessarily subscribing to the tautologies of neo-Marxist theory. . . . The picture is rather one of statesmen who were powerless to control the self-propelled course of imperial expansion, which began with more or less informal methods and then called for the use of formal power in one case after another, often against the wishes of the politicians concerned.

" . . . On the other hand, a new theory should not, as is frequent in the Western world, content itself with regarding imperialism as a thing of the past: it must take account of the after-effects of imperialism in the world as we know it, not least the disturbing fact that the gap between rich and poor nations is growing steadily wider. Many may even develop nostalgia for the days of formal colonial rule, when the European powers were, at least in principle, responsible for developments at the periphery, whereas today they are formally relieved of the burden. But the question remains of how far these developments are rooted in the era of formal imperialism, and whether the forms of economic, cultural and political dependence which have survived the end of colonialism are not partly to blame for the 'development of underdevelopment' in many parts of the third world. Any modern theory of imperialism must face the question of how far the international capitalist system contains latent or manifest imperialist tendencies, or even whether it is manifestly imperialist."

From J. A. Hobson, *Imperialism: A Study* (1902; London: George Allen & Unwin, 1961; sixth impression of the 3rd rev. ed. of 1938), pp. 356, 358, 360; Joseph Schumpeter, *Two Essays by Joseph Schumpeter: Social Classes, Imperialism,* Heinz Norden (tr.) (Meridian Books, 1951), pp. 97–98; Hanna Arendt *The Origins of Totalitarianism* (Harcourt, Brace & World, 1966), pp. 125, 158–59; Wolfgang J. Mommsen, *Theories of Imperialism,* P. S. Fall (tr.) (London: Weidenfeld & Nicolson, 1980).

segregation. Other races, viewed as less evolved, were often said to be like children, which justified all sorts of policies as needed discipline—policies and justifications much like those used toward the lower classes at home. Natives, like the workers and peasants of Europe, were often described as ignorant, dirty, lazy, and uncooperative. Racial mixing and sexual encounters felt so threatening that harsh laws and elaborate rules of social behavior restricted every circumstance of contact and speech. Ostensibly designed to protect the purity of white women, in fact these practices made the subordination of women explicit. At the same time, Europeans often cited the higher position of women in Western society as evidence of its superiority over others (not surprisingly, the contradictions of imperial society played a part in the rising feminist movement). Cultural attitudes combined with power and fear to keep rulers separate from the people they ruled.

◆ IMPERIALISM AND EUROPEAN SOCIETY

With rare exceptions, imperialism was not the central political or social issue within European countries. Nevertheless, imperial activity drew support more broadly than from just those groups that most immediately benefited from it, and issues surrounding imperialism became part of political debate on other matters.

Social Programs   Across Europe, the role of government was expanding. Governments increasingly engaged in collecting statistics, providing for public health, building schools, and establishing welfare programs; they found it natural to undertake similar measures in their colonies. In fact, such activities were often easier to launch there on a smaller scale, and officials with colonial experience proved useful in directing them back home. Organizing hospitals in the tropics taught doctors and nurses lessons about health care in the slums. The system of courts, police, and prisons being built across Europe and in the United States (which had pioneered in creating them to rehabilitate criminals) offered useful techniques for maintaining order in the colonies.

The argument for hospitals, schools, or railroads were similar at home and abroad; criticism or praise for imperial examples became part of the debate about domestic programs and extended beyond those of the state. Britain's best-known organization in the campaign for public education was the British and Foreign Schools Society. Overcoming isolation and ignorance in the colonies was much like making good citizens in the nation. In both cases the goal was to combat local dialects, provincial outlooks, corruption, and lack of civic spirit.

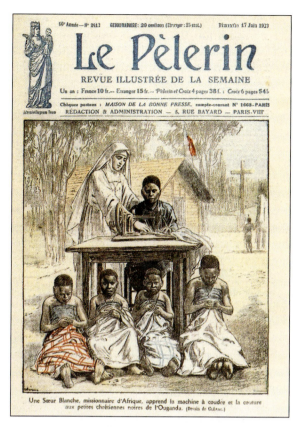

▲ This illustrated French Catholic weekly presented the popular European view of imperial influence: a saintly (and beautiful) member of the White Sisters teaches a well-behaved group of newly converted Ugandan girls to use a sewing machine. Faith, order, civilization, and technology went together. At home, too, Catholic orders emphasized the importance of teaching poor girls a useful trade.
Mary Evans Picture Library

Religion and Class Religious missions increased enormously throughout Europe in the nineteenth century. Many of the hundreds of new religious orders and missionary societies initially created in response to the social problems of industrialization also sent increasing numbers overseas to convert the heathen. For churches often at odds with the culture of their day and in conflict with the state, imperialism offered a dramatic outlet and a welcome reassurance of their importance in modern life. British, Swiss, and German missionaries were competing for souls on the Nigerian coast well before the area was targeted by any foreign office. Sermons, special collections, and Sunday

School programs allowed churches to feel themselves to be part of a dramatic and colorful extension of Christian charity and influence.

Imperial rule had particular meaning for members of the aristocracy, especially in Britain and France. In Britain the younger sons of aristocratic families had a long tradition of government and military service. With democratization and the rise of a civil service, their best chances for the experience of governing or of military command were in the empire. In France, where the Republic turned anticlerical after 1875, Catholic and monarchist nobles were largely excluded from public positions at home but could find them in the colonies. Aristocrats, after all, expected to feel distant from the people they ruled, and they were comfortable with a language of subordination applicable to both European and colonial societies.

While conservatives often used empire to argue for the necessity of inequality, labor leaders and radicals were equally quick to note parallels of another sort. They compared the treatment of strikers and radicals to the brutality of imperial repression. An effective way to protest the living conditions of workers and peasants in Wales, Scotland, southern Italy, or eastern Germany was to say they were treated like colonial subjects. On the left, imperialism was often directly attacked. Anatole France, one of France's most popular authors, told a protest meeting in 1906, "Whites do not communicate with blacks or yellow people except to enserf or massacre them. The people whom we call barbarians know us only through our own crimes."[5]

Propaganda for Empire The propaganda for empire spoke directly to nationalism and contained other ideological messages as well. Descriptions of encounters with native peoples were rich in images of Europeans mistaken for gods and of a superiority in knowledge and technology that made dominance inevitable and beneficial. They tended to equate European qualities with masculine virtues (rationality, decisiveness, dominance) and those of other societies with feminine ones (intuitive sensitivity, passivity, subordination). Like the discoveries of science, exploration and conquest

---

[5]Cited in Robert Aldrich, *Greater France: A History of French Overseas Expansion* (New York, 1996), p. 112.

were high and noble adventure; geographical societies became prominent in every European country, proudly acclaiming the association of new knowledge with increased power.

Mass-circulation newspapers, a relatively new phenomenon, gloried in imperialism, writing of adventure and wealth and of Christianity and progress in the virile language of force. Press reports made popular heroes of daring men like Henry M. Stanley, who followed the rivers of South Africa and penetrated the interior of the Congo, and Pierre de Brazza, who traveled up the Congo River, overcoming hardship and danger after dismantling a steamship so it could be carried around the rapids.

The Appeal of Imperialism Exploration was thus presented as an expression of progress, the brave adventurer as the personification of individual initiative. If the explorers also gained wealth, that completed the parable. The missionaries who risked their lives to build a chapel in the jungle and convert the heathen made for appealing stories of sacrifice, while social Darwinists could hardheadedly expound on the inevitable struggle between races and its benefits for civilization. As European societies became more bureaucratized, empire provided tales of individual action in which great risks resulted in gain, glory, and conquest.

In the face of class tensions and domestic conflict at home, colonial expansion offered all citizens a share in national glory and gain. Rudyard Kipling's poems of imperial derring-do in exotic lands hail the simple cockney soldier; whatever his lot at home, he was a ruler abroad. Imperialism, like nationalism, cut across social divisions. It aided the political resurgence of the right, especially in Great Britain and Germany, allowing conservative groups strong in the army, the Church, and the aristocracy to ally themselves with commercial interests in a program of popular appeal that promised increased employment as well as glory.

Significantly, imperialism never achieved comparable political effect in France, the nation with the second largest of the European empires. French nationalism retained ideas associated with the Revolution that often conflicted with those of imperialism, and patriots were preoccupied with

avenging the loss of Alsace and Lorraine to Germany. In addition, the right, including the soldiers and priests so central to the empire, fumbled its effort at mass appeal in the Dreyfus affair (discussed in the next chapter).

Imperialism in Britain In England, too, liberals were critical of empire. They had generally joined the call for the reform of British rule in India following the great uprisings of 1857, and that precedent made it easier in 1867 to pass the important act that gave Canada the self-governing autonomy of dominion status. Liberals rejected many of the techniques of imperial expansion, including the use of ambiguous treaties and the hasty reliance on force; William Gladstone, their leader, won the election of 1880 after campaigning against the immoral and un-Christian imperialist policies of the Conservatives. Yet a little more than a year later, the Liberal government occupied Egypt, for Gladstone could not withstand the public outcry once incidents occurred that were deemed a threat to British interests and a challenge to British honor.

The Conservatives, led by Benjamin Disraeli, embraced empire in principle as well as practice. When the debt-ridden Khedive of Egypt (who ruled autonomously although still nominally under the Ottomans) had to sell a large bloc of Suez Canal shares in 1875, Disraeli snatched the chance to get them for Britain and thus gain a voice in Egyptian affairs and counterbalance French influence there. As prime minister, Disraeli had Queen Victoria declared Empress of India in 1876, a flamboyant title that caught the popular imagination. Imperialism proved politically popular even as it began to draw the British into armed conflicts around the world.

The Boer War The most costly of these conflicts—in blood, money, and prestige—was the Boer War (1899–1902) in South Africa. Ultimately a conflict between the Dutch-speaking white farmers, called *Boers*, and the British government, its origins were complex. Britain had acquired the Cape Colony from the Dutch during the wars of the French Revolution. The Boers, who had lived in South Africa for centuries, resented Britain's organization of the Cape Colony; in the Great Trek of 1835–1837 the Boers had literally moved

▲ This engraving of 1897 typically shows Cecil Rhodes as popular hero. Leaving the Cape Town railway station, his carriage is drawn by a private army (called the Matabili boys after the Zulu warriors) through a crowd meant to depict the romance and color of empire.
The Granger Collection, New York

away, across the Orange River, where they established two (frankly racist) republics that were almost constantly at war with neighboring African peoples.

From the Cape Colony, British forces, too, were often at war, most significantly with the powerful Zulus. The situation became more explosive in the 1870s and 1880s with the discovery of diamonds and gold in the Boer republics. The rush was on. Prospectors poured in, mining companies amassed enormous wealth, railroads were hastily completed, and African blacks were forced to work for meager wages or be driven away. Ambitious Englishmen on the scene urged expanding the territory under British rule. The most notable of them was Cecil Rhodes, who had gained a near monopoly of the world's diamond production before he was thirty. He became prime minister of the Cape Colony and used his position to scheme and propagandize for a South African federation dominated by the British.

By 1890, the Boer republics were swarming with British citizens and surrounded by British colonies. Conflicts between the two groups grew more heated, and in 1899 the Boers declared war. British forces rapidly occupied the major cities of the Boer republics, but it took two years to subdue the Boers' skillful guerrilla resistance. The rest of Europe watched that slow progress with surprise and then shock as farmhouses were destroyed and homeless Boers herded together in guarded areas called concentration camps. In Great Britain, however, the Boer War produced patriotic fervor. British victory allowed the establishment a few years later, in 1910, of the Union of South Africa, a partial fulfillment of Rhodes's ambitions.

◆ CONQUESTS OF THE NEW IMPERIALISM

Despite the general popularity of imperialist ideas, few wholehearted imperialists held high political office even in Great Britain. Nevertheless, in just a few decades European nations attached vast territories in Africa and Asia to their empires.

The Process of Empire Building   Colonial conquest remained less the result of long-range schemes than of a series of decisions that appear almost accidental when viewed singly. Now, more frequently than before, individual explorers, traders, or officers—acting independently of their home governments—established claims in a given region through treaties with native leaders whose agreement was won by fear, the lure of profit, the promise of investment, or the hope of help against some nearby enemy.

Once involved, European interests proved difficult to dislodge. When enforcing contracts and maintaining order, Europeans on the scene often exceeded their instructions and then sought the backing of their governments after the fact. Anxious not to appear weak in the eyes of voters or of other powers, the governments acquiesced. Applying their own laws and practices to other cultures, Europeans were surprised when natives failed to honor Western rules, and they responded with increased force. Efforts to maintain order led to further treaties and formal institutions that transformed trading concessions and protectorates into colonies. Even those Europeans drawn to non-Western cultures by curiosity, in the name of religion, or humanitarian purposes had a disruptive effect, for they introduced alien ideas, institutions, and technology as overwhelming as sheer wealth and power. There is, in fact, a whole other history of imperialism now being written from the perspective of the indigenous peoples that shows how native political, economic, and religious organization was disrupted by the arrival of outsiders. To confident Westerners, such unstable conditions left no alternative but further European control.

The Conquest of Africa   Prior to 1875 European involvement in Africa had produced only limited territorial claims (see map 25.1)—despite the growing pressures of traders, missionaries, and officers, despite the vigorous exploration of the Congo sponsored by King Leopold II of Belgium, and despite conflicts like those between the British, Zulus, and Boers. Twenty years later, seven European states had partitioned almost the entire continent.

The Suez Canal was completed in 1869, with France and (after 1875) Britain the largest shareholders. Determined to protect their investments, the two countries established joint control over Egyptian finances. In 1882 a nationalist revolt by the Egyptian army against both the khedive and foreign influence threatened this arrangement. The British government decided to mount a show of strength (the French Parlement refused to allow France to take part), and the Royal Navy bombarded Alexandria to teach Egyptians that contracts must be honored.

In the resulting chaos, the British attempted to restore order. That quickly led to the occupation of Egypt, which remained a British protectorate until after World War II. Later, British troops joined Egyptian forces in bloody fighting in the Sudan, which added the Anglo-Egyptian Sudan to the British Empire. In Tunisia a similar pattern of increased foreign investments followed by a financial crisis and intricate diplomatic maneuverings brought about French occupation in 1881. Both events accelerated the European competition for African Empire.

Competition South of the Sahara   In sub-Saharan Africa, European nations found themselves drawn piecemeal into scores of treaties that prescribed arrangements for societies they little understood and defined boundaries in areas whose geography they barely knew. Africa had become a site of competition among European states; and European governments, even when reluctant to accept responsibility for all that their ambitious citizens did, were afraid to disown any local advantage, however gained.

The International Association for the Exploration and Civilization of Central Africa, founded in Brussels in 1876, quickly became a private operation of Leopold II. The association paid less attention to its lofty aims of furthering science and ending slavery than to the vast territorial claims it might make by sponsoring Stanley's explorations. From their outposts along the west coast, the French, English, Spaniards, and Portuguese responded with a hurried push inward into what are now Senegal and Nigeria.

Finding themselves drawn into a scramble for Africa, European states sought through diplomacy to lessen the danger that clashes in Africa could lead to war in Europe. At Berlin in 1885 they established rules for one another. The most important was that coastal settlement by a European nation would give it claim to the hinterlands beyond. Straight boundary lines drawn from haphazard coastal conquests cut across little-known indigenous cultures. They constrained the anarchy of European ambition, as did agreements allowing Germany and Italy to occupy the remaining bits of Africa not already claimed by a European state. At Berlin the powers also agreed to prohibit slavery; and five years later they banned liquor and limited arms in the zone between the Sahara and the Cape Colony. Humanitarian considerations had not been wholly forgotten, and by the turn of the century, the ruthless exploitation of the Belgian Congo was recognized to be an international scandal.

The Fashoda Crisis France's gains in West Africa were the most extensive of all, and in 1898 a group of soldiers pushed two-thirds of the way across the continent at its widest point to arrive at Fashoda, on the Nile. They got there a few days before British forces that were moving into the Sudan. Both nations considered their troops' encounter at Fashoda a matter of national honor, and imperialists plotted on maps how dominance over Africa was at stake. The French imagined holdings stretching from west to east across the continent, controlling the headwaters of the Nile. The British talked in terms of territory and maybe even a railway from the Cape of Good Hope to Cairo, a north-south axis through the continent. For weeks Great Britain and France were on the brink of war over the obscure outpost at Fashoda, which neither nation's general staff had sought. The confrontation ended when the French, facing serious political divisions at home, chose to give way.

Chronology
MAJOR MOMENTS IN THE SCRAMBLE FOR AFRICA

(compare maps 25.1 and 25.2)

1869	Suez Canal completed
1876	King Leopold's International Association for the Exploration and Civilization of Central Africa
1881	France occupies Tunisia
1882	Great Britain occupies Egypt
1885	Creation of Belgian Congo
	Berlin Conference
1895	France establishes French West Africa
1898	Fashoda Crisis
1899–1902	Boer War
1906	France and Spain divide Morocco
1910	Union of South Africa

By 1912 only Liberia and Ethiopia were formally free of European domination. The officials who bravely planted their flags and wrote out treaties for chieftains to sign set about pacifying the countryside. They established formal rule, imposed their laws, built roads, and promised wide-ranging benefits; everywhere the political, social, cultural, and religious life of Africans was submerged under a European order based on raw power used for prestige and profit, whatever its other intentions.

India India remained the jewel of the British Empire, the envy of all imperial powers. As Britain's trading partner, India stood on a par with France (only the United States ranked higher in British commerce). India's wealth and the prestige of its culture made it the very symbol of empire. Many of the leading figures of British political life made their reputations in the India service, and their techniques of administration through local lords and British courts were often proclaimed as models of enlightened rule. The British invested heavily in an efficient

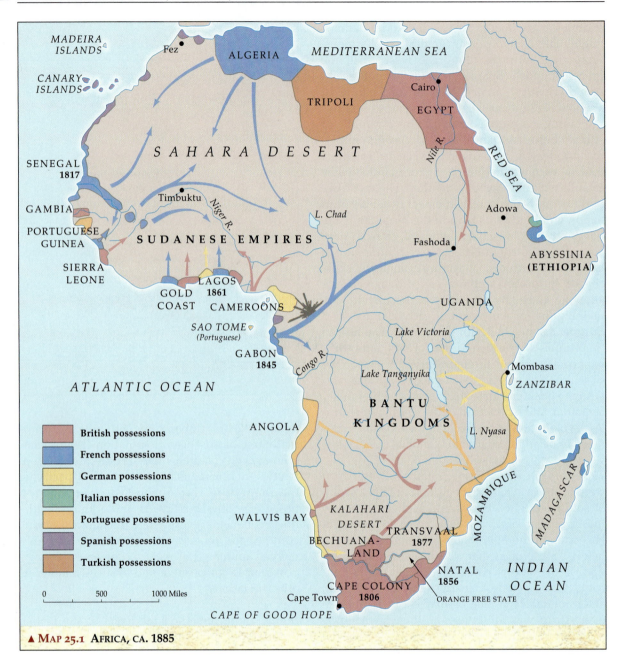

▲ **MAP 25.1** AFRICA, CA. 1885

administration and built railroads; yet the growth of trade and industry did not prevent devastating famines in the 1890s. Despite often effective efforts to win over local elites and concessions to local government, the British faced growing, organized, nationwide demands for a native voice in political life.

Southeast Asia East of India and south of China, only Siam (Thailand) preserved its independence from European control. It did so through its willingness to modernize—that is, to adopt European forms of political and economic organization—and because of the countervailing pressures from the three European powers in neighboring realms,

▲ Map 25.2 Africa, 1914

who in effect constrained one another. The Dutch were established on Java, Sumatra, and Borneo as a result of treaties with the British, who after the Napoleonic wars restored much of the territory previously in the hands of the Dutch East India Company. Revolts against the Dutch (in 1825, 1849, and 1888) resulted each time in the consoli-dation and strengthening of Dutch rule. The British annexed upper Burma in 1886 and part of Malaya in 1896 and benefited, on a northern strip of Borneo (called Sarawak), from the reign of an English rajah, who in 1841 acquired lands his de-scendants would hold until 1946.

▲ **A latecomer to African Empire, Germany shared the general sense that Europeans were bringing civilization to a primitive world, the results of which were lampooned in this German cartoon on the effects of Teutonic order in Africa.**
The Granger Collection, New York

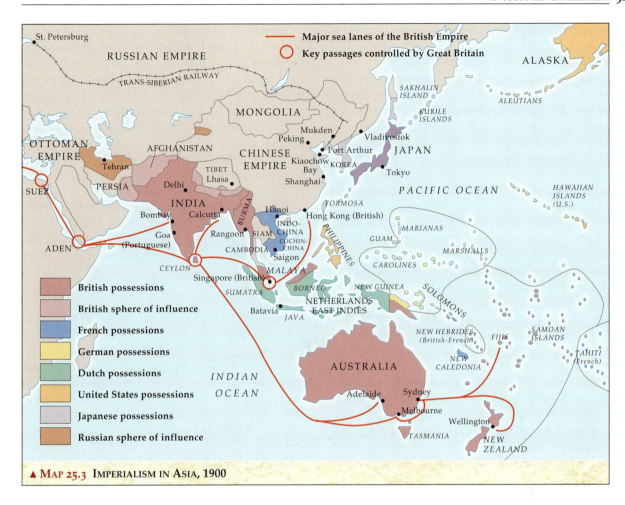

St. Petersburg

—— Major sea lanes of the British Empire
○ Key passages controlled by Great Britain

British possessions

British sphere of influence

French possessions

German possessions

Dutch possessions

United States possessions

Japanese possessions

Russian sphere of influence

▲ MAP 25.3 IMPERIALISM IN ASIA, 1900

French influence in Cambodia and Cochin China steadily increased during the 1860s despite the indifference of the governments in Paris. Whenever Christians were attacked or a trader murdered, the local commander pressed native rulers for further political concessions without waiting for instructions from home. Even the modest goal of providing territory held by the French with a secure frontier—a European conception that ignored social realities—usually led to war and the extension of French power into another ancient realm. France in this way eventually found itself at war with China in 1883; though the parliament voted down the government of Premier Jules Ferry, France's leading imperialist, the war nevertheless resulted in an enlarged French protectorate, which was reorganized in 1887 as French Indochina. By the 1890s France had begun

the kind of full-scale program to build roads and schools and headquarters that marked a well-run colony.

China The weakness of China and the strengthening of Japan were the central realities of Asian political history in the second half of the nineteenth century. Both proud nations had tried to keep intruding Europeans at a distance; both failed, but with contrasting results. Western missionaries and traders were especially disruptive in the huge Chinese Empire, its administrative system threatened by inefficiency and by provincial warlords. Thus, French gains in Indochina, the extension of Russian interests in Manchuria, the arrival of more and more missionaries, and China's further trading concessions were all part of a continuing process. Again and again, a local riot, a missionary murdered, or a contract broken would provoke military intervention from the great powers and demands for new privileges.

European governments competed in the systematic exploitation of these new opportunities. In 1898 China's inland waters were opened to foreign shipping (mainly British), and the Germans laid claim to Kiaochow Bay, as Germany and Japan entered the lists of those with claims on China. Chinese efforts to raise revenues, reform administration, and stimulate railroads required, in turn, further loans from Western nations, accompanied by further concessions to them. Another round of violence began with the rebellion in 1900–1901, known as the Boxer Rebellion after the Western nickname for one of the local militias involved. The rising resulted in the killing of more than two hundred Westerners, mainly missionaries and traders but also some diplomats. The Western powers responded with a heavy military intervention, led by Russia and Germany, which forced the Chinese government to grant further concessions and pay a large indemnity. Ironically, the only defense against European imperialism even in a great and ancient nation like China appeared to be a Westernization that deepened European influence. Chinese movements demanding reform culminated in the revolution of 1911, led by Sun Yat-sen, the establishment of a constitutional Republic, and years of further turmoil.

Japan Once Japan—which for centuries had preserved its isolation—had been pressured into permitting trade with the West and protecting foreigners, the country experienced the familiar pattern of misunderstandings, broken agreements, antiforeign feeling, and renewed Western demands. But domestic political transformation came quickly in Japan. A new generation of leaders joined with the emperor, after a brief civil war, in carrying out the Meiji Restoration (1868). An essentially feudal system that had lasted seven centuries was ended, and by the end of the century Japan had embarked on a systematic policy of adapting Western industry, technology, education, laws, and governmental institutions, including a constitutional system (much influenced by Germany's).

The resultant economic growth, efficient administration, and modern army enabled Japan, like the imperialists of the West, to attack China and win easy victories in the war of 1894–1895. Japan's gains included Formosa (Taiwan) and the control of Korea, demonstrating that successful imperialism, like the ambitions and power from which it stemmed, need not be limited to Europeans.

The United States As European powers snatched Pacific islands, the United States established a naval base at Pearl Harbor in the Hawaiian islands, and Americans invested in sugar plantations there. Soon the Hawaiian monarchy was overthrown by a group calling for annexation to the United States, and American marines were sent to protect American citizens. Congress and President Cleveland hesitated, but annexation took place in 1897 under President McKinley. A year later the Spanish-American war revealed that the United States, too, had adopted an imperialist path. The war was an overwhelming military response to a dubious incident (the sinking of the American battleship, *Maine*), and it was fanned by sensational journalism that stirred patriotic outrage with exciting tales of heroism and one-sided battles. Victory came quickly, and the United States, having gone to war in support of a Cuban revolt against Spanish rule, acquired Puerto Rico and the Philippines from Spain. The Western system of power relations encircled the globe.

SUMMARY

◆

Europe's expanding economy and growing population, its scientific discoveries, technological achievements, and social theories carried European power and influence around the world. Initially, the flow was primarily one-way: European technology, dress, etiquette, ways of doing business, wage payment, religion, and political ideas spread everywhere. Confident of their superiority, Europeans were slower to learn from non-Western cultures, but gradually they would borrow from the art, philosophy, and food of the societies so quickly overpowered. The dynamism of European civilization was changing the world and preparing the way for an explosion. Wherever they went, Europeans taught the possibility of freedom, the lure of profit, and ways of marshalling power; the people who learned those lessons were the ones most resentful of being conquered. Imperial expansion benefited from and helped to mask dangerous tensions within European society; it did not resolve them. And the tension from imperial competition between Europe's leading nations raised the specter of war.

QUESTIONS FOR FURTHER THOUGHT

◆

1. In what respects was the second industrial revolution different from previous examples of economic growth? Was its social impact equally unprecedented?

2. The demographic transition is shorthand for one of the fundamental changes in modern history. What relative weight do you give to psychological, cultural, economic, and political factors in explaining that change?

3. Is there a connection between the discoveries in the natural sciences and the prominent theories in the social sciences?

4. The impact of Western imperialism is still felt—and debated—today; but what was the impact of imperialism on European society?

RECOMMENDED READING

Sources

Darwin, Charles. A number of volumes provide good selections from Darwin's writings, which demonstrate his gifts for observation and his reflectiveness. Some eight volumes of his *Correspondence* have appeared in the new edition edited by F. Burckhardt and Sydney Smith, which began in 1985. These letters show him to have been a well-connected and self-aware intellectual.

Lugard, Frederick J. D. *The Rise of Our East Africa Empire.* 2 vols. 1893. This colorful account provides a superb example of the mixture of qualities in a dynamic English imperialist: curious and arrogant, well-intentioned and domineering.

Studies

*Avineri, Shlomo. *The Social and Political Thought of Karl Marx.* 1971. There are dozens of excellent introductions to Marx's thought; this one stands out for the clarity and freshness of its treatment.

*Barzun, Jacques. *Darwin, Marx, and Wagner.* 1958. This famous essay finds a good deal to connect three of the most famous thinkers of midcentury.

Bowler, P. *Evolution: The History of an Idea.* 1989. Combining recent work in the history of science with more general intellectual history, this book traces the various conceptions of evolution in different fields.

Burrow, J. W. *Evolution and Society: A Study in Victorian Social Thought.* 1968. A distinguished essay on the origins of anthropology and the scientific study of society in Britain.

Cameron, Rondo. *France and the Economic Development of Europe, 1800–1914.* 1961. Demonstrates the importance of capital and engineers for the economic growth of Europe and the important role played by France in the development of central and Eastern Europe.

Clark, Ronald W. *The Survival of Charles Darwin.* 1984. A detailed biography that also discusses the impact of Darwin's work.

Curtin, Philip D. *The World and the West: The European Challenge and the Overseas Response in the Age of Empire.* 2000. The impact of European imperialism is studied here in terms of the response from the rest of the world.

*Fieldhouse, D. K. *The Colonial Empires: A Comparative Study from the Eighteenth Century.* 1982. A valuable introduction to this complicated subject that combines older and newer approaches in looking at imperialism around the world.

Headrick, Daniel R. *The Tools of Empire: Technology and European Imperialism in the Nineteenth Century.* 1981. The author discusses an array of fascinating examples in arguing convincingly for the importance of technology in European domination.

*Himmelfarb, Gertrude. *Darwin and the Darwinian Revolution.* 1968. Relates Darwinian ideas to the intellectual currents of the age, not just in geology and other sciences but in liberal thought as well.

Hobsbawm, Eric. *The Age of Empire, 1875–1914.* 1987. An interesting interpretive essay emphasizing England that argues for the importance of imperialism in domestic life.

Kennedy, Paul. *The Rise of the Anglo-German Antagonism, 1860–1914.* 1980. This massive study of international relations includes economic and political factors as well as imperialism in accounting for the rising tension between the two nations.

Kiernan, V. G. *European Empires from Conquest to Collapse, 1815–1960.* 1981. A good survey of European imperial activity around the globe.

Kindelberger, Charles. *Economic Growth in France and Britain, 1851–1950.* 1964. Comparing the two economies reveals a good deal about the role of the state and social structure in the economic history of each.

*McLellan, David. *Karl Marx: His Life and Thought.* 1977. Considers the more youthful writings as well as *Das Kapital,* bringing out their essential unity.

Milward, Alan S., and S. B. Saul. *The Development of the Economies of Continental Europe, 1850–1914.* 1977. Excellent study of the second great wave of industrialization, which shows the significant difference between this later continental experience and the earlier English one.

*Mommsen, Wolfgang J. *Theories of Imperialism.* P. S. Falla (tr.). 1977. A careful assessment of the dominant approaches that argues the need for a new theory without producing it.

*Owen, Roger, and Bob Sutcliffe (eds.). *Studies in the Theory of Imperialism.* 1972. Telling essays evaluate current and older theories, while case studies treat particular historical examples; a heterogeneous collection, both Marxist and non-Marxist.

Porter, Andrew. *The Nineteenth Century.* Vol. 3 of the *Oxford History of the British Empire.* 1999. Provides a remarkably comprehensive study of the history and impact of the British Empire from just before the French Revolution to World War I.

Reddy, William M. *Money and Liberty in Modern Europe: A Critique of Historical Understanding.* 1987. A critical look at the social impact of the expansion of capitalism in England, France, and Germany, probing the nature of the inequality that resulted.

*Robinson, Ronald, John Gallegher, and Alice Denny. *Africa and the Victorians: The Climax of Imperialism.* 1961. An influential study that has affected all subsequent writing through its emphasis on the importance of the domestic history of the societies subjected to imperialist pressure and its argument for the continuity in European imperialism.

Rotberg, Robert I. *Africa and Its Explorers: Motives, Methods, and Impact.* 1970. A lively account that

incorporates modern scholarship on European imperialism.

———. *The Founder: Cecil Rhodes and the Pursuit of Power.* 1988. A biography that uses psychology and the astounding events of Rhodes's life to explain the dynamic of imperialism in Africa.

Simmel, Bernard. *The Liberal Ideal and the Demons of Empire.* 1993. A penetrating study of the contradictory relations of liberalism to empire by a leading expert on the ideas behind British imperialism.

Wiener, Martin. *English Culture and the Decline of the Industrial Spirit, 1850–1980.* 1981. Argues that English society and culture never really held the values or accepted the social practices necessary to sustain economic growth.

*Available in paperback.

▲ *Claude Monet*

GARDEN AT SAINT-ADRESSE

This early and famous painting by Claude Monet, which partakes of the Impressionists' delight in scenes of outdoor leisure and in seascapes, also conveys the calm satisfaction of middle-class life against a background of the commerce plying the English Channel that made such a lifestyle possible.

The Metropolitan Museum of Art. Purchased with special contributions and purchase funds given or bequeathed by friends of the Museum 1967. (67.241). Photograph ©1989 The Metropolitan Museum of Art

THE AGE OF PROGRESS

*T*oward the end of the nineteenth and the beginning of the twentieth century, European society entered a new, distinctly modern era. Most observers hailed it as an age of progress, marked by expanding production and trade, a rising standard of living, greater democracy, new opportunities for education and employment, and greater leisure. More people than ever lived in the growing cities, and the arts had never been more inventive or varied.

It was also a time of tension and conflict. Although millions shared in a popular commercial culture, many thoughtful people worried about lower standards and coarser public conduct. As exciting, innovative styles in the arts and letters ostentatiously rejected traditional forms as "academic," the arts fostered public questioning of where this civilization was headed. Many organized movements, both radical and religious, stepped up their attacks on this confident society, and new intellectual currents questioned the basis for that optimism.

Politics reflected other tensions. Public life was now dominated by large-scale institutions—business corporations, government agencies, political parties, labor unions, national associations, newspapers, and churches. In the long run these institutions may have encouraged accommodation and compromise; more immediately, they amplified conflicts among workers and employers, interest groups, and ideological opponents. Each country, through its own distinctive political struggles, wrestled with ways to contain and temper these conflicts. An age that would be remembered for its optimism and peaceful prosperity was also a time of division and conflict.

CHAPTER 26. THE AGE OF PROGRESS							
	Social Structure	Body Politic	Changes in the Organization of Production and in the Impact of Technology	Evolution of Family and Changing Gender Roles	War	Religion	Cultural Expression
I. THE BELLE EPOQUE	■			■			■
II. ATTACKS ON LIBERAL CIVILIZATION	■	■				■	■
III. DOMESTIC POLITICS	■	■					

I. The Belle Epoque

With a touch of nostalgia, the thirty years or so before 1914 has come to be called the *Belle Epoque*, a phrase evocative of the Paris of the 1890s, the city of lights where the Eiffel Tower was new, the grand boulevards were crowded with cafés, and great department stores propagandized for consumerism. In all the great cities of Europe, a sense of spectacle and dynamism accompanied the drearier realities of urban life. Women found better opportunities for work and education and campaigned for political rights. Most of all, perhaps, the *Belle Epoque* is remembered for achievements in the arts.

◆ POPULAR CULTURE

Men and women had carried their culture with them as they moved to cities, and the dialects, songs, and stories of rural regions continued to be heard in specific sections of the major cities. Nevertheless, traditional festivals and games, once tied to the local region, faded in importance in the face of a dynamic and commercial popular culture. Millions of Europeans came to share an urban life of public ceremonies, strolls through parks, relaxation and light entertainment. Regular leisure for the masses was part of an essentially new way of life that offered something for every taste and pocketbook.

The Business of Entertainment Folk songs about work, the life of the soldier or sailor, and young love continued to be sung but more often now by

paid singers in pubs or cafés or beer halls that featured singing and dancing. Music halls combined adaptations of opera, theater, and symphony with

▼ Department stores, like this one in Paris — a combination of theater and commercial display — were the seductive symbols of consumerism and prosperity.
©Tallandier

▲ **The street life and vaudeville of Paris provided an international model, and all Europe's great cities delighted in an urban life that provided attractions for every class.**
Christie's Images/Bridgeman Art Library

forms borrowed from the circus and vaudeville. The entertainments available in outdoor gardens (there were more than two hundred such places in London alone) and less-expensive theaters also used elements of folk and high culture.

More people could now afford to pay for entertainment, and it was an important business whose clientele included families from the lower-middle and working classes (see "G. B. Shaw Explains the Appeal of Popular Theater," p. 930). Performances designed to appeal to different social classes— revues, operettas (those by Gilbert and Sullivan are the best known), melodramas, and comedy routines (especially popular at the beach resorts now opening up to families from the lower-middle and working classes)—reached an ever larger part of the population. By the turn of the century silent motion pictures won a still greater audience.

Professional Sport Something similar happened with sport. Its roughest forms (free-for-alls and animal baiting) had been banned and were replaced by more regulated activities (the Marquis of Queensberry rules for boxing, for instance, date from 1867). Many traditional games faded away, leaving a trace in ball games like cricket, soccer, and rugby. By midcentury, these ball games had become the sports of elite English secondary schools and had earned increasing notice in the press. Then teams formed in cities (the industrial cities of Birmingham and Liverpool each had more than two hundred cricket teams by the 1890s) with players from the working classes, and the best of these teams began to be paid. Leagues were formed, and their matches became important communal events.

G. B. Shaw Explains the Appeal of Popular Theater

The famous playwright George Bernard Shaw was even better known as a drama critic. In this review published in the April 9, 1898, issue of The Saturday Review, *a prestigious general magazine, he contrasts the high culture of the theaters in London's West End, where internationally admired artists such as Sarah Bernhardt performed, with the more vaudeville-like popular theater.*

"The Britannia Theatre is in Hoxton, not far from Shoreditch Church, a neighbourhood in which the *Saturday Review* is comparatively little read. The manager, a lady, is the most famous of all London managers. . . . Over 4000 people pay nightly at her doors; and the spectacle of these thousands, serried in the vast pit and empyrean gallery, is so fascinating that the stranger who first beholds it can hardly turn away to look at the stage. Forty years ago Mrs. Sara Lane built this theatre; and she has managed it ever since. It may be no such great matter to handle a single playhouse . . . ; but Mrs. Lane is said to own the whole ward in which her theatre stands. Madam Sarah Bernhardt's diamonds fill a jewel-box: Mrs. Lane's are reputed to fill sacks.

" . . . The enthusiasm of the pit last night, with no stalls to cut it off from the performers, was frantic. There was a great throwing of flowers and confectionery on the stage; and it would happen occasionally that an artist would overlook one of these tributes, and walk off, leaving it unnoticed on the boards. Then a shriek of tearing anxiety would arise, as if the performer were wandering blindfold into a furnace or over a precipice. Every factory girl in the house would lacerate the air with a mad scream of 'Pick it up, Topsy!' 'Pick it up, Voylit!' followed by a gasp of relief, several thousand strong, when Miss

Topsy Sinden or Miss Violet Durkin would return and annex the offering. I was agreeably astonished by Miss Topsy Sinden's dancing. Thitherto it had been my miserable fate to see her come on, late in the second act of some unspeakably dreary inanity at the West End. . . . At the Brittania Miss Sinden really danced, acted, and turned out quite a charming person. I was not surprised; for the atmosphere was altogether more bracing than at the other end of the town. These poor playgoers, to whom the expenditure of half a guinea for a front seat at a theater is as outrageously and extravagantly impossible as the purchase of a deer forest in Mars is to a millionaire, have at least one excellent quality in the theatre. They are jealous *for* the dignity of the artist, not derisively covetous of his (or her) degradation. . . . Altogether, I seriously recommend those of my readers who find a pantomime once a year good for them, to go next year to the Britannia, and leave the West End to its boredoms and all the otherdoms that make it so expensively dreary."

From George Bernard Shaw, "The Drama in Hoxton," in *The Saturday Review*, April 9, 1899, reprinted in George Rowell (ed.), *Victorian Dramatic Criticism* (London: Methuen, 1971).

Professional soccer teams attracted huge, noisy, paying Sunday crowds, and the game spread across Europe. Most of the European professional teams famous today were (like the older American baseball teams) founded around the turn of the century. Their games became an important part of civic life, and teams depended on their ability to appeal to workers as well as to members of the middle class, while the upper-middle classes took to individual games like golf and tennis, which had recently adopted new sets of rules.

Britain's elite schools had emphasized athletics, believing they inculcated the "manly virtues"

of perseverance, sacrifice for the team, and playing by the rules. Sport, it was said, trained leaders (especially the sort of leaders empire required) and fostered religion, a "muscular Christianity" that was also embraced by schools in the United States, Canada, and Australia. But sports soon demonstrated the capacity to promote communal identity on a much broader civic and national scale. Athletic competition could invoke both individualism and nationalism, as it did in the modern Olympic games, established in 1896 through the efforts of Baron Pierre de Coubertin of France.

The Uses of Leisure Increased leisure was made possible by the "English week" (Sundays and half of Saturdays off) and laws restricting working hours that were adopted in most of Europe. For all the talk of manliness, the changing position of women was also fundamental to the new use of leisure. As women's opportunities to attend the theater or café concerts increased, impressarios catered to their tastes. Strolls in public parks, picnics, and boating provided occasions for young couples to be unchaperoned. So did women's participation in sports, which raised heated debates about their physical capacity as well as the propriety of their wearing more revealing athletic garb in public. Despite all the warnings and doubts, women increasingly took part in such activities; and the bicycle had a further revolutionary effect, stimulating changes in fashion and offering unprecedented freedom.

Limited hours of work (and long tram rides home) left employees with time to read newspapers, and the papers quickly discovered ways to increase their circulation. Appealing to a broader public, several newspapers now approached daily sales of a million copies. The most popular of them publicized professional sport and fostered a less literary style of writing, abandoning the tone of sober reflection on public affairs characteristic of older papers. Instead, the new kind of newspaper gave more space to sensational accounts of crime and disasters (and imperial adventures) and sought out colorful human interest features.

Like the millions of popular novels (now more specialized into romances, adventure stories especially for children, and penny thrillers), such writing candidly sought a wide audience rather than a learned one. For the first time in Western history, in the wealthier nations at least, a majority of the adult population could read and write. By the 1880s governments almost everywhere, recognizing the importance of literacy to politics and industry, had made education universal and compulsory and had reduced or eliminated school fees.

In 1850 Prussia was the only major nation in which a majority of the adult population could read and write; by 1900 more than 90 percent of the adult population of Germany, France, and Great Britain was literate, and the proportion elsewhere was climbing rapidly. Mass schooling was usually limited to a few years of the most elementary subjects, and aside from special supplementary instructions in workers' classes, night schools, and special vocational institutes, few of the poor had any opportunity for further training. Young men and, to a much lesser extent, young women from the middle class were expected to have a few years more instruction; the amount and kind of education received was one of the clearest distinctions between the middle class and those below it. Nevertheless, the schooling available to everybody would be steadily extended and access to secondary school, technical school, and university gradually increased.

◆ "THE WOMAN QUESTION"

From the 1860s on, women everywhere had begun to organize in behalf of their own, distinctive interests. While they pressed for further change, the existence of these organizations also reflected important changes already taking place in the workplace, in social attitudes, and in the educational opportunities available to women.

Women's Movements Often divided over goals and tactics, these movements tended to fall into three types. The first and largest were led by middle-class women and often reflected their experience in charitable work and education. Usually cautious in outlook, they could effectively demonstrate the contradictions between a social reality that subjected millions of women to desperate poverty and sometimes brutal conditions and a cultural ideal of female purity and motherhood. The meeting of the International Congress of the Rights of Women on the occasion of the Paris exposition of 1878 brought together representatives from twelve countries, including the United States. Women's issues were becoming a regular part of the public agenda.

By the 1880s and 1890s, this growing awareness led to a second, politically more radical type of movement, less intent upon protecting women and more explicitly concerned with equal rights. Particularly in Germany, England, and France, these movements realized that their demands required fundamental social change, and they often looked toward the traditional left for support. But they met a mixed response. Working men, who were the strength of Britain's Labour party and the continental socialist parties, feared competition from women, who were traditionally paid less. And many feminist leaders worried that to seek special laws regulating women's work would tend to preserve paternalistic attitudes and close off new opportunities.

A third response centered in the growing women's trade union movement, which was concerned primarily with the immediate problems of pay and working conditions. Employers' resistance, low pay, the nature of the jobs most working women were permitted, and a lack of sympathy from men's unions made it difficult to establish strong women's unions. When a British trade union leader declared it men's "duty as men and husbands . . . to bring about a condition of things where wives should be in their proper sphere at home," he spoke for most of his sex of every class (and quite possibly for a majority of women).

Working Women The fact remained that in the late nineteenth century most women in industrial nations worked for wages from their early teens until they married and increasingly afterward, once their children were no longer infants, as an often essential contribution to family income. The increase in the number of women workers was especially noticeable in countries in which industrialization was more recent, such as Germany, Italy, and the Scandinavian countries. The proportion of women who worked for pay was highest in France—about 40 percent. (The proportion of married women who worked was twice as high there as in England.)

Jobs remained tightly tied to gender. More women in England and Germany were employed as domestic servants than in any other field. The next most common employment for a woman was as a laundress, seamstress, chambermaid, or waitress. Only about one-fifth of working women were employed in factories, where they were usually assigned tasks associated with domestic skills. In the textile industries the proportion of women workers steadily rose to become the majority everywhere. Paid less than men in any case (from one-half to two-thirds as much for comparable work), women were less numerous in the burgeoning industries of the second industrial

▲ Middle-class women were the leaders in feminist movements, and efforts to organize women workers concentrated on industrial work; but far more women earned money in menial drudgery, like these women in a French laundry.
Edimedia, Göteborg Konstmuseum

revolution than in more stagnant ones in which pay was lower; and far more women than men did piecework, fabricating buttons or cardboard boxes in shops or at home. The garrets of every city were filled with women living in tiny rooms where they worked late into the night making hats, artificial flowers, and lace; a measure

▼ New developments like the small electric motor created new jobs for women, as in this German metal-working plant.
©Bettmann/Corbis

establishing a minimum rate for piecework in England was an unusual protection, even in 1910. Many women found jobs in the growing service sector—washing, ironing, and mending clothes—the classic employment for the young woman newly arrived in the city.

New Opportunities Some significant changes in women's employment were helpful to the women's movement generally. With the spread of elementary schooling, women slowly took over as bookkeepers, office clerks, and secretaries, occupations in which prestige, opportunities for advancement, and pay declined as they came to be women's work. Some professions also opened to women, especially nursing (primarily provided by nuns in Catholic countries) and teaching in elementary school. By the end of the century three-quarters of the elementary school teachers in England were women, as were more than half the teachers in Sweden and France and one-fifth of those in Germany.

The expanding field of social work began to pay women, often the sort of middle-class women whose earlier charitable work had pioneered in creating the field. Small shops and, more slowly, the great department stores also hired women as clerks, preferably women from the lower-middle class who were trained to speak and dress in the ways considered proper by a bourgeois clientele. A few of the famous stores provided dormitories for their women employees, although the city life of single women who supported themselves and lived alone continued to worry moralists and titillate readers of the sensational press.

Public Policy These developments, along with the women's movements and the formidable resistance to them, made "the woman question" a persistent topic of debate in newspapers, from pulpits, and in learned essays. The very awkwardness of the phrase suggested some embarrassment and confusion. Feminists found themselves combating custom and widespread attitudes as well as the prejudices of supposed experts, doctors who cited women's physical weakness and psychological instability and social Darwinists who declared that civilization required women to concentrate on their biological function. Nevertheless, dominant attitudes did begin to change.

Women's colleges were established at Oxford and Cambridge in the 1870s; and in Italy, where universities had never been closed to women, Marie Montessori's lectures at the end of the century on "the new woman" were widely hailed. Outstanding achievements by individual women (and their number was growing) in science, medicine, education, literature, art, economics, and social reform challenged stereotypes; it was far less unusual now for women to attend school beyond the elementary grades, to take part in demonstrations, and even to speak at public meetings.

As women lived longer and bore fewer children, legal and cultural constraints that assumed their lives would be circumscribed by marriage and motherhood became harder to defend. By 1910, most European nations had passed laws protecting women workers and increasing women's rights to dispose of property (France in

▼ **This advertisement in a German magazine was typical in selling not just an inexpensive means of transport but the joys of youth, style, and a new freedom for women.**
May Evans Picture Library

1884 and 1910 granted wives control of the money they earned, independent of their husbands); to share in decisions affecting their children; and to take part in civic life (the ban forbidding women to attend public political meetings in Germany was lifted in 1908). Wherever suffrage was universal for men, demands that women be allowed to vote were becoming louder.

◆ THE ARTS

The creative arts continued to flourish, benefiting from high prestige and ever larger and more sophisticated audiences. Yet the forms and styles employed grew so diverse that the arts hardly seemed to speak for a single civilization. One reason for the change (and the one most welcomed) was the trend toward national styles. The use of folk elements and distinct traditions gave an instantly recognizable national identity to English or Russian novels and French, German, or Russian music. Another reason for the variety of artistic styles was the tendency of artists to act as social critics, thereby bringing into the realm of aesthetics the issues of politics and values that troubled society. Thus, the tension between the individual and society, between the artist's personal perceptions and the unstable conventions of a world undergoing rapid change, remained a central theme of nineteenth-century art.

▼ *Auguste Renoir*
LE MOULIN DE LA GALETTE
Renoir's festive scene of the outdoor Sunday dance at *Le Moulin de la Galette,* **an outdoor café in Paris that catered to the working class and the lower-middle class as well as to artists, is characteristic of the Impressionists' interest in urban life.**
Erich Lessing/Art Resource, NY

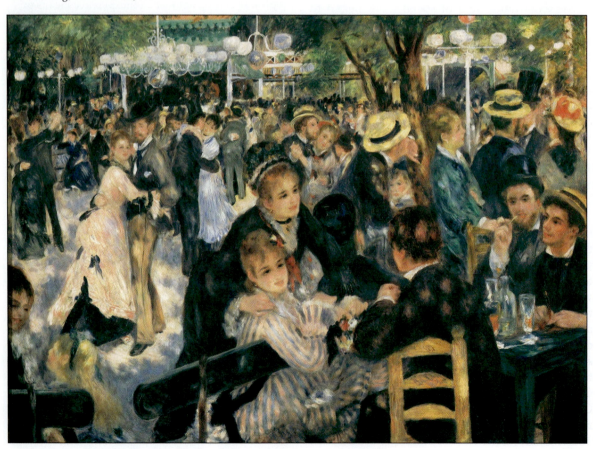

Divergent Schools   These concerns and then the reaction against them in favor of a "purer" art led to a bewildering variety of competing movements. "Naturalism," the "Pre-Raphaelites," "Impressionism," the "Decadents," "Symbolism"—such self-conscious labels for new artistic movements were frequently proclaimed with angry manifestos against previous art and present culture.

Naturalists claimed that the artist, like a scientist, should present life in objective detail after careful research. This aim was particularly suited to the novel, and Émile Zola, with his precise descriptions of industrial and Parisian life, was a master of the school. Determinism, the view that behavior was determined by social circumstance or blood inheritance, was a favorite theme in this Darwinian age. It proved especially effective on the stage, where the protagonist's destiny inexorably unfolded and gradually won new audiences to realistic drama in the plays of Henrik Ibsen of Norway, August Strindberg of Sweden, and Anton Chekov of Russia.

The realistic painters of midcentury had turned to scenes from ordinary life yet tended, like England's pre-Raphaelites (who took their name from the pious and simpler art of the early Renaissance), to believe that much of a painting's importance lay in the message it conveyed and, therefore, in its subject matter. For them, art was supposed to be uplifting.

Toward a More Subjective Art   A new generation of painters broke with this tradition to concentrate on capturing the effects of light and color, making the artist's brilliance in analyzing and re-creating such effects in itself a purpose of painting. When the academic judges of the annual Paris Salon rejected most of this new work, the government authorized a Salon des Refusés in 1863 and 1867, where the public could decide for itself (most visitors declared the judges had been right). Yet these are the painters we remember, artists who for a decade, beginning in 1874, exhibited as a group and called themselves *impressionists*. Many of them, including Edgar Degas, Auguste Renoir, Claude Monet, and the post-impressionist Paul Cézanne were recognized in their own lifetimes as ranking among the great artists of Western history. Today their works remain the most reproduced

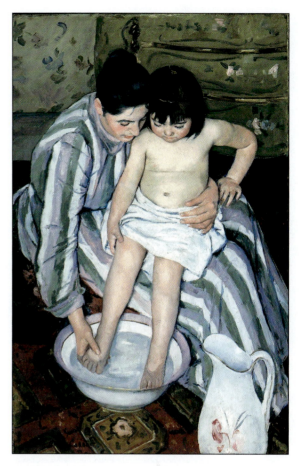

▲ *Mary Cassatt*
THE BATH
The American, Mary Cassatt, was the first woman painter to achieve recognition as a member of the impressionists. The unusual composition, which emphasizes the relationship between mother and daughter, is characteristic of the experimentation found in many impressionist works (with composition, the effects of thick paint on the surface, and strong patches of color) that pointed in directions that would be explored by the next generation of painters.
Art Institute of Chicago. Robert A. Waller Fund, 1910.2. Photograph ©1998, The Art Institute of Chicago. All Rights Reserved.

and widely enjoyed of Western art. Yet painters only slightly younger, like Paul Gauguin and Vincent van Gogh, quickly turned to still newer, more challenging, and more personal styles.

Poetry, like painting, became an increasingly private expression, often obscure, indifferent to

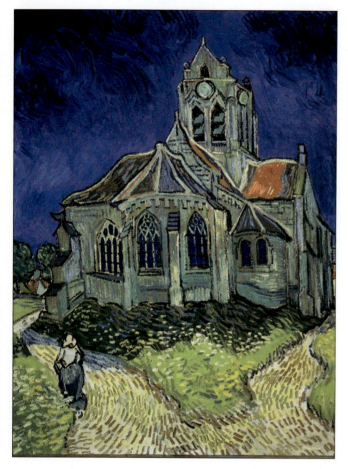

▲ *Vincent van Gogh*
Much influenced by the impressionists, Vincent van Gogh was one of the important artists to move away from their emphasis on cohesion and control in favor of vigorous strokes that made a dazzling, and often fervently mystical, personal statement. By 1890, when he painted this picture of a village church, impressionism was being superseded.
Erich Lessing / Art Resource, NY

conventional morality, and constructed according to complex aesthetic doctrines. The fashionable fascination with death, languid despair, and perfumed aestheticism was called *decadent* by its critics, a label the artists willingly accepted until that term gave way to *symbolism*. A movement of French poets that spread throughout Europe, symbolism interpreted the things one sees and describes as signs of a deeper and more spiritual reality. Art, like life itself, was to be complexly understood on several levels of meaning at once,

and individual style became a personal conquest, a private bridge between the artist's identity and external society.

Art and Society   Architecture, the most immediately social of all the arts, was the least innovative. Perhaps the theme so central to most nineteenth-century art, the tension between the individual and society, raised issues less conducive to innovation in so functional and public an art form as architecture. Even when they achieved real beauty, the great buildings of the nineteenth century were eclectically dressed in the styles of other periods. Churches evoked the spiritual coherence of the High Middle Ages; banks and public buildings expressed in stone the civic virtues of Greece and Rome. Even apartment houses usually imitated some earlier epoch, as if to make new wealth feel more secure. Only at the very end of the century were the structural and aesthetic possibilities hidden in railroad sheds, bridges, and exhibit halls developed into a new architectural style that included the skyscraper. Even as that was happening, the international style known as *art nouveau* turned its back on the practical and efficient industrial world of the turn of the century and

▼ *Edvard Munch*
DANCE OF LIFE
In Norway Edvard Munch's use of Symbolism pointed the way to German Expressionism, using color and line to convey the anxiety underlying ordinary life as in this bitter comment on the tragedy of the *Dance of Life*.
Nasjonalgalleriet, Oslo, Norway / Bridgeman Art Library

▲ *Georges de Feure*
Porcelain Vase
With playful elegance, art nouveau was even more influential in the design of household objects than in architecture. Graceful curvilinear suggestions of natural objects were echoed in the shape of vases, gates, and furniture in porcelain, metal, and wood. Georges de Feure, who made this vase, had a whole room of porcelain on display at the Paris Exposition of 1900.
The Metropolitan Museum of Art, Purchase, Edward C. Moore, Jr. Gift, 1926. (22.228.9). Photograph by Schecter Lee. Photograph ©1986 The Metropolitan Museum of Art

delighted in applying ornamental arabesques to everything from wrought iron to poster lettering and printed cloth.

In the decade preceding World War I, far more radical changes (changes that would shape the art of the twentieth century and will therefore be discussed in chapter 28) further separated the artist from the broad public. That separation, like the quality of popular entertainment and mass journalism, seemed to some commentators an ominous new threat to Western culture. For most contemporaries, however, European culture at the end of the century was characterized primarily by

an extraordinary commitment to education and to the dissemination of knowledge, encouraging evidence of progress that seemed to fit with political liberty and industrial prosperity.

II. Attacks on Liberal Civilization
◆

This prosperous Europe with its constitutional liberties could claim to be fulfilling much of liberalism's promise; yet liberalism came under a heavy critique. Many intellectuals joined with artists in expressing contempt for middle-class society. Radicals sought the end of the capitalist system, and conservatives and Christians mounted new attacks on liberal values. These attacks had their intellectual foundations in well-developed systems of thought, but they had their greatest impact in organized movements that clamored for public attention and fought for political power.

◆ WORKING-CLASS MOVEMENTS

Although Marx had done most of his work in the library of the British Museum, he and Engels intended to lead an effective social movement. Their influence grew greatly toward the end of the century, although never so complete as Marxists expected.

The First International   When in 1864 a group of English labor leaders called a small international conference in London, Marx readily agreed to attend as a representative of German workers. The International Working Men's Association, usually called the First International, was founded at that meeting, and Marx dominated it from the start. He did his best to replace traditional radical rhetoric about truth and justice with the hard language of Marxism. During the eight years the First International lasted, he gradually succeeded in expelling those who disagreed with him.

The French members were generally followers of Louis-Auguste Blanqui and Pierre Joseph Proudhon, socialists for whom Marx had little use. He dismissed the Blanquists, with their fondness for violence and dreams of conspiracy, as romantic revolutionaries; his earliest socialist writing had criticized Proudhon's plans for workers' cooperatives and his sympathy for anarchy.

Marx also antagonized the English members of the International who did not accept his emphasis on revolution or his claim that the Paris Commune of 1871 (discussed later in this chapter) was "the glorious harbinger of a new society."

Mikhail Bakunin   Marx's most important conflict, however, was with Mikhail Bakunin. A Russian anarchist, Bakunin had established himself in 1848 as one of Europe's more flamboyant revolutionaries (see "Bakunin on Why He Opposes the State," p. 939). Later sentenced to exile in Siberia, he escaped in 1861 and eventually joined the International in 1867. Bakunin respected Marx and understood his materialist philosophy, while Marx seems to have felt some of the fascination of Bakunin's personality. But Bakunin supported nationalism and praised the revolutionary spirit of countries like Italy and Spain, whereas Marx insisted that the revolutionary cause was international and most certain to triumph where industrialization was farthest advanced. The Russian's delight in conspiracies and plots seemed childish to the German expatriate, and Bakunin, who distrusted any state, found a dangerous authoritarianism in Marx and Marxism.

The 1872 meeting, at which Bakunin was expelled, was the First International's last, for Marx and Engels then let the association die. Its membership had never been large or even clearly defined. Yet it played a part in building a workers' movement by disseminating Marxism, by teaching others to view each strike or demonstration as part of a larger conflict, by stressing the international ties of workers in a period of nationalism, and by exemplifying the advantages of militant discipline. In these ways and in its intolerance of doctrinal error and its intense polemics, the First International helped set the tone of the growing socialist movement.

Socialist Parties and Trade Unions   Between 1875 and World War I, socialist parties became an important part of political life in nearly every European country. Except in Great Britain, most socialist parties were at least formally Marxist. As they began to win elections, socialists disagreed over whether to follow a more moderate policy aimed at electoral success or to adhere rigidly to the teachings of Marx. The most common compromise combined moderate policies with flaming rhetoric, and the Second International, formed in 1889 with representatives from parties and unions in every country, sought to maintain doctrinal rigor and socialist unity. The Marxist critique of liberalism and capitalism was spread through books, newspapers, and magazines; in parliamentary debate; and in every election.

Labor organizations outside Germany were not often consistently Marxist, but trade unions everywhere were class conscious, frequently tempted by anarchism, and suspicious of politics. Their

▼ The nation was shocked when an anarchist bomb exploded in the French Chamber of Deputies in 1893, shown in this illustration in *Le Petit Journal*, France's most popular newspaper.
Mary Evans Picture Library

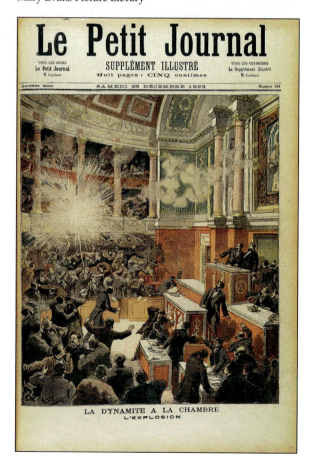

BAKUNIN ON WHY HE OPPOSES THE STATE

A professional revolutionary, Mikhail Bakunin took part in the Polish revolution of 1863 and spent most of the next six years in Italy organizing workers there. In 1870 he took part in an uprising in Lyons aimed at creating a regime like that of the Paris Commune, which he greatly admired. In the spring of 1871 he was in Geneva, where he published three lectures "To the Swiss Members of the International," part of which is given here. Always eager to present his interpretation of European history and his arguments for anarchism, he was an important figure in the International Working Men's Association until his conflicts with Marx led to his expulsion in 1872.

"This ruination and general oppression of the working masses, and partly of the bourgeois class, had for its pretext and as its acknowledged goal the grandeur, power, and magnificence of the monarchical, nobiliary, bureaucratic, and military State, a State which had usurped the place of the Church and proclaimed itself a divine institution. Accordingly, there was a State morality entirely different from, or rather wholly opposed to, the private morality of men. Private morality has an everlasting basis that is more or less recognized, understood, accepted, and achieved in every human society, insofar as it is not vitiated by religious dogmas. This basis is nothing but human respect, respect for human dignity and for the right and freedom of every human individual. To respect [these principles] is a virtue; to violate them, on the contrary, is a crime. State morality is wholly opposed to this human morality. The State presents itself to its subjects as the supreme goal. Virtue consists of serving its power and grandeur, by all means possible and impossible, even contrary to all human laws and to the good of humanity. Since everything which contributes to the power and growth of the State is good, everything contrary to them is bad, be it even the noblest and most virtuous action from the human point of view.

" . . . The contradiction lies in the very idea of the State. Because the worldwide State has never been realized, every State is a limited entity comprising a limited territory and a somewhat restricted number of subjects.

" . . . This is why we are passionate opponents both of the State and of every State. For so long as there exist States, there will be no humanity; and so long as there exist States, war and its horrible crimes and inevitable consequences, the destruction and general misery of the peoples, will never cease.

"So long as there are States, the masses of the people will be *de facto* slaves even in the most democratic republics, for they will work not with a view to their own happiness and wealth, but for the power and wealth of the State. And what is the State? People claim that it is the expression and the realization of the common good, universal rights and freedom. Well, whoever so claims is as good a liar as someone who claims that God Almighty is everyone's protector. Ever since the fantasy of a Divine Being took shape in men's imagination, God—all gods, and among them above all the God of the Christians—has always taken the part of the strong and the rich against the ignorant and impoverished masses. Through His priests, He has blessed the most revolting privileges, the basest oppressions and exploitations.

"The State is likewise nothing but the guarantor of all exploitation, to the profit of a small number of prosperous and privileged persons and to the loss of the popular masses. In order to assure the welfare, prosperity, and privileges of some, it uses everyone's collective strength and collective labor, to the detriment of everyone's human rights. In such a set-up the minority plays the role of the hammer and the majority that of the anvil."

From Mikhail Bakunin, *Mikhail Bakunin: From Out of the Dustbin: Bakunin's Basic Writings, 1869–1871*, Robert M. Cutler (tr. and ed.), (Ardis Publishers, 1985).

membership soared, with millions of workers paying dues in the industrialized countries, and the strike became the common expression of social protest. Skilled artisans, threatened by new modes of production yet strengthened by their own traditions of cooperation, often continued to be the leaders in militant action; but it was the successful organization of workers in larger factories that led to a great wave of strikes, larger, better organized, and more orderly than any that had come before.

Anarchism Most people did not distinguish clearly among the various radical movements, and newspapers were quick to associate socialists and labor leaders with the anarchist "propaganda of the deed," violent acts that made headlines. In the 1880s and 1890s, bombs were thrown into parades, cafés, and theaters in cities all over Europe. Acting on their own, individual anarchists assassinated the president of France in 1893, the prime minister of Spain in 1897, the empress of Austria in 1898, the king of Italy in 1900, and the president of the United States in 1901. Such incidents were followed by the arrest of known radicals, spectacular trials, and denunciations of leftists.

But bomb throwers and assassins were only a tiny part of the broad anarchist movement. Anarchism's intellectual tradition was continuous from the time of the French Revolution. Its most famous figure after Bakunin was Prince Peter Kropotkin, an exiled Russian aristocrat. Kropotkin was a theorist whose gentleness and compassion made him a kind of spiritual leader, but his prescriptions for what he called anarcho-communism did not unify the movement. Some anarchists stressed individualism, some pacifism, and some the abolition of private property. All rejected imposed authority and denounced the state as a repressive machine serving the interests of wealth.

They won their largest following among the poor who felt crushed by industrialization: immigrants to the United States, peasants in southern Spain, artisans and some industrial workers in Italy and France. Anarchism was an influential element in the opposition to bureaucratic centralization and to militarism. It appealed to artists and writers who shared the anarchists' contempt for bourgeois values, while it contributed heroes and martyrs to the growing mystique of the radical left.

Socialism, anarchism, and trade unions all fostered feelings of brotherhood and addressed the sense of justice and common interest that had developed within working-class life. Expressed in songs and speeches at meetings, demonstrations, and strikes, these shared values had developed over generations to be reinforced now by militant organizations but also by changes that made the conditions of labor in different industries more similar and by housing patterns that created working-class districts. One of the functions of

radical movements, then, was to sustain this solidarity by linking the immediate issues of the workplace to broad principles and to national politics. The result was a powerful challenge to the established system. Nevertheless, the left remained far from united. Different interests often divided skilled from unskilled workers, those in established trades from those employed in new industries, male from female workers, and labor unions from political parties.

◆ THE CHRISTIAN CRITIQUE

Many Protestants, especially in Great Britain and the United States, felt a natural affinity with liberalism; yet attacks on liberalism came from the pulpits of every Christian denomination. Some Protestants were drawn to a Christian socialism, and even conservative Protestant ministers excoriated the tendency to mistake selfishness for individualism, moral indifference for toleration, and materialism for progress. As official churches closely connected to the state and to governing elites, the Lutheran churches of Germany and Scandinavia, the Church of England, and the Russian Orthodox Church generally supported nationalism and the established social system. Even so, churches often found themselves opposing the growing claims of the state, especially in education and welfare, and both Protestants and Catholics engaged in social work were likely to denounce the injustices of capitalist society as forcefully as socialists did.

Roman Catholic Opposition Since the French Revolution, the Roman Catholic Church had found itself at odds with many modern trends, and it was particularly hostile to liberalism. In 1864 Pope Pius IX issued an encyclical, *Quanta Cura*, accompanied by a syllabus of "the principal errors of our time." Taken from earlier statements by the pope, its eighty items were written in the unbending tones of theological dispute. The syllabus was a list of false propositions; for example, that "it is no longer expedient that the Catholic religion should be held as the only religion of the State, to the exclusion of all other forms of worship."

Catholics more politic than the pope were quick to point out that declaring such statements not to be general truths is not the same as advocating religious intolerance, but such subtleties were easily lost. The syllabus denounced total faith in human reason, the exclusive authority of the state, and attacks on traditional rights of the Church; but its most noted proposition was the last, which declared it false to think that "the Roman Pontiff can, and ought to, reconcile himself, and come to terms with progress, liberalism and modern civilization."

The Vatican Council of 1869–1870, the first council of the Church in three hundred years, confirmed the impression of intransigence. It was a splendid demonstration of the Church's continued power, and prelates came from around the world to proclaim the dogma of papal infallibility. It declared that the pope, when speaking *ex cathedra* (that is, formally from the chair of Peter and on matters of faith and morals), is incapable of error. This belief had long been a tradition, and its elevation to dogma confirmed the trend toward increased centralization within the Church and affirmed the solidarity of Catholics in the face of new social and political dangers. Even as the council met, the outbreak of the Franco-Prussian war allowed Italy to take the city of Rome from the pope and make it the Italian capital. But throughout Europe political leaders wondered whether Catholics who now followed an infallible pope could be reliable citizens of a secular state.

Church and State The expanding role of government, especially in matters of education and welfare, made conflicts between church and state a major theme of European life. Theories of evolution, positivism, and biblical criticism put defenders of traditional beliefs on the defensive and made them seem opponents of science. Politicians, on the other hand, worried about the influence that the clergy might exercise in elections, especially in rural areas, among national minorities, and among men who had never voted before.

In the United Kingdom, the Church of England had steadily been stripped of its special privileges in moves opposed at every step by the clergy, by most peers, and by many conservatives. And religious differences continued to inflame the Irish question. As chancellor of the new German state, Bismarck launched and then abandoned attacks on the Catholic Church as his government relied more and more on the Catholic Center party. In Russia the Orthodox Church became, in effect, a department of state, used to strengthen the dominance of Russians in the multinational empire; while the Austrian government, in contrast, broke its close ties (and its concordat) with the Roman Catholic Church in an effort to lessen nationalist opposition to rule from Vienna. The conflict between church and state was most open and bitter, however, in Spain, Italy, and France, where it was the central political division of the 1880s and 1890s.

Generally, these conflicts subsided somewhat after the turn of the century. Relatively secure states, having established the breadth of their authority, tended to become more tolerant; anticlericalism came to seem outmoded as governments faced the rising challenge from the left. The churches, too, became more flexible, in the style of Pope Leo XIII (r. 1878–1903), who established an understanding with Bismarck and encouraged French Catholics to accept the Third Republic.

Social Action At the same time, Christianity displayed renewed vigor. There was a general revival of biblical and theological studies among Protestants and Catholics, marked in the Roman Catholic Church by emphasis on the theology of St. Thomas Aquinas, whose arguments for the compatibility of faith and reason brought greater clarity and confidence to Catholic positions. Christian political and social movements learned to mobilize enormous support and became more active in social work (the Protestant Salvation Army was founded in 1865). This engagement in charity, religious missions at home and overseas, education, labor unions, and hundreds of special projects not only strengthened Christian social influence but gave concreteness to the outspoken denunciations by religious leaders of immoral and unjust conditions.

In his social encyclicals, especially *Rerum Novarum*, issued in 1891, Leo XIII added a powerful voice to the rising cry for social reform. He restated Catholic belief in private property, the sanctity of the family, and the social role of religion, but he went beyond these well-known views to speak to modern industrial conditions. The Catholic Church, he wrote, recognizes the right of workers to their own organizations and to "reasonable and frugal comfort"; but the state, he warned, should not favor any single class, and society must not consider human beings as merely a means to profit.

Strongest in rural areas and with more support among women than men, Christian churches knew a lot about those who had not necessarily benefited from modern social change. The churches now made more effort to reach workers and the middle class, urban groups whose special needs had often been overlooked in the past, and they spoke more readily for those discontented groups that tended not to rely on close ties to the state. By 1910 Christianity was more respectable among intellectuals, more active in society, and more prominent in politics than it had been since the early nineteenth century. Whether of the political left or right, Protestants and Catholics found in Christian teaching a whole arsenal of complaints against liberalism and industrial capitalism.

◆ BEYOND REASON

Until World War I European political thought remained predominantly liberal, but some of its optimism was fading. Liberals themselves worried more about problems of community and social justice, and others questioned the power of human reason and argued for leadership by a small elite.

Georges Sorel and Henri Bergson The Frenchman Georges Sorel shared the growing suspicion that public opinion owed more to prejudice than to reason. Like many intellectuals, he felt contempt for middle-class society, but he argued that its overthrow would not come in the way predicted by Marx. His most important book, *Reflections on Violence* (1908), postulated rather that historic changes like the rise of Christianity and the French Revolution come about when people are inspired by some great myth beyond the test of reason. As a myth for his times, he proposed the general strike, a possibility then much discussed by European unions. Sorel thus contributed to the widespread syndicalist movement, which called on workers' organizations, or *syndicats*, to bring down bourgeois society. He rejected bourgeois rationalism in favor of violence as an expression of the will that could create powerful political movements. Like many contemporary writers in Italy and Germany, he found the energy for change in humanity's irrationality.[1]

Sorel's countryman, Henri Bergson, the most eloquent and revered philosopher of his day, expounded gentler, more abstract theories; yet he, too, pictured much that is best in human understanding as arising not from reason but intuitively from subjective and unconscious feelings. Bergson was close to contemporary movements in the arts, psychology, and religion; and he believed society needed the new spirit of energy and common endeavor that could be achieved through spontaneity. That concern to translate feeling into action led away from liberalism's emphasis on the importance of law and formal procedures.

Friedrich Nietzsche The revolutionary challenge that such ideas contained was clearest in the works of Friedrich Nietzsche. He, too, emphasized human will in a philosophy that lashed contemporary civilization on every page. His disdain for ideas of equality and democracy was balanced by his hatred of nationalism and militarism; he rejected his society not only for what it was but also for what it meant to be. The only hope for the future was the work of a few, the supermen who would drop the inhibitions of bourgeois society and the "slave morality" of Christianity. Nietzsche's tone had the violence of a man trying to bring everything crashing down, but he was no mere nihilist. He was a brilliant analyst of culture and of language, who wrote his passionate aphorisms as a man in terror for himself and his world. A deeply original thinker who would prove vastly influential for twentieth-century thought, he was a child of his times in his concern for civilization, in his emphasis on history, and above all, in his anger.

Antisemitism Like Nietzsche's philosophy, antisemitism, which he detested, was part of the rising current of opposition to liberal society. Antisemitism in the 1890s was more than a continuation of centuries-old prejudices, and it was

---

[1]Vilfredo Pareto and Sorel, both trained as engineers, are usually grouped together with Robert Michels as leading theorists of the new political "realism."

remarkably widespread. Venomous assertions of Jewish avarice and lack of patriotism were used to discredit the entire republic in France and the opponents of imperial policy in Great Britain. Sixteen deputies from antisemitic parties won seats in the German Reichstag in 1893, and Germany's prestigious Conservative party added antisemitism to its program (see "The Argument of Antisemitism," p. 944). The lord mayor of Vienna from 1895 to 1910 found antisemitism invaluable in his electoral victories, and antisemitism was an official policy of the Russian government from the terrible pogroms of 1881 on.

There is no simple explanation for a phenomenon seemingly so contrary to the major trends of the century, but scholars note that Jews were often perceived as a symbol of liberal, capitalist society. They had received their civil rights at the hands of Napoleon and in liberal revolutions, lived primarily in urban environments, and found their opportunities for advancement in the expanding professions and businesses of the nineteenth century. They were prominent leaders in many of the most venturesome enterprises, important scientific discoveries, and striking social theories. Nationalism, especially in Germany, had come to stress folk culture and race; by attacking Jews, conservatives could make the liberal, capitalist world itself seem alien to national traditions. Crude adaptations of Darwinism gave racial theories a pseudoscientific panache,[2] and indeed quack science generally flourished, for credulity was encouraged by the fact that much of academic science, especially physics, was no longer comprehensible to the layperson. Theories of conspiracy gave concrete and simple explanations for the baffling pace of social change, offering the hope that by circumscribing specific groups—and especially Jews—society could resist change itself.

For Jews, a different set of issues arose, as to whether modernizing change included a place for the practice of their faith. Late-nineteenth-century antisemitism was no mere continuation of medieval prejudices. In Germany, Austria, and France, it emerged within a new politics of mass appeal; its prominence in France was especially shocking. Restrictions against Jews were official and public in Russia and Romania and had been lifted slowly and reluctantly in Germany and Austria, but French Jews had long been recognized as equal citizens. For Theodor Herzl, who became the leading spokesperson of Zionism, the lesson was clear: Jews must have a homeland of their own, not just a place of refuge in Palestine but a national state of their own.

The Revival of the Right   Neither irrationalism nor antisemitism belongs inherently to a single political persuasion, but both were used primarily by the political right in the decades preceding World War I. Rightist movements revived notably in these years, building among those social groups that felt most harmed by the changes of the century: aristocrats, rural people, members of the lower-middle class whose status was threatened, and many Christians. Often incongruously, they defended established constitutions—the House of Lords in Britain, the concordat with the Roman Catholic Church in France, three-class voting and government independent of the Reichstag in Germany, limited suffrage and an intrusive monarchy in Italy, the authority of the tsar in Russia.

They added to this conservatism contemporary concerns about the shallowness of middle-class culture and the evils of unchecked capitalism. A reinvigorated right tried, frequently with success, to use patriotism and national strength as their battle cry, learning to make the effective mass appeal that had often eluded it in the past. They declared socialism the menace of the hour and the natural consequence of liberal error, while Marxists denounced both liberals and conservatives as defenders of reactionary capitalism.

Thus, critics from the right and the left gained by addressing the discontents that liberalism tended to ignore and by criticizing the modern changes that most people still labeled progress. So many simultaneous assaults created grave political crises in many states. How those assaults were dealt with in each country reshaped the political

---

[2] An important example is Houston Stewart Chamberlain's *The Foundation of the Nineteenth Century,* published in Germany in 1899. A Germanophile Englishman, son-in-law and intense admirer of Richard Wagner, who had become more antisemitic, Chamberlain traced all that was best in European civilization to its "Aryan" elements. The work was widely admired until the collapse of the Nazi regime.

THE ARGUMENT OF ANTISEMITISM

Antisemitism became more organized and more vocal in most European countries in the 1880s. Despite important variations of tone and tactic in each nation, certain myths and themes were common to most of these movements. In 1883 a German publication calling itself The Journal for the Universal Rally for Combatting Jewdom (Zeitschrift für die Allgemeine Vereinigung zur Bekämpfung des Judentums) *repeated many of these themes. The article was presented in the form of a petition to Chancellor Bismarck, calling for a ban on Jews holding important offices and a restriction on their immigration.*

"Wherever Christian and Jew enter into social relations, we see the Jew as master and the native-born Christian population in a servile position. The Jew takes only a vanishingly small part in the hard work of the great mass of our people; in field and workshop, in mines and on scaffolding, in swamps and canals—everywhere it is only the calloused hand of the Christian that is active. But it is above all the Jew who harvests the fruits of this labor. By far the greatest portion of capital produced by national labor is concentrated in Jewish hands. Jewish real estate keeps pace with the growth of mobile capital. Not only the proudest palaces of our cities belong to the Jewish masters (whose fathers or grandfathers crossed the borders of our fatherland as peddlers and hawkers), but the rural estate—this highly significant and conserving basis of our state structure—is falling into Jewish hands with ever greater frequency.

"Truly, in view of these conditions and because of the massive penetration of the Semitic element into all positions affording power and influence, the following question seems justified on an ethical as well as national standpoint: *what future is left our fatherland if the Semitic element is allowed to make a conquest of our home ground for another generation as it has been allowed to do in the last two decades?* If the concept of 'fatherland' is not to be stripped of its ideal content, if the idea that it was our fathers who tore this land from the wilderness and fertilized it with their blood in a thousand battles is not to be lost, if the inward connection between German custom and morality and the Christian outlook and tradition is to be maintained, then an alien tribe may never, ever rise to rule on German soil. This tribe, to whom our humane legislation extended the rights of hospitality and the rights of the native, stands further from us in thought and feeling than any other people in the entire Aryan world.

"The danger to our national way of life must naturally mount not only when the Jews succeed in not only encroaching upon the national and religious consciousness of our people by means of the *press*, but also when they succeed in obtaining state offices, the bearers of which are obliged to guard over the idealistic goods of our nation. We think above all of the professions of *teacher* and *judge*. Both were inaccessible to Jews until very recently, and both must again be closed if the concept of authority, the feeling for legality and fatherland, are not to become confused and doubted by the nation. Even now the Germanic ideals of honor, loyalty, and genuine piety begin to be displaced to make room for a cosmopolitan pseudoideal."

From Richard S. Levy (tr. and ed.), *Antisemitism in the Modern World* (D.C. Heath, 1991).

system that would guide it through the challenges ahead. Despite ominous signs of division and disaffection and major policy failures, despite giant strikes and an arms race, most observers believed that the international trend by 1910 was for governments to accept more responsibility for social justice, politics to become more democratic, and society to grow more tolerant. Overall, Europeans had never been so free to move about as they wished and say what they liked.

III. Domestic Politics

In many respects political systems were more similar at the end of the nineteenth century than they had been since before the French Revolution, and everywhere they faced some of the same issues. Yet each nation evolved its own distinctive response and its own way of balancing the pressures for continuity and change, the interests of business and agriculture, the values of old aristocracies and new elites, the claims of workers and factory owners, the demands of democracy and differences of wealth and status.

◆ COMMON PROBLEMS

There were certain issues that every political system had to deal with. One was who should participate in political life. The trend was to increase suffrage until every adult male had the right to vote, and extending that right to women had become a divisive issue in many countries by the turn of the century. Each political system also found its own ways of constraining democracy, through royal prerogatives, a conservative second chamber, or limits on what legislatures could do.

The state—the center at which political parties, economic interests, and ideologies competed—had become the focus of patriotism, a sponsor of culture, an agent of economic growth, and a source of public welfare. But its precise role in these matters was often hotly contested, especially its responsibility for social welfare (including education, housing, and public health) and its economic policies as they affected banks, commerce, and labor unions. Powerful groups such as the church, the military, or the aristocracy sought to enlist the state on their side; sometimes these competing interests could be balanced (as in tariffs that protected both industry and agriculture) or resolved through compromise (as in reforms that preserved social distinctions but expanded access to public schooling and to positions in the civil service). Often these conflicts reinforced older ideological divisions that threatened to undermine the political system itself.

Large-Scale Organizations As governments took on increased responsibilities for public health, social welfare, transportation, the post, and the telegraph, the role of government expanded. Government agencies carried out their duties by means of bureaucratic procedures within formal hierarchies. Businesses tended to become bigger and more bureaucratic; often a few large companies dominated whole national industries from steel and shipping to retail sales. Smaller firms thus tended to organize in associations that could

represent their interests in dealings with government and with other interest groups.

Workers, too, were increasingly organized in national trade unions that negotiated for particular industries. In every industrial country from the 1880s on, there were great strikes in which the two well-organized sides battled while competing for political protection and public support. Political parties also tended to adopt some form of national organization and a permanent staff, especially where universal male suffrage made such efforts worthwhile. And the German Social Democratic party, with its Marxist program, national organization, and thousands of local centers for recreation and instruction, was the most impressive example of all.

Professional associations set standards, lobbied governments, and conferred prestige on the physicians, lawyers, engineers, and teachers that belonged to them. Like political parties, associations offered a means whereby scattered groups and new interests could make their presence felt in public life. This institutionalization of society was in many respects a source of stability, providing rapidly expanding activities with norms, internal discipline, and a means for negotiating conflicts. But the very size of these organizations amplified their disagreements and encouraged intransigence as a means for keeping followers in line, deepening social divisions.

Not surprisingly, nearly every country struggled with the very definition of national community and whether some groups—ethnic minorities, foreigners, Catholics, Jews, anarchists, or socialists—should be excluded as alien or of uncertain loyalty. Identifying such groups, which evoked extreme patriotism and aroused passionate fears, could become extremely disruptive; and the way each society responded to this challenge became an important measure of its political system. Peaceful resolutions were possible: When Norway voted for separation from Sweden in 1905, the decision was accepted on both sides, and the two nations lived thereafter in harmony, among the most democratic in the world. In this period comparative politics became a formal academic subject, in part because the similarities among European political systems made their differences more revealing.

◆ FRANCE: THE THIRD REPUBLIC

In France political conflict revolved around the form of government following the fall of the Second Empire.

Monarchy or Republic Shortly after Louis Napoleon surrendered in the Franco-Prussian War of 1870, Parisian crowds cheered the proclamation of a republic, and new leaders sought to mobilize the nation as an earlier republic had done in 1792. German forces quickly surrounded Paris, but Léon Gambetta, the most dynamic of the republicans, made a daring escape, flying off in a balloon to set up headquarters and organize resistance outside the capital. French forces, strengthened by newly recruited peasants, even made some gains until, overmatched, they were pushed back in December.

Paris remained under German siege. Refusing to surrender, its citizens held out for four months. They cut down the trees of the boulevards for fuel, slaughtered pets, and emptied the zoo as a starving city continued to resist during a winter as severe as any on record. But heroism and patriotic fervor could not defeat a modern army, and at the end of January Paris capitulated. German troops marched into a denuded and quiet city.

France's newly elected assembly met at Versailles and quickly accepted peace on German terms. The assembly, divided between monarchists (elected as proponents of peace) and republicans, could not agree, however, on the form of government. It compromised by naming Adolphe Thiers, a moderate politician who had been prominent in the July Monarchy thirty years earlier, as chief of the "Executive Power," thereby postponing the issue of whether France was to have a king or a president.

The Paris Commune Thiers knew that his government must establish control of Paris, which had been cut off from the rest of France. As a first step, he decided to disarm the city's National Guard. When troops from Versailles tried to remove some cannons, however, they were confronted by an angry crowd. Shots were fired; by day's end, two generals lay dead. Faced with insurrection, Thiers withdrew his army, determined first to isolate the revolution and then to crush it.

▲ Scenes of the Paris Commune and the destruction that resulted were in great demand afterward. One dramatic moment was the execution of Generals Clément-Thomas and Lecomte by the communards on March 18, 1871. That scene was reconstructed a few months later in this composite photograph. Created for its commercial possibilities (in books and on postcards, for example), the image echoed traditional scenes of comparable historical episodes.
Roger-Viollet/Getty Images

The municipal council of Paris, in another echo of the French Revolution of 1789, declared the city a self-governing commune and prepared to fight. While German armies idly watched, the French engaged in civil war.

Many of the well-to-do had left Paris during the armistice, but the poor and the radical remained. Hardened by months of siege, their resentments mounted as the government at Versailles stopped payments to the National Guard, the only income for many Parisians, and suddenly ended the moratorium on the payment of personal debts (including rents) that had been in effect while Paris was under siege. The Paris Commune included moderate and radical republicans, some followers of Pierre Joseph Proudhon and Louis-Auguste Blanqui, militant socialists in the tradition of Saint-Simon and Fourier, and a few members of the Marxist First International. Its program, favoring democracy and federalism, was not very specific on other matters, and it had little time to experiment.

Civil War The conservative assembly in Versailles sent its armies to assault the Paris Commune, and the mutual hatred in this civil war was exacerbated by the recent anguish of siege and defeat as well as by the long-standing differences, ideological and social, between rural France and the capital. The two camps fought for competing visions of what the nation should become, and they fought with rising fury. On both sides hostages were taken and prisoners shot (the communards executed the archbishop of Paris), and it took almost two months of bloodshed before government troops broke into the city in May.

Even then the fighting continued, barricade by barricade, into the working-class quarters, where the group commanded by Louise Michel was among the last to fall. The most famous of hundreds of militant *citoyennes,* she would later tell her captors, "I belong entirely to the Social Revolution." Solid citizens shuddered at revolutionary excess (and especially at the part played by women), but on the whole, the victors were more brutal. Tens of thousands of Parisians died in the streets, and summary courts-martial ordered execution, imprisonment, or deportation for tens of thousands more.

Throughout Europe, the commune raised the specter of revolution. From the first, Marxists hailed it as a proletarian rising, the dawning of a new era, though Marx was indignant with the communard's lack of revolutionary daring and their respect for property and legality. Former communards became the heroes of socialist gatherings for the next generation, and to this day the cemetery where many of them were executed remains a shrine honored by socialists and communists.[3] Historians have been at great pains to show how little socialism, still less Marxism, there was in the Paris Commune (it respectfully left the Bank of Paris intact); yet myth has its historical importance, too. This indisputably was class conflict, and the rage on both sides was more significant than mere differences of program. After 1871

a proletarian revolution became a credible possibility to radical and conservative alike, and working-class movements across Europe pointed to the martyrs of the Commune as evidence of the selfish cruelty of bourgeois rule.

The Founding of the Third Republic Remarkably, a stable republic gradually emerged from this unpromising beginning. The administrative structure of the French state remained, stronger than any political group, and Thiers used it effectively. The loan needed to pay the indemnity to Germany was soon oversubscribed. As elections produced victories for moderate republicans, monarchists feared that their chance was slipping away. They ousted Thiers, put a monarchist in his place, and looked for a chance to restore the monarchy. They never found it.

The monarchists themselves were divided between the conservative supporters of the grandson of Charles X and those who favored the grandson of Louis Philippe. The two factions differed on issues of democracy, social policy, relations with the Church, and even symbolism (the more conservative claimant refused to accept the tricolor, the flag of French patriotism, because it was the flag of revolution). Meanwhile, moderate republicans continued to gain in popularity, and in 1875 the assembly passed a law declaring that "the president of the republic" should be elected by the two legislative houses. The Third Republic was thus quietly established, without ringing phrases, as the government that, as Thiers put it, divided Frenchmen least.

There was a Chamber of Deputies, elected by direct universal male suffrage, and a Senate, indirectly elected by local officials. In elections the following year, republicans captured two-thirds of the seats in the Chamber and almost half those in the Senate. The presidency, which had been so strong under Thiers, was still in monarchist hands, but its authority continued to decline. That established a further precedent: The Republic would have a weak executive. Made acceptable by having crushed the Commune and by having a conservative Senate, this republic was a regime of compromise; it would last longer than any French regime since 1789.

Successive republican governments guaranteed political freedom and deferred to the middle

---

[3] A century later a Russian sputnik proudly carried to the moon not only a Soviet flag but a red flag from the Commune of 1871.

class while France's public institutions preserved the remarkable administrative continuity that had characterized them since 1800. Economic growth, less dramatic than in Great Britain or Germany, was also less disruptive. France had found its own balance between the demands for order and the need for change.

Conflicts and Crises For twenty years, from 1879 to 1899, the leading politicians were moderate republicans who found in lack of daring the best guarantee of stability and in anticlericalism their most popular plank. Strong defenders of free speech and individualism, they recognized unions but initiated few projects of public works or social welfare. They made elementary education in state schools compulsory and established restrictions on the Catholic Church that were intended to weaken its political influence, policies that carried the parliamentary conflicts between left and right into the villages of France.

In 1889 General Georges Boulanger gained the popularity that the republic's more cautious leaders lacked through speeches expressing concern for workers and patriotic denunciation of Germany. There was danger that Boulanger would attempt a coup d'état. Even after that danger had passed, scandals threatened the republic's stability. Companies planning a canal through Panama went bankrupt, and investigations uncovered political graft. There followed a stormy campaign against republican politicians, liberal newspapers, and Jewish financiers. Only when the regime seemed close to toppling did its defenders pull together.

The Dreyfus Affair The Third Republic's great trial came with the Dreyfus case. In 1894 a court-martial convicted Captain Alfred Dreyfus, a Jew and a member of the General Staff, of providing the German military attaché with secret French documents. Although the sensational press shouted Jewish treachery, the issue only became the center of public attention three years afterward, when evidence appeared implicating another officer as the guilty party.

The army's principal officers, refusing to reopen the case, spoke darkly of honor and state secrets, and the right-wing press hailed their patriotism. The controversy escalated with charges

and countercharges in parliament and the press, a series of sensational trials, and huge public demonstrations. The nation was divided. The majority of Catholics, monarchists, and conservatives joined in patriotic indignation against Jews and socialists who were allegedly conspiring to sell out France and weaken a loyal army. The left—intellectuals, socialists, and republicans—came to view Dreyfus as the innocent victim of a plot against republican institutions.

Figures like the novelist Émile Zola, who was twice convicted of libel for his efforts, led in demanding a new trial. The military courts, however, were reluctant to admit past mistakes. A court-martial in 1898 instead acquitted the man who forged the principal evidence against Dreyfus and a year later it convicted Dreyfus a second time but "with extenuating circumstances," a confusing ruling that led to a presidential pardon. The defenders of Dreyfus won the battle for public opinion, though barely,[4] and that victory set the tone of subsequent French politics, cementing traditions of republican unity on the left and greatly reducing the political influence of the Church and monarchists. Years of polemics and confrontation, however, left deep scars.

A Stable Republic From 1900 until World War I, government was in the hands of firm republicans who, despite their cautious position on social issues, called themselves the Radical party. They set

---

[4]A few Dreyfusards continued collecting evidence and finally won acquittal in a civil trial in 1906. Dreyfus was then decorated and promoted to the rank of major.

about purging the army of the most outspoken opponents of the republic, and they launched new attacks on the Church that subsided only with the passage of a law separating church and state in 1905. Yet they administered with restraint. Solicitous of the "little man," of small businesses and peasant farmers, they solidified support for the republic. Indeed, part of the Third Republic's achievement was its ability to draw radical politicians to moderate policies. A socialist even entered the cabinet in the aftermath of the Dreyfus affair (thereby earning the condemnation of the Second International for cooperating in a bourgeois state). The prime minister from 1906 to 1909

was Georges Clemenceau, a man once considered a militant leftist, who now shrewdly combined policies of reform and conciliation. The trade union movement doubled its membership, but frequent strikes never culminated in the revolutionary general strike so much talked about. On the eve of world war, France, prosperous and stable, appeared to have surmounted its most dangerous divisions.

◆ GERMANY: THE REICH

Bismarck had given Germany a constitution that established representative institutions but left power in the hands of a conservative monarchy, and throughout its history the Reich would be haunted by the question of whether this awkward system could hold together or must veer sharply toward autocracy or democracy. Until 1890 Bismarck dominated German public life with an authority few modern figures have equaled. Scornful of criticism, he won many enemies but remained untouchable until William II ascended the throne in 1888. Twenty-nine years old, bright but ill-prepared, William was infatuated with all things military, anxious to make himself loved, and eager to rule. He disagreed with parts of Bismarck's foreign policy and opposed the antisocialist laws, but theirs was primarily a conflict of wills. In 1890 the emperor, impatient with Bismarck's paternal arrogance, forced his resignation.

The Army and the Conservative Leagues Bismarck's policies had allowed for great concentrations of political and economic power in a rapidly expanding society, one in which court, army, bureaucracy, and business were treated as semiautonomous interests. Holding the system together while balancing the demands of parliament and public opinion was the growing challenge Bismarck's successors faced. They sometimes tried to match his dazzling foreign policy, and they followed him in attending to the army. Bismarck had won a sizable electoral victory in 1887 on the issue of enlarging the army over the parliament's objections, and military appropriations were a source of intense conflicts between right and left again in 1893, 1898, and 1911–1913; each time the army grew larger, the government's statements became more nationalist, and society seemed more divided.

Germany's conservatives had also learned from Bismarck the value of appealing to the public, and they did so through the strident propaganda of political leagues—the Landlords', Peasants', Pan-German, Colonial, and Naval Leagues—organized in the 1890s. Well-financed by Prussian Junkers and some industrialists, these leagues campaigned for high tariffs, overseas empire, and the military, with attacks on socialists, Jews, and foreign enemies. As pressure groups, they won significant victories, including the naval bill of 1898, which proposed to create a fleet that could compete with Britain's. In addition to building railroads, roads, and schools, the government extended the comprehensive social welfare programs begun under Bismarck, and William II was hailed as "the Labor Emperor" for supporting social security, labor arbitration, the regulation of workers' hours, and provisions for their safety.

The Social Democrats But Bismarck's hope that such measures would weaken the socialists was not realized. The well-organized Social Democrats

◄ **At a mine entrance in the Ruhr in 1912, striking German mine workers read an official proclamation warning that the police are authorized to shoot.**
Ullstein Bilderdienst

continued to gain in the 1890s, and they became the largest party in the Reichstag in 1912 (and the strongest socialist party in Europe) despite the distortions of the electoral system. Socialists also dominated Germany's vigorous labor unions, which had 2.5 million members by 1912, and the Social Democratic party sustained an influential subculture that had its own newspapers, libraries, and recreation centers.

In theory, at least, the Social Democrats remained firm revolutionaries, formally rejecting the revisionism of Eduard Bernstein, who in his book *Evolutionary Socialism* (1897), argued for less emphasis on economic determinism or revolution and a greater focus instead on improving working conditions and strengthening democracy. The subject of international debate, Bernstein's criticism of Marx and his alternative theory implied a less militant socialism willing to cooperate with other democratic parties, and it was an important moment in the history of socialism when Germany's powerful Social Democrats chose instead to make a rigorous Marxism their official policy.

An angry rigidity had developed in Germany's politics. The last peacetime chancellor (and the first of bourgeois origin), Theobald von Bethmann-Hollweg took office in 1909. A cautious bureaucrat who presided over a government rife with cabals, he tried to placate parliament and hold in check a royal court in which people spoke openly of using the army against radicals. Bethmann-Hollweg's mild programs for political reform came to nothing. The continent's most powerful nation remained dominated by Prussia, where voting continued to be by the three-class system, and Germany's chancellor remained responsible to the crown and not to the Reichstag.

◆ ITALY: THE LIBERAL MONARCHY

Italy's liberal monarchy was committed to modernizing the nation while balancing the budget and steadily sponsoring modest reforms, but the political system in which only the well-to-do could vote and in which the government kept its parliamentary majority by means of political favors made it hard to win broad popular support.

The Crisis of the 1890s　As a hero of Italian unification and former radical, Francesco Crispi, prime minister in the late 1880s and 1890s, tried to change that. His policies—which included anti-clericalism, a trade war with France, and imperial adventure—proved divisive instead. To end a protest movement among Sicilian peasants, Crispi resorted to martial law, and in 1894, he launched an invasion of Ethiopia to establish an Italian protectorate there. Two years later, he had to resign when 25,000 Italian troops were nearly wiped out at Aduwa by well-prepared Ethiopian forces four times their number.[5]

Domestic unrest increased both in the poverty-stricken agrarian south and in the rapidly industrializing north, where anarchist bombs, socialist demonstrations, and waves of strikes culminated in riots that reached revolutionary scale in Milan in 1898. The government restored order but at the cost of bloodshed, the suppression of scores of newspapers, and a ban on hundreds of socialist, republican, and Catholic organizations. Many conservatives argued for still firmer measures; yet the Chamber of Deputies, although frightened, refused further restriction of civil liberties, a stand supported in the elections of 1900. In Italy, as in France at the same time, the political campaign of a revitalized right was defeated by parliament and public opinion.

Limited Liberalism　The political system acquired a broader base of support under Giovanni Giolitti, prime minister from 1903 to 1914. He acknowledged the right to strike, nationalized railroads and life insurance, sponsored public health measures, and in 1911 supported universal male suffrage. Giolitti also encouraged Catholics to enter the national politics they had boycotted since 1870, and he, too, acquiesced in an imperial venture. Italy went to war against the Ottoman sultan in 1912, took Rhodes and the other major Dodecanese Islands in the eastern Mediterranean, and landed at the port city of Tripoli in Libya, all of which the sultan ceded. The year of war inspired an enthusiasm that Italian governments had rarely enjoyed. Although the economic problems of the south remained grave and the discontent of more and more militant workers went largely

---

[5]Subsequent governments held on to Eritrea as an Italian colony.

◄ *Umberto Boccioni*
RIOT IN THE GALLERIA, 1910
**Social tension in an era of
prosperity: The excitement and
uncertainty of a riot contrasts with
the stable warmth of an elegant
café.**
Scala / Art Resource, NY

unappeased, the Italian economy, less developed than that of the great industrial powers, experienced the fastest growth rate in Europe during the decade ending in 1914. In the elections of 1913, the first under the broadened suffrage, Giolitti's compromises would prove an easy target for critics from the left and the right, and they were the notable winners. Still, Italy appeared firmly set on a liberal, democratic course.

◆ RUSSIA: DEFEAT AND REVOLUTION

In Russia the pressures for political change were held in check for a generation by official policies that centered on a program of "Russification," meant to create a united nation. But defeat in war and the first stages of industrialization produced a revolution.

Reaction Alexander III had become tsar in 1881 on his father's assassination, an event that he believed resulted from too much talk about further reform following the abolition of serfdom. He sought instead to achieve stability by using the Orthodox Church and the police to extend an official reactionary ideology through public life, and he gave nobles an increased role in regional councils, the *zemstvos*, and in rural administration. Local governors were authorized to use martial law, to restrict or ban the religions and languages of non-Russian peoples, and to persecute Jews.[6]

---

[6]One of history's famous forgeries, the *Protocols of the Elders of Zion*, was published (and written) by the Russian police in 1903. The protocols purported to be the secret minutes of a Jewish congress that revealed a conspiracy to control the world.

These policies were continued with equal conviction but less energy by Tsar Nicholas II, who ascended the throne in 1894. As unrest increased in cities and in the countryside, many in the government searched for other ways of achieving the solidarity that repression had failed to create.

The Russo-Japanese War War, and the patriotism it evokes, was thus welcomed in 1904, when Japan suddenly attacked the Russians at Port Arthur on the Yellow Sea. Russia had leased Port Arthur from China in 1898 as part of its expansion into East Asia and Manchuria. For years these moves had troubled the Japanese, and Russia had neither kept its promises to withdraw nor acknowledged Japan's proposals for establishing mutually acceptable spheres of influence. The war was a disaster for Russia. Surprise attack was followed by defeats in Manchuria, the fall of Port Arthur, and then the annihilation of a large Russian fleet that sailed around the world only to be sunk in Japanese waters. In the peace treaty, signed at Portsmouth, New Hampshire—the United States, like Japan, wished to demonstrate its status as a world power—Russia ceded most of its recent gains, including Port Arthur and the southern half of Sakhalin Island, and recognized Japanese interest in Korea.

The Revolution of 1905 So dramatic a defeat increased pressure for major reforms just as the Crimean War had done fifty years before, but this time the pressure came from deep within Russian society. Peasant agitation had been on the rise since a terrible famine in 1891. Secret organizations were growing among the non-Russian nationalities, and workers drawn to St. Petersburg and Moscow by industrialization had begun to form unions. The Social Revolutionaries, a party combining the traditions of populism and terrorism, grew more active; the Marxist Social Democrats, hitherto composed of rather disparate groups, now organized in exile and strengthened their ties within Russia.

In this atmosphere liberal members of the *zemstvos* held a national congress in 1904, though forbidden to by the government, and insisted on civil liberties. Then in January 1905 striking workers in St. Petersburg marched on the Winter Palace to petition the tsar for a national constitution and the recognition of labor unions. The workers carried icons and sang "God save the tsar," but when they

◀ **On Bloody Sunday in January 1905, protesters, led by a priest and carrying a petition to the tsar, marched to the Winter Palace, where they were fired on by Russian soldiers. That bloodshed, following rising demands for a representative assembly, marked the beginning of the Revolution of 1905; thousands of people died that day.**
Sovfoto

had assembled, the army opened fire, killing scores and wounding hundreds more.

"Bloody Sunday" led to agitation so widespread that in March the tsar promised to call an assembly of notables and announced immediate reforms: religious toleration, reduced restrictions on Jews and non-Russian nationals, and cancellation of part of the payments peasants owed for their land. Agitation for a constitution only grew stronger, expressed through urban strikes, peasant riots, and mutinies in both the army and navy. In August the tsar conceded more, declaring he would consult a national assembly, the Imperial Duma. Many close to the throne were shocked by so radical a step. A public wanting something more concrete responded with a wave of strikes.

A Russian Constitution   For the last ten days of October, Russia's economic life came to a halt, the most effective general strike Europe had ever seen. It won from the tsar the October Manifesto, which granted a constitution. Crowds danced in the streets, but proponents of change were divided. Those willing to work with this constitution, which guaranteed freedom of speech and assembly but was vague on much else, became known as Octobrists. Liberals who insisted on a constituent assembly and broader guarantees formed the Constitutional Democratic party, called Cadets for short. Further to the left, socialists and revolutionaries rejected compromise, and the St. Petersburg Soviet, a committee of trade union leaders and socialists, called another general strike. It was only partially successful, and an emboldened government arrested the leaders of the Soviet in December and bloodily defeated the Moscow workers who revolted in protest.

The Fundamental Laws announced in May 1906 defined the limitations of the tsar's concessions. He would keep the power of veto, the right to name his ministers, and full command of the executive, the judiciary, and the armed forces; the national legislature would have an upper house in addition to the Duma, with half its members appointed by the tsar. Elections under this new system, however, brought the Cadets a large majority, which demanded representative government. Nicholas then disbanded the legislature and held new elections, but they produced an even

more radical assembly; it, too, was disbanded. Only a new electoral law favoring the propertied classes ensured conservative majorities in subsequent legislatures.

The Revolution of 1905 had nevertheless brought important changes. Russia now had parliamentary institutions and organized parties, the power of the aristocracy had been greatly reduced, and the nation was clearly set on a modern course. The prime minister from 1906 to 1911, Peter Stolypin, reformed education and administration and strove to stimulate the economy by turning away from the *mir* system of communal lands in favor of the full private ownership of land, and he created land banks and a program of social insurance. With the aid of foreign capital, the pace of industrialization rapidly increased. While discontent among workers and poorer peasants remained serious and radical movements were sternly repressed, the Cadets were finding it possible to work with the new system. Liberals throughout Europe rejoiced that the giant of the East had at last begun to follow the path of Western progress.

◆ AUSTRIA-HUNGARY: THE DELICATE BALANCE

The political problems of Austria-Hungary were revealed not so much in crises as in stalemate. Creation of an autonomous regime in Hungary led to conflicts with the rest of the empire, and these political and nationalist issues were exacerbated by the divergent economic interests of the Empire's industrializing and agrarian regions. The conservative instincts of the imperial court, the aristocracy, and the bureaucracy stymied further reforms.

Shifting Stalemates   These groups, the pillars of the empire, settled on a cautious prime minister, Count Eduard von Taafe, who held office from 1879 to 1893. Taafe's parliamentary supporters included Czechs and Poles. But they wanted concessions that Taafe's other supporters would not accept, so that inaction was the safest course. Social change brought further disagreements. The spread of education, for instance, heightened conflict over what language should be used in schools. In response to workers' agitation, Taafe proposed welfare measures but repressed socialists, antagonizing both left and right. After his fall, governments came to rely more on decree powers and support from the crown than on parliament. After universal manhood suffrage was introduced without conviction in 1907, the Christian Socialists and the Social Democrats became the two largest parties, but neither was acceptable to the leaders of the empire. Kept from imperial office, they competed in the city of Vienna, where the Christian Socialists gained sway by combining social programs with demagogic antisemitism.

Within Hungary, Magyar notables maintained their dominance over other nationalities by requiring that the Magyar language be used in government and schools, by tightly controlling the electoral system, and by subverting the bureaucracy through corruption. Their policies protecting large landowners and seeking greater independence from the imperial government weakened the empire. In 1903, when Hungary's leaders demanded greater autonomy for their own army, they touched one issue about which Emperor Franz Joseph I cared too much to yield. He suspended the Hungarian constitution, ruled without parliament, and frightened the Magyars into submission by threatening to subject them, a minority in their own country, to universal male suffrage. Magyars and the empire needed each other; and Magyar politics, admired in the 1840s as a model of liberal nationalism, had turned by 1906 into the defensive strategy of a threatened aristocracy. For mutual survival the leaders of Austria and Hungary avoided risky changes and dangerously relied instead on imperial foreign policy to strengthen from the outside a political system in trouble at home.

◆ SPAIN: INSTABILITY AND LOSS OF EMPIRE

Spain developed a remarkable tradition of parliamentarism in which governments were careful to keep the support of the army, the Church, big business, and regional interests. By emphasizing the economy, a liberal coalition held power from 1854 to 1863, years in which Spain experienced on a smaller scale the waves of speculation, railroad building, economic growth, and ostentation associated with the Second Empire in France.

Revolution and Restoration This growth brought new demands that old alliances, palace intrigue, and electoral manipulation could not check. Rising discontent led in 1868 to the flight of the unpopular Queen Isabella II and to revolution. The leaders of the revolution were political moderates who quickly agreed on a constitutional monarchy with universal manhood suffrage, trial by jury, and freedom of religion and the press. It proved easier to adopt a new constitution, however, than to find a new king. Candidate after candidate declined to become entangled in Spanish politics and the sort of international complications that precipitated the Franco-Prussian War. The Italian prince who finally did accept the throne gave it up after three years in the face of rising opposition from left and right. The subsequent republic lasted only two years before the military installed Isabella's son on the throne as Alfonso XII.

He began his reign in 1875 with a new constitution closer to the one in effect at midcentury than to the more democratic ones that had succeeded it. In a parliamentary system based on limited suffrage, the Conservative and Liberal parties alternated in power with little change in policy, a system that by keeping the state weak masked the bitter divisions between regionalists and centralists, Catholics and anticlericals, the poor and the propertied. As in Russia and Austria, however, industrialization exacerbated these tensions. Unable to establish a consistent program for the colonies, the government met unrest in Cuba with alternating policies of repression and laxity. Cuban resistance became guerrilla war, and in 1898 the United States entered the conflict with an imperialist enthusiasm of its own. As a result of the Spanish-American War, Spain was forced to withdraw from Cuba and to cede Puerto Rico, Guam, and the Philippine Islands to the United States.

Those losses led to a great deal of soul searching. A group of Spanish intellectuals known as the generation of 1898 brought new vitality to Spanish public life, but neither the caution of conservatives nor the mild reforms of liberals could stem the increasing dissension in which the Church denounced the liberals while growing anarchist and socialist movements attacked the whole establishment. In 1909 these conflicts burst forth in a week of violence in Barcelona during which churches were burned and looted and private citizens were murdered. Yet the authorities soon restored order. Spain's unadmired moderate regime remained less divisive than the alternatives.

◆ GREAT BRITAIN: EDGING TOWARD DEMOCRACY

From Russia to Spain, European nations had adopted parliamentary systems, and until the end of the century, Britain provided the model of how such a system was supposed to work. In Britain legislation addressed the most pressing social issues, however cautiously. Parliament gradually reduced legal inequalities, opening the civil service to those who passed competitive examinations, removing legal disabilities on Jews, and eliminating special taxes on behalf of the Church of England. At the same time, order was maintained through respect for law, toleration, and social deference. There were serious domestic tensions, but they were attenuated by a thriving two-party system.

The Liberal and Conservative Parties   The creation of modern political parties led by two brilliant leaders facilitated Britain's adaptation to change. William Gladstone was instrumental in transforming the Whigs into the Liberal party, and Benjamin Disraeli led in making the Tories into the modern Conservative party. Gladstone was a skilled parliamentary tactician sympathetic to liberal reformers and even radicals, for whom political liberalism was a moral cause. Somewhat hesitantly, he made increased suffrage, which had been talked about for a generation, a central plank, but his complicated bill was defeated in Parliament.

Instead, Disraeli persuaded his startled party to support a simpler, more generous reform, which passed in 1867. It doubled the electorate by extending the right to vote to all men who paid property taxes directly or indirectly through rent (about one adult male in three). Equally important, imperial policies and major programs of reform now became a regular part of the competition for popular favor. The parliamentary clashes of Gladstone and Disraeli became a dramatic part of British public life.

Political Reforms   The enlarged electorate after the 1867 reform gave the Liberals a great victory, and for six years Gladstone's first ministry fundamentally altered the relations between government and society. State aid to elementary schools, both religious and secular, brought Britain closer to universal education. The Liberals also reformed the army (even the purchase of commissions was abolished, despite great resistance from the House of Lords) and disestablished the Anglican Church of Ireland (so that an overwhelmingly Catholic population no longer paid taxes to support a Protestant church). Recognizing the festering poverty and discontent in Ireland, new laws restricted the abuses of absentee landlords and provided peasants some protection against eviction.

The Conservatives, returned to power in the elections of 1874, were more willing than the Liberals to expand the authority of the state. A public health act established a national code for housing and urban sanitation, and new measures allowed striking workers to picket, making unions more effective. These social concerns, often called Tory democracy, which offered a British parallel to the policies of Bismarck and Napoleon III, became the cornerstone of the revived Conservative party.

Gladstone in turn adopted the principle of universal male suffrage, which became law in 1885. Men with an independent place of residence could now vote, and it says much about the life of the poor that this one requirement—which excluded domestic servants, sons living with parents, and those with no permanent address—was enough to exclude roughly one-third of all adult males. Gladstone's perpetual compromises, however, were losing their appeal. Imperial issues were his undoing. His renewed efforts in behalf of Irish peasants failed to satisfy Irish nationalists who wanted an independent parliament of their own, and when Gladstone acquiesced to Irish home rule in 1886, his party split. A group of Liberals led by Joseph Chamberlain allied with the Conservatives. A radical in social matters, Chamberlain had adopted the popular cause of imperialism, which would help the Conservatives stay in office for sixteen of the nineteen years between 1886 and 1905.

Rising Social Tensions   While projecting British power around the world, Conservative governments remained active at home. In 1888 and again in 1894 they restructured local government, a traditional source of the aristocracy's political power, making country councils elective and thus more democratic. They extended the reforms of the civil service and, in an act of 1902, established a national education system that for the first time included secondary schooling. Yet these important changes did not address the needs of the working class, whose rising dissatisfaction was marked by the dramatic strikes of London match girls in 1888 and dockworkers the next year. The strikes, which won public sympathy, were part of a "new unionism" that included unskilled workers in a more militant labor movement. Social conflict became public in Britain as never before.

In 1900 a combination of union representatives and some prominent intellectuals formed the Labour party on a platform of democratic socialism. Both the Labour and Liberal parties campaigned for social programs that the Conservatives resisted, relying instead on the popular appeal of empire to keep them in power. In 1906 the Liberals won the most one-sided electoral victory since 1832. They immediately established systems of workers' compensation, old-age pensions, and urban planning. These measures—and the expanding arms race—required new revenues, and in 1909 David Lloyd George, the Chancellor of the Exchequer, proposed a "people's budget." A skilled orator who delighted in the rhetoric of class conflict, he promised to place the costs of social welfare squarely on the rich.

Constitutional Crisis   An aroused House of Lords rejected Lloyd George's budget, an unprecedented act that forced a constitutional crisis and new elections. The king's threat to appoint hundreds of additional peers finally forced the upper house to accept not only the hated budget but also a major change in the constitution. By law, the Lords could no longer veto money bills or any measure that passed the Commons in three successive sessions.

The peers' intemperate outburst, which cost them so much, was part of a general rise in social tension. From 1910 to 1914 strikes increased in frequency, size, and violence; a general strike became a real and much-talked-of threat. Women campaigning for the right to vote interrupted public

◄ **London's dockworkers had gained national sympathy with their orderly demonstrations in the great strike of 1889 and had won some of their demands, but the agitation and unrest continued. Here, during a subsequent strike, police guard a convoy of food trucks making their way to city markets.**
©Bettmann/Corbis

EMMELINE PANKHURST ON WOMEN'S RIGHTS
◆

Emmeline Pankhurst founded the Women's Social and Political Union in 1903. As the militant leader of the British suffragettes, she won headlines and eventually significant support for her cause with her disruptive tactics and powerful speeches. Her fame was international by the time she went on a speaking tour in Canada in 1912, where on January 14 she gave a long speech from which this passage is taken. Delighting her audience with stories of the resistance she had met, she focused on the right to vote but made clear that her vision of women's roles was much broader.

"There has been a great deal of talk lately of new legislation for those who are about to enter into marriage. Women should have a say as one of the contracting parties. There are the questions of divorce and of the training of children. Who knows better of these matters than do women? There are also the trades and professions which are at the present time open to women. It is only right that we should have some say in the legislation concerning us. We have heard much of the English divorce law. It is a disgrace to any civilized country. The only redeeming feature of the matter is that the bulk of men are better than the law allows. But there is the minority, and the law should be severe for them. They are as bad as the law allows them to be. If woman only had weight in politics this would be rectified soon. She will serve to call more attention to such questions of national welfare. If we are to have any divorce law at all, and that is a much-debated question, it should be a law that is equal both for man and woman. Unless women get the vote we have no guarantee that it will be so.

" . . . Men are responsible if they allow the present condition of things to continue. Women have the power to work out their own salvation. But as it is, if a woman is ruined, if a child is injured, man is responsible for it all. It is a responsibility I would not care to have, and, as things are, I would not be a man for all the world. If women fail as men have failed, then they will bear the burden with them. But since men cannot protect and shield us, let us share the duty with them, let us use our power so that woman may be a participant, not to tyrannize over man but to take a share in the responsibilities of ruling, without which there is no real representative government. What we really are interested in in this fight is the uplifting of the sex and better conditions of humanity than men can secure. In the legal home there is but the man. What we want is the combined intelligence of man and woman working for the salvation of the children of the race. This will make for the world a better time than ever before in its history. It will raise mankind to heights of which now it has little conception. We must only make this last fight for human freedom that as the class distinction disappeared so that sex distinction may pass, and then you will get better things than men can by themselves secure."

From Emmeline Pankhurst, "The Last Fight for Human Freedom," speech given in Canada in 1912, in Brian MacArthur, *Twentieth-Century Speeches* (New York: Viking, 1992).

meetings, invaded Parliament itself, smashed windows, and planted bombs. Arrested, they went on hunger strikes until baffled statesmen ordered their release. Such behavior from ladies was shocking in itself; but as the movement gained strength, recruiting women (and some men) from every social class, its outraged attack on smug male assumptions reinforced the rising challenge to a whole social order (see "Emmeline Pankhurst on Women's Rights").

Nor was the threat of violence limited to the left. In 1914 the Commons for the third time passed a bill granting Irish home rule, which made it immune to a veto in the House of Lords. The Protestants of northern Ireland, with support from many in England, openly threatened civil war. Squads began drilling, and the British officer corps seemed ready to mutiny rather than fight to impose home rule on Protestant loyalists.

The outbreak of world war generated the national unity that neither imperialism nor social reform had been able to achieve. But if the death of Queen Victoria in 1901 had symbolized the end of an age of British expansion, the ascent of George

V to the throne (r. 1910–1936) marked the opening of new and terrible conflicts. Edward VII's brief reign (r. 1901–1910) would soon be remembered a little sadly as the Edwardian era, a happy time of relaxed confidence in prosperity, progress, and peace.

SUMMARY

In the period from 1870 to 1914 every European nation had faced major political crises; yet as political systems worked to balance class conflict and clashing interests, the trend toward greater democracy and large-scale organization seemed irresistible. For good or ill, there had been few major upheavals, save in backward Russia, and no European war, facts that contemporaries often cited as proof of progress. In most countries there was greater freedom of expression, more political participation, more leisure, increased literacy and education, and better health care than in the past. In general, productivity and prosperity, already at levels never achieved before, continued to rise. Science and technology promised still greater wonders. Even in retrospect, the level of creativity in the arts and scholarship and the growth of knowledge and professional standards in every field remain impressive.

Yet the civilization that achieved all this was bitterly denounced not only for its manifest injustices, which stood out in contrast to its achievements, but more fundamentally for its lack of coherent values, for its materialism, for the ugliness of industrial society, and for the privileged position of a middle class portrayed as self-serving and philistine. Perhaps European society was evolving toward solutions of these deficiencies, as many believed. Or maybe the positive trends were less significant than the effects of imperialism, domestic social conflict, and the arms race. In 1914 the very compromises that had held society together and kept the peace exploded—not in revolution, but in total war.

QUESTIONS FOR FURTHER THOUGHT

1. Why are periods of history often remembered for certain characteristics although equally important ones pointed in a very different direction? Why is the era preceding World War I, which was full of conflict, still remembered as the Belle Epoque?

2. How could the spread of parliamentary government, increased freedom, and prosperity produce such powerful and diverse criticism?

3. What explains the fact that the countries of Europe, with very different social structures, levels of economic development, and political systems all experienced major political crises toward the end of the nineteenth century and apparently resolved them with similar institutions and compromises by the beginning of the twentieth century?

RECOMMENDED READING

Sources

*Hélias, Pierre-Jackez. *The Horse of Pride: Life in a Breton Village.* June Guicharnaud (tr.). 1980. A compelling memoir of a preindustrial society about to be transformed at the turn of the century.

MacDougall, H. A. (ed.). *Lord Acton on Papal Power.* 1973. A leading figure in Britain's intellectual life and a thoughtful historian, Lord Acton was a committed Catholic who was also an outspoken opponent of the doctrine of papal infallibility proclaimed at the Vatican Council in 1871. This collection of his public writings and private correspondence with important contemporaries provides a touching glimpse of Acton's anguish as well as the widespread attention these issues received.

Snyder, Louis L. *The Dreyfus Case: A Documentary History.* 1973. These well-edited documents convey the passions that this famous affair evoked and the broad implications that all sides saw in it.

Weintraub, Stanley. *The Yellow Book: Quintessence of the Nineties.* 1964. The stories and articles in this collection are all taken from the most daring literary quarterly of the day; nearly every piece is an exercise in the rejection of Victorian proprieties, and in that respect characteristic of the new movements in the arts.

Studies

Berghahn, Voker R. *Germany, 1871–1914: Economy, Society, Culture, and Politics.* 1993. A thematic survey unusual in its breadth, particularly attentive to public culture and social structure.

Berlanstein, Lenard R. *The Working People of Paris, 1871–1914.* 1984. Looks at the important changes in the lives of wage earners, in the nature of work, and in the workplace, as well as their impact on working-class movements.

Boxer, Marilyn, and Jean Quataert. *Socialist Women: Socialist Feminism in the Nineteenth and Twentieth Century.* 1978. Looking at the important figures, the book explores the tortured ambivalence among socialists toward feminism in all the major countries.

Canning, Kathleen. *Languages of Labor and Gender: Female Factory Work in Germany, 1850–1914.* 1996. Connects social changes in the nature of work to changes in women's lives and to the shifting discourse on gender.

*Craig, Gordon. *Germany: 1866–1945.* 1978. A well-written and capable analysis that stresses the failure of liberalism to overcome preindustrial forces as a key to public life.

*Dangerfield, George. *The Strange Death of Liberal England.* 1935. A skillfully and argumentatively written description of a society in crisis that has influenced subsequent interpretations of the period.

*Derfler, Leslie. *Socialism since Marx: A Century of the European Left.* 1973. Thoughtful discussion of the movements that stemmed from Marx, showing their variety, creativity, and contradictions.

*Evans, Richard J. *The Feminist Movement in Germany, 1894–1933.* 1976. Establishes the importance of these movements and their connection to German politics and parties more generally.

*———. *The Feminists: Women's Emancipation in Europe, America, and Australia.* 1979. The similarities and differences in feminist campaigns reveal a good deal about the dominant ideologies, social structure, and politics of their respective societies.

*Gay, Peter. *The Education of the Senses.* 1984. A sensitive treatment of sexuality during the Victorian Age and the first part of a major study of the values of the bourgeoisie, written from a Freudian perspective.

Gillis, John R. *Youth and History: Tradition and Change in European Age Relations, 1770 to the Present.* 1981. An original study of youth transformed by social change that highlights the late nineteenth century as a pivotal period.

*Gullickson, Gay L. *Unruly Women of Paris: Images of the Commune.* 1997. A richly illustrated study of the hysterical press accounts of the role of women in the Commune.

*Hughes, H. Stuart. *Consciousness and Society: The Reorientation of European Social Thought, 1890–1930.* 1958. A gracefully written and indispensable analysis of the currents of modern thought in this time of transition from midcentury certitudes.

Johnson, Douglas. *France and the Dreyfus Affair.* 1966. A standard account of the affair that explains its extraordinary impact.

*Joll, James. *The Anarchists.* 1964. Provides a particularly clear discussion of the ideas and motives of very disparate groups, all claiming to be anarchist.

*———. *The Second International, 1889–1914.* 1966. A general history of the socialist movement in this period, with striking portraits of the major figures.

Kern, Stephen. *The Culture of Time and Space 1880–1918*. 1983. An imaginative study of ideas and experiences related to technological and cultural change reflected in art, literature, politics, and social life.

Lidtke, Vernon. *The Alternative Culture: Socialist Labor in Imperial Germany*. 1985. A significant analysis of how German socialists created Europe's most organized working-class subculture.

*Löwith, Karl. *From Hegel to Nietzsche: The Revolution in Nineteenth-Century Thought*. 1964. A sober essay on the pessimistic and irrationalist transformations in modern thought and the powerful insights that resulted.

Lyons, Francis S. *Ireland since the Famine*. 1971. A broad social history of a society in crisis.

*Mayeur, Jean-Marie, and Madeleine Rebérioux. *The Third Republic from Its Origins to the Great War, 1871–1914*. J. R. Foster (tr.). 1984. A balanced synthesis of recent scholarship on the establishment of a stable republic amidst social conflict.

Miller, Michael. *The Bon Marché: Bourgeois Culture and the Development of the Department Store*. 1981. A fascinating study that explores the department store as a significant cultural institution.

Moses, Claire. *French Feminism in the Nineteenth Century*. 1984. Reveals the vigor of a feminist movement quite different from its British and German counterparts.

*Mosse, George L. *The Crisis of German Ideology*. 1964. Looks for the currents of Nazi ideology in the views of nation and race embodied in the popular ideas and movements of the late nineteenth century.

Pugh, Martin. *The Tories and the People, 1880–1935*. 1985. A study of the basis for and limitations of the Conservatives' mass appeal.

*Pulzer, Peter G. *The Rise of Political Anti-Semitism in Germany and Austria*. 1964. A clear and balanced survey of a difficult topic that shows the remarkable scope of antisemitism.

Ralston, David B. *The Army of the Republic, 1871–1914*. 1967. Treats a question of central importance to the establishment of democracy: the problem of the military in France both before and after the Dreyfus affair.

Rearick, Charles. *Pleasures of the Belle Époque*. 1985. Captures the cultural and social vitality of the period, emphasizing popular culture and the uses of leisure.

*Robertson, Priscilla. *An Experience of Women: Pattern and Change in Nineteenth-Century Europe*. 1982. A social and intellectual history of middle- and upper-class women in Western Europe, useful for the breadth of its coverage.

*Romero, Patricia W. *E. Sylvia Pankhurst: Portrait of a Radical*. 1987. This biography of Britain's feminist leader gives a good sense of the development of the movement overall.

*Schorske, Carl E. *Fin-de-Siècle Vienna: Politics and Culture*. 1980. Unusually sensitive and imaginative assessment of one of the important moments in European cultural history.

Seton-Watson, Christopher. *Italy from Liberalism to Fascism*. 1967. A thorough general, political account of Italy in its first period of rapid industrialization.

*Shattuck, Roger. *The Banquet Years*. 1968. A brilliant study of the role of artists in late-nineteenth-century Paris, showing the connections among social attitudes, institutions, and the birth of modernism in the arts.

Sheehan, James J. *German Liberalism in the Nineteenth Century*. 1978. An important assessment of a much disputed and critical issue, the place of liberalism in German intellectual and political life.

Stone, Norman. *Europe Transformed, 1878–1919*. 1984. An insightful and fresh new survey of the period, outlining the weaknesses of the liberals.

Tannenbaum, Edward R. *1900: The Generation before the Great War*. 1976. Interesting essays on the major facets of society.

*Wagar, Warren W. *Good Tidings: The Belief in Progress from Darwin to Marcuse*. 1972. A wide-ranging account of the period's principal yet beleaguered concepts.

*Weber, Eugen. *Peasants into Frenchmen: The Modernization of Rural France, 1880–1914*. 1976. A provocative treatment stressing the resistance of rural France to the pressures for change and the lateness of their arrival.

Wehler, Hans-Ulrich. *The German Empire 1871–1918*. Kim Traynor (tr.). 1985. A comprehensive structural analysis that synthesizes the most recent empirical research.

*Wohl, Robert. *The Generation of 1914*. 1979. Theories of generations in conflict are related to the intellectual and political discontent preceding World War I in this important book.

*Available in paperback.

▲ A British surgeon and painter, Henry Tonks, was sent to the front in 1917 to paint this scene of a dressing station at the Somme, where officers classify the wounded while the artillery barrages go on.
Imperial War Museum, London

WORLD WAR I AND THE WORLD IT CREATED

In 1914 Germany, Russia, Austria-Hungary, France, and Great Britain were suddenly at war—a war different from any that had gone before, a war that permanently altered society and politics, and a war that even in retrospect stands as the dividing point between two eras. Interpreting its origins is thus crucial to any understanding of modern history and is still the subject of controversy. Historians have given few subjects closer study than the system of alliances and the diplomatic moves that led to World War I. We understand the role of events, the arms race, and strident nationalism in leading to catastrophe.

The larger question is whether these fatal steps were themselves a result of long-term trends—economic expansion, imperialism, social divisions, ideological conflicts, and democratic politics. Once it came, the war strained every resource of the belligerents and mobilized civilian life as never before. As it ended, the victors were shaken, their societies and politics different. The losing states crumbled, opening the way to still more dramatic political changes. The complicated peace settlement, which changed the map of Europe and tried to make democracy universal, was meant above all to ensure that there would not be another world war.

	Social Structure	Body Politic	Changes in the Organization of Production and in the Impact of Technology	Evolution of Family and Changing Gender Roles	War	Religion	Cultural Expression
CHAPTER 27. WORLD WAR I AND THE WORLD IT CREATED							
I. THE COMING OF WORLD WAR	▓		▓		▓		
II. THE COURSE OF THE WAR	▓	▓	▓	▓	▓		
III. THE PEACE		▓					
IV. POSTWAR DEMOCRACY	▓	▓	▓	▓			

I. The Coming of World War

◆

International relations held center stage in the period from 1870 to World War I for a variety of reasons. The balance of power established at the Congress of Vienna in 1815 had been overturned by the unification of Italy and Germany and by Prussia's defeat of Austria in 1866 and of France in 1870. The heightened sense of insecurity that followed led to an intricate web of alliances requiring constant attention. At the same time, imperialism, economic competition, and an escalating arms race multiplied the arenas in which national interests might clash. In addition, every threat, insult, or setback was magnified in daily journalism and domestic politics, for nationalism sold newspapers and made political careers. Foreign ministries worked to keep these conflicting pressures under control through diplomacy conducted by gentlemen, largely in secret and according to elaborate rules.

◆ BISMARCK'S SYSTEM OF ALLIANCES

From the 1860s to 1890, Bismarck dominated international relations. His diplomacy was essential to the creation of the Second Reich, and he led Europe's major nations in addressing a series of long-term issues, particularly the decline of Ottoman power, the resulting power vacuum in the Balkans, and competing Russian and Austrian ambitions there. His first concern was to make the new German nation secure from any potential foreign threat. Although intended to increase secu-

rity, the treaties Bismarck fostered ultimately stimulated a dangerous arms race.

The Congress of Berlin, 1878   Bismarck established his mastery at the Congress of Berlin in 1878. Once again, as at the time of the Crimean War twenty years earlier, Russia had expanded its influence in the Balkans by defeating Turkey in war and by forcing the sultan to cede territory across the Caucasus Mountains to Russia, to allow creation of an enlarged Montenegro and Serbia,

▼ **Bismarck dominated the Congress of Berlin in 1878 much as he dominates this portrait, which shows him being congratulated by the Russian delegate, with Count Andrassy of Austria-Hungary on the left.**
AKG London

and to grant full independence to a large and autonomous Bulgaria, which everyone believed would be a Russian puppet. This was more than the other European powers would allow. The aim of the Congress was to restrain Russian ambitions while finding a response to Balkan nationalism and Ottoman weakness that avoided further war.

With few German interests directly involved, Bismarck presented himself as an "honest broker" and skillfully orchestrated agreements in which everyone got something. The settlement granted autonomy to a greatly reduced Bulgaria (thus lessening Russia's gains) and recognized the independence of Serbia, Romania, and Montenegro (acknowledging rising nationalism).[1] Austria-Hungary, nervous about a challenge from new and nationalist Balkan states, was authorized in compensation to occupy Bosnia and Herzegovina, which nevertheless remained formally under Ottoman rule. In addition Britain's occupation of Cyprus was confirmed, and Tunis was in effect promised to France. The balance the Congress of Berlin achieved among competing nations had come at the expense of a weakening Ottoman Empire and by extending the dominion of the major powers—a pattern characteristic of imperialism.

Germany's Alliances Fresh from this triumph, Bismarck persuaded Austria-Hungary to a mutual defense pact. Austria was worried by Russia's ambitions and grateful for Germany's support at the Congress, and the secret pact became the foundation of German foreign policy. The two nations promised that should either be attacked by Russia the other would come to its defense. But Bismarck sought further insurance, and so in 1881 he audaciously persuaded Russia (eager to escape diplomatic isolation) to join Germany and Austria-Hungary in promising to remain neutral in the event of war between any of them and a fourth power. To these understandings, Bismarck then added a third, the Triple Alliance of Italy, Germany, and Austria-Hungary. This renewable

five-year pact was first signed in 1882. In creating this treaty, Bismarck took advantage of Italy's resentment of France for occupying Tunis in 1881. While imperial competition worked in his favor, Bismarck's goal was the diplomatic isolation of France, for he feared the continuing bitterness in France over the loss of Alsace-Lorraine to Germany in 1870.

Formally, these treaties were defensive, although the secrecy surrounding them fostered a sense of insecurity (see "The Terms of the Triple Alliance," p. 966). They gave Germany an international influence rare in peacetime, but holding them together took great skill. Italy and Russia had more reasons for conflict with Austria-Hungary than with any other nation, and it was hard to keep them tied to Germany. In fact, Russia and Austria-Hungary let their alliance lapse in 1887 because of their disagreements in the Balkans, and Bismarck could only partially repair the damage through a separate Reinsurance Treaty in which Germany and Russia promised to remain neutral toward each other if one of them was at war. For Italy, Austria-Hungary was not only the traditional enemy Italy had fought to achieve unification but the occupier of Italian-speaking lands in the region of Trieste. To persuade Italy to renew the Triple Alliance in 1887, Bismarck had to recognize a range of Italian ambitions in the Balkans, Africa, and elsewhere.

◆ THE SHIFTING BALANCE

Germany's system of alliances was already showing strains when the Kaiser dismissed Bismarck from office in 1890. Without him, that system disintegrated and German diplomacy became erratic and even abrasive.

German Diplomacy after Bismarck Bismarck's successors understood the importance of Germany's alliances but tended to overlook the new factor that could draw other nations together: common fear of Germany. When Germany's new leaders let the Reinsurance Treaty with Russia lapse, France pressed Russia for an understanding. By 1894, that became a full alliance. France and Russia promised that each would support the other if either were attacked by Germany or by another member of the Triple Alliance that was

---

[1] The tsar's nephew was elected to the Bulgarian throne. Rumelia, the southern part of Bulgaria, remained under Turkish rule as a separate province. The provinces of Wallachia and Moldavia had been joined in 1862 to form Romania and received their own prince two years later. A Hohenzollern, he became King Carol in 1881.

THE TERMS OF THE TRIPLE ALLIANCE

◆

These articles are from the treaty of 1912 in which Austria-Hungary, Germany, and Italy renewed the Triple Alliance for the fifth time since 1882. This version essentially continued earlier ones, except for articles VI through XI, not printed here, which dealt rather vaguely with the Balkans, Ottoman territories, Egypt, and North Africa. With respect to those regions, the signatories reassured each other that they preferred to maintain the status quo but promised mutual understanding and even support if Austria-Hungary or Italy found it necessary temporarily to occupy territory in the Balkans or if Italy had to take measures against French expansion in North Africa. The promises of support to Italy indicated the higher price now required to keep Italy in the Alliance.

"ARTICLE I. The High Contracting Parties mutually promise peace and friendship, and will enter into no alliance or engagement directed against any one of their States.

"They engage to proceed to an exchange of ideas on political and economic questions of a general nature which may arise, and they further promise one another mutual support within the limits of their own interests.

"ARTICLE II. In case Italy, without direct provocation on her part, should be attacked by France for any reason whatsoever, the two other Contracting Parties shall be bound to lend help and assistance with all their forces to the Party attacked.

"This same obligation shall devolve upon Italy in case of any aggression without direct provocation by France against Germany.

"ARTICLE III. If one, or two, of the High Contracting Parties, without direct provocation on their part, should chance to be attacked and to be engaged in a war with two or more Great Powers nonsignatory to the present Treaty, the *casus foederis* will arise simultaneously for all the High Contracting Parties.

"ARTICLE IV. In case a Great Power nonsignatory to the present Treaty should threaten the security of the states of one of the High Contracting Parties, and the threatened Party should find itself forced on that account to make war against it, the two others bind themselves to observe towards their Ally a benevolent neutrality. Each of them reserves to itself, in this case, the right to take part in the war, if it should see fit, to make common cause with its Ally.

"ARTICLE V. If the peace of one of the High Contracting Parties should chance to be threatened under the circumstances foreseen by the preceding Articles, the High Contracting Parties shall take counsel together in ample time as to the military measures to be taken with a view to eventual cooperation.

"They engage, henceforth, in all cases of common participation in a war, to conclude neither armistice, nor peace, nor treaty, except by common agreement among themselves.

"ARTICLE XII. The High Contracting Parties mutually promise secrecy as to the contents of the present Treaty."

From Sidney Bradshaw Fay, *The Origins of the World War* (Macmillan, 1930).

---

aided by Germany. Such an accord between the Russian autocracy and the French republic had seemed politically impossible, despite Russia's having already turned to France for loans and arms purchases. Now the tsar greeted French delegates while a band played the "Marseillaise," previously outlawed in Russia as a song of revolution.

In response, German diplomats were determined to reassert Germany's importance in world affairs. They attempted to reach some understanding with Great Britain but also to demonstrate to the British how much they needed German friendship. When in 1896 the South African Boers defeated a small private army organized by Englishmen, Kaiser William II sent a telegram congratulating the president of the Boer republic. The British public responded with anger. The kaiser's talk of the "yellow peril" during a period of turmoil in China, when he instructed his soldiers to behave like the barbaric Huns of old, did nothing to enhance his reputation for stability. Neither did the talk of a "natural" alliance between the Teutonic and Anglo-Saxon races when at the same time Germany was exploring a continental coalition against Great Britain. The concrete issue was the expanding German navy, and some negotiated limit seemed possible until the Germans demanded a formal alliance first. The British concluded that the German fleet was aimed at them.

Anglo-French Understanding Relations between Great Britain and France had centered on their colonial competition, in which they had seemed ready to risk war. Instead, they settled for defined spheres of influence. Following the confrontation at Fashoda in 1898, the French set about turning humiliation into good relations. They accepted British domination in Egypt in return for Britain's recognition of French interests in North Africa, particularly Morocco. Further understandings followed, culminating in the Anglo-French Entente Cordiale of 1904, in which France and Great Britain eliminated their major issues of imperial conflict. Those issues stretched from Asia to the Atlantic (from Siam to Newfoundland) and across the African continent (from the Niger River to North Africa). Formally a mere understanding, the Entente implied much more, as the exchange of public visits between Edward VII and the president of France was meant to demonstrate.

Germany's diplomatic position remained strong, and German leaders reasoned that an assertive foreign policy would demonstrate that strength. But the tenor of international relations was changing. As armaments increased and treaties proliferated, each power became more obsessed with its own security, and public opinion grew more sensitive to questions of national honor.

Testing Alliances: Three International Crises From 1905 to 1911 three diplomatic crises—each of which initially seemed a German victory—in fact drew Germany's opponents closer together. The first of these crises arose over Morocco. France, with well-known designs on Morocco, had carefully won acquiescence from the powers except for Germany. The German chancellor, Bernhard von Bülow, demanded that an international conference settle Morocco's future. He aimed to demonstrate that France was isolated, and in fact his warnings forced the resignation of Théophile Delcassé, France's foreign minister and the architect of

French policy. When in 1906 the conference met at Algeciras, it confirmed that Morocco had special international status but recognized the primacy of French interests. The crisis was a disaster for German diplomacy. Only Austria-Hungary loyally voted with its ally. Italy, Russia, Great Britain, and the United States (now a regular participant in such international agreements) supported France, and Germany's threatening tactics led French and British officials to begin talks about their mutual military interests.

The second crisis arose over the Balkans. Austria was concerned that Serbia, led by a new king and a radical nationalist government, had become a dangerous antagonist. Austria also feared that Turkey's influence in the Balkans would grow following the 1908 revolution in Turkey—led by a group known as the Young Turks, who were determined to modernize their nation. In response, Austria-Hungary decided to annex Bosnia and Herzegovina. That move, which threatened Serbia, in turn outraged Russian Slavophiles. They were nationalists who believed that Russia should defend the interests of Slavs everywhere, and they demanded an international conference. Britain and France agreed. Germany supported Austria-Hungary, although angered by the sudden annexation.

Diplomatic crises were becoming tests of alliances (and significantly, Italy expressed resentment at not being consulted by Austria-Hungary rather than loyalty to the Triple Alliance). There had been earlier signs that Italy might drift away. In 1902 France recognized Italian ambitions in Libya, and France and Italy pledged neutrality if either was attacked by a third power (i.e., Germany). Although the Triple Alliance was renewed in the same year, Italy now sat on the fence between the Franco-Russian and the Austro-German alliances. Only time would tell on which side Italy might end up.

The third major crisis once again involved Morocco, which France now wanted to annex. It had consulted all the European powers, and talks with Germany seemed to be going well when suddenly in 1911 the Germans sent the gunboat *Panther* to the Moroccan port of Agadir (a show of power and a classic imperialist gesture) and then asked for all of the French Congo as the price for accepting France's annexation of Morocco. Both the demands and the method seemed excessive, and in Great Britain David Lloyd George publicly denounced them. Once again, eventual compromise (France would cede parts of its Congo lands and bits of its other African territories adjacent to German colonies) counted for less than the rising tension and growing international distrust of the Germans.

The Arms Race   The standing armies of France and Germany doubled between 1870 and 1914, and all able-bodied men had some military responsibilities from the age of twenty to their late fifties. In 1889 Great Britain adopted the principle that its navy must equal in size the two next-largest fleets combined, and in 1906 it had launched the *Dreadnought,* the first battleship armed entirely with big guns. By 1914 Britain had twenty-nine ships of this class afloat and thirteen under construction. The German navy had eighteen, with nine being built. With the dangers of a European arms race ever more apparent, especially the growing naval competition between Britain and Germany, the major powers agreed to two great conferences on disarmament and compulsory arbitration. The conferences met at The Hague in 1899 and again in 1907, but no country was willing to sacrifice any of its strength. At the second conference German delegates bluntly rejected any limitation on their sovereign right to make war, while at that very moment Kaiser William complained to the British press that England should be grateful to Germany for having remained neutral in the Boer War. This time, British recriminations against the outspoken Kaiser reflected an important shift in policy as well as anger.

The Triple Entente   In 1902 Britain ended its long tradition of refusing peacetime alliances and did so by signing a treaty with Japan, the rising power in the East. It was a first step toward reducing conflicts over imperial claims. That agreement was followed in 1907 by an accord among France, Russia, and Japan. It delimited each nation's areas of interest and, by guaranteeing the integrity of China, sought to reduce their competition there. Such understandings opened the way for further agreement between Great Britain and Russia, old imperial antagonists. They resolved points of contention reaching from the Black Sea to Persia, Afghanistan, and Tibet. The treaty between Britain and Russia, each already allied with France, brought into being the Triple Entente as an informal coalition of France, Russia, and Britain. It was clearly intended to counterbalance the Triple Alliance of Germany, Austria, and Italy, and its implications became clear when Britain decided in 1912 to withdraw its battleships from the Mediterranean, leaving the French navy to defend Britain's interests there while the British fleet concentrated on the German threat in the North Sea.

◆ THE OUTBREAK OF WORLD WAR

The Triple Alliance and the Triple Entente glared menacingly at each other, increasing their armament, and measuring every international event as a gain or loss for their side.

The Balkan Threat   Turmoil in the Balkans was thus a test of strength for the two sides. The ferment there of nationalism, modernization, militarism, and shaky parliamentarism echoed Europe-wide trends, but it was complicated by centuries of oppression, by disputed boundaries (most of recent invention), and by social, ethnic, and religious rivalries. The competition between Russia and Austria-Hungary quickly became enmeshed in these conflicts, and so did the Balkan ambitions of Germany (with railway and economic interests in the peninsula) and of Italy.

Italy's defeat of Turkey in 1912, when Italy gained Libya and important Mediterranean islands, triggered what came to be known as the first Balkan War. In the fall of that year Bulgaria, Serbia, and Greece also declared war on Turkey. In a few months they drove the Ottomans from all their remaining holdings in Europe except Constantinople. After a partial truce and months of border skirmishes, the great powers hammered out the terms of peace at the end of May 1913.

One month later Serbia and Greece, quickly joined by Romania and Turkey, declared war on Bulgaria, the big winner in the previous war. This conflict ended in a few weeks, but local anger and international concern did not. The great powers pressured the belligerents to accept peace, but they were watching each other more closely still.

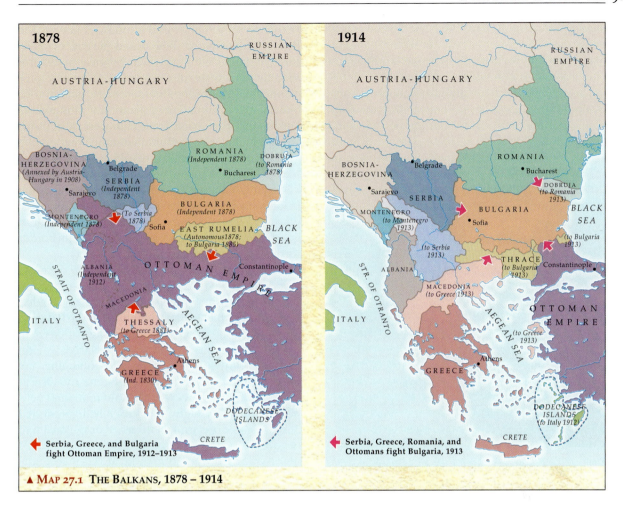

▲ MAP 27.1 THE BALKANS, 1878 – 1914

The Assassination of an Austrian Archduke In this atmosphere of growing distrust, tension between Austria-Hungary and Serbia increased. Groups of Serbian nationalists agitated in behalf of their fellow Slavs living under Austrian rule in Bosnia and Herzegovina, and Austria threatened to use force against Serbia if it did not abandon some of its nationalist claims. Against this background, Archduke Francis Ferdinand, the heir to the Austrian and Hungarian thrones, chose to parade in Sarajevo, the capital of Bosnia, on June 28, 1914. If the archduke wished to display Habsburg authority, others were eager to demonstrate against Austria. As the archduke's car moved down the street, a bomb just missed him. Then other conspirators lost their courage and failed to fire as his car passed by. At that point his driver made a wrong turn, started to back up, and yet

another young Bosnian revolutionary fired point-blank, killing both the archduke and his wife.

The leaders of Austria-Hungary, convinced that the Serbian government was involved, believed it essential to respond strongly. They dispatched a special emissary to Berlin, where he was promised Germany's full support, and on July 23 Austria sent an ultimatum to Serbia. Meant to be unacceptable, it gave Serbia forty-eight hours in which to apologize, ban all anti-Austrian propaganda, and accept Austria-Hungary's participation in investigations of the plot against Francis Ferdinand.

Serbia replied with great tact, accepting all terms except those that diminished its sovereignty and offering to submit even these to arbitration. Great Britain proposed an international conference, to which France and Russia reluctantly agreed, and Germany hinted that Serbia and

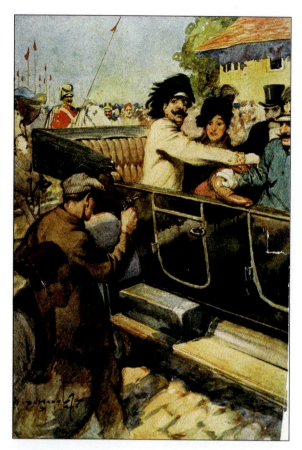

▲ The assassination of Archduke Francis Ferdinand and his wife in Sarajevo, painted as a dramatic moment when a single act affected the course of history.
© Corbis

Austria-Hungary alone should settle the matter. Another crisis seemed about to pass when, on July 28, Austria-Hungary declared war on Serbia.

Stumbling into War   The system of alliances, increasing armament, bluster, and compromise had become a trap. Austria-Hungary was in reality not yet ready to fight. Germany and Great Britain still hoped the Austrians would limit themselves to occupying Belgrade, the Serbian capital, and then agree to an international conference. But Russia could not appear to abandon its role as protector of the Slavs nor let Austria-Hungary unilaterally extend its sway in the Balkans.

On July 29 Russia ordered partial mobilization, making clear that its move was aimed at Austria-Hungary only. The following day, however, the Russians discovered they lacked the organization for a partial call-up and so announced a general mobilization instead. On July 31 Germany proclaimed a state of readiness, sent Russia an ultimatum demanding demobilization within twelve hours, and requested France to declare what it would do in case of a Russo-German war.

France answered that it would act in its own interests and then mobilized but held its troops ten kilometers (about six miles) from the German frontier to prevent any incidents. The Germans, who had planned next to demand that France guarantee its neutrality by surrendering its border fortresses, were unsatisfied.

On August 1 Germany mobilized and declared war on Russia. Convinced this step meant war on the Western front as well, Germany also invaded Luxemburg and sent an ultimatum to the Belgians demanding the unobstructed passage of German troops. On August 3 Germany declared war on France and invaded Belgium. The following day Great Britain declared war on Germany. Of Europe's six major powers, only Italy remained neutral. Within forty-eight hours each belligerent had 2 million soldiers under orders. World War I had begun.

◆ THE ORIGINS OF WORLD WAR

The question of what caused the Great War—or, more simply, who was to blame—would become an important issue in European affairs. Four years later the victors in that war blamed Germany so insistently that they would write its guilt into the peace treaty. Most historians have considered that assessment to be one-sided. German scholars rejected it with special force, which explains the furor some forty years later (after another world war) that greeted the research of the German historian Fritz Fischer. He found evidence that Germany's leaders had, in fact, looked forward to war and nurtured almost boundless ambitions for military dominance. But the question remains without a final answer, for the causes adduced depend very much on how long-range a view one takes.

The Response to an Assassination   The immediate cause, the assassination of the archduke, almost did not happen. The tensions that made it so significant had deeper roots, however: in Balkan struggles for independence, in Austria-Hungary's declining power, and in each nation's fears for its safety. Human judgment was also involved, and individual leaders and governments can be blamed for Austria-Hungary's untoward haste in attacking Serbia, Germany's irresponsible support of Austria-Hungary, Russia's clumsy and confused diplomacy, and France's eagerness to prove loyalty to the Russians. British leaders were at fault as well. Not wanting to admit that they were already attached to one side, they failed to warn the Germans that an attack on France meant war with Britain.

The Limits of Diplomacy   Such an analysis, however, may make statesmen seem to have been more autonomous and therefore more to blame than they were. The system of alliances that was intended to achieve security had been hardened by habit, military imperatives, and domestic poli-

tics. The fears that cemented these commitments were reflected in: Britain's conviction that empire required supremacy at sea; France's eagerness to revenge the defeat of 1870 and regain Alsace-Lorraine; Russia's 150 years of territorial expansion; Italy's need to show itself a great power; Austria's dependence, since Metternich, on foreign policy to sustain a shaky regime; and Germany's fear of encirclement and use of prestige abroad to reduce conflict at home.

The arms race itself contributed to the outbreak of war. Strategy was a factor, too. Germany's victory over France in 1870 had been understood to prove the superiority of the Prussian system of universal conscription, large reserves, and detailed military planning. Furthermore, it was believed that technology gave an attacker overwhelming advantages. It took immense organization and many days to locate millions of reservists, get them to their proper units, equip them, and then effectively deploy them.

▼ **By 1912 this Krupp factory at Essen was devoted to the arms race that was consuming an increasing proportion of Europe's energy and wealth.**
AKG London

Mobilization, which in the eyes of some diplomats was a cumbersome but effective show of seriousness, was considered by military men in each country to be an essential act of self-defense. By 1914 it had become tantamount to war. Even slight disadvantages in numbers, weapons, speed, or tactics might prove fatal. Thus, each increase in personnel and weapons was quickly matched, often with enormous effort; France, for example, had only 60 percent of Germany's potential manpower and yet equaled its rival through more burdensome conscription. The arms race, justified by the fear that it was meant to allay, fed on itself.

Public Opinion Such expenditures of money and resources had to be justified to parliaments. Ultimately, these enormous forces, like foreign policy, rested on domestic politics. In every country flag-waving could win votes and nationalism seemed a way to overcome domestic divisions. Special interest groups associated with the military and imperialism joined with political groups fearful of socialist gains in dramatizing issues of national honor as a way to appeal to the masses. This pattern was especially strong in Germany, where economic growth and social change threatened the political system that preserved the dominance of Prussia and of the Junker class.

Few Europeans really wanted war, yet everywhere there was popular joy at its outbreak. After decades of economic, demographic, and imperial competition, after decades of threats and fears, armed conflict was almost a relief; and it generated a sense of unity and common purpose that was a welcome contrast with ordinary public life. In immediate terms, world war could have been avoided; in a larger sense, it was a product of the very structures it nearly annihilated.

▼ **Summer hats in the air, an August crowd in London's Trafalgar Square cheers the declaration of war on Austria, as it had a week earlier the announcement of war with Germany. Similar scenes occurred throughout that week of 1914 in France and Germany.**
© Corbis

◄ In Berlin during August 1914, German volunteers march down the street hailing their good fortune; they will soon fight for their country.
Ullstein Bilderdienst

▼ Newly mobilized French recruits pose in front of the flower-decked train that will carry them off to military duty.
©Tallandier

II. The Course of the War

For decades European military staffs had prepared detailed plans for the situation they now faced. The French intended to drive into Alsace and Lorraine in coordinated dashes that reflected their almost mystic belief in the spirit of a patriotic offensive. German strategy began from the desire to avoid fighting on two fronts simultaneously: A detailed plan adopted years earlier called for assigning minimal forces to hold the Russians in the East and to slow the expected French attack in Alsace. Then Germany's main armies would pour through Belgium and on to Paris. The German aim was to knock France out of the war before Russia could bring its massive armies into play and before British aid could make a difference. That strategy envisioned the German army as a coiled spring to be released the moment war began, and it required the invasion of neutral Belgium, further labeled Germany as the aggressor, and determined Britain's entry into the war. Both sides believed they were ready. The Triple Alliance was reduced to two, Germany and Austria-Hungary, referred to as the Central Powers. Italy announced its neutrality when war broke out, declaring the attack on Serbia an offensive action that did not meet the terms of the Triple Alliance. Against the Central Powers stood Britain, France, and Russia, referred to as the Allies.

◆ THE SURPRISES OF THE FIRST TWO YEARS

In 1914 the belligerents all assumed the war could not last long. It was thought that modern economies, intricately connected by trade, would be unable to sustain a long conflict and that modern weapons would make for brief wars of rapid movement (as in 1870). But in a few months it began to be clear that the war being fought was not the one planned, though commanders were slow to admit it. Increased firepower gave defensive forces unexpected strength. Cavalry was ineffectual, for rifles could now hit horses from great distances; infantry, loaded down with equipment, could not go far very rapidly; and the common soldier proved able to absorb more punishment than anyone had thought possible.

The German Offensive After making some slight gains, the French offensive in Alsace was stopped, with heavy losses on both sides. The Germans were more nearly successful. The French command had underestimated by half the forces they would face at the outbreak of war, and in the first weeks the Germans drove to within thirty miles of Paris. But the German army was as battered as the defenders, its casualties as high, and its lines of communication and supply dangerously stretched.

These factors, added to unanticipated Belgian resistance, infuriated and worried German commanders; for their elaborate plans, first drawn up by Count Alfred von Schlieffen in 1891 and regularly modified thereafter, relied on a different outcome. The Schlieffen plan was based on a series of assumptions: that there was no decisive strategic objective on the Eastern front (which proved true), that Russia would be slow to mobilize (less true than expected), and that modest German forces would therefore be sufficient to hold the Russians

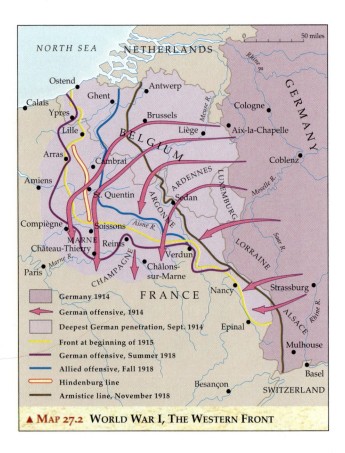

▲ MAP 27.2 WORLD WAR I, THE WESTERN FRONT

off while Germany gained an overwhelming advantage on the Western front by throwing two-thirds of its forces against the French (French forces, however, had grown larger and stronger in the decade before the war broke out).

The plan called for the German armies wheeling through northern France to capture Paris and knock France out of the war. For so great and quick a victory, the general staff was willing to violate Belgian and Dutch neutrality and leave the Eastern front largely to Austrian forces, for which they had little respect. Despite initial successes, a number of things went slightly wrong. When a small British force arrived sooner than expected and Russian armies made unanticipated advances, the indecisive German chief of staff, Helmuth von Moltke (nephew of the field marshal who had led Germany to victory in 1866 and 1870), modified the Schlieffen plan. He ordered troops intended for the Western front to the East and sent extra forces to Alsace in hope of a breakthrough there. The German army cut east of Paris instead of running beyond it as planned. After each bloody encounter, the enemy retreated but was not routed, and German officers were surprised they took so few prisoners.

French and Russian Offensives On the other side, the French commander in chief, Joseph Joffre, remained imperturbably confident of the ultimate success of a great French drive. In September the French launched a counteroffensive along the Marne River that saved Paris and hurled the Germans back to the natural defenses of the Aisne River. There, despite repeated Allied attacks, the Germans held. In the next few months the armies tried to outflank each other but succeeded only in extending the front northward to the sea. With changes of only a few miles, the battle lines that were established at the end of 1914 would remain those of the Western front for the next four years. France had not been knocked out of the war, but Germany held the important industrial and agricultural area of northeastern France, a tenth of its territory, and nearly all of Belgium.

On the Eastern front, Russian armies scored important gains in early August, taking eastern Galicia from Austria-Hungary and beginning an invasion of eastern Prussia in the north. Moltke talked in panic of a general retreat until the battle of Tannenberg late in August. There generals Paul von Hindenburg and Erich Ludendorff, who became Germany's greatest war heroes, surrounded and destroyed a Russian army and then pushed on almost to Warsaw before being stopped.

In the south, Austria-Hungary halted the Russian advance with German aid and took Belgrade despite the strong resistance of the Serbian army. By the end of 1914, Germany and Austria-Hungary had made impressive gains at every hand. They had also gained from Turkey's entry into the war in late October on the side of the Central Powers (and against its old enemy, Russia), which threatened Britain and France through the eastern Mediterranean all the way to Suez.

The War of Attrition On the Western front especially, the great armies found themselves bogged down in a terrifying kind of siege warfare. Artillery became increasingly important, and shells were fired at rates unimaginable a few months before, devastating the pockmarked land and making any movement difficult. Dug into trenches and clinging to specially created concrete huts called pillboxes, neither side could be uprooted. Military units worked out complex systems of communication by laying cables, building bridges, and maintaining roads and railways. For the first time, poison gas was used, but the German troops could not follow up the momentary gains their new weapon permitted (and the British were no more successful when they experimented with gas some months later).

Again and again, the Allied armies attempted to mount a great offensive, only to be stopped when German reinforcements arrived and with gains of only a few miles and hundreds of thousands of men lost. Battles were now numbered— the Second Battle of Ypres (April–May 1915), the Second Battle of Artois (May–June), the Second Battle of Champagne (September–November), the Third Battle of Artois (September–October)—and after a year's bloodshed, the Western front remained essentially the same.

Italy Joins the Allies   Nothing broke the stalemate, neither desperate new offensives nor Italy's entry into the war. Both sides had been negotiating with Italy; Britain and France could make the better offer. In April 1915 Italy signed a secret agreement, the Treaty of London, and committed itself to the Allies. In return Italy was promised considerable territory along its border with Austria-Hungary, important Dalmatian islands, and expansion of its colonial holdings. Italy declared war in May and soon advanced to a line along the Isonzo River. Eleven battles would be fought along that line in the next two years.

Costly Offensives   Early in 1916 the Germans launched another all-out offensive to knock France out of the war. They stormed the fortifications at Verdun. Their aim, knowing the French

▼ **The ruins of Verdun stood like a broken tombstone after the siege that bled both armies.**
AP/Wide World Photos

would be determined to hold, was more to bleed the enemy than to take territory. For days shells poured down, and then the Germans attacked in overwhelming numbers. From February to July 1916 the fighting continued at full pitch. German forces captured two outlying forts, but the French managed a brief counterattack. Verdun held; and though the French losses, more than 300,000 men, weakened the subsequent Allied offensive, Germany casualties were only slightly less.

The Allied attack in the Battle of the Somme, from July to November, brought still heavier casualties and a maximum advance of seven miles. The doctrine of the offensive, like general morale, was sinking in mud and gore. If tactics could not guarantee victory, then attrition, systematically exhausting men and resources, was the alternative.

There was more movement on the Eastern front but no decisive result. The Central Powers (Germany, Austria-Hungary, and the countries on their side) launched an offensive through Galicia in May 1915, drove forward a hundred miles, and followed that with a general offensive in July. By late September—while their new ally, Bulgaria, pushed into Serbia—the Central Powers were massed on a line from Riga in the north to the easternmost part of Hungary. Russia lost Poland and Lithuania.

▼ **Massive German forces cross the Schara river, the opening of the drive into Galicia in May 1915 that would carry the Central Powers into Russia.**
AKG London

The following year, however, in one of the few really well-conducted Russian campaigns, General Alexis Brusilov regained a large part of those losses. The effort cost Russia a million men and used up the capacity to do more. Although the Russian offensive brought Romania into the war on the Allied side, Austria-Hungary took Bucharest at the end of the year.

The Naval War   Naval strength, so significant to the arms race, proved more important in terms of supply lines than combat. The single large-scale attack by sea, the dramatic landing of Allied forces on the Gallipoli peninsula in April 1915, was a failure. The Allies were grateful to withdraw in December without having either opened the Dardanelles as a pipeline to Russia or forced the Ottomans out of the war.

Britain's naval blockade of Germany was more effective. As the blockade began to hurt, Germany countered in 1915 by announcing a submarine blockade of Britain; but the angry reaction of neutrals, led by the United States, forced Germany to abandon the tactic. The sinking of passenger ships—most sensationally the *Lusitania*, killing more than a thousand civilians—gave way in 1916 to attacks on armed merchant ships and then, in the face of American warnings, to the renunciation of "unlimited" submarine warfare. The one great naval battle of the war, at Jutland in May 1916, was indecisive. British and German fleets lost the same number of ships, though three British battle cruisers were sunk to only one German capital ship. The British retained a two-to-one naval superiority, however, and after Jutland the feared German fleet stayed in its harbors.

◆ ADJUSTMENT TO TOTAL WAR

By every measure, this was war on an unprecedented scale, and adjustment to its demands strained the very fabric of society. The first response was national unity. The German parliament unanimously voted the funds for war, the public convinced that theirs was a just and defensive war. The French hailed their "sacred union," and a leading socialist joined the cabinet. In Great Britain the Liberal government soon gave way to

Chronology

THE WESTERN FRONT, 1915–1916

1915

Feb. 16–Mar. 30	Battle of Champagne, French attacks.
Apr. 22–May 25	Second Battle of Ypres, Germans gain, using gas, halt.
May 9–June 18	Second Battle of Artois, French short advance.
Sept. 22–Oct. 15	Second Battle of Champagne and Third Battle of Artois, broad Allied attack, limited gains.

1916

Feb. 21–July 11	Battle of Verdun, nearly 350,000 casualties on each side.
Aug. 29	Hindenburg and Ludendorff replace von Falkenhayn.
July 1–Nov. 18	Battle of the Somme, British lose about 400,000 men; French, 200,000; Germans nearly 500,000.
Dec. 12	Nivelle replaces Joffre as commander of French armies.

a coalition that included Conservatives, and in Russia the government seemed almost popular.

Domestic Mobilization There was also immediate dislocation. At first, factories closed and unemployment rose despite conscription; a labor shortage followed as war production became crucial. Everywhere, agricultural output dropped, contributing to the food shortages of subsequent years. Prices rose rapidly, and consumer hoarding further strained faltering systems of distribution. Just as the rules of warfare were bent or shattered by unlimited submarine warfare, poison gas, and a blockade that included consumer goods, so governments expanded their powers to move workers, censor the press, control railroads and shipping, and direct the economy. Unprepared for the ever greater amounts of ammunition and sup-

plies required by the war, governments quickly learned to use paper money, rationing, and central planning.

In Great Britain the government requisitioned supplies and forced industry to new efficiency. Despite voluntary enlistments that raised the largest army in British history, it had to adopt conscription in 1916, a step Winston Churchill would call "the greatest revolution in our system since the institution of feudalism under William the Conqueror." Rebellion in Ireland that Easter was quickly put down; yet it was a serious diversion for British troops and a disturbing reminder of how cruelly war tested every weakness in the social structure.

Germany, deprived of critical raw materials, developed the most fully controlled economy of any of the combatants, under the brilliant direction of Walther Rathenau. Private firms were organized into sectors of production so that the most important could be favored, inefficient firms closed, and national planning enforced. The chemical industry created rubber substitutes, culled aluminum from local clays, manufactured fertilizers from nitrates in the air, and made textiles from wood pulp. Substitutes, which made *ersatz* an international word, included chestnut flour and clover meal used in the "war bread" that, like meatless days and conscription, soon made civilians feel the burden of all-out war. German officials were less sensitive to civilian needs, and far less efficient in meeting them, than Allied leaders.

In the first weeks of German advances, France lost half of its iron ore and coal fields and more than half its heavy industry; yet as commissions established quotas and allocated supplies, production steadily increased. Although Joffre exercised virtually dictatorial powers and censorship was severe, the tradition of political dispute was in large part preserved. In France, as in Great Britain, civilian authority had begun to reassert itself by 1915.

Great Britain, France, and Germany adjusted effectively to the new challenge of fielding vast armies while increasing industrial production and maintaining intricate logistical networks. The Austro-Hungarian and Russian empires could not match these feats. Their industries were less well developed; supplies and trained personnel were often lacking. Equally important, neither government knew how nor dared try to squeeze from the economy the quantities of food, ammunition, and clothing that war required. Russian armies increasingly showed the effects of fighting ill-fed and ill-shod, with inadequate weapons and ammunition, and without good communication. (Orders to Russian troops were broadcast uncoded, and the German ability to intercept them contributed to Ludendorff's reputation as a great tactician.) In adversity, Austria-Hungary could not rely on the continued loyalty of subject peoples, and soldiers were carefully dispatched to zones far from their native lands so as not to be fighting against people who spoke their own language.

Social Effects By the winter of 1916–1917, the strains were visible to all. Everywhere on the bloodied continent, Europeans were thinner, more shabbily dressed, overworked, and grieved by the endless losses of husbands, sons, and homes. Poor crops and overloaded transportation systems further reduced the diet; this winter was Germany's "turnip winter," when the best prepared of the domestic war economies could barely keep its people healthy. Society itself was subtly altered from the first month, when Belgian refugees poured into France, until years after the war. The strains of war were changing society. As the queue became a kind of public rite and rationing a way of life, distinctions of social class blurred. Each government awkwardly tried to restrict the consumption of alcohol and worried about rising rates of illegitimacy.

Women on the Home Front The role of women in the workplace took on added meaning. Women were essential in sustaining what was now called the "home front" while the men fought on the battle front, and even most feminists became active supporters of their nation's war effort. In every country, women left home and domestic service to work in industry, transportation, and business. Though war propaganda reinforced traditional gender stereotypes by emphasizing the enemy's brutality toward women and the maternal care that nurses provided the wounded, governments were soon eager for women to go to work. British women were asked in 1915 to take any jobs they could, and by 1917 the government denied contracts to employers unwilling to hire women (see "Meet the 'Khaki Girls,'" p. 980). Thus, women

◀ **At a Vickers factory in England, women labored with patriotic seriousness at the task of preparing artillery shells.**
© Hulton-Deutsch Collection/Corbis

Meet the "Khaki Girls"

The two women who wrote this brief article, published in June 1917 in The Englishwoman, *a lady's magazine, present it as an upbeat account of the dedication of women workers, but it is also a document about class distinctions.*

"We got out of the tram and walked up the short, muddy path, past the sentry, who with fixed bayonet guards the entrance to A$_3$, the 'shop' in which we work. It was twenty minutes past two—ten minutes before the hour for the shift to begin—so there were plenty of our fellow-workers passing through the door. Among the three hundred girls employed on this shift there are not more than four or five lady-workers, so the crowd was made up of 'khaki girls', the colloquial name given to the industrial hands, originating from the fact that when women were admitted last July to the munition shops they wore khaki overalls, which since have been replaced for economical reasons by those made of black material.

"We had grown accustomed to the sight of the endless procession of girls pouring into the factory . . . all of the same type, rather wild, yet in their quieter moods giving an impression of sullen defiance, ready to answer you back if you should happen to tread on their very tender corns. So long, though, as you keep off those corns, and do not let these wayward creatures feel you are intruding nor provide yourself with anything which they have not, even though it be merely a newspaper to sit upon in preference to a dusty board, they will show their good nature to you—and they have plenty. Then there is their good humour and their gay spirits. No matter how strenuous the work, nor how wearing the hardships, they will always give out from this wonderful gaiety of spirits, and keep the ball rolling with their sense of humour—obvious and childlike—running as it does mostly to nicknaming, pelting the mechanics with orange peel, or skipping with a rope of steel shavings cut from the shell on the lathe.

"Every one of them carries a brown or green despatch-case. Most of them are flashily dressed: a cherry-coloured coat, a black-and-white check skirt, a satin blouse trimmed with swansdown, a hat, small in shape but too large to fit, so it drops over one eye, and down-trodden boots, is typical of what they wear. Some of them are exceedingly pretty; they are all heavily powdered, and in some cases rouged. Their hair is dressed with great care, and even if it does fall about their eyes it is not untidiness, but an effect purposely arranged by the aid of the small mirror—often a beautiful thing to look upon, either encrusted with shells or mounted on scarlet plush—carried in that despatch-case which is the essential part of a khaki girl's equipment, since it contains the food with which she is obliged to provide herself.

"We stood in the doorway a moment looking at the sun shining down upon the river. 'Do you think the Zeppelins will come tonight?' one of us said to the other. 'It will be a good night for them.' 'There's no moon.' 'Nor wind—and they were at Paris last night.'

"Then we went to our work, and the absorption of screwing plugs into shells, turning them on the lathe, taking them out and gauging them, working to exceed the standard number, swallowed up every other thought."

From Brenda Girvin and Monica Coxens, "Meet the 'Khaki Girls,'" *The Englishwoman*, 1917.

got jobs in the new munitions factories and other war-related industries that previously had employed only men. The French government forbade hiring men for jobs that women could do; and in Germany the Krupp steelworks, which had no women employees in 1914, counted twelve thousand by 1917. In Great Britain, the number of women workers soared to 5 million by 1918. In the munitions industries especially, the number of women workers rose steadily to become one-third or more of the total. Women also ran farms, became firefighters and bus conductors, and worked in offices. On the front, they served as nurses.

Women's contributions outside the home were publicly acknowledged, and for some women wartime activities brought increased independence. Women became more likely to live on their own and go out in public alone. Inevitably, questions arose about unequal pay and whether men might be permanently displaced; the debate over the proper role of women, which the suffrage movement had stimulated before the war, intensified.

Although general labor agitation remained below prewar levels, signs of growing discontent among workers had to be taken seriously. Trade unions were treated with new respect, and officials began to talk of the benefits to be granted after the war to those making such heavy sacrifices now. Even the kaiser spoke of ending the three-class voting system in Prussia and hinted at a government that would be responsible to parliament, while the House of Commons, in a notable reversal, declared its support in principle for women's suffrage. Meanwhile, month upon month of bloodshed in muddy, disease-filled trenches took a psychological as well as physical toll. Morale was sinking.

New Generals Having gained the initiative on the Eastern front, the Central Powers in December 1916 indicated their willingness to discuss a settlement, but their terms were wholly unacceptable to the Allies. The war would continue, and the belligerents looked to new leaders. In France Joffre's intolerance of civilian leaders brought his downfall in December 1916; he was replaced by the tactful and dashing General Robert Georges Nivelle, who planned a massive new offensive. This one, he promised, would break through German defenses.

In Germany two heroes of the Eastern front had been promoted. Hindenburg received overall command and with Ludendorff took charge of campaigns in the West in the fall of 1916. To destroy the shipping on which Britain depended, Germany returned to unlimited submarine warfare in January 1917. Aware that such a step might bring the United States into the war, the Germans calculated that Britain would have to sue for peace before American power could make a difference.

Political Changes The political changes were more revealing. Lloyd George, made minister of war in June 1916, became prime minister in December. Eloquent and energetic, once a radical orator who had terrified the upper classes, he now seemed the kind of popular and decisive leader who could galvanize the British war effort. After

▼ **In March 1917 women demonstrated in Petrograd, demanding that the rations of soldiers' families be increased.**
Sovfoto

French morale hit a dangerous low, that country made the fiery Clemenceau premier again in November 1917.

Change came to Russia too—through revolution. In March 1917 popular protest forced the tsar to abdicate (see Revolution in Russia, p. 1006), and a new provisional government proclaimed sweeping democratic reforms while promising to continue the war. Both sides knew that Russia was now more vulnerable than ever but that its immense resources had yet to be effectively tapped. For the Allies these changes in Russia gave the war itself new meaning. Now democracies, led by politicians with ties to the left, were fighting together against authoritarian governments. A war that involved the people more fully than any before took on an ideological meaning. The Allies' sense of democratic purpose was strengthened in April when the United States—resentful that Germany was sinking its ships and making overtures to Mexico that included promises of the return of former Mexican lands now part of the United States—declared war on Germany.

◆ THE GREAT TRIALS OF 1917–1918

In the fighting itself, neither new leaders nor shared ideals seemed to make much difference (see "Wilfred Owen Describes Trench Warfare," p. 983). Relentlessly, the war went on. Russia's collapse aided the Central Powers; American entry into the war was a gain for the Allies. Not until late in the summer of 1918 did the outcome begin to be clear.

Fighting in the West   On the Western front, Nivelle launched his great offensive in April and May 1917 despite multiple handicaps. The Germans had strengthened their defenses; disagreements arose between the British and French commands; and some French troops, dispirited by two years of endless death on the same desolate terrain, mutinied, refusing to fight. The Second Battle of the Aisne and the Third Battle of Champagne took a toll as great as their predecessors and made even slighter gains. Nivelle was replaced by General Henri Philippe Pétain, the hero of Verdun, who began a concerted effort to raise morale, but it would be months before France dared another offensive.

▲ **Desolation surrounded weary Allied soldiers as they made their way across the mud on the battlefield at Ypres.**
Imperial War Museum, London

The British went ahead with plans for an attack in the north, spurred by the desperate need to knock out at least some of the submarine bases from which German U-boats were sinking such enormous tonnages that the Admiralty openly wondered how many months Great Britain could last. The noise of battle could be heard in England, and hundreds of thousands of men fell, but the British fared no better in the Third Battle of Ypres (July–November) than the French had in their spring offensive. British morale, too, was shaken; yet stalemate continued. Germany's submarine warfare had come close to its goal, but Allied losses dropped to a tolerable level in mid-1917 with the development of the convoy, in which fleets of armed ships accompanied merchant vessels across the ocean. With America's entry into the war, the tonnage those convoys delivered grew still greater.

Allied Defeats: Russia and Italy   Elsewhere, the picture was different. On the Eastern front, Russian advances in July soon turned into almost constant retreat, and in November the communists gained control of the government. They invited all nations to join in peace without annexations or indemnities, then entered into independent negotiations with the Central Powers. The most populous of the Allies had been defeated.

WILFRED OWEN DESCRIBES TRENCH WARFARE

◆

Wilfred Owen's moving poems about World War I were published after he was killed in action in 1918, and they continue to be widely read. His first tour of duty had ended when he was sent home suffering from "shell shock." Some months later, he was back in France. On January 4, 1917, he wrote his mother that "on all the officers' faces there is a harassed look that I have never seen before," adding, "I censored hundreds of letters yesterday, and the hope of peace was in every one of them." He was back in the fighting a few days later, when he wrote her this letter.

Tuesday, 16 January 1917
[2nd Manchester Regt, B.E.F.]

"My own sweet Mother,

" . . . I can see no excuse for deceiving you about these last 4 days. I have suffered seventh hell.

"I have not been at the front.

"I have been in front of it.

"I held an advanced post, that is, a 'dug-out' in the middle of No Man's Land.

"We had a march of 3 miles over shelled road then nearly 3 along a flooded trench. After that we came to where the trenches had been blown flat out and had to go over the top. It was of course dark, too dark, and the ground was not mud, not sloppy mud; but an octopus of sucking clay, 3, 4, and 5 feet deep, relieved only by craters full of water. Men have been known to drown in them. Many stuck in the mud & only got on by leaving their waders, equipment, and in some cases their clothes.

"High explosives were dropping all around us, and machine-guns spluttered every few minutes. But it was so dark that even the German flares did not reveal us.

"Three quarters dead, I mean each of us 3/4 dead, we reached the dug-out, and relieved the wretches therein. I then had to go forth and find another dug-out for a still more advanced post where I left 18 bombers. I was responsible for other posts on the left but there was a junior officer in charge.

"My dug-out held 25 men tight packed. Water filled it to a depth of 1 or 2 feet, leaving say 4 feet of air.

"One entrance had been blown in & blocked.

"So far, the other remained.

"The Germans knew we were staying there and decided we shouldn't.

"Those fifty hours were the agony of my happy life.

"Every ten minutes on Sunday afternoon seemed an hour.

"I nearly broke down and let myself drown in the water that was now slowly rising over my knees.

"Towards 6 o'clock, when, I suppose, you would be going to church, the shelling grew less intense and less accurate: so that I was mercifully helped to do my duty and crawl, wade, climb and flounder over No Man's Land to visit my other post. It took me half an hour to move about 150 yards.

"I was chiefly annoyed by our own machine-guns from behind. The seeng-seeng-seeng of the bullets reminded me of Mary's canary. On the whole I can support the canary better.

"In the Platoon on my left the sentries over the dug-out were blown to nothing. One of these poor fellows was my first servant whom I rejected. If I had kept him he would have lived, for servants don't do Sentry Duty."

From Harold Owen and John Bell (eds.), *Wilfred Owen: The Collected Letters* (Oxford University Press, 1967).

Able now to engage more troops on the Italian front, Germany and Austria-Hungary launched a concentrated attack there in October, scoring an overwhelming victory at the Battle of Caporetto. Italy's armies collapsed as tens of thousands died, surrendered, or deserted. But the Italians regrouped along the Piave River; Britain and France rushed in reinforcements, and the Austro-German onslaught was slowed and then stopped.

The Last Year Although the Russians stopped fighting in February 1918, the Central Powers did not. They continued their eastward march until Russia signed the Treaty of Brest Litovsk in March. Russia surrendered Russian Poland, the Baltic provinces, the Ukraine, and Transcaucasia. Germany had acquired invaluable wheat and oil when it needed them most and a respite on one front. But merely patrolling such immense gains

Chronology

♦

The Western Front,
1917–1918

1917

April 6	United States declares war on Germany.
Apr. 9–20	Battle of Arras; Second Battle of the Aisne; Third Battle of Champagne; major Allied assaults bring minimal gains.
May 15	Pétain replaces Nivelle as mutinies break out in French army.
July 31–Nov. 10	Third Battle of Ypres; British assault costs 400,000 casualties.

1918

Mar. 21–Apr. 5	Great German offensive, major gains, finally checked.
Mar. 26	Foch named commander of all Allied armies in France.
May 27–June 6	Third Battle of the Aisne, major German attack, initial gains, then slowed; first major engagement of American troops.
July 15–Aug. 7	Second Battle of the Marne, German attack and Allied counterattack, Germans forced back over Marne.
Sept. 26–Oct. 15	Battle of Argonne; Fourth Battle of Ypres; slow Allied advance.
Nov. 11	Armistice.

required great numbers of badly needed troops, and the incredibly harsh terms of the treaty stiffened resistance elsewhere. Both Lloyd George and U.S. President Wilson now formally stated Allied war aims that expressed their confidence in victory and put revolutionary emphasis on the right to self-government.

On the Western front, the Germans, their reserves of personnel and resources nearing exhaustion, opened a great offensive. Attacking sector after sector from March through June, they made the greatest advances seen there in four years. It was a triumph of careful strategy, improved tactics, heavy artillery, and gas. To correct the weakness of divided command, the Allies named General Ferdinand Foch supreme commander of all their forces; and they retained their reserves while the Germans exhausted theirs. Enemy guns once more bombarded Paris before the Allied counteroffensive began in July. Slowly, then faster, the Germans were driven back over the familiar and devastated landscape. By the end of August, German armies had retreated to the Hindenburg line, a defensive position established at the beginning of 1917. The Allies continued their push in battles of the Argonne and Ypres in September and October, gaining inexorably—even if less rapidly than hoped or expected.

The Collapse of the Central Powers   On other fronts the Central Powers collapsed dramatically. In the Middle East, Turkish and German troops were defeated by British and Arab forces led by T. E. Lawrence, whose exploits in mobilizing Arab opposition to Turkey became part of the romantic lore in which this war was poorer than most. In October the sultan was deposed, and a new government sued for peace. Combined Serbian, French, British, and Greek forces under French leadership drove up the Balkan Peninsula. Bulgaria surrendered at the end of September, and the Allies moved toward Romania.

The Austro-Hungarian Empire was disintegrating. Czech, Yugoslav, Romanian, and Polish movements for independence, encouraged by the Allies, gained strength throughout 1918. Austria-Hungary attacked once more on the Italian front but withdrew after heavy losses. Its armies, defeated at Vittorio Veneto at the end of October, began simply to dissolve as the various nationalities left for home and revolution. Czechoslovakia and the kingdom later called Yugoslavia both declared their independence. In November Austria-Hungary surrendered unconditionally to the Italians.

At the end of September, Ludendorff had demanded that Germany seek an armistice, but that required political changes as well. Twice in 1917 Kaiser William II had promised to make his cabinet subject to a majority in the Reichstag; and in October 1918 he appointed Prince Max of Baden

▲ MAP 27.3 TERRITORIAL GAINS, 1914–1919

as chancellor to begin this transformation from above. Ludendorff resigned his command at the end of October, and Germany asked for peace on the general terms set forth by President Wilson. But Wilson now insisted on the evacuation of occupied territories and a democratic German government with which to negotiate.

The German Republic Accepts an Armistice
While German leaders hesitated, they faced the threat of revolution at home. A liberal believer in parliamentary government, Prince Max repre-

sented a compromise that might have worked earlier but now could not in the face of uprisings in the name of peace, democracy, and socialism. Germany threatened to break apart. Prince Max pleaded with William to abdicate and, when revolt spread to Berlin, simply announced that the kaiser had done so. William II abdicated on November 9 after a mutiny in the German fleet and revolution in Munich. The government was handed over to Friedrich Ebert, the leader of the Social Democrats; a German Republic was proclaimed and an armistice commission sent to meet with Foch. The commission agreed to terms on November 11. By then Allied troops were approaching German borders in the West and had crossed the Danube in the East, taken Trieste on the Adriatic, and sailed through the Dardanelles. In the meantime, revolution was sweeping across central Europe.

◆ THE EFFECTS OF WORLD WAR I

The war itself had some of the effects of revolution. Among the defeated nations, governments were overturned and shaky new ones established. Even among the Allies, war had forced such changes that no one could be sure what the postwar world would be like. Society had to be put together again.

The New State of Affairs   Throughout central Europe, political conflict adopted the techniques of force. In Germany radical groups staged a number of local revolts, creating an air of instability sustained by *Freikorps* ("free corps"), merce-nary squads made up of former soldiers available to any movement that could pay them for street fighting and marauding. To the east of Germany, new regimes and sometimes whole new nations replaced the defeated states.

The victorious governments, having shown the capacity to mobilize society for war, would now be held more responsible than in the past for society's peacetime needs, as evidenced in a spate of postwar legislation on housing, education, and pensions. Clemenceau, Lloyd George, and Wilson, the spokesmen of victory, had all been vigorous reformers, but now they watched with apprehension the revival of the radical left.

Life in wartime had affected social classes differently. Even where there was no open revolution, the aristocracy and other traditional elites had been weakened by the general democratization of political life and by the decline in purchasing power that resulted from inflation, reduction in the value of land, and increased taxes (especially in England). A middle class confident in 1914 found itself exposed and vulnerable after the

▼ It would take years to recover from the damage to roads and bridges and private housing in Belgium and northeastern France. The French village of Craonne, where Napoleon once won a battle and which was the scene of fighting in 1917 and 1918, looked like this in 1919.
© Collection Roger-Viollet/Getty Images

war, its savings threatened, its possibilities limited, its values challenged. Those on salary or fixed income suffered more from inflation than those on workers' wages; middle-class life became less lavish, and there were fewer servants (some 400,000 English women left domestic service in the course of the war). Workers, particularly the skilled, were on the whole relatively well off. Although rates of pay usually lagged behind inflation, the years of full employment and more jobs for women had increased family income; and trade unions used their greater influence to maintain shorter hours and higher pay. Peasants, though declining in number, were also often better off, helped by the demand for food and by inflation, which made it easier to pay off their debts.

The Change in Social Mores   Even ordinary manners and dress were different. Gentlemen, forced to use public transportation, had abandoned their top hats; women's clothes grew simpler and their skirts shorter. Women of the working class took to wearing cosmetics and high-heeled shoes and smoking and drinking in public, as did their middle-class sisters. Such changes in customs, even more than the increase in violent crime and juvenile delinquency, shocked moralists who associated them with casual encounters between the sexes, increased illegitimacy, and the popularity of dance halls.

Public appearance thus added to the economic and political disruptions of wartime in suggesting a new openness and uncertainty, a more fluid society in which old standards could not be recaptured. Millions of refugees constituted more tangible displacement, and millions of other Europeans (especially peasants and women) were not eager to return to their old way of life. Of course most people more or less did, and by the 1920s prewar constraints of class and gender were largely back in place, despite some relaxation.

The psychological impact of war, harder to demonstrate than the social changes, may have been just as important. Throughout society, there was a tendency following the war to expect instability. Intellectuals suffered what one historian has called "minds scorched by war"; and among the populace, a cynical distrust of leaders and institutions seems to have spread after years of wartime promises. There was a cleavage, too, between those who had fought and those who stayed home, those whose lives were transformed and those who had more nearly maintained business as usual. Bitterness about these inequalities of sacrifice surfaced in public denunciations of war profiteers and in a more inflammatory political rhetoric. At the same time, with a kind of selective nostalgia, many regretted the loss of that sense of common purpose and national unity that war had brought, and some even yearned again for the thrill of combat.

Economic Effects   Military needs had stimulated the rapid development of certain technologies. When World War I began, the cavalry was a major element of every army, pack horses and horse-drawn wagons the principal form of transport from rail lines to the front. By war's end, the practical importance of automobiles and airplanes, radio, and the chemical industry had become clear to all. In many factories the effort to speed up industrial production altered the nature of work as tasks were reorganized in ways thought to be more rational and efficient but that workers found increasingly impersonal and demanding.

Although some sectors of the economy gained from their wartime importance, the overall losses were dramatic. World trade had been disrupted and Europe's place in it transformed. In 1914 Europe was the world's greatest lender of money; in 1918 its nations were debtors. The physical destruction of property, aside from the billions lost in war matériel, was greatest in Belgium and France. In France alone, thousands of bridges and factories as well as a million buildings were destroyed. Total European production in the 1920s would fall below the level of 1913.

▼ MILITARY FATALITIES IN WORLD WAR I (MAJOR POWERS)	
Germany	1,900,000
Russia	1,700,000
France	1,400,000
Austria-Hungary	1,200,000
British Empire	900,000
Ottoman Empire	700,000
Italy	600,000
United States	100,000

The Dead and Wounded   The effects of the war required enormous adjustments from individuals, institutions, and society as a whole. So did the war's simplest accomplishment: the killing of 10 to 13 million people, perhaps one-third of them civilians. Moreover, for every soldier who died, two or three were wounded; millions were maimed for life. The casualty figures tell much about the history of the first third of the twentieth century. Among the armed forces, casualties ran about 50 percent for the major combatants except France, which suffered higher losses. Able to mobilize some 7 percent of its population, Russia could only estimate fatalities. Germany mobilized some 16 percent and France, 19 percent. In each country whole classes from the elite schools were virtually wiped out. For France, with its older population and low birthrate, the war was a demographic catastrophe in which a large part of an entire generation disappeared on the Western front. And throughout Europe, the one-armed, the one-legged, and the blind would live on, supported by pensions and performing menial tasks, in silent testimony to the cost of total war.

With all these losses before them, the leaders of exhausted nations sat down to make a lasting peace. The gigantic effort that victory required had increasingly been fueled by the vision of a better world in which governments would use their enhanced powers to ensure greater justice and fuller democracy. With Wilson as its moralistic voice, democracy—meaning popular participation in public life and opportunity for all—seemed a guarantee of peace. And democracy, Wilson urged, would put an end to the old secret diplomacy that juggled spheres of influence and national interests without regard for public opinion.

III. The Peace

From the Rhine to Russia so many governments were new and so many boundaries undecided that, by default as well as victory, the Allies seemed free to construct the new Europe of peaceful democracies their wartime statements had foreshadowed. Instead, the diplomats assembled at the Peace Conference in Paris found their task complicated by the very extent of victory and beset by more interests than they could satisfy. So great an opportunity and so grand an undertaking fed the extremes, first of hope, then of disillusionment. Meanwhile, away from Paris, more direct means were being used to shape the postwar world.

◆ THE REVOLUTIONARY SITUATION

The revolution in Russia was the most important of the revolutions that resulted from World War I, but there were many others. Among the defeated nations, only Bulgaria's government survived. From Asia Minor to Ireland, nationalist movements sought to capture power.

New Nations in Eastern Europe   The peoples suddenly released from Habsburg and Russian rule fought to define the boundaries of their new nations. In the Baltic lands, Lithuanian, Estonian, and Latvian republics marked their independence by war with Russia. Lithuania was also at odds with the new republic of Poland; and Poland faced conflict on all its other borders—against Russians, Ukranians, Czechs, and Germans. The creation of Czechoslovakia and the new kingdom of Yugoslavia led to renewed warfare as Hungary attacked Czechoslovakia, while in the Balkans Romania attacked both Hungary and Yugoslavia, just the kind of hostility that had preceded World War I.

Communist Expectations   Russia's communists had good reason then to hope that revolution would sweep from East to West, and Marxists throughout Europe looked to the miraculous events in Russia as the beginning of the socialist future they had so long imagined. In March 1919 delegates from a score of countries met in Moscow to establish the Third International. Communists were active in the Baltic states, and in 1919 Lenin's friend Béla Kun led a communist government in Hungary until Romanian armies ended his brief reign. There was also communist agitation in Vienna, where the provisional government of truncated Austria, all that was left of the Habsburg Empire, looked forward to union with the new German republic.

Marxists, however, had long set their eyes on highly industrialized Germany, finding revolutionary promise in its class tensions and strong socialist movement. Germany's defeat and a shaky new German republic appeared the fulfillment of old portents. In January 1919 a communist revolt broke out in Berlin, and in the following spring another uprising managed for a few weeks to make Bavaria a Soviet republic. Both were quickly defeated by remnants of the German army. Russia remained the center of the communist world.

◆ THE PEACE TREATIES

President Wilson's Fourteen Points had won acceptance as a basis for defining a new European order. The points dealt mainly with territorial adjustments but idealistically proclaimed the self-determination of peoples to be a matter of policy.

Wilson's call for free trade and open seas had long been part of the liberal canon. His attention to the dangers of colonial warfare, the need for disarmament, and the benefits of open diplomacy was more radical but echoed the common belief that such policies would have averted world war. Wilson's final point, and the one closest to his heart, called for a League of Nations to guarantee the safety of all. The American president's talk of "impartial justice," a "peace that will be permanent," and covenants that will be "sacredly observed" caught the imagination of the world.

The Paris Conference At the Paris Peace Conference, which opened in January 1919, all parties agreed not to repeat the mistakes of the Congress

▼ **When Woodrow Wilson paraded through the streets, Parisians cheered the representative of a new democratic era as well as an ally in victory.**
The Granger Collection, New York

of Vienna a century earlier. No defeated nations would take part in the early discussions; no German Talleyrand would divide the Allies. The atmosphere was one of sober business, organized around commissions of expert advisers. Thirty nations had joined the Allies, at least formally,[2] but the major decisions would be taken by the five big powers: France, the United Kingdom, Italy, Japan, and the United States.

In practice, since most questions did not directly concern Japan, primary authority resided in four men: Clemenceau, Lloyd George, Premier Vittorio Orlando, and Wilson. Disagreements among the Big Four soon became the center around which the negotiations turned. All were elected leaders, sensitive to public opinion, faced with grave domestic problems, and worried by the turmoil in central and Eastern Europe. Experienced politicians, they knew they had to hurry.

The Treaty with Germany   To settle by May the complicated terms for peace with Germany was a remarkable achievement. Haste itself probably made the treaty more severe than it might otherwise have been. Commissions, assuming their proposals would be subject to later bargaining, tended to begin with maximum terms, but these were often simply written into the treaty itself.

The territorial provisions were not extremely harsh. Germany lost territory and colonies but remained a great state. Except for Alsace-Lorraine, however, the new boundaries were a source of continuing difficulties. France did not get the left bank of the Rhine as it had wanted. Instead, the Allies were to occupy the Rhineland for fifteen years; and the coal-producing regions along the Saar River, while remaining under German sovereignty, would be supervised by France until a later plebiscite by universal suffrage determined the final disposition. Plebiscites would also decide whether Germany surrendered part of Schleswig to Denmark and part of upper Silesia to Poland.

The Polish provinces of eastern Prussia, where Germans formed about 40 percent of the popula-

tion, were immediately ceded to Poland. That created the controversial Polish corridor to the sea, which awkwardly separated eastern Prussia from the rest of Germany. Although a majority of the population within the corridor was Polish, its outlet was the German port city of Danzig, restored to its ancient status as a free city. Poland would always feel insecure with an arrangement the Germans never accepted.

Germany was to have no large artillery, submarines, or military air force, and no more than 100,000 men under arms—requirements that would have been less controversial if they had led to the general disarmament the treaty implied. The lists of matériel Germany had to deliver to the Allies were more punitive: horses and railway carriages, quantities of coal, most of its present ships, and some new vessels to be specially built.

Reparations   The required reparations were more burdensome still. Despite fine talk of not requiring an indemnity, the Allies declared that Germany should pay for civilian damages. The claims of Belgium, a neutral attacked without warning, were easily justified; and Clemenceau could argue that the most destructive fighting had occurred in Belgium and France. But Lloyd George had campaigned on a platform of making Germany pay. He insisted, over American objections, on including Allied military pensions as civilian costs—a demand that made Germany liable for sums unspecified and without foreseeable end. And Germany was required to accept "responsibility" for losses from a war "imposed . . . by the aggression of Germany and her allies." The "war guilt clause" became a subject of controversy in every country and a source of bitter resentment, official and private, in every part of Germany.

In German eyes, the treaty was an intolerable *Diktat* that German delegates had no chance to discuss until it was already drafted, when only minor objections were accepted. Faced with these terms, the German government resigned, and the parliament at first rejected the treaty's stipulation of German guilt. But when the Allies held firm, parliament angrily acquiesced. The treaty was signed on June 28, 1919, the fifth anniversary of the assassination at Sarajevo, in the Hall of Mirrors at Versailles, where Bismarck and Kaiser Wilhelm I had announced the German Empire

---

[2]The newly created nations of Yugoslavia, Czechoslovakia, and Poland were treated as Allies; the new republics of Austria, Hungary, and Germany as the defeated Central Powers.

forty-eight years before. The symbolism was complete.

Italian Aims   For the Big Four, Italy's expectations were especially difficult, and Italian insistence on them particularly irksome. The Treaty of London of 1915 had promised Italy much of the Slavic-speaking lands of the Dalmatian coast, and the Italian delegates expected to get them. Wilson was determined to prevent further violations of the principle of nationality beyond allowing Italy, for strategic reasons, to have the Tyrol south of the Brenner Pass through the Alps, although that former Austrian land was German-speaking.

Using a press interview, Wilson in effect spoke directly to the Italian people, asking them to reject the position taken by their representatives at the conference. The Italian delegation withdrew in protest, to a great outpouring of nationalist feeling at home. Eventually, Italy was given the Istrian Peninsula and some islands but not Dalmatia. For years to come, resentment over the promises not kept at Paris would be a disruptive issue in Italian domestic politics.

The Other Treaties   With the signing of the Treaty of Versailles, the Big Four dispersed, leaving the details of the remaining settlements to their foreign offices. The treaty with Austria in September was closely modeled on the treaty with Germany, but reparations and demilitarization, including naval restrictions, hardly seemed appropriate for the shaky little landlocked Austrian republic. Boundaries for the other new states were settled on the basis of nationality in some cases and strategic needs in others.

Treaties with Bulgaria in November and with Hungary in June 1920 gave Bohemia to Czechoslovakia on historical grounds, while Hungarian claims to a larger historical kingdom were largely

▲ **MAP 27.4 TERRITORIAL SETTLEMENTS, 1919–1926**

Legend:
- Allied Occupation Zone
- Demilitarized Zone
- New states created in 1919
- Areas ceded by Austria-Hungary
- Areas ceded by Bulgaria
- Areas ceded by Germany
- Areas ceded by Russia
- Plebiscite areas

ignored. Hungary lost almost three-quarters of its former lands. Although Bulgaria surrendered relatively little territory, resentment over its borders was also great. Every state of Eastern Europe could cite some injustice it had suffered, usually with exaggerated statistics and with tales, too often true, of inhumane treatment. Railways, economic ties, "natural" boundaries, historical claims, and nationality simply did not coincide. It would fall to the new League of Nations to make these arrangements work.

Much remained to negotiate. The fate of many territories was determined later, sometimes by plebiscite. The promise of just treatment for minorities, an expression of the Allies' decent intent, would confront the sensitivity of new states about protecting their sovereignty. Many of the arrangements were just not workable. The reparations required from Austria-Hungary, for example, were divided among the new states carved out of the former Habsburg Empire, which left some of them paying reparations to others, a perpetual source of dissension.

The Unstable Settlement in The Middle East

The final treaty, with Turkey, was not signed until August 1920, and much of it never went into effect. The Allies' aims had been contradictory all along, and the postwar situation spawned indigenous movements in the former Ottoman Empire as complex and uncontrollable as those in Eastern Europe. The Russian and Habsburg empires no longer competed for influence there, and the Soviet government's release of earlier secret Allied plans for partitioning the Ottoman Empire reinforced suspicions that Britain and France were more commited to an old imperialism than to any new arrangements.

A nationalist revolt in Turkey had brought the reforming Mustafa Kemal to power, and he succeeded in ensuring Turkey's territorial integrity. Arabia's independence was also recognized, although internal conflict there created further opportunities for European influence. The pressing need to create political order on the eastern shores of the Mediterranean was met by a solution defined as temporary. France was to have a supervisory authority in Syria, and a vaguely defined area—carved from Palestine, Trans-Jordan, and Iraq—would be subject to British authority. Aside from recognizing the presence of Britain and France in the Middle East, the treaty settled little, and lasting boundaries would be determined only through the conflicts and diplomacy of the next few years.

British intentions in separating Palestine from Trans-Jordan were especially confusing. Anti-imperialist sentiment was strong in the Middle East, where it was often connected to Islam.

During the war, the European powers had competed with each other in showing sympathy for the region's nationalist movements; and the Allies had encouraged Arab nationalism. In 1917 the British foreign secretary, Arthur Balfour, had also promised that a "national home" for Jews would be created in Palestine. In accord with the propaganda and humanitarian concern of that difficult year, the Balfour Declaration also guaranteed the rights of Muslims. In short, British intentions for Palestine remained uncertain, and their subsequent statements provided little clarification.

Colonial Mandates

In their effort to codify French and British interests, these arrangements did lead to an important innovation. Colonial territories were declared "mandates" of the League of Nations and assigned to classes. The parts of the Ottoman Empire newly placed under British or French rule were Class A mandates, states considered on the verge of self-government. Most of the reassigned African territories (primarily former German colonies) were Class B mandates, ones in which European rules were to guarantee freedom of religion, prohibit trade in liquor and arms, refrain from subjecting natives to military training, and encourage commerce. Class C mandates were primarily Pacific islands, to be ruled essentially as colonies.

In every case, the mandate power had to submit annual reports to the League of Nations for review. Like much else in the treaties, the system of mandates can be seen both as an expression of conscience toward the rest of the world and as a device for absorbing former German colonies while legitimating continued European dominance.

Europe's Diminished Position

Taken together, all these arrangements confirmed Europe's importance in world affairs and the dominance of Britain and France among the European powers. Yet these provisions also reflected changes in Europe's position. The French and British could take pride in the contributions of wealth and people they had received from their empires, but imperialism was weakened by the war. Its assumptions and ideals were under challenge around the world, and the very system of mandates was a response to widespread criticism of European rule. The independence of former colonies was now recognized as an official and desirable goal. China and Siam (Thailand) had been able during the war to eliminate many of the treaties that had granted special rights to European states, and powerful movements in India, South Africa, Madagascar, and Egypt were demanding self-government.

Economically, while Europe had been enormously weakened, its suppliers (including countries with a single valuable crop, like Chile or Cuba) had prospered. The two that benefitted most were Japan and the United States. Japan sold munitions and weapons to the belligerents, especially Russia, and quickly replaced German traders throughout East Asia. American production reached new heights in sector after sector (steel production doubled), and by war's end the United States had a huge new merchant fleet. The United States, increasingly willing to intervene in South America, economically, politically, and militarily, now dominated that continent while its financiers directed the flow of world capital.

In the conflict everyone called "The Great War," the battles that mattered most had all taken place in Europe, but it had been a world war in the sense that its effects were felt around a globe that was getting smaller. The improved communications that carried supplies more rapidly across the seas (the Panama Canal opened in 1914) and on railroads from Japan to Russia and across Africa (the railroad from the Cape of Good Hope to Cairo was completed in 1918) also opened the possibility of communications and trade independent of Europe.

Disillusionment   Not since 1848 had liberal conceptions so thoroughly dominated European politics. There was much to hope for in the call for self-determination and plebiscites, the League of Nations, the system of colonial mandates, and the establishment of representative regimes throughout central Europe. By 1920, however, the limitations of what had been accomplished at Paris were all too apparent. Many of the agreements reached there reflected a cold assertion of national interest and a realistic appraisal of power, but the Allies had propagandized standards of high principle and injected ideology into international affairs.

Living in a time of revolutionary changes that they largely welcomed, the leaders who forged the peace were not revolutionaries. They never managed to find a place for Russia at the conference. They took little account of the social and economic complexities of Eastern Europe. Believ-

ers in democracy, they were baffled by the turmoil it created. They stimulated nationalist movements but recognized the dangers of nationalism. Slogans that sounded radical in November 1918 gave way to frightened insistence on order a few months later. None of the leaders of democracy yet fully understood how much had changed.

Disillusionment came quickly. In March 1920 the Senate of the United States rejected the treaties for the final time. Having claimed moral leadership, America would in the end not enter the League of Nations. In the process, it added France to the list of aggrieved states, for France had abandoned demands that Germany be weakened further in return for a joint guarantee against German aggression from the United States and Great Britain, which it did not get. China refused to sign the treaties because of terms that gave Japan, in addition to other gains, extensive rights in China. Japan was offended by the conference's rejection of a formal declaration that all races are equal.

The reparations were denounced in a brilliant and influential pamphlet in which the English economist John Maynard Keynes castigated the Carthaginian peace the victors had exacted.[3] He argued that the Allies owed one another more money than Germany could pay and that reparations would merely slow Europe's economic recovery. His analysis helped undermine confidence in the terms of peace, but his prescriptions—cancellation of international war debts and recognition that the international economic system was essentially artificial—were as utopian in their way as any of Woodrow Wilson's points. Keynes's criticisms, like those that for decades would ring from party platforms in every country, tended to exaggerate how much of the postwar world could be shaped by worried statesmen quarreling in Paris.

IV. Postwar Democracy
◆

From Finland to the Balkans, most of the states of Eastern Europe were new, and most of them had

---

[3]John Maynard Keynes, *The Economic Consequences of the Peace,* 1920; and the famous rebuttal, Etienne Mantoux, *The Carthaginian Peace: Or the Economic Consequences of Mr. Keynes,* 1946. The reference is to the harsh peace terms that Roman senators demanded upon the defeat of Carthage in the Third Punic War, 149–146 B.C.

democratic constitutions. The disappearance of the Russian, Austrian, and Ottoman empires opened the way for systematic modernization using the administrative institutions and practices they left behind. There were some hopeful signs. Schools, for example, were built by the thousands and functioned fairly effectively despite issues of language and nationality. But stability was threatened by economic, social, and ethnic conflict.

◆ THE NEW GOVERNMENTS

Economic Issues   The newly independent states of central and Eastern Europe had to construct a reliable administrative system while dealing with the destruction and dislocation left by war. In addition, economies far less efficient than those of Western Europe were further disrupted by national tariffs intended to protect local producers but that made conditions worse by breaking up the prewar flow of goods.

Extensive help from the new League of Nations proved essential as growing populations, widespread illiteracy, and lack of capital plagued economic development. Only Austria and Czechoslovakia had advanced industries that could compete in European markets; elsewhere, land remained the central economic issue.

Independence brought the eviction of "foreign" landlords, the breakup of large estates in the Baltic countries, and land reform in Bulgaria, Romania, and Czechoslovakia. These measures, less effective than expected, fostered accusations in each region of special treatment for favored nationalities. In Poland and still more in Hungary (where 40 percent of the peasants were landless and 90 percent held less than 3 hectares, or 7.4 acres), the great estate owners of the aristocracy succeeded in protecting their interests.

Ethnic Conflict   The resulting resentments favored peasant parties, soon dominant in Eastern Europe, which tended to combine agrarian radicalism with distrust of urban values, of modernizing changes, and of parliaments. Social conflicts were reinforced by ethnic and religious differences. The German minorities in Poland, Czechoslovakia, Hungary, and Bulgaria were generally among the resented well-to-do. Town-country antagonisms often put the rural Slovaks at odds with the Czechs of industrialized western Czecho-

slovakia. Anti-Semitism was especially virulent in Poland and Romania, where it was partly an expression of rural hostility toward village moneylenders and urban values. In Yugoslavia the claims of Greek Orthodox Serbians to be the "national" people angered the Roman Catholic Croatians and Slovenes. Macedonians—their homeland divided among Yugoslavia, Greece, and Bulgaria—agitated in all three countries and produced chaotic insurrection in Bulgaria from 1923 to 1925.

Such circumstances encouraged military intervention in politics, as in the new Greek republic and in the authoritarian rule in Hungary of Admiral Miklós Horthy, regent for an empty throne, who abolished the secret ballot in rural areas. But most of the governments of Eastern Europe worked more or less within their constitutions; Czechoslovakia, under President Tomás Masaryk and Foreign Minister Eduard Benes, became a model of the order, freedom, and prosperity that democracy was supposed to bring.

The Weimar Republic   The German provisional government had been established just in time to sign the armistice. Its officials referred proudly to the German "revolution" and promulgated decrees promising democracy, freedom of speech, a return to the eight-hour workday, and improvements in social security. Frightened of a communist revolution, the government quickly reached an accommodation with the army, which was already encouraging the legend that it had not lost the war but had been stabbed in the back by politicians and radicals at home. General Wilhelm Groener, who replaced Ludendorff as Hindenburg's principal aide, promised to assist the government provided it would not meddle in the army's affairs.

President Ebert accepted those terms, and when an uprising of left-wing Marxists, the Spartacists, gained control of most of Berlin in January 1919, the army crushed the revolt and shot its leaders. Lenin's best hope for a communist revolution in Germany died with them. One of those murdered was Rosa Luxemburg, who had drafted the Spartacist platform calling for a proletarian revolution. An effective leader and impressive intellectual, she had urged the Spartacists to avoid useless violence and had recognized that most workers remained loyal to Ebert's social

◄ **Friedrich Ebert took the oath of office as provisional president of Germany in February 1919; note the absence of men in uniform.**
Ullstein Bilderdienst

democratic government. But she would not abandon her party when hotter heads chose armed conflict. Her death was a lasting blow to the radical left, the government's reliance on the army a blow to Germany's new democracy.

Committed democrats nevertheless, Germany's new leaders held elections in January 1919 for a constituent assembly. It met in Weimar, with nearly three-quarters of the delegates intent on installing a republic. They wrote a thoroughly democratic constitution that joined proportional representation to universal suffrage. The president, directly elected for a seven-year term, would nominate the chancellor, or prime minister, who would have to be approved by the Reichstag. The Reichsrat, the upper house, would still represent the single states but with reduced powers. In the new Germany, government would be responsible to parliament, minorities would be fairly represented, the aristocracy would hold no political privilege, and civil rights and private property would be guaranteed. With women voting, the Social Democrats in power, and a broad spectrum of parties, German politics was launched on a new course.

German Inflation   The gravest problem of these years was inflation. Early in 1923 French and Belgian forces occupied the Ruhr district following Germany's failure to make the coal deliveries required as reparations. The local populace responded with passive resistance, a kind of general strike that made the occupation fruitless. The resulting dislocation and scarcity drastically

▼ **By November 1923 German children could play with their nation's worthless paper money.**
AKG London

GERMAN INFLATION

The German statistical office published this description of the effects of inflation in 1923. Obviously concerned that foreigners did not understand how bad the effects of inflation were, the account also expresses the rising insecurity of the middle class.

"The greater part of the population has been forced down far below their old standard of living, even with regard to the most important necessities of life.

"Consequently the foreigner, for example, who has visited Germany since the war, would do well to ask himself whether, in the overcrowded first-class railway carriages, he has found many Germans, or whether in the best seats at the theatre Germans are in the majority. He would do well to inquire whether in fashionable places of entertainment the German or the foreign public predominates, and if he does see Germans present spending their money for light entertainment, let him consider whether these are the majority of the German people. He must not forget either that many people today are influenced by the psychological fact that saving is no longer of any use: 100 marks today will perhaps be only 50 marks tomorrow. He who before the war, for example, had saved 5,500 marks could purchase for that amount furniture for a middle-class flat of three rooms as well as clothing, for a married couple with two children. In the middle of February 1923 (with an average dollar rate of 27,819 for February) the same person, for the same articles, would have had to spend 26.3 million marks in paper money. The man who did not spend the 5,500 marks, but preferred to save it together with the interest thereon might have over 7,000 marks today, with which, however, he cannot even buy a shirt! Who would care to 'save' under such conditions? Does the stranger realize, moreover, that such violent changes in the valuation of German money have meant for many thousands of German savers the annihilation of their savings? Does the stranger see the formerly well-to-do men and women of the middle class who today with a heavy heart carry their old family jewellery to the dealer, in order to prolong their physical existence a little longer? He who before the war could spend the interest on 1 million marks was a rich man, even up to 1919 he could still live upon it with reasonable comfort; today he is poor, for with his 50,000 marks interest he can today barely provide his own person with the necessities of life for a week! Does the stranger see the women and girls from the higher circles, even up to the highest, who are compelled to take up some occupation or who help to eke out the family income by working in their homes for a miserable wage? Does the stranger see the 1½ millions of war cripples, who are struggling desperately to earn their living, because the pensions that the State can afford to pay them are utterly inadequate?"

From Sidney Pollard and Colin Holmes (eds.), *Documents of European Economic History*, Vol. 3: *The End of Old Europe, 1914–1939* (St. Martin's Press, 1972).

accelerated the already serious inflation. The German government, which from 1920 on found it easier to print more money than to raise taxes, continued that practice in 1923 as its expenses rose (it provided payments to the striking workers of the Ruhr) and its revenues declined.

The German mark, valued at 4 marks to 1 U.S. dollar in 1914 and 9 to 1 in 1919, was exchanged at 500 to 1 by 1922. Its subsequent fall was cataclysmic. One dollar was worth 18,000 marks in January 1923, 350,000 marks in July, nearly 5,000,000 in August, and inflation accelerated after that. New money was run off the presses at top speed, and old notes with additional zeros printed on them were rushed to the banks before they, too, became valueless. Prices changed within hours, always upward. By November a newspaper could sell for nearly 100 billion marks (see "German Inflation," above).

By the end of the year a restructuring was begun. The government imposed stringent new financial measures, aided by foreign loans, a moratorium on reparations, and subsequently a new schedule of payments. Some fortunes had been made during the inflation, especially by speculators and financiers; many large industries and property owners had fared quite well. Small businesses were more often hurt, as were nearly all wage earners. Savings held in cash had been wiped out, but a slow recovery began.

Domestic Conflict　At the height of the Ruhr crisis, a little-known man named Adolf Hitler led a nationalist *putsch,* or coup, in Munich. Notable for Ludendorff's participation, it was quickly defeated, and the plotters' punishment was ludicrously light. Ludendorff was acquitted, and Hitler was given a five-year sentence in comfortable prison quarters, where he composed *Mein Kampf (My Struggle)* during the thirteen months he actually served. Such attacks on the new government were becoming less frequent, however. Its moderate policies and general prosperity brought relief from the assassinations and revolts of the earlier years, and it was reasonable to believe in 1924 that Germany was on the road to stability.

But the divisions in German society were sharpening, and there was no significant group with primary loyalty to the existing regime. The leading statesman was Gustav Stresemann, who sat in every cabinet, usually as foreign minister, from 1923 to his death in 1929. A nationalist of the center-right, he acquiesced in the army's violations of the disarmament clauses, but the right denounced him for his conciliatory tone toward former enemies and for bringing Germany into the League of Nations. German workers felt little was being done for them. The middle class could not forgive the inflation. The political extremes were growing at the expense of the center. When President Ebert died in 1925, a rightist coalition elected General von Hindenburg as his successor, defeating the candidate supported by both the Center and the Social Democratic parties; significantly, the 2 million votes given the Communist nominee would have made the difference.

◆ THE ESTABLISHED DEMOCRACIES

Except for Italy, where Fascism came to power, democracy at first fared rather well in the postwar years. Belgium, despite the ruins left by the war and conflicts over language and religion, recaptured its place among Europe's most prosperous and freest countries. Although the Netherlands faced nationalist unrest in its colonies, especially the East Indies, such problems hardly threatened democratic institutions at home. The Scandinavian countries, while often at odds among themselves, sustained effective democracies.

Social Changes　European society had not been radically reformed, although in every country the most militant Marxists felt strengthened by the presence of the Soviet Union as an international homeland for the proletariat. But the founding of Communist parties and allegiance to the Soviet Union split and weakened the left in domestic affairs. Economic recovery, though slower than expected, brought a general prosperity by the mid-1920s that contributed to the electoral victories of moderate and conservative parties. Constitutional democracy was the European norm, and many were convinced that even the Soviet Union and Italy would in time return to that standard.

Generally, the central government now spent a higher proportion of national wealth; although most of that went to the military, to interest on the national debt, and to pensions (all costs left from the war), some of it was used to lay the basis for broader measures of social security for all. Politically, both business interests and labor unions exercised a more direct influence, supporting efforts to achieve economic stability. Yet despite periods of prosperity and a genuine boom in certain industries, the 1920s did not provide the steady growth of the prewar decade. Economic uncertainty, increased by inflation and unemployment, tended, like the disillusionment over reparations or the specter of Bolshevism, to favor caution.

Changes in Women's Lives　Women's suffrage, once hotly debated, had been adopted in the Scandinavian countries (Finland, 1906; Norway, 1907; Denmark, 1917; Sweden, 1919) and in Great Britain (right after the war, as promised) and was part of the new constitutions of Austria and Germany. The effects on public life were less dramatic than either advocates or opponents had predicted. Politics was not transformed and the family not harmed, but there was significance in the spreading sense that for women to vote was a natural extension of democracy.

The most fundamental social changes of the period were usually not the result of deliberate policy. Employment in services such as sales and office work increased more rapidly than in industry, and the number of domestic servants continued to decline. These changes affected unmarried women especially. In most countries more women were gainfully employed than before the war (at those jobs thought suitable for women) despite a sharp decline from the wartime peak and despite the strong tendency for women to leave work upon marriage. Everywhere, women received more years of schooling than before, and the number of (middle class and still primarily male) youths enrolled in universities increased sharply. A rising standard of living and the automobile, especially in France and Britain, began to alter middle-class life.

Limited Recovery in France Life in France quickly returned to prewar patterns. The nation had become par excellence the land of the middle class, the artisan, and the peasant proprietor fiercely attached to a tiny plot of land. Though the expected cornucopia of reparations never materialized, ordinary people accomplished miracles of reconstruction, carefully making their new buildings look as much as possible like those destroyed. The Chamber of Deputies elected in 1919 at the height of patriotic pride in victory was the most conservative since the founding of the Third Republic; and politics, too, focused on restoration.

The depreciation of the franc, for a century one of the world's stablest currencies, was the principal concern of President Raymond Poincaré's conservative program. Inadequate taxation during the war (it took great political courage to raise taxes in France) lay at the root of the problem, and budgetary contraction was the preferred solution. The rigid focus on a stable franc and military security reflected the psychological as well as the economic and demographic costs of war.

In the subsequent prosperity, competent leaders presided over governments content with policies that permitted domestic stagnation and encouraged inflexibility in foreign affairs. Poincaré's concern for national honor and a stable currency appealed to a cautious middle class much as the complicated maneuvers of Aristide Briand, the leading figure of the 1930s, did to parliamentarians, but neither encouraged their followers to face more difficult long-term issues of working conditions, social inequality, cultural change, or international peace.

The Altered Circumstances of the United Kingdom In the United Kingdom, also, the elections of 1919—the first in which women (those over thirty years old) were allowed to vote—produced an overwhelming victory for leaders who promised to extract enough from Germany to make winning the war worthwhile. Lloyd George remained prime minister, but his government was essentially conservative. The breakup of the wartime coalition exposed the Liberal party's decline, and in 1924 new elections brought the Labour party briefly to power. Except for recognizing the Soviet Union, Labour did little to recall its leftist origins. For most of that decade, Britain was led with dull caution by the Conservatives and Stanley Baldwin, who inherited problems of unemployment, Irish nationalism, and a changing empire.

A crisis in the coal industry led to a ten-day general strike in 1926 that became a lightning rod for social division. Frightened by the bitter class conflict, many of the well-to-do volunteered in maintaining essential services, thus helping to break the strike. That response and the antilabor legislation that followed did much to deepen the resentments of British workers and heighten the angry rhetoric of public life.

Irish Independence The Irish question was equally explosive. The promise of home rule had been suspended during the war, and the Easter

▼ Demonstrations and parades were banned in Dublin and Belfast, where an armored car stands ready to put down any trouble; violence had become an expected part of political struggle in Ireland.
© Corbis

Rebellion of 1916 had been firmly suppressed. In 1919, however, the most militant Irish nationalists, led by the Sinn Fein (meaning "We Ourselves") party, refused to take their seats in the House of Commons and met instead at Dublin in a parliament of their own, the Dail Eireann. There, they declared Ireland an independent nation.

To this defiance the London government responded slowly and ineptly, finally choosing to suppress the Sinn Fein party and with it Irish independence. The government then sent armed reinforcements in numbers sufficient to spread the fighting without ending it, troops that soon became the most hated symbol of British repression. Violent civilian resisters called themselves the Irish Republican Army, and against civilian terrorists, the British could look only foolish or brutal. By the 1920s the two sides were fighting a bloody war.

With pressure mounting at home and abroad for some settlement, the British government in 1920 passed an Ireland act, creating two Irish parliaments, one in the predominantly Catholic areas of the south and west, and the other in the predominantly Protestant counties of the northeast. Sinn Fein warred against this division of the island during almost two more years of fighting. Nevertheless, in December 1922 the Irish parliament sitting in Dublin in the Catholic south proclaimed, with British acquiescence, the existence of the Irish Free State, which included all Ireland except the six northern counties of Ulster. As Northern Ireland, these counties maintained the traditional union with Great Britain in an uneasy peace, its terms the basis for further tension and conflict that has continued through two more generations.

The British Commonwealth   Only in imperial affairs did flexible compromise still seem to work. Canadian complaints led the Imperial Conference of 1926 to a significant new definition of all dominions as "autonomous communities . . . equal in status . . . united by a common allegiance to the crown and freely associated as members of the British Commonwealth of Nations." Autonomous in all domestic and foreign affairs, dominions accepted ties to the British crown as the expression of their common traditions and loyalties. Given legal sanction by the Statute of Westminster in 1931, this conception of empire proved a skillful adaptation to new conditions crowned by the stability, prosperity, and loyalty of dominions such as Canada, New Zealand, and Australia.

◆ INTERNATIONAL RELATIONS

From 1924 to 1930 the conduct of international relations reflected some of the idealism of the Paris Peace Conference. The League of Nations, formally established in 1920, successfully resolved a number of disputes, despite the absence of the United States, Britain's greater concern for its empire, and France's tendency to use the League for its own security. The League's special commissions helped restructure the disjointed economies of new states, aided refugees, and set international standards for public health and working conditions. To further the rule of law the League also established the Permanent Court of International Justice, and in the late 1920s its decisions were treated with great respect.

Debt Payments   Crises over debt payments were dealt with directly by the major powers. As Germany fell behind in its payments, the Allies took the position that they, in turn, could not pay their war debts to the United States. Some compromise was essential, and in 1924 the nations involved accepted the proposals of an international commission of financial experts, headed by the American banker Charles G. Dawes. The Dawes Plan fixed Germany's reparations payments on a regular scale, established an orderly mode of collection, and provided loans to Germany equal to 80 percent of the reparations payment Germany owed in the first year of the plan.

The Dawes Plan did not admit any connection between Allied debts to the United States and German reparations to the European victors, but it did end the worst of the chaos. For the next six years, Germany, fed by loans largely from the United States, made its reparations payments on schedule. The issue seemed forever resolved with the adoption of the Young Plan in 1929, which finally set a limit to Germany's obligations (fifty-nine years), reduced annual payments, and ended foreign occupation of the Rhineland. Under the leadership of American bankers, the interests of international capital had come to shape policy in the name of economic necessity.

The Locarno Era International efforts to outlaw war foundered on definitions of aggression, but they led to a series of treaties in 1925 known as the Locarno Pact. In the major agreement—entered into by Germany, Belgium, France, Great Britain, and Italy—all parties accepted Germany's western frontier as defined by the Versailles Treaty and promised to arbitrate their disagreements. In addition, France pursued a more traditional diplomacy, signing a mutual-defense alliance with Poland and Czechoslovakia. A continental war caused by German aggression now seemed impossible.

The optimism of the Locarno era was capped by the Kellogg-Briand pact of 1928. The French had suggested that the American entry into World War I be commemorated by a friendship pact, and the Americans proposed to include others as well. More than a score of nations signed the pact, which contained no troubling provisions for enforcement while it renounced war "as an instrument of national policy."

Disarmament From 1921 on, some League commission was always studying the problem of disarmament. Given the enormous cost of capital ships (Britain no longer aspired to maintain a fleet twice the size of any other), naval disarmament seemed especially promising. At the Washington Conference of 1921–1922, called by President Warren G. Harding, the United States, Great Britain, Japan, France, and Italy agreed after some difficulty to fix their relative strength in capital ships at current levels,[4] not to expand their naval bases, and even to scrap some of their larger vessels. Never again did discussions of naval disarmament prove so fruitful. At Geneva in 1927 and London in 1930, Italy (citing the special needs of its geography) and France (arguing that all forms of disarmament should be discussed together) refused to accept a treaty. By 1935 Japan would reject even the Washington accord.

Attempts to limit land and air arms were even less successful. League commissions could not agree on which were offensive weapons, on

whether a professional army was comparable to a reserve force, and on whether limitations should be expressed in terms of budgets, weapons, or personnel. German and Russian proposals that their own military weakness be made a standard for other nations, one to be achieved by disarming, only aroused suspicion. After much preparation, these League commissions called a conference on general disarmament in 1932. By then, the dream of arms restrictions was more remote than ever. Discussions continued at length, but before agreements were reached, Hitler had come to power in Germany, and a new arms race ensued.

The Beginning of a New Era To contemporaries, and for historians since, World War I was the beginning of a new era. The war itself was understood to have resulted from a dangerous system of alliances, secret diplomacy, and the arms race. Creation of the League of Nations, agreements like the Locarno treaties, and conferences on disarmament were unusual examples of an extensive effort to learn from history and to correct the errors of the past. Postwar international relations differed in other respects, too; for the nations of Europe, weakened economically and militarily, were now deeply in debt, their hold on empire weakening.

Multiple new states with contested boundaries, in which nationalism was often the strongest communal bond, wrestled with the unfamiliar complications of democracy. In those countries and in the established democracies, the relationship between politics and the general public had changed. Old elites were less trusted, the techniques of mass mobilization now more familiar and available to every party, and groups once treated as peripheral (such as workers, farmers, women, and veterans) were now more assertive. Disillusionment with politics was deep after years of propaganda; yet more was expected of government following its wartime accomplishments, and the range of issues politicians engaged grew wider. Revolutionary new political movements threatened to change the rules of politics altogether.

Economic conditions were different, too. The war and the terms of peace left enormous problems of physical destruction, burdens of debt, broken trade patterns. The flood of former soldiers

---

[4]The current level was defined as parity between the United States and Great Britain at 525,000 tons apiece in capital ships, 315,000 tons for Japan, and 175,000 tons each for France and Italy.

seeking jobs while war industries shrank (an immediate effect of demobilization) was followed by long-term changes involving new technologies and the reorganization of production to incorporate American techniques of mass production for mass markets.

In these circumstances the radical ideas and shocking cultural movements of the 1890s had new relevance. Nearly all Europeans had personal experience of lives disrupted—families broken up, women adding new roles to demanding old ones, jobs gained and suddenly lost, savings wiped out, property destroyed, invading armies, civil war, or sickness and death. All these changes at once, from the international to the personal, marked a new era.

Summary

The nations of Europe had stumbled into the most destructive war in their history, forcing them to harness the political systems, organizational skills, and technology that had made them powerful. The war had probed every social weakness, eliminated the German, Austro-Hungarian, and Russian empires, and left the victors only marginally better off than the losers. In the course of the war and as part of its justification, the winning alliance had promulgated universal values of democracy; and though these values were tainted in the practical decisions of the peace, they were to some extent embraced across the continent. Gradually, stability and prosperity did return to much of Europe. If broader hopes for social justice and international cooperation lost their luster, the institutions that expressed them remained in place. Their responses to the new challenges arising in the postwar world would determine the chances for domestic and international peace.

Questions for Further Thought

1. Could wiser policies have prevented the outbreak of world war?

2. What factors determine victory in modern warfare?

3. Never have leaders forged a more elaborate peace settlement or tried harder to avoid the mistakes of the past, yet historians still debate the efficacy of those efforts. What is your assessment? Are there lessons to be learned that should be applied in the future?

4. To most observers, the Europe of the 1920s seemed radically different from what it had been just ten years before. What do you see as the most fundamental changes and which of them gave reason for optimism or grave concern?

Recommended Reading

Sources

Chapman, Guy. *A Passionate Prodigality.* 1966. No war stimulated a richer literature, and this searing account of the personal experiences of an English soldier, first published in 1933, is among the best of these works.

*Nicholson, Harold G. *Peacemaking, 1919.* 1965. The retrospective analysis of an experienced diplomat who was a disillusioned participant at the Versailles Conference.

*Remarque, Erich Maria. *All Quiet on the Western Front.* First published in Germany in 1928, this novel with its realistic (and antinationalist) depiction of the war became the subject of great controversy there, and its moving rejection of modern warfare made it a best-seller throughout Europe and in the United States.

Studies

Becker, Jean-Jacques. *The Great War and the French People.* 1985. Shows the multiple ways in which the war was a turning point in French life.

Cannadine, David. *The Decline and Fall of the British Aristocracy.* 1990. Traces the extraordinary erosion of the position of a dominant class from the Lloyd George budget of 1906 through World War I and the changes that have followed.

Carsten, F. L. *Revolution in Central Europe, 1918–1919.* 1972. An important treatment of these significant outbreaks following the war.

Downs, Laura L. *Manufacturing Inequality.* 1995. A study of class relations and social attitudes in the organization of women's work in British and French factories.

Falls, Cyril B. *The Great War.* 1961. A skillful account of the war by a noted military historian.

Feldman, Gerald D. *Army, Industry, and Labor in Germany, 1914–1918.* 1966. A fundamental analysis of the war's effects on institutions and power in Germany.

*Ferro, Marc. *The Great War, 1914–1918.* 1973. This stimulating, outspoken essay emphasizes the economic and social impact of the war.

*Fischer, Fritz. *Germany's Aims in the First World War.* 1967. The reassessment that became a center of controversy among Germany historians.

Fridenson, Patrick (ed.). *The French Home Front, 1914–1918.* Bruce Little (tr.). 1992. A valuable collection of essays by social historians on the effects of wartime on the lives of industrial workers.

*Fussell, Paul. *The Great War and Modern Memory.* 1975. A lively study of the cultural impact of the war, denouncing modern warfare in all its aspects.

*Grayzel, Susan B. *The Women's Identities at War: Gender, Motherhood, and Politics in Britain and France during the First World War.* 1999. Shows both how conventional views of women were challenged by the war but subsequently the established gender system prevailed.

*Herrmann, David G. *Arming of Europe and the Making of the First World War.* 1997. Uses new archival evidence to show the importance of military considerations in the diplomacy that led to world war.

*Joll, James. *The Origins of the First World War.* 1984. Draws upon the vast literature dealing with a question that was once extremely controversial to establish a balanced perspective.

Kennedy, Paul (ed.). *The War Plans of the Great Powers, 1880–1914.* 1979. Places the arms race in the context of imperialist and political pressures that underlay the planning process leading up to the war.

Kocka, Jürgen. *Facing Total War: German Society 1914–1918.* Barbara Weinberger (tr.). 1984. A leading social historian's assessment of the domestic impact of the war on Germany.

Marwick, Arthur. *War and Social Change in the Twentieth Century: A Comparative Study of Britain, France, Germany, Russia, and the United States.* 1975. Develops the case for the revolutionary effects of World War I and World War II on the domestic economy of modern society.

*Mayer, Arno J. *Politics and Diplomacy of Peacemaking: Containment and Counterrevolution at Versailles, 1918–1919.* 1967. Argues that fear of Bolshevism shaped the terms of peace more than publicized principles did.

Miller, S. (ed.). *Military Strategy and the Origins of the First World War.* 1985. These essays assess the role of the military in the decisions that led to war.

Williams, John. *The Home Fronts: Britain, France, and Germany, 1914–1918.* 1972. Pulls together a variety of evidence of the war's domestic impact.

Williamson, S. R., Jr. *The Politics of Grand Strategy: Britain and France Prepare for War, 1904–1914.* 1969.

Winter, J. M., and R. M. Wall. *The Upheaval of War: Family, Work, and Welfare in Europe, 1914–1918.* 1988. An insightful assessment of the effects of the war on domestic society.

Winter, Jay. *Sites of Memory, Sites of Mourning: The Great War in European Cultural History.* 1996. A powerful study of the impact of the war on European culture.

Winter, Jay, and Jean-Louis Robert. *Capital Cities at War: Paris, London, Berlin, 1914–1919.* 1997. An important new study of the social history of the war.

---

*Available in paperback.

▲ This idealized image of Lenin addressing the people conveys the power of Lenin's oratory skills and the sense that his leadership began a new era. The portrait of impassioned workers, soldiers and sailors, men and women — all inspired by their leader — and the careful placement of Stalin just behind Lenin reveal the painting as the subsequent official view of the Soviet government. One of the marks of the new era in Europe was, in fact, the effective propaganda of single-party states.
Sovfoto

Chapter 28

THE GREAT TWENTIETH-CENTURY CRISIS

*T*he 1920s and 1930s opened an era of intense hope and great fear. As the prosperity and consumerism of the 1920s gave way to economic depression, Europe's liberal governments had difficulty responding. Domestic divisions grew sharper, reinforced by the example of radical alternatives; for, although most of the revolutions in the aftermath of World War I had failed, new political systems emerged in communist Russia and Fascist Italy. Relatively isolated at first, these new regimes became influential models. The possibility of communist revolution and the potential of fascist nationalism reshaped political life throughout Europe.

Cultural life was unsettling, too. A flourishing popular culture, flippant and commercial, undermined nineteenth-century standards of propriety (and the confidence that went with them). Europe's most interesting artists and intellectuals disdained the prosperity of the 1920s, and provocative theories, in both the physical and social sciences, invited skepticism about absolute truths and traditional values. Politics and culture both struggled with questions about the nature of modern mass society.

There were also immediate reasons for discontent among workers who had expected the postwar world to bring greater improvements in their way of life, among peasants who found it hard to make a living from small but often inefficient holdings, among ethnic groups resentful of sudden minority status as a result of the boundary changes in Eastern Europe, among nationalists angry that their new states had not gained more territory, and among all those who disliked the altered lifestyle of the postwar era. Then economic depression drove home the failures of capitalism, the limitations of liberalism, and the weaknesses of democracy.

Two nations seemed to rise above the economic crisis: Communist Russia under Stalin and Nazi Germany under Hitler. Their apparent escape from the Great Depression, their capacity to mobilize popular support, and their brutal use of force contrasted with the hesitant compromises of more democratic governments. In the 1930s that contrast sharpened as they began applying their dynamism to international relations.

CHAPTER 28. THE GREAT TWENTIETH-CENTURY CRISIS							
	Social Structure	Body Politic	Changes in the Organization of Production and in the Impact of Technology	Evolution of Family and Changing Gender Roles	War	Religion	Cultural Expression
I. Two Successful Revolutions	██	██	██	██	██	██	
II. The Distinctive Culture of the Twentieth Century			██	██			██
III. The Retreat from Democracy		██	██				██
IV. Nazi Germany and the U.S.S.R.	██	██	██				
V. The Democracies' Weak Response	██	██				██	██

I. Two Successful Revolutions

In Russia and in Italy the aftermath of war was revolution. Both nations had begun rapid industrialization in the 1890s, and both were sorely tested in the world war that followed. Revolution in Russia began while the war was still going on, and it continued for several years before the outcome was certain. Revolution in Italy occurred quickly a few years after the war. Each resulted in a new kind of political regime, and only gradually did it become clear that Russian communism and Italian fascism might change the face of Europe.

◆ REVOLUTION IN RUSSIA

When world war broke out in 1914, Russia's parliament (the Duma) and local councils (or *zemstvos*) had helped coordinate the war effort. But when the Cadet party maintained its insistence on further liberal reforms, the tsar suspended the Duma. Resentful that political aims should be pursued in wartime—they still did not see that a more representative government could strengthen the war effort—the tsar and his officials grew increasingly isolated from the country. More comfortable as a military strategist than as a head of state, Tsar Nicholas II grandly departed to command his army, leaving Tsarina Alexandra and those closest to her to oppose any program for reform. Her chief confidant was Grigori Rasputin, an ignorant and corrupt mystic whose influence symbolized the decadence of this regime.

The February Revolution Throughout 1916 signs of Russia's failures had accumulated. Production and transportation were undependable, war refugees filled the roads, inflation soared, and food shortages became critical. All this came on top of years of rising anger among peasants eager for land and workers determined to change their lot. Without realizing the depth of this social strife, officials were well aware of how serious the situation was. Even in the highest circles, there was talk of deposing the tsar. In November in the reconvened Duma, Pavel Milyukov, a noted historian and the leader of the liberal Cadets, courageously delivered a biting attack on the government. In December a group of nobles murdered Rasputin. Strikes spread, and in March 1917, when strikers filled the streets of Petrograd,[1] their economic demands quickly broadened to include political issues. The army could not be

---

[1] St. Petersburg was a Germanic name, and in 1914 Nicholas had changed it to the Russian *Petrograd*. The capital until 1918, the city would become Leningrad in 1924 and St. Petersburg again in 1991.

relied on to oppose them. Once again, much as in 1905, a soviet of workers (now called the Soviet of Workers' and Soldiers' Deputies) became the voice of revolution, and they joined with a Duma committee in seeking a provisional government. They prepared to resist any tsarist force that might be sent against them. None came. The military situation was desperate, the government in disarray, and the tsar unpopular. With nowhere to turn, Nicholas II abdicated, and the February Revolution[2] was hailed with joy and relief throughout the country.

The provisional government's central figure was Milyukov; its only socialist was Aleksandr Kerensky, a member of the Social Revolutionary party and vice-chairman of the Petrograd soviet. The new government quickly established broad civil liberties, an amnesty for political prisoners, and the end of religious persecution. It also proposed granting a constitution to Finland, which Russia ruled, and independence to Russian Poland. Declaring its support for an eight-hour workday and for the abolition of class privileges, it left most other social issues to a constituent assembly, which it promised to call soon.

In fact, the parties of revolution sharply disagreed on these issues. The Cadets, who dominated the provisional government, came to accept the idea of a republic, political democracy, and distribution of land with compensation to former owners. To their left, the Social Revolutionary party and the Menshevik wing of the Social Democratic party, which was especially strong in the soviets forming across the nation, demanded more drastic reforms. These parties were divided, too, however. Some of their members were willing to postpone these further reforms until after the war, which, like the Cadets, they still meant to win. The more radical of them stressed an early end to the war, without yet advocating an immediate armistice. For the time being, the soviets, watching from the outside and ever ready to criti-

cize, allowed the provisional government its chance. To the left of all these factions stood a small group known as the Bolsheviks.

The Bolsheviks In 1898 Russian Marxists had secretly formed the Social Democratic party, which functioned mainly in the conspiratorial world of exile. At the party's second congress, held in Brussels and London in 1903, it had split into two groups, called the Bolsheviks (majority) and Mensheviks (minority); in fact, the Bolsheviks rarely had a majority, but these nicknames stuck. Their differences were theoretical, organizational, and personal. The theoretical issues, which engaged Marxists everywhere, were fought with the special intensity of revolutionaries far from home and power. On the whole, the Mensheviks placed greater emphasis on popular support and parliamentary institutions, which implied cooperation with other parties. The Bolsheviks stressed instead the need for a disciplined revolutionary party to instruct and lead the masses, which might otherwise be likely to settle for immediate gains rather than the European revolution that would bring about socialism. Led by Georgi Plekhanov and V. I. Lenin, the Bolsheviks denounced as enemies all who did not join them. Only later would these party battles waged in foreign cities prove significant for Russian history.

The ideas of socialism that spread in Russia after 1905 were not so much those of the Bolsheviks as those of the Mensheviks and the Social Revolutionaries, who were less consistently Marxist and were closer to the peasants. Although Plekhanov tried on his own to heal the breach in the Social Democratic party, Lenin's conception of iron discipline allowed little room for compromise; and he soon consigned Plekhanov to the Mensheviks.

Lenin's Tactics Removed from events in Russia, Lenin continued from Switzerland to organize selected followers, denounce the heresies of others, and develop his theoretical view of the special role a militant party should play in a country that, like Russia, was just achieving modern capitalism. The party could achieve its aims, he argued, only by recognizing the revolutionary potential in the peasants' hunger for land (most Marxists considered the peasantry a socially backward class and land ownership opposed to socialism). Thus, the

---

[2]These events occurred on March 8–12 according to the Gregorian calendar used throughout the West. Russia, however, had never abandoned the older Julian calendar (which continues to be the calendar of the Orthodox Church). The revolutions of March 8–12 and November 7, 1917, according to the Gregorian system were dated thirteen days earlier according to the Julian, and they continue to be called the February and October revolutions.

Bolsheviks, although they lacked a large following in Russia, had a theory of how to make a revolution.

Lenin considered World War I a civil war among capitalists, and in a sense that theoretical stand gave Lenin his chance, for it suggested to the Germans that his presence in Russia as an agitator might be useful in undermining the Russian war effort. In April 1917 the Germans arranged to send Lenin by sealed train through Germany and Scandinavia to Russia. Lenin, however, had something grander than mere agitation in mind; once again it began from a practical solution to a doctrinal problem.

Marxists were ambivalent in their attitude toward the February Revolution, which they welcomed as progressive but tended to disdain as a bourgeois revolution and not a victory of the proletariat. Lenin offered another interpretation: Revolution in Russia was part of a larger revolution about to sweep all of Europe. Socialists had no

interest in the capitalist war, which Russia's provisional government continued to support, but Bolsheviks could seize the chance to push the revolution beyond its bourgeois phase to a "second stage" in which the soviets would be the true representatives of the proletariat. That in turn dictated the tactics the Bolsheviks should follow: They must gain the leadership of the soviets, and then Russia could join in the international revolution that was imminent. Historians have emphasized Lenin's tactical flexibility, but in April his views seemed impossibly dogmatic even to radicals. It was the force of his personality, his political skill, and his oratory that kept him leader of the Bolsheviks.

Summer Crisis While the soviets were building a national organization that claimed authority over railroads, telegraph lines, and troops, the provisional government was falling apart. Its members disagreed over war policy and land

▼ The armed civilians in the foreground are Red Guards, demonstrating their might and protecting the Bolshevik leaders addressing a large crowd of workers.
Sovfoto

reform; its police and officials were abandoning their posts. Workers continued to strike, and nationalist movements erupted in Latvia, Georgia, and the Ukraine. Army morale was sinking when in March the Petrograd soviet issued its famous Order Number 1: Officers would be chosen by their men and the army run by elected committees. The order was adopted in most military units, and a good part of the army simply melted away. In the face of a losing war effort, disruptive nationalism, and class conflict, a radical change in political leadership was imperative. Milyukov resigned, four more socialists joined the cabinet, and Kerensky, an energetic leader and effective orator, became the cabinet's leading figure.

The Kerensky government was quickly attacked from left and right. The Bolsheviks criticized Kerensky at the first all-Russian Congress of Soviets in June but gained support from just over 100 of the 800 plus delegates. In July they attempted a coup in Petrograd. That was decisively defeated, and many of the coup leaders were arrested. Lenin fled to Finland.

Kerensky, still focused on the war, believed he could achieve a more effective and stable government with just one successful military offensive. Although prepared as carefully as possible, the offensive failed. His call for a national congress of all interests (and not just the soviets) was intended to show that the soviets were isolated. It revealed instead how deeply divided the nation was over war aims and social policy. Cities were torn by strikes and demonstrations as the situation at the front grew more perilous. In the countryside, rioting peasants demanding land burned manor houses and murdered landlords.

Convinced that a strong military hand was what the nation needed, the army's commander in chief, General Lavr Kornilov, led an attack on Petrograd in September. Kerensky asked the soviets (and thus the Bolsheviks as well) to defend the government. Most of Kornilov's men had refused to follow his orders, and the threat passed quickly. But in the meantime Bolshevik leaders had been released from prison, and Bolshevist propaganda was gaining ground with simple slogans promising peace, land, and bread—issues at the heart of daily life and ones for which the provisional government had no clear solutions.

The Bolsheviks won control of the soviets in Moscow and Petrograd, electing Leon Trotsky chairman of the latter. Trotsky, who had worked with Lenin in exile, had until recently stood somewhat aloof from party conflicts. Now firmly in Lenin's camp, he proceeded to organize the armed forces in Petrograd. With the Social Revolutionaries supporting peasant expropriation of land, the provisional government was left politically alone in a city it could not control, trying to rule a nation in chaos and still at war.

The October Revolution   To the dismay of many in his party, Lenin, who had reentered Russia, boldly decided to seize power. When the second all-Russian Congress of Soviets met on November 7, he confronted it with a new government. Kerensky began countermeasures a few days before that date, but it was too late. On November 6, Red Guards (squads of armed workers), sailors, and soldiers captured the Winter Palace and strategic points throughout the city. A simultaneous movement in Moscow won control of the city in a week. Lenin announced to the Congress that the Bolsheviks held power and sent out a young officer to take command of the armies. At each stop along his route, the troops enthusiastically cheered his announcement of the Bolshevik coup. Their commanders could only acquiesce. Kerensky, who had escaped from the capital, tried to muster support, but the one group of Cossacks who moved on Petrograd was soundly defeated. The world's first communist government had taken office (see "Two Accounts of Revolution in Russia," p. 1010).

"All power to the soviets!" had been one of the Bolsheviks' most effective slogans, and the Congress readily approved the one-party cabinet Lenin presented it. The rudiments of a new form of government emerged: The Congress of Soviets replaced parliament and elected a Central Executive committee to advise the Council of People's Commissars, or cabinet. From the very first, Bolshevik rule did not depend on any elected body. Elections for the promised constituent assembly, held at the end of November, would be the last open competition among parties for more than seventy years. The Bolsheviks won a quarter of the seats, other socialist parties more than 60 percent, conservatives and liberals the rest. As the

TWO ACCOUNTS OF REVOLUTION IN RUSSIA

◆

The culmination of the Russian Revolution came on November 7, 1917, when the Communists captured the Winter Palace, which was then the seat of the Kerensky government. Eyewitnesses saw the event very differently. The first account is by Pitirim Sorokin, a young member of the Social Revolutionary party, who would soon go into exile and have a distinguished career as a professor of sociology at Harvard. In his memoir, Leaves from a Russian Diary, *he recalled that day. The second description is from* Ten Days That Shook the World, *the famous book by John Reed, an American journalist who admired the Bolsheviks.*

"Lying ill all day on my bed, I listened to the steady booming of the cannon and the spatter of machine-guns and crack of rifles. Over the telephone I learned that the Bolsheviki had brought up from Kronstadt the warship *Aurora* and had opened fire on the Winter Palace, demanding the surrender of members of the Provisional Government, still barricaded there. At seven in the evening I went to the Municipal Duma. With many matters before us, the immediate horror that faced us was this situation at the Winter Palace. There was a regiment of women and the military cadets were bravely resisting an overwhelming force of Bolshevist troops, and over the telephone Minister Konovalov was appealing for aid. Poor women, poor lads, their situation was desperate, for we knew that the wild sailors, after taking the Palace, would probably tear them to pieces. What could we do? After breathless council it was decided that all of us, the Soviets, Municipalities, Committees of Socialist Parties, members of the Council of the Republic, should go in procession to the Winter Palace and do our utmost to rescue the Ministers, the women soldiers, and the cadets. Even as we prepared to go, over the telephone came the despairing shout: 'The gates of the Palace have been forced. The massacre has begun. . . . Hurry! The mob has reached the first floor. All is over. Goodbye. . . . They break in. They are. . . . ' The last word . . . from the Winter Palace was a broken cry."

From Pitirim Alexandrovitch Sorokin, *Leaves from a Russian Diary*, exp. ed. (1920; Beacon Press, 1950).

"Carried along by the eager wave of men we were swept into the right-hand entrance, opening into a great bare vaulted room, the cellar of the east wing, from which issued a maze of corridors and staircases. A number of huge packing cases stood about, and upon these the Red Guards and soldiers fell furiously, battering them open with the butts of their rifles, and pulling out carpets, curtains, linen, porcelain plates, glassware. . . . One man went strutting around with a bronze clock perched on his shoulder; another found a plume of ostrich feathers, which he stuck in his hat. The looting was just beginning when somebody cried, 'Comrades! Don't touch anything! Don't take anything! This is the property of the People!' Immediately twenty voices were crying, 'Stop! Put everything back! Don't take anything! Property of the People!' Many hands dragged the spoilers down. Damask and tapestry were snatched from the arms of those who had them; two men took away the bronze clock. Roughly and hastily the things were crammed back in their cases, and self-appointed sentinels stood guard. It was all utterly spontaneous. Through corridors and up staircases the cry could be heard growing fainter and fainter in the distance, 'Revolutionary discipline! Property of the People'"

From John Reed, *Ten Days That Shook the World* (1919).

---

assembly met on its second day, the military guards told it to adjourn.

Lenin provided a basis for such ruthlessness in his pamphlet "The State and Revolution," written in Finland in the summer of 1917. It used the Marxist conception that the state is the coercive organ of the ruling class to argue that, once the Bolsheviks held power, the proletariat would be

that ruling class. The dictatorship of the proletariat, Lenin reasoned, was the only way to lead backward Russia through the transition to that higher historical stage that Marxists envisioned in which a state would no longer be necessary. The nationalization of land and factories would achieve socialism. Communism would follow once everyone learned to work for the good of society and once production met the needs of all. Until then, the single party, the "vanguard of the proletariat," would be model and guide. That party, as Lenin envisioned it, would sustain its enthusiasm through open discussion in which differences would be reconciled and criticisms would keep officials on their toes. By this combination of theory, attention to such immediate issues as bread and land, and ruthless but flexible tactics, Lenin placed himself beside Marx as a founder of modern communism.

◆ TOWARD A COMMUNIST SOCIETY

Millions of workers, soldiers, and peasants had joined in pulling down the old system, and the Bolshevik leaders were determined to snatch their historical moment. The day after taking the Winter Palace, the new government decreed that land, livestock, and farm equipment belonged to the state but could be "temporarily" held by peasant committees, thereby legitimizing the rural revolution that was taking place anyway.

Initial Policies   No peasant was to work for hire, and committees of the poor would supervise the allocation of land and produce. Workers' committees would share in factory management, and everyone would be paid according to the work done (the state's new leaders assigned themselves laborers' salaries). All social titles and military ranks were abolished. "People's tribunals" and workers' militias replaced tsarist courts and police. Church and state were separated; the equality of the sexes was decreed and followed by regulations allowing divorce by mutual consent, measures that enhanced the reputation of Russian communism among progressives in Western Europe. Even the alphabet was reformed and the Gregorian calendar adopted.

In the next few months, railroads, banks, and shipping concerns were nationalized; foreign trade became a state monopoly, and Russia's debts were repudiated. The various nationalities of Russia were declared equal and granted the right of secession; Finland took advantage of that decree to separate from Russia in December 1917, while the Bolsheviks struggled to prevent the Ukraine and the ethnic groups of the Baltic regions from following suit.

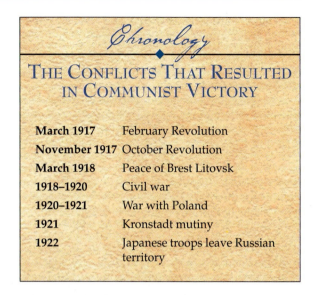

Chronology

THE CONFLICTS THAT RESULTED IN COMMUNIST VICTORY

March 1917	February Revolution
November 1917	October Revolution
March 1918	Peace of Brest Litovsk
1918–1920	Civil war
1920–1921	War with Poland
1921	Kronstadt mutiny
1922	Japanese troops leave Russian territory

Revolutionary measures also made way for a reign of terror. A new secret police, the Cheka, differed from tsarist police in determination more than method. The citizens who sat on the new committees and tribunals often combined revolutionary enthusiasm with personal vengeance, and tens of thousands lost their property, their rights, and their lives for "mistaken" alliances, "false" ideas, or "suspect" gestures. Such practices, which helped the regime solidify support, also threatened to undermine the regular procedures of government.

Ending the War with Germany   The most pressing issue was to find a way out of the war. The Bolsheviks had asked all nations to accept peace without annexations. When rebuffed, they shocked the world by publishing secret Allied agreements that revealed the cynicism of their territorial ambitions. Then in February 1918 a delegation headed by Trotsky, having failed to arrange terms of peace with Germany, proposed a policy of no peace, no war: Russia would just stop fighting. The Germans advanced to within 100 miles of Petrograd, and in March the Russians accepted the Treaty of Brest Litovsk. Russia surrendered more than 1 million square miles of territory to Germany, including a third of its arable land, a third of its factories, and three-quarters of its deposits of iron and coal. It granted the independence of Finland, Georgia, and the Ukraine; left to Germany the disposition of Russian Poland,

Lithuania, Latvia, and Estonia; and ceded parts of Transcaucasia to the Ottoman Empire. The Communists paid this high price for peace, confident that revolution in Germany would soon nullify the kaiser's gains.

The peace treaty, like the course of the revolution itself, exposed the discontent among non-Russian nationalities, and in July a new constitution tried to meet that problem by declaring Russia a federation—the Russian Soviet Federated Socialist Republic (R.S.F.S.R.). Great Russia, extending through Siberia, was the largest member. Ostensibly, political power rested with the local soviets, organized by occupation and elected by the votes of all men and women except for members of the clergy, former high officials, and those classified as bourgeois "nontoilers." These soviets elected delegates to the congress of soviets of their canton, the smallest administrative unit, and each of these congresses in turn sent delegates to a congress at the next administrative level. The system, which continued by steps up to the all-Russia Congress, allowed considerable control from the top. The constitution did not mention the Russian Communist party, as it was now named, although it was the real center of political authority. Its Central Committee elected the smaller Politburo, which shared ruling power with the governing Council of People's Commissars. Lenin was the dominant figure in both.

Civil War The Bolsheviks were still surrounded by enemies. In March Allied troops in small numbers had landed in Murmansk, Archangel, and Vladivostok to prevent the supplies they had shipped to Russia from falling into German hands, but those detachments might also be used to support a change of regime (a move some Allied officials favored). In addition, the Soviet government had reluctantly permitted a Czech brigade of some 30,000 men to go by rail from the Eastern front to Vladivostok in order to sail around the world to the Western front and fight against the Germans. On the long train journey, the Czechs clashed with some Hungarian prisoners of war; the fighting spread, and the Czechs, aided by Russian anti-Bolsheviks, captured one train station after another. Allied leaders decided to seize this opportunity and ordered the Czechs to move back along the railway toward the center

of Russia, in effect creating new bases for anti-Soviet military action. At the same time, a number of tsarist generals, among them the army's former commander-in-chief, Kornilov, were preparing to lead a small but excellent army of Cossacks against the Bolsheviks. It was the beginning of a civil war that would last for two terrible years.

While Trotsky undertook to organize the new regime's army, anti-Bolsheviks of every stripe, including the Social Revolutionaries, organized in hundreds of villages and towns. Across Russia, food riots, battles over land, skirmishes between workers and bourgeois, and ethnic hatred added to the violence. With the economy near collapse, the Bolsheviks adopted "War Communism," a program to extract from a country in chaos just enough men and supplies to fight a civil war through propaganda, requisitioning, police repression, and terror. With the firm leadership of Lenin, the military talent of Trotsky, and above all the mistakes of their enemies, they would eventually win.

By mid-1919 the major remaining threat came from armies under the command of former tsarist officers. One army pushed from the Urals toward Moscow but was stopped before it got there. Another took Kiev in August and reached within 300 miles of Moscow by October, while a third stood only 30 miles from Petrograd. These armies were weakened, however, by their conflicting ambitions; and they did little to win popular support. The areas under their control experienced a terror less efficient but at least as brutal as that conducted by the revolutionaries. With each defeat, more of the anticommunist soldiers melted away until hardly more than marauding bands were left. By the end of 1919, they were in general retreat. Their most important group withdrew to the Crimea early in 1920 and stubbornly fought on before finally heeding Allied advice and evacuating their remaining soldiers in November 1920.

The Last of the Fighting The Communists had to fight against Poland as well. As provided by the Versailles treaty, an Allied commission had determined the Russo-Polish border, placing it along a line that assigned to Poland most areas in which Poles were a clear majority. Poland wanted more and insisted on its boundary of 1772, well to the east, citing cultural and historical arguments.

▲ Uncomfortable with the pomp of conventional armies, the Bolsheviks were nevertheless proud of the forces that had won the civil war. Here Trotsky reviews the Moscow Brigade of the Red Army.
Novosti/Sovfoto

Rejecting Russian offers of compromise, Poland sent an army into the Ukraine in March 1920. Within a month it took Kiev, but the Ukrainian nationalists who had fought the Russians were unwilling to fight for the Poles. In August the Red army, by now a relatively efficient military machine, launched an assault that soon threatened Warsaw. An effective Polish counterattack led in 1921 to a compromise settlement after all, one by which Poland gained considerable non-Polish territory in the Ukraine and in the adjacent region of White Russia. Once Russia's western border was settled, it was possible to agree on a boundary with Turkey as well. It ignored local independence movements and assigned Armenia and Georgia to the Soviet federation, Kars and Ardahan to Turkey. Fighting continued in Asia until 1922, when Japan withdrew from eastern Siberia. By then, the Soviet Union was firmly in Communist hands.

Continuing Turmoil Under War Communism, regimentation and bloodshed were the means of survival, and by using them, the Communist party had become increasingly powerful; yet most of the countryside was still subject to the whims of local party officials and roving bands of armed men. Cities were partially empty, a million Russians had gone into exile, tens of millions more had died, manufacturing produced less in 1920 than in 1913, foreign trade had almost ceased, and poor harvests raised the specter of famine. Requisitions spurred resistance, and black markets flourished. Thus, the mutiny of sailors at the

Kronstadt naval base in March 1921 was an ominous sign.[3] These sailors were the sort of men who had made the October Revolution possible; though their revolt was soon quelled and their demands for political liberty rejected, Lenin recognized the need for change.

The New Economic Policy   Lenin announced the New Economic Policy (NEP), a major turning point in the development of Communist Russia. To many, the NEP seemed a departure from Marxism, but Lenin saw Russia's problems as the result not of flaws in Marxist theory but of having stormed the "citadel of capitalism" too fast. Russia suffered from old habits hard to uproot and from a lack of the technical experts and managers that a modern economy required. With noteworthy pragmatism, Lenin proposed a moderate course that earlier the Bolsheviks would have opposed.

Under the NEP, peasants were no longer subject to requisitions but rather to a tax in kind. Businesses employing fewer than twenty workers could be run as private enterprises, and nationalized industries could be leased to foreigners as a way of training Russians in efficient methods. Fiscal reforms guaranteed a stable currency, helping Russia's external trade to emerge from the pattern of barter into which it had fallen. Recovery was slow. Millions died in the famine of 1920–1921 despite the extensive aid of the American Relief Administration, and not for another six years would production reach prewar levels.

Communist Rule   Abandoning the hope of creating communism all at once, the NEP was nevertheless the reaffirmation of Communist determination. Every social institution was recruited to help create a stable new society. Cooperatives and trade unions, newspapers and public meetings taught efficiency and pride in class and na-

tion, as did the school system, which was improved and extended. Its curriculum stressed official doctrines; workers' children were favored for admission to selective schools, and teachers were urged to abandon old-fashioned rote learning. Women were encouraged to work outside the home and were provided a whole series of programs aimed at their special needs as mothers. The problems of ruling over multiple nationalities had eased somewhat with the cession of so much territory in the Treaty of Brest Litovsk, and three-quarters of the remaining population could be called Russian. Officially non-Russian nationalities were given more recognition than ever before, as the Communist government reassembled much of the Russian empire, and the Orthodox Church, while kept under tight supervision, was permitted to function.

In practice, the Communist party, which remained a restricted elite, was the most important instrument of rule. Organized in a hierarchy that paralleled the bureaucracy, it reached into every aspect of public life—factories, hundreds of new centers for adult education, and youth associations—propagandizing and encouraging, pressuring and explaining. In 1922 cultural activities were placed directly under the Ministry of Education, and the Western artistic movements recently welcomed were discouraged in favor of books and art that met the current definition of communist aesthetics: realistic in style, popular in appeal, and useful to the new order. Issues of practical policy were thrashed out within the government and the party, but to be on the losing side could be politically and sometimes personally fatal. Although the Communist government would never abandon the fear of foreign attack established during the civil war, it gave signs of seeking normal diplomatic relations; by 1924, the year of Lenin's death, every major power except the United States had recognized the new regime. An object of fear to liberals and conservatives, the new communist state became a source of inspiration and hope for the far left throughout the world.

---

[3]Denounced as part of an international counterrevolutionary conspiracy, the members of the Kronstadt base who were captured after the mutiny was crushed were subject to executions and deportations, and for seventy years the event was cited in Soviet histories as an example of the kinds of forces arrayed against the revolution. In 1994 Boris Yeltsin announced the rehabilitation of these rebels, and the event was used as evidence that the brutality of Communist rule had begun with Lenin's ruthlessness.

◆ ITALIAN FASCISM

Italy, too, experimented with a new form of government. Economically the least developed of the major Western powers, Italy and Russia had begun extensive industrialization at about the same time in the late nineteenth century, and there were many parallels between the two countries, despite Italy's more urban society, greater freedom, stronger constitutional tradition, and more responsive governments. With the end of the war, Italy was racked by inflation, unemployment, and talk of revolution. In many places peasants simply confiscated the land they had long been promised; when industrialists met a series of strikes with lockouts in 1920, workers answered by occupying factories, and many in the upper classes feared a communist revolution. Social conflicts that the state had largely ignored for twenty years now challenged the established system. The peace treaty, too, was disillusioning. Although granted considerable territory, Italy got less than expected, and its treatment by the other Allies was often humiliating. Disposition of the Dalmatian port of Fiume was still being argued in 1919 when a private expedition led by Gabriele d'Annunzio dramatically captured it for Italy. The nation's most famous living poet, d'Annunzio ruled Fiume for more than a year at the head of an "army" of the unemployed, whose nationalist frenzy and vulgar slogans were for many a welcome contrast to the wordy frustration of diplomacy. Eventually, the Italian government evicted him, but he had shown the effectiveness of direct action in a nationalist cause.

The Victory of Fascism The Fascist movement was born amid these crises. The term *fascio,* meaning "bundle," comes from an ancient Roman symbol of authority—a bundle of sticks, individually weak but strong in unity. Echoes of imperial Rome were part of the Fascist mystique. The movement centered around Benito Mussolini, whose polemical skills won him promotion to the editorship of the Socialist party newspaper until he was expelled in 1915 for favoring Italy's entry into the war. Mussolini, who established another paper, became one of Italy's noisiest nationalists, using the rhetoric of the left to denounce liberalism and parliamentary indecision and the slogans of nationalism to castigate Marxists. Fascism grew from this diverse heritage. Both a movement and a party, it employed propaganda, symbols, and activism in new ways, making party militants in their black shirts seem a civilian army.

At first the Fascists had little electoral success, but the changes in Italian politics offered them multiple opportunities. The elections of 1921 were the first in Italy with universal male suffrage, and two newer, well-organized mass parties overshadowed the traditional leaders and groups. The Catholic Popular party demanded major reforms, but much of its real strength came from rural and conservative groups. The Socialists, for all their increased strength, were weakened by the split with their left wing, which formed a Communist party, inspired by the Bolsheviks' success in Russia.

The Fascists, who had won no seats in 1919, gained thirty-five in the new Chamber; and the aging Giolitti, who had been a dominating prime minister in the prewar era, tried to patch together a personal coalition that included the Fascists in a "national bloc" of candidates. Giolitti thought the Fascists could thus be domesticated to parliamentary ways. Instead, they used the electoral campaign to demonstrate their style. Fascist squads in black shirts planted bombs, beat up opponents, and disrupted meetings, enjoying violence and intimidation while denouncing Marxists as a threat to order. And they benefited from the sympathy of many in the police and administration as well as the support of many property owners.

The Weakness of Opposition When left-wing unions called a general strike in 1922, raising fears of revolution, Mussolini's Black Shirts grew more threatening and started taking over town councils by force. While politicians struggled to find a parliamentary majority, the Fascists staged a march on Rome in October. Motley squads of party militants moved on the capital in a grand gesture of revolt while Mussolini cautiously waited in Milan. Belatedly, parliamentary leaders called for martial law, but King Victor Emmanuel III refused. Mussolini dashed to Rome, where the king invited him to form a cabinet; the largely symbolic revolt had been enough to capture power. Claiming the office both as a matter of perfect legality and by right of conquest, Mussolini at age thirty-nine became prime minister of a coalition government. In the elections of 1924, Fascists won a massive victory. Intimidation and fraud contributed to this success, but most Italians were willing to give the new party a chance.

It soon became clearer what a Fascist regime would mean. Giacomo Matteotti, a Socialist who bravely stood before the entire Chamber to enumerate Fascist crimes, was subsequently murdered in gangland style. As public condemnation mounted, Mussolini's government seemed about to topple, but the opponents of Fascism were no more able to unite now than when they had been stronger. The Fascists gradually isolated first the Socialist and then the Popular party, which was weakened by the Vatican's distaste for its program of social reform. By 1925 all the opponents of Fascism had been expelled from the legislature, and newspapers either printed what they were told or risked suppression. The Fascist period had begun.

To many in and out of Italy, it seemed merely that the nation at last had a strong, antisocialist leader. Some distinguished Italians were associated with the regime in various ways, men such as d'Annunzio, the sociologist Vilfredo Pareto, the composer Giacomo Puccini, the playwright Luigi Pirandello, and some of the avant-garde Futurist artists. Even moderates found it hard to believe that a party whose program contained so many contradictions—Fascists praised revolution and promised a strong state, defended property and called for social change, advocated order and used violence—could be dangerous for long.

Fascist Rule   Mussolini moved slowly to institutionalize his power. A series of special laws passed by 1926 declared the Duce (leader) of Fascism the head of state with the right to set the Chamber's agenda and to govern by decree. For twenty years, nearly all the laws of Italy would be issued

▼ **Mussolini and his bodyguard of black-shirted party members in paramilitary uniforms give the Fascist salute. The propaganda and rituals developed by Italian Fascists would be imitated across Europe.**
AP/Wide World Photos

in that way. Opposition parties were outlawed, scores of potential opponents arrested, and the civil service and judiciary purged of anyone thought too independent. Italy's newspapers were filled with pictures of Mussolini overawing visitors, captivating vast throngs, leaping hurdles on horseback, flying airplanes, harvesting grains. No story was too silly: The Duce recited the cantos of Dante from memory, he worked all night (the light in his office was carefully left on), he inspired philosophers and instructed economists, American razor blades were inadequate to the toughness of his beard, and his speed in race cars frightened experts. Slogans such as "The Duce is always right" and "Believe, Obey, Fight" soon covered walls throughout Italy. The victory of an Italian athlete or the birth of a child to a prolific mother became an occasion for hailing the new order as Mussolini's propaganda pumped pride and confidence into a troubled nation.

Despite considerable skepticism, the good news and sense of energy were welcome. Mussolini's sensitivity to the masses brought to Italian government a popular touch that it had lacked. By 1931 when the government demanded that all professors sign a loyalty oath, only eleven refused. With most people frightened into silence and organized resistance shattered, the regime had little to fear from some secret Communist groups and an underground centered in France.

The authoritarian single party, completely subordinate to the Duce, reached into every city and town with its own militia, secret police, and tribunals. Recruited in its early years mainly from among the unemployed and alienated, the Fascist party soon won hundreds of thousands of new members eager for the advantages it offered, until by the 1930s the party decided to accept members more selectively in an effort to achieve internal discipline. There were associations for Fascist teachers, workers, and university students. In youth organizations for every age group over four years old, the next generation wore black shirts, marched, and recited official slogans. Citizens were to replace the handshake with the extended right arm of the Fascist salute,[4] and regulations established the Fascist names to give one's children and the form of address to use with one's friends.

Fascist doctrine, never wholly consistent, denounced the principles of the French Revolution and of majority rule but hailed "the people." The much-advertised principle of authority was

▼ These ten-year-old boys were not, official propaganda declared, just playing at being soldiers but were ready with half-size rifles and lunch kits to defend their country. Millions of Italian children were enrolled in five organizations: one for boys and girls 6 and 7 years old, two separate ones for boys and girls from the ages of 8 to 13, and two more for those from 14 to 17. For the four years after that, they could belong to the Young Fascists.
© Corbis

---

[4]The salute was a stylized form of the greeting used in ancient Rome and portrayed in the statue of Marcus Aurelius that since the Renaissance had stood on the Capitoline Hill in Rome, where Michelangelo designed a piazza to frame it. The salute quickly became an international symbol.

FASCIST DOCTRINE

◆

The most carefully constructed single statement of Fascist doctrine was the article "Fascism: Doctrine and Institutions," written in 1932 for the Enciclopedia Italiana, *one of the most impressive intellectual works accomplished under the Fascist regime. Although the article was officially listed as by Mussolini himself, most of it was written by Giovanni Gentile, a noted philosopher who was an early supporter of Fascism.*

"It [Fascism] is opposed to classical liberalism which arose as a reaction to absolutism and exhausted its historical function when the State became the expression of the conscience and will of the people. Liberalism denied the State in the name of the individual; Fascism reasserts the rights of the State as expressing the real essence of the individual. . . . The Fascist conception of the State is all-embracing; outside of it no human or spiritual values can exist, much less have value. Thus understood, Fascism is totalitarian, and the Fascist State—a synthesis and a unit inclusive of all values—interprets, develops, and potentiates the whole life of a people.

" . . . First of all, as regards the future development of mankind—and quite apart from present political considerations—Fascism does not, generally speaking, believe in the possibility or utility of perpetual peace. It therefore discards pacificism as a cloak for cowardly supine renunciation in contradistinction to self-sacrifice. War alone keys up all human energies to their maximum tension and sets the seal of nobility on those peoples who have the courage to face it. . . .

"Fascism denies the materialistic conception of happiness. . . . This means that Fascism denies the equation: well-being = happiness, which sees in men mere animals, content when they can feed and fatten, thus reducing them to a vegetative existence pure and simple.

"After socialism, Fascism trains its guns on the whole block of democratic ideologies, and rejects both their premises and their practical applications and implements. Fascism denies that numbers, as such, can be the determining factor in human society; it denies the right of numbers to govern by means of periodic consultations; it asserts the irremediable and fertile and beneficent inequality of men who cannot be leveled by any such mechanical and extrinsic device as universal suffrage.

" . . . The State, as conceived and realized by Fascism, is a spiritual and ethical entity for securing the political, juridical, and economic organization of the nation, an organization which in its origin and growth is a manifestation of the spirit. The State guarantees the internal and external safety of the country, but it also safeguards and transmits the spirit of the people, elaborated down the ages in its language, its customs, its faith. The State is not only the present, it is also the past and above all the future. Transcending the individual's brief spell of life, the State stands for the immanent conscience of the nation."

From S. William Halperin (ed.), *Mussolini and Italian Fascism* (Van Nostrand, 1964).

reduced to simple obedience to the Duce. Authority itself was deemed purer when arbitrary. There was said to be a Fascist style in art and philosophy, sport and war. A candid irrationalism suspicious of intellectuals and traditional culture stressed the virtues of intuitive "thinking with the blood" and joy in war. As the antithesis of the decadent materialism of the democracies, Italy would influence the world and reclaim the heritage of imperial Rome (see "Fascist Doctrine").

The Corporate State The most discussed element of Fascism, the corporate state, was partly facade, partly an institutional expression of ideology. The intent was to organize each sector of production into a huge confederation, or corporation. Each corporation encompassed a syndicate of employers and one of workers, each headed by party members appointed by the government. Corporations were to establish industrywide policies and wage scales, and by 1926 the system was sufficiently in place to outlaw strikes, lockouts, and

▲ **The techniques of modern art combined with evocations of ancient Rome in Fascist posters like this one for an exhibition in 1933 on the eleventh anniversary of the Fascist revolution.**
Index s.a.s.

independent unions. In 1934 the number of corporations was set at twenty-two.[5] The Duce, as president of each corporation, appointed its council of delegates, which then also sat in the National

---

[5]A corporation covered an entire sphere of production, from raw materials to manufacture and distribution, and the corporations were divided into three groups: 1) grains, fruits and vegetables, wines, edible oils, beets and sugar, livestock, forestry and lumber, and textiles; 2) metals, chemicals, clothing, paper and printing, construction, utilities, mining, and glass and pottery; 3) insurance and banking, fine arts and liberal professions, sea and air transportation, land transportation, public entertainment, and public lodging.

Council of Corporations. These institutions, which never attained real autonomy, were further undercut by the strength of established interests and by Mussolini's habit of legislating by decree. They were presented, however, as the Fascist alternative to liberal forms of representation, replacing conflict with coordination and eliminating class conflict.

The new order in its twenty years did not remake Italy, which never became as orderly, efficient, or docile as Fascists wished. A quiet and safely intellectual opposition was tolerated, exemplified by the relative freedom allowed the world-famous philosopher, Benedetto Croce. The twentieth century would witness greater tyranny and worse brutality, but freedom in Italy was crushed, the jails filled, hundreds of prominent figures exiled to dreary southern towns or desolate islands.

Domestic Policies Fascist economic policy sought *autarchy,* a self-sufficient national economy, and emphasized industrialization and technology. Initial distrust of big business soon lessened, but the government remained active in economic affairs and often favored nationalization. For reasons of prestige, the value of the lira was set to equal the French franc, which hurt Italian exports and required restrictions that led to a painful devaluation. In the interest of self-sufficiency, the government launched its famous battle of grain in 1926, which succeeded (with enormous hoopla) in doubling grain production at great cost in efficiency.

Output per capita declined in the Fascist era. Generally, the industrial giants in steel, automobiles, rubber, and chemicals found it easy to deal with (and often to manipulate) Fascist bureaucracy. At the same time, the Institute for Industrial Reconstruction (IRI) established in 1933 provided subsidies to weak industries and often ended up owning them, a significant extension of government ownership. By 1940 real wages were down in both industry and agriculture.

Efforts to keep peasants on the land and to increase the birthrate at most merely slowed the contrary trends. But the regime did score some notable achievements, which it vigorously advertised. It suppressed the activities in Sicily of criminal groups called *mafia,* drained the malaria-infested marshes near Rome, built new railroads, and launched some superhighways. Enormous building projects contributed to employment. Workers benefited from the creation of centers with recreation halls, meeting rooms, and libraries in most towns and programs for vacations at seaside or mountain resorts. Family bonuses gave the poor an increased sense of security, and educational reforms put more people in school for longer periods.

The Lateran Agreements Fascism's most publicized accomplishment was its accommodation with the Vatican. Although Mussolini and most of his early followers were thoroughly anticlerical, the Fascist government adopted many measures the Church would welcome, putting crucifixes in classrooms and raising the budget for clerical salaries and church repairs. The Lateran treaties of 1929 ended sixty years of conflict between Italy and the Church. They recognized the tiny area of Vatican City as an independent state, and related agreements established religious teaching in public schools, guaranteed that marriage laws would conform to Catholic doctrine, promised to restrict Protestant activities, and determined the indemnity the Church should be paid for its losses during Italian unification. A dispute that had seared the consciences of millions of Italians was at last resolved. Abroad, the agreement suggested that Fascism had won special favor from the papacy, an impression little dimmed by an encyclical of 1931 that warned against the worship of the state or by subsequent conflicts between Fascists and Church officials. Although these conflicts were bitter, the Catholic Church was on the whole more generous toward Mussolini's regime than it had been toward the preceding liberal government.

Within the country, potential opponents of Fascism were baffled by Mussolini's apparent successes and, surrounded by propaganda, felt isolated and uncertain of what to believe. Indeed, most Italians probably shared some pride in their nation's heightened prestige. Outside Italy, important groups in all European and many South American nations sang the praises of Fascism's "bold experiment" that ended petty squabbling, ran the trains on time, kept order, and eliminated the threat of communism.

II. The Distinctive Culture of the Twentieth Century

The exciting intellectual and cultural movements of the 1920s built on those of the prewar period. Many of the works that marked new directions in science, philosophy, and the arts had appeared in the decades just before and after the turn of the century. These new trends, disquieting then, gained momentum to became dominant in many fields after the war. Psychology, literature, and art explored the irrational and surreal. The sciences uncovered complexities in nature that made uncertainty a theoretical principle, and theories of society adopted a tough-minded "realism" that spoke of power and interest more than values. Norms of behavior that had been considered the essence of civilization just a generation earlier were now called into question.

◆ FREUDIAN PSYCHOLOGY

No one disturbed accepted views more deeply than Sigmund Freud, a Viennese physician whose clinical studies had taken him gradually from an interest in neurology to the study of psychiatry. Freud followed the method—close and detailed observation—of medical science, and his writings were as careful in their logic as in their literary elegance. Freud had done his most important work before 1914, and in many ways he was old-fashioned. For the most part, he accepted as socially necessary the norms of respectable behavior promulgated by the nineteenth-century middle class. He was deeply influenced by ideas of evolution, and his metaphors and assumptions betray the liberal economist's appreciation of self-discipline and calculated self-interest. His attention to the phenomenon of hysteria and his use of hypnosis built on the work of others to create a startling view of the human mind, which he insisted could be universally applied. His great impact, however, came in the twentieth century.

The Unconscious In treating neurotics, Freud found that they often experienced relief of their symptoms by recalling forgotten events under hypnosis. He concluded that the recollection itself was crucial, not for its accuracy but as an expression of the psychic reality with which the patient had been unconsciously struggling. Within the unconscious, conflicting urges contended in what Freud labeled the *id*. Here universal basic desires (similar to instincts) seek satisfaction, and Freud found the most troublesome and psychologically significant desires to be sexual. The *ego* tries to channel and control these desires, directed to do so by the *superego,* which (rather like the conscience in more traditional conceptions) imposes a socially conditioned sense of what is acceptable behavior. Thus, mental life is marked by perpetual tension between the id and the superego.

This conflict, uncomfortably mediated by the ego, is unconscious, for one of the mind's responses is to repress from consciousness the id's desires. Most people remain unaware of their own deepest motivations. Repression, however, causes an enormous mental strain that often finds an outlet in neurotic behavior. As the patient comes to face and understand what is being repressed, neurosis is relieved.

Psychoanalysis   From this conception of the human psyche, Freud developed an elaborate, subtle, and shocking theory that ascribed sexual lusts to every person at every age. The idea of infant sexuality was especially offensive to contemporaries, but so was the notion of the Oedipus or Electra complex, through which the boy's angry competition with his father (or the daughter's with her mother) could produce a child's unconscious guilt-ridden wish for the death of one parent in order to possess the other. Few in Freud's time could tolerate this ascription of base desires

▼ **Although Freud believed his theories had universal, scientific validity, his consultation room in Vienna unmistakably reflected the cultivated taste of a central European of the upper-middle class in the late nineteenth century, from its tiled stove and afghans to its pictures and ancient sculptures.**
Edmund Engelman

to decent people. Freudian theory proclaimed that such decent people were merely the most repressed. Similarly, religion provided satisfaction for infantile and obsessive needs. Even the greatest human achievements in art and science were the result of sublimation, by which Freud meant the diversion of the id's primitive demands to other, higher purposes.

Psychoanalysis, the name Freud gave his body of theory and his therapeutic technique, calls on the analyst not to pass judgments but rather to help the patient discover aspects of self that proper society held to be quite simply unmentionable. By implication, these ideas and therapeutic techniques called for a shift in aesthetic and intellectual standards. Freud considered whatever seemed real to the psyche to be important; dreams and slips of the tongue were serious expressions of psychic conflict. Hypnosis and free association (in which patients are encouraged to let their thoughts ramble) were valued as modes of expression in which hidden connections emerged without the intervention of narrative or logic. Freud pioneered new ways of comprehending life and literature on several levels at once and provided the model for doing so.

Wider Implications In the 1920s the broad implications of Freud's discoveries gained wider public recognition despite continued hostility. If repression leads to neuroses, one extrapolation went, then greater sexual freedom and, above all, greater candor will produce healthier people. This inference remains perhaps the most widespread popular notion drawn from Freudian teaching, though it was not a view he held. Related to this view is the belief that guilt is evil, a kind of Christian perversion of human nature. Freudian insights encouraged literary and personal introspection and supported the view that childhood is the most important phase of life. Although his theories stimulated new visions of a freer and happier life, Freud's dark conclusion was that "the price of progress in civilization is paid in forfeiting happiness." Civilization, then, is based on the repression of primitive and still very powerful drives, which may burst forth at any moment. Freud, who feared the explosion he foresaw, died in 1939, driven into exile by the antisemitism of the Nazis.

Freudians strove to maintain these doctrines whole as science and therapy, treating deviations as heresies; but there would be many deviations. The best known came from the Swiss psychologist Carl G. Jung, who soon broke from Freud and developed his theory of the collective unconscious, the common psychic inheritance of whole peoples, which they most commonly expressed in the symbols and rituals of religion. Jung's somewhat looser and more mystical perspectives have fascinated religious thinkers, attracted theorists of nation and race, and influenced philosophers and artists. More generally, the concepts and vocabulary of psychoanalysis penetrated much of Western culture, apparent in art and literature, journalism and advertising.

◆ THE HUMANITIES

Art and Literature Some artists in the postwar period—the Surrealists, with their dreamlike canvases, are an example—applied Freudian ideas directly, and in his manifesto of Surrealism (1924), the writer André Breton proclaimed that art must liberate the subconscious. Quite independent of Freud, explorations of human irrationality fairly exploded in prose and poetry. The novels of Marcel Proust, Franz Kafka, and James Joyce most clearly mark the change in style and content.

Marcel Proust died in 1922, soon to be hailed as one of the great stylists of the French language. His long novel, *Remembrance of Things Past,* built an introverted and delicately detailed picture of upper-class Parisian life into a monumental and sensitive study of one man's quiet suffering, which became a model of interior monologue, of the novel in which the subject is not action seen from the outside but feelings observed from within.

Franz Kafka, who wrote in German though born in Prague, died in 1924, leaving instructions for his manuscripts to be burned. They were not, and they came to be accepted as quintessentially modern, with their realistic and reasonable descriptions of fantasies that convey the torture of anxiety. In *The Trial* the narrator tells of his arrest, conviction, and execution on charges he can never discover, an exploration of the psychology of guilt that foreshadows the totalitarian state.

▲ Like many German Expressionists, Otto Dix challenged the public with a series of paintings that simultaneously lampooned and celebrated the decadence of life in Berlin in the Weimar era.
AKG London

James Joyce's international fame came with the publication of his novel *Ulysses* (1922), the presentation on a mythic scale of a single day in the life of a modest Dubliner, written in an exuberant, endlessly inventive game of words in which puns, cliché, parody, and poetry swirl in a dizzying stream of consciousness.

Virginia Woolf, who used related devices in her novels, was less widely read at the time, but her work would become very influential a generation later. A political activist and feminist who was prominent in England's intellectual circles, her book *A Room of One's Own* (1929) subtly explored the value of a female perspective and the ways in which women were discouraged from intellectual independence. Not all of the most important writers turned away from the objective tone and chronological clarity of traditional narrative. But even those who made use of more familiar techniques—like Thomas Mann in Germany, André

THE FUTURIST MANIFESTO

The futurist movement was announced in typically provocative language in the "Manifesto of Futurism," written by Filippo Marinetti and published in the Paris newspaper Le Figaro *in 1909.*

MANIFESTO OF FUTURISM

"1. We intend to sing the love of danger, the habit of energy and fearlessness.

"2. Courage, audacity, and revolt will be essential elements of our poetry.

"3. Up to now literature has exalted a pensive immobility, ecstasy, and sleep. We intend to exalt aggressive action, a feverish insomnia, the racer's stride, the mortal leap, the punch and the slap.

"4. We say that the world's magnificence has been enriched by a new beauty; the beauty of speed. A racing car whose hood is adorned with great pipes, like serpents of explosive breath—a roaring car that seems to ride on grapeshot—is more beautiful than the *Victory of Samothrace*.

"5. We want to hymn the man at the wheel, who hurls the lance of his spirit across the Earth, along the circle of its orbit.

"6. The poet must spend himself with ardor, splendor, and generosity, to swell the enthusiastic fervor of the primordial elements.

"7. Except in struggle, there is no more beauty. No work without an aggressive character can be a masterpiece. Poetry must be conceived as a violent attack on unknown forces, to reduce and prostrate them before man.

"8. We stand on the last promontory of the centuries! . . . Why should we look back, when what we want is to break down the mysterious doors of the Impossible? Time and Space died yesterday. We already live in the absolute, because we have created eternal, omnipresent speed.

"9. We will glorify war—the world's only hygiene—militarism, patriotism, the destructive gesture of freedom-bringers, beautiful ideas worth dying for, and scorn for woman.

"10. We will destroy the museums, libraries, academies of every kind, will fight moralism, feminism, every opportunistic or utilitarian cowardice.

"11. We will sing of great crowds excited by work, by pleasure, and by riot; we will sing of the multicolored, polyphonic tides of revolution in the modern capitals; we will sing of the vibrant mighty fervor of arsenals and shipyards blazing with violent electric moons; greedy railway stations that devour smoke-plumed serpents; factories hung on clouds by the crooked lines of their smoke; bridges that stride the rivers like giant gymnasts, flashing in the sun with a glitter of knives; adventurous steamers that sniff the horizon; deep-chested locomotives whose wheels paw the tracks like the hooves of enormous steel horses bridled by tubing; and the sleek flight planes whose propellers chatter in the wind like banners and seem to cheer like an enthusiastic crowd."

Excerpt from F. T. Marinetti, "The Founding and Manifesto of Futurism," in R. W. Flint and Arthur A. Coppotelli (eds. and trs.), *Marinetti Selected Writings* (Farrar, Straus and Giroux, 1971).

Gide in France, and D. H. Lawrence in England—tended to explore topics and attitudes offensive to convention.

The Other Arts In all the arts, shock became one of the points of creative expression. Dada, a movement that originated during World War I, put on displays, part theater and part art exhibition, of noisy nonsense and absurd juxtapositions that were intended to infuriate the Parisian bourgeoisie. Italian Futurists, poets and playwrights as well as artists, promised to build a new art for a technological age—"The world has been enriched by a new beauty: the beauty of speed"—and in their manifesto of 1909 had issued a call to "burn the libraries . . . demolish the venerated cities" (see "The Futurist Manifesto," above and the painting by Boccioni, p. 952). The Fauves in France and the Expressionists in Germany and Scandinavia gloried in their reputation for wild and often brutal candor in the style and content of their paintings as well as in their conduct.

Works of art became more difficult to comprehend. Cubist and expressionist painters, like composers using the twelve-tone scale and dissonance, deliberately eschewed the merely decorative or pleasant and seemed eager to incorporate violence and amorality. Even when more sober traditions prevailed—as in the carefully constructed, cerebral poetry of William Butler Yeats and of the younger Ezra Pound and T. S. Eliot—foreboding and obscurity intertwined. Today the richness and profundity of the greatest of these works are readily apparent; but to contemporaries, they were more threatening than attractive, dangerously widening the chasm between "serious" art and the popular culture most intellectuals disdained.

Philosophy The philosophical work most widely read in the 1920s was Oswald Spengler's *Decline of the West*, which had appeared in 1918. Spengler treated whole civilizations as biological organisms, each with a life cycle of its own, and presented his study of Western culture as an achievement of German philosophy. But his fame rested on the dire prediction of his title: World War I had begun the final act of Western civilization (see "Spengler's View of History," p. 1026). José Ortega y Gasset's *The Revolt of the Masses*, published in 1930, was hardly more optimistic. The masses, he warned, were destined to use their rising power to destroy civilization's highest achievements. Scores of other writers joined in scorn for modern culture as vapid and directionless.

The most striking innovation in philosophy, however, came from another tradition entirely and was monumentally set forth in *Principia Mathematica* (1910) by Bertrand Russell and Alfred North Whitehead. It became the cornerstone of analytic philosophy, which holds that philosophers should concern themselves only with what is precise and empirically demonstrable. On the continent a group known as the Vienna Circle developed a related system, logical positivism. The work of Ludwig Wittgenstein, especially his *Tractatus Logico-Philosophicus* (1921), influenced both schools of thought.

Wittgenstein attempted in a series of numbered propositions "to set a limit to thought." By insisting on such rigor and seeking through symbolic logic to attain the precision of mathematical reasoning, analytic philosophers tended to exclude most of the general questions of ordinary life. The issues that theologians and moral philosophers had argued about for centuries were too imprecise to merit debate. Like the earlier positivists, analytic philosophers consciously emulated the nat-

ural sciences, but their stress on the lean language of mathematics led away from positivist confidence in knowledge. The philosopher's task was to analyze every statement, stripping away those connotations and values, however appealing, that do not convey precise meaning. "My propositions," Wittgenstein concluded in the *Tractatus*, "serve as elucidations in the following way: anyone who understands me eventually recognizes them as nonsensical." Philosophy, too, generated doubt and turned to its own specialized challenges.

◆ THE SCIENCES

Science had also moved beyond the layperson's comprehension since the late-nineteenth century. Even when the achievements of science were apparent to everyone, they often rested on theoretical advances that overturned established certainties. And the fields in which scientists worked became ever more highly specialized.

The Nature of Matter One line of scientific investigation stemmed from an experiment by two Americans, Albert A. Michelson and Edward W. Morley, in 1887. By demonstrating that the speed of light leaving earth was the same whether the light traveled in the direction of the earth's movement or against it, they challenged the established theory that the universe was filled with a motionless substance called "ether," which was thought necessary because waves could not function in empty space. The implications were fundamental, and exploring them led Albert Einstein to his theory of relativity, which he set forth in two brief papers published in 1905 and 1915. They were of the highest philosophical as well as scientific interest: Space and time are not absolute, he said, but must be measured in relation to the observer and on the most fundamental levels are aspects of a single continuum.

As Einstein developed his theory of relativity, physicists were also achieving a new understanding of matter. Wilhelm Roentgen's discovery of x-rays in 1895 had given the first important insight into the world of subatomic particles. Within two years the English physicist J. J. Thomson showed the existence of the electron, the subatomic particle that carries a negative electrical charge. The atom

SPENGLER'S VIEW OF HISTORY

◆

Oswald Spengler was an obscure German teacher before the publication of The Decline of the West *in 1918. A philosophy of history in two substantial volumes, it presents an original and systematic analysis of world history. The erudition is remarkable, and Spengler elaborately categorized the societies of Asia and Europe while discussing all sorts of topics, beginning with the meaning of numbers and ideas of destiny. The study's central device, however, is to analyze the arts as the symbolic expression of entire civilizations. The passage quoted here is from the last two paragraphs in the book. The final chapter—which follows chapters on the state, politics, and money—is entitled "The Form-World of Economic Life (B): The Machine." Although conceived and largely written before the outbreak of World War I, the work was inevitably read as a commentary on the postwar world and prediction of the future.*

"The *private* powers of the economy want free paths for their acquisition of great resources. No legislation must stand in their way. They want to make the laws themselves, in their interests, and to that end they make use of the tool they have made for themselves, democracy, the subsidized party. Law needs, in order to resist this onslaught, a high tradition and an ambition of strong families that finds its satisfaction not in the heaping-up of riches, but in the tasks of true rulership, above and beyond all money-advantage. *A power can be overthrown only by another power,* not by a principle, and no power that can confront money is left but this one. Money is overthrown and abolished only by blood. *Life* is alpha and omega, the cosmic onflow in microcosmic form. It is *the* fact of facts within the world-as-history. Before the irresistible rhythm of the generation-sequence, everything built up by the waking-consciousness in its intellectual world vanishes at the last. Ever in History it is life and life only—race-quality, the triumph of the will-to-power—and not the victory of truths, discoveries, or money that signifies. *World-history is the world court,* and it has ever decided in favour of the stronger, fuller, and more self-assured life—decreed to it, namely, the right to exist, regardless of whether its right would hold before a tribunal of waking-consciousness. Always it has sacrificed truth and justice to might and race, and passed doom of death upon men and peoples in whom truth was more than deeds, and justice than

power. And so the drama of a high Culture—that wondrous world of deities, arts, thoughts, battles, cities—closes with the return of the pristine facts of the blood eternal that is one and the same as the ever-circling cosmic flow. The bright imaginative Waking-Being submerges itself into the silent service of Being, as the Chinese and Roman empires tell us. Time triumphs over Space, and it is Time whose inexorable movement embeds the ephemeral incident of the Culture, on this planet, in the incident of Man—a form wherein the incident life flows on for a time, while behind it all the streaming horizons of geological and stellar histories pile up in the light-world of our eyes.

"For us, however, whom a Destiny has placed in this Culture and at this moment of its development—the moment when money is celebrating its last victories, and the Cæsarism that is to succeed approaches with quiet, firm step—our direction, willed and obligatory at once, is set for us within narrow limits, and on any other terms life is not worth the living. We have not the freedom to reach to this or to that, but the freedom to do the necessary or to do nothing. And a task that historic necessity has set *will* be accomplished with the individual or against him.

"*Ducunt Fata volentem, nolentem trabunt.*"

From Oswald Spengler, *The Decline of the West*, Charles Frances Atkinson (tr.) (Alfred A. Knopf, 1970).

was not the basic unit of matter. By the turn of the century Pierre and Marie Curie, among others, had found radium and other materials to be radioactive; that is, they emitted both subatomic particles and a form of electromagnetic radiation. Soon, largely through the work of the English

physicist Ernest Rutherford, radioactivity was identified with the breakdown of heavy and unstable atoms. These discoveries made it possible to link the structure of atoms with Dmitri Mendeleev's periodic table of elements. Elements with similar chemical properties were also similar

▲ Einstein's face remains one of the best-known icons of the twentieth century, a symbol of humanity, universal genius, and Jewish exile.
Ottawa Karsh/Woodfin Camp & Associates

in their atomic structures. A simpler and clear understanding of matter seemed in the offing.

Quantum Physics But continuing research soon revealed phenomena that Newtonian physics could not explain. In 1902 the German physicist Max Planck challenged Newtonian assumptions by announcing that energy in the subatomic world was released or absorbed not in a continuous stream but in discrete, measurable, and apparently irreducible units, which Planck called quanta. Energy, in effect, possessed many of the properties of matter.

This finding implied that matter and energy might be interchangeable, and Einstein incorporated the insight into his theory of relativity in the famous equation $E = mc^2$. Energy (E) is equivalent to mass (m) times the square of the speed of light, a constant (c), which means that, at least in

theory, small quantities of matter could be turned into enormous amounts of energy. In this respect Newtonian physics was wrong; matter could be transformed after all. In 1919 Rutherford produced changes in the structure of the nitrogen atom by bombarding it with subatomic particles, and other atomic changes were soon produced in the laboratory.

Uncertainty Principle By the mid-1920s, however, physicists had to face troubling anomalies. Planck's quantum theory, though verified in numerous experiments, considered particles to behave in probabilistic rather than absolutely regular patterns—a concept Einstein himself could never wholly accept. Furthermore, electromagnetic radiation, including visible light, seemed to behave like a flow of particles in some circumstances and in others as a wave—a regular disturbance of particles in which the particles themselves do not advance. Nor, the German physicist Werner Heisenberg argued, was it possible at the same time to determine a particle's position and its momentum, for at the subatomic level measurement interfered with the variables measured—a disturbing effect that Heisenberg appropriately named "the uncertainty principle." Conceptions of matter had been transformed in just a few years. Inside atoms there was mostly empty space and particles that did not behave with absolute regularity; and in both the subatomic world and the stellar universe, the position and purpose of the observer fundamentally affected what was observed.

The new theories proved powerful tools, but physicists who chose to philosophize about such matters now spoke in humbler and more tentative tones. Physics became one of the most prestigious, highly organized, and expensive of human activities, recognized rather than understood by the public through its applications: x-ray technology, the electron microscope, and eventually the controlled fission of atomic energy. Newtonian principles, physicists insisted, still obtained in most cases, as solid and predictable as ever. But there was a loss. The Western world had long looked to the sciences for confirmation of its philosophy and even its theology. In the twentieth century no popularizer would build a general outlook on society from the latest scientific discoveries as Voltaire had once done from the ideas of Newton.

▲ A school of handicrafts, art, and architecture, the Bauhaus defined a modernist aesthetic. Buildings like this one designed by Walter Gropius in 1925 pioneered the functional, international style that would dominate the most admired architecture of the next fifty years. Part of the explosive creativity of the Weimar years, the school broke up with the advent of Hitler when many of its members left Germany, most for the United States.
AKG London

The Biological and Social Sciences   Although the new work in other fields of science was less revolutionary, it often had immediate impact. Knowledge of the mechanisms of heredity furthered scientific breeding of animals and the creation of plant hybrids that would greatly increase the productivity of agriculture. The isolation of viruses opened a new field of study, and medicine gained a new armory that led to invaluable drugs with the discovery of penicillin in England by Sir Alexander Fleming and Sir Howard Florey in 1928.

The understanding of society was deeply affected by two giants of modern sociology, the Frenchman Émile Durkheim and the German Max Weber, whose work is central to modern social science. Durkheim's use of statistical tools and Weber's use of the "ideal type" to analyze how societies function remain influential, as does

their concern with the customs and beliefs that hold society together. Both, for example, emphasized the importance of religion, although they were concerned not with its metaphysical truth but with its contribution to the development of the state and of capitalism. Both stressed the threat to society when group norms broke down, and both saw a danger of that breakdown in modern trends. Through this emphasis on the function of communal values rather than their validity and on the role of myth and ritual in all societies including our own, anthropology, sociology, and history have tended to share psychology's insistent relativism.

◆ PUBLIC CULTURE

To the public at large, developments in science and the arts were associated with the prosperity and brash excitement of the twenties. Science meant the spread of automobiles, radios, and airplanes; new trends were known through colorful stylish advertising, risqué literature, and vibrant theater. The surprising crisp architecture and applied design of Walter Gropius' Bauhaus school in Germany, with its emphasis on relating form to function, began to win a following, and there was curiosity about the still more daring endeavors in France of Le Corbusier to envision a wholly modern city as a machine for living.

Cinema   The distortions of time and perspective through flashbacks and close-ups were less disturbing when conveyed in motion pictures than through words or on canvas. On the silent screen, even the frothiest romance or adventure story could contain subliminal themes of social or national concern, reflecting the experiences of World War I through themes of abandonment in France and of betrayal in Germany.[6] Motion pictures became more popular and more profitable than any form of entertainment had ever been. Movie theaters were built on the most elegant streets of Paris, London, and Berlin, gaudily combining the exoticism of a world's fair with reassuring luxury. Egyptian and Greek motifs, marble columns, fountains, mirrors, and statues reinforced the fantasies on the screen. The Gaumont Palace built in Paris in 1919 became an international model, with its 5,000 plush seats and an orchestra pit for eighty musicians. Berlin's three hundred cinemas included the Sportspalast, redone for motion pictures in 1920, which boasted of being the largest movie theater in the world. By the mid-1920s, Britain, France, Germany, and Italy each counted their movie theaters in the thousands.

Crowds of people from every stratum attended the same movies, and women came, even without male escorts. Influenced by the movies, middle-class and working-class families in the 1920s were more likely to be talking about the same things, and women especially could more easily imagine a different and better life. Reviews and movie magazines helped to provide the publicity essential to success in a business that relied on stars and

▲ Gaudy movie palaces like this Parisian theater, one of the first, became prominent monuments in every city, offering the masses an exotic luxury previously associated with the great opera houses.
©Tallandier

vast distribution networks. American companies did all this very effectively, filling screens around the world. The United States made more films than any other country. Japan was second and Germany third, with Europe's largest film company.

The rapid transition to talking pictures between 1929 and 1930 underscored national differences, and every country had some ministry empowered to restrain the presentation on the screen of sex and violence. In 1919 an English Watch committee condemned a film of the

---

[6]Paul Monaco develops this interpretation in *Cinema and Society: France and Germany during the Twenties* (1976).

Johnson-Jeffries fight, fearing it could "demoralize and brutalize the minds of young persons." Sunday showings were an issue for years. Politics was present, too. Many countries restricted or banned German films in the 1920s; France, generally the most tolerant, in effect proscribed films made in the Soviet Union where, with Lenin's encouragement, the director Sergei Eisenstein brilliantly showed how well suited the medium was to depicting official views of the revolutionary power of the masses.

Consumerism While moralists worried about the cynicism of mass entertainment and the amoral excess of nightlife in cabarets and theaters, millions joined a kind of dizzying celebration. Middle-class families bought their first car; millions from every class, their first radio. Sophistication was a kind of shibboleth, used to justify lipstick, short skirts, alcohol, and one brash fad after another but also to underscore the cosmopolitanism that valued American jazz, openly learned from African art, and welcomed the new. For perhaps the only time, Berlin rivaled Paris as a European artistic center, more famous as the home of acid satire in art and theater than for its thriving cultural institutions of a more traditional sort. Modernism turned its back on gentility.

III. The Retreat from Democracy

◆

Within less than a decade after the Paris Peace Conference, democracy was in retreat across Europe. By 1929 authoritarian regimes had violated or eliminated the liberal constitutions of Hungary, Spain, Albania, Portugal, Lithuania, Poland, and Yugoslavia as well as Italy. By 1936 political liberty had also been suppressed in Romania, Austria, Bulgaria, Estonia, Latvia, and Greece as well as Germany. Most of these countries were among the poorest in Europe, but their political difficulties illustrate the broader trend. Divided over issues of social reform, nationality, and religion—differences amplified by new and angry socialist and peasant parties—they suffered increased disruption with each economic crisis and foreign threat.

◆ AUTHORITARIAN REGIMES

Authoritarian leaders often flirted with fascism on the Italian model, only to find it dangerously uncontrollable. They sought through decisiveness and force to achieve stability in societies riven by social conflict and where religious and ethnic loyalties could be readily fanned into anger and hatred by ambitious politicians.

The Monarchies of Central and Eastern Europe Hungary was among the first to turn to authoritarian rule. Behind a constitutional facade, the Magyar aristocracy relied on a rigged electoral system to maintain its political dominance, protect its privileges, and stifle land reform. Under Admiral Horthy, who became head of state in 1920, the regime made sure that any threats of democracy were kept in check. Hungary was drawn toward Italy both as another opponent of the peace treaties and as a model of order. In the 1930s fascist trappings increased, and successive governments became more antisemitic; yet Hungary never became a full-fledged modern dictatorship, and the government dissolved the most threatening fascist parties in 1939.

Romania's liberal government began to give way even before Carol II was called to the throne in 1930. King Carol admired Mussolini and secretly subsidized the Iron Guard, a fascist organization whose political violence and antisemitism imitated the worst of fascism in other countries. The government stripped most Jews of land and citizenship, tightened censorship, and imposed martial law, but the disruptions that followed and pressure from Britain and France brought a shift in policy. By 1938 the king led the way in suppressing fascist activities.

In Yugoslavia, King Alexander I assumed dictatorial powers in 1929 in an effort to tame the divisive forces of Croatian, Slovenian, and Serbian nationalism. But as these conflicts continued, he tried a restricted parliamentarianism. The regent, who directed affairs after Alexander's death in 1934, pursued a similar course, drawn at first to the example of Germany and Italy, and then deciding by 1939 that Yugoslavia's international position and internal stability would best be served by a federal and democratic system.

◄ The men of Romania's fascist Iron Guard movement marched in green shirts, its women's corps in green skirts.
© Corbis

In Bulgaria a military coup ended parliament, parties, and free speech in 1934, and the regime moved closer to fascism as it sought both urban and rural support. But by 1936 the king was restricting the military, banning some fascist groups, and talking of constitutions.

Fear of Germany and the need for French support was one reason these regimes turned away from fascism, but there was another. Authoritarians, attracted to fascism because of its ability to mobilize a mass following in the name of order, were soon threatened by this very ability to rouse support, by the ambitions of fascist leaders, and by the backlash against fascist tactics.

The Republics of Poland, Greece, and Austria

Although republican regimes were more neces-

sarily in touch with public opinion, they faced similar conflicts over land reform and labor. Their political systems, too, were subject to the mutual fears of left and right and to international pressures. Poland especially suffered from having powerful neighbors, and Poles disagreed on whether their national interest lay with Germany, Russia, or France. Socialists and Catholics, conservative landowners and radical peasants, looked in different directions for outside support as they battled each other, and the resulting instability brought Marshal Jozef Pilsudski to the fore. A former socialist, he took power in a military revolt. Once his supporters had gained a majority in parliament, in 1930, he resigned, but Poland continued to be ruled by men from the military. Unable to quell the noisy conflicts of fascists and socialists and without a popular base, they persisted in trying to strengthen a nation badly hurt by the worldwide economic depression of the 1930s.

The Greek republic, founded in 1924, lasted little more than a decade. As liberals gradually lost ground and monarchists gained, republicans attempted a coup but failed to prevent a plebescite in 1935, which the monarchists manipulated and which led to King George II's return to the throne. When liberals made gains in the 1936 elections, General Joannes Metaxas proclaimed himself dictator and clung to power in fascist style by balancing severe censorship and the abolition of political parties with extensive social welfare, public works, and armament.

In Austria the republic was undermined by the sharp division between a Catholic German countryside and a cosmopolitan imperial Vienna that no longer had an empire to administer. The Socialists, out of power since 1926, had little strength beyond the city, while the Christian Socialists—whose nineteenth-century programs of welfare, nationalism, and antisemitism had influenced the young Hitler—moved steadily toward fascism. In the 1920s both parties had established paramilitary organizations, and their violent clashes became a regular part of Austrian politics. Chancellor Engelbert Dollfuss drew Austria closer to Fascist Italy and ruled by decree, suspending parliament, outlawing communists, and by 1934,

▼ **Police in Vienna prepare to confront socialists in 1927. The socialists were protesting the release of men believed to have murdered a socialist. In the ensuing riots, the palace of justice was burned and a hundred people were killed, part of the cycle of violence shaking the Austrian republic.**
© Corbis

banning all parties except his own Fatherland Front. The Socialists responded with a general strike, and the government replied by bombarding Karl Marx Hof, the public housing that Viennese socialists had been so proud of, an act that symbolized the end of Austrian democracy. A new constitution, elaborately corporative and claiming inspiration from papal encyclicals, was announced in 1934 but never really put into operation. Events in Germany, where Hitler and the Nazis had come to power, now overshadowed everything else in Austrian politics. In July a group of Austria's Nazis assassinated the Austrian chancellor. Although the Anschluss, or union with Germany, that they thought would follow did not come immediately, Austria's authoritarian government, having repressed the left, had little basis from which to resist growing Nazi pressure.

Alternative Regimes in Spain With its overstaffed army, discontented workers, militant anarchists, and socialists, Spain was already a strife-torn nation in 1921 when its army in Spanish Morocco was routed by Berber tribesmen. The resulting turmoil at home temporarily ended in 1923 when General Miguel Primo de Rivera issued a *pronunciamento* in time-honored style and assumed office as de facto dictator. Without a clear program, he used the themes of modern antiliberalism and Mussolinian techniques, dividing the left with extensive welfare programs and establishing a political party of his own. Experiments with corporatism followed, but by 1926 intellectuals, business people, the Church, and the army were restive. As economic depression hit and the government faltered, King Alfonso lost his taste for Primo de Rivera's attempt at a fascist constitution, and the dictator went into exile. The king, who now presented himself as the protector of liberty, tried another military government, which experimented in turn with both martial law and the promise of constitutionalism, but all the old problems remained. When republicans and socialists triumphed in the municipal elections of 1931, Alfonso also chose exile.

The second Spanish republic briefly held its divergent supporters together with progressive labor legislation and welfare programs ill-adapted to Spain's economy. It granted autonomy to Catalonia but left unresolved other regional conflicts and the critical problem of effective land reform. Its policies separating church and state and secularizing education infuriated half of Spain without satisfying the anticlericals. Neither a conservative government nor a leftist coalition could keep opposition from growing more radical, both on the far left and on the right, where a movement called the Falange (in direct imitation of Italian Fascism), founded by José Antonio Primo de Rivera, the dictator's son, grew stronger. Systematic street violence was commonplace by 1936, when a group of army generals announced their revolt. That began the Spanish civil war, which set the stage for World War II.

International Fascism Whether they won power or not, Europe's fascist movements had much in common. Generally influenced by Italian Fascism, they looked and sounded similar. They liked uniforms, starting with a shirt of one color. Cheap to buy and easy to adopt, it made a group of supporters (however few or poor) look like a movement, a historical force. They used paramilitary organization that promised decisive action to remake society through discipline and force. They created drama in the streets—noise, marches, colorful demonstrations, symbolic acts, and real violence—that undermined conventional standards of public behavior while advertising fascism as something new and powerful. They borrowed heavily from working-class movements and used all the devices of democratic politics, while seeming to stand outside the corrupting process of compromise and responsibility. Populist tactics were thus attached to the promise of order.

Fascists nostalgically evoked the enthusiastic patriotism of World War I to offer simple solutions to real problems. The disruption and inequity of capitalism, class conflict, a faltering economy, and aimless governments were the fault of enemies— liberal politicians, Marxist revolutionaries, Jews, and foreigners. Those enemies, although ridiculed and denounced in fascist propaganda, were credited with hidden powers that only the force of fascism could overcome. Fascism promised to create a united, orderly, prosperous community.

There was more to these movements than their simple myths, camaraderie, and sinister attraction to violence. Fascists addressed real fears. They spoke to a rural society that felt threatened by urbanization, to small-business people threatened by the competition of large corporations and to all business people threatened by workers' demands and government intervention, to a middle class threatened by socialism, to the privileged threatened by democracy, to the unemployed threatened by continuing economic depression, to the religious threatened by a secular society. Everywhere, they played on fear of a communist revolution.

The Appeal of Fascism   Fascists could do all this by borrowing freely from ideas current throughout Europe. They used socialist criticisms of liberalism and capitalism, conservative values of hierarchy and order, and intellectual denunciations of modern culture. They amplified a widespread contempt for parliamentary ineffectiveness, used doctrines of race made familiar by war and imperialism, and laid claim to the nationalism that every government liked to invoke. At the same time, as admirers of technology and organization, fascists promised to create more modern societies. And they laid claim to corporatism, which Mussolini's Italy advertised as the wave of the future.

Corporatist thought had a long and respectable history. Organizing society as well as parliament according to occupation promised to do away with the selfish competition of interests and parties characteristic of liberalism, to preserve social hierarchy, and to eliminate class conflict. The idea of so integrated a society gained attractiveness in the years of economic depression and prestige with Pope Pius XI's encyclical *Quadragesimo Anno* ("In the Fortieth Year") issued in 1931 on the fortieth anniversary of Leo XIII's *Rerum Novarum*. The new encyclical went further in rejecting the injustices of capitalism and the solutions of Marxism, and it called instead for harmony based on religion and cooperation through corporative organization. Many anxious people found in that papal pronouncement a sympathy for fascism that seemed to justify overlooking its deeply antireligious qualities.

The appeal of fascism was not limited to poor nations. Its ambiguities made it applicable everywhere. In Britain, Sir Oswald Mosley, once considered a likely Labour prime minister, founded the British Union of Fascists. In Belgium, fascism benefited from the antagonism between Catholics and anticlericals and between French-speaking Walloons and Dutch-speaking Flemings, who were increasingly sympathetic to fascism and to the Nazis. In the Netherlands a National Socialist movement rose to prominence in the 1930s, and there were a number of fascist and protofascist movements in France, including *Action Française*,

◀ **Sir Oswald Mosley reviews a women's unit before a large Fascist parade in London, 1936.**
©Bettmann/Corbis

which had become prominent in the furor of the Dreyfus case. Led by Charles Maurras, its denunciations of the bourgeois republic were echoed by fascist parties everywhere; but *Action Française* lacked the mass appeal of full-fledged fascism and was overshadowed in the 1930s by other movements of uniformed young militants eager to take to the streets.

◆ THE GREAT DEPRESSION

Above all, fascist and Marxist movements benefited from a worldwide economic depression that undermined social and political stability and seemed to many the death knell of capitalism.

The Stock Market Crash On October 24, 1929, the price of stocks on the New York Exchange began to plummet. Suspecting that speculation had pushed stock prices too high, nervous investors sold their shares. Day after day tens of millions of dollars in paper assets disappeared. Such panics were not new, and they had spread from New York to Europe in the previous century. Now, however, the United States was the world's wealthiest nation and greatest creditor, and this panic settled into full-scale depression as banks failed, businesses cut back, consumption declined, factories closed, and unemployment rose. Its banks and exchanges shaken, the European economy suffered further from the decline in world trade and the withdrawal of American investments and loans. Financial panic hit Europe in May 1931 when Austria's largest bank nearly went under. That started a run on Austrian and German banks and then spread as it had in the United States to other sectors of the economy and to other nations.

The late 1920s had been years of boom in the United States and of general prosperity in much of Europe, but the Great Depression exposed deep-seated problems. Not all industries had recovered after the war. Coal and textile industries had long been sliding toward chronic depression. Former trade patterns had not revived, especially among the underdeveloped new countries of Eastern Europe, and economic difficulties were increased by Germany's inflation and Russia's withdrawal from commerce. Europe, which lost huge amounts of foreign investments during the war,

had not regained its prewar percentage of world trade (about half), and American investments in Europe increased dramatically throughout the 1920s. Too much of the international economy rested on the unproductive passing of paper from the United States to Germany as loans, from Germany to the Allies as reparations, and from the Allies to the United States as payment of war debts; and the United States raised tariffs in 1922 and again in 1930 to levels that made it nearly impossible for Europeans to earn dollars by selling to Americans. Much of the prosperity of the 1920s rested on new processes and on new products, such as automobiles and synthetic fabrics, which proved vulnerable to the withdrawal of American investment and the decline in consumer confidence. The Great Depression underscored how uneven and artificial much of the preceding prosperity had been and showed that for Europe a decade had not been long enough to overcome the effects of World War I.

The Repercussions By 1932 the world's industrial production was two-thirds of what it had been in 1929. Unemployment climbed to more than 13 million in the United States, 6 million in Germany, and nearly 3 million in Great Britain. Among leading industrial nations, only France, with its balanced economy and lower fertility rate, escaped a crisis of unemployment. Since the war, and especially in democracies, governments were expected to provide solutions to economic problems. They looked first for international help. Because the reparations system had broken down amid the world economic crisis, European nations declared that they could no longer make debt payments to the United States. The United States refused to acknowledge the connection. Instead, President Hoover proposed that all intergovernment payments be suspended; his proposal, quickly accepted in 1932, was supposed to be temporary but in fact marked the end of both kinds of payments.

Other crises loomed. Austria's banking system had been saved from bankruptcy with British loans; but the deepening depression and other financial burdens forced Great Britain to abandon the gold standard, which meant it no longer guaranteed the value of the pound sterling. The important bloc of countries that traded in sterling

▲ **Unemployed workers from Glasgow set out for London on a "famine march" in 1934.**
Mary Evans Picture Library

followed suit. Tantamount to devaluation, these moves threatened chaos for international monetary exchanges and trade; and so the League of Nations sponsored a World Economic Conference that met in London in 1933. Begun with visions of high statesmanship, it ended in failure. When the United States also went off the gold standard, the structure of credit and exchange that had been one of the signal achievements of liberal finance fell apart. For a century nations, like so many bankers, had supported international financial stability by honoring these rules of liberal economics, and that historic era had ended.[7]

---

[7]Karl Polanyi elaborated on the significance of abandoning the gold standard in a famous essay, *The Great Transformation: The Political and Economic Origins of Our Time.*

National Responses In this crisis democracies responded first to domestic pressures. Austria and Germany sought a customs union, which was opposed by France and rejected by the World Court. Nearly everyone raised tariffs and import quotas, further reducing trade, while domestic programs protected political interests. Liberals were at a loss as to what else to do, and socialists were no better prepared to solve the problems of declining commerce, insufficient capital, and—most pressing of all—unemployment. Socialists could find some vindication in the evident weakness of capitalism, but their favorite nostrum, the nationalization of industry, was barely relevant. In practice, they adopted rather orthodox measures of budget reduction while supporting whatever palliatives for unemployment could be suggested, though the dole, the most common one, strained the budgets they wanted to balance.

Most government policies, then, did little to help and may have made the situation worse; bankers and financiers, desperate to stem their losses, gave little attention to the international or social effects of their actions. And the millions of unemployed were more helpless still, standing in line for the dole, eating whatever they could get, taking any bits of work available. Growing communist parties let no one forget that while a whole international system had been collapsing, Soviet production advanced at a steady pace.

Gradually, economic conditions did improve; and by 1937, production in Germany, Britain, and Sweden was well above the 1929 level, though below that in the United States, Italy, Belgium, and France. Subsequent government intervention to shore up industries and provide employment did alleviate distress and improve morale. It also changed economic and political life and, at least in democracies, was often as socially divisive as the Depression itself. Democracies faced the dual threat of communism and fascism with a heavy burden of economic and social failure.

IV. Nazi Germany and the U.S.S.R.

In the 1930s Nazi Germany and the Soviet Union acquired unprecedented power over their own populations and used it in ways that changed the world. Understanding how these regimes evolved, their techniques of rule, and the policies they pursued remains a central challenge of twentieth-century history.

Totalitarianism Dictatorship has been recognized since ancient times as a specific political form. The most important dictatorships of this century, however, were different enough from previous examples to merit a separate term. They relied on a single political party, absolute devotion to a leader, domination of mass communications, direction of the economy, and the ruthless use of force—all in the name of an explicit, official ideology. The term *totalitarianism* refers to the combination of these characteristics and describes a system of rule more than specific policies, a system inclined to use oppression and terror to force citizens to participate in the regime's activities and belief system. In principle totalitarianism seeks to shape every aspect of life and to crush "enemies" identified by their race, occupation, region, or religion. Such a vision and the institutions that would attempt to carry it out did not develop all at once but evolved, primarily in Communist Russia, Fascist Italy, and Nazi Germany.

Useful as the concept of totalitarianism is, it has also come under heavy criticism for a number of reasons. In practice, none of the totalitarian regimes achieved total control. They often gave way before customs and institutions they could not afford to offend and negotiated with entrenched interests. Inefficiency and duplication were characteristic, even endemic, for these regimes were not monolithic. Officials and party members often bickered among themselves. No totalitarian ideology was entirely coherent or unanimously embraced, and there were important differences among totalitarian systems. The values promulgated and policies pursued in Soviet Russia were not at all the same as those of Nazi Germany. Italy's claim to be totalitarian was largely propaganda, and that is the point. *Totalitarianism* is a useful term not for describing how these regimes actually functioned but rather for describing the ambitions and techniques that made Europe's leading twentieth-century tyrannies a fundamentally new political form.

◆ HITLER'S GERMANY

The Nazi regime won power in a democracy with an advanced economy and a strong administrative tradition. It played upon selected elements of German history, from militarism and nationalism to the weakness of the Weimar Republic, and it took advantage of the social shocks Germany had recently suffered: defeat in war, failed revolutions, inflation, clashing ideologies, and a depression that brought the most extensive unemployment in Europe.

The Rise of Hitler As a young man, Adolf Hitler was undistinguished, his ambition to be an artist thwarted when the Academy in Vienna rejected his application. Service in World War I had been a kind of salvation, providing comradeship and some accomplishment: He was promoted in the field. In Munich after the war, he found brief employment spying on the small German Worker's party, which the army considered dangerous. He also took to addressing political rallies in the beer halls, where he learned the potential of a movement that combined the personal loyalty of a paramilitary corps with mass appeal and where he molded the speaking style that would make him the most powerful figure in Germany.

His speeches combined crude accusations, a messianic tone, and simple themes repeated in a spiraling frenzy. Race and universal struggle were the core of his message. Germans were victims of vast conspiracies mounted by foreign powers, capitalists, Marxists, Freemasons, and (above all) Jews—the gutter antisemitism that Hitler had absorbed in Vienna. Jews were behind war profits, reparations, inflation, and depression; but Marxism was also Jewish, and communists were agents of the Jewish conspiracy. Internationalism and pacifism were Jewish ideas intended to destroy Germany as the bastion of Western civilization.

To Hitler, Western civilization was Aryan, an old term for the prehistoric peoples of Eurasia that he used to describe race. Germans and Nordic peoples were the purest Aryans, Jews their enemy. Life was a desperate struggle won by the ruthless, and Germany's destiny was victory over enemies who threatened the nation by means of the Versailles Treaty, economic disasters, communists, Jews, moral decay, and abstract art. All attacked the Germanic *Volk*, the German people whose primitive virtues must be welded into an irresistible force.

The Growth of the Nazi Party Hitler named his party the National Socialist German Workers' party. *Nazi* was its acronym. The party was one of many such nationalist movements when in 1923 Hitler led them in the Munich *Putsch*, or rising. After it failed and Hitler was sent to prison, the book he wrote there, *Mein Kampf*, won little notice, for it was a turbulent, repetitive outpouring of his political views interlarded with demoniac statements about how human beings are manipulated by fear, big lies, and simplistic explanations. In prison and after his release in 1925, Hitler worked to reorganize and strengthen the party. To

the SA, his street army of brown-shirted storm troopers, he added the SS, an elite corps in black uniforms who served as his bodyguards and special police. The party picked up some ideas and useful phrases from Moeller van den Bruck, a literary figure respected in conservative circles, whose book *The Third Reich* advocated a corporative and nationalist regime. And the party established its own newspaper, edited by Alfred Rosenberg, who expanded Hitler's racist ideas in *The Myth of the Twentieth Century,* published in 1930, a work that despite its turgidity was significant as part of the effort to establish a formal ideology.

Even with an ideology and with organizations in place, the Nazis had limited success. The party's membership of 60,000 in 1928 was not enough to have much weight in German politics. It had some notable assets, however. General Ludendorff had joined Hitler in the 1923 *Putsch,* and other officers might be expected to lend support. Some circles of Bavarian conservatives and Rhineland industrialists showed interest in the movement, and in 1929 the Nazis gained national prominence with a petition against the Young Plan. The Plan's aim was to put a final limit on reparations, but the Nazis opposed all reparations and declared it high treason not to renounce the war-guilt clause of the Versailles Treaty. Four million Germans signed.

If Hitler's intensity and bad manners offended many, others felt the fascination of a personality that radiated power. He soon gathered a group of absolutely loyal men: Hermann Göring, an air ace; Joseph Goebbels, journalist and party propagandist; and Heinrich Himmler. They worked ceaselessly to enlarge the party, orchestrate impressive rallies, and terrorize their opponents. The Nazis were gaining attention and support. In 1930 they became the second-largest party in the Reichstag, and the following year a group of Rhineland industrialists promised the Nazis financial support.

By the 1930s, the party was broadly based, and the issue of what social groups were first drawn to the Nazis has been the subject of historical controversy, because different interpretations of Nazism follow from the answer. Workers were probably the biggest single group of members, but most workers continued to favor socialists and communists. Disproportionately large numbers of Nazi supporters were small-business people and tradespeople, civil service employees, and (to a lesser extent) farmers—all groups fearful of losing income and status.

In the Depression, promises of recovery, higher agricultural prices, and more employment (tens of thousands found jobs in the SA and SS) had concrete appeal. Many people were drawn to the call to rebuild the army and to save society from socialism. In 1931 an array of right-wing nationalists joined the Nazis in a manifesto denouncing the "cultural Bolshevism" of the Weimar Republic and hinting that, once they seized power, the Nazis would protect only those who had joined them now. The Nazis spoke simultaneously like a government in office and like an underworld gang, and they demonstrated their seriousness by beating up Jews and socialists.

Collapse of the Weimar Republic The Social Democrats led the government that faced the Great Depression and did the best they could with a shaky parliamentary majority and an uncooperative president. In 1930 the government resigned, to be replaced by the Center party and Heinrich Brüning, a cautious man with little popular appeal. President von Hindenburg allowed this government to enact measures by decree, something he had denied the Social Democrats. But a nation in crisis was in political stalemate, with an unalert, reactionary president and a Reichstag incapable of producing a stable majority. It, like the country, was divided among multiple parties, each with its own agenda of outrage. Hindenburg's sporadic interventions only made the situation worse; repeated elections raised the heat but brought no resolution.

The elections of 1930 gave Nazis more than a hundred new seats from which they contemptuously disrupted parliamentary proceedings. His confidence growing, Hitler became a candidate for president in 1932, when Hindenburg's term expired. Worried politicians persuaded the nearly senile field marshal to run for reelection. Ludicrously cast as the defender of the constitution, the eighty-four-year-old Hindenburg won handily, but Hitler got more than 13 million votes. When Brüning proposed a financial reform that included expropriation of some East Prussian estates, Hindenburg dismissed him and turned to

Franz von Papen, a friend of important army officers and Junkers.

Hoping to create a right-wing coalition, von Papen lifted Brüning's ban on the SA and SS, named four barons and a count to his cabinet, and declared martial law in Prussia so he could unseat the socialist government there. The outcry led Hindenburg to call another election. This one resulted in a Nazi landslide. With 40 percent of the Reichstag's seats, the Nazis were by far its largest party. Hindenburg avoided naming Hitler chancellor by refusing to grant him the full decree powers he insisted on. The nation was sent to the polls again, and although the Nazis lost a little, they remained the largest party.

Hitler Takes Office Hindenburg then named another chancellor, General Kurt von Schleicher, a conventional army officer. He made an easy target for the Communists, the disgruntled von Papen (who thought he saw his chance to regain power), and the Nazis. Von Papen, confident he could use Hitler but contain him, persuaded the men around Hindenburg to appoint Hitler the head of a coalition government. In fact Hitler was the only leader acceptable to the right who could also command a popular following. Of the twelve men in Hitler's cabinet, only two others were Nazis. Hitler, the leader of an unsuccessful *Putsch* only ten years before, took office late in January 1933. As the anti-Weimar parties of left and right gained ground, the political system lost its flexibility. The number of votes for Marxist parties remained nearly constant, but the Communist share of them grew; and the Nazis increasingly garnered the votes of the right.

Hitler almost immediately called another election. Previous campaigns had been ugly, but this one was marked by systematic terror, especially in Prussia, where Hermann Göring was now minister-president and the police acted like electoral agents. The climax came with the burning of parliament, the Reichstag fire that the Nazis loudly blamed on the Communists. Hindenburg agreed to issue special laws—Ordinances for the Protection of the German State and Nation—that ended most civil liberties, including freedom of the press and assembly. The voters gave the Nazis 44 percent of the seats, enough, with the Nazis' nationalist allies, for a bare majority. Hitler pressed on. Communists were expelled from the

Reichstag, conservatives wooed with calls to nationalism, and the Center party enticed with promises to respect the privileges of the Catholic Church. By March Hitler dared demand a special enabling act that gave him, as chancellor, the right to enact all laws and treaties independent of constitutional restraints for four years. Of the 566 deputies left in the Reichstag, only 94 Social Democrats (out of 121) voted no. Blandishment and terror had done their work, but the tragedy went deeper: German politics offered no clear alternative to Hitler.

Consolidating Nazi Rule Hitler's regime moved quickly to destroy the potential for opposition. It established concentration camps, first on private estates and then in larger and more permanent institutions. The new order appeared to enjoy all but unanimous support. A campaign to boycott Jewish businesses was followed in April by laws eliminating most Jews from public service and limiting Jews to 1.5 percent and women to 10 per-

cent of university enrollment. On May Day 1933, workers arrayed by occupation marched beside Nazi banners and slogans. By July all parties except the National Socialist had been outlawed, and soon all competing political organizations disappeared.

In the elections of November 1933, the Nazis won more than 90 percent of the vote. They restructured government, purged the civil service and judiciary, outlawed strikes, and clamped stricter controls on the press. In a few months Hitler had achieved fuller power than Mussolini had managed in years, and in the next few years Nazi policies on racial purity would be extended step by step throughout public life by ordinances, official policies, and police brutality.

Hitler's most serious potential rivals were within his own party, and his solution was barbarically simple. On a long weekend in June 1934, leaders of the Nazi left wing were shot or stabbed. Among hundreds of others, so were General von Schleicher and his wife, some Catholic leaders,

▼ **Nazi party troops march out of the rally on Nuremberg Party Day, 1933, carrying victory banners proclaiming "Germany Awake."**
AKG London

some socialists, and some taken by mistake. Hitler admitted to seventy-four deaths; subsequent estimates raise the figure to as many as a thousand. The Night of the Long Knives proved that any horror was possible; and the purge, like the noisy accusations of homosexuality that accompanied it, established the tone of Germany's new order. When Hindenburg died in August, Germans voted overwhelmingly to unite presidency and chancellorship in the person of Adolf Hitler, who took the official title of *Führer* ("Leader").

Administrative and Economic Policies The federal states lost their autonomy through a policy of *Gleichschaltung,* or coordination, and all government employees were made appointees of the Führer. New people's courts heard secret trials for treason, now very broadly defined, and rewritten statutes allowed prosecution for intent as well as for overt acts. Arrest and detention without charge or trial became a regular practice. At the same time, the Nazi party was restructured to parallel the state, with administrative *Gaue*

◄ Under Hitler, labor battalions also marched. By 1938 this "shovel brigade" could parade through the streets of Eger, a German town near the Czech border, on its way to extend the road from the newly annexed Sudetenland.
© Corbis

("regions") headed by a party Gauleiter. The party also had its own office of foreign affairs and its own secret police, the Gestapo, which infiltrated both the bureaucracy and the army.

Economic policies scored impressive successes. Unemployment dropped steadily thanks to great public works projects—government offices, highways, public housing, reclamation, and reforestation. Many of these projects used special labor battalions, in which one year's service was soon compulsory. Later the burgeoning armaments industry and growing armed forces eliminated the problem of joblessness entirely. By spending money when more traditional governments thought it essential to balance their budgets, the Nazis reduced unemployment more effectively than any other Western nation.

Paying the Cost   Such programs were expensive, and they were paid for in several ways. A currency scheme largely designed by Hjalmar Schacht, a brilliant economist, required that payments for foreign trade be made with special marks whose value changed according to the products and the nations involved. Goods that Germany bought were paid for in marks redeemable only through purchases in Germany. Tantamount to barter, this system increased Germany's self-sufficiency and its influence in countries that depended on German markets. Additional revenues came from property confiscated from Jews, high taxes, forced loans, and carefully staged campaigns urging patriotic Germans to contribute their personal jewelry to the state. Ultimately, costs would be covered by printing paper currency, with effects long hidden by a war economy and the exploitation of conquered lands. By 1945 the mark had fallen to about 1 percent of its 1933 value.

Labor policies met related goals. Strikes were outlawed and the mobility of workers regulated. The National Labor Front, which represented all workers and management, froze wages and directed personnel in the interests of business and government. Industrialists were relieved of the uncertainties of the Weimar years.

Winning Approval   Meanwhile, the regime advertised the new benefits provided workers, including the summer camps and special cruises that were part of the Nazi program of Strength

Through Joy. Nazi propaganda also reassured those ordinary people fearful of contemporary trends by denouncing modern art, the decadence of Berlin nightlife (and especially of homosexuality), and new roles for women. Special benefits to new families aided young couples in a depressed economy. Along with improved prenatal care and special honors for the most prolific mothers, such measures were part of the Nazi obsession with biology.

Initially, women were discouraged from working outside the home as a way to reduce unemployment among men, but the concern with women went far deeper. Wifely subordination was presented as a principle of social order and the foundation of the family. Women could not be lawyers or judges and could not constitute more than 10 percent of the learned professions. Social policies, schools, and clinics reinforced propaganda praising the role of Aryan women as breeders of a pure race. Severe penalties for performing abortions on healthy Aryans were accompanied by forced sterilization of the "unfit." Boys and girls were required to join the Hitler Youth. Despite the insistent propaganda, there is evidence that poor pay and lack of freedom were resented but evidence, too, of an oppressive enthusiasm for a great leader who brought order and hope.

The military had clear reasons for gratitude. Disregarding the disarmament clauses of the Treaty of Versailles (which Germany formally repudiated in 1935), Hitler pushed rearmament from the first. With the return of universal compulsory service in 1935 and the creation of an air force, Germany was soon spending several times as much on arms as Britain and France combined. If regular officers resented Nazi paramilitary organizations and looked down on the Nazis as their social inferiors, they nevertheless accepted the oath of personal loyalty Hitler required. Strengthened by his diplomatic successes, Hitler asserted control more directly in 1938, removing the minister of war, the chief of staff, and more than a dozen generals amid public tales of private vice. At the same time the foreign minister, an old-style nationalist who had served since 1933, was replaced by Joachim von Ribbentrop, a good Nazi and no aristocrat at all. The army and foreign service, strongholds of traditional conservatives, were under the Nazi thumb.

The Nazis and the Churches The churches presented a different challenge. A concordat with the Vatican in 1933 gave the state some voice in the appointment of bishops while assuring the Church of its authority over Catholic orders and schools. Protestant denominations agreed to form a new body, the Evangelical Church, under a national bishop whom Hitler named; but when the bishop declared a need to "Aryanize" the church, dissidents formed the separate Confessional Church. The Minister for Church Affairs was authorized to confiscate ecclesiastical property, withhold funds, and have pastors arrested; but in practice the state kept religion in line more through the local harassment of individual clergy. Some priests and ministers cooperated with the regime—enthusiastically supporting war, race, and Reich. Most resisted at least the more outrageous demands made of them, and some individuals spoke out courageously. In 1937 Martin Niemoeller, the leader of the Confessional Church, was arrested for his opposition to Nazism; and Pope Pius XI condemned both the deification of the state and Nazi racial doctrine. In the following years some Catholic churches were burned, and members of religious orders were frequently tried on morals charges.

Antisemitism Antisemitism was central to Nazi ideology and practice, and the Nuremberg laws of 1935 codified and extended previous regulations. Jews (anyone with one or more Jewish grandparents was considered a Jew) were declared to be mere subjects but no longer citizens. The Law for the Protection of German Blood and Honor prohibited marriage or sexual intercourse between Aryans and Jews, "Gypsies, negroes or their bastards." Subsequently, Jews were expelled from one activity after another, required to register with the state, and ordered to give their children identifiably Jewish names.

In 1938 the murder of a German diplomat by a young Jewish boy touched off a new round of terror. Many Jews were arrested, and the SS led an

▼ The six-pointed star and the word *Jude* scrawled on this Berlin department store in 1938 were a warning to good Aryans not to shop there.
© Corbis

GOEBBELS' POPULIST VIEW OF GERMAN CULTURE

◆

As minister of propaganda in the German government, Joseph Goebbels was also president of the Reich Chamber of Culture, an organization divided into separate sections for the various arts and for film, radio, and the press. Artists had to belong in order to exhibit, perform, or be published. The speech quoted here was an address given by Goebbels to the annual Congress of the Chamber and of the Strength Through Joy organization held in Berlin in November 1937. Goebbels' efforts were at their peak, and he reported proudly on the campaign against decadent art (which included much of the modern art most admired today), on the abolition of art criticism, and on the new recreation homes for veterans and the elderly, saying, "Nothing similar has even been tried ever or anywhere else in the world."

"My Führer! Your excellencies!

"My racial comrades!

"Organization plays a decisive role in the lives of people. . . . For every organization must demand that its members surrender certain individual private rights for the benefit of a greater and more comprehensive law of life. . . .

"The purging of the cultural field has been accomplished with the least amount of legislation. The social estate of creative artists took this cleansing into its own hands. Nowhere did any serious obstructions emerge. Today we can assert with joy and satisfaction that the great development is once again set in motion. Everywhere people are painting, building, writing poetry, singing, and acting. The German artist has his feet on the ground. Art, taken out of its narrow and isolated circle, again stands in the midst of the people and from there exerts its strong influences on the whole nation.

" . . . True culture is not bound up with wealth. On the contrary, wealth often makes one bored and decadent. It is frequently the cause of uncertainty in matters of the mind and of taste. Only in this way can we explain the terrible devastations of the degeneration of German art in the past. Had the representatives of decadence and decline turned their attention to the masses of the people, they would have come up against icy contempt and cold mockery. For the people have no fear of being scorned as out of step with the times and as reactionary by enraged Jewish literati. Only the wealthy classes have this fear. . . . These defects are familiar to us under the label 'snobbism.' The snob is an empty and hollow culture lackey. . . . He goes in black tie and tails to the theater in order to breathe the fragrance of poor people. He must see suffering, which he shudderingly and shiveringly enjoys. This is the final degeneration of the rabble-like amusement industry. . . . The Volk visits the theater, concerts, museums, and galleries for other reasons. It wants to see and enjoy the beautiful and the lofty. That which life so often and stubbornly withholds from the people . . . here ought to unfold before their eyes gleaming with astonishment. The people approach the illusions of art with a naïve and unbroken joyousness and imagine themselves to be in an enchanted world of the Ideal. . . . The people seek joy. They have a right to it.

" . . . 'Hence bread and circuses!' croak the wiseacres. No: 'Strength Through Joy!' we reply to them.

"This is why we have thus named the movement for the organization of optimism. It has led all strata of the people by the million to the beauties of our country, to the treasures of our culture, our art, and our life. . . . The German artist of today feels himself freer and more untrammeled than ever before. With joy he serves the people and the state. . . . National Socialism has wholly won over German creative artists. They belong to us and we to them.

" . . . In this hour, we all look reverently upon you, Führer, you who do not regard art as a ceremonial duty but as a sacred mission and a lofty task, the ultimate and mightiest documentation of human life."

From Salvator Attanasio et al. (trs.), Speech of Goebbels, in George L. Moesse, *Nazi Culture: Intellectual, Cultural, and Social Life in the Third Reich* (University of Wisconsin Press, 1966).

orgy of violence (named *Kristallnacht*, the "night of broken glass") in which Jews were beaten and murdered, their homes and businesses smashed, and synagogues burned. A fine of 1 billion marks was levied on the Jews of Germany, and they were barred from the theater and concerts, forbidden to buy jewelry, forced to sell their businesses or property, denied access to certain streets, and made to wear a yellow star. Worse would come.

For most Germans, life went on much as before but a little better, and there was a new excitement in the air. From the beginning, the Nazis' publicity had been flamboyant, their posters striking, and their rallies well staged; after the movement came to power, propaganda became a way of life. Torchlight parades, chorused shouts of *Sieg Heil!* ("Hail to victory!"), book burnings, the evocation of Norse gods, schoolyard calisthenics, the return to Gothic script—a thousand occasions offered Germans a feeling of participating, of being swept up and implicated in some great historical transformation. At the Reich Chamber of Culture, Joseph Goebbels saw to it that cinema, theater, literature, art, and music all promoted Nazism (see "Goebbels' Populist View of German Culture," p. 1045). Things primitive and brutal were praised as Aryan; any who opposed or even doubted the Führer ceased to be German. Warfare was for this new regime its natural condition.

◆ STALIN'S SOVIET UNION

Communists held that dictatorship in the Soviet Union was incidental and supposedly temporary. The reality proved different. Communist rule became more systematically brutal and bloody after Lenin's death, but in the last decade historians have uncovered substantial evidence in newly opened Russian archives that Lenin had already laid the groundwork for such policies.

The Succession to Lenin No one knew who Lenin's successors would be when he died in 1924 or even how the succession would be determined. For more than a year, Lenin had been ill and nearly incapacitated, but his prestige had precluded any public scramble for power, and many expected a more relaxed government by committee to follow. In a famous letter, Lenin had as-

sessed two likely successors: Trotsky, whom he called overconfident but the best man in the Politburo, and Stalin, whom Lenin found "too rude" though an able organizer.

Over the next three years, Russia's leaders publicly debated complex issues of Communist theory and practical policy. Trotsky led those who clung to the traditional vision that revolution would spread across Europe, and he favored an uncompromisingly radical program at home and abroad. Stalin declared that the Soviet Revolution must survive alone, a "revolution in one country." No theoretician, and little informed about the world outside Russia, Stalin was not wholly at ease in these debates with more intellectual and experienced opponents. But they, in turn, underestimated his single-minded determination. When the Politburo formally adopted his position in December 1925, his victory rested on more than ideas.

The Rise of Stalin As general secretary of the party's Central Committee, Stalin was the link between the Politburo and the party organization below it, and he could count on the loyalty of party officials, many of whom he had appointed. He played effectively on personal antagonisms and on resentment of Trotsky's tactless arrogance. When the Politburo elected three new members at that December meeting, all were Stalin's associates. He then effectively eliminated his opponents. When leading figures publicly sided with Trotsky, Stalin labeled the break in party solidarity a threat to communism. Trotsky and Grigori Zinoviev—the head of the Comintern, the organization of the Third International intended to lead communists around the world, whose prominence made him dangerous—were expelled from the Politburo in 1926 and from the party in 1927.

The left was broken, and the following year Zinoviev recanted his "mistake" in having supported Trotsky. Nikolai Bukharin, perhaps the party's subtlest theoretician and a leader of the right, recanted too. Trotsky, who refused to change his mind, was deported, continuing from abroad his criticism of Stalin's growing dictatorship. None of these veterans of the October Revolution had attempted to oust Stalin; even Trotsky, who built the Red Army, never tried to use it against him. Old Bolsheviks fervently accepted the need for party loyalty, and Stalin made sure that the open debates of those early years would not recur.

The First Five-Year Plan: Agriculture   In aims and enforcement, the First Five-Year Plan reflected some of the qualities that had brought Stalin to the top. It shamelessly incorporated ideas Stalin had denounced just months before, but it was thoroughly his in the bold assumption that Russia could be transformed into an industrial power by mobilizing every resource. By 1928, when the plan was launched, Russian production had regained prewar levels in most sectors. Lenin's New Economic Policy had depended heavily on private entrepreneurs in commerce and peasant owners in agriculture. The task now was to create a socialist economy, and the first step was to collectivize agriculture.

Using the improved techniques and the mechanization that peasants had on the whole resisted, Soviet agriculture could produce enough both to feed industrial workers and to export grain that in turn would pay for importing the machinery that industrialization required. The problem was that Russian peasants continued to withhold their goods from market when agricultural prices fell. Some 4 or 5 percent of them had the means to hire labor and lend money within their villages, which gave them a further hold over the local economy.

As famine threatened, the government mounted a sweeping campaign of propaganda and police action against these wealthier peasants, calling them *kulaks*—the old, pejorative term for grasping merchants and usurers. Their grain was seized (informers were given a quarter of any hoard uncovered), hundreds of thousands of people killed, and untold numbers deported to till the unbroken soil of Siberia. Peasants destroyed crops and animals rather than let the government have them.

The explosive antagonisms of rural society raged out of control, and Stalin had to intervene in 1930 to halt a virtual civil war. By then, more than half the peasants belonged to collective farms, but the strife had badly hurt production, which contributed to serious famine in 1932–1933. A kind of compromise followed. Even on collective farms peasants were permitted individual plots and privately owned tools. Larger machinery was concentrated at Machine Tractor Stations, which became the rural base for agricultural agents and party officials. By 1933 output was sufficiently reliable to permit the state to concentrate on the most massive and rapid industrialization in history.

The First Five-Year Plan: Industry   According to the five-year forecast, industrial production was to double in less than five years, and in some critical areas, such as electrical power, it was to

◀ **Farmers, women as well as men, drive imported tractors out of one of the Soviet Union's Machine Tractor Stations to work fields in which such mechanization had been rare.**
Sovfoto

increase sixfold. More than 1,500 new factories were to be put into operation, including large automobile and tractor plants. Projects on a still grander scale included a Dnieper River power station and a great coal and iron complex in a whole new city, Magnitogorsk. These goals were met somewhat ahead of schedule, and there was only slight exaggeration in the government's proud claim to have made Russia an industrial nation almost overnight.

To pay for that achievement, indirect taxes were levied, wages allowed to increase only slightly, planned improvements postponed, peasants displaced, and peasant land collectivized. Food and most consumer items were rationed, with allotments varying according to one's contribution to the plan. Success required much more than money. Unskilled or poorly trained, laborers were unaccustomed to the pace now required: Turnover was high; output and quality, low. The state resorted to a continuous work week and moved special "shock brigades" of abler workers from plant to plant. Women and young people were urged into industrial jobs. "Socialist competition" pitted groups of workers and whole factories against each other for bonuses and prizes; piecework payment, once a hated symbol of capitalism, became increasingly common. Violators of shop rules were fined; malingering, pilfering, and sabotage (often loosely defined) became crimes against the state. "Corrective" labor camps, initially a mode of prison reform, became another way to get more work done. Special courses within factories and enlarged technical schools trained new managers and engineers to replace the foreigners who were still essential to efficient industrial production.

In effect, an entire nation was mobilized, and the need for social discipline replaced an earlier emphasis on revolutionary enthusiasm. In schools, the formal examinations, homework, and academic degrees, recently abolished, began to return; classroom democracy gave way to greater authority for the teacher. The state stressed the importance of the family and praised the virtues of marriage, and the earlier emphasis on freedom for women gradually gave way to an emphasis on their contribution to Soviet productivity. Divorce was discouraged, and regulations on abortion, which had been legalized in 1920, became increas-

ingly restrictive. Associations of writers, musicians, and artists worked on propaganda for the plan. Mass organizations of youth and workers met for indoctrination, and within the party, criticism or even skepticism was akin to treason. Hundreds of thousands of party members were expelled, and new recruits were carefully screened. "Overfulfillment" was triumphantly announced in 1932; the miracle of industrialization came with creation of a Russian totalitarianism.

Growth in the 1930s   The Second (1933–1937) and Third (1938–1942) Five-Year Plans continued the push for industrialization at somewhat lower pressure. Consumer goods were more available, and rationing was eliminated by 1936. Standards of quality rose, and dramatic improvement in transportation, especially domestic aviation,

▼ **Villagers watch with anticipation for the first light bulb in Bryansk Province to be switched on, an achievement of the First Five-Year Plan.**
Novosti/Sovfoto

▲ **This Soviet poster of 1930 hails the International Day of Women Workers, part of the government's extended campaign to encourage women to work in factories.**
Edimedia

made previously remote territories accessible. By 1939 Soviet Russia ranked third among the world's industrial producers behind only the United States and Germany, producing twenty-four times more electrical power and five times more coal and steel than in 1913. Literacy among people older than school age rose from below 50 percent in 1926 to more than 80 percent in 1939. As millions moved to cities, the number of higher schools, libraries, and hospitals doubled or tripled. In these years one-seventh of the population moved to the cities, making the country more

urban than ever before. More than 90 percent of peasant households were on collective farms serviced by the Machine Tractor Stations.

Announcing that the stage of socialism had been reached, the Soviet Union adopted a new constitution in 1936. The changes it made were mainly formal. Direct voting by secret ballot replaced the cumbersome indirect elections for the Soviet of the Union. The other house, the Soviet of the Nationalities, represented the republics, which on paper had considerable autonomy. The two houses together elected the Council of Ministers (the term *Commissars* thus passed away) as well as the Presidium, which legislated and whose chairman was head of state. The constitution recognized the Communist party as "the vanguard of the working people" and provided social and political guarantees that Communists hailed as the most democratic in the world. Ninety-six percent of the population voted in the next elections, 98 percent of them for the list the party presented.

Stalinism   A more confident government showed signs of relaxing its campaigns against potential enemies. Some political prisoners were amnestied in 1935, and a more controlled political police, the NKVD, replaced the sinister secret police. The campaign against religion abated. Opportunities for advancement in this expanding economy were great. White-collar classes got more respect, officers were restored to the army and navy, and supervisors were reinstalled in factories. Expression of opinion remained tightly controlled, however. Writers, Stalin commented ominously, were "engineers of human souls." Although harassed less than during the First Five-Year Plan, intellectuals had long since learned the necessity of caution. The Russian Academy of Science, an important source of money and prestige, was never far from politics.

At the center of Soviet society stood Stalin, adulated as leader in every activity. Works of art were dedicated to him, factories named after him. His picture was everywhere. Patriotism overshadowed the socialist internationalism of an earlier generation, and Stalin was placed with Ivan the Terrible and Peter the Great as one of the molders of Russia. Although he held no official position other than party secretary, he demonstrated his awful power in the great purges of the late 1930s.

Directed against engineers, Ukrainian separatists, former Mensheviks, and party members accused of being counterrevolutionaries, the purges were touched off by the assassination in 1934 of Sergei Kirov, a member of the Politburo who had been a close associate of Stalin's (in fact, Stalin himself was probably behind the assassination). Party and state mobilized to root out a great conspiracy. Zinoviev and members of the "left opposition" were twice tried for treason and were executed in 1937.

Other public trials followed: party leaders and army officers in 1937, members of the "right opposition," Nikolai Bukharin and other old Bolsheviks, in 1939. To the outside world, the indictments seemed vague and the evidence unconvincing. Yet the accused consistently confessed—the effect of torture perhaps, or the wish to protect their families, or maybe the final act of faith by men who were convinced of the inevitable course of history and believed that anyone resisting it was "objectively" a traitor. A reign of terror swept the country, feeding local vendettas until Stalin called a halt in 1939. The dead were countless; jails and labor camps were bursting with prisoners, perhaps 10 million. More than twice that many had gone into exile. Soviet totalitarianism had grown to be ominously like that of Germany and Italy, except for the values it professed.

V. The Democracies' Weak Response

Confident Communist, Fascist, and Nazi regimes had moved dramatically to meet the challenge of the Depression and to forge social unity while tightening their hold on power. Europe's democracies responded more uncertainly, forever compromising and unable to disguise the social and ideological dissension that politics could not overcome.

◆ DIVISIVE SOCIAL CHANGE

The Economy Economic recovery by the mid-1930s did not lessen these divisions, even though standards of living were rising again. Agriculture became more productive by becoming more mechanized and scientific, but those changes required increased capital (thus favoring larger holdings) and employed fewer laborers. Workers benefited from better transportation, mechanical refrigeration, cheaper clothes, and more leisure; but it took organized conflict for them to pry better wages from employers.

Many employees now enjoyed a shorter work week, but work itself was more subject to "American" efficiency on speeded-up assembly lines, forcing workers to repeat the same tasks at a pace set by factory managers (and known as Fordism, after the production methods of Henry Ford in Detroit). This form of production and the use of elaborate time and motion studies intended to reorganize work in ways that would further increase productivity (called Taylorism, after studies by the American efficiency expert, Frederick W. Taylor) seemed to suggest that efficiency meant treating human beings like machines.

The middle classes recouped much that inflation and depression had undermined, but not their former confidence. While small businesses and craft industries remained insecure, larger corporations benefited first from the economic upturn and tended to form more powerful cartels, combining many firms within a single field so as to gain control of the entire production process from raw materials to marketing. And businesses large and small feared labor unions and socialist parties that were sounding increasingly militant.

Cultural Life Even cultural life lacked the healing qualities once expected of it. The scholars, scientists, and artists exiled from the new regimes in Russia, Italy, and Germany went to London, Paris, and especially the United States. They brought knowledge, methods, and artistic achievements that stimulated an explosion of creativity, and they brought their fears and disillusionment. Cultural movements seemed all the more foreign, politicized, and ideological. The new media did much to bridge the chasm between rural and urban life, but mass entertainment was not given to thoughtful discourse and moral uplift. The distinction between high and popular culture sharpened, and to many intellectuals culture itself was threatened as never before by the frothy commercialism of talking motion pictures and radio.

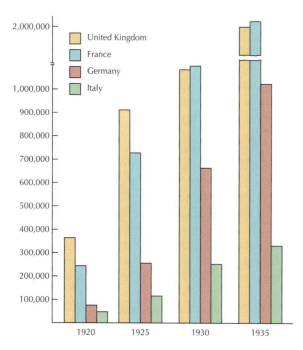

▲ NUMBER OF MOTOR VEHICLES
The number of automobiles in a society reflects its general wealth, adaptation to a consumer economy, and changing patterns of communication. (Note that the United Kingdom, France, and Italy each had about 40 million people; Germany had 65 million.) This graph gives evidence of impressive prosperity and change; by 1935 France and the United Kingdom had one vehicle for every 20 people.

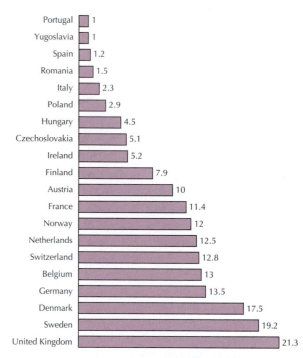

▲ APPROXIMATE NUMBER OF RADIOS LICENSED FOR EVERY 100 PEOPLE IN 20 SELECTED COUNTRIES (1938)
Radio was an important new instrument of communication and propaganda. These statistics suggest that most families in the United Kingdom had a radio, that nearly everyone could sometimes listen to the radio in Finland and Austria, and that from Italy to Portugal, millions of people heard the radio only on special occasions when speakers blared in public places.

Social scientists, poets, and novelists probed the theme of alienation, denounced faceless mass society, and engaged in radical politics.

In Paris, the Spanish painter Pablo Picasso became the dominant figure of twentieth-century art, restlessly experimenting with one new style after another. His most political work, *Guernica*, was a searing comment on war prepared for the Spanish pavilion at the Paris World's Fair of 1937 (see p. 1051). Some artists defended the "experiments" of Hitler and Mussolini; far more joined Marxist groups, convinced that only socialism could create an acceptable society and preserve culture. The energy of the propaganda that advertised the transformation of Soviet society or the happy order, well-lit factories, and vacation resorts of Germany and Italy underscored the contrast between the ideologically coherent and purposeful societies of a single party and the aimless dislocation and dissension in the democracies.

◆ THE ARGUMENT FOR LIBERTY

Against the strident claims of radicals and fascists, four major groups of intellectuals—Marxists, Christian thinkers, liberals, and economists—expressed a revived commitment to freedom. The most prominent of these thinkers were the Marxists. The Russian Revolution had enthralled millions of Europeans with visions of economic progress in a backward nation and of social equality and high culture in a mass society. This appeal grew as capitalist economies

▲ *Pablo Picasso*
GUERNICA
Pablo Picasso used the still new stylistic techniques he had mastered to protest the bombing of the Spanish town of Guernica by German planes in 1937. The huge, dark canvas, a political act in opposition to Franco and the Spanish Nationalists, foreshadowed modern warfare's brutal impact on civilian life. Kept in the United States for nearly fifty years, the painting can now be exhibited in a democratic Spain.
©2002 The Estate of Pablo Picasso/Artists Rights Society (ARS), New York

staggered, and it reached a peak with the promulgation of the Soviet constitution of 1936. At the same time, socialists and even communists insisted on the importance of justice, equality, and liberty, asserting that dictatorship in the Soviet Union was a special case.

Christians and Liberals In Christian thought, traditional arguments against the idolatry of the state gained new meaning. The Protestant Karl Barth and the Catholic Jacques Maritain built on firm theological orthodoxy to stress the importance of individual freedom and social justice. Similar concerns emerged in the influential work of the Russian Orthodox Nikolai Berdyaev and the Jewish scholar Martin Buber.

From a more secular perspective, noted poets and novelists such as W. H. Auden, Thomas Mann, and André Malraux wrote powerfully in behalf of human dignity and social justice, warning of the dangers of power and the evils of war. Most vigorous in the politics and universities of Britain and France, liberals were also heard even

in Fascist Italy. In his important *History of European Liberalism*, Guido de Ruggiero argued that liberal values, modified yet again, offered a practical path to stability and progress; and Benedetto Croce made liberty the central theme of his historical and philosophical writings.

Keynesian Economics Economic theory also contributed to the argument for political freedom through the work of John Maynard Keynes, whose book *The General Theory of Employment, Interest, and Money* appeared in 1936. Keynes rejected classical views of economic man and the self-regulating economy. Few people, he argued, consistently act in their own financial interest, for no one is free of ideas, values, and tastes that shape actions. Nor do iron economic laws inexorably dictate a pattern of booms and busts. To Keynes, massive unemployment was not only intolerable but proof that capitalism must not be left to its own devices.

At the same time, he dismissed Marxism as outmoded. Instead, he offered a sophisticated theory that called on governments to smooth out the economic cycle. When the economy lagged, the government should lower interest rates to encourage production and should finance public works and social welfare to stimulate consumption. As the economy expanded, the opposite policies should check inflation and excessive speculation. Keynes advocated granting government a more active role while preserving free markets. In effect, he gave a theoretical foundation for practices already partially adopted under Swedish socialism, the French Popular Front (see later in this chapter), and the American New Deal, President Franklin D. Roosevelt's program of social and economic reform inaugurated in 1933. An advocate of capitalism, Keynes defended it by denying that its social evils were inevitable; most capitalists denounced him as a socialist.

Few thinkers were neutral. With socialist anger, Auden, the British poet who chose to live in America, warned capitalists that "the game is up for you and for the others."[8] T. S. Eliot, the American poet who chose to live in Britain, proposed still tougher choices in a voice of Christian outrage: "The term 'democracy' . . . does not contain enough positive content to stand alone. . . . If you will not have God (and He is a jealous God) you should pay your respects to Hitler or Stalin."[9]

◆ DOMESTIC POLITICS

The Great Depression and rising international dangers undermined the traditional programs of democratic parties, left and right. Conservative parties pursued balanced budgets with results that embittered the unemployed. Liberals reluctantly accepted tariffs and subsidies that had few positive results. Socialists, weakened by competition from communists, antagonized workers by accepting weak welfare measures in the interest of better-balanced budgets. Issues of foreign policy had an even more paradoxical effect. Conservatives, historically supporters of military strength,

---

[8]W. H. Auden, "Consider This" and "In Our Time," in *A Little Treasury of Great Poetry,* Oscar Williams (ed.) (New York: Charles Scribner's Sons, 1947), p. 689.

[9]T. S. Eliot, *The Idea of a Christian Society* (New York: Harcourt Brace, 1960).

were now inclined to downplay the dangers arising from Italy and Germany. Parties of the left, arguing that fascism must be resisted, tended to abandon their antimilitary rhetoric. As Finland and Czechoslovakia, whose economic growth and political freedom had made them models of the new postwar nations, felt the pressure from their stronger neighbors, the cause of democracy increasingly depended on Britain and France.

Cautious Compromise in Great Britain   Ramsay MacDonald became the British prime minister after a Labour victory in 1929. Following the advice of experts, he made drastic cuts in welfare and unemployment payments, measures that divided his own party. He then formed a national government with members from all three parties, in effect a conservative government in disguise, and was expelled from the Labour party amid bitter recriminations. His government adopted controls on foreign exchange and increased tariffs, policies that split the Liberals. When MacDonald resigned in 1935, tired and unloved, his coalition government had overseen a slow recovery of the British economy, redefined imperial relations, and initiated some cautious steps toward government planning. But it had done so by pursuing conservative policies, and it had devastated the proletarian movement to which MacDonald had devoted his life.

He was succeeded by Stanley Baldwin's Conservative government, his third time as prime minister. Baldwin campaigned as a strong supporter of the League of Nations, in which he actually had little interest; and, with a complacency that masked indecision, he steered clear of political extremes. The parliament elected with him, which would continue to sit through 1945 as the longest-lived in modern history, would later reveal a wealth of talent, testimony to the continued vitality of British political life.

In retrospect, even the crisis of 1936 could be seen as a comforting assertion of tradition. King Edward VIII, who had acceded to the throne, insisted on marrying an American divorcée. He was forced to abdicate, and the transition to George VI went smoothly, quelling talk of the end of the monarchy. At the time, however, British institutions appeared weak. As international affairs grew more ominous, Britain's uncertain foreign policy further undermined the capacity of continental states to resist the expansionist policies of Germany and Italy. Doubts about Britain's role increased in 1937 when Baldwin turned the prime ministership over to his earnest Chancellor of the Exchequer, Neville Chamberlain, who was convinced he could avoid the danger of war through caution and compromise.

Weak Government in France   France experienced the Depression later and less severely than other highly industrialized countries, but when the decline came, it lasted. The left won the legislative elections of 1932, as the economic slump began to be felt, but found it difficult to construct a reliable majority, for the Socialists refused to participate in bourgeois governments. The result was unstable governments committed to reducing expenditures and protecting established interests. Outside parliament, rightist factions, including the fascist Croix de Feu (Cross of Fire), grew increasingly noisy. On February 6, 1934, their uniformed militants led demonstrations against parliament that resulted in more bloodshed than Paris had seen since the Commune of 1871; many believe that the Third Republic nearly died that day. France seemed more bitterly divided than at any time since the Dreyfus affair at the turn of the century.

The exposure of a gigantic investment swindle perpetrated by one Serge Stavisky, who had important political connections, became the basis for a strident campaign against the republic by proto-fascist groups using the now familiar devices of uniforms, antisemitism, propaganda, and demonstrations. To meet the emergency, a former president of the republic, Gaston Doumergue, was recalled from retirement to take the premiership and empowered to govern by decree. The sober old man, supported by every party except the royalists and the Marxists, held office for nine calming months before giving way to a parliament that insisted on its prerogatives but little else.

The elections of 1936 brought a dramatic change. Moderate republicans, Socialists, and Communists formed an antifascist Popular Front (cooperation made possible by the decision of the Comintern directed from the Soviet Union to permit Communist alliances with other parties). Such rare solidarity brought the three parties a resounding victory and France its first Socialist premier, Léon Blum. He was a learned, humane intellectual and a Jew—attributes his enemies distrusted. Even as it took office, the new government faced a wave of strikes by workers determined to collect the fruits of their victory. They occupied factories, and many conservatives took that to be the revolution they dreaded. Eventually the strikes ended as the government pushed through legislation that provided for a general 12 percent increase in wages, two-week paid vacations, a forty-hour work week, and compulsory arbitration. Other reforms were soon added. Public works were launched, the Bank of France (long distrusted by the left) restructured, the arms industry nationalized, veterans given increased pensions, and small businesses offered subsidies. Each of these measures, like the devaluation of the franc, which in 1937 could no longer be avoided, frightened the business classes. New programs were hard to finance, and the economy proved more accessible to regulation than to stimulation. Blum's government—one of the Third Republic's most admired and most hated—had hardly begun the tax reforms its plans required when, after a year in office, it was defeated in the conservative senate. The Popular Front itself soon broke up. Subsequent governments were less daring amidst political feuds and public slander. Meanwhile, France's carefully constructed international position was collapsing.

◆ THE FAILURES OF DIPLOMACY

The internationalism of the twenties had faded, and the sense of unreality in international affairs was underscored by the absence of the Soviet Union, which was effectively ostracized, and by the limited participation of the United States, which was absorbed in domestic affairs.

Efforts at Cooperation   The League of Nations had little independent authority. China protested to the League when Japanese troops occupied the major cities of southern Manchuria in 1931; after two years of deliberations a league committee recommended that Japan be ordered to withdraw. Japan withdrew from the League instead and in

1933 renounced the limitations on its naval strength that were part of the international agreements that had seemed so promising a decade earlier. Then Germany withdrew from the London conference on disarmament and from the League of Nations as well.

To counterbalance the threat of Germany's rapid rearmament, the Little Entente—an alliance of Czechoslovakia, Yugoslavia, and Romania, each also allied to France—drew closer together, and Greece and Turkey joined this French sphere in 1934. But Hungary and Bulgaria, authoritarian states attracted to Italy and impressed by Germany's resurgence, did not. For a while, Italy seemed the key to the balance of power in Europe. When Italian troops were rushed to the border in 1934, Austrian Nazis abandoned their attempt to force the unification of Austria and Germany through a coup d'état; and in 1935, after Germany publicly renounced the disarmament clauses of the Versailles Treaty, Mussolini used his heightened prestige to form the so-called Stresa Front with France and Great Britain.

But in fact the great powers quickly went their separate ways. France signed a mutual assistance pact with the Soviet Union, which was loudly opposed by many at home, worried Britain, and frightened Poland. Britain and Germany negotiated an agreement that the German navy, excluding submarines, should not exceed 35 percent of the British fleet—dealings that outraged France. Italy and Germany meanwhile prepared to take advantage of these international differences.

Italy and Germany Test Their Strength In October 1935 Italy invaded Ethiopia, seemingly an old-fashioned imperialistic venture preceded by carefully arranged understandings with Britain and France. But the racist propaganda and enthusiastic bombing of defenseless populations signaled something new. Europeans were shocked, and the League of Nations labeled Italy an aggressor and banned the sale to Italy of essential war materials. Most of Europe seemed united in this crucial test of the League's peacekeeping powers. Although the embargo angered Italy and caused some hardship, it did not stop the war, partly because the most important commodity of all, oil, was not included.

More important, some leaders in France and Britain considered Italy's friendship more important than the League, including the two foreign ministers: Pierre Laval, a slippery politician who had drifted steadily to the right, and Sir Samuel Hoare, an experienced conservative diplomat. Secretly, they arranged a settlement that would, in effect, give Italy most of Ethiopia. When the plan leaked to the press, public outrage forced both men to resign; but they had delayed efforts to add oil to the list of sanctions and undermined confidence in the two democracies. By May 1936, Ethiopia had capitulated, Italy could celebrate the lifting of the embargo, and all could see the ineffectiveness of the League of Nations.

Germany then began to exploit its opportunities. Everyone knew that Germany was rebuilding its fighting forces, and when German troops marched into the demilitarized Rhineland in 1936, there was no compelling international response. Italy this time did nothing. France, unwilling to act alone as it had in 1923, consulted the British, who urged acquiescence. The German troops were cheered by their countrymen in the Rhineland just as they had been the year before when France had turned over the Saar following a plebiscite overwhelmingly in favor of German rule. The fascist powers wanted radical changes in the international balance, and they had the initiative. Britain and France were internally divided, their leaders kept off balance by Germany's protests against the Versailles Treaty, by exuberant propaganda, and by shifting demands. Eastern European nations were torn between fear of the Soviet Union and fear of Germany.

The Spanish Civil War Civil war in Spain drove home the sense that all of Europe was divided between the fascist right and the Marxist left, destined for a life-and-death struggle. In 1936 the army's best units, stationed in Spanish Morocco, rose up against the Spanish republic. General Francisco Franco soon emerged as their leader. The insurgent officers counted on support from Italy, Germany, and Portugal, where Antonio de Oliveira Salazar had already established his dominance over a single-party, corporative, conservative, and Catholic state. Little interested in doctrines or ideologies, Franco recognized the utility of a modern mass appeal and a disciplined movement. His supporters were called the Nationalists. Dominated by the army, they appealed to the monarchists and fascistic Falangists (while somewhat aloof from both), to most of the clergy, and to all who favored desperate measures to escape from anarchy and communism. Italy and Germany quickly proffered their support and formed the Rome-Berlin Axis. Germany and Japan asserted their mutual sympathy and opposition to communism in the Anti-Comintern Pact. The Nationalist cause had become ideological and international.

The Spanish government's supporters included republicans, socialists, communists, anarchists, labor groups, and Catalan and Basque nationalists, a loose and badly split coalition. Known as the Loyalists, they saw themselves as the defenders of democracy against fascist aggression and of social justice against reaction; and they looked to the democracies for support. They received little except from the thousands of idealistic young men who went to Spain to fight as volunteers in national units like the Lincoln Brigade and the Garibaldi Brigade (which had its greatest moment

when it defeated troops of the regular Italian army sent by Mussolini).

The Course of the Conflict Most of the Spanish navy remained loyal to the republic, and one of the insurgents' first problems was to get their armies from Spanish Morocco to the mainland, where many garrisons had risen in support of the Nationalists. Italian and German planes soon provided the needed transport, and the help of the fascist powers—in the form of military advisers, planes, tanks, and ammunition, as well as significant numbers of Italian troops—remained essential. Mussolini welcomed the chance to enhance Italian prestige, and Hitler used the opportunity to test new German military technology.

Only the Soviet Union gave reliable if limited aid to the Loyalists—until 1938, when Stalin decided to cut his losses. Blum's government in France favored the Loyalists but feared the domestic and international consequences of openly aiding them; Britain's Conservative government shared France's caution, but with a deeper distaste for the radicals of Madrid and a greater hope for good relations with Italy. The democracies thus chose neutrality. Under pressure, Germany

▼ A French gendarme leads members of the International Brigade who, with the fall of the Spanish republic, made their way across the French border to safety.
Robert Capa/Magnum Photos

and Italy pretended to as well. All joined in an international commission to prevent foreign intervention. It merely sustained the legalisms that starved the republic, honoring international law while undermining it. As aid to the Nationalists flowed in from the fascist powers, Britain and France looked the other way.

Foreign aid, trained troops, better military organization, and modern weapons made the victory of Franco's forces almost inevitable. They nearly won Madrid and the war itself in the summer of 1936, but the Loyalists held on and in a last-minute counterattack broke the Nationalists' assault. For more than two years, despite poor equipment and internal conflict, the republicans fought on, heartened by occasional victories. As the war progressed, the Loyalists became increasingly dependent on the Soviet Union for supplies, and that dependency plus the Communists' organizational skills made them increasingly influential.

To the disgust of his Axis supporters, Franco conducted a war of attrition. Not until the spring of 1939, when Soviet supplies had ceased to come and Britain had signed special treaties of friendship with Italy, did the Spanish republic finally fall. Thousands of refugees wearily crossed into France while Franco filled Spain's capacious prisons with potential enemies, undid the republic's social measures, and restored the power of the Church over education. Franco then joined the Anti-Comintern Pact and took Spain out of the League of Nations. The civil war had taken more than a million Spanish lives, many at the hands of firing squads and mobs. The bombing of the town of Guernica by German aircraft in 1937 made people shudder before the vision of what war now meant for civilians, and the tales of atrocities on both sides fed the angry arguments between left and right throughout Europe and the United States. The one clear lesson was that the Western democracies, fearful and divided, had accepted defeat while the Axis acted.

SUMMARY

For European societies the 1920s and 30s were a period of innovation in cultural expression, social organization, and political mobilization. Where economic disaster, social failure, and political conflict were greatest, the response brought official ideologies, systematically enforced and apparently deeply believed. Using skillful mass propaganda disseminated on an unprecedented scale, governments found new ways to organize whole societies in the name of unanimity and efficiency, exercising powers rarely equaled even in wartime. That organization of society made the vague decencies of democracy with its social and ideological conflicts and the hypothetical opportunities of free markets seem limp in comparison. The anger, intolerance, and raw violence in European domestic life soon extended to international relations, creating a situation that clearly could not last. Optimists hoped that these crises might dissipate; pessimists could only wait for them to explode as states increased their military strength.

QUESTIONS FOR FURTHER THOUGHT

◆

1. What are the significant similarities and differences between the revolutions in Russia and Italy, in the tactics that brought communists and fascists to power, and in the regimes they created?

2. On almost every front, cultural developments appeared to undermine established beliefs and values, but looking back from today's perspective, is that a correct assessment?

3. Did the 1930s reveal inherent, and maybe universal, weaknesses in democracy and free markets or were those weaknesses the result of specific, and unusual, circumstances and the inadequacies of particular leaders?

4. Soviet Russia and Nazi Germany each set out to transform society and won fervent support at home and abroad. As models, each is now largely discredited, but are there aspects of their appeal and their policies that remain influential?

RECOMMENDED READING

◆

Sources

*Adamthwaite, Anthony P. (ed.). *The Making of the Second World War.* 1979. A valuable collection of documents on the events and policies leading to war with a useful introductory essay.

Ciano, Count Galiazzo. *Diary, 1937–1938.* 1952. *Diary, 1939–1943.* 1947. The diaries of Mussolini's son-in-law and, eventually, foreign minister are often self-serving, but they give a vivid picture of the intrigue and confusion at the center of the Fascist regime.

Engel, Barbara Alpern, and Anastasia Posadskaya-Vanderbeck (eds.). *A Revolution of Their Own: Voices of Soviet Women in Soviet History.* 1997. Interviews with eight women born before the Russian Revolution reveal the difficulties and gains experienced by women from different backgrounds under Russian communism.

Ortega y Gasset, José. *The Revolt of the Masses.* 1957. First published in 1932, this essay by one of Spain's leading philosophers and historians, an important work in its own right, is also a significant document of the disquiet that intellectual elites felt over the effects that increased specialization and mass society were having on the traditional culture of the West.

Reed, John. *Ten Days That Shook the World.* Available in many editions, this classic account of the Russian revolution was first published in 1922. John Reed went to Russia as a journalist and radical. His enthusiastic and perceptive report on the revolution captures both the excitement of the moment and the communist revolution's dramatic and international appeal.

Studies

Adamson, Walter. *Avant-Garde Florence: From Modernism to Fascism.* 1993. An insightful and provocative assessment of the links between prewar avant-garde literary movements and fascism.

*Allen, William S. *The Nazi Seizure of Power: The Experience of a Single German Town, 1930–1935.* 1965. A much-used microcosmic study.

*Arendt, Hannah. *The Origins of Totalitarianism.* 1958. This important study begins with a profoundly pessimistic application of hindsight to the imperialism and antisemitism of the late-nineteenth century to make the case for Nazi totalitarianism as a phenomenon rooted in Western history.

Bessel, Richard. *Life in the Third Reich.* 1987. Essays by leading historians using recent research to provide fresh interpretations of various aspects of Nazi rule.

*Bracher, Karl D. *The German Dictatorship.* Jean Steinberg (tr.). 1970. A major synthesis of work on the origins, structure, and impact of the Nazi movement.

Broszat, Martin. *The Hitler State: The Foundation and Internal Structure of the Third Reich*. 1981. Uses the methods of social history to show the complexity and confusion of Nazi rule, emphasizing its operation in daily life.

*Bullock, Alan. *Hitler: A Study in Tyranny*. 1971. The best biography of Hitler and one that gives an effective picture of Nazi society.

Carsten, F. L. *The Rise of Fascism*. 1967. The careful synthesis of a distinguished scholar that looks at the varieties of fascist regimes.

*De Felice, Renzo. *Interpretations of Fascism*. Brenda Huff Evertt (tr.). 1977. A very thoughtful review of the interpretations of Italian Fascism.

Fitzpatrick, Sheila. *The Russian Revolution, 1917–1932*. 1982. A valuable, fresh overview that emphasizes social conditions.

*——— (ed.). *The Cultural Revolution in Russia*. 1978. Essays treating varied aspects of the effort to create a new culture.

Gay, Peter. *Weimar Culture: The Outsider as Insider*. 1968. A wide-ranging essay arguing that the vigorous cultural life of Weimar Germany was shaped by those viewed as marginal to Germany's traditional culture.

Kater, Michael H. *The Nazi Party: A Social Profile of Members and Leaders, 1919–1945*. 1984. An impressive analysis of the relevant statistical data on the social origins of Nazi party members.

*Kershaw, Ian. *The Nazi Dictatorship: Problems and Perspectives of Interpretation*. 2000. A significant assessment that provides an excellent introduction to and interpretation of a vast literature.

*Kershaw, Ian, and Moshe Lewin (eds.). *Stalinism and Nazism: Dictatorships in Comparison*. 1997.

Kindleberger, Charles P. *The World in Depression, 1929–1939*. 1973. A study of the origins of the Depression and of responses to it in different countries.

*Kolb, Eberhard. *The Weimar Republic*. P. S. Falla (tr.). 1988. A comprehensive account of the difficulties and failures of Germany's experiment with democracy.

Koonz, Claudia. *Mothers in the Fatherland: Women, the Family, and Nazi Politics*. 1987. Shows the importance of gender policies to Nazi ideology and rule.

Lebovics, Herman. *Social Conservatism and the Middle Classes in Germany, 1914–1933*. 1969. Looks at individual figures to explore the development of an ideology of conservatism that prepared many members of the middle class to be sympathetic to the Nazi movement.

Lee, Stephen J. *The European Dictatorships: 1918–1945*. 1987. A comprehensive and systematic comparison of Communist Russia, Fascist Italy, and Nazi Germany.

Lewin, Mosche. *The Making of the Soviet System: Essays in the Social History of Interwar Russia*. 1985. Explores the complex roots and real limitations of the regime in a period of revolutionary change.

Mack Smith, Denis. *Mussolini*. 1981. An informed, skeptical account by the leading English scholar of modern Italy.

*Nettl, J. P. *The Soviet Achievement*. 1967. Effectively tackles the difficult task of assessing both the economic development of the USSR and its social cost.

*Nolte, Ernst. *Three Faces of Fascism*. Leila Vennewitz (tr.). 1965. A learned effort to place the intellectual history of fascism in France, Germany, and Italy in the mainstream of European thought.

*Nove, Alec. *An Economic History of the USSR*. 1982. A compact survey through the Brezhnev years, which concentrates on the formation of economic policies.

Peukert, Detlev J. K. *Inside Nazi Germany: Conformity, Opposition, and Racism in Everyday Life*. 1987. Makes use of a great deal of recent research to explore the effects of Nazi tyranny on ordinary life and the difficulties of opposition to it.

*Pipes, Richard. *The Formation of the Soviet Union*. 1964. A clear, comprehensive, and very critical treatment of Soviet rule.

*Schoenbaum, David. *Hitler's Social Revolution: Class and Status in Nazi Germany, 1933–1939*. 1966. A topical discussion contrasting theory and practice in the social policies of the Third Reich.

Tannenbaum, Edward R. *The Fascist Experience: Italian Society and Culture, 1922–1945*. 1972. A wide-ranging effort to recapture the meaning in practice of Fascist rule.

Thompson, John M. *Revolutionary Russia, 1917*. 1989. A good overview of what the revolution meant for ordinary life throughout the country.

*Tucker, Robert C. *Stalin as Revolutionary, 1879–1929: A Study in History and Personality.* 1973. Sensitively explores the shaping of Stalin's character as a key to his use of power.

*Ulam, Adam B. *Lenin and the Bolsheviks.* 1969. Combines the study of ideas and of policy to explain Lenin's triumph.

Weinberg, Gerhard L. *The Foreign Policy of Hitler's Germany.* 1970. A major study by a leading American diplomatic historian that helps explain Hitler's early successes.

*Woolf, S. J. (ed.). *Fascism in Europe.* 1981. Essays on the countries that offer major examples of fascist movements.

▲ **A women's unit pulls in one of the barrage balloons used for defense in the Battle of Britain. The weighted cables dangling beneath the balloons prevented low-level flights by German bombers.**
Imperial War Museum, London

THE NIGHTMARE: WORLD WAR II

World War II was the centerpiece of a long trial of European civilization. The outbreak of war followed a series of international crises, but in a larger sense it resulted from the kinds of governments brought to power by the social tensions of the era. For more than a decade a kind of ideological civil war undermined established institutions and exposed every weakness in the social fabric. New communist, Fascist, and Nazi regimes carried those conflicts into international affairs, challenging the status quo and the democracies that defended it. The result was World War II, a war more total and more worldwide than its predecessor. The war required massive organization, challenged national economies, and altered social relations. At first Germany gained everywhere, its preparations farther along, its tactics more ruthless. Slowly the Allies gained the upper hand, and the terrors of the battlefield were exceeded by the deliberate, systematic horrors of genocide, torture, and concentration camps. When peace finally came, Europe was a continent devastated, where millions had lost homes, family, health, and hope. It was a struggle just to make society function, and the achievement of stability and prosperity by the 1950s was a European miracle.

	Social Structure	Body Politic	Changes in the Organization of Production and in the Impact of Technology	Evolution of Family and Changing Gender Roles	War	Religion	Cultural Expression
CHAPTER 29. THE NIGHTMARE: WORLD WAR II							
I. THE YEARS OF AXIS VICTORY							
II. THE GLOBAL WAR, 1942–1945							
III. BUILDING ON THE RUINS							
IV. EUROPEAN RECOVERY							

I. The Years of Axis Victory

◆

The civil war in Spain made the international situation frighteningly clear. Germany and Italy were allied, rearming, and aggressive. France and Britain, more dependent on each other than allied, reluctantly rearming, still hoped to avoid war. The countries of Eastern Europe were effectively paralyzed, and the Soviet Union was an enigma, for no one knew whether it would eventually take sides or could fight effectively if it did. Once war began, German forces went from victory to victory.

◆ THE PATH TO WAR

For eighteen months Hitler orchestrated a series of escalating demands that culminated in the outbreak of World War II in September 1939.

The Anschluss   In February 1938, with the outcome of civil war in Spain still uncertain, Hitler began to pressure Austria. He summoned the Austrian chancellor, Kurt von Schuschnigg, to the Führer's secluded mountain retreat at Berchtesgaden and subjected him to a humiliating harangue. Schuschnigg promised to include Austrian Nazis in his cabinet. On returning home, he felt braver and decided to hold a plebiscite in the hope that public opinion would rally to save Austria's independence. Hitler, furious, massed the German army on the Austrian border, and Schuschnigg realized his position was hopeless. He had previously disbanded the Socialist party, the strongest opponent of union with Germany,

and Italy warned that this time it would not oppose the German moves as it had a few years earlier. The friendless Austrian chancellor was replaced by Artur von Seyss-Inquart, a Nazi, who invited German troops to restore order. They did so on March 13, and Nazis indulged in the vulgar, public humiliation of Viennese Jews and intellectuals. Within a month Austria's annexation to Germany was almost unanimously approved in a plebiscite run by the Nazis. The dream of union with Germany, *Anschluss*, had been fulfilled; Hitler's popularity at home rose still higher, and German influence spread more deeply into the Balkans. Britain and France merely protested.

Czechoslovakia   Two weeks after the Austrian plebiscite, Hitler demanded autonomy for the Sudetenland, an overwhelmingly German-speaking section of Czechoslovakia. Once again, the claims that the Versailles settlement had been unfair and that Germans were being abused rallied support at home and weakened opposition abroad. Although this challenge to the Czech republic was far more daring—Czechoslovakia was a prosperous industrial state protected by a respectable army, well-fortified frontiers, and mutual-aid treaties with both France and Russia—the parallel with Austria was lost on no one. Supported by its allies, Czechoslovakia mobilized, and Hitler ordered the Sudeten Nazis to quiet down. But Czechoslovakia was vulnerable, and Hitler was adept at fanning ethnic resentments. The republic, dominated by the more prosperous Czech region, was barely able to maintain the loyalty of the Slovaks; a pro-Nazi party had won more votes than any other in the 1935 elections, and the great powers remained divided. Britain's prime minister, Neville Chamberlain, wanted to parlay directly with Germany, believing that no nonnegotiable British interest was at stake in the Sudetenland, and he rejected suggestions from the United States and the Soviet Union that they meet to consider ways of restraining the Nazi dictator. Many in France and England, deeply alarmed at how close to war they were, doubted that fighting for Czechoslovakia's sovereignty over a German population was worth the risk. Throughout the summer, Sudeten Nazi leaders negotiated with the Czech state in an atmosphere heated by demonstrations there and in Germany.

In August, Chamberlain, with French concurrence, sent his own emissary to mediate while German troops held maneuvers on the Czech border, and Hitler pointedly toured Germany's fortifications in the west. Hitler's speeches became more bellicose, and Chamberlain decided, once again with French support, to visit the Führer at Berchtesgaden. When they met on September 15, Hitler raised the stakes, demanding that Germany annex the Sudetenland. Britain and France advised Czechoslovakia to submit. Desperately, the Czechs sought some escape, but only the Soviet Union was ready to support Czech resistance. In a week Chamberlain flew back to Germany with the good news that Czechoslovakia had agreed to Hitler's terms, only to find them changed again: German troops must occupy the ceded territory immediately. The Czechs would have no time to move factories and military supplies or provide for citizens who wished to evacuate. A shocked Chamberlain said no, and for five days the world listened for war.

The Munich Agreement Then Mussolini persuaded Hitler to meet with the Duce and the prime ministers of Britain and France. They met on September 29, 1938, in Munich, where just fifteen years earlier Hitler had failed to capture the town hall. Now he dealt in terms of nations. During an afternoon and evening of discussions, Hitler was granted all he asked. Neither the Soviet Union nor Czechoslovakia was consulted. The next day Czechoslovakia submitted to Hitler's terms and accepted last-minute demands from

Poland and Hungary for additional pieces of Czechoslovak territory that they had long coveted. At a single stroke, Czechoslovakia surrendered one-third of its population, its best military defenses, and much of its economic strength. Central Europe's strongest democracy was reduced to a German dependency, and a keystone of France's continental security was shattered. As the French prime minister's plane circled the Paris airport on his return from Munich, he watched the crowd below with dread. But it cheered him, and in Britain, Chamberlain became a hero. Peace, the papers echoed, had been preserved.

Poland and the Hitler-Stalin Pact German might, Hitler's speeches, virulent antisemitism, goose-stepping troops marching through central Europe, and news of what life was like in the newly annexed lands and in Germany itself—all gave Jews, ethnic groups the Nazis labeled inferior, peoples living along the German borders, and whole nations reason to be terrified. Early in 1939 German troops occupied all of Czechoslovakia (except for an additional piece taken by Hungary) and annexed the seaport of Memel from a frightened Lithuania. The pretext of absorbing only German peoples had now been abandoned.

Chamberlain, believing that not even Nazis could want world war, was one of many in Europe who hoped concessions would appease Hitler; but most people in England and France were resigned to the fact that Germany could only be stopped by force. Italy, inspired by Hitler's success, began a noisy campaign to get Nice and Corsica from France and in the summer of 1939 invaded and annexed Albania. The Rome-Berlin Axis was formally tightened into the "Pact of Steel," and Germany kept European chancelleries quaking with demands for nonaggression pacts. Late in August the leader of the Nazi party in German-speaking Danzig declared that his city, which the Versailles treaties had carved from Polish territory and made a free city, must be returned to the fatherland. The denunciations of the Versailles boundaries that poured from Germany, along with claims that Germans living within the Polish corridor were being persecuted, made it clear that Poland was next. As they had all summer, Britain and France renewed their pledges to protect Poland.

▲ **Hitler and Mussolini on the way to the train station after the Munich conference. Count Galeazzo Ciano, the Italian foreign minister, is on Hitler's left; Hermann Göring is on Mussolini's right; General William Keitel, Rudolf Hess, and Heinrich Himmler are among those behind them.**
Ullstein Bilderdienst

The summer's most important contest was for some alliance with the Soviet Union, and Hitler won that, too. Germany and the Soviet Union announced a nonaggression pact. The USSR had made overtures to Britain and France, suggesting that the territorial integrity of all the states between the Baltic and Black seas be guaranteed. The Western powers, reluctant to grant a communist nation such extensive influence, had responded weakly. Since 1935 the Soviet Union had advocated disarmament, supported the League of Nations, supplied Loyalist Spain, and offered support to Czechoslovakia, but Stalin feared that the democracies would welcome a war between Germany and the Soviet Union. In May 1939 he replaced his foreign minister, Maxim Litvinov, the eloquent spokesman for a pro-Western policy,

with Vyacheslav Molotov, a tougher and less cosmopolitan old ally. Hitler offered the Soviet Union a free hand in Finland, Estonia, Latvia, eastern Poland, and part of Romania should Germany seek any changes in its own eastern border. That became the basis for a nonaggression pact between the international sponsor of antifascist fronts and the creators of the Anti-Comintern Pact, a masterpiece of cynicism (and very old-fashioned diplomacy) that shocked a world still unaccustomed to totalitarian flexibility.

The last days of August resounded with formal warnings and clarifications from the major powers. On September 1, Germany invaded Poland. Britain and France mobilized, sent Germany an ultimatum, and declared war on September 3, 1939. One year after surrendering democratic

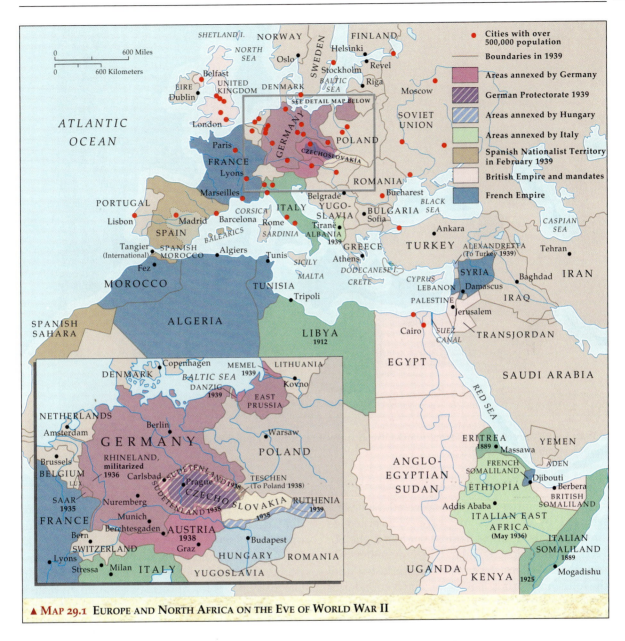

▲ MAP 29.1 EUROPE AND NORTH AFRICA ON THE EVE OF WORLD WAR II

Czechoslovakia, they would fight for authoritarian Poland.

◆ THE COURSE OF THE WAR, 1939–1941

One argument for the policy of appeasement was that it enabled Britain and France to buy time. They had been vigorously strengthening their armed forces, and the domestic consensus that war required was slowly taking shape. But much

remained to be done; Germany had gained, too, in territory and power, and now there was no time left.

Blitzkrieg and Phony War For two years the Axis scored one victory after another. Having carefully prepared the invasion, Germany attacked Poland with overwhelming force in September 1939, the first *blitzkrieg*, or "lightning war." Poland fell in less than a month, and Hitler

▲ **Warsaw, October 5, 1939: German tanks, fresh from their lightning destruction of the Polish army, pass in review before Adolf Hitler.**
AP/Wide World Photos

suggested that the war could now end. Few were tempted by his hints of peace. Concerned to strengthen its frontiers against Germany, the Soviet Union attacked Finland in November and met such fierce resistance that the war lasted until the following spring. Having regained boundaries close to those of the last tsars, Russia could afford to wait. The Western powers had been waiting, too. Hitler refrained from attacking along the French border, and the Allied commanders resolved not to risk precious planes too soon or to repeat the pointless assaults of World War I. This was the period of the so-called phony war, during which arms production and mobilization speeded up, the world waited, and little happened. The strain was bad for morale.

With the Soviet Union standing aside from the conflict, French communists now said the war was a mistake; their party was suppressed. Paul Reynaud, energetic and determined, replaced

Daladier as premier, and the Allies prepared to defend Norway, an obvious German target. But on April 9, 1940, Germany attacked Denmark, taking it in a day, and captured Norway's most important strategic points in short order, giving Germany bases for numerous assaults on British ships and cities. In Britain, Chamberlain resigned after a wide-ranging and often angry parliamentary debate, and Winston Churchill became prime minister of an all-party government on the day that the Germans attacked on the Western front. A Conservative who believed in empire and an opponent of appeasement, Churchill was a political maverick given his chance in the face of disaster. His decisiveness and eloquence made him one of England's greatest leaders.

The Fall of France On May 10, and without warning, German troops flooded the Netherlands and Belgium. The Dutch, who had expected to

▲ **French refugees with all the possessions they can carry clog the roads, expecting to be able to escape the German armies in 1940 as their parents had twenty-five years before.**
© Collection Roger-Viollet/Getty Images

escape this war as they had all others since the Napoleonic wars, surrendered in five days. The better-prepared and larger Belgian army held out for eighteen days. On May 14 a skillfully executed German offensive broke through the Ardennes forest, thought to be impervious to tanks, reached Sedan, and drove to the English Channel, trap-

ping the Belgian and British forces fighting there along with much of the French army. The German air force, the Luftwaffe, controlled the skies, and the Allies' proudest achievement in the battle for France was the evacuation from the port town of Dunkirk of 340,000 troops pinned against the sea. They left for Britain in a motley flotilla of naval vessels, commercial ferries, and private sailboats, a symbol of heroism and inferior preparation.

The Allied defense of France was broken. German forces renewed the attack on June 5 and took Paris in a week. Anxious lest he miss the war entirely, Mussolini attacked France on the tenth, and France surrendered on June 16, 1940. The armistice was signed in the railway car used for Germany's surrender in 1918. More ironic still, the man who chose to sign for France was the World War I hero of Verdun, Marshal Henri Philippe Pétain.

Germany's Victory over France   Hitler seemed invincible and the blitzkrieg some terrible new Teutonic force, a totalitarian achievement other societies could not hope to equal. In fact, however, many of the tactical ideas on which it rested were first put forward by British and French experts, including a French officer, Charles de Gaulle. The blitzkrieg was the result not so much of new technology as new strategy. It combined air attacks with rapid movements of motorized columns to overcome the advantages that defensive positions had previously enjoyed. Tanks roared through and behind enemy lines, a maneuver requiring speed and precision that were nearly forbidden in older theories. In the flat terrain of Poland, Germany's panzer tank divisions quickly encircled the enemy; in France, they often assaulted troops so far in the rear that they were not yet prepared for battle. The aim was less to capture ground than to break up communications, using air power to disorient and terrify the retreating army. Even the machine-gunning of French roads clogged with civilian refugees and the bombing of Rotterdam had their place in the campaign to demoralize.

French strategy had relied too much on the defensive strength of the Maginot Line, a system of fortifications extending from the Belgian border to Switzerland, and on the assumption that Germany would respect the neutrality of Belgium and the Netherlands. The French had powerful tanks of their own but had been slow to deploy them; their air force was momentarily weakened because it was changing models. During the phony war, morale sagged with memories of the previous war and policy was undermined by politics rife with suspicion of the British, of the army, of the politicians, and of the left. Pétain, who believed France must now make its way in Hitler's Europe, blamed the Third Republic, and for a moment the nation turned to the octogenarian marshal with stunned unanimity.

He accepted terms of surrender that put three-fifths of the country under Nazi occupation and allowed French prisoners of war to be kept in Germany. The unoccupied southeastern part of France could have its own government, and that was established at Vichy. There a reconvened parliament maneuvered by Pierre Laval named Pétain chief of state. The new regime, known as Vichy France, relied on a confused coalition of militant fascists and the traditional right and would never really be independent of Germany. After adopting bits of corporatism and some fascist trappings, it settled into a lethargy of its own, an often willing collaborator in Hitler's new order, ruling a truncated state as rife with intrigue, personal ambition, and shifting alliances as the Third Republic it so heartily denounced.

The Battle of Britain Great Britain now stood alone. Unprepared for such enormous victories so soon, German officers planned their invasion of Britain while, beginning in June 1940, their bombers roared over England in sustained attacks that many believed would be enough to force surrender. Instead, in September the projected invasion was postponed, while the air attacks continued. The German navy had suffered enough damage in encounters with the British to favor caution, and by the spring even the air raids were letting up.

The waves of German planes flying across the channel sustained losses far greater than those of Britain's Royal Air Force. British fighter planes, particularly the newer designs, proved at least the equal of the German; and they were aided by new techniques of antiaircraft defense, including radar, an English development that was the most critical addition to military technology in these

▲ In the hopfields of Kent in southeastern England, the pickers and their families took refuge in trenches during the air raids.
The Image Works

years. At first the air raids concentrated on ports and shipping, then on airfields, and finally on cities, leaving great burning holes in London and completely destroying the industrial city of Coventry. But the diversity of targets dissipated the economic and military effects of the bombing, and the terror from the skies seemed to raise morale in a nation ever better organized and more fiercely determined to carry on. Merely to survive from June 1940 to June 1941 was a kind of victory in what Churchill memorably called Britain's "finest hour."

The Balkans With all the continent from Norway to Sicily and the Atlantic in their own hands or under friendly dictators in Spain and Portugal, the Axis powers looked eastward. In October 1940 Italian forces moved from Albania into Greece only to be pushed back, and Hitler had to bail out Mussolini by sending in German troops and further squeezing the Balkan states, which were rapidly losing their independence. In June 1940 the Soviet Union, stretching the terms of its pact with Germany, took Bessarabia from Romania. Hungary and Bulgaria then took some of Romania for themselves, and Hitler announced that he would protect the rest of the country. In fact all three Eastern European nations, already implicated in Hitler's mapmaking, were closely tied to Germany. It was no great step for them to join the Axis, welcome German troops in March 1941, and cooperate with Germany in invading Yugoslavia, which had hesitated too long over whether to join the Axis, and in attacking Greece, which had fought Mussolini too well.

The invasion was launched in April 1941 and swept through both countries within the month. Some Greek and British forces pulled back to Crete, only to be forced out almost immediately by German gliders and paratroops, the first time those forces had been used in war. The Allies retreated to Egypt, where British forces had held off an attack from Italy's neighboring colony of Libya. The Axis now threatened to dominate the Mediterranean, too.

The Invasion of the Soviet Union Having conquered so much, Hitler decided to complete his domination of the continent. On June 22 German forces attacked the Soviet Union. The Soviets had long feared such a move, yet they appeared genuinely surprised, at least by the timing and the size of the German invasion (see "Stalin Appeals to Patriotism," p. 1070). The assault, in three broad sectors, was the largest concentration of military power that had ever been assembled, and once more the blitzkrieg worked its magic. Germany's armored divisions ripped through

Russian lines and encircled astonishing numbers of troops. It looked to many observers as if the Soviet Union might collapse. German armies crossed the vast lands Russia had acquired since 1939, taking Riga and Smolensk in July, reaching the Dnieper in August, claiming Kiev and the whole Ukraine in September. Then the pace slowed, but while one German force lay siege to Leningrad in the north, a second hit Sevastopol in the south and moved into the Crimea. By December still another had penetrated to the suburbs of Moscow. There the German advance stopped temporarily, halted by an early and severe winter, by strained supply lines, and (at last) by sharp Russian counterattacks. The territory now held by Germany had accounted for nearly two-thirds of Russia's production of coal, iron, steel, and aluminum, as well as 40 percent of its grain and hogs.

As the war engulfed all of Europe,[1] German power at the end of 1941 was at its height, encompassing between 7 and 10 million soldiers, a superb air force, and a navy that included more than 150 submarines, which would sink nearly 400 Allied ships in the summer of 1942. Italy added sizable forces that were especially important in Africa. And yet Axis dominance was short-lived.

II. The Global War, 1942–1945

From the 1930s on, the fascist powers had held the initiative in politics, international relations, and war. Germany's invasion of the Soviet Union extended the war across Europe to Asia (after the Allied retreat had carried it to North Africa). Japan's attack on the United States in 1941 continued the pattern of Axis surprises, but it also marked the beginning of a significant change. War in the Pacific made this a truly global war—involving Asia, the Middle East, and North Africa—and the addition of American power helped tip the balance toward the Allies, whose industrial capacity was far greater than their enemies'. Axis propaganda was losing effect in the face of the realities of German rule, which gave weight to Allied claims that they

---

[1]Only Sweden, Spain, Portugal, Switzerland, and Eire remained even technically neutral by grace of geography.

STALIN APPEALS TO PATRIOTISM

◆

Stalin, apparently in a state of shock, was silent for the first week after German forces invaded the Soviet Union. Finally, on July 3, 1941, he spoke by radio to the Soviet people. His address acknowledged initial defeats, invoked the example of Russian victories over invaders in the past, and emphasized that the Allies were fighting together against Nazi tyranny. But he also called in striking detail for ordinary citizens to continue the fight by destroying anything that might be helpful to the invader (which became known as the "scorched earth" policy) and by constant sabotage.

"Comrades! Citizens! Brothers and Sisters! Men of our Army and Navy!

"I am addressing you, my friends!

"The perfidious military attack on our fatherland, begun on 22 June by Hitler's Germany is continuing.

"In spite of heroic resistance of the Red Army, and although the enemy's finest divisions and finest air-force units have already been smashed and have met their doom on the field of battle, the enemy continues to push forward, hurling fresh forces into the attack.

"Hitler's troops have succeeded in capturing Lithuania, a considerable part of Latvia, the western part of White Russia, and a part of the western Ukraine.

" . . . A grave danger hangs over our country.

"How could it have happened that our glorious Red Army surrendered a number of cities and districts to the Fascist armies?

"Is it really true that German Fascist troops are invincible, as is ceaselessly trumpeted by boastful Fascist propagandists? Of course not!

"History shows that there are no invincible armies, and never have been. Napoleon's army was considered invincible, but it was beaten successively by Russian, English, and German armies. Kaiser Wilhelm's German army in the period of the first imperialist war was also considered invincible, but it was beaten several times by Russian and Anglo-French forces.

"The same must be said of Hitler's German Fascist army today. This army has not yet met with serious resistance on the Continent of Europe. Only on our territory has it met serious resistance, and if as a result of this resistance the finest divisions of Hitler's German Fascist army have been defeated by our Red Army, it means that this army, too, can be smashed and will be smashed as were the armies of Napoleon and Wilhelm.

"There can be no doubt that this short-lived military gain for Germany is only an episode . . . , while the tremendous political gain of the USSR is a serious and lasting factor that is bound to form the basis for development of decisive military successes. . . .

"In case of a forced retreat of Red Army units, all rolling stock must be evacuated, to the enemy must not be left a single engine, a single railway car, nor a single pound of grain or a gallon of fuel.

"Collective farmers must drive off all their cattle and turn over their grain to the safekeeping of state authorities for transportation to the rear. All valuable property including nonferrous metals, grain, and fuel which cannot be withdrawn must without fail be destroyed.

"In areas occupied by the enemy, guerrilla units, mounted and foot, must be formed, diversionist groups must be organized to combat enemy troops, to foment guerrilla warfare everywhere, to blow up bridges, roads, damage telephone and telegraph lines, and to set fire to forests, stores, and transports.

"In occupied regions [the Germans] must be hounded and annihilated at every step and all their measures frustrated.

"This war with Fascist Germany cannot be considered an ordinary war. It is not only a war between two armies, it is also a great war of the entire Soviet people against the German Fascist forces.

"The aim of this national war in defense of our country against the Fascist oppressors is . . . aid to all European peoples groaning under the yoke of German Fascism.

"In this war of liberation we shall not be alone.

"In this great war we shall have loyal allies in the peoples of Europe and America, including German people who are enslaved by Hitlerite despots.

"Our war for the freedom of our country will merge with the struggle of the peoples of Europe and America for their independence, democratic liberties. It will be a united front of peoples standing for freedom and against enslavement."

Speech of Joseph Stalin on July 3, 1941, quoted in Brian MacArthur (ed.), *The Penguin Book of Twentieth-Century Speeches* (New York: Viking, 1992).

SEQUENCE OF GERMAN EXPANSION

1939	Austria, Czechoslovakia, Poland
1940	Denmark, Norway
1940	Low Countries, France
1940–41	Balkans
1942	Vichy France
1942–43	Russian Front

Axis powers, 1939

Greater Germany, 1942

German advances, 1938–42

Axis Allies

Occupied by the U.S.S.R., 1939–40

Allies

Neutral countries

Boundaries as of January, 1939

▲ **MAP 29.2 THE HEIGHT OF AXIS POWER, 1942**

were fighting for civilization as Russia, the Americas, and the British Empire set out to reconquer Europe.

◆ THE TURN OF THE TIDE

The United States Enters the War Despite its deep partisanship for France and Britain, the United States had remained technically at peace, even as the American government sold weapons to private firms for transfer to Great Britain and traded fifty old American destroyers for the lease of British bases in the western Atlantic. The United States, which Roosevelt called "the arsenal of democracy," also extended loans to Britain and then the Soviet Union. In August, Churchill and Roosevelt met at sea to draft the Atlantic Charter, which envisioned a world "after the destruction of the Nazi tyranny" that included collective security and self-determination for all nations, a world in which "all the men of all the lands may live out their lives in freedom from fear and want."

Ideological commitment, however, did not bring the United States into the war. Japan did

Chronology

MAJOR MOMENTS OF WORLD WAR II

March 1938	*Anschluss:* Germany annexes Austria.
September 1938	Munich Agreement, Germany takes Sudetenland.
August 1939	Hitler-Stalin Pact.
September 1939	Germany invades Poland, beginning of World War II.
April 1940	Germany invades Denmark, Norway.
May 1940	Germany invades Belgium, France, Netherlands.
June 1940	France surrenders.
October 1940	Italy invades Albania and Greece.
April 1941	Romania, Bulgaria, Hungary, and Germany invade Yugoslavia.
June 1941	Germany invades the U.S.S.R.
August 1941	Atlantic Charter
December 1941	Japan attacks Pearl Harbor.
August 1942– February 1943	Battle of Stalingrad.
November 1942	Allies land in North Africa.
January 1943	Casablanca Conference.
July 1943	Allies land in Sicily, Mussolini ousted.
November– December 1943	Teheran Conference.
June 1944	Allies land in Normandy.
February 1945	Yalta Conference.
May 1945	Germany surrenders.
July–August 1945	Potsdam Conference.

the assault on Indochina with sanctions. Anticipating more, Japan gambled that the United States could be rendered nearly harmless in one blow, an attack on the American Pacific fleet at Pearl Harbor. The raid, on December 7, was devastating, and the United States declared it an act of war. All sides immediately recognized that the wars in Asia, Europe, and North Africa were one. Germany and Italy declared war on the United States three days later. Unless the Allies were driven from the seas, the industrial and military power of the United States might make a decisive difference in a war fought around the world.

Stalingrad Winter snows raised the specter of a continuing two-front war, which Hitler had sworn to avoid. For all its losses, Russia's Red Army was intact, and its scorched-earth policy in retreat left the German army little to live on. To secure its massive victories, Germany had to knock Russia out of the war. But the siege of Leningrad, the attacks on Moscow, and even a drive into southern Russia in the summer of 1942 that took Sevastopol (and desperately needed grain) did not accomplish that goal. The crucial battle of the Eastern front took place at Stalingrad (now Volgograd) from August to October 1942. A breakthrough for the Germans at that strategic center would open the way to the oilfields of southern Russia.

By September the Germans had penetrated the city and fighting continued from building to building. The heroic defense gave Russia time to amass more troops than the Germans thought were available, and in the meantime Germany's supplies dwindled. A Russian counterattack encircled the German army, which Hitler frantically ordered to stand its ground. When it finally surrendered, in February 1943, less than one-third of its 300,000 men were left. The giant Russian pincers had cost the Germans more than half a million casualties. Stalingrad was the turning point of the war on the Eastern front.

Air Power and the Invasion of North Africa In the West, too, the Axis position was eroding. The losses that German submarines inflicted were less crippling after 1942, and Allied air supremacy extended to the continent, where thousands of tons of explosives were dropped on Germany each month in 1942, a rate that would increase fivefold in 1943. The Americans bombed strategic targets

that. Its attack on Manchuria in 1931 had been followed by a series of aggressive actions, from war with China starting in 1937 to the conquest of French Indochina in 1941. Tension between the United States and Japan increased with each new act of Japanese aggression, and America replied to

▲ **American servicemen survey the ruins on an airfield at Pearl Harbor; the United States had entered the war.**
National Archives

during the day; the British preferred nighttime area bombing, with a city itself as the target. The inferno created by the firebombing of Hamburg in 1943 was a horror to be exceeded two years later in a yet more massive raid that leveled Dresden, a cultural center without important industry. The Germans were unaware, of course, that the secret codes they believed unbreakable had been cracked in London as early as 1940, giving the Allies an advantage that would be more important as the war progressed.[2]

---

[2]The code was cracked in a project named Ultra, using devices that foreshadowed the computer. The secret of Ultra was not revealed until long after the war, and historians are still assessing its impact. The information that the Allies gained through Ultra appears to have been especially important in the Battle of Britain, the protection of Atlantic shipping, later in the war in Egypt, and (above all) in the Normandy landing.

The Allies also regained control of the Mediterranean. Fighting had spread to Libya and Somalia as soon as Italy entered the war, and battle lines then ebbed and flowed as each side balanced military needs elsewhere against the chance for victory in North Africa. In April 1941 Germany sent significant reinforcements, and General Erwin Rommel, the German "desert fox," began a drive toward the Egyptian border. In October 1942 his *Afrikakorps* reached El Alamein but was defeated there, allowing Britain's General Bernard Montgomery to launch a counteroffensive as British and American forces landed in Morocco and Algeria. That November invasion, the largest amphibious action yet attempted, and the campaign that followed was an important test of green American troops and of Allied coordination under an American commander, General Dwight D. Eisenhower. It succeeded, and by May 1943 and after heavy losses, the Axis powers had been pushed out of Africa.

Halting the Japanese Advance in the Pacific
After costly stands at Bataan and Corregidor, the United States lost the Philippine Islands early in 1942. By March, the Japanese had conquered Malaya and Indonesia, defeating the British and the Dutch in costly naval and land battles. The rest of the war against Japan would be fought primarily by Australia and the United States. Stopping further Japanese expansion in the summer of 1942 was thus an important turning point. Although a naval engagement in the Coral Sea in May brought no clear-cut victory to either side, the United States was better able than Japan to replace its losses. A month later the Japanese suffered heavy losses at Midway in a naval battle they had sought, and in August American forces launched a relatively small invasion of their own in the Solomon Islands. Each side poured in reinforcements, and the fighting on Guadalcanal, which was especially bloody, continued for six months before the Japanese were defeated. The war was far from won, but these victories ended the threat that Japan might invade Australia or cut off supply lines from India to the Middle East. The Allies could feel comfortable with their agreement that the war in Europe should have priority—an acknowledgement of fear that the Soviet Union might not survive without massive help, of the importance of European industrial power, and of the bonds of Western culture.

◆ COMPETING POLITICAL SYSTEMS

War on this scale required the coordination of entire economies and cooperation from every sector of society. After their slow start, Britain and the United States achieved that with impressive effect. The Soviet Union proved far stronger than expected, and Germany, the state that in theory was most devoted to militarism, managed in practice less well than its enemies.

The Allied Effort at Home As bombs rained down on Britain, support for the war effort was nearly unanimous. Civilians accepted sacrifice and welcomed the end of unemployment. One-third of all males between 14 and 64 were in uniform, and unmarried women were mobilized. More women were employed in industry than ever before in both Britain and the United States. British wives and mothers were hailed as heroines supporting their men (and some women) in the armed forces. Even children and the elderly took part in volunteer activities related to the war. With tight rationing and government control of the economy, no society mobilized more thoroughly. Civilians accepted blackouts and suffered air raids and the evacuation of 3.5 million women and children to the safer countryside. Even with that effort and that bravery, Britain increasingly depended on American aid. With its economic resources fully mobilized, the United States by the end of 1942 was producing more war matériel than all its enemies combined. Ships, planes, arms, and munitions from American factories and food from American farms flowed across the oceans to Britain and the Soviet Union.

Even before 1939 Stalin had adopted the policy of industrializing the more backward regions east of the Urals, a safe distance from Russia's western border, and in the months preceding Hitler's attack in 1941 hundreds of factories were moved there piece by piece. Despite its enormous losses of productive capacity, the Soviet Union was able throughout the war to produce most of the military supplies it needed. Central planning, rationing, military discipline, and the employment of women were not such a dramatic change in this communist regime, but the acceptance of rationing, the increased hours of labor, the destruction of homes, the death of loved ones, and the loss of men and territory required patriotism of a rather old-fashioned and bourgeois sort. Patriotism became the dominant theme of Soviet public life.

Nazi Rule Until 1943 German civilians did not experience hardships comparable to the sacrifices of the Soviets or the lowered standard of living of the British. Nor was German output much greater than at the war's outset. The illusion, fed by military success and propaganda, that the war would soon be over encouraged interim measures. Competing elements of the Nazi party worked at cross purposes with each other and the government. Mutual distrust made it difficult for the Nazis to cooperate consistently with science and industry. Only when Albert Speer was given increased powers over the economy did coordination improve. In mid-July 1943 German production was twice what it had been in 1939, despite Allied bombing. A year later it was three times the pre-war level.

Germany certainly benefited from its vast gains of territory rich in resources, industry, and personnel, but the system that took so naturally to ruthless conquest was less well adapted to ordinary life. The Nazis alienated those they conquered with their labor conscription, racial policies, and oppressive brutality. A high percent-age of Ukrainians, for example, had welcomed liberation from Russian rule, but brief acquaintance with Nazi treatment of the "racially inferior" Slavs discouraged their cooperation. Nazi rule was most severe and most destructive in Eastern Europe and less harsh among the "Aryan" populations of the Nordic lands. In France food rations provided only about half the minimum that decent health requires. Germany's most crucial need was for workers, and slave labor was an answer in accord with Nazi racial theory. About 1 million French workers and eventually some 5 million Slavs were shipped like cattle to labor in Germany. By 1944 the 8 million foreign workers in Germany constituted one-fifth of the workforce.

▼ The laborers' barracks at Buchenwald at the end of the war.
© Corbis

Genocide   The hysteria of racial hatred dominated rational planning. Brutalized and starving workers could hardly be efficient. Transporting and guarding slave laborers became an enormous, corrupting, and expensive enterprise. Many millions of people died in forced labor, perhaps 3 million Soviet prisoners of war were killed, and millions more Slavs in occupied territory were starved to death. These deaths, evidence of massive brutality and consonant with Nazi ideas about inferior races, could be said to have had some connection with the exigencies of war, as could the German practice of killing large numbers of civilian hostages in occupied lands as a means of demoralizing resistance while reducing unworthy populations. Hounding Jews and Gypsies, cramming them into concentration camps, and killing them had less to do with the brutality of war (the massacre of prisoners taken on the Eastern front may have been a precedent) than with the implementation of Nazi racial theory. Throughout the fall of 1941 mobile SS squads executed Jews who had been rounded up on the Eastern front. Men and women, old and young were lined up, made to undress, and marched toward ditches to be shot by the SS (one squad reported having killed more than 200,000 people). The orders, equipment, and reports this slaughter required establish that many people had to have known about it.

The Holocaust   In January 1942, at a secret meeting of high officials held just outside Berlin, it was agreed that the systematic and efficient extermination of Jews should be made a general policy, "the final solution of the Jewish question" (see "A Gas Chamber," p. 1077). By 1945, nearly 6 million Jews and as many other people (Poles, Gypsies, and Magyars especially) had died in concentration camps like Buchenwald and Dachau and the more recently constructed death camps like Auschwitz. Some of these camps were also supposed to be centers of production: A Krupp arms factory, an I. G. Farben chemical plant, and a coal mine were part of the Auschwitz complex. But the chief product of Auschwitz was corpses, at a rate that reached twelve thousand a day.

The extermination camps remain the ultimate nightmare of modern history. Beating and torturing prisoners of war was not new, though rarely so common as under the Nazis, but the industrial organization of death in Nazi camps raises terrifying questions about modern civilization. Hundreds of thousands of people were involved in operating those camps and in rounding up men, women, and children to be shipped to them. At first, the victims were primarily Slavs and Jews from the conquered lands of Eastern Europe; then Jews from Western Europe were hunted down and added to the flow. They came by trainload, huddled in boxcars, hungry, thirsty, frightened, and confused. Upon arrival at the camps, the weakest and least "useful" (the ill, the elderly, children, and often women) were sent to showers that proved to be gas chambers. The others were given uniforms, often with patches that distinguished into neat categories the common criminals, political prisoners, homosexuals, communists, Jehovah's Witnesses, Slavs, and Jews. Many were literally worked to death or were killed when they could work no longer. The prisoners themselves, reduced to blind survival, were caught up in this dehumanized world of beatings, limited rations, constant abuse, and contempt. Neither submission nor animal cunning guaranteed another day of life. Many inmates nevertheless managed haunting gestures of human feeling through a story told, a song sung, a bit of food shared.

German clerks and bureaucrats kept elaborate records of names, stolen possessions, and corpses, which were efficiently stripped of gold fillings and useful hair before being turned to ashes that could be used as fertilizer. Doctors invented new tortures under the guise of medical experiments to benefit the Aryan race. The sadistic pseudoscience of these doctors elaborated on the paranoid dream of purifying the Aryan race. Forced sterilization and euthanasia of the chronically ill, the physically handicapped, and the mentally retarded had been advocated and practiced by Nazis since they first came to power. In *Mein Kampf* Hitler had referred to Jews as a plague and like a bacillus weakening the Aryan race. Racial laws had extended that point to all aspects of social life, and brutal treatment helped to make prisoners seem inferior, even subhuman. Organized killing carried this denial of humanity one step further.

Yet even the SS guards—like the camp commandants, the people who arranged for trains,

A GAS CHAMBER

At a meeting of high Nazi officials on January 20, 1942, Reinard Heydrich, Plenipotentiary for the Preparation of the Final Solution of the European Jewish Question, spoke proudly of the liquidation of the Jews already accomplished and of the concentration camps already established but called for a further step. "We have the means, the methods, the organization, experience, and people. And we have the will. This is a historic moment in the struggle against Jewry. The Führer has declared his determination . . . [and sees destruction of the Jews] as exterminating fatal bacteria to save the organism. . . . We will work effectively but silently." Nazi extermination camps indeed followed strikingly similar procedures, and the following description of the Birkenau camp is typical of hundreds of survivors' testimonies. It was written by a French doctor, André Lettich, who was a member of the "special commando" squad, whose job it was to empty the crematoria of corpses and make them ready for the next round.

"Until the end of January 1943, there were no crematoria in Birkenau. In the middle of a small birch forest, about two kilometres from the camp, was a peaceful looking house, where a Polish family had once lived before it had been either murdered or expelled. This cottage had been equipped as a gas chamber for a long time.

"More than five hundred metres further on were two barracks: the men stood on one side, the women on the other. They were addressed in a very polite and friendly way: 'You have been on a journey. You are dirty. You will take a bath. Get undressed quickly.' Towels and soap were handed out, and then suddenly the brutes woke up and showed their true faces: this horde of people, these men and women were driven outside with hard blows and forced both summer and winter to go the few hundred metres to the 'Shower Room'. Above the entry door was the word 'Shower'. One could even see shower heads on the ceiling which were cemented in but never had water flowing through them.

"These poor innocents were crammed together, pressed against each other. Then panic broke out, for at last they realised the fate in store for them. But blows with rifle butts and revolver shots soon restored order and finally they all entered the death chamber. The doors were shut and, ten minutes later, the temperature was high enough to facilitate the condensation of the hydrogen cyanide, for the condemned were gassed with hydrogen cyanide. This was the so-called 'Zyklon B', gravel pellets saturated with twenty per cent of hydrogen cyanide which was used by the German barbarians.

"Then, *SS Unterscharführer* Moll threw the gas in through a little vent. One could hear fearful screams, but a few moments later there was complete silence. Twenty to twenty-five minutes later, the doors and windows were opened to ventilate the rooms and the corpses were thrown at once into pits to be burnt. But, beforehand the dentists had searched every mouth to pull out the gold teeth. The women were also searched to see if they had not hidden jewelry in the intimate parts of their bodies, and their hair was cut off and methodically placed in sacks for industrial purposes."

From J. Noakes and G. Pridham (eds.), *Nazism, 1919–1945: A Documentary Reader*, Vol. 3: *Foreign Policy, War, and Racial Extermination* (University of Exeter Press).

and the business people who bid for contracts to build gas ovens—employed euphemisms rather than acknowledge what was really happening. The residents of nearby towns rarely discussed what was carried in the trains rumbling by or asked about the odor that settled over the countryside from crematoria smokestacks. Nor did the Allies quite believe or choose to act on the stories that filtered out of Germany about atrocities on a scale too terrible to comprehend.

Resistance Movements Millions of Europeans came to rely on the British Broadcasting Corporation for news and for encouragement in occupied lands, where every act of opposition—a speech not applauded, a whispered joke—took on symbolic significance. Gradually, against great odds, organized resistance movements formed. Some developed around neighborhood groups; many were connected to prewar political parties. Always composed of a small minority, these partisan

◄ **The scene that greeted the Allies on entering Lansberg concentration camp. American forces required several hundred German civilians in the area to come look at it as well.**
© Corbis

movements achieved particular strength in Denmark and Norway, the Netherlands, France, and Yugoslavia. Many of them received material aid and guidance from governments-in-exile operating from London, the most notable being the Free French, headed by General De Gaulle.

Nazi reprisals for acts of resistance were meant to be horrible. When Czechs assassinated the new Reich Protector of Bohemia and Moravia in June 1942, the Germans retaliated by wiping out the village of Lidice, which they suspected of hiding the murderers: Every man was killed; every woman and child deported. On a single day in 1943, the Germans put 1,400 men to death in a Greek village. Hundreds of towns across occupied Europe have their memorials, a burned-out building or a ditch where clusters of civilians were massacred.

Yet the underground movements continued to grow, and their actions became a barometer of the course of the war. In France, partisan activities expanded from single exploits—smuggling Allied airmen out of the country, dynamiting a bridge, or attacking individual German officers—to large-scale operations closely coordinated from London. Norway's resistance helped force the

THE HISTORIANS' DEBATE ON GERMAN GENOCIDE

◆

Over the past decade historians of Germany, particularly in Germany itself, have sustained a heated debate about the ways of understanding Nazi genocide. Among the issues in this debate, known as the Historikerstreit, *are the role of racial theories, the example of the Soviet Union, and whether genocide had distinctly German roots. The citations here, from three well-known scholars, illustrate these positions.*

HENRY FRIEDLANDER

"Historians investigating Nazi genocide have long debated who gave the order to commit mass murder, when it was issued, and how it was transmitted. Although the specific mechanism has been a matter of contention between rival groups of historians . . . , there now appears to be a general agreement that Hitler had a deciding voice, although no one has ever discovered, or is likely to discover, a smoking gun. Recently historians have focused on the specific dates when the idea to launch the physical annihilation of the European Jews was first advanced and when the decision to do so became irrevocable. . . . My own approach is somewhat different. I am not particularly interested in exact dates. Instead, I want to trace the sequential development of mass murder.

"I define Nazi genocide, what is now commonly called the Holocaust, as the mass murder of human beings because they belonged to a biologically defined group. Heredity determined the selection of victims. Although the regime persecuted and often killed men and women for their politics, nationality, religion, behavior, or activities, the Nazis applied a consistent and inclusive policy of extermination only against three groups of human beings: the handicapped, Jews, and Gypsies.

"The attack on these targeted groups drew on more than fifty years of political and scientific arguments hostile to the belief in the equality of man. Since the turn of the century, the German elite, that is the members of the educated professional classes, had increasingly accepted an ideology based on human inequality. Geneticists, anthropologists, and psychiatrists had advanced a theory of human heredity that had merged with the racist doctrine of *völkisch* nationalists to form a political ideology of a nation based on race. The Nazi movement both absorbed and advanced this ideology. After 1933 they created the political framework that made it possible to translate this ideology of inequality into a policy of exclusion, while the German bureaucratic, professional, and scientific elite provided the legitimacy

the regime needed for the smooth implementation of this policy."

From Henry Friedlander, "Step by Step: The Expansion of Murder, 1939–1941," *German Studies Review* 17, October 1994.

ERNST NOLTE

"Auschwitz is not primarily a result of traditional anti-Semitism and was not, in its essential core, mere 'genocide'; rather, it was, above all, a reaction—born out of anxiety—to the annihilations which occurred during the Russian Revolution. This copy was far more irrational than the earlier original (because it was simply an absurd notion to imagine that 'the Jews' had ever wished to annihilate the German bourgeoisie or even the German people), and it is difficult to attribute to it even a perverted ethos. It was more horrifying than the original because it carried out the annihilation of human beings in a quasi-industrial manner. It was more repulsive than the original because it was based on mere suppositions, and was almost completely free of that mass hatred which, within the midst of horror, remains nonetheless an understandable—and thus, to a limited extent, reconciling—element. All this supports the notion of singularity, yet does not alter the fact that the so-called annihilation of the Jews during the Third Reich was a reaction or a distorted copy—and not a first act, not the original."

From Ernst Nolte, "Between Historical Myth and Revisionism," *Yad Vashem Studies* 19, 1988.

HANS-ULRICH WEHLER

"Nolte's thesis concerning the fatal consequences of the Bolsheviks' anxiety-producing class warfare is directed above all against a well-grounded interpretation: that Hitler and National Socialism were products of German and Austrian history. Only after factors rooted in that past have been assessed should the broader European context be considered. Nolte has sought to undermine this hard-won insight by displacing the "primary historical guilt" onto Marx, the Russian Revolution, and the extermination policy of the Bolsheviks. I shall emphasize below the main points of the opposing view—a view that is better grounded empirically and more convincing in its interpretive approach than Nolte's theory:

"—Hitler and countless other National Socialists had internalized a fanatical anti-Marxism long before the First World War: that is, before the Russian Revolution, the civil war, and class warfare in the new Soviet Union could confirm and strengthen their hatred of the 'Reds.'

"—Social Darwinism in its vulgar (racist) form was one of the strongest forces driving the highly ideological 'worldview' of Hitler and many other Nazis well before 1917. Contemporary developments thereafter only served as confirmation to these confused minds.

"—The poisonous morass of German and Austrian anti-Semitism was the source of the crazed ideas associated with the Nazi hatred of the Jews. The new racist, political anti-Semitism that flourished in the late 1870s quickly led to the explicit idea of extermination. For example, in its Hamburg resolutions of September 1899, the German Social Reform Party claimed publicly and without any embarrassment that 'in the course of the twentieth century, the Jewish question must be solved . . . once and for all by the complete separation and (if necessary for defensive purposes) the definitive extermination of the Jewish people.' What was new in the 1930s was 'only' that Hitler and his cohorts took this program literally—and brought with them the will to carry out the deed itself.

"—The Nazis effortlessly adopted the widespread, fully developed antidemocratic, antiliberal, and antiparliamentary political ideology that had already been fully developed by the German Right before 1917/18.

"—The Nazis were able to exploit the deeply corrosive anticapitalist resentments of the Protestant, provincial bourgeoisie and of peasant society. They were also able to counter the difficult conflicts of a modern class society with the hypertrophied idealization of an oft-evoked *Volksgemeinschaft* (national community).

"—National Socialism benefitted from long-term conditions in Germany: the antagonisms of Germany's social structure, an authoritarian mentality, the peculiarities of Prussian militarism, the Protestant subservience to the state, the national susceptibility to charismatic leaders, a particular kind of political philosophy, etc. Hitler's regime also profited from more recent conditions that stemmed from the experiences of the period 1914–33. Among these were 'the experience of war,' 'the nation in arms,' the 'total war' of 1916–18, the beginning of the defeat, the renunciation of all war aims, the stab-in-the-back myth, the 'disgraceful peace' at Versailles, the war reparations and postwar hyperinflation, and the destructive force of the Depression. These events belong to a long list of favorable factors with fatal consequences.

"Above all, the traditions and burdens of Germany's past influenced the course of National Socialism. Only after these have been identified should historians proceed to analyze the influence of the wider European and world-historical context."

From Hans-Ulrich Wehler, "Unburdening the German Past? A Preliminary Assessment," in Peter Baldwin (ed.), *Reworking the Past: Hitler, the Holocaust, and the Historians' Debate* (Beacon Press, 1990).

Germans to keep 300,000 troops there and away from more active fronts. In Yugoslavia, two groups of partisans maintained an active guerrilla war, although the British decision to support the group led by Tito all but ensured his control of the country at the end of the war. After the Allied invasion of Italy, partisan groups there maintained an unnerving harassment of Fascist and Nazi forces. Even in Germany itself some members of the army and the old aristocracy began to plot against Hitler, and in July 1944 a group of conspirators planted a bomb under the table as the Führer conducted a conference with his staff.

Hitler escaped serious injury, but the sense that he was doomed had spread to the heart of Germany.

These partisan movements were important for more than their immediate contribution to the war. The memory of their bravery eased the painful reality of defeat, and in countries like France, Italy, and Norway, where many had acquiesced in fascist regimes, the militant opposition of the resistance could be taken to express the real will of the people. In fact many of the major political parties of the postwar era were formed in the resistance, and the ideas of democracy, freedom, and equality that circulated so passionately then would be repeated in constitutions and party platforms later. Most resistance fighters were young men, but many women, too, experienced the camaraderie of activism as secret couriers, provisioners, and occasionally group commanders. By joining in the resistance, women were being drawn into the rudimentary renewal of national political life.

◆ ALLIED STRATEGY

By 1943 the Axis was on the defensive although it had the advantage of shorter, direct lines of supply. While Hitler continued to imagine that some daring thrust or miracle weapon would bring him victory, the Allies continued to disagree as to how they should attack Hitler's "fortress Europe."

A Second Front   The Soviet Union had repeatedly urged opening a second front on the continent, and most of the American military command favored an immediate invasion. The British warned against the high cost of such an expedition, and with Roosevelt's support, Churchill prevailed. The Allies invaded North Africa instead, ending the threat to Egypt. When that was not followed by landings on the continent, the Soviets suspected that they and the Germans were being left to annihilate each other. The Americans continued to favor such an attack, but the British argued for tightening the blockade of Germany and for making more limited assaults in the eastern Mediterranean and southern Europe, on what Churchill called the "soft underbelly."

More than military strategy was at stake. The Allies had been less specific about their long-range goals than during World War I, and they were divided. Stalin looked forward to regaining the Polish territory lost in 1939 (Poland could be compensated with territory taken from a defeated Germany). The British correctly warned that Soviet expansion into Poland would be unacceptable to the Americans and recalled the earlier communist aim of revolution across the continent (as well as imperial Russia's efforts before that to expand into Eastern Europe). The British hoped to place Anglo-American troops in such a way that, after the war, they could have a voice in the disposition of Eastern Europe. In London the exiled leaders of the Eastern European countries agitated for their own nationalist goals, alarmed by Stalin's references to the need for "friendly" governments along Russia's borders.

The Casablanca Conference   With such issues before them, Roosevelt and Churchill met at Casablanca in January 1943. There they decided (to the Soviets' disgust) to invade Sicily and agreed to demand the unconditional surrender of Italy, Germany, and Japan, an expression of moral outrage against fascism that was also meant to prevent the Soviet Union and the Western Allies from making any separate deals with the enemy. Welcomed by Allied public opinion at the time, the refusal to negotiate with the Axis was subsequently criticized for strengthening their desperate defense after defeat was inevitable.

The Invasion of Italy   In July a mammoth amphibious assault carried Anglo-American forces into Sicily. A victim of his own propaganda, Mussolini had consistently overestimated Italian strength. As the invaders advanced, the Fascist Grand Council in a secret session voted Mussolini out of office. The Duce was arrested, and Marshal Pietro Badoglio was named prime minister. A coalition of monarchists and moderate Fascists then sought an armistice. But Committees of National Liberation had sprung up throughout Italy; composed of anti-Fascists from liberals to communists, these Committees wanted nothing to do with Badoglio, a Fascist hero of the campaign in Ethiopia, or with the king, who had bowed to Mussolini for twenty years. Again the Allies were divided. Britain favored the monarchy and feared leftist influence in the Committees. The Americans leaned toward the Committees but agreed that representatives of the Soviet Union should be excluded from the Allied military government that would be installed in Italy. Stalin accepted that decision, knowing that arguments about spheres of influence would be useful elsewhere; and he encouraged Italy's communists to be flexible in cooperating with the arrangements the Anglo-Americans preferred.

In September Allied forces in Sicily invaded southern Italy, where they were well dug in by the end of the month. The German army, however, had snatched control of the rest of the peninsula.

Although the Allies captured Naples in October, their campaign in Italy soon bogged down in difficult terrain and in the face of fierce German resistance. In a daring rescue, German paratroops snatched Mussolini from his mountaintop prison and took him to northern Italy, where he proclaimed a Fascist republic that was blatantly a German puppet. At the same time, Italy's antifascist partisans were becoming increasingly effective. Italians, their country a battleground for foreign armies, were caught in civil war.

The Free French   Italy was not the first place in which the Allies indicated they might compromise with tainted regimes. At the moment of the North African invasion, Admiral Jean François Darlan, a former vice premier of Vichy France and commander of its armed forces, happened to be in Algiers. Eisenhower's staff quickly agreed to make him governor-general of French Africa provided his forces would not resist the Allied invasion. De

Gaulle was outraged. He had claimed to represent a free France since his first call for continued resistance in 1940 when, from London, he organized French forces fighting with the Allies. His hauteur, his insistence on a voice in Allied policy, and his success in winning support in the French colonies had made his relations with Britain and the United States difficult at best. The assassination of Darlan in December 1942 eased the situation, and Germany's decision to occupy all of France in response to the Allied invasion of North Africa reduced De Gaulle's fears that the Allies might choose to deal with the Vichy regime. Watching events in Italy, the European governments-in-exile shared Stalin's concerns about the consistency and true aims of Allied policy.

The Teheran Conference   Finally, at the end of November 1943, Roosevelt, Churchill, and Stalin met for the first time, at Teheran. The conversations were not easy. Previously, the British had

▼ **Stalin, Roosevelt, and Churchill, meeting for the first time at Teheran, reached an understanding that laid the groundwork for Allied cooperation in pursuing the war.**
© Corbis

mediated between the United States and the Soviet Union, but now the Americans took a middle position. The Allies reached a tentative understanding that the Soviet Union would accept a border with Poland similar to the one proposed in 1919, and they left open the question of what kind of government a liberated Poland might have. Their unity thus preserved by postponing the most difficult issues, the Allies could plan vigorous prosecution of the war. Stalin promised to declare war on Japan as soon as Germany surrendered, and Churchill's proposal for an invasion of the Dardanelles was rejected. The British and Americans agreed instead to land in France in the following year.

◆ THE ROAD TO VICTORY

The Italian Front   The Allies progressed slowly in Italy, taking five months to fight their way past a costly new beachhead at Anzio. In December 1943, King Victor Emmanuel III announced that he would abdicate in favor of his son, and Badoglio gave way to a cabinet drawn from members of the Committees of National Liberation. Italy then officially joined the Allies. The Germans, however, held the advantage of entrenched positions on one mountain ridge after another. Northern Italy became another German-occupied country in which Jews were rounded up for death camps and captured Italian soldiers were sent to slave labor in Germany. The Allies slowly pushed northward, aided by partisan risings, while the main forces were held aside for the invasion of France. Only in May 1944 did Anglo-American armies finally seize the old Benedictine abbey of Monte Cassino, north of Naples, after a destructive bombardment. Rome, the first European capital to be liberated, was taken in June. German resistance converged on the so-called Gothic Line, running from Pisa to Rimini. Not until it was pierced in September 1944, after months of bloody fighting, could further drives lead to the capture of Ravenna (in December) and Bologna, Verona, and Genoa (in April 1945). By then German resistance had ceased.

The Soviet Union   Soviet successes were more spectacular. In the spring of 1943 the Germans could still launch an offensive of their own, but it slowed within weeks. In July the Soviet army began a relentless advance that continued, with few setbacks, for almost two years. With armies now superior in numbers and matériel, Soviet forces reached the Dnieper and Kiev by November. In February 1944 they were at the Polish border. They retook the Crimea in the spring, Romania surrendered in August, and Finland and Bulgaria fell a few weeks later. Soviet power loomed over Eastern Europe.

The Western Front   For months Germany was subjected to constant pounding from the air, and the Germans knew an invasion across the English Channel was imminent. They believed it would come in the area around Calais, the shore closest to England, as a series of calculated feints seemed to indicate. Instead, on June 6, 1944, the Allies landed in Normandy. The largest amphibious landing in history, it put 150,000 men ashore within two days, supported by 5,000 ships and 1,500 tanks. In a complex series of landings Eisenhower's Allied force poured onto the French beaches. Made possible by overwhelming control of the air and helped by a poorly coordinated German defense, the landings nevertheless suffered heavy losses. Within a few months, more than a million men disembarked. In July they broke through the German defense and began a series of rapid drives through France. A second amphibious attack, in southern France in mid-August, led to swift advances inland that were greatly aided by well-organized French resistance groups. On August 24 the Parisian underground rose against the Germans, and French forces under Charles de Gaulle quickly entered the cheering city. Brussels fell a week later, and ten days after that, American troops crossed the German frontier.

Germany had launched its "miracle" weapon in June, the relatively ineffective V-1 pilotless plane, which was followed in September by the far more dangerous V-2 rocket. Had the Nazis recognized its potential earlier, the effects might have been devastating. The V-2 flew faster than the speed of sound and was almost impossible to intercept; but these rockets were hard to aim and too few and too late to be decisive. More threatening was a counterstroke through the Ardennes in December that rocked the Allied line back. The Battle of the Bulge, the last offensive the Germans would mount, cost about 70,000 men on each side before the Allies regained the initiative in January 1945.

▲ In February 1944 an American sergeant who spoke German, believing he faced six or seven Germans, called on them to surrender — fifty-six came forward.
© Corbis

The Yalta Conference   When Allied leaders held their last wartime meeting, at Yalta in February 1945, Russian troops occupied part of Czechoslovakia and stood on the German frontier of Poland. The decisions of the Big Three at Yalta, which were widely hailed at the time, later became the most controversial of World War II. The hurried meeting dealt with four broad issues, each a measure of the Allies' mutual distrust. They agreed to create a United Nations Organization. The Soviet Union asked for sixteen votes, one for each of its republics, to counterbalance the votes of the British Commonwealth and of Latin America, which the United States was expected to dominate. That request was reduced to three, and the

Soviet Union got the veto it demanded but with some slight restrictions on its use. The USSR promised to declare war against Japan within ninety days of Germany's defeat in return for the territories Russia had surrendered to Japan in 1905 and for a sphere of influence in Manchuria.

A more contentious issue was the treatment of Germany. Each of the Big Three was assigned a zone of occupation, and Russia reluctantly agreed to the American and British plan to carve a zone for France from the areas under their control. Russia's demands for huge reparations and "labor services" were so troubling that specific terms had to be postponed. The form of Italy's government was in fact now largely set, as was De Gaulle's

▲ **MAP 29.3** **THE ALLIED VICTORY IN WORLD WAR II**

ascendance in an independent France. The main issue was Soviet dominance in Eastern Europe. The creation of new governments for the liberated nations, the most difficult issue of all, could not be postponed much longer; yet every proposal exposed fundamental differences between the Soviet Union and the Western powers.

In most of the countries they occupied, the Soviets were tolerating broad coalitions that included all the old antifascist parties, but they would not allow a role for the Western powers,

even restricting Allied observers. When Churchill visited Moscow four months earlier, he had proposed a division of interests: The Soviet Union would have predominance in Romania and the largest influence in Bulgaria, Britain would have a free hand in Greece, and the two powers would recognize their equal interests in Yugoslavia and Hungary. Such crude understandings offered few guarantees, however, though Stalin remained silent when Britain intervened in the civil war raging in Greece in order to rout the leftists.

Stalin in turn exercised a free hand in Poland after the Polish underground arose against the Germans in August 1944. As Soviet troops approached Warsaw, the Russians simply halted their advance until the Germans had wiped out the resistance fighters, who were closely tied to the anticommunist Polish government in London. The Yalta Conference did not in fact adopt cynically drawn spheres of influence, but the Conference's formulas, with their references to democratic governments and free elections, would in the end be interpreted by those who held the guns.

The Final Months As the Allies pushed into Germany from all sides, it became clear that Berlin would be the final battleground. Fearing that Hitler planned a last desperate stand at his retreat at Berchtesgaden in the southern German mountains, Eisenhower halted the eastward advance of American and British armies at the Elbe River. The Russians took Berlin, where Hitler had en-

sured the maximum destruction by ordering a defense to the death. The Führer committed suicide on April 30, 1945, and his aides burned his body, which has never been found. Four days later a group of German officers signed the final unconditional surrender. The war in Europe was over.

World conflict would continue in Asia for four months more. It was expected to last much longer, even with the Russian help that had seemed so necessary when promised at Yalta. Despite massive bombing and repeated naval victories, Allied progress through the islands and jungles of the Pacific toward Japan had been laborious and bloody. Americans conquered Guam, landed in the Philippines, and took Iwo Jima but at great cost. The tactic of landing on some islands while skipping others, often leaving Japanese forces isolated and useless, created bases from which Allied planes threatened the Japanese fleet and the mainland itself. Eventual victory was no longer in doubt. During the three months following Germany's surrender, air raids obliterated

▼ **Charles de Gaulle, the epitome of French resistance, greeted by Parisians on the day of the city's liberation in August 1944.**
Robert Capa/Magnum Photos

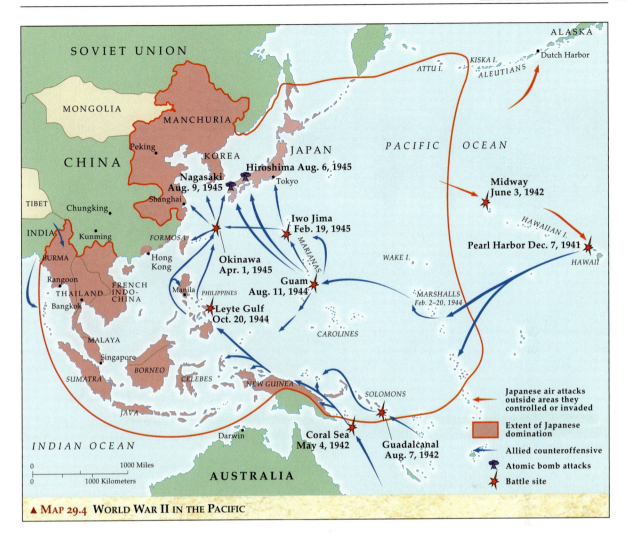

▲ MAP 29.4 WORLD WAR II IN THE PACIFIC

Map labels: ALASKA, Dutch Harbor, KISKA I., ATTU I., ALEUTIANS, SOVIET UNION, MONGOLIA, MANCHURIA, Peking, CHINA, KOREA, JAPAN, PACIFIC OCEAN, Hiroshima Aug. 6, 1945, Nagasaki Aug. 9, 1945, Tokyo, TIBET, Chungking, Shanghai, Midway June 3, 1942, INDIA, Kunming, FORMOSA, Iwo Jima Feb. 19, 1945, HAWAIIAN I., BURMA, Hong Kong, Pearl Harbor Dec. 7, 1941, Rangoon, Okinawa Apr. 1, 1945, MARIANAS, WAKE I., HAWAII, THAILAND, FRENCH INDO-CHINA, Manila, PHILIPPINES, Guam Aug. 11, 1944, Bangkok, MARSHALLS Feb. 2–20, 1944, Leyte Gulf Oct. 20, 1944, MALAYA, CAROLINES, Singapore, BORNEO, CELEBES, SUMATRA, NEW GUINEA, SOLOMONS, JAVA, Darwin, Coral Sea May 4, 1942, Guadalcanal Aug. 7, 1942, INDIAN OCEAN, AUSTRALIA, 0 1000 Miles, 0 1000 Kilometers

Legend: Japanese air attacks outside areas they controlled or invaded; Extent of Japanese domination; Allied counteroffensive; Atomic bomb attacks; Battle site

Japan's navy, industrial plants, and large parts of its cities: Nearly 200,000 people were killed in Tokyo in just one week. But still the Japanese would not surrender.

On August 6 the new president of the United States, Harry Truman (Roosevelt had died in April), authorized the use of a new weapon that had been developed after years of secret research, the atomic bomb. In one blow, half of the city of Hiroshima disappeared from the face of the earth. A quarter of its 320,000 inhabitants were killed. On August 9 the Americans dropped an even more powerful atomic bomb on the city of Nagasaki. On August 8 the Soviet Union declared war on Japan; and on September 2, 1945, Japan surrendered unconditionally. The atomic bomb, an extraordinary achievement of science and tech-

nology made possible by great wealth and scores of European scientists driven to sanctuary in the United States, permitted a great democracy to end World War II by unleashing a new order of terror upon humanity. Later, many people would question the morality of using so terrible a weapon. Even in the jubilation of victory, leaders reordering a shattered world now knew that another war might bring the end of civilization.

III. Building on the Ruins

For most Europeans the immediate postwar period brought little improvement in their living conditions, and for years individuals, institutions, and governments struggled with the effects of

▲ **Hiroshima, the victim of one of science's great achievements. The world had entered a new era of warfare, and for a generation the Japanese would suffer from the environmental destruction and the effects of radiation.**
AP/Wide World Photos

death, destruction, and the displacement of millions of people. Overcoming such fundamental problems on so vast a scale was the central achievement of the next decade. Euphoria was brief even among the victors and the newly liberated, as people set about their daily tasks in an uncertain world of economic hardship, social dislocation, and political division. As European nations gained in political stability and economic strength, they remained distinctly subordinate to the United States and the Soviet Union in a world divided by the Cold War. They had no choice but to give up their colonial empires.

◆ IMMEDIATE CRISES

The Devastation   In contrast to World War I, a majority of the fatalities in World War II were civilian. About 4 million men died on battlefields; and for every soldier killed, two more were either wounded or taken captive. Civilian losses are harder to categorize, and often there was no one to do the counting. The Germans killed between 12 and 20 million people in occupied countries and concentration camps. Across Europe millions more civilians died just for being where armies chose to bomb or shell or shoot. In all, the European casualties in World War II were five or six times greater than in World War I (only for Britain and France were they lower). The Soviet Union lost some 27 million people; Poland, about 6 million (including 3 million Jews); Germany, nearly 5 million. So the total European casualties of World War II—dead, wounded, or crippled by inhumane treatment—remain an estimate, a number hard to comprehend in its gruesome total or ghostly imprecision: some 45 to 55 million people.

Europe's industrial capability in 1945 was perhaps half what it had been in 1939, and only parts of such major cities as Frankfurt, Dresden, Brest, and Toulon were still standing. The

▲ Citizens of Dresden, nearly a year after the war ended, making their way through the rubble from Allied saturation bombing.
© Corbis

continent's most important ports, bridges, and rail lines had been all but destroyed. Agriculture was also hard hit. Large areas of farmland in France, Italy, and Germany could not be cultivated; the number of cattle in France had been reduced by half. In the winter of 1945–1946, starvation was a threat in many places, and in some, such as Vienna, thousands died of famine. Disease was an ever-present danger, too, although penicillin helped limit the epidemics that erupted. The rationing of food and clothes (and illegal black markets) continued in many countries into the 1950s, and Europeans looked to the United States and the Soviet Union for relief as Allied troops occupied the continent.

Refugees   In addition to the millions without jobs or housing, there were more refugees in Europe than ever before in history. Some 8 million slave laborers in the Third Reich and millions in concentration camps were put on trains headed back to where their homes had been. There were German prisoners of war and Allied prisoners in Germany. More than 7 million Soviet citizens in Germany, including defectors, had no place to go. Some 2 million Poles and Czechs returning from prison in the Soviet Union joined millions of Ukrainians and Poles who moved west to stay on the other side of the shifting border with the USSR. Romanians drove out Hungarians; Czechs expelled Hungarians and Germans. Millions of

Germans whom the Nazis had transplanted to Poland in the interests of Germanization were forced to leave, and many of the 1.5 million Poles the Nazis had evicted wanted to go back home. The question of where national boundaries should be drawn, which had so troubled the peacemakers of Versailles, was settled now by first drawing the lines and then pushing inconvenient nationalities across them.

Most of the refugees who carried their few belongings along unfamiliar roads were civilians, perhaps 60 million in all, a majority of them women and children who had lost their homes and livelihood. Separated from kin and possessions, they struggled to survive in strange lands that were impoverished by war. We will never know how many died or were abused or robbed. Governments tried to make nice distinctions between the homeless (those in or near their own country) and displaced persons (who were mostly stateless—some 12 million were so registered in 1945), and they tried to separate criminals from others. Abandoned factories and warehouses, even former concentration camps, were used to house refugees. When facilities were specially built, they were usually crude barracks without plumbing or electricity and were meant to be temporary. Bit by bit the fortunate were assigned a destination, but "unaccompanied children," the disabled, and the aged were harder to place. In 1960, fifteen years after the war had ended, there were still 32,000 refugees in 107 camps in Europe, sharing tiny quarters and communal toilets.

The Terms of Peace: Potsdam No great peace conference took place after World War II. When the leaders of the Soviet Union, Great Britain, and the United States met at Potsdam for two weeks in July 1945, they hardly knew each other. President Harry Truman had been in office only three months following the death of Roosevelt, and in the midst of the meeting Clement Attlee replaced Churchill, who had been defeated in the British elections.

The Potsdam meeting outlined the future of Germany but left details for the future. The Allies readily agreed that all Nazi institutions must be abolished, German arms production prohibited, and German industry controlled. Democracy and free speech were to be restored. In the meantime

Germany was divided into four zones of occupation, and so was Berlin, isolated in the Soviet zone. Germany's eastern border was moved westward to the Oder and Neisse rivers, enlarging Poland. During the next year, the foreign ministers of the four principal Allies (now including France) drafted treaties for the other defeated states, but their meetings soon became a forum for quarrels between the Soviets and the other three. Italy, Romania, Hungary, Bulgaria, and Finland each ceded minor territories to its neighbors. Austria, like Germany, remained divided into four occupied zones and without a formal treaty.

The Potsdam Conference had also laid down the terms for peace with Japan. The Soviet Union would get some territory, and the European nations would regain their Asian colonies. But the prime beneficiaries were China and, above all, the United States, whose troops already held most of the strategic islands in the Pacific and were to occupy Japan.

War Crimes Trials Within Europe, rooting out fascism was a major concern. In countries the Nazis had occupied, there were summary executions of collaborators and some public prosecutions, notably in France, where Pierre Laval and Marshal Pétain were tried. In Germany itself, however, the numbers involved made denazification difficult. Millions of forms were filled out and hundreds of trials held, but the drive against former Nazis soon waned. Determined to establish some lasting standard, the Allies created an international tribunal to try Hitler's closest associates for crimes against humanity. The trials, held in Nuremberg in 1945 and 1946, were also intended to inform the German people of the full horror of Nazi rule. The appalling revelations of those solemn hearings were followed by restrained judgments—only twelve of the twenty-two prime defendants were condemned to death, and three were acquitted.

International Agencies The belief in international law that underlay the Nuremberg trials and the United Nations Organization was tempered by a determination to learn from the past. This peace would not be punitive, and devastated nations, defeated enemies as well as those liberated from German rule, must be helped. Even before

III: BUILDING ON THE RUINS **1091**

▲ **Göring, Hess, and von Ribbentrop (the first three on the left in the prison's dock) listen to the proceedings at the beginning of the Nuremberg trial for war crimes.**
© Corbis

the UN had its charter, its first agency, the United Nations Relief and Rehabilitation Administration (UNRRA), was created, late in 1943. UNRRA played a major role in reconstructing postwar Europe, organizing relief of food and medical supplies, and coordinating international loans. To avoid the dangerous inflation that had followed World War I, a conference at Bretton Woods, New Hampshire, in 1944 created the International Monetary Fund and an International Bank for Reconstruction and Development (later the World Bank). Those institutions, with nearly $20 billion in assets, furthered reconstruction and capital investment by supporting stable currencies. They would become influential mechanisms for shaping the international capitalist economy.

But the main instrument of peace was to be the United Nations, and a few months after the Yalta meeting, fifty-one countries approved the United Nations Charter at a special conference held in San Francisco. The charter established a General Assembly of all members to determine policy, a decision-making Security Council of eleven nations to supervise "the maintenance of international peace," and various economic, social, and legal agencies. Permanent Security Council seats were reserved for the United States, the Soviet Union, China, Great Britain, and France, each with a right to veto any council action; the remaining six seats were filled by election from among the other member states. The fact that the United States and the Soviet Union belonged to the UN was a promising contrast to the League of Nations, but the conflict between them dominated international relations even within the UN, where the superpowers competed for the support of Asian, African, and Latin American nations.

◆ EUROPE DIVIDED

The conflict between communists and opponents of communism divided Europe, domestically between the national parties of Left and Right, then more deeply between two sets of values and ideology, and ultimately between Eastern European nations dominated by the USSR and Western ones allied with the United States. With the fall of fascism, communists enjoyed the prestige of having played a central part in most resistance movements, and communist calls for social justice and greater democracy resonated with postwar idealism. Quickly, however, nearly every disagreement between communists and anticommunists became part of a larger power struggle.

Eastern Europe: New Communist Regimes At war's end, Soviet troops occupied Eastern Europe from the Adriatic to the Baltic. The three formerly independent states of Estonia, Latvia, and Lithuania became Soviet republics, and Russia annexed territory from East Prussia, Poland, Hungary, and Romania. In the ostensibly autonomous nations of Eastern Europe, the Soviets discouraged independent revolutions like those that had followed World War I but skillfully used social issues and crude coercion to establish governments friendly to them. Communist parties had considerable support throughout the region, and the common pattern was to build on that base, excluding prominent anticommunists from the governing coalition, then using propaganda campaigns and sudden arrests to drive noncommunists from a share of power. The result was a single-party dictatorship on the Soviet model that consolidated its position through purge trials and use of the secret police (see "Churchill Sees an Iron Curtain," p. 1093).

The USSR had an economic as well as a political purpose. Its production had sunk to less than two-thirds of prewar levels, and the new Five-Year Plan of 1946 openly depended on ransacking occupied areas, especially in the eastern zone of Germany. Early in 1946 the Russians forced a merger of East Germany's Social Democratic party with the smaller Communist party, and Soviet control was soon complete. After expropriating much of German industry and restricting trade with the West, the Russians gradually allowed increased industrial activity in the eastern zone and in 1949 gave it independent status as the German Democratic Republic. Germany had been divided in two.

In Romania the communists forced King Michael into exile late in 1947. Poland, where the communists were weakest, had been promised free elections, but repressive measures weakened the Peasant party in the elections of 1947. It was soon purged, and the largest party of Independent Socialists subordinated to the communist Workers' party. The government could then put a Russian in command of the army and attack the Catholic Church. The president and the foreign minister of Czechoslovakia, Eduard Beneš and Jan Masaryk, were the heirs of a notable democratic tradition. But the Communists were the largest party, and when in 1948 they threatened to take over the country, Beneš gave way and Masaryk died in a mysterious fall from a window. Hungary's coalition government, which had an anti-Communist majority, lost to the Communists in a dubious election in 1949. In each of these cases Britain and the United States protested, with little effect, and the new regimes established close links with the Soviet Union. By 1950 Albania and Bulgaria were also solid members of the communist bloc.

Only Yugoslavia followed a different course. Marshal Tito easily won the 1945 national election, and communists dominated the government, but Tito resisted Soviet efforts to influence his foreign and domestic policies. After having joined the Cominform, which had replaced the Comintern and was similarly designed to coordinate international communist activity, Yugoslavia broke with its neighbors in 1948, using ties with the West to resist economic and political pressure from the East—an example to others of how small states could use the tense balance between the superpowers.

Western Europe: The Politics of the Past Despite well-intentioned talk of radical change, most

CHURCHILL SEES AN IRON CURTAIN

◆

On March 5, 1946, Winston Churchill gave a speech at Westminster College in Fulton, Missouri, that immediately received worldwide attention. After years of official emphasis on the cooperation among the wartime Allies, its directness was shocking. In effect, it announced the Cold War.

"A shadow has fallen upon the scenes so lately lighted by the Allied victory. Nobody knows what Soviet Russia and its Communist international organization intends to do in the immediate future, or what are the limits, if any, to their expansive and proselytizing tendencies. I have a strong admiration and regard for the valiant Russian people and for my wartime comrade, Marshal Stalin. There is deep sympathy and goodwill in Britain—and I doubt not here also—towards the peoples of all the Russias and a resolve to persevere through many differences and rebuffs in establishing lasting friendships. We understand the Russian need to be secure on her western frontiers by the removal of all possibility of German aggression. We welcome Russia to her rightful place among the leading nations of the world. We welcome her flag upon the seas. Above all, we welcome constant, frequent and growing contacts between the Russian people and our own people on both sides of the Atlantic. It is my duty, however, for I am sure you would wish me to state the facts as I see them to you, to place before you certain facts about the present position in Europe.

"From Stettin in the Baltic to Trieste in the Adriatic, an iron curtain has descended across the Continent. Behind that line lie all the capitals of the ancient states of Central and Eastern Europe. Warsaw, Berlin, Prague, Vienna, Budapest, Belgrade, Bucharest and Sofia, all these famous cities and the populations around them lie in what I must call the Soviet sphere, and all are subject in one form or another, not only to Soviet influence but to a very high and, in many cases, increasing measure of control from Moscow. " . . . An attempt is being made by the Russians in Berlin to build up a quasi-Communist party in their zone of Occupied Germany by showing special favours to groups of left-wing German leaders. At the end of the fighting last June, the American and British Armies withdrew westwards, in accordance with an earlier agreement, to a depth at some points of one hundred and fifty miles upon a front of nearly four hundred miles, in order to allow our Russian allies to occupy this vast expanse of territory which the Western Democracies had conquered.

"If now the Soviet Government tries, by separate action, to build up a pro-Communist Germany in their areas, this will cause new serious difficulties in the British and American zones, and will give the defeated Germans the power of putting themselves up to auction between the Soviets and the Western Democracies. Whatever conclusions may be drawn from these facts—and facts they are—this is certainly not the Liberated Europe we fought to build up. Nor is it one which contains the essentials of permanent peace."

Reprinted in Brian MacArthur, *The Penguin Book of Twentieth-Century Speeches* (New York: Viking, 1992) and available in many other places.

Western countries returned to prewar patterns of parliamentary life and multiple parties (although Spain and Portugal remained defiant dictatorships). The new constitutions of France and Italy spoke of the right to work, guaranteed social as well as civil rights, and at last gave women the vote. West Germany's federal structure and its two dominant parties, the Christian Democrats and the Social Democrats, recalled the pre-Nazi Weimar Republic. Everywhere social programs received much attention, but reconstruction took precedence over reform.

Ironically, at war's end Germany's industry was in better shape than that of any other continental nation, and the Allies soon relaxed restrictions on its economic activity. Early in 1949 they acknowledged the division of Germany and recognized the western sectors that Britain, France, and the United States had occupied as the Federal Republic of Germany. For the next fourteen years, Konrad Adenauer, the head of the Christian Democrats, served as chancellor. Mayor of Cologne from 1917 to 1933, he was seventy-three years old in 1949, a firm and conservative leader closely allied with the United States, who promoted an atmosphere of efficient calm.

Italy, too, became a republic when a majority of the electorate voted in 1946 to replace a monarchy tainted by Fascism. As the largest party, the Christian Democrats gave Alcide De Gasperi, prime minister from 1945 to 1953, a solid basis from which to govern. A wily politician, he successfully ostracized the Communists—the largest Communist party in the West—and took advantage of a split among Socialists to bring Italy into close alliance with the United States. Winning the crucial elections of 1948, with the help of heavy American pressure, he launched a program of moderate reform intended to lessen poverty in southern Italy and to stimulate industry in the north. Italian politics had returned to the unheroic tradition of parliamentary maneuver the Fascists had overturned.

France's Fourth Republic looked much like the Third. The new constitution kept the president subordinate to the legislature as in the past, and the domineering De Gaulle was soon pushed from office as provisional president. Although an effective program of massive reconstruction got quickly under way, the problems of unstable governments, labor agitation, and communist intransigence got more attention. The parliamentary maneuvers necessary to win thin and uncertain majorities soon fostered disillusionment with the Fourth Republic.

Without constitutional change, Britain's postwar politics in many respects brought greater change than did the newer continental governments. Churchill was defeated in the elections of 1945, as the nation turned away from wartime unity and sacrifice. With an enormous majority, the Labour party under Clement Attlee launched a massive program of nationalization, taking over the Bank of England and a wide range of major industries, including coal, transportation, electricity, and iron and steel. It also instituted extensive welfare programs and established public housing, national insurance, and free medical care for all. True to its principles, the Labour government also began Britain's withdrawal from the empire to which men like Churchill had been so attached.

The Cold War   A turning point came in 1947 when distrust between the Soviet Union and the United States hardened into a worldwide military, political, and ideological conflict quickly dubbed the Cold War. As Russia tightened its grip on Eastern Europe, the American president announced the Truman Doctrine, promising military and economic aid to nations in danger of communist takeover. His immediate concern was the civil war in Greece, where local communists were aided by neighboring Yugoslavia. The United States also sought bases in Turkey, for Britain could no longer sustain its power and influence in the eastern Mediterranean, and the United States replaced Britain as the leading anticommunist force there. American money and supplies poured into Greece, and this combined with Yugoslavia's break with Russia enabled the Greek government to crush the opposition by 1949. Turkey, slowly moving toward democracy, received similar assistance. Opposing communism and Soviet influence had become the focus of American policy.

A few months after the announcement of the Truman Doctrine, Secretary of State George Marshall unveiled an imaginative plan to stimulate European recovery and overcome the postwar economic crisis in which communism was likely to prosper. The United States would offer massive economic aid to all nations still recovering from the war. Remarkably, communist governments were eligible, too, but Russia forbade their participation and established its own Council of Mutual Economic Assistance (Comecon) instead. Even aid was a Cold War issue. In the West, Communist parties opposed the Marshall Plan despite its obvious benefits, and the United States used its growing influence to see that communists were excluded from coalition governments in France and Italy. That happened in 1947, and West Germany banned the party itself in 1956. The two halves of Europe followed the lead of their powerful patrons.

Escalating Confrontation   Fearful of the growing German economy and of American support for anticommunist movements everywhere, the Soviet Union tightened its hold over the states of Eastern Europe. Suddenly, in June 1948, the Soviets closed off overland access to Berlin, which they saw as a dangerous outpost of Western power. War seemed imminent. The United States responded with an extraordinary airlift: For nearly a year, until the Soviets backed down, a steady stream of flights ferried in all of West Berlin's supplies.

▲ The world was as impressed as the children of Berlin by the airlift that carried supplies to the city and completed 277,264 flights in a year.
Fenno Jacobs/Black Star

When the Soviet Union tested its own atomic bomb in 1949, the United States announced that work had begun on the even more devastating hydrogen bomb. But the loss of a monopoly on atomic weapons made ground forces that did not depend on using them an essential deterrent to Soviet aggression. Consequently, in 1949 the North Atlantic Treaty Organization (NATO) was created to coordinate the military planning of the United States, Canada, and ten Western European nations,[3] which now received U.S. military aid. The Soviets replied with the Warsaw Pact of communist states in 1955.

At first, the Cold War was primarily a conflict over Europe, waged as a competition for public opinion as well as international power. But with Eastern Europe isolated behind what Churchill called an "iron curtain" and communists excluded from political power in the West, the focus of the Cold War shifted. When the communist North Koreans invaded South Korea in 1950, the United States at once asked the United Nations to intervene, and the UN (with the USSR temporarily absent) called for an international army to stop the North Koreans. The Cold War was now worldwide. Having marked the lessened autonomy of the European nations, it spread to colonial issues and conflicts in the Middle East and Asia (see "The Soviet Union Denounces the United States While Calling for Arms Reduction," p. 1098).

---

[3]Great Britain, France, Belgium, the Netherlands, Luxemburg, Italy, Portugal, Denmark, Norway, and Iceland were the European members. Greece and Turkey would be added in 1952; West Germany, in 1955.

▲ MAP 29.5 COLD WAR ALLIANCES AND CONFLICT

◆ DECOLONIZATION

Although many Allied leaders believed that with some concessions they could restore their empires, the contrary pressures proved too strong. During the war, Japan had taken Indonesia from the Dutch, Indochina from France, and much of Malaysia from Britain. The Vichy government had lost touch with much of France's empire during the war, and both Stalin and President Roosevelt let De Gaulle know they did not favor France's return to Vietnam. Indeed, the United States was traditionally unsympathetic to European empires, and the Soviet Union not only denounced imperialism but frequently aided colonial uprisings.

The Opposition to Empire Nationalist movements opposed to colonial rule had been developing since before World War I, especially in Algeria, India, Indonesia, and Vietnam. These movements gained strength with their experience in combat during two world wars and with the wartime concessions won from their European rulers. European-educated statesmen and intellectuals—like Jawaharlal Nehru in India, Léopold Sedar Senghor in Senegal, Sékou Touré in Guinea, and Franz Fanon and Aimé Césaire from the West Indies—built a powerful following at home and appealed to European intellectuals and reformers through writings that explored the profound destructiveness of imperialism. The language and tactics of these movements stressed liberty and self-determination while exposing injustice and selfish interests. Within the Netherlands, France, and Britain, the opponents of imperialism (primarily from parties on the left) grew stronger, their positions reinforced by the public's greater interest in having money spent on reconstruction at home.

For all that, withdrawal was piecemeal and often reluctant. Even in the Middle East, where during the war Britain and France had promised independence to Lebanon and Syria, the two imperial powers continued to jockey for position before withdrawing in 1946. Trans-Jordan became independent. Foreign troops left Iraq and Iran, and negotiations began for British forces to depart from Egypt and the Sudan. Great Britain also undertook the creation of separate Jewish and Muslim states in Palestine, despite Arab hostility, removing their troops in May 1948, amid mounting terror campaigns from both sides. Arab forces invaded the day the British left but were driven back. The United Nations, eager to provide Jews a refuge following Nazi persecution, endorsed the creation of an Israeli state, and UN mediators were able to bring about a shaky truce that confirmed Israel's existence.

The Global Pattern Where imperial rule was direct and of long standing, colonial officials offered concessions that somehow always came a little too late or led to demands for more. When they used force, opposition tended to increase, not only on the scene but around the world. News of effective resistance in one colony stimulated new protests and risings in others around the world. Efforts to censor the news and renewed campaigns against subversive agitators only increased their following and cost support of native local elites. Eventually it became clear that once fighting broke out, colonial rule was unlikely to survive, for the subject peoples were generally more determined and more willing to risk their lives than their former rulers.

But pulling out of empire was not easy. Mohandas K. Gandhi gained worldwide admiration for his personal qualities and his spiritual message, and that contributed greatly to the movement that forced Britain to grant independence to India in 1947. Neither Gandhi nor the British, however, could prevent the violent conflict between Hindus and Muslims that led to an independent Pakistan. Sri Lanka (Ceylon) and Burma gained their independence from Great Britain in the following year, but a major communist revolt broke out immediately afterward. Conflict in Malaya lasted from 1947 until complete British withdrawal in 1960, and Indonesia similarly won freedom from the Dutch in 1949 only after years of combat. Although France had officially recognized Vietnam as a free state in 1945, the French continued for a decade to fight for dominance over Indochina. The campaign for independence became entangled with revolutionary movements and Cold War interests. India tried to steer a middle course, and Pakistan committed to the West, but in Vietnam the French-educated communist leader Ho Chi Minh organized a brilliant guerrilla campaign to unify the nation. The United States then encouraged France to defeat him, a costly war that ended only with the capture of a major French base at Dien Bien Phu in 1954 and French withdrawal from Vietnam. The Vietnamese communists got strong support from Russia and China, the most formidable of the newly communist states, where after long civil conflict the communists under Mao Zedong consolidated power in 1949. As a counterweight, the United States promoted the economic revival of a now democratic Japan and gave strong economic and military

The Soviet Union Denounces the United States While Calling for Arms Reduction

Andrei Vishinsky, the Russian delegate to the United Nations, spoke to the General Assembly on November 1, 1948, proposing steps toward arms reduction and control of atomic weapons. The address was testimony, however, to the global range of the Cold War. Most of it consisted of a lengthy denunciation of the policies of the United States, which was accused of undermining the United Nations; of intervening against democracy and peace in Korea, Greece, Indonesia, and Palestine; and of harming Europe's economy with the Marshall Plan while forming a military alliance with the nations of Western Europe aimed at the "freedom-loving" states of Eastern Europe.

"The policy of the USSR is a consistent and constant policy of expanding and strengthening international cooperation. This follows from the very nature of the Soviet State. A socialist State of workers and peasants deeply interested—a State, I repeat, which is deeply interested in the establishment of the most favorable conditions for peaceful creative work in the building of a socialist society. The foreign policy of the Soviet Union pursues the course of co-operation among all countries prepared for peaceful cooperation. The USSR consistently fights against any plan and measures and designs intended to create a gap, a cleavage, among peoples. It fights for the realization and implementation of democratic principles which were born out of the war.

"Such is not the case with the present foreign policy of the United States. After the termination of the recent war, the Government of the United States has changed its foreign policy: from a policy of fighting against aggressive forces, the United States has passed over to a policy of expansion. It is now attempting to realize plans for world domination. It is in open support in various countries of the most reactionary and monarchofascist regimes and groups and rendering to them systematic aid with money and armaments for the suppression of democratic national liberation movements in these countries; organization of military alliances or blocs, the construction of new military air and naval bases as well as the expansion and reconstruction in accordance with the newest military technical requirements of old bases established during the war with Germany, Japan, and Italy; furthermore, unchecked propaganda of a new war against the Soviet Union and the new democracies of Eastern Europe; a wild race of armaments; a true worship of the cult of the atomic bomb and allegedly a means of escape from all the dangers and misfortunes threatening the capitalistic world: these are the principal aspects, the characteristic features, of the foreign policy of the United States of America at present.

"Such a policy is inciting the psychosis of war, sowing restlessness and fear among the broad masses which strive for peace and peaceful creative labor. Such a policy has nothing in common whatsoever with a policy of peace.

"[A] . . . map by the ESSO Company of New York is of the same insolently arrogant and war-inciting nature. This map is published by the Standard Oil Company of New Jersey. It is called, quite provocatively, 'The Map of the Third World War.' That is what they are publishing in the United States—the Map of the Third World War! They are handing them out to motorists. This map, with provocatively militant appeals, carries the heading: 'Pacific Theatre of Military Operations.' The map is an example of the malicious war propaganda against the Soviet Union and the new democracies of East Europe.

" . . . The reactionary circles of the United States and the United Kingdom as well as of countries such as France, Belgium, and others, do not confine themselves to slander and abuse alone. This campaign is now being headed not only by amateurs from the family of retired politicians, statesmen, Senators and Members of Parliament, but also by persons now holding high official posts in the Governments of the United States, the United Kingdom, France and some other countries.

" . . . On the instructions of the Soviet Union Government the delegation of the USSR proposes to the General Assembly, for the purpose of strengthening the cause of peace and removing the menace of a new war which is being fomented by expansionists and other reactionary elements, the adoption of the following resolution:

" . . . as the first step in the reduction of armaments and armed forces to reduce by one-third during one year all present land, naval, and air forces. . . .

" . . . to prohibit atomic weapons as weapons intended for aims of aggression and not for those of defense;

" . . . to establish within the framework of the Security Council an international control body for the purpose of the supervision and control of the implementation of . . . [these] measures. . . . "

Speech by Andrei Y. Vishinsky to the United Nations, November 1, 1948, from *Vital Speeches of the Day*, Vol. 15, No. 2 (New York: City News Pub. Co., 1949).

◄ **Lord Mountbatten, war hero and England's last Viceroy of India, speaks to India's Constituent Assembly on the day India became independent, August 18, 1947.**
Hulton Archive/Getty Images

support to Taiwan (a large island off China still held by the Chinese nationalists). The Americans also promoted a Pacific equivalent to NATO in the Southeast Asia Treaty Organization (SEATO), in which Britain, Pakistan, Australia, New Zealand, and various Asian states joined with the United States in common defense. The Cold War, like decolonization, had a global reach.

In Africa, European officials, business people, and residents did what they could to prolong European rule with grants of autonomy and promises of aid, but they could only delay the inevitable. Britain acceded to Ghana's independence in 1957, but resistance and conflict were much greater where there were many residents of European descent. The fight over Algerian independence created a crisis in France (see below). Kenya won independence from Britain in 1963 only after years of costly warfare, and Britain had to use force in 1979 to overturn white-supremacist rule in Rhodesia, which the new rulers renamed Zimbabwe. Most African states had won formal independence by the 1960s, although Portugal held on to its colonies longer at the price of a decade of fighting. That ended only in 1974 when a military coup in Portugal forced it to abandon its empire. Its prize colony, Angola, was almost immediately caught up in a civil war in which the

United States supported one side and the Soviet Union the other. Conflicts within the former colonies also tended to draw European states back into the political life of former colonies as local leaders appealed to old interests, and African nations often preferred to work with the European country from which they had gained independence rather than embrace the firm Cold War alignment that tended to come with American or Soviet aid.

Thus, Britain and France continued to influence affairs in their former colonies, especially in Africa, by taking advantage of diplomacy, economic interests, common languages, and similar educational, legal, and administrative institutions. Through the Commonwealth of Nations, Great Britain gathered its former colonies in an often influential international club, even if it could not always resolve conflicts between its own members (and even if Ireland refused to join on gaining independence in 1949). The *Union Française* even gave French-speaking former colonies a voice in France's domestic politics, but it hardly functioned as an empire, despite valuable connections with local elites. Cold War competition, which increased the amount of economic and military aid available, also helped keep corrupt and dictatorial regimes in power by playing the superpowers against each other. Foreign intervention did not end with the passing of European empires.

IV. European Recovery

By the early 1950s, European society had taken on a new look of health and stability. That in itself was an impressive achievement. Amid a remarkable economic revival, political life settled into familiar national patterns. An easing of international tension made it possible to agree on a peace treaty for Austria and the withdrawal of occupation forces in 1955, and the USSR granted diplomatic recognition to West Germany despite its having joined NATO. This welcome recovery remained circumscribed, however, by postwar realities. Reinvigorated economies depended heavily on old industries, new state programs, and the policies of the two superpowers. Political stability remained vulnerable to sharp ideological divisions and crises of regime. European nations had not regained their prewar autonomy.

◆ ECONOMIC GROWTH

Across Europe, economic growth from 1947 to 1957 was extraordinary, and it was connected to a distinctive European emphasis on the role of the state. National governments not only played a central economic role but developed social policies that set new standards for equity and well-being.

Postwar Gains   Despite the shortages of capital and supplies, the postwar situation provided some opportunities. European nations had access to a backlog of unexploited technology, including atomic power, the jet engine, television, antibiotics, and frozen foods. The very need to rebuild factories and transportation networks made it easier to adopt the most efficient methods and newest machinery. Similarly, the tragic displacement of millions of people increased the available skilled labor. Demographic developments also reflected Europe's remarkable resilience. Birthrates had actually increased during World War II in nonbelligerent nations and in England and France (in contrast to World War I) and declined less in Germany than during the previous war. This European "baby boom," though not so large as the

simultaneous one in the United States, lasted until 1963, helping to replace some of the losses of war and to expand domestic markets.

Stimulus from the Soviet Union and the United States   The recovery of Eastern Europe depended heavily on the Soviet Union. A strenuous effort enabled it to exceed prewar industrial output by 1953, and its leaders confidently predicted that the USSR would surpass the United States. As the economy expanded, however, the costs of administration increased disproportionately, and the inefficiencies of centralized management became more pronounced. Without a free market, planners had difficulty judging costs and performance. Agriculture was a major disappointment, and the cereal harvest of 1953 was only slightly larger than in 1913.

The Soviet Union nevertheless provided an important market and economic stimulus for the countries of the Communist bloc, which organized their economies along the Russian model. All but Poland collectivized farmlands, and all instituted five-year plans to achieve rapid industrialization. In varying degrees, these governments adopted some elements of a mixed economic system—"goulash socialism," as Hungary's compromise came to be called. The state retained ownership of most means of production, but managers operated within the structure of a largely free market and increased the production of consumer goods. Initially most successful in the already advanced economies of Czechoslovakia and East Germany, the model was generally adopted throughout Eastern Europe, which although dramatically less prosperous than the West, experienced the highest economic growth rate in its history by the 1950s.

The Western European nations looked for help to the United States. In 1946 the United States extended $4.4 billion in long-term credit to Great Britain and, subsequently, $1.2 billion to France. A year later the United States acknowledged that Europe's economic problems existed on a scale that threatened to undermine recovery and announced the Marshall Plan. Over the next four years, more than $15 billion was channeled into Europe under the direction of the Organization for European Economic Cooperation (OEEC), which eighteen Western states established for this purpose. That was followed by the European Payments Union, which regulated currency exchanges from 1950 to 1958. Europe's rapid recovery was made possible by this financial stability, by the planning the Marshall Plan required, and by the importation of goods from the United States the Plan provided for (which also benefited the American economy). In the three years from 1948 to 1950, the combined gross national product of the OEEC participants increased at an astonishing annual rate of 25 percent. By 1952 the gross product was approximately half again what it had been in 1938, and per capita income was a third higher. Western Europe had never been wealthier.

The Economic Role of the State   The increased economic importance of the public sector resulted in part from the extension of wartime measures and from immediate social needs after the war, but it also reflected a changed attitude toward government's role. Britain and France nationalized much of their heavy industry and their banking systems immediately after the war, and in Italy the new state inherited from Fascism the ownership of huge conglomerates that directed hundreds of firms in some of the critical sections of industry. West Germany alone made no effort to expand the number of state-owned industries, but there, too, the government had an important role (as it had during the war) in coordinating economic growth. State ownership gave no assurance of efficient management, good labor relations, or a high return on capital, but it encouraged governments to develop economic policies to guide both public and private enterprises in the interests of overall growth.

With the Monnet Plan (1946–1950), France set the model of loose but effective economic direction from the state (building on policies developed under the Vichy regime). Its advanced methods of national accounting and its highly trained corps of "technocrats" proved especially effective. Comparable plans were devised from Britain to Israel, especially in Scandinavian and Mediterranean countries. In West Germany the largest banks and a private trade association played a somewhat similar role through their close ties to government.

Nearly all European governments established programs to protect ordinary citizens and their families against sickness, impoverished old age, and unemployment. Great Britain provided the earliest and (Sweden excepted) probably the most complete example of what has come to be called the welfare state. Its cornerstone was the National Health Service, inaugurated in 1948, which assumed nearly the total cost of medical, dental, and hospital care for every citizen. Such programs were themselves an outcome of the war effort, which had lessened inequality in Britain (the diet of the very poor had actually improved). Continental governments also provided universal health care, family allowances with payments for minor children, housing programs, and a growing array of social services. By reducing insecurity, these measures also stimulated consumption. To meet their cost, states raised taxes and became more efficient in collecting them, in the process accumulating large reserves that they used for investment according to their economic plans.

◆ NEW POLITICAL DIRECTIONS

Greater well-being tended to favor more conservative policies. Only in Scandinavia did socialists continue in office. In Britain the Conservatives regained power in 1951 and kept it for the next thirteen years, ending rationing and lowering taxes but not undoing most of Labour's social program. In 1953 the coronation of Queen Elizabeth II was celebrated as the symbol of a new era of prosperity. Italy's Christian Democrats turned more to the right while keeping Communists isolated, and West Germany under Adenauer became a model of stable prosperity. Political changes in France and the Soviet Union were more dramatic.

The Crisis of France's Fourth Republic   France's multiparty system tended not to produce strong governments; yet in many respects the Fourth Republic performed very well. In 1954 an able prime minister of the center-left, Pierre Mendès-France, announced a dynamic program of political reform and social modernization and at the same time set about extricating France from Indochina. To some on the right, that seemed dangerous weakness, and the reform measures further antagonized an angry movement of small shopkeepers and farmers—people bypassed by the benefits of modernization. The electorate shifted away from the

▲ In January 1957 French paratroopers, searching for terrorists on the outskirts of Algiers, frisk a civilian in Arab clothing.
© Corbis

center toward Charles de Gaulle, the very symbol of strength and order, and to the communist left.

Given these social strains, the colonial crisis in Algeria proved fatal. From 1954 to 1958 the Algerian problem brought down more French governments than any other issue, and the uprising against French rule was growing. A French colony since 1830, Algeria had a sizable French population that had lived there for generations, and their insistence that Algeria should remain French had a patriotic appeal to many people in France. The question of what to do added another bitter, ideological division. Supporters of French rule emphasized the loyalty of French settlers and the atrocities committed by Algerian nationalists. French army officers who had been fighting colonial uprisings in Africa and Asia since 1945 saw

themselves, in the spirit of the Cold War, holding the line alone against worldwide communist plots. They took tougher measures in Algeria and denounced treacherous "politicians" ready to make concessions to Algerian nationalists. Leftists and intellectuals, however, were more outraged by the atrocities committed by the French army and at a democracy that would wage war against Algerians seeking to govern themselves.

The Fifth Republic When a group of French army officers seized political control in Algeria in 1958 and threatened to move against the French government, the National Assembly turned to De Gaulle as the man to unify the country and pacify the military insurgents. Saying he would once again serve the nation, he accepted extraordinary powers for six years (and led France for the next ten). De Gaulle then supported a new constitution, which was overwhelmingly approved by popular referendum in September 1958. It established the Fifth Republic as a presidential regime with a chief executive indirectly elected for a seven-year term. De Gaulle was chosen president two months later, and Gaullists became by far the largest party in parliament, where the Communists were reduced to a handful.

The president moved cautiously on the Algerian question, about which he had been shrewdly ambiguous. He quietly weakened and dispersed the leaders of the military revolt, only gradually revealing his willingness to accept Algerian self-determination, something three-quarters of the voters approved in a referendum held in January 1961. Infuriated, the most intransigent officers formed a secret army that for the next eighteen months employed terrorist tactics in both Algeria and France. Having arranged peace with the Algerian rebels, De Gaulle declared war on the army rebels, and by the end of 1962, they had disbanded. Algeria was independent, and France enjoyed the stability its voters had wanted.

The Soviet Union   After thirty years of dictatorship, Joseph Stalin died of a stroke in 1953. The shock and sense of loss in the Soviet Union was compounded by the problem of succession, something its communist government had faced only once before. It went surprisingly smoothly, and a form of collective leadership emerged. Only in 1956–1957 did it become clear that Nikita Khrushchev was the dominant figure. The competition for leadership involved two principal issues. Stalin's last years had brought heavy repression (with terror), ugly antisemitism, and a party line enforced on everything from socialist realism in the arts to the fallacious genetic theories of Trofim Lysenko. Many Russians wanted an end to such policies. The second issue was the standard of living, which had been sacrificed to the demanding goals of the latest five-year plan. Even Stalin had hinted that it might be time to increase consumption as well as build industry. Khrushchev had seemed conservative on the need for change, and his triumph showed again that control of the Communist party remained the key to power. Still, the infighting that brought him to the top, which included sudden dismissals and even executions, was followed not by purges but by the reassignment of his opponents to less prominent positions.

With a speech to the Twentieth Party Congress in 1956, Khrushchev established his surprising new direction. He attacked the "cult of personality" under Stalin, naming many of Stalin's excesses, his paranoid distrust, his interference in the conduct of war, and his responsibility for the purge trials of the 1930s. Nothing like it had occurred before. Myths that for a generation had been central to the nation's enormous sacrifices were suddenly unmasked. Khrushchev's charges circulated widely in secret and then more openly, with unsettling effects in the Soviet Union, Eastern Europe, and communist movements everywhere. Streets and squares were renamed; statues and pictures disappeared. With the thaw following Stalin's death,[4] a freer and more open society appeared in prospect. Although Khrushchev quickly clamped down on criticism amid rising complaints about domestic problems and rumblings from within the Soviet bloc, restraints were never again so rigid or arbitrary as they had been under Stalin. When the Soviet Union celebrated the fortieth anniversary of the Russian Revolution in 1957 by launching the world's first space satellite, Sputnik, the USSR's status as a state both powerful and stable seemed dramatically confirmed.

◆ THE INTERNATIONAL CONTEXT

Although Britain and France were on the Security Council and Scandinavians served as the UN's general secretaries until 1961, the United Nations reflected a redistribution of international power in which Europe was no longer dominant. Economic strength made Western European nations prominent in such international economic organizations as the International Monetary Fund and the Organization for Economic Cooperation and

---

[4]The metaphor of the thaw, which has come to be generally applied to these changes in domestic and foreign policy, is derived from a novel of that title written by the noted Russian fiction writer and journalist Ilya Ehrenburg.

Development (OEEC), in foreign aid, and in arms sales but did not lessen their subordination to the superpowers. Often restive individual nations sought to follow distinctive paths.

Forays at Independence　Not that the superpowers always had their way. To strengthen European defenses against the Soviet Union, the United States wanted Germany to rearm. That was something the French could hardly welcome and that the USSR was determined to prevent. Instead, France proposed a European Defense Community (EDC), in effect, a European army strengthened by German participation without the risks of a separate German army. The proposal was accepted by most of the European members of NATO and pushed by the United States. The British, however, were leery of permanent continental engagement, and growing doubts in France increased with resentment of unusually heavy American pressure. In 1954 the French parliament rejected the EDC.

Great Britain asserted its independence during a crisis in relations with Egypt, once a part of their empire. Gamal Abdel Nasser's government was distrusted in the West for its nationalism, its radical domestic program, and its willingness to accept aid from nations in the Communist bloc. When the Western powers, following the United States, refused aid for the construction of a high dam across the Nile at Aswan, Nasser nationalized the Suez Canal, still owned by a British-controlled company. Britain responded strongly and, after efforts at compromise broke down, conspired with Israel and France to take military action. Israel attacked Egypt in October 1956 and occupied the banks of the canal, aided by an Anglo-French bombardment. Because both the Soviet Union and the United States opposed the entire venture, the United Nations was able to force a ceasefire within a week and the withdrawal of foreign troops shortly afterward. This return to old imperialist tactics merely demonstrated that such tactics no longer worked and that British and French action required American acquiescence. That remained true even though Britain soon became the third nation to possess a hydrogen bomb and France would later be the fourth.

The Soviet Bloc　The Communist governments of Eastern Europe had closely mimicked Soviet rule in the ruthless use of secret police and internment camps, in the idolization of Stalin, and in general policy. But resentment of the USSR's exploitation became more public after Stalin's death. Within three months, the workers of East Berlin took to the streets in a general strike, protesting the increased production quotas they blamed on the Soviet Union. Russian tanks rushed in to put down the revolt, but it had long-lasting effects. Walter Ulbricht became the new leader of East Germany and offered a program of higher wages and better living conditions even while strengthening the dictatorship. Although still tightly tied to the Soviet Union, East Germany expanded its trade with West Germany and developed a voice of its own in the councils of communist countries.

A workers' protest in Poland in 1956 even won support from nationalists within the Communist party. Once again Soviet forces intervened and this time to public jeers. The Polish Communist party then elected its secretary, Wladyslaw Gomulka, in preference to the pro-Russian candidate. Gomulka retained power until 1970 by convincing the Soviets of his loyalty while arguing that socialist states needed to follow distinctive national paths. Poland demanded and got a share of the war reparations that Germany paid, negotiated economic aid from the United States, and mitigated its repression of the Catholic Church and of Polish intellectuals.

Risings in Hungary ended more tragically. Riots in October 1956 were fiercely anti-Russian, and the Soviet troops at first withdrew from Budapest, seemingly disposed to accept Hungary's increased autonomy. Then Imre Nagy, who had been arrested the year before for "right-wing deviationism," became premier. Bowing to popular pressure, he agreed to replace the alliance with Russia with a policy of neutrality. The Soviet leaders pressured, threatened, and finally sent their army to crush the revolution. It did so in ten days of bitter fighting while rebel radio stations pleaded for the Western aid that many Hungarians expected. None came, and Hungary suffered a heavy-handed, repressive Soviet occupation.

▲ Soviet tanks occupy the streets of Budapest; the uprising of October 1956 had been crushed.
© Corbis

Nagy himself was eventually executed, and a new wave of refugees left the country; yet his successor, Janos Kadar, slowly led the country on a more national course.

Washington denounced Russian imperialism but remained preoccupied with the crisis over the Suez Canal within its own alliance, in effect acknowledging a Soviet sphere of influence. The USSR would not allow satellite regimes to defy Soviet policy. Yugoslavia remained the great exception, and improved relations with Khrushchev did not affect Yugoslavia's trade with the West nor its experiments at decentralization. Albania, isolated from the Soviet sphere by geography, and the most backward country on the continent, formed closer ties to communist China as a kind of challenge to the USSR. Romania, like Bulgaria among the most Stalinist of the satellite regimes, distanced itself slightly by seeking better relations with the West. Little more was possible.

Bipolar Stability The Warsaw Pact and the NATO alliance institutionalized the armed confrontation between the superpowers in Europe. For some thirty years their competition shaped international relations, at times becoming a rigid opposition and at others allowing some flexibility. In 1961 East-West tension was literally cast in stone when East Germany built a long gray wall across the center of Berlin, eventually extending it along East Germany's entire western border. As a symbol and as a device to keep East Germans from leaving, the wall fostered international distrust. There was a still more ominous crisis in 1961, when the United States sponsored an invasion of Cuba aimed at the overthrow of Fidel Castro. It failed, and in the following year the Russians began to base missiles on Cuba. War seemed imminent until, as the Americans massed their fleet, the Soviets withdrew their missiles. There was, after all, a mutual interest in not disturbing the balance of power, and the Soviet Union was facing a growing rift with China that made diplomatic exchanges with the United States more attractive.

Literally in the middle, European governments used their influence to favor East-West negotiations at summit conferences and on specific issues. They promoted agreements on space exploration in 1967, the beginning of the Strategic Arms Limitation Talks in 1969, and on the principles of human rights at the Helsinki Conference in 1975. Through trade, loans, and technical agreements, the governments of Western Europe encouraged those of Eastern Europe toward whatever autonomy from the Soviet Union they were willing to attempt.

National Interests   Individual states continued to probe ways to serve their interests. West Germany gradually asserted some of the political weight that its wealth implied. Less committed to the Cold War than Adenauer had been, Willy Brandt skillfully negotiated a new opening to the East. The resulting treaty between West Germany and the Soviet Union, signed in 1970, was a milestone that earned Brandt the Nobel peace prize. While allowing for a peaceful reunification of Germany as a possibility, it accepted West Germany's eastern boundary, pointed to a normalization of the status of Berlin (still divided between Soviet and Western occupation), and paved the way for extensive relations between West Germany and the governments of Eastern Europe. By 1981–1982 this increased trade culminated in the agreement to build a natural gas pipeline from Russia to Germany, Italy, and France.

Great Britain emphasized its close ties to the United States rather than to Europe, and the Scandinavian countries tended to position themselves as friends of nonaligned countries and mediators between the superpowers. The most flamboyant search for an independent policy was De Gaulle's. Resentful of American policy toward France, he set upon a course that by 1966 led to the withdrawal of French forces from NATO command (and of NATO forces from French soil), although France remained a member of the alliance. France also strengthened its relations with Eastern Europe and increased its aid to developing nations. Greater independence from American policy appealed to many others in the West, especially on the left, and in 1981 nearly half a million young people in Bonn and perhaps another million in other capitals marched to demand that Europe be freed of the nuclear weapons of either side.

SUMMARY

◆

Europe's war, like its ideological divisions, had spread around the world, and it had taken a worldwide mobilization to defeat the Axis. The exhausting triumph over Fascism and Nazism was costly. Afterward, European nations recovered with astonishing speed and on the whole adjusted realistically to the loss of empire and of their former international preeminence. The Cold War's ideological and geographical division of Europe became a familiar if often uncomfortable fact of life. Neither communism nor democratic capitalism managed to create the societies they promised, and neither prosperity nor carefully contrived political stability necessarily resolved old conflicts. Europe had recovered from the war, but its economic, social, and cultural place in the modern world remained unclear.

QUESTIONS FOR FURTHER THOUGHT

◆

1. Initially, new technologies and tactics made a crucial difference in the course of the war, but was the later course of the war reminiscent of, even a continuation of, World War I?

2. How would you compare the problems of reconstruction after World War II and the responses to them to the period of reconstruction after World War I? What was learned from that recent history?

3. To what extent were American and Western European policies partly responsible for the Cold War?

4. How do you explain the remarkable elements of historical continuity in European society and politics before and after the war?

RECOMMENDED READING

◆

Sources

*Churchill, Sir Winston S. *The Second World War.* 6 vols. 1948–1954. Each volume of Churchill's detailed account can be read singly, and all are rich in documents. His masterly prose (he was awarded the Nobel prize for literature in 1953) recaptures the drama and meaning of the century's greatest war.

*Frank, Anne. *Diary of a Young Girl.* 1947. The unvarnished thoughts of a Jewish girl hiding in Amsterdam during the Nazi occupation, valuable as historical evidence and as a moving expression of human dignity.

Hitler's Table-Talk. Hugh Trevor-Roper (ed.). 1988. Isolated in his headquarters, Hitler liked at mealtime to discourse on all sorts of topics with his closest aides. From 1941 to 1944 he allowed notes to be taken on these discussions, and this book is a translation of the transcript, edited by his secretary, Martin Bormann. Hitler's opinionated ramblings and reminiscences have a chilling fascination.

Monnet, Jean. *Memoires.* 1978. The chief architect of the European Community here reveals the intellectual roots of his vision and the personal style that made him so effective.

Studies

Allsop, Kenneth. *The Angry Decade: A Survey of the Cultural Revolt of the 1950s.* 1969. Captures very well the postwar disillusionment that undermined political and social consensus.

*Aron, Raymond. *The Imperial Republic: The United States and the World, 1945–1973.* 1974. A leading French thinker of the time analyzes the period of American dominance.

Brown, Colin, and Peter J. Mooney. *Cold War to Détente, 1945–1980.* 1981. A largely narrative account of relations between the superpowers.

Calvocaressi, Peter. *The British Experience, 1945–1975.* 1978. A comprehensive study of British life in a period of imperial decline and economic difficulty.

Carr, Raymond. *The Civil War in Spain.* 1986. A comprehensive and unusually balanced study that effectively uses recent research to put the events of the war in the context of Spanish history and international relations.

Chambers, John Whiteclay, II, and David Culbert (eds.). *World War II, Film and History.* 1996. A study of the formation of popular images.

*Clendinnen, Inga. *Reading the Holocaust.* 1999. A beautifully written discussion of what the Holocaust meant to perpetrators and victims as reflected in memoires and fiction.

Colton, Joel C. *Léon Blum: Humanist in Politics.* 1966. The biography of this appealing figure is particularly useful for the period of the Popular Front.

*Crossman, Richard H. (ed.). *The God That Failed.* 1950. The moving testimony of former Marxists about their lost faith during the era of Stalin; in itself a document of the Cold War.

*Crouzet, Maurice. *The European Renaissance since 1945.* 1971. An optimistic essay on the politics, society, and culture of postwar Europe reflecting the hopes that underlay the years of prosperity and the growth of the European Community.

*Dahrendorf, Ralf. *Society and Democracy in Germany.* 1969. A German sociologist assesses the special qualities of German society and its implications for the postwar West German republic.

Dawidowicz, Lucy S. *The War against the Jews, 1933–1945.* 1976. An extensive and thoughtful consideration of the twentieth century's greatest horror.

*DePorte, A. W. *Europe between the Superpowers.* 1979. A stimulating assessment of Europe's place in the postwar bipolar system.

Fejto, François. *A History of the People's Democracies: Eastern Europe since Stalin.* 1971. A careful study of the conflicts and variety among Eastern European states under Soviet dominance.

Geyer, Michael, and John Boyer (eds.). *Resistance against the Third Reich, 1933–1990.* 1994. Sober assessments of the strengths and limits of German opposition to Nazism.

Grosser, Alfred. *The Western Alliance: European-American Relations since 1945.* 1983. A clear-headed account of how international relations have worked in practice.

*Hoffman, Stanley, et al. *In Search of France.* 1965. A group of distinguished scholars attempt to define the unique patterns of French political and social life and to explain the significance of the Fifth Republic.

Iriye, Akira. *Cultural Internationalism and World Order.* 1997. Thoughtfully surveys efforts to foster international cooperation from the nineteenth century to the present that adds to the understanding of the world wars, the international agencies founded after each, and the Cold War.

Knox, MacGregor. *Mussolini Unleashed, 1939–41: Politics and Strategy in Fascist Italy's Last War.* 1982. A thorough and insightful analysis of Fascist foreign policy and strategic aims as well as of the regime's many weaknesses in pursuing them.

La Feber, Walter. *America, Russia, and the Cold War.* 1967. Consistently argues for the responsibility of the United States in creating the Cold War.

Jackson, Julian. *France: The Dark Years, 1940–1944.* 2001. The most comprehensive and balanced account.

Lagrou, Pieter. *The Legacy of Nazi Occupation: Patriotic Memory and National Recovery in Western Europe, 1945–1965.* 1999. A comparative study of how France, Belgium, and the Netherlands dealt with the impact of Nazi occupation as they undertook postwar reconstruction.

*Laqueur, Walter. *Europe since Hitler.* 1982. One of the ablest surveys of the foundations of contemporary Europe that sees Europe as a whole.

*Liddell-Hart, Basil H. *History of the Second World War.* 1980. The crowning work of this renowned strategist and military historian.

*Maier, Charles S. *In Search of Stability: Explorations in Historical Political Economy.* 1987. Essays relating economic interests to the ambitions, limitations, and bitter divisions of European politics between the wars.

*——— (ed.). *The Origins of the Cold War and Contemporary Europe.* 1978. Essays by leading scholars seeking not so much to lay blame for the Cold War but to study its connection to domestic societies.

*Mason, Tim, and Jane Caplan (eds.). *Nazism, Fascism, and the Working Class.* 1995. Ten essays engage leading historical interpretations on fascism and social class.

Middlemas, Keith. *Power, Competition, and State.* Vol. 1: *Britain in Search of Balance, 1940–1961.* 1986. A clear assessment of the pressures that shaped British society and politics.

Milward, Alan S. *The Reconstruction of Western Europe, 1945–1951.* 1984. Concludes that the economic boom of the 1950s and 1960s began as early as 1945, through the role of government policy in establishing international economic interdependence.

*———. *War, Economy, and Society, 1939–1945.* 1977. Examines the interdependence of economic planning and military strategy and its implications for the postwar period.

*Neff, Donal. *Warriors at Suez.* 1981. Well-researched and comprehensive, this dramatic account by a journalist focuses on the political leaders of the nations involved in the highly significant crisis of 1956.

*Paxton, Robert. *Vichy France: Old Guard and New Order, 1940–1944.* 1972. Stresses the continuity and lasting significance for French society and institutions of this twilight period.

*Payne, Stanley G. *The Franco Regime, 1936–1975.* 1987. A fair-minded account that sees the bases of Spain's subsequent transformation in Franco's later years.

Postan, Michael M. *An Economic History of Western Europe, 1945–1964.* 1967. A noted economic historian analyzes the roots of European recovery.

Rioux, Jean-Pierre. *The Fourth Republic, 1945–1958.* 1987. A close look at and a critical assessment of the politics of the period.

Sherwin, M. J. A. *A World Destroyed: The Atomic Bomb and the Grand Alliance.* 1975. A scholarly and balanced account of this controversial and complicated subject.

*Ulam, Adam B. *Expansion and Coexistence: The History of Soviet Foreign Policy, 1917–1973.* 1974. An expert appraisal of the consistent patterns and political pressures underlying Soviet policy.

Weinberg, Gerhard. *A World at Arms: A Global History of World War II.* 1994. Remarkably balanced and learned synthesis, attentive to political and economic as well as military aspects of the war.

Wilkinson, James D. *The Intellectual Resistance in Europe.* 1981. A wide-ranging and sensitive assessment of the content and legacy of the resistance and its place in contemporary thought.

*Winter, Jay, and Emmanuel Sivan. *War and Remembrance in the Twentieth Century.* 2000. A collection of essays on the cultural and psychological impact of war as a major element of modern history.

---

*Available in paperback.

▲ In November 1989 the East German government suddenly granted free access to West Berlin; the spontaneous celebrations that followed became the symbol of one of history's great turning points. The breach of the Berlin Wall seemed a victory as great as any commemorated by the Brandenburg Gate in the background.
D. Aubert/Corbis Sygma

THE NEW EUROPE

In the last third of the twentieth century, Europe entered on a new course, and 1957 marked a quiet turning point. The Soviet Union's achievement in launching Sputnik confirmed the equilibrium between the two superpowers and allowed renewed emphasis on raising the standard of living in the USSR and the Eastern European nations firmly in the Soviet orbit. In Western Europe the struggles over Algeria and Egypt were the last flurry of old imperial dreams and brought a new constitution in France and new policies and leaders in Britain. In retrospect, however, the event of 1957 with the greatest importance for the future was a treaty signed by six nations meeting in Rome. That agreement would grow into the European Union (EU), which has steadily expanded in authority and membership. To some of its members, the EU remains merely a set of international agreements. To others the new institutions constitute a fundamental change in the body politic.

Despite the economic "miracles" of the 1950s, there was good reason to wonder whether European economies could match the economic transformation occurring in North America or meet the demands of global capitalism. That Western Europe was able to do that requires explanation. At the same time, the social changes accompanying this transformation created new strains and highlighted issues of the environment, immigration, and persistent unemployment. Political systems had to deal with these challenges amidst increasing demands for greater democracy and social justice. The nations of Western Europe weathered the domestic crises of the 1960s and 70s with new policies and awkward compromises. Communist governments responded first with repression; then in the 1980s they, too, tried desperate compromise. Its outcome was their sudden collapse—a sweeping and unexpected transformation that affected all of Europe and much of the world.

This new Europe of open markets, international institutions, and easy movement across boundaries fosters a lively, self-aware culture. Affected by increased leisure, the growth in higher education, and the spread of mass media, it critically addresses new questions about the role of women, the meaning of identity, and the nature of culture itself.

CHAPTER 30. THE NEW EUROPE							
	Social Structure	Body Politic	Changes in the Organization of Production and in the Impact of Technology	Evolution of Family and Changing Gender Roles	War	Religion	Cultural Expression
I. THE NEW INSTITUTIONS		▓	▓				
II. POSTINDUSTRIAL SOCIETY	▓		▓	▓			▓
III. THE POLITICS OF PROSPERITY	▓	▓	▓	▓			
IV. THE END OF AN ERA	▓	▓					
V. CONTEMPORARY CULTURE				▓		▓	▓

I. The New Institutions

◆

Paradoxically, the bloodshed of World War II made it easier to see Western Europe as a cultural unit.[1] The Allies had talked a lot about the shared values of Western civilization. Postwar recovery in Western Europe featured transnational programs like the Marshall Plan, and the Cold War engendered further measures of cooperation, as in NATO. Thus, economic and military needs, cultural change, and an older idealism came together in the creation of new European institutions. Some doubt the durability of these new ventures; some see them as beginning a historic transformation, a new body politic. All agree that today, at least, they are a central fact of European life.

◆ CAUTIOUS BEGINNINGS

The Council of Europe Movements calling for some kind of European integration sprang up in many parts of Europe in the postwar period, and in 1948 a conference met in The Hague to consider the possibilities. A thousand delegates from twenty countries gathered for the meeting, which was chaired by Winston Churchill, who had spoken a few years earlier about the need for a United States of Europe. Division that continues to this day appeared from the first. Some (initially led by France and Belgium) wanted to create a European body with real political power, while others (primarily Great Britain and the Scandinavian countries) favored a kind of continuing conference.

The Council of Europe founded in the following year was a compromise. The foreign ministers of the member states, meeting in private, would constitute the Council. There would also be a merely consultative assembly, whose delegates eventually came to be selected by their national parliaments. Headquarters were established in Strasbourg; ten nations joined.[2] The new organization had no binding powers over its members; yet it did come to exercise some influence. A declaration of human rights, drawn up in 1950, went into effect in 1953 to safeguard "the ideals and principles of . . . [the members'] common heritage," and a European Court of Human Rights held its first hearing in 1960. Maintaining individual freedom and the rule of law was a requirement that excluded all the nations of Eastern

---

[1]Geographers list nineteen nations as belonging to Western Europe: Austria, Belgium, Denmark, Finland, France, Greece, Iceland, Ireland, Italy, Lichtenstein, Luxemburg, the Netherlands, Norway, Portugal, Spain, Sweden, Switzerland, the United Kingdom, and Germany. All of these countries save Finland now belong to the Council of Europe, which also includes Cyprus, Malta, and Turkey.

Belgium, Denmark, Iceland, Germany, Italy, Luxemburg, the Netherlands, Norway, Portugal, Turkey, the United Kingdom, Canada, and the United States belong to NATO. France and Greece are also NATO members, although their armed forces no longer are under NATO command.

[2]Belgium, France, the Netherlands, Luxemburg, the United Kingdom, Ireland, Italy, Denmark, Norway, and Sweden.

Europe as well as Spain, Portugal, and Greece while they were ruled by dictators.

Remarkably, the decisions of the Council and its Court of Justice have been obeyed by member states (Britain, for example, abolished corporeal punishment in schools as the result of a Council judgment). By 1970 eight more nations had joined, and the Council has gained authority over the years, playing an active part in aiding the nations of Eastern Europe before and after the breakup of communist regimes there. Today, some forty-one nations, from Russia to the Atlantic, including all the smallest ones, belong to the Council. Its assembly meets regularly in Strasbourg to establish general policies, where complaints against any member state are adjudicated. The aspirations it represents (the Council's anthem is Beethoven's "Ode to Joy") have made its flag a popular symbol on buildings and private automobiles across the continent.

The Coal and Steel Community Stronger transnational institutions proved hard to establish, however, and so two leaders who envisioned a more integrated Europe decided to begin with small steps. Jean Monnet, a leading French economist, and Robert Schuman, France's foreign minister, proposed creation of the French-German Coal and Steel Authority, and it was established in 1950. France was rich in iron ore and Germany in coal. For nearly a century the desire to control both had been a source of conflict. Now the Authority guaranteed each of them access to these resources. A year later, propelled by the euphoria of recovery, Italy and the three Benelux countries (Belgium, Luxemburg, and the Netherlands) joined to establish the European Coal and Steel Community (ECSC), which was given the power to coordinate the production and distribution of the coal and steel critical to industrial growth. That became the kernel of a common market.

As the ECSC demonstrated its economic value and as its authority increased, further steps became possible just as Monnet and Schuman had hoped. In the Treaty of Rome the six members of the ECSC created a new agency to coordinate the development of atomic energy (EURATOM) and agreed in gradual steps to eliminate tariffs between each other and to establish a common tariff toward goods from other nations. This was the European Economic Community (EEC). Its prospects were anything but certain. Britain refused to take part, and De Gaulle was less internationalist than his predecessors. Nevertheless, six nations that had often been at war now declared that they were "determined to lay the foundations of ever-closer union among the peoples of Europe . . . and to ensure economic and social progress by common action."

EEC vs. EFTA A dramatic rivalry followed. Reluctant to accept permanent political ties to the continent or to loosen its Commonwealth connections, Great Britain fostered the creation of the European Free Trade Association (EFTA). This looser association, which set more limited goals (free trade among its members, for example, but not a common tariff) and had very limited powers of enforcement, was joined by Sweden, Norway, Denmark, Austria, Switzerland, and Portugal. That put the two economic alliances in direct competition. Sweden, with the most socialist economic system, and Switzerland, with the most thoroughly free market system, already had the highest per capita incomes in the industrial world.

In the ensuing years the difference in growth rates proved telling. The United Kingdom remained last among major European countries while the states of the EEC enjoyed the highest increase in per capita productivity, more than 4 percent a year. By 1968 (sooner than its organizers had expected) all tariffs within the European Community had been abolished, and continued economic growth made it ever more attractive. The year before, the EEC's three organizations had been folded into a single entity, the European Community (EC). Its name, like its goals, now frankly reached beyond the merely economic.

The European Community After extended negotiations, Great Britain, Ireland, and Denmark joined the EC in 1973.[3] Twice before, Britain had sought membership, but with special concessions (to protect it from the Community's agricultural

---

[3]In a surprising referendum, Norwegians voted not to join the European Community, one of many signs of resistance to the EC's centralizing tendencies and to its domination by France and Germany—concerns that have been strongest in the Scandinavian countries and in Britain.

ICELAND

EU
EUROPEAN UNION

Members

Associate member

EFTA
EUROPEAN FREE TRADE ASSOCIATION

Members

Dates shown for members
added since 1960

NORWAY

SWEDEN
(1995)

FINLAND
(1995)

ESTONIA

RUSSIA

LATVIA

LITHUANIA

(RUS.)

NORTHERN
IRELAND

IRELAND
(1973)

DENMARK
(1973)

BELARUS

UNITED
KINGDOM
(1973)

NETHERLANDS

POLAND

UKRAINE

BELGIUM

GERMANY

LUXEMBOURG

CZECH REP.

SLOVAKIA

LIECHTEN-
STEIN

FRANCE

AUSTRIA
(1995)

HUNGARY

MOLDOVA

SWITZERLAND

SLOVENIA

CROATIA

ROMANIA

PORTUGAL
(1986)

BOSNIA-
HERZEGOVINA

YUGO-
SLAVIA

BULGARIA

SPAIN
(1986)

FMR. YUG. REP. OF
MACEDONIA

ITALY

ALBANIA

GREECE
(1981)

TURKEY

MOROCCO

CYPRUS

TUNISIA

ALGERIA

0   200   400 Miles

LIBYA

EGYPT

▲ **MAP 30.1B** EUROPEAN UNION AND EUROPEAN FREE TRADE ASSOCIATION, 1996

policies and to preserve its Commonwealth interests), only to be blocked by De Gaulle's opposition and by a general concern that separate arrangements could undermine the EC's coherence. Together, the nine members of the European Community surpassed the United States in the production of automobiles and steel, and by 1979 in total gross national product (GNP) as well. Fuller integration among the nine member-states came slowly, however.

Once again, the momentum for growth came more from evolving practices than dramatic decisions. The EC's executive is the Commission, to which each member nation appoints at least one member and the larger countries more. Members of the Commission are independent of any national government. The programs adopted by the Commission often set new precedents and have led to a large bureaucracy at its headquarters in Brussels. The heads of government of the EC countries began in 1972 to hold meetings several

times a year as the European Council, in itself an important step toward more coordinated policies. Every six months the head of a different government serves as president, and a tendency developed for presidents of the European Council to seek some new accomplishment to mark their term, another stimulus to expanded activity. New legislation proposed by the Commission must be approved by a Council of Ministers, specialists in the relevant fields, such as agriculture or finance, appointed by and responsible to the member governments. Clearly intended as a check on the EC's autonomy, the Council of Ministers was nevertheless empowered in the 1980s to set some policies by majority vote rather than unanimity.

At the same time the European parliament has gradually become more assertive. Despite its very limited powers, the creation of an elected parliament was hailed as "the birth of the European citizen." In 1979 the citizens of each member nation began voting directly for delegates to the

▼ **Flags of the member states fly outside the Brussels headquarters of the European Union.**
Steve Vidler/eStock Photo

Community's parliament, where the representatives sit according to political party rather than nationality.[4] Over the years parliament has begun to assert itself and to supervise the Commission more closely. The process of integration continued, with creation of a mechanism for regulating exchange rates and through the rulings of the EC's court. Thus, uniform regulations have spread to many fields (on standards of product quality, insurance, and environmental issues, for instance) and common legal rights (in the case, for example, of migrant workers).

Agricultural policy was especially controversial. The EC's subsidies, which had strong domestic support from farmers, resulted in costly stockpiles of unsold produce. Because Britain imports most of its food and has a smaller farm population, it contributed far more toward these costs than the EC spent in Britain. Its vigorous protests forced adjustments and then some reform of agricultural policies in 1981; but the issue was complicated by the further enlargement of the Community to include Greece in 1981 and Spain and Portugal in 1986, all countries with competing agricultural interests. Special grants to poorer regions—including the northwestern part of the British Isles, southern Italy, and the poorer members generally (Ireland, Portugal, Spain, and Greece)—have helped to bring those regions closer to the EC's general level of prosperity. As the Community gained a voice in matters traditionally considered the exclusive concern of national governments, especially social issues, domestic opposition to the EC tended to become more vocal.

◆ TOWARD EUROPEAN UNION

The Single Europe Act   The record of small steps and acrimonious debate even on minor issues

contrasted with the lofty rhetoric of the EC's supporters, and the Community's intangible impact was frequently ignored by politicians and dismissed by journalists. There was thus some surprise when Jacques Delors, the unusually effective president of the Commission in 1986, succeeded in winning support for the Single European Act, an agreement to create a single market. It declared that by the end of 1992 there would no longer be any restrictions within the Community on the movement of goods, services, workers, or capital. These terms were met, with minor exceptions, and they brought striking changes in the lives of ordinary people. Most of the border checkpoints between member states on the continent have disappeared. All citizens of the member states carry a community passport, crossing national boundaries without restriction. Any of them can open a bank account, take out a mortgage, receive medical care, or practice a profession anywhere in the EC, for in principle at least the licenses and university degrees of one country are recognized in all the others. Such measures strengthened established programs for educational exchange (hundreds of thousands of students now regularly study in another European country).

The Single European Act required that vast arrays of national regulations be made uniform. Social practice, however, was as important as any new directives. Anticipating European integration, businesses, government agencies, and schools set about on their own to bring their practices in line with those of the EC, forming ties with colleagues in other countries. Organizations and individuals began to think and operate in terms of the Community as a whole; and sensing this momentum, the leaders of the EC pressed for more.

The European Union   The Maastricht Treaty of 1992 changed the name of the EC to the European Union (EU) to indicate its greater integration, enlarged the powers of its parliament, and called for a coordinated foreign policy and the adoption of a common European currency by 1999. The public found all these changes and requirements a little overwhelming. Attitudes toward the EU tended to turn more negative wherever domestic economies faltered, and public opinion on the complex Maastricht treaty was so evenly divided in most countries that many questioned support

---

[4]The complexities of representation are exemplified by the fact that France, Great Britain, Italy, and West Germany were given eighty-one representatives each (a large enough number to ensure that Scotland and Wales had more representatives than did Denmark or Ireland). The Netherlands and Belgium were each allotted 25, but Belgium preferred 24 (so that the Flemings and Walloons would have equal representation), which meant a gift of 1 representative to Denmark, which has 16. Ireland has 15 representatives; Luxemburg, 6; Greece, 24; Portugal, 24; and Spain, 60.

Chronology

THE MAKING OF THE EUROPEAN UNION

1950 Germany and France form the Coal and Steel Authority.

1951 Italy and the Benelux nations join.

1957 The Treaty of Rome creates the European Economic Community of six nations.

1965 The EEC becomes the European Community.

1973 Great Britain, Ireland, and Denmark join the EC.

1979 Citizens elect the EC parliament.

1981 Greece joins the EC.

1986 Spain and Portugal join the EC.

1987 The Single Europe Act.

1992 Maastricht Treaty calls for European Union, common currency.

1995 Austria, Finland, and Sweden join the EU.

1999 Common currency, central bank takes effect.

for the EU itself. Within member states, opposition to the EU was joined by those opposed to any surrender of national sovereignty, by opponents of the EU's bureaucratic regulations, by those fearful of foreign immigrants, and by a variety of special interests. Advocates of the EU, on the other hand, have tended to include the most prominent political leaders, economic interests, and intellectuals.

In 1995 Austria, Finland, and Sweden joined the EU, and, remarkably, all of the 15 member states except Greece met the Maastricht Treaty's stringent requirements. That willingness to raise taxes and cut budgets is testimony to widespread faith in the future of the EU. Great Britain, Denmark, and Sweden opted, however, not to join the common currency on the first wave. In the rest of the EU, banks, businesses, and governments began in 1999 to keep accounts in Euros, and in 2002 the traditional coins and bills emblazoned

with national symbols gave way to currency in Euros (only the coins have national emblems, on one side). A uniform currency is leading to more uniform prices and intense competition, although the Euro proved less successful on money markets. Expected to be a strong competitor of the dollar, the Euro lost one-quarter of its value against the dollar in its first year. That aided European exports but increased the impact of rising oil prices even while the growth rate of EU economies, which had been well behind that of the United States, passed that of the United States in 2000.

By the end of the century, thirteen additional nations were in line to join the EU, leading to further prolonged negotiations as each state struggled to meet the EU's requirements for limited national debt, low inflation, political freedoms, and accommodation to hundreds of complex regulations. Decision making remains cumbersome, however, and reform difficult. New regulations in 2000 broadened the range of issues that could be decided by a majority vote rather than unanimity and brought the number of votes assigned each member nation more in line with its population, but more fundamental changes had to be postponed. The EU's authority has continued to grow nevertheless. Its idealism is represented in EU policies requiring that all members protect freedom of speech and movement and have a system of equal justice (with no death penalty) and in its many pronouncements on such matters as human rights, opposition to racism, protection of children, and "the full participation of women in civic, political, social, and economic life."

II. Postindustrial Society

The European Union's importance in Europe today rests on a half-century of economic growth and on the political and social changes that accompanied it. Standards of living rose, despite important setbacks, and every nation grew richer than it had ever been before. But the ways of creating wealth changed and so did lifestyles. Industrial production no longer dominated the economy, for the service sector employed more and more people in office work, sales, and

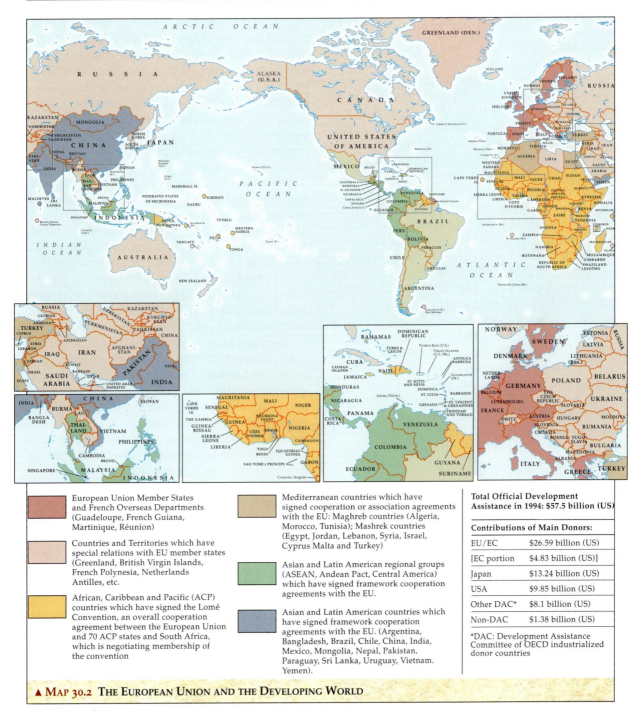

European Union Member States and French Overseas Departments (Guadeloupe, French Guiana, Martinique, Réunion)

Countries and Territories which have special relations with EU member states (Greenland, British Virgin Islands, French Polynesia, Netherlands Antilles, etc.)

African, Caribbean and Pacific (ACP) countries which have signed the Lomé Convention, an overall cooperation agreement between the European Union and 70 ACP states and South Africa, which is negotiating membership of the convention

Mediterranean countries which have signed cooperation or association agreements with the EU: Maghreb countries (Algeria, Morocco, Tunisia); Mashrek countries (Egypt, Jordan, Lebanon, Syria, Israel, Cyprus Malta and Turkey)

Asian and Latin American regional groups (ASEAN, Andean Pact, Central America) which have signed framework cooperation agreements with the EU.

Asian and Latin American countries which have signed framework cooperation agreements with the EU. (Argentina, Bangladesh, Brazil, Chile, China, India, Mexico, Mongolia, Nepal, Pakistan, Paraguay, Sri Lanka, Uruguay, Vietnam. Yemen).

Total Official Development Assistance in 1994: $57.5 billion (US)

Contributions of Main Donors:	
EU/EC	$26.59 billion (US)
[EC portion	$4.83 billion (US)]
Japan	$13.24 billion (US)
USA	$9.85 billion (US)
Other DAC*	$8.1 billion (US)
Non-DAC	$1.38 billion (US)

*DAC: Development Assistance Committee of OECD industrialized donor countries

▲ **Map 30.2 The European Union and the Developing World**

personal services. Societies so structured have come to be called, a little misleadingly, *postindustrial*, to indicate the importance of these changes with their emphasis on new technologies. Exuberantly embraced in North America and by the elites of Western Europe, the transformation was slower and encountered greater difficulty in Eastern Europe. Everywhere, it brought painful dislocations, unemployment, and greater inequality as well as greater wealth.

◆ EUROPE'S ADVANTAGE

The coal fields of Britain, West Germany, and Eastern Europe and the iron ore fields of France and Sweden were once critical to industrialization, and they have been supplemented by other sources of energy such as natural gas and oilfields in the North Sea. Except for the Soviet Union, however, much of Europe has historically been disadvantaged by its limited natural resources. That is now less crucial. Economies today create wealth primarily through efficient production and services; and Europe, like the United States, excels in the factors that matter most: great amounts of capital and institutions to facilitate its rapid movement, advanced technology, experienced managers, skilled and willing workers, efficient marketing, rapid communication, high levels of education, adaptable societies, and high consumption.

Infrastructure During the 1960s every European nation launched new road-building projects, and by 1980 the most important of them had been completed. Superhighways now run from Stockholm to south of Valencia and from Naples to Hamburg. Railroads, valued for passenger travel as well as for transport (and usually considered a service to be provided by the state) have been extensively modernized. In 1981 French trains,

▼ **High-speed electric trains poised for their dash from Paris to Lyons.**
Liaison International/Getty Images

which hold world speed records, began to carry passengers from Paris to Lyons at 165 miles per hour. A tunnel under the English Channel, a project considered for centuries, opened in 1994 to provide direct automobile and rail links between Britain and the continent. Water transport along Europe's coasts, rivers, and canals is relatively inexpensive, and air travel, dense throughout the continent, is especially important across the expanses of Russia.

In the face of American and Japanese competition, Western European nations remain among the technological leaders in electronic communication, especially wireless telephones and satellite communication. On average, one-third of EU households are connected to the internet. Europe's banks and stock markets, important sources of stability, began in the 1980s to become more flexible and in the 1990s to join international and global mergers. In 2000 the Frankfurt and London stock markets joined forces. Until the 1980s, in much of Western Europe as well as the communist nations outside the USSR, economic growth rested on mixed economies, with an important role for state planning in the West and some room for private enterprise in Eastern Europe. Since then, a strong trend toward privatization has brought more rapid growth and painful social adjustments that include cost cutting, rising unemployment, and international competition. The emphasis on productive efficiency, new products, marketing, and personal consumption that once seemed characteristically American now dominates most of Europe.

In the West agricultural productivity has increased as well, while the number of people who work on the land has continued to decline (in Ireland, until very recently one of the West's least developed nations, 60 percent of the workforce was employed in agriculture in 1960 and less than 8 percent are today). Modern farming, too, requires new investment and mechanization. With only about 3 percent of the world's farmland, Western Europe produces nearly one-third of the world's dairy products and 15 percent of the world's eggs, potatoes, and wheat (of which France is one of the world's largest producers).

Education Modern societies require citizens to be more highly educated than ever before. That

▲ The skyscrapers of Frankfurt, one of Europe's greatest commercial centers, loom over the statue of Schiller, Germany's great eighteenth-century playwright.
Liaison International/Getty Images

has led to extensive and controversial reforms that in the late 1960s and early 1970s often led to angry demonstrations and even riots. Traditionally in Europe, secondary education has been the great mark of social difference. A small fraction of students went to secondary schools noted for their demanding and usually classical curriculums. These schools were the gateway to a university. A larger proportion of students went to vocational secondary schools, and half or more of the youths beyond the ages of twelve and fourteen went directly to work. Despite efforts to make this segregation an effect of academic performance, in practice social class made a critical difference.

Educational reforms intended to make the system more democratic were offensive to defenders of the older curriculum, while not going far enough to satisfy student radicals, but they instituted important changes. In the West enrollments in the more prestigious forms of secondary education doubled and trebled, and a trend toward "comprehensive" schools more like the American high school allowed many of the graduates of those schools to go on to higher education. The number of university students has increased enormously, and more women than men now receive postsecondary education in most developed countries. In communist societies the children of workers and party members had priority for admission to such schools, but total enrollments increased more slowly than in the West before 1989. This expansion in the years of schooling and access to it requires increased state expenditure and families able to support children for a longer period before they begin to work. It helps to make social mobility become a more universal goal and makes education the subject of intense debate about fairness, culture, and employment.

Educational systems have tended to become more similar across Western Europe, although important differences in national traditions remain. Despite creation of hundreds of new institutions of higher education, often with American-style campuses, enrollments in many countries swelled beyond capacity. Among European nations, the Scandinavian countries, France, Italy, Belgium, and the Netherlands have the highest proportion of young adults in some form of postsecondary education, with the proportion somewhat lower in Great Britain and Germany.

The Changing Roles of Women As women's lives changed even more than men's, European institutions have gradually adapted. Women have become more prominent in all the professions and in politics. Most European women over the age of fifteen engage in economic activity (the proportion ranges from about half in Italy, Spain, and Ireland to more than 80 percent of them in the Czech Republic, Poland, and the Scandinavian countries). Women make up from one-fifth to half of all managers in most countries, especially in smaller enterprises and rarely in top positions. Labor unions thus pay more attention to their needs: in Italy, for example, pressing employers to grant released time with pay to take special courses. Women constitute from one-half to nearly two-thirds of professional and technical workers. European governments and employers have made child care available to most women, in effect, encouraging mothers to have careers. On the average, however, women workers continue to earn less than men (between two-thirds as much in Britain and four-fifths as much in France).

Young women expected to have a freedom of movement that their mothers did not as they trained, traveled, worked, and socialized outside their families. The availability of contraception and, by the 1970s, abortion (changes more accepted in Europe than in the United States) added to this sense that women had the right to plan their life course. Gender discrimination nevertheless remains a serious problem and source of tension. The EU and many governments have adopted strong statements for equality and against sexual harassment, but their effect is limited, making the difference between ideal and reality all the more apparent as women wrestle with the pressure of multiple responsibilities.

Urban Planning Postindustrial society is heavily urban, and Europe has long experience in making its well-organized cities function well. The threat was clear: As urban agglomerations expanded across the surrounding suburbs, the inner core of older cities tended to lose population as people with greater wealth and leisure sought more space and privacy. The new highways, extended subways, and bus lines that push the cities outward rarely keep pace with the congestion of traffic at their heart. As similar-looking skyscrapers rise in the city centers and in new business centers around what had been the periphery, similar residential districts sprawl across the outskirts. One-fifth of the population of France lives within an hour's drive of Paris, and nearly that proportion

of Britain's population is similarly close to London. Volgograd stretches for forty-five miles along the river after which it was named, and some fourteen cities of the former Soviet Union have a population of more than a million.

European states were accustomed to spending money to maintain city services, but governments were unsure how best to build. In the 1950s new housing in both the East and West tended to look like dreary concrete barracks and often provided few of the services necessary to create a sense of community. In nearly every country, whole new cities, often bleak and artificial, surround the metropolis: Five towns of 24,000 people each were placed around Paris; twenty-four such towns surround Moscow. Since the 1970s the trend has shifted to new urban hubs on a smaller scale, carefully planned to have shopping, recreational, and cultural centers of their own as well as some light industry so that much of the working population need not commute. Many of these ventures—those in Scandinavia were among the first—have proved to be attractive models, widely imitated, mixing large and small modern buildings, pleasant streets, and restful green spaces. War damage forced German governments into expensive projects of urban renewal, and from the 1960s on governments across much of Western Europe have invested in refurbishing urban centers and creating some of the world's most interesting experiments in urban planning, often with stunning effects.

Cities like Rome and Vienna found that banning traffic from the narrow, medieval streets of their old centers made them more attractive (and expensive) for shops and housing. Loud laments were heard at the razing of Les Halles in Paris, handsome wrought iron sheds built in the Second Empire to provision the capital with food, but the gains in efficiency and improved traffic were undeniable. The exciting new cultural center built in the 1970s as part of the area's renewal has become the most visited site in Paris. In London, the produce sellers of Covent Garden also had to give way to a cultural center, and Billingsgate, the fishmarket that gave the language a word for verbal abuse, closed in 1981. Everywhere, new projects are under way in the expectation that, like the stunning Guggenheim museum in Bilbao or bridge in Lisbon, they will keep Europe's great

▲ The glass structures that replaced Paris' central market evoke the iron and glass pavilions built a century earlier but now contain shops, museums, and a media center. New apartment buildings stand in the background. Leveling the crowded old mercantile buildings surrounding the market also provided a view of the gothic church of St. Eustache that had not been seen for centuries.
Charles Graham/eStock Photo

cities among the most livable and attractive in the world.

Social Welfare Although the gap between the wealthiest and poorest segments of society is less in Europe than in the United States, large pockets of unemployment and poverty remain. In communist Europe professional people and officials lived at a much higher standard and with far greater freedom of choice than workers or peasants, an important element in the unpopularity and ultimate downfall of those governments. The full impact of these inequalities is softened throughout Europe by complex provisions for social security, minimal fees for education, universal medical care, many provisions for the elderly, and a wide variety of family benefits and services. Not surprisingly, rates of infant mortality have declined and longevity rates have improved in West-

ern Europe to be among the most favorable in the world. Because birthrates in Europe are now generally the lowest in the world and the elderly are an ever-increasing proportion of the population as people live longer, social expenditures necessarily increase.

In the 1970s unemployment had begun to rise, depressing regions dependent on declining industries as well as those that had never enjoyed industrial prosperity. By the 1990s, endemic unemployment had become one of Europe's most pressing social problems, generally averaging more than 10 percent and hitting young people and immigrants the hardest. On the whole, programs of special subsidies and tax incentives have had disappointing results. With taxation already relatively high, governments have had little new to offer, while demands for lower taxes became a mainstay of the political center and right.

Subsidized housing had mixed results. Although relatively cheap in communist Europe, good housing remained scarce, leading to long waiting lists for cramped apartments. In the West, where much new housing was subsidized by governments (in the 1980s about one-third of new housing in Germany, one-half in Great Britain, two-thirds in Sweden and France), the result was segregation in isolated and dismal surroundings.

◆ NEW ISSUES

Foreign Workers   A massive movement of people began to alter European society in the 1960s. With jobs available in the industrial zones, many men and somewhat fewer women moved from the less developed to the more prosperous regions. At first, it seemed a continuation of older patterns, but immigrants now crossed national boundaries more freely than in the past. Southern Italians went to northern Italy but also to Switzerland and Germany; Spaniards, Portuguese, and North Africans to France; Yugoslavs and Turks to Germany; African and Caribbean blacks, Indians, and Pakistanis to England. These people, too, con-tributed to Europe's economic miracle although they were most often employed as domestic servants, street sweepers, and the least skilled industrial workers. By the 1970s foreign immigrants made up 17 percent of the workforce in Switzerland, some 8 percent in Germany, and only slightly less than that in France.

Often different in physical appearance, language, and culture from the majority of those around them, immigrants were drawn together and forced by poverty to live in slums that quickly became ghetto subcultures resistant to and misunderstood by the larger society. Lacking the full protection of citizenship, resented by native workers competing for jobs and higher pay, despised as sources of crime and heavy welfare costs, these migrants re-created some of the gravest social problems of the early nineteenth century, now exacerbated by prejudices of race and color. Many gradually came to see themselves as permanent residents, and many acquired citizenship, as their children automatically did (except in Germany). This second generation went to local schools and for the most part adopted local ways, yet these families often remained partially

▼ **Many German cities have districts, like this one in Cologne, that look almost as if they were in Turkey.**
Regis Bossu/Corbis Sygma

A Turkish Girl Arrives in Germany

◆

Aynur, a young Turkish girl, published in a Turkish newspaper a very personal and frank account of her life in Germany. She had gone to Germany with her mother to live with her father, who had worked there several years. Leaving her village elementary school behind, she went to a Turkish school in Germany and lived there into her teens. As she adopted new ways, she became alienated from her family, found German friends only among groups of homosexuals and drug addicts, and eventually made several visits to Turkey in search of old ties to her extended family and native culture. She ends her account with the comment, "On my birth certificate it is written that I am a 'Turk.' But in the full sense, more correctly, with my thinking, I am not completely a Turk. I do not want to be a German either." In the passage quoted here, she describes her first days in Germany.

"A bustle of activity commenced as soon as the plane landed in Berlin. Everyone wanted to disembark. I looked for the sun as soon as we went out, but it wasn't to be seen. I thought I was before a gray wall. The weather was cloudy and rainy. Later on I started looking for blond people. I always thought that all Germans were blond.

"We took a taxi. I was watching out of the window. I was trying to see the white houses which I had dreamed about. All around were large brick buildings. There were no people in sight on the wide boulevards. I was constantly asking my father, 'Which one looks like our house?'

"Finally we got out of the taxi. I was looking around to find the house that they lived in. My father, pointing to a somewhat larger door, said, 'You enter here.' An old door, all the edges of which were broken, and a somewhat large building from which the plaster was falling. After we entered through the large door and went through the small concrete courtyard, we started climbing the stairs. The holding-on places were broken.

"Suddenly all of my illusions were shattered. Pessimism and dejection overcame me. We climbed until the fourth floor. My father opened the door. A small hallway, a living room, and a kitchen. That was all there was to the home. The toilet was outside, they said.

"I asked myself, 'Is this our house?' I withdrew to a corner and started to investigate the living room. In the middle a faded rug was laid. Around it stood a few old armchairs. The only new thing was a fairly large television that stood in the corner. Forgetting everything, we started playing with the television. At each press of a button, a different film appeared.

"Six of us started to live together in the one-room house. This situation did not strike me as odd. In our village, too, we used to live all together. Since I had not had any different living experience, this did not seem unusual.

"My older sister and I did not get out of the room for a period of three months. We were afraid, and moreover, our father was not giving us permission. Our only tie to the outside was a window facing the courtyard. Children were playing in the courtyard. My only wish was to play with them. From time to time I was able to talk through the kitchen window with our neighbor's daughter, who was a year older than I. I was impatiently waiting for her return from school. My first friend in Germany was this girl.

"Her hair was cut very short. She looked like a very modern girl. We went down together to the courtyard entrance to play. I gained a little courage. After that I started going to their home.

"We used to wear skirts over pajamas in our village. My father had bought slacks for us in Istanbul. From then on we wore slacks under our skirts instead of pajamas. Slowly I began to imitate my friend. When no one was at home, I would take off my skirt and walk around in my slacks. At other times, I would take off my slacks and walk around in just my skirt. My older sister was not able to dare to do this. She would sit at the window as my lookout.

"For a long time when we went outside, we wore slacks under our skirts."

From Akural Aynur (tr.), in Ilhan Basgöz and Norman Furniss (eds.), *Turkish Workers in Europe* (Turkish Studies Publications, 1985).

dependent on government programs and were the first to feel the effects of any economic downturn. Their plight and the prejudice against them were problems for which most European societies were ill prepared (see "A Turkish Girl Arrives in Germany," above).

The Environment Economic growth also brought pollution that contaminated the air, waterways, and countryside as it poured from factories and automobiles and littered the landscape. Monuments and scenic places revered for centuries came to be seriously threatened. Western Europe was slow to respond, and in Eastern Europe the problem was ruthlessly ignored. The Rhine became one of the most polluted international waterways, and high concentrations of mercury were recorded in Geneva's Lac Leman. Escaped industrial gases caused illness and death in the outskirts of Milan, and the magnificent palaces of Venice were discovered to be slowly sinking, apparently because the earth beneath their pilings gives way as underground water is pumped up on the mainland for industrial use. Acid rain is destroying Germany's Black Forest, and it is now dangerous to bathe in or eat fish from much of the Baltic and Mediterranean seas. The remaining monuments of ancient Greece and Rome and the ornate facades of Gothic churches in city after city crumble and crack from the vibrations and fumes of modern traffic.

Governments intent upon stimulating growth were reluctant to impose the restrictions and to undertake the expense that protecting the environment required until strong ecology movements in Germany, Britain, the Low Countries, and France forced their hand. Political parties, known everywhere as the Greens, focused on these environmental issues, and several international agencies now enforce European standards against pollution. Although much more remains to be done, the gains have been impressive. Stern regulations eliminated the smog that had plagued London since the sixteenth century, killing thousands of people as recently as 1952. The Thames has become a clean river for the first time in centuries. In the 1960s and 1970s, nearly every building in Paris was stripped of the somber, dark patina of soot accumulated through 150 years of industrialization (to begin darkening anew from automotive exhaust). By the 1980s, citizens' movements, well-organized programs for recycling, and strict regulations were changing the landscape across Europe, and European states had become leaders in international measures to protect the environment. Green parties have remained small, even in Germany, where the movement is strongest, but the larger parties have adopted much of the Green's program.

III. The Politics of Prosperity

In retrospect, the basis for Europe's greater integration and economic transformation was established by 1957, but that prospect was often called into question between then and 1989. At the time, the tensions of the Cold War in a divided continent and domestic social and political conflicts were more obvious. Two periods of crisis stand out, one culminating in 1968 and the other beginning in 1973; both challenged established economic and political systems.

◆ WAVES OF PROTEST

Greater well-being seemed to strengthen moral outrage. Many Western Europeans were appalled by the rising commercialism and inequality that accompanied prosperity. Many Eastern Europeans were determined to win some of the advantages that their Western neighbors enjoyed. A number of otherwise very different movements sought alternatives.

The Revolutions of 1968 For a few weeks in May 1968 the students of Paris seemed to recapture the revolutionary spirit of 1848, with their barricades of paving stones and trees, imaginative posters, and mocking slogans. In Germany, Italy, Great Britain, and the United States as well, students briefly acted as an independent political force in 1968 and 1969. Inspired by the movements of national liberation in Africa and Asia and outraged by the war in Vietnam, they denounced imperialism as a product of capitalist societies that used consumer goods to mask inequality and injustice.

More specifically, they excoriated the rigidities and inadequacies of the educational system to which they were subject. Their elders noted with surprise that these angry protesters were in fact the beneficiaries of expanded educational opportunities and increased prosperity. As revolutions, these movements failed. Labor unions and the traditional left were suspicious of privileged college students; liberals and conservatives were offended by rudeness and violence. In elections

▲ **After weeks of student demonstrations in Paris, police used buses to cordon off the Sorbonne shortly before storming the university and evicting the students in June 1968.**
© Corbis

following these upheavals, the majority of voters turned to parties that emphasized order. These protest movements nevertheless stimulated important reforms, especially of education; and their style of protest, their challenges to middle-class values, and their questioning of authority have remained important elements in public discourse and in a distinctive youth culture. Ever since,

movements of social criticism have used the organizing skills and tactics of satire and street theater that worked so well in 1968 to win the attention of a complacent society. The Greens are very much the heirs of those student activists.

In Czechoslovakia the optimism of 1968, when Alexander Dubček came to power, was short-lived. As Communist party secretary, he was able to adopt a program of liberalization including greater autonomy for Slovakia and freedom of speech, assembly, and religion. Students were noisily enthusiastic for this "communism with a human face," but Moscow saw it as an intolerable danger. In the largest military operation in Europe since World War II, troops from the Soviet Union, East Germany, Hungary, and Poland invaded Czechoslovakia in August. Dubček was soon ousted; of his springtime program, only Slovakian autonomy was allowed to stand.

The Women's Movement   Women were prominent in the student demonstrations across Europe and the United States, but many discovered that male radicals, despite their rhetoric of equality in matters of race and class, tended to allocate subordinate roles to women. Simone de Beauvoir's *The Second Sex* and Betty Friedan's *The Feminine Mystique* helped women identify the problem.

When her book first appeared in 1949, Beauvoir was well established in French intellectual circles but best known as the intimate friend of Sartre, the most admired intellectual of the day. *The Second Sex*, a memoir of her own experiences, made her famous. The book gained power in the context of the 1960s, for it reflected on the ways in which society tends to make women ancillary to others (institutions, families, husbands). Beauvoir wondered whether equality for women, even if possible, would be enough to overcome this subordination to other interests or whether women did not need to establish their own distinctive voice. Her questions and her candor pushed the women's movement in new directions.

The Feminine Mystique appeared in 1963. Betty Friedan, an experienced American journalist and mother of three, wrote about what she saw as the split between the idealized vision of the perfect homemaker and the reality of women's lives. In the years after World War II, women were expected to find personal fulfillment as wives and mothers. Instead, Friedan identified women as suffering from "the problem that has no name" and a profound crisis in identity. Along with *The Second Sex, The Feminine Mystique* became a handbook of the women's movement in the 1960s and 1970s. The new politics centering on women's needs and women's rights became one of the important developments of the latter half of the twentieth century.

Terrorism Rather than abandon fading hope for revolution, some radical groups turned to terrorism. The skills and equipment necessary for a terrorist campaign were not hard to come by in the semisecret world of international crime, espionage, and arms deals that flourished during the Cold War. Although terrorists were few in number, modern urban society is vulnerable to their anonymity and surprise tactics. These small groups did not aim to capture power but rather to provoke the authorities into repressive acts that would alienate the public. German terrorists shot at business leaders as well as politicians until caught by severely efficient police. Basque terrorists shook several Spanish governments with their bombs and murders but accomplished little more.

In Italy, Marxist and neo-Fascist underground bands competed in kidnappings and bombings accompanied by revolutionary proclamations. In 1978 the best-known of the radical groups, the Red Brigades, climaxed a series of attention-getting exploits by kidnapping Aldo Moro, a prominent politician. Police searched for him in vain as the nation held its breath until his bullet-riddled body was found in an abandoned car. Across the political spectrum, the public responded with outrage against terrorism rather than anger at the state. Although the Red Brigades remained active, they were on the wane by the time their leaders were arrested a few years later. Such incidents, like the shooting of Pope John Paul II by a Turkish terrorist in 1981, provoked outcries about the alienation and violence of modern society but did little to change it.

Terrorism was more effective where local hatreds gave it a popular base. Irish Protestants, determined to maintain British rule in Northern Ireland, had long clashed with their Catholic neighbors who wanted Northern Ireland to be part of the Irish Republic. Neither side had much

▲ **A local sign warns residents of sniper attacks in this Northern Ireland town where IRA sharpshooters had killed seven soldiers.**
© Oistin MacBride/Corbis

faith in the British government's proposed compromises permitting local rule, proposals never tested because terrorism reached the level of continuous war. Underground organizations on each side killed hundreds of innocent people. Although a majority of people said they favored some workable solution, loyalty to neighbors, nationalism, and recollections of past injustice, discrimination, and repression permitted violence to prevent a resolution. Even by the end of the century, the truce established in the 1990s remained uncertain.

More distant religious strife brought terrorists to the continent, too. Supporters of the Palestine Liberation Organization, seeking a Palestinian state, killed Israeli athletes at the Munich Olympic Games in 1972, and in the 1970s Muslim terrorists placed bombs in Paris stores. Terrorists gained little for their various causes, but heightened urban fear made tough security measures and heavily armed police a prominent part of European city life.

Eurocommunism   By the 1980s, communist parties in Western Europe realized that they had to broaden their appeal. Italy's Communist party, the largest outside the Soviet bloc, was especially innovative. It sponsored dozens of publications aimed at women, students, and intellectuals as well as at workers and held great public celebrations that had elements of an industrial exhibit and a rock concert with lectures and seminars on the side. The spectacle and the content were impressive, and the party grew less inclined to hold up the Soviet Union as the model of the future. Throughout Western Europe years of electoral and union activity had led communist parties to form coalitions and take positions on scores of practical issues. Arguing for social justice and political freedom invited commitment to pluralism and democracy. The French and Italian parties had objected to the Soviet invasion of Czechoslovakia in 1968, and the Italian party even accepted NATO. Criticizing Soviet policies in Eastern Europe opened prospects for an alternative program.

That alternative came to be known as Eurocommunism, and Italy's Communist party was its model and major proponent.[5] It proclaimed its commitment to civil rights, multiple parties, and free elections; and its increased electoral successes stimulated a trend toward Eurocommunism on the left. The French Communist party, traditionally among Europe's most rigid, and a newly revived Spanish Communist party adopted Eurocommunist positions despite pressure from the Soviet Union to preserve the unity of communism and remain loyal to Soviet leadership. By the sixtieth anniversary of the Russian Revolution in 1977, Eurocommunism represented a schism within the communist movement. But suspicion

of communist parties ran deep, and even limited electoral stimulated opposition on the right.

The End of Dictatorship in Greece   While the Western European Left was moderating its goals, opposition to anti-Communist dictatorships grew stronger. In Greece army officers had overthrown the unstable parliamentary system and eventually the monarchy itself in 1967, but in 1973, civilian leaders were able to force the restoration of democracy. To strengthen a fragile but modernizing economy, Greece's repressive military rulers had needed to draw closer to Western Europe, where they found little inclination to deal with dictators. Weakened at home by conflict with Turkey over control of Cyprus, the military regime gradually increased freedom as it recognized its own unpopularity. Conflict between left and right remained strident in Greece, but the country was clearly on a course leading toward democracy and economic growth. That was confirmed by the acceptance of Greece as a member of the European Community in 1981.

The End of Dictatorship in Portugal   Portugal and Spain had been ruled by dictators since the 1930s. In Portugal the Salazar regime, which had paralleled Franco's long period of rule in Spain, continued in milder form even after Salazar became incapacitated in 1968. While opposition remained stymied at home, it grew stronger in Portuguese Guinea, Angola, and Mozambique, where Portugal relied on brute force to hold on to its empire. Condemned in the United Nations, by African states, and by most European nations, the overtaxed government was suddenly seized in April 1974 by a group of army officers promising full freedom and civil rights for Portugal and self-determination for the colonies. The response was overwhelming. Crowds danced in the streets and cheered smiling soldiers whose rifles were decorated with flowers.

The euphoria could not last. A poor and backward country, Portugal faced raging inflation and declining production. While peasants claimed the land they had long coveted, socialist and communist unions competed for support among the workers, business groups struggled to defend their interests, and many prominent businesspersons left the country. For two years new cabinets

---

[5]Communist parties had traditionally attracted nearly one-third of the electorate in Italy, one-fifth in France and Finland, one-eighth in Spain, and much less elsewhere: about 5 percent in Sweden, 4 percent in Denmark, 3 percent in Belgium, 2 percent in Greece and the Netherlands, and less than 1 percent in West Germany and Great Britain. The parties in Portugal, briefly powerful after the revolution there, and in Finland were the two least inclined to Eurocommunism.

fell after a few months in the face of revolts from left and right. Nevertheless, the nationalization of banks and industry was followed by free elections in 1975 and 1976 and relatively moderate socialist governments that brought Portugal closer to other countries in Western Europe. With elections that gave Portugal its first democratically elected civilian president in sixty years, Portugal was able to join the European Community in 1986.

The End of Dictatorship in Spain The political transformation in Spain was more gradual. Franco retired in 1973 but skillfully kept his influence until his death two years later. In 1969 he had called on Juan Carlos, the grandson of Spain's last king, to take the empty throne, in effect as Franco's heir. Juan Carlos showed himself more committed to democracy and more adept than expected. Increased freedom of speech did not lead to a recurrence of the civil war that so many people feared, and the voters approved a new constitution in 1978. Many dangers remained, but an attempted military coup failed, and greater regional autonomy reduced agitation from separatists.

Suddenly, a society long dormant came alive. A stagnant economy caught fire in the 1970s and 1980s under the premiership of the extremely popular socialist Felipe Gonzales. Although his decision to join NATO was not popular, his success in joining the European Community in 1986 and ending Spain's fifty years of relative isolation was widely cheered. The prosperous democracies of Western Europe, capitalist but committed to programs of social welfare, were the models other Europeans wanted to follow.

◆ CAPITALIST COUNTRIES: THE CHALLENGE OF RECESSION

When economic growth slowed, political conflict sharpened. Traditional political programs lost relevance, and weakened governments struggled with problems deeply embedded in their social and economic systems. Nearly everywhere the crisis brought a change of government as opposition parties gained power.

The Energy Crisis European economies were instantly vulnerable when in October 1973 the oil-exporting nations (mainly in the Middle East) banded together in a cartel to raise international prices. Europe imported nearly two-thirds of its energy in the form of petroleum, and only the Soviet Union could meet its own energy needs through domestic production. In response to higher prices, Western nations redoubled efforts to develop domestic sources of energy. Over the next decade the exploitation of North Sea oilfields made Norway self-sufficient and Britain nearly so, and the Netherlands developed Europe's largest fields of natural gas. But Europe's energy consumption continued to rise, and greater self-sufficiency depended heavily on nuclear energy. By 1976 more than half the world's nuclear power plants operating or under construction were in Europe, where France became the world leader. These measures and the collapse of oil prices in 1986 eased the immediate economic crisis, but its effects remained.

Opposition to reliance on nuclear power, long led by the Greens, increased after the meltdown of a nuclear reactor at Chernobyl in the Soviet Union in 1986. Radioactive clouds swept over much of central Europe, creating concern for safety that increased in the following years as the full extent of the casualties within the Soviet Union came to be known.

Stagflation The high cost of energy added to inflationary pressures. Among major capitalist nations, only West Germany consistently managed to hold the rate of inflation below 5 percent a year. It rose to more than 20 percent in Britain and Italy in 1975–1976 (30 percent in Portugal) and undermined planning, savings, and trade, while squeezing salaried employees and many workers. This widespread inflation called into question practices on which prosperity had seemed to rest: deficit financing by governments, increased imports, and business reliance on raising prices to maintain profits. Efforts to change these policies initiated conflicts and class conflicts over social programs, especially in Britain and Italy. Economists identified a new condition, *stagflation,* the paradoxical combination of economic stagnation and rising prices, and worried about a more familiar one, recession.

Where strong anti-inflationary measures were imposed, as in Britain, unemployment rose, and in Europe generally became higher in the 1980s than at any time since World War II (although it

▲ France invested more heavily in nuclear energy than did any other country. Well run and efficient, the French plants provoked little public opposition, but not even a mural of a child at the beach could make the giant stacks seem to belong in their bucolic surroundings.
Liaison International/Getty Images

would rise higher still a decade later). Europe was undergoing a major and painful economic transition. Its now-aging industries faced increased competition from the Japanese and from new plants in other parts of the world, and the state's capacity to respond was limited. The public supported social programs but opposed still higher taxes, leaving little room for maneuver, and an unexpected rise in regionalism brought new accusations that central governments disadvantaged local interests. Thus, long-accepted national policies were called into question amid new divisions. Although each country evolved its own response, the central issues were similar.

Opening to the Left: France The student revolt in May 1968 shook De Gaulle's government. It weathered the storm through firmness and promises of reform because student radicals had frightened French voters, but the Fifth Republic

was never the same. The government passed education reforms, broadened social programs, and made the civil service more responsive; but when a referendum on De Gaulle's vague but far-reaching plans for decentralizing the state was defeated in 1969, he resigned. The next two presidents from the center-right differed from him more in style than policy, winning close elections with promises of stability and moderation, while the opposition criticized the political system as isolated from public opinion in its reliance on highly trained experts, however brilliant. Although most French voters were centrist, the division between a more or less Marxist left and a technocratic right dominated politics.

In 1981 the socialist leader of that opposition, François Mitterrand, won the presidential election by attempting to bridge that divide. He promised a new emphasis on issues of culture, leisure, and urban life but maintained his alliance with the

Communists and supported the traditional demands of the left for the nationalization of many industries and for a more equitable distribution of income. On election night there was dancing in the streets and optimistic talk of a post-Gaullist era. The new government began with dramatic measures, nationalizing many heavy industries and most banks, raising wages and benefits, and increasing social expenditures. The daring gamble failed to stimulate an economy hurt by business distrust, the fall of the franc, and an unfavorable international economy. Within a few years, sepa-rated from the Communists, Mitterrand adopted policies of austerity, deflation, and investment in high technology that were more like those of his predecessors than his own platform. As the right gained in elections, France found a socialist president leading a government of the center that was concerned with economic modernization, military strength, and support of the European Community. As to the new social problems—large pockets of endemic unemployment, drug addiction, and racial conflict—politicians had few solutions.

Opening to the Left: Italy   In 1983 Bettino Craxi became Italy's first Socialist prime minister. A wily politician who had rebuilt the Socialist party, his arrival in power was the culmination of two long-term political trends. The Christian Democrats had dominated Italian politics since the founding of the republic in 1946, relying on a system of semisecret negotiations and labyrinthine deals. The Communists continued to be excluded from these coalitions as were the Socialists until 1963. While the economy boomed—Italy had enjoyed the longest period of economic growth of any European nation—this domination was acceptable. As restiveness increased, so did restiveness with this closed and often corrupt system. Meanwhile the growing respectability of the Communist party helped it win local offices in much of the north, especially in the newly established regional administrations and in most of Italy's largest cities. Having gained a reputation for probity and efficiency, they argued for a "historic compromise," in which Communists and Christian Democrats would govern together in the interests of stability and reform.

Some such solution seemed all but inevitable until Craxi set the Socialists on the opposite course and made his party indispensable to a governing coalition. He became prime minister and brought a new decisiveness to government, but the hoped-for reforms gave way to more immediate economic issues. His government brought stability, an impressive achievement in a tension-filled nation undergoing rapid social change, but one that fell far short of the significant changes promised.

A Shift to the Right: West Germany   In West Germany political issues tended to be overshadowed by the satisfying fact of prosperity as the Federal Republic surpassed the United States in world trade. Even the significant shift in 1969 to a government led by the Social Democrats did not lessen the commitment to encouraging investment, expanding trade, and preventing inflation. Often surprisingly conservative in their economic policies, the Social Democrats pursued democratization in other ways, carrying through educational reforms, expanding social services, and requiring large firms to have elected labor repre-

sentatives on a central board of directors. Then in 1982 an unfavorable economic climate helped the Christian Democrats to regain office under Helmut Kohl, who would remain prime minister for longer than anyone since Bismarck. Kohl's government was more closely tied to the United States and friendlier to business but almost as eager as its predecessors to maintain good relations with the East. Like France and Italy, Germany looked more and more to the European Community to provide a program for the future and to shape its international role.

A Shift to the Right: Great Britain   Continuity had characterized British policy for thirty years until Margaret Thatcher became prime minister in 1979. When the Conservatives were in power, they favored the private sector but largely accepted the extensive welfare programs and mixed economy they inherited. Constrained by the plight of the British economy, Labour governments in their turn reduced public expenditures and pressured trade unions to accept wage limits, while improving transport and expanding higher education.

Britain's overwhelming problem was the economy, and neither North Sea oil nor membership in the European Community solved it. Businesses failed to modernize plants or raise productivity at the pace of other industrial nations. Inflation depressed the rate of investment. Analysts found it easier to lay the blame—on the enormous cost to Britain of World War II, unimaginative and weak business managers, an inadequate educational system, the selfish conservatism of labor unions, and the high costs of welfare and defense—than to prescribe remedies. In office as the recession got worse, the Labour party lost the 1979 election.

Margaret Thatcher   A doctrinaire advocate of free enterprise, Mrs. Thatcher reversed the course of British domestic policy, and the two major parties became more ideological. Out of power, Labour was dominated by its left wing, a fact that divided opposition, helping the Conservatives to stay in office. The results of Thatcher's decisive policies were impressive. The British economy restructured, and productivity rose in the late 1980s, increasing prosperity and reducing still high unemployment. That restructuring, combined with reductions in social services, including education, also increased social inequality.

Even her opponents—and she was widely disliked—grudgingly admired Thatcher's outspokenness and fearless consistency, and there was no arguing with economic growth. She strengthened her position by appealing to nationalist fervor in 1983 when Argentina suddenly attacked the Falkland Islands (which Britain had held and Argentina had claimed for more than a century), and she took much of the credit for Britain's victory. In 1990 she won her third consecutive election, something no prime minister had done for 160 years. But her unbending defense of unrestrained capitalism and her view of Britain's

national interest made for abrasive relations with many leaders at home and with the European Community. A revolt in her own party forced her to resign soon after her last electoral victory. Her less divisive successor kept his party in power until Labour's overwhelming victory in the elections of 1997, but the Thatcher years remain a turning point in modern British history.

◆ COMMUNIST RULE: THE PROBLEM OF RIGIDITY

Khrushchev's Effort The Soviet Union's most impressive achievement, admired throughout the world, had been its industrial growth. By the 1960s its economy was second in overall

▼ Soviet science and industry gained enormous prestige with the first successful orbit of a space vehicle in 1957. Later, the atmosphere of détente made it possible to hold exhibits like this one in Los Angeles in 1977.
AP/Wide World Photos

production and wealth only to that of the United States. It sent the first person into orbit around the earth in 1961; and as the world's largest producer of steel, iron, and, more recently, oil, the USSR was apparently gaining in the economic competition with the West. Brashly confident, Khrushchev, who declared that the Soviet Union "would bury" the United States, promised that his government was now able to give more attention to consumer products and adequate housing. Like his campaign of de-Stalinization, such policies opened the possibility of a new evolution in Soviet rule, but that proved difficult.

Khrushchev's plans to increase agricultural production failed, and the issue of whether to invest in consumer goods or heavy industry reopened long-standing conflicts within the highest circles. Many Kremlin leaders worried as well about the growing restiveness in Eastern Europe and the rift with China, which since 1956 had consistently denounced the Soviet Union's international policies as a betrayal of communism. When, in the process of solidifying his authority, Khrushchev antagonized the military, they and his opponents in the Politburo and the Central Committee felt strong enough to speak against him. In 1964 they voted him out of office and sent him into quiet retirement.

Signs of Failure   The orderly transition was promising in itself, but Khrushchev's successors, led by Leonid Brezhnev, were tough party technicians who held a firm grip on power and offered no fresh solutions. The cold-blooded invasion of Czechoslovakia, the continuing agricultural crisis (which required the purchase of American grain in 1972 and 1975), and the need to import industrial technology, particularly from Italy and France, were all signs of a system failing to adapt to change.

Evidence of arbitrary repression continued to tarnish the country's international image. Throughout the West the press revealed the plight of Soviet Jews, subject to discrimination and attack and intermittently permitted to emigrate. When Boris Pasternak's novel *Doctor Zhivago* exposed the seamy aspects of Soviet life and earned him the Nobel prize for literature in 1958, Pasternak was not permitted to go to Stockholm to receive it. Significantly, the case of Alexander

Solzhenitsyn in 1970 caused still greater international furor. He, too, was prevented from receiving the Nobel prize he won that year for his story of the *Gulag Archipelago*, a haunting account of the terrors of Soviet concentration camps. Four years later he was arrested and deported, joining a chorus of Russian writers and scientists whose criticisms were widely published outside the USSR and increasingly well known at home.

Gorbachev's Gamble   When Brezhnev died in 1982, he was succeeded by elderly and ailing party figures who exemplified the bureaucratic grayness of Soviet rule. Thus, the appointment in 1985 of Mikhail Gorbachev to be general secretary of the Communist party marked a new era. At fifty-four, the youngest man to lead the Soviet Union since Stalin, Gorbachev gradually revealed a personality and daring that led him in startling new directions. He spoke openly about problems of inefficiency and alienation (absenteeism and alcoholism among the workforce reached alarming levels), and he recognized the importance of radical reform in order to meet the growing demand for consumer goods and to sustain the arms race with the United States. The cost, and risk, of that competition went up as the president of the United States, Ronald Reagan, poured more money into new weapons. Meanwhile, the contrast between East and West in both agricultural and industrial production had grown more striking, and the USSR's earlier achievements in heavy industry now counted for less economically than the newer technologies and services in which it lagged.

Gorbachev confronted these problems on three fronts. He set about to restructure Soviet society by decentralizing decision making, which required more open communication, greater authority for local managers, and a reduction in the role of the Communist party. Gorbachev had to overcome entrenched resistance at all levels, but his efforts made *perestroika* (political and economic restructuring) and *glasnost* (greater openness) international words and won him admirers around the world.

Internationally, his foreign policy made him the most popular figure in Soviet history. He campaigned against the threat of nuclear war; and at a summit meeting with Reagan in 1986, Gorbachev suddenly proposed breathtaking reductions in nuclear arms that nearly won Reagan's acquiescence before aides hurriedly dissuaded him. Gorbachev also knew that he must end the war in Afghanistan. Soviet troops had gone there in 1979 to support a Communist government entangled in a bloody guerrilla war against rebels heavily supported by the United States. The war was a dangerous drain on Soviet lives, wealth, and morale, and in 1987 Gorbachev began a staged withdrawal.

Remarkably, he also extended glasnost to Eastern Europe. Gorbachev realized that those governments, too, needed to restructure; and he was glad to end costly barter arrangements with the Comecon nations, which permitted them to buy Soviet oil at prices below the world market in exchange for Eastern European products that the Soviet Union did not want. But once launched, glasnost was hard to contain. When some of the East European nations began to request that Soviet troops leave their territory and to replace their Communist regimes, Gorbachev accepted those changes, too. However necessary, such concessions troubled hostile hard-liners at home, and each step toward reform revealed the need for more and the resistance from officials.

Ethnic Conflict in the USSR   A still greater danger to Soviet stability arose from the explosion of nationalist unrest in 1988. Demonstrations and violent clashes occurred around the perimeter: on the Eastern frontier (in Georgia, Moldavia, and the Ukraine), among the Baltic republics (Latvia, Lithuania, and Estonia), and in the southern republics. The Baltic states created at the end of World War I had lost their independence in World War II, becoming part of the Soviet Union by

▼ For years Gorbachev was mobbed by enthusiastic well-wishers whenever he visited Western Europe and the United States; his trip to West Germany in 1990, where he was accompanied by Chancellor Kohl, was one of his last triumphal tours.
R. Bossu/Corbis Sygma

war's end. Demonstrations there now revived passionate memories of independence, and formerly rubber-stamp representative bodies began to act like parliaments. While they wrote new laws and constitutions, Gorbachev offered general promises, argued for the benefits of membership in the USSR, restrained his own army, and delayed any final stand on their status.

In the southern republics, Azerbaijanis and Armenians engaged in open war, inflamed by conflicts that were ethnic (Azeri and Armenians had fought for centuries), religious (Shia Muslims and Armenian Orthodox Christians), social (the Armenians had generally been wealthier and better educated), political (involving territorial claims and relations with Moscow), and economic (Azerbaijan's oil industry, its principal source of wealth, was declining). Eventually, Soviet troops attempted to separate the combatants but did not try to exercise sovereign authority over them.

Russians constituted the largest ethnic group in the multinational USSR, and theirs was the largest republic. They had long enjoyed privileged status throughout the federation. Now, Russian nationalists fanned the fears of losing that status with a campaign in the name of culture (with appeals to the Orthodox Church), order (attractive to the military and some party members), and race (including virulent antisemitism). Nationalism was as grave a challenge to Gorbachev as bloated bureaucracy and stores with empty shelves. The bonds of ideology, institutions, and custom that had held a great state together were beginning to look weak.

Pressure for Change in Eastern Europe In 1968 the "Brezhnev doctrine" had declared that a "threat to socialism" in one country was a threat to all. He had followed the invasion of Czechoslovakia with efforts to strengthen the economic ties binding the Comecon countries, but the nations of Eastern Europe were looking westward for increased trade and badly needed loans. Romania, not content with its allotted role as a Soviet granary, had launched its own course of industrialization and an independent foreign policy that made its brutal dictator, Nicolae Ceauşescu, welcome in the West. East Germany, the second industrial power among communist states (and the seventh in Europe), oscillated between

friendly overtures toward and suspicious rejection of West Germany much as it alternated between concessions and repression at home, where there were riots against the government in the early 1970s.

The pressures for change were stronger still in Czechoslovakia, Hungary, and Poland, where cultural ties to Western Europe remained strong and the Catholic Church became an outlet for growing restiveness. Riots against the police took place in Hungary, which had one of the strongest and most consumer-oriented economies of Eastern Europe. Riots in Poland in 1976 forced postponement of a projected rise in food prices, and four years later strikes led to the recognition of Solidarity, an organization of independent trade unions, whose leader, Lech Walesa, became a national hero. With support from the Catholic Church, the Solidarity movement grew strong enough to prompt a change of government. In a world in which public protest was dangerous and rare, events in Poland gained significance. But there was no telling where they would lead. The new head of the Polish Communist party, General Wojciech Jaruzelski, resorted to martial law and clamped down on Solidarity. East European governments continued to rely on force in the face of rising public resentment.

Yugoslavia was the maverick among communist states. Its limited market economy and its independence from the Soviet Union had once suggested another kind of communism. Weakened by Tito's death in 1980 and by contention among its member republics, Yugoslavia could not manage the reforms necessary to shake its economy out of a prolonged economic downturn. There was, in fact, no model of how to make desired changes and preserve communist rule. Soviet presence remained the central fact of life in Eastern Europe.

IV. The End of an Era

◆

International relations, domestic politics, culture, and trade had all been shaped by forty years of Cold War. In one of history's sudden great turns, communist governments fell across Europe, bringing new regimes in the East and easing domestic divisions in the West by undermining

**BOUNDARY CHANGES
SINCE 1989**

☐ Former boundary of Soviet Union

☐ Former boundary of Czechoslovakia

☐ Former boundary of Yugoslavia

☐ Former boundary between
East & West Germany

All other boundaries as of 1994

▲ MAP 30.3 EUROPE SINCE WORLD WAR II
◆ www.mhhe.com/chambers8ch30maps

ideologies of left and right. Market economies and mass, parliamentary democracies were the order of the day.

◆ THE MIRACLES OF 1989

Although the contradictions had become obvious, no one expected communist rule to collapse completely. Eastern Europe governments had for years eased up on controls and repression when greater efficiency or popular anger seemed to require it. When, however, those steps exposed institutional blockage and threatening dissent, communist governments had moved to stifle reform and silence opposition. In 1989 they did not, and one by one communist regimes were swept away.

Poland   In Poland, despite martial law, Solidarity continued its underground propaganda with wit and daring. It turned the visit of the pope, who was Polish, into the occasion for more demonstrations. Placards and pamphlets, rumors and clandestine radio broadcasts nourished rising agitation. And the government did not call out the army. Gorbachev had told the United Nations in 1988 that the Soviet Union would allow its allies to go their own way. Now that policy was tested. Sensing Walesa's popularity and the power of Solidarity, Jaruzelski relaxed martial law and released some political prisoners. But public anger and frustration increased, and the economy worsened. In February 1989 the government, in a major concession, acknowledged Solidarity's legitimacy, but Solidarity demanded free elections. The government hesitated, and Gorbachev signaled that Poland was on its own. In April, when elections took place, Solidarity won almost all the seats in the parliament. Stunned and frightened, Communist party members did not know what to

▼ **Lech Walesa addressed workers outside a factory in Zyrardow, not far from Warsaw, in October 1981. The scene, reminiscent of the long history of labor movements except for the television cameras, marked the rising power of the Solidarity movement.**
Giansanti/Corbis Sygma

do. After various formulas for compromise failed, Solidarity took over the cabinet in August, the first noncommunist government in the Soviet bloc.

Hungary Hungarians were well aware of events in Poland, for the irrepressible flow of information was an important factor in the events of 1989. Political discussion, like economic activity, was already freer in Hungary than other Eastern European countries, and by April even some party officials joined in public discussions of the need for free speech, civil rights, and the protection of private property. At the annual May Day celebrations, international communism's grandest occasion, opponents dwarfed the official celebration, and a huge demonstration in June dared to honor the uprising of 1956. Even some members of the government chose to attend. In October the Hungarian Communist party flexibly changed its name to the Socialist party and promised free elections for the following year. The power of people aroused seemed irresistible.

East Germany Many old-line Communist leaders remained convinced that a good show of force would restore order and keep the party in power. In October Erich Honecker, the head of East Germany's Communist party and its prime minister, took that tack. His soldiers beat and arrested demonstrators in East Berlin. A week later, however, he resigned, for Gorbachev announced that he disapproved such use of force; worse, the East German republic was walking away. Every day hundreds of people, especially the young and those with marketable skills, abandoned their country. Most went to Hungary, where they mobbed the West German embassy, seeking visas. Embarrassed Hungarian and West German governments arranged for special trains to carry them west, and more people came, pushing and shouting and climbing over embassy walls.

On November 9, 1989, Honecker's successor announced that East Germany's border with West Berlin would be opened that very day. The guards could not believe their orders. Then late that night they shrugged and stepped aside as hoards of people pushed through the gates of the Berlin Wall. Hundreds, then thousands, cheered and waved from atop that symbol of oppression before strolling past the well-stocked shops of West Berlin. The celebrations continued in front of the television cameras for days, even after work crews began dismantling the wall. Thousands continued to come each day, some just testing what it felt like to be that free and looking in store windows, others seeking a different life in West Germany. Throughout East Germany, meetings that would have been illegal a few weeks earlier took place in churches and public squares as the police watched and then withdrew. The government's promises for reform and official pleas for order were drowned in revelations of past corruption and talk of uniting the two Germanies.

The Final Round in Eastern Europe For a while the harsher East European governments—in Czechoslovakia, Bulgaria, and Romania—remained unscathed by the changes around them, but that isolation did not last. Crowds of protesters were filling Wenceslas Square in Prague, 40,000 people in October, then 200,000 after a riot in which police beat up demonstrating students. A few days later 300,000 came to shout, sing, and jingle keys as a good-humored suggestion that it was time for the Communists to leave. In now familiar rites, slogans were scrawled everywhere, posters covered the walls, and new political groups formed. By December 1989 the best organized of these, Civic Forum, had won power and elected as president of Czechoslovakia its leader, Vaclav Havel, the popular playwright whose works had long been banned (see "Havel's Inaugural Address," p. 1141).

Even Bulgaria and Romania, with less-developed economies and weaker traditions of political participation, could not escape the historic pressure. They met it very differently. Bulgaria's Communist party took its cues from the Soviet Union and in November forced from office Todor Zhivkov, party secretary for thirty-five years and head of state for twenty-seven. He was jailed and plans for free elections announced. Romania, in contrast, suffered weeks of bloodshed. When in December crowds gathered in Bucharest, the government gave the order to shoot. Still the crowds formed and violence increased. Romania's dictator, Ceauşescu, tried to make his escape but

HAVEL'S INAUGURAL ADDRESS

◆

Vaclav Havel was perhaps the most widely admired of the new leaders of Eastern Europe, and his literary skill and philosophic bent made him a particularly effective spokesperson. In his inaugural address on January 1, 1990, as president of the Czech Republic, he commented on the historical meaning of the dramatic changes that brought him to office.

"My dear fellow citizens, for forty years you heard from my predecessors on this day different variations of the same theme: how our country flourished, how many million tons of steel we produced, how happy we all were, how we trusted our government, and what bright perspectives were unfolding in front of us.

"I assume you did not propose me for this office so that I, too, would lie to you.

"Our country is not flourishing. The enormous creative and spiritual potential of our nation is not being used sensibly. Entire branches of industry are producing goods which are of no interest to anyone, while we are lacking the things we need. A state which calls itself a workers' state humiliates and exploits workers. Our obsolete economy is wasting the little energy we have available. A country that once could be proud of the educational level of its citizens spends so little on education that it ranks today as seventy-second in the world. We have polluted our soil, our rivers and forests, bequeathed to us by our ancestors, and we have today the most contaminated environment in Europe. Adult people in our country die earlier than in most other European countries. . . .

"But all this is still not the main problem. The worst thing is that we live in a contaminated moral environment. We fell morally ill because we became used to saying something different from what we thought. We learned not to believe in anything, to ignore each other, to care only about ourselves. Concepts such as love, friendship, compassion, humility, or forgiveness lost their depth and dimensions, and for many of us they represented only psychological peculiarities, or they resembled gone-astray greetings from ancient times, a little ridiculous in the era of computers and spaceships. Only a few of us were able to cry out loud that the powers that be should not be all-powerful, and that special farms, which produce ecologically pure and top-quality food just for them, should send their produce to schools, children's homes, and hospitals if our agriculture was unable to offer them to all. The previous regime—armed with its arrogant and intolerant ideology—reduced man to a force of production and nature to a tool of production. In this it attacked both their very substance and their mutual relationship. It reduced gifted and autonomous people, skillfully working in their own country, to nuts and bolts of some monstrously huge, noisy, and stinking machine, whose real meaning is not clear to anyone. It cannot do more than slowly but inexorably wear down itself and all its nuts and bolts."

From Brian MacArthur (ed.), *The Penguin Book of Twentieth-Century Speeches* (New York: Viking, 1992).

was caught and executed by firing squad on Christmas day. Fighting continued for a week between the army and special police loyal to Ceaușescu. Everywhere Romanians waved flags with a conspicuous hole in the center where the Communist hammer and sickle had been. The last communist government west of the Soviet Union (except for Albania) had fallen.

Rarely has there been so sudden a political collapse and on such a scale. Economic failure and resentment of Soviet dominance explain a good deal. Workers and Catholics in Poland, party members and entrepreneurs in Hungary, students and intellectuals in Czechoslovakia mobilized their fellow citizens with surprising speed and skill. For years radio and television had conveyed the knowledge that life was better in the West, despite all the efforts at censorship; and in the fall of 1989 images of cheering or rioting crowds spread the contagion of revolt. In the face of such diffuse anger, officials remarkably ready to quit and citizens determined to push revealed shockingly widespread cynicism about these regimes. The frequent comparisons to the revolutions across

▲ **May 1990: Having pulled a statue of Lenin to the ground, Romanian workers remove the cable from his neck.**
© Corbis

Europe in 1848 made sense. Young men and women, especially students, echoed the events of 1968 and revealed the impact of an international youth culture in their clothes and music, their sense of theater and use of mockery, and their slogans. As crowds lost their fear, a massive contempt and a universal hunger for freedom washed away the pomp of officialdom, the claims of party ideology, and the power of the police.

Freedom illumined not only the appalling failures and corruption of the fallen regimes but also the problems still to be faced. Within months, unaccustomed freedoms resurrected old divisions—ethnic, social, and ideological. All at once, the Eastern Europe of 1990 looked much like that of

the 1920s. Moderate conservatives gained the lead among Hungary's multiple parties and expressed nationalist resentment at the treatment Romania accorded Hungarians living in its territory. Czechoslovakia was soon debating yet again the relations of Czechs and Slovaks. As Poland risked the drastic medicine of sudden conversion to a market economy, rifts appeared within Solidarity. In Bulgaria, Communist party members won most of the seats in free elections, and in Romania leaders who claimed no longer to be Communists showed little willingness to allow real democracy. East Germans voted for those who promised the most rapid assimilation into the German Federal Republic.

◆ THE DISINTEGRATION OF THE USSR

A hero in Western Europe and the United States, Gorbachev was never so popular at home. Efforts to create more of a market economy threatened jobs. Attempts to make one sector more efficient were stymied by related sectors that operated in the old ways. The new price structure increased inflation, uncertainty, and hoarding. Many party members and the army resented the erosion of their own authority and the weakening of the Soviet Union's international position.

The Opposition to Gorbachev Seeking a strong political base, Gorbachev called for a huge Congress of People's Deputies as a step toward greater democracy. It met in 1989 and elected Gorbachev president of the Soviet Union. It also rejected the constitution's assertion that the Communist party must be preeminent (like all Soviet leaders since Stalin, Gorbachev's power had previously come from his position as party secretary). Discussions were more open than ever before. Deputies attacked old abuses, denounced the KGB, and gave vent to a rising chorus of competing ethnic demands. Solzhenitsyn warned against allowing Western decadence to infiltrate Russian society. Caught in the middle, Gorbachev clamped down on the media and allowed the army to threaten that it might restore order in the Baltic republics.

Among the opponents of this authoritarian turn, Boris Yeltsin, the head of the Communist

▲ Lithuanian crowds hold up a banner that says "Ivan Go Home" and cheer as a Soviet soldier is burned in effigy. This demonstration in April 1990 followed two years of similar agitation.
© Corbis

party in Moscow, stood out. An outspoken populist, he reached ordinary people as Gorbachev never had, and in 1991 he was elected by popular vote president of the Russian republic, the largest in the Soviet Union. Other enemies of Gorbachev were active, too. When Gorbachev took his August vacation in the Crimea, hard-liners in his own government, in the military, and in the KGB staged a coup. Tanks filled the streets, and the coup leaders announced that Gorbachev had been replaced. Beyond that, they seemed to have no plan. Yeltsin held firm against the coup with remarkable support from public opinion. Crowds pleaded with the soldiers not to act, miners in

Siberia went on a strike, demonstrators marched in city after city, and some army officers declared their support of Yeltsin.

Within two days, the leaders of the coup were in prison and Gorbachev was back in Moscow, but he was now overshadowed by Yeltsin. He had no party, for across the nation, people pulled down the symbols of communism, closed and sometimes looted Communist party offices. Only eight of the fifteen Soviet republics responded to his call for a meeting. In October 1991 Russia, Ukraine, Belarus, and Kazakhstan declared that the Soviet Union had ceased to exist. No significant group fought to save it, and it was replaced

BOUNDARY CHANGES SINCE 1989

—— Former boundary of Soviet Union

⫽⫽⫽ Former area of Soviet Union

—— Former boundary of Czechoslovakia

—— Former boundary of Yugoslavia

---- Former boundary between East & West Germany

All other boundaries as of 1998

SIGNIFICANT NATIONALIST MOVEMENTS

1 France (Brittany)

2 France (Corsica)

3 Great Britain (Scotland)

4 Great Britain (Wales)

5 Italy (Sardinia)

6 Italy (Tyrol)

7 Spain (Basque Region)

8 Spain (Catalonia)

AREAS OF VIOLENT CONFLICT OR OPEN WAR

1 Armenia-Azerbaijan

2 Georgia-Abkhazia

3 Moldova

4 Bosnia-Herzegovina, former Yugoslavia

5 Northern Ireland

6 Persian Gulf War

7 Israeli-Palestinian conflict

8 Kurdish-Turkish-Iraqi conflict

9 Chechnya

ETHNIC-BASED DISPUTES

1 Hungarian populations in Slovakia

2 Hungarian poulations in Romania

3 Russian populations in Crimea (Ukraine)

4 Russian populations in Georgia

5 Russian populations in Azerbaijan

6 Russian populations in Baltic States

▲ **MAP 30.4** ETHNIC AND TERRITORIAL CONFLICT IN EUROPE AND THE MIDDLE EAST

by the looser Confederation of Independent States. Gorbachev resigned, a victim of the revolution he had unleashed.

◆ EUROPE WITHOUT COLD WAR

The fall of communism and the collapse of the Soviet Union meant the end of the Cold War. The policies of fifty years had to be rethought, as did the hard-headed assumptions on which they had rested. No one could know the implications of such fundamental changes, but it was clear that domestic politics, economic policies, and international relations would all now be different.

German Unification The fall of communism affected Germany right away. Chancellor Kohl pushed for the immediate unification of East and West Germany, moving faster than many Germans thought wise, outmaneuvering the opposition parties, and capturing popular enthusiasm. By the end of 1989, he had gained the support of the United States and then of France, in effect, forcing a reluctant Britain to join in negotiations aimed at winning Soviet acceptance of German unification. Many were frightened at the prospect, but Kohl reassured the West with the promise that an enlarged Germany would be fully integrated into the European Community. The Soviet Union feared the increase in NATO's strength, but such concerns were rooted in an era quickly passing. In August 1990 the victors of World War II—the Soviet Union, the United States, Britain, and France—signed a treaty with the two Germanies. In return for the promise to respect its boundary with Poland and to limit the size of its combined army, Germany could unify and remain in NATO as Europe's richest and most powerful state.

For Germans, however, the benefits were not immediate. The East German economy, which had been the most productive in Eastern Europe, revealed enormous weakness. Its outmoded and inefficient industry could not compete in the dynamic economy of the West, and unemployment rose. East Germans, suffering high unemployment, resented what felt like subordinate status, and West Germans struggled with the unexpectedly high cost of unification as well as a flood of German immigrants. Confidently, parliament voted to make Berlin once again the capital

of a united Germany, launching a building boom there that has made it one of Europe's most exciting and dynamic cities. Nevertheless, by 1998 German unemployment hit a postwar high at 12.6 percent, and in the election of that year the Christian Democrats lost to the Social Democrats. Shortly after that Helmut Kohl, the hero of unification, was disgraced by revelations of corrupt practices in party finance, and the Christian Democrats chose Angela Merkel to lead them in opposition. She was the first woman to lead a major German party.

New Political Alignments and Immigration The collapse of communist regimes had important repercussions elsewhere, too. Italian politics since World War II had been shaped by the presence of a powerful Communist party that was excluded from power. Increasingly moderate, it responded to the events of 1989 by making a final break with old-line communism and changing its name. The Christian Democrats, however, lost their principal reason for being, which had been to keep the Communists out of power. When charges of corruption uncovered a vast network of graft, the Christian Democratic party and their Socialist allies both simply disintegrated. In the next parliament, two-thirds of the deputies had never held any elective office and most belonged to new parties with new leaders. Public contempt for the old political class and a new electoral system (reducing the effects of proportional representation) opened the way for a restructuring of the political system.

Throughout Europe, politics was altered by the enfeeblement of the Marxist left, by the weakening of the anticommunist right, and by resentment of foreigners. Shifting toward the center enabled parties of the center-left to gain office in Italy (1996), France and Britain (1997), and Germany (1998). While preserving systems of national health care and increasing access to higher education, all of them followed policies of balanced budgets and the privatization of government-owned industries.

On the right, noisy new groups, often with neo-fascist tendencies, played on the fear of foreigners, gaining attention and many votes from Russia through the West. Heightened by unemployment and by the increased number of immigrants from Eastern Europe, Turkey, the Middle East, and Africa, antiforeign feeling fed on the competition for space and ill-paying jobs. In Italy a new party, the Northern League, gained ground in the prosperous north by combining in one program opposition to immigration and denunciation of the central government's corruption and high taxes. In France unemployed industrial workers who had voted communist in the past were often sympathetic to the xenophobic but influential campaigns of the National Front. Aimed especially at Muslims from North Africa, these campaigns made immigration a national issue that influenced governmental policies. And in Germany, where hundreds of thousands of people made their way from the faltering economies of Eastern Europe, incidents in which gangs of skinheads and neo-Nazis burned immigrant housing were an ominous reminder of Germany's past. These movements, most of which never gained more than a small minority of votes, were denounced by the left and by most figures of authority, especially in France. When, in 2000, an Austrian party led by Joerg Haider, who had expressed admiration for Hitler, gained a share in the ruling coalition, the other EU nations joined in refusing formal cooperation with the Austrian government. Although that effort had limited effect, it raised new concern that the EU might infringe on national sovereignty, especially in smaller nations.

The Transition from Communism   The governments of Eastern Europe turned out to have heavier debts and more outmoded industries than even the critics of communism had suspected, and industrial pollution on an enormous, sometimes life-threatening, scale was a difficult problem for new governments in strapped economies. Unsure of the loyalty or competence of their own administrations, they attempted painful reforms while subject to unfamiliar public criticism. The capitalism suddenly unleashed was often socially disruptive, and the search for a new sense of community encouraged appeals to ethnic identity.

Poland undertook the most radical shift to a market economy, and economic indicators showed dramatic improvement. Ordinary citizens often suffered, however, and former Communists gained in the elections of 1993 by promising to

slow the transition. Russia, Hungary, Poland, and the Czech Republic pleaded for more foreign aid and foreign investment. The relentless drive to capitalism in prosperous Czech regions and the cynical ambitions of Slovak politicians had forced the breakup of Czechoslovakia, creating the Czech Republic and Slovakia, although opinion polls indicated a majority in each country would have preferred to stay together. Elsewhere, too, economic strains reinforced ethnic and religious conflict, something nationalist parties were quick to use, especially in Romania.

The Breakup of Yugoslavia   Former Communists, in fact, proved particularly adept at stirring ethnic resentments, especially in the former Soviet Union and, most tragically of all, in Yugoslavia. Ethnic differences had not prevented Yugoslavia's six republics from effectively functioning together even after the death of Tito. By the 1980s Croatia and Slovenia, economically the most developed Yugoslav republics, openly attacked the economic and political policies of the Serbian-dominated government of Yugoslavia. As demands for reform grew stronger with the fall of communism elsewhere, Serbian communists resisted by raising support at home through appeals to Serbian nationalism. In 1990–1991 Slovenia and Macedonia joined Croatia and Bosnia-Herzegovina in declaring their independence. But large numbers of Serbs lived in sections of the latter two lands. Efforts to expel them and their own armed resistance, supported by the Yugoslav government under Slobodan Milosevic, created civil war. Regional, economic, and ideological differences transmuted into ethnic hatred as each side, recalling past injustices, committed new atrocities. Truces were signed and broken. Uncontrolled local units could count on support no matter what horrors they committed. Slaughter and rape destroyed whole villages. By 1993 Serb forces had recaptured about one-third of Croatia and nearly two-thirds of Bosnia-Herzegovina, a republic in which Serbs, Croatians, and Muslims had once been proud of living peacefully together.

Despite these horrors and the risk that war could spread, NATO and the EU responded weakly, denouncing ethnic violence but not wanting to be drawn into a Balkan war. Slowly, the United States assumed a cautious leadership,

Former border of Yugoslavia

Border of Bosnia-Herzegovina

Dayton Agreement inter-entity boundary
(November, 1995)

Bosnian Serb territory, after Dayton

Croat-Muslim Federation portion of Bosnia,
after Dayton

▲ MAP 30.4 INSET

pressuring the contending parties to accept a truce signed in 1995 in Dayton, Ohio. American and even some Russian troops then joined European and UN forces as peacekeepers with limited roles. Although Milosevic faced opposition at home, militant nationalism and alert police squelched voices of moderation. Meanwhile, ethnic Albanians grew increasingly restive in Kosovo, a Yugoslav province historically tied to Serb identity. Milosevic followed a familiar pattern, tightening control, using nationalist rhetoric, and in 1998 launching an assault to drive the Albanians out. It was called ethnic cleansing, and it pushed more than 600,000 refugees out of the country. NATO forces, led by the United States, responded in March 1999 with an air assault that lasted three months before the Serbs withdrew. Yugoslavia, its infrastructure badly damaged, was reduced to Serbia and a discontented Montenegro. The uneasy peace in the Balkans depended on the presence of foreign troops keeping ethnic groups

apart, while most of those accused of war crimes remained out of reach.

Hope for a more principled outcome revived in the fall of 2000, however, when Milosovic was forced from power. His efforts to manipulate elections had brought the opposition parties, students, and farmers together in demonstrations reminiscent of Warsaw and Prague a decade earlier. Police and propaganda lost effectiveness, and Europe's last communist government fell. Its shaky replacement looked to the EU for economic and political support. Yugoslavia had to deal with a devastated economy and do so—like much of Eastern Europe—with ramshackle institutions, administrators and police from the previous regime, and a populace in poverty, harboring tragic memories and bitter resentments only partially repressed. Tensions eased, however, in a more open regime. It allowed Milosovic to be tried for war crimes in the Hague, and in 2002 Serbia and Montenegro agreed to split while keeping their diplomatic and military services in common. Yugoslavia was no more.

Transition in Russia Only Yugoslavia faced more serious ethnic conflicts than Russia, and no former communist country found the transition to free markets more difficult. As president, Yeltsin postponed as much as he could and tried to moderate disputes within the new Confederation of Independent States while he pushed for drastic economic reform. The effects, though limited, were painful. Unemployment rose, the ruble all but collapsed, and production fell to about half what it had been a few years before. Managers did not know how to adjust to a market economy; many officials resisted change altogether. As repression eased, corruption spread, criminal gangs flourished, and ugly groups of nationalists grew louder.

Free elections in 1991 produced a Congress of People's Deputies in which Yeltsin's opponents—communists, nationalists, members of the military, and representatives of regional movements—outnumbered his supporters. Yeltsin compromised when possible and ignored the Congress when he could. As parliamentary resistance stiffened and his own popularity declined, Yeltsin risked a national presidential election in the spring of 1993 and won. A few months later Yeltsin declared the parliament dissolved. Several hundred delegates refused to obey. Holed up in their offices, they

▲ **The Soviet army surveys the streets of Moscow in October 1993 after having preserved Yeltsin's hold on power by storming the parliament's White House, where opposition leaders had barricaded themselves.** Liaison International/Getty Images

collected arms and called on the people and the army for support. The army remained silent, but the delegates were heartened when groups of Yeltsin's opponents gathered outside the parliament building. Amid calls to bring the government down, shots were fired from within, until the army bombarded and then stormed the building. A hundred or more people died, more bloodshed than Moscow had seen since 1917.

Reliance on the military, like Yeltsin's measures against parliament and his indifference to the rulings of the supreme court, was troubling proof that Russia had not achieved a constitutional system or the rule of law. Although seemingly rather indifferent, the public supported Yeltsin when forced to choose, and he surprised pollsters by winning reelection in 1996. By then the economy was improving slightly, and Russia could take its place in meetings of the nations with the largest economies. Ill and exhausted, Yeltsin named

Vladimir Putin his successor and stepped down on the last day of 1999; it was, he noted, the end of the millennium. Putin, a former KGB officer who had entered politics in 1990, won the presidential election in March 2000. Combining insistence on order, cryptic statements in favor of democracy, shrewd deals at home, and assertion of Russia's importance abroad, he brought an air of firmness to a still unstable polity.

International Implications The end of the Cold War affected international affairs around the world. The United Nations, no longer hobbled by a Security Council in which the United States and Russia nearly always disagreed, began to function more in the way envisioned at its founding, pacifying local conflicts and providing humanitarian aid. When Iraq invaded Kuwait in 1991, Russia supported the American-led attack on Iraq. Unable to play on superpower competition, all sides in the Middle East had to reassess their positions. Without Soviet support, the Muslim states could only lose by diplomatic intransigence, and once Israel was no longer a Cold War bastion, it could be less certain of unending American aid. After decades of stalemate, Palestinians and Israelis agreed in 1993 to negotiate on limited autonomy for Palestine. Just as some resolution seemed imminent in 2000, however, fear and violence flared again, threatening to undo the peace process.

Ironically, the diplomatic implications of the Cold War's end were less clear in Europe, where that confrontation had begun. The future of NATO was a major issue, and its failure to act in Yugoslavia increased public doubts about its continued usefulness. The United States, with British support, insisted it was still needed; Germany and France appeared tempted by the idea of a more autonomous European force. Reacting to its initially feeble response to the Balkan crisis, the EU agreed in 2000 to create its own rapid-response force to serve as peacekeepers in just such situations. NATO also decided to expand, including nations once in the Soviet bloc (Hungary, Poland, and the Czech Republic were to be the first to join and others indicated a wish to do so). That would assure American involvement on the continent and protect East European nations from Russia. It might also prevent those nations from fighting each other over boundaries that had changed many times in the recent past and often been a cause of war. There were risks, however, in isolating Russia, selecting certain states to become NATO members, and requiring them to invest in the modern arms NATO membership required. Meanwhile, the slowly moving negotiations to dismantle nuclear warheads in the three former Soviet republics that harbored them remained an encouraging sign of the changes brought by the end of the Cold War. So did Russia's agreement to take part in NATO deliberations.

A New War on Terrorism   The overarching international reality was that the United States had become the world's only superpower. While maintaining close relations with the United States, members of the European Union sought collectively and individually to establish some independence in world affairs. Greater tensions arose in areas beyond Europe. In Asia, Latin America, and the Middle East, issues were often defined as reactions to U.S. policy even though that policy was not always consistent or clear. Efforts to unseat or at least discipline the Iraqi regime had limited effect, were often distrusted in Europe, and fed rising resentment in the Muslim world. America's hesitant interventions to end civil war and foster democracy in Africa, the Caribbean, and the Balkans had mixed results and garnered more criticism than support at home. But if the "Vietnam syndrome" made the United States cautious about military intervention, America's economic power and pervasive mass culture were felt everywhere.

On taking office in January 2001, the administration of George W. Bush appeared to be setting a new course. With little consultation of other nations, the United States declared its determination to stand alone in rejecting international agreements, those on the environment and nuclear arms, among many others. It also broke from previous administrations by announcing that it would not undertake "nation building" in unstable societies and would no longer serve as the active intermediary in the Israeli-Palestinian conflict. These and similar measures brought denunciations from Russia and cries of protest from Europe against American "unilateralism."

Then on September 11, 2001, nineteen men highjacked four domestic flights. One plane crashed, one flew into the Pentagon, and the other two deliberately smashed into the twin towers of the World Trade Center in New York City. The effects were catastrophic. The planes, loaded with fuel for transcontinental flights, were incendiary bombs, setting fires that blasted people out of the buildings and melted steel girders, causing the towers to crumble in a fountain of debris. Some three thousand people died from these assaults on symbols of American economic and military strength. Almost from the beginning television carried images around the world of the largely futile rescue efforts in an inferno of flames and smoke that lasted for days. Expressions of sympathy and outrage poured in from nearly every nation, and the public learned that this devastating act of terrorism had apparently been the work of a network of Muslim extremists. Their headquarters were in Afghanistan, where they were led by

▲ **The wreckage of the World Trade Center in New York City. Searing images of airplanes shooting into the twin towers and of the resulting destruction burned into the American consciousness.**
SipaPress

Osama bin Laden, a wealthy Saudi opposed to the Saudi Arabian government, which he denounced as a repressive agent of the American infidel. In Afghanistan he cooperated with the fanatically intolerant Taliban regime that gained control of most of the country in the aftermath of the Afghan war against the Soviet Union.

Religion, geopolitics, a global economy, and global communications came together in the training camps Osama bin Laden maintained. His group was responsible for at least three major attacks on American forces and embassies in the Middle East and Africa starting in 1993. While he escaped American efforts to hunt him down, he gained sympathy in the Muslim world by fanning resentment of American policy in the Middle East, especially its support for Israel, and by denouncing America's "immoral" culture and selfish eco-

nomic power. With a network of agents and funds scattered across Europe and into Asia, he had accomplished the first important attack on American soil since the war of 1812.

Americans responded with patriotic fervor, and President Bush declared the focus of his administration to be the war against terrorism around the world. NATO, for the first time in its history, invoked a treaty clause that considered an attack on one member as an attack on all. Britain and France offered their armed forces as did other members of NATO. Russia announced its willingness to join (recalling that it considered the Chechnyan rebels to be terrorists, too). The United Nations unanimously supported the United States (which had recently agreed to pay most of its back dues), while Muslim nations and leaders cautiously distanced themselves from the Afghan government and the terrorists it harbored. As the United States assembled its military force, governments everywhere began to freeze bank accounts the terrorists might use and to round up Middle Easterners suspected of ties to terrorists. Amid remarkable international cooperation and many hopeful signs, people everywhere wondered what else they had to fear. No one knew quite how this new kind of war would be fought, how extensive it might become, or how long it would last.

V. Contemporary Culture

The burst of artistic creativity that followed World War II embraced new trends and styles in all the arts. At the same time, the global expansion of a dynamic popular culture is one of the hallmarks of the second half of the twentieth century. Gradually interwoven into modern social thought, these developments have contributed to new ideas about culture that have spread through the humanities and social sciences and influenced modern social movements.

◆ POSTWAR CREATIVITY

With the end of the war, European artists could reflect more freely on the searing experiences of repression and bloodshed that had darkened the previous decade. They could take part in artistic movements that had been banned under fascist governments, and they could catch up on the new ideas and styles coming from America, where the many European artists and intellectuals who fled the continent had helped to make New York the cultural capital of the Western world. Figures already famous in the 1930s, like the painter Pablo Picasso and the poet T. S. Eliot, could now be simultaneously honored as founders of modern art and savored with a freshness usually reserved for the newly discovered. The works most admired in the 1950s and 1960s showed considerable continuity with the avant-garde works of the prewar period.

Authors wanting to show how ordinary people had experienced dictatorship, war, and postwar dislocation favored a style noted for its directness and telling detail. Called neorealism, this style flourished especially in Italy, where the novels of Ignazio Silone and Alberto Moravia gave incisive, often bitter, yet affectionate accounts of the daily struggles of people buffeted by movements and events beyond their control, and where the films of Roberto Rossellini and Vittorio de Sica combined the harsh eye of the candid camera with sympathy for the minor characters who are society's victims and its strength.

These forms gradually gave way to ones that built on more radical prewar art and presented several points of view simultaneously, challenging any assumption of a single reality. In Germany the plays of Bertolt Brecht used such devices for a firm Marxist purpose (in 1949 Brecht left the West to live in East Berlin), and the savagely satirical novels of Heinrich Böll extended the once-shocking surrealism of Franz Kafka to convey central Europe's experience of the twentieth century. Stimulus from outside Europe was also important. The most admired sculptor, the English artist Henry Moore, was directly influenced by African art in designing huge reclining figures that combined clean lines, solid masses, and provocative empty spaces.

Adapting Traditional Values   The arguments for human decency needed restatement following the horrors of genocide, totalitarianism, and war. Existentialism, one of the most influential movements of the postwar period, offered a radical solution to the problem of ethics. Life may be absurd and meaningless, the French philosopher Jean-Paul Sartre reasoned, but to take any action is to make a decision, and doing so is to make a personal moral choice. Building on the prewar work of Karl Jaspers and Martin Heidegger in Germany, Sartre constructed a radical individualism that centered on moral responsibility. Even in the worst of circumstances, the sum of the choices made give each life its moral meaning. The soldier could refuse to torture; the civilian could choose to resist custom or authority. Underneath its relentless pessimism, Sartre's existentialism—set forth in essays, dramas, and criticism—held out the possibility of moral heroism.

Christian voices shared in the postwar anguish over values. Leading theologians—also

▲ Prelates from around the world stand as Pope Paul VI is carried on his throne into St. Peter's during the Vatican Council. Amid Renaissance splendor, the leaders of the Catholic Church set about the task of *aggiornamento*.
AP/Wide World Photos

mainly men of an older generation, like Jaspers, Karl Barth, and Jacques Maritain—were studied with renewed interest. The Protestant Paul Tillich and the Catholic Pierre Teilhard de Chardin achieved a large following with their systematic claims for Christianity's relevance to modern life. This confidence, reflected in the postwar vigor of Christian political parties, illuminated the pa-

pacy (1958–1963) of Pope John XXIII. He was extraordinarily popular, admired by Protestants as well as Catholics and by peasants and workers as well as intellectuals. Determined to recast the Church's position in the modern world, he called the Vatican Council known as Vatican II, which opened in 1962. Devoted to *aggiornamento*, the Council sought to bring the Catholic Church up to date not just organizationally but in social policy as well. It made the leadership of the Church far more international, directed attention to the concerns of developing nations, made respect for Jews a formal policy, and expressed belief in religious liberty. Putting more emphasis on individual understanding than institutional uniformity, it ordered that Masses be conducted in the vernacular instead of Latin. These changes encountered resistance, and with Pope John's death before the Council was completed, the Church turned to more cautious consolidation of doctrine and structure.

◆ THE EXPLOSION OF POPULAR CULTURE

American Influence   A very large part of the commercial entertainment that Europeans watch and listen to comes from the United States. American dominance in the motion picture industry, apparent in the 1930s, has grown since World War II. Although European governments have tried a variety of measures to reduce the proportion of American productions in their movie theaters and on television, they have failed. In the 1950s over half of the movies that Europeans attended were from the United States, and by the 1990s the figure was more than 80 percent. American films had some commercial advantages. They could be offered cheaply because the large American market had already covered most of their production costs. American movie companies were masters at distribution, and the American government was willing to pressure other countries to provide access to American films. American productions have had similar success on European television, as privately owned television networks compete with government-run networks by filling a majority of their airtime with inexpensive American reruns.

In fact, American television productions have demonstrated remarkably wide appeal. The television series *Dallas* was as popular and well known in Europe as in the United States, and Italian judges have found themselves explaining to defendants more familiar with *Perry Mason* than with their own justice system that "your honor" is not a term used in Italian courts. By the 1990s, soap operas from Brazil (especially popular in Portugal and Spain) and Australia (especially popular in Great Britain) were added to American shows as regular fare on European television networks owned by Italian, French, and German media tycoons. Theme parks, too, have spread from the United States to Europe. Denmark has its Legoland; and *Parc Asterix*, based on a series of French comic books, is located on the outskirts of Paris, not far from the European Disneyland.

An International Youth Culture   Much criticized on both sides of the Atlantic, such commercial entertainment had been especially troubling to many European intellectuals who feared that their societies would follow the American example. Conservatives worried that American-style democracy undermined the values that supported high culture; Marxists believed that ruthless capitalism made culture a commodity, mass produced, cheap, and aimed at the lowest taste. The signs that something more was at stake—the creation of an international youth culture—became clearer in the 1950s with the international appeal of rock and roll and the fashions that went with it.

American jazz had been popular in Europe since the 1920s, especially in France, and after the war, the presence of American troops and the programs of Armed Forces Radio did much to disseminate American popular music. The new

▼ In Poland in 1987, fans at a rock concert celebrate in international style.
Christophe Kazor/Corbis Sygma

musical culture did not come exclusively from the United States, however. The Beatles, who combined American influences with those of the British music hall, were by far the most influential popular music group of the 1960s and, along with the Rolling Stones, helped to create a transatlantic style that was at home on the continent and in Latin America as well as in Britain and the United States. By the 1980s an international tour was a normal part of star status in pop music. In each country, performances were usually preceded by local groups, adding to the sense of a single culture with national variants. When in 1997 the Irish band U2 performed in Rome and Sarajevo, or when Bob Dylan and gospel singers appeared with the Pope at a eucharistic congress, national origin hardly seemed to matter.

New Directions   The arts had never been more international than after World War II, and they were necessarily affected by the energy of new forms of popular culture. One response was to turn away from the fast-paced plots of American cinema in favor of a more reflective mood. The novels of Alain Robbe-Grillet and the films of Jean François Truffaut and Ingmar Bergman were contemplative personal essays, held together by the sensitivity and imagination of a single creator and by images simultaneously surreal and real. Identified in France as the *nouvelle vague* of the 1960s, this style had its counterpart in all the arts.

Experiment and Shock   The desire to convey individual and fleeting perceptions encouraged further experimentation with varied forms of narrative in literature and a freer use of surrealistic images in the visual media. The highly personal and even autobiographical films of Federico Fellini incorporated swirling images of circuslike fantasy. In painting, highly disciplined abstract expressionism gave way to a great variety of styles that often made use of popular culture and referred to urban consumerism. New styles, such as Pop Art and Op Art were deliberately garish and disturbing in treating recognizable objects satirically. Younger artists found original ways to transform the familiar into something new, using common objects and materials of every sort to produce strange forms and creating gigantic "environmental" sculptures consisting of lines traced across deserts or plastic wrapping stretched around whole buildings.

At the same time that popular music tended to become more complex and artistically serious, noted composers of classical or art music were drawn to experiments using everyday noises and musical sounds carefully arranged on spliced tapes, a form known as *musique concrète,* and with electronic music in the manner of the American John Cage and the German Karlheinz Stockhausen. Even when it employed traditional instruments, the dissonances and strange rhythms of avant-garde music won only a tiny audience, but it shared the general determination to breach artistic conventions. In their need to stimulate a public already bombarded by images and sensations, visual artists also used technology for aesthetic purposes. Taking advantage of the ambiguity of random noise, flashing lights, plastics forms, and mechanical motion, they further eroded the distinctions between art and advertising.

Postmodernism   The change of attitude as the arts tended to become less austere and less concerned with the formal principles that academies taught and critics favored was dramatically obvious in architecture. Modern architecture, influenced by the Bauhaus school (see p. 1029), had developed an international style that favored the pure and simple, geometric forms and unadorned walls of glass. By the 1970s, however, newer styles rejected that aesthetic and instead deliberately featured unexpected shapes, pitched roofs with gables, echoes of many older styles, and whimsical ornamentation. Because the element that this eclectic architecture most obviously shared was its rejection of modernism, it came to be called *postmodern,* a term soon applied to many other fields as well.

A preference for playful attitudes and individualistic innovation more than a formal school of thought, postmodernism reflected important cultural tendencies. Labeling regularity, rigid logic, and the control of nature or human beings as modern made postmodernism a convenient way to describe a new direction in the arts and social sciences.

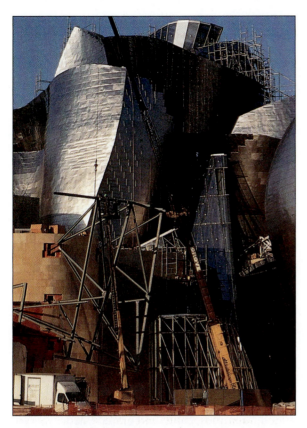

▲ **A monument of a postmodern and international age, this Guggenheim museum was designed by the American architect Frank Gehry and opened in 1997 in Bilbao, Spain, a city once known primarily as a grim industrial town.**

J. Pavlovsky/Corbis Sygma

◆ SOCIAL THOUGHT

Following World War II, the major schools of social thought had generally assumed that rational analysis could explain social behavior with a certain objectivity that would lead to beneficial policies. From the 1970s on, however, students of society have been increasingly inclined to show instead how programs for social improvement, how claims to objective knowledge, and how the promotion of high culture may actually be exercises that preserve the dominance of elites.

Modernization and Marxism Social and political thought in the 1950s used historical and social analysis to prescribe solutions for current prob-

lems. Theories of modernization traced a line of development from the era of absolute monarchy to a modern age of liberal democracy, and in doing so sought to explain what went wrong in nations like Germany, Italy, and Spain that had not sustained democracy. The answers to these historical questions were then offered as a guide for developing nations around the world as the means to democratic stability.

Writings on modernization, especially pervasive in the United States, influenced the social sciences throughout the West. They demonstrated the connection between political freedom and economic growth and showed that these developments in turn were intricately related to social changes, such as literacy and urbanization. Discussions of modernization tended to advocate for all societies the values, legal systems, and social practices identified as characteristic of Western Europe and the United States. Studies of modernization fostered greater attention to the non-Western world and favored interdisciplinary research that used sophisticated social scientific theories and methods (including quantitative analysis and opinion surveys). By the 1970s, however, these theories had come under heavy attack for creating an idealized description of Western (often American) society and then applying it everywhere, for stressing consensus and compromise while largely ignoring social conflicts and injustice, and for serving as a Cold War ideology in competition with Soviet Marxism.

Marxist thought, which also incorporated ideas of progress, provided the principal alternative to theories of modernization. Varieties of Marxism less rigid than Soviet communism were influential throughout European intellectual life, especially in England and Italy in the late 1960s and 1970s. In their flexibility and subtle insights, these neo-Marxist analyses made lasting contributions to the understanding of society and culture, especially through ideas associated with the so-called Frankfurt school and with Antonio Gramsci. A group of innovative and Marxian social scientists and philosophers had flourished in Frankfurt under Germany's Weimar republic until Hitler forced its leaders into exile. Although their writings were rigorous and difficult, they gained a wide readership in the postwar period. And their analyses, whether of the arts or social structure, interlaced modern sociology and psychology (especially Freudian ideas) with a profound distaste for mass culture and contemporary society. One of their members, Herbert Marcuse, became a hero to leaders of the student revolts of 1968 because of his powerful criticism of the commercialism and illusory freedom of modern society.

The pervasiveness of Marxist thinking also owed a great deal to the work of Antonio Gramsci. Like the more doctrinaire Hungarian Georg Lukács, Gramsci was a communist intellectual who took culture seriously, not simply as a reflection of society's material structure but as the collection of values that held it together. One of Italy's leading Communist activists, Gramsci was imprisoned by the Fascist authorities; most of his writing consists of notebooks and letters written in prison during the 1920s and 1930s and published after the war. Gramsci, while recognizing the importance of religion and the arts, sought to explain why peasants and workers accept inequality. He developed the concept of cultural hegemony, exploring how the values and styles invented and promulgated by elites come to be shared across social classes and thus shape the thought and action of entire societies. Radicals, Gramsci argued, must provide an alternative culture that matches the qualities of the culture they wish to overturn.

Cultural Studies   English, French, German, and American scholars applied these ideas to their own histories and to current political debates, exposing a bias toward the status quo in liberal ideology and elitism in much current scholarship. The field of cultural studies has evolved from this line of attack on dominant ideologies while distancing itself from Marxism and gaining momentum from worldwide changes in politics as well as culture. Decolonization invited a new look at how imperialism functions and provoked renewed interest in how non-Western societies wrestle with Western cultural and economic domination. The self-serving assumptions built into European assessments of non-European cultures (a topic that dominates anthropology today) had become easier to identify. Movements in behalf of ethnic minorities—African Americans in the United States and other ethnic groups in the United States and Europe—undermined claims that society's established institutions and authorities were neutral. Cultural studies has also made popular culture the object of serious study, especially in Britain, welcoming its irreverence and finding within it a yearning for freedom and the creative expression of marginalized people alienated from consumer society.

Michel Foucault   The methods, insights, and vocabulary of cultural studies owe a great deal to the work of the Frenchman Michel Foucault, perhaps the most influential thinker of the 1980s, particularly in the United States and England. Foucault was trained as a philosopher, and his work achieved international resonance much as Sartre's had done a generation earlier. Foucault consistently acknowledged his debt to Nietzsche and was clearly influenced by Marx, the new social history,[6] and the work of the French anthropologist Claude Lévi-Strauss. Lévi-Strauss believed that every aspect of a supposedly primitive society—its kinship systems, customs, rituals, and myths—can be understood as the extension of unstated, complex, and integrated structures of thought. These hidden structures, he declared, reflect the nature of the human mind, a view that led him to an admiration of premodern societies comparable to that felt by many modern artists.

All these currents were present in Foucault's thought, but most of all he built on the rising science of semiotics, the study of the signs by which human beings communicate. In Foucault's hands, semiotics provided the means for reinterpreting modern history and civilization. His periodization was conventional: Modernity emerged in the late eighteenth century and was heralded by the French Revolution. But he upended the conventional interpretations of what modernity meant. Medicine, psychology, and prison reform were not simply the progressive results of increased

---

[6]French historians centered around the journal *Annales* began before World War II to develop approaches to social history that influenced historical study around the world in the 1960s and 1970s and continue to make important contributions to the social sciences and humanities. Foucault himself was close to although not part of the *Annales* group.

Foucault on Sexual Discourse

◆

One of Michel Foucault's last major works was The History of Sexuality, *which explored the topic from ancient Greece to the present. In the selection here he touches on several of his major themes.*

"But there may be another reason that makes it so gratifying for us to define the relationship between sex and power in terms of repression: something that one might call the speaker's benefit. If sex is repressed, that is, condemned to prohibition, nonexistence, and silence, then the mere fact that one is speaking about it has the appearance of a deliberate transgression. A person who holds forth in such language places himself to a certain extent outside the reach of power; he upsets established law; he somehow anticipates the coming freedom. This explains the solemnity with which one speaks of sex nowadays. When they had to allude to it, the first demographers and psychiatrists of the nineteenth century thought it advisable to excuse themselves for asking their readers to dwell on matters so trivial and base. But for decades now, we have found it difficult to speak on the subject without striking a different pose: we are conscious of defying established power, our tone of voice shows that we know we are being subversive, and we ardently conjure away the present and appeal to the future, whose day will be hastened by the contribution we believe we are making. Something that smacks of revolt, of promised freedom, of the coming age of a different law, slips easily into this discourse on sexual oppression. Some of the ancient functions of prophecy are reactivated therein. Tomorrow sex will be good again. Because this repression is affirmed, one can discreetly bring into coexistence concepts which the fear of ridicule or the bitterness of history prevents most of us from putting side by side: revolution and happiness; or revolution and a different body, one that is newer and more beautiful; or indeed, revolution and pleasure. What sustains our eagerness to speak of sex in terms of repression is doubtless this opportunity to speak out against the powers that be, to utter truths and promise bliss, to link together enlightenment, liberation, and manifold pleasures; to pronounce a discourse that combines the fervor of knowledge, the determination to change the laws, and the longing for the garden of earthly delights. This is perhaps what also explains the market value attributed not only to what is said about sexual repression, but also to the mere fact of lending an ear to those who would eliminate the effects of repression. Ours is, after all, the only civilization in which officials are paid to listen to all and sundry impart the secrets of their sex: as if the urge to talk about it, and the interest one hopes to arouse by doing so, have far surpassed the possibilities of being heard, so that some individuals have even offered their ears for hire.

"But it appears to me that the essential thing is not this economic factor, but rather the existence in our era of a discourse in which sex, the revelation of truth, the overturning of global laws, the proclamation of a new day to come, and the promise of a certain felicity are linked together. Today it is sex that serves as a support for the ancient form—so familiar and important in the West—of preaching. A great sexual sermon—which has had its subtle theologians and its popular voices—has swept through our societies over the last decades; it has chastised the old order, denounced hypocrisy, and praised the rights of the immediate and the real; it has made people dream of a New City. The Franciscans are called to mind. And we might wonder how it is possible that the lyricism and religiosity that long accompanied the revolutionary project have, in Western industrial societies, been largely carried over to sex."

From Michel Foucault, The History of Sexuality, *Vol. 1:* An Introduction, *Robert Hurley (tr.) (Vintage Books, 1990).*

knowledge but instruments of a new social discipline. The scientific observation of other people, however neutral or objective it claims to be, is a means of controlling behavior through shared *discourse*—a crucial Foucauldian term. By *discourse* Foucault means a framework of understanding used consciously and unconsciously that automatically excludes some possibilities and urges others. To talk about certain behavior as an illness, for example, is a form of power, and power is one of Foucault's central concerns. Discourse functions within society to make power diffuse and pervasive, independent of public intent. Foucault's ideas (like his witty, perceptive, and involuted style) provided a new and effective way to challenge not just the acknowledged evils of modern society but the laws, institutions, practices, and conception of knowledge on which society rests. Without proffering solutions, Foucault's works offer an arsenal of weapons with which to unmask intellectual claims to authority or objectivity (see "Foucault on Sexual Discourse," p. 1158).

Poststructuralism   A further powerful attack on the apparent neutrality of scientific categories and logical reason is heavily indebted to French intellectual Jacques Derrida. Like Foucault, Derrida uses the tools of semiotics and philosophy and has more followers in the United States than in Europe. The two have been called the philosophers of 1968 because of their ties to the student movement of those years. Derrida studies literature by concentrating on the text and subjecting it to a technique he named *deconstruction.* For deconstructionists, texts contain linguistic signs that are not straightforward—not *transparent*, to use their term—but instead carry multiple associations with individual words, with style and syntax, and with all the literary, cultural, social, and personal contexts from which a given text has emerged. Necessarily, the signs on the page must be (mis)translated in the mind of the reader. Thus, no text has one stable meaning but communicates differently to different people and on many levels at once. Deconstruction, the exploration of multiple and hidden signification,

directly denies the existence of absolutes and any pretense to objectivity.

These currents of contemporary thought, obviously related to postmodernism, are often referred to as *poststructuralism* because they have moved beyond logical structures, scientific models, and fixed categories. Under the influence of poststructuralism, the techniques of literary analysis have become important to contemporary writings about society. Social custom, forms of courtesy and dress, organizations and law, education and religion can all be studied like a text for the multiple messages they convey.

Gender Studies   In no field has the large body of poststructuralist theory had greater impact than in gender studies, which looks beyond biological or sexual differences to the social construction of different roles for men and women, differences fabricated from custom, from views about the nature of women and men, and above all, from seemingly neutral dichotomies such as strength/weakness, rationality/irrationality, and public/private, which when associated with male/female become constraints on the roles thought proper for women. Such studies have made it necessary to rethink and rewrite a great deal of history, anthropology, and sociology. If the theoretical base has been heavily European, its application has been more extensive in the United States, where the structure of universities, the rapid opening of careers to women, and public preoccupation with oppressed groups has fostered the development of gender studies. In Europe, too, however, similar reinterpretations of society and culture have given new strength to feminist movements and to campaigns in behalf of groups previously marginalized (see "A Reflection on Contemporary Feminism," pp. 1159–1160).

Europe's admired, established culture and the institutions that sustain it have come under attack from many quarters, and those attacks have made their own contributions to culture. That established culture, which remains at the core of education, religion, and much of public life, meanwhile draws millions of people each year to museums and concert halls.

A Reflection on Contemporary Feminism

◆

Julia Kristeva arrived in Paris in 1966 as a twenty-six-year-old Bulgarian scholar trained in linguistics. She quickly became an important contributor to the semiotics movement in France, noted for her remarkable knowledge of European philosophy, Marxism, and influential Russian scholarship in semiotics. An active participant in the events of 1968, she subsequently trained in the leading French school of psychoanalysis and developed her own practice. In addition to widely acclaimed scholarly works, essays, and novels, she writes frequently on women's issues. Provocative and controversial, her studies are nevertheless representative of European feminist writings in several respects: their engagement with European philosophy from Plato through Hegel and Nietzsche; their sophisticated use of psychoanalysis and literary criticism, including deconstruction (she has been particularly close to Derrida); their analysis of the contemporary historical context; and their search for a new feminism through close attention to immediate, practical, and personal issues. Following are excerpts from "Women's Time," an essay first published in French in 1979 and subsequently reprinted many times in many languages.

When the women's movement began as the struggle of suffragists and existential feminists, it sought to stake out its place in the linear time of planning and history. As a result, although the movement was universalist from the start, it was deeply rooted in the sociopolitical life of nations. The political demands of women, their struggles for equal pay for equal work and for the right to the same opportunities as men have, as well as the rejection of feminine or maternal traits considered incompatible with participation in such a history, all stem from the *logic of indentification* with values that are not ideological (such values have been rightly criticized as too reactionary) but logical and ontological with regard to the dominant rationality of the nation and the state.

It is unnecessary to enumerate all the benefits that this logic of identification and spirited protest have offered and still offer to women (abortion rights, contraception, equal pay, professional recognition, and others). These benefits have had or will soon prove to have even more significant effects than those of the Industrial Revolution. This current of feminism, which is universalist in scope, *globalizes* the problems of women of various social categories, ages, civilizations, or simply psychic structures under the banner of Universal Woman. In this world, a reflection about generations of women could only be conceived of as a succession, a progression that sought to implement the program set out by its founding members.

A second phase is associated with women who have come to feminism since May 1968 and who have brought their aesthetic or psychoanalytic experiences with them. This phase is characterized by a quasi-universal rejection of linear temporality and by a highly pronounced mistrust of political life. Although it is true that this current of feminism still has an allegiance to its founding members and still focuses (by necessity) on the struggle for the sociocultural recognition of women, in a *qualitative* sense, it sees itself in a different light than did the prior generation of feminists.

The "second phase" women, who are primarily interested in the specificity of feminine psychology and its symbolic manifestations, seek a language for their corporeal and intersubjective experiences, which have been silenced by the cultures of the past. As artists or writers, they have undertaken a veritable exploration of the *dynamics of signs*. At least on the level of its intentions, their exploration is comparable to the most ambitious projects for religious and artistic upheaval. . . . For more than a century, anthropologists and sociologists have attracted our attention to the society-sacrifice that works behind "savage thought," wars, dream discourse, or great writers. . . . Today's women have proclaimed that this sacrificial contract imposes itself against their will, which has compelled them to attempt a revolt that they perceive to be a resurrection. Society as a whole, however, considers this revolt to be a refusal and it can result in violence between the sexes (a murderous hatred, the break-up of the couple and the family) or in cultural innovation. In fact, it probably leads to them both. In any event, that is where the stakes are, and they are of enormous consequence. By fighting against evil, we reproduce it, this time at the core of the social bond—the bond between men and women.

... That women have assumed commercial, industrial, and cultural power has not changed the nature of this power. ... Some may regret that the rise of a libertarian movement such as feminism may wind up reinforcing conformity, and others will celebrate this consequence and use it to their advantage. ... In our world, the various marginal groups of sex, age, religion, ethnic origin, and ideology represent a refuge of hope, that is, a secular transcendence. All the same, ... the problem of the countersociety is becoming an enormous one.

The majority of women today feel that they have a mission to put a child into the world. This brings up a question for the new generation that the preceding one repudiated: what lies behind this desire to be a mother? Unable to answer this question, feminist ideology opens the door to a return of religion, which may serve to pacify anxiety, suffering, and maternal expectations.

From Julia Kristeva, *New Maladies of the Soul*. Copyright ©1995 by Columbia University Press. Reprinted with the permission of the publisher.

Summary

Without the harsh simplicity of bipolar conflict, European affairs looked more complex after the collapse of the Soviet Union and the end of the Cold War, but that complexity also reflected the astounding gains of fifty years of peace. The promise of well-being was never more universal or real. To be sure, capitalism brought dangerous dislocation across the continent, and freedom allowed ethnic conflict. But political and ideological differences were now less important and the distinction between Eastern and Western Europe less relevant. Intellectual creativity has generated excitement but no clear consensus; questions of values remain painfully unresolved. Whereas social equality has yet to be achieved, increased wealth has been accompanied by the signs of alienation revealed in drug abuse and xenophobia. There are troubling indications every day of the anger, frustration, and disillusionment many people feel. Nevertheless, Eastern Europe is freer than ever before in its history and Western Europe more united than it has ever been. A half-century ago few people expected that by the end of the twentieth century, in an increasingly global society, Europe would remain a favored continent, enviable in its wealth, liberty, and culture.

QUESTIONS FOR FURTHER THOUGHT

◆

1. How do you explain the growth of the European Union despite hesitant beginnings, frequent disagreements, and continual setbacks that all along the way have led most commentators to predict its failure?

2. Are postindustrial society and the new economy really so different from the past?

3. Why have European dictatorships fallen?

4. What do you see as the strengths and weaknesses of contemporary culture? Is it likely to produce a backlash comparable to that of the 1930s?

RECOMMENDED READING

◆

Sources

Ash, Timothy Garton. *The Magic Lantern: The Revolution of '89 Witnessed in Warsaw, Budapest, Berlin, and Prague.* 1990. An eyewitness account by a particularly keen and informed observer.

de Beauvoir, Simone. *Memoirs of a Dutiful Daughter.* James Kickup (tr.). 1959. *All Said and Done.* Patrick O'Brian (tr.). 1974. Important to the history of contemporary feminism, Beauvoir's memoirs also give a sense of the intellectual life of the times.

*Ellul, Jacques. *The Technological Society.* John Wilkinson (tr.). 1964. One of the most striking and influential of contemporary attacks on the effects of technology.

Gorbachev, Mikhail. *Perestroika: New Thinking for Our Country and the World.* 1989. This presentation of Gorbachev's vision of the future is as revealing for the issues it does not address as for its specific recommendations.

Studies

*Albertini, Rudolf von. *Decolonization: The Administration and Future of the Colonies, 1919–1960.* Francisca Garvie (tr.). 1982. A solid account that focuses on Britain and France and is especially valuable for its historical depth.

*Ardagh, John. *France in the 1980s.* 1987. A fascinating examination of the fabric of daily life, with an eye on the development of the first forty years after World War II and of France's position in Europe.

*Ash, Timothy Garton. *The Polish Revolution: Solidarity.* 1984. Rich in insights into the social roots, techniques, ideas, and effectiveness of a moment that captured worldwide attention.

Berger, Suzanne (ed.). *Organizing Interests in Western Europe: Pluralism, Corporatism, and the Transformation of Politics.* 1981. Important assessments of the political balance of power by some of the leading American social scientists.

*Burgess, Michael. *Federalism and the European Union.* 2000. Reviews the history of the European Union to make the case for the continuing importance of the national states within it.

*Caplan, Richard, and John Feffer. *Europe's New Nationalism: States and Minorities in Conflict.* 1996. Essays on regions from Scotland to Eastern Europe that discuss the important historical issues raised by some of the less-familiar outbursts of nationalism since the end of the Cold War.

*Craig, Gordon. *The Germans.* 1983. A noted historian's insightful, handsomely written, and critical assessment of German society.

*Fink, Carole, Philipp Gassert, and Detlef Junker (eds.). *1968: The World Transformed.* 1998. Essays on the worldwide phenomenon of the protest movements from China and the United States to Eastern Europe, attentive not only to global influences and their use of common themes but to the variety of specific issues, including race, women, and consumerism.

*Heidenheimer, Arnold J., Hugh Heclo, and Carolyn Adams. *Comparative Public Policy: The Politics of Social Choice in Europe and America*. 1975. Studies the background and implications of the varied approaches to social policy, written as the limitations of these programs were becoming apparent.

Hennessy, Peter, and Anthony Seldons. *Ruling Performance: British Governments from Attlee to Thatcher*. 1987. Contrasting perspectives on British politics in radically different governments.

Hoffmann, Stanley, and Paschalis Kitromilides. *Culture and Society in Contemporary Europe*. 1981. An anthology of essays by leading intellectuals attempting to evaluate the interplay of tradition and modernity in Europe.

*Hooper, John. *The Spaniards: A Portrait of the New Spain*. 1987. An engaging look at the extraordinary changes in post-Franco Spain.

Hoskins, Geoffrey. *The Awakening of the Soviet Union*. 1990. An excellent overview of how change came to a society that had resisted it for so long.

*Hughes, H. Stuart. *Sophisticated Rebels*. 1990. An intellectual historian considers the nature of dissent in the West as well as in Eastern Europe during the critical years of 1988 and 1989.

*Hulsberg, Werner. *The German Greens: A Social and Political Profile*. 1988. A systematic treatment of the strongest of the European environmental movements.

*Jarausch, Konrad H. *The Rush to German Unity*. 1994. Uses recently opened archives to provide a historian's assessment of the complicated events that united the two Germanies.

*Jay, Martin. *The Dialectical Imagination: A History of the Frankfurt School and the Institute of Social Research, 1923–1950*. 1973. A rewarding study of some of the most influential thinkers of modern social science written with a keen understanding of the intellectual background and prejudices from which they wrote about modern society.

*Jenkins, Keith. *The Postmodern History Reader*. 1997. Selections from more than thirty historians suggest the variety of ways that current intellectual trends have affected the writing of history.

Katzenstein, Mary F., and Carol M. Mueller (eds.). *The Women's Movements of the United States and Western Europe*. 1987. These collected essays make for a book with wide coverage that underscores some striking national differences.

*Kavanagh, Dennis, and Anthony Seldon (eds.). *The Thatcher Effect*. 1989. A variety of critical appraisals of Thatcher's policies.

Kennedy, Paul. *Preparing for the Twenty-First Century*. 1993. A historian's skeptical look at power relations in the near future.

Lewin, Moshe. *The Gorbachev Phenomenon*. 1988. A brilliant analysis written as the phenomenon was unfolding that relates current events to the developments in Soviet society over the previous fifty years.

*Maier, Charles S. *Dissolution: The Crisis of Communism and the End of East Germany*. 1997. Connects domestic and international politics to ideology and social conditions to explain the collapse of communism and the German unification.

*Mandelbaum, Michael. *The Nuclear Revolution: International Politics before and after Hiroshima*. 1981. A thoughtful study, making good use of parallels from the diplomacy of earlier eras to assess the implications of the nuclear age for international relations.

Marrus, Michael R. *The Emergence of Leisure*. 1974. A historical study that identifies one of the important characteristics of modern life as an important historical trend.

Merkl, Peter H. *The Federal Republic at Forty*. 1989. A distinguished political scientist evaluates the German republic that has lasted far longer than the Weimar Republic.

*Modood, Tariq, and Pnina Werbner. *The Politics of Multiculturalism in the New Europe: Racism, Identity, and Community*. 1997. Essays present multiculturalism as the result of the change in domestic politics.

*Panayi, Panikos. *An Ethnic History of Europe since 1945*. 2000. Compares the experience of ethnic minorities across Europe.

*Parker, Geoffrey. *The Logic of Unity*. 1975. Usefully analyzes the forces for European unity from a geographer's perspective.

Poster, Mark. *Existential Marxism in Postwar France*. 1975. An able analysis of an intellectual movement that had a wide impact on its generation.

Riddle, Peter. *The Thatcher Decade: How Britain Has Changed during the 1980s.* 1989. An unusually positive assessment of the long-term effects of the Thatcher period on British society.

Silber, Laura, and Allan Little. *The Death of Yugoslavia.* 1995. A moving, penetrating, and unusually balanced account.

Williams, Raymond. *Communications.* 1976. A leading British writer and historian reflects on the role of communication in modern societies.

*Available in paperback.

EPILOGUE: THE PRESENT IN HISTORICAL PERSPECTIVE

To some extent we all think historically, for the history of the world in the last two hundred years has made awareness of change an essential part of our outlook. We assess the present by contrasting it with the past; our fears and hopes for the future are largely based on historical trends that seem to forecast conditions to come. Publicists announce "revolutions" in everything from world politics and technology to manners and fashions. Politicians justify their decisions by confidently predicting what "history will say"; conservatives and radicals claim to know "the lessons of history." Obviously, much about the way we think about the world depends on our understanding of the past.

I. The Present and the Past

◆

Historical understanding begins with a sense of historical perspective. When the Berlin Wall came down and Europe's communist regimes collapsed, everyone recognized in those dramas a major historical watershed. These great changes were all the more striking because they were unintended, not the aim of any policy but the effect rather of a surge of popular feeling among millions of Eastern Europeans wanting the freedom and prosperity enjoyed in Western Europe. Such sudden change, facilitated by modern mass communication and peacefully achieved, made it easy to believe, in both East and West, that a wholly new era had begun and that the world had entered an age of disarmament, liberal governments, and capitalist economies.

◆ LOOKING FOR LESSONS

Assumptions of such total change need to be tempered with historical perspective, which suggests four reasons for caution. The first is simply that great transformations are difficult, and the strains they create can have unexpected results. The Reformation, the expansion of Europe, the French Revolution, industrialization, and the revolutions of 1848 brought important changes, many of them very different from initial expectations.

Second, historical perspective tempers assumptions about sweeping change, for there is often surprising continuity in social life. Established patterns matter. Differences persist even today between those parts of Europe that belonged to the Roman Empire and those that did not, between those Christian missionaries converted in the Early Middle Ages and those converted later, between those peoples who experienced the Protestant Reformation and those who did not. If the nations of central and Eastern Europe were to be ranked today according to the relative strengths and weaknesses of their economies and political systems, they would stand in relation to each other much as they did seventy years ago, following World War I and the collapse of the Habsburg Empire.

Many observers, of course, have noticed this; and facile analogies to the past have become as common as simplistic assumptions that everything is different. Such analogies are a third reason for caution. Commentators on current events in Eastern Europe point to parallels with Russia in the nineteenth century and the arguments then between Slavophiles and Westerners, to the surge of nationalism in the nineteenth century that led to the unification of Italy and Germany, and to ethnic and religious conflicts in Europe going back to the Middle Ages. Such examples can be invaluable when used analytically to explore how contemporary issues evolved and how societies evoke the loyalties that enable them to function. The examples are inherently selective, however, and easily manipulated. Historical awareness, which should lessen surprise at the renewed vigor of nationalism in Eastern Europe, includes recognition of how readily political leaders and intellectuals reconstruct the past, how they recall past glories as if they should have lasted forever and past injuries as if they must still be avenged. Self-serving histories—and all societies create them—can achieve the power of founding myths that refer more to current feeling than to any past reality.

Finally, historical understanding recognizes that human history is always contingent on many elements; identifying trends does not predict outcomes. In this century the impact of individual decisions by intellectuals, demagogues, revolutionaries, popes, and political leaders has continued to be great and unpredictable. Gorbachev came to power as part of a process of adaptive reform that seemed likely to strengthen the Soviet Union. Almost no one imagined that his daring determination would have such effect that the Soviet Union would soon cease to exist. Good historical thinking leaves room for unforeseeable decisions, for unexpected results, for the interplay of multiple forces, trends, and interests, and for sheer accident.

Living with the Past Societies depend on the past, constructing it to establish memories of common and noble purpose, using tradition as a

▲ **The new Jewish museum in Berlin, dedicated in 2001 and designed by Daniel Liebskind, has the shape of a broken Star of David.**
AP/Wide World Photos

source of stability. There are always elements of the past, however, that fail to fit the dominant consensus, and there are always groups whose memories or interests demand a different interpretation. History is therefore controversial, and that is particularly true at present. The fall of communist governments opens new vistas into how they functioned, who served them, and what they achieved. The end of the Cold War exposes the shallowness of much anticommunist propaganda and the harm done in pursuit of suspected communists. The disintegration of imper-

ial systems and the rise of new nations require new historical understanding to better connect past to present. Increased awareness of global connections—economic, cultural, and political—has stimulated an essentially new field of global history.

As a given outlook becomes prominent, it builds a supportive reading of the past. St. Augustine provided a Christian interpretation of the decline of Rome. Today's commitment to human rights leads to a deeper look into the history of slavery, industrial labor, and serfdom. Ethnic consciousness fosters a patriotic version of the past and investigation into how a specific group came to be defined and treated differently.

In addition to the historical narrative that is a source of pride, every society must deal with aspects of the past it would be comforting to forget. President George W. Bush at first called the campaign against terrorism a *crusade,* but the response revealed that the term, which in the European tradition evokes heroic cooperation for a glorious cause, is still recalled by Muslims as referring to religious war and centuries of Western aggression.

Nothing in recent European history burdens modern memory more heavily than the extermination of Jews. The need to respond has led to many memorials and museums, including the impressive Holocaust Museum in Washington, D.C., which evokes events that in a narrow sense were not part of American history. But uncertainty remains about how to treat such a painful past, expressed in conflicts over whether a Christian cross has any place at Auschwitz or what memorial might be appropriate in Vienna. After many false starts and disagreements, a Museum of Jewish History has opened in Berlin. A massive architectural statement, its great slabs surround three paths the visitor can take: one descends into a void representing the Holocaust, one leads to a disorienting Garden of Exile with pillars that are neither vertical nor horizontal, and one leads into displays on the history of Jews in Berlin. Every museum, like memory itself, is an interpretation of history, and history, ever comforting and ever painful, remains subject to controversy.

Seeing the Past through the Present Historical understanding is constantly renewed by new research based on new methods and, even more important, on new questions. A major source of those questions is contemporary experience. The social concerns of the twentieth century stimulated new schools of social and demographic history that have fundamentally altered our vision of the European past. Decolonization and increasing international trade fostered fresh analysis of the historical relations between economies at different levels of development, from the Middle Ages to the present. That research has revised the understanding of imperialism and of capitalism in both the present and the past.

From the 1950s through the 1980s, the harsh realities of the Cold War caused many commentators and politicians to look at history in terms of power politics, the rise and fall of superpowers, and the differences between East and West. The studies that followed illuminated aspects of history often overlooked and affected interpretations of the Cold War itself. With the end of the Cold War, we see more clearly the effects it had on domestic parties, social programs, and basic freedoms around the world, raising new questions about even the recent past and contemporary policy.

As societies today struggle with issues concerning the roles of women and the position of ethnic minorities, historians have found new ways to investigate the importance of gender and race in other eras. That research, which dramatically altered views of the past, becomes in turn a potent element in current debates.

Periodization These changing views of the connection between present and past are especially clear in terms of periodization. In the 1950s and 1960s, it was common to say that the world had entered the Atomic Age, because the promise of atomic energy and the fear of atomic warfare seemed to shape an era. In the 1990s references to the Atomic Age had become rare because both that promise and that fear had faded. Similarly, the promise that World War I would make the world safe for democracy is now remembered primarily as a bitter irony; but should stable democracies in fact become the European norm, that achievement might well be seen as having been at work since 1918. Some observers see 1968–1970 as a turning point, when failed revolutions, a new kind of social criticism, and the oil crisis undermined confidence in established institutions, consumerism, and perpetual economic growth.

Many historians, diplomats, and politicians once identified the decline of Europe as one of history's major trends. In that light a new era could be said to have begun with World War I or a generation later when a continent tragically dominated by the Axis plunged into a war that destroyed Europe's international power and left it subject to Soviet and American domination. In 1940 France dropped from the ranks of the world's most powerful states; Germany did so five years later; and in the 1950s even victorious Great Britain could no longer sustain an international position comparable to that of the United States and the Soviet Union. The economic crises of the postwar period and the loss of colonial empires seemed to confirm a process of relative decline in Western Europe's strength. Thus, in the 1950s Arnold Toynbee's widely admired, multivolume *Study of History* echoed the earlier gloom of Oswald Spengler in proclaiming that a millennium of European preeminence in world history had come to an end.

Shifting dates just a few years, however, could produce a periodization that points to a new era in European history beginning in the 1950s and marked by rapid social change, unprecedented prosperity, and the trend toward European union. Neither periodization is wrong; each fits a different set of questions. The questions asked of historical evidence may evolve from prior research, from a body of theory, or from current concerns. The findings that result lead to new understanding and, in turn, new questions. To think about European history in terms of current issues can thus be fruitful both for historical research and for insight into the present. Many of the world's pressing problems, after all, have roots in the history of Europe; and Europe's future will be molded through its response to worldwide trends.

Its very complexity makes historical analysis not merely good training but essential to assessing our own condition. The twentieth century was an era of ethnic slaughter, totalitarian brutality, and two world wars. It also witnessed unprecedented wealth, freedom, and well-being. How these contrasting aspects may be related is central to understanding the world in which we live.

◆ EUROPE AND THE WORLD

A Global Era Today, the extent of communication, technology, and trade seems to be creating a new kind of global society. That, too, has a relevant past. Recent research by archaeologists and historians has uncovered extensive connections of commerce and culture even in the ancient world and in the early Middle Ages. There is now impressive evidence that metals, olive oil, wine, and new technologies moved along routes that reached from Asia to Europe. Restless Europe created the basis for a global era through the crusades, the voyages of discovery, the conquest of the New World, the spread of Dutch and British trade in the seventeenth century, the building of empires in North America and India a century later, direct rule in the age of imperialism, and the extension of Western interests in the competition of the Cold War. This expansion involved knowledge of the world and its peoples, bloodshed, idealism, and greed. There is no reason to think that the process of building a global society will be simpler or have political and cultural effects that are any less mixed.

To many, globalization is synonymous with Americanization. America's economic power has been felt in Europe since World War I, became more prominent after World War II, and is experienced now through multinational corporations even more than governments. Some Europeans have seen the United States as foreshadowing their own future ever since its founding, and that feeling has been strengthened by Europe's own democratization, the widespread use of English, the prominence of America's commercial culture, and the power of American technology. Many in Europe see globalization as a cultural, economic, and environmental threat.

Despite its great wealth, Europe will not again dominate the world as it once did. At the most, it will be one of many poles of wealth and power. Having learned to exercise their diplomatic influence in the interstices of Cold War competition, European nations have become accustomed to limited influence in circumstances like those in which many states of the former Soviet Union now find themselves.

▲ Advertisements for American and Japanese corporations dominate the patriotic symbols of Britain's past in London's Picadilly Circus.
© Corbis

Cultural Exchanges In part because Europeans have been more consistently interested in other societies—as objects of exploration, study, conversion, and exploitation—than people from any other region, European ideas, institutions, and techniques have spread around the world and are so much a part of local history that in many places they are no longer merely European. In the last fifty years European societies have become far more open to extra-European influences through commerce, mass communications, and formal study but also through the massive presence of Americans, Asian tourists, and immigrants from the Middle East, Africa, and the Caribbean.

These enriching cultural encounters have produced a long history of misunderstandings, abuse, and resentment that is part of world politics today. They have also led to concern every-where that local ways will be overcome by the homogenizing impact of global contact. While it is true, for example, that urban life around the world has become more similar (from its conveniences to its problems of traffic and pollution), it is also true that Western influence, even when reinforced by brute force, the power of wealth, and new technologies, has not obliterated cultural differences. Within Europe itself local cultures have often found ways to preserve much of their identity while adapting to outside pressures; regional differences have survived the laws, armies, and roads of ancient Rome; the demands of national states; the intrusion of railroads, newspapers, and universal schooling; and the impact of telephones, television, and computers. European cities may be crowded with restaurants that offer American fast food in addition to

Chinese, North African, Middle Eastern, Indian, and Vietnamese foods, and eating habits do seem to be changing. Yet national and regional cuisines have lost neither their identity nor their popularity.

II. The Modern Economy

◆

Economic growth, once primarily a Western pre-occupation, is now a universal goal. The power of the Japanese economy and the extraordinary growth of other Asian economies may be as significant for Europe (and as great a competitive challenge) as the economic expansion of the United States has been. Many experts expect this pattern of growth to extend through much of the rest of Asia, including the giant economies of China and India, and to much of Latin America and the Middle East. Development on this scale would have enormous implications for Europe, implications extending beyond the fact of Europe's high productivity, its historic ties to the non-Western world, its investments there, or its role as a principal source of economic and technological assistance.

◆ NATIONAL STANDING

As the pioneer of an expansive capitalism, Europe has long experience of the fact that comparative economic advantages rarely last. The decline of the great commercial centers of the Middle Ages was followed by the relative decline of Renaissance Italy, then Spain, and then the Netherlands as the centers of shipping, banking, and textile production moved north. Shifts in relative economic strength speeded up with industrialization. England had the world's most productive economy and was the world's greatest trader for much of the nineteenth century, only to be overtaken by Germany and the United States.

Recent Developments Such trends are sometimes reversible, however. As late as 1960 almost no one expected France and then Italy to surpass Britain in per capita income, nor would anyone have anticipated the recent rapid growth of Spain. Sudden economic transformations remain possible despite the advantages that accrue from tradition, capital, technology, infrastructure, and education—advantages demonstrated in Germany's impressive recovery from defeat in two world wars.

Although the resources and technologies that matter most today are far different from those that were important in the past, Europe's wealthiest regions at the end of the twentieth century include many that were the wealthiest centuries ago. If, as some predict will happen, information replaces production as the principal source of wealth, European societies may be well situated for future growth. Certainly all nations now hope to take part. In Eastern Europe the collapse of communism left room for the kind of speculation and raw entrepreneurship associated with the American wild west. Disastrous pyramid investment schemes that shocked society in Romania and brought down the government of Albania were also touching evidence of how far ahead of harsh reality the myths of capitalist wealth had spread.

Trade and Wages A more immediate challenge arises from the tendency of international corporations to shift production from older centers to developing countries in which wages are lower. Even if neoliberal theories are correct in predicting benefits for all in the long term, the immediate social impact is serious. High and seemingly permanent unemployment is already a major problem across the continent. The historic pattern that led to higher wages and increased consumption may have been broken, for labor unions were weakened by changes in the workforce and by international competition that favors low-wage areas. The policies traditionally favored by the left to raise workers' incomes become less relevant when governments declare their helplessness before the pressures of global trade. The balance of power among capital, labor, and the state seems to have shifted.

While the majority of Western Europeans have enjoyed increased freedom and a rising standard of living, a significant minority suffers unemployment, segregation, and discrimination. Thus, many Europeans worry about the creation of a permanent underclass and what some have called "the two-thirds society," societies in which two-thirds of the population continues to prosper, enjoying increased wealth and leisure, while a bottom third is left out forever. Even mild economic downturns in a world in which economic growth is expected to continue can have serious social and political consequences. The revolutions of 1848, the political crises at the end of the nineteenth century, the revolutions in Russia, the rise of fascism, and the fall of communism were all related to economic crises. Thus the concern that a downturn, especially when large segments of the population are already hard-pressed, would challenge the social principles and the political stability of modern Europe as seriously as industrialization and the Great Depression did in the past.

The Limits of Growth   In fact, perpetual growth may be doomed by demographic and ecological constraints. Industrial expansion in nineteenth-century Europe benefited from growing populations, but now demographic factors are more likely to have a negative economic effect. In Europe, as people live longer and families are smaller, the population grows older; and an aging population requires more services and produces less. Currently, birthrates are so low in a number of European countries that their population is actually declining while population growth continues to be strong in Africa and Asia, with enormous implications for international relations as well as domestic economies.

The still graver issue is how much growth the environment can sustain. Italy suffered for centuries from the erosion of a mountainous terrain that had been stripped of trees in order to supply the shipbuilders of ancient Rome and of the medieval maritime republics. In the seventeenth century the Spanish economy was severely harmed by the effects of overgrazing. Since the Renaissance, cities have tried to regulate pollution, and in the sixteenth and seventeenth centuries states

tried to control practices likely to cause flooding or threaten the animals that nobles liked to hunt. Until the end of the eighteenth century, however, Europeans usually understood environmental disaster as an act of God, like epidemics and natural catastrophes such as earthquakes and volcanic eruptions.

Europe was fortunate in the nineteenth century that, as its supply of timber or grain or other critical resources seemed about to run short, unexploited sources of energy, new agricultural techniques, and the expansion of trade permitted a timely readjustment. The rest of the world may not be so lucky in the future, and predictions of environmental catastrophes no longer seem so exaggerated. Western European societies today spend a great deal of money to combat the pollution they create. The far graver effects of pollution in Eastern Europe, still being discovered, will be a burden at least through the next generation. Environmental issues challenge the status quo and suggest policies that run counter to the immediate interests of specific groups and sometimes of whole regions. They divide traditional political parties and push governments into new areas of activity, and they are often so international that responsibility is diffused and responses are necessarily complicated. The many important environmental movements in Europe have enjoyed only limited political success, despite their strong appeal, especially to young people; but they offer added reasons for a distrust of politics, formal institutions, and established interests.

III. The Functions of the State

The modern state is a European invention that has spread around the world. From the Carolingian and Norman monarchies of the Middle Ages and the city-states of Renaissance Italy to the present, the steady growth of the state has shaped European history. The national monarchies of Spain, France, and England made the state an instrument for creating military might, dispensing uniform justice, and supporting a national culture. With the French Revolution and Napoleonic rule, the role of the state increased enormously, its intrusive efficiency expanding as it more fully engaged the entire citizenry. The demands of nationalism, democracy, and two world wars added still more to the state's power and the range of its activities. So did fascism, communism, and programs of social welfare. International organizations have also proliferated in this century, but in all of them, member states have tenaciously defended their individual sovereignty. Yet many thoughtful observers now suggest that the state may be losing some of its functions and much of its autonomy.

◆ ECONOMIC POLICIES

Modern economic life has added to the responsibilities of the state, which is expected to provide a stable currency and banking system, an environment favorable to investments and trade, and the education, detailed statistical information, and means of communication that postindustrial societies require. These demands of course are not entirely new.

Directed Economies   The city-states and monarchies of the Middle Ages sponsored guilds and free cities, where duties and taxes were reduced, in order to stimulate the economy. The fact that the states of the early modern period adhered to theories of mercantilism, restricting imports and encouraging exports through regulation, is a reminder of how ideological economic policy often is.

The last twenty years have seen an enormous growth in the power of international corporations eager to shift capital and plants for economic advantage, independent of national states. The governments themselves, especially those in the most developed economies, have tended to accept the argument that reducing trade barriers is beneficial to all. In the early phases of industrialization, governments abolished guilds as organizations that stifled competition and protected the privileged and inefficient; but those same ordinances also made labor organizations illegal, a situation recti-

fied only after generations of conflict. Today the free movement of goods and capital tends also to create an international labor market, undermining the state's role as protector of employment and wages.

By the 1970s most informed observers outside the communist world suspected that Soviet-style planning was not working well. A very different kind of planning, looser, more general, and reliant on free markets was very much in favor, however. In France, a planning office with a large staff of experts and a consultative assembly representing business, labor, and governmental agencies created long-range programs and drafted legislation for parliamentary action. Most other European countries had, and to a large extent still have, comparably comprehensive arrangements. Nearly all sought to manage their economies, indirectly through tax and fiscal policies and sometimes directly through nationalized industries and subsidies.

Now the trend is away from such intervention. Members of the European Union are prepared to surrender much of their fiscal sovereignty to a new central European bank at the same time that they are abandoning many older policies intended to give direction to the economy. West Germany's economy became Europe's largest while limiting the government's direct role in economic affairs. In England the Conservative party under Margaret Thatcher launched a systematic campaign to limit the government's economic role and to dismantle the welfare state. Governments in France and Italy are selling off state-owned industries; and the nations of Eastern Europe are, to varying degrees and often at great social pain, allowing prices, wages, production, and distribution to be largely determined by the free market.

Social Policies   When socialist parties first gained power during the Great Depression, they found themselves applying the policies of economic liberalism, balancing budgets and reducing deficits. In 1996 and 1997, parties that were once socialist won elections in many European countries, including Britain, France, and Italy.

Concerned to stimulate competition and contain social expenditures, they have followed budgetary policies not very different from those of their opponents.

The social activism of European governments was aimed at much more than the economy, for it sought to create a more just and egalitarian society. Large-scale programs for housing, welfare, health, and education implied some reallocation of wealth from the well-to-do to the less fortunate. In practice, the middle of society probably benefits as much as the poor, and the accompanying tax burden is in fact too great to fall on the rich alone.

Now, both the cost and many specific policies of the welfare state have come under attack; yet few Europeans seem to favor reducing social programs to the level of such programs in the United States. Unemployment is lower in the United States and in Britain than on the continent, but the disparity between rich and poor is also much greater in America, and Britain has a higher proportion of the population at or below the poverty level than do continental nations. Thus, the tension between the goal of social equity and the desire to encourage investment and to meet international competition remains unresolved, the fault line of contemporary politics.

◆ DIMINISHING THE STATE

Arguably, these debates about what functions the state should perform are beginning to undermine the state's position as the dominant social organization.

Bureaucracy The state, and its bureaucratic mode of organization, became a pervasive model adopted throughout society. In principle organized for well-defined tasks, bureaucracy was expected to deal with specific problems rationally and objectively and was supposed to be managed by people selected for their talent and technical training. Each nation developed its distinctive bureaucratic style reflecting its own history—the independent role of the aristocracy in England, the service tradition of the Junkers in Prussia, the centralized expertise of royal and Napoleonic government in France (adopted in many other countries) and so forth.

The institutions with which governments deal—political parties, businesses, unions, education systems, hospitals—have tended to be organized in similar bureaucracies and in theory maintaining similar standards of fairness and expertise. In practice, of course, no government agency is removed from special interests and political prejudices. This bias makes bureaucracy itself a central issue in modern society. Bureaucratic organization can subvert official policies and inhibit social flexibility. Its procedures tend to be especially resented in democracies and its cost unpopularly tangible in the tax rate.

In the past decade many Europeans, finding fault with bureaucracy, have become increasingly critical of the state's prominence. The state has become an object of suspicion, not so much for being the captive agent of the ruling class (the classic Marxist reason) or as a threat to individual liberty (the traditional liberal fear) but simply as a concentration of power dedicated to its own interests. To some extent a similar criticism is applied to other large organizations—business corporations, political parties, and universities. A distrust of institutions is an important element in what are known collectively as the New Social Movements (NSMs). Like environmentalism and feminism, NSMs that have had the greatest effect operate beyond ordinary politics and look beyond the state, preferring to found new groups, influence public opinion, and affect individual lives.

Federalism Criticism of the state has strengthened the call for increased federalism. Regional movements appeal to traditional differences in customs and dialects and at the same time make very modern arguments about their distinctive and neglected economic needs and about the obtuseness of distant officials. Even in effective democracies, the political process often seems far removed from the people, a sort of private game of interests. The breakup of the Soviet Union was a criticism of centralized communist rule as well

▲ **British troops in Kosovo keep Albanian demonstrators from storming the bridge that separates the Albanian sector of Mitrovice from the Serbian sector, where French forces held back the Serbs.**
© Nik Wheeler/Corbis

as an expression of local nationalisms. Though not so thoroughly federal as Germany, France has created regional governments, and Spain has granted increased regional autonomy. In 1997 an Italian assembly worked on creating a federal structure, and the Scots voted for devolution granting increased local rule and a parliament of their own (which they had rejected a few years before). In accepting the advantages of smallness, national governments shed some of their historic functions (especially in areas such as urban planning, cultural subsidies, social services, adult education, recreation, programs to attract investment, and tourism).

The Military   While the economic and social roles of the modern state are being challenged, so is its most traditional function as the locus of military power. With war in Europe unlikely and the Cold War ended, European states have reduced their military budgets. British and French forces played an active if subordinate role in the Gulf War against Iraq and an even more subordinate one in Afghanistan. Perhaps in the future national pride in the military can be satisfactorily expressed through limited peacekeeping missions. The major European nations have joined in missions that helped to undermine the white government of South Africa, to bring about conversations between Catholics and Protestants in Northern Ireland, negotiations between Palestinians and Israelis, and pacification in the Balkans. But European democracies have clearly not been eager to take major risks to quell brutal fighting in

◄ **Burning a poster of the cover of Salman Rushdie's** *Satanic Verses*, **Kuala Lumpur, March 1989.** The Saint Louis Art Museum. Purchase: Gift of Mr. and Mrs. Joseph Pulitzer, Jr., by exchange.

Rwanda and Burundi, and they were embarrassingly slow to respond to the crises that followed the breakup of Yugoslavia. To correct that, members of the European Union propose to create an international peacekeeping force of their own. That troubles the United States, which prefers an emphasis on NATO, which it dominates. Military strength may be less important to the European state than ever before.

The European Union   In this light the European Union takes on considerable historical interest. There are many reasons for the remarkable momentum behind its growth. The most recognized, of course, is its impressive economic success. A reason often overlooked is its moral and social appeal as the embodiment of a new kind of polity, socially progressive and antinationalist. Ireland elected its second consecutive woman president in 1997, and of the five candidates, four were women. When asked why women had such prominence, the influence of the European Union on Irish culture was one of the first explanations the candidates gave. As the former communist states of Eastern Europe prepare to make their case for membership in the EU, they seek to establish that they meet the standard of modern democracy that the EU is thought to represent, including free speech, civil rights, and equality for women and minorities.

In some respects the European Union is absorbing many of the traditional functions of the state. National governments have made sacrifices that many believed politically impossible in order to meet the criteria for joining the European single currency, the Euro. Adopting the Euro, however, means that each nation surrenders control over its own currency, a sovereign power that states have manipulated for millennia and a symbol of authority from the ancient world to the present. Great Britain, without a written constitution, now has in effect a written bill of rights, the result of decisions by the European court. A great deal of the legislation that issues from Brussels on everything from insurance to safety in the workplace and standards for food is adopted by national legislatures with minimum review.

Perhaps, then, the European Union will replace the national state in many realms. On the other hand, the fear that it might do so was one of the principal objections to the Maastricht treaties heard throughout the member countries. Denunciations of EU bureaucracy and its voluminous rulings are even louder, especially when established practices are criticized from abroad, as when the farmers of Normandy are told they must make Camembert cheese with pasteurized milk or British companies are told that chocolate bars should not contain vegetable oils. Not having found a way to make its institutions democratic, the EU does not yet have the legitimacy of the democratic state.

IV. Questions of Values

Ironically, at the very time that certain values seem to be widely accepted as human rights that are applicable everywhere, there have been strong criticisms of the assumptions on which those ideals rest. They question whether one society or group has the right to impose its standards on another and deny that European values have timeless and universal meaning. Greater liberty, knowledge, and prosperity increase the burden of difficult choices that individuals must make.

◆ HUMAN RIGHTS

The belief that its principles should be universal has been characteristic of Western thought. Greek philosophy searched for truths applicable to everyone, and Roman law was extended wherever Roman civilization could reach. Christianity has always emphasized the need to carry Christian teachings to all peoples, and in the last two centuries Europeans have variously but confidently proposed capitalism, liberalism, Marxism, and democracy as ideals to be universally embraced.

Specific Issues   Within the European Union and among nations that aspire to join there is effective unanimity on the importance of human rights ranging from freedom of speech and religion to the rights of labor and opposition to the death penalty (no state that employs the death penalty may belong to the E.U.). The Council of Europe and its Court of Justice have similarly set very explicit standards so that, for example, Croatia began in 1996 to remove restraints on a free press in order to be allowed to join the Council.

Many people in Europe (and many more in the United States) criticize Eurocentrism and emphasize cultural diversity as an important value in itself. Such concerns induce self-consciousness about advocating human rights around the world. The very conception of such rights may be "fundamentally a product of the liberal imagination, reflecting the complacent cultural imperialism of the modern Western world."[1]

In 1989 Salman Rushdie, an Indian Muslim educated in England, published *Satanic Verses*, a novel that the Ayatollah Khomeini considered blasphemous in its references to Muhammad. To Khomeini the book was the latest of many assaults from Western culture on an Islamic way of life. Supported by the other leaders of Iran, he pronounced a death sentence on Rushdie and on all who, knowing the book's contents, participated in its publication. Rushdie was forced into

[1]Stephen Shute and Susan Hurley (eds.), *On Human Rights: The Oxford Amnesty Lectures, 1993* (New York; Basic Books, 1993).

hiding. Western intellectuals and political leaders expressed outrage and reaffirmed their commitment to freedom of expression. Crowds of militant Muslims demonstrated in the streets of England, India, Pakistan, the Middle East, and North Africa to protest against insults to Islam and the imposition of Western values. Rushdie lives in guarded seclusion.

The Problem of Choice   These issues are not just differences between East and West, for there is conflict within Europe and America between those who give absolute priority to individual rights and those who place social values first, between those who insist on the right of individuals to make moral choices, even wrong ones, and those who insist that society and the state must embody and enforce some absolute truths. The movement to accord to women all the opportunities for education, careers, and independent activity permitted to men can thus be seen as a logical extension of individual rights. To some it will mean the dangerous destruction of a tradition that built the family around the distinctive domestic role of women. Such conflicts between social needs and personal aims were explored in Classical Greek drama, wrestled with by the Church fathers, and recast during the Renaissance and the Reformation. The great intellectual battles of the Enlightenment were often fought on just these issues, and they have remained divisive ever since.

Several factors, however, have made these disputes especially difficult today. Mobility, education, science, and market economies have broadened the range of personal choices. Matters such as diet and dress that were once simply determined by custom have become personal statements, and people are expected to make wise choices about their lifestyle and their occupation, about where they live and how they spend their leisure. Furthermore, decisions about even such intimate choices as marriage and divorce, contraception, and abortion are surrounded by public discussion and debate—in which religious leaders, moralists, and feminists disagree because these are issues of both personal identity and social ethics. In practice the wide availability of contraception has made possible vast changes in human relations and has allowed women a freedom that seemed impossible at the beginning of the century. Many people are also convinced, however, that these changes have devalued human life and the sanctity of marriage. Knowledge of genetics will exacerbate ethical issues of choice.

The Family   These concerns are among the reasons for widespread fear that the institution of the family is being undermined, despite the likelihood that belief in the importance of the family may be as high as it has ever been. There is little reassurance in the fact that alarm over threats to the family has been heard from thousands of pulpits for centuries; that serfdom, slavery, and poverty have also endangered the family; and that the Christian view of human nature and the Freudian view of the human psyche both acknowledge that the constraints of family life are difficult to accept. Despite all the pessimistic predictions, the family has survived. It has survived the effects of industrialization, which separated household members for nearly all their waking hours, moved millions of people to new places, and deprived the family of the traditional social support of relatives and village custom. Indeed, the expectations of the family have steadily increased since the eighteenth century. The Victorian conception of the Christian family raised the norms for loyalty and comity, and they have risen higher since then. Marriage in the twentieth century is expected to be a mutual choice and a delightful partnership in which child rearing lasts longer and is more intensive than ever before.

Warnings that society is losing its ethical compass are difficult to assess in historical terms. For some commentators, the spread of acquired immune deficiency syndrome (AIDS) became the basis for denunciations of sexual promiscuity, homosexuality, and the ease with which people and disease now move across continents. A quite different assessment of modern values follows from those observers who emphasize instead the extensive scientific research on AIDS in Europe and the United States and the widespread determination that the victims of this disease should not be treated the way lepers were for centuries.

Social Responsibility   Many people now argue that feelings of alienation, which Marx attributed primarily to the faulty organization of production, have become more general, affecting not just craftsmanship but attitudes toward society and work in general, taste in entertainment, and the prevalence in modern Western societies of crime and drug addiction. Or perhaps this behavior is not so different from the alcoholism of Hogarth's London or the centuries of peasant revolts, highway robbery, cockfighting, prostitution, and public hangings in the past.

Critics often assert that the contemporary world has experienced a sharp decline in civic responsibility, and they point to examples like weak neighborhood ties and gratuitous vandalism. This tension between individualism and social responsibility, familiar in the United States, is at the center of intense public concern in Europe and underlies the debate between neoliberal advocates of free markets and defenders of the welfare state. The issue is particularly acute in former communist societies. There, individualism is for many a new battle cry that is especially attractive to the young, but one that can be used to excuse racketeering and worse. A poll of teenagers in Russia in 1997 asked them to list the careers that most attracted them. Of the thirty-six choices, contract killer finished in the middle, cosmonaut dead last. Understandably, the press worried about a return of the nihilism that was strong in Russia exactly a century earlier.

A generalized sense of responsibility may be growing, nevertheless. Environmentalism asks individuals to sacrifice some personal convenience for a larger good; and from France to Finland half to two-thirds of all glass is recycled, which means that every day millions of people make an extra effort in behalf of a social benefit they never see. Similarly the spreading ordinances against smoking or boycotts against manufacturers who hire underpaid workers all give more weight to a social good than to individual pleasure.

No question has raised the issue of social responsibility more dramatically than the Holocaust, a source of continuing anguish. In 1997, more than fifty years after the event, a court trial in France hammered home the fact that many French people had cooperated with the Nazis in rounding up Jews to be sent to concentration camps, and official organizations of French police and attorneys apologized for having once acquiesced in anti-semitism. Swiss banks confessed to still holding the funds that Jews had deposited on their way to death or exile. Fresh accounts appeared about the profits that Swiss interests had garnered from cooperation with Nazi Germany, and in Sweden newly published documents revealed that major firms had carefully assured their German contractors that they employed no Jews. The Roman Catholic Church apologized for the indifference of many Catholics to the plight of the Jews, and the pope appointed a commission to study anti-Judaic prejudice in the Church. Memories that whole societies had conspired to repress have become the occasion for wrestling with the nature of moral responsibility.

Communists, too, have found soul searching necessary, and many of them took the occasion to praise a book written by a group of French historians, most of them Marxists, attempting to assess how many human beings communism had killed around the world. On the eightieth anniversary of the Russian revolution, the European press was filled with comment on its estimates: 85 million people killed (half of them in China), including 15 million killed in the Soviet Union between 1917 and 1953. The commentators could all remember, and many had marched in, earlier commemorations of the Russian revolution when across Europe thousands sang songs and carried banners expressing their hope in revolution. The modern citizen has reasons both for hope and for disillusionment.

V. The Nature of Community

Conflicts over social justice, moral values, and culture make for deep disagreements over what a social contract might contain or whether society

▲ *Anselm Kiefer*
BURNING RODS
Kiefer's paintings often move beyond abstraction to evoke the history of the ancient Hebrews, Nazi Germany, and the contemporary world. 1984–87. Mixed media on canvas. The St. Louis Art Museum. Purchase: Gift to Mr. and Mrs. Joseph Pulitzer, Jr., by exchange.
Andrew Testa/Panos Pictures

rests at all on the kinds of principles that Locke and Rousseau described and on which liberalism was founded.

◆ COHESION AND CONFLICT

Freedom, some people argue, has gone too far, and prosperity has proved to be morally dangerous. Yet highly organized societies leave individuals feeling powerless and manipulated despite the apparent array of choices before them. Significantly, social control, a central concern in the writings of the Frankfurt school and Michel Foucault, has become a favorite subject for social research, which finds it operating through advertising and education as well as through religion

and custom, laws and institutions. The effect, these critics argue, is to keep the disadvantaged docile and to obscure issues of social justice. Suddenly, the question of what kind of social contract should be extended to foreign immigrants or to citizens who merely lack the skills most in demand has become one of the burning issues of modern Europe.

Religion Around the world, nationalism and vibrant religious movements demonstrate the power of community feeling, raising the question of whether Europeans will once again turn to such movements as they have in the past and whether postindustrial societies can satisfy the desire for social solidarity. Although fundamentalist religious movements remain weak in most of Europe, there is a significant Catholic fundamentalist movement in Italy; a Protestant one in Northern Ireland; Muslim ones in Britain, France, and Russia; and Orthodox ones in the former Soviet Union. Religious clashes have been endemic in Europe—part of medieval battles against heretics and Muslims, warfare between Protestants and Catholics, and modern conflicts between church and state.

Religion can mobilize opposition to current social trends, as in the frequent campaigns against immoral ways, whether of dress or drugs; opposition to the state, as in the Solidarity movement in Poland; and opposition to other social groups, as in the enduring conflict in Ireland. Under John Paul II, elected pope in 1978 (and the first non-Italian pope in 455 years), the Roman Catholic Church has become more resolutely conservative and outspoken on theological, institutional, and moral issues while remaining a vigorous critic of modern materialism and the injustices of capitalism. Conceivably, religious issues could heighten some of the conflicts in contemporary European society as they did in the 1920s and 1930s, even though church attendance in most European countries is the lowest it has ever been.

Identity   Ethnic conflict, too, has rarely been absent in European history, and Yugoslavia in the 1990s provided frightening proof that it remains possible for political leaders to inflame ethnic hatreds for their own purposes. Such efforts are in fact under way in much of Eastern Europe, and parties opposed to foreigners have gained attention and votes in France, Germany, and Italy. Western societies, which have generated the most powerful ideas and most effective movements opposed to racism, have also spawned virulent racist movements. The memory of Nazi genocide must affect any assessment of Western civilization and any evaluation of modern history, and nationalist movements anywhere in Europe are bound to evoke that fear. Nazism did strengthen the sense of German national identity, and national sentiment remains strong throughout Europe. As the Falkland war, the union of East and West Germany, and bloodshed in the Balkans show, political leaders can play no stronger card than an appeal to national loyalty.

In the last half-century, Western Europeans have been drawn closer together and gotten to know each other better than ever before. The question is whether a fulfilling sense of community can come either from pride in a more integrated Europe or from regional loyalties that encourage a symbolic nationalism without a state. Polls indicate that 51 percent of the people living in EU countries feel that being European is part of their identity (men more than women, the young more than those older, and citizens of the founding six nations more than those in countries that have joined more recently).

◆ SPLINTERED CULTURES

Sharing culture once implied proximity; now it occurs among people similar in class or age more readily than place. Eurovision allows national networks to participate in Europe-wide transmissions, and styles in music and dress have become more global than European. Formal or high culture has also become more international than in the nineteenth century, in part because exiles from Hitler's Europe and Stalin's Russia made cultural life more international and transatlantic.

Whose Culture?   Nevertheless, at negotiations on the General Agreement on Tariffs and Trade in 1994, the countries of the European Union supported France in insisting that their mass media must reserve some support for European productions. That argument was not about the content or function of popular culture but where it originated and who profited.

Research in the sciences and humanities conducted in Europe now often has a distinctively and perhaps increasingly European rather than national flavor. Scholars from one part of Europe teach and work in another, and research teams include people from several European countries. In the arts individual performers, orchestras, and works of art move freely across Europe's national borders, and student exchanges within the European Union have become the norm. No previous civilization supported so much scholarship, so many centers of learning, or so many artists.

Contemporary observers are less confident, however, than those Enlightenment thinkers who more than two centuries ago compared ancient and modern culture and decided that the moderns had the advantage. At the beginning of the twenty-first century, the proportion of Europeans certain of modern progress is probably lower than a century earlier. Instead, revelations of mass murder under a Soviet regime that proclaimed humane values and sustained an admirable high culture serves as a reminder that the expanded capacities of modern society include the capacity for evil. The role of culture is much clearer as a basis for opposition than as an expression of commitment. It was in the euphoria of liberation that Czechoslovakia picked a playwright as president.

Popular and High Culture Part of this unease about the role of culture stems from the troubling separation nowadays between popular and formal culture. The great literary works of all ages continue to be taught in schools and universities and are still read with pleasure. More people than ever before hear classical music and visit museums and art galleries. Yet commercial entertainment, ubiquitous and international, conveys quite a different set of values; and the morally earnest culture of the nineteenth century, of which so much was expected, threatens to become merely academic, a matter for special study by experts. The very forms that defined that culture—long novels and epic poems, symphonies, operas, impressive museums—are, by current standards, discouragingly demanding of attention, time, and money. Ironically, this older bourgeois culture was lavishly supported under communism; but now state subsidies for elite culture, though far more common in Europe than in the United States, are questioned everywhere.

The music, art, and literature that the twentieth-century avant-garde proudly called modern and that it used to attack the established high culture from which it grew never achieved a broad popularity. Doubt about human rationality and disdain for elites have made anti-intellectualism respectable, and there has been a remarkable revival of interest in the occult. Computers, after all, can also be used to plot astrological charts. For centuries, Europeans have taken culture to be the most significant expression of society, and we tend to identify historical eras by their characteristic cultural achievements. If that is done in the future, what will be said of this era?

The Consolation of History Because every era tends narcissistically to believe that its problems are unique, that very assumption deserves to be doubted. Europe today faces no threat comparable to the barbarian invasions of ancient Rome or the Black Death. If social change now is rapid, we have learned to expect and even anticipate it; the changes that followed the fifteenth century or those in the hundred years after 1780 may well have been more shocking and harder to absorb. We should not let nostalgia make it seem that earlier ages enjoyed a confidence and comforting unanimity denied to us. Rarely in Western history has a single philosophy or set of values enjoyed undisputed hegemony. The view that other eras were informed by a single spirit is largely the product of distance, which makes outlines clearer and fissures more obscure. The competing claims of throne and altar and the disputes about forms of transubstantiation were once as socially shattering as issues about public and private ownership, ethnic minorities, or abortion and euthanasia are today.

And there are encouraging lessons to be learned. Good causes can be served by ordinary people with all the normal human flaws. The resistance movements that fought fascism and are rightly honored throughout Western Europe were often formed around old conflicts and resentments. If the future is uncertain, as futures always are, that is partly because what human beings choose to do does make a difference. History takes a turn at the intersection of long-term trends and accident, where personalities interact within larger frameworks of ideas and social structures.

European history demonstrates that the past is inescapable but also that memory is malleable, that radical transformations can be consonant with great continuity. That being so, the western tip of the Eurasian peninsula can be expected to generate in the future the conflicts, dangers, discoveries, institutions, customs, ideas, and dreams that have made the Western experience such a compelling experiment.

Appendix

RECOMMENDED FILMS

Chapter 1

Ancient Civilizations. Color. 1978. National Geographic Society. Looks at archaeology of Mesopotamia, Egypt, Greece, Rome, and China.

*Ancient Egypt. 51 min. Color. 1971. Time-Life Video. Kenneth Clark on Egyptian culture and society.

Ascent of Man: Lower Than the Angels. 52 min. Color. 1974. BBC. Explores the evolutionary changes of humankind at the dawn of civilization.

Yesterday's Worlds: The Missing City Gates. 29 min. Color. National Educational Television. A description of the Assyrians and their civilization.

Yesterday's Worlds: Treasures from the Land of the Bible. 29 min. Color. National Educational Television. The Dead Sea Scrolls and ancient Palestine.

Chapter 2

Minoan Civilization. 53 min. Films for the Humanities and Sciences (BDU3289).

Greek Epic. 40 min. Films for the Humanities and Sciences. Explores *The Iliad* and *The Odyssey* and examines the nature of the epic.

The Glory That Was Greece: The Age of Civil War. 36 min. B/W. Time-Life Films. The revolt against Persia and the Greek victories in the Persian Wars.

Chapter 3

The Classical Age. 57 min. Films for the Humanities and Sciences.

The Athenian Trireme. 55 min. Films for the Humanities and Sciences.

Antigone. 88 min. B/W. 1962. Fleetwood. Sophocles' play with English subtitles.

Art of the Western World. Vol. 1, 1. *The Classical Ideal*, Part I. 28 min. Color. 1989. Educational Broadcasting Corporation, funded by Annenberg/CPB Project. Presents art and architecture within the context of history.

Plato's Apology: The Life and Teachings of Socrates. 29 min. Color. 1962. Encyclopedia Britannica Educational Corporation. The teachings of Socrates as presented in Plato's famous dialogue.

Chapter 4

The Etruscans. 27 min. Films for the Humanities and Sciences (BDU132).

Pompeii: Daily Life of the Ancient Romans. 45 min. Color. Films for the Humanities and Sciences. Uses artifacts from Pompeii to recreate Roman life.

I, Claudius. 780 min. Color. 1976. Series depicting the history of the Roman Empire from Emperors Augustus to Claudius.

Julius Caesar: The Rise of the Roman Empire. 22 min. Color. 1962. Encyclopedia Britannica Educational Corporation. Examines the successes of Julius Caesar.

Chapter 5

Cyber Rome. 39 min. Films for the Humanities and Sciences. A tour of Rome, about A.D. 200, in virtual reality.

Intimate Details of Roman Life. 27 min. Color. Films for the Humanities. Everyday life in the early Empire.

Testament: Thine Is the Kingdom. 52 min. Color. Films for the Humanities. Christianity under Diocletian and Constantine.

Chapter 6

Beowolf. 38 min. Color. Films for the Humanities. Detailed contextual survey of the epic.

The Book of Kells. 26 min. Color. Films for the Humanities and Sciences. Identifies the faces and figures in the drawings of the book and explains the symbolism.

The City of God. 39 min. Color. Film for the Humanities and Sciences. Surveys the resurgence of the Church, development of the Vulgate Bible, Pope Gregory the Great, Romanesque architecture, and the significance of pilgrimages.

The Lindisfarne Gospels: A Masterpiece of Anglo-Saxon Book Painting. 35 min. Color. Films for the Humanities and Sciences. Explains the creation of the gospels.

Medieval Manuscripts. 30 min. Color. Films for the Humanities and Sciences. Surveys the work behind the making of manuscripts and the key role that monasteries played in the preservation of Western culture.

Chapter 7

Charlemagne. 240 min. 1995. British miniseries.

Constantinople: City in the Middle Ages. 17 min. Color. 1992. Britannica Films.

Islam: The Prophet and the People. 34 min. Color. 1975. Texture. A biography of Muhammed and a history of the Islamic people.

The Vikings. Ten 30-min. episodes. Color. 1980. Films for the Humanities. Surveys the life and culture of the Vikings.

The World of Islam: Islamic Art and Islamic Science and Technology. 30-min. episodes. Color. Films for the Humanities. Surveys Islamic artistic and scientific contributions in the Middle Ages.

Chapter 8

Castle. 60 min. Color. 1983. Unicorn Projects. Study of castle construction in Wales.

*The Crusades. 200 min., 5-part series. Color. 1995. A&E Home Video. Terry Jones explores the subject of the crusades during the eleventh and twelfth centuries.

The Crusades: Saints and Sinners. 25 min. Color. 1967. Learning Corporation of America. Examines the First Crusade based on contemporary accounts.

Medieval London: 1066–1500. 20 min. Color. Films for the Humanities and Sciences. Traces some major events in London from 1066 to 1500, including the rebuilding of Westminster Abbey in the Gothic style, the first stone bridge across the Thames, and the occurrence of the Black Death.

The Middle Ages: The Rise of Feudalism. 20 min. Color. Encyclopedia Britannica Educational Corporation. Surveys the development of feudalism using contemporary documents.

Chapter 9

Acts of Faith: Jewish Civilization in Spain. 52 min. Color. Films for the Humanities and Sciences. Examines the Jewish civilization in Spain and its remnants.

Art of the Western World. Vol. 1, *1. A White Garment of Churches—Romanesque and Gothic*, Part II. 28 min. Color. 1989. Educational Broadcasting Corporation, funded by Annenberg/CPB Project. Presents art and architecture within the context of history.

*Becket. 149 min. Color. Paramount. Tells the story of Henry II's conflict with Thomas Becket.

Cathedral. 60 min. Color. 1985. Unicorn Projects. Account of the building of a thirteenth-century cathedral.

Hildegard of Bingen. 52 min. Color. 1997. Oblate Media and Communication Corporation. Explores the life of this famous medieval woman.

Illuminated Lives: A Brief History of Women's Work in the Middle Ages. Color. 1982. National Film Board of Canada.

*Lion in Winter. 1968. Color. Portrays the conflict between Henry II and his family at their Christmas court.

Chapter 10

Mongols: Storm from the East. 200 min., 4-part series. Color. Films for the Humanities and Sciences.

Medieval Realms. Britain from 1066–1500: From the Collections of the British Library. CD-ROM. Films for the Humanities and Sciences. Includes manuscripts; historical documents and maps; pictures of buildings and artifacts; extracts from wills, chronicles, letters, and charters; music; and spoken word recordings.

The Trinity Apocalypse. Films for the Humanities and Sciences. Illustrations from this thirteenth-century manuscript with transliteration of the original text.

Chapter 11

*Civilization: Romance and Reality. 50 min. Color. 1969. BBC. Kenneth Clark on the achievements of the later Middle Ages in France and Italy.

Faith and Fear. 40 min. Color. 1976. McGraw-Hill. Examines religion in the period of the Black Death.

The Fall of Constantinople. 34 min. Color. 1970. Time-Life Films. Examination of Constantinople's demise; filmed on location.

Henry V. 138 min. Color. 1989. Portrayal of Shakespeare's classic telling of the battle of Agincourt.

Joan of Arc. 26 min. Color. 1976. Learning Corporation of America. Recreates the era and personality of Joan of Arc using modern interview techniques.

York Mystery Plays: The Annunciation and Joseph's Trouble About Mary. 25 min. Color. Films for the Humanities and Sciences. Reconstruction of two fifteenth-century mystery plays.

Chapter 12

Renaissance: The Artist. 55 min. Color. 1994. PBS.

The Seventh Seal. 96 min. B/W. 1956. Allegorical film portraying a "man, his eternal search for God, with death his only certainty."

Civilization: The Hero as Artist. 52 min. Color. 1970. Time-Life Films. Kenneth Clark on the High Renaissance.

I, Leonardo da Vinci. 52 min. Color. 1965. McGraw-Hill. Uses his journals and writings.

Tradesmen and Treasures: Gothic and Renaissance Nuremberg. 60 min. Color. Bayerischer Fund with the Metropolitan Museum of Art. Uses art and artifacts to explore fourteenth-, fifteenth-, and sixteenth-century Nuremberg.

Chapter 13

Renaissance: The Dissenter. 55 min. Color. 1994. PBS.

A Man for All Seasons. 120 min. Color. 1966. Stunning version of the Robert Bolt play about Thomas More's refusal to help Henry VIII in breaking with the Roman Catholic Church and starting the Church of England.

Return of Martin Guerre. 111 min. 1982. Color. Evocation of village life in seventeenth-century France.

Chapter 14

Renaissance: The Prince. 55 min. Color. 1994. PBS.

The Black Robe. 101 min. Color. 1991. Vivid depiction of Catholic missionaries and Indians in the Great Lakes.

The Six Wives of Henry VIII. Six 90-min. episodes. Color. BBC. Life at court and the demands it placed on women.

Chapter 15

Carnival in Flanders. 92 min. B/W. 1936. Uses film to recreate the works of the great masters dealing with carnival time in the life of a village.

Renaissance: The Warrior. 55 min. Color. 1994. PBS.

Art of the Western World. Vol. 2, 5. *Realms of Light—The Baroque,* Parts I and II. 56 min. Color. 1989. Educational Broadcasting Corporation, funded by Annenberg/CPB Project. Presents art and architecture within the context of history.

Cromwell. 141 min. Color. 1970. Richard Harris as Cromwell and Alec Guiness as Charles I.

*Elizabeth R. 540 min. 1972. Color. BBC. Chronicle of Elizabeth I's life and reign.

Gunpowder and the Transformation of Europe. 20 min. Color. Houghton Mifflin. Warfare and technology in Europe from the fourteenth to the eighteenth centuries.

Chapter 16

Renaissance: The Scientist. 55 min. Color. 1994. PBS.

Rembrandt. 90 min. B/W. 1936. Charles Laughton stars in this satisfying portrait of the Dutch painter.

The Ascent of Man: The Starry Messenger. 50 min. Color. Time-Life Films. Jacob Bronowski on the scientific revolution.

Civilization: Grandeur and Obedience. 52 min. Color. Time-Life Films. Kenneth Clark on the Baroque.

Civilization: The Light of Experience. 52 min. Color. 1970. Time-Life Films. Shift in worldview experienced in the late seventeenth century.

Chapter 17

The Rise of Louis XIV. 100 min. 1966. Chronicles Louis XIV's ascent to power.

Let Joy Reign Supreme. A film about Louis XV starring Philip Noiret.

*Barry Lyndon. 187 min. Color. 1975. Depiction of Thackeray's novel has excellent coverage of eighteenth-century warfare.

Peter the Great. 380 min. Color. 1980. Maximilian Schell and international cast in the television miniseries.

Chapter 18

The Ascent of Man: The Drive for Power. 52 min. Color. 1974. Time-Life Films. Eighteenth-century economic changes; presented in the Jacob Bronowski series.

Last of the Mohicans. 114 min. Color. 1992. Superb reenactments of a French and Indian war siege.

The Market Society and How It Grew. Two 29-min. episodes. B/W. 1963. National Educational Television. Robert Heilbroner on Adam Smith and the development of market economy.

Chapter 19

Amadeus. 158 min. Color. 1984. Spectacular presentation of Mozart's life and times.

Civilization: The Pursuit of Happiness. 52 min. Color. Time-Life Films. Kenneth Clark on eighteenth-century music and art.

Civilization: The Smile of Reason. 52 min. Color. Time-Life Films. Kenneth Clark on the Enlightenment.

Ridicule. 102 min. Color. The doings of high society under Louis XVI. Brilliant.

Chapter 20

Danton. 135 min. Color. 1992. Powerful film by Polish director Andrzej Wajda on the personality and political differences between Danton and Robespierre; Gerard Depardieu as Danton.

La Marseillese. 130 min. B/W. 1937. French with English subtitles. A celebration of the revolutionary spirit in 1792.

The Battle of Cholet: 1794. 30 min. Color. Films for the Humanities. Revolt in the Vendèe.

Chapter 21

The Battle of Austerlitz; The Battle of Trafalgar; The Battle of Waterloo. 30 min. each. Color. Films for the Humanities. Probably the single most important battles of the era.

The Hundred Days: Napoleon from Elba to Waterloo. 53 min. Color. 1969. Time-Life Films. Filmed on location.

Napoleon. 4 hours. Color. PBS. A documentary by David Grubin, especially strong on Napoleon's rise and on his major military campaigns.

Chapter 22

The Crystal Year. 30 min. B/W. 1965. National Educational Television. England in 1851.

Pride and Prejudice. 226 min. Color. BBC. An effective adaptation of Jane Austen's famous novel that gives a good picture of genteel village life in England.

Silas Marner. 100 min. Color. BBC. Country village relations during the early industrial revolution.

Chapter 23

Civilization: The Worship of Nature. 52 min. Color. 1969. BBC. Kenneth Clark on the nineteenth-century belief in the divinity of nature.

Great Expectations. 124 min. Color. 1974. BBC. A somewhat condensed version of Dickens' classic novel that captures the bustle of industrial England.

When Ireland Starved. Four 26-min. episodes. Color. Films for the Humanities. The Irish famine, why it occurred, what was done, and what resulted; uses contemporary reports and illustrations.

Chapter 24

1848. 22 min. B/W. 1949. Radim Films. Daumier graphics show Paris in 1848.

Bismarck: Germany from Blood and Iron. 30 min. Color. 1976. Learning Corporation of America. Bismarck's word to describe German unification.

The Leopard. 205 min. 1963. A superb adaptation of Lampedusa's great novel of nineteenth-century Sicily.

Chapter 25

Europe, the Mighty Continent: Hey-Day Fever and A World to Win. 52 min. each. Color. 1976. Time-Life Films. Europe in 1900 and in the decade before the First World War.

Zulu. 138 min. Color. 1964. Classic account of battle between Zulu army and a small group of British soldiers; filmed on location in South Africa.

Chapter 26

Art of the Western World. Vol. III, 7. *A Fresh View of Impressionism and Post-Impressionism.* 56 min. Color. 1989. Educational Broadcasting Corporation, funded by Annenberg Project CPB.

The Battleship Potemkin. 75 min. B/W. 1925. Eissenstein's classic film study of the Odessa Mutiny of 1903 is also an important document of early Soviet propaganda that captures the enthusiasm of the revolution.

La Belle Epoque: 1840–1914. 60 min. Color. ABC Video in association with the Metropolitan Museum of Art. Evokes this time of wealth and pleasure for the upper classes.

Chapter 27

All Quiet on the Western Front. 130 min. B/W. 1930. Beautiful film from the novel.

The Grand Illusion. 95 min. B/W. 1937. Jean Renoir's magnificent essay against the Great War that portrays differences of social class among the French and sympathetically suggests differences in cultural attitudes between the French and Germans.

Verdun. 30 min. B/W. 1965. Indiana University. The battle.

Chapter 28

Between the Wars. Eight 60-min. episodes. Color. 1978. Anthony Potter Production. Different aspects of these two decades.

Triumph of the Will. 110 min. B/W. 1935. Leni Riefenstahl's powerful film of the 1934 Nuremberg rally.

The Twisted Cross. 53 min. B/W. 1956. NBC. Study of Hitler's rise to power. Includes newsreel film.

Chapter 29

The Bicycle Thief. 90 min. B/W. 1949. A classic neorealist film about the postwar struggle for survival in Rome

D-Day. 50 min. B/W. 1962. Films, Inc. German and Allied footage of the landings.

Open City. 103 min. B/W. 1945. The beginning of the great wave of Italian postwar films; work on this film began as the Germans were evacuating the city. A moving presentation of the official myth of the resistance:

supported by the honest poor and led by a heroic communist and a heroic priest.

Shoah. 570 min. Color. 1985. Claude Lanzmann's stunning documentary, based on interviews with people involved in rounding up Jews and sending them to the death camps and with survivors.

*Stalingrad. 135 min. 1993. German antiwar film that traces the WWII Stalingrad campaign. Follows structure of *All Quiet on the Western Front.*

Chapter 30

The Battle of Algiers. 135 min. B/W. 1965. Casbah. An important film of the revolt against French colonial rule.

Europe on the Brink. 1992. CNN. The fall of the Berlin Wall and the Soviet Union, and the changes in Eastern Europe.

Frontline: The Struggle for Russia. 1992. PBS. Documentary exploring Boris Yeltsin's presidency.

Gandhi. 188 min. Color. 1982. The struggle for Indian independence from colonialism.

Text Credits

Chapter 1

(13) Reprinted from *The Code of Hammurabi*, Robert F. Harper, trans., Gordon Press, 1904, 1991. Reprinted with permission. **(26)** Scripture quotations from Exodus, 15, are from the *Revised Standard Version of the Bible*. Copyright © 1946, 1952, 1971 by the Division of Christian Education of the National Council of the Churches of Christ in the USA. Used by permission. **(27)** Scripture quotations from Jeremiah, 11, are from the *Revised Standard Version of the Bible*. Copyright © 1946, 1952, 1971 by the Division of Christian Education of the National Council of the Churches of Christ in the USA. Used by permission.

Chapter 2

(48) From *Black Athena* by Martin Bernal, Rutgers University Press, 1987, pp. 17–23, abridged. Reprinted by permission. **(48)** Excerpt from *Black Athena Revisited* edited by Mary R. Lefkowitz and Guy MacLean Rogers. Copyright © 1996 by the University of North Carolina Press. Used by permission of the publisher. **(53)** From Guy Davenport, *7 Greeks*. Copyright © 1995 by Guy Davenport. Reprinted by permission of New Directions Publishing Corp. **(65)** From *Herodotus, Book VII*, M. H. Chambers, trans., pp. 101–104. Copied with permission from Ayer Co. Publishers, Inc., N. Stratford, NH 03590.

Chapter 3

(78) From *The Last Days of Socrates* by Plato, translated by Hugh Tredennick, Penguin Classics 1954, Second revised edition 1969. Copyright © 1954, 1959, 1969 by Hugh Tredennick. Reproduced by permission of Penguin Books Ltd. **(86)** Abridged from *The Peloponnesian War* by Thucydides, translated by Rex Warner, Penguin Classics, 1954. Copyright © 1954 Rex Warner. Reproduced by permission of Penguin Books Ltd.

Chapter 6

(200) Excerpt from *The Rule of St. Benedict in Latin and English with Notes* edited by Timothy Fry, Liturgical Press, 1980, pp. 261–265. Reprinted with permission.

Chapter 8

(266) From William Fitz Stephen, *Norman London*, Italica Press, pp. 52, 54. Used by permission of Italica Press, in cooperation with The Historical Association, London. **(270)** C. W. Hollister et al., *Medieval Europe: A Short Sourcebook*. Copyright © 1992 by McGraw-Hill. Reprinted by permission of The McGraw-Hill Companies. **(276)** From *Basic Documents in Medieval History* by Norman Downs. Copyright © 1959 by Krieger Publishing Company. Reprinted with permission.

Chapter 9

(295) From *The Middle Ages: Sources of Medieval History*, Fifth Edition, by Brian Tierney et al., pp. 172–175. Copyright © 1992 by McGraw-Hill. Reprinted with permission from The McGraw-Hill Companies.

Chapter 10

(335, 354) From *Women's Lives in Medieval Europe: A Source Book* by Emilie Amt, pp. 195–196, 264–265. Reprinted with permission from Routledge. **(352)** From *Medieval Europe: A Short Source Book* by Warren Hollister et al., pp. 215–216. Copyright © 1994 McGraw-Hill. Reprinted with permission from The McGraw-Hill Companies.

Chapter 11

(365) From *Medieval Europe: A Short Source Book* by Warren Hollister et al., pp. 215–216. Copyright © 1994 McGraw-Hill. Reprinted with permission from The McGraw-Hill Companies. **(376)** Excerpted from "Did Women Have A

Renaissance?" by Joan Kelly in *Becoming Visible*, Third Edition by Bridenthal et al. Copyright © 1998 by Houghton Mifflin Company. Reprinted by permission. **(387)** From *The Trial of Jeanne D'Arc*, edited by G. G. Coulton and Eileen Power, translated by W. P. Barrett. Copyright © 1931 by Routledge. Reprinted by permission from Taylor & Francis.

Chapter 12

(417) From D. S. Chambers, ed., *Patrons and Artists in the Italian Renaissance*, University of South Carolina Press, 1970, pp. 128–130, 147–148. Reprinted with permission.

Chapter 13

(442) From Lucien Febvre and Henri-Jean Martin, David Gerard, trans., *The Coming of the Book: The Impact of Printing 1450–1800*, Verso, 1976, pp. 178–179, 184–185. Reprinted by permission. **(467)** From E. Allison Peers, *The Life of Teresa of Jesus*, Sheed & Ward, 1960, pp. 258–260, 273–274. Reprinted with permission.

Chapter 14

(475) Adapted from J. H. Elliott, *Imperial Spain, 1469–1716* by Edward Arnold, The Hodder Headline PLC Group, 1964, p. 175. Reprinted by permission. **(484)** From *The Conquest of Paradise: Christopher Columbus and the Columbian Legacy* by Kirkpatrick Sale, pp. 209–210, 362. Reprinted by permission of Alfred A. Knopf, Inc.

Chapter 15

(543) Adapted from J. H. Elliott, *Imperial Spain, 1469–1716* by Edward Arnold, The Hodder Headline PLC Group, 1964, p. 175. Reprinted by permission.

Chapter 16

(557) Excerpt from *The Crime of Galileo* by Giorgio de Santillana, University of Chicago Press, 1955, pp. 11, 14–15. Reprinted by permission of the publisher. **(577)** From *The Economy of Europe in an Age of Crisis, 1600–1750* by Jan de Vries, Cambridge University Press, 1976, p. 5. Reprinted by permission.

Chapter 17

(599) From William F. Church, *The Greatness of Louis XIV: Myth or Reality?* Copyright © 1959 by D. C. Heath and Company. Used with permission from Houghton Mifflin Company.

Chapter 18

(654) Adapted from *British Economic Growth 1688–1959* by Phyllis Dean and W. A. Cole, Cambridge University Press, 1964, p. 49. Reprinted by permission. **(655)** Adapted from Philip Curtin, *The Atlantic Slave Trade: A Census*, The University of Wisconsin Press, 1969. Reprinted with permission from the publisher.

Chapter 19

(671) Specified excerpts from *The Habsburg and Hohenzollern Dynasties in the late 17th and the 18th Centuries* by C. A. Macartney. Copyright © 1970 by C. A. Macartney. Reprinted by permission of HarperCollins Publishers. **(680)** Excerpt from Jean-Jacques Rousseau, *The Social Contract*, Book I, David Campbell Publishers. Reprinted by permission.

Chapter 20

(707, 715) From R. R. Palmer, trans., *The Coming of the Revolution*. Copyright © 1989 by Princeton University Press. Reprinted by permission of Princeton University Press. **(707)** Excerpt from *Origins of the French Revolution* by William Doyle, 1988. Reprinted by permission of Oxford University Press.

Chapter 22

(796) Excerpt from *Documents of European Economic History*, Vol. I, edited by Sidney Pollard and Colin Holmes. Copyright © 1969 Sidney Pollard and Colin Holmes. Reprinted with permission from Palgrave, St. Martin's Press. **(798)** From Thomas S. Ashton, "The Standard of Life of the Workers in England, 1790–1830," *Journal of Economic History*, Vol. 9, 1949. Reprinted by permission of Cambridge University Press. **(799)** From Ronald M. Hartwell, "The Rising Standard of Living in England 1800–1850," *Economic History Review*, 1961. Reprinted by permission of the author. **(800)** From Philip A. M. Taylor, ed., *The Industrial Revolution in Britain: Triumph or Disaster?* D. C. Heath, 1970. **(786)** From "Production in Belgium, France, and the United Kingdom," and "Emigration from Europe," in *European Historical Statistics, 1750–1970* by B. R. Mitchel. Copyright © 1975 by Columbia University Press. Reprinted with permission from the publisher. **(799)** From Eric J. Hobsbawn, "The British Standard of Living, 1790–1850," *Economic History Review*, 1957. Used with permission.

Chapter 25

(891) From P. Bairoch et al., *The Working Population and Its Structure*, Gordon & Breach, 1968. Reprinted with permission. **(909)** Reprinted by permission of the publisher from *Imperialism and Social Classes* by Joseph Schumpeter, pp. 128–129, Cambridge, Mass.: Harvard University Press. Copyright © 1951 by Meridian Books, the World Publishing Company. **(910)** Excerpts from *The Origins of Totalitarianism* by Hannah Arendt. Copyright © 1951 and renewed 1979 by Marty McCarthy West. Reprinted by permission of Harcourt, Inc. **(910)** Extract taken from *Theories of Imperialism* by Wolfgang J. Mommesen, P. S. Fall, trans., Weidenfeld & Nicolson Ltd., London, 1980. Reprinted by permission.

Chapter 26

(939) From Robert M. Cutler, trans. and ed., *Mikhail Bakunin: From Out of the Dustbin: Bakunin's Basic Writings, 1869–1871*, Ardis Publishers, 1985. Reprinted by permission. **(944)** From Richard Levy, ed., *Antisemitism in the Modern World*.

Chapter 27

(966) Reprinted with permission of Simon & Schuster from *The Origins of War* by Sidney B. Fay. Copyright © 1930 by Macmillan Publishing Company; copyright renewed © 1958 by Sidney Bradshaw Fay. **(983)** Reprinted from Harold Owen and John Bell, eds., *Wilfred Owen: The Collected Letters*. Copyright © 1967 Oxford University Press. Reprinted by permission of Oxford University Press. **(997)** Excerpt from *Documents of European Economic History*, Vol. I, edited by Sidney Pollard and Colin Holmes. Copyright © 1969 Sidney Pollard and Colin Holmes. Reprinted with permission from Palgrave, St. Martin's Press.

Chapter 28

(1024) Excerpt from "Manifesto of Futurism" in *Marinetti: Selected Writings* by F. T. Marinetti, edited by R. W. Flint, translated by R. W. Flint and Arthur A. Coppotelli. Translation copyright © 1972 by Farrar, Straus & Giroux, Inc. Reprinted by permission of Farrar, Straus & Giroux, Inc. **(1026)** From *The Decline of the West: Volume I* by Oswald Spengler, translated by C. G. Atkinson. Copyright © 1926 by Alfred A. Knopf, a division of Random House, Inc. Used by permission of the publisher. **(1045)** From Salvator Attansio et al., trans., Speech of Goebbels, in *Nazi Culture: Intellectual, Cultural and Social Life in the Third Reich* by George L. Mosse, University of Wisconsin Press, 1996. Reprinted by permission.

Chapter 29

(1079) From Ernst Nolte, "Between Historical Myth and Revisionism," *Yad Vashem Studies, XIX*, 1988. Copyright © 1988 by Yad Vashem Martyrs and Heros Remembrance Authority. Reprinted with permission. **(1077)** From *Nazism, 1919–1945: State, Economy and Society 1933–1939*, Volume II, revised edition, 2000, edited by J. Noakes and G. Pridham. Copyright © 1988 by the University of Exeter Press. Reprinted with permission. **(1079)** From Henry Friedlander, "Step by Step: The Expansion of Murder, 1939–1941," *German Studies Review*, XVII, October 1994. Reprinted with permission from the German Studies Association. **(1080)** From *Reworking the Past* by Peter Baldwin. Copyright © 1990 by Peter Baldwin. Reprinted by permission of Beacon Press, Boston. **(1093)** Speech by Winston Churchill given at Westminster College, March 5, 1946, from *The Penguin Book of Twentieth Century Speeches*, edited by Brian MacArthur. Copyright © the Estate of Sir Winston S. Churchill. Reproduced with permission of Curtis Brown Ltd., London, on behalf of the Estate of Sir Winston S. Churchill. **(1098)** Speech by Andrei Y. Vishinsky to the United Nations, November 1, 1948, from *Vital Speeches of the Day*, Vol. 15, No. 2. Reprinted with permission from The City News Publishing Company.

Chapter 30

(1125) From *Turkish Workers in Europe*, edited by Ilhan Basgoz and Norman Furniss, Akural Aynu translator, 1985. Reprinted by permission of Indiana University Turkish Studies Publications. **(1158)** From *The History of Sexuality* by Michel Foucault, Random House, 1978. Originally published in French as *La Volonte De Savior*. Copyright © 1976 by Editions Gallimard. Reprinted by permission of Georges Borchardt, Inc., for the author. **(1159)** From "Women's Time" by Julia Kristeva, in *New Maladies of the Soul* by Julia Kristeva. Copyright © 1995 by Columbia University Press. Reprinted by permission of the publisher.

Main Index

*Index notes: Main themes are indicated in **bold type.** Page numbers in *italics* indicate illustrations and their captions; page numbers followed by *m* indicate maps; page numbers followed by *t* indicate tables; page numbers followed by *n* indicate notes.